CATHOLIC AUTHORS

Catholic Authors

CONTEMPORARY BIOGRAPHICAL SKETCHES

1930-1947

EDITED BY **MATTHEW HOEHN**, O.S.B., B.L.S.

Librarian of St. Benedict's Preparatory School
Newark, N. J.

861

NEWARK • **ST. MARY'S ABBEY** • *MCMXLVIII*

74-304

Imprimi potest
✠Patrick M. O'Brien, o.s.b.
Abbot

Nihil obstat
Joseph H. Brady, s.t.d.
Censor Librorum

Imprimatur
✠Thomas J. Walsh, s.t.d., j.c.d.
Archbishop of Newark

Newark, N. J., October 10, 1947

PREFACE

I N JANUARY, 1939, work was begun on this volume, the underlying purpose of which is to afford the reading public an
intimate introduction to contemporary Catholic authors. It
attempts in no wise to appraise critically the literary standing
of the writers presented, nor to stamp all the works discussed as entirely representative of Catholic thought and doctrine. Every effort
has been made to obtain dependable information. To that end more
than five thousand letters were sent to authors, editors, librarians,
publishers, and, whenever possible, to relatives and friends of the
authors. Each completed sketch was submitted to the biographee,
if living, for verification, and only in a few instances did the sketch
fail to return. Foreign authors are included if at least one of their
works has been translated into English.

A list of more than sixteen hundred authors, comprising those
who have died since 1930 as well as those who are still living, was
sent to each of several librarians, editors, and literary critics who independently selected the authors they thought qualified. From these
check lists our 620 Catholic authors were chosen. As a rule more
space has been devoted to well-known authors than to beginners;
·in many instances, however, the amount of available data has determined the length of the sketch. Only by shortening the bibliographies has it been possible to include so many biographical
sketches.

While compiling this book the editor had in mind particularly
librarians who are happy to have biographical material on hand
to satisfy the needs of their varied clientele. He will be pleased if
the volume proves useful to teachers, students, and such other
readers as may wish to be informed about the person behind each
of the books they read.

The editor wrote up more than two hundred of the biographies
and is indebted to the following contributors for the sketch or
sketches they have written for this book: Catherine M. Neale, Mary
Armstrong Sullivan, Katherine Bregy, Helen Iswolsky, Julie Ker-

nan, Dorothy Dixon, Sister Jane Marie, Sister Jerome Keeler, O.S.B., John Garrett Underhill, Francis Meehan, C. J. Eustace, Paul Martin-Dillon, the Reverend Bonaventure Schwinn, O.S.B., Shaemus O'Sheel, W. J. White (Ireland), Franz Mueller, Harry L. Binsse, James Tobin, Elmer Ellis, William Titterton (England), Alice McLarney, the late Reginald Ferrier, Sister Miriam, R.S.M., Sister Miriam of the Temple, C.N.D., Teresa Varni, Ella Marie Flick, the Reverend Justin Mahoney, O.S.B., Hertha Pauli, Mary Toomey Giesselmann, Patricia O'Neil, Anne Ford, Naomi Gilpatrick, Grace MacGowan Angerstein, Clara Kircher, Ida H. Chamberlain, Anne Murphy, the Reverend John Considine, M.M., E. Carroll Skinner, the Reverend Thomas B. Cannon, S.J., Sigmund Uminski, Riley Hughes, Elise Lavelle, Patricia McNulty, the Reverend Joseph Fenton, the Reverend Edmond Benard, Regina Kelly, Francis McCullagh, Clifford Laube, Sister Mary Justitia, B.V.M., and to a few others who do not wish their names published.

The list of those who have cooperated in other ways is endless. The editor wishes to make special mention of the Right Reverend Abbot Patrick O'Brien, O.S.B., for permitting the compilation of this book, and also of the monks of St. Mary's Abbey for meeting the expense of its manufacture. To Sister Catherine Regina of Marylawn Academy, the Central Catholic Library in Dublin, the Gallery of Living Catholic Authors, the British Information Services, the Irish Legation, the French Press and Information Service; to Miguel Espinos, Consul General of Spain, and John Van Horne, Cultural Relations Attaché of the American Embassy in Spain; to Louise Wijnhausen, Julie Kernan, Jacques Maritain, Theodore Maynard, Joseph J. Reilly, the Reverend George Timpe, P.S.M., George Shuster, the Reverend Adalbert Callahan, O.F.M., Margaret M. Link, the late E. K. Rand, Reverend Joseph Plumpe, Reverend Gerald Flynn, O.S.B., Reverend Daniel Ready, O.S.B., Reverend Sigmund Toenig, O.S.B., Mildred Maher, Mary Flynn; to the publicity directors of colleges and to publishers, the editor is indebted for their assistance. Thanks are due to the Reverend Justin Mahoney, O.S.B., who read the manuscript and gave advice. Unfortunately there remains insufficient space in which to mention the hundreds of other persons who have helped gather data and clarify some doubtful points.

The editor is deeply grateful to the typists who for about three years volunteered their services one night a week—namely, Margaret Degen, Hilda Riester Heinrich, Mary Burns Herbert, Mildred Hoehn Ritter, Cecilia Koermaier, Audrey Martin, Agnes Koermaier Oelkers, Mildred Riester, Marie Schweitzer Healy— and to the typists who helped in the project's early stage—namely, Theresa Land, Grace MacGowan Angerstein, and Dorothea Bozza.

The funds to finance the preparation of this work were raised through the Catholic Literary Institute, Inc., of Newark, N. J., formed for the purpose of fostering an interest in Catholic literature. The executive members are Mrs. Edward Fitzpatrick, Mrs. Robert Fitzpatrick, Mr. and Mrs. Ernest Tibbitts, Miss Katherine McLaughlin, Mrs. Peter L. Hughes, Mary McCormick Dunn, Mr. Charles Deubel, Mr. Joseph Hanson, the Reverend Thomas Long, O.S.B., Mr. James McKenna, with the editor, the Reverend Matthew Hoehn, O.S.B., as chairman. More than fifty members worked on card-party committees and on other benefits. The Parent-Teacher Association of St. Benedict's Preparatory School generously donated fourteen hundred dollars toward the general expenses and has shown an abiding interest in the success of the work. St. Mary's Abbey advanced ten thousand dollars to have the manuscript printed. The book would not have been possible without the help of these organizations. To the members the editor wishes to express his heartfelt thanks.

Matthew Hoehn, O.S.B., B.L.S.

CONTENTS

Contents

Contents

Contents

CATHOLIC AUTHORS

Achmed Abdullah 1881-1945

Born in Yalta, Russia, in 1881, Achmed Abdullah was the son of the late Grand Duke Nicholas Romanoff and Princess Nourmahal Durani, a granddaughter of the Amir of Afghanistan and, on her father's side, a descendant of the prophet Mohammed. Though his father was a member of the Russian Orthodox Church, the boy was brought up in the Moslem religion of his mother.

Achmed Abdullah, also known as Prince Nadir Khan Durani, was educated at Eton, at a Jesuit preparatory school in Paris, at the Berlin Gymnasium, at Oxford, and at the University of Paris. He attended the college of El Azhar in Cairo, Egypt, where he received a doctorate in Koranic Law. Later he served as a British army officer in India, China, South Africa, the Balkans, Gibraltar, France, and Mesopotamia, and as official interpreter of the first Younghusband expedition into Tibet.

Captain Abdullah, who was short and stocky, wore a monocle because he needed it, and his clothes were faultless. He hated injustice and disliked critics who praised the nasty and disparaged the decent, regarding them as victims of a psychological disease. Genuinely modest, he detested being taken for a high-brow.

The scene of many of his books was the Orient, where he had spent much time. The diversity of his talent is illustrated by his numerous works. *The Honourable Gentleman* was translated by the Chinese University of Peking, which considered it "one of the few honest books in fiction form on Chinese life." This novel won for its author recognition by the French Academy. *Shackled* was being translated into Russian by Maxim Gorky, who died before he completed the task. Gorky spoke of *Shackled* as "one of the most notable books of the last decade and written by one of our greatest masters of the written word."

Other books by Abdullah are: *Chansons Couleur Puce* (poems in French); *Wings: Being Tales of the Psychic* (short stories); *A Buccaneer in Spats; Night Drums; Alien Souls* (short stories); *The Swinging Caravan* (short stories), which came out in nine different languages; *The Wild Goose of Limerick; The Year of the Wood Dragon; Lute and Scimitar* (translations of Oriental songs, ballads, and other poems), which revealed Abdullah as a linguist, translator, and authority on the ethnology and folklore of the peoples of Afghanistan and Turkestan; *Steel and Jade; The Cat Had Nine Lives* (adventures and reminiscences), his autobiography! *Never Without You;* and, in collaboration with Faith Baldwin, *Ruth's Rebellion* and *Broadway Interlude.*

Deliver Us from Evil, his first Catholic book, was dedicated to Jean Wick, his late wife, and the Reverend Martin J. Scott, S.J., "whose example—for they never argued, preached, tried to convert me—showed me the road to that amazing truth and beauty which is the Catholic Faith." This volume was published in 1939, a few years after he entered the Church. He said: "I am inclined to be a 'militant' Catholic, and—here is where religion pays for itself—I find most of my plots in perusing the lives of the saints, lives that contain every temptation, every greatness, every conflict, every climax, since the beginning of time." *The Shadow of the Master,* written in collaboration with Fulton Oursler, appeared in 1940.

One of Abdullah's most successful plays was *Toto,* a sardonic comedy, in which the late great actor Leo Dietrichstein played for three years. His adaptation of *The Lives of a Bengal Lancer* was perhaps his best-known motion picture.

Captain Abdullah's first wife—Jean Wick, who was also his literary agent—died in January, 1939. In 1940 he married the former Rosemary Dolan of Denver, Colorado.

His death occurred on May 12, 1945, his sixty-fourth birthday.

M. H.

Reverend Karl Adam 1876-

The usual photograph of Father Karl Adam shows him in wing collar and black bow necktie, with a knee-length frock coat. Although this garb is distinctly clerical for the part of Germany in which he teaches, often he has been taken for a layman.

Karl Adam, one of the ten children of Clemens and Babette Sturm Adam, was born at Pursruck in Bavaria (the Upper Palatinate) in 1876. He was educated at the Gymnasium in Amber; at the philosophical and theological seminary in Regensburg; and at the University of Munich, from which he received his doctorate in 1904.

At the age of twenty-four (1900) Father Adam was ordained to the priesthood, then did parish work for two years. His scholarly and theological interests soon claimed him and he began publishing specialized studies in the history of dogma; these have never been translated and are of interest primarily to other specialists, who, naturally, have described them as his best work. His later and more popular volumes have been translated into many languages and have had tremendous influence in every sort of religious atmosphere. Two of the earlier works are *Tertullian's Conception of the Church* (1907) and the *Eucharistic Teaching of St. Augustine* (1908). In 1915, during World War I, Dr. Adam became a professor at Munich. Two years later he moved to the chair of moral theology at the University of Strasbourg. After another two years he went to the University of Tuebingen, where he held the chair of dogmatic theology. (The University of Tuebingen, a state university, has two theological faculties—one Catholic, the other Protestant.) In January, 1934, Father Adam got into difficulties with the Nazi government for his outspoken address on "The Eternal Christ," in which he criticized the so-called "German religion" as defined by Professor Hauer. At once the Nazis launched an attack upon him. Young rowdies heckled him, his house was riddled with bullets, and his life was threatened. Finally his right to lecture was denied him. He fled to the Bishop of Rottenburg and only after some time, when the storm had died down, could he return to Tuebingen and again speak in public. In his many lectures and writings he continued to stress the Christian faith and explain how Nazism was at variance with it.

Adam's great popular work was done principally in three books, all of them available in English translation. Of these the most widely read and influential is *The Spirit of Catholicism,* which has appeared in almost every European language, as well as in Latin and Japanese, and in 1946 reached its eleventh edition. The other two are *Christ Our Brother* and *The Son of God* (in German, *Jesus Christus*); the latter has been enlarged in its seventh edition. These three books concentrate on Christ Himself and on the doctrine of the Mystical Body—that doctrine which particularly suits the problems of our day, when a principal of unity is so badly lacking to mankind and when so many purely human or material bonds of unity have been proposed for man's salvation. His main field is the theology of St. Augustine, on whom he is an authority. He has a great love for tradition and for the Fathers of the Church.

Father Adam is a man of great dynamic force whether he writes or lectures. His style captivates both readers and audience. His class and public lectures are always overfilled. He exerts a tremendous influence on non-Catholics. He is much interested in a union between Catholics and Protestants and gave three lectures on the subject at Stuttgart in 1947. He is still lecturing at Tuebingen University in spite of the fact that he is over seventy years old. The most commonplace and drab objects or experiences suddenly take on a vital and brilliant light when he speaks about them. He may be called the greatest of living German-speaking theologians.

Teaching catechism to children and serving as Chaplain of the Royal Bavarian Cadet Corps helped to make Karl Adam's writings clear, exact and compact. A great inspirer of youth, he was a leader in the German Catholic youth movement. He is very likeable, human and has a keen sense of humor. His house is open to all alike and his charity is well known. He reacts strongly against sentimentality in every form. Dr. Adam's whole mind is concentrated on Christ.

William Macdonough Agar 1894-

The things that have interested William Macdonough Agar most are science itself, the fundamental relationship between philosophy, science, and the Christian religion, and the improvement of man's lot on this earth through the democratic way of life. A scientist by profession, all his earlier writing was in the nature of scientific articles. His first contribution in the way of a book was a compilation, along with two other scientists, called *Geology from Original Sources,* and also a small part of a geological textbook. *Catholicism and the Progress of Science* was published in 1940 and *The Dilemma of Science* in 1941.

William Macdonough Agar was born in New York City, February 14, 1894, the son of John Giraud and Agnes Louise (Macdonough) Agar. He was educated at the Newman School, Lakewood, New Jersey. After his graduation there in 1912, he went to Princeton University and received his B.S. in 1916.

World War I interrupted his education for nineteen months. Enlisting in February 1917, he served in the American Ambulance Service Section 16, on the French Front, but resigned to join the American forces in September 1918. He attained the rank of Sous Chef and won the decoration Croix-de-Guerre. He then joined the American Air Service. After training in Italy he was detailed on special duty, testing, instructing, and delivering planes. After a brief service on the Italian Front he returned to the United States to the army testing field in Dayton, Ohio. He was mustered out on December 9, 1918. He returned to Princeton University for graduate work, receiving his M.A. in 1920 and his Ph.D. in 1922.

Soon after leaving Princeton University he married Alida Stewart Carter on May 6, 1922, and they have four children. He then went to Butte, Montana, as one of the geological staff of Anaconda Copper Company. He resigned in the summer of 1923 to accept an appointment at Yale University, and left there to go to Columbia University in 1928, where he remained until 1935. From 1935 to 1940 he was headmaster of the Newman School, Lakewood, New Jersey. Since resigning from this position he has been active in the field of adult education as a lecturer and writer.

M. H.

Reverend Calvert Page Alexander, S.J.   1900-

Interest in Catholic literature of the present day led the Reverend Calvert Alexander, S.J., to write his book *The Catholic Literary Revival.* His newspaper and magazine work also gives him a place in the literary field, together with his brothers, Roy and Jack, who have confined their writings to the press, the former now with *Time* and the latter a contributor to the *New Yorker,* the *Saturday Evening Post* and *Life.* Father Alexander's work, appropriate to his calling, is with the *Jesuit Missions,* of which he has been editor since 1938.

He was born in St. Paul, Minnesota, in 1900 and, his family moving to St. Louis, Missouri, he was educated there at the Harrison Public School, the St. Louis University High School, and St. Louis University. His mother's illness and the family finances necessitated his leaving college in his sophomore year, and he obtained a job on the St. Louis *Globe-Democrat* as reporter, in 1920. Accepting a better position on the St. Louis *Star-Times,* he was for a time associated with this newspaper, as were also his two brothers. Later he returned to the editorial staff of the *Globe-Democrat.* In 1924 he was able to answer his religious vocation and entered the Society of Jesus. Completing his course at St. Louis University, he received his A.B. in 1926 and his M.A. in 1928. From 1929 to 1933 he taught at the St. Louis University High School.

While a scholastic, he wrote *The Catholic Literary Revival,* which has become a standard reference work for the period. There was great need of such a book and Father Alexander ably presents his subject. He says in his Introduction that he attempts "to trace the development of Catholic literature through three successive and rather well-defined phases in its growth," corresponding to three stages in the cultural history of Europe: the Victorian, 1845-90; from the end of the nineteenth century to World War I; and the postwar period. At first overshadowed by the confident prosperity of society, against which it protested, Catholic literature received more recognition in the second phase, and finally assumed a position of importance. Critical studies of the representative writers are given, types of literature and various phases of the movement are treated, and selective bibliographies are appended. The book is one of The Science and Culture Series, and was published in 1935.

Ordained priest at St. Mary's, Kansas, in 1936, Father Alexander taught for a while at Marquette University and in 1938 was appointed editor of *Jesuit Missions* and Director of the National Office of Jesuit Missions, news center of the world-wide mission activities of more than seven hundred American Jesuits.

On June 11, 1947, he and Father Hubbard, S.J., completed a 35,000 mile trip around the world, studying and filming Catholic missions. Father

Alexander went specifically to discuss and to study mission problems and needs with mission leaders both clerical and lay. He has been a consultant on the publishing of books of Jesuit missioners, as well as the organizer and founder of the Mission Seminary School, the Institute of Social Studies held at St. Louis University.

C. M. N.

Rudolf Allers 1883-

"Though born a Catholic and educated, or at least trained, in the Catholic religion, I had not developed a real faith. I always liked to read theology, however, and, even while a psychiatrist, found time to study several treatises on various problems of theology," writes Dr. Rudolf Allers. The sequel to this part of his religious history is that his experimental research and his study of abnormal neurotic personalities brought him more and more into contact with philosophical and metaphysical problems, and ultimately led him back to the Church. His closer contact with Catholic scholars contributed to strengthening his admiration for scholastic philosophy. What really made him a follower of Scholasticism was "the discovery of the immanent truth of this philosophy and of the possibility of using it for the sake of clarifying many a problem of science."

Dr. Allers was born in Vienna, Austria, January 13, 1883, the son of Mark Allers and Augusta (Grailich) Allers. Because his father, a physician, divided his work between Vienna, where he did research in winter, and a famous health resort in Bohemia, in summer, Dr. Allers received his early education at home. When eleven years old, he passed the final examination of the Volksschule in Vienna and became a student of the Gymnasium. After eight years of study, he passed the examination with honors and then matriculated at the Medical School of the University of Vienna, from which University he received his M.D. in 1906. Continuing his research in biological chemistry, he became an assistant in a laboratory of biological chemistry in 1907. In April 1908 he was appointed assistant at the Clinic for Nervous and Mental Diseases of the German University at Praha. It was in this year (1908) that he married Carola Meitner of Vienna. They have one son.

In April 1909 he became an assistant in the Psychiatrical Clinic at Munich, Bavaria, under Dr. Emil Kraepelin, one of the founders of modern psychiatry.

When the war broke out in 1914, Dr. Allers worked as a physician. His work varied. At first he was a surgeon in Vienna; then he was sent to Poland, and finally to a field hospital at the Polish-Russian frontier. In 1917 he was called back to Vienna to become a member of the staff in the War Ministry which had been established for research, and remained there until the end of the war. For his services as a physician he was given the Golden Cross of Merit with the Crown and the Medal of the German Red Cross.

In 1918 he took charge of the Department of Medical Psychology and Sense-Physiology of the Institute of Physiology at the Vienna Medical School. Here he had to work under difficult conditions. In these postwar years there was a lack of funds, of instruments, of fuel, and of other things. Often the temperature of the classroom was thirty-eight or forty degrees. Much of the apparatus had fallen into decay. There was no money to buy more. One had to depend rather on "invention and imagination than on ready-made complicated mechanical means."

Dr. Allers' interest had always turned on psychology. It was one of the reasons which made him choose the profession of psychiatry. He is also interested in philosophy. It has been the endeavor of Dr. Allers to show that "psychology cannot reach its own aims without being, on the one hand, philosophical and without staying in close contact with practice on the other hand."

Dr. Allers' technical works have not been translated. His first book written in English is *The New Psychologies* (1932). His other works in English are: *Psychology of Character* (1930); *Practical Psychology in Character Development* (1934); *Sex Psychology in Education* (1937); *Self-Improvement* (1939), and *The Successful Error* (1940).

Besides lecturing at the Catholic Summer University at Salzburg and teaching in various institutions, Dr. Allers acted for seven years as an expert in the Ecclesiastical Court especially in matrimonial cases.

He reads and writes German, English, French, Italian and Latin. His great passion is reading. Since February 1938, he has been professor of Psychology at the Catholic University of America.

M. H.

Peter Frederick Anson   1889-

The son of a British admiral and a collateral descendant of Admiral Lord Anson, "the Father of the British Navy," Peter Anson's chief interest is everything that has to do with seafaring, especially Scottish fishermen, in the midst of whom he lives. This interest was developed by living fourteen years of Benedictine life on Caldey Island, off the coast of Wales, and also by spending much time at sea with fishermen and other classes of seamen—British and foreign. He was one of the founders of the Apostleship of the Sea in 1920 and organizing secretary from 1920 to 1924.

Art and architecture, especially church architecture, also interest him. He is often asked to give advice about the decoration of churches and to supply designs.

With the other members of the Anglican Benedictine community of Caldey, he was received into the Catholic Church in 1913. Finding it impossible, owing to a bad breakdown in health, to remain with his

Benedictine brethren, he was clothed and professed a member of the Third Order of St. Francis, at Assisi, in 1924.

As an artist, he held the first exhibition of his drawings, and water colors of shipping in London, 1922. He has since exhibited at the Royal Academy, London, the Royal Scottish Academy, Edinburgh, and elsewhere. He is a founder of the Society of Marine Artists and prefers drawing to writing.

Peter Anson was born in Portsmouth, England, in August 1889, the son of Admiral Charles E. Anson and Evelyn (Ross) Anson. He was educated at Wixenford, Wokingham, then with private tutors, and later at the Architectural Association Schools, London.

Peter Anson has been a weekly contributor to the *Universe* since 1929. He has been the Scottish correspondent for the *Catholic Herald* since 1937. He illustrated Abbot Hunter-Blair's *A Medley of Memories* and his *Last Medley of Memories*.

He is the author and illustrator of *The Pilgrim's Guide to Franciscan Italy* (1927); *Fishing Boats and Fisher Folk on the East Coast of Scotland* (1930); *Mariners of Brittany* (1931); *Fishermen and Fishing Ways* (1931); *A Pilgrim Artist in Palestine* (1938); *The Quest of Solitude* (1932); *The Pilgrim's Sketch Books* (1934); *The Catholic Church in Modern Scotland* (1937); *The Story of the Apostleship of the Sea* (1938); *The Caravan Pilgrim* (1938); *The Scottish Fisheries—Are They Doomed?* (1939); *Benedictines of Caldéy* (1940); *Harbour Head* (his autobiography) (1945); *British Sea Fishermen* (1944), and *A Roving Recluse* (1946).

He is also a frequent contributor to the *Dublin Review, Pax, Franciscan Annals, The Month, Geographical Magazine, Fishing News* and others. His home is at Macduff, Banffshire, a small fishing port on the north coast of Scotland.

M. H.

George Elliot Anstruther 1870-1940

A busy working journalist, a prolific author of historical and controversial books and pamphlets, Mr. Anstruther was much in demand as a public speaker—notably in the East End of London—being the possessor of an easy and fluent style. His speeches always informative and reflecting a wide scholarship, were characterized by a sense of intense earnestness and conviction. Another weapon in his repertory as a speaker was a sharp but kindly Cockney wit.

He was born in London in 1870. In 1896 he married Lydia Mary Richardson. Two sons and two daughters were born of the marriage, one of the sons becoming a Dominican priest. In 1926, Mr. Anstruther attended the International Eucharistic Congress at Chicago, Illinois, as the lay speaker from England.

Evidence of Mr. Anstruther's organizing ability was shown in his work as Honorable Secretary of the Permanent Committee of the National

Catholic Congresses. He was also organizing secretary of the Catholic Truth Society from 1909 to 1920.

Editorial work occupied much of his time. From 1906 to 1909 he edited *The Universe;* from 1920 to 1936 he was Assistant Editor of the *Tablet.* Subsequently he served as Associate Editor of the *Catholic Herald,* the position he held up to his death on March 20, 1940. In all his literary work he was meticulously accurate.

He was an indefatigable worker in Catholic societies, notably, as the Honorable Secretary of the Historical Research Society, and The Guild of Our Lady of Ransom.

A great walker in his youth—he thought nothing of walking from London to Oxford—he gained much intimate knowledge of London from covering great distances just for the sake of exploring.

His books include: *William Hogarth; Catholic Answers to Protestant Charges; What is Orangeism?; The Protestant Platform; Caroline Chisholm; Edith O'Gorman and Her Book; A Hundred Years of Catholic Progress; Philip Fletcher,* and *The Blindness of Tomorrow.*

In 1938, in recognition of his work for the Church, Pope Pius XI bestowed upon him the Knighthood of St. Gregory the Great.

M. H.

Herbert Antcliffe, Jr. 1875-

With the intention that his eldest son follow him in his profession, Herbert Antcliffe, Sr. placed his son Herbert in the office of a large firm of accountants at Sheffield, his native city. In the words of Herbert Antcliffe, Jr., "nature, however, protested and in spite of my utmost efforts, I made no progress, while the long columns of figures with which I had often to deal made me physically sick." He was accordingly allowed to devote his studies to literature and music.

Herbert Antcliffe, Jr. was born on July 30, 1875. He was named Herbert after his father who in turn was named Herbert after George Herbert, the poet. He studied literature at the University of Sheffield, and music under his uncle, Worsley Staniford, a well-known organist and composer. He secured positions as organist and choirmaster in various churches, his spare time being devoted to reading history, both ecclesiastical and musical, on which subjects he frequently lectured. The preparation of these lectures and some visits to the continent of Europe, were intellectually the road which led him into the Catholic Church in 1914.

His first two books, published almost simultaneously, were a short study of the German composer Johannes Brahms (who had recently died) and *Living Music*—a popular introduction to the methods of modern music. Then followed *Schubert; How to Enjoy Music; Music in Europe Since Wagner; Short Studies on the Nature of Music; The Successful*

Music Teacher; Art, Religion and Clothes. He contributed to *Grove's Dictionary of Music and Musicians.*

As an historical writer, he endeavors to correlate musical history with general history, being one of the earliest workers of his generation to take up this subject. It has since been followed by other writers.

On the occasion of the fortieth anniversary of the coronation of Queen Wilhelmina of the Netherlands, Her Majesty appointed him a Chevalier of the Order of Orange Nassau, the only other foreigner in the list being Dr. F. M. Huebner, the well-known German writer on philosophy.

In January, 1939 he was elected President of the Foreign Press Association in Holland. He has always been active in improving the artistic relations between England and Holland. For five years he was under the Nazis in The Hague. In 1945 he was re-elected President of the Foreign Press Association in Holland.

In recognition of his services in propagating British music (and incidentally other British culture) in March 1939 King George VI granted Antcliffe a Civil List pension of one hundred pounds per year. These pensions are voted by Parliament and given on the personal nomination of the sovereign, to persons who have won distinction in civil life, particularly in literature and the arts.

M. H.

Reverend John Peter Arendzen 1873-

A clear thinker, and an exponent of difficult argument, the possessor of an eloquence which enlivens any technical matter, Dr. Arendzen is at his best when dealing with speculative issues, and answering objections. For many years his "Question Box" has been a feature in the *Catholic Gazette.*

His book *The Holy Trinity,* a theological treatise for modern laymen, is a feat of skill. Noted also for their clearness are his three books in The Treasury of the Faith Series, *Eternal Punishment; The Church Triumphant,* and *Extreme Unction.* These small works are very popular.

The Reverend John Peter Arendzen, the son of P. J. Arendzen, the famous Dutch etcher, and E. Stracke, was born at Amsterdam, Holland, on January 6, 1873. His theological course was taken at Oscott College, England, from 1891 to 1895. After his ordination in 1895, he went to the University of Bonn for two years, receiving a Ph.D. in Semitic philosophy. He studied at the University of Munich for his D.D. degree which he received in 1900. Christ's College, Cambridge conferred an A.M. on him for his research done there. He is an expert in Arabic.

Since 1937 he has been the Spiritual Director of St. Edmund's College, Ware and a Canon of the Metropolitan Chapter of Westminster since

1938. He is the one surviving member of the first three foundation members of the Catholic Missionary Society.

His works include: *Gospels: Fact, Myth or Legend; Prophets, Priests and Publicans; What Becomes of the Dead?; Whom Do You Say? Men and Manners in the Days of Christ; Things Temporal and Timeless; Reason and Religion,* and *Faith and Commonsense.* Twenty-nine articles were written by him for the *Catholic Encyclopedia* and he is frequently called upon to write for learned journals.   **M. H.**

Donald Attwater   1892-

Since about 1925 when he began to depend wholly on his pen for a living, Donald Attwater has written tirelessly and exquisitely on a variety of subjects, principally religious.

He was born on December 24, 1892, in Essex County, England, the eldest son of Walter J. Attwater, solicitor, and Lucy Alexandra (Roberson) Attwater, both of Faversham in the County of Kent. He was brought up as a Wesleyan Methodist until his tenth year, when he became an Episcopalian. He was educated at private schools and at a public school (in the English sense). He left school at sixteen to study law. He attended no university and has no degrees.

Upon the death of his father he had to abandon law and go to work in a publisher's office. When he was eighteen years of age he entered the Catholic Church "in the belief that Christ founded a visible Church. The Roman Church seemed on historical grounds to be that Church."

In 1913 he married Dorothy Bickle of Camborne, Cornwall, and went to live in Wales which was their home until 1934. They have one son and two daughters.

From 1916 to 1919 he was a soldier in the ranks, in the artillery, serving mostly in the Near East, India and Palestine. It was here that he became interested in the Eastern Churches and became "a specialist in the study of the Christian Orient," as The *Catholic World* calls him.

Donald Attwater himself gives the formative influences and background of his life:

"(1) A thorough grounding in the fundamentals of Christian faith and life in my home, my Protestant parents, being religious folk, active in public works for social justice and order. I got nothing but good from my Protestant upbringing.

"(2) The spiritual and intellectual influence of a Benedictine monastery for which I worked from 1914 to 1916 and from 1920 to 1923 in close association with the monks.

"(3) A rural upbringing, and an adult life of twenty continuous years (less three as a soldier) in remote country places, far removed from any city.

"(4) The discovery of a non-Thomist, non-Latin, non-juridical Catholic tradition in the East.

"(5) A continuous inability to earn more money than will just keep me and my family, that is, a sharing of the almost day-to-day economic uncertainty of so many of my fellow men."

He has also stated: "I hate all politics of all kinds, whether international, municipal or ecclesiastical . . . I believe that all organizations for good are useless—even pernicious—unless their first undertaking is to impress on the persons composing them their individual responsibility to seek first the Kingdom of God and His righteousness."

He is the author of: *Father Ignatius of Llanthony* (1931); *The Catholic Church in Modern Wales* (1935); *The Catholic Eastern Churches* (1935); *The White Fathers in Africa* (1937); *The Dissident Eastern Churches* (1937); *The Golden Book of Eastern Saints* (1938); *A Dictionary of Saints* (1939); *A Dictionary of the Popes* (1939); *Life of St. John Chrysostom* (1939); *Names and Name Days* (1939), and *Eastern Catholic Worship* (1945).

He is concise and lucid in all his writings. He was the Editor in Chief of *The Catholic Encyclopedic Dictionary* (1931); *Pax, The Quarterly Review* of the Benedictines of Caldey, 1922-28; joint editor with Father Thurston, S.J. of Volumes VII-XII of *Butler's Lives of the Saints* (1932-38).

He translated from Middle English, Langland's *Piers Plowman;* from the French he translated several works of Nicholas Berdyaev, one work of Solovyev *(God, Man and the Church)*, one of Gheon and some others.

He is a contributor to the principal English and American Catholic papers.

In 1937 he visited the United States and is anxious to return.

M. H.

Eugene Bagger 1892-

Eugene Bagger, who "has some profound thoughts, and when need be is not above using a hammer to drive them in," was born in Budapest, Hungary, on March 21, 1892. Of Jewish parents, the future journalist, author, linguist, and philosopher was sent to the State Gymnasium at the age of ten. Equivalent of the French lycée, the Gymnasium was an eight year combination of preparatory school, high school, and college. Throughout those eight years he was at the head of his class. As a student of Latin and history he evinced a curiosity about Catholicism. The reading of Chesterton's works, together with a teacher's influence, effected his conversion at seventeen—a conversion, however, which proved only superficial. His Catholicism was not strong enough to withstand familiarity with Freudian psychoanalysis and current intellectual fads, and he became negligent. Three years after matriculation he left the University of Budapest, without his degree. His father died meanwhile, so the young man had to go to work. He obtained a position on a Budapest newspaper owned by the father of one of his friends. This was in the year 1911, when he was nineteen. In the next two years he acquired some standing as a rising young journalist with his signed half-literary, half-news stories of the kind that characterized Continental newspapers. By 1913 he got tired of it, resigned and went to Copenhagen to study Scandinavian literature; he had learned Danish at the age of sixteen to be able to read Ibsen in the original. From Copenhagen he visited England and Ireland. After the outbreak of the first World War he published, in Copenhagen newspapers, several articles advocating the cause of the Entente against Prussian militarism, and also self-determination for the "oppressed" nationalities, so-called, of the Austro-Hungarian Empire. This blocked his return to his native country. Today he recognizes that the issues at stake in the first World War were not as clear-cut as he then thought. He still believes that the Western Allies were, on the whole, in the right against Prussia, but he realizes that Austria-Hungary was in the right against Russian imperialism and he realizes also that the destruction of the Hapsburg Empire by the Allied victory merely paved the way for the destruction of European civilization by the "mechanized neo-barbarism" of the totalitarian heresy in its Nazi and Communist versions.

In December 1914 he sailed for the United States. At first he worked for a Hungarian socialist newspaper in New York City, and then for another Hungarian daily in Cleveland, Ohio. Subsequently he joined the staff of the Cleveland *Press,* and after the armistice he became editorial writer on the New York *Tribune. The New Republic, Century Magazine,* and other high-brow periodicals also accepted his contributions. He became an American citizen in 1920.

Toward the end of 1921 he resigned from the *Tribune,* to do freelance journalism. At this time a friend, "an older man well-versed in the ways of this world, came to me . . . and said, why not write a book? I said why not indeed, but what sort of book, and who would publish a book written by a nonentity like myself? My friend said, 'I shall tell you.' And he did." A few days later Mr. Bagger signed a contract with George Palmer Putnam, the publisher. Late in 1922 this book, about currently eminent Europeans, appeared, and scored some success.

A newspaper assignment took him to Vienna in March 1923, but in October he was again in New York. In January he was once more on his way to Europe, having secured a roving commission as a feature writer for the Sunday Magazine of the New York *Times.* In London he interviewed some prominent British scholars and scientists concerning the decay of Western civilization as announced by Spengler's then famous work *The Decline of the West.* Next, he returned to Vienna to write the first biography in English of Francis Joseph, Emperor of Austria and King of Hungary. This book, published by Putnam's in 1927, he now disavows as an "unsound work, a regrettable monument of my temporary aberration into unhistoric doctrinaire liberalism; an unfair attack on the old Austrian Emperor—who knew his job as a ruler better than I knew mine as a biographer—and an unintelligent account of the Hapsburg Empire which has been the last bulwark of our traditional Catholic culture on the eastern marches of Europe."

In 1927 he quit his work for the New York *Times* and took up his abode on the coast of Provence. He wrote a play and had it accepted by a Paris producer. But this play was never performed, the producer having gone into bankruptcy. For the next few years his output was limited to a few articles published in *Harper's,* and a kind of column in the Paris edition of the Chicago *Tribune.* He planned a biography of Stendhal but eventually condensed the results of his research into an essay which, under the title "The First of the Moderns" was published in the *Atlantic Monthly* in 1934.

While living at Le Trayas, a little village on the Provençal coast, he took up in a rather haphazard way the study of philosophy, which eventually led to his return to the Church. On this subject he likes to quote Chesterton's saying, "There are two ways of getting home and one of them is to stay there. The other way is to walk round the world till you come back to the same place." "Mine," he adds, "was the long way." He recognized in the lack of fixed principles and standards in modern philosophy the source of the disintegration of Western civilization and finally discovered that the Catholic Church and the philosophy of Saint Thomas Aquinas contain all the answers. The turning point of his spiritual and intellectual development came when he read Maritain's *Three Reformers.* He says he owes his reconversion to these three, Luther, Descartes, and Rousseau, "for it was by the study of their works that I came to understand the radical absurdity, the self-defeating dialectic, of the world-view of Modernity, of all that happened in the spheres of religion and philosophy since the sixteenth century."

After the fall of France in 1940 he returned to the United States and incorporated the story of his spiritual and intellectual pilgrimage in a philosophical autobiography entitled *For the Heathen Are Wrong*—"an account of the end of our time in terms of one man's life." In this book he also analyses the fall of France, in which he sees the epitome and symbol of the fall of modern civilization, as the inevitable result of the One and Indivisible Revolution which began in the religious sphere with Luther, in the philosophical sphere with Descartes, in the moral sphere with Rousseau, and in the political sphere with the Jacobins. "There are many things in this book which I should say differently if I had a chance to write it again. Above all, I am sorry that I went too far in expressing my hatred of the Germans. Today I realize that the sins of Nazi Germany are fundamentally the sins of us all. The third Reich and its bigger and more dangerous successor, Communist Russia, are the punishment visited, in the natural order by Providence on our apostate culture. Hitler was, and Stalin is, the hammer of God; we are the anvil." His wife, an Englishwoman, and her two sons from her first marriage are also converts to the Faith.

He is currently working on two books, one being the sequel to *For the Heathen Are Wrong,* the other a selection from the works of the Swiss Catholic philosopher Gonzague de Reynold which he edits, translates and introduces. He sums up his view of history in two sentences:

"No human institution can endure if it be not supported by the hand of Him Who supports all. 'Sine tuo numine, nihil est in homine, nihil est innoxium.' "

M. H.

Charles Sears Baldwin   1867-1935

 With fifteen years of service as a professor of English at Yale (1895-1911) and the last twenty-four years of his life teaching at Barnard College and Columbia University, Charles Sears Baldwin thought of himself not as a writer or a scholar, but always as a teacher. Born in New York City in 1867, he died there in 1935. As a boy of seventeen, he entered Columbia College on Madison Avenue and received his A.B. in 1888. He did his graduate work also at Columbia, where he was one of the earliest to whom Columbia granted the Ph.D. degree in English, and one of the first instructors appointed to teach English in Barnard College.

Most of his life an Episcopalian, Dr. Baldwin became a convert to Catholicism in March 1934. He came to know and love the Catholic Church through the literature of the Middle Ages. As Dr. William Haller in the Columbia University *Quarterly* for December 1935 puts it, "He gave his allegiance to that ideal of an ordered, unified, Catholic civilization resting upon faith which he found best expressed in medieval literature and mystically embodied in the historic Christian Church. He was of the communion of St. Thomas, Dante, Erasmus and St. Thomas More."

Dr. Baldwin's forte in teaching was an emphasis on how to express one's thoughts clearly and concisely. His principal books are concerned with (1) the art of writing and speaking: *College Manual of Rhetoric* (1902), *Composition, Oral and Written* (1909), (1924); (2) the history of literature: *Three Medieval Centuries of Literature in England 1100-1400* (1932); (3) scholarly treatises on the history of rhetoric: *Ancient Rhetoric and Poetic* (1924), *Medieval Rhetoric and Poetic* (1928), and a recent work published posthumously, *Renaissance Literary Theory and Practice* (1939); (4) reviews, some verse, a few essays, some collected in *Essays Out of Hours* (1907), and *God Unknown* (1920).

M. H.

Reverend Rudolph G. Bandas 1896-

Father Bandas is one of those writers on theological, philosophical and biblical subjects who are so constantly necessary and useful in the teaching task of the Church. He is a native of Minnesota, having been born at Silver Lake, Minnesota, in 1896. He received all his college and seminary training there—at the University of Minnesota, St. Thomas College (A.B. 1917) and St. Paul Seminary (S.T.B. 1921). His graduate work was done both at Louvain and at the Angelico in Rome; from both he received doctorates, and from the former, the much-prized Masterate in Sacred Theology—a higher degree than the doctorate, of which only about seventy persons have been recipients in the last hundred years.

Having completed his extended training in the sacred sciences, Father Bandas returned to teach at St. Paul Seminary and has greatly enlarged his sphere of influence through his most valuable studies in his various fields of interest. He has likewise contributed extensively to *Thought, The American Ecclesiastical Review, The Pastoral and Homiletic Review.*

Dr. Bandas is professor of dogmatic theology and catechetics at the St. Paul Seminary. Besides holding several positions in the archdiocesan curia, he is also Archdiocesan Director of the Confraternity of Christian Doctrine, Catholic Students' Mission Crusade, the Catholic Youth Council, and the National Organization for Decent Literature. He is Chairman of the Seminary Catechetical Department of the National Center of the Confraternity of Christian Doctrine and Associate Editor of *Our Parish Confraternity.* In June 1945 he succeeded the Most Reverend James L. Connolly, Coadjutor Bishop of Fall River, as rector of the St. Paul Seminary.

Dr. Bandas is the author of the following books: *The Master Idea of St. Paul's Epistles* (1925); *Catechetical Methods* (1929); *Contemporary Philosophy and Thomistic Principles* (1931); *Practical Problems in Religion* (1934); *Catechetics in the New Testament* (1934); *Biblical Questions, Old Testament* (1934); *Biblical Questions, New Testament* (1935); *Religion Teaching and Practice* (1935); *Modern Questions* (6 vols.) (1941).

A recent achievement of his was the publication of a complete course in religion from the kindergarten through high school and college, for Catholic students attending public schools and secular institutions.

Reverend Albert R. Bandini   1882-

Since 1907 Father Albert Bandini has been a resident of the United States and a naturalized citizen since 1916. He had come to the United States at the invitation of Bishop McQuade of Rochester to whom he was recommended by priests of the Rochester diocese who were sent to Florence, Italy, to study Italian. These priests had met Father Bandini in Florence and learned of his reputation as a student of the classics.

Father Bandini was born in Florence, Italy, on October 22, 1882 and was educated at the Archdiocesan Seminary. After his ordination to the priesthood in 1905 he was appointed Assistant Pastor at Quintole near Florence. Two years later he resigned to accept Bishop McQuade's invitation to teach Latin and Greek at St. Andrew's College, the preparatory seminary at Rochester, New York.

Feeling that he should do more for his people, he left Rochester and was accepted by Archbishop Ireland. From 1910 to 1914 he was Pastor of Our Lady of Mt. Carmel Church, Minneapolis, Minnesota.

When at Rochester, Father Bandini met the late Archbishop of San Francisco, Edward J. Hanna, then a seminary professor. Later when Professor Hanna became Auxiliary Bishop he invited Father Bandini to California and he has been there ever since. His first assignment was at St. Gertrude's Church, Stockton, California, where he served as Assistant Pastor from 1915 to 1920. From 1921 to 1927 he was Pastor of St. Michael's Church also in Stockton, California, and from 1927 to 1932 he was Pastor of St. Joseph's Church at Cotati, California. Since then he has been Pastor of St. Rose of Lima Church at Crockett, California. For his activities in behalf of Italian culture in the United States, he was awarded a medal by the Italian Government.

Father Bandini translated into English "terza rima" Dante's *Divine Comedy*. The last three Cantos of the "Paradiso" were published in *The Book of Christian Classics* edited by Michael Williams. He also published a volume of essays entitled *Life Is Too Short*, a play *Catherine of Siena* and other short works. Besides, he has contributed to the *American Ecclesiastical Review, The Catholic World, Commonweal,* and other publications.

Recently he has taken up music with more earnestness than formerly and he has published several pieces, especially an *Ave Maria* which has merit. He has also lectured on literary and social questions. He has given much thought to the subject of universal peace and has published a few pamphlets on it.

One of the founders of the Italian Catholic Federation of California in 1924 he served as its Grand Chaplain and for several years as its president. He edits their monthly bulletin. Although he studied law and was admitted to the California Bar he has not practised that profession.

Father Bandini is a Knight, Order of the Crown of Italy, and Knight, Holy Military Order of St. George.   M. H.

Maurice Baring 1874-1945

Author of more than fifty books, Maurice Baring became widely known as a novelist, poet, dramatist, historian, critic, journalist, and diplomat.

An interesting account of him as a journalist has been contributed by Captain Francis McCullagh, who writes: "The war correspondents who awaited assignment to various parts of the Russian Front in the spring of 1904 were a mixed group—Russian, American, British, Irish, German, Italian, French, and Danish. One day we were told that a new colleague was to join us, an Englishman, the Honorable Maurice Baring, youngest son of Lord Revelstoke. Baring was tall, and timid. Gentleness, sincerity and even humility were written all over him—in his smile, in his blue eyes, in his hearty handshake. His dress had certainly never been put together in Bond Street. It seemed to be of Russo-Chinese manufacture partly hidden by a shapeless overcoat with the wool inside. On his head towered a papakha that looked like an episcopal miter. On his feet were Russian top-boots. His two horses were far inferior to mine which had been sent me by a Tientsin racing man.

"About six months afterwards he asked me to bring him to the camp of Mishchenko, the famous Cossack leader, on the edge of No Man's Land, but for some reason or other Mishchenko did not like him. Perhaps it was because Baring knew so well the Russian language, Russian history, Russian literature, and even the songs and fairy tales of the Cossacks that the old man was afraid to open his mouth. Perhaps it was because Mishchenko was anti-English and did not like the help that John Bull had given to the Japanese. At all events he ceased talking while Baring was his unwelcome guest, and, as he was usually an inexhaustible talker, the whole staff was alarmed. Next day no food was cooked, whereupon Baring took the hint and left, very quietly. Nevertheless, when describing this visit, long after the war, in *The Puppet Show of Memory,* Baring speaks nothing but good of Mishchenko. Very few correspondents would have been so forgiving."

In his book *Lost Lectures* (1932), Baring states he had suffered all his life from the fact that all the high-brows thought he was a low-brow and all the low-brows thought he was a high-brow.

Maurice Baring was born April 27, 1874, the fourth son of the first Lord Revelstoke. He was educated at Eton and Trinity College, Cambridge. His father was the former Edward Charles Baring, a partner in the London mercantile firm of Baring Brothers & Co.

His productions whether in drama, poetry or romance would remain quite unintelligible if one did not go back to his early years, his education and training. The environment in which he lived had much to do with what he wrote.

His earliest years were spent either in Berkeley Square where his family passed the winter or at Coombe Cottage where the summers were usually spent. In these formative years, he played with dolls, "but not as girls do, mothering them and dressing them. Mine were little tiny dolls, and could not be dressed or undressed and they were used as puppets. I made them open Parliament, act plays and stories, and not infrequently take the part of the French Merovingian kings. This was the beginning of the school-room period," he wrote in his autobiography, *The Puppet Show of Memory*. The idea and very name of puppet so influenced his life that his remotest memories are recalled through them. "Our house," he writes in *The Puppet Show of Memory*, "was saturated with an atmosphere of music. My mother played the violin and was a fine concertina player, and almost before I could walk I had violin lessons from no less a person than Mr. Ries. Until I was three I was called Strad."

In 1884 his education at home ceased and he was sent to a school near Ascot. In 1889 he went to Eton. He liked Eton because they treated one "like a grown-up person." His favorite haunt was the library. It was there, during his last year, that he made, by himself, the discovery of English poetry. He read the works of Shelley and the poems of Keats. There also he made the friendship of Arthur Benson through one of his pupils. Mr. Benson was most kind and took an interest in him. On Sunday afternoons he would come to Mr. Benson's rooms and read poetry. Benson in these meetings, stimulated Baring's reading tremendously.

In 1891 Mr. Baring had a little book of poems privately printed at Eton called *Damozel Blanche* consisting of ballads and lyrics. This was his first book of poems printed. Another book of poems was privately printed after he had left Eton and was given as a Christmas present to his mother.

After spending a year in Germany, on his return to England he left Eton for Cambridge. There he passed a preliminary examination for the diplomatic service which he was already proposing to adopt for his career. It was not until 1898 that he passed his last examination. The time intervening was spent travelling. In this same year (1898) he was nominated to be attaché to the Paris embassy; transferred to Copenhagen in 1900; became third secretary in the same year; transferred to Rome in 1902 and then was employed in the Foreign Office from 1903 to 1904.

Disliking diplomacy as a career, he resigned. He went to St. Petersburg and then to Moscow in Russia. While there the Russo-Japanese War broke out. He accepted an offer from the *Morning Post* (now defunct) to be their military correspondent. At the end of 1907 he returned to London, dividing his time between journalism and writing books.

Baring's first experience with the Catholic Church was by accident in 1884 when he was ten years of age. At Contrexeville, where he was staying, he met a charming old curé; with him he visited a Catholic Church for the first time. The impression did not last. While in Paris in 1899 he attended a low Mass in the Church of Our Lady of Victories.

The silence and the attitude of the worshippers overwhelmed him. He was also awed while assisting at a solemn Mass in St. Peter's during the celebration of Pope Leo XIII's jubilee in 1902. In 1909 he was received into the Catholic Church by Father Sebastian Bowden at the Brompton Oratory. Of his conversion, Mr. Baring called it "the only action of my life which I am quite certain I have never regretted." Though brought up in the Protestant tradition he never adhered, with conviction, to any denomination. His intellectual life crowded out religious curiosity.

In 1914 he served with the British Expeditionary Force. He was promoted to Staff Lieutenant in 1915 and a month later Captain. In 1916 he was made a Staff Captain and the following year a Major. From January to April 1918 he was the Personal Secretary to General Sir Hugh Trenchard. He was demobilized in 1919. In 1925 he was granted an honorary commission as Wing-Commander in Reserve of Air Force Officers. For the last three years of his life he was bedridden from a form of paralysis. He died at Beaufort Castle, Scotland, on December 15, 1945.

Mr. Baring wrote the following books: *The Black Prince* (1902); *With the Russians in Manchuria* (1905); *Sonnets and Short Poems* (1906); *A Year in Russia* (1907); *Proserpine* (1908); *Russian Essays and Stories* (1909); *Landmarks in Russian Literature* (1910); *Dead Letters* (1910); *Collected Poems* (1911); *The Russian People* (1911); *The Grey Stocking and other Plays* (1912); *Letters from the Near East* (1913); *What I Saw in Russia* (1913); *Lost Diaries* (1913); *The Main-Springs of Russia* (1914); *An Outline of Russian Literature* (1914); *The Puppet Show of Memory* (1922); *Punch and Judy and other Essays* (1924); *Collected Poems* (1925); *Cat's Cradle* (1925); *Daphne Adeane* (1926); *Tinker's Leave* (1927); *The Coat Without Seam* (1929); *In the End Is My Beginning* (1931); *Sarah Bernhardt* (1933); *The Lonely Lady of Dulwich* (1934), and *Have You Anything to Declare?* (1936).   F. M. and M. H.

Lillian Barker

Starting out with two ambitions—to sing and to write Lillian Barker became a writer through her singing. Her singing teacher in Atlanta, Georgia, where she was born and reared, advised her to go to New York to study for opera. This advice she took, but instead of continuing her musical career she developed her flair for writing when assigned by French and Italian papers to "cover" musical events in Manhattan. The reviews were so well received she decided to try her hand at straight reporting. Returning South, she held jobs in various cities as reporter, interviewer and feature writer. Then she went to Washington, D.C., and worked for the *Washington Post*. Because of her fluency in French and Italian she got many assignments to interview celebrities. With her reputation as star reporter and linguist well established, she later became a foreign correspondent for leading newspaper syndicates, "covering" European capitals. From 1928 to 1929, she was stationed in Paris; in 1930 in Rome. While in Paris, she took special courses in French and literature at the Sorbonne.

Returning to New York in 1931, she resolved to devote all her time to writing fiction. Innumerable short stories and serials were written. Three of these were published in book form: *Cabaret Love* (1933); *The Wheel of Love* (1933); *Spanish Blonde* (1938).

The birth of the Dionne Quints, May 28, 1934 lured her back to newspaper work again. When she learned that their mother was a devout Catholic and spoke only French, she made up her mind to go to Callendar, Ontario and write her biography for the Chicago *Tribune*—New York News Syndicate. Although reporters in general were already being turned away from the Dionne home, Miss Barker, through her sympathy, tact and command of French, persuaded Elzire Dionne, the world's most famous mother to tell her story. Miss Barker is the only writer ever to be the farmhouse guest of the Dionne family. She shared in the family life, talked to the neighbors and friends—and observed the Quints. She has covered twenty-five Dionne assignments including the presentation of the parents and the quintuplets to the King and Queen of England in Toronto in May, 1939. The confidante of the Dionnes, she has become their official biographer. Her book *The Quints Have a Family* was published by Sheed and Ward. The Dionne parents have also twice visited Lillian Barker in her New York apartment.

Because of her knowledge of the Quints, her dynamic personality and charm, Miss Barker is in demand as a lecturer. Although she doesn't like lecturing, she does it to offset the vicious propaganda about the Dionne family. She feels it her duty to tell the world the truth.

In 1936 she went to Hollywood, California as a scenario writer, and worked for Universal Pictures Corporation.

Miss Barker has also done comic strips and has "ghosted" biographies.

M. H.

Right Reverend Arthur Stapylton Barnes
1861-1936

The late Monsignor Arthur Barnes was born in Kussonli, India, May 31, 1861. He was the second son of the late George Carnac Barnes, Foreign Secretary to the Government of India and the late Margaret Diana Chetwynd Stapylton. He was educated at Eton, The Royal Military Academy, Woolwich, Oxford and Cambridge. From 1877 to 1879 he served as a lieutenant in the Royal Artillery. He was ordained in the Church of England. In 1895 he was received into the Catholic Church by Cardinal Merry del Val at Rome. Three years later he was ordained a priest. He served as Catholic Chaplain at the University of Cambridge, 1902 to 1916, at Oxford from 1918 to 1926. He was co-editor of the *Dublin Review*, 1915-1917.

He has written the following books: *St. Peter in Rome* (1900); *The Man of the Mask* (1908); *The Early Church in the Light of the Monuments* (1913); *Bishop Barton and Anglican Orders* (1922); *The Catholic Schools in England* (1926); *The Martyrdom of St. Peter and St. Paul* (1933), and *The Holy Shroud of Turin* (1934).

Monsignor Barnes died November 13, 1936.   M. H.

Reverend Alfred Barrett, S.J. 1906-

Father Barrett was born in August 1906 in Flushing, Long Island, New York, the son of the late Alfred M. Barrett, Public Service Commissioner of New York. Although he has published only one slender book of poems, the quality of that slim little book is such as to warrant recognition. The book, *Mint by Night* was hailed by almost all critics as being the work of an outstanding talent, giving great promise for the future.

After the completion of his preliminary studies at Xavier High School, New York in 1924, Father Barrett entered the Society of Jesus at St. Andrew-on-Hudson. He received his Bachelor of Arts degree from St. Andrew-on-Hudson in 1930 and his Master of Arts degree from the same college in 1931. After advanced studies at Woodstock he was ordained in 1937. From 1931 to 1934 he was Professor of Poetry at Canisius College, and from 1940 to 1945 he was chaplain of the Catholic Poetry Society of America. From 1939 until he received his commission as First Lieutenant in the Army in 1942 he was Associate Editor of the *Messenger of the Sacred Heart*. Assigned to the 35th Coast Artillery Anti-aircraft Battalion, he was the 101st Jesuit to enter the Armed Forces of the United States as Chaplain. On August 21, 1943, he was promoted to the rank of Captain. He spent 18 months in Texas with the Army Air Force; then two years overseas in England and France. He was discharged in February, 1946, as a Major.

Father Barrett is the eldest of nine children; three of his sisters are Sisters of St. Joseph, one is a Carmelite nun, and one brother is a member of the Order of Preachers. He is an instructor in Literature in Fordham College and Director of the Fordham *Monthly*, the oldest extra-curricular student activity at the University. In 1947 he was appointed director of the publication division of the Department of Communication Arts at Fordham University.

Father Barrett says that his favorite sources are "the Fathers of the Church and the metaphysical poets of the seventeenth century. Of moderns I am especially interested in Father Hopkins and Eileen Duggan." His poetic style is precise and illuminating. Egerton Clarke, the English critic, has said: "The Thomist verbal economy and conciseness of vision, as well as phrase, are abundantly evident in Father Barrett's work. His thought is profound; his expression simple and above all, economical." This concise, gritty verse is of an extremely high order. One can only hope that Father Barrett will, later on, attempt some poem frankly ambitious in length and matter. He is working on a drama of the Passion, *The Garden of Olives,* in which he hopes to externalize the agonizing vision of Our Lord in the manner of such modern followers of the Grecian tragedies as T. S. Eliot and Violet Clifton.

Besides his one book of poems, *Mint by Night* (1938), Father Barrett is also the author of several booklets including *The White Plume of Aloysius; A Short Life in the Saddle,* and *Captain of His Soul.*

Reverend James Francis Barrett   1888-1934

As a novelist, Father Barrett's aim was to portray the principles of Christian doctrine. He wrote to edify rather than to make money.

Father Barrett was born in Bridgeport, Connecticut, on September 1, 1888. He received his grammar school education at the Sacred Heart School, and his secondary education at Bridgeport High School. Upon graduation, he went to St. Thomas Seminary, Hartford, Connecticut. His higher studies for the priesthood were pursued at St. John's Seminary, Brighton, Massachusetts, and at St. Mary's Seminary, Baltimore, Maryland. Previous to ordination he was a prefect at St. Thomas Seminary, Hartford for one year. He was ordained to the priesthood on June 26, 1914 by the late Bishop Nilan.

The next three months he served as temporary chaplain at St. Francis Hospital, Hartford. He was then assigned as curate at the Immaculate Conception Church, Hartford, where he spent the entire sixteen years of his curacy. For several years he was principal of the parochial school.

All of his writing had to be done in leisure moments. In his books vice is punished and virtue rewarded. Of his four novels the two best known are *The Loyalist* and *The Winter of Discontent.*

In his first novel, *The Loyalist,* Father Barrett stressed the point that the founders of our country had a guide in the Catholic Church. He also makes it clear that Catholics are taught to be true to their country and true to their fellow citizens.

His second published novel *The Winter of Discontent* shows the folly of sin—that one reaps what he sows.

His third book was a text, *Elements of Psychology for Nurses.* While Father Barrett's studies in psychology were brought out in three volumes, the second volume is the most popular and is now being used in one hundred twenty-six educational institutions.

The Creature Man, his last book, was completed a few weeks before his death.

In 1930 he was made pastor of St. Patrick's Church, Farmington, where, for four years he attended zealously to the spiritual needs of the faithful. He died on May 29, 1934.

M. H.

Charles Barry *see* Charles Bryson

Philip Barry 1896-

Philip Barry, one of the most gifted dramatists of our contemporary American Theatre, was dubbed "poet and paradox" by a recent critic because of the variety, and even the contrasts, found in his work.

The skeleton facts of Mr. Barry's life are in themselves interesting. He was born in Rochester, New York, in 1896, with a goodly heritage of Celtic blood and Catholic faith behind him. Yale gave him his A.B., after which he served for a few months during 1918-1919 in the Code Department of the United States Embassy in London, returning to this country to do postgraduate work at Harvard. Here, in Doctor George Pierce Baker's celebrated "Workshop 47," his first play *You and I* won—and quite obviously merited—the first prize in 1922. This three-act comedy ran for six months in New York.

It showed already the brilliant dialogue, poetic imagination and subtle understanding of human nature which were to distinguish his later work.

Entering the professional theater through this academic door, Barry continued for several years to write plays which the critics praised but the audiences somewhat neglected. *The Youngest* (1924), *White Wings* (1926), *In a Garden* (1925), were some of these—also *John,* a dramatic study of Saint John the Baptist. Then, in 1927, he probably decided to give the public what it wanted, and his *Paris Bound* became a spectacular if slightly scandalous success. But in spite of the sophistication which goes along with the so-called "cocktail school of drama," this comedy of manners was at root a defense of the sanctity and reality of the marriage bond. Neither here nor in the pathetic story of *Tomorrow and Tomorrow* would he tolerate divorce as a solution; the only criticism which can be validly brought against these plays is that they may be too pitifully tolerant of infidelity. Beyond all such cavilling is *Holiday* (1929), that delightful and very American comedy of a woman who knew what she really wanted, and of mismated lovers reassigned before the bell tolls.

In 1930 Mr. Barry ventured into the field of psychological and psychoanalytical drama with *Hotel Universe,* a study of frustration in which he experiments very tellingly with time and eternity, the conscious, subconscious and superconscious mind. The following year brought his *Animal Kingdom,* an excoriation of the selfish wife. And in 1933 came that play of richly Catholic motivation, *The Joyous Season*—a penetrating and highly artistic study of a Catholic family disintegrating because of worldliness, but brought back to integrity by the human and super-human wisdom of the young daughter nun home for a Christmas visit. This blending of the author's realistic and mystical sides is again apparent in the tremendous if less coherent vindication of free will which goes by the challenging title of *Here Come the Clowns* (1938), in many ways Philip Barry's most interesting drama so far.

After the financial failure of the latter, he seems to have gone on playing alternately from the brittle and the fanciful sides of his genius. The very successful *Philadelphia Story* was followed by *Liberty Jones,* a patriotic allegory or "Ballet with Words for City Children," with verse, music and dancing—and this in turn by the recent sophisticated comedy with political overtones, *Without Love.* His admirers still wait for even greater work which will be a fusing of all of his powers.

Mr. Barry was married in 1922 to Miss Ellen Semple, and rejoices in two sons, Philip and Jonathan. While he considers Jupiter Island in Hobe Sound, Florida, as "home," he naturally spends much time in New York City, where he is a member of the National Institute of Arts and Letters, the American Society of Dramatists, the Authors' League, and the Yale, University, Century, Players, Coffee House and other clubs. Fishing is one of his hobbies—and international statesmanship, especially resolving the English-Irish-American triangle, one of his heart interests.

K. B.

Right Reverend William F. Barry   1849-1930

As a writer Canon Barry was one of the best-known men of the past half century. He lived until the end of 1930, and published a book in that same year, but his flavor and style is of an earlier day, and his name is rapidly becoming but a name. This is sad, for his achievement was heroic in its proportions, and much that he wrote still holds interest for a reader not frightened by that ponderosity of style which so appealed to Victorian men of letters.

Even if his books are no longer widely read, his life remains interesting because of its intimate contact with so long a span of history. William Barry was born in London in 1849 of Irish parents and educated at Oscott near Birmingham. From there he went to the English College and the Gregorian University at Rome at the time of the dramatic sessions of the Vatican Council. He saw the events of September 20, 1870—and lived to see the Lateran Pact, truly something that happened to few priests. He was ordained priest in

Rome in 1873. Shortly after his return to England he was for a short time an assistant priest at Saint Chad's Cathedral in Birmingham. He was then designated as vice-president and professor of philosophy at the new theological Olton College (formal opening, 1873). Within two years Canon Barry was writing for the *Dublin Review,* where he more and more found a sympathetic editor and public. The *Dublin Review* seldom went to press without an article from his pen. He later wrote: "I now had the *Dublin* as a free estate, where I could take up as much room as I chose." In 1885 he had easy access to the *Contemporary Review,* which normally would not have been described as having a Catholic bias. He had arrived. Then came his first novel, *The New Antigone,* published pseudo-anony-mously. There followed a succession of works of history, theology, philos-ophy, fiction, belles lettres. The fiction, which is not at all unreadable today, principally concerned itself with the projection of a Christian light upon the most un-Christian life and manners of that day. It pas-sionately called for economic justice to the poor which was a new idea in the novel in 1887. It held up to scorn in Christian eyes the vanities in-duced by a thoroughly materialistic attitude toward life, which was the most dubious of the achievements of Victoria's day—an achievement for which we are still paying.

The genuine honesty and scrupulousness of the man are shown in his historical works treating of the Papacy. Here he erred. if anything, by treating the popes too harshly, certainly not by minimizing their historic failings. His strict integrity is also shown in his life of Renan, whose views he might not share but whose talents he vastly admired. It is a further tribute to his fairness of spirit that he should have been asked to give, in 1897, the centenary addresses on Edmund Burke both in Dublin and London, for Burke is a Protestant hero perhaps more than a Catholic.

His critical essays deal with English, French, Italian, and German authors. His book *The World's Debate* is a defense of the Allies against German accusations. His *Tradition of Scripture* is a Bible compendium for Catholic students. When Newman was raised to the cardinalate in 1879, Barry in the chair of divinity at Oscott was chosen to write the con-gratulatory address of the college. His articles in *The Catholic Encyclo-pedia* are numerous.

Along with his writings, he administered one parish for twenty-five years and another for sixteen years. He had a genius for friendship. He was an omniverous reader.

Canon Barry was a valiant man, who wrote much and well and deserved the respect of his peers. Other books of his include: *Two Stand-ards* (1899); *Arden Massiter* (1900); *Place of Dreams* (1901); *Wizard's Knot* (1901); *Dayspring* (1903); *Higher Criticism* (1906); *Papacy and Modern Times* (1911); *Memories and Opinions* (1927); *Roma Sacra* (1927); *Triumph of Life* (1928), and *The Coming Age and The Catholic Church* (1930).

H. B.

George Barton   1866-1940

The late Philadelphia newspaperman, prolific writer of detective thrillers and columnist, George Barton, liked to tell his friends that he considered his weekly contribution to the *Catholic Standard and Times* entitled "Walks and Talks," under the pen name of The Rambler, the most representative of his writings.

Born in Philadelphia, January 22, 1866, he was a son of George and Maria (Gormley) Barton. He was educated in the public schools of the city. In 1893 he married Sophia McCauley. He was the father of four children, and he used humorously to say that he considered himself rather patriotic because he was married on Flag Day, his first son was born on the 4th of July and his second boy saw the light of day on Washington's Birthday.

At nineteen Barton began his newspaper work with the Philadelphia *Inquirer* as a bit news reporter; later he became an editorial writer for the Philadelphia *Bulletin* and later still returned as editorial writer for the *Inquirer,* where he remained until his death.

A man of diversified talent, his writings cover many fields. As special writer he wrote up inaugurations in Harrisburg and in Washington, wrote a series of juveniles, each devoted to a different sport—baseball, football, basketball, and rowing. Larger works comprise *Angels of the Battlefield,* the history of the work of the nuns in the Civil War (1898), *Barry Wynn,* a story of the United States Congress (1912), and *Columbus, the Catholic.*

All through his newspaper life he wrote detective stories, writing some two hundred in all. Some ten years ago when the *Literary Digest* put out ten volumes of *100 of The World's Best Detective Stories,* they included in them four of Barton's.

He greatly loved Philadelphia, its history and its beauty. Two of his books, *Little Journeys Around Philadelphia* and *Walks and Talks Around Old Philadelphia,* portray vividly the attractive spots of his home city. History was one of his favorite topics, especially Catholic history. He was a member of The Philadelphia Catholic Historical Society, and for many years a member of its Research Committee.

George Barton is recalled as a jovial man of medium height, white-haired with rosy cheeks and a frank way of talking. He died in Philadelphia, March 16, 1940.

E. F.

Very Reverend John Mackintosh Tilney Barton 1898-

Monsignor Barton is the son of Tilney Wallace Barton, a solicitor of the Supreme Court, who later became Official Receiver in Bankruptcy for the Salisbury district. His mother, Marian Helen Jowitt Barton, became a Catholic in 1906. Tilney Barton did all in his power to prevent his son's following his mother into the Church, including a successful application to make him a ward of the court. As a result of these efforts the boy did not make his first Confession and Holy Communion until April 1914 when he was almost sixteen. In 1915 he decided to become a priest. Mr. Barton never became reconciled to his son's vocation and they have not met since 1915.

Monsignor Barton was born at Parkstone, Dorsetshire, England, May 20, 1898. He attended Dane Court School in that place. In 1912 he won an entrance scholarship in Classics and History to Harrow. He was at Harrow for three years until his father removed him as a result of World War I. He entered St. Edmund's College, Ware, the Westminster diocesan seminary, in September 1915, and remained there until 1920. He received tonsure in 1916, minor orders in 1917, and when he reached the canonical age of twenty-one in 1919, the subdiaconate. His only fellow-ordinand in the last case was Ronald Knox, the well-known Oxford convert. He was too young to be ordained with his class so in 1920 he went to Rome where he studied at the Angelico University for two years. On June 24, 1921 he was ordained by Cardinal Bourne, from whose hands he had received all the orders from tonsure up. In 1921 he received the degrees S.T.B. and S.T.L. (cum laude) and in 1922 his Doctorate of Divinity (magna cum laude). In September 1922 the Cardinal sent him to Jerusalem where he became a guest of the renowned Biblical School of St. Etienne, where the famous Père Lagrange was a lecturer. In 1924 he returned to St. Edmund's as Professor of Hebrew and Old Testament Exegesis. In 1926 upon the departure of Ronald Knox he was made Professor of Scripture. A year later he returned to Rome and studied under Père Vosté, O.P. at the Collegio Angelico. In June 1928 he proceeded to the degree of Licentiate of Sacred Scripture as the result of a public examination held at the Holy Office and at the Vatican by the Consultors of the Pontifical Biblical Commission. He then returned to his professorship at St. Edmund's. He was named English Consultor for the Pontifical Biblical Commission, and ex-officio examiner for the Papal degrees in Holy Scripture, in 1935. Pope Pius XI made him a Privy Chamberlain in 1936, and Pope Pius XII renewed the nomination later. He has been appointed a member of the editorial board of the Catholic Biblical Association of America, and to the board of the New English translation made by Monsignor Ronald Knox.

In August 1936 Archbishop Hinsley asked him to head a new house of higher studies at Edmonton, and he left St. Edmund's which had been his home for so many years. Besides his professorship there he had served as Chief Librarian for seven years (1929-1936). In 1937 the foundation was moved from Edmonton to a much better house at West Drayton, Middlesex, and he became administrator of the parish there. Parish duties take up much of his day but he finds time for scriptural studies and has a number of books in preparation or contemplation.

Throughout World War II, he was the officiating Chaplain to the R.A.F., West Drayton Station.

In 1940 he undertook the editorship, for Burns, Oates and Washbourne, of a series of scripture textbooks.

In 1943 he was invited by the Hierarchy to organize a course of theological and scriptural studies by correspondence for nuns and other non-clerical students.

In 1944 he was elected a Fellow of the Society of Antiquaries (F.S.A.), a coveted distinction. In the same year, His Grace, the Archbishop of Westminster appointed him a pro-synodal Judge of the Westminster diocesan court. In 1945 he was elected a Fellow of the Royal Society of Arts (F.R.S.A.).

One of his chief interests for a number of years has been the Eastern Churches, and he has been Vice-Chairman of the St. John Chrysostom Society since 1934. Criminology is one of his hobbies.

He is the author of: *Holy Ghost; Religion of Israel; Semitic Religions;* and joint author of *New Testament and Divorce.* He edited: Père Lagrange's *Catholic Harmony of Four Gospels;* Dom Chapman's *Matthew, Mark and Luke;* and brought out a new edition of Cardinal Wiseman's *Lectures on the Blessed Eucharist.* He translated D. Buzy's *Life of St. John the Baptist* and adapted from the French of Père Sévérien Salaville's *Introduction to the Study of the Eastern Liturgies.*   M. S.

Henri Marie Alfred Cardinal Baudrillart
1859-1942

The promotion in 1935 to Commander of the Legion of Honor, of which he was made an officer in 1931, designated Alfred Cardinal Baudrillart as a "man of letters, member of the French Academy." This prince of the Church made notable contributions to Catholic literature, especially as historian and biographer, and was also an apostle of Christian education and of the Catholic press.

He was born in Paris, France, in 1859, of distinguished ancestry. His great-grandfather, Silvestre de Lacy, was secretary for life of the Academy of Inscriptions and Belles-Lettres, and a learned Orientalist. His grandfather, also named Silvestre de Lacy, was a great journalist and a member of the French Academy. The father of

Cardinal Baudrillart was Henri Baudrillart, distinguished member of the Academy of Moral and Political Science.

Alfred Baudrillart was educated at the Ecole Bossuet, the Lycée Louis le Grand, where he won highest scholastic honors, and at the Ecole Normale Supérieure. In 1881 he became professor of history at Laval University at Caen, and later held this chair at the College Stanislas in Paris and at the Institut Catholique. Under commission by the Ministry of Public Instruction he several times visited Spain for special study of Franco-Spanish history in the early eighteenth century, and he embodied the results in a monumental work on Philip V (1700-48), twice awarded the Grand Prix Gobert. He received the degree of Litt.D. in 1890 and in the same year entered the Congregation of the Oratory. Ordained priest in 1893, he was one of the outstanding members of the Congregation until its suppression in 1906. Father Baudrillart became rector of the Institut Catholique, Paris, in 1907, and vicar general in 1908. At the Institut he introduced additional lecture courses on apologetics, church history and philosophy and also encouraged science, so that the laboratories attract eager students as well as the lectures on scientific progress. As rector of the Institute he helped and encouraged the electrical researches of Edouard Branly, which were carried on there and which paved the way for the discoveries of Marconi.

Cardinal Baudrillart was a prolific writer, having published numerous historical books and articles that were widely translated. He was also a fine orator. Three lectures on the Renaissance and seven on the Reformation and the comparative influence of Catholicity and Protestantism form his valuable authoritative work, *L'Eglise Catholique, la Renaissance, le Protestantisme,* which reached a fifth edition in 1904 and was translated into English by Mrs. Philip Gibbs in 1908, under the title, *The Catholic Church, the Renaissance and Protestantism.* Among his other works are a book on charity in the early Church, *Charité aux premiers siècles du Christianisme* (1903), and lives of St. Severin (1908); Frederic Ozanam (1912); Monsignor d'Hulst (2 vols., 1921) and St. Germain d'Auxerre (1929). With Guibert and Lesetre he founded and remained the editor of the *Revue Pratique d'Apologetique,* which is dedicated to the exposition of Catholic truth.

On the fiftieth anniversary of the episcopal consecration of Cardinal Gibbons (1918), he was one of the French Commission sent to the United States to convey felicitations to the American prelate.

During World War I he acted as chaplain in the French army and was both priest and friend to the wounded and the dying. In addition, he wrote more than seventy articles in various reviews, and organized and directed the Catholic Committee for French Propaganda in Foreign Countries, the purpose of which was to overcome a lack of sympathy for France. His *Campagne Française* is an explanation and defense of this work.

For his "high merit and eminent services" he was elected to the French Academy, May 2, 1918, and was received into the Institution April 10, 1919. In recording this honor François Veuillot said: "Among the clergy, hitherto suspect, at the head of our Catholic University, but yesterday menaced, the French Academy has found and crowned a great

Frenchman. . . ." He succeeded the Catholic soldier and orator, Count Albert de Mun, and his discourse upon reception into the Academy was a eulogy of his predecessor.

In 1921 he was made Titular Bishop of Himeria and consecrated at Notre Dame de Paris by Cardinal Dubois. Four years later he was named assistant at the pontifical throne, and in 1928 he was promoted to Titular Archbishop of Melitene. In 1935 he was created cardinal, and Pope Pius XI conferred the red hat on him in December of that year. Cardinal Baudrillart was a member of the Congregations of Rites, of Seminaries, and of the Basilica of St. Peter and one of the best known representatives of the Church of France, eminent as religious apologist, publicist, orator, educator and writer.

C. M. N.

Émile Baumann 1868-1942

"The Catholic faith is the blood in my veins," wrote Baumann in the preface of *Trois Villes Saintes*. This short sentence is an epitome of all his works, for he was without question one of the most Catholic of our contemporary French writers, ready to speak loudly and openly when his faith was concerned. As a moralist, he was stern and unrelenting, but the grandeur of his thought cannot fail to impress and inspire anyone who is willing to accept his complex plots, his rugged style, and his ungloved handling of vice.

He was born in Lyons in 1868, and spent his early years in this city. His ancestors had been Lutherans, but through the marriage of his grandfather with a Catholic girl, had been converted and became staunch defenders of the faith. Émile and his brother Léon, five years younger than he, who later entered the Dominicans, received their first lessons from a devout mother, and were then sent to the Jesuit school in the city. They read the Bible and the Fathers of the Church, and imbibed a knowledge and understanding of Christian doctrine and practice beyond their years.

Émile became an agrégé at Roanne, then professor at the University of Algiers, and later at Roche-sur-Yon, at Sens, and at Mans. In 1890 he was married and had one son who died in the Vendée when only twenty years old. His second marriage was with Elizabeth de Groux, daughter of Charles de Groux, the famous artist. In Algiers he had met Saint-Saëns, and consecrated his first work to him, *Les Grandes Formes de la musique*. It was published in 1905 and reflects the love for music which had characterized the Baumanns through several generations.

About two dozen volumes, including biographies, philosophical studies, essays, and novels comprise Baumann's literary production. His *Saint Paul*, written in 1924 after a trip to Palestine, is possibly the finest of all his works, for it presents in language both dramatic and poetic, the colossal figure of the great apostle of the Gentiles.

His seven novels may all be classed as thesis novels, for they are written around some dogma or moral lesson that he wished to teach. His definite aim is to show the ugliness of sin and the sureness with which it is justly chastised, and it is in no timid and half-hearted manner that he undertakes to carry out this mission. Hence there is strength and persuasion in what he writes, but also lack of artistry arising from exaggeration and poor construction. His doctrine is sound, his intention good, and his sincerity unquestionable, but even from the point of view of Catholic moral teaching, Baumann seems too severe and devoid of that sense of far-reaching mercy which characterizes the Gospel of Christ.

His plots are often complex, threading through unnecessary incidents and useless details. His characters are a curious compound of idealism and realism, showing the power of the flesh which lusteth against the spirit. Some of them are unnatural monsters, while others are too evidently the mouthpiece of the author. His style is forceful rather than beautiful, for it lacks the clarity and grace which are so characteristically French. Its severity and harshness, however, often fit the characters and subject-matter.

Baumann died in 1942.   J. K.

William H. Baumer, Jr. 1909-

It was at the suggestion of a friend that William Baumer began writing books on army life and West Point. As a student at that famous school and later one of its teachers, participating in many extra-curricular activities, Baumer is fully qualified to write on that subject.

William Baumer was born in Omaha, Nebraska, November 27, 1909, the son of William Henry and Winifred (Mitchell) Baumer. He was graduated from Creighton Preparatory School in 1927, and then attended Creighton University for two years. While a sophomore, his father came home one day and asked which of his two sons would like to go to West Point. The appointment was assured if either of them could qualify. Since William had done better in his class than his brother, he was selected. In 1933 he was graduated from the United States Military Academy at West Point.

"The urge to write first showed itself when as a West Point cadet I turned out copy on sports for the cadet magazine and added running accounts of sports for the Public Relations Officer at West Point," he recalls. Working in the press box at football games followed—one week with Ted Husing, another with Westbrook Pegler, another with Grantland Rice, etc. His job was to identify the players for press and radio. "From that contact with men who wrote and spoke, I first found the urge to do likewise." Thus he follows in the tradition of the many American writers whose introduction to writing came through journalism.

"Pitchforked" after graduation into the duty of mess officer in the Civilian Conservation Corps at Camp—now Fort Dix, New Jersey (1933-1936), he covered the activities of the camp for The New York *Times.*

Aftei Infantry School at Fort Benning, Georgia, 1936-1937, he taught English at a West Point "prep" school for enlisted men in Fort Snelling, Minnesota, but was back at West Point again in 1938 teaching history, working for an M.A. degree in public law and government (which he received from Columbia University in 1941), and engaging in publicity writing during his spare time.

"My first sale was to *The Sign,*" he writes, "and then they followed in orderly procession." Besides contributing to *The Sign, America, Hygeia,* and *The Seventh Regiment Gazette,* William Baumer is the author of several books, namely: *Sports As Taught and Played at West Point* (1939); *21-35 What the Draft and Your Army Training Mean to You* (with S. F. Griffin) (1940); *How to be an Army Officer* (1940); *He's in the Army Now* (1941); *Not All Warriors* (a series of portraits of 19th century West Pointers who became famous in other than army careers) (1941), and *West Point: Moulder of Men* (1942).

In 1936 William Baumer married Alice Hull Brough. They have two children, Winifred Joan, and Natalie, both born at West Point, New York.

He was called away from the Military Academy to report for service, with the rank of Major, in May 1942, to the War Plans Division of the War Department.

T. V.

René Bazin   1853-1932

Up until his death in 1932, there had been a steady growth in power in the works of René Bazin. The leaven of this power was his stanch Catholicity. Criticized for not following the genre of his time, his deepening faith gave him courage and strength to write of life from a truly Christian and Catholic point of view. He was one of the few brave authors of his time who refused to follow realism and sensualism. René Bazin insisted on the spiritual side of man's nature. He saw man's soul behind every action. He himself said, "I desire to portray the sweetness, purity, and beauty of French family life and not to perpetuate a gross libel upon it. . . . I am also anxious to dispel the illusion that the French are a godless people." He preferred to make a deliberate choice of portraying virtue and its possible triumph over evil, in contradistinction to that other Catholic school, which chooses from moral grounds, rather to depict vice with its necessary punishment, or as leading to final ruin. In this his critics found fault, but not with his literary craftsmanship, his creative imagination, his brilliant style, his clear structure, his faithfulness in painting a landscape and his exquisite taste. He was also accused of being too much of an optimist and of missing the dramatic moment, of not being a profound thinker, not being capable of arousing intense emotions within the reader, but never for lacking honesty. The novels are healthy and stimulating.

René Bazin was born in 1853 at Angers, France, of an old Catholic bourgeois family. His father was an Angevin and his mother a Parisian. Because of delicate health he was brought up in the country where he lived close to nature. He was zealous in learning from nature. His books give a true picture of his love of the earth and show what a keen observer he was. Though he lacked much of the formal education of his companions, he became a law student at the Catholic University of his native city. From there he went to the University of Paris to continue his education. Upon completing his studies, he returned to Angers as Professor of Criminal Law in 1878. He held this position until his death in 1932. He married Aline Bricard. They had two sons and six daughters.

In 1884 his first novel *Stephanette* appeared. The book won the admiration of Ludovic Halévy who advised the editor of the *Journal des Débats* to secure Bazin as a contributor. This journal published most of his works before they appeared in book form.

René Bazin was a prolific writer. At least forty books flowed from his pen. About twenty-five of these are novels. These usually treat some social problem. Perhaps the most popular are his *Ma Tante Giron* (1886), a story very similar to Halévy's *L'Abbé Constantin: Une Tache d'encre (The Ink-Stain)* (1888), which was crowned by the French Academy, and *Humble Amour* (1894). In his book *De Toute son âme (Redemption)*, Henriette Madiot, a young girl of the people exemplifies by her life the glory of sacrifice and of consecration to God. *La Terre qui meurt (Autumn Glory)* deals with the drain of the villages to fill the cities of France. He also wrote several travel books and some biographies of special Catholic interest such as the life of Pope Pius X. René Bazin's last work was a novel, *Magnificat*. It came out in May 1931. It presents the distress of a young Breton girl in love with a young man who has heard the divine call to the priesthood and whose decision came after a long and bitter struggle. It is significant that the High Mass of Requiem for René Bazin at the Church of Saint Barthélemy was sung by the rector of the seminary of Nantes, who appears as one of the characters in the *Magnificat*.

When René Bazin was received into the French Academy on April 28, 1904, to replace Ernest Leguove, a magnificent tribute was paid to his work by the celebrated critic Brunetière.

René Bazin was a Knight Commander of the Order of St. Gregory the Great, and was President of the Corporation des Publicistes Chretiens.

R. B.

Arthur Charles Frederick Beales   1905-

One of the brilliant young men to be received into the Church in 1935 is A. C. F. Beales, known as "Rudolf" by his many friends, from a supposed likeness to the film-star Valentino.

It was partly due to his reading of history and partly to the prayers of Freda Morris of Twickenham, whom he married in 1936, that he entered the Catholic Church.

Born in London, in 1905, Arthur Beales was educated at the Latymer Upper School and the University of London, King's College, where in 1925 he received his B.A. (Honours in History and first in Class I), and his M.A. in History (with distinction) in 1927. A year later he obtained the University of London Teacher's Diploma. From 1928 to 1930 he was Assistant Master at the Haberdasher's School, Hampstead and a lecturer in history at University College, Swansea in 1931. Since 1935 he has been a lecturer in education at the University of London, King's College.

While Mr. Beales has built up a reputation as a historian, he is best known as a broadcaster, a leader of Catholic Action and as the author of the "Penguin" best seller *The Catholic Church and International Order.* His other books are: *The History of Peace* (1931) and *The Guide to the Teaching of History in Schools.* He edited the English version of the official commentary on the Pope's Peace Points.

As Joint Honorary Secretary of the "Sword of the Spirit Movement" he was constantly in close touch with His Eminence, the late Cardinal Hinsley and frequently went to receive his instructions direct. He retired from office as Joint Honorary Secretary on October 28, 1944 and was elected a member of the Executive Committee.

Mr. Beales is often in demand as a lecturer.

                                                                    M. H.

Piaras Béaslaí 1883-

An Irish patriot who has served his country not only with the sword but very largely with the pen, Piaras Béaslaí was born in England of Irish parents; his father was for many years editor of the *Catholic Times* of Liverpool. His father was a native of Kerry and he spent some of his childhood in that country. Piaras Béaslaí was educated at St. Francis Xavier College (Liverpool) and from adolescence was steeped in the Irish nationalist movement, which included for him a special devotion to the Irish language. He was for years prominent in the affairs of the Gaelic League serving as a member of the Executive and later as Vice-President. He was founder and first president of "An Faínne" (League of Irish Speakers) and also of "Na h Aisteoiri" (Gaelic Players, producing plays in Irish) and first president of its successor, "An Comhar Dramuióchta." For some years he edited *Fainne an Lae,* organ of the Gaelic League. Piaras Béaslaí was also, on the side of direct political action, a founder and leader of the Irish Volunteers (1913) and a member of its Executive. Naturally he played a prominent part in the Easter Week insurrection of 1916, and spent long periods in Irish and English prisons. Twice he escaped. He served with the Irish Republican Army, being especially charged with its official, secretly published *An t Óglách,* until the truce of July, 1921. He was elected to the Dail Eireann as Deputy for East Kerry, (1918-1923) and served in the Irish National Army till 1925 as Major-General. His published books cover a wide range, most of them being in Irish and some of them translations into that language from other literatures.

He is the author of *Michael Collins and the Making of a New Ireland* (2 volumes) (1926); *Michael Collins, Soldier and Statesman* (1937); *Bealltaine* (1916), a volume of poems in Irish; *Eigse Nua Ghaedhilge* (a critical history of Gaelic poetry in two volumes, in Gaelic); *Astronar* (a novel); *An Danar, An Bhean Chródha* (tragedies); *Cluiche Cartai, Fear an Sgeilin Grinn* and nine other original comedies (all frequently produced).

He himself lists as his favorite amusements: "Walking, cycling, swimming, the drama, the study of languages and wildflowers."

H. B.

Catherine Beebe 1899- *and* Robb Beebe
1891-

The Beebes have their workshop built into their home and overlooking their garden in Ridgewood, New Jersey. It is not at all unusual to find Mrs. Beebe busy on stories for a school reader for one publisher while her husband is drawing the pictures for another reader for a different publisher. This is the work they like best to do, stories and pictures for and about children, and it finds its happiest expression in their own books that they do together, the "Beebe Books" that Catherine writes and Robb illustrates.

It seems that they were always striving toward this ideal of together doing books in which the child would find himself and his playmates reflected—books that he himself could read and understand and enjoy. Catherine Beebe's poetry, short stories, articles, advertising copy—all had been for and about children. Robb Beebe had also specialized, in his magazine and advertising illustrations, in juvenile subjects.

They finished the text and drawings for their first book together in 1937. They felt that it was good, but would any publisher think so? To their surprise and delight it was accepted by the first editor to whom it was shown. There are now thirteen published Beebe books and one in manufacture. Another is almost ready, both in story and picture, to be submitted to their publishers. The three Beebe children, as well as their seemingly numberless playmates and friends have been an invaluable laboratory.

Seven of the Beebe books were done especially for Catholic children for the Beebes with their love of the Faith have drawn upon the inspiration, authority and beauty of Holy Mother Church for the subject matter of these volumes. The Beebes are converts, having been received together into the Church of St. Jean Baptiste in New York City.

They were born in Ohio, Catherine Herman in Cleveland in 1899, where she was educated in the public schools and by the Ursuline Sisters, and Robb Beebe in 1891 in Ashtabula, where he attended the public schools. It was after he had gone to Western Reserve University and the Cleveland School of Art in Cleveland that Mr. Beebe met his future wife. Their romance was interrupted by the first World War in which he served in the Marines. They were married in June, following the Armistice.

They are ardent in support of the Crusade for Decent Literature and the spread of good reading. They frequently give informal talks to parent-teacher and library groups as well as to the children themselves. In Ridgewood, the home of their final choice, they take keen interest in parish and civic activities.

They have written and illustrated the following books: *Do you Like* to *Open Packages?; Happily Ever After; A B C's for Catholic Boys and Girls; Little Patron of Gardeners; A Wish for Timothy; Just Around the Corner; The Calendar; Bob's Bike; We Know the Mass; The Children's Saint Anthony; Our Baby's Memory Book; The Christmas Story* and *The Children's Saint Francis.*

Herbert Clifford Francis Bell   1881-

Professor Bell was born at Hamilton, Ontario on August 4, 1881. His father was a lawyer and an Anglican of Irish stock; his father's family, originally from Tennessee, were among the earliest settlers of Ontario, and were Presbyterians. He received his education at the Universities of Toronto, Pennsylvania, and Paris, settling permanently in the United States in 1903, and being naturalized in 1919. He says of himself: "During my early years as a student and teacher of history I spent most of my time on the history of the British West Indies, but apart from a *Guide* to documentary materials written for the Carnegie Institution, I published only articles. I simply did not find material for what seemed to me a sufficiently interesting book. In the early twenties I shifted over to nineteenth century English history. That led me to Palmerston." Professor Bell's two-volume work on Palmerston is considered standard. He continues: "The Palmerston book took all the time I could spare from other work for twelve years. I am now at work on two other books in this same field: a study of the connections between 'Popery' and politics, and an account of the decline and fall of the Whigs."

In 1945 his book *Woodrow Wilson and the People* appeared, of which he says: "I have really tried to write the sort of book about Wilson that I think he would have wanted to have written about him. He was always so intensely anxious that he should be understood by the people, not merely by any class or section of them." In reviewing the book for The New York *Times,* Henry Steele Commager writes: "Mr. Bell's interpretation is unquestionably the most satisfactory that has so far appeared."

Professor Bell has held positions at Wisconsin, Bowdoin, and Wesleyan (where he is now) and has been a visiting professor at Yale and Pennsylvania. Bowdoin and Holy Cross have given him honorary doctorates. He does considerable lecturing and contributes articles and book reviews to various periodicals.

Although he had for some time felt that he "had to be a Catholic or nothing," Professor Bell was not received into the Church until 1934. He also writes: "At the beginning of World War I, I was interned in Germany for a while as a British subject. I got out on parole, and in 1917, after training at Plattsburg and the War College, went with the A.E.F. to France, where I had an interesting but not at all heroic career as an intelligence officer. I received a citation from General Pershing and (quite undeservedly) stars for three battles. . . . The hobbies which remain to me are horseback riding, camping, and fishing, but I get very little time for them. I enjoy the great privilege of being an oblate of Prinknash Abbey."

H. B. .

Hilaire Belloc 1870-

To try to cover in small compass the achievement of a figure like Belloc is to try the impossible. He has been blessed not only with a keen and brilliant mind coupled with abounding energy, but he has also been blessed with many years in which to make use of his talents, and the result is so great a bulk of accomplishment that it fatigues the ordinary mortal even to contemplate it.

The bare skeleton of Hilaire Belloc's life is simple enough and is well known to most of those who have followed his career. He was born in 1870 at La Celle, St. Cloud, France, his father being a distinguished French lawyer, his mother a granddaughter of the English scientist Priestly. When the elder Belloc died, the family moved to England. Hilaire went to school at the Oratory, Edgbaston, where Cardinal Newman was the presiding genius. After he had finished school, he returned to France to do his military service; then back to England and to Balliol College, Oxford, in 1892. The University soon recognized his preeminent talents; Benjamin Jowett, the great translator of Plato, influenced him in the direction of history. In 1895 he took his degree with first class honors in that field. His ambition was to re-write the Catholic history of his two fatherlands. In 1896 he married an American, Elodie Hogan of Napa, California, a marriage blessed with four children, two sons and two daughters. There followed a career in London as journalist and author which only ceased after a stroke in 1946.

In 1903 Mr. Belloc became a British subject and in 1906 was elected a Liberal member for Salford in the House of Commons where he held a seat until 1910. He refused a third term as a waste of time. From this experience he amassed material for his book, *The Party System* with Cecil Chesterton as collaborator. With the cessation of his political activity at Fleet St., he became a squire and farmer at Horshan.

He has several times visited the United States, where he has been guest lecturer at both Notre Dame and Fordham Universities. His personal appearance is much more English than French; as he has grown older his stockiness has become more pronounced, so that he is in many ways the image of John Bull himself—thick-set, and sturdy as a rock. World War II has meant personal tragedy for him—in it he lost his son Peter, who while stationed in central Scotland, died of pneumonia in a hospital. The celebration of his seventy-first birthday in August, 1941 was a great occasion, in which the most distinguished of English writers and statesmen joined in honoring a man who has won the admiration of all his countrymen and of thousands in other lands as well. On that occasion, former Information Minister Duff Cooper presented him, with a silver cup made in 1815.

Belloc's literary output has been enormous. In addition to hundreds of magazine and newspaper articles, he has written more than a hundred books, and books of every variety. He once said in an interview: "The shortest time I spent on a book was on a novel. I wrote it (*The Change in the Cabinet*) in a week. I began it Palm Sunday, 1909 and finished it Easter Sunday, 1909." In the Dedication (to Maurice Baring) of his book *The Cruise of the Nona* which he wrote in two weeks, he ventures the suggestion that books ought to be numbered like the streets of America. Thus the *Cruise of the Nona* would be Belloc 106. He has written biographies, history, essays, travel books, novels, volumes on military science, poetry. Naturally all that he has done has not been at the same high level, but his best work both in prose and verse can rank with the best produced in English in the last two-score years.

With Maurice Baring, Belloc edited the *North Street Gazette,* which died after the first number, but it was perhaps the indirect begetter of another newspaper, which had a longer life, the *Eye-Witness,* which later became the *New Witness.* The *Eye-Witness* was first edited by Belloc and then by Cecil Chesterton. The two papers were responsible for the exposure of the sale of honors and for generally debunking the party system in the process of which was started the League for Clean Government. But the most significant thing about the *Witnesses* was the development of the theory of Distributism—the protection of liberty by the distribution of ownership.

Catholics can be grateful to have had such a champion to defend them before the English-speaking public; for two things especially they owe him a debt of gratitude—his work in history and in apologetics. Throughout the nineteenth century English history was written and generally accepted after a very partizan fashion. The Whig interpretation of the past was the only interpretation most Englishmen (or Americans) knew, and this interpretation had become solidified until it commanded uncritical acceptance. Its principal assumptions were a strong antipathy to the Catholic Church and the belief that England's greatness grew out of her Anglo-Saxon origins and her Protestant religion. Henry VIII and Elizabeth were the great national heroes; Catholics had ever been bloody, intolerant and backward. British industry and commerce were man's greatest creation, and liberal capitalism was by-and-large the happiest regime under which men could live. It was against this version of history that Belloc fought, and he fought with consummate skill. Today the Whig view of history is dead, and although many historians may not go so far as Belloc in their interpretations, their thought has been marked by his work. He has constantly been subject to criticism by the academically minded, who have taken violent exception to his informal methods—dispensing almost entirely with references and footnotes and careful documentation. But they have been forced to modify their own views by the very books they affect to scorn, and it is a question whether any other method than that Belloc used would have effected as much. In apologetics his achievement is similar. At the beginning of this century there was very little respect either in England or America for the Catholic intellectual position. By his controversy and apologetic writings Belloc more than any other man has changed all this. As "This Publishing Business" of Sheed & Ward in May 1939 issue has put it, "What Belloc writes goes *home:* they could no more ignore him than they could ignore a tiger on the doorstep."

Las Vergnas, in his book *Chesterton, Belloc, Baring* states: "He hurls his facts into the fray like so many jagged stones." When Chesterton was alive, George Bernard Shaw referred to them as ChesterBelloc—defining this term as an animal with four legs, capable of doing infinite harm.

Yet it is probably not for his historical, biographical or apologetic writings that Belloc's name will live. Nothing dies quicker than interest in a dead controversy, and most of his writing in these fields is strictly controversial. The better he has succeeded in making his point, the quicker what he wrote will die. But there are other fields in which he has written that have a far more durable interest. His travel books are not likely soon to sink into oblivion. Of these *The Path to Rome* is perhaps the best known. It is an account of the adventures of a pilgrim who has vowed to go to Rome on foot. His essays and verse seem now to have achieved a firm place in literature. Several of the essays have quaint titles: *On Nothing and Kindred Subjects* (1908); *On Everything* (1909); *This and That and The Other* (1909); *On Anything* (1910); *On Something* (1910); *On* (1923). His best verse is perhaps *Bad Child's Book of Beasts* published in 1896. There is a simplicity coupled with strength and originality in his style, an emotion and humanity and sadness which seem long likely to win readers. And his verse for children, which is also very much verse for adults, attains a quality unique in the contemporary literary world. In Hilaire Belloc, England (and France) produced not only a great defender of the Faith but also a great master of letters in the finest Christian tradition of the West.   H. B. & M. H.

Reverend Edmond Darvil Benard   1914-

A Preface to Newman's Theology immediately marked its young author as an authority on the religious teaching of the great Victorian. Only a few weeks before the work on Newman had appeared, the brief monograph *The Appeal to the Emotions in Preaching* was acclaimed as an outstanding modern contribution to the study of homiletics. Either work would have assured Doctor Benard of a prominent place among the Catholic writers of our time.

Doctor Benard was born in Boston, Massachusetts, on August 9, 1914. After graduating from Holy Name Grammar School in Springfield in 1928, he entered St. Michael's Cathedral High School in that same city. While at Cathedral, he was a member of the debating team for three years, and left a record of excellence as a debater which has never been surpassed. At the age of fifteen, he won the prize as the champion high school orator of the eastern United States, and was awarded a trip to Europe in the summer of 1930. Graduating from Cathedral with highest honors, he matriculated at Holy Cross College, in Worcester, Massachusetts.

During his college days, Doctor Benard was Editor in Chief of the *Tomahawk,* the college newspaper, a member of the staff of the literary magazine, the *Purple,* and chairman of the college debating council. The enthusiasm for excellence in the craftsmanship of speaking and writing which he acquired and exercised at Holy Cross still characterizes his work.

Valedictorian of the Holy Cross class of 1936, Doctor Benard entered the Grand Seminary of Montreal, the school of sacred theology for the University of Montreal, to prepare for the priesthood. He received his licentiate in theology (summa cum laude) in 1940, and the doctorate (summa cum laude) in 1942. In 1941 he received priestly ordination at the hands of his Excellency, the Most Reverend Thomas M. O'Leary, Bishop of Springfield.

After completing his course in sacred theology at the University of Montreal, he entered the Catholic University of America, where he received the degree of Master of Arts in Philosophy in 1942. In the fall of 1943 he joined the Faculty of Sacred Theology at the Catholic University of America, and has been promoted to assistant professor (1947).

During his days at Montreal, Doctor Benard had written frequently and brilliantly for *Le Seminaire,* the theological review of the University. In January 1944 he became secretary of the editorial board of the *American Ecclesiastical Review,* to which he has been a frequent and valued contributor.

Doctor Benard's contribution to American Catholic letters is outstanding for two distinct reasons. He is a brilliant and tireless student. He has definite lessons to deliver for the profit of his fellow workers for Christ in our country. His erudition is solid and conscientious. He does not read carelessly. Furthermore, he is one of the writers who really knows the craft of literary composition. There is not one careless phrase in all the writings he has produced.

At the University, Doctor Benard is in charge of classes in apologetics and homiletics and of a special class in the theology of Newman. It is along these paths that his intellectual interests lie. The Catholic Church in the United States is truly fortunate to have this gifted young priest, consecrating his life to the defence of Christ in His Mystical Body, and in instructing his younger confreres in the art of presenting our Lord's message effectively to His people.

J. F.

Jacinto Benavente   1866-

Recognized alike by critics and public as the lead-ing Spanish dramatist of the twentieth century, Jacinto Benavente was born in Madrid, Spain, August 10, 1866. His father, Dr. Mariano Bena-vente, an eminent specialist in children's diseases, had moved there from Murcia, the most African of European cities.

Jacinto spent his childhood in Madrid, mak-ing also occasional visits to Paris. He received his education at San Isidro Institute and attended the University of Madrid where he was enrolled in the Faculty of Law. When his father died in 1885 he determined to devote himself to literature and in particular to the drama. José Echegaray, the leading playwright of the previous generation, had been a patient and intimate of his father and through his influence the youth had seen many plays and had met many theatrical people. He trav-eled extensively, appeared as an amateur actor and also professionally and for a time toured with a circus, cultivating a curious interest in clowns. His financial position freed him from economic worries while his travels familiarized him with the languages of western Europe.

His career as a writer began in 1893 with a book of poems entitled *Versos.* A year later his first play, *El Nido Ajeno,* was performed. *Gente Conocida (In Society)* was his first pronounced success (1896).

Benavente has written more than one hundred and fifty plays that have been produced, covering the entire range of the theatre with the exception of poetic drama. His non-dramatic works include his *Cartas de Mujeres (Ladies' Letter Writer);* five series of *Table Talk; Marginalia; Conferences,* and *The Popular Theatre.* He is perhaps the most acute literary critic who has appeared in modern Spain.

Among his outstanding plays the two best known are *Los Intereses Creados* and *La Malquerida.* The former was the first production of the New York Theatre Guild (1919) and also of the Everyman Theatre, London (1920). *La Malquerida* was played in New York and throughout the country by Nance O'Neil under the title *The Passion Flower,* reaching a total of 866 performances (1920-1922). *Saturday Night (La Noche del Sábado)* was the first production of Eva Le Gallienne's Civic Repertory Theatre (1926). Walter Hampden and Frances Starr have appeared in Benavente plays. Miss O'Neil presented *Field of Ermine* in Boston and in Chicago. *His Widow's Husband* was one of the successes of the original Washington Square Players. Other notable plays are the peasant drama *Señora Ama;* the court satire *La Princesa Bébé; La Escuela de las Princesas; La Gobernadora,* staged by the Harvard Dramatic Club; the provincial comedy *La Inmaculada de los Dolores; La Fuerza Bruta,* and the powerful drama *Cuando los Hijos de Eva no son los Hijos de Adán.*

Benavente is a penetrating psychologist and a keen analyst of women. He wrote: "I do not make my plays for the public, I make the public for my plays." . . . "He who thinks every day cannot think the same thing every day." When asked in 1939 whether he was a Catholic, he replied: "Yes, and now more so than ever." He was travelling in Loyalist territory at the outbreak of the Spanish Civil War and for a time stood in grave peril of his life. His last play was acted in Madrid in 1942 and he has been repeatedly honored publicly by the Franco Government. In 1913 he was elected to the Spanish Academy and was awarded the Nobel Prize for Literature in 1922.

The authorized translation of his works into English is by John Garrett Underhill. Plays, 1st Series: *His Widow's Husband, The Bonds of Interest, the Evil Doers of Good, La Malquerida* (1917); Plays, 2nd Series: *No Smoking, Princess Bebe, The Governor's Wife, Autumnal Roses* (1919); Plays, 3rd Series: *The Prince Who Learned Everything Out of Books, Saturday Night, In the Clouds, The Truth* (1923); Plays, 4th Series: *The School of Princesses, A Lady, The Magic of an Hour, Field of Ermine* (1924); *The Smile of Mona Lisa* (1915); *Brute Force* (1935); *At Close Range* (1936).

J. G. U.

James Lincoln Benvenisti 1890-

An old practitioner of the trade of journalism, Mr. Benvenisti's name first began to be known in America at the beginning of the late war (World War II), when his spirited articles in *The Commonweal* on wartime England first began to attract attention. Through the period of the "phoney war" to Dunkirk, through the London blitz and the flying bombs, he continued to give American readers a graphic and often humorous account of life in what gradually came to be America's most advanced operational aerodrome.

These articles were written at odd moments while the writer was engaged in various types of work connected with the war effort. The most exacting of these activities came immediately after Dunkirk, when Mr. Benvenisti seized the opportunity to gain an experience which had hitherto been denied him, namely of becoming a manual worker in a factory. He got himself trained as a centre lathe turner and began to work on night shifts in an aircraft works, and has left on record a vivid description of what he and countless others went through during that period. For a great part of the time he was on night shift from eight-thirty at night until seven-thirty in the morning, with two half-hour meals breaks, for six nights a week. "I have known" he writes "that faint but horrible nausea that overtakes some of us between two and three o'clock, and what is almost worse, the strange subconscious anticipation of it just before one starts work. I have learned to value as a precious boon the chance to snatch a few moments' rest on a hard floor under a bench during a meal break." While he was thus strenuously engaged on night shift, however, Mr. Benvenisti used the daytime hours for journalism, interviewing and reporting, with the result that he got virtually no sleep at all, and in due course suffered the breakdown in health which was obviously inevitable. A change of occupation was needed and he was offered a job as a lecturer to the troops, a job which he found eminently congenial and in which he achieved a very high degree of success. Mr. Benvenisti expounded to them the whole idea of freedom and democracy and the making clear of the power and responsibility which the ordinary individual citizen carries in his hands.

From the end of 1942 till a few weeks after V.J. Day, Mr. Benvenisti delivered over 1,000 lectures to the fighting services up and down the country, and he is still carrying on with this work on a more restricted scale. He has also in some measure extended it to cover civilian audiences, for he lectures three evenings a week at the Evening Institutes which are run by the London County Council's Education Authority.

James Lincoln Benvenisti was born in America, in Atlantic City, New Jersey on August 7, 1890, but as an infant he was brought by his parents to England, and his home has been there ever since. He received an Honours Degree at Oxford, and in the first World War served first with the Gunners and then with the original Royal Flying Corps which became later the Royal Air Force. In 1931, the company of which his father was chairman was forced into bankruptcy during the depression. He felt that in this case the law had been used to defeat common justice, and started to investigate the attitude of the Church in such matters. As a result of his studies he wrote his first book, *The Iniquitous Contract,* seeking to prove that the debenture was an usurious instrument.

In 1934 he began to write articles for *G.K.'s Weekly* and in 1937 started a weekly column for that review entitled, "From a Distributist's Notebook." Later the title was changed to "Under the Bushel." He also contributed a column to the *Catholic Herald,* "J. L. Benvenisti Tells." In the same paper he has suggested as a framework for the future, a Chart of Human Value, which he claims is capable of being accepted by every person of every creed who subscribes to our central principle of personality value. Mr. Benvenisti has been a contributor to the *Economist,* and a frequent contributor to *The Financial News.*

If Mr. Benvenisti now has a doctrine to expound it is that world unity is impossible, and with it permanent international peace, without a far higher degree of international economic equality than can be brought about by the ordinary means of commercial exchange. If that economic equality is to be secured in the necessary minimum measure, it is imperative that countries with large surpluses should be willing to export those surpluses without the hope of any quick direct return and on much more generous conditions than those hitherto prescribed by normal commercial practice. He has recently been expounding this doctrine at some length in the pages of *The Commonweal.*

Apart from *The Iniquitous Contract* mentioned above, Mr. Benvenisti has also published *The Absent Minded Revolution,* but having recently adopted a war orphan he is tending more and more to devote his time to the writing of adventure stories for the entertainment of this and other little boys. His first adventure story is scheduled for publication in 1947. M. S.

Reverend Francis E. Benz 1899-

Father Francis E. Benz was born at St. Paul, Minnesota, on May 3, 1899, the son of Frank A. and Sophia (Junius) Benz. His first attempt at writing was in the field of poetry while a student in high school. Two of his poems were published in the school magazine. Subsequent poems were never submitted to any publication, except one, "Mother" which was printed more than a million times.

In 1919 when a senior in college, he worked for the *St. Paul Dispatch and Pioneer Press* as a reporter from 5:00 P.M. to about 1:00 A.M. A few months later he covered college sports but left the paper in September to enter the St. Paul Seminary.

As a seminarian, he found time to write a column for the diocesan paper and to cover the seminary news. He also wrote some articles for various magazines.

After his ordination to the priesthood in 1925, he became interested in youth activities and attended some literature and journalism classes at the University of Minnesota and Columbia University in New York.

In 1933 he became the founder, editor and publisher of *The Catholic Boy,* a magazine for Catholic boys.

A novel, *The Red Flame of Sound* was published. Then Father Benz began writing biographies for Catholic boys and girls. *Pasteur: Knight of the Laboratory,* a biography of the famous Catholic scientist, Louis Pasteur, was the first of these. His next book was *On to Suez,* a biography of Ferdinand de Lesseps, the engineer and builder of the Suez Canal. Then came a non-technical book on the invention of the telephone and the life of Alexander Graham Bell. The title of this book is *Talking Round the Earth.*

In 1942 Father Benz began a publication for girls and called it *The Catholic Miss of America.* In March of the same year, he took over *The Catholic Woman's World,* changing the name to *Poise.* In September, he began the publication of *The Catholic Student,* a magazine for boys and girls nine and ten years of age. He also edits a magazine for boys and girls six and seven years of age. In September 1943 he launched the last of the series of monthly magazines for Catholic boys and girls in the eight-year-old group. During the same month he began publication of *Heroes All,* a comic or picture magazine for Catholic boys and girls.

Father Benz is also the author of: *History of Tabloid Journalism* (1932), and a series of lives of saints for children, viz. *Maid of Sacred Sword; Another Altar Boy; Seven Sons of a Saint,* and *America's First Altar Boy.*
                                                     M. H.

Georges Bernanos   1888-

"No—I'm not an 'author'," declares Georges Bernanos. "Had I been a real one, I never should have waited till I was forty before I published my first book." It was in 1926 that this book, *Sous Le Soleil De Satan* appeared, bringing him sudden celebrity as a writer and a psychologist. Several literary juries considered it for a prize, but it failed to obtain a majority anywhere. The author was working as an inspector for an insurance company at the time. "I began to write," he says, "to try to escape from this disgusting era."

His first prize came in December 1929 when he received the Prix Femina-La Vie Heureuse for *La Joie* the sequel to *L'Imposture.* The Grand Prix du Roman of the French Academy was given to him in 1936 for *Le Journal d'un curé de Campagne.* This is perhaps his best known work; it has been translated into five languages. Father C. C. Martindale, S.J., said of it: "This book, then, by a layman, has been as good as a retreat for at least one priest. We hope it will be read in America. But an effort will have to be made by the reader. If he be comfortable, he must remember that the author who was (we understand) brought up in no such comfortable circumstances, sees vividly what we, from our padded chairs, can hardly imagine."

Bernanos was born in Paris on February 20, 1888. He spent, however, the best days of his childhood and youth in an old estate in the country belonging to his father in the little village of Fressin (Pas de Calais), in a countryside of great woods and pasture land, which he has since made more or less the setting for nearly all the characters of his novels. His family came originally from Spain, but long ago struck root in several French provinces. He is profoundly French and attached to all that is ancient and great in France. His mother came from Berry. His teachers were the Jesuits at Vaugirard College, where he was, by the way, a schoolmate of General de Gaulle.

His other schools were the Institut Catholique and the University of Paris. He received a licentiate in law and licentiate in letters from the University of Paris. In World War I he served as a corporal in the French Cavalry, and received a chest wound. The Croix de Guerre is his decoration. Married in 1917, the Bernanos have three sons and three daughters; the eldest son went to England in 1941, serving there in the Air Force; but he came back to Brazil very ill. His second son left in 1942 and was in the navy on a submarine chaser. His youngest son is only twelve years old (1947). His wife's family Du Lys d'Arc claims kindred with Joan of

Arc. This saint is for the author a symbol of France. Bernanos is a Royalist, and was "discovered" by Leon Daudet, the director of L'Action Francaise.

In 1936 Bernanos was living at Palma in the Balaeric Islands. His experiences of the Spanish Revolution at this spot impelled him to write *les Grandes Cimetières Sous la Lune* (Diary of My Times). This fiery book provoked much discussion inasmuch as he attacked the Catholics for favoring Franco in the Spanish Civil War of 1937-1939. "The Spanish experience," he writes, "is probably the principal event of my life." In 1937 he returned to France, to Toulon, where he fell ill. The next year he and his family moved first to Paraguay and then to Brazil. They remodelled a farm on the rolling uplands of Minas Geraes province, "far from the railroad and the highway with no other company than that of our horses and cows." It was there he wrote *Nous Autres Français* and *Scandale de la Verite*. When France capitulated Bernanos came nearer to civilization. His little farm was quite solitary but communication was more available. He became popular in the country and a friend of Foreign Minister Aranha. In 1946 he returned to France. He is a stout, heavy-shouldered man with grey hair and mustache. He walks with two canes, and limps badly from an old motorcycle accident. An old cavalryman, he is happiest on horseback.

Bernanos is known for his electrifying portrayal of evil, and the struggle of the soul with it. His vivid picture of the devil makes his ideas incomprehensible to much of the modern world. He once told an interviewer, "I have seen the devil, as I see you, since my childhood." He is a propagandist in his writings and says, "I humbly endure the shame of having so far only spattered with ink the face of injustice, whose incessant outrages are my zest for life."

He writes, "If I wanted to tell my friends in a few words the essential thing of which my religious and moral education consisted, I should say that I have been brought up with not only respect and love but also with the most liberal understanding possible of the past of both my country and my religion."

The author is grateful to his pen for having enabled him to support his "numerous" children in some comfort, but he finds writing hard work. "I am no author. The sight alone of a blank sheet wearies my spirit, and the sheer physical isolation imposed by such work is so distasteful to me that I avoid it as much as I can. I sit scribbling in cafés, at the risk of being taken for a drunkard—and that no doubt is what I should really be, if our mighty government did not burden so ruthlessly with taxation the cup that cheers. I write at café tables because I cannot long be deprived of the human face and voice, which I have tried to render with dignity. Let clever folk suppose that I sit 'observing' my fellow men. I observe nothing. Observations never lead to much. I scribble in cafés, just as I used to scribble in railway carriages." He has travelled far since the days when as an insurance inspector he was forced to fit in his writing as he made his tours by train from his modest home in Bar-le Duc. His railway scribblings, however, rocketed him to fame.

Bernanos was able to write regularly for the Brazilian press and for a few underground French magazines. *Time* magazine in its October 14, 1946, issue states: "Georges Bernanos is France's most distinguished Catholic author—and his own Church's sharpest critic." In an interview with the Most Reverend Edwin V. O'Hara, Bernanos explained his severe attacks on Catholics as an attempt to awaken Catholics to their responsibilities.

He is the author of: *Sous le Soleil de Satan* (Star of Satan) (1926); *Saint Dominique* (1927); *L'Imposture* (1927); *La Joie* (1928); *Jeanne D'Arc* (1929); *La Grande peur des Bien-Pensants* (1932); *Un Crime* (a Crime) (1935); *Journal d'un Curé de Campagne* (Diary of a Country Priest) (1936); *Nouvelle Histoire de Mouchette* (1937); *Les Grands Cimetières sous la Lune* (Diary of My Times) (1938); *Scandale de la Verité* (1938); *Nous autres Francais* (1939); *Lettre aux Anglais* (Letter to the English) (1942); *Monsieur Ouine* (1943); *Le Chemin de la Croix-des-Ames* (1943 and 1944), and *The Open Mind* (1945), translated by Geoffrey Dunlop.

M. S.

Louis Bertrand 1866-1941

Louis Bertrand, French writer and historian, was born at Spincourt (Meuse) on March 20, 1866. His background was conservative and royalist and his childhood—not a particularly happy one—was passed in the little village of Lorraine where he was born. He attended the Collège de Bar-le-Duc, and at seventeen went to Paris where he entered the Lycée Henri IV. Andre Bellesort, whose friendship for him dated from those times, described him at that age as distant and shy and says that reared in a religious and reactionary milieu, Bertrand, like many others of his generation, was exposed in student days to influences of moral anarchy. He was a royalist among republicans, and must have defended his views for Bellesort tells us that one day a professor said to him, *"Monsieur Bertrand, vous êtes un ancêtre* (M. Bertrand, you are an ancestor). However this may be, young Bertrand does not seem to have taken great interest in politics; he devoted himself to learning how to write. He greatly admired Flaubert, imitating and laboriously studying his style and construction. Later, as annotator and editor of Flaubert, he acknowledged his debt to his works and especially to Salambô.

Passing through the École Normale, Louis Bertrand was appointed, in 1888, to a professorship at the Lycée of Aix but was not happy there, and in 1891 obtained a post as professor of rhetoric at the Lycée of Algiers. Africa was for him a revelation; in this sunny climate he was delivered from his pessimism and enthusiastically devoted himself to the study of the history and inhabitants of the region. His observations made him more and more conscious of his Latin origins. "We are Latins"; he would say, "it is as Latins that we should think and act." He saw the French, Italians and Spanish who were colonizing Africa as a new and enterprising people, and he considered them as the prototype of what the united and regenerated Latin race would one day become.

Louis Bertrand spent eight years in Algeria without writing a line. "This was," he said, "my best school and the most fruitful period of my life." Little by little the plan of his future work took form, and in 1899 he wrote his first novel *Le Sang des Races,* the story of a Spanish muleteer transplanted and acclimated to North Africa. One of his great masters was Cervantes, traces of whom he found in Algeria.

Just as Africa awakened in him a new love and appreciation for his native France, it also brought him back to his Christian belief. He had gone through the period of disillusion and doubt which was the lot of many young Frenchmen of his day, but was led back to his Catholic faith by the study of African and Spanish traditions. It is not surprising that his first and perhaps his finest biography was of St. Augustine. Taking the *Confessions* in hand, he visited every spot connected with that great saint, endeavoring to reconstruct his life and surroundings. The critic J. Calvet states that Louis Bertrand was the originator and the master of contemporary hagiography which treats a saint's life as a work of art and at the same time as a work of faith. He worked as a novelist interested in complicated souls and vast backgrounds. Another great biography, that of Theresa of Avila likewise abounds in wonderful descriptive passages and proofs of psychological powers.

Louis Bertrand remained in Algiers until 1900. In 1897, two years after the publication of his first novel, he obtained the degree of *docteur-es-lettres* from the University of Algiers. On his return to metropolitan France he divided his time between Paris, a retreat he called "Chalet la Cina" near Nice, and numerous voyages in search of material. He was a hard worker and a prolific writer as the list of his books will show. All his travel books and almost all his novels celebrate the fecundity and the greatness of Mediterranean culture. His work presents a remarkable unity. His critical writings, *La Grece du Soleil* and the manifesto he called *Le Mirage Oriental,* denounce "the debacle of local color" in an Orient which is "neither the fairylike country described by our poets nor a land thirsting for modern civilization as our Utopians like to imagine." If he sounded the deathknell of poetic illusion, it was to make place for a reality which was the renaissance of Latin races in French Africa. He also believed that from Africa would flow renewed strength to the old civilization of France.

In 1926 he was elected to the French Academy to fill the chair left vacant by the death of Maurice Barres. He died at Cap d'Antibes, France, on December 6, 1941. He was unmarried.

Some of the works of Louis Bertrand are: *Le Sang des Races* (1899); *La Cina* (1901); *Sanguis Martyrum* (1917); *Mademoiselle de Jessincourt* (1911); *Louis XIV* (1923); *Gustave Flaubert* and *Les Villes d'Or* (1921). English translations of his works are: *The Art of Suffering,* translated by E. F. Peeler; *History of Spain,* translated by Warre B. Welles; *Louis XIV,* translated by Cleveland B. Chase; *St. Augustine,* translated by Vincent O'Sullivan. J. K.

Reverend Francis Salesius Betten, S.J.
1861-1942

It was out of practical necessity that Father Betten became an historian, in order to do something to counteract the conspiracy against the truth he found in most of the text books he had to use. So also his becoming a Jesuit was due to his reading about Bismarck's "Kulturkampf"; he wished to join the Order that had been driven out of Germany, though at that time he had never seen one of its members.

Born at Wocklum in Germany in 1861, the son of Francis Salesius and Clara Mertens Betten, he systematically prepared himself for the novitiate by attendance at the Paderborn Gymnasium, and entered the Society in Holland sixty years ago, studying afterwards in Austria and England. Oddly enough, his first interest in America, to which he did not come until 1898, was aroused by Father Finn's books for boys, several of which he translated into German. In the United States, teaching history at Canisius College, St. Louis University, John Carroll University, Cleveland and finally Marquette, he became convinced of the crying need for a textbook for schools and colleges that would be unobjectionable from the Catholic point of view. This need he supplied in his *Ancient World* (first edition—1916), which has had great success. It was a drastic revision of a previous work by W. M. West, and was issued with West's permission. Another text-book, *Ancient and Medieval History* (1928), had an equally wide appeal. Both works were done with characteristic Germanic thoroughness, as indeed is all of Father Betten's work. Among his other books are: *The Roman Index of Forbidden Books Briefly Explained* (1909); *Historical Terms and Facts* (1924); *The ABC of the History of Church Architecture* (1931); *St. Boniface and St. Virgil* (1927); *From Many Centuries*, a collection of twenty historical papers of interest to students (1938). Father Betten's had been a long life of remarkable devotion to his dream of providing colleges and high schools with good history text-books. If it involved some sacrifice of the delights of pure scholarship, there can be no question as to its disinterested usefulness.

Daniel Binchy 1899-

The distinguished Catholic scholar of Ireland, Daniel A. Binchy was born on June 3, 1899 at Charleville, County Cork, Ireland. He was educated at Clongowes Wood College; University College, Dublin; Munich; Berlin; Paris, and The Hague. His degrees, M.A. and Dr. Phil. were received from the National University of Ireland and Munich respectively.

From 1924 to 1932 he was professor of Jurisprudence and International Law at University College, Dublin. In 1926 he was a member of the Council of the Royal Irish Academy. From 1929 to 1932 he served as the first Irish Free State Minister to Germany.

Since 1934 he has been professor of Roman Law, Jurisprudence and legal history (including ancient Irish Law) at the University College, Dublin.

His principal work is *Church and State in Fascist Italy* (1941). This well-documented history stresses the Lateran treaties of 1929 between the Papacy and the Fascist Government of Italy. The *Times* [London] *Literary Supplement* calls it "a model of contemporary history." Dr. Binchy also wrote *Crith gablach, An Early Irish Legal Tract* (1940), papers on Old Irish Law, and articles for several Irish, English, and German reviews.

M. H.

Hugh (Aodh) de Blacam   1890?-

Since 1909 Hugh (Aodh) de Blacam has been a prodigious writer. He is fluent in both Gaelic and English; equally at home in prose and in verse. Under the pen name, "Roddy the Rover," he contributes a daily article to the *Irish Press.* "The World of Letters," the literary section of the *Irish Monthly* has been his output for many years. His books include novels, juveniles, biographies— in fact, there is hardly a literary form in which he has not been published. Lately he has shown an increasing interest in hagiography and drama. Mr. De Blacam has combined these two forms by recently publishing a number of plays based on the lives of saints. Through the drama, the most vivid of mediums, he is endeavouring to express his faith and mind. "The Faith and the lives of saints," he says, "are subjects which excite the creative mind. As the greatest of paintings here find themes, so what wonder that drama does the same." The playwright would have institutions such as dioceses, religious orders, and colleges dramatize the lives of their local saints or founders. Such plays, he believes, should be given as the Passion Play of Oberammergau is given. Thus the saints would be made to live before the eyes of generation after generation, and each generation would enrich such traditional productions with new lines, music and effects. In this way, he would have the dramatic muse made once more the handmaid of Faith.

In the second decade of the century Aodh de Blacam was active in the Sinn Fein Movement. In 1919 his inflammatory *Towards the Republic* was published. His political activities brought his imprisonment in 1922. He has described himself as "a thorough-going Nationalist," and a cause dear to him is the return of the six counties to the Irish Nation. In the English magazine, the *Nineteenth Century and After,* he once declared "the separation of my people from the National State, the branding of them as un-Irish, embitters me more than any other wrong that ever our nation endured. We Northerners could forgive anything save this."

Mr. De Blacam has worked hard for the upbuilding of a new Ireland but has not forgotten to cherish the splendid traditions of his ancient land. Such works as *The Black North,* for which President DeValera wrote a foreword, and *Gentle Ireland* (1935), narrate her history and customs, for her citizens and for aliens. *The Story of Columcille,* based on Gaelic literary and oral sources, has been adopted by schools throughout Ireland. The chief colleges of the country use *Gaelic Literature Surveyed* (1929). His influence has been further felt through his editorial work for such organs as *The Irish Commonwealth,* the *Irish Press,* and *The New Irish Magazine.* Countless contributions have appeared in the American and English presses, too. *The Authors' and Writers' Who's Who* lists his special subjects as Gaelic Literature, Irish History and Folklore, and Spanish Literature. Certainly, a vast scope.

The Irish writer was born about 1890 in London, England, of Ulster Protestant stock. His first impressions of Catholicism were gained in his youth from the Irish colony in that city. In 1913 he became a Catholic. He married the author of the *Rhymer's Wake,* Mary MacCarvill, in 1915. They have two children. They make their home at Sruhan House, Ravensdale, County Louth, Ireland.

Besides the works previously mentioned, he is the author of: *Credo* (1922); *Druid's Cave* (1919); *First Book of Irish Literature* (1934); *Flying Cromlech (The lady of the Cromlech-English title)* (1930); *Holy Romans,* (1920); *Life Story of Wolfe Tone* (1935); *Ship That Sailed Too Soon; Tales of the Gaels* (1922); *Uncle Pat's Plybook; From a Gaelic Outpost; Saint Patrick: Apostle of Ireland* (1941); *The Saints of Ireland* (1942); *The Golden Priest* (1937).   M. S.

Reverend Paul Lendrum Blakely, S.J.
1880-1943

Valued as the chief editorial writer of *America,* the Jesuit weekly, Father Paul Blakely, S.J., was a member of its staff for twenty-nine years. During this period, he wrote nearly seven thousand editorials for *America,* about twelve hundred articles, most of them for *America,* though he frequently wrote for other periodicals. Many of his articles appeared under the pseudonym "John Wiltbye." A second pseudonym, "Cricket Wainscott" was used when "Wiltbye" and Blakely were already signed to articles.

A son of Kentucky, he came of a family distinguished in the annals of that state through several generations of lawyers, journalists and soldiers. He himself was born in Covington, on February 29, 1880, the second child of the late Colonel Laurie John Blakely, who served in the Confederate Army and of the late Lily Hudson (Lendrum) Blakely. He received his early education from tutors and in private schools in Covington. In 1891 he entered St. Xavier High School, Cincinnati, Ohio, and after finishing his preparatory schooling attended St. Xavier College. After entering the Society of Jesus at St. Stanislaus Novitiate, Florissant, Missouri, in 1897, he completed his philosophical and theological courses at St. Louis University, Missouri. His B.A. degree was received from St. Xavier, Cincinnati, Ohio, in 1898; his Master of Arts degree from St. Louis University in 1904; his Ph.D. degree from Fordham in 1919 and the honorary degree, D.Litt. was conferred upon him in 1926 by Holy Cross College.

He taught Latin, Greek, and English at the University of Detroit, from 1900 to 1902 and from 1906 to 1909 was Professor of Literature at St. Louis University. In July 1914 he was named Associate Editor of *America*. For twenty-nine years, he continued in his role as critic and investigator of social and political evils. He was particularly interested in the labor question and in the encyclicals of Pope Leo XIII and Pope Pius XI, in their application to the economic structure of the United States. An ardent believer in Jeffersonian democracy, he never wearied of bringing home to the individual citizen his personal responsibility for the maintenance and preservation of the American Constitution. He was a champion of human rights.

A hatred of tyranny and oppression as well as of sham and hypocrisy, gave to his writing an alertness, sometimes a flavor of irony, which never failed to stimulate the reader. His interests were varied: sociology, education, constitutional law and school legislation. He was also an authority on the War for Southern Independence. Nevertheless, it was in his treatment of a purely literary subject that he was most happy. He wrote in a clear, incisive and, occasionally humorous style.

Though an authority on secular subjects, Father Blakely ever remained the spiritual-minded priest, intent on the work of His Master, as his three volumes of reflections on the Sunday Gospels testify: *Looking on Jesus* (1939); *Then Jesus Said* (1940); *We Wish to See Jesus*.

Though in frail health for several years, Father Blakely continued to work until the day before his death, February 26, 1943.

Two of his sisters are Mother Jane Frances Blakely and Sister M. Agatha Blakely of Cardome Visitation Academy, Georgetown, Kentucky.

P. B.

Melesina Mackenzie Blount (Mrs. George Norman)

It is under the pen name of Mrs. George Norman that Melesina Mackenzie Blount is better known, especially in America.

"Most writers," she says, "feel an urge, I suppose, to write from the dawn of (their) time. Daisy Ashford, the Catholic author of that now world-famous classic *The Young Visiters,* wrote it, as the spelling of the title might indicate, at the age of nine. I started at that of eleven but produced not a masterpiece, but the embryo of a novel whose name *Francine* I felt must ensure it a romantic success. The penny copy-book, however, was either confiscated by the nuns of the Sacred Heart Convent where I "commenced author" or was lost in my transference to another school, that of the English Convent at Bruges, surely the most charming, cultural and picturesquely lovely of Seminaries for Young Ladies. It had the quaintest customs: the pupils were 'the pensioners,' our main corridor was The Pant (I imagine from the old English word pantiles). We habitually addressed each other as 'Ladies' (Mesdames), the nuns used hour-glasses for clocks and so on. That was so then—now I fear it has become an up-to-date, a streamlined establishment. There at any rate, seven happy years were to go by for me, and there I was taught to write, not *Francines,* but as good English as the first-rate nun-teacher, herself an author of no mean quality, could impress upon my often wandering inner sense. If I never mastered the art of proper punctuation, that was due to an inherent inability of my own, not my teacher's.

"In those now long past days careers for women may be said not to have existed, the life of the average young English girl home from school was entirely domestic and social, made up of very light home duties such as turning out a drawer or so for mother in the morning, 'paying visits' with her of an afternoon—from three o'clock onwards one had to be dressed and ready for this, or for receiving visits on other days; then a rare 'party' or theatre and no cinemas at all, for there weren't any. And all the time one was conscious of an urge to do something, that there was something, somewhere, one could *do.* All educated up and nothing to do. Whether this quiet home-life with time for development and plenty of it, was not as well worth while as the feverish 'doing' one now looks back to as having missed, is a question. The net result for me, however, was that though I had 'written' largely at school, it did not even occur to me for at least three or four years that I could write in the old Georgian house, my home on the river Thames at Richmond, one of the historic and beauty spots of England. That I ever started is due to my winning a competition in *The Gentlewoman,* under a pen-name for which I have always had a shy and fatal partiality. It was not until I had married that I wrote a series of sketches that turned into a book; this beginning was in the most famous and literary of British evening papers, the old *Westminster Gazette* with a record of brilliant editors. After that I wrote a dozen or so of novels; the last five of which had a definitely Catholic interest, and then in 1929 a biography of Father Pro, the Mexican martyr, *God's Jester,* still finding a public interested in the romance and heroism of the life. Now I write chiefly on French Catholic authors and the intellectual Catholic revival in Europe!"

"Intermittently I did a certain amount of free-lance articles. I had discovered the lure of Fleet St. for it has atmosphere, something so alluring that even the amateur, nervously conscious of her status on such professional and expert ground, is drawn almost against her will. Just off Fleet St. is that home of ancient peace, The Temple. Nearby is Maiden Lane (named, no doubt, after Our Lady), and less than a mile away there are (or were alas before the Blitz) Paternoster Row, Amen Corner and other old Catholic street names. In Maiden Lane also is the Catholic actor's church, dim and quiet after the turmoil close by. In both Temple and church the rash amateur I felt I was would retire for comfort after the nervous strain of confronting her editors. On the other hand, perhaps mistakenly, I have never frequented literary sets, never for instance joined the famous Authors' Society or haunted literary lunches, or clubs, etc., where The Critics, it is hoped, may be met. The Catholic Writers' Movement started in 1940 by a dynamic group in New Zealand, does, on the other hand, interest me so much that I became a Foundation Life Member. This movement aims at enrolling all Catholic authors on an *international* basis; it does not seek to supersede existing societies such as that which New Zealand organisers term 'the magnificent Catholic Press Association of the U.S.A.,' but aims, rather, at affiliation."

Mrs. Blount is the author of: *Sylvia in Society; Lady Fanny; The Town on the Hill* (1927); *Hylton's Wife* (1929); *Brigit* (1930); *God's Jester* (1929); *King's Mountain* (1931); *Night of Spring* (1933).

Right Reverend Hugh Francis Blunt
1877-

The love Monsignor Hugh Blunt has for poetry was engendered in him in his youth. A product of the New England schools, much time was spent on the fundamentals and the appreciation of poetry. The poems of Longfellow and other New England poets had to be memorized. Monsignor Blunt ascribes to this training his first love of books.

Hugh Francis Blunt was born at Medway, Massachusetts, January 21, 1877, the son of the late Patrick and Ann Mahon Blunt. Both his parents were born in Ireland, but migrated to this country in their teens.

During his grammar school days, Hugh was an altar boy and he attributes to that fact his first desire to become a priest. When he finished grammar school, in 1892, he entered Boston College, twenty-five miles away, making the trip every day. By the end of the year his health gave way under the strain, so he transferred to St. Laurent College, near Montreal. At St. Laurent the English classics were stressed and the students drilled in writing. It was here that Hugh Blunt broke into print with a full page story in one of the Catholic papers.

In 1896 he left St. Laurent to enter St. John's Seminary, Brighton, Massachusetts, to study for the priesthood and was ordained in 1901. He was appointed temporarily to the Church at Stoneham, Massachusetts but later was made assistant at St. Peter's Church, Dorchester, Massachusetts. Despite a busy life with his priestly duties, he did much writing. Many of his poems were published in *Donahue's Magazine*.

Monsignor Blunt's first book *Poems* was published in 1911. In this same year, he became chief editorial writer for the Boston *Pilot*—a post he held until 1919.

In 1914 he was appointed Pastor of the Church at South Braintree, Massachusetts and after three years was sent to East Cambridge to edit the now defunct *Sacred Heart Review*. Monsignor Blunt was one of the first writers for the *Magnificat*, which Sister Ignatia of the Sisters of Mercy founded and still edits in Manchester, New Hampshire.

In 1919 Monsignor Blunt was awarded the Marian Poetry Prize by the *Queen's Work* magazine. Ten years later he won the Catholic Press Poetry Prize.

Monsignor Blunt has been pastor of St. John's Church, Cambridge, Massachusetts, since 1929. He prides himself especially on his parish school which, including a high school, registers nineteen hundred pupils.

In December 1944 he was one of the fifteen priests of the Boston Archdiocese who were raised by Pope Pius XII to the rank of monsignor.

Besides writing poetry, and prose, and contributing to almost every Catholic magazine here and abroad, Monsignor Blunt composed six hymns in honor of the Little Flower. He is also a lecturer and orator of note.

His books include: *Poems* (1911); *Songs for Sinners* (1912); *Great Wives and Mothers* (1912); *Fred Carmody* (1914); *The Dividers* (1920); *My Own People*, poetry (1921); *Great Penitents* (1922); *The Book of the Mother of God*, poetry (1925); *Spiritual Songs* (1925); *Homely Spirituals* (1926); *Great Magdalens* (1927); *Witnesses to the Eucharist* (1929); *Give This Man Place* (1934); *The Road of Pain* (1937); *Seven Swords* (1938); *Old Nuns and Other Poems* (1938); *Mother Seton*, play (1939); *Mary's Garden of Roses* (1939); *Mary Poems* (1939); *Listen, Mother of God* (1940); *The New Song* (1941); *Life with the Holy Ghost* (1944); *Our Lady and the Angels; The Quality of Mercy* (1945).

Monsignor Blunt's chief hobby during many years has been the collecting of books about Newman. His Newman library, which he gave to Regis College, is perhaps the most complete in the country, containing almost a thousand titles.

M. H.

William Joseph Blyton 1887-1944

Until the advent of World War II, William Joseph Blyton was principally occupied working his small farm in Surrey, England. He was a leading spirit of the Marydown Catholic land colony there. He succeeded in making unfertile acres bring forth abundantly. What writing he did was in his odd hours, for Catholic papers, on farming and on religious subjects.

When the war came, the government sent out its inspectors to tell farmers simple things about the land. Douglas Woodruff, at the time of his death in 1944 wrote of William Blyton in the London *Tablet:* "What finally drove him from the land again was not nature but man; the intolerable war-time pressure of the official on the countryman. He had not left the inkpots of Fleet Street to spend his days filling up forms and taking instructions." After three years, Mr. Blyton decided to sell the land he so loved and for which he had done so much. He returned to Fleet Street—to journalism. He was at one time London editor of the Manchester *Daily Dispatch.*

Mr. Blyton was born in 1887, the son of Samuel Felix and Catherine Blyton. In 1912 he married Elsie Hull. One son and three daughters were born of the marriage. In 1923 he was received into the Church. From 1926 to 1932, he was editor of the *Ransomer.* He wrote several books with the country tang, and they are delightful. His novels about country life are often fierce propaganda for Catholic simplicity. He is the author of: *The Law of Self Sacrifice; The Modern Adventure* (1930); *Gale Warning* (a novel) (1931); *Country Airs* (1935); *The Rolling Years: A Farmer's Log* (1936); *English Cavalcade* (1937); *We Are Observed* (1938); *Arrows of Desire* (1938); *Anglo-German Future* (1939). He is also the writer of several Catholic Truth Society booklets, and he contributed to the *Dublin Review, Hibbert Journal, Countryman, Cornhill* and other magazines.

M. H.

Mother Margaret Bolton, R.C.   1873-1943

For many years the Directress of methods of teaching religion in the American province of the Cenacle, a society founded for the purpose of teaching Christian Doctrine, Mother Bolton markedly influenced the teaching of religion in the United States. She had been insistent in her demand that sound pedagogical principles be applied in this field of teaching, and had urged the teacher of religion to make use of methods developed by modern educational research; and she had not only trained teachers; she had furnished the teacher and pupil with suitable texts. The desperate need for more interesting, stimulating, and compelling texts forced the educator into authorship.

In her books for children, Mother Bolton avoided the sentimental and the infantile. Based on modern pedagogical principles, her books not only teach the child his religion, but also aid his general education. Mother Bolton believed that a child who has been taught by *The Spiritual Way* stands in little danger of losing his faith, in maturity. A reviewer said of the four volumes of this series, "One closes the volumes with an almost Augustinian sigh; too late have I known thee, too late have I loved thee. But he is comforted with the thought that the children trained in the spirit of these textbooks will surely accomplish the things their teachers have only dreamed." Pope Pius XI praised *The Spiritual Way*.

Mother Bolton was a member of an enclosed community. Many other religious communities made it known that they desired to know more about her way of presenting the truths of our Faith; and the requests of several American bishops for her to be allowed to come to their dioceses to teach her methods induced Pope Pius XI to give Mother Bolton permission to go to any diocese when the bishop requested that she teach there. Pope Pius XII had renewed this permission.

Besides teaching the young and training teachers, Mother Bolton had also devoted herself to the instruction of converts. Through her classes in which she had regularly given presentations of Catholic doctrine to non-Catholics interested in religious education, she had made Catholic doctrine better understood and appreciated by those who had no desire for conversion.

Mother Bolton was born in Richfield Springs, a small town in New York, in 1873. Her parents, John and B. Anne Lannen Bolton, were her principal religious instructors in youth, for while the town had a church, there was no resident priest. In 1892 she graduated from the State Normal School in Albany. She continued her education with courses in English, psychology and elementary teaching at Columbia University (1899-1906). Theology she studied at the Cenacle (1914-1922). She began her long teaching career in the grade school at Patchogue, New York, when she was nineteen, and taught English in the New York City schools (1896-1906) and in the Training School for Teachers (1906-1913). At Fordham University she was associate professor of Religious Teaching (1928-1933). She has given courses in teaching Religion at Boston College, Loyola University (Chicago), Providence Teachers' College and St. John's University.

Besides *The Spiritual Way* series, Mother Bolton is the author of *Meditations for God-Loving Children* (1924); *The History of the Most Wonderful Promise Ever Made; A Little Child's First Communion* (1931); *Foundation Material for Catholic Action* (1938); *A Way to Achievement;* and *God's Hour in the Nursery* (1947).

Mother Bolton died February 27, 1943.   M. S.

Reverend John Louis Bonn, S.J.   1906-

Reverend John Louis Bonn, S.J., is another name that must be added to the lengthening list of creative writers among American Jesuits. Born at Waterbury, Conn., on October 28, 1906, he graduated from Boston College in 1929 and received the Master's degree from that institution in 1930. He was ordained priest on June 21, 1935, and received the licentiate in theology from the Gregorian University, Rome, in 1936. Greatly interested in the theatre as well as in poetry, he has been Dean of the Boston College School of Drama and Professor of Poetry at Boston College since 1937. Besides contributing to magazines, he has published one collection of poems and two prose works.

As distinguished a poet as Sister M. Madeleva, C.S.C., has described Father Bonn's *Canticle and Other Poems,* which appeared in 1936, as "compact of poetic power, wide scholarship, mystical insight," and she finds him reminiscent of Keats, Blake, and Emily Dickinson, but not derivative. Aline Kilmer pronounced the book "major poetry." He translates from the Gaelic, the Latin of the Venerable Bede, the Spanish of St. John of the Cross, and the French of St. Theresa of Lisieux. His lines have great freshness and power, and he is what might be called a poets' poet. But the poetry in this first collection is not such as is likely to become widely popular.

Father Bonn published *So Falls the Elm Tree* in 1940. It is the life story of Mother Ann Valencia, foundress of St. Francis' Hospital in Hartford, Connecticut. Instead of adhering to the conventional pattern of biography, Father Bonn has taken the rich materials afforded by the interior and exterior events in the life of this valiant woman and woven them into what in his Introduction he calls a "novel-biography." The book tries hard, he says, "to be that better fiction which is holier than fact —the fiction that sacrifices fact to the fundamental meanings of the facts, that sees things as symbols, that dares enter in under the sacred veil of things." Most readers will admit that it succeeds.

And Down the Days (1942) was a Catholic Book-of-the-Month Club selection. Taking its title from a line of Francis Thompson's *The Hound of Heaven,* it is a novel-biography of that strange and amazing woman, Elsa St. John Eckel, daughter of the notorious Maria Monk. Father Bonn brings to the telling of her story the same imaginative and dramatic gifts he displayed in *So Falls the Elm Tree.*

The sources for his books of verse were at first the classics; now they are social themes. The sources for his books of prose are people. Nearly always he takes his characters from real life. He prefers to write from midnight to dawn.

During World War II he was a chaplain in the United States Navy. He has since returned to Boston College and is Director of Drama and Moderator of the Boston Blackfriars. B. S.

Henry Bordeaux 1870-

When Henry Bordeaux was admitted to the French Academy in 1919, he was the youngest of the Forty Immortals. Now he is one of the Old Guard, looking back over years filled with literary activity, marked by many honors that came to him in the form of prizes awarded for his books, or distinctions such as the *Croix de Guerre* and *Officier de la Légion d'honneur.* His life was apparently unclouded by any great misfortune until the national disaster of 1940 came upon his beloved France to sadden all those who are loyal to her traditions.

He was born in Thonon, Haute-Savoie, in 1870, the son of one of the magistrates of the town. His childhood was peaceful and happy, passed among the beauties of nature that surround Lake Geneva. He attended the school of the Brothers of Mary, and then went to the College Stanislas and the Sorbonne in Paris. He studied law and received his degree from the Faculté de Droit in preparation for what he then intended to make his life work. He was always a great reader and even as a student began to write verses and to contribute articles to periodicals. In 1896 he was called back to Savoy on the death of his father, to take his place as head of the family. He took up the practice of law in the village and accepted the position of mayor for four years. At the time this set-back seemed disastrous to his career, but the experiences he gained then were later on valuable to him as a novelist.

In 1901 he married Mlle. Odile Gabet, and giving up the practice of law, devoted himself entirely to literature. During the World War I he served his country as captain and major, and was twice decorated for conspicuous bravery. He has three daughters, and before World War II, spent his winters in Paris and his summers in his chalet de Maupas in Savoy.

His most important works of criticism are *Les Ecrivains et les moeurs,* *Le Vie au théâtre,* and *Portraits d'hommes.* They prove him to be a clear thinker with considerable insight into drama and poetry and a rather marked preference for the seventeenth century classicists and his own contemporaries. So also in his biographical studies (Georges Guynemer, Barbey d'Aurevilly, St. Francis de Sales, etc.), he evinces sympathetic understanding and wise moderation in his evaluation of human endeavors.

The great bulk of his work, however, is made up of novels. Those best known in this country are probably *La Maison,* a defense of the sacredness of the home, *La Peur de Vivre,* the story of a courageous woman who was not afraid of life, and *Les Roquevillard,* a picture of the ruin brought on a whole family through the wrong-doing of one member. These three, with their wholesome traditionalism, are typical of the method and thought of the author.

Bordeaux can tell a good story, one that is worth reading just for itself, and in addition he consciously saturates it with large doses of moral teaching and Catholic philosophy. His main characters are usually very distinct and well-drawn, but the minor ones are sometimes shadowy and blurred. His style is clear and balanced, running along with the smooth gentle motion of a limpid stream. He is undoubtedly one of our most prolific writers, having produced an average of more than one work a year. In fact, he is too facile, for although he gives us books that are interesting and well-written they are lacking in that depth of thought and artistic perfection which characterize the world's greatest literature.

His works translated into English are *La Croisée des Chemins* (Parting of the Ways); *La Maison* (The House); *Les Yeux qui s'ouvrent* (Awakening); *La Peur de Vivre* (Fear of Living); and *La Neige sur les Pas* (Footprints Beneath the Snow).

Lucille Papin Borden 1873-

The novelist Lucille Papin Borden was born in Saint Louis, Missouri—a city founded by her great-great-grandfather, the Marquis Pierre Liquest de Laclede, in 1764. Her mother's family was of English Catholic descent, so her education was naturally enough entrusted to the Mesdames of the Sacred Heart at Maryville in her native city. In 1898 she married Gerald Borden of New York —who has served as Private Chamberlain under four Popes and is now also one of the Master Knights of Malta—and together they have spent richly rewarding years divided between Rome, Paris, London, the Pyrenees, the English countryside and along the shores of the Saint Lawrence in Canada.

It was not until the closing months of the first World War that

Lucille Borden—whose literary father used to regret that she would "never make a writer"—suddenly began to publish. A short story, "written to comfort those who were suffering," as she says, was listed with several stars in O'Brien's annual collection, and when the unexpected request for a novel arrived, she promptly composed *The Gates of Olivet*, using for material the miracles of Lourdes with which she was devotedly familiar. It has been reprinted annually since 1919, and was followed in 1923 by *The Candlestick Makers*, designed to offset popular birth-control propaganda. After this Mrs. Borden turned to the Catholic historical novel which she had often discussed with her friend Monsignor Benson, creating such works as *Gentleman Riches*, *Silver Trumpets Calling*, The Italian stories *Sing to the Sun* and *White Hawthorn*, *Starforth*, *The King's Highway* and the imaginative meditations of *Once in Palestine*. She has also done translations from the French, articles and verse—all achieved with beautiful Catholic spirit and smooth and cultured artistry. In 1943 she published, *From the Morning Watch*, and in 1945 *Francesca Cabrini: Without Staff or Scrip*.

At present Mr. and Mrs. Borden divide their time between a New York residence and their beloved "Anchorhold" at Bar Harbor. Recently awarded the decoration Pro Ecclesia et Pontifice by the present Holy Father, she flings in the face of a sad world her memories of long, active, and "heavenly happy," years.

K. B.

Paul Bourget   1852-1935

Poetry, criticism, novels, short stories and dramas have flowed from the pen of Paul Bourget. It is as novelist, however, that he won fame and will be best remembered.

Paul Bourget was born in 1852 at Amiens, in northern France, on the Somme River. His father, Justin Bourget, was a professor of mathematics. His mother was of German descent and was from Lorraine. To her, Bourget gives the credit for his poetic and philosophic bent; he ascribes his aptitude for clarity and analysis to his father. His education began at Strasbourg and continued at Clermont-Ferrand, Sainte-Barbe and Louis-le-Grand. The changing from one school to another was caused by his father, a professor of mathematics, transferring from one lyceum to another and taking the family with him. Looking back on these unsettled years, Bourget saw in them the source—at least in part—of the conflicts in his own character which, he felt, were also due somewhat to the diverse heredity of his parents.

At an early age, he read Shakespeare, Dickens, Walter Scott, Balzac, Stendhal and Baudelaire. Later Pascal, William James and Walter Pater influenced him. He was an avid reader and had a retentive memory.

Philosophy, Greek and Latin were his favorite studies at Sainte-Barbe. After receiving his licentiate degree in 1872 he began to teach at École Bossuet. He spent the following year travelling in Italy and Greece, and then decided to give up teaching as a profession. His decision cost him his allowance from his father. He tried to support himself by writing, but for ten years eked out a meagre existence, living in an attic. Besides writing poetry and magazine articles he taught backward students for a few hours a day. These years taught him, with great understanding, to bend down to human suffering.

In 1883 Paul Bourget's first story appeared, *L'Irreparable*—a study of a woman's character. It is—like all of his works—a psychological study. He displays the soul in its strength and in its weakness, and depicts the growth and development of passion. At times unlawful love is unduly stressed, and for this he has been criticized. He has been accused, too, of spreading discouragement and pessimism. He frequently develops the theme that children have to suffer for the sins of their parents. His plots are always well constructed and the interest is sustained. L'Abbe Dimnet said of him, "compared with most contemporary novelists he towers above them."

Bourget had been baptized a Catholic but in his youth and early manhood had been tainted with Agnosticism and Materialism. After his book, *Le Disciple* appeared in 1889, he identified himself with the conservative Catholic group. The chief character in the above mentioned book is Pope Adrian the Sixth, and although Bourget does not allow his hero to reach correct conclusions it is evident that the author himself accepts the utter dependence of man upon God, as the source of Good and Punisher of Evil. From then on he proceeded to revise some of his earlier writings and to stress the importance of religion. Catholic principles thereafter dominate the theme. His *Le Démon de Midi* will probably be of lasting value. It is one of his most popular novels in French. This "straying savant in literature," as Maurice Barrés called him, wished to cure and save.

In 1890, he married Mlle. David of Antwerp, Belgium. She died in 1932. In August, 1893 he visited the U.S. and spent nine months here. His impressions of this country are given in his book *Outre-Mer* (1895).

In this same year (1895) he was made a Member of the French Academy. Other honors were conferred upon him. He was appointed Curator of the Palace of Chantilly (1922) and in 1923 he was made Commander of the Legion of Honor. During his last illness in 1935, he was visited by His Eminence Cardinal Verdier, Archbishop of Paris.

He averaged a novel a year. He wrote in all more than seventy books. Sixty of these are listed in Macmillan's *Who Was Who*, 1929-1940. His first volume of poems appeared in 1875, under the title *La Vie Inquiete*. Among his books translated into English are: *A Cruel Enigma* (1887); *A Love Crime* (1887); *The Disciple* (1889); *A Woman's Heart* (1891); *The Land of Promise* (1895); *A Tragic Idyll* (1896); *The Screen* (1901); *The Blue Duchess* (1902); *The Weight of a Name* (1908); *Two Sisters* (1912); *The Night Cometh* (1916), and *The Goal* (1924).

M. H.

Right Reverend Patrick Boylan

A scholar and philologist of international reputation, Monsignor Patrick Boylan was a former vice-president and professor of scripture and oriental languages at St. Patrick's College, Maynooth. Later he assumed a professorship of Eastern languages at the University College, Dublin, and became Chairman of Irish Censorship of the Publications Board. Since 1939 he has been Vicar-General of Dublin and a Domestic Prelate. In 1941 The Holy Father appointed him Consultor of the Commission for Biblical Studies. He is president of the Catholic Library Association.

His books include: *The Psalms* (a study of the Vulgate Psalter in the light of Hebrew text); *Thoth, the Hermes of Egypt; The Epistle to the Hebrews* (a translation and brief commentary); *The Epistle to the Romans* (translation and commentary); and *Epistles and Gospels* (a commentary).

Reverend Neil Boyton, S.J. 1884-

The varied and colorful experiences of Father Neil Boyton have furnished the material for most of his books. A pleasant boyhood spent at Coney Island, New York, where his father invented and built the amusement device. Shooting the Chutes, gave him the data for two of his boys' books, *On the Sands of Coney* (1925), and its sequel, *Killgloom Park* (1938). *A Yankee Xavier* (1937), is a biography of Mr. Henry P. McGlinchey, S.J., who accompanied him in 1916, when he was sent as a Jesuit scholastic to teach in St. Mary's High School, Bombay, India. A victim of tropical fever, Mr. Boyton had to return to the United States and was sent to Georgetown University. His year in India, however, supplied him with notes for two books, *Cobra Island* (1922), and *Where Monkeys Swing* (1924).

His duties as a Chaplain at Camp Columbus, Leonardtown, Maryland, in the summer of 1922 helped him to write *Whoopee* (1923). Later, as a Scout Chaplain for eight seasons, he gathered material for *The Mystery of St. Regis* (1937); *Paul in the Scout World* (1940), and *Saints for Scouts* (1941).

Neil was the first of five sons born to his parents, Captain Paul Boyton and Margaret (Connolly) Boyton. His father had been with the Barnum and Bailey Circus and Neil spent a memorable week with the show. His mother was a lover of books and imparted this love to Neil.

His father's work kept the family on the move. From New York City, where Neil was born on November 30, 1884, he went to Milwaukee, Wisconsin and then to Chicago, Illinois. Here he attended St. Vincent's

Reverend Neil Boyton, S.J.

Parochial School and Melrose Academy. One year (1894-1895), had been spent at Notre Dame University as a minim. Returning to Chicago, he attended his first Jesuit School, St. Ignatius on the West Side. His schooling then continued at St. Michael's Parochial School in Brooklyn and later at St. Francis Xavier's High School in Manhattan. When he was graduated in 1904, he went to St. Louis, where his father had the Chutes concession on The Midway of the St. Louis World's Fair. In the fall, he entered St. Louis University. When the Fair closed his father took the family for a cruise on a houseboat down the Mississippi River.

In the fall of that year, Neil matriculated at Holy Cross College, Worcester, Massachusetts and was graduated in 1908. Less than twenty-four hours later, he was busy as an assistant manager at Steeplechase Island, Bridgeport, Connecticut, where his father was manager.

On December 7, 1909, Neil entered the Society of Jesus' Novitiate of St. Andrew-on-Hudson, Poughkeepsie, New York, and took his first vows on December 8, 1911.

While he was studying at Woodstock, Maryland, and teaching at St. Joseph's High School, Philadelphia, Pennsylvania, he wrote verse and short stories for various Catholic magazines. Some of these short stories were printed in book form under the titles: *In God's Country* (1923); *In Xavier Lands* (1937), and *On Hike to Heaven* (1942).

During World War I, Mr. Boyton, S.J., taught at Georgetown University where he had been sent upon his return from India. In the summer of 1919, he was sent to Woodstock, Maryland, to start his theological studies. Under a war privilege, he was ordained at the end of his second year of theology on June 29, 1921. His First Mass was read the following day at Dahlgren Chapel, Georgetown University, with his father and his brother, Claude Paul, as altar boys.

Two years later his superiors sent him to Georgetown Preparatory School, Garnett Park, Maryland, where he taught first year high school until 1928. While there he wrote his North American Indian Missionary stories: *Mangled Hands* (1926); *Mississippi's Blackrobe* (1927), and *Redrobes* (1936).

In 1928 Father Neil Boyton was transferred to Regis High School, New York City, where he taught for three years. From 1931 on he taught Latin and English at Loyola School, in New York City. In the summer of 1945 he was assigned to St. Ignatius Church as assistant pastor.

Father Boyton is also the author of *The Blessed Friend of Youth* (1929) (a biography of St. John Bosco); *That Silver Fox Patrol* (1944), and *The Summer Jerry Never Saw* (1945).

M. H.

Katherine Marie Cornelia Brégy 1888-

Since early girlhood this Philadelphian of French descent has devoted herself to a quest for the "beauty of holiness" as expressed in poetry. Neither her father—a distinguished judge—nor her mother had been brought up in the Catholic religion; but the Faith was "in the blood" through her forefathers the Comtes de Brégy or Brégi, so that she has always thought of herself as a "revert" rather than a "convert."

An autobiographical article describes Katherine Brégy as "rather a quiet, dreamy child, mildly given to dolls with elaborate names and elaborate garments, very much given to questions and not at all to outdoor sports," growing up in a dignified judicial home full of books, pictures and pets. Her early schooling was at a fashionable seminary of Presbyterian bias in her native city—where, however, her love of poetry and history soon attracted her to the ancient Catholic Church, and she was stirred deeply by the *Idylls of the King* and Mark Twain's life of *Joan of Arc*. At the age of fifteen she had already decided to become a Catholic, although her formal reception came some few years later.

While a student at the University of Pennsylvania Miss Brégy wrote a paper on Robert Southwell which was published in the *Catholic World*. This opened up the little known field of the more mystical Catholic poetry in which she was to become a specialist. An early visit to London brought her into the friendship and under the inspiring influence of Alice and Wilfrid Meynell and in due time she became one of the circle made vivid in this country by Joyce Kilmer. Her first book of appreciations, *The Poets' Chantry*, was much praised on both sides of the Atlantic, and has been followed at too long intervals by the equally discriminating critical volumes, *Poets and Pilgrims* and *From Dante to Jeanne d'Arc*, as well as by two collections of original verse, *Bridges* (1930) and *Ladders and Bridges* (1936).

In 1927 Katherine Brégy won, in international competition, the Leahy Prize of $1,000 for the best short essay on Dante, and a sonnet of hers captured the gold medal for Pennsylvania in a recent poetry contest at the New York World's Fair. But in the main her work has never been on the popular side, although she has had what she calls "episodes of straight teaching" and of newspaper writing. Even more personally than through her books, magazine articles and reviews, she spreads her literary gospel on the lecture platform, where her specialties are contemporary—especially Catholic—English, French and American poetry and drama.

Clothed in her "perpetual purples" Miss Brégy might give the impression of a gracious woman of the world rather than a serious and spiritual critic, but she herself would probably find no contradiction in these feminine contrasts. She has received the honorary degree of Litt. D.

from D'Youville College, Buffalo, and was the first woman to be so honored by Holy Cross College, Worcester; while her devotion to French culture won the decorations of Officier d'Academie and Officier de l'Instruction Publique, from the Third French Republic.

She is a member of the Poetry Society of America, the Philadelphia Art Alliance, the Catholic Association for International Peace, and is past-president and at present vice-president of the American Catholic Poetry Society.

Reverend André Bremond, S.J. 1872-

Henri Bremond's seven-years-younger brother André is today probably better known to Americans than is the great historian of seventeenth century French religious thought.

Father André Bremond was born in 1872 at Aix-en-Provence and educated there at Sacred Heart College, entering the Society of Jesus in October, 1889, at St. Stanislaus's College, St. Leonard's-on-sea, England.

In 1923 he went to the Island of Jersey to teach philosophy in the French scholasticate of the Society. In 1937 he taught a course on Aristotle at the Fordham summer school. The journey to America and the course he gave at Fordham University, were, he writes: very striking and interesting events. His teaching at Fordham was the occasion for his agreeing to write two popular books on which rest his American fame. One day at Fordham, the "head of the literary department at Benziger's called and asked me point-blank if I had anything to give him for print. I happened to have some papers on 'prehistoric philosophy' with the addition of some chapters, they could be shaped into a small book introductory to the study of philosophy. Such was the origin of *Philosophy in the Making*. An English adaptation of my French book *Rationalisme et Religion* was made at the same time at the request of Father Husslein, the editor of The Science and Culture series and appeared under the title of *Religions of Unbelief*." Other books are: *Le Dilemme Aristotélician* (1933); *La Piété Grecque* (1914), and in collaboration with his brothers, Henri and John, *Le Charme d'Athènes*.

His other literary work has been largely in French scholarly reviews. At one time he was joint editor of the great philosophical review *Archives de Philosophie*. He made contributions to the English and American reviews *New Verse, Month, Thought* and the *Journal of Religion*.

Father Bremond says of himself: "I have earned a certain reputation as a raconteur of tales (borrowed with free adaptation from such classics as Wells, Wallace, Chesterton and Wodehouse) . . . a gift which has stood me in good stead with boys young and elderly." And he adds, "I dare say my best work has been as a professor." H. B.

Reverend Henri Bremond   1865-1933

The great work for which the Abbé Bremond will long be remembered is the eleven volumes of his unfinished *Literary History of Religious Thought in France*. It was planned to comprise fourteen volumes. He died soon after the completion of the eleventh volume. Three volumes were translated into English between the years 1928 and 1937. In 1936 Charles Grolleau brought out a general index under the title: *"Index Alphabétique et Analytique à l'Histoire Littéraire du Sentiment Religieux en France de Bremond*. Abbé Dimnet appraises Bremond's work as a "monument of psychological acumen as well as erudition." The French Academy awarded it The Grand Prix in 1922 and the following year elected its author to membership. He was received at the French Academy May 22, 1924.

Henri Bremond was born in 1865 at Aix-en-Provence. His forebears had been lawyers, and loyal to the Church. His two brothers entered the Society of Jesus and the three daughters of his only sister became Benedictine nuns.

After graduating from the College of Aix, he went to England to join the Jesuits in 1882. He was sent to Wales for his philosophical and theological studies. In Great Britain he cultivated a scholarly interest in English literature. While he liked the works of George Eliot and Charles Dickens he was especially influenced by Newman. Later he wrote a penetrating study on the mentality and character of Newman. Abbé Bremond was ordained in 1892.

Upon his return to France, he engaged in the teaching of philosophy in various schools of the Society of Jesus. Then he was sent to Paris to work on *Études Religieuses,* the well-known monthly of the Jesuits in France. Through his illuminating articles, which were simple and sincere, he won many friends. One of these was Abbé Dimnet. It was Bremond's article on Newman's *Sermons* that gave the urge to Dimnet to write to him. And thus a friendship of thirty-odd years was started—the last ten years of which were spent together, sharing an apartment in Paris, Abbé Bremond having left the Jesuits in 1904.

In his earlier years as a secular priest Abbé Bremond was constantly changing his living quarters. He rented rooms for only a few weeks. It was not until 1924 that he finally settled down at 16 rue Chanoinesse, with Dimnet. Bremond was satisfied with little furniture. The provençal furniture that he accumulated he put into four garrets.

Henri Bremond was likewise an intimate friend of Maurice Barrès, a prominent literary figure. They first met in 1900. In 1923 Bremond wrote an article on Maurice Barrès for *Le Correspondant*. Although he read voraciously, he kept about twenty-five volumes in his room. Most of his work was done in public libraries. His writings which were voluminous, were crowned four times by the French Academy. His special field was history.

His books in English are *Blessed Thomas More* (1904); the three volumes of *The Literary History of Religious Thought in France,* viz. *Devout Humanism,* Vol. 1; *Coming Mysticism,* Vol. 2; and *Triumph of Mysticism,* Vol 3; *Mystery of Newman* (1905); *Prayer and Poetry, a Contribution to Poetical Theory* (1927), and *Thundering Abbot* (1930), which recounts the story of Armand de Rancé, reformer of La Trappe, and is told with skill, wit and learning.

His book *Sainte Chantal,* a biography of St. Jeanne de Chantal, was condemned and put on the Index. The book was withdrawn by the author. That Abbé Bremond was loyal in his filial devotion to the Holy See, there is no doubt. A special blessing of Pope Pius XI reached him in his last hours.

The *Petit Journal* lamented the passing of "one of the most eminent souls of our time . . . a great man of letters who was also a model priest."

This Officer of the Legion of Honor, Doctor of Literature, honoris causa, of Oxford, historian, member of the French Academy and littérateur died in 1933.

H. B.

Reverend Robert Edward Brennan, O.P. 1897-

Psychology classes at Providence College, where Father Brennan is chairman of the department of philosophy, and, more recently, lectures at the Thomistic Institute, of which he is director, know him for his mild, flexible, yet unerringly directive manner of teaching. The Thomistic Institute of Providence College, established six years ago by Father Brennan, is a unique foundation. It draws its teachings and its principles from the pure wellsprings of St. Thomas, its pattern and inspiration from the medieval system of guilds, and its temper from the ideals and human approach of its director. The Institute is an organization attempting to apply the teachings of St. Thomas to modern professional and business life through the formation of guilds for such groups as nurses, doctors, lawyers, and teachers. The topics discussed are up-to-date and soundly practical. "The analysis of contemporary problems must be wrought in the same spirit and with the same temper that distinguished Aquinas in his dealing with his own age," Father Brennan tells his guild-members. The guilds are part of the parent and coordinating body, the Thomistic Institute, which is devoted to research and publications of the College faculty. All this is primarily "an adventure into the realm of the intellectual, an experiment in speculation."

Father Brennan was born in 1897 in Lima, Ohio. His education was entirely in Catholic schools. In 1918 he entered the Dominican novitiate in Somerset, Ohio, proceeding to further study at St. Rose Priory, Springfield, Kentucky; and finally to the Dominican House of Studies at the Catholic University, Washington, D. C. Here he specialized in psychology and prepared for the priesthood, being ordained in 1925. He received his Doctorate in philosophy at the Catholic University in the same year, and his Lectorate in theology in 1926. In 1944 the degree of Master in Sacred Theology, the highest obtainable in the Dominican order, was conferred on him.

Father Brennan's first assignment was to the missions in Kienningfu, Fukien, China, where he spent five years. He soon mastered the Chinese language, teaching it to the Chinese children and compiling his *Chinese-Latin Manual of Prayers*. He was made Director of Catholic Schools in the district belonging to the American Dominican Fathers. At length malaria and sunstroke, the latter occasioned by too much horticultural enthusiasm, got the better of him; and he returned in 1931 to teach psychology at Providence College. A few years back, his knowledge of Chinese was put to good use when he was called suddenly to a Boston hospital to hear the confession of a Chinese woman and to prepare her for death.

Besides his directorship of the Institute and a full schedule of teaching undergraduate courses in psychology, Father Brennan has found time for the publication of books and articles. In 1937 he published, as the first book to appear under the name of the Thomistic Institute, *General Psychology*, which he subtitled "An Interpretation of the Science of Mind based on Thomas Aquinas." His next volume, *Thomistic Psychology*, was published in 1941. Mortimer Adler has called this book "the pioneer's work" in the promulgation of a unified psychology which will incorporate "all the truths we now know about human nature, both philosophical and scientific." *History of Psychology* appeared in 1945.

Father Brennan had long interested a group of Thomists, both from the United States and abroad, in the publication of a symposium which would cover critical problems in the whole field of Thomistic philosophy. After five years of collaborate effort, this work has just recently appeared. Entitled *Essays in Thomism*, it represents the contribution of sixteen of the foremost living Thomists in the English-speaking world. Father Brennan is now engaged in writing a *Thomistic Cosmology*, which will complement his work in psychology and give a rounded analysis of the whole philosophy of Nature. Meanwhile, the work of the Thomistic Institute goes forward in vigorous crescendo, showing "the appeal that philosophy can have for all peoples, and how it can help in the solution of everyman's problems."

R. H.

Reverend James Brodrick, S.J.   1891-

Confining himself to writing on subjects pertaining to the Society of Jesus (of which he is a member) and the celebrated members of that Society in the past, Father Brodrick has written only six books but they are voluminous.

He was born in 1891 in Athenry, County Galway, Ireland, the son of Peter and Julia (Rushe) Brodrick. It is a town in the far west of Ireland whose ancient walls and towers are still standing. It is called Athenry which means the "Town of the Kings" but there have been no kings there for a long time. Poverty drove his people to England. He was educated at Stonyhurst College, Lancashire and St. Beuno Beuno's College, Wales. He received his M.A. degree from London University in 1919.

After he went to England in 1910, he joined the Jesuits. He was ordained a priest in 1923.

The six books he wrote are: *Life and Work of St. Robert Bellarmine* (2 vols) (1928); *Economic Morals of the Jesuits* (1934); *St. Peter Canisius* (1935); *The Origin of the Jesuits* (1940), and *The Progress of the Jesuits* (1947). He does some writing for *The Month* and *The Tablet* (London). His books are highly documented and thus let the past speak for itself.

M. H.

Heywood Broun   1888-1939

One of the ablest Bible-quoters in United States journalism, Heywood Broun's parable about Christmas was read over the radio by President Roosevelt on Christmas Eve, 1937. While at Harvard, Broun took a course in the Bible as English literature in which the effect of the Bible on the styles of various writers was emphasized.

Broun was brought up in a wealthy Episcopalian family and from the beginning was tender, sentimental, religious, a friend of the downtrodden. Because of his leanings towards communism and membership in the Socialist Party—until he resigned in 1931 —almost everybody was surprised to hear he had become a Catholic. The first hint that he gave of his interest in the Catholic Church was in his column "It Seems To Me" of March 2, 1939, the day following the election of Pope Pius XII. After about ninety hours of instruction by Monsignor Fulton Sheen, Mr. Broun was baptized on May 23, 1939. A few days later he became the first person to be confirmed by Archbishop (now Cardinal) Francis Spellman as Ordinary of New York.

In an interview with an editor of *The Tidings,* Los Angeles, he said, "I sorely needed the companionship of Jesus Christ—that was the compelling cause of my conversion to the Catholic Church." Other motives, according to Monsignor Sheen, were a visit he made to the Shrine of Our Lady of Guadalupe in Mexico, the election of Cardinal Pacelli as Pope Pius XII, which convinced him there was only one moral authority left in the world and that is the Papacy, the fear of death, and lastly, he said, "There is nothing more ridiculous than individualism in either economics, politics, or religion."

Heywood Campbell Broun was born in Brooklyn, New York, on December 7, 1888, the son of Heywood Cox Broun and Henriette (Brose) Broun. His father was of Scotch descent. As a boy Heywood Campbell Broun attended the Horace Mann School in Manhattan where he was voted the best all around man in his class. He then went to Harvard in 1906 but never was graduated because of difficulty with elementary French. At Harvard his classmates included Stuart Chase, Jack Reed, Walter Lippmann and Hamilton Fish.

In 1912 he joined the re-write staff of the New York *Tribune* and soon was moved to the sports department and assigned to write baseball. He became a brilliant reporter of this sport and he never lost his flair for writing about the game. His baseball stories for *The Tribune* have been called the best ever written. When the dramatic critic of *The Tribune* died Heywood Broun succeeded him. In this field he showed himself likewise competent. Then in 1921 he was given a column to write. He insisted that he be given complete independence in writing it. The column was called "It Seems To Me." The column became very popular and was most widely read. It was really the beginning of Broun's career.

For eighteen years this column ran, first in *The World,* then in Scripps-Howard's *Telegram,* later in *The World-Telegram,* when the publisher Howard merged the two papers in 1931. The New Deal caused a feud between his employer Roy Howard and himself which finally terminated his relations with *The World-Telegram* when his contract ran out December 14, 1939. The next day he began working for the New York *Post.* By his transfer, Heywood Broun lost considerable money, being paid much less than his $39,000 a year salary with the *World-Telegram.* Mr. Broun had been with the Scripps-Howard newspapers since 1928. On Friday, December 15, his first column appeared in the New York *Post.* It was also his last. He was stricken with pneumonia and died December 18, 1939—mourned by Jew, Protestant, and Catholic alike.

A prodigious writer in spite of his pose of indolence, he figured that he had turned out close to 21,000,000 words during his thirty-one years as a newspaper man. "I have averaged 2000 words a day for thirty years," he said. He could be devastating in print although he was by nature extremely genial, gregarious, sympathetic, and very polite. He took pleasure in meeting his worst enemies socially.

Somehow he found time to paint pictures, run for Congress, run a weekly newspaper (The Connecticut *Nutmeg*), organize The American

Newspaper Guild of which he was president from its beginning, and to lecture on the drama at Columbia University in 1920 and at the Rand School in 1921.

His first wife was Ruth Hale whom he married in 1917. They were divorced in 1933. She died a year later. His second wife, a Catholic, is Constantina Maria Incoronata Fruscella Dooley, a former actress.

Mr. Broun is the author of *A. E. F. With General Pershing and American Forces* (1918); *Seeing Things At Night* (1922); *The Sun Field* (1923); *Sitting On The World* (1924); *Gandle Follows His Nose* (1926); *Anthony Comstock, Roundsman of The Lord* (with Margaret Leech) (1927); *Christians Only* (with George Britt) (1931).   M. H.

Alfred J. Brown   1894-

Walking for walking's sake has always been in the blood of Alfred J. Brown. When as a soldier, in the first World War, he obtained his first "leave," he astonished the rest of the regiment when they learned he spent his time walking. "There is, of course," said Mr. Brown, "a world of difference between 'route-marching' and walking for fun." Joined by his friend "Ouse," G. C. Heseltine, author of *Great Yorkshiremen,* etc., they "walked from Ilkley to Kettlewell, then over Great Whernside and down Nidderdale, finishing at the Camp at Harrogate. That walk has colored my whole life. It opened my eyes to the glory of Yorkshire." About seven years later he wrote his first Yorkshire book *Four Boon Fellows.* Mr. Brown thinks that is his best book, despite the fact that most London publishers rejected it. Mr. Hugh Dent, of J. M. Dent & Sons, wrote him a charming letter to say that as a Yorkshireman he felt the book ought to be published but as a publisher he had grave doubts. He published it, however.

About this time, Mr. Brown began writing essays and sketches on his walking experiences in Yorkshire. These were sent to *Country Life* and accepted by its editor, the late Edward Hudson. Mr. Hudson asked Mr. Brown to do him a book about Yorkshire. *Moorland Tramping* was the result, which has been his most successful book. Later a second volume, *Tramping in Yorkshire, N. and E.* was published. Through these books, Mr. Brown became known as a writer of walking books. *Broad Acres* is a collection of some essays, sketches and verse about different aspects of Yorkshire. A novel, *Golden Fleece* is in manuscript.

Mr. Alfred Brown was born in 1894 in the West Riding, Bradford, England, and is exactly the same age as J. B. Priestly who was also born in Bradford. He was educated at St. Bede's Grammar school in Bradford, and privately. In 1927 he married Marie-Eugenie Bull. They have three daughters and one son.

Apart from authorship, he is a director and foreign traveller for a merchant house in England and before the second World War spent half the year travelling about Europe.

During World War I, Mr. Brown was invalided from the army as "totally incapacitated" for further service due to an attack of diphtheria, which made him ill for several years, four of which he spent in a hospital.

While he was convalescing, he read and wrote verse. When he regained his strength, he went to Belgium for a short walking tour and wrote his first book, *Joyous Entry*, "on the strength of that scanty experience." Shortly afterwards "the story of my post-hospital days—somewhat embellished—formed the background of my first novel *The Lean Years*, which was published under the pseudonym, 'Julian Laverack.' " Mr. Brown served in the Royal Air Force in World War II.

Douglas Jerrold of Eyre & Spottiswoode accepted his manuscript dealing with some of his RAF experiences from 1940 on.   M. H.

Reverend Stephen J. Brown, S.J.   1881-

A good part of Father Stephen Brown's life has been spent as a librarian and since 1929 he has been a lecturer in bibliography in the School of Library Training of the National University of Ireland. In 1922 he founded the Central Catholic Library in Dublin, of which he is now the Honorary Librarian. Thus his interest in books and libraries has been perennial.

Father Brown was born in Hollywood, County Down in 1881, but the family moved shortly afterward to County Kildare. He followed his education at Clongowes Wood College from 1892 to 1897 and at the Royal University of Ireland. In September, 1897, he entered the Jesuit Novitiate at St. Stanislaus College at Tullamore. He studied philosophy at Maison St. Louis with the French Jesuits at Jersey, Channel Islands.

He taught at Clongowes Wood College for six years before and three years after his ordination, which was in 1914. Theology he studied at Milltown Park, Dublin where he is now stationed. From 1919 to 1921 he had special Scripture studies at Hastings, England with the French Jesuits. He was professor of Sacred Scripture at Milltown Park from 1921 to 1924 and from 1926 on, spent several years at Rathfarnham Castle in Dublin.

After five years of effort he succeeded in 1936 in inducing the government to inaugurate a system of supplying books to the hospitals throughout Ireland and became Chairman of the Hospital Library Council. He was one of the Irish delegates to the International Conferences at Oxford in 1925, at London in 1936, at Dublin in 1937 and at The Hague in 1938.

While Father Brown felt quite early the urge to write, it was not until 1910 that he had a book published. This was *A Reader's Guide to Irish Fiction*, written with the purpose of doing something useful for Ireland

and to preserve the memory of hundreds of fine books. This book was revised and enlarged in 1916 under the title *Ireland In Fiction*.

The Realm of Poetry appeared in 1921. Based on notes of a nine years' period of teaching, the book "was written in the hope of making its readers sharers in an experience which has been for the writer, as for countless other men, a source of unfeigned delight." The nature and inner meaning of poetry are deftly handled, helping toward the appreciation of the best poetry.

Six years later *The World of Imagery* was published. Considerable portions of the first seven chapters of this book appeared in the Irish Ecclesiastical Record. Chapters one and six appeared in the American periodical *Thought*.

To prevent deserving books from being forgotten, Father Brown took an interest in Bibliography. In 1928 he published *The Preacher's Library* in which pulpit literature was recorded. His *Catalogue of Novels* and *Tales by Catholic Writers* passed through seven editions. Other volumes by Father Brown are: *An International Index of Catholic Biographies* (1935); *Catholic Mission Literature* (1932); *Divine Song Book* (1926); *Guide to Books on Ireland* (1912); *International Relations From a Catholic Standpoint* (1932); *Introduction to Catholic Booklore, Catholic Juvenile Literature, Poison and Balm* (1938); *From God to God: an Outline of Life* (1940); *Poetry of Irish History* (1927); *The Press in Ireland* (1937); *Studies in Life By and Large* (1942), and *A Survey of Catholic Literature* (1943).

In 1943 Father Brown was named Chairman of the recently-organized Book Association of Ireland. The purpose of this organization is to promote the reading, publication and circulation of books of Irish interest which have little or no appeal to the National Book Council of England. "The association will direct its attention chiefly to books in the Irish language, books by Irish authors, books published in Ireland and works of special Irish interest wherever published." M. H.

Reverend Henry J. Browne, S.J. 1853-1941

Much of Father Browne's life was devoted to the classics and he was blessed with a long life indeed. Most of his writing, naturally enough, had been of a technical sort, dealing directly with the problems of teaching Greek and Latin in secondary schools. *The Road to Rome,* a compilation which he edited and for which he wrote a short autobiographical sketch is his only generally popular book. But in his special field he had honor and success. He took a leading part in founding the Classical Association of Ireland and was its president in 1913; he served on official government committees working on the relationship between archaeology and classical instruction, between museums and education. In this connection he visited the United States and spoke at some of the leading American universities to give a report on the work done; he had experimented in the melodic rendering of Greek choral rhythms, giving demonstrations at Columbia and Chicago Universities. After many years of distinguished service he was made professor Emeritus of Greek at the University College, Dublin.

Father Browne was born in 1853 at Birkenhead, the second son of J. Wilson Browne. He was educated at King Edward's High School, Birmingham and New College, Oxford. He pursued his theological studies at St. Beuno's College, N. Wales, where he was also ordained a priest. He entered the Irish Province of the Society of Jesus in 1877.

When the Catholic Truth Society of Ireland brought out his *The City of Peace* it suppressed his name. It was, as the preface states, mainly a reprint of St. Joseph's Sheaf, of which Father Browne was editor then and for twenty-five years. His books are: *Our Renaissance—Essays on the Reform and Revival of Classical Studies* (1917); *Handbook of Homeric Study* (1905); *Handbooks of Greek and Latin Composition* (1903). He also edited the *City of Peace* (1903); contributed to *History of Religions* (1910); *The Catholic Evidence Movement* (1924); and *Darkness or Light?* (1925).   H. B.

Lillian Browne-Olf   1880-

Raised in an anti-Catholic environment and born of strongly anti-Catholic parents, Lillian Browne-Olf became a Catholic in 1938. She had been baptized a Congregationalist, but had long since separated from that sect, and in her search for a way of life consistent with the urge for personal freedom and her ardent desire for world peace had sampled many of the prevalent "isms" of the day.

While still a child she went with her mother to hear Father Chiniquy of "Fifty Years in the Church of Rome" fame. Although her reaction to "this nice ruddy-faced, white haired gentleman" was not unpleasant, she could not but feel that the disclosures made by him and *The Menace* and like publications of "escaped nuns" and suchlike "revelations" were "laid on a bit too thick."

Her suspicions were aroused while studying the history and appreciation of art, under Dr. Von Mach of Harvard. But all her former prejudices received their first real jolt when she began studying history first-hand by travel in Europe. Four extended tours in Europe were the true source of her conversion. Her indignation was great when she saw the devastation done to monasteries and cathedrals in England by Henry VIII and by Cromwell, and in Paris and rural France by the Revolutionists. These revealing facts gave her the urge to rectify the intellectual wrongs done to her in childhood.

In 1929 she had her first audience with the late Pontiff, Pius XI. Again in 1930 and in 1931 she repeated these experiences at the Vatican. One day while in San Paolo fuori le Mura, looking up at the medallions of all the popes, she determined to write a life of the reigning pontiff whose niche on the architrave was as yet, empty. Her *Pius XI: Apostle of Peace*, published by Macmillan in 1938 was the result. She was still a non-Catholic—"at least officially." Her book, *Their Name is Pius,* deals with the modern popes who bore that name—from the time of the French Revolution to the present and is a study of the conflicts of these pontiffs with the various "isms" prevalent during their pontificates. It is the struggle of Christ against anti-Christ and points out the cause of World War II whose roots go far back to Pius VI's time. The research for this book was done at the Vatican Library. In 1943 *The Sword of St. Michael: The Life of St. Pius V* was published.

Mrs. Browne-Olf was born in Bradford, Massachusetts, the youngest daughter of Francis Myron and Sarah Amanda (Lavers) Browne, on February 14, 1880. She attended Bradford High School and Bradford Academy. At these schools she took all the prizes in literature. She studied a year at Wellesley College, leaving to be married. She has one son.

Mrs. Browne-Olf collaborated with John Hayes Holmes on an Anthology, *The Grail of Life.* She translated from the Italian Dr. Rocco Lazazzera's *The White Cavalier.* She is also a free lance writer and a poet. "Ever since I can remember I have been interested in World Peace and International understanding." For two seasons she was Leader of the local branch of the National Committee on the Cause and Cure of War.

Mrs. Browne-Olf lives in Chicago.   I. C.

Josephine Van Dyke Brownson   ?-1942

Granddaughter of "the father of American philosophy," as Orestes A. Brownson was known, and daughter of Major Henry F. Brownson, editor of his father's works and recipient of the Laetare Medal in 1892, as was his daughter in 1939, Josephine Van Dyke Brownson carried on an illustrious family tradition in literary, educational and religious leadership.

She was educated at the Sacred Heart Convent in Detroit, Grosse Pointe, Michigan and the Sacred Heart Convent in Albany, New York. She received her A.B. from Michigan University and an LL.D., from the University of Detroit.

"All my life," she says, "my hobby has been to teach religion to neglected children." Stated with typical modesty, this became her life work, from whence stemmed her writings: *Catholic Bible Stories from the Old and New Testament* (1919); *Stopping the Leak* (1928); *Learn of Me* (series of eight books for the first eight grades in religion); *Living Forever-on Church and Sacraments* (for high schools); *Come Unto Me*

(1938); *Feed My Lambs* (1938); *Come and See* (1939); *To the Heart of a Child* (1934), and *Thou Art Peter* (1938).

Giving courses in Old Testament religion to teachers at the Detroit University led to her founding, in 1906, the Catholic Instruction League in Detroit. In 1939, when Miss Brownson was awarded the Laetare Medal —the only descendant of a former medalist to receive this honor, bestowed annually by Notre Dame University, since 1883, upon an outstanding lay Catholic—more than four hundred teachers and thirteen thousand students were under her supervision. She is the eleventh woman to receive the award since 1934.

"Miss Brownson was one of the first Catholics in any country to organize on an extensive scale the catechetical instruction ordered by Pope Pius X in his encyclical 'Acerbo Nimis' published in 1905," said the Reverend John F. O'Hara, C.S.C. then President of Notre Dame University in announcing the award.

Formerly an instructor of mathematics at Cass Technical High School, Detroit, she resigned her position in 1936 to devote her time to religious instruction. She was a leader also in social work. She was a member of the commission that was sent to Venezuela in 1939 to advise the government there on social service technique.

Recognition of her work in the cause of Catholic Action was made by the late Pope Pius XI, when he conferred upon Miss Brownson the Papal Decoration "Pro Ecclesia et Pontifice," in 1938.

After a year's illness, Miss Brownson died in 1942.   I. C.

Jean Bruchesi 1901-

The Under-Secretary of State of the Province of Quebec, Jean Bruchesi, is a writer not only on International Politics and French History, but also on classical subjects. Born at Montreal, Canada, on the 9th of April, 1901, Jean Bruchesi is the son of Charles Bruchesi, K.C. and Elmira Desnoyers. An uncle, Mgr. Paul Bruchesi, was Archbishop of Montreal from 1897 to 1939.

He followed his classical studies with the Sulpicians and afterwards with the Jesuits. Then he studied law at the University of Montreal. In 1923, he was one of the Secretaries of the Canadian Economic Mission in France headed by Senator Beaubien. He obtained his Master's degree in law in 1924 and was admitted to the Bar that same year. Returning to France the following year, as winner of a Province of Quebec scholarship, he remained in Paris from 1924 to 1927. While there he studied Political Science, History and International Law, becoming the originator of many Franco-Canadian manifestoes. Having secured a diploma from l'Ecole Libre des Sciences Politiques (Diplomatic Section) he was, in 1927, placed in charge of a course in general history at the Faculty of Letters of the University of Montreal.

The next ten years were divided between teaching, writing and travelling. In 1929, he was appointed Professor of Political Science and of External Politics at the Faculty of Social, Economical and Political sciences of the University of Montreal. In 1931, he took over the chair of Trade Relations. During these years, he was Professor of Canadian History at the Marguerite-Bourgeoys College and at l'Externat Classique de St. Sulpice.

Jean Bruchesi early became a contributor to the principal papers and reviews of Canada, and is a noted lecturer. He has, on several occasions, represented the University of Montreal in Europe, and was a member of the Canadian delegation to the Convention of the Universal Postal Union, at Cairo, Egypt, in 1934. Besides being a recognized teacher, Professor Bruchesi has at various times edited Canadian reviews. Among his services in this field has been that of the editorship of Foreign Politics of *Le Canada* (1928-1931), Chief Editor of *La Revue Moderne* (1930-1936) and first Chief Editor of *L'Action Universaire* (1935-1937).

Along with newspaper work he is a member of various Canadian and French societies connected with writing or teaching: The Canadian Authors Association, the Poets of Quebec Society, the Montreal Historical Society. He founded La Société des Ecrivains Canadiens in 1936. He was elected a member of the *Royal Society of Canada* in 1940, and of the *Polish Institute of Arts and Sciences in America* in 1941, and of *La Société des Dix,* in 1943.

Jean Bruchesi contributed a chapter to the following works: *Les Canadiens Francais et leurs voisins du Sud; French Canadian Backgrounds* (in English); *Montréal Economique.*

Besides his writings in newspapers and reviews, Mr. Bruchesi has published several literary and historical works: *Coups d'ailes* (poems) (1922); *Oscar Dunn et son temps* (1928); *Jours Eteints* (vol. of essays relating to his sojourn in France) (1929); *A booklet on Mistral* (1930); *Aux Marches de l'Europe* (1931) (political and historical studies of the Central and Eastern Countries of Europe which he visited in 1929); *L'Histoire du Canada pour Tous* (1934-1936) (2 vol. history). An abridged version of this work is now (1945) being translated into English and Portuguese. Also: *L'Epopée Canadienne* (1935) (History of Canada for youth); *Rappels* (1941) (historical and literary essays); *De Ville-Marie à Montréal* (history); *Le Chemin des Ecoliers* (an educational subject) (1944). *L'Histoire du Canada pour Tous* was prized by the French Academy. Two other of his books, *Jours Eteints* and *Aux Marches de l'Europe* won the prize of l'Action Intellectuelle, the first in 1929, the other in 1931.

Jean Bruchesi has been a reader of French, English and American Classics. His tastes are wide. His love of history and international law led him to civil service, but his interest in classical writings has induced him to continue his contributions to literature and to keep in touch with all the new movements of learning. Mr. Bruchesi was appointed Under-Secretary of State of the Province of Quebec, on May 1st, 1937. In 1930, he married Miss Berthe Denis, daughter of Mr. Wilfrid Denis, Prothonotary and Registrar of the County of Nicolet. They have two daughters, Anne and Nicole.

Reverend Charles Bruehl 1876-

"My life has been absolutely colorless and commonplace. It is so featureless that I do not even remember it. Thus there is nothing to say which might interest anybody." Thus writes the Professor of Sociology at St. Charles Seminary, Overbrook, Philadelphia. It is difficult to take him literally, and yet it is indeed true that the life of a teaching priest is not likely to be filled with external excitement. Dr. Bruehl went to the University of Louvain, where he came greatly under the influence of Cardinal Mercier. His great interest has ever been the problems of society, particularly its economic problems as it is at present organized, and his books show a deep concern with social reform along corporative lines. Dr. Bruehl is a very modest, quiet man, devoted to the truth and to the welfare of the poor. His thought has stimulated thousands to question the value of capitalism as a basis for a true Christian life.

Dr. Bruehl was born in Herdorf, Germany May 8, 1876. He was educated at Pensacola, Florida; Cleveland, Ohio, and in Germany. He pursued his philosophical and theological studies at St. Charles Seminary, Overbrook, Philadelphia, Pa.; the University of Munster and the University of Louvain where he received his Ph.D. degree in 1904. He was ordained in 1902. He was an assistant at St. Boniface Church, London, England; at Glasgow, Scotland, and later at St. Ignatius Church, Philadelphia, Pennsylvania. In 1909 he became professor of theology at St. Francis Seminary in Wisconsin. After teaching there for five years, from 1909 to 1914, he went to St. Charles Seminary at Overbrook, Philadelphia, Pennsylvania, where he has been teaching since. He was a lecturer in psychology at the Catholic Summer School in Cliff Haven, New York.

He is the author of: *Meine Reise nach Schottland* (1904); *Psychoanalysis* (1924); *Birth Control and Eugenics* (1928); *The Pope's Plan for Social Reconstruction* (1939); *Ethics* (1940), and *This Way Happiness* (1947). He also contributes to reviews.

H. B.

John Gilland Brunini 1899-

The poet and editor, John Gilland Brunini, was born in Vicksburg, Mississippi on October 1, 1899. He was educated at St. Aloysius High School there, and at Georgetown University, where he received his B.A. degree in 1919. At ceremonies marking the University's sesquicentennial in 1939, at which he was given the honorary degree of M.A., Mr. Brunini read a commemorative ode. Becoming a resident of New York City on leaving college, Mr. Brunini served for four years with the United Fruit Company and had charge of all incoming cargo brought by the company into the port. Then from 1924 to 1928, he was reporter, feature editor and critic on various New York newspapers. Later he joined the staff of *The Commonweal,* serving as associate editor until 1931. He then became associated with the Catholic Poetry Society of America, of which he has been, since 1932, the Executive Director. In 1934, when that Society's publication, *Spirit, A Magazine of Poetry,* was launched, Mr. Brunini became its first editor, continuing at that post ever since.

As editor, Mr. Brunini has done much to lift the level of contemporary poetry above mediocrity, and to stem the tide of the pietistic approach to matters religious. On one side of this editorial dilemma he holds: "Because Milton in Il Penseroso uses a simile of a nun, this does not mean that he admired nuns or that he really sympathized with the spiritual well-spring of their lives." On the other side, he has long fought for the conviction "that art must rest on norms which are stable and which must be jealously guarded even in the face of the allure of expediency and conformity." Against the cry of many modern poets that the world is chaos and that they must register their own agreement with this "realization," he demands that the poet, like all men, is bound to seek a spiritual center; if he lacks one, he cannot cover up "by the use of strange and clever technical devices." To record chaos by the chaotic is to make a pretence of thinking, is to reveal sterility. In *Spirit,* in the CPSA Bulletin and in countless letters of criticisms to those who submit poetry to the magazine, Mr. Brunini, in season and out, has taught that poetry is a fine art which must serve beauty, and beauty is God.

In his own poetry, only one volume of which has appeared, *The Mysteries of the Rosary* (1932), Mr. Brunini's poetry reflects modern tendencies and the modern tempo, yet he observes but does not share in its confusion. Some of his poems are religious; most of them concern the mood of the city and of the contemporary scene.

In addition to his editorial work, and his contributions of articles, book reviews and short stories to many publications, Mr. Brunini has found time to serve in many civic enterprises. He was Director of Religious Participation at the New York World's Fair and Executive Director of the Fair's Temple of Religion. In June 1945 he became Executive Director of the Park Association of New York. He has served, too, in war related activities—first as Chairman of Manhattan Neighborhood Defense Councils, then as Manhattan Salvage Chairman and lastly as Executive Assistant to the New York Civilian Defense Volunteer Office. With a group of associate judges, he edited the two anthologies of poems from *Spirit*, published by the Catholic Poetry Society; *From the Four Winds* (1939) and *Drink from the Rock* (1944). His latest book is *Whereon To Stand* (1946).   J. T.

Charles Bryson (Charles Barry, pseudonym) 1887-

In his autobiography, *Unsought Adventure*, Charles Barry says his life has "never been adventurous—merely curious." He was born in Belfast, Ireland in 1887, the eldest son of a family of four boys and three girls. At the age of ten he left Belfast to enter St. Macarten's College, Monaghan where he won a scholarship. Deciding to become a missionary priest, he entered All Hallows, Dublin, but didn't like logic as expounded in Latin with a Kerry brogue. He then tried out his vocation with the Passionists in England, and finally with the Benedictines of the Congregation of Solesmes. At the latter place, he became interested in Plain Chant, Archaeology and Liturgy. This Benedictine Abbey was later used as the background of his book, *The Corpse on the Bridge*.

Deciding that he had no vocation to the priesthood and determined that he would no longer be a burden on his father and knowing that he was not yet equipped for a career, he went to Paris at the suggestion of a friend, where he could earn and learn at the same time. Within a few days he was installed as an assistant teacher in a school in a fashionable quarter. Then through an American, whom he knew slightly, he obtained a job as tutor and companion to a young American around the world on a tour. His next job was a "navvy" on the Pennsylvania Railroad and this job was followed by serving as a waiter in a restaurant at Coney Island. When the season ended, he returned to Paris to study. Then he became holiday tutor to a youthful marquis of the Napoleonic nobility. Succeeding in this, he soon had his time fully occupied as visiting tutor in several of the aristocratic families of the Quartier Saint Germaine. His vacations were spent travelling all over Europe and learning languages for which he had a peculiar facility. He can speak French, German, Italian, Russian, Polish, Serbian, and Rumanian with considerable fluency.

After the declaration of war in 1914, he joined the Russian Army—serving in a battery of the Imperial Horse Artillery. Despite the fact that he was not a Russian, he was commissioned as an officer. Then followed a transfer to the Staff of a Cavalry Brigade, later to the Army Corps and finally to General Headquarters of the Russian front, where he was wounded.

When the Russian Revolution broke out, he left the Russian Army and obtained a commission in the British Army. He was appointed to the British Military Mission in Rumania. Then he became Chief Military Control Officer of the Allied Expeditionary Force to Archangel. He mustered out in 1920.

Work as an official of the International Labor Office, League of Nations, followed, where he wrote, in collaboration with Pardo, the first publication ever issued by the League, *Labor Conditions in Soviet Russia.* He was appointed Editor of the International Labor Office Publications under Dr. Royal Meeker, former Librarian of Congress.

He left Geneva for work as a newspaper man and then went into the country to write detective stories. His writing was interspersed with radio talks on various subjects, interpreting for various Government departments at international conferences.

Mr. Barry's first book of fiction was written for a wager. The title was *The Smaller Penny.* A fellow newspaperman bet him that he couldn't write a detective story around that particular penny. Although he won the bet, it was a long time before he collected, for the book was refused by nineteen publishers before it was brought out. Since then he has sold it five times to publishers, with the proviso that in case of liquidation of the firm all rights revert to him. The last firm must have looked up the book's record, for they changed its name to *The Red Star Mystery.* This publisher is still in business.

Other books by Mr. Barry are: *The Clue of the Clot; The Witness at the Window; Death in Darkness; The Wrong Murder Mystery; The Shot From the Door; Death of a First Mate; Death Overseas; Poison in Public; The Detective's Holiday,* and *A Case for Tressider.*

The honors that have been conferred on Mr. Barry are: Member of the Order of the British Empire, Order of St. Anne, Order of St. Stanislaus, Order of St. Vladimir, St. George's Cross, Knight of the Order of the Star of Rumania and Officer of the Order of the Crown of Rumania.

Mr. Barry lives on the Isle of Wight. M. H.

Alan Michael Buck

The story of Alan Buck's early childhood is told in his first book, *When I Was a Boy in Ireland.* The circumstances which led to its publication are interesting. He writes, "I had the pleasure of meeting Mr. Henry Kellett Chambers, playwright and former *Literary Digest* editor. One day, browsing through his library, I came across a book, one of a series of childhood tales in foreign lands, entitled, *When I Was A Girl in Australia.* I noticed at the time that Ireland had not been included in the series and in discussing the matter with Mr. Chambers he suggested that I fill what I felt to be the gap. Instead of writing the book forthwith, however, I sat down and wrote the publishers, telling them a white lie, to wit, that

I had completed a book which I believed would be suitable for their series, and asking them if they would be interested in reading it. A letter reached me by return mail, requesting the manuscript at once. Well, there I was. I had committed myself and was enmeshed in a trap of my own weaving. (I believe there is a moral there.) For the next three weeks, I locked myself up and with the help of countless cups of black coffee, aspirin and cigarettes, knocked out the story and sent it off with a prayer for its acceptance. My prayer was answered and I found myself launched as an author."

Alan Buck was born in England but raised in Ireland on his parents' farm, one mile distant from the town of Tramore. His father was Pennsylvania Dutch; his mother was from Tipperary, Ireland. When he was eight years of age, his parents sent him to Mount Saint Benedict, a boarding school. While on vacation, he visited a schoolmate in Cork City. While there he went to see Blarney Castle. "Kissing the Blarney Stone," he said, "was for me a frightening experience. Always, I have been upset looking down from on high, and when I tell you that to obtain the gift of a nimble tongue, I was let down through an iron grill over a yawning chasm of space to touch with my lips the famous stone underlying a turret ridge, you may have an inkling of how I felt. No, I would not repeat the undignified experience."

When Mount Saint Benedict School was closed, Alan went to the Waterpark School in Waterford City, in charge of the Christian Brothers. When he completed his studies there, he decided to become a wireless operator. He took the nine months course at the Atlantic Radio College in Dublin but failed in the examinations. He then decided to go to America.

Alan Buck was in the United States Army. He joined up in September 1939, soon after he returned from a trip to Ireland, where he had written what he considers to be his best work, *The Harper's Daughter*. He believed at the time that America would be in the war sooner than she expected. "Having led a sedentary life," he wrote, "I thought I had better get in on the ground floor and learn all that I could while the going was good. I was sent to Hawaii two months later and was due to return to the mainland on the eighth of December, 1941. I need hardly add that after that Sunday morning of the seventh, this was out of the question, and I still find myself in the Pacific area on an island where there is plenty of excitement, but which must remain nameless for the time being."

On November 5, 1944 he married Agnes Marie Katski of Red Bank, New Jersey. In 1945 he was honorably discharged from the Army.

Other books by Alan Buck are: *The Hound of Culain,* being the adventures of Cuchulain, the Hound of Culain "a boar for valor, half god, half man—most courageous of warriors, most beautiful of heroes," and *My Saint Patrick* (1937), a biography of the Saint.

M. H.

Nancy Buckley

Nancy Buckley was born in San Francisco, California and received most of her formal education at the Sacred Heart Convent. Further study brought her to the University of California where she specialized in journalism and literature. She spent some twelve years in Europe, returning to her native city in 1940 after taking courses at the Sorbonne, at Oxford and in Athens where she studied art.

Nancy Buckley has published three books of poems: *Laughter and Longing, Wings of Youth,* and *Cameos.* A fourth collection of her verses, *Wings Against the Wind,* she is now preparing for the press. Her poems, rarely more than twenty lines in length and many of them much shorter, have appeared in a wide variety of magazines including *The Delineator, The Ladies Home Journal, Good Housekeeping, Town Topics, Sunset, The Overland Monthly, The Catholic World, The Ave Maria, The Magnificat, The Grail.* One of her short stories, "Little People from Home," achieved the distinction of being named in an edition of Edward J. O'Brien's annual winnowing of fiction. Her first novel, *Sandals of the Moon,* now awaits publication.

Miss Buckley's prose and verse have won numerous prizes and awards, notably from the San Francisco Open Forum, the Poetry Society, the League of American Pen Women. Several of her lyrics have been set to music by distinguished artists, including Charles Wakefield Cadman and Edward Morris of the New York Symphony. She enjoys telling deep-browed critics and starry-eyed poets that her most lucrative recognition came as the result of her winning a competition for a fire prevention slogan.

Singularly skilled in the technique of verse-writing, Nancy Buckley really sings; but her song is something much more than technical virtuosity. Her songs come from deep within. Usually they are vibrant and joyous; occasionally they are pensive and lightly touched with shadow; more rarely, as in "In a Tea Room," they sparkle with satire. But always they sing. Her poems, wrote Hildegarde Hawthorne, "are fresh and sweet as a bird's singing in May." And the heart of them, whether expressly or by implication, is the living Catholic Faith of the singer.

F. M.

John Bunker 1884-

If ever a man has had a wide variety of intellectual interests, that man is John Bunker. But preeminently he is a poet. If his name is to live through years to come, there is no doubt but that he would wish it to live through his poetry.

Mr. Bunker was born in 1884, raised, and at present lives in Cincinnati, a city proud of its old cultural traditions and its achievements in the arts. After leaving Xavier University, he served a year as a reporter on the Cincinnati *Commercial-Tribune,* meanwhile studying law in night school. Then for five years he was associated with the Mechanical Engineering Department of the Cincinnati Board of Education. In 1917 he came to New York, where he entered upon a brilliant career of teaching, editing and writing. He lectured at New York University, the Catholic Summer School of America, Manhattanville College of the Sacred Heart. He did editorial work for the George H. Doran Company, Henry Holt, and John Lane. He wrote for most of America's higher quality magazines: *Scribner's, Harper's, The Nation, The Bookman, New York Times Book Review, The Catholic World, The Commonweal, The Unpopular Review,* and a host of others.

In 1919 John Lane Co. brought out his book of poems *Shining Fields and Dark Towers.*

In 1920 he married Dorothy T. Schmidt, a professional dancer and teacher of rhythmic expression, and the Bunkers have had five children— three boys and two girls. In 1921 Mr. Bunker returned to Cincinnati and entered the advertising business with the Frederick A. Schmidt Real Estate Company, later founding his own general advertising agency of which he is at present president.

He has continued his literary interests as shown by numerous poems, essays, and critical articles in the periodical press. In 1930 he edited the *Selected Poems of Thomas Walsh,* for which he wrote also the Introductory Memoir, and in the May-June number of *The Poetry Review* (London) he published a long poem "Shelley's Birthday." His latest work was a remarkable poem "Revolt," on which he had been at work for a number of years, and which, when published, created a considerable stir in literary circles. With great strength and eloquence it deals with the moral condition of the contemporary world. He himself describes it as his "longest and most ambitious work." It reflects a mind keenly sensitive to the world's stress and moulded by a wide and catholic experience of life.

H. B.

Addison Burbank 1895-

If there is anything in a name, Addison Burbank was destined for a literary career and not that of a naturalist as was his renowned uncle, Luther Burbank. At the time of his birth in Los Angeles, California, his father, a newspaper editor and publisher and his mother, a poetess, were reading the works of Joseph Addison. They wanted a literary son and named him "Addison" in the hope that the name would work a magic over the infant in the future. In his cradle days there were signs —but not of essays. Instead, Addison had begun to draw. His first drawings were of chickens, very lively chickens. In a sense, they were prophetic, for when he became a magazine illustrator he was noted for his drawings of "chickens" or what we would now call hepcats.

At San Jose High School, he edited and illustrated the school papers, *The Herald* and *The Bell,* and during a term at Santa Clara University he drew for *The Redwood.*

After the death of his father, Addison Burbank succeeded him as president of the Sentinel Publishing Co., Winston-Salem, North Carolina, publishers of *The Daily Sentinel* and the weekly *Western Sentinel.* During these years he gained reportorial experience and wrote a daily column dealing largely with the history of the Moravians in North Carolina. His talent for art came to the fore again after he had sold his paper.

He became an illustrator in order to earn money while he studied. He successively attended the Hopkins Art Institute, San Francisco; Chicago Art Institute; the Grand Chaumiere and Colarros's, Paris, France, and was a pupil of Howard Giles and Harvey Dunn.

While living in Europe, he painted in Spain, Italy, and France. He exhibited in Paris and gave his first one-man show of water-colors at the Ferargil Galleries in New York City, on his return in 1927. He won the first award for mural painting in oil for the Florida Building, Century of Progress Exposition, Chicago, 1933. During the years 1936-1937 he lived and painted in Guatemala, C. A. While there he exhibited water-colors at the Academia de Bellas Artes, Guatemala City, under the auspices of the Guatemalan Government. He wrote and illustrated *Guatemala Profile* (1939), and *The Cedar Deer,* a Guatemalan juvenile (1940). After a border-to-border trek of Mexico he wrote and illustrated *Mexican Frieze* (1940). Mr. Burbank has also illustrated numerous books by other authors, including those of Covelle Newcomb and Marion Ley. With Covelle Newcomb, his wife, he brought out *Narizona's Holiday* in 1946.

The turning point in his dual career came with his Guatemalan experience, for it was at this time that his eyes were opened to the great work done by the Spanish Dominican, Bartolome de Las Casas, and other missionaries in saving the lives and the arts of the Indians. Las Cases became the spiritual inspiration which led Mr. Burbank into the Roman Catholic Faith. He was received August 15, 1942, by the Reverend James M. Gillis, C.S.P. He believes that art must emanate from experience and reflection, and that what the artist feels strongly enough will find expression and create its own form.

Pauline Wilcox Burke   1884-

Inheriting a manuscript collection and several relics of President Andrew Jackson inspired Mrs. Burke to write a two-volume biography of her great-grandmother. It appeared in 1941, the year of the death of her husband, the late Moncure Burke, who was for thirty-four years clerk and deputy clerk of the United States Court of Appeals for the District of Columbia and who aided her in writing the biography, *Emily Donelson of Tennessee.*

The manuscript collection, comprising one hundred and fifteen original items, has since been presented to the Division of Manuscripts, Library of Congress. The book "is a running story of the Jacksonian era, rooted in pioneer history of the city of Nashville, Tennessee."

Mrs. Burke is the great-granddaughter of Major Andrew Jackson Donelson and his wife Emily Tennessee Donelson who were first cousins, and nephew and niece respectively of Mrs. Andrew Jackson—Rachel Donelson (Robards) Jackson.

Mrs. Burke is engaged on a biography of Andrew Jackson Donelson, who after being private secretary to President Jackson was the United States Charge d'Affaires to the Republic of Texas, 1844 to 1845; Minister to Prussia 1846 to 1849 and nominee for Vice President with Millard Fillmore in 1856 on the Know-nothing ticket.

Pauline Wilcox (Mrs. Burke) was born on July 5, 1884 in Georgetown, Washington, D. C., the daughter of Andrew Donelson and Ida Seymour Wilcox.

At the age of eight she attended the Georgetown Visitation Convent, and later spent six years at the Convent of the Sacred Heart, "Eden Hall," Torresdale, Philadelphia, Pennsylvania. From the latter school Pauline Wilcox was graduated in June 1903, being valedictorian of her class. From 1903 to 1905 she attended Trinity College, Washington, D. C., as a "special student." Then she spent a year travelling in Europe, studying Spanish and Italian.

On her tour through Spain, she spent a fortnight at Avila, over the fifteenth of October, when there were colorful celebrations in honor of St. Teresa. Several days were spent at Lisieux, the home of St. Thérèse of the Child of Jesus. Here Mrs. Burke had the privilege of several visits with the Saint's sister, Mother Agnes of Jesus, and also gave an order for a copy of a portrait of the Little Flower made by her sister, Celine.

This portrait done in oil is now in the Convent of the Carmelites, Philadelphia, Pennsylvania. The winter of 1906-1907 was spent in Rome where the author had the privilege of several audiences with Pope Pius X and attended Mass said by him in his private chapel.

In 1927 Mrs. Burke again visited Europe and was received in audience by Pope Pius XI on several occasions.

Mrs. Burke has been a contributor of manuscripts to several historical books. These include *The Correspondence of Andrew Jackson,* edited by Dr. John Spencer Bassett and after his death by Dr. J. Franklin Jamieson; *The Portrait of a President* by Marquis James has two of her portraits as illustrations and she also gave Mr. James some manuscript material; and Dr. Douglas Freeman has used some of her manuscripts in his *Lee's Lieutenants* (vols. 1 and 2) recently published.

Mrs. Burke presented to the National Museum, the Smithsonian Institution, the collection on the mannequins of Mrs. Donelson which is in the collection of the costumes of the mistresses of the White House.

M. H.

Michael Burt 1900-

Author, critic, radio dramatist and journalist, Michael Burt is prouder of being the London correspondent of the *Irish Rosary* than he is of being the author of his five Anglo-Indian novels.

Michael Burt was born in 1900, the son of the late Major G. M. Burt, of Worthing, Sussex. He was educated at Ridley and the R.M.C. (Royal Military College). He served with the Indian Army and Royal Signals from 1918-1931. He was received into the Catholic Church in 1929. In 1935 he married Elsie Mary Day, a Sister in Q.A.I.M.N.S. (Queen Alexandra's Imperial Military Nursing Service). His best book is *Hill Quest.* He gives vivid pictures of native life and the reactions of the English soldiers. He also has a stirring plot and a homely human atmosphere.

Some of his novels are: *The Road to Roundabout; Secret Orchards; Catch-'Em-Alive-O,* and *Pyre for a Pilgrim. Walking in Sussex* is a travel book. He also wrote *A Tale from Timbuctoo* and other radio plays.

He is a contributor to *Chamber's Journal, Cornhill, Windsor Magazine* and other periodicals.

He is a jolly member of "The Keys." "The Keys" is an organization of Catholic journalists and writers who meet to dine, talk and help each other. Their most distinguished president was Sir Richard Terry. Among the other members are Charles Barry, William Titterton, Denis Gwynn, Reginald Dingle, Edward and George MacDonald and David Walker of Balkan fame. This organization was responsible for the establishment of the Westminster Catholic Press Bureau.   M. H.

Katherine Burton   1884-

One needs to be in the company of Katherine Burton but a short time to catch the spark of her enthusiasm and to be impressed by her magnetic personality. A delightful conversationalist, she is well-read on many topics. That she is observant and can philosophize one can readily see by reading her articles in magazines, particularly *The Sign,* for which she conducts a woman's page "Woman to Woman." The range of topics is very wide. One month it may be the condemnation of the modern Christmas spirit, another month it may be the development of the thesis that great authors write from an inner compulsion, but the merely talented usually write because it is a way of making a living. Sometimes the whole page may be devoted to the discussion of a Catholic novelist like Kathleen Norris, or it may be a plea for prayers for those, such as Jehovah's Witnesses, who, ignorant of the Catholic Church's teaching, spread lies and try to undermine her and her work.

Mrs. Burton was born in Cleveland, Ohio, in 1884 and is the daughter of John and Louise (Bittner) Kurz. After attending Lakewood High School, she entered Western Reserve University and graduated from there with an A.B. degree. Her first year out of college was spent teaching in a private school in a mining town where her oldest pupil was thirty-two and her youngest twenty, just her own age. She taught Latin, Greek, German, Botany, Geology, and the study of the Pennsylvania Statesmen.

In 1910 she married Harry Payne Burton, an editor. They have two sons and one daughter.

In 1926 her first book appeared, *The Circus Lady,* a biography of Josephine DeMott, the seventy-year-old rider. This book was ghost-written. From 1928 to 1930 Mrs. Burton became associate editor of *McCall's* magazine. She held the same position on *Redbook* from 1930 to 1933.

In 1930 Mrs. Burton came into the Church. The story of her conversion is told in *America,* the Jesuit weekly, July 29, 1939. In 1933, she gave up her position as Associate Editor of *Redbook Magazine* to do free-lancing.

Her second book did not appear until 1937. Under the title *Sorrow Built a Bridge,* there is told the story of Rose Hawthorne, the youngest of Nathaniel Hawthorne's three children who after becoming a Catholic became Mother Alphonsa, a Dominican Nun, and opened a home for the cancerous poor. This book has gone through ten editions. Two years later *Paradise Planters* (1939) was published. It is the history of the New England social experiment of the '40's. Her main idea in the book is to show how at Brook Farm—Emerson, Hawthorne, Thoreau, and the rest, were really actuated by religion and not by sheer philosophy or humanitarianism.

To write *His Dear Persuasion,* which came out in 1940, Mrs. Burton went to Emmitsburg, Maryland, "to absorb the atmosphere of the place, for I have already spent much time on the study of Mother Seton's beautiful life," she said, in an interview. Another book, *In No Strange Land* was written in 1942. It is a book of brief biographies of some of the more outstanding American converts to the Catholic faith during the nineteenth century, although a few of them belong to our own twentieth. Among the biographies it contains are those of Levi Silliman Ives, the Protestant Episcopal Bishop of North Carolina; Orestes Brownson, the philosopher and essayist; Isaac Hecker, the founder of the Paulists; Rose Hawthorne, the daughter of the great writer; and eleven others.

Celestial Homespun, a life of Isaac Hecker, founder of the Paulist Fathers, was published in 1943; *Mother Butler of Marymount* appeared in 1944 and so did *No Shadow of Turning,* a life of James Kent Stone (Father Fidelis of the Cross, Passionist). *His Mercy Endureth Forever,* a history of the Apostolate of the Sisters of Mercy, appeared in 1946.

M. H.

Reverend Paul Bussard 1904-

One of the younger stars in the group of American writers on the Liturgy is Father Paul Bussard. His thesis was on a liturgical subject, and he has devoted much of his great energy to spreading popular devotion for and interest in the official prayer of the Church. His work with the Leaflet Missal has been particularly fruitful, making available to many who would find a regular Missal too complicated the specific Mass for any given occasion.

Father Bussard says that his favorite among his books is *Staircase to a Star,* and the reason he assigns is that "it attempted a new sort of apologetics; influencing attitudes rather than intellectual persuasion, with the aid of a dialogue set in nature musically. Brother Leo said, 'It is like a symphony with a number of basic themes upon which is imposed a structure of tonal decoration . . .' I don't know Brother Leo personally, but this is astute criticism, because some of the essays were written with actual pieces of music in mind. He is the first critic to have noticed it, and I am properly pleased." Father Bussard's biggest job is being editor of the *Catholic Digest,* a monthly which has won for itself a position of esteem and a measure of financial success unusual among Catholic periodicals. Speaking of his education, he has paid high tribute to the Benedictines of the Abbey of Maria Laach in Germany in whose liturgical academy he spent a year. "Out of fifty monks in the monastery, forty of them had Ph.D.'s . . . for the seven students in the Academy there were fourteen professors."

Father Bussard was born at Essex, Iowa, on November 22, 1904, the son of William and Catherine (Howard) Bussard. He was educated at St.

Thomas College, 1919 to 1922, at the Catholic University of America, 1932 to 1934 and 1935 to 1937. In 1937 he received his Ph.D. The year 1934 was spent at German Universities.

H. B.

Right Reverend (Edward) Cuthbert Butler, O.S.B.   1858-1934

Abbot Butler is remembered at Downside Abbey principally for his good example in the spiritual life. He lived a life of prayer. This close communion with God manifested itself not only in his life but also in his writings. For sixty-five years he had been associated with St. Gregory's and for sixteen of these he was its superior.

Edward Joseph Aloysius Butler was born in Dublin, Ireland on May 6th, 1858, the son of the late Edward Butler, a barrister-at-law and Mary, sister of the late Sir Francis Cruise, M.D. In 1869 he entered the school at Downside and remained there till June 1875. During his latter years at Downside, he sought advice from Msgr. Lord Petre, who was living there at the time, and the Prior, Dom Bernard Murphy, about his vocation. His parents advised him to leave Downside for a while to see if this desire to be a Benedictine persisted in a different locale. He, therefore, went to the Catholic University College in Kensington and did some travelling. In 1876 at the age of 18, he decided to become a Benedictine and went to Belmont in the diocese of Newport and Menevia for his Novitiate.

All through his life his text book for the spiritual life was Fr. Augustine Baker's classic *Sancta Sophia*. Abbot Butler regarded his early acquaintance with *Sancta Sophia* "as one of the chief graces of my life. It gave me a definite theory of the spiritual and monastic lives, and a high ideal to aim at. A high ideal is a great thing, it is to a man's life what a sound philosophy is to his intellect." Abbot Butler specialized in ecclesiastical and monastic history, when he returned to Downside in 1880. There he remained for fifteen years teaching, reading and studying the records of monastic history. He had the gifts of concentration and perseverance. The years 1888 to 1892 were spent as Headmaster of the Downside School.

In 1896 Dom Cuthbert Butler received into the Church his only convert, the Vice-Principal of Wells Theological College, Henry Havelock Ramsay, who later became his successor.

When Prior Ford decided to open a Downside house of studies at Cambridge in 1895, Dom Cuthbert Butler was chosen as its first head. He moved there in October 1896. He often looked back on these eight years (1896-1904) at Cambridge as the happiest of his life, for he had the desire and ability to be a scholar. In 1898, he and his first companion, Dom

Benedict Kuypers, editor of the *Book of Cerne* received their Bachelor of Arts degrees. They were the first priests to receive a degree from one of the old universities since the time of Queen Mary. In this year appeared his first Volume of *Lausiac History of Palladius*. To prepare for the second volume, Abbot Butler had to examine manuscripts in foreign libraries.

In the spring of 1898 he went to Venice to spend three weeks with the Benedictines of S. Giorgio Maggiore. He worked in the library from 9 A.M. to 12 noon and from 12:30 to 4:00 P.M. the closing hour of the library. The Greek text of Palladius was published in 1904, the year he left Cambridge. Then he went to Maria Laach in order to perfect his German for studies in early Church history and the New Testament. In 1905 he was back at Downside, writing articles on monastic history for the *Encyclopedia Britannica*. The following year, he was elected Abbot.

By his kindness, his clear comprehension of principle, his distinguished appearance and his learning, he won the admiration and respect of all. He was tall, had a high forehead, walked falteringly and had a powerful voice.

One of his acts as Abbot in which he took pride was restoring the Novitiate at Downside. Though his ambition in life to become a novice-master had never been realized, he now had an opportunity to help form monks. In his conferences with them, he made them familiar with the Confessions of St. Augustine, the Fathers of the Desert, Newman's essays on the Benedictines and especially Father Baker's *Sancta Sophia*. He loved the liturgy and introduced the daily sung conventual Mass at Downside.

In 1914 when Abbot Gasquet was raised to the Cardinalate, Abbot Butler, as First Assistant to the Abbot President, automatically became President of the English Benedictine Congregation and held this office until 1921. This new honor did not prevent him from digging in the garden for an hour or so, two or three days of the week.

The following year he retired as Abbot and went to Ealing. This residence brought him in close proximity to the British Museum and other London libraries. He could devote more time now to writing. Along with his literary efforts he did some open-air preaching for the Catholic Evidence Guild. Most of his time, however, was devoted to writing.

He refused a titular abbacy for some time after he resigned, but yielded later to take the titular abbacy of St. Augustine's Canterbury and at the death of Cardinal Gasquet that of St. Alban's. He died in 1934.

He is the author of *St. Benedict's Rule* (editio critico-practica) (1912, 1927); *Benedictine Monachism* (1919, 1924); *Western Mysticism* (1922, 1927); *Life of Bishop Ullathorne* (1926); *Story of the Vatican Council* (2 vols.) (1930); *Religions of Authority and Other Essays* (1930); and *Ways of Christian Life* (1932).

Besides contributing to the *Encyclopedia Britannica,* he also wrote many articles for the *Catholic Encyclopedia* and the *Downside Review* For the *Cambridge History* he wrote the chapter on Monasticism.

At the time of his death, Abbot Butler was working upon a long article, with the title "The Pageant of the Popes" in which he was to present "the most significant figures and periods of the papacy from the earliest to our own times."   **M. H.**

Right Reverend Fernand Cabrol, O.S.B.
1855-1937

Internationally renowned as an authority on liturgy and archaeology, Abbot Fernand Cabrol died in June 1937. He was born at Marseilles, France in 1855, and educated at Marseilles College. In 1877 he was professed at the Benedictine monastery of Solesmes, and was ordained to the priesthood five years later. He became Prior of Solesmes in 1890 and held that office for six years. When Solesmes Abbey founded the monastery of St. Michael's, Farnborough, England in 1896, through the generosity of the Empress Eugénie, wife of Napoleon III who resided in England after the downfall of her husband's government, Dom Cabrol became the first Prior. In 1903 when the monastery was raised to an Abbey, he became the first Abbot.

In 1908 he was President of the French Section of the Eucharistic Congress of Westminster. Abbot Cabrol was intrusted with several scientific missions in France, Italy, Switzerland and Germany, in order to study the manuscripts and prepare the materials for *La Paleógraphie Musicale.*

Through his efforts there has been a growing interest in liturgical prayer, the use of Holy Week books and particularly the use of the Missal by the laity. For his services to the Red Cross in World War I he was honored by the English Government. The O. B. E. (Order of the British Empire) was conferred upon him in 1920. In 1932 the French Government made him Officier d'Academie and Chevalier de la Legion d'Honneur in 1935.

His great work is the *Dictionnaire d'Archeólogie chrétienne et de Liturgie* begun in 1907 in collaboration with Dom Henri Le Clerc.

Some of his books translated into English are *Books of the Latin Liturgy* (1932); *Holy Sacrifice* (1937); *Holy Week* (1928); *Lay Folks Ritual* (1918); *Liturgical Prayer: Its History and Spirit* (1925); *Liturgical Prayerbook* (1927); *Mass of the Western Rites* (1934); *My Missal* (1931); *Prayer of the Early Christians* (1930); *St. Benedict* (1934), and *The Year's Liturgy* (1939).

                                                                    M. H.

Gertrude Callaghan (Mrs. James W. Donoghue)

Although she only began publishing her poems when urged to do so by her friends in 1921, Gertrude Callaghan (Mrs. James Donoghue), author of *Inheritance* (1924), and *Witch Girl* (1926), cannot remember a time when she did not like to write. In her own words writing, to her, "was so much easier than arithmetic."

Born in New York City, she received a convent education followed by travel in foreign lands. She was married in Marseilles, France in 1927 to James W. Donoghue who is now Judge Donoghue of the Municipal Court in Bronx County, New York.

Her work is poetry. Her verses first appeared in current magazines and periodicals and were gathered into a volume. About her first ventures she says, "They were pretty bad." Others did not think so however. Her poems are included in Thomas Walsh's *The Catholic Anthology* (1927); Braithwaites (1925-26); Rittenhouse's *Third Book of Modern Verse* (1927).

Gertrude Callaghan is of the belief that very young poets spoil their work by being in too great a hurry to see their poems in print. She still hopes someday to write something to "efface her own early writings."

Like many other poets she loves simplicity, beauty of nature, "quiet things in quiet places." Her summers are spent at Martha's Vineyard, Massachusetts.   E. F.

Morley Edward Callaghan 1903-

While "cubbing" on the Toronto *Daily Star,* Morley Callaghan, then just out of college, met Ernest Hemingway who encouraged him to write.

Mr. Callaghan was born in Toronto, Ontario in 1903, the son of Thomas and Mary (Dewan) Callaghan, both of Irish descent. He was educated at St. Michael's College of the University of Toronto and graduated in 1925 with an A.B. degree.

His interest and success in public speaking at the University of Toronto, inspired him to study law. He chose the Osgoode Hall Law School. His time is devoted to writing and he is best known for his short stories. For at least twelve years in succession his stories were included in Edward O'Brien's "The Best Short Stories." Strange to say, Mr. Callaghan's first stories were published in the American-owned Paris magazines—*The Quarter* and *Transition.* He also wrote for Ezra Pound's periodical *The Exile,* edited in Italy. These attracted the attention of the editor of *Scribner's* magazine who published two of Callaghan's short stories.

In 1929 he married Loretta Florence Dee and went to Paris for his honeymoon trip. There he joined the select group of writers which, for a time, directed the trend of American fiction.

His first novel appeared in 1928 with the publication of *Strange Fugitive.* The story centers about a foreman in a Toronto lumber yard who, tired of home life, leaves his wife for a year. During that time he makes a fortune in bootlegging. Desiring to quit his life of dissipation he decides to return home to his wife but is frustrated in his attempt by a gangster who kills him. A book of short stories appeared in 1929 under the title *Native Argosy.* In 1930 appeared *It's Never Over.* The principal character of this story is Fred Thompson who is hanged for murdering a policeman. The disgrace that befell the relatives leads to many unhappy events in their lives. *Broken Journey* followed in 1932 and *Such Is My Beloved* in 1934. A story of what happened to one group of people living in an American city during the business depression came out in 1935 under the title *They Shall Inherit the Earth. Now That April's Here* and other satires (1936), contains thirty-five short stories. *More Joy in Heaven* was published in 1937. The story that he likes the best is *Two Fishermen.*

Mr. Callaghan is "short and stocky, with black curly hair and blue eyes which light up when he smiles, which is often." He is looked upon as Canada's most promising author.   M. H.

Reverend Adalbert John Callahan, O.F.M.
1905

Father Adalbert is an historian and his favorite field is the history of his order, the Friars Minor. Most scholars have confined themselves to the foundations of the order in the thirteenth century. Americans have, of course, been fascinated by Franciscan history in California and the Southwest. Father Adalbert has, however, devoted his labors to the history of the Holy Name Province, which comprises most of the Eastern states. The spirit of the little poor man of Assisi inspires his sons in modern America just as much as it did the friars in the glorious thirteenth century and in the adventurous days of discovery and exploration in the Southwest. In *Medieval Francis and Modern America* (1936) Father Adalbert has told the story of eighty years of love and labor in a territory stretching from Massachusetts to South Carolina. We are all familiar with the famous chain of missions which lay along the California coast. Father Adalbert depicts the no-less-extensive accomplishments of the Franciscans in the Eastern states.

Perhaps the most renowned friar of Holy Name Province is the saintly Father Leo Heinrichs, slain at the altar in Denver, Colorado, whose cause for beatification is being urged at Rome. His Excellency, the Most Reverend Amleto Giovanni Cicognani, the Apostolic Delegate, has told the story of Father Leo's assassination in *Sanctity in America*. Clients of Father Leo will find Father Adalbert's account of him in the chapter entitled "A Martyr of the Eucharist."

The Friars Minor have always associated lay persons in their works through their great Third Order. Father Adalbert has been most active in fostering the Tertiary movement. He was commissary Provincial of the Third Order from 1936 to 1937. In 1934 he founded *The Tertiary Record,* the monthly of the tertiaries affiliated with St. Francis Monastery,

New York City. He also founded, in 1936, *The Tertiary News Letter* as the official publication of the entire Third Order Province.

Father Adalbert was born in Passaic, New Jersey, on December 26, 1905, the son of James and Elizabeth (Grady) Callahan. Although most of Father Adalbert's education has been under Franciscan auspices, for four years he was under the tutelage of the Benedictine monks of Saint Mary's Abbey, Newark. He was graduated from their Saint Benedict's Preparatory School in June 1924, and in the following August was received into the Friars Minor at Paterson, New Jersey. His B.A. and M.A. degrees were awarded by Saint Bonaventure College, Allegany, New York, in 1929 and 1930; his S.T.B. by Catholic University in 1932. He was ordained June 9, 1931 by Bishop Thomas J. Shahan in the National Shrine of the Immaculate Conception, Washington, D.C. He has been stationed at St. Francis and at Holy Cross monasteries in New York City. In 1937 he was appointed professor of economics and sociology at Siena College, Loudonville, New York. In 1936 he founded *The Provincial Annals,* the quarterly historical publication of the Holy Name Province of the Friars Minor. He is now (1946) stationed at the Franciscan monastery in Paterson, New Jersey.   M. S.

Very Reverend Charles Jerome Callan, O.P.
1877-

In an atmosphere of plain living and high thinking Charles Callan, the future Biblical scholar was reared. He was born December 5, 1877, on a farm in the town of Royalton, Niagara County, New York. His parents were John Francis Callan and Mary Somers. He was a delicate child, unable to do any heavy farm work or even to read or study much. That frail health, although pursuing him through life has helped rather than hindered his tremendous intellectual output, as it has to a great extent prevented him from engaging in other arduous priestly duties, thus enabling him to concentrate on scholarship. The father of the Callan family was a famous public reader and speaker. Father Callan's mother, "a queenly woman in appearance and noble in character," was a gifted musician, and she also read aloud a great deal to her large family. Culture was not lacking in the only Catholic household of that vicinity.

The young Charles Callan was educated in the public schools of his town and nearby Lockport. Even as a boy his literary attempts found their way into the local newspapers. A sermon heard at a Dominican's first mass made an extraordinary impression on him. To use Father Callan's own words, "it seemed to me as if the world and all its glory had suddenly turned to ashes. . . . The charge was instantaneous and complete, mentally, morally, religiously."

During the next three years, one of which was spent at the Lockport High School, and two at the Jesuit Canisius College in Buffalo, New York, Charles Callan's thoughts flowed into Ignatian channels, but divine Providence caused him to meet the Dominican who had said that particular first Mass. That priest argued that the boy would never be able to stand the rigors of Jesuit life, and that preaching would be secondary to teaching. As a matter of fact Father Callan's subsequent Dominican life has been spent in teaching and in study, and only rarely has he preached outside the parish church where he has lived.

At the Dominican novitiate in Springfield, Kentucky, Brother Jerome Callan (as he became) met a fellow novice who was destined to be associated with him in life and in letters ever since. This fellow novice, priest, and scholar, is the Very Rev. John Ambrose McHugh, O.P. They were ordained together in Somerset, Ohio, in 1905. Graduate study followed in Washington, Rome, and Fribourg, Switzerland, where Father Callan received, in 1907, the degree of Lectorate in Sacred Theology. From 1908 to 1915 these two Fathers both taught at the Dominican House of Studies in Washington. Since 1916 they have been editors of the *Homiletic and Pastoral Review,* New York; but even their great attainments in scholarship are not considered as important to Father Callan as their association with the Catholic Foreign Mission Society at Maryknoll, where they have been professors since 1915. They have helped educate and train all the members of that remarkable institution with the exception of the founders, Bishop Walsh and Father Price, and about a half dozen priests who were ordained before entering Maryknoll. To Father Callan and to Father McHugh, this association is "the greatest achievement and blessing of lives."

During these years the two Dominicans have lived at, and administered to, the parish of Holy Rosary, Hawthorne, New York. To quote Father Callan, "their active days of prayer, writing, study and teaching have rarely been interrupted save for brief family visits in the summer." Therefore it has been possible for Father Callan to turn out the startling number of volumes that are to his credit, not to mention those written in collaboration with Father McHugh.

Father Callan's first book, *Out of Shadows* (1912) and another early one, *The Lord is My Shepherd* (1915) show the fine gold of Biblical scholarship in essay form. Except for another volume of essays published in 1926, Father Callan's work has been almost wholly confined to scriptural exegesis, dogma, moral theology, devotion and the liturgy. Various commentaries on the New Testament have been written by him, either singly or jointly with Father McHugh.

In 1920 Archbishop (later Cardinal) Hayes appointed these two Dominicans to draw up a Preaching Program for the Archdiocese of New York, which thereafter became the official sermon plan for twelve consecutive years.

In 1920 to 1921, with the encouragement of Archbishop Hayes of New York, the two Fathers also compiled and finished a monumental four-volume work for preachers, entitled *A Parochial Course of Doctrinal*

Instructions Based on the Catechism of the Council of Trent for all Sundays and Holydays of the Year.

As editors of the superb "Spencer Translation of the New Testament from the original Greek," they were naturally asked to serve on the editorial board for the revision of the Douai Bible.

Father Callan's achievements in ecclesiastical scholarship have been crowned with papal as well as university honors. In 1925 Gonzaga College, Washington, D.C. made him a Doctor of Letters, and in 1931 the Angelico University in Rome conferred upon him the degree of Master of Sacred Theology. Furthermore, for the first time in the history of the Church in the United States, a native American was appointed Consultor of the Pontifical Biblical Commission in Rome when Pope Pius XII bestowed this honor upon Father Callan in July 1940.   A. M.

Dom Bede Camm, O.S.B.   1864-1942

Perhaps few people fulfill more perfectly the ideal of the Benedictine scholar than did Dom Bede Camm. He belonged to that line of Downside men who have had among their recent glories Cardinal Gasquet and Abbots Butler and Chapman.

Dom Bede Camm was like so many distinguished English Catholics, a convert to the Faith. He was born at Sudbury Park, Sudbury-on-Thames, Middlesex, the eldest son of John Brooke Camm and his wife Caroline. He was educated at Westminster School and Keble College, Oxford. After two years at Oxford, he was shipwrecked in the Bay of Biscay, an experience which filled him, he said "with a consuming desire to consecrate to God the life which He had thus wonderfully given back to me." After Oxford, he studied for the Anglican ministry for which he was ordained at Rochester, England in 1888 at the age of twenty-four.

His first appointment was as curate of St. Agnes's Church in Kennington Park. Two years later, however, he was received into the Church at the Benedictine Abbey of Maredsous in Belgium. There that same year (1890) he received the habit and was professed in 1891. Four years later he was ordained to the priesthood in the Lateran Basilica at Rome (1895), and then was stationed at Erdington Abbey, near Birmingham until 1912. In 1913 he was appointed to prepare the Anglican Benedictine monks at Caldey and the nuns of St. Bride's, Milford Haven, for their reception into the Church as communities.

In his book *The Call of Caldey* (1937) he tells how his relations with the Caldey Community began. On Caldey Island, on February 28, 1913, he said the first Mass offered there since the Reformation; "that Mass was one of the happiest in my life," he wrote. He was appointed Novice-Master to the Monks. This work accomplished, he became affiliated with

Downside Abbey, and after a period as army chaplain with the British forces in Egypt during World War I, he became head of Benet House, the Benedictine House of Studies at Cambridge University, remaining there until his retirement to Downside in 1931. His health was then beginning to fail and he could do but little active work. His love for architecture and archaeology was rewarded in 1922 by the degree of F.S.A.

Father Camm has a long line of books to his credit. Among these are: *A Benedictine Martyr in England* (1897); *In the Brave Days of Old* (1900); *A Day in the Cloister* (1900); *Blessed Sebastian Newdigate* (1900); *Lives of the English Martyrs* (1904-5); *Rood-Screens and Rood-lofts* (in collaboration with Mr. F. Bligh Bond, the architect); *Tyburn Conferences* (1906); *Birthday Book of the English Martyrs* (1909); *Heroes of the Faith* (1909); *William Cardinal Allen* (1909); *Forgotten Shrines* (1910); *Pilgrim Paths in Latin Lands* (1923); *Good Fruit of Tyburn Tree* (1929); *Nine Martyr Monks* (1931); *Life of Blessed John Wall* (1932); *The Foundress of Tyburn Convent* (1935), and *Anglican Memories* (1935). He was also the editor of *The St. Nicholas Series.*

Like his fellow Benedictine, Dom Norbert Birt, he had specialized in Elizabethan history, and of this field had taken the story of the Elizabethan martyrs as specially his own. Less the purely research student than the Jesuit, John Hungerford Pollen, his writings happily combine sound scholarship with popular interest. The subject he had chosen to deal with is so rich in material as to be almost inexhaustible. Dom Bede Camm dealt with it in such a way as to encourage a greater determination to bring England back to the Faith of the martyrs rather than to raise rancor towards those who did the persecuting. His enthusiasm for the cause of the English martyrs sprang from his great zeal to spread the Catholic Faith in England. He studied the lives of the martyrs and spread devotion to them as much as he could. In many other ways, too, he served the Church.

Dom Bede Camm died on September 8th, 1942.

Joseph Campbell   1879-1944

Joseph Campbell (Seosamh Mac Cathmhaoil) poet, dramatist, editor and educator, was born in Belfast, Ireland in 1879, of a large Catholic family which stood out in the midst of Protestant surroundings. He was educated at St. Malachy's College in that city and later became engaged in rural teaching. At the turn of the century, caught up by the resurgence of the Irish literary movement, he began in simple unaffected verse to record his impressions of his own people. Under his Gaelic name his writings appeared in Arthur Griffith's *United Irishman*. He was associated with the Ulster Literary Theatre from its first days. This group produced his play, *The Little Cowherd of Slaigne*. Another, *Judgment,* was produced in Dublin, in 1912, by the Abbey Theatre.

While in Ireland, he was closely associated with Frank Biggar, to whom he dedicated his first book, with James Cousins, Herbert Hughes, the composer, Rutherford Mayne and Seumas O'Sullivan. At a *feis* held in Antrim, while serving with the Ulster Gaelic League, he met Padraic Colum and Roger Casement, with both of whom he was to remain friendly. Later he moved to Dublin, where he worked for one of the agricultural societies and talked poetry and drama and politics with all the leaders of the revival, from Joseph O'Neill, the Norse scholar, to William Butler Yeats. A period of residence in London followed, during which he served as secretary of the Irish Literary Society there, when Barry O'Brien and Albert Percival Graves were its presidents. He returned to Ireland to take an active, underground part in the rebellion which ended in 1916 and which cost him many close friends. Failure to agree with the decisions of the Cosgrave government resulted in a political sentence of a year and a half in prison, during which he wrote, but did not publish, a Jail Journal. All this while, Colum was his staunchest friend. On his release, *persona non grata* to the new leaders, he came to America.

Here he lectured for several years, founding the School of Irish Studies in 1925, which, three years later, became affiliated with Fordham University. His work was devoted to the spread of Irish culture, history, literature, drama and the arts, and was modeled on the ninth century school of Cluain-Eraird. He was fortunate in obtaining such lecturers as the poets Theodore Maynard, Horace Reynolds and Margaret Widdemer, Professors A. duPont Coleman, John Gerig, Frederick N. Robinson, Cornelius Weygandt, Henry Seidel Canby, Shaw Desmond, Ernest Horrowitz, Edward J. Kavanagh and Joseph J. Tynan. He remained at Fordham until 1937, when he withdrew to devote his attention to a concurrently functioning Irish Foundation, of which he was also the director, and to publish the short-lived *Irish Review*.

In spite of tremendous enthusiasm and a brilliant personality on the lecture platform—his speaking and singing voice had a bardic perfection—he was not happy during his long stay away from his own country. His work did not bear the fruit which he expected, and he was saddened and disappointed that a city which he thought was a centre of Irish-Catholic culture in the new world did not rally to the support of its artistic origins. In 1935, he wrote that he would struggle on for three more years, and then retire to devote himself solely to writing, "which, perhaps, is where I belong." Attempts to interest wealthy Irish book collectors to leave their libraries to Catholic institutions, and to establish a building for his Foundation and reading rooms in several large libraries, further disillusioned him, and he returned to Ireland shortly before the outbreak of the war. There he continued with some short stories and brief Gaelic poems, several of which were published in the *Irish Times*. He informed Padraic Colum that he was planning at least three new books, *Mountain Tops, Tower of Marl* and *Triads of Fearfeada,* before his death in Wicklow, on June 9, 1944.

Most of his published writing was completed before 1920. His first book of poems was *The Garden of the Bees* (1905), followed by *The Rushlight* (1906); *The Man-Child* (1907); *The Gilly of Christ* (1909); *The*

Mountainy Singer (1909); *Irishry* (1913), and *The Earth of Cualaan* (1917). A charming collection of travel sketches, jotted down during a walking tour of Donegal, appeared in 1911 as *Mearing Stones*. This book, *The Rushlight,* and *Agnus Dei,* a slight volume by his wife Nancy, were illustrated by the poet, whose pencil drawings are strong, sharp and suggestive of the early art of Paul Henry. His only recent volume of comment, *Irish Culture,* was edited, with E. J. Kavanagh and J. E. Tobin, in 1928.

Most of the anthologies which have reprinted his work have featured his single poem, "The Old Woman," which, while representative, is not necessarily his best. Mr. Campbell wrote of simple things, the Irish folk and the Irish faith, or a shepherd on the hills where "the constellations ring His forehead like a king"; of the fiddler and his "dreamer's mind" who "hears things in the wind"; the ploughman, amid "smoking lines of sunset earth against a clump of pines"; the mountainy singer—himself—"the voice of the peasant's dream." He saw his country inwardly as well as outwardly, color and soul, dress and spirit. He loved this land. "One hears on all sides of greyness, emigration, degeneracy, but one has only to look about to see that the cry has no mouth," he wrote. Until the end, he fought for his beliefs, certain that the world would desire to know the beauty of a tradition he hugged to his poetic heart; that, "The strength you sweat shall blossom yet in golden glory to the sun." Only in his last days was the hurt great, that not every one wanted what he ached to offer. Along with the poetry of Colum, with whose poetic outlook he was closely akin, his work stands among the best of his nation for their unsophisticated naturalness. For the cheaper publicists and the men of easy reputation he had neither respect nor patience.

J. T.

Roy Campbell   1902-

When a man has published thirteen books, eleven of them books of poetry, it is rather surprising to find his occupation given in *Who's Who* as "horse merchant." But Roy Campbell does run a horse and mule business, and considers poetry his recreation.

Royston Dunnachie Campbell was born in Durban, Natal, Union of South Africa, of Scottish ancestry, on October 2, 1902. His grandfather's family were among the first settlers of Natal. This grandfather, William Campbell, was a great controversialist and proclaimed his ideas in striking verse. Roy's father, Dr. Samuel George Campbell was a brilliant scholar and athlete. His mother was Margaret Dunnachie Campbell. "There have never been shopkeepers, lawyers, politicians, or parsons in the family, only soldiers, scholars, athletes, poets, doctors, and farmers."

While still a boy Campbell left Natal on a whaling schooner. He joined the Sixth South African infantry when fifteen, but was sent back to the Durban High School. After a very short time at Oxford, he went to the South of France, where he joined some fishermen and spent about a year, on and off, sailing boats going from port to port. Returning to London, England, he met and married, while yet in his teens, Mary Margaret Gorman. "Naturally my father cut me off for marrying without his consent, but from this time on I date all the major events of my life." Sick of city life the young couple went to a remote fishing village in North Wales. For fifteen dollars a year, they rented a stable, which they converted into a cottage. Their first child, Teresa, was born in this cottage. "We lived at first on about five pounds a month, spending half of it on books, for I had soon the whole country set with traps and springes. For vegetables I toured the whole district at night. Over the fire we read Dante, Pope's Homer, Dryden's Virgil, Paradise Lost, Donne, Mickle's Camoens, Cervantes, Rabelais, and the Englisabethans: living for a year under the continual intoxication of poetry." Here he wrote *The Flaming Terrapin.*

When both fathers discovered themselves to have been old college chums the young Campbells were invited home to Africa. There he edited a monthly, which was abandoned after a row. While in South Africa he wrote *The Wayzgoose,* a satire. They returned to England, and thence to Provence. In Provence he took part in all the native sports, especially bull fighting and water jousting. He won the steer-throwing championship of Provence in 1932 and 1933 and jousted for Martiques 1928-1931.

Campbell expounds his love of the bull ring in his prose work *Taurine Provence.* He declares, "Bull fighting is the only sport which is at the same time a great art, and in which man opposes a terrific adversary with inferior weapons." He believes "the poet and the athlete do the same thing in different spheres." While extolling the athlete he does not praise the physical in opposition to the intellectual—he has flayed modern British intellectuals in *The Georgiad* and in *The Flowering Rifle*—rather he condemns the opposition between them set up by modern life. He desires the development of the total man, both body and soul.

Roy Campbell loves Spain as "a country to which I owe everything as having saved my soul." He and his family were baptized by the parish priest at Altea in 1934. Mrs. Campbell had been brought up an Anglo-Catholic; he more or less a "bush-Baptist." "I don't think that my family and I were converted by any event at any given moment. We lived for a time on a small farm in the sierras at Altea where the working people were mostly good Catholics, and there was such a fragrance and freshness in their life, in their bravery, in their reverence, that it took hold of us all imperceptibly." While they were living in Toledo, the Carmelite prior, who was martyred later, took them to Cardinal Gomá, Archbishop of Toledo, for Confirmation as they had several times hidden the Fathers in their house when it was dangerous to do so. They escaped from Toledo in a lorry.

Campbell fought for the Nationalist cause in the Spanish Civil War, and was war correspondent for the London *Tablet* during this time. He saved the Carmelite archives of Toledo during the siege. Twice he was before a firing squad but was saved. Out of the war came *The Flower-ing Rifle,* which some critics regard as one of the world's great epics. Speak-ing of the war he said, "To have witnessed and shared in some of this would have enabled a dumb ox to write inspired poetry." General Quiepo de Llano mentioned him with honour in his despatches of April 1937.

In 1942 he left Spain to join the Intelligence Corps in England and became a sergeant. He was sent to East Africa. There among other things he wrote two sonnets on Camoens.

He is the author of: *The Flaming Terrapin; The Gum Trees; Mith-raic Emblems; Pomegranates; The Georgiad; The Flowering Rifle; Choos-ing a Mast; Flowering Reeds; Adamastor; The Wayzgoose; Taurine Prov-ence; Sons of the Mistral,* and *Broken Record* (autobiography). He also translated three plays by Helge Krog, from the Norwegian.

M. S.

(James) Francis Carlin (MacDonnell)
1881-1945

In 1917 Francis Carlin, a floorwalker at Macy's Department Store, had the poems which he had written in his spare time privately printed by an Irish printer. He sent a copy to Mr. T. A. Daly, then associate editor of the Philadelphia *Record.* Mr. Daly, who was attracted to the book by its dedication, read it while waiting for a taxi-cab. He wrote a review of it for his paper and then telephoned to Christopher Morley. Morley imme-diately went in search of a publisher, and suc-ceeded in getting Henry Holt & Company. The book, *My Ireland* was an immediate success. Two years later while superintendent of the fourth floor at Macy's, Carlin wrote *Cairn of Stars.* He was proclaimed an Irish poet although he had never seen Ireland until he was 23 years of age.

James MacDonnell, who used the pen name of his maternal grand-father, Francis Carlin (a weaver in County Tyrone, Ireland, who won local fame as an impromptu versifier) was born in Bay Shore, Long Island, New York, April 7, 1881 and had lived all his life in the vicinity of New York City. His father, who was a coachman, died of pneumonia while his three sons were very small. His widow took in washing to support her family. James was educated in the parochial schools of Norwalk Con-necticut. The late Sister M. Joseph of Laurelton Academy, Milford, Con-necticut, who taught him, remembered that he had a talent for art, and that after work he haunted the public library. A librarian introduced him to Ruskin. He was working in a shoe shop at the time and although he could devote only ten minutes a day to reading, he read all the works of

Ruskin. "Ruskin," said Francis Carlin, "sent me to the woods—to the streams. Through him I began to see things in Nature."

He recounted the other literary influences of his youth. "It was the reading aloud of the Catholic Bible in our home that first put the wonder on me, as well as the rhymes and riddles of my grandfather whose name my pen now bears."

James left school before finishing the eighth grade. He wished to be a Christian Brother, but the family was poor, so he let the education go to his brother, John, who became an Assistant District Attorney in New York.

"When I was about twenty-three," he once said, "I was sickly, and so I was sent to Ireland for a spell, my mother thinking the Irish air would do me good. The first day I was there I followed the plow and talked to the plowman, and I found a kinship with the very clods of the earth, and my heart was full of something I wanted to say. I threw away all my medicines. I never took another drop of medicine in Ireland. It was the Irish land that cured me." His mother had planted the love of Ireland in his heart. This visit helped to produce the rich harvest that followed. On his return home he became a dry-goods salesman at Macy's Department Store in New York City.

He revisited Ireland when he was twenty-eight or twenty-nine and then he began to write. In 1924 he disappeared. No one knew what became of him. Christopher Morley and Tom Daly "had urged him to keep away from pink teas, poetry societies and association with more formal literary figures; fearing that all such influences would steal away from him his untutored poetic gift." Morley and Daly said in 1939, "He took us much too literally." He turned up at Father Leonard Feeney's ordination at Weston College in 1928. Later Christopher Morley advertised for him in *The Saturday Review of Literature,* and in 1937 Father Feeney wrote about the mystery in *America.* In 1939 his discovery made the first page of the New York *World-Telegram.* He had been living in New York all along.

Some of the poems written during this time appeared later in the *Catholic World* and *The Messenger of the Sacred Heart.* During the sixteen years of his hidden life, the Bible was his principal study and his forty boxes in storage filled with data, give evidence of this fact. He would have continued his obscurity only his money gave out. He went looking for a job that would give him the needed $10.00 a week to take care of his moderate wants and to finish the work which he called, "Biblical Construction." In December he went back to Macy's as a checker in the receiving department but was laid off on May 18, 1940.

Francis Carlin died in St. Francis Hospital on March 11, 1945, after a brief illness.

M. S.

Montgomery Carmichael   1857-1936

Having lived in Italy for many years, Carmichael only naturally reflects Italian life in his books. They are bathed in the immortal atmosphere of the historic lands of Tuscany and Umbria. It is an intimate life that he depicts. His writings show he loved Italy and knew it well. His books also evince a knowledge of Italian art. His long residence in Tuscany brought about his conversion to the Catholic Church. As early as 1892, Montgomery Carmichael became British Vice-Consul at Leghorn, the seaport city of Tuscany, Italy. He was consul from 1908 to 1922 and Consul-General to the Republic of San Marino and His Britannic Majesty's Consul for Tuscany (except Florence) Umbria and the Marches, from 1912 to 1922.

Montgomery Carmichael was born in 1857 at Birkenhead, England, and was educated at Brewood, Bonn and Munich. In 1887 he married Miss Maud Parker, a daughter of J. W. Parker, the publisher of *Fraser's Magazine*. They had one son.

Montgomery Carmichael's first book, *Sketches and Stories Grave and Gay* was published in 1896. Then came *In Tuscany* (1901), in which he deals with the Tuscan temperament and Tuscan types. His first work of fiction, *The Major-General*, a story of modern Florence, came out the same year. *Lady Poverty*, also published in 1901 is a translation from a medieval original.

What is regarded as Carmichael's most representative novel, *John William Walshe* was published in 1902. This book deceived many. Instead of being considered as a novel, which Carmichael intended it to be, many readers thought it was a biography. It is a soul study of exquisite spirituality and consummate scholarship. Its lines cling to the heart.

Montgomery Carmichael in his earlier years may have been esoteric for all but the initiate. But during the last decade of his life, he appeared to have broken away from the preciousness of his former style and developed a more austere and cryptic prose.

Essay after essay flowed from his pen to the pages of the *Dublin Review, The Catholic World* and *Thought*. He was well-versed in the history of mysticism, on St. John of the Cross and St. Teresa, as well as St. Francis. In one of his last articles "The Layman," he conceives the possibilities of a new movement comparable to the Friends of God of the fourteenth century. Yet his scholarship is not limited to religious literature —he had wandered through many an obscure English pathway—for example, his paper on the Catholic interests of the poet, William Cowper. His other books show the Italian influence: *On the Old Road Through France to Florence* (1904); *Inscriptions in the Old British Cemetery of Leghorn* (edited by him in 1906); *Francais Masterpiece* (1909); *The Solitaries of the Sambucca* (1914), and *Christopher and Cressida* (1924).

A. M.

Alexis Carrel 1873-1944

The achievements in the field of medical science of Alexis Carrel read like a modern day fairy tale. He first attracted wide attention in 1912 through his spectacular experiment with the cultivation of a fragment of embryo chicken heart muscle in a test tube.

In 1934 Dr. Carrel again attracted attention through his joint announcement with Charles A. Lindbergh of their ingenious germ-proof *perfusion pump,* designed to keep alive organs of animals in an artificial circulation medium that served as a blood substitute. When the high expectations originally held out for this "artificial heart" failed to materialize, Dr. Carrel discontinued the experiments in 1939.

Carrel, a Frenchman, is claimed by both America and France. He was Born June 28, 1873 in Sainte Foy les Lyon, France, son of Alexis Carrel, silk merchant, and his wife Anne (Ricard) Carrel. He was educated at the University of Lyons where he graduated as a doctor of medicine. From 1896 to 1900 he was an intern at the hospitals in Lyons and from 1900 until 1902 conducted classes in the University there.

His peculiar genius began to assert itself in student days. At the University of Lyons he early acquired such surgical skill that he could tie together with his index and middle finger two pieces of cat-gut inside a small cardboard box, uniting them so securely that no one could untie them with both hands. He also sewed five hundred stitches into a single sheet of cigarette paper.

After leaving school his research experiments were so far-fetched and so seemingly impractical that his teachers in Lyons lost interest in him. He was looked upon as a clever trickster rather than a promising physician.

Like an explorer who had not as yet discovered his trail, but knew in his heart he was heading in the right direction, Carrel set forth for Canada with a vague idea of cattle raising. His thoughts still turned towards animals and no doubt animal experiments. Fortunately somewhere along the line he drifted back to science and "found himself" at the Hull Physiological Laboratory in Chicago. Here he soon won professional recognition and fame by his discovery of a new way of sewing together the ends of an artery and by his success in removing a dog's goiter and putting it back upside down for thyroid functioning.

In 1905, aged thirty-two he accepted a post on the staff of the newly organized Rockefeller Institute for Research in New York City. He went there on the special invitation of Simon Flexner, and in 1912 won the Nobel prize ($40,000) for success in suturing blood vessels and the transplanting of organs. Other honors followed in rapid succession. He won the Nordhoff-Jung Cancer Prize in 1931; the Newman Foundation Award of the University of Illinois in 1937 and the Rotary Club of New York Service Medal in 1939. He held degrees from the Universities of Columbia, Brown and Princeton.

Just before World War I (1913), Carrel married Anne de La Motte, attractive widow of the Marquis de la Mairie, who had been his laboratory assistant. When war broke out in France they both offered their services. He joined the French Army and his wife drove an ambulance. He was in service from 1914 till 1919, was made a major and won the Cross of the Legion of Honor. With a chemist, Henry D. Dakin, Carrel perfected the famed Carrel-Dakin antiseptic solution for the treatment of infected wounds and was credited with the saving of lives of many wounded allied soldiers.

In appearance Dr. Carrel was a stocky man, broad of face and broad of brow. He had a pink complexion and piercing kindly eyes. He was a typical Frenchman in appearance and mannerisms. In his *Man The Unknown* (1935) are to be found his experiences, philosophy and intuitions as a doctor and as a man. The book offers opportunity for a better understanding of human beings and of life. Just before his death, he completed a book on the influence of prayer, entitled *The Prayer*. A writer on biological and surgical subjects, he had contributed to medical and lay magazines in Europe and in America. Since his work was one to catch the fancy of the man on the street, his name was much publicized.

In 1939, having reached the Rockefeller Institute age of retirement, Dr. Carrel with several others gave up all official connection with the Institute but as *Member Emeritus* he continued his research in his private laboratory there.

Having saved so many lives through his research work in World War I, Dr. Carrel in 1940 again set out for Europe to make a health survey in the war-infected countries. He did special research on the action of cold and malnutrition on the young. He was in France studying the effects of famine and starvation when the blitzkrieg ended the war for France. From France he went to Spain. In February 1941 he accompanied the writer James Wood Johnson on a tour of France and Spain to see what five years' war had done to the children of those countries. Mr. Johnson gives us an excellent insight into the work of Dr. Carrel in two articles written for the *Saturday Evening Post* entitled *We Saw Spain Starving,* and *Ah Madrid! Rumors, Suspicion, Fear!*

In 1944, after the allied occupation of France, he was suspected of having collaborated with the enemies of France during the tenure of the Vichy regime. One week before his death this accusation which had caused him great grief was officially denied. Two weeks before his death on November 5, 1944 he had received the last rites of the Church.

E. F.

Reverend Patrick Joseph Carroll, C.S.C. 1876-

Since 1934, Father Patrick Carroll has been editor of *Ave Maria*, the Catholic Home Weekly, now (1947) in its 82nd year.

His connection with that periodical began in 1898 when he had his first poem "The Wrecks of Departed Years" printed in it. Later he wrote a weekly story for the *Ave Maria;* these were put into book form. The first story was *Round About Home,* the title of which was suggested by a picture in the *Dome*—the Notre Dame yearbook. The picture showed boys swimming, playing baseball and lolling on the grass. It bore the caption *Round About Now.* That decided him to call his West Limerick sketches *Round About Home.*

Father Carroll was born in County Limerick, Ireland, in 1876, the son of Joseph and Johanna (Maloney) Carroll. He was educated at the University of Notre Dame in Indiana and at the Catholic University of America (1897-1900). In 1896 he entered the Congregation of the Holy Cross. He was professed in 1898 and ordained in 1900. He served as president of Sacred Heart College, Watertown, Wisconsin and St. Edward's University in Austin, Texas. From 1926 to 1928 he was vice-president of Notre Dame University. Previous to his professorship at Notre Dame in 1922, he was rector of St. Joseph's Church in South Bend from 1913-1922. Then followed four years of teaching. His term as vice-president lasted two years, 1926-1928.

Father Carroll is the author of *Songs of Creelabeg* (poetry) (1916); *Memory Sketches* (1920), (dealing with the country people of Ireland); *The Man-God* (1927), (a Life of Christ as a text for schools and colleges); *Heart Hermitage, and Other Poems* (1928); *Patch* (1930)—which was published in serial form in the *Ave Maria,* under the title "Memories of an Irish Boy." Patch is the hero of the story. *Michaeleen* a sequel to *Patch* appeared one year later. *Bog:* a novel of the Irish rebellion in 1916 and after, was published in 1934. The following year, a story of love, adventure and mystery laid in contemporary Ireland was published under the title, *Mastery of Tess.* Those with a religious theme, *Many Shall Come,* and *Smoking Flax* came out in 1937 and 1939 respectively. Father Carroll likes *Many Shall Come* as his best book of fiction. His *Ship in the Wake* (1916), is a play for college boys and the book *Vagrant Essays* (1936), deals with unrelated subjects which are, however, always to the point and packed with good common sense. *Patch of Askeaton Days* appeared in 1943.

Father Carroll is also a lecturer on Irish history and literature.

M. H.

Paul Vincent Carroll   1900-

At twenty-one years of age Paul Vincent Carroll emigrated to Scotland, from Ireland where he was born on July 10, 1900 at Blackrock near Dundalk.

He was educated at his father's school until he was thirteen, and later at St. Mary's (Marist) College, Dundalk; and in 1916 went to St. Patrick's Training College for teachers in Dublin. At the Abbey Theatre in Dublin he learned the rudiments of the drama and there chose his profession. For seventeen years, however, he taught in Catholic schools in Scotland. He resigned in 1937.

In 1923, he married Helena Reilly, a gown designer, and now has three daughters. All three attended the Notre Dame boarding school.

Carroll wants to be called an Anglo-Irishman. He says, "I have no politics. I do not believe in a Gaelic-speaking smug Irish Republic. I believe that the future greatness of Ireland lies in her full cooperation with a spring-cleaned British Commonwealth of Nations. I am not a republican doctrinaire. I believe the monarchy is the best form of government for Britain."

Strongly influenced by Chesterton, Carroll loves the paradox. He also loves satire. Swift, too, has been a potent factor in his writing. With W. B. Yeats, who was his first love in poetry, he believes that the coming of the monstrosity of the mass-man is part of our modern tragedy. In drama, Mr. Carroll feels indebted to Ibsen and Synge. The latter taught him color and rhythm.

In 1932, Carroll won the Abbey Theatre prize for the best play of the year with *Things That Are Caesar's*.

It was not until 1937, however, that he won recognition as a professional dramatist. In this year, the American theatre approved the acclaim given *Shadow and Substance* by the Abbey Theatre where it was produced in 1937. (It was written in 1936.) In 1938 it was produced in New York, and in London in 1943. This play received the Casement Award of the Irish Academy of Letters, and the American Foreign Award of 1937-1938. It deals with the clash between classical thinking and the popularization of education; with the royal conception of Christ as a King versus the simple illiterate faith of the lowly and the untutored.

The White Steed, written in 1938, was rejected by the Abbey Theatre in Dublin and refused production by all theatres in Ireland. In the words of Paul Carroll: "It deals with the clash between clerical fascism and the old liberal Catholicism of wayward love, divine mercy and pity and the redeeming grace of God." It was pronounced by George Jean Nathan "the best play of the Broadway (New York City) season 1938-1939."

His other plays are: *The Old Foolishness; Kindred; The Strings, My Lord, are False;* and *The Wise Have Not Spoken*.

Mr. Carroll deplores the decline in acting and the "panzification" of Shakespeare. He also deplores "the decline in declamation and of the spoken beauty of English and would welcome a return to high Shakespearean glamour as a means of ousting the present dreadful 'clipped' drawing room English of the modern theatre."

He believes we should have more laughter, more color, more intelligent glamour and happiness in the lives of ordinary people. He detests outdoor sports and hates the drivelling sentiment associated with animals, especially dogs. He loves children under fourteen, "after which their beauty and intelligence begin to decay."

He is looking forward to the time when we shall have a civic theatre in every city of Great Britain, when the drama will be recognized as a powerful moulding force, culturally and intellectually, and run in close correlation with the Church.

Although Mr. Carroll is critical of clerical interference in the arts, he says, "I am convinced that Catholicism, as a religion, and as a philosophy of life and living, has nothing whatever to fear from the assaults of materialists and vendors of shibboleths."   M. H.

Barbara Barclay Carter

Barbara Barclay Carter was born in Santa Barbara, California, a daughter of John Alexander Carter and Lucia Barclay, whose father had been Anglican Bishop of Jerusalem. Brought to England while still a small child, she was educated there till she was eighteen. Three years later, after a period of secretarial work that included employment in the International Labor Office in Geneva and with the Irish Republican Envoy in Rome, she resumed her studies in Paris, at the Sorbonne and Catholic Institute, specializing in mediaeval history in which she had the honor of passing first in the University. Having taken her degree of Licenciée-ès-Lettres, at the Sorbonne and the first year "Auditorat" diploma in Scholastic Philosophy at the Catholic Institute, she returned to London, becoming a contributor to various reviews and newspapers.

Since a small child, she had had the firm intention of becoming a writer. Her first appearance in print (save for a "poem" in French, in honor of King Albert of Belgium during the last war), was in the shape of two short stories in the *Cork Examiner* and the Dublin *Freeman's Weekly.*

Her first book *Ship Without Sails,* was published in 1931. This book, a reconstruction of the latter years of Dante's life, had obsessed her imagination for some years. She had included Italian literature in her studies at the Sorbonne in order to deepen her knowledge of Dante, and every year her vacations were spent in retracing his wanderings through Northern Italy. The form of a novel was chosen partly because it imposed itself, but also partly because in many biographies of Dante so large a part was played by conjecture that a fictional approach appeared a more honest and rewarding form. This approach indeed found a solution for more than one problem that had troubled biographers; with imaginative consideration, apparent discrepancies in early documents could be reconciled, and in at least one instance she anticipated findings now generally accepted among Dante scholars. The title was taken from Dante's description of himself as a "ship without sails, without rudder," with a cross-reference to the ship in which Lancelot (with whom there is evidence that Dante identified himself) came to the Castle of the Holy Grail.

In later years, she wrote various studies on Dante, which appeared in the *Dublin Review, Contemporary Review, Hibbert Journal* and the Notre Dame *Review of Politics;* to the first two she also contributed articles on other subjects of literary or historical interest. Her second book, however, was of a wholly different character, *Old Nurse* (1936), a study of her own childhood against the background of her old nurse's world, an adorable little country town in Wales, where she herself spent her school vacations after her mother's death. A third work is a play on Abelard, which is awaiting a more propitious time in which to try its fortunes.

At the Sorbonne, she had first come into contact with the Christian Democratic movement through Marc Sangnier and his "Jeune Republique" (then the object of ferocious attacks from the partizans of Charles Maurras and the *Action Française*). Soon after returning to London, she interviewed Don Sturzo on behalf of the *Daily Herald.* This was the beginning of what was to be a lasting collaboration. Acting at first as his interpreter, she became his regular translator and was brought into ever closer contact with Christian Democracy in its international manifestations. London Correspondent for *l'Illustrazione Vaticana, El Matl* (Barcelona), *l'Aube* (Paris) and *La Cité Nouvelle* (Brussels), all of Christian-Democratic tendency, in 1936 she was one of the founders of a British branch of the movement, the People & Freedom Group (the name is taken from the mediaeval Florentine slogan, revived by Savonarola in the XVth century and again by the Swiss Christian Democrats in the XIXth century), of which the Chairman was Mrs. Virginia Crawford, in youth the favorite disciple of Cardinal Manning, and she herself Hon. Secretary. When in 1938 the Group founded its own paper *People & Freedom* (which became a quarterly in 1939 and a monthly in 1940) she became its editor.

In the fall of 1939 the Group published a composite book, *For Democracy,* in which leading Christian Democrats from several countries (they included Mendizabal, Joseph Clayton, Father Gosling, Maurice Vaussard) collaborated under Don Sturzo's direction. To this she contributed the introductory chapter "What we mean by Democracy." This book had an enthusiastic reception from the press, Catholic and non-Catholic, and was the subject of a leading article in the Manchester *Guardian* as a "service to the democratic cause."

From the spring of 1940 to the late summer of 1944, during the German occupation of Europe, *People & Freedom,* with its Swiss namesake, remained the only expression of Christian Democracy on the political plane, while the People & Freedom Group in London formed a rallying-point for Christian Democrats in the exiled Governments. It was thus able to bring into being the International Christian Democratic Union, with the one Hon. Secretary serving for both organizations.

On the appropriate date of July 4, 1944, she entered the service of the American Government (having retained her American citizenship in spite of long residence in Europe) and held the office of Consultant on Italian developments to OSS. Besides all Don Sturzo's books, she has translated Soderini's *Leo XIII*, Maria Montessori's *Secret of Childhood* and Fanfani's *Catholicism, Protestantism and Capitalism*. Miss Carter's interest in the development of the inner life within the Church is instanced by her enrollment among the lay oblates of the renowned English Benedictine Abbey of Buckfast. A more ephemeral interest is her main hobby of bee-keeping which she pursues in a London back garden and she is extremely proud of having passed the "Junior Craftsman" examination of the British Bee-keepers' Association.

George Carver 1888-

Professor George G. Carver is one who, while creating little individually, has done much to advance the cause of Catholic literature. Born in Cincinnati, Ohio, in 1888, he studied at the Universities of Alabama, Chicago, and Miami. He served as instructor in English at Pennsylvania State College from 1916 to 1918, then joined the A.E.F. and saw brief service overseas. From 1919 to 1924 he taught at the University of Iowa. Next he went to the University of Pittsburgh as assistant professor, becoming associate and in 1931 professor of English, which post he still holds.

George Carver declares that all his life he has "wanted to write," but circumstances decreed that most of his writing should be critical or editorial work connected with his teaching. Those excellent anthologies, *The Catholic Tradition in English Literature,* and *Representative Catholic Essays* are cases in point—also *The Stream of English Literature,* done in collaboration with Katherine Brégy and the late Sister M. Eleanor. Also, he has published a few essays and short stories, one of which brought him the stimulating friendship of William Marion Reedy.

Professor Carver is a member of Phi Beta Kappa and Phi Kappa Sigma fraternities, and is interested in music. He was married in 1919 to Eva Gertrude Schultz of Chicago, and is the father of one son. Confessing to the uneventfulness of many professorial lives, he declares: "My family, my students and my writing comprise my interests. A pleasant home, congenial occupation and freedom to be forever learning are enough for me." He is a convert to the Catholic Faith. K. B.

Robert J. Casey   1890-

Because of its length, a list of the published works of Robert J. Casey compares favorably with the catalogue of a publishing house. Likewise, during the quarter century that he has been writing copy of the sort given permanent form between covers, Casey has explored a vast field. War, mystery, travel, romance, satire, verse, and even the technical side of radio have been grist to his mill. Then too, he has ventured into the field of semi-biography, for in *Such Interesting People* he has been compelled (however reluctantly) to reveal much of his own life and career while at the same time describing the eccentricities of scores of his friends, acquaintances and fellow workers.

For the sake of convenience, here is part of the Casey bibliography with his works presented, not in order of their appearance, but according to classification:

War: *I Can't Forget; Torpedo Junction; Battle Below,* and *This Is Where I Came In.* Mystery: *The Secret of No. 37 Hardy Street; The Secret of the Bungalow.* Travel: *Four Faces of Siva; Baghdad and Points East; Easter Island; The Lost Kingdom of Burgundy.* Romance: *The Gentleman in Armor.* Satire: *The Voice of the Lobster.* Verse: *The Vest Pocket Anthology.* Technical: *Manual of Radio Interference.*

It will be noted that none of these works indicates Catholicity. Casey has never undertaken to write what would ordinarily be called a "Catholic" book, but that he is himself a practical Catholic, who is not only unafraid, but proud, to proclaim his religion openly, becomes apparent in the pages of his books whenever the subject gives suitable occasion for a profession of faith.

It should likewise be stressed that Casey's philosophy is always sound and rests on the firm basis of the Scholastic system taught him during his student days with the Jesuits at St. Mary's College, Kansas.

Ever since he received his Bachelor of Arts degree from St. Mary's College in 1910, Bob Casey, as he is best known, has worked as a reporter, feature writer and foreign correspondent on daily newspapers of metropolitan standing. This career was interrupted by World War I when Casey entered the United States Army and spent months as an artillery captain with the American Expeditionary Force in France. With him, the writing of books has been purely a sideline, although *I Can't Forget* and *Torpedo Junction,* both of which deal with the second World War, grew naturally out of his work as a war correspondent for *The Chicago Daily News. The Cannoneers Have Hairy Ears* resulted from Casey's experience as a soldier during the first *World War.*

A native of Beresford, South Dakota, Robert Joseph Casey was born March 14, 1890, the son of James and Mary A. (Wilson) Casey. Being mechanically inclined, Casey entered the Armour Institute of Technology at Chicago, but transferred to St. Mary's College, Kansas where he received a classical training according to the Jesuit Ratio Studiorum. He was no sooner graduated from college than he married his childhood sweetheart, Miss Marie Driscoll of Rapid City, South Dakota, and after a few months during which he worked in the office of a saw mill at Beresford, he went to Des Moines, Iowa, where he got his first newspaper job as a reporter on the *Register* and *Leader*. Later he worked in Houston, Texas and then Chicago beckoned.

It is as a Chicago newspaper man that Casey has won a world-wide reputation for himself. The *Inter Ocean* and The *Journal,* both of which suspended long since, knew him well, and in 1920 he joined the staff of The Chicago *Daily News*. From that time on he has been regarded as a star reporter and books have flowed from his typewriter in a steady stream.

When the war clouds began to hang heavy over Europe in 1939, the Chicago *Daily News* sent Casey abroad to get some first-hand information of what was happening. He chose Luxembourg as his point of vantage. He even penetrated a short distance within Germany. He saw World War II break and Luxembourg overrun and Paris taken. He was with the refugees from that city as they made their way southward. He was an eye-witness to the bombings in Bordeaux and then, crossing Spain to Portugal, he eventually reached England.

In London he went through weeks of that reign of terror created by the Nazis and then he went to Egypt when the British and Nazis were struggling for possession of the Near East. He was injured by being pushed from a railroad train in Cairo and was ordered back to Chicago. It was during the long, roundabout voyage to the United States that Casey wrote the greater part of *I Can't Forget.*

Soon after his arrival in this country he was sent to Alaska, for even then the Chicago *Daily News* anticipated trouble with Japan. It was not long after Casey's return from the North that Pearl Harbor was attacked. Casey was immediately sent to Hawaii, arriving in Honolulu just eleven days after the Pearl Harbor debacle. He was the first correspondent to enter that area from the outside. On board a ship of Admiral Halsey's task force he saw all the fighting in the Pacific during those days when the United States was trying to get its feet on the ground. When at long last he returned to the United States, Casey wrote *Torpedo Junction.*

Robert J. Casey is perhaps the only correspondent who had been in every fighting zone and had seen the war from every angle. Bob Casey is what has been called "a newspaper man's newspaper man." He is first of all an accurate reporter who overlooks no details. He is a graphic writer, an expert in sketching character and he never fails to find the human interest in every situation. Nor does he overlook the humor which to the discerning abounds even in the midst of tragedy.

Leland Stowe has written that Casey's benign Irish face and ready tongue are sufficient to gain him entree wherever he goes. To know Bob Casey is to love him, a fact which always makes him the most popular man in any gathering.   P. M.

Catherine Sister Mary   *see* Mary Catherine, Sister

Mrs. George Catlin   *see* Mildred Criss

Algernon Cecil   1879-

A descendant of Queen Elizabeth's famous Lord Treasurer, Lord Burghley, and of his equally famous son, Robert Cecil, first Earl of Salisbury, Secretary of State for Elizabeth and James I, Algernon Cecil was born on January 31, 1879 and entered the Catholic Church in 1915. Unlike many converts, and most unusual for an author, he has as yet published no book about his conversion. Yet, we know the bare outline of his experience, for, in the Introduction to *A Dreamer in Christendom* he writes, "What is set down here might as well, perhaps, have been cast in the mould of a 'journal intime,' but that the writer happens to prefer a more impersonal to a more egotistical manner of treatment. The diary and the essay are in fact more closely related than we commonly admit." Then in the essay, "Religio Historici," he describes a change of religion which "comes about neither under the influence of taste, nor of reaction, nor of intimacies too sacred to pry into, but as the result of a conscious, natural, or, if this be the better expression, supernatural growth in the mind of certain opinions and falling away of others; the whole process going on without haste or rest over a term of years and involving no wholesale, eager arson of those things that were once adored nor sudden indiscriminate admiration of things that once were burnt. In a case of this kind reason may fairly be presumed to have had its due, and more particularly if the conversion should have occurred just about that time of a man's life when such power of judgment as he has is, as one might say, at the full."

With his ancestry Mr. Cecil was drawn by the history of the Tudor period and the heroic figure of Henry VIII's Lord Chancellor early attracted him. His book, *A Portrait of Thomas More*, was the result of a love maturing over a quarter of a century. He is interested in the close interweaving of More's inner life and outer life. In *Metternich* he admires a statesman; in his life of More, he can admire the statesman and marvel at the saint. It is above all as a saint that he depicts More.

Mr. Cecil is a barrister. His father, Lord Eustace Cecil was a Crimean veteran, and at one time Surveyor-General of the Ordnance. His mother was Lady Gertrude Scott, daughter of the second Earl of Eldon. He is a nephew of the late Lord Salisbury. He attended Eton and New College, Oxford. He received his A.B. with first class honors in history in 1901, and his M.A. in 1905. He was president of the Oxford Union, "the cradle of statesmen" in 1901. He became a Barrister-at-Law, Inner Temple, 1905. During the first European War he was attached to the Intelligence Division of the Admiralty and subsequently to the Historical Section of the Foreign Office. He has practically written a history of the Foreign Office in *British Foreign Secretaries.* In 1923 he married Lady Guendolen Fanny Godolphin-Osborne, eldest daughter of the tenth Duke of Leeds. She died in 1933. There were no children. In honor of his wife, "Allegra" he wrote *A House in Bryanston Square*—the house in which he and his wife lived and which was destroyed by a German bomb in World War II. J. J. Dwyer in *The Tablet* for January 6th, 1945 writes: "the reader is conducted through the House from the doorstep to the skylight, in a symbolic tour of inspection, with the author as his guide, so that No. 43 Bryanston Square is made the framework which holds together many diverse aspects of experience, much criticism of society and politics, and in particular the author's adventures among masterpieces of sacred and profane love. In this pilgrimage the reader enjoys contact with a mature and powerful mind and follows with alacrity a guide who seems to have read and remembered nearly everything." In 1938, Algernon Cecil was elected a Knight of Honour and Devotion of the Sovereign Order of St. John of Jerusalem (Knight of Malta).

He is the author of *Six Oxford Thinkers* (1909); *Essays in Imitation* (1910); *Life of Robert Cecil, First Earl of Salisbury* (1915); *The World We Live In* (1925); *A Dreamer in Christendom* (1935); *British Foreign Secretaries* (1927); *Metternich* (1933); *A Portrait of Thomas More, Scholar, Statesman, Saint* (1937); *Facing the Facts in Foreign Policy* (1941), and *A House in Bryanston Square* (1944).

M. S.

Maria Cristina Chambers

At the age of twenty, María Cristina Chambers became the first woman of Mexican birth to write fiction in English. Although she was born in Mexico, she has lived in the United States since her fourteenth year. Her maiden name was Mena, and as María Cristina Mena she published her first story in the *Century Magazine.* The editor at the time, was the late Robert Underwood Johnson, the poet, who later became American Ambassador to Italy. It was he who launched María Critina Mena on her literary career.

Mrs. Chambers began to write when she was about ten years old. She recalls with pleasant memories how she liked to hide in corners and write verses which no one ever saw. From her earliest years she read the classics written in English, French, Italian, and her native tongue, Spanish.

Mrs. Chambers never concerned herself about the "methods" of how to write. "I have never read, much less studied, the so-called 'methods' for learning how to write. I do not believe an aspirant for authorship needs any more than to learn from observation and much reading of good authors; that writing is something that is born and grows naturally through much working at it and particularly from one's own original and very personal feeling and thinking," writes Mrs. Chambers.

Her first story for *Century Magazine* won a contract for a series of stories of Mexican life and these appeared every three or four months for about five years. There were about sixteen stories in all.

Mrs. Chambers considers as her "most representative" work, a short story she wrote called "John of God, the Water-Carrier," which was published by the *Criterion,* of London, England. This monthly magazine was then edited by Thomas Stearns Eliot. That same year, 1928, Edward O'Brien selected the story for his volume *Best Short Stories of 1928.*

All her short stories were written for adults. Her first story for boys and girls is *The Water Carrier's Secrets.* The interest of this story centers on Juan de Dios, John of God, the eldest son of a large family in Mexico, who follows the career of his father as a water-carrier for the surrounding neighborhood. He worked hard and prospered. The adoption of a daughter by his father gave Juan greater incentive to work harder. He decided then that when he had enough money and he was old enough, he would marry Dolores, the adopted girl.

"I've written this book—my first juvenile—with 'the hand on the heart' as we say in Mexico. It is my small contribution and very large wish for a better understanding by the youth of the United States—my adopted country—of Mexico—the country of my birth," writes Mrs. Chambers.

Mrs. Chambers is planning to do a series of short stories dedicated to the youth of the United States for the purpose of showing the life of Mexico in all its phases. In November 1943 she published a novel dealing with the fifteen-year-old son of the governor of a Mexican State. She hopes to write a series of articles on the churches of Mexico and some essays portraying the soul-experiences of the Mexican people in their struggle to remain good Catholics. In 1945 she wrote *Bullfighter's Son* and *The Three Kings* appeared in 1946.

Mrs. Chambers' stories have been translated into Spanish by the famous Mexican author and poet, Manuel Sales Cepeda, of Yucatan. Besides the *Century* and *Criterion Magazines,* her stories appeared in the *Cosmopolitan Magazine, American Magazine,* and the *Household Magazine.*

Mrs. Chambers is the widow of Henry Kellett Chambers, the well-known dramatic author and journalist. At the time of his passing (1935) he was one of the editors of the *Literary Digest,* a post he held for fifteen years.

M. H.

Caroline Augusta Chandler   1906-

In the past few years many American medical men have been a joy to publishing firms. Caroline Chandler adds a feminine name to the lengthening list of doctor-authors. In 1939, she started writing a medical page for *The Catholic Woman's World,* of which she has since become Associate Editor. These articles were favorably noticed, and she was invited by Dodd, Mead and Company to write for their *Career Books series* a work on woman doctors. Her story, *Susie Stuart, M.D.,* which is largely autobiographical, should certainly increase the enrollment of women in medical schools.

Doctor Chandler is a descendant of the Chandler family which settled in Roxbury, Massachusetts in 1634. The child of Andrew Hartupee and Lucille Brown Chandler, she was born in Ford City, Pennsylvania, December 7, 1906. She became a Catholic while she was a student at Mt. Aloysius Academy, Cresson, Pennsylvania. She attended the University of Pittsburgh (1924-1927), and received a B.A. from Barnard in 1929. Four years of study at Yale School of Medicine, where she was the only woman in a class of forty-odd, followed. She was elected to the board of the Yale Journal of Biology and Medicine 1931-1933. While still a student she won her first spurs in her chosen field—medical research. She received her degree *cum laude.* She was awarded a research fellowship at Harvard Medical School (1934-1936). She did her research in pediatrics and was assistant on the Medical Service in the Children's Hospital, Boston. From 1936 to 1937 she was assistant in bacteriology and immunology at the Harvard School of Public Health. In 1936 the National Federation of Business and Professional Women's Clubs gave her the Lena Lake Forrest Fellowship for research on influenzal meningitis. From 1937 to 1939 she did research work in obstetrics, and bacteriology under Dr. Hans Zinsser; was assistant in bacteriology at Harvard Medical School, and volunteer assistant in bacteriology at the Boston Lying-in Hospital. In 1939 she went to Baltimore to Johns Hopkins University and did research in pediatrics for two years. At the same time she was made assistant dispensary pediatrician at Johns Hopkins Hospital. Since 1941 she has been assistant visiting pediatrician at the hospital. The same year she was appointed instructor in preventive medicine at Johns Hopkins University. She is a member of the National Board of Medical Examiners of U. S.

A priest and a scientist have influenced Doctor Chandler in her writing. The priest is Leonard Feeney, S.J., the poet and essayist, whom she knows personally; the scientist, Hans Zinsser, the famous immunologist and the author of the best seller *Rats, Lice and History,* who died in 1940. Doctor Chandler worked in the laboratory at Harvard under Dr. Zinsser for three years. Under his supervision and in collaboration with Dr. Leroy Fothergill and Dr. John Dingle she did research on the influenza bacillus and influenza bacillus meningitis.

Besides her monthly page in *The Catholic Woman's World,* Doctor Chandler is a frequent contributor to the scientific and medical journals. In 1944 *Susie Stuart: Home Front Doctor* appeared.

M. S.

Margaret Chanler   1862-

Most authors begin to write very early in life. In the case of Margaret Chanler, literature came at the end of a long life crowded with other experiences such as travel and devotion to the many forms of art. It was to record these that in 1934, when she was seventy-two, she wrote her first book, *Roman Spring.*

Her father, Luther Terry, the painter, left Connecticut for Rome in 1833, and there in 1861 he married the widow of Thomas Crawford, the mother of Francis Marion Crawford and Mrs. Hugh Frazer by a previous marriage. It was in Rome that Margaret Terry was born and there she spent the early years of her life, and it was there that she married her cousin Winthrop Chanler in 1886. Eight children and twenty-four grandchildren and two great-grandchildren have blessed their union.

Not until 1883 was she received into the Catholic Church (from Anglicanism) though she was afterwards to write, "I cannot remember the time when Catholicism was not the true religion for me."

She professes to be "invincibly ignorant of politics," yet she numbered Theodore Roosevelt, Henry Cabot Lodge and Henry Adams among her friends, although most of her friendships were with artists and literary people. In this connection must be mentioned Edith Wharton, Jean Paul Richter, the archaeologist and historian of art, Monsignor Duchesne, The Abbé Liszt, Saint-Gaudens, John La Farge and Stanford White.

If her upbringing was cosmopolitan to a degree—so much so that in her early years in America she felt herself a foreigner—it had the great advantage of giving her the widest sort of culture, and a perfect knowledge of French, German and Italian. But to all her artistic interests she added a special love for horses. It was a sound balance to the learned, artistic and fashionable societies in which she lived.

Her *Autumn in the Valley* (1936) followed up the success of her previous book of reminiscences, which had been a best-seller for months, and continued the story of her many friendships. Again we see some of the people of the earlier book, and some whose portraits were not fully drawn. Edward Lear, who is generally credited with the invention of the Limerick, is one of these; Mrs. Jack Gardner, the artist "Bob" Chanler,

Henry James and Prince Borghese are others. Though the book carries us
to many cities—Rome, London, Newport, Washington and Paris—much
of it is concerned with the new quiet life in Sweet Briar Farm, Geneseo,
New York. The two books together give us an amusing and intimate
picture of a brilliant generation of which Mrs. Chanler is one of the few
survivors. It was a world of more leisure than our own, and it gave an
opportunity for the cultivation of friendships. For this Margaret Chanler
had a special genius, as she has also for setting down her pictures of a
day not to be recovered. It reaches back to "Uncle Sam" Ward and
Julia Ward Howe, to Longfellow and even to Pio Nono.

In 1937, Mrs. Chanler published her translation of Gertrude von Le
Fort's *Hymns to the Church*. It was a remarkable feat of transferring to
the English medium not only the matter but the tone of the original.
It was all the more remarkable in that this was done by a woman then
seventy-five years old.

Right Reverend John (Henry Palmer) Chapman, O.S.B. 1865-1933

The Benedictine tradition of erudition and scholarship has been particularly upheld in recent
years by not a few outstanding monks of the historic English Congregation of the Order. Recognized as a scholar of high calibre and an outstanding critic in ecclesiastical studies, Abbott John
Chapman was one of the foremost men of that
congregation. Although only six volumes have
issued from his pen, he was the author of a continuous output of monographs, essays and tracts
on historical theology and church history. The
non-Catholic world of historical writers recognized
in him an able student and a most powerful controversialist.

Like numerous other great English Catholic religious leaders, he
came to the Faith from an early training received under Anglican auspices.
The son of Venerable F. R. Chapman, Archdeacon of Sudbury and Canon
of Ely, Henry Chapman was born in Ashfield, Suffolk in 1865. Educated
first by tutors at home, he went in 1884 to Christ Church, Oxford and took
a First in Greats, and then a second in theology. After pursuing theology
at the college at Cuddesdon, he was ordained a deacon in the Anglican
Church in 1889 and held for a short time a curacy at St. Pancras.

Being drawn towards an acceptance of the truth of the Catholic religion, he shortly gave up his living in the Anglican ministry and was
received into the Catholic fold at the London Oratory in 1890. He was
attracted to the Jesuits and spent six months in their novitiate but decided
his vocation lay in the monastic life. He entered the Benedictine novitiate
at the Abbey of Maredsous in Belgium and was professed there in 1893,

taking the religious name of John. Two years later in 1895 he was ordained priest. He was sent by his superiors to the English monastery of Erdington, which is attached to the Congregation of Beuron as was Maredsous at that time. In 1912 he returned to Maredsous but not for long, the next year he was made temporary Superior of the former Anglican community of Caldey. This group of monks had just come into the church and wished to retain their corporate life as Benedictines. Father Chapman guided them through their novitiate period until they were professed. Then came an appointment to serve on the Pontifical Commission for the Revision of the Vulgate under Cardinal Gasquet. This work brought Father Chapman to Rome, where he lived at San Calisto. With the advent of the first World War Father John enlisted in the British forces, but being beyond the age for active combat duty, he was given work ministering to the interned prisoners of various nationalities in Switzerland.

After the war's end he obtained a transfer to the English Congregation and became affiliated with Downside Abbey. He continued, however, his work on the Vulgate in Rome until 1922 when he was recalled to England to become the Claustral Prior at Downside. This office he held until, after the death of Abbot Ramsay in 1929, he was chosen by the Chapter as Abbot of Downside.

All through his life he was a voracious reader. Especially did he like to read the works of the Fathers and the great theologians. His knowledge of Greek and Latin were of immense help to him.

Abbot Chapman is the author of: *Bishop Gore and the Catholic Claims* (1905); *Notes on the Early History of the Vulgate Gospels* (1908); *John the Presbyter* (1911); *Studies in the Early Papacy* (1928); *St. Benedict and the Sixth Century* (1929); and *The Four Gospels*. He contributed to *Hastings' Dictionary of Religion and Ethics* and the *Catholic Encyclopedia*. Much of what he wrote was controversial. His best book is perhaps *Bishop Gore and the Catholic Claims*. He worked hard for three years on *Notes on the Early History of the Vulgate Gospels*. *John the Presbyter* was written to combat the theory of Harnack and others that the author of the Fourth Gospel was not John the Apostle but a "John the Presbyter," referred to by Papias. *St. Benedict and the Sixth Century* was written while he was Prior at Downside. Abbot Cuthbert Butler disagreed with some of his views in this book and stated them in the *Downside Review*. For this periodical, Dom Chapman reviewed many books.

Dom Chapman was also a musician and a lover of art. Through his efforts Downside acquired an exquisite organ and gorgeously carved choir stalls. Though too ill to be present at the opening of the Worth Foundation he lived to see the realization of the project which he had conceived and executed. After four years of service as Abbot he died on Nov. 7th, 1933.

M. H.

Very Reverend Michael Andrew Chapman
1884-

When the paper *The Acolyte: To Serve the Priest* was launched on January 3, 1925, Father Michael Andrew Chapman was its first editor and served in that capacity for ten years. In January 1945 just ten years after his retirement from publication work, he returned to this field as an associate editor of *The Priest.*

Father Chapman was born at Auburndale, Massachusetts on September 9, 1884 of Protestant parents. He was educated at Boston Latin School and Cheshire Academy. He then attended St. Stephen's (later Bard) College, Annandale-on-Hudson, Central Theological Seminary of the Protestant Episcopal Church, Columbia University. Ordained to the Protestant Episcopal ministry in 1909 he held various charges and was Honorary Consultor to the Anglican bishop of Quincy. After his conversion to the Faith in 1918 he studied at Mt. St. Mary's Seminary, Emmitsburg, Maryland and Catholic University. He was ordained to the priesthood in the Catholic Church by the late Bishop Alerding on May 26, 1923. His first appointment was assistant at Holy Angels', Gary, Indiana until June 1924 when he worked on the staff of *Our Sunday Visitor,* Huntingdon, as Associate Editor with residence at St. Mary's. In June 1925, he was appointed pastor of St. Joseph's, Roanoke; then in June 1926 he went to the Cathedral, Fort Wayne where he remained until 1935 when he was given a pastorate in Huntingdon, Indiana.

He is the author of: *The Faith of the Gospel; The Epistle of Christ; The Prayer of Faith; The Heart of the Father; Sundays of the Saints; Judas and Jude; A Garland of Saints for Children; Peregrinus Gasolinus; Peregrinus Goes Abroad; Open My Heart,* and *The Mass of the Cross.*

His articles on the Liturgy and church decoration and furnishing appear currently in *Liturgical Arts* and *Parish Administration.* From 1933 to 1935 he gave lectures to non-Catholics and gave missions and retreats for young people. His hobbies are photography and sculpture.

M. H.

Reverend Angelico Chavez, O.F.M. 1910-

Poetry and painting are the two avocations to which Fray Angelico Chavez, O.F.M. devotes his time when free from his duties as a Franciscan missionary in the Southwest.

Born at Wagon Mound, New Mexico, on April 10, 1910 the son of Fabian and Nicolasa (Roybal) Chavez, he was educated in the public grade school, in charge of the Sisters of Loretto, at Mora, New Mexico, from 1917 to 1924. He learned from his history book the work of the Franciscan padres in California and the Southwest and felt a call to follow in their footsteps. In 1924 therefore, when fourteen years of age, he began his studies for the priesthood at St. Francis Seminary, Mt. Healthy, Ohio, and remained there until 1929. Even at this early date in his training, he succeeded in having original verse and prose printed in Catholic periodicals. In 1929 he entered the novitiate and was given the religious name of Fra Angelico, after the great medieval painter, Fra Angelico of Fiesole. He uses "Fray" (Spanish form) in his pen name. He omits O.F.M. when he writes because he thinks initials disfigure a name. He concludes if his work is no good the Order will not suffer; if his work is successful, people will soon find out to what Order he belongs.

In 1930 he continued his philosophical studies at Duns Scotus College in Detroit, Michigan; then the four years of theology in the Franciscan House of Studies in Oldenburg, Indiana and was ordained priest on May 6, 1937 at Santa Fe, New Mexico. He was given charge of the Indian missions at Santo Domingo, Cochiti, and San Felipe and also worked among his own people as preacher of missions in Spanish.

The poems which he wrote during his seminary days together with others written while a missionary were published at the instance of some well known authors of that vicinity. The title of the volume, *Clothed With the Sun* was taken from the Apocalypse. It is also the title of one poem in the book to *Our Lady*. Besides, it denotes the theme of poems shot through with the sun of the Southwest and of religious life. This book, which is now out of print, John Gillard Brunini hailed, in *Spirit*, as "excellent poems, with unique music and distinction of phrasing." Jessica Powers in the *Commonweal* said he "may be called one of the great hopes of Catholic poetry." In 1940 he published *New Mexico Triptych*, three stories akin to "those quaint three-paneled medieval altar-screens which often carried the Crucifixion in the center, flanked by pictures of other sacred mysteries. In *New Mexico Triptych* we are shown the Nativity, the Crucifixion, and the Madonna, as seen through the simple faith of the early Southwest Spanish-American natives." The illustrations are his own. His third book *Eleven Lady-Lyrics and Other Poems*, which included war poems, was published in 1945. Many of these poems have been published in *Spirit, America,* and *Commonweal,* and three of them appear in the British anthology Moult's *Best Poems* of 1938, 1940, and 1941.

His most ambitious work, as a painter, is the Stations of the Cross in the church of Peña Blanca, New Mexico. The murals, eight feet by thirteen, cover the walls, thus greatly brightening the old church. The faces of the characters are portraits of the townspeople. These paintings which artists came to see have been described in *Travel* magazine for March, 1943 as well as in a London paper.

In May, 1943 he reported at the Chaplains' School, Harvard University. He served at Camp Chaffee in Arkansas with an Armored Division before going to Hawaii. Later he took part in the invasion of Guam and Leyte with the New York 77th (Statue of Liberty) Division. In May 1946 he was honorably discharged from the Army. **M. H.**

Gilbert Keith Chesterton 1874-1936

Familiarly known to the world as "G.K.," Gilbert Keith Chesterton was celebrated as a literary commentator, novelist, essayist, poet, pamphleteer, propagandist, lecturer, and illustrator.

In the opening chapter of his autobiography, he says: "I am firmly of opinion that I was born on the 29th of May, 1874, on Campden Hill, Kensington." He was educated at St. Paul's School and in 1892 enrolled in the Slade School of Art at University College, London. Considerable success was achieved as an artist or illustrator. He illustrated his own first book, *Greybeards At Play* and continued to illustrate some of his other books and some of Hilaire Belloc's.

During the years following his study at the Slade School, he cast about for work suitable to his genius. He began to find himself only in 1900 when he brought out *Greybeards at Play,* a collection of humorous poems. *The Wild Night and Other Poems,* mostly in the Swinburne manner, was published during the same year and evoked a crop of enthusiastic reviews and aroused much curiosity as to who G.K.C. was. These successes led to his becoming a regular contributor to the London *Daily News* in 1901, a connection he maintained during the rest of his life. In this year also, on June 28, he married Frances Blogg, an Anglo-Catholic, who led him from Unitarianism to Anglicanism. She was five years older than Chesterton and was the daughter of a diamond merchant. The marriage ceremony was performed by Conrad Noel at the Kensington Church.

During the first year of their married life, the Chestertons lived in a house in Edwards Square, Kensington, then they moved to the Overstrand Mansions, Battersea, where they resided until 1909 when they moved to Overroads, a country home in Beaconsfield. It was at Beaconsfield in the Chapel of the Railway Hotel, the first public church in town, that he was received into the Church in 1922, by Reverend John O'Connor, the

Father Brown of Chesterton's detective stories. Two other priest friends were present at his baptism: Ronald Knox, of Oxford, and Ignatius Rice, O.S.B., of Douai. When Chesterton was asked why he became a Catholic he answered, "To get rid of my sins." Though the Chestertons greatly desired children, none were born to them. Their secretary and adopted daughter, Dorothy Collins, was afterwards converted by them. Chesterton's death in 1936 at Beaconsfield, was followed by his wife's in 1938.

His towering height and his weight of nearly three hundred and fifty pounds impressed people, and prompted several humorous stories. One of these was told by Brigid de Vine in the *Universe*. Gilbert Keith Chesterton met George Bernard Shaw in a restaurant and was struck by Shaw's thinness. "To look at you," said Chesterton, "people would think there was a famine in England." "And to look at you," rejoined Shaw, "they would think you were the cause of it."

Chesterton had a charming personality as striking as his rotundity. When he said something that amused him there was no doubt of the fact, for his chuckles of laughter rippled over his huge body.

His sense of wit differed from that of George Bernard Shaw in that there was the absence of satire and cutting stabs. He was a constant source of puns and paradoxes. He defined paradox as "Truth standing on her head to attract attention" (*Paradoxes of Mr. Pond*), and the emphasis was on "truth."

Though Mr. Chesterton loved merriment, laughter, companionship, he walked with God. What he himself has said of himself is true: "I could not be anything but Catholic." The Catholic Church was to him the one window through which he could gaze upon reality in what concerns the most important of all things to man—the nature of man and his destiny. In Chapter four of his *Autobiography* (p. 75) he says: "I am very proud of my religion: I am especially proud of those parts of it that are most commonly called superstition. I am proud of being fettered by antiquated dogmas and enslaved by dead creeds (as my journalistic friends repeat with so much pertinacity), for I know very well that it is the heretical creeds that are dead, and that it is only the reasonable dogma that lives long enough to be called antiquated."

For a rapid access to his thought one might read *Orthodoxy, St. Francis of Assisi, The Everlasting Man,* and *St. Thomas Aquinas.* His books were nearly always dictated, which accounts for the conversational tone.

Until the publication of Maisie Ward's biography in 1943 it might be said that no really adequate account of Gilbert Keith Chesterton had appeared. Even the little volume by his closest friend, Hilaire Belloc, *On the Place of Gilbert Chesterton in English Letters* is furiously disappointing. W. R. Titterton, so long associated with him on *C. K.'s Weekly* and, before that, on the *New Witness* gives, in *G. K. Chesterton—a Portrait,* what is mainly an account of Chesterton's bohemian Fleet Street days. The Frenchman, Raymond Las Vergnas, in his *Chesterton, Belloc, Baring* (1938), offers an acute study. A good account is in the anonymous *G. K. Chesterton, a Criticism,* written thirty years ago by Gilbert's brother Cecil; but of course that is only of the early years.

In 1930 Chesterton lectured at Notre Dame, University, South Bend, Indiana, which conferred the LL.D. on him. Besides giving many other lectures in various cities, he debated with Clarence Darrow in New York City before an audience of 4000 in Mecca Temple on the question: "Will the World Return to Religion?" At the close of the debate a vote was taken. The result was 2,359 for Chesterton's point of view and 1,022 for Darrow's.

When one comes to the writings of Chesterton, it is necessary to select and classify. The novels make excellent reading for their art and excitement, and are written primarily to point a moral. Though *The Napoleon of Notting Hill* is a swiftly moving "yarn" and though in Father Brown, Chesterton created one of the great characters in detective literature, not in these is he really found. One exception may be made. *Manalive* (1930), though far from being his best book, does contain his doctrine in parable form. It is concerned with the problem of reviving the romance of common things and the need for appreciation. It is only by surprise that enjoyment of life can be kept alive, and only by humility that surprise can live.

His travel books, *The New Jerusalem, What I Saw in America,* and *The Resurrection of Rome* contain magnificent passages and would have to be considered in any general treatment of his work, into which they fit as part of a harmonious whole, but they are only incidental to the main body of his output. The same thing is true of his dazzling *Short History of England.* As for his plays, *Magic* and *Dr. Johnson,* they were brief excursions into a field not really Chesterton's at all. They state once again his central theme, but they do it less effectively than his other work.

Essays form the greater part of Chesterton's prolific and varied writings, of which he produced more than thirty volumes. Most of these were written for journals and so vary in subject according to the nature of the organ and the time of the year in which they appeared. Maurice Evans in his *G. K. Chesterton* states (p. 109) "at his best he (Chesterton) is unsurpassed by any essayist of the century."

Heretics (1905) is a study of those contemporary writers whom Chesterton considered most dangerous to truth. In *Orthodoxy* (1908), he proves that "The central Christian theology (sufficiently summarized in the Apostles' Creed) is the best root of energy and sound ethics." This book is probably his best, and though written long before he became a Catholic, is unimpeachably orthodox, so far as it goes. It traces his progress from agnosticism to Christianity. It was the ridiculous attacks of the Atheists that made him a Christian apologist. Not until *The Everlasting Man,* written shortly after his conversion, was the rounded doctrine presented to the world. It is another masterpiece.

The sociological studies of Chesterton have been relatively neglected. People read *What's Wrong with the World* and *The Outline of Sanity* (1936), but unfortunately fail as a rule to take them seriously. But the time will come when Chesterton's diagnosis of the ills of society—and he prescribes as well as diagnoses—will be recognized as of first-rate importance. Because he was a poet and a humorist and the creator of Father

Brown, people imagined that Chesterton could not be an important thinker. He was always original and interesting. He was, however, more important for his body of thought than for anything else. His unique style was good only because it was the adequate expression of the thing he had to say. It could be said in no other way—or not so well.

It was for this reason that his poetry must be rated high, the best of it perhaps even higher than all except the very finest passages of his prose. It is his philosophy in quintessence, but it is always lyrical. Truth here, to use Wordworth's phrase, is carried alive into the heart by passion. If Chesterton began as the *Wild Knight,* he ended as the *Crusader* with *Lepanto* and his epic-ballad, *The Ballad of the White Horse.* But hardly less is he the crusader in some of his satirical poems, especially the utterly devastating one directed against F. E. Smith, the future Lord Birkenhead. Of all his poems undoubtedly *The Ballad of the White Horse* is the grandest and the finest. It still awaits complete recognition.

Chesterton was also one of the best of critics. Yet, as he confessed of his book about Browning (1903), it is mainly about his own ideas, with an occasional introduction of Browning's name. Even better pieces of criticism are his *Charles Dickens* (1906) and his *William Cobbett.* Here he is in complete sympathy with his subject. At the same time we must remember his *George Bernard Shaw* (1909) was a great success, though Chesterton announces in the briefest preface in the history of literature: "Most people say either that they agree with Shaw or that they do not understand him. I am the only person who understands him, and I disagree with him." In spite of this, Shaw and Chesterton, the protagonists of a hundred debates on the platform and in print, had the greatest personal affection for one another. The little survey, *The Victorian Age in Literature* (1913) is breathtaking.

We have to remember about Chesterton that only about a third of what he printed in periodicals was ever published in book form. He wrote with the greatest of ease. His conversation was always brilliant, and about any subject he knew exactly what he wished to say. But precisely because of his astonishing abundance, he talked (or if one insists, he *wrote*) about much that was of merely ephemeral interest. He was constitutionally incapable of allowing any fallacy to pass unrefuted, which was why he was drawn into endless battles with cranks and fools who are mostly forgotten. Out of his humility Chesterton was prodigal of his gifts. Nor need we say that he wasted himself. The lie does indeed rot, but he had to uproot it at once. The measure of his goodness is that he never made an enemy by his controversies, nor had an enemy for any other reason. He was in competition with no man, for what he was doing was unique, something that no other man could so much as think of attempting. When he wrote his *Autobiography* (which appeared posthumously) he told his readers little about himself. The book turned at the slightest pretext to stories about his friends or into the exposition of ideas. His whole hilarious and happy life was in fact devoted to thought, however fantastic might be its expression. There lies his true greatness. It is by study of his thought that we reach the man.

A bibliography of his works is given on p. 671 et seq. of Maisie Ward's *Gilbert Keith Chesterton.*

Top Meadow, G. K. Chesterton's house at Beaconsfield was bought by the Converts' Aid Society in 1945, as a place of refuge for converts in the first difficulties of their reception.

Hector Chevigny 1904-

Looked upon as one of the real pioneers in the radio writing field, Hector Chevigny is also regarded as one of the early developers of presentation techniques now widely employed in American broadcasting.

In his formative years, Chevigny had no intention of writing for a living and never prepared for that work. His early ambition was to practise medicine and he majored in science. For various reasons that course became impossible. For a few years he floundered badly, fighting poverty and vainly endeavoring to find a foothold in business. Writing was never an effort. For some obscure reason, he felt that writing could not be his life-work because it came too easily to him. Finally he realized it was his métier. He accepted his "fate" and applied himself diligently to writing.

Hector Chevigny was born on June 28, 1904 at Missoula, Montana, the son of Angelina Ménard and Jeffrey Chevigny de la Chevrotière, Montana pioneers. His family is French-Canadian and stems in the New World from the brother of Madame de la Peltrie (nee Chevigny), who accompanied the famed Mère Marie de l'Incarnation, the founder of the first community of Ursuline nuns in New France.

He was educated at St. Joseph's Grammar School, Missoula, Montana, and the Montana common schools. When eleven years of age he developed blindness as a result of a severe case of scarlet fever, but his sight was restored in two years by surgery.

A five-year gap in his formal education was spent on a relative's ranch near Frenchtown, Montana, where he heard vivid stories of the fur-trade. He attended both Gonzaga Preparatory School and Gonzaga University in Spokane, Washington. From the latter, he received his A.B. degree in English in 1927. He worked his way through college, working as a night-telephone operator in a large hospital and later as editor of the Spokane *County News,* a farm journal. He was the founder of the *Gonzagan,* the Gonzaga University Quarterly. For it, he wrote a column under the heading "Cretinoid Criticisms." Even in those days he was an exceptionally good writer.

When he moved to Seattle, he worked for some months as assistant to the music and dramatic editors of the Seattle *Post-Intelligencer.*

In 1928 he began to write a daily feature, for the American Broadcasting System. When that crashed financially, he went to K O M O, the NBC station as its first staff-writer. After spending four years with this system, he spent two years as staff-writer with KOL of the CBS in Seattle. In August, 1936, he was appointed Director of the Script Division at KNX, Hollywood. Mr. Chevigny then organized the western writing staff for CBS and assisted in planning the original program structure. Later he was put in charge of all writing for CBS in the West. He has written more than five hundred radio plays, the majority of which were for nation-wide commercial sponsors. He was a leader in the fight for good music on the West Coast and for an increased use of the drama. He has lectured extensively on broadcasting.

In 1929 Mr. Chevigny married Claire Roze Graves. They have two children, Antoinette and Paul Graves.

In 1937 he published *Lost Empire, the Life and Adventures of Niko-lai Rezánov*. Rezánov was the designer of the charter of the Russian American Company which controlled Alaska from 1799 until its purchase by the United States in 1867. Mr. Chevigny's research was done from the Russian standpoint.

In 1942 *Lord of Alaska: Baranov and the Russian Adventure* was published. It records the life and deeds of Aleksandr Baranov, the son of a Russian storekeeper living on the Finnish border in the Eighteenth century. His experiences as trader, warrior, governor, ship-builder and son-in-law of an Indian chieftain are dramatically told. Chevigny's latest book, *My Eyes Have a Cold Nose* (1946), tells the story of his blindness suffered in 1943 and how he has gone on with his profession of radio writing.   M. H.

Wilfred Rowland Mary Childe 1890-

At the time he was first drawn to the Church, Wilfred Childe was writing for *The New Witness*, which was then edited by Gilbert K. Chesterton. Childe attributes his conversion, after the grace of God, to the antiquity and unity of the Catholic Church. The artistic beauty of her churches in the many lands through which he travelled also impressed him. When he returned to England, comparing the Church of England with the Church of Rome, he became a Catholic in 1914. His recreation consists in bemoaning the "Refor-mation."

Mr. Childe was born at Wakefield, England in 1890. He is the eldest son of the late Henry Slade Childe (Justice of the Peace), and Kate, daughter of Henry France of Thornes, Yorkshire, England. He was edu-cated at Harrow School and Magdalen College, Oxford. Since 1922 he has been lecturer in English literature at Leeds University.

His best poems are strictly traditional in their calm beauty. Among his books of verse are: *The Little City* (1911); *The Escaped Princess* (1916); *The Hills of Morning* (1920); *The Gothic Rose* (1922); *The Garland of Armor* (1923); *The Ballad of Jak and Anne* (1924); *Ivory Palaces* (1925); *The Country of Sweet Bells* (1927); *The Happy Garden* (1928); *The Golden Thurible* (1931); *Fountains and Forests* (1935); *Selected Poems* (1936); *Contributions to Edwardian Poetry* (1936); and *Neo-Georgian Poetry* (1937). His prose works include: *Dream English, a Fantastical Romance* (1917); and *Blue Distance* (1930).   M. H.

Most Reverend Amleto Giovanni Cicognani
1883-

A life of unremitting activity has been the lot of His Excellency, the Most Reverend Amleto Giovanni Cicognani, Titular Archbishop of Laodicea in Phrygia, who was appointed the sixth Apostolic Delegate to the United States, May 22, 1933. He had been here in 1924 and 1931 on special missions. As Monsignor Cicognani, he made his first visit to the United States as an official of the Sacred Consistorial Congregation. He came to organize the work of the Scalabrini Fathers— Missionaries of St. Charles Borromeo. His second visit was made seven years later, while serving as Assessor of the Sacred Congregation for the Oriental Church—this time to reorganize the offices of the Catholic Near East Welfare Association.

His Excellency was born February 24, 1883 at Brisighella, Province of Ravenna, Italy, the second son of William and Ann (Ceroni) Cicognani. He was educated in the Seminary of Faenza and the Athenaeum of the Pontifical Roman Seminary. Ordained in 1905, he became a Doctor in Theology 1907; received his Ph.D. in 1908; his J.U.D. in 1910. Honorary degrees have been conferred on him by Holy Cross College, St. John's University, Notre Dame University, University of Portland, Catholic University of America, Fordham University and Duquesne University.

Other appointments were: Advocate of the Sacred Roman Rota (1914); Minutante to the Sacred Consistorial Congregation (1922); Undersecretary to the same Congregation (1928); Secretary of the Commission for Cardinals for Oriental Canon Law until March 1933; Consultor in Rome to the Sacred Congregation of the Council, of Propaganda Fide, and of Extraordinary Ecclesiastical Affairs. He also taught Canon Law at the Pontifical Institute of St. Apollinaris from 1921 to 1932.

His first book *Il Gran del Vangelo* (1915) was translated into Spanish by P. F. Mier in 1931, as *La Caridad* and into English by Rev. Joseph T. Schade (1931) as *The Great Commandment of the Gospel in the Early Church.*

An authorized version of his widely known work *Ius Canonicum* was brought out in this country under the English title *Canon Law.* It is in three parts. The first is: an *Introduction to the Study of Canon Law;* the second is *History of the Sources of Canon Law;* and the third is a *Commentary on Book 1 of the Code.*

Another of his books is: *Addresses and Sermons* (1938). This book contains sixty-seven discourses of the Apostolic Delegate to the United States from 1933 to 1937. Some of the topics included are: Catholic Action, Catholic Physicians and Hospitals, The Holy Name Society, The Catholic Press, Catholic Education, and the Priesthood. *Sanctity in*

America published in 1939, has gone into a second edition (1941). He also wrote *The Priest in the Epistles of St. Paul.*

During his office as Apostolic Delegate nine new dioceses and the new Arch-diocese of Washington were set up in the United States. Four existing dioceses were elevated to the rank of Archdioceses thereby creating five new ecclesiastical provinces: viz., Los Angeles; Detroit; Louisville; Newark, New Jersey, and Denver. He also superintended the establishment of the Apostolic Delegation to the United States in its new home on Massachusetts Avenue in Washington.   M. H.

Eleanor Grace Clark   1895-

A convert to the Catholic religion since 1925 Dr. Eleanor Grace Clark is now (1945) writing a book on the Counter-Renaissance in an attempt to show others a better and surer way *in,* than the tedious and hazardous way she took. "It is designed," she says, "to be a kind of Catholic Primer for adults. In other words, it is in an attempt to write an honest introduction to English culture in general, English literature in particular. It was only by accident that I discovered that the ground plan and foundation of English literature was Catholic Christianity. As a young student I thought of Beowulf as early and crude paganism—crude, but nice and hearty—of Chaucer as late and refined paganism—the World, the Flesh and the Devil under a charming veneer of Christianity; and Shakespeare as the modern spirit entirely emancipated from the shackles of the institutional Church! I never even guessed that some very intelligent Christian monk was trying in the Beowulf to do with early Germanic pagan lore precisely what the Deuteronomists had done with the pre-Mosaic epos of the Hebrews; or that Chaucer was trying in the Canterbury Tales to lead his Prince (or Princes) into paths of righteousness exactly as Isaiah had guided or tried to guide the rulers of his generation. Of Bede or Benedict Biscop I knew nothing; of Richard Rolle of Haupole less than nothing; I fancied Miles Coverdale was a Protestant and that the King James version was the first (and best!) complete English Bible! Though a Ph.D. in English my ignorance of the fountains of English was all but absolute. Of the whole tradition of Christian pedagogy—from Clement of Alexandria through the great Mediaeval Schoolmen—Lanfranc, Anselm, Alcuin, etc. to the great Renaissance teachers—Eliot, Recorde, Erasmus, More, etc.—I was totally unaware. I spent years fussing with meters, analogies, sources, etc. without having any idea why any of it was important. I came out of a Classics course in college without the foggiest notion of Greek "religion" and hence without any understanding of the ultimate issues of Hebraism and Hellenism.

"My own tale of ignorance would not be so bad if it were not—I am convinced—so significant of the vast corruption of our whole educational system. I am by no means unusual in having failed to realize that Chaucer was a prophet first and poet second—like all the prophet-poets, from Isaiah and Jeremiah to Skelton!"

Eleanor Grace Clark was born at Neenah, Wisconsin on July 6, 1895, the daughter of Nimshi Frederick and Eleanor Aalene (Dunham) Clark. From Wayland Academy she went to Oberlin College where she received her A.B. in 1918 and her M.A. in 1919. Her Ph.D. was received in 1928 at Bryn Mawr. She did post-graduate work at Oxford, London, and Edinburgh Universities. For two years she was Head of the English department at St. Helen's Hall, Portland, Oregon, and then taught for a year at Friends School in Moorestown, New York. From 1923 to 1930 she served as tutor and then associate professor in English at Bryn Mawr. Since 1930 she has been associate professor of English at Hunter College in New York City.

Among her teachers and guides she lists the late Charles Henry Adams Wager, who first introduced her to English literature and to Catholic Christianity; Ellen Gates Starr, Oblate of St. Benedict, who introduced her to Catholic art and gave her her first lessons in Catholic living (secularly speaking); Mother Mary Ita, S.H.C.J. who initiated her into the arcana of monastery thought; Raymond Wilson Chambers, professor of English at University College, London, who led her into the deeper ways of Catholic scholarship; President Hutchins of Chicago University, and at Hunter College, its president, Dr. George N. Shuster; its Dean of Women, Hannah Egan, and its Librarian, Dr. Joseph Reilly.

She is the author of: *Pembroke Plays* (1928); *Elizabethan Fustian* (1938); *Raleigh and Marlowe* (1941), and *The Bitter Box* (1946).

Egerton Clarke 1899-1944

From 1933 to 1939, Egerton Clarke was children's Librarian of Messrs. Burns Oates and Washbourne, the Catholic publishers. In 1939 he was art editor of the publishing firm of Hutchinson's.

Egerton Clarke was born in 1899, the son of the Reverend Percy Carmichael Clarke, an Anglican Chaplain living at Dinard, Brittany. He was educated at St. Edmund's School, Canterbury and at Keble College, Oxford. When 23 years of age (1922) he was received into the Church. During World War I he served with the 5th Devon Regiment from 1917 to 1918.

In 1926 he married Teresa Kelly of Dublin. Two sons and one daughter were born from the marriage.

The author of many books of poems, he was a vice-president of the Catholic Poetry Society. Up until his death in October, 1944 he was secretary of St. Hugh's Society for Catholic boys of the professional classes.

He is the author of: *The Death of Glass and Other Poems* (1923);

The Ear-ring (1923); *The Popular Kerry Blue Terrier* (1927); *The Death of England and Other Poems* (1930); *The Seven Niches: a Legend in Verse* (1932), and *Alcazar* (1937). He was also a contributor to periodicals.

M. H.

Isabel Constance Clarke

Isabel Constance Clarke is a daughter of the late Colonel Francis Coningsby Hannam Clarke, C.M.G. Royal Artillery, and was born near Plymouth in Devonshire. Except for drawing classes she was educated entirely at home but nevertheless succeeded in passing such examinations as the Oxford and Cambridge local ones. She began to scribble at a very early age and from the time she was twelve obtained prizes for essays and stories in children's magazines. It may have been her father's constant preoccupation with writing that influenced her, for although a very busy officer and for some years a professor of Military Law at the Staff College, Camberley, he still found time to translate a number of military books and pamphlets from the French, Russian and German, of which copies still remain in her possession. While compiling a book on *Staff Duties,* he often called upon his daughter, then in her early teens, to write at his dictation, since he had injured his right arm in an accident. He also instructed her in the elements of proofreading, all of which was of great use later on.

For many years, with the exception of two slim volumes of verse, Isabel Clarke's name appeared only under stories, essays and verse, in magazines and weekly journals, and the novels met with no success until the publication of *Prisoners' Years* in 1912. It appeared simultaneously in London and New York and was serialized in both countries. Since then Isabel Clarke has published nearly sixty books which include fifty novels with another in preparation. Her biographies have also met with considerable success. They are: *Haworth Parsonage; A Picture of The Brontës; Elizabeth Barrett Browning: A Portrait; Shelley and Byron; A Tragic Friendship;* and *Six Portraits* (which include those of Mme. de Staël, Jane Austen, George Eliot, Mrs. Oliphant, John Oliver Hobbes (Mrs. Craigie) and Katherine Mansfield. The last-named 'Portrait' is being published in New Zealand in brochure form. Isabel Clarke lived in Rome for twenty-six years, leaving only a few weeks before Italy, to her great grief, declared war against her country. Many of her novels have a Roman or Italian setting and perhaps *It Happened in Rome* (1925), *Carina,* and *Roman Year* (1935) have been the most successful of these; Venice is described in *The Light on the Lagoon,* and Amalfi in *The Altar of Sacrifice.* Converts have sometimes written to tell her that they had been greatly influenced by her novel *Children of the Shadow.* But she herself always believes that her fourth novel *Fine Clay* was the one that established her reputation as a Catholic author. It was mentioned in pulpits at the time of its publication in 1914, and since then has gone through many editions and is still selling in its cheaper forms. Isabel Clarke's novel *Welcome* with its Jamaican setting has proved popular in England and has lately been released by Longmans, Green of New York, "Welcome" is the name of a great sugar plantation and is the background for this love story.

More than twenty years ago, Miss Agnes Repplier had this to say about the novels of Miss Isabel Clarke: "Miss Clarke's work is necessarily work within limits, because she subordinates all the elements of story-telling to one controlling motive. But, on the other hand this motive is so powerful and illuminating that it lifts her books high above the insipidities of the average novel. Miss Clarke's novels deserve to be widely known and well read." At the time this was written Miss Clarke had published twenty novels. Since then she has written over thirty more. Miss Repplier also said: "Her novels are the medium through which she expresses her supreme sense of the power and the sweetness of faith." The late Reverend Michael Earls, S.J. said of her, as a loyal and devoted student in the school of Catholic letters: "She knows the full grammar of her craft, all her exercises are true to the philosophy of life."

Her chief recreations are reading, sketching and bridge, and she exhibited a water-colour landscape at the Visitors' Show in the Institute of Jamaica, Kingston, in 1943. She has no rival writer in her own family, but her brother, the late Robert Coningsby Clarke, was well-known as the gifted composer of many popular songs. She made Jamaica, British West Indies her home during World War II. Miss Clarke has travelled extensively in Ceylon, France, Greece, Switzerland and North Africa. She escaped from France in a collier with seven hundred British refugees and had the unpleasant experience of a submarine attack in the Mediterranean.

Some of her other publications are: *The Secret Citadel* (1913); *Whose Name Is Legion* (1915); *Children of Eve; Strangers of Rome* (1928); *Silence is Golden* and *Where the Apple Reddens* (1946).   **M. H.**

Paul Claudel 1868-

At the time Presidents Coolidge and Hoover were in office and for part of President Roosevelt's term, Paul Claudel was France's Ambassador to the United States.

Bostwick in his book, *A Life with Men and Books,* described him then as "a bluff, stocky, rather heavy-featured man, who looks more like a country grocer than an ethereal poet." Claudel is not a poet easy to read. He has a speech peculiar to himself.

Paul Claudel was born in August 1868 at Villeneuve-sur-Fere-en-Tardenois, Aisne, France, a small village of about 300 inhabitants where his grand uncle was a priest. The son of Louis Prosper Claudel, a Registrar of Mortgages, he spent his childhood in a series of small towns: Bar-le-duc, Nogent-sur-Seine, Wassy, Rambouillet, Compiègne. His mother was Louise (Cerveaux) Claudel. He was educated by private tutors and at provincial schools. When his family moved to Paris in 1882, where his sister Camille was studying sculpture under Professor Rodin, Paul studied at the Lycée Louis-le-Grand, under Burdeau, professor of philosophy. He then went to Law School and later attended the School of Political Sciences.

His return to the Church was full of surprise. Though he had been baptized a Catholic, he was indifferent and afterwards definitely hostile to religion until he began to read the works of Arthur Rimbaud. He has himself told the story of his conversion. It occurred on Christmas Day, 1886, when he and some of his friends were on their way to Notre Dame Cathedral in Paris, not out of reverence for the feast but merely in the hope of getting some inspiration from the splendor of the ceremonies. Then, as suddenly as his namesake on the road to Damascus, he was struck by grace, though he did not yield completely until four years later. Since 1890 he has been a most militant and uncompromising Catholic. As this occurred at a time when official advancement in France usually depended on a man's taking a very different attitude, it is a proof—in view of the ambassadorial rank he reached—not only of his professional competence, but still more of high courage.

For more than twenty years he worked quietly. His books were brought out in special edition and only a limited number of copies were printed. His first dramas tell of man's great struggle to dispense with God. As Claudel's faith strengthens and grows brighter, sadness gives way to joy. His *Tete d'Or* is the principal one of his dramas. It reflects rather the extravagant romanticism of his youth than the symbolism of his later and Christian years. This was followed by a dozen other plays, of which the best known to English readers are *The Tidings Brought to Mary* and *The Satin Slipper*. The first of these was produced by the New York Theatre Guild in 1923 and though not a notable box-office success greatly moved such audiences as saw it performed. Here Claudel proved that he had a great sense of the theatre. *The Satin Slipper,* coming late in his life in 1929 sums up all that he has tried to say, that "all things minister to a divine purpose and so to one another, be it events or personalities." *The Satin Slipper* was played in Paris during 1944, with the greatest success at the Comedie Francaise. Paul Claudel personally supervised all the rehearsals and was pleased with the whole production.

All his plays—like his lyrical poems and his philosophical writings— form a whole. His works are often difficult and yield only to patient study, a study which well rewards those who are prepared to make the effort. As Jacques Riviere says of him: "Each drama is a verse of the immense poem of life." This is true even of his *Book of Christopher Columbus,* a lyrical drama in two parts, interpreting the life of the dis- coverer and cross-bearer and showing once more the futility of human endeavor against divine appointment. It is this concept of Providence, overruling human waywardness (often by external events rather than by personal choice), which runs through all his work and makes it a har- monious whole. It is for this reason that Claudel may be called the most integrated of all contemporary writers. All life points to God, he says, but man must seek God by the road of renunciation unless life is to be, for him, a failure.

His work has been strongly influenced by Aeschylus, three of whose plays he has translated into French. The other main influence, in matters of literary form, has been that of Pindar. He has not belonged to any school and therefore has suffered from the criticism of those who are unable to put a convenient label upon him. Nevertheless he has had a considerable effect upon contemporary letters, though he has never been what could be called a popular author. Having had a profession that gave him a secure standing in the world, he has been able to preserve a complete independence and to write merely for those who are willing to listen.

If Claudel acknowledges his indebtedness to Rimbaud, this does not seem to extend either to style or subject matter. It was rather that Rimbaud, who "tried to express the inexpressible," gave him a clue as to what his own work was to be. Though sometimes his shorter poems are simple and even homely, in general they are difficult to understand, and the versification is his own. This is a kind of free verse, reminding one however more of the cadence of the psalms than of our contemporary eccentricity; but rhyme and assonance are not always avoided and sometimes the French alexandrine is used to good effect. In general, what Claudel seeks is the rhyming of ideas instead of what we understand by rhyme, and inner harmony takes the place of formal meter.

Besides his poetry, Claudel has published three volumes in prose. Of these *La Connaissance de l'Est* has been translated into English as *The East I Know*. It is a series of sketches which are the fruit of his diplomatic service in China and Japan, and as it is simple and picturesque, many people who avoid the poetic and the mystical Claudel have read it with enjoyment.

Paul Claudel came to the United States in 1893 as Assistant-Consul in New York. The following year he became Director of the Consulate in Boston. In 1895 he returned to France and was sent to China where he returned in 1901 and again in 1906.

Paul Claudel was Ambassador to Japan from 1921 to 1925. For six years, from 1927 to 1933, he was Ambassador at Washington, D.C. Then he was recalled to be Ambassador at the Belgian Court. He was there when King Albert died and for two years of Queen Astrid's reign. He retired from the diplomatic service in 1936, as Dean of the French diplomatic corps.

Paul Claudel represented France at the Coronation of Pope Pius XII, after which he assumed no further official functions.

In 1906 he was married to Reine-Marie Perrin, the daughter of Mr. de Fourvieres, the well-known architect. Two sons and three daughters were born. One of the sons, Pierre Paul Claudel, lives in New York.

Paul Claudel now lives at his country place not far distant from Lyons and Grenoble. While there he has written a number of books, not yet published. His books in later years have dealt with religious and biblical problems.

Claudel is a great religious poet. His work is a long pilgrimage towards God. When people can be brought to study him by degrees they find themselves permeated with his ideas. As these become more familiar the barrier of obscurity will also disappear, and then Claudel will come completely into his own.

In 1946 he was chosen a member of the French Academy.

Among his books translated into English are: *The East I Know;* translated by Teresa Frances and William Rose Benet (1914); *The Tidings Brought to Mary,* a mystery, translated by Louise M. Sill (1916); *The Hostage,* a drama, translated by Pierre Chavannes (1917); *Tete d'or,* a three-act play, translated by John S. Newberry (1919); *Three Poems of the War,* translated by Edward J. O'Brien (1919); *The City,* a play, translated by John S. Newberry (1920); *Letters to a Doubter,* translated by Henry L. Stuart (1925); *Stations of the Cross,* translated by John J. Burke (1927); *The Book of Christopher Columbus,* a lyrical drama in two parts (1930); *The Satin Slipper: or, The Worst is not the Surest,* translated by Reverend John O'Connor (1931), and *Bitter Leaven, Ways and Crossways,* translated by Rev. John O'Connor (1936).

Joseph Clayton   1868-1943

Joseph Clayton, English author, Fellow of the Royal Historical Society, convert to Catholicity, was born in London, April 28, 1868. He was the son of Francis Clayton, manager of the now extinct daily *St. James Gazette.* His grandfather was a wholesale newspaper agent in London.

He received his early education in London day schools, later going to Worcester College and thence to Oxford. While at Oxford, he played chess for the University Club.

For a short time following graduation he taught in private and elementary schools in Leeds. For two years 1912-1914, he was chairman of the local managers of public elementary schools.

Entering commercial life, he became a clerk in a leading merchant's office in London. As a young man he was interested in labor and wrote a book on trade unions. Following this line of thought, he also accepted employment as a general laborer and gas stoker in London to gain experience. During these years he took some part in early British labor and socialist movements, acting as secretary to the newly formed Independent Labor Party in Leeds, lecturing for the Fabian Society and acting as election agent and organizer. He served in the Peace Guard who fought the mob in the Boer War times. In 1898 he married Margaret Souter. They had no children. Both of them were militant suffragists.

Clayton began writing for the press in 1896, contributing to numerous papers and reviews. During these years he was the author of two novels, *Grace Marlow* and *The Under Man*. His journalistic career included his editorship of *Labor Chronicles* (1896-1898), and *New Age* (1906-1907), of which he was also proprietor.

Before entering the Catholic Church, Clayton was known as an Anglo-Catholic biographer of some merit. *Father Dolling, Father Stanton of St. Alban's Holborn,* and *Bishop Westcott,* were written during his Anglican years.

In 1910 (February 12) he was received into the Church by Father Bede Jarrett, O.P. Following his conversion he became a regular contributor to the widely known Catholic periodicals, *Blackfriars, Studies, Irish Rosary,* and also contributed articles to the *Catholic Encyclopedia.*

In 1939 Rev. Joseph Husslein, S.J., general editor of the "Science and Culture Series," delegated Mr. Clayton to undertake the task of writing *Pope Innocent III and His Times.* With the same zeal which characterized his research on earlier Anglo-Catholic works, he went to work on his new commission. *St. Anselm, Protestant Reformation in Great Britain,* and *Luther and His Work,* are all Science and Culture Series books. His Catholic works also include *St. Hugh of Lincoln, Sir Thomas More,* and *The Historic Basis of Anglicanism.* His book, *Pope Innocent III and His Times,* written in 1941 as the January volume of the above-mentioned culture series, is the first English account of that interesting pontiff's life.

Some of his other books are: *Bishops as Legislators; Leaders of the People; The Rise of the Democracy; Robert Kett and The Norfolk Rising of 1549; Cooperation and Trade Unions; Economics for Christians,* and *Rise and Decline of Socialism.*

In October 1914, Mr. Clayton enlisted in the London Irish Rifles, served in the Rifle Brigade in India and Burma from 1915 to 1917, and in France (Labour Corps) from 1917 to 1918. He was released from the army in 1919.

He was elected a Fellow of the Royal Historical Society in 1920, and professed in the Third Order of St. Dominic in 1923.

He lectured at the Catholic Summer School in Cambridge from 1928 to 1929; at the Pax Romana Congress in Cambridge in 1929, and in Seville, Spain in 1930.

His particular bent was history—medieval and modern. He has been known throughout his entire life as a Christian socialist and a democrat in politics. His writings are known for their clear, brief style. An humble and unostentatious man, when approached for biographical data in 1939, he wrote across the brief file of dates and names: "I am rather elderly, and at present too tired to write more."

He died at Chipping in 1943.

E. F.

Cyril Clemens 1902-

A request from a women's club for a paper on Mark Twain launched Cyril Clemens, a cousin of the humorist, on a writing career when he was twenty years old. Until that time he had read hardly anything by Twain. Son of Dr. James Ross and Katherine (Boland) Clemens, Cyril Clemens was born in St. Louis, July 14, 1902, and received his education at St. Louis University, Stanford, and Georgetown University. Three books on various aspects of Samuel Clemens, *My Cousin Mark Twain; Mark Twain the Letter Writer,* and *Mark Twain and Mussolini,* established his writing ability. *Young Sam Clemens; Josh Billings Yankee Humorist* and *Petroleum Vesuvius Nasby* presented new angles on Americans who thought in the lighter vein. *An Evening with A. E. Housman* and *A Chat with Robert Frost* tell of his friendship with two contemporary poets. *Lytton Strachey* gives a short account of the great biographer. *My Chat with Thomas Hardy* appeared in 1944.

A chance meeting with Dan Beard, Boy Scout founder, led to another biography, *Uncle Dan,* followed by *Literary Education of Franklin D. Roosevelt.* Admiration for G. K. Chesterton resulted in *Chesterton As Seen by His Contemporaries.* Mr. Clemens edited *Wit and Wisdom of Mark Twain; Gold Rush Days,* and has been editor-in-chief of the *Mark Twain Quarterly* since 1936. He has contributed to *The Commonweal; America; The Catholic World; The Ave Maria; The Rotarian; The Dalhousie Review* and other magazines.

Since 1927, Clemens has been president of the International Mark Twain Society whose Mark Twain Medal he has personally presented to Marconi, Belloc, Bernard Shaw, Alfred Noyes, Charles Evans Hughes, Robert Frost, and Franklin D. Roosevelt.

His favorite recreation is meeting people—preferring men to museums, as the latter remain, but the former do not. Clemens likes sea travel, walking, and chess. His hobby is autograph collecting. In 1933 he married Nan B. Shallcross, and has one son, Samuel. He lives in a small house surrounded by trees at Kirkwood, Missouri.

I. C.

"Clementia"   Sister Mary Edward, R.S.M. (Agnes M. Feehan) 1878-

This popular author never had any ambition to be a writer, yet her books are a joy to a second generation of girls. All through her school life she disliked composition and theme-writing—chiefly because of the uninteresting subjects assigned. In a sense she was driven to writing. As a teacher of music and dramatic art she did not have the time to spend in selecting and revising published material to suit the elocution classes she happened to be teaching so she began to write her own plays. Later she was on duty in the evening with junior boarders—children from six to twelve years of age. To amuse them she told stories until her stock of those she had read in her own childhood was exhausted. Then she began to "make up" a story. When she saw how it held the children she decided to write it, and so her first book, *Uncle Frank's Mary,* came into being. She taught for many years, but in 1918 her health failed and she was obliged to give it up. For many years she had devoted her time to writing juvenile fiction and drama. Influenced by her own early life, her favorite theme is the portrayal of Catholic home life as she thinks it should be lived.

"Clementia" was born in St. Louis, and educated at St. Vincent's Seminary in that city and at St. Patrick's Academy, Chicago. Her parents were, Edward L. Feehan, M.D. and Anna Hughes Feehan, the former a brother of Chicago's first archbishop, the Most Reverend Patrick A. Feehan. In 1901 she entered the Community of the Sisters of Mercy, St. Patrick's Academy, Chicago. Her sister, May A. Feehan, is also a writer. Her brother-in-law, C. Bosseron Chambers, the artist, painted the frontispieces for a number of her books.

Her books are: *Uncle Frank's Mary* (1916); *Quest of Mary Selwyn* (1917); *Bird-A-Lea* (1920); *Mostly Mary* (1921); *Mary's Rainbow* (1922); *The Selwyns in Dixie* (1923); *Berta and Beth* (1924); *Bab Comes into Her Own* (1925); *New Neighbors at Bird-A-Lea* (1932), and *Wilhelmina* (1939).

M. S.

Reverend Cornelius C. Clifford 1859-1938

All who have ever passed through Whippany, New Jersey, even those who never knew Father Cornelius Cyprian Clifford, will remember his church. It is a little church, seating at the most two hundred but it has a medieval atmosphere that attracts visitors from far places. Its miniature statues are decorated by well-known artists, friends of the pastor, and the picturesque little building has a touch of antiquity enhanced by mementoes from foreign countries which grace the walls, fetched home by Father Clifford himself from his wandering lecture tours all over the world. In 1933 he was awarded the first Gold Medal conferred by the Liturgical Arts Society. This Society was organized to stimulate interest in ecclesiastical art and architecture. The Board of Directors decided to make an annual award to the most eminent contributor to its general aims, and the first to receive the award was Father Clifford.

And Father Clifford was just as colorful as his church. Widely known as lecturer, professor, author, he was a brilliant man. He taught at Columbia for twenty-six years, until his death. Aside from his teaching lectures, which were many, he delivered many private lectures in the homes of prominent laymen, including the late Clarence H. Mackey.

The Reverend Cornelius Clifford, educator, leader in literary and cultural centres, was born in New York City, August 24, 1859, a son of Jane Rae and Cornelius Clifford. The brilliant lecturer was of Irish ancestry on his father's side and Scotch on his mother's. He was educated in the public schools and College of the City of New York; received his B.A. at Fordham University in 1879 where he was "Honors Man" and won both the Hughes Medal for philosophy and the James Gordon Bennett Medal for biography.

Upon graduation from Fordham he entered the Society of Jesus, in 1879. He studied theology at Woodstock, Innsbruck and Louvain. He was ordained (English Province of the Society of Jesus) in 1898 at Wimbledon. A year later, he withdrew from the Society with the permission of the superior. From 1885 until 1887 he was Master of Juniors at Frederick, Maryland, and served in the same capacity from 1892 until 1895 at Manressa House, Roehampton, England. From 1896 until 1898 he was headmaster at Wimbledon, and from 1899 he was a lecturer in history and logic. At Manressa House, Roehampton, England, he prepared candidates for orders and prepared and selected students for Oxford. For some time he was stationed at St. Beuno's College in North Wales.

Returning to America, Father Clifford taught church history and philosophy at St. Thomas College, St. Paul, Minnesota. In 1900 he edited *The Visitor* of Providence, Rhode Island, and three years later directed the parochial school of the Church of the Assumption in Morristown, New Jersey. In 1907-09 he lectured in metaphysics and church history at the Immaculate Conception Seminary of Seton Hall College. In 1909 he went to Whippany, New Jersey. Two years later he began his lectures at Columbia University, which post he held until his death December 4th, 1938, at the Church of Our Lady of Mercy at Whippany, New Jersey.

During his twenty-nine years as pastor in Whippany, New Jersey, Father Clifford became known as a writer for Catholic magazines, a lecturer and a brilliant preacher. *Introibo,* published by the Cathedral Library Association 1903, and *The Burden of Time* in 1904, two exegetical and homiletic studies on the Introits of the Roman missal and the scriptural lessons of the Roman Breviary, launched him into writing. He was a regular contributor during this period for the *Month, The Catholic World, Tablet, Spectator* (London), *Ecclesiastical Review* and the *Annals de Philosophie Chrétienne.*

During his early years Father Clifford traveled in Austria, France, Germany, Belgium, Scotland, and Ireland. He was a very interesting talker and even in his old age, people came to his little rectory just to listen to his brilliant talk. E. F.

Sir Hugh Clifford 1866-1941

Regarded as one of the great colonial administrators of the British Empire, Sir Hugh Clifford spent the first twenty years of his career in the Malay States. There he took part in many armed expeditions to restore order. He became known as a scholar and writer on the East and in particular as an authority on Malaya.

He was born in London in 1866, the eldest son of the late Major-General Honorable Sir Henry Clifford and Josephine (Anstice) Clifford. He was educated at Woburn Park under the 13th Lord Petre. He could have entered Sandhurst but instead joined the Malay States Civil Service as a cadet in 1883. One year later, in Malay, he passed the final examinations. In 1887 he was sent on a special mission to the Sultan of Pahang. He succeeded in getting a promise of a Treaty. From 1887-1888 he was Governors' Agent at Pahang, and the following year Superintendent. While an Acting Resident in Pahang, he took a leading part in suppressing the Pahang Rebellion in 1892. In 1894 he was made Commissioner to the Cocos—Keeling Islands. He served also as Colonial Secretary of Trinidad, Tobago and Ceylon. He administered the governments of Trinidad, Ceylon and the Gold Coast. Later he became Governor of Nigeria, Ceylon and of the Straits Settlements.

In 1929, as High Commissioner for the Malay States and British Agent for Borneo, he resigned, owing to Lady Clifford's serious illness. Lady

Clifford, whom he had married in 1910, was the widow of Henry de la Pasture. Minna Gilbert a Becket, who had been his first wife, died in 1907 after a happy union lasting since 1886.

In 1900 he was made a Companion of St. Michael and St. George; in 1909 he was credited a Knight Commander of St. Michael and St. George; in 1921 he was created a Knight of the Grand Cross of St. Michael and St. George and in 1925 he was created a Knight Grand Cross of the order of the British Empire.

He is the author of: *In Court and Kampong* (1897); *Studies in Brown Humanity* (1898); *Since the Beginning* (1898); *In a Corner of Asia* (1899); *Bush-Whacking* (1901); *Heroes of Exile* (1906); *Malayan Monochromes* (1913); *The German Colonies* (1918), and *In Days That Are Dead* (1926).

M. H.

Violet Mary Beauclerk Clifton   1883-

Mrs. Clifton is an Englishwoman who has spent very little of her life in England. Much of her time has been devoted to travelling and she has lived abroad many years. Her travels, unburdened by prejudices, have permitted her sympathies to grow simply and naturally. Lord Dunsany wrote of her, " 'nil humanum mihi alienum est' might well be taken by her for a motto." Her father was in the English diplomatic service and when she left school in Brussels at seventeen she accompanied him to Peru to be his official hostess. His duty often took him to Ecuador and Bolivia and she went with him. After three years in South America she returned to England because of illness following an accident. She visited India before she rejoined her father. She had already lost her belief in God, "because of a man of science" and on this visit to the East became interested in oriental religions.

After her return to Peru she met Talbot Clifton. They went to England to be married in 1907. Her husband, Hugh Talbot Clifton, the Squire of Lytham, Lancashire, was a great traveller and explorer— before he was twenty he had been around the world twice. Marriage did not cure his wanderlust and Mrs. Clifton was his companion on almost all his travels and explorations. Little time was available for writing. Oliver St. John Gogarty, who dedicated *As I Was Going Down Sackville Street* to her, compares her with Lady Lavery, "who was an excellent painter, but, for her husband's sake, she suppressed her talent." Mrs. Clifton has enjoyed her many journeys. In dedicating *The Islands of Queen Wilhelmina,* a record of two hunting trips to the Dutch East Indies, to her five children, she writes, "My hope is that they, too, with increasing amazement may be gladdened by the beauty of the earth."

Mrs. Clifton is a leisurely and painstaking writer. Before she published her play, *Sanctity,* about St. Elizabeth of Hungary, she wrote four versions. "For over twenty years I have contemplated the figure of Elizabeth. As, away from Eastern influences I moved toward Rome her light guided me—I have brooded upon Elizabeth in jungles of Mentawei; in villages of Nias; on coral of Lirdeng. In the Island of Islay was written the most of this play."

Her parents were William Nelthorpe and Jane Rathborne Beauclerk. She was born in 1883 at Rome, where her father was studying sculpture. She was educated in Brussels. Her husband had become a Catholic during a stay in California in 1897. Ten years after their marriage, she followed him into the Church. Her biography of her husband, *The Book of Talbot*, was awarded the Tait-Black Memorial Prize, the most valuable literary prize in Great Britain, by the University of Glasgow in 1934. In some respects this book is her own autobiography. She received three decorations for her services to her country in the first European War. In World War II her daughter, Aurea, was an ambulance driver for the Red Cross in France before the occupation, and her son, Michael, was on a mine-sweeper. Her eldest son, Harry de Vere Clifton, who became Squire of Lytham at his father's death in 1928 has inherited her writing ability, and has published *Dielma and Other Poems*.

She is the author of: *Pilgrims to the Isles of Penance* (1910); *The Islands of Queen Wilhelmina* (1925); *Book of Talbot* (1933); *Sanctity* (1934), and *Charister* (1938).   M. S.

Reverend Moses Michael Coady   1882-

The Extension Department of St. Francis Xavier University, Nova Scotia, dates back to 1928 and since its inception, Dr. Moses Coady has been its Director.

Born on a farm at N. E. Margaree, Nova Scotia on January 3, 1882 he was late in starting school. When he was graduated from the Margaree Forks High School, he went to normal school and became principal of Margaree High School, a position he held for two years. Dr. J. J. Tompkins taught him Latin by correspondence during this period and instilled in him a love for the classics. To increase his knowledge of the classics, he entered St. Francis Xavier College and was graduated with an A.B. degree in 1905. Then he went to Urban College in Rome to study for the priesthood. Here he received a Ph.D. in 1907 and a D.D. in 1910 and then returned to teach at St. Francis Xavier University. For some years he attended the Catholic University of America in Washington, D. C. to take courses in education. He received an Honorary LL.D. from Boston College and the University of Ottawa in the years 1938 and 1944 respectively.

It was during the years from 1920 to 1924 that he first displayed his interest in adult education. When he was sent as Antigonish County representative of the Nova Scotia Teachers' Federation, he strongly urged the reorganization of that union and founded and edited the Nova Scotia Teachers' Bulletin. Both are still thriving.

In 1928 on the recommendation of the MacLean Royal Commission on the Fisheries of the Maritime Provinces, Dr. Coady was asked to organize the fishermen of these provinces. He devoted an entire year to this work and founded the United Maritime Fishermen. He then promoted an adult educational program which he based upon a foundation of economic cooperation for eastern Nova Scotia. Later the three Maritime Provinces were included. In 1936 a grant was made to St. Francis Xavier Extension Department for an intensive program of education among the fishermen of the Maritimes and the Magdalens. This grant has been renewed annually.

Because of the success of his work he has been in demand, as a lecturer, both in Canada and the United States. To describe the Antigonish Movement, its principles, philosophy and achievements, he wrote *Masters of Their Own Destiny*. It was published in 1939. It endeavors to teach people the aim, technique and benefits of cooperation, principally through credit unions, cooperative stores, lobster factories and sawmills, to lay the foundation for the appreciation of Shakespeare and grand opera. A pamphlet, giving a brief account of the Antigonish Movement was also published in 1939 under the title *Mobilizing For Enlightenment*. In 1943 he collaborated with Father MacCormack of the Extension staff in a series of ten broadcasts for the CBC which was published under the title "The Antigonish Way of Adult Learning."

M. H.

Reverend Joseph Bernard Code   1899-

We have all seen various lists of "America's Ten Greatest Women," and more often than not have been disappointed by the names. Surely among the most remarkable women the country has ever seen have been some of the nuns who founded and guided the various religious communities of the nation. But even among Catholics the lives of these women are too little known. *The Catholic World* once said of Father Code that it would seem to be one of his missions in life to reclaim from oblivion remarkable women who have actually made history. He has introduced sixteen of these heroines to us in *Great American Foundresses*. To make them even more widely celebrated he has condensed this book, and published it as *The Veil Is Lifted* for use in schools. Monsignor Fulton Sheen says, "He has lifted the veil to let some of the goodness of the nuns shine upon the children of men." His evocation of these sturdy pioneers should inspire our youth with courage, fortitude and missionary zeal.

Father Code is of pioneer stock himself, not only of Iowa, where his people settled before 1850, but of Maryland and Virginia ancestry as well. This partially explains his interest in the history of this country, especially of the Church's part in it. Future biographers of the members of the American hierarchy will be grateful to him for his *Dictionary of the American Hierarchy.* On November 6, 1789, the Holy See established the American hierarchy when it appointed John Carroll first bishop of the United States. In the years since then many new dioceses have been set up. As the Apostolic Delegate, the Most Reverend Amleto Giovanni Cicognani writes in his introduction to the dictionary, "It is a development which finds a counterpart only in the first three centuries of the Church when all about the Mediterranean basin a great number of dioceses arose in a remarkably short time." About five hundred men have ruled over this rapid expansion of the Church, and the biographical data of all these occupants of the episcopal thrones are to be found in Father Code's book. Truly it is a treasure-house for historians, and will not be left unhandled on the library shelf.

Father Code is best known to many for his numerous works concerning Mother Seton. He has preached at many religious gatherings honouring her, and has lectured on her life throughout the country. In 1931 he was chosen to head the first International Federation of Catholic Alumnae pilgrimage to Rome, where he presented to the late Pope Pius XI a gigantic petition for favorable consideration of the cause of canonization of Mother Seton.

Keokuk, Iowa, is Father Code's birthplace. His parents were John Matthew and Helen Kennedy Code. He received an A.B. from St. Ambrose College, Davenport, Iowa, in 1920. He attended St. Mary's Seminary in Baltimore where he was awarded an M.A. in 1923 and an S.T.B. in 1924, and the Sulpician Seminary at the Catholic University of America in Washington, D. C. He was ordained in Davenport, May 31, 1924. He was a member of the faculty and the librarian at St. Ambrose College 1924-1931. He has studied at Columbia University, and at the Universities of Paris, Oxford, Heidelberg, and Louvain, where he received the Doctorate in Historical Sciences in 1935.

Queen Elizabeth and the English Catholic Historians secured his election to the fellowship of the Royal Historical Society of England in 1935. In 1936 Father Code became a member of the faculty of The Catholic University of America, Managing Editor of *The Catholic Historical Review,* and Assistant Secretary of the American Catholic Historical Association. In 1941, Bishop Rohlman of Davenport, to whose diocese Father Code belongs, announced his appointment as chaplain of the Imperial House of Austria, which was in exile in the United States and Canada, and in June 1942 his appointment as Catholic professor of religion at the State University of Iowa.

His books are: *Elizabeth Seton* (1927); *Great American Foundresses* (1929); *Mother Seton and Her Sisters of Charity* (1930); *The Veil Is Lifted* (1931); *Guy DeFontgalland* (1934); *Letters of Mother Seton to Mrs. Juliana Scott* (1934); *Queen Elizabeth and the English Catholic Historians* (1935); *The Spanish War and Lying Propaganda* (1938), and *Dictionary of the American Hierarchy* (1939). M. S.

Elbridge Colby 1891-

In order to force himself to keep abreast of the literature on military matters and on the Far East, Colonel Elbridge Colby has been writing book reviews regularly in those fields. His writing and much of his historical research has been carried on in Vermont, Georgia, Maryland, Virginia, Panama, China, Minnesota, and Washington, D. C.,—this in addition to inspecting the guard after midnight and saying "squads right" to countless men and boys in uniform. For Colonel Colby has remained in the Army since World War I. Military reading and writing are his hobbies.

Colonel Colby was born in New York City on October 4, 1891, the son of Charles Edwards and Emily Lynn (Carrington) Colby. He received his A.B., *magna cum laude,* from Columbia College in 1912; his A.M. from Columbia University in 1913, and his Ph.D. from the same institution in 1922. During the years, 1912 to 1914 and 1915 to 1916 he was a Proudfit fellow at Columbia University. The years 1920 to 1921, 1932 to 1933 were spent at the Infantry School, and the year 1928 at the Chemical Warfare School.

Following in the footsteps of his father, who was a professor at Columbia University, Colonel Colby became an instructor in English at the University of Minnesota from 1914 to 1915, and in rhetoric from 1916 to 1917. From 1919 to 1920 he was instructor in English and rhetoric. Since 1939 he has been associate professor in English at George Washington University. Other teaching assignments were at the Department of Experiment, Infantry School, 1921-1922, and assistant professor of Military Science and tactics at the University of Vermont, 1933-1938.

In World War I, Colonel Colby served as a lieutenant in the U. S. Army from 1917-1919. From 1920-1935, he was a captain; from 1935-1940, a major; from 1940-1942 a lieutenant colonel, and since then a colonel. He also served in the historical section of the Army War College from 1938-1941.

For many years he has written military articles for the *Infantry Journal,* and the *Military Engineer*—the latter awarded him the Toulmin Medal of the American Society of Military Engineers in 1938 for the best article in that magazine for that year. This article, which was about Marlborough, now comprises a chapter in his 1943 book, *Masters of Mobile Warfare.* The other two masters are Frederick the Great, and Napoleon. The purpose of this book is to show that "although mechanization enabled armies to move faster than ever before, the basic principles had not changed from the time of great generals in the past."

In 1942 Colonel Colby published his book *Army Talk.* The *Field Artillery Journal* calls it "a first-rate compendium of the important military section of our speech." He is also the author of *Small Problems for*

Trench Warfare (1918); *Echo Device in Literature* (1920); *Bibliography of Thomas Holcroft* (1922); *Education and the Army* (1922); *The Profession of Arms* (1923); *Swimming Soldiers* (1924); *Life of Thomas Holcroft* (1925); *American Militarism* (1934), and *English Catholic Poets* (1936).

He is interested in postage stamps of the Far East. He contributes to Scott's monthly journal and is the Manchurian stamp editor of the American Philatelic Society journal, *The China Clipper.* He is also interested in swimming. For more than fifteen years he did volunteer service with the Red Cross Life Saving Corps, serving as instructor at Red Cross aquatic schools, and he gave life saving instructions in the Army at Fort Howard, Maryland, Fort Benning, Georgia, and Tientsin, China.

Colonel Colby has been a frequent contributor to *Harper's, Current History, American Mercury,* the *Encyclopedia of the Social Sciences, Dictionary of American History,* and *Dictionary of American Biography.*

He contributes anonymous editorials on public questions to a weekly journal, the name of which, like the connections, remains secret.

Colonel Colby is a convert from the Episcopalian Church, since 1914. Three years after that he married Margaret Egan. They have one son.

In 1935 he was awarded the gold medal of the Serbian Red Cross; the Order of Mercy (Jugoslavia) the same year, and the university Medal of Columbia University in 1940. **M. H.**

Mary Colum

Since 1914 Mary Colum has been a resident of the United States. She came to this country from Ireland with her husband, Padraic Colum, whom she married in 1912. Mary Colum was born in Ireland, the daughter of Charles Maguire, of Derryhollow, County Fermanagh and Maria (Gunning) Maguire. A graduate of the National University of Ireland, she also attended the Sorbonne, Dominican College, Dublin and the Pensionnat Sacré-Coeur, Vaals, Holland.

While still a young girl her work as a writer and book reviewer attracted the attention of such men as William Butler Yeats, A. E. (George William Russell) and James Joyce, and she took part in the literary discussions of the little group of Irish writers who have since become famous, among them her husband, the poet and dramatist, Padraic Colum who was one of the founders of the Abbey Theatre.

She is considered to be one of America's best critics. She believes that "critics—because they have to be familiar with writing of all kinds—are best developed during their formative period when they are surrounded by writers, saturated in literature, rocked and dandled to its sounds and syllables from their earliest years, as composers have to be rocked and dandled to the sounds of music."

Most of Mary Colum's writing has been for periodicals. She has contributed to *Dial, Scribner's, New Republic, Saturday Review, Yale Review, The Catholic World, The Nation, The Spectator, The Irish Statesman* under A.E.'s editorship, the *Irish Review* and the *United Irishman.* Frequently she reviews books for the New York *Times* and has been widely quoted. From 1933 until 1940 Mary Colum conducted the "Life and Literature" department in the now defunct *Forum,* and her monthly articles were considered to be the best of their kind. During recent years, she has been on the staff of Columbia University, lecturing there in literature.

She was awarded the Guggenheim fellowship in literary criticism in 1930 and also in 1938. For distinction in literature, Georgetown University, Washington, D. C., presented her with the John Ryder Randall gold medal and in 1941 the American Institute of Arts and Letters gave her a $500.00 award for literary criticism.

She has written only two books. *From These Roots* appeared in 1937. In this work she "presents a creative interpretation of modern literature —the ideas out of which it has sprung, its historical development and present day direction. Because of its original insight, its grasp of fundamentals, and the clarity and freshness of its style, it was immediately recognized as one of the important critical works of our time."

Her autobiography, *Life and the Dream,* was published in 1947.

M. H.

Padraic Colum   1881-

Padraic Colum is now an American citizen and has lived for a quarter of a century in or near New York City, yet one could scarcely point to a body of work more arrestingly Celtic than his. In fact it epitomizes what he himself once defined as the essence of Celtic genius—its combination of fantasy and realism.

Mr. Colum sometimes likes to startle listeners by declaring that his birth, in 1881, occurred in the "workhouse" at Longford, Ireland. This happens to be true, as his father was at that time the official director of the institution. And it was surely a happy fatality which permitted the observant, imaginative boy to grow up in the much-travelled main road between Leinster and Connaught, hearing the tales of peasant men and women, and of the wanderers—many of whom he was to immortalize in the printed page. The young Colum taught for awhile at the historic St. Enda's School and served for awhile as clerk in Dublin, becoming affiliated very early with the movement of the Irish Literary Revival. His earliest work was contributed to the *United Irishman* at the suggestion of Yeats and his connection with the Irish National Theatre came about through acting in the

Deirdre of "A. E." (George Russell), who was to become his lifelong friend.

At twenty, Padraic wrote probably the first of those peasant dramas which the Abbey Theatre was to make famous, *Broken Soil,* later rewritten and published as *The Fiddler's House.* It shows the conflict between what Cornelius Weygandt (in *Irish Plays and Playwrights*) describes as those "primordial things, the love of wandering, the love of the land and the love of woman." Another play called *The Land* proved a great success in 1905. Five years later came *Thomas Muskerry,* in which Colum concentrated upon "three characters that stood as first types in my human comedy, the peasant, the artist, the official." It had been his plan to develop this Celtic "human comedy" in a series of plays, but he left the Abbey Theatre because of disagreement with some of its policies and came to live in the United States in 1914, shortly after his marriage to that admirable critic, Mary Maguire (Colum). The dramas just mentioned were published in 1916 as *Three Plays,* and with the briefly beautiful *Miracle of the Corn* and the oriental fantasy *Mogu the Wanderer,* compile practically all of his dramatic achievements up to the present.

Meanwhile Colum's undoubted poetic genius had borne striking fruit in the *Wild Earth* (1909). Here was elemental poetry, from the invocation of its opening lines—

"Sunset and silence! A man; around him earth savage, earth broken;
Beside him, two horses, a plough"—

to the homesick plaint of the "Old Woman of the Roads" or the haunting "Cradle Song" of the peasant mother. Since then his poetic work, from the *Dramatic Legends* of 1922, to the *Collected Poems* of 1932, has touched many points of Irish life and Irish dreaming. His pages tell of saints and poor scholars and peasants, of the bird and animal "Creatures" to which a whole volume was dedicated; while a group of Hawaiian lyrics were the fruit of his visit to those islands made at the invitation of the Hawaiian Legislature for the purpose of surveying the native myths and folk lore. His recent *Story of Lowry Maen,* a long verse narrative of Irish Kings in the Bronze Age, shows Padraic Colum as fundamentally a scholar as well as a poet.

This combination is responsible also for the great variety of his work in prose. He has rewritten many of the great legends and mythological stories of the world in his *Orpheus,* and in those delightful tales for children which have included *The King of Ireland's Son, Adventures of Odysseus, The Golden Fleece, The Girl Who Sat by the Ashes, The Boy Who Knew What the Birds Said, The Children Who Followed the Piper,* etc. The Celtic note rings through *My Irish Year, the Legend of St. Columba,* and *The Road Round Ireland;* the note of gentle fantasy through his exquisite story of *The White Sparrow;* the note of personal opinion and reminiscence in the essays of *A Half-Day's Ride.* In 1943 he published *Frenzied Prince: Heroic Stories of Ancient Ireland.*

Padraic Colum taught at many American strongholds, including Columbia, Wisconsin and Miami Universities, the New York City College, and Rollins College. He is a member of the Academy of Irish Letters and served for several years as president of the Poetry Society of America. His lectures and recitals are greatly in demand and he has edited one of the best anthologies of Irish verse.

Admitting that his own dearest aim has been to "continue the note of the Celtic folk poets," Padraic Colum may be said to have followed and achieved this dream through his poetry and drama, his prose and his own personality and conversation. And, as he has lived through a highly experimental age, his expression has naturally included many experimental forms.   K. B.

Helena (Mrs. Thomas) Concannon 1878-

Since 1912, Helena Concannon has lived in Salthill, Galway, in a house named by Patrick Pearse "Lios na Mara" (the dwelling by the sea) because of its location on the edge of Galway Bay.

Helena Concannon (née Walsh) was born on the 28th of October, 1878 at Maghera, County Derry, Ireland. She received her primary education at the National School in Maghera and her secondary education at Loreto College, Dublin. For her university training she attended the Royal University of Ireland, the Sorbonne in Paris, the University of Berlin, and took a postgraduate course in Rome. From the Royal University of Ireland she received her B.A. and M.A. degrees, taking First Class Honors in Modern Literature in 1900 and 1902 respectively.

In 1906 she married Thomas Concannon, the brother of the late James Concannon, founder of the Concannon Vineyards, Livermore, California, United States of America.

In 1915 her book *Life of St. Columban* was awarded a prize of $1,000 offered by the late Monsignor Shahan, Rector of the Catholic University of America for the best life of the Saint to be published in connection with the fifteenth centenary celebration at Bobbio in 1915. Her book *The Poor Clares in Ireland* was awarded the National University Prize for Historical Research and earned for her the degree Doctor of Literature. In 1932 she was awarded the Tailteann Gold Medal for the best work on St. Patrick issued during the Patrician year (1932). She published the book under the title *St. Patrick: His Life and Mission.*

In 1933 Dr. Concannon was elected to Dail Eireann as Representative of the National University of Ireland. After the passing of the Irish Constitution, when the University "seats" were transferred to the Senate, she was elected Senator, heading the poll at four successive elections. She attends the Senate meetings regularly and takes an active part in its discussions, particularly when they concern matters of social or educational import. In June 1945 she wrote: "I lead a very busy life which involves frequent journeys to Dublin—lasting under 'emergency' conditions the greater part of a working day."

Besides the books already mentioned she has written: *The Defence of Gaelic Civilization* (1919); *Women of '98* (1919); *Daughters of Banba* (1922) (awarded the Tailteann Medal for Literature); *Defenders of the Ford,* (studies of Irish Boyhood) (1925); *A Garden Of Girls* (historical studies of the education of Catholic Girls) (1928); *White Horsemen* (Jesuit Martyrs of North America) (1930); *Irish Nuns in Penal Days* (1931); *At the Court of the Eucharistic King* (an historical account of the first Convent of Perpetual Adoration in Ireland—the Franciscan Convent, Drumshanbo, County Leitrim) (1931); *Blessed Oliver Plunket* (1935); *The Queen of Ireland* (Ireland's devotion to Our Blessed Lady) (1938), and *The Curé of La Courneuve* (Pére Lamy) (1944) with an introduction by his Grace, Most Reverend Dr. McQuaid, Archbishop of Dublin.

Senator Helena Concannon has also written many pamphlets issued by the *Irish Messenger of the Sacred Heart,* Dublin. They include *Ireland's Fight for the Mass; The Mass: Ireland's Treasure; The Jesuits in Ireland; Our Lady of Fatima; St. Paschal Baylon* and others. She has contributed many articles to Catholic magazines both in Ireland and the United States.   M. H.

Burton Confrey 1898-

Teaching is the field of Dr. Burton Confrey; hence seventeen of his books deal with Catholic education. *Travel Light,* a fiction book whose leitmotif is Catholic youth in war service, has also as its narrative motivation the acts of men with a Catholic sense.

Dr. Confrey was born at La Salle, Illinois, on February 1, 1898. He received his bachelor's degree (Ph.B.) at the University of Chicago and then served in World War I in the infantry, in the psychological laboratory, and Chemical Warfare Service. When the war was over, he returned to the University of Chicago on a graduate scholarship in General Literature and received his Master's degree in 1920. In succeeding years he taught at the Universities of Chicago and Minnesota. During the first eight years of the "Religious Bulletin" he was a teacher at the University of Notre Dame, and from that publication got the inspiration for his work in the correlation of the means of achieving a Catholic heritage. For three summers, he lectured at the Catholic Summer School, Cliff Haven, on Lake Champlain. He is now teaching at St. John's University in Brooklyn.

His favorite theme is that a "curriculum to be truly Catholic must normally be attached to the life of the Church—the liturgy, which has for its purpose the glory of God and the sanctification and edification of souls."

His first book was a doctoral dissertation. As partial requirement for his Ph.D. degree (Catholic University, 1931) he wrote *Secularism in American Education: A History,* which shows how education in our country has dropped its intimate connection with religious teaching, although all the large Eastern universities except Pennsylvania were founded to train young men for the ministry. *Faith and Youth* was published in 1932. *Initiating Research in Catholic Schools* (1938) is out of print: Its purpose was to train college freshmen "to read economically and effectively, take notes, and so on."

Other books are: *Social Studies* (1934), written "to inculcate a Catholic sense—the ability to see eye to eye with the Church in all matters of faith and morals"; *Catholic Action, A Textbook for Colleges and Study Clubs* (1935); *Original Readings for Catholic Action* (1936); *Readings for Catholic Action* (1937); *Method in Literature For Catholic Schools* (1938); *Sensory Training For Catholic Schools* (1938); *Spiritual Conferences For College Men* (1939); *Stenciled of God* (1939); *Techniques for Students* (1939); *Moral Mission of Literature* (1933); *Method in Literature* (1938); *Educational and Vocational Supervision For Catholic Schools* (1940), and *Following the Liturgical Year.* Included in this last mentioned book are some two hundred and fifty "counselors" each a page in length, which he had written and posted on the school bulletin board of a college of which he was dean. These "counselors" were daily reminders, "to aid the students in applying the lessons of the Church liturgy to life in their homes, in the classroom, and in the community."

Dr. Confrey has written over five hundred articles and short stories, principally for Catholic periodicals. He is an honorary member of L' Institut Historique et Heraldique de France; of the Eugene Field Literary Society; of the International Social Studies, honorary society Pi Gamma Mu, and of the Gallery of Living Catholic Authors.

M. H.

Reverend Francis J. Connell, C.SS.R.   1888-

Dogmatic and moral theology are the special fields of Father Francis J. Connell, priest of the Congregation of the Most Holy Redeemer. He taught dogmatic theology at Mt. St. Alphonsus Seminary, Esopus, New York, from 1915 to 1921, and from 1924 to 1940. Since 1940 he has been teaching moral theology at the Catholic University of America, where he is an associate professor.

Francis J. Connell was born in Boston, Massachusetts, January 31, 1888. His parents were Timothy and Mary (Sheehan) Connell. He attended the public schools of his native city and was graduated with highest honors from the Boston Latin School in June, 1905. In the fall of the same year, he entered Boston College under the Jesuits, where he spent two years. It was at this time that he first wrote for publication, contributing several articles to the college paper *The Stylus* at the invitation of the gifted writer, Father Michael Earls, S.J., who was then a scholastic at the College.

In the fall of 1907, Francis Connell entered the novitiate of the Congregation of the Most Holy Redeemer (C.SS.R.) and a year later took his vows as a member of that congregation. From 1908 to 1914, he was engaged in his philosophical and theological studies at the Redemptorist Seminary, Mount St. Alphonsus, at Esopus, New York. He was ordained to the priesthood on June 26, 1913. After a brief period of parochial activity in the parish of Our Lady of Perpetual Help, Brooklyn, New York, in 1915 he was appointed professor of dogmatic theology at Mount St. Alphonsus, Esopus, New York, which post he held until 1921.

It was not until 1920 that he ventured into print with an article entitled "Our Lady and the Sacraments," in the *The American Ecclesiastical Review*. On receipt of this article, the Reverend Dr. H. Heusser, the venerable editor of the periodical, invited Father Connell to contribute at regular intervals a digest of the noteworthy theological articles appearing in European clerical magazines. Accordingly, since that time, Father Connell has published twice each year in the *Ecclesiastical Review* an article entitled "Recent Theology."

From October 1921 until June 1923, Father Connell was in Rome, taking a postgraduate course in theology at the International Pontifical University of the Angelico under the Dominicans. At the completion of his course, he received the doctorate of sacred theology (S.T.D.) *summa cum laude*. On his return to America he spent a year in missionary work, and in the fall of 1924 returned to Esopus to assume again the professorship of dogmatic theology. He also taught pastoral theology and liturgy. In 1940 he left Esopus to teach moral theology at the Catholic University of America, where he still teaches.

Since 1929, Father Connell has spoken frequently on the radio. He gave an address on the "Catholic Hour," on August 4, 1930, and a series of talks the following spring, which have been published by the National Council of Catholic Men under the title, "The Constitution and Government of the Church." He has also lectured several times at the Forum of Columbus Council, Knights of Columbus, Brooklyn, New York. Father Connell has also lectured to non-Catholic groups on the teachings of the Church, for he is convinced that the most effective means to break down prejudice and to make converts is a clear and kindly exposition of Catholic doctrine.

Father Connell is the author of a biography of his late uncle, the Reverend Michael Sheehan, C.SS.R., *A Modern Apostle* (1925); he translated *Our Lady of Perpetual Help* (1927); a devotional work by Reverend B. D'Orazzio, C.SS.R.; and he also translated *Mixed Marriages and Their Remedies* (1932), by Reverend F. Ter Haar, C.SS.R. In 1935 he brought out *De Sacramentis Ecclesiae*, a Latin textbook for clerical students. He contributes to several periodicals.

M. H.

James Brendan Connolly   1868-

For more than forty years James Brendan Connolly has been writing for a living. Most of his writing is done mornings after breakfast, "a three-hour stretch usually with now and then a lay-off," he writes.

"Jim" Connolly was born in South Boston, Massachusetts, on October 28, 1868, the sixth of John and Ann Connolly's ten sons. His parents were natives of the Aran Islands in Galway Bay, were married there, and while still young, came to live in South Boston.

His brother, Michael, the Admiralty Commissioner for the port of Savannah, got Jim a job with the U. S. Engineer Corps, then at the work of improving the rivers and harbors of the southeast Atlantic coast. Jim left the Engineer Corps for a special engineering course at Harvard College. He discontinued his studies, however, when he was refused permission to compete in the revival of the ancient Olympic Games at Athens. He had been the amateur hop, step, and jump champion and record-holder before that. He won his event at Athens.

He came home a hero, but now he had to think about earning a living. He began writing for two Boston daily papers and two monthly sports magazines. Just as he was making a name for himself as a special writer, the Spanish War broke out. Enlisting with the Ninth Massachusetts Infantry, he served through the campaign of '98 in Cuba. After the Spanish troops in Cuba surrendered, the Ninth was sent home and mustered out.

Jim Connolly's next adventure was working on a cattle boat to England. He returned to America the same way when his money ran out.

The following job was with the Gloucester Athletic Club as physical director, but in the spring he quit it to re-visit England. He went on to Paris to see the Paris Exhibition and competed in the second Olympic Games, winning second place in his event. While wondering what he would do for his next meal, he ran across Bob Garrett, a wealthy friend. Garrett bought his steerage passage ticket home.

While in Gloucester with the athletic club he met several sea-captains. His experiences with them on fishing trips inspired a series of stories, which were sent to *Scribner's* magazine, and were immediately accepted.

Out of Gloucester (1902), is a collection of his first six stories. It was immediately republished in England. Also republished in England were eight subsequent volumes of his short stories, one book of personal experiences, and three novels. These volumes were written between trips overseas.

Scribner's and *Harper's* magazines both commissioned him to make

Arctic trips. He fished with Finnish fishermen on the Siberian coast and the Lapp fishermen out of Hammerfest. He made a whaling trip to 76 degrees north, with the famous Norwegian Captain Morgan Ingrebrystken. He also sailed with English fishermen in the North Sea and German fishermen in the Baltic Sea.

In 1906 he revisited Greece to get the atmosphere for his novel about the Olympic Games, for *Scribner's.*

President Theodore Roosevelt gave him authority to go aboard any American navy ship any time anywhere and stay as long as it suited him. He saw navy life from ward rooms and admirals' cabins as a guest; and from the fo'c'sle end as an enlisted man. He was with the American naval rescue party after the disastrous Kingston, Jamaica, earthquake; and was mentioned for meritorious service in Jamaica by the commanding American Admiral Davis, in his despatches.

In 1914, he was *Collier's* correspondent in Mexico, when we landed troops at Vera Cruz. That same year he entered a story in the Collier short story contest. Eight thousand manuscripts were submitted anonymously in that competition. His story, *The Trawler* (1914), won first place.

During World War I he was *Collier's* naval correspondent for European waters, seeing service with our U-Boat-hunting destroyer fleet out of Queenstown in 1917. He came home for Christmas, 1917, with pneumonia; got over it and went back as a correspondent in the Bay of Biscay air and surface patrol in 1918.

In 1921, he was named Commissioner for the American Committee for the Relief in Ireland, his mission being to visit Ireland and report on the story put out by London that American Relief money was being spent for arms and munitions for the Irish Republican Army. He was able to nail that London report as a canard. On his return he severely indicted the British conduct of the war in a series of articles for the Hearst Press.

Altogether he has written 23 volumes of short stories, novels, personal experiences, and several hundred newspaper and magazine articles on widely varying subjects.

He is a member of the Army of Santiago de Cuba, a Spanish War veteran, a member of the National Institute of Arts and Letters, a Knights of Columbus, and a Gloucester Master Mariner. He now lives in Boston (1946) with the wife he married forty-two years ago and a daughter, Brenda.

Some of his books are: *Out of Gloucester* (1902); *The Seiners* (1904); *Deep Sea Toll* (1905); *Head Winds* (1916); *The U Boat Hunters* (1918); *Book of Gloucester Fishermen* (1927); *Gloucestermen* (1930); *Navy Men* (1939); *The Port of Gloucester* (1940); *Canton Captain* (1941); and his autobiography, *Sea Borne* (1944).

M. H.

Reverend Terence L. Connolly, S.J. 1888-

Terence L. Connolly was born in Attleboro, Massachusetts, in 1888 and attended the primary and secondary public schools of Pawtucket, Rhode Island. As he joined the Jesuits on August 15, 1908, his subsequent education was accomplished as a member of the Society of Jesus, with degrees of B.A. and M.A. coming from Woodstock College, and Ph.D. from Fordham University.

Father Connolly's preoccupation with literature has naturally been reflected in his teaching assignments. After serving as professor of English at Fordham and dean of English at Georgetown, he now heads the English department at Boston College. The fact that he is also curator of the distinguished Francis Thompson Collection at the same institution throws an interesting sidelight on Terence Connolly's activities, for he was largely instrumental in the college's acquisition and expansion of this treasure-trove of Thompsoniana (originally assembled by Seymour Adelman). In 1932 he edited, with copious notes and a commentary, the *Complete Poems* of Francis Thompson. Six years later he edited the *Mystical Poems of Nuptial Love* by Coventry Patmore; and he has been responsible for translations or new editions of John Norris' *Picture of Love Unveiled;* of *St. Bernard On The Love of God;* and for correctives to Long's *History of English Literature; An Introduction to Chaucer and Langland* and a treatise on *The English Renaissance in the Age of Elizabeth.*

With over-great modesty, Father Connolly describes himself not as an author but as a "literary drudge." Probably no one else would label as hackwork the scholarly devotion with which he has introduced or interpreted to students and general readers those "crested and prevailing" names in our literary heritage.   K. B.

Reverend John Joseph Considine, M.M. 1897-

Father Considine has been identified with missionary activities. In the fall of 1924, the year after his ordination, he was sent to Rome. One of his first tasks there was "to prepare a series of statistical graphs for Pope Pius XI on Protestant world missions." In the Holy Year of 1925, a mission exhibit building was opened on the Vatican grounds. The Maryknoll exhibit was in charge of Father Considine.

From this experience, he wrote a book giving an account of the Holy Year mission exhibit. The project about which this book was written has become permanent at the Vatican. The following nine years Father Considine spent in Rome where Maryknoll opened a House of Studies.

During this time, Father Considine played a large part in establishing the *Fides News Service,* a world-wide organization for the dissemination of mission news. For seven years he was director of the *Fides News Service.* With other representatives from the Vatican, he was sent on a diplomatic mission to Ethiopia where he served as secretary (1929).

In his book, *Across A World* (1942) he reviews "Catholic endeavor for the advance of the Faith in Asia and Africa, as I saw it during a journey from Rome out through Asia and then across the Dark Continent." It is a book crammed full of information about the missionaries, of the people in strange lands, and it is studded with interesting anecdotes. Thomas Kernan collaborated with Father Considine on this book.

Father Considine was born at New Bedford, Massachusetts on October 9, 1897. His parents are John William and Alice (Murphy) Considine. He attended the elementary schools at New Bedford, Massachusetts, and then went to Holy Family High School. In September 1917 he entered Maryknoll. From 1922 to 1924 he studied at the Catholic University of America and was awarded the J.C.B. and S.T.L. degrees. He was ordained to the priesthood in 1923. From 1924 to 1934 he was the procurator general in Rome. As a Representative of the Fides News Service, Father Considine toured the missions a short while before returning to Maryknoll, New York, where he became a council member of the Catholic Foreign Mission Society of America in 1934.

Other books by Father Considine are: *When The Sorghum Was High* (1940), a biography of Father Gerard A. Donovan of Maryknoll, who was martyred for the Faith in 1938; *March Into Tomorrow* (1942), a short history of the work of the Maryknoll missioners in Western Asia; *World Christianity* (1945); and *Call For Forty Thousand* (1946).

After serving as Assistant General of the Maryknoll missionaries and associate editor of *The Field Afar,* Father Considine has been elected Vicar General of the Maryknoll Society.   M. H.

Robert Bernard Considine 1906-

While journalism is the special field of Robert Considine, he is also the author of *MacArthur, the Magnificent* (1942), and co-author with Captain Ted W. Lawson of *Thirty Seconds Over Tokyo* (1943) and *Where's Sammy?* (with Sammy Schulman) (1943).

More than a half a million copies of *Thirty Seconds Over Tokyo* have already been sold. It was the Book-of-the-Month-Club selection and was the longest continued story that ever ran in *Collier's Weekly.* In 66 United States papers, it was the cartoon feature and is one of the MGM's movies, costing some three million dollars. Robert Considine wanted to call this book *Flight From Shangri-La* but followed his wife's suggestion by naming it, *Thirty Seconds Over Tokyo*. He thinks her arresting title had much to do with the success of the book. He married Mildred Anderson on July 21, 1931. They have three children.

Robert Considine was born in Washington, D. C., on November 4, 1906, the son of James W. Considine and Sophie (Small) Considine. He was educated at St. Aloysius grade school, and Gonzaga High School, which he left at the beginning of his junior year in 1923, to work as a messenger boy in the Census Bureau of the government and later as a typist in the United States Treasury Department. From 1927 to 1930 he was a special student in journalism and creative writing at George Washington University.

His first newspaper work began in 1929 with the Washington *Post* for which paper he wrote a weekly column about tennis, then inadequately covered. Being an ardent tennis player, he won the District of Columbia Public Parks championship, from 1925 to 1930; National Public Parks Doubles Championship (with George Jennings of Chicago) in 1929 and the District of Columbia, the City of Washington and the Maryland Indoor Championship in 1930. Robert Considine complained to the local sports editors, one of whom was Shirley Povich, then sports editor of the Washington *Post,* that the paper carried no news about tennis. Shirley Povich put him to work writing the weekly round-up of tennis news, for which he was paid $5.00 a week. To him, Dan Parker, Jack Lait of the New York *Mirror,* and Seymour Berkson of the *International News Service,* Robert Considine owes much of his training as a reporter. The job on the *Post* enlivened his interest in journalism and made his work as senior clerk in the State Department seem boring.

In 1930 Robert Considine resigned "from the overpowering ennui of routine government clerical work," as he put it, to accept a job as high-school sports writer for the Washington *Post.* In 1932 he became a baseball writer. A year later he transferred to the Washington *Herald* and was made sports editor, columnist, editorial writer, feature writer, and drama critic. He succeeded Damon Runyon as sports columnist for the New York *American,* and *Universal Service,* Hearst syndicate, in January 1937. In June of the same year, he joined the staff of the *Daily Mirror* and *International News Service* and has been working for these two ever since, as sports columnist, trial reporter, and feature writer. In June 1943 he became a war correspondent and spent six months in England and Ireland.

His first fiction story appeared in the *Cosmopolitan* magazine. His first movie script is the "Church of the Good Thief" based on Reverend Ambrose R. Hyland's chapel at Dannemora Prison.

Regarding his habit of writing, Robert Considine said: "I write fast; seldom rewrite: Am chronically lazy: Am so reluctant to tie myself to a desk—for non-newspaper writing—that I usually wait until the wolf has not only appeared at the door but has gnawed his way half through. Then mad industry: During one such siege in the fall of 1940, turned out in one month five articles—which appeared in *Collier's, Saturday Evening Post, Cosmopolitan, Esquire* and *Look.*"

M. H.

Reverend Bertrand Conway, C.S.P.   1872-

Noted for his convert making, Father Bertrand Conway, C.S.P., is spiritual director of The Catholic Unity League which he founded in 1917. Up to 1946 it has guided twenty-one hundred and fifty converts to the Catholic Church. The League's activities include requests to honest non-Catholic professors to contradict publicly false statements made in class; furnishing lay defenders material to answer attacks upon the Church in the daily press; bringing back to Catholicism convicts in jails and penitentiaries and supplying spiritual reading books. It was founded as a Loan Library for Catholics and non-Catholics.

Father Conway was born on May 5, 1872 and was educated in the public schools of New York, at St. Charles College in Ellicott City, Maryland, at St. Paul's College, Washington, D. C., and at the Catholic University of America, also in Washington, D. C. From the last named institution he received his S.T.B. and S.T.L. degrees. He received his A.B. and A.M. at St. Mary's Seminary in Baltimore. He was ordained on December 28, 1896. Two years later he started out on his long career as a missioner. Since 1931 he has been Treasurer of the Paulists.

He is the author of *The Question Box* of which 3,000,000 copies have been distributed; of *The Virgin Birth* and *Studies in Church History*. He has contributed articles to *The Catholic World, The Missionary, America, Women's Home Companion* and the *Ecclesiastical Review*. He translated into English Vacandard's *Inquisition* and D'Hulst's *The Christian Family*. From 1898 to 1945 forty-eight hundred and twenty-five of his reviews appeared in *The Catholic World*.   M. H.

Right Reverend John Montgomery Cooper
1881-

Descended from English pioneers who settled in America in 1684 Right Reverend John Montgomery Cooper, Ph.D., has devoted much of his life to contributing to the knowledge of anthropology through field work among the vanishing original Americans—Indian tribes of the North, the James Bay Region, Labrador, Quebec, Ontario and the Mackenzie Valley; also through source research into the culture of the Tierra del Fuego people and others of South America. Since 1915 he has made twelve expeditions into the Indian territories. Souvenirs of his experiences—replicas of dwellings, craft and handwork—surround him in his office at the Catholic University of America, Washington, D. C., where he has been a member of the faculty since 1909 and Professor of Anthropology since 1928. Here he writes books and scientific papers in the field which has accorded him world recognition.

The son of James Joseph and Emma (Toulou) Cooper, Dr. Cooper was born October 28, 1881 at Rockville, Maryland. He studied at Calvert Hall and St. Charles College in Baltimore, and at the American College in Rome. His Ph.D. was awarded him by the Roman Academy of St. Thomas and his S.T.D. by the Propaganda College in Rome. Dr. Cooper was ordained in 1915. From 1905 to 1918 he was assistant pastor of St. Matthew's Church, Washington, D. C. He was made a Domestic Prelate on June 5, 1939. Dr. Cooper is a Past President of the American Anthropological Association and of the Anthropological Society of Washington, a member of the National Research Council and Chairman of its Committee on Survey of South American Indians, the Secretary and Editor of the Catholic Anthropological Conference and a member of other international scientific groups.

Dr. Cooper's published works include: *Analytical and Critical Bibliography of Tribes of Tierra del Fuego; Northern Algonquian Supreme Being* (1934); *Traps of the Northern Algonquian and Northern Athapaskans; Temporal Sequence—and the Marginal Cultures; Religion Outlines for Colleges* (1920-1934); *Children's Institutions* (1931); *Play Fair* (1923); *Content of the Advanced Religion Course* (1923); *Birth Control* (1923), and *Snares and Deadfalls of Northern Algonquians* (1938). He has made numerous contributions to anthropological, psychological, sociological, educational and Catholic publications. From 1918 to 1920, he was in charge of camp and community activities of the National Catholic War Council. In 1939 the Mendel Medal of Villanova College was awarded Dr. Cooper in recognition of outstanding achievement in science.

I. C.

Daniel Corkery   1878-

Writing in the *Irish Monthly,* July, 1918, Alice Furlong called Daniel Corkery an "Irish Trollope," who foreswore the natural advantages a writer derives from dealing with country folk in a setting of rural beauty or with aristocrats in a setting of luxury and pomp, to "clothe his genius in tweeds" and picture the middle class in their prosaic homes and occupations. Eighteen years later Sean O'Faolain in the *Dublin Magazine* said that Corkery's early stories were "authentic city-folklore," but that Corkery had turned unsoundly romantic when he wrote of the peasantry and of Ireland's past. To which Corkery's admirers retorted that as an organizer of Irish Volunteers, from 1913 to 1916, and a guerilla fighter against the

Black and Tans, from 1918 to 1921, he had a matchless opportunity to learn the truth about country people and to sense the romantic traditions of the Gael.

Daniel Corkery was born in Cork in 1878, and educated by the Presentation Brothers in his native city. His literary adventures began with the writing of one-act plays for the Cork Dramatic Society, an amateur group composed of young enthusiasts of the Irish Literary Revival. Publication in 1916 of his volume of short stories entitled *A Munster Twilight* established him as a force in that movement, and as a master of the short story form. His one novel, *The Threshold of Quiet* followed in 1917. It was the first novel, says O'Faolain, of the Irish Renaissance, theretofore the work of the dramatists and poets. O'Faolain compares this novel with the work of Musset, and Miss Furlong notes its "curiously spiritual atmosphere." *Hounds of Banba* (1921) is a collection of stories which again prove Corkery's mastery, and, what is more important, reveal convincingly the courage and idealism of a people fighting for their liberties and their culture.

Turning to the theatre again, Corkery published *The Yellow Bittern and Other Plays,* and also the *Labour Leader* (a three-act drama) in 1920. *The Yellow Bittern* is a masterly miracle-play; *King and Hermit* and *Clan Falvey* give some color to O'Faolain's strictures. *The Labour Leader* (1920) (produced at the Abbey Theatre) is powerful but somewhat confused in thought. *Resurrection,* a play honored by being published in *Theatre Arts* (1924) is the truest and strongest of all his dramatic work as a picture of Irish character against the background of Ireland's cause. In 1925 he published his best-known book, *The Hidden Ireland,* a critical study of Gaelic poetry as it persisted even to the end of the 18th and beginning of the 19th centuries, when the bardic schools and "big houses" were overthrown and the poets had to work as day laborers or wander homeless, but before the Union, the Famine and the "National" school system tore out the roots of Gaelic culture. Over-romantic or not, this book is a prime contribution toward the Irish people's recovery of their great past.

Since 1930 Daniel Corkery has been Professor of English at University College, Cork. From 1933 to 1938 he was a member of Dail Eireann, and since 1938 has been a Senator of Eire. His recreation is sketching. Other books are: *I Bhreasail* (poems) (1921); *The Stormy Hills* (stories) (1929), and *Synge and Anglo-Irish Literature* (criticism) (1931).

S. O.

Herbert Ellsworth Cory   1883-1947

For outstanding service as a Catholic and as a citizen the De Smet medal bestowed annually upon an outstanding Catholic layman of the Pacific northwest was awarded in 1940 to Doctor Herbert E. Cory, the head of the Department of Liberal Arts of the University of Washington. Gonzaga University of Spokane had established this award as a memorial to Father Peter De Smet, S.J., pioneer missionary, who came to the Northwest in 1840 in response to the urgent request of the Flathead Indians.

One of Dr. Cory's unusual services as a citizen was his keeping open house for the young men and women of Seattle, whether matriculated at the University or not. After a strenuous day of teaching, nightly Dr. Cory welcomed these young people who came to discuss their problems and perplexities. He said of this hospitality, "I feel that this is but one of the minute ways that I can thank God for the precious gift He has given me—my life as a Catholic. But seven years ago I was like these youths, floundering uncertainly between the materialistic code of the day and longing for a truly rational solution of the problems which beset us all today."

Like Father De Smet, Dr. Cory went to the Northwest in response to a request. In 1923 the University of Washington invited him to start a series of courses to help students to gain their intellectual bearings. These were to offset the effects of early specialization. A student in one of the undergraduate courses was James B. McGoldrick. This student entered the priesthood and had the happiness of baptizing his former professor in 1933. Father McGoldrick is now dean of Seattle College. Dr. Cory wrote of his conversion: "I became a Roman Catholic on purely intellectual grounds. As I look backward over the years I am amazed at the obstinacy with which, in the face of innumerable and unusual opportunities I resisted the truth." He had published his spiritual autobiography, *The Emancipation of a Freethinker*.

Providence, Rhode Island is Dr. Cory's birthplace. His parents, Benjamin Herbert and Ella Cook Cory, were descendants of early Puritans who landed at Boston and later settled at Providence. His parents were Congregationalists and the boy was raised one, too. His mother, however, outgrew Congregationalism and entered the Anglican communion. She was about to start instruction in Catholicism when she died in 1920. Herbert Cory went to the famous Peace Street Grammar School and the equally famous Providence Classical High School. This education led to a love of Greek and Latin. Dr. Cory thoroughly believed in the study of the classics as a foundation for life. At Brown University he took his A.B. in 1906. At Harvard he spent four years in graduate studies in English Literature and received his Ph.D. In 1910 he joined the faculty of the University of California, where he remained for eight years. He continued his English research and in 1917 produced *Edmund Spenser: A Critical Study.* For two years while at the University of California he was editor of the *University of California Chronicle.* In August 1918 he came east to Washington, D. C. to become a member of Felix Frankfurter's War Labor Policies Board. In his spare time he went to Baltimore two or three times a week to do research in biology and psychology at Johns Hopkins University. He studied here for five years and in the biological laboratory lost his agnosticism and developed reasoned proofs for the existence of God. Dr. Cory explained, "When I went to Johns Hopkins as a student once more after teaching for a number of years, I realized in observing life under a microscope that it cannot be explained by mere chance. There must be a Supreme Being that holds not only our lives in balance, but also the tiniest spark of life and today all the sciences are inevitably moving closer toward a confirmation of our faith."

In 1922 Dr. Cory married Ethel Duncan Morton of New York City. She died ten years later and in 1933 he married Mary (Maloney) Austin of Juneau, Alaska. Lacking children of their own, Dr. and Mrs. Cory had adopted five, two girls and three boys. Although his own education had been completely secular and all his teaching had been done in secular universities Dr. Cory stated, "I would never send one of my children to any secular university." He says of his teaching, "By teaching in secular universities I trust that I may help others who are now as puzzled as I once was."

He is the author of: *The Critics of Edmund Spenser* (1911); *Spenser: the School of Fletcher and Milton* (1912); *Edmund Spenser, A Critical Study* (1917); co-author, *Essays in Exposition* (1917); *The Intellectuals and the Wage-Workers* (1919); *Progress, Delusory and Real; The Emancipation of a Freethinker* (1941), and in preparation, *The Significance of Beauty in Nature and Art.*

He died Saturday, February 1, 1947.   M. S.

Ida Friedrike Coudenhove (Mrs. Carl Görres)
1901-

In the last decade, translations have appeared from the distinguished German of Ida Coudenhove and have won acclaim. She began writing when very young. She intended to enter the convent but was convinced by Father Peter Stone, S.J. that she could do better work for the Church by her writings. Her book *The Cloister and the World* emphasizes a single perfection for all Christians. It points out that Joan of Arc gained her sanctity by the very secular job of routing the English and restoring order in France. Ida Coudenhove believes that the vocation to holiness in the world is not only real, but common rather than exceptional. If the laity are to be enticed into trying to be saints, the humanness of the saints must be stressed. Modern hagiography is beginning to do this and a notable example is the discussion of Elizabeth of Hungary's humaneness in *The Nature of Sanctity.* "We are not human enough to be saints," declares the author.

Ida Coudenhove was educated first in the College of the Sacred Heart in Pressbaum near Vienna, then in the Lyceum of the Loretto nuns in St. Pölten, Austria. When 20 years old, she entered the novitiate there but the Lord had other plans about her vocation so she left the convent in 1925. In her book *Mary Ward, an Historical Romance,* about the saintly though not canonized foundress of that congregation, she says: "I have tried to acknowledge something of the deep and, I trust, undying gratitude to the spirit of the House." She intended *Mary Ward* "to revive the memory of one of the most extraordinary women of the seventeenth century, indeed perhaps of the whole history of religious orders, and to re-tell, in a reliable, if romantic tale, the wonderful and enthralling adventure of her strangely tragic life."

About 1925 she joined the then authentic German Youth Movement in its Catholic League, called Neuland in Austria. In Germany, she worked for many years as one of the leaders of the girls. She believes this Catholic movement is *"the* origin of the religious revival in Germany and Austria."

From 1925 to 1932 she trained for social work in the Caritas College for Social Work in Freiburg, Breisgau and studied sociology and history at the Universities of Vienna and Freiburg. She broke off her studies to take the post of Secretary for Catholic girls work in the Diaspora—Diocese of Meissen. After three years she married Carl Josef Görres. They have no children.

She was born on December 2, 1901 in Ronsperg in Bohemia. Count Heinrich J. M. von Coudenhove-Kalergi was the author's father. While engaged in diplomatic work for his government, he married a Japanese, Mitsu Aoyama. When the Countess was baptized she took the name Maria Thecla. Count Richard Nicolaus von Coudenhove-Kalergi is Ida Coudenhove's brother. He is president of the Pan-European Union and author of *Europe Must Unite* (1940); *Pan Europe* prefaced by Nicholas Murray Butler (1926); *The Totalitarian State Against Man; Crusade For the Future* (1943), and other works.

Ida Coudenhove is the author of *The Nature of Sanctity* (1933); *Burden of Belief* (1934); *The Cloister and the World* (1935); *Mary Ward* (1939). Other books are *Zwei deutsche Heilige,* a contribution to the very lively debate in the first years of the Nazi regime about "nordic spirit and Christianity." It is a sketch of the Blessed Henry Suso, O.P., the great German mystic of the 14th century and St. Radegund, German princess, prisoner of war of the Merovingian King Chlothar. In 1940 she wrote *Des Andern Last, ein Gespräch über die Barmherzigkeit* a vindication of Christ's charity, alms, works of mercy, etc., against the claim of the totalitarian state of having rendered all that kind of thing obsolete and superfluous. In 1942 she wrote a rather bulky book *Das Verborgene Antlitz* about St. Thérèse of Lisieux. It is considered to be her best work.

The first edition was totally destroyed by an air raid on Freiburg in the autumn of 1942. It has been republished since 1945.

During the last three or four years of the war her books were not allowed to be sold in Germany. They could be exported. T. S. Eliot's play "Murder in the Cathedral" was translated by her into German verse and awaits publication.

M. S.

Frederick Cowles 1900-

Literary critic, lecturer on subjects connected with travel, archaeology and gypsy lore, Frederick Cowles is a librarian by profession. He commenced writing at an early age and by the time he was thirteen was contributing regularly to papers and magazines. He served in World War I and afterwards became a journalist. From 1922 to 1926 he was assistant librarian at Trinity College, Cambridge and since 1926 he has been chief librarian of Swinton and Pendlebury, Lancashire, England.

Frederick Cowles was born in Cambridge, England, in 1900, and was educated privately in England and Malta. He is a descendant on his father's side from a well-known English Jacobite family and one of his ancestors fought under Prince Charles Edward. On his mother's side he has Spanish gypsy blood in his veins, a fact which has led him to take a keen interest in the gypsy race. He is a prominent member of the Gypsy Lore Society and has lived with gypsies in Spain, Hungary, and France.

His private library contains a unique collection of books on witchcraft and sorcery, and many early printed books. His collections include many fine manuscripts, autograph letters, coins, bookplates, prints, and engravings. He is interested in the revival of pilgrimages to the ancient shrines in England and has written and lectured on the subject. As a member of the Ancient Monument Society he has worked for the preservation of ecclesiastical relics and old houses.

To increase the popularity of the public libraries, he has adopted classes for the unemployed, organized debating societies and even founded a successful amateur dramatic society.

In 1932 he married Doris Mary, (daughter of Wilfrid Grimshaw, Commander, Order of the British Empire). They have one son, Michael Wilfrid. Mrs. Cowles is a well-known artist and has illustrated many of her husband's books.

Mr. Cowles is a Fellow of the Royal Society of Literature; Fellow of the Royal Society of Arts; Fellow of the Society of Antiquaries of Scotland and an Hon. Member of the Institut Littéraire et Artistique de France. In 1936, he was awarded the Silver Laureate Medal of the Institut.

He is the author of two books of Essays and Criticism, Men of Old Cambridge and Some Contemporary Writers. He wrote nine books of travel: The Road to Canterbury; Dust of Years 'Neath English Skies; Pilgrim Ways; More Pilgrim Ways; The Magic of Cornwall; Not Far From the Smoke; Signposts to Romance; Let's Go to Bavaria (under the pseudonym of Michael Sutton). He wrote three books of fiction: The Horror of Abbot's Grange; The Night Wind Howls; The Ghosts' High Noon, and two books of verse: Midsummer Madness and The English Heritage. His books for children are : Harlequinade; The Magic Map; The Fairy Isle; Michael in Bookland; The Enchanted Thistle; The Joyous Pilgrimage, and Romany Wonder Tales. His latest books are: Gypsy Caravan; This Is England, and Round the Gypsy Fire. Forthcoming books are: Memory Dances; Signposts to Romance; Hide and Seek, and The Enchanted Thistle.

He is a contributor to The Publishers' Circular, The Library World, The Manchester Guardian, The Universe, The Catholic Herald, The Catholic Fireside, and others and is the editor of: The Bookland News, Swinton and Pendlebury Public Libraries Bulletin and The Hub.

In World War II he served as Captain and was engaged mostly in welfare work and education in the Forces. Since 1939 he has given thousands of lectures to men and women in the Services, including many to United States Forces stationed in England.

M. H.

Pierre Crabitès 1877-1943

In 1911 President Taft selected a young New Orleans lawyer, Pierre Crabitès, to be this country's representative at the Mixed Tribunals in Egypt. The Mixed Tribunals was once described by Sir Maurice Amos, the former Judicial Adviser of the Egyptian government as "with the exception of the Roman Catholic Church, the greatest international organization in the world." In 1876 this court was set up at the request of the Egyptian government and with the consent of fourteen Christian powers to remedy the deplorable state of the civil law as it regarded foreigners. The composition of the court is partly native and partly foreign, but with the foreigners a majority. It has jurisdiction over all civil suits in which at least one party is a foreigner. The language of the court is French and all the pleadings are filed in French.

The appointment to this court made Judge Crabitès a resident of Cairo for twenty-five years and opened many fields for his writing. He had written two books about the rulers of Egypt. In Ismail, The Maligned Khedive, lawyer Crabitès was indulging in "the keenest of intellectual pleasures, the defence of a just cause." This volume won him a personal standing at Abdine Palace. His late majesty, King Fuad, received him in audience more often than his official rank required, and also gave him unrestrained access to the Royal Archives of Abdine Palace for material for several books. He wrote of King Fuad, "His Majesty's kindness to me is another evidence of that love for historical truth which is so characteristic of him." Fuad's son, the present king, Farouk, (1946) continued his father's kindness and entertained him privately when he revisited Egypt in 1939. With His Majesty's permission he dedicated to him his last book, *The Spoliation of Suez*.

A favorite theme with Judge Crabitès had been women's property rights. When he first assumed his duties in Egypt he was amazed to see Egyptian women come into court and plead their own cases. This Occidental found that the veiled woman of the harem possesses much greater property rights than her Western sister, and is never slow to defend them. These rights were secured to her by the Prophet himself, and this led the judge to look upon Mahomet as one of the greatest champions of women's rights the world has ever known. The Moslem women do not give dowers, they receive them; half in cash, and half reserved as a guarantee in case of divorce. The law "permits the wife to do with her assets whatever she pleases without consulting her husband, who in such matters has no greater rights than a perfect stranger." Further study made him conclude that the Islamic woman has these great rights only because of her matrimonial insecurity. She may be divorced at the caprice of her husband, and so has to be secure in her property rights. These great property rights are an indication of the decay of the marital bond. So, while a pleader for more lenient laws regarding women's property, to cover special cases, Judge Crabitès deplored a modern tendency to demand absolute freedom in property matters for women, as a sign of increased marital instability and hence a portent of deterioration.

Pierre Crabitès was born in New Orleans; his parents were Pierre and Martha Patton Crabitès. He attended school in his native state and in 1895 received his A.M. from Immaculate Conception College, New Orleans. He got his LL.B. from Tulane University in 1898, and two years later was admitted to the bar. He practised in Louisiana until he went to Egypt. Loyola University of New Orleans honoured him with an LL.D. in 1918. In the spring of 1924, while in Cairo, Judge Crabitès fell while trying to board a street car, the wheels of which crushed one of his legs below the knee, necessitating amputation. Three years later he fell downstairs in his home and fractured the kneecap of his other leg. In 1936 when he was the senior American Judge of the Mixed Tribunals he resigned, and returned to the United States.

Until the outbreak of World War II he had been a special lecturer at the Louisiana State University Law School. The whole world of the Levant was especially opened to the judge because of his mastery of Arabic. His command of other languages has made him at home on three continents. Yet sitting at his desk in his home on a small island in the Nile at Cairo, looking out over that river to the pyramids on the far horizon he wrote, "I observe in the Nile not the River of Mystery, but the African Mississippi. I cannot help it. I was born in New Orleans and everything in the world revolves, in my mind, around that bewitching city."

Not long after the outbreak of World War II, Judge Crabitès was sent on a special mission to Cairo and remained there during the tense period of Rommel's drive through North Africa. When he returned to Washington in 1942, he was appointed Special Aide to the United States Minister to Iraq and arrived there in July. It was at Iraq that Judge Crabitès died in 1943.

He is the author of: *Ismail, The Maligned Khedive* (1933); *Gordon, The Sudan and Slavery* (1933); *American Officers In the Egyptian Army* (1938); *The Winning of the Sudan* (1934); *Ibrahim of Egypt* (1935); *Benes, Statesman of Central Europe* (1935); *Clement VII and Henry VIII* (1936); *Victoria's Guardian Angel* (1937); *Unhappy Spain* (1937), and *The Spoliation of Suez* (1940). He translated from the French Aston Kevork's *Armenia and the Americans* (1920).

M. S.

Mairin Cregan (Mrs. James Ryan)

The mountains of Kerry have about them some peculiar magic and charm, absent from all other bits of rugged country. At least, that is the considered opinion of Mairin Cregan, who was born in the rough hill country near the McGillicuddy's Reeks. Mairin Cregan, who in private life is the wife of Dr. James Ryan, presently Minister for Agriculture in the cabinet of Prime Minister De Valera of Eire, is one of the outstanding contributors to the resurgence of literary production which has marked the "New" Ireland since the Revolution. Her forte is books especially appealing to children.

The Ryans live at Kindlestown House, Delgany, County Wicklow, about 16 miles from Dublin, with their three young children, Evin, Nuala (short for Fionuala) and Saemus. The mother, Mairin, was educated by the Saint Louis nuns in Ireland. She has always had an intense interest in music and in the development of the theatre. She has made a special study of Irish folk-music and has followed the new plays very closely. A drama, *Hunger Strike,* flowed from her pen. For the past few years, the readers of Irish newspapers and magazines have been familiar with her many appealing short stories.

Her first full-length book is *Old John* (1936), a charming fairy tale about an old Irish shoemaker who lived at the edge of the wood with his family—a dog, a hen and a goat. How she came to write it, let her tell in her own words. "When Evin and Nuala were younger they were always wanting stories read to them, Grimm and Hans Andersen, especially. I was so tired reading the same thing over and over for them that I began making up stories, which is much easier on the voice than reading aloud. *Old John* got started somehow and, because it was easier to keep on one subject, I added something to the tale every evening. When I changed to other stories the children used to say, 'Yes, we like that, but have you any more to tell about Old John?' So it went like that. Later on when I had forgotten it, they remembered it all. Then my husband suggested that I should write it down and the children helped remind me of the plot. After 'Old John' was written it lay in my desk for over a year. Then Mr. James Carty of the National Library in Dublin read it and liked it. He said, 'You should send it to the Macmillan Company. They will understand it.'" And they did! The book was published in New York.

On December 8, 1943, Mairin Cregan received the Downey Award, presented annually by the Pro Parvulis Book Club for Catholic Children, for her latest book, *Rathina*. The award is given for the finest children's book written in the American tradition. *Rathina* is a delightful family story, set in the countryside outside of Dublin. The focal interest is in the young daughter's training of a horse, who, though separated from her by many miles, wins the Grand National in England. It was translated into Swedish by Frederik Ramel and part of it was broadcast from Stockholm. The British Broadcasting Company broadcast it as a Serial Dialogue Story.

Rathina was published in New York, too, and the award was accepted, in the author's absence, by Mr. Brennan, Minister to the United States from Eire.

J. M.

Mildred Criss (Mrs. George Catlin) 1890-

Mildred Criss Catlin, one of our happiest writers of juvenile literature, was born in Orange, New Jersey, in 1890, and was educated privately at Hollins College, Virginia—a strictly Baptist institution, although her family affiliations were Episcopalian. Later she studied at Mlle. La Salle's school in Geneva, Switzerland and Paris, France. While in France, she lived in the homes of "charming French Catholics," who offered a striking contrast to any religious life she had hitherto known. However, her own religious connections hovered for a long time between attachment and detachment. She became interested in Christian Science, but was surprised to find that its most helpful doctrines had been long anticipated by the Catholic Church. Later on, while studying and teaching the Bible under

Episcopalian auspices, she was again surprised to discover that only from a kindly Catholic priest could she obtain answers to many difficult questions.

Still, "inherited prejudice" held her back, and it was not until coming into the friendship of Dr. Selden P. Delaney in New York that she was seriously disturbed by the claims of Catholicism. Abbé Dimnet helped in "breaking down the Anglican foundations," and she was received into the Catholic Church in 1928—a few months before Dr. Delaney himself.

Mildred Criss was married in 1936 to George Lewis Catlin of Boston (a very early marriage to Benjamin McGuckin having been pronounced null by the Church). Her first publications were the *Poems* of 1922 and 1923; but in 1928 she apparently found her true metier in books for children. A good deal of her beloved Europe went into *Little Cabbages; Malou; Martine and Michel; The Red Caravan*, and *Madelein's Court;* while her *Mary Stuart, Young Queen of Scots* (1939) and *Isabella, Young Queen of Spain* (1941) brought to adolescents and their elders a kind of biography mingling charm and scholarship.

In 1943 she published *Pocahontas: Young American Princess* and *Dom Pedro of Brazil* in 1945. Mrs. Mildred Criss Catlin's home is at Whitefield, New Hampshire but she lived in Washington, D. C. during World War II.

K. B.

Reverend Clement H. Crock   1890-

The sale of 42,000 books establishes Father Crock as a popular writer on Catholic dogma. A busy pastor of St. Benedict's Church, Cambridge, Ohio, in the past eleven years (1935 to 1946), he has published seven books. His best known works are the four books forming a complete homiletic library: *The Commandments in Sermons; The Apostles' Creed; Grace and the Sacraments; Virtue and Vice*. He is also the author of three series of Lenten Discourses: *The Characters of the Passion; The Principles of the Church; Prayer and Its Effects*. Father Crock came to writing by the long hard road of missionary experience and by the special invitation of his brother clergy. He has been a priest twenty-nine years—a writer but eleven.

Pastor in the rural sections of Ohio with 350 converts to his credit, traveling on horseback twenty miles a day, ten miles between missions, hearing confessions in four languages, his books are of necessity practical books. Along with being a priest, acting as carpenter, painter, plumber, gardener, and janitor also falls to his lot.

His writing began in 1935 when Pope Pius XI gave the world his famous encyclical on preaching. A group of his fellow priests came to

Father Crock and asked him to prepare some sermons on the Commandments. In preparation for the venture (covering a two-year period) he attended the Eucharistic Congress in Carthage, visited the Holy Land, the Passion Play, the shrines at Lourdes and at Lisieux, went to the Congress in Dublin, spent one summer in Rome reviewing part of his theology, and another summer at the Catholic University, Washington, D. C. under Fathers Walsh, O.S.B., Smith, O.P., and Kirsch, O.M.Cap., in a special study of the Sixth Commandment. His first attempt was so successful that one bishop in the midwest ordered 165 copies of his book for Christmas gifts to his priests.

Father Crock writes not only with priests and confessors in mind but with doctors, lawyers, statesmen, businessmen and women with problems to solve. He is a spiritual man and desires to give to souls in search of truth the theologically correct information for which they are seeking and to give it to them in language they can readily understand.

Clement H. Crock was born on a farm at Fulda, Nobel Co., Ohio, April 2, 1890, sixth in a family of eleven. He was educated at St. Joseph's College, Collegeville, Indiana and Mt. St. Mary's Seminary of the West, Cincinnati, Ohio. He was ordained in June 1917 for the diocese of Columbus.

His first post was Bellaire, Ohio, where he spent fourteen months. He was sent by his bishop as pastor to Churchtown, Ohio in 1918. From here he went to Our Lady of Mercy Parish, in Lowell, Ohio with Beverly, Ohio as a mission. In 1922 he was transferred to St. Philomena's, Caldwell, Ohio, with Belle Valley as a mission. About seven nationalities comprise these two missions calling for as many different languages. During his stay in Caldwell he organized a school. At the request of his Bishop, the Mother House of the Ursuline Sisters was established there.

In 1928 he was assigned, by the Bishop, to his present parish (1946), St. Benedict's, Cambridge, Ohio. He has a congregation of about two hundred families and has organized a complete parochial high school with extensive athletic activities.

Father Crock during the years 1917 to 1935 put such care into his sermons, always writing them out, keeping a careful file of clippings taken from all sources of reading covering these years, that when requested to write, it was in these well laid foundations he discovered the beginnings of his popular books.

Besides his books, Father Crock has been a regular contributor to the *Homiletic and Pastoral Review* for a number of years, and reviewed about fifteen manuscripts for publishers of books, several of which are now in print.

In addition to his parochial duties and extensive writings, Father Crock served as auxiliary army chaplain for Fletcher General Army Hospital of Cambridge, which has a capacity of 1,740 patients, 30 percent of whom are Catholic. He supervised and furnished a beautiful Eucharistic chapel in 1943 at this hospital. For five months he acted as the sole Catholic chaplain, often saying three Masses on Sundays for the benefit of the patients (soldiers) and personnel.

E. F.

Archibald Joseph Cronin   1896-

Beginning his career as an author in 1931 "to lighten, not to enlighten the world," A. J. Cronin has been writing best-sellers or near best-sellers ever since.

Cronin was born July 19, 1896 in Cardross, Dunbartonshire, Scotland, of Scotch-Irish parents, Patrick and Jessie (Montgomerie) Cronin. Like Francis Chisholm, the main character in *The Keys of the Kingdom,* he was an only child, was left fatherless early in life, and knew what it was to suffer for his creed at the hands of bigoted villagers. Father Francis is modeled after Cronin's uncle, a priest, who helped him to secure his education.

He attended the Cardross Village School and Dunbarton Academy. Although literature was his best subject, he decided to make medicine his career, and entered Glasgow University in 1914. His studies were interrupted in 1916 by the first World War. For two years he served as surgeon sub-lieutenant in the Royal Navy Volunteer Reserve.

Following the war, he returned to the University and graduated in 1919. He also made a trip to India that year as ship's surgeon on a liner. During the following two years he held various hospital appointments. In 1921 he married Agnes Mary Gibson, also a physician and a graduate of Glasgow.

After four years of private practice in South Wales, Dr. Cronin was appointed medical inspector of mines for Great Britain in 1924, and the following year published his report on first-aid conditions in the mines, for which Glasgow awarded him his M.D. with honors. He spent another year studying pulmonary disabilities in the coal fields for the Ministry of Mines, and then began practice in London.

Between 1926 and 1930, Dr. Cronin built up a fine practice for himself in London's fashionable West End. Then his health broke down, and he spent the summer of 1930 at a farm in the Scottish West Highlands, indulging himself in his long-suppressed desire to try his hand at a novel. For three months he wrote at white-heat, often getting up in the night to set down his ideas. He had laid the scene of his story in the Highlands of his boyhood, and, though writing was and still is torture to him, the fascination of his tale was more than he could resist.

He wrote a quarter of a million words that summer, and then, weary of the whole thing, shipped the manuscript off to a publisher chosen at random. He was ready to go back to medicine if the work should prove a failure. The book, *Hatter's Castle,* was accepted and proved an immediate success. It was the first "first novel" to be accepted by the English Book Society for the book-of-the-month.

That was in 1931. A year later Cronin's second novel, *Three Loves* appeared, followed by *Grand Canary* (1933); *The Stars Looked Down* (1935); *The Citadel* (1937); a play, *Jupiter Laughs,* which was produced on Broadway in 1940, and the controversial *Keys of the Kingdom* (1941). In 1944 *The Green Years* was published. *Keys of the Kingdom* was severely criticized by some Catholic critics as theologically unsound and an unfair picture of churchmen. Others were just as loud in their praise of it as a sympathetic story of mission life, with a fine moral. American critics, polled by the Book-of-the-Month-Club, designated it as the outstanding book of the year. The moving picture version appeared in 1944.

The author has three sons, Vincent Archibald Patrick, Robert Francis Patrick and Andrew James. He is a life governor of the Sussex General Hospital, an honorary Doctor of Literature of Bowdoin College, a member of the council of the Author's Society, of the Royal College of Physicians, and the Garrick Club.

His hobbies are golf, tennis, gardening and fishing. In his youth he was an ardent footballer. His favorite authors in the romantic tradition are Robert Louis Stevenson, Walter Scott and Joseph Conrad, and among the realists, Balzac, de Maupassant and Flaubert. He does not admire the stream-of-consciousness school, and among modern authors his favorites are Arnold Bennett, Sinclair Lewis and Somerset Maugham.

In 1941 the author came to this country in the service of the British Ministry of Information, and rented a home in Blue Hills, Maine and later lived in Greenwich, Connecticut. In September, 1945 he returned home on the Queen Mary.   P. O.

Reverend John F. Cronin, S.S.   1908-

One of the first teachers to initiate a full-time course in economics at an American Seminary, Reverend John F. Cronin, S.S., Ph.D., found it necessary to write his own book on the subject, *Economics and Society.* Although primarily a text book, the handling of the social encyclicals of Popes Leo XIII and Pius XI in such a manner as to make them understandable to the layman, has given his first full-length subject a wide circle of readers. His book *Economic Analysis and Problems* appeared in 1945.

Father Cronin was born in Glens Falls, New York on October 4, 1908. He studied at Holy Cross and Basselin Colleges and was granted his S.T.B. and Ph.D. degrees by the Catholic University of America in 1935. Ordained to the priesthood in 1932, he entered the novitiate for a year in preparation for joining the Society of St. Sulpice. In 1934, he was assigned to St. Mary's Seminary, Baltimore, Maryland, as teacher of philosophy and economics. In addition he has taught at the Catholic University Summer School, lectured at two National Catholic Social Action Conferences, spoken on the Catholic Hour (Radio) Programs and lectured at the Public Affairs Institute of the University of Virginia.

He is Director of the Institute of Catholic Social Studies, Catholic University of America Summer School; permanent arbitrator for the Men's Clothing Industry of Baltimore and was a member of the General War Rationing Board of Baltimore. In 1946 he was appointed assistant director of the Department of Social Action, National Catholic Welfare Conference.

Editor of the five pamphlets in his field of social economics: *Rugged Individualism; Prices in the United States; Government—Tyrant or Protector; The Social Problem of Money,* and *The Living Wage Today,* Dr. Cronin has also written for leading Catholic periodicals, including *The Commonweal, The Sign* and *The Christian Front.* Cardinal Newman's works have been his chief philosophical inspiration, but his great interest is in the problems and struggles of the average man.

In 1944 he was awarded a $1,000 prize in an essay contest dealing with post-war employment problems.   I. C.

Franz Theodor Csokor   1885-

Franz Theodor Csokor, Austrian author and dramatist, by birth a Czech, and when last heard of an exile in Poland, is, according to Percival Wilde "an extremely able writer."

He was born in Vienna (Austria) September 6, 1885, of a distinguished old family. He was educated at the University of Vienna where he majored in the History of Art.

At the age of twenty-one he wrote his first play *Thermidor* which was later produced in Vienna, Budapest, and Petersburg.

His most important works are: *Ballade of the Town (Ballade von der Stadt)* an historic piece dramatizing the fate of a town during a thousand years—this play obtained first prize from the Berlin Broadcasting Company in competition with 4,000 other plays—and *League of the Rights of Men (Gesellschaft der Menschenrechte)* a play describing the struggle for liberty and defeat of the German Democrats in 1834, assembled around the young deceased German poet George Bücher, author of *Danton's Death* (Danton's Tod).—This last production is well known in the United States through the performance of Max Reinhardt. It ran in Berlin from 1928 to 1932. The author himself says of it, "It is full of tragic parallels to the events of today."

In 1930 he wrote, *A History Play of Present Times.* It had a stirring effect wherever produced. It tells the story of a major from a little Catholic town in the "Rhine" who comes into conflict with the Nationalists.

His dramas portray the origin and nature of the tragic movements in Austria. They are full of poignant life. They reveal simple Catholic life in the little war-torn villages of Europe, with the dead dreams and lost hopes of their once joyous youths.

In 1937 Csokor's play Third of November 1918 depicting the fall of the Austro-Hungarian Army during World War I, met with the greatest success of his writing career. For this play he received the famous Burge Theatre prize which only five European poets have received.

In the sad days of Nationalistic trouble, Csokor gave up his home and all he so dearly loved and went to Poland to live. "I wasn't afraid for my person (I am Aryan)" he writes, "but it was impossible for me and my conscience to remain."

In his exile he has finished two great religious plays *The General of God* depicting the tragic soldier, Saint Ignatius Loyola, and *Jadwiga*, Poland's Jeanne d'Arc and greatest Queen.   E. F.

Alice Curtayne

Alice Curtayne was born in Tralee, Ireland, her schooling being accomplished at the convent of her home town and that of the Sainte Union in Southampton. She spent three years in Italy continuing her education and working at a secretarial post. When this latter brought her back to Liverpool, she became much interested in the work of the Catholic Evidence Guild and prepared herself to be one of its outdoor speakers. It was through Guild activities that she became a friend of Frank Sheed, and it was through his encouragement that she turned to writing. Her first publication was a life of *St. Catherine of Siena* (1929) done in the newer, "human interest" manner now generally accepted by hagiographers. It immediately attracted very favorable attention and remains her best known work, although followed by *A Recall to Dante* (1930); *Laborers in the Vineyard* (a translation from Papini in 1931); and biographies of *St. Anthony of Padua*, *St. Brigid of Ireland* and *Sarsfield*. She has also written a volume of essays, *Borne on the Wind* (1933), and a less successful novel, *House of Cards* (1939). *Lough Derg, St. Patrick's Purgatory* appeared in 1945.

In 1935 Alice Curtayne was married to Stephen Rynne, a farmer-author, with whom she lives at the historic old farm, Downings House, in the pleasantly named village of Prosperous in County Kildare. Between the upbringing of her three children, assisting her husband in poultry and bee-keeping as well as in Irish research, her own literary work and occasional lecturing and a practical all-round interest in the problems of modern Ireland, Alice Curtayne would seem to have achieved a happily crowded and well rounded life.   K. B.

Father Cuthbert, O.S.F.C.   1866-1939

Considered to have been the most outstanding Capuchin of the century in the English speaking world, Father Cuthbert died in his cell at St. Lawrence College in Assisi, Italy, March 22, 1939.

He was born Lawrence Anthony Hess, in Brighton, England, October 27, 1866. His father, James Hess, was German; his mother, Angelina Lorind, English. He was educated at St. Mary's School, Woolhampton and in the Capuchin Order. In 1889, he was ordained to the priesthood.

For fifty-eight years, he was with the Order, having entered it in 1881. Father Cuthbert claimed that he was perhaps the youngest religious to make profession since the Council of Trent. At the time of his profession it was important to know the exact hour of birth so that fifteen years might be complete. His mother told him it was exactly seven o'clock in the morning. When the superior heard this fact, he allowed Father Cuthbert to make profession at seven-thirty o'clock on his fifteenth birthday. During his years in the Order he held various responsible positions. From 1911 to 1930, he was the principal of the Franciscan House of Studies at Oxford, where he received an honorary M.A. degree. From 1930 until his death he was president of the Capuchin Franciscan College of St. Lawrence at Assisi, the first to hold that office.

Other activities included organizing the Franciscan Missions amongst Catholic hop-pickers, 1905 to 1922; serving as Minister Provincial of the English Province of Friars Minor, Capuchin, 1922 to 1925; and from 1930 on filling the important post of president of the Capuchin Commission for Franciscan Research Studies. It was no easy task to leave his native England, at the age of 64, to take up residence at Assisi.

In 1914 Oxford University celebrated the seventh centenary of the birth of the Franciscan Roger Bacon. Through the efforts of Father Cuthbert a statue of Roger Bacon was erected near the site of his grave.

Father Cuthbert was a prolific writer and a profound student of the life of St. Francis and of Franciscan history. His *Life of St. Francis of Assisi* is one of the best in English.

The learned author of international fame was always the simple friar at heart. He firmly believed that his true vocation was to win souls to God by preaching the Gospel, following the footsteps of his Father, St. Francis. And like St. Francis he had a magnificent charity and compassion for the poor, the afflicted and the outcast. For his golden jubilee in 1931 through the generosity of his friends in England and America, Father Cuthbert gave a dinner to three hundred poor people in Assisi and distributed clothes and shoes to the value of several hundred dollars.

His love for St. Francis can be gleaned from some of the titles of his

books: *St. Francis and You, An Appeal to Franciscan Tertiaries* (1899);
St. Francis and You, to which is added, *The Conversion of Modern
Democracy* (1901); *On The Spiritual Significance of Evangelical Poverty
with The Lady Poverty* (1902); *St. Francis and Poverty* (1910); *Life of
St. Francis of Assisi* (1912); *The Romanticism of St. Francis and Other
Studies in the Genius of the Franciscans* (1915); *The Capuchins: A Con-
tribution to the History of the Counter-Reformation* (1929).

In all these works, Father Cuthbert explains that in these times as
in the time of St. Francis, the inward peace and joy, true liberty and
tranquillity of mind can be found by living up to the teachings of St.
Francis. To that end, Father Cuthbert labored throughout his life and
with all his strength to restore to society the principles of discipline of St.
Francis.

He is also the author of: *Catholic Ideals in Social Life* (1905 and
1911); *A Tuscan Penitent* (1907); *God and The Supernatural* (1920);
In Christ: An Exposition of the Christian Life (1933), and *The Mystery
of the Redemption* (1939). He edited *The Capuchin Classic Series* and
wrote for many magazines.

He died of pneumonia in 1939. His body rests on the hillside overlooking the tomb of the Little Poor Man of Assisi. M. H.

Reverend James J. Daly, S.J. 1872-

The son of John and Mary (Curtis) Daly, the Reverend James J. Daly, S.J., was born in Chicago,
Illinois, in 1872, and educated there at St. Ignatius
High School and St. Ignatius College. He entered
the Jesuit novitiate in 1890. Pursuing higher stud-
ies at St. Louis University, he took his M.A. there
in 1906, one year after his ordination in St. Louis.
He began his editorial career as literary editor of
America in 1909, continuing in that capacity until
1911; from 1920 to 1924 he was assistant editor of
The Queen's Work; and with the publication of
Thought he became its literary editor till 1939.
He has taught at many Jesuit colleges and universities and is now Professor Emeritus of English at the University of Detroit. His several books
include: a *Life of St. John Berchmans;* two volumes of essays, *A Cheerful
Ascetic,* which initiated The Science and Culture Series, and *The Road
to Peace,* one of the Religion and Culture Series; a book of verse, *Boscobel
and Other Rimes,* which is pleasing, whimsical and colorful; and *The
Jesuit in Focus.* The last was written on the occasion of the 400th anniversary of the Jesuits as a tribute by one "who is so fortunate as to have
lived for fifty years in the Society of Jesus." In this valuable book he
portrays the true spirit of the Order as revealed in its Constitution and
Rules and in the Spiritual Exercises, and as manifested in the lives of
the novice, scholastic, priest and brother; slanders and misrepresentations

are refuted, persecutions and suppression are discussed dispassionately and in faultless English. The same impeccable style marks his essays, whether discussing Francis de Cordona, "the cheerful ascetic," and other interesting people, or the supernatural life, of which he conveys an understanding and appreciation as "the road to peace."

C. M. N.

Maureen Daly 1921-

Maureen Daly was born in Castlecaufield, County Tyrone, Ireland on March 15, 1921, the third of the four daughters of Joseph Desmond and Margaret Mellon (Kelly) Daly. At the age of three she came to the United States with her family to live at Fond du Lac, Wisconsin, where her father had established a business. Miss Daly attended the public grade school and St. Mary's Springs Academy there and Rosary College in Chicago, Illinois, under the Sisters of St. Dominic. While at college she majored in English and Latin, edited the *Rosary College Eagle* and wrote for a number of magazines. She began to write at sixteen "and then it was not ambition but inhibition that spurred me on," she said. She was a high school senior at the time and felt she had to put down on paper her experience of skating with a boy for the first time and "to relieve the tense, hurt feeling inside of me" because he had promised to call but never did. This story, *Sixteen,* won first prize that year in the national short story contest for high school students sponsored by *Scholastic* magazine. It was chosen by Harry Hansen to appear in the O. Henry Collection of Best Short Stories for 1938. Miss Daly was the youngest writer ever to attain this honor. It was selected as "Encore of the Month" by *Redbook* magazine; was made into a radio script and reprinted in several textbooks and anthologies.

Her first full-length novel *Seventeenth Summer* (1942) was the winner of the Dodd, Mead Intercollegiate Fellowship Award. This story deals with a boy and a girl both seventeen years old, and is told in a simple, sincere and entertaining manner. As one reviewer said: *"Seventeenth Summer* is possessed of considerable humor and a kind of sturdy common sense." Miss Daly herself said: "What I have tried to do, you see, is just write about the things that happened to me and about which I knew— things that meant a lot to me." It took nine months to write *Seventeenth Summer.* It is now (1945) in its 23rd edition.

She is extremely proud of the literary efforts of her youngest sister, Sheila who, at the age of seventeen has had over 15 short stories accepted by national magazines. Maureen has contributed to *Vogue, Mademoiselle, Cosmopolitan, Redbook* and other magazines. A collection of articles for teen-agers originally printed in the Chicago *Tribune* and other newspapers was published in 1944 under the title *Smarter and Smoother* and had gone into its ninth printing by July 1945. For three and one-half years she had written a column for young people for the Chicago *Tribune* and syndicate papers. Her first page as editor of the *Ladies' Home Journal's* "Sub-Deb" department appeared in the October 1945 issue.

Miss Daly admires particularly the works of Sigrid Undset and G. K. Chesterton.

Thomas Augustine Daly 1871-

As a young reporter, T. A. Daly delighted his friends with a story of an Italian baseball game, so well told and often repeated that he was urged to write in the same vein. *Mia Carlotta* followed, and then other verse inspired by the Italian immigrant and faithfully portraying his romantic nature, artistic sense and true nobility of character. Thus Daly became known as the "Dago poet." While a student at Fordham University from 1887 to 1889 he played short stop on the team and was one of the editors of the *Fordham Monthly* to which he contributed his first lyrics. His previous education had been received in the public schools of Philadelphia, where he was born in 1871 and at Villanova College which he attended from 1880 to 1887. He left Fordham at the conclusion of the sophomore year to take a clerical position, but he received an honorary M.A. from his Alma Mater in 1901 and an honorary Litt.D. in 1910. Notre Dame gave him an honorary degree of LL.D. in 1917 and Boston College in 1921.

His first newspaper work was with the Philadelphia *Record* as reporter and editorial writer. He then became general manager of the *Catholic Standard and Times* of Philadelphia from 1898 to 1915. Successively, columnist with the Philadelphia *Evening Ledger* and associate editor of the *Record,* he became a columnist with the *Evening Bulletin* in 1929, which position he now maintains.

In 1896 he married Nannie Barrett of Philadelphia, frequently the inspiration and subject of his verse. His "Songs of Wedlock" are testimony to his sacred regard for matrimony, of which he writes tenderly. Five sons and three daughters were born; and to his little girl, Brenda, crippled at birth, who later died, "one soul a lure for snaring three," he wrote an outstandingly beautiful poem, "To a Thrush." The bird's song is heard on that May morning when the child is born, and both prelude and epilogue begin with these lines:

> "Sing clear, O throstle,
> Thou golden-tongued apostle
> And little brown-frocked brother
> Of the loved Assisian!
> Sing courage to the mother,
> Sing strength into the man . . ."

Not only are human joys and sorrows eloquently expressed in his verse, but he also dwells on the beauties of nature, as in his twelve songs for the various months. Poems included in Joyce Kilmer's *Anthology of Catholic Poets* are "October," "The Poet," "To a Robin," "To a Plain Sweetheart" and "To a Thrush." Christopher Morley wrote an introductory letter to Thomas Daly's *Selected Poems,* published in 1936. In prose he has written *Herself and the Houseful,* an amusing story of a large family, and (with Morley) *The House of Dooner*." His dialect poems are the familiar *Canzoni, Carmina, Madrigali, McAroni Ballads* and *McAroni Medleys,* delightfully capturing all aspects of Italian immigrant life. It is an Italian word that best conveys the quality of T. A. Daly's writings; they are *simpatico.* His versification is melodious, and the constant strain is an abiding faith, with variations of tender sentiment and delightful humor.

C. M. N.

Very Reverend Martin Cyril D'Arcy, S.J.   1888-   .

One of the eminent Catholic philosophers in the world today as well as one of the most noted English-speaking Jesuits, the Very Reverend Martin Cyril D'Arcy, S.J., was born in Bath, England, in 1888. His father, Martin Valentine D'Arcy was a well-known barrister-at-law. Very Reverend Father D'Arcy attended the Jesuit College of Stonyhurst and Campion Hall, Oxford, of which latter he was made Master in 1933. The list of his honors is long: at Oxford he took first class honors in Humanities, won the Charles Oldham Prize in 1915 and the John Locke Scholarship in 1918, and received his M.A. degree in 1919 and the Green Moral Philosophy Prize in 1923. Theology he studied at the Gregorian University in Rome, where he was ordained in 1921. His Ph.D. and S.T.D. were bestowed upon him at the same university in 1926. After teaching at Stonyhurst, he was stationed at Farm Street Church, London, and became lecturer in philosophy at Oxford.

Having been invited to preach the Lenten course at Our Lady of Lourdes Church, New York City, Father D'Arcy came to the United States in 1936. While here he was much in demand as preacher and lecturer, and Georgetown University gave him the honorary degree of LL.D. In the summer of 1939 he again came to New York as a delegate to the Pax Romana Conference. Because of the war he remained through the winter of 1940. He was appointed to fill a vacancy as Dean of the Department of Philosophy at Fordham University Graduate School. And again he was much sought for in the pulpit and lecture hall. He received the honorary degree of D.Litt. from Fordham. In the latter part of 1941 he again visited the United States and remained during the early part of 1942. He is now (1947) in the United States.

A frequent contributor to periodicals such as *The Hibbert Journal, The Criterion* and *The Colosseum,* Father D'Arcy is also the author of many books on philosophical and theological subjects which reveal his brilliancy of mind and erudition. *Christian Morals* is based on a series of broadcast talks given by him, and his *Nature of Belief* even elicited praise from "the gloomy Dean" Inge.

Among Father D'Arcy's other works are *The Idea of God; Catholicism;* published in 1928, and in 1931 *God and the Universe,* a symposium. Also he wrote *The Spirit of Charity* (1929); *Mirage and Truth* (1935); *The Problem of Evil* (1922); *Thomas Aquinas* (1930); *Death and Life* (1942); and *Belief and Reason.*

As Master of Campion Hall, Father D'Arcy is one of the Heads of Colleges, an academic body that makes up the governing board of the University. Campion Hall is the first Catholic college to be affiliated as an integral school of the University of Oxford since the Reformation.

He was appointed Provincial of the English Province of the Society of Jesus, and took over the duties of his office on Thursday, August 2, 1945.

C. M. N.

Christopher Henry Dawson, 1889-

At Hartlington Hall, in Yorkshire, Christopher Dawson now makes his home. His childhood there, with his parents, Lt. Col. H. P. and Mary (Bevan) Dawson, daughter of the Archdeacon of Brecon, was steeped in religious and social tradition. He has been a student and a detached observer of life both in its contemporary phases and in the historical records of the past. Born in 1889, at Hay Castle, he was educated at Winchester, the most religious of the English public schools, and at Trinity College, Oxford. Leaving there in 1911, he studied economics with Professor Gustave Cassel in Sweden and then returned to Oxford for post-graduate studies in history and sociology.

At this time he became acquainted with the work of Ernest Troeltsch and thereafter devoted himself entirely to the study of the relation between religion and culture. He came to know the Bible thoroughly and through it "the fundamental unity of Catholic theology and the Catholic life." The early reading of the lives of the Catholic mystics and saints had greatly impressed him as did also a later visit to Rome, when he was nineteen. These various influences led him to recognize the limitations of Anglicanism, to which he had been so closely bound, and to embrace

Catholicism. He was received into the Church at St. Aloysius', Oxford, in 1914. Two years later he married Valery Mills; they have one son and two daughters.

After years of thorough study and careful preparation he published in 1928 the first of a group of five books in which he plans to cover world history: *The Age of the Gods; The Rise of the World Religions; The Making of Europe; The Breakdown of European Unity,* and *The Modern World.* The third, which he subtitles *An Introduction to the History of European Unity,* appeared in 1932; and it was translated into French by Louis Halphen in 1934. *The Age of the Gods* is a study in the origins of culture in prehistoric Europe and in the ancient East. *The Making of Europe* interestingly relates how upon the ruins of the ancient world were laid the foundations of Europe, deriving its political unity from Rome, its religious unity from the Catholic Church, its intellectual culture from the classical tradition preserved by the Church, and embracing the barbarians in its human material. The author shows how A.D. 400 to 1,000, erroneously known as the "dark ages," created the ground of all future cultural achievements. Dawson is an omnivorous reader, and in both books he makes use of the vast material provided by archeological and historical investigation and presents facts in their proper perspective, the relation of man to God. He is essentially a philosophical historian. He has a wide and deep vision, a remarkable memory and erudition.

In *Enquiries into Religion and Culture* he takes into account the organic development of European, Islamic, Indian and Chinese cultures and sees religion as the energizing influence in every sphere of human activity. This book of essays has an underlying unity in its main thesis.

The Modern Dilemma: The Problem of European Unity is one of the Essays in Order, a series of which he is a general editor. *Religion and the Modern State* considers the menace of "the organized materialism of the social state" and the necessity of reformation of the individual for the reformation of society. Communism, National Socialism or Capitalism, he says, cannot be regarded as "a final solution to the problem of civilization or even as a tolerable one." His book *The Judgment of the Nations* "nearly resembles *Religion and the Modern State* but it is longer and more important." In it he urges a world order intermediate between the single state and the world organization.

He convincingly proves that only a return to the spiritual traditions of Christianity will save civilization, for culture, having lost its spiritual roots, is dying. The Catholic Church offers a program vital to the world today. In the words of Dawson: "Today she stands as she did under the Roman Empire, as the representative in a changing world of an unchanging spiritual order. That is why I believe that the Church that made Europe may yet save Europe, and that, in the words of the great Easter liturgy, 'the whole world may experience and see what was fallen raised up, what has grown old made new, and all things returning to unity through Him from Whom they took their beginning.' "

Dawson is an outstanding figure in present-day literature. It is interesting to note that in a Sheed & Ward survey, he, more than any other European Catholic author of today, is recommended to American readers.

He is also known as a lecturer. He lectured on the Philosophy of Religion at Liverpool University, 1933 to 1934 and on the History of Culture at University College, Exeter in 1935. He also gave the British Academy annual master mind lecture in 1934, on Edward Gibbon. In 1945 he was appointed to give the Gifford lecture at Edinburgh University for 1946. Since 1940 he has, with notable success, been editor of the *Dublin Review*.

C. M. N.

Dorothy Day 1897-

In the titles of her two books *Union Square to Rome* and *House of Hospitality* is the keynote to the life of Dorothy Day. Converted from Communism to Catholicism, she has since devoted her life to providing hospitality for the poor, giving liberally of her own labors in order to shelter, feed and cheer those in need. The initial step in reaching the workingman, for whom she had had since girlhood a live sympathy, was the editing of a monthly paper, *The Catholic Worker*, sold for a penny so that through its pages the principles of social justice and a realization of the sanctity of labor could reach as many as possible. It began publication in May, 1933, and in 1946 had a circulation of 60,000. Then developed the idea of houses where those unable to buy food could be given a free meal and, if necessary, provided lodging. No questions are asked and thousands benefit by this charity as they have by her printed word.

Having no personal means, she herself relies on charity and prayer for the necessary funds to carry on, and with her co-workers practices voluntary poverty, sharing with those in need. In addition to the house in New York City, where 600 are still fed daily, in 1943 there were 32 houses of hospitality opened under the guidance of Dorothy Day, in several other states. An account of them and of the whole Catholic Worker Movement is given in *House of Hospitality*. Because many workers were drafted during World War II, its houses of hospitality were reduced to 7. There are farms in Easton, Pennsylvania; Upton, Massachusetts; one near Cleveland, Ohio, and one near Detroit, Michigan.

Her first book *From Union Square to Rome,* recounts her early years and her conversion. She was born in Brooklyn, New York, in 1897, and then with her family lived in California until the earthquake of 1906 brought them East. In Chicago she was baptized and confirmed in the Episcopal Church and educated in the public schools. She then studied at the University of Illinois from 1914 to 1916, when she came to New York and began reporting for *The New York Call*.

She joined the Socialist Party and later became a member of the

Industrial Workers of the World and then of Communist organizations. Though she did not sign up as a member of the Communist party, she became associated with the movement through her writings in radical publications. She was successively associated with *The Masses, The Liberator* and *The New Masses,* and reported for dailies in Chicago, New York, New Orleans and other cities. She gave up religion but retained her belief in God. The steps which led her into the Catholic Church are recorded in her book. She is a Benedictine Oblate.

The years following her conversion (1927) were spent in writing for periodicals and reporting in New York, California, Florida and Mexico. In 1933 she came to New York and with the aid of Peter Maurin undertook the Catholic Worker Movement, with which she is still identified.

C. M. N.

Reverend Henry Day, S.J.   1865-

Although busily engaged in preaching, Father Henry Day has found time to write eight books.

He was born on the 29th of May, 1865, the seventh son of the late Right Honorable Sir John Charles Day, Judge of the High Court. His early education was received at Beaumont College, Old Windsor, Berkshire, England. From there he entered the Society of Jesus in 1884 and was ordained in 1894.

For the first twenty years of his priesthood, he was actively engaged in the Lancashire missions, and was successively on the staff of St. John's, Wigan, St. Francis Xavier, Liverpool, and the Holy Name, Manchester.

His sermons on "Christianity and Socialism," "Modern Unbelief and Feminism," attracted much attention at the time and through them he received invitations to address non-Catholic audiences.

When the war broke out in 1914, Father Day volunteered for active service and was one of the first Catholic chaplains to be accepted and sent to the front. He served in Egypt, Gallipoli, Macedonia, and France. He was decorated with the Serbian White Eagle, was mentioned in dispatches and was awarded the Military Cross. For a few years after the war, he continued to be associated with the army as territorial chaplain.

From 1921 on he has been active on the missionary staff of the English Province of the Society of Jesus.

His publications are: *Marriage, Divorce and Morality* (1912); *Catholic Democracy, Individualism, and Socialism* (1914); *A Cavalry Chaplain* (1922); *The New Morality* (1924); *The Love Story of the Little Flower* (1927); *Macedonian Memories* (1930); *On a Troopship to India* (1937), and *An Army Chaplain's War Memories* (1937).   M. H.

Roy Joseph Deferrari   1890-

Doctor Deferrari is a firm supporter of the papal desire that Catholics have their education under Church auspices, even at the graduate level. He declares that, "while the Catholic may, through his previous Catholic training, develop under non-Catholic teachers a sound, scholarly mind in many fields of study, nevertheless Catholic surroundings are almost necessary for the development of a sound research specialist in any field. The search for truth in all its ramifications is nothing more than the study of life—past, present, and future— and in all this the Church is intimately concerned; and while the Church does not and cannot contradict truth, it does and must contradict the false under the guise of truth. Falsehood of this kind, in greater or less degree, often in a most subtle manner, is scattered throughout all fields of knowledge. Hence the necessity for the guiding hand of the Church in every phase of graduate study, in the training of the student in methods of research."

Roy J. Deferrari was born in Stoneham, Massachusetts, June 1, 1890. His parents were Augustino and Mary Crovo Deferrari. He is an alumnus of Dartmouth College, class of 1912. His A.M. was obtained in 1913, his Ph.D. in 1915, at Princeton. In 1939 Providence College bestowed on him an LL.D. His marriage to Evelyn Mary Biggi took place December 30, 1920. They have two children, Austin John and Mary Evelyn.

Doctor Deferrari has been successful both as a scholar and as an administrator. Classical philology has been his field of research and he has written many articles, pamphlets and books concerning it. As a reviewer of books in the field, his opinions are much in demand. He has been editor of the sixty-five volumes of Catholic University Patristic Studies, of the ten volumes of Catholic University Studies in Mediaeval and Renaissance Latin, and of the five volumes of Catholic University Classical Studies. The American Council of Learned Societies in 1943 authorized a grant of $500.00 to the scholar to prepare a Latin-English lexicon of the works of St. Thomas Aquinas.

At Princeton he was an instructor in Classics from 1915 to 1917. During the first World War he served as instructor in military studies at the Princeton University Ground School. In 1917 he became associate professor of Classics at Catholic University, and has been affiliated with the University ever since. In 1922 he was made Professor of Greek and Latin. During these years, until administration claimed too much of his time, he also gave advanced Latin courses at Trinity College. His career as administrator started in 1931 when he was appointed Dean of the Graduate School of Arts and Sciences. In 1937 he was given the offices of Secretary-General and of Director of the Summer Session. He edited, in

1940, *Vital Problems of Catholic Education in the United States,* and in 1941, *Catholic Education in the United States,* to which he contributed an essay on "Origin and Development of Graduate Studies under Catholic Auspices." He has commended the magnificent job Catholics have done in the field of education, but has not hesitated to point out weaknesses at certain levels, viz., the pre-school child, the junior college, training schools for elementary school teachers, and university support. A diocesan training school for nuns with a faculty drawn from all the orders is a solution he has suggested for the problem of elementary teacher training.

The influence of Catholics in the intellectual life of the country is not at all in keeping with their numbers and their ability, according to Doctor Deferrari. He believes that concentration, for the time being, of all our efforts on one university would help to correct this disproportion. He is particularly interested in Catholic educational development at the university level for, "History reveals that every anti-religious movement of the last few centuries has come through some university campus. The counter-tide must be through the same channels. The most insidious perils to faith and morals lie in the intellectual world when pride wells up in men whose learning is not tempered by faith."

In 1946 Professor Deferrari, with 26 other American educators, was received by Emperor Hirohito of Japan.

He is the author of: *Selections from Roman Historians* (1916); *A First Latin Book for Catholic Schools* (1921); *The Letters of Saint Basil,* 4 vols., (1926-1934); *Concordance of Prudentius* (1931); *A Concordance of Ovid* (1939); *A Concordance of Lucan* (1940), and *A Concordance of Statius* (1941).

         M. S.

Joseph Peter de Fonseka   1897-

As one of the best known writers east of Suez, Joseph Peter de Fonseka has been a contributor to the press of Ceylon, both secular and Catholic for over twenty-five years.

The conviction that his life's work is journalism has made his output impressive in volume as well as varied in range and interest. Known in Ceylon as the "Chesterton of Ceylon" he has been described in the magazine *Month* as the Douglas Woodruff of the Island.

A native of Ceylon (Singhalese),—having been born there in 1897—he is one of a noted family whose members held important offices in the Portuguese, Dutch and British administrations of the ancient island of Ceylon. Generations of his forbears held the post of Mudaliyars (Chieftains of the People). His name is a Singhalese variation of the Portuguese surname, familiar in the Iberian peninsula as "de Fonseca." It is indicative of an adherence to the Catholic Faith about four or five centuries old, since the Portuguese in those times were in the habit of giving their family names to their converts.

De Fonseka was educated at St. Joseph's College, Colombo and at London University. From the latter institution, in 1927, he was awarded a Master of Arts degree in the faculty of Medieval and Modern Languages. From 1927 to 1931 he remained in England and became associated with G. K. Chesterton, for whose genius and personality he had a great admiration and whom he claims as one of the guiding forces of his life. During these years he did considerable work in Fleet Street and contributed to Chesterton's *G. K.'s Weekly*. He also took part in the activities of the Distributist school of political and social regeneration connected with the names of Chesterton and Hilaire Belloc. While in England he made the acquaintance of a wide circle of writers which includes E. V. Lucas, Robert Lynd, Walter de la Mare, Sir Philip Gibbs, John Galsworthy, Sir John Squire and Humbert Wolfe.

One of the best informed authorities on the life and work of G. K. Chesterton, he edited in 1929 a collection of thirty-seven of Chesterton's prefaces under the title of *G.K.C. as M.C.* and a book of the same writer's essays called *Come To Think Of It,* in 1930.

Since 1931 de Fonseka has lectured in English at St. Joseph's College, Colombo and has given much time to writing for the press. For six years he has contributed a weekly article to the *Ceylon Catholic Messenger* which Francis J. Sheed has described as an astonishingly high level periodical. Several of his articles appeared in America's *Catholic Digest.*

In Ceylon, de Fonseka was co-founder and co-editor of the monthly paper called *Social Justice,* which gained many readers by its brilliant presentation of the social theory of the Papal encyclicals and received praise from many Catholic authorities abroad. He is also a principal contributor to the *New Review,* the Jesuit monthly of India.

A series of which de Fonseka is especially proud has been his articles which gave a journalistic slant on the New Testament. As a lecturer he recently drew attention by "preaching a layman's sermon" to the professors and students of the Papal Seminary which was reproduced in the Ceylon *Clergy Monthly.*

On December 23, 1946 he was appointed a Chamberlain of Honour of the Sword and Cape to His Holiness Pope Pius XII.

M. H.

Richard Dehan (Clotilde Graves) 1863-1932

The playwright, journalist, and novelist Clotilde Graves, who wrote under the pen name of Richard Dehan, was born at Barracks, Buttevant, Co. Cork, Ireland, on June 3, 1863. She was the third daughter of the late Major W. H. Graves, 18th Royal Irish Regiment, and Antoinette (Deane) Graves. She was educated at the Convent at Lourdes and studied art. To support her parents she played small parts on the stage and drew for comic papers. In 1896 she was received into the Catholic Church. Sixteen of her plays were produced in London and New York between 1887 and 1913. Richard Dehan was a born story-teller.

Her novel, *Between Two Thieves* (1912), is a story of the Crimean War. The "two thieves" are Louis Napoleon and a British contractor. Although the author apparently wishes to inculcate the lesson of the abounding mercy of the Saviour, the novel is an example of offensive realism that ill becomes a Catholic writer. The *Dop Doctor* (1910) is a terribly real novel of the Boer War and was reprinted thirty times. In the United States, it was published under the title *One Braver Thing.* *Eve of Pascua* (1920) is a collection of sixteen short stories, of which the first gives its title to the volume. The stories range from the tragic to the farcial. *The Lovers of the Market Place* (1928) describes the English scene as it was in the 'seventies. *The Pipers of the Market Place* (1924) is known for its fine delineation of character. It is a story of the sacrifices a mother makes for her children's future in loyalty to her worthless husband.

Other books by Clotilde Graves are: *The Lovers' Battle* (1902); *The Headquarter Recruit* (1913); *The Cost of Wings* (1914); *The Man of Iron* (1914); *Off Sandy Hook* (1915); *Earth to Earth* (1916); *Under the Hermés* (1917); *That Which Hath Wings* (1918); *A Sailor's Home* (1919); *The Villa of the Peacock* (1921); *The Just Steward* (1922); *The Sower of the Wind* (1927); *Shallow Seas* (1930); *The Man in the Mask* (1931), and *Dead Pearls* (1932). She wrote the following plays: *Nitocris* (1887); *The Drury Lane Pantomime Puss in Boots* (1888); *Dr. and Mrs. Neill* (1894); *A Mother of Three* (1896); *A Matchmaker* (1896); *The Bishop's Eye* (1900); *A Maker of Comedies* (1903); *The Bond of Ninon* (1906), and *A Tenement Tragedy* (1907).

After a long illness, Clotilde Graves died in Middlesex, England on December 3, 1932.

M. H.

Michael de la Bedoyere 1900-

An ancestral mixture of French and English seems to produce literary talent. Michael de la Bedoyere is an excellent example of this. His parentage is three-quarters British, one-quarter French (of the Breton nobility). And his British inheritance ran to Anglican bishops and political wits. He is the grandson (on his mother's side) of Dr. Anthony Wilson Thorold, successively Anglican bishop of Rochester and Winchester. He is the great-nephew of Right Honorable Henry Labouchere, P.C., Victorian statesman, journalist and wit. He is the nephew of Algar Labouchere Thorold, a convert to the Church, who for many years was Editor of the *Dublin Review*.

De la Bedoyere was educated at Stonyhurst College, whence he entered the Society of Jesus. He remained there for some years until he decided he did not fit because he had neither the health nor the vocation. He took his degrees with first class honors in politics, philosophy and economics at Oxford, and then taught for a year (from 1930 to 1931) at the University of Minnesota. Until 1935 his principle literary work was devoted to the study of modern political theories and experiments in the light of Catholic teaching, and his attitude largely was to insist that Catholics must be active as Catholics, in the world in which they live, in their citizenship, culture, business, loyalties, without, however, falling into the trap of sectarianism. "They must not divide their lives into a Sunday compartment which is religious and a weekday compartment which is secularist." He also has tended to emphasize the weakness of the democracies, which has led some critics to consider him too friendly to the enemies of democracy, though there is nothing explicit in what he has written to justify this criticism. This emphasis, however, goes with a strong defense of radical social reform.

In 1935 de la Bedoyere became closely associated with the re-foundation of the *Catholic Herald,* an established Catholic weekly which had fallen on evil days and had been bought by a group of young men who wished to publish a paper primarily interested in the Catholic attitude on secular matters rather than ecclesiastical news. In April, 1936, he became its editor, and he has succeeded in making the influence of the *Herald* widely felt. But the pressure of editing a weekly paper has cut down his output in other fields. Yet he views this preoccupation with day-to-day affairs as an excellent preparation for future books on the relationship between the Christian outlook and our contemporary secularist civilization. Much of the paper is written by Mr. de la Bedoyere himself. In private life farming and painting provide for him a valuable balance to thinking, speaking and writing.

In 1930 Mr. de la Bedoyere married his first cousin, Catherine Thorold, the daughter of Algar Thorold. They have five children.

His books are: *The Drift of Democracy* (his first published work) (1931); *Catholicism and the Modern Mind; Lafayette: A Revolutionary Gentleman; George Washington: An English Judgment; Society:* in *European Civilization, its Origin and Development* (Vol. V); *A Catholic Looks at the World; Christian Crisis* (1940); *Christianity in the Market Place* (1943), and *No Dreamers Weak* (1945).   H. B.

Reverend Selden Peabody Delany   1874-1935

After thirty years in the Anglican ministry the Reverend Selden P. Delany became a Catholic priest. The difficulties and doubts of the years he devoted to God's service in the Anglo-Catholic Church are related in *Why Rome?* The book was written while he was still an Anglican, and he determined to make no change in his ecclesiastical position until he had finally resolved his doubts. "From the very beginning of my ministry," he said, "I have suffered qualms of conscience on the subject of the papacy." Writing in order to clarify his own mind, he proceeded step by step to his final argument in favor of the Petrine claims and the invalidity of Anglican orders. The last was most difficult to accept, but he found consolation in Father Woodlock's *Constantinople, Canterbury and Rome* and realized that "the work for souls God had performed through my ministry has been real." Unwilling to hurt those who had trusted him, he ministered to them as long as he conscientiously could and then sought to carry on his work for souls as a Catholic priest.

"Nothing in my life has been harder," he wrote, "than to part company with my many friends." He had indeed a genius for friendship, as was said of him by Monsignor Joseph McMahon who received him into the Catholic Church in 1930. He was then fifty-six years old, for he had been born in 1874 in Fond du Lac, Wisconsin. In his childhood he was a Presbyterian, but while in his junior year at Harvard he took a course in early Christian history and thus came to know of the apostolic ministry. This and association with his High Church Episcopalian classmates influenced him in becoming confirmed by the Episcopal Bishop of Massachusetts and, deciding he had a vocation for the priesthood, he went to the Western Theological Seminary in Chicago after taking his A.B. at Harvard in 1896. He was ordained to the Episcopal ministry in 1899. Thereafter he served churches in Roxbury, Massachusetts; Menasha, Appleton and Milwaukee, Wisconsin, and finally New York City, where he assisted his very good friend, Dr. Barry, at the church of St. Mary the Virgin. He succeeded him as rector there in 1929. During the preceding eleven years he was editor of the *American Church Monthly,* and he wrote *Difficulties of Faith, The Value of Confession* and *The Parish Priest*. He held back from the "heroic adventure" of marriage, thinking that some day he might want to become a Catholic priest. And this sacrifice bore fruit when despite his years he was permitted to study for the priesthood at the Collegio Beda, Rome, where he was ordained in 1934.

He then returned to America. Ill health made parochial duties difficult and he was appointed chaplain at the convent of the Religious of Jesus and Mary, at Highland Mills, New York. On July 5, 1935, a brief time after ordination, he died in New York City.

Rome from Within gives Father Delany's impressions of the Church after five years as a Catholic. Another book, *Married Saints*, for which he gathered material during three summers in England, was published posthumously. It admirably illustrates that sanctity may be attained in the married state as well as in a life of celibacy, and includes many eminent for piety and virtue not yet enrolled in the Calendar of Saints. Especially interesting are chapters on Lucie Felix-Faure Goyau (1866-1913), Elizabeth Arrighi Leseur (1866-1914) and three Italian apostles of Catholic Action: the lawyer Giambattista Paganuzzi (1830-1910); the professor of economics, Giuseppe Toniolo (1845-1918); and the physician, Ludovico Necchi (1876-1930). Father Delany thus brings the lesson of sanctity close to our own times when it is so greatly needed.

C. M. N.

Reverend Hippolyte Delehaye, S.J. 1859-1941

A fellow Jesuit described the life of Father Delehaye, the renowned hagiographer, as one long uninterrupted succession of days devoted to writing and research.

Hippolyte Delehaye was born at Antwerp, Belgium, in the year, 1859. He was educated there, at Louvain and at Innsbruck. In 1876 he entered the Society of Jesus and was ordained in 1890.

On the completion of his studies at Louvain and Innsbruck he became a member of the staff of St. Michael's College, Belgium. In 1886, while at St. Michael's College, he wrote his first published historical study on Henry of Ghent in the *Messager des sciences historiques,* of Ghent.

His work on the *Analecta Bollandiana,* the quarterly review of the Bollandists began in 1888. Three years later he became associated with the editors of La Societé des Bollandistes (Acta Sanctorum).

Father Delehaye spent his life as a member of the Society of Bollandists, of which he was president, in hagiographic research. Besides making inventories and catalogues of manuscripts for the use of hagiographers he also wrote monographs on the lives of the saints.

The first World War, 1914-1918, interrupted the work of the Bollandists. Father Delehaye was among those imprisoned by the Germans when they invaded Belgium. When the war was over, there was only one other collaborator to reorganize the work. It was at this time that he became president of the Bollandist Society; he held this office until his death on April 1, 1941. He is remembered for his scholarly work and his helpfulness to others.

Among his writings are: *Cinq leçons sur la methode hagiographique,* a helpful book for a beginner in hagiography; *Legendes hagiographiques* (1905). Some chapters of this study first appeared in the *Revue des Questions historiques* (July 1903). The second edition, except for two or three unimportant changes, is a reprint of the first edition. It was the second edition that was translated into English by Virginia M. Crawford in 1907. The purpose of this book is "to indicate briefly the spirit in which hagiographic texts should be studied, to lay down the rules for discriminating between the materials that the historian can use and those that he should hand over as their natural property to artists and poets, to place people on their guard against the fascination of formulas and preconceived systems." Delehaye's life of *St. John Berchman's* was translated from the French by Henry C. Temple in 1921. *The Work of the Bollandists* was published by the Princeton University Press in 1922.

Other works are: *Origines du Culte des Martyrs* (2nd ed.) (1933); *Les Saints Stylites* (1923); *Les légendes grecques des saints militaires* (1909); *Les versions grecques des actes des martyres persans sous Sapor II* (1905). Father Delehaye achieved fame for his *Propylaeum ad acta Sanctorum Novembris* in which he published the abridged collection of the lives of the saints of the Church of Constantinople. He also edited in full for the first time in 1902 the *Synaxarium Ecclesiae Constantinopolitanae.*

His native country Belgium made him a member of L'Académie Royale de Belgique and a like honor was conferred upon him by France and England in nominating him to the Institut de France and the British Academy, respectively.   M. H.

Raoul de Roussy de Sales (Jean Jacques François) 1896-1942

Although he could trace his ancestry back nine hundred years among the French and Spanish aristocracy, the late Raoul de Roussy de Sales, Chevalier of the Legion of Honor, never publicly used his title of "Count," a fact which may be considered symbolical of his intense realistic devotion to France as a modern nation, then fighting for its life and its freedom.

Son of Count Jean and Countess Rose Lily (Rheims) de Roussy de Sales, Raoul was born in Paris, March 5, 1896. His death in New York, December 3, 1942, closed a short life packed with activity. After his student days in Paris and England, he promptly followed his literary bent by contributing literary and musical criticism to

French and British papers. He served with the American Red Cross in France during the first World War, and from 1922 to 1931 was assistant general secretary of the League of Red Cross Societies.

In 1932 de Roussy de Sales came to the United States as a representative of *Revue de Paris*, and two years later he became correspondent for *Paris-Midi* and *Paris-Soir;* his despatches to the latter paper were signed "Jacques Fransales." In 1936 he was appointed American correspondent for *l'Europe Nouvelle*, and in 1937 he was named chief diplomatic correspondent for the Havas News Agency, whereupon Washington became the scene of his principal activities, theretofore carried on in New York. His connection with Havas ended with the Nazi occupation of Paris. Meanwhile he served as president of the Association of Foreign Press Correspondents in the United States from 1937 through 1939, and for "outstanding services" was made a life member of that Association. In 1936 he had received the Strassburger Award, with the citation that his writings had promoted French-American friendship.

In addition to his work as a correspondent, de Roussy de Sales contributed regularly to the *Atlantic Monthly* and to the New York *Times*, and lectured extensively throughout the United States. Doubtless the fact that he had an American grandmother, and the fact that he married an American—the former Reine Marie Melanie Tracy, by whom he had one son—contributed to the growth of an unbounded and affectionate admiration for this country, and led to that intensive study of the American social and political structure which, says the New York *Times*, "helped to shape his own democratic way of thinking." He was one of the contributors to a book entitled *You Americans*.

Upon the temporary conquest of France, he turned all his energies to opposing the subservient Vichy regime and to urging French resistance to the Nazis. He became Chancellor of the Fighting French Delegation to this country. He edited *They Speak For A Nation*, a collection of letters from French men and women of all classes, revealing their reactions to the national disaster. He also edited, from the verbose mass of Hitler's speeches, a volume entitled *My New Order*, exposing the brutality of Nazi ideology. But de Sales' fame rests chiefly on his book *The Making of Tomorrow* (published in the Spring of 1942) which Wilson Follett in the *Atlantic Monthly* described as "an attempt, shrewd and in some of its aperçus, profound, to analyze the elements of the world situation that are fundamentally new." Charles Willis Thompson wrote in *The Catholic World:* "In a literary style most vivid, graceful and enthralling, M. de Sales expounds with great force, ideas that are not always well-founded, but are always arresting and commanding." Let the author speak for himself in the last words of his book: "We believe that a world is in the making before our eyes. The aims for which we toil seem very distant and sometimes dim, but we know that there is no hope of reaching them except through victory."

Raoul de Roussy de Sales carried on his many activities while engaged in an almost lifelong fight against chronic illness. His publisher, Curtice Hitchcock, called him "a really great person," in whom were blended "ironic wit, clarity of vision and of expression, wide information, and charm of manner." S. O.

Monica Enid Dickens 1915-

Monica Enid Dickens is the great-granddaughter of Charles Dickens, the famous novelist. She was born in May, 1915, in London, the daughter of Henry Charles Dickens, a barrister-at-law and Fanny (Runge) Dickens. When she was seven years of age she went to the Norland Place School in Holland Park where she stayed till she was thirteen. Having won a scholarship for St. Paul's Girls School in London, she went there until she was eighteen. Then she journeyed to Paris to study French, dressmaking and cooking. In the same year in which she was presented (1935), she attended Miss Fogerty's dramatic school but was expelled because she was "unable to act." Finally she decided to take a job as cook-general, deeming herself as unqualified for any other occupation. "I had about a dozen jobs within a year," she writes, "until I met a man from a publishing office who was amused by the idea and said, 'Why not write a book about it?' I had never written a word, so it was his risk." President Cass Canfield of Harper Brothers announced he had bought the book *One Pair of Hands* because he said, "She has an easy pen and the same interest in the lower half of the people, that Dickens is so well known for."

At the beginning of World War II, Miss Dickens wrote her first novel, *Mariana,* published in the United States as *The Moon Was Low.* Then she entered the King Edward VIIth Hospital, Windsor, as a probationer-nurse in training. Upon the completion of her first year of training she got an urge to write about her experiences. "After one or two chapters," she writes, "I saw that it would never do for me to be still there when the book was published, so I left." When this book *One Pair of Feet,* was finished Miss Dickens went into a government training school for engineering. In December, 1942 she got a job as an aero-inspector at Sunbeam Talbot's Limited, No. Kensington, London.

In January, 1943 she completed another novel called *Edward's Fancy,* a story of life in war-time England. *The Happy Prisoner* appeared in 1947. She says "I never want to be anything else but an author," and gives these reasons: "First, one works in one's own time, and then an author is never lonely. One makes all sorts of friends, some of whom one never sees. I have many pen-friends in the States and in Canada." Miss Dickens visited the United States once and is anxious to return. Besides contributing articles to the Sunday *Chronicle,* London, she also writes scripts for the British Broadcasting Company.

In generalizing about her life she writes, "My parents are the most understanding and amusing couple I know. I cannot imagine being enough in love with anyone to want to leave home."

M. H.

Reverend Ernest Dimnet 1866-

One of the few Frenchmen to attain literary distinction by his writings in English, Abbé Ernest Dimnet has contributed to English and American reviews since 1899 and has written several popular books. He was born in 1866 at Trelon, in the Ardennes, which is close to the Channel and the Belgian border. There he owns a little house, from which he had to flee before the German invasion in 1914 and again in 1940. In a letter to the New York *Times* he vividly described the "endless column of misery" on the roads of Northern France in May, 1940.

Dimnet was educated at Cambrai Cathedral School and Theological Seminary, at Lille University and the Sorbonne. He was ordained priest in 1893 and became professor at Douai (when the English Benedictines were there), and later at Lille University and the College Stanislas, Paris, where he taught English literature, 1902 to 1923. Meanwhile he was French correspondent of the *Pilot* (1899 to 1903), the *North American Review* (1904 to 1909) and the *Saturday Review* (from 1909 on). He received an honorary doctorate from Lille and was made honorary Canon of Cambrai in 1920. He had been invited to give the Lowell Lectures in Boston, Massachusetts, in 1919, and was the representative of France at the Williamstown Institute of Politics in 1923. Since then he has come annually to America to renew his many friendships and to lecture.

In Paris he occupied a flat with the Abbé Bremond until the death of the latter in 1933. There, among his associates of the early twentieth century, was Tyrrell, with whom a strong sympathy and friendship sprang up. Modernism, of which Tyrrell was an exponent, was condemned in 1907 in the encyclical, "Pascendi," and in the same year a book Dimnet had written, *La Pensée Catholique dans l'Angleterre Contemporaine,* was placed on the Index. It has long been out of print and the Abbé refers to it as a "religious inventory," after which he "felt happy and secure" in his religion. His real interest, he says, is in religious psychology and he has "never written a word that can be called theological."

In 1910 he published *Les Soeurs Bronté* which was translated into English by Louise M. Sill in 1927, and is highly esteemed in the history of literature. *Figures de Moines* was crowned by the French Academy in 1908. An English firm contracted for *France Herself Again,* which appeared prophetically on the eve of the first World War. It was the success of this book that induced the President of Harvard, in October 1919, to invite Abbé Dimnet to give a series of Lowell Lectures. His most successful book is *The Art of Thinking,* based on notes made over a period of fifteen years, on how an article set his mind working. He added memoranda and in 1924 outlined four lectures on the *Art of Thinking.* The book was written in 1927, but difficulties in obtaining a publisher post-poned its appearance until 1928. It became a best seller, and twelve years later elicited letters to the author expressing appreciation.

In a somewhat reflective mood, *My Old World* recounts his early years. *My New World* relates events of the twentieth century. It teems with interesting people and incidents in Paris before the War, the War itself and after-years in America. Both are autobiographical. An engaging style distinguishes all Dimnet's books, and personal charm as well as a delightful mind make him a popular lecturer.

In 1945 Abbé Dimnet again came to the United States. Upon his arrival, aboard a Pan-American Airways clipper at La Guardia Field, he stated that he had been unable to write anything during the five years in Nazi occupied France. Another visit was made in 1947.   C. M. N.

Enid Dinnis   1873-1942

Having "made the discovery that the Church is a living reality, not a fancy name for a school of morality," Enid Dinnis, born in London in 1873, daughter of an Anglican clergyman, was "received into the City set on a Hill" in 1897. She was in-structed by Canon Fleming of St. Mary's, Moor-fields, and then spent several months in Belgium, at the Ursuline convent at Thildonck, where she was further grounded in the Faith and so well absorbed Catholine truth and doctrine that she was taken for an "old Catholic." Returning to England in 1898, she contributed light articles and *vers de société* to *Punch* for about ten years, keeping strictly to a secular line of writing. Her first religious poem was published in *The Dublin* in 1909. Many others followed. Thereafter she gave her pen to "the only thing worth writing and singing about," the supernatural, of which "to the convert, Catholicism presents itself as the embodiment."

Her first book was *Mr. Coleman, Gent.* (1914), which deals with the Popish Plot of Titus Oates. Other historical novels are *The Three Roses,* the story of King Henry VI, saint and peace-maker, and *Bess of Cobb's Hill,* portraying the humble serving maid, Elizabeth Barton, as God's instrument. In the weaving of historical fact into fiction she successfully combats much false history.

The supernatural is combined with a touch of realism in the short stories for which she is especially known. The first collection was *God's Fairy Tales,* which had appeared in magazines, as did many of her writ-ings before their publication in book form. Then appeared the book, *Mystics All,* to the whimsical title of which she attributed the designation of mysticism that has been misapplied to her writing. Monsignor Hugh Benson's stories had suggested to her the vehicle for such flights of the imagination as are contained in this and the subsequent books, *Once*

Upon Eternity, More Mystics, and many others. A rare spiritual quality characterizes all her stories, and they are in great part inspired by her early association with the poor, her father having moved to an East End parish when she was three. In the simple and humble she recognized souls touched by the special grace of God, seeing His hand in all things. From the Middle Ages she drew material for *The Anchorhold* and *The Shepherd of Weepingwold. Meadowsweet and Thyme* is a volume of verse.

Living near Richmond, in a pleasant suburb on the Thames, she made a hobby of librarian work in a Catholic library. She died in November, 1942 at the age of sixty-nine. C. M. N.

Edward Doherty 1890-

"Anybody can write ninety per cent of the stories you see in the newspapers. You don't have to have an education for that. You simply tell the facts. But don't you write that way, kid. You be different. You write human interest stuff, and you'll be somebody some day. There's tragedy, pathos, humor, or belly laughs in most everything that happens. If you haven't put them in your story, you haven't told the story. You're just another hack reporter, and there are too many hacks in the game now." Thus Ambrose Breece, the Criminal Courts reporter of the Chicago *City Press,* remarked to the six-dollar-a-week copy boy Eddie Doherty. Eddie Doherty followed the advice of his tutor so well that he was once offered thirty-nine thousand dollars a year, and was advertised as the "Star Reporter of America."

Edward Doherty is the eldest son of Police Lieutenant Edward Doherty and Ellen Rodgers. He was born in Chicago in 1890 and was one of ten children, five boys and five girls. He graduated from St. Viator's school when he was twelve. He wished to be a priest, and in January 1914 entered the Servite monastery at Granville, Wisconsin. "The Sisters in the school, the priests I served at the altar, my parents, my brothers, all the rowdy kids I 'palled' with tried to dissuade me. But they couldn't." He enjoyed his days at Granville, but after two years he left, with the blessing of the Father General of the Order.

After he left the seminary he went to business school for a year. He worked as a stenographer for a chain store firm, and then as a timekeeper in a boiler shop. He hated being shut up in an office all day. He wished to be a newspaperman; finally his father got him a job with the *City Press.*

He advanced from copy boy to the switchboard, and then on to be a night police reporter. His salary, too, advanced from six dollars a week to twelve. After three years at the *City Press* he went to the Chicago *Examiner,* then the *Record-Herald,* and later to *the* newspaper of

Chicago, the Chicago *Tribune*. He left the *Tribune* for the *Herald* where he spent two years at the rewrite desk. Next he tried an afternoon paper, the *American*. Here he wrote his first column, *Atoms and Items*. He wrote another for the Saturday funny section, *Up and Down*. His pay check was up to forty dollars.

In December 1914 he married Marie Ryan, his childhood sweetheart. Their son, Edward junior was born July 11, 1917. On July 18, Edward senior went before the examining board of the second army officers' corps and took the physical and mental tests. He passed with flying colors, but was turned down when it became known that he had a week-old son. The war was over for him; gone his hopes of reporting in France. In the fall of 1918 Marie Doherty died of influenza. Much embittered by his wife's death; he drifted from the Church.

Afterwards, when he returned to work, he found many changes. The paper had hired four women reporters. One of these was Mildred Frisby. She and Edward Doherty were married in a minister's home in the summer of 1919. Their son, John James was born in April 1920 and baptized in St. Viator's Church. Edward Doherty has dedicated his autobiography, *Gall and Honey* to Marie and Mildred, the two women who meant so much in his life.

He helped to establish the Joseph Medill School of Journalism. He was working for the Chicago *Tribune* again; one of the few men it ever reemployed. Many newspapermen were taught to write by older members of the staff. "Department stores had schools for their clerks. Many big corporations had begun training their employees for better jobs. Why couldn't the Chicago *Tribune* start a school for its reporters? That night I wrote a note to J. N. Patterson, suggesting he create such a school. He answered immediately. 'Dear Mr. Doherty. Regarding your idea of a school of journalism for Chicago *Tribune* men. Go and do it.' " The *Tribune* gave him a bonus of a thousand dollars for the school idea.

Shortly after the birth of his son he decided to go to Mexico to work for the Tampico *Tribune,* the only English paper in Mexico.

Mexico lost its charm for him when his son contracted scarlet fever, and he returned to the United States. A short time later the Chicago *Tribune* opened a news bureau at Hollywood and placed him in charge. His wife started to write a column "Hollywood Society" under the name "Mildred Spain." After three years in the West the Dohertys' went to New York. She became a movie critic. In 1927 he was put on the staff of *Liberty* magazine at a salary of $17,500. He wrote articles, fiction stories and serials. He took three trips abroad to secure stories for *Liberty*. On one trip he interviewed Mussolini. He returned to Hollywood and wrote for RKO and Columbia. By this time *Liberty* had become a MacFadden magazine. The editor, Fulton Oursler, made a contract with Doherty for fifteen stories a year. He wrote in all over a thousand articles for *Liberty,* a record probably unexcelled. He was likewise a reporter on the Chicago *Sun* (until 1946). He intends to enter public relations.

While with *Liberty* he was sent to Detroit to see Father Coughlin. Doherty made a bargain to start going to church again in return for an interview. He could not return to the sacraments because of his marriage outside the church. Then a *Liberty* reader suggested that he write a story about Martin de Porres. After the article, *Hurrying Heaven,* appeared he was given a relic of Blessed Martin. Mrs. Doherty became very much interested in the Dominican lay brother and read all she could find about him. "She'd ask to take the relic, and she'd leave me for half an hour or more at a time, to come back with heaven in her eyes." "Someday," she promised, "we'll be married in the Church, but first I want to be baptized, to be a Catholic—if I can." An accident, a fall of only eight feet, in the California hills in 1939 killed her before she kept her promise. In 1943 he married the Baroness Catherine de Hueck, the founder of Friendship House, in Harlem, New York.

He wrote the screen story of the five Sullivan brothers, lost at sea when the Juneau was sunk. He is likewise the author of: *The Rain Girl; The Saint of Paralytics; Gall and Honey; The Murders on the Roof; The Shackled Cinderella; Splendor of Sorrow,* and *The Pied Piper of Peru* (1945). *My Russian Wife* was written from September to December 1946 at Combermere, Ontario where Friendship House has its training center for new staff workers.   M. S.

Reverend Martin W. Doherty 1899-

When *The House on Humility Street* was published in 1943 and attracted favorable attention, especially among priests who had been students at the North American College in Rome, there were those who believed that a new Catholic author had suddenly appeared on the literary horizon. The name of the Reverend Martin W. Doherty of Gervais, Oregon, became significant and what was considered his initial effort as a writing man, augured well for the future.

But the assumption of Father Doherty's admirers was wrong. This priest was not a new author although *The House on Humility Street* was his first published book. He had been writing for publication since those days when, fresh from his high school studies at DePaul Academy, Chicago, he took his first job as a copy boy on the Chicago *Herald* and a city editor named Walter Washburne discovered that the big blond boy he had hired to run errands in the news room not only had a keen sense of humor but could set down his observations in a way that made them newspaper features of the sort a lot of people liked to read.

From then on until young Doherty entered St. Viator's College at Bourbonnais, Illinois, a feature by "Marty the Copy Boy" appeared almost daily in the Chicago *Herald*. "Marty at the Ball Game," "Marty at the Turkish Bath," "Marty Takes a Bus Ride"—these are samples of the fare with which "Marty" Doherty entertained a large audience of Chicago readers over a considerable period.

Marty's particular branch of Clan-na-Doherty was by no means unknown throughout Chicago newspaper circles. Marty was the son of James Edward and Ellen (Rodgers) Doherty, the former a police lieutenant who had won honors back when the Haymarket riots made the first page of every big newspaper in America.

Martin was one of the younger members of a large family, having been born in Chicago on July 24, 1899. He gave fine promise of giving additional luster to the journalistic tradition of the Doherty family, but down in his soul the fires of a priestly vocation were burning.

That is why, despite the prestige he achieved at an early age, he left his newspaper job and went to St. Viator's College. But as so often happens, he began to have doubts about his vocation before he had completed his classical studies. As a result he returned to Chicago and joined the reportorial staff of *The Evening Post* where his old mentor, Walter Washburne, had become city editor after the *Herald* became extinct.

Again Marty Doherty began to write for the information and entertainment of the Chicago public, although the idea of priesthood persisted in his mind. From the *Post* he went to the *Herald-Examiner* and then to the *Tribune* where he was assigned to the East Chicago Avenue police station as a police reporter.

After making up his mind definitely that he could become a priest, he went to St. Mary's College, Kentucky, where he brushed up his philosophy and taught at the same time. Then he entered St. Paul's Seminary at St. Paul, Minnesota, to take up the study of theology. While he was there, the Most Reverend Alexander Christie, Archbishop of Portland in Oregon, came in search of some likely seminarians who would consider adoption at his hands. Martin W. Doherty was one of the first to volunteer and he was accepted. Then the dream of his life came true for Archbishop Christie decided to send him to the North American College in Rome to complete his studies.

The account of his experiences as a Roman seminarian is set down in *The House on Humility Street*. They make intriguing reading, but Divine Providence decreed that Martin Doherty was not to be ordained in Rome as he had planned. Illness interfered and Seminarian Doherty was brought back to the United States where, after recovering from the digestive trouble that had caused him to leave Rome, he re-entered St. Paul's Seminary where he was ordained priest on June 13, 1926.

But even ordination could not keep him entirely away from the newspaper business. Returning to Chicago to celebrate his first Mass in his home parish church and to visit his family before leaving for his mission in Oregon, Father Doherty arrived just when the great International Eucharistic Congress was about to open under the patronage of Cardinal Mundelein. Walter Washburne, who had played such an important part in the life of Father Doherty planned that his paper should cover this event in the most thorough manner possible. He wanted a man who, knowing both newspaper work and Catholic liturgy, could act as editor in charge of the force of reporters detailed to write the news of the Eucharistic Congress. Arrangements were made and the Reverend Martin Doherty, having just celebrated his first Mass, went to the office of *The Evening Post* and again sat down at the desk he had occupied a few years before.

Father Doherty has, during his eighteen years of priesthood, done a lot of important work in the Archdiocese of Portland in Oregon. He was a curate in several Portland churches, he was pastor of a parish that covered two or three counties and for some time he has been pastor at Gervais, one of the most historic parishes in the Northwest, where he occupies a rambling old rectory originally built as a priory for the Benedictine Fathers who now have the great abbey at Mt. Angel.

There was never a time when he was not doing writing of some sort. Various Catholic magazines have frequently welcomed his articles. He conceived the idea of a book to refute a travel book about Rome in which the seminarians of the Eternal City were depicted in an untrue and unjust light. On the advice of newspaper friends this was changed from a refutation to a straight story of one Roman Seminary—the North American College. Its title is derived from Via dell' Umilta (Humility Street) on which the college is located. **P. M.**

Reverend Albert Harold Dolan, O.Carm.
1892-

The Little Flower has been the constant inspiration and interest of Father Albert Dolan, O.Carm. To her he dedicated his special life work and of her he writes untiringly and beautifully. Born in Fond du Lac, Wisconsin, in 1892, he was educated at St. Lucy's Academy, Syracuse, New York, Niagara University, and the North American College, in Rome. He then pursued his studies for the priesthood at St. Augustine's Seminary, Toronto, from 1913 to 1918. In the latter year he entered the Carmelite Order. Professed in 1919 and ordained in Toronto the same year, he became a teacher and prefect of discipline at Mt. Carmel College, Chicago. In that city in 1924 he founded the Society of the Little Flower, which has now spread throughout the country, maintaining national headquarters in Chicago. Father Dolan was stationed there as National Director until ill health necessitated his giving up this responsibility in 1931. Since then he has been Eastern Director of the society with headquarters at Englewood, New Jersey. The society spreads devotion to the Little Flower, bringing countless thousands under her care and protection.

Father Dolan's sermons given at the novena in St. Cecilia's Church, Englewood, in 1932, were so popular that they were published in book form as *St. Thérèse Returns*. Therein he vigorously defends the fundamental Catholic teachings most frequently attacked today, submitting them to the light of the life and words of the Little Flower. At Lisieux Father Dolan had the extraordinary privilege of visiting the interior of the cloister, and he also met and talked with the sisters of St. Thérèse, who gave him the original painting of her and the precious relics now enshrined at Chicago. These experiences he related in *The Living Sisters of the Little Flower, Our Sister Is in Heaven,* and *Where the Little Flower Seems Nearest.* He has also written of the Little Flower's mother.

When he was in France in 1926 a pamphlet on the intercessory power of the saint, which he bought at a railroad newsstand, so impressed him that he translated it for his own private use. In later years he decided to preach on the interesting idea that God's love for Thérèse and her love for Him were as two streams descending and mounting and when they mingled forming the "shower of roses" which the Little Flower promised to let fall on earth. The resulting book, *Roses Fall Where Rivers Meet,* was based on the pamphlet, which was lost—he was unable to find the author, to whom however he gives due credit. So appealing is the volume that it bears repeated reading.

In addition to his writings on St. Thérèse, Father Dolan has numerous pamphlets to his credit, such as: *All the Answers concerning Marriage and Birth Control; Enjoy the Mass; The Carmelite Life.* His *Modern Messenger of Purity* has reached its eighth edition and proved eminently practical and helpful. A recent companion booklet is *Happiness in Marriage.* Other pamphlets are: *Homiletic Hints,* the sub-title of which is "The Preparation, Building and Delivery of a Sermon"; *Half-Way to Happiness,* and *The Friends and Enemies of Happiness.*

Father Dolan also edits *The Sword.*

In 1944 Father Dolan brought out two books: *Why We are Catholics,* with the sub-title "A Defense of Fundamental Catholic Beliefs," and *Scapular Facts* described as "A Handbook of Practical Information concerning Our Lady's Scapular."   C. M. N.

Dorothy Donnelly (Mrs. Walter Donnelly)
1903-

"The spark that really set off my first book, *The Bone and the Star* (1944)" says Dorothy Donnelly, "was the casual use, by a young 'intellectual,' of the term 'Christian Myth,' as if enlightened people could understand Christianity in no other way than as myth. It was then that I saw clearly a work that I should try to do. What it amounted to in the end was to show that there is no contradiction in truth and that consequently no one need be afraid to face truth in any field of science. Examined critically the truths discovered by science are shown to be perfectly compatible with the truth of revelation. I divided the book into two sections. The first one looked at important things from the viewpoint of science, the second travelled over the same ground and looked at things from a theological viewpoint." The title is taken from line 6 on page 134 in the book and is a general reference to material things signified by the "Bone" and spiritual ones, signified by the "Star." Mrs. Donnelly spent a year in reading and planning before she began the actual writing of the book, which took a year and a half. Mortimer Adler says of the book . . . "an extraordinarily synthetic and imaginative study of primitive man, looked at from points of view of Christian theology and modern science." Father Frank McPhillips, the chaplain of the students at the University of Michigan, praises it as "a splendid antidote to the materialism students acquire from some anthropology lecturers." Mrs. Donnelly is interested in bringing into the light various kinds of internal evidence and in expressing them in as interesting and objective and beautiful a way as possible. She believes that if this is successfully done it is the best way to reach the modern mind. "What is needed" she says "is a searchingly critical attitude toward what we read and hear."

The mother of three children, seven, nine and eleven years old, she must do her writing in the evenings. From the time she was a small girl she always wanted and intended to write, but never had much time. Her first bit of writing to be published was a sketch, done very much in the modern manner, which appeared in the experimental magazine *Transition* (or transition with a small *t* as it was written for some time), published in Paris by Eugene Jolas. The magazine published the work of James Joyce, Gertrude Stein, Kay Boyle and many others. Five of her sketches, poetic in content and approach, appeared in *Transition;* the last one, called "Dream of the End of Time," was published in the last number of the magazine to appear, the tenth anniversary number.

Dorothy Donnelly was born in Detroit, Michigan, on September 7, 1903, the daughter of Alexander and Theresa Boillotat. She was graduated from the University of Michigan with the degrees A.B. and M.A. In 1931 she won the major Avery Hopwood award of $1,500 in the field of the essay at the University of Michigan. After her marriage to Walter Donnelly in that same year, she finished work on her master's degree. In the spring of 1932 she and her husband travelled in Italy, Switzerland and France. She has contributed articles to *The Catholic World, The Commonweal* and *America.* She intends to gather some of these and other essays for publication in book form.   M. H.

Reverend Francis Patrick Donnelly, S.J. 1869-

The future Jesuit, poet, author and educator, Francis Patrick Donnelly, was born December 10, 1869. His birthplace, Pittston, Susquehanna County, Pennsylvania, lies in the northeastern section of the state in the region known as "the cradle of Catholicism in the early days of Pennsylvania history." A large colony of Irish immigrants gathered there early in the last century and their "sturdy faith shone like a beacon light in the wilderness of their new home." In this section Father Donnelly's parents were born and spent their lives. From his mother, a school teacher, he inherited a love of reading and study and though he lost her when only eight years old she remained a deep influence on his life. A pious aunt took charge of the young family at the mother's death and also encouraged serious reading in young Francis. His pocket money went into books and his free time was spent hidden away in secluded nooks reading. His father urged the study of music for the boy and, though during the three years devoted to it, most of the practice time was spent absorbed in reading books rather than notes, he nevertheless learned enough to enable him in later years to put his songs to the music of others. Songs about Ireland and patriotic lyrics came readily from his pen and he has given us many in charming style and all well fitted to some old sweet familiar air.

When he was about twelve a reading of O'Kane Murray's *History of the Catholic Church in the United States* made known to him the great heroes of the early missionary days. He wondered what S.J. following the names of the great Brebeuf, Lalemant, Jogues and Marquette meant. Of added interest he found on another page statistics of religious orders with the Jesuits listed first, for having more men and houses than the others, and the young hero-worshipper decided then to belong to that Society. Through a pious servant he obtained a litany to St. Ignatius Loyola and for two years recited it faithfully that he too might in time write S.J. after his name.

In 1884 with his brother he went to the Augustinian college at Villanova. There he met a fellow student, Tom Daly, and between those two poets a life-long friendship has flourished. After a year at Villanova, Francis Donnelly went to Fordham where he remained until in 1888 his prayers bore fruit and he entered the Jesuit novitiate at Frederick, Maryland. From then on he followed the usual course of Jesuit training and he was ordained in 1903 at Woodstock, Maryland by the late Cardinal Gibbons.

Except for the year when he was assistant editor of *The Messenger of the Sacred Heart,* and the year 1915 when he was rector of Gonzaga College, Washington, D. C., Father Donnelly's years have been spent in the class room as professor of rhetoric in the various Jesuit schools. The Litt.D. was conferred on him by Holy Cross College in 1929, by Fordham in 1934, and later by Georgetown University.

Father Donnelly's literary gifts are divided between poetry, educational text books and many songs. In 1902 he published *Model English I* and in 1919 *Model English II.* In 1934 he brought out *Jesuit Principles of Education in Practice* and in 1938 *Literature, the Leading Educator.* His books of devotion are well known: *The Heart of the Gospel; The Heart of Revelation; Mustard Seed; Chaff and Wheat; Holy Hour in Gethsemane; Grains of Incense; The Heart of the Mass; The Heart of the Rosary; Cicero's Milo* is a rhetorical commentary, and *The Heart of the Church.* These are but some of Father Donnelly's valuable contributions to poetry, devotion, scholastic writings and songs of love of God and country. At the celebration at Fordham, in 1938, of his golden jubilee as a Jesuit, *The Song of the Society* and others of his compositions were sung.

C. M. N.

Lord Alfred Douglas 1870-1945

"My life (much against my will) has been distinctly melodramatic," wrote Lord Alfred Douglas in a letter to the editor of this volume. And in his *Autobiography* (1929), he wrote, "I am a man who is always being libelled. . . . I suppose the two main reasons why I have been so unkindly and harshly treated in England are that I am a Scotsman and that I am a poet."

Lord Alfred Douglas was born on the twenty-second of October, 1870 in a house called Ham Hill near Worcester. His father, the eighth Marquis of Queensberry, is chiefly remembered in the sporting world as the author or compiler of the Queensberry rules of boxing, the guide for good sportsmanship in the prize ring. As a boy, Lord Alfred Douglas hardly ever saw his father. He remembered him as being selfish and an agnostic. He described his mother as "so beautiful that just after her marriage when she and her sister went driving in London in the park, people stood on chairs to see them." He also said of his mother that she was "the most unselfish, the most incredibly good and sweet and kind and patient, and also the most valiant and loyal, woman that ever drew the breath of life. . . . Good as she was, she lacked the one thing to make her a perfect mother, which she has obtained since. I mean that she was not definitely religious." She became a Catholic in her 80th year.

The happiest days of his childhood were passed at Kinmount, which is about four miles from Annan. He left this place when ten years of age to go to London. At home his brothers and sister called him "Bosie," a name that stuck to him all his life. It is just a variation of "boy" and means "little boy." In his tenth year he went to a private school called Lambrock, a school "populated by sprigs of nobility." After he had been there about a year the school more or less broke up, so he moved to another school called Wixenford. From Wixenford he went to Winchester, being then just fourteen. He edited the school paper called the *Pentagram* —"the only literary or journalistic venture out of which I ever made a profit" he wrote in 1914. At Christmas, 1888 he entered Magdalen College where he remained four years. During his second year at Oxford he contributed to the *Oxford Magazine* (the official journal of the University) a poem which won the praise of Mr. Herbert Warren, the President of Magdalen. This was Lord Alfred Douglas' first serious poem and is now included in the *City of the Soul*. It was called "Autumn Days."

Always a lover of the best in literature, he had read most of the best English poetry and all the standard novels by the time he had finished his second year at Oxford. In his third year at Oxford he met Oscar Wilde, through his friend Lionel Johnson, the Wykehamist poet. A friendship developed between Oscar Wilde and himself 'which later brought the gravest disasters not only upon himself but also upon those nearest and dearest to him. Nevertheless Douglas stated, "while with him I wrote some of my own best poetry." His book *Oscar Wilde and Myself* (1914) sets out the whole details of his relationship with Oscar Wilde. Douglas left Oxford without a degree. When the time came for his examination in the Honours School, Lord Alfred Douglas happened to be ill and was unable to attend. The authorities offered to confer an honorary degree if he would return in the vacation and pass two papers. His father advised him against it.

In 1899 Douglas published his first book of verse, *The City of the Soul*. It was published anonymously. The critics, who were unaware of its author's identity praised it. It sold so well, a second edition was called for before the end of the year. Against the advice of his publisher, Mr. Grant Richards, Douglas insisted his name be put on the title page of the second edition. . . . From that time on the sale of the book ceased. When Thompson reviewed *The City of the Soul,* he knew Douglas wrote it. He hailed Douglas as a colourist in poetry, that is as belonging to the school of Keats. Thompson claimed, however, that *The City of the Soul* lacked thought. Padraic Gregory disagrees with him. Thompson does admit Douglas has a "rich sense of language" a "true gift of mellifluous versification" and "cunning and iridescent diction." He was out of favor, however, on account of his association with Oscar Wilde and the many libel suits against him. Twice he was convicted for libel, once for libelling his father-in-law, Colonel Custance, by accusing him of defrauding his daughter, and once for libelling Winston Churchill, by accusing him of writing a deliberately false account of the battle of Jutland with the object of enabling a group of Jews to make a financial coup on the American stock markets. For doing this he was sent to prison for six months. While imprisoned, he wrote what he considered to be his finest poem "In Excelsis." In his *Autobiography* (1929) he made a confession of his faults in a straightforward and truthful manner. His book *Without Apology* (1938) may be described as a footnote to the *Autobiography*. In it, he stated that he no longer believed the accusation against Mr. Churchill, "though of course at the time when I published the accusation (which I made in a speech at the Memorial Hall in London and also in my paper *Plain English*) I was convinced of its truth and published it entirely out of patriotism."

Because of these charges he was ostracized, and was prevented from getting the literary recognition that he deserved.

In 1902 he married Olive Custance, a distinguished poet. The romance began when she wrote to Douglas and expressed her admiration for his poetry. He replied in suitable terms. Despite their shyness, the romance ripened rapidly and was only impaired when Douglas went to America for a visit. On his return, he learned that Olive Custance had become engaged to his friend George Montagu. He invited Olive to dinner, assured her of his love for her and asked her to run away with him to be married as the only way out. She did. One son was born of the marriage.

In 1911 Lord Alfred Douglas became a Catholic. He was converted by reading history and especially Pope Pius X's encyclical against Modernism. His poetry was always written under strong emotional stress. He claimed to be the only English poet since Byron whose poetry has been translated into French and published in his lifetime.

For more than three years, he edited *The Academy*. His publications include: *Sonnets* (1909); *Collected Poems* (1919); *In Excelsis* (1924); *Complete Poems* (1928), (New edition in two volumes); *Sonnets and Lyrics* (1935). Light Verse: *Tails with a Twist; The Duke of Berwick; The Placid Pug; The Pongo Papers*. Biography: *Oscar Wilde, a Summing Up* (1940). Also: *Collected Satire* (1927); *The True History of Shakespeare's Sonnets* (1933).

He died at his farm in Sussex on March 20, 1945. M. H.

Helen Douglas-Irvine ?-1947

Miss Helen Douglas-Irvine writes: "I was born in Scotland, in the country, at Grangemuir, Pittenweem, Fife, and am the daughter of a Scottish father and an Irish mother. My father was born a Douglas but had to take the second surname of Irvine when, before my birth, he inherited my early home and some property in Tobago in the West Indies from his mother's family, whose name was Irvine and who had been sugar-planters in Tobago for a couple of generations. My father had spent a good many of his younger years in Tobago and most of my mother's girlhood had been passed in Pau in France. Thus my parents had the habit of wandering, and they continued to wander with their large family—five sons and three daughters of whom I was the youngest—during my childhood. Before I was twelve years old we had lived at Montreux in Switzerland, at Heidelberg in Germany, in the Austrian Tyrol, and in Versailles where I spent my most impressionable years. In Versailles I went to school to the Institut Supérieur des demoiselles Chenu et Frezzola: I have described that school in my *Mirror of a Dead Lady*. I finished my schooldays in England, at the Clifton High School, and afterwards, since my parents had returned to Scotland, I took the M.A. degree, with Honours in History, at St. Andrew's University. In my grown-up years I first gave myself up to historical research: before the last war I was on the staff of the *Victoria Counties' Histories of England* and wrote *The Royal Palaces of Scotland* and a *History of London* as well as a small source-book called *Mediaeval Markets and Fairs*. In November 1914 I went to Serbia as clerk to the First Scottish Women's Hospital, stationed in Kragujevatz, a town which has lately figured in the news as the place of a massacre of patriot schoolboys. Until the retreat of the Serbian army this hospital received sick and wounded soldiers, both Serbian soldiers and their many prisoners, subjects of the countries then included in the Austro-Hungarian army. Serbs and prisoners were treated exactly alike in the hospital. In 1916 I went to Rome, to fill the place, on the staff of the International Institute of Agriculture, of an Englishman called to the colours. I edited the English edition of the review of agricultural economics published by the Institute in several languages. In 1920 I was transferred to the agricultural section of the International Labour Office, where I worked for one year. After these two latter experiences I wrote an agrarian history called *The Making of Rural Europe*. I first went to Chile, where two brothers of mine were settled, in 1922, and from that time I have spent much time there, making it my home from 1931 onwards. I have written much for the *Times* and other newspapers about Chile and also about Peru and Argentina which I have visited. I turned from journalism and history to fiction, mainly because I had all my life wanted to write fiction, but partly also because I lived in Chile in a remote country place, and was out of touch with current affairs and cut off from the libraries which enable historical research. I have published three novels and one book of long-short stories of which the scenes are mainly laid in Chile and Peru—*Magdalena; Fray Mario; Mirror of a Dead Lady,* and *Angelic Romance*. I think *Fray Mario* is probably the best book I have written; certainly it has been the most successful. But I have a private preference for *Mirror of a Dead Lady,* perhaps because so much of my own experience was reproduced in it. This book has not had the sale it might have had if the whole stock of it had not perished when the premises of my publishers, Longmans, were twice bombed in 1941.

"After the outbreak of this war (World War II) I joined the staff of the Postal Censorship in Liverpool and there used the knowledge of languages I have acquired during my wandering life. Last August I resigned from the Censorship and have since done propaganda writing of various kinds, especially scripts for the Latin-American programme of the B.B.C. During the last few months, in which the tension of our anxiety about the war has relaxed a little, I have found I could again do imaginative work, and I am now working at a novel of which the scene is laid in Victorian England.

"The authors of fiction whom I enjoy most are Jane Austen, Henry James and Stendhal.

"Of all my experiences, it is my early years in Versailles, the four years I had the incredibly good fortune to spend in Rome, and my happy years in beautiful Chile which have influenced me most.

"I love all animals, horses and dogs best, I love fine buildings, and I love the sea, the hills and wild flowers. My favourite recreations are reading, riding, arranging flowers, and conversation."

Miss Helen Douglas-Irvine was received into the Catholic Church in 1917. For two and a half years she was Editor of *The Catholic Citizen* (London).

In 1945 her novel *Torchlight Procession* was published. Long interested in the life of St. Catherine, she was engaged in a translation of the works of this great medieval mystic when she died in Chile in 1947. She was buried in Dunnoo, Fife.

Most Reverend Richard Downey 1881-

A first rate journalist before he became a priest, Archbishop Downey maintains in some of his books and public utterances the journalistic habit of polemic attack. Extraordinarily learned, he does not wear his knowledge as a robe but uses it as a sword, occasionally as a bludgeon.

Archbishop Downey has long been in demand as a speaker. His sparkling wit makes him an excellent after-dinner speaker. He is never at a loss for a humorous phrase. On one occasion when called upon unexpectedly to speak at a banquet His Grace said "I hate extempore speeches." Generally speaking they are not worth the paper they are written on."

His Grace was born in Kilkenny in 1881. He was educated at St. Edward's College, Liverpool, at London University, St. Joseph's College, Upholland and the Gregorian University in Rome. He was ordained a priest at Upholland. From 1915 to 1918 and again from 1925 to 1928, he was Extern Examiner in philosophy to the National University of Ireland. In 1922 and in 1925 he preached and lectured in America on philosophical subjects. He was professor of philosophy for Oblates, Oratorians and Carmelites at Bayswater Novitiate from 1918 to 1926. From 1926 to 1928 he was professor of dogmatic theology and Dean of the Departments of Theology and Philosophy at Upholland.

In 1928 he was consecrated Archbishop of Liverpool and was made Metropolitan of the Northern Province with the suffragan sees, Hexham, Lancaster, Leeds, Middlesbrough and Salford. He has fearlessly defended the rights of Catholics.

In 1939 his home at Woolton became an air raid post.

He is the author of: *Some Errors of H. G. Wells; Personal Immortality; Divine Providence; The Blessed Trinity; Pulpit and Platform Addresses; Critical and Constructed Essays; Civic Virtue; A Plea for Justice; The Question of Reunion.* He contributed to the Cambridge Summer School volumes, *The Religion of the Scriptures; The Papacy; St. Thomas Aquinas; The Incarnation;* and *The Church.*

He is a co-founder and first editor of *The Catholic Gazette.*

M. H.

Reverend Charles Hugo Doyle 1904-

While spending a year in bed in a hospital, Father Charles Doyle's attention was drawn to a contest advertised in one of the local newspapers. The children in the various schools of the city were asked to send in the names of the men they con- sidered the most outstanding in statesmanship. What impressed him was the fact that a Catholic high school for girls conducted by Sisters voted for Hull, Roosevelt, Chamberlain and other lay- men. Only one girl out of over three hundred mentioned the name of Pope Pius XI. There and then he decided that our Catholic children knew nothing about the Pope and so he decided to supply a book to inform them. He made a translation from the French of a book on Pope Pius XI. Before he left the hospital, Pope Pius XI had died and Pope Pius XII had been elected. During the long hours in bed, he followed every radio broadcast of the election. And this knowledge endeared him to the Pope and gave him the urge to make him better known.

For children, Father Doyle wrote *Our Holy Father Pope Pius XII,* illustrated in color by Addison Burbank and A. Donald Rahn. During the year 1943-1944, this book was chosen one of the best ten for children by the Catholic Committee of the National Conference of Christians and Jews. *We Have A Pope* is a life of Pope Pius XII for eighth grade and high school students. *The Life of Pope Pius XII* is a full length biography. Other works published are *Do You Know Jesus?,* a study of the Mystical Body for little tots, and *Let Us Know The Pope,* a booklet.

Charles Hugo Doyle was born in Kingston, Ontario, Canada on April 12, 1904, where he attended St. Mary's School and Regiopolis College. He entered St. Joseph's Seminary in Edmonton, Alberta, in September 1922 and completed his philosophical studies there. His theological studies were followed at St. Augustine's Seminary, Toronto, Canada and he was ordained on December 22, 1928.

Having begun his seminary studies in the Canadian West, Father Doyle saw the great need there for priests, so volunteered for missionary work in the archdiocese of Edmonton. After spending one year as assist- ant at Vegreville, Alta, Father Doyle was appointed pastor of Brosseau, Alta, and one year later, pastor of Blessed Sacrament Church, Wainwright, Alberta. In the short space of three years, Father Doyle built a school, church and convent in this latter place and at the same time was editor of the *Western Catholic,* the diocesan weekly.

Illness caused him to be hospitalized in Kingston, Ontario for a year. He then came to New York for further treatment. Because of his knowl- edge of French, Father Doyle was appointed assistant at St. Teresa's Church, North Tarrytown, New York where there is a small group of

French speaking families. He hopes for the day, however, when he can return to the Canadian West.

M. H.

Charles Du Bos 1882-1940

In Charles Du Bos we find a Frenchman who lost the faith of his fathers only to regain it paradoxically through his intimate association with and love of English poetry.

Born in Paris in 1882, he studied at the Gerson School and then at Oxford. His mother was an Anglo-American, and he was linked both by family and cultural ties to the Anglo-Saxon world. He spoke English perfectly, and there was something typically English in his clear-cut features, his clothes, and the short briar pipe he was continually smoking. However, after his university days, he spent most of his life in France, except for the journeys which occasionally took him to Italy, Germany, Switzerland, Holland, and later to America. On his return from Oxford, in 1902, he started his literary career in Paris where he was lecturer at the popular universities. He was married in 1907. The following year, he began his "Diary," an intimate journal in which he wrote of his literary, philosophical and artistic experiences and research, as well as of the religious crisis which made him a practicing and fervent Catholic. During the war of 1914, unable to do military duty, he and André Gide established the *Foyer Franco-Belge,* a club for soldiers. After the war, he filled, for several years, the post of director of the American Library in Paris.

Charles Du Bos was a contributor to the *Nouvelle Revue Française,* at the time when this review, under the management of Jacques Rivière, was the center of Paris literary and cultural life. In 1930, he published with Jacques Maritain, Paul Claudel, François Mauriac, Gabriel Marcel and l'Abbe Altermann the Catholic periodical *Vigile.*

For many years, Charles Du Bos was the friend of André Gide with whom he directed the "Pontigny Decades," a meeting of intellectuals from all nations held every year at the country home of Professor Desjardins. There literary, philosophical and spiritual problems were discussed at length, and the Pontigny meetings exercised a profound influence on French intellectual life.

When Charles Du Bos turned to the Church, there occurred a gradual estrangement between him and André Gide, and Du Bos identified himself with the Catholic writers and thinkers such as Jacques Maritain and Mauriac. But he still presided every year at the Pontigny meetings. He was known as a prolific writer, a great scholar and a profound lecturer. He had a passion for debate which he directed with incomparable skill.

At most meetings of Parisian intellectuals he would be heard leading the discussion in his quiet, clear voice, waving his extinguished pipe like a conductor waves his baton. Even those who disagreed with him, had a profound respect for his deep devotion to ideas; his intellectual integrity and complete disinterestedness became proverbial.

After his "Diary," he was almost entirely absorbed in literary criticism; besides his articles in various reviews and the lectures he gave for students, he wrote seven volumes of literary essays entitled *Approximations,* devoted to French, English and German writers and poets, from Flaubert and Baudelaire to Proust and Valéry, from Shakespeare to Shelley, Browning, Keats and Coventry Patmore, from Goethe to Hoffmannsthal. He spoke German fluently and was considered one of the best French linguists.

The works of Du Bos have been called an oasis in the midst of our troubled times. His passion for English poetry led to a deeper, richer knowledge of English literature than that of any other French critic of his time. Shakespeare, Keats, and Dante are acclaimed by him as the three greatest poets in the world. Literature he defines as "life becoming conscious of itself when in the soul of a man of genius it finds its plentitude of expression." He argued that "creative joy, transcending the pain of experience, forges the link between poet and reader through which medium literature becomes the meeting ground of two souls. And accepting the reality of that medium we must admit the existence of God."

Besides his "Diary" and his monumental *Approximations* (the last part, forming a sequel to volume seven, remained unpublished at his death), he wrote *Reflections on Mérimée, Dialogue with Marie Gied,* and *François Mauriac and the Problem of the Catholic Novelist.* His first and only work in English, *What is Literature?* was published a few months before his death in the spring of 1940. Agreeing with Thomas Aquinas that "the Beauty of God is the cause of the being of all that is," he recognizes in his little book the sacramental quality of creative literature.

Du Bos was not only a highly gifted and brilliant critic, he was also a profound psychologist, and for him the experience of a poet is something more than a purely literary achievement. It is a spiritual adventure, a mystical trend, the overcoming of suffering and turmoil in the name of supreme harmony and beauty.

Du Bos himself was familiar with suffering. During the last ten years of his life, he was almost continually an invalid and endured the most severe physical pain. Yet his life was entirely devoted to the work; even during the most cruel spells of his illness he never ceased dictating his books, studying and lecturing. He was known for his inexhaustible generosity, and when the German and Jewish intellectuals, driven out of their country by Hitler, came to Paris, Du Bos offered them both hospitality and spiritual comfort. His homes at Versailles and in Paris were open to writers, philosophers and publicists of all nationalities; but his guests had one thing in common, the deep resentment of totalitarian doctrines and the devotion to the humanist ideal.

His life was centered round the Eucharist. In spite of his frail health, he was a daily communicant, and those who have seen him at early Mass will never forget his fervor, his concentration, his intentness on every word pronounced during the Holy Sacrifice.

In 1937, Charles Du Bos came to America where he occupied a chair in the University of Notre Dame. He made a place for himself in the American educational world and left the memory of a spirituality enriched by genius. Just as in Paris, his home at Notre Dame became the hospitable centre of intellectual life, where members of the faculty and students assembled on Sundays. He often visited the neighbouring college of St. Mary's, where he had many friends and was warmly greeted by the President, Sister Madeleva, the great Catholic poet. It was at St. Mary's that Du Bos and his family attended Mass; his daughter was a student at the college, and the Sisters of the faculty still show to the visitor the "Du Bos' pew," from whence so many fervent prayers daily ascended.

In the summer of 1940, Charles Du Bos returned to France for the holidays with his wife and daughter. His health was seriously undermined and he had to spend the last weeks in America in a hospital. After his arrival in France, his condition grew worse, and he died August, 1940.

During his life, this remarkable critic was not sufficiently appreciated in France, because of his great modesty, his fear of publicity and vainglory. His essays were too serious, too deep for the public at large and did not receive easy recognition. But after his death, the Paris press was unanimous in declaring him one of the outstanding literary critics and thinkers of his time.   C. M. N.

Jacques Ducharme 1910-

A young author of promise, Jacques Ducharme was born in Holyoke, Mass., in 1910. He is the great grandson of the first French Canadian to settle there, and it is with sympathy as well as charm that he writes of the early French Canadian migration to New England in *The Delusson Family*. After receiving his B.A. at Assumption College, Worcester, Massachusetts, the only completely French school in the United States, he studied at the Sorbonne, Paris. He began writing, about 1935, during the summer when he was unemployed. But it was only after several years, during which he travelled, taught school and tried various crafts, that he published his first novel, *The Delusson Family*.

It was the outgrowth of his family's history in Canada and New England. It was the Catholic Book Club choice for July, 1939.

Mr. Ducharme's second book is *The Shadows of the Trees*, a nonfiction book. The title of the book is taken from a quotation of *The Kennebec*, by Robert P. Tristram Coffin. *The Shadows of the Trees* is an account of the role the Franco-Americans have played in New England.
                                         C. M. N.

Reverend Owen Francis Dudley 1882-

After only four years in the Anglican ministry, the Reverend Owen Francis Dudley made his submission to the Church of Rome in 1915. Born in 1882, he had studied for the Anglican ministry at Lichfield Theological College, obtained the Licentiate of Theology of Durham University and was ordained in 1911. Following his reception into the Catholic Church he went to Collegio Beda in Rome to study for the priesthood and was ordained in September, 1917, by Cardinal Bourne in Westminster Cathedral, London. He was then appointed British Army chaplain, saw service on the French and Italian fronts and was wounded.

Joining the Catholic Missionary Society in August, 1919, Father Dudley during the succeeding years has labored indefatigably throughout the British Isles, expounding true Catholic philosophy as against the false in "town hall, theatre, Hyde Park or mining clubroom." This last he describes with keen relish as "a large hall, open all day, next the church. At night you enter a din of music and a thick mingle of beer and shag. In the center, on a platform, a band crashes out popular songs, the crowded tables all around roaring back a raucous chorus. Great scene!" To this strenuous work Father Dudley adds "motor-missioning" which he calls "great fun . . . packed with human interest . . . one gets to love the scene each night . . . humanity in the raw—hungry, restless, seeking."

Not content with this active apostolate, Father Dudley has become known as not only "a dynamic thinker but a powerful novelist," using his pen "to bring Catholic philosophy and theology before the public in a popular form." His trilogy, *Will Men Be Like Gods?*, *Shadow on the Earth*, and *The Masterful Monk*, deal with humanitarianism, the problem of evil and the Catholic moral code, and have been serialized, translated in various languages and transcribed in Braille.

Two further novels followed, *Pageant of Life* and *The Coming of the Monster*. His latest addition to the Masterful Monk series, *The Tremaynes and the Masterful Monk* was published in September, 1940.

Father Dudley visited the United States in 1939 while on a tour of thirteen months which took him to New Zealand, Australia and the West Indies as well. It was made at the invitation of various archbishops and bishops, and, as in England, he addressed people of all types and color from varied pulpits and platforms.

He was elected superior of the Catholic Missionary Society in 1933 and reelected in 1936. The Society, founded in 1902 by Cardinal Herbert Vaughan, is a society of priests set apart by their bishops for the work of the conversion of England and Wales. After Father Dudley's visit to Australia similar work was started there, some of the Missionary Fathers of the Sacred Heart dedicating themselves to the cause of the conversion of the non-Catholics of Australia.

World War II had given Father Dudley new chances to reach comfort and strengthen souls in the hospital wards of London and in the bomb-shattered debris. He wrote during the war: "Our area has suffered terribly. The mission house and rectory have been wrecked by high explosives. All around is a haunted scene of death and desolation. We are all alive and uninjured however—Deo Gratias."

In 1947 he resigned from the position of Superior of the Catholic Missionary Society. C. M. N.

Reverend Thomas Gavan Duffy 1888-1941

The Seven Last Words by Father Thomas Gavan Duffy is one of the "New Hope Series" of books written by the late Father Thomas Gavan Duffy, Irish patriot and Australian statesman who had been for twenty-five years a missionary in India, until his death in 1941.

Reverend Thomas Gavan Duffy, son of the late Sir Charles Duffy K.C.M.G. renowned in history as one of the brilliant leaders of the Young Ireland Party, was born in 1888. He was educated at Stonyhurst, Thurles and Paris, ordained priest of the Paris Foreign Missions and joined the Indian Mission Field in 1911.

Father Thomas Gavan Duffy labored in one of the most difficult mission fields—South India. It was said of him that although the climate there made sluggards of the best in thirty years, it never conquered him.

All Father Thomas Gavan Duffy's writings were in connection with missions and catechists. Twenty-five years ago he came to America on "loan" from the Paris Foreign Mission Society to assist in training the first Maryknoll fledglings, from 1915 to 1916. His boys of that period recall "the vision of a rich, red, well groomed Vandyke beard borne by an earnest apostle" moving over the hilltop that was early Maryknoll.

Tindivanum, where Father Thomas Gavan Duffy established his remarkable catechist-training school, was called the West Point of India. Five hundred in number, his pupils were known, as was his school, for order and discipline. Under his strong hands the easy-going Tamil candidates were turned into very satisfactory assistants to the missionaries. In his book *The Second Ten Years of Hope* he tells much of this story of the catechists.

"The Hope Series," consisting of sixteen books by Father Thomas Gavan Duffy has become well known to all interested in mission work in foreign lands. *Yonder,* one of the most popular of the series, is now out of print.

Great emphasis on the building of a native clergy during the past twenty years eclipsed the drive launched by Father Thomas Gavan Duffy for trained lay helpers but the need of them in great numbers still remains and his name is forever linked with creating world interest in catechists and in their training.

The best known among his books are: *Yonder; Scout Songs; The First Ten Years; The Second Ten Years; Let's Go* and *The Other Way Home*. Besides his Mission books Father Thomas Gavan Duffy was the author of *The Price of Dawning Day*, an historical novel laid in Annam, the land of martyrs where Theophane Venard won his crown. It was much admired by the late Archbishop Goodier. There are also two collections of poems; *God's Little Hope*, and *Wayfarer For Christ*.   E. F.

Eileen Duggan

New Zealand's poet-laureate, Eileen Duggan, is the product of two countries. Her parents came from the poetic south of Ireland, Kerry, the land of bards. But Miss Duggan herself was born on a farm in Marlborough County, New Zealand. Her native place bears the musical Maori name of Tua Marina. These three streams, the Celtic, the New Zealand and the Maori, are all united in her work.

Her early years were spent in the village school. She then attended Marlborough College and was awarded the Jacob Joseph scholarship. She obtained her M.A. degree from Victoria University College in Wellington in 1918, and took First Class Honours in history. She lectured in that subject at the University for a brief period, but soon abandoned teaching for writing. Her first poems were written when she was still at college, and were collected into a brochure in 1921 by the editor of the New Zealand *Tablet*. This has now become a collector's item. In these early verses the Celtic inspiration is uppermost. George Russell (AE) had a premonition of her greatness when he reviewed Eileen Duggan's *Poems* in his *Irish Homestead*. Her Ireland, he said, "appears bluer in the distance, like all distant things." He commented on her "full endowment of sensitiveness," hoped she would never descend to easier things to gain a wider public, and advised her to keep her place, writing of the things close to her knowledge.

Her second book, published in 1929, and now also out of print, was a collection written primarily for children. It is called *New Zealand Bird Songs* and contains some of her most beautiful poems about the native song-birds. Each bird is given its Maori name. There is Tui, "swinging on a flax-flower, mad with the honey and the noon in his throat"; the now extinct Huia, "kind to its mate of the curving bill"; the sheep-stealing Kea; a sea of sleepy gannets; the Moas who "had lost the sky"; and the Bellbird which calls to the exile from every foreign spire. Her poem on the Fantail in the house is a challenge to all superstition, Celtic or other. Not an omen but an honour is the bird's flying through, for "He had the whole sweet countryside, and yet he came to you."

Miss Duggan has, unwittingly or not, followed the advice of AE. Her output is always limited by her severe criticism of her own verses. She never publishes anything that does not meet the highest standards of poetry. As a result, she has progressed steadily to greater reticence, to a craftsmanship as chaste, as restrained and as exacting as that of Alice Meynell. Her *Poems* of 1937 gained the prophesied recognition and won for her a place in the King's Honours List. Miss Duggan is now the holder of an Order of the British Empire. She values the title not for itself, but for the sanction it places upon a message so consciously Christian as hers.

Though she has nothing of the propagandist, as Walter de la Mare insists in his Introduction, poetry to Miss Duggan is not a withdrawal. It is a positive revelation of virility both in thought and language. She has come to reject all but the strong and picturesque words of her Gaelic heritage, but these she uses with courage and acumen. She writes of a wind that "clouted the nose of our chimney"; of the "soft dousing rain"; of the "footloose mountains that taunted Magellan"; of the "wizened rose"; of the hare that "flashed a frosty scut"; and of Augustine that he was "once his mother's cark." Nor does she lack courage in attacking the modern sins. Concentration of wealth alone causes misery: "If earth is gaunt, in plenty seek the cause." The remedy is equally repellent for the poor "are fobbed off with a mealy-mouthed dole." Birth control she dismisses in a few swift and telling lines: of all creation man alone revolts "against the primal instancy of life." *Poems* went into a second edition in Great Britain in 1939 and has had two American editions.

Miss Duggan's latest book, *New Zealand Poems,* was published for the centenary of her country in 1940, and has a greater number of poems of New Zealand and the Maoris. In spite of the difficulties of war-time publishing, two British editions and one American edition were issued. She sings of her country, "whose parted name blows like a winter horn across the wilderness of shifting sky," in two odes of magnificent sweep and feeling. Its youth is "unassailable, like a great moment or a fleeting glance; its peasantry is "our feldspar, definite as deeds." The musterer, the drayman, the bushwoman, the cow-girl are all in her poems.

She has sung the lament of the blacksmith's wife and the prayer of the bushfeller's. Side by side with these are poems of pure religious inspiration as virile as the songs of her peasants. She has written, too, of the abstract things of the spirit, of conscience that is "a fence"; of idealism, of faith that is "a blind hound nosing the knee." In all her work there is utter freedom from sentimentality, a disciplined realism that is at once satisfying and remote. When asked to define poetry she replied, characteristically, "Define it and you lose it."

Miss Duggan's prose is as artistic and original as her poetry, but too much of both still lies fugitive in periodicals and newspapers. She is at ease in the critical essay, and has written a most penetrating study of G. K. Chesterton. She has also written short stories, historical sketches and biographical studies of the writers of her country. She is keenly interested in the missionary activities of the South Pacific, and has edited and translated various books and pamphlets on the work of the Church in the Solomons. Always her prose is arresting and distinguished.

It is difficult to place Miss Duggan in any one tradition. She is indebted, on her own admission, to all poets save the eighteenth century formalists and the modern symbolists. She has the pure lyric demanded of modern poetry and deep insight into the things of the earth. But her final verdict on nature is factual and not romantic. Earth will neither mock nor mourn over the sorrows of man: "She will be indifferent as when she was born." Harder than scorn is this her "heedlessness," for she is "Careless conquered, careless free, Cool to all distress."

The work of Eileen Duggan is known to Americans largely through the pages of *The Sign, America,* and *The Commonweal.* But she writes both prose and poetry for various British and Australasian periodicals. She is an Academy member of the Gallery of Living Catholic Authors, Vice-President of the Catholic Writers' Movement, and honorary member of the international P.E.N. She is by choice a solitary, strongly averse to all forms of publicity. She lives quietly with her sister in Wellington and is content to allow her work to take its share of praise or censure without benefit of biography.

S. M.

Finley Peter Dunne   1867-1936

Finley Peter Dunne was the journalist who created the character "Mr. Dooley," and by means of syndicated articles in Irish dialect exercised a profound influence on American life from 1898 to 1910.

Peter Dunne was born in Chicago July 10, 1867. His parents' home was on West Adams Street across from St. Patrick's Church where his father's brother, Dennis, served as priest. A cousin Father P. W. Riordan, who later became Archbishop of San Francisco, baptized the infant.

After Peter Dunne graduated from West Division High School, he went to work on Chicago newspapers, finding his most profitable experience on the morning *News.* Here he wrote editorial paragraphs, and for one summer reported baseball. From the *News* he went to the *Times,* where his brilliance made him city editor at twenty-one years of age. This was followed by political reporting on the *Tribune* and the *Herald,* and finally he became chief editorial writer for the *Evening Post,* the most literate paper in the city.

When the *Post* introduced a Sunday edition, Dunne did humorous Irish dialect articles to help fill out the larger paper. These became the "Mr. Dooley" articles late in 1893. "Mr. Dooley" was a character Dunne placed in a little saloon located on Archer Avenue, "Archey Road," in the center of Irish life in Chicago. Here Mr. Dooley dispensed wisdom and humor with his other refreshments. At first his principal listener was a real person, John McKenna, but in time it became a fictional creation, Martin Hennessy, laborer, and more or less typical Irish born citizen of Archey Road and Bridgeport.

These weekly articles—which Dunne took to the *Journal* when he joined it as managing editor in 1897—were wide favorites in Chicago, and while they were sometimes merely laugh provoking, they were frequently effective editorials and occasionally inspired sermons. The tone of good-natured satire made them a potent weapon for influencing public opinion, and Dunne used them to attack public evils that afflicted the city. In 1898 his circle of readers became not only national, but international when Mr. Dooley's remarks on Dewey's victory at Manila became a sensation, and syndication of the articles followed in many newspapers in the United States and Britain. Book publications followed: *Mr. Dooley in Peace and in War* (1898); *Mr. Dooley in the Hearts of His Countrymen* (1899); *Mr. Dooley's Philosophy* (1900); *Mr. Dooley's Opinions* (1901); *Observations of Mr. Dooley* (1902); *Dissertations by Mr. Dooley* (1906); *Mr. Dooley Says* (1910), and *Mr. Dooley on Making a Will and Other Essays* (1919).

The popularity of the essays was astounding. They were read in Cabinet meetings of at least three Presidents, and were recited by numerous amateur monologists. Through them Dunne exercised a wide influence on American life, taking particular pleasure in puncturing a bag of windy conceit, and in bringing the healing power of laughter into public controversies that were becoming too warm for rational consideration.

In 1907 Dunne joined with a distinguished group of writers to edit the *American Magazine*. Here he published some of his finest Mr. Dooley essays, and also wrote "In the Interpreter's House," an unusual literary feature which attracted considerable interest. When he retired from this position in 1913, he had completed all his writing of importance. He served as editor of *Collier's* weekly during the illness and following the death of Robert Collier, and in 1926 revived the Mr. Dooley essays in *Liberty* magazine for a period of six months.

Dunne married Margaret Abbott in 1903. Four children were born to them: F. P. Jr., Philip, and the twins—Leonard and Margaret. The second son, Philip, has achieved a substantial reputation as a scenario writer for Twentieth Century Fox.

Finley Peter Dunne died on April 14, 1936 in New York. He was buried from St. Patrick's Cathedral and his body placed in the F. P. Garvin Mausoleum in Woodlawn cemetery. The City Council of Chicago designated May 29th as "Scribes' Day" as a tribute to all writers who had contributed to the world's good, and specifically to honor Dunne. On that day a memorial Mass was celebrated at St. Bridget's Church on Archer Avenue, and a delegation of students from St. Patrick's School laid a wreath on the site of the old Dunne home on West Adams Street. The press of the country hailed the passing of America's greatest humorist since Mark Twain.   E. E.

Reverend Peter Masten Dunne, S.J. 1889-

Peter Masten Dunne was born in San Jose, California, on April 16, 1889, the son of Peter Joseph and Josephine (Masten) Dunne. After passing through the parochial school of the city he went where his father had gone, to Santa Clara College, now the University of Santa Clara. Those were the old days when the courses ran as first, second, and third academic; and then philosophy and science. After five years at the college, Father Dunne entered, in July 1906, the Jesuit novitiate at Los Gatos in the delightful California foothills a few miles from both San Jose and Santa Clara. The usual Jesuit routine and course of studies were now pursued with the result that he obtained an A.B. degree in 1913 from Gonzaga University in Spokane, Washington, and the following year an M.A. degree from the same institution. He taught at St. Ignatius High School, San Francisco, from 1914 to 1916 and at Santa Clara Preparatory School, from 1916 to 1919. The following four years, 1919 to 1923, he studied theology under the supervision of the French Jesuits at Hastings, England. He was ordained to the priesthood in 1921.

Just before leaving for Europe Father Dunne became acquainted with Dr. Herbert Eugene Bolton of the University of California who that very year was getting out his *Historical Memoir of Primería Alta,* a document he had discovered in the National Archives in Mexico City. This was an account of the missionary activities of the famous Jesuit explorer, ranchman, and cartographer, Eusebio Francisco Kino, written by the padre himself. From England Father Dunne had correspondence with Bolton concerning this publication and procured the two-volume work. This was the stimulus which led the modern Jesuit into the ancient paths trod by his confrères of old. Dunne then wrote to Bolton: "If the old time Jesuits did such fine things in the mission field of Northern Mexico and in Arizona why should not their modern confrères know of these high deeds and write about them." Forthwith the modern padre began to study Spanish and to read up on the annals of the missionaries of the West Coast. Some day, he thought, he might be able to write about them. That was in 1919.

There was to be a long wait. Back in the United States Father Dunne was appointed associate editor of the national Catholic weekly *America,* 1924 to 1925; and he utilized this time by becoming a member of the graduate school of Columbia University, department of history. Sent back to California, the padre was now given a teaching position at his first home in the Society, the seminary at Los Gatos, from 1926 to 1930. A first historical love was the Renaissance and Reformation period of European history. He had cultivated this field for years. Now he began writing on it and on the historical method to try to correct what he considered the nar- row and unscientific method and spirit prevalent in a large number of Catholic historical works. He had a good deal of fun doing this and received lots of criticism. A series of articles on the causes of the Protestant Revolt was returned by the editors of a certain Catholic historical periodical. They averred the articles did not represent the Catholic viewpoint. But thirteen years later these and other articles were printed by the same periodical now under younger editors. Father Dunne has written more than sixty articles (not counting book reviews) for various Catholic and non-Catholic publications. During this time he published the biography of a nun, *Mother Mary of St. Bernard* (1929).

At last Father Dunne had the opportunity to sit at Bolton's feet. The Jesuit Provincial Superior requested him to obtain a doctor's degree in history and he could think of no place better than the University of California, and with Bolton who was now busily engaged in writing his classic biography of Father Kino. With the previous year spent at the graduate school of Columbia University, the degree was obtained at the end of 1934. Father Dunne was Bolton's most recent Jesuit pupil and introducing the Doctor before a Jesuit group he called himself a Benjamin at forty-five. In that same year (1934) he became chairman of the department of history at the University of San Francisco and still holds this post. Since 1939 he has been on the Board of Editors of the *Pacific Historical Review*.

The padre could now write on the Jesuit missions and a book of his soon appeared from the University of California press: *Pioneer Black Robes on the West Coast* (1940) and then in 1944 another: *Pioneer Jesuits in Northern Mexico*. *A Padre Views South America* appeared in 1945.

Reverend Michael Earls, S.J. 1875-1937

A gay-hearted Crusader of Christ, the Reverend Michael Earls, S.J., was for many years associated with the College of the Holy Cross, to which he gave devoted service. He was born at Southbridge, Massachusetts, 1875, the eldest of ten children, and attended grammer school there. In order to obtain funds to continue his education he worked in the new mill and taught school at night, preparing for college along the banks of the Memramcook, St. John's, New Brunswick. He went to Holy Cross College in 1893 and after three years received his A.B. From 1896 to 1897 he studied literature at Georgetown University which awarded him an M.A. He then acted as tutor to Clyde Waggaman, from 1897 to 1898, spending most of the year in France and other countries of Europe.

In 1898 he entered the Grand Seminary at Montreal, Canada, but deciding to be not only a priest but also a religious he went to the Jesuit novitiate at Frederick, Maryland, in 1899, and took his first vows on the feast of St. Michael, Sept. 29, 1901. After his philosophical studies at Woodstock, Maryland, he taught in Boston College High School and Boston College. While there he was moderator of the literary magazine, *The Boston College Stylus,* and also lectured on Irish poetry and music before various Catholic clubs and parish groups, and wrote and produced "The Chorister's Christmas Eve."

Returning to Woodstock for his theology, he was ordained there in 1912. From 1913 to 1915, Father Earls taught rhetoric at Holy Cross College and was moderator of *The Holy Cross Purple,* college literary monthly, in which his first writings appeared. After his tertianship at St. Andrew-on-Hudson, N. Y., he went again to Holy Cross, to remain for many years. He was Professor of Rhetoric from 1916 to 1926, Father Minister of the community, 1926-1929, during which time he began the beautification of the campus, and then conducted classes in elective English from 1929 to 1931.

Appointed superior of Manresa Institute, South Norwalk, Connecticut, in 1931, he remained there until 1933, when he became an assistant parish priest at St. Mary's Church, Boston. In 1935, Father Earls returned to Keyser Island, Connecticut, to devote himself to writing, many books having already come from his pen. In that year appeared his last volume of verse, *The Hosting of the King.* His first volume, *The Road Beyond the Town* was published in 1912. Two volumes of short stories, *Melchior of Boston* and *Stuore,* had preceded this. He also wrote two novels, *The Wedding Bells of Glendalough* and *Marie of the House d'Anters.* Other collections of poems are *Ballads of Childhood; Ballads of Peace in War; From Bersabee to Dan;* and *In the Abbey of the Woods.* A book of essays entitled *Under College Towers.*

Father Earls was not long at Keyser Island, for that same year, 1935, he was recalled to Holy Cross and appointed Faculty Director of the Alumni Association, in which capacity he traveled up and down the country addressing local meetings. After boarding a westbound train for Cleveland, Ohio, in 1937, he collapsed, from a heart attack and was removed to St. Vincent's Hospital, New York City, where, despite the skilled attention of his devoted friend, Dr. Raymond Sullivan, he died on January 31.

Within those last two years he had found time to complete a volume of essays, *Manuscripts and Memories* (1936), and he left also an unfinished manuscript.

C. M. N.

Helen Josephine Parry Eden 1885-

Pen and brush were Helen Parry Eden's tools for self-expression early in life. Daughter of Sir Edward Abbot Parry, a former County Court Judge at Lambeth and in Manchester, and himself a writer, she was educated at the Roedean School and at Manchester University, where she was History Scholar in 1902. From her very early childhood she had written poetry and in 1903 she received the Vice-Chancellor's Prize for English verse. She then took up painting and for two years studied under Byam Shaw and Rex Vicat Cole at King's College, London. In 1907 she married Denis Eden, an artist, who has now for many years exhibited at the Royal Academy. Together they were received into the Catholic Church by the Reverend Dr. Arendzen at Saffron Walden in 1909. They have a son and two daughters and make their home in Oxfordshire. Their son Captain Peter M. G. Eden is married to Hermia Sowerby, granddaughter of Alice and Wilfred Meynell.

Mrs. Eden's poetic bent found joyous expression with motherhood. To her little girl, "Betsey," she writes many of the poems in her first book, *Bread and Circuses,* published in 1914, and around the child revolve the poet's thoughts. In the midst of these frolicsome fancies is the striking verse, "Sorrow," one of her most representative poems, which is included in Joyce Kilmer's *Anthology of Catholic Poets* with "The Confessional," "A Purpose of Amendment" and "An Elegy." Kilmer considered Mrs. Eden's "the noblest devotional poetry written since the death of Francis Thompson." He notes also the "irresistibly mirth-compelling things" within the volume. Chesterton said he had read it many times "and it has become part of my existence in a peculiar way."

Next came the slim volume, *Coal and Candlelight* (1918), of which the title poem is an idyll of mother and babe. Also included are a few war poems, some vers de société and chaste religious verse. Here is an exquisite fineness of expression that never encroaches on sentimentalism. A devout intimacy with holy things characterizes the telling of the legend of the founding of the Servites, in *The Rhyme of the Servants of Mary* (1919), narrative verse. Mrs. Eden is a tertiary of the Order. Her fourth book was *A String of Sapphires:* Being Mysteries of the Life and Death of the Blessed Lord and Saviour Jesus Christ, Put into English Verse for the Young and Simple (1921). To Monsignor Benson's *Child's Rule of Life* she confesses a debt for the suggestion, but her Gospel ballads embracing the complete life of Our Lord are uniquely beautiful. They are for all ages and especially is the book ideal for the child.

After an interval of several years, during which she contributed book reviews to *Punch,* verse to various periodicals, and prose legends, chiefly medieval, to *Blackfriars, The Golden Hind, The English Review, The Westminster Gazette, The Catholic World* and *The Commonweal,* these last were collected into a volume, *Whistles of Silver* (1933), for the Science and Culture Series. The title is taken from Hakluyt's Voyages: "On the contrary part there was no warlike Musicke in the Spanish Gallies, but only their whistles of silver." The story based on this appears last in the volume. The text is admirably illustrated both in conception and execution by her husband, Denis Eden. Most of the stories are preceded by a poem appropriate to the theme but independent of it. The charm of Italy and France and England are all revealed in these quaint tales, among them Three Legends from *Biblioteca Ignotana.* In the *Idyll of Pusey Terrace,* locally mispronounced "Pussy," cats, for which Mrs. Eden has a great fondness, play a part. In 1943 she published *Poems and Verses.*

C. M. N.

Mother Mary Eleanore, C.S.C. (Katherine Mary Brosnahan) 1890-1940

Colonial ancestry was the background of Katherine Mary Brosnahan. She was part Irish, part Pennsylvania Dutch. Her ancestors came over with William Penn—she is a Daughter of the Revolution of 1776 "and proud of it." Betsy Ross and Samuel L. Clemens are on the same family tree. Born in Pierceton, Indiana, in 1890, she was educated in the public schools until at eighteen she went to St. Mary's College, Notre Dame. She entered the novitiate of the Congregation of the Holy Cross in her junior year. During that year her father had published a little volume of her poems entitled *Thoughts.* In religion she became Sister Mary Eleanore and obtained several degrees: A.B., St. Mary's College (1915); M.A., University of Notre Dame (1917); and Ph.D., Notre Dame (1923). During this time she wrote verses and articles and for her doctorate a textbook, *The Literary Essay in English.* From then until her death in February, 1940, Mother Eleanore wrote constantly and published a number of books, at the same time continuing her work as an educator. She held the high posts of dean of English at St. Mary's College and superior and principal of St. Mary's high school, Michigan City, Indiana. In the summer of 1934 she studied at the University of Illinois and in 1935 took a summer course at Cambridge, England. She was sent to France and Rome in 1937 for the centenary of the founding of the community. In July, 1937, Mother Eleanore was elected to the office of General Secretary of her Congregation which she held up to the time of her death. With this office she acquired the title of "Mother" and thereafter she was called "Mother Eleanore." Of her books Mother Eleanore said, they "all have a decided religious flavor." Her choice of titles is most pleasing, among them: *Troubadours of Paradise; Certitudes; Through the Lane of Stars; On the King's Highway,* the story of her Congregation, and *Love Folds Its Wings,* a book of poems. The year before her death she published *Mary,* a popular manual of Marian theology, history and devotion.

To her childhood's small-town life Mother Eleanore attributed her hobbies, birds and flowers, and her life's work among the young gave her particular pleasure in writing for children. Also, a Protestant mother and home environment had given her an understanding of the difficulties Protestants have with our religion, so as to make Catholic dogma most acceptable to them in her writings.

Mother Eleanore's death on February 17, 1940, at fifty, brought to a close a most valuable life in which she was active as author, poet, educator, lecturer and administrator in her congregation.   C. M. N.

Ethel Augusta Cook Eliot 1890-

Ethel Cook Eliot cannot remember a time when she was not writing. At the age of ten she was filling big blank-books with elaborately plotted stories inspired by Howard Pyle's *King Arthur* and to a less degree by his *Robin Hood.* When there were no more Pyle books left to read, she began creating plots, places, even characters, for herself. In her memory of this early scribbling she finds no dividing line between the satisfactions of reading and the satisfactions of writing. Both were joyously intense exercise of the imagination.

She was born in North Gage, New York, the fourth of six children of a Congregational minister. Her school years were spent in Pittsfield, Massachusetts. In her last year at high school, *Harper's Monthly* published a poem she had written, and this somehow opened the way to editorial work with the McClure Publications in New York. Running the children's page in the *Ladies' World,* and later editing *The Story-Tellers' Magazine,* she found time also for special articles and other free-lance writing.

In 1915 she married Samuel Atkins Eliot, Jr., son of the President of the Unitarian Association and grandson of President Charles W. Eliot of Harvard. Her husband became professor of drama at Smith College, and since 1918 they have lived at Northampton. Two daughters and a son were born. In 1925 Mrs. Eliot was received into the Church.

Mrs. Eliot's first books were fairy stories, influenced by George MacDonald but full of a mythology entirely her own. They are *The House on the Edge of Things; The Little House in the Fairy Wood; The House Above the Trees,* and (much the best known) *The Wind Boy.* Hundreds of letters still attest the joy that *The Wind Boy* gives to both children and parents. It is most appreciated by potential mystics without religious direction. These were followed by half a dozen "Junior Books" for high school age, of which the best known is *The Vanishing Comrade.* Most recent are four novels: *Ariel Dances; Green Doors; Her Soul to Keep,* and *Angels' Mirth.* These have all been published in England as well as America. Of *Her Soul to Keep* the New York *Times* said, "If this is propaganda it is powerful propaganda," and the London *Times* said, "A rooted religion has trained her (Mrs. Eliot) to be aware of God. She is not, however, concerned to exploit these perceptions in themselves; they flow in the flux of her narrative."

These two quotations from critics are typical of the reception of Mrs. Eliot's novels by the lay press at home and in England. The Catholic press has been just as appreciative. Mrs. Eliot feels that writing by a Catholic cannot possibly be anything but Catholic writing, for there is only one mind and heart to draw it out from, and that is Catholic. She never worries about whether what she writes will be called propaganda or not. She simply knows that she could not have written one page of these novels as she did write them unless she were herself a Catholic. Monsignor Thomas F. Cummings, D.D., pastor of St. Mary's in Northampton, awakened her interest in Catholicism, instructed her and received her into the Church. She has nothing to say, thus far, about her conversion except that a Catholic's life is Catholic life. Its beginnings, as with natural life, seem dim and dull in comparison with its progressions.

Reverend Gerald Ellard, S.J.   1894-

 From early years when he served as an altar-boy, the Reverend Gerald Ellard, S.J., had a strong attraction to the liturgy of the Church. During his years of development as a Jesuit he had opportunities to enlarge this interest and to lay the foundation for his future place in the liturgical movement. Through various stages of study, research at home and abroad, and constant writing and lecturing he has become an authority on a subject Pope Pius XI often dealt with, the function of corporate worship "for the formation of the social conscience."

Born in Commonwealth, Wisconsin, in 1894, Father Ellard entered the Society of Jesus in 1912 at Denver, Colorado, and was ordained in St. Louis in 1923. From Gonzaga University, Spokane, Washington, he received his A.B. degree in 1918 and his M.A. in 1919, and from St. Louis University he received a second M.A. in 1925.

The years 1927 to 1931 were spent in Europe where he had the great advantage of close association with outstanding liturgists, and visited abbeys and parishes in countries where the liturgy flourished. He also attended two liturgical retreats, a Dutch Liturgical Day and a Belgian Liturgical Week. He wrote of these experiences in articles contributed to *Orate*

Fratres of which he is an associate editor. In 1931 he received his Ph.D. degree at the University of Munich, where he had specialized in liturgical history. The Medieval Academy of America published his dissertation, "Ordination Anointings in the Western Church before 1000 A.D." (1932).

Not only by writing and study has Father Ellard become an authority on liturgical formation, but also as lecturer, retreat master and instructor in the class room. Since 1931 he has taught courses in liturgy in its various social aspects at the Sodality Summer Schools of Catholic Action. Since 1932 he has been assistant professor of liturgical theology at St. Mary's College, Kansas.

In 1933 Father Ellard brought out his great work, *Christian Life and Worship,* which received enthusiastic press notices here and in England and was also favorably noted in France, Germany, Rome and the Far East. In 1940 *Men at Work at Worship* was published. Father Ellard began to outline this work as early as 1927, and in the interval before publication perfected his presentation through first-hand contacts and continued study and lecturing. The book is a most interesting exposition of the progress of the liturgical movement, showing how it has revolutionized the lay method of participating in public worship in Europe, and also its effects on Catholic worship in the United States. The author chronicles the development of the young movement in this country during the past fifteen years.

His volume, *The Dialog Mass,* was issued in May, 1942, with a preface by Archbishop Curley. The book is the most ample treatment the subject has received, providing historical, canonical, liturgical and pastoral considerations, together with abundant surprising data on the current use of Dialog Mass in this country. Father Ellard has been associated with the Liturgical Weeks and is also a frequent contributor to publications here and abroad.   C. M. N.

Reverend Zephyrin Engelhardt, O.F.M.
1851-1934

Twenty years of missionary activity in Wisconsin, Michigan and California helped Father Zephyrin Engelhardt, O.F.M., acquire his intimate knowledge of the Indians. The Menominee Indians in Keshena, Wisconsin, an Algonquian tribe—where he was sent soon after his ordination to the priesthood—were his first charges. Later he was appointed superior and director of the Holy Child Indian School at Harbor Springs, Michigan. Here in 1897 he wrote his first book *The Franciscans in California,* during "the spare time of four years."

Two years later (1899), he published another one volume work under the title *The Franciscans in Arizona.* He himself set the type and did the printing for these two volumes on a little printing press he had bought second-hand. Here he also issued in the Ottawa language a four-page leaflet of the life of Kateri Tekakwitha, the Lily of the Mohawks, and published a monthly magazine entitled *Anishinabe Enamiad* (Praying Indian). In 1900 he took up his permanent residence at the Old Mission of Santa Barbara in California.

Born Charles Anthony Engelhardt in Bilshausen, Hanover, Germany in 1851, the son of Anthony and Elizabeth Engelhardt, he was brought by them to this country, arriving in New York on December 8, 1852. Later his parents moved to Kentucky and Charles attended the parish school at Covington. In 1869 he entered the Franciscan Seminary at Cincinnati, Ohio and was clothed with the Franciscan habit on September 22, 1872. After his philosophical studies at the Franciscan Monastery at Quincy, Illinois and his theological studies at the Franciscan Monastery in St. Louis, Missouri, he was ordained to the priesthood in 1878. He taught at the Franciscan day college of St. Joseph in Cleveland, Ohio and then began his long career as a missioner which was interrupted for a short time for him to serve as assistant to the Commissary of the Holy Land at Washington, D.C. Here he edited a monthly magazine *Pilgrims of Palestine,* now known as *The Crusader's Almanac.* For some time also he administered to the Pomo Indians in Lake and Mendocino Counties, California and while among them he collected a vocabulary of the Pomo language, a copy of which is held in high esteem by the Smithsonian Institution.

From 1903 he devoted himself to historical research exclusively. His aim was, he said "to furnish from original sources full and accurate information in plain language and as concisely as clearness would permit." He bravely set out to write up the local history of each of California's twenty-one missions but died on the completion of the sixteenth volume. He followed the chronological order in his treatment of the matter in preference to the topical method. His documents were always quoted in full. He was indefatigable in his search through many archives, visiting libraries and other sources of information in the United States and Mexico, gathering manuscripts and documents for his monumental work, *The Missions and Missionaries of California,* which he completed in the year 1930. In Volume IV of this work he wrote in the preface: "Though it will never be known what hardship and toil the collecting and reducing of the vast material involved, honest workers are welcome to avail themselves of it all in the interest of truth and justice." Untiring in his labors, he hoped God would let him die "in harness"—and He did. He died April 27, 1934, and was buried in the old Indian cemetery of Santa Barbara Mission where he had hoped to find a resting place. Dr. Herbert Bolton, Professor of History at the University of California in appraising his work as an historian of the early Spanish and Mexican missions said, "He is without a peer in the field and doubtless will long remain the standard authority."

Besides the works already mentioned, he is author of: *San Diego Mission* (1920); *San Luis Rey Mission* (1921); *San Juan Capistrano Mission* (1922); *Santa Barbara Mission* (1923); *Mission Dolores and the Beginnings of San Francisco* (1925); *San Gabriel Mission and the Beginnings of Los*

Angeles (1927); *San Fernando Mission* (1927); *San Miguel, San Antonio and Soledad Missions* (1929); *San Buenaventura Mission* (1930); *San Juan Bautista Mission* (1931); *Missions Santa Ines and Purisima Concepcion* (1932); *Mission San Luis Obispo* (1933), and *Mission San Carlos Borromeo* (1934). He contributed twenty-four articles on subjects and personalities for the *Catholic Encyclopedia* and wrote for numerous magazines and papers.   M. H.

Brother Ernest (Ryan), C.S.C.   1897-

Born in Elyria, Ohio, Brother Ernest Ryan, C.S.C., studied at St. Mary's school and in January, 1918, entered the postulate of the Brothers of Holy Cross, at Sacred Heart College, Watertown, Wisconsin. He received the habit and was given the name of Brother Ernest on March 19 of that year. After completion of his novitiate he continued his studies at Notre Dame, where he received his Ph.B. In 1931 he went to the Catholic University at Washington, D.C., to study for a degree in Library Science, and upon completion of his course he taught in the summer sessions there for four terms. He received his M.A. at Portland University. He was the founder, and is at present (1947) Editor of *Junior Books,* a national magazine, devoted to reviews of books for Catholic youth, for parents, teachers and librarians, at Notre Dame, Indiana.

While a student at Notre Dame, Brother Ernest wrote verse and short stories, and during the first year of his teaching career his juvenile novel, *Orphan Eddie,* was published privately and sold one thousand copies within six months. He then wrote several novels for *The Sentinel of the Blessed Sacrament, The Annals of Our Lady of Lourdes,* and in 1932 published *The Knightly Lady* serially in *The Daily American Tribune.* In 1938 he brought out a memorial edition of *Captain Johnny Ford* that was very popular and has been reprinted several times by the Ave Maria Press. *Dick of Copper Gap, Boys of the Covered Wagons, The Adventures of Tommy Blake,* and *Eddie of Jackson's Gang* followed. According to the author's purpose the main characters of his books are motivated entirely by religion. He is now writing a series of books on the saints, of which *That Boy!* the story of St. Gabriel, C.P., illustrated by Brother Hilarion, C.S.C., was the first (1940); *The Boy Who Saw the World,* the story of St. Francis Xavier, with the same illustrator (1941), was the second; *The Giant Saint,* the legend of St. Christopher, illustrated by Herbert Heywood (1942), the third; *The Boy Who Threw Away His Gold,* the story of St. Francis of Assisi, same illustrator (1943), the fourth; *Young Prince Gonzaga,* story of St. Aloysius, illustrated by Brother Etienne, C.S.C. (1944), the fifth; *The Dragon Killer,* story of St. George, universal patron of Boy Scouts, illustrated by Sister M. Edna, C.S.C. (1945), the sixth.

Besides his books for boys, Brother Ernest has written *Our Brothers,* a book explaining the life and work of some sixty religious orders of Brothers in the United States. His educational writings include *Equipping the Teacher of Religion,* which is the result of ten years' research, experiment and study; and *Religion and Living,* a book made up of his series of articles on methodology which appeared in *The Catholic School Journal* and was considered very favorably by educators. Other than books, his interests are: classical music, flowers, stamp collecting, making pen etchings and painting with pastels. He was made an honorary member of the Eugene Field Society in 1940; served as Merit Badge Counselor for the Portland Area Council of the Boy Scouts of America; was chairman of the Portland Local of the National Catholic Library Association in 1942; founded the St. Joseph County Catholic Library Association in 1942; made an honorary member of the International Mark Twain Society in 1945, and honorary member of the Catholic Library Society of Hawaii in 1945.

On March 19, 1943, Brother Ernest celebrated his silver jubilee as a religious.   C. M. N.

Cecil John Eustace 1904-

A resident of Canada since 1925, C. J. Eustace was born in England, at Walton-on-Thames, in 1904. As a boy he met many of the leading financial and political figures of Edwardian and Georgian days. He was named after Cecil Rhodes with whom his father was associated in financial enterprises in South Africa. He was educated at Marlborough House School, Hove, 1911 to 1915, and at Felstead College, near Cambridge, and had planned to specialize in science at Cambridge, but instead became a farm apprentice for a year in Northampton, where he took part in the sporting and social life. Upon arrival in Canada, he was at first with the Bank of Montreal, then edited *Bookseller and Stationer,* a publisher's trade paper, and in 1929 became editor of the first book club in Canada, The Eaton Book Club. Since 1931 he has been educational editor with J. M. Dent & Sons, in Toronto, where he makes his home. He married in 1930 and is the father of two sons and one daughter.

In 1929 he left the Anglican Church, in which he had been reared, and became a Catholic. This spiritual experience is recorded in *Romewards,* which was the Catholic Book Club choice for February, 1933. It was printed in England and Canada as well as in the United States, and was very successful.

Eustace's short stories have made him well-known—he entered the fiction field in New York in 1927, and many English and Canadian reviews carry his articles and stories. His best story to date, "Obsession," appeared first in the *Canadian Forum,* was reprinted in the *English Review* and was included in O'Brien's *Best Short Stories* for 1929, with three stars. In all, it sold eleven times. It was translated into Scandinavian, and finally published in the first *English Review Book of Best Short Stories* (1934). He was also represented in "Best Short Stories" of 1930 and 1931.

His conversion to the Church aroused his interest in philosophy and theology as a means of broadening his spiritual life. St. Thomas became his special study, and he gratefully acknowledged the profound effect of the books of Maritain and Garrigou-Lagrange upon his mental growth. His *Mind and Mystery* (1937) is a philosophical commentary which was well received. *Catholicism, Communism, and Dictatorship* (1938) is a clear exposition of the problems confronting Catholics under totalitarian governments. It is stimulating reading and an excellent manual for study clubs. In 1943 *House of Bread* was published, with the sub-title "A Catholic Journey." It is an autobiographical account written for converts and prospective Catholics.

C. J. Eustace has been writing ever since he can remember and has numerous unpublished scripts as well as new books and stories in the making. He writes a weekly column in the *Catholic Record* of London, Ontario, the *Northwest Review* of Winnipeg, and *The Western Catholic* of Edmonton, Alberta, Canada. He has contributed at various times to *The Commonweal, Thought* and *The Sign.*

His other books include: *The Scarlet Gentleman* (1927); *Damaged Lives* (1934), and *An Infinity of Questions* (1946), in which he suggests "the relation between mysticism and art through the brilliant studies of five women of our day."   C. M. N.

Virgil B. Fairman *see* Reverend Andrew F. Klarmann

Mabel Adelaide Farnum

The literary career of Mabel Adelaide Farnum began at the age of fifteen, when her first published work appeared in *The Sunday Companion,* a magazine for Catholic youth, published in New York. This was a serial of the life of Christ, which appeared weekly in the magazine pages during the entire school year. Other magazines asked for her work, so that for the next few years she wrote children's stories continuously in both serial and short-story form, as well as essays.

Her first poem was printed when she was eighteen Father Hugh Blunt, the well-known writer, encouraged her efforts in both story-writing and poetry, and she was especially pleased that the priest-author added for lines to her first poem. A little later Father Walter Dwight, S.J., accepted her first sonnet for *America*. Father Dwight promoted the work of the young author in a most gracious manner, and subsequently published a series of her sonnets, also other poems, in the Jesuit weekly. One of Miss Farnum's poems, entitled "Mary's Lament" won a place of honor in a poetry contest sponsored by *The Queen's Work,* then a story magazine. Father Garesche, who was editor at the time, asked Miss Farnum to do a short story for him. Although she was desirous of keeping on in poetry without interruption, she complied with his request. Unknown to her, this story was entered in a national short story contest conducted by that magazine. The judges in the contest were Kathleen Norris, the well-known writer, and two prominent newspapermen, one a member of the Chicago *Tribune* and the other a member of the staff of the New York *Times*. Three thousand writers from all over the United States competed. The first prize, the Marian Medal, was awarded to Miss Farnum's short story, *The Strange Man.* Eleven years later she won first prize in a national short story contest sponsored by *Extension Magazine.* This story was titled *The House Numbered Nineteen.* A poem *Good Friday Night,* was awarded a place of honor in a poetry contest conducted by *The Far East.*

Miss Farnum continued writing short stories for *The Queen's Work* under the editorships of Father William Agnew, S.J., later president of Creighton University, and Father Henry Spalding, S.J., well-known writer of boys' books. A serial story printed in the columns, titled *The Town Landing,* appeared in book form. Stories by this author were also regularly appearing in ten leading Catholic magazines, including *The Catholic World* and *Ave Maria*. The late Father Daniel Hudson, C.S.C., beloved apostle of the Catholic press, sent message to Miss Farnum, saying: "You write equally well for children and for adults."

A letter from His Eminence Cardinal O'Connell brought happiness to the author when he graciously wrote her, in speaking of her book for youth, *The Town Landing,* "You have entered the field in which René Bazin is the great master. Something in your book constantly reminded me of him." Other tributes highly prized by Miss Farnum included one from Monsieur Henri Bordeaux, of the Academie Française who wrote a letter-preface for a collection of her essays yet to appear: "I read your essays with intense interest, often with deep emotion. You have well expressed the great principles taught me by my illustrious master, Paul Bourget."

Sixteen books to date have come from Miss Farnum's pen. The first, *The Wounded Face,* which as a serial ran in the Boston *Pilot,* was published when its author was still at school age. With the exception of four, these books are for young people. Two of them, *Our Little Vatican City Cousin,* and *The White Knight,* present the story, in fiction form, of two illustrious Pontiffs, Popes Pius XI and X.

Attracted to the field of biography and history, especially in relation to hagiography, Miss Farnum's latest three books tell the story of heroic apostles in the Church, two of them canonized saints. In 1938 there appeared in book form *A Carrack Sailed Away, The Voyage of Master Francis Xavier.* For this book the author studied the Portuguese language sufficiently to enable her to get a more complete background for her work and also to imbibe more of the atmosphere of the times and incidents related in the book.

Successor to this was *Street of the Half Moon,* an account of the Spanish noble, Pedro Claver, which appeared in 1940. For data the author visited the old Spanish city by the Caribbean where St. Claver lived and worked for the abandoned slaves, studying her matter with the Jesuits who care for the church which enshrines his precious relics.

Another historical and biographical work in dramatic form is *The Seven Golden Cities—Fray Marcos and The Coronado Adventure.* This is the story of a pioneer friar of four hundred years ago, who made a journey from Old Mexico to our Southwest in search of mythical golden cities which the government of Spain hoped to exploit and Christianize. For the data on this book the author worked for several autumn vacation periods in New Mexico, whither Fray Marcos travelled; with the friars she visited and explored certain sites introduced into the story. While her book deals with Franciscan exploration and pioneering, faithful allies in the work were Jesuit professors of the various universities in the United States, notably St. Louis, Loyola (Chicago) and San Francisco. In 1945 *The Wool Merchant of Segovia,* a life of St. Alonso Rodriguez, S.J., famous lay brother, appeared and in 1946 *The Sacred Scimitar,* a thrilling record of Father John de Brito's amazing missionary endeavors. Her latest book is *American Saint—Mother Cabrini—A Story for Youth.*

M. H.

Reverend Walter Farrell, O.P. 1902-

Under the aegis of Father Walter Farrell, O.P., a fresh impetus has lately been given to Thomistic studies in this country. It seems impossible to talk about Walter Farrell without talking about Thomas Aquinas. "If Thomas," he writes, "were to drop into a twentieth century club or a twentieth century pub for that matter, he would of course, be judged by twentieth century standards." To show us how to judge ourselves by the standards of St. Thomas has been Father Farrell's superb task. This contribution to the renaissance of Christian humanism is medieval in its daring— akin to that fourteenth century follower of the Angelic Doctor, the unknown author of *Everyman,* who boiled down the Summa to dramatic tabloid.

Since St. Thomas's great work is a four-part guide to the universe, Father Farrell conceived the brilliant and simple idea of giving everyone in America a four-part companion to that guide. "But it is important to remember," he tells us, "that it is the *Summa* reduced to popular language and not merely another book about St. Thomas or about the Summa." Yet what is modestly termed "popular language" is a transparent and sinewy prose which repeatedly bends to beauty for the sake of truth.

The four volumes of the *Companion to the Summa* are the result of the lectures Father Farrell gave to the Catholic Thought Association in New York. Commuting from Washington, D. C. to New York, for four years, Father Farrell gave twenty lectures each year on the *Summa* to this Association. When the series of lectures was completed, he submitted the material that now comprises Volume II of the *Companion to the Summa* and which he deemed the most readable, to Mr. Sheed to see if he would print it. Mr. Sheed accepted it. Volume II was printed in 1938. Volumes III, I and IV were published in 1940, 1941, and 1942 respectively. For Volume I the Gallery of Living Catholic Authors presented him with an illuminated scroll in testimony of the 1942 Catholic Literary award for the outstanding book of the past year. After thanking the Gallery of Living Catholic Authors, at a tea in his honor on November 11, Father Farrell stated his best volume was Volume IV. He also reiterated what he says in the foreword of his books, that all the good things in the books are taken from St. Thomas. The "double purpose of the whole work is an introduction to Thomas and a defense of the truths, natural and divine, by which human life is lived."

Walter Farrell was born in Chicago on the twenty-first of July 1902. His parents were James William Farrell and Minnie S. (Morgan) Farrell. He attended parochial schools conducted by the Dominican Sisters of Adrian, Michigan. After five years at Quigley Preparatory Seminary, he entered the Dominican order and was ordained to the priesthood in Washington, D. C. on June 9, 1927. From 1928 to 1930, because he manifested interest and ability in philosophy and theology, Father Farrell was sent to the University of Fribourg and received an S.T.D. degree. In 1930 he was appointed professor of theology at the Dominican House of Studies, Washington, D. C. In 1939 he was made Regent of Studies for the Eastern Province of St. Joseph. Returning to Rome in 1940, he was honored with the rarely given Dominican degree of S.T.M. (Master of Sacred Theology).

In 1942, Father Farrell volunteered his services as a Chaplain in the United States Navy and then went to the Navy Chaplains' Training School. He served as chaplain from 1943 to 1946. He is now Regent of Studies at the Dominican House of Studies in Washington, D. C.

Father Farrell is also the author of *Natural Moral Law According to St. Thomas and Suarez.*

A. M.

Robert Farren 1909-

Robert Farren, better known at home in Ireland by the Gaelic form of Roibeárd O'Faracháin, was born in Dublin, Ireland on April 24, 1909, seven years to the day before the insurrection which was led by Pádraic Pearse, Thomas MacDonagh, and Joseph Plunkett. For at least three generations on both sides his people have been natives of Dublin. The name Farren has been, for a few centuries, associated with the English stage, and includes such famous actors and actresses as Elizabeth and William Farren. The Farrens have, however, been known in Ireland for at least two centuries, for Eoghan Ruadh O'Suilleabhain, a Gaelic poet of the eighteenth century mentions the name; it occurs, too, among the regimental names in the American War of Independence.

After completing his primary education in St. Mary's National School, Dublin, Robert Farren entered St. Patrick's College, Drumcondra, for training as a National Teacher, and later took the degree of M.A. in Scholastic Philosophy in the National University of Ireland, with a thesis on "The Poetic Experience" discussed according to the philosophy of St. Thomas. He spent ten years from 1929 to 1939 teaching in primary schools, and was for two of those years also assistant editor of Capuchin Publications, Dublin, and foundation editor of the Gaelic annual, *Eire*. On undertaking the latter work he received from Dr. Douglas Hyde, President of Eire, Gaelic scholar and poet, a letter expressing the President's pleasure at the appointment.

In the year 1936 Robert Farren published his first book of poems, *Thronging Feet*, the motto of which was David's "Credidi, ergo locutus sum" (I believed, therefore have I spoken), and in which was expressed an enthusiastic belief in Catholic truth. The book had somewhat more than the ordinary success of poetry, though some reviewers professed to find the influence of Francis Thompson and Gerard Manley Hopkins in it. In fact, the author had not then read any poem of Hopkins, and very little of Thompson, and the main influence in his work was that of Gaelic poetry.

Before and after the publication of this first book Farren had published poems, articles, and stories in American, Irish and English periodicals, notably in *Spirit* and *The Commonweal*. His next book was *Fíen gan mhoirt (Wine Without Lees)*, a collection of original stories in Irish. This was in 1938. In 1939 Sheed and Ward published his second book of poems, *Time's Wall Asunder*, which continued and developed the notes of the earlier work, and revealed an interest in humorous and satirical poetry. In 1939, also, the poet was appointed Director of Talks at Radio Éireann, the broadcasting house of Éire. (At that time the director of Irish broadcasting was Dr. T. J. Kiernan, now Minister for Éire to the Vatican.) In 1940 he was invited to join the Board of Directors of the famous Abbey Theatre, Dublin, mother of the Little Theatres of the World. He has continued to fill both positions since then and has recently been approved by the Minister for Education as a senior member of the Board which directs the production of plays in Gaelic at the Abbey Theatre.

In 1942 Sheed and Ward published Farren's most ambitious work, *The First Exile*. It is a long poem (running to 3,500 lines), in varied metres, portraying the life of Colmcille (or Columba), one of the greatest of the Irish saints and one of the three patrons of Ireland, as well as evangelist of Scotland. The poem is based on Adamnan's life of the saint, one of the choice treasures of medieval biography, and on the Gaelic life by Manus O'Donnell, published by the University of Illinois. The poem a leading Irish critic is willing to accept as "the masterpiece of modern Irish poetry." A section of it has already been broadcast from Radio Éireann, and the same section, arranged for the stage, was produced at the Abbey Theatre early in 1943. (Incidentally, a one-act play in verse, dealing with the 1916 rebellion, was produced over Robert Farren's name in the same theatre to mark the twenty-seventh anniversary of the Rising.) *Rime, Gentlemen, Please* appeared in 1945. The book contains short Irish lyrics and "Lost Light" a poetic play about the year 1916.

The personality of St. Colmcille has fascinated the poet from the age of twelve, and the idea of expressing it in a book took shape in his mind very early. In 1937 he began reading for the work and in the same year began to write it. After six months' work it was interrupted by preparation for the degree of M.A., which involved severe philosophical study; but it was resumed towards the middle of 1939, after *Time's Wall Asunder* had been completed. Unremitting daily labour during the next three years brought it to a conclusion in August 1941. The delays of war have held up publication but the book is now ready. The most prominent of Irish poets, Austin Clarke, said after reading *The First Exile:* "This is not just a poem by Robert Farren; it is something which has happened to Irish literature. All the currents which flowed, one in this writer, one in that, have met in this poem."

Another phase of this poet's work has been the restoration in Ireland of the lost art of reciting poetry. With Austin Clarke, who was formerly an adjudicator at the Oxford Poetry Festival in England, he has chosen and trained young men and women in this lovely and difficult art, and broadcast, and produced in theatres, choral speech programs, and poetic plays. The work which Yeats laboured at in the Abbey Theatre—the establishment of a poetic theatre, he hopes to continue there as well as on the air.

John Villiers Farrow   1904-

Love of travel and a desire for adventure have taken John Farrow to distant places. He is best known for his story of another who went far afield to labor, in Molokai, *Damien the Leper.* This book was most successful and established Farrow as an author. His first literary product was an *English-Tahitian Dictionary* which he brought out in 1932, translating his native tongue into that of an island he knew well. The South Seas are familiar to him. He cruised and traded around the islands in his own schooner. He was born in Sydney, Australia, in 1904, the son of Colonel Joseph Rashmere Villiers Farrow. He was educated privately in Australia, England and on the Continent. Then he saw adventure as both soldier and sailor, serving through two South American revolutions and rounding the Horn in a sailing ship. He also joined several scientific expeditions, and is a Fellow of the Royal Geographic Society.

Motion pictures have always interested him. In France and Austria he wrote and directed many screen plays and is now (1947) a cinema director in Hollywood. He married the screen star, Maureen O'Sullivan, of Roscommon, Ireland, in 1936. They have four children. His home is in Bel Air, California.

With the advent of war, Farrow, well-known as deep water yachtsman, joined the Canadian Naval Forces (1940) and was given a lieutenant's commission and duties as controller of naval information and then in mine-sweeping. Later he won distinction serving as a lieutenant commander.

He found opportunity, however, to continue his writing, and in 1942 his book on the Popes, from St. Peter to the present Pontiff, was completed. This book, *Pageant of the Popes,* was begun immediately after the success of his *Damien the Leper.* Strange to say he could do more work on it while on sea duty than at Hollywood. He was stricken with the dreaded typhus germ in the South Atlantic. The dreary months spent recuperating in a small Dutch hospital in Curacao saw the completion of the manuscript after almost five years. Mr. Farrow was released from active naval service and instructed to take a long rest. Instead he returned to Hollywood and directed "Wake Island," which won the award for the best movie of the season. Other moving pictures that he directed were: "Commandos Strike at Dawn" and "China."

His book on Father Damien was written at the time the interest of all the world was aroused in the Belgian priest whose remains were then being transferred, with befitting honor, and by special ship, from the South Sea island of Molokai, where he had heroically devoted his life to the care of lepers, half way across the world to Belgium, to repose in his native land and there to await the preliminary procedures of the cause of his beatification. In the year of publication of *Damien the Leper* (1936), Farrow was created a Knight of the Holy Sepulchre by Pope Pius XI. He was also made an honorary member of the Belgian Societe Royale Humanitaire. Other decorations are Chevalier of the Order of Nichan Iftikhar (Tunis), the Order of the Crown of Rumania and the Order of St. John of Jerusalem.

"For the outstanding book of 1942," he was awarded the annual Catholic Literary Award of the Gallery of Living Catholic Authors for his *Pageant of the Popes*.   **C. M. N.**

Michael Cardinal Faulhaber   1869-

Fearless opponent of Nazism, Michael Cardinal Faulhaber is a masterful preacher and erudite writer, having effectively used his oratory and pen in defense of justice for church and nation. He was born in Klosterheidenfeld, Bavaria, in 1869, of a family of millers and bakers. From 1887 to 1888 he served in the Bavarian Army. He studied for the priesthood at Würzburg Seminary, was ordained in 1892 and received his degree of S.T.D. from the University of Würzburg. When only twenty-four he was appointed prefect at the Kilianeum Seminary and from 1895 to 1898 was given further scope for his intellectual ability in studies abroad. He went to Italy, England and Spain, engaging in research at the Vatican and at Oxford. Upon his return he was appointed to the faculty at Würzburg, and after four years, at the age of thirty-four, he became professor of Old Testament exegesis at the University of Strassbourg. Many books on religious history were written at this time, and he contributed articles to *The Catholic Encyclopedia*.

In 1911 he was consecrated Bishop of Speyer and administered this see during the greater part of World War I, aiding German soldiers and intervening on behalf of Allied prisoners. In 1917 he became Archbishop of Munich and Freising, and for his loyal services as prelate, King Ludwig III of Bavaria conferred upon him the rank of nobility. When the revolution broke November 6, 1918), Archbishop Faulhaber was suspected of harboring the King and machine guns were mounted outside his home. In constant danger of death, he nevertheless preached against the socialist philosophy, and under the Bavarian Soviet Republic in 1919 he daily passed the Red Guards unmolested on his way to the cathedral. In 1921 he was created Cardinal by Pope Benedict XV.

In the spring of 1923 Cardinal Faulhaber visited the United States to lecture on behalf of impoverished Germany, and American help was given. He assured President Harding that the Germans were anxious to obtain work to earn their bread but were unable to do so. In the face of famine he exhorted his people to courage. The Cardinal was not sympathetic to the Weimar Republic, but under Hindenburg, Stresemann and Bruening conditions improved. From the very beginning, at the time of the Beer Hall Putsch in 1923, he was an opponent of the Nazis, and when they came to power in 1933 shots were fired through the windows of his palace. He preached that New Year's Eve against the myth of Teutonic superiority, and his sermons during Advent, on Hebrew revelation as an integral part of the Christian religion, and the falsity of Teuton paganism, were translated into English by George D. Smith and published in 1934 under the title of *Judaism, Christianity and Germany.* Another book published in English is *Women of the Bible* (translated in 1938), a treatise on the position and true character of womanhood, with examples from Sacred Scripture.

Under the Nazi regime Cardinal Faulhaber had consistently defended the rights of the Church. He is the spiritual leader of fifteen million German Catholics, and his palace is open to all seeking his aid. "Extreme nationalism," he declares, "is the enemy of world peace and the real heresy of the twentieth century."

Just a few days before the unconditional surrender of Germany, the Cardinal told Dr. Max Jordan, the war correspondent: "We shall go to work as soon as we can." About one-half of the church buildings in his diocese were destroyed by bombing.   C. M. N.

Reverend Leonard Feeney, S.J.   1897-

Individuality and a rare whimsical quality distinguish the writings of the Reverend Leonard Feeney, S.J., whether poetry or prose. He entered the Society of Jesus in 1914, at the age of seventeen, having been born in Lynn, Massachusetts in 1897. His early years at home and at school, taught by the Sisters of St. Joseph, at Lynn, and by the Jesuits, at Boston College High School, are delightfully recounted in *Survival Till Seventeen.* There are stories about "Heaven in a Pond," the Chinese laundryman, the corner grocer, and Sunday evenings in the Feeney family. His parents were born in Ireland but raised in the United States, and Leonard was their eldest child. After his novitiate at St. Andrew-on-Hudson, Poughkeepsie, New York, later studies at Woodstock and Weston Colleges, and teaching at Canisius High School and Holy Cross College, Father Feeney was ordained at Weston by Bishop Dinand, S.J., in 1928. Tertianship at St. Beuno's College, North Wales, was followed by studies in art and esthetics at Wadham College and Campion Hall, Oxford, and summer courses at the Sorbonne, Paris. While in England he was engaged also as lecturer and preacher.

Upon his return to the United States, he was successively lecturer in English and professor of English literature at Boston College until 1936, when he became literary editor of the weekly, *America,* which position he held until 1940. At present (1947) he is teaching at the Jesuit Seminary at Weston College, Weston, Massachusetts. He is in demand as a lecturer, and his topics and their treatment are refreshing. "Preservation of Personality" he chose as his subject on one occasion, but his purpose was not to tell how to be fascinating, he said, for charm must come through impulse; personality he considers an art, not a science.

Certainly Father Feeney is gifted with a personal charm which seems to pervade his writings. His poems comprise four books: *In Towns and Little Towns; Riddle and Reverie; Boundaries,* and *Song for a Listener.* Here is the profundity of simple things treated with a light touch. Here are wit and originality. Father Feeney calls his poems "The Pygmies":

> "I count my pygmies, one by one,
> The nearly finished, half-begun,
> Bedraggled poems I have written,
> Companioned by a clock and kitten,
> On littered desk, by candle-light,
> Locked in my chamber late at night,
> When folks in bed were long tucked in,
> And maybe I had better been."

His essays are equally witty and original. In addition to *Survival Till Seventeen,* he has published *Fish on Friday* and *You'd Better Come Quietly.* In "Some Outlines" in the last book, there is a beautiful simplicity in his familiarity with divine things. A great admirer of Mother Seton, Father Feeney faithfully portrays her in the biography *An American Woman: Elizabeth Bailey Seton. Your Second Childhood* appeared in 1945. He also contributes to magazines.

Father Feeney is a former president of the Catholic Poetry Society of America, and is an Academy member of the Gallery of Living Catholic Authors.   C. M. N.

Reverend Joseph C. Fenton   1906-

The careful research and crystal clear presentation which characterize the works of the Reverend Dr. Joseph Fenton have gained for him a recognized place of honor among Catholic theologians here and abroad. Born in Springfield, Massachusetts, in 1906, Father Fenton's preliminary education was at Holy Name Grammar School of that city and at Cathedral High School from which he graduated in 1922. His college years were spent under the Jesuits at Holy Cross College, Worcester, Massachusetts, where he received the B.A. degree in 1926. His gift of the pen was recognized while at Holy Cross and he was on the staff of *The Purple,* and also wrote for *The Tomahawk.*

His years of preparation for the priesthood were spent at the Grand Seminary, Montreal, from 1926 to 1930, until he was ordained priest in St. Michael's Cathedral, Springfield, Massachusetts by Bishop O'Leary. From the University of Montreal he received the degrees of S.T.L. and J.C.B. The year following (1931) found him in Rome where he obtained his S.T.D. from the Angelico. His doctoral dissertation, *De Natura Theologaie Catholicae,* was directed by Father Reginald Garrigou-Lagrange, O.P., renowned Roman professor.

Returning home, the young priest, from 1931 to 1934, served as curate in his home diocese of Springfield. Then for a year he taught philosophy at St. Ambrose College, Davenport, Iowa, and from 1935 to 1938 was professor of dogmatic theology at St. Bernard's Seminary, Rochester, New York. Since then Dr. Fenton has been at the Catholic University of America, teaching fundamental dogmatic theology and compiling a history of Post-Tridentine theology. From June 1943 to 1945 he was dean of the School of Sacred Theology of the Catholic University. He is now associate professor of dogmatic theology. He was administrative assistant to the late Bishop Joseph M. Corrigan when the latter was rector of the university and dean of the School of Sacred Theology. He became acting dean when Bishop Corrigan died. His book, *The Theology of Prayer,* is based on St. Thomas Aquinas, Sylvius, Vallgornera, and Joseph of the Holy Spirit and shows with scientific accuracy and clearness the Catholic doctrine of prayer.

His *Concept of Sacred Theology,* a masterly exposition of the nature and dignity of that science, was published in 1941. A year later, *We Stand With Christ,* an able and complete defense of the rational credibility of Catholic dogma, marked him as one of the outstanding authorities on Catholic apologetics. In 1943, his *The Calling of a Diocesan Priest* was welcomed as a valuable addition to the literature on the sacerdotal vocation.

With the issue of January, 1943, Dr. Fenton became editor of *The American Ecclesiastical Review.* His articles in that periodical on Ecclesiology have contributed greatly to progress in that field of sacred knowledge. He is also widely known for his contributions to *Columbia, America,* the old *Fortnightly Review,* the *Catholic Educational Review,* and *Le Seminaire* of Montreal.

He is Secretary of the Catholic Theological Society of America.

D. D.

Reverend Joseph H. Fichter, S.J. 1908-

The main trend of the special studies of Father Joseph Fichter, S.J. has been toward social philosophy.

Joseph Fichter was born in Union City, New Jersey, June 10, 1908, the third child of six (five boys, one girl) of Charles John Fichter and Victoria (Weiss) Fichter. After graduating from the high school of the Josephinum Pontifical College, at Columbus, Ohio, he was engaged until 1930 in the residential building business with his brother, Harry C. Fichter, a contractor at Tenafly, New Jersey.

In August of that year, he entered the novitiate of the New Orleans Province of the Society of Jesus at Grand Coteau, Louisiana. He made his first vows in September 1932. Two years of college work affiliated with Loyola University of New Orleans and the year of 1934 to 1935 at St. Louis University obtained for him in June 1935 the A.B. degree. The following year he taught at the Jesuit High School in New Orleans and then taught for a year from 1936 to 1937 at Spring Hill College, Mobile, Alabama. From 1937 to 1939 he studied again at St. Louis University, receiving his M.A. in sociology in February 1939. Then he went to St. Mary's College, St. Mary, Kansas, for four years, 1939 to 1943, for his theological studies; being ordained priest there in June 1942. The year of tertianship, 1943 to 1944, was spent at St. Robert's Hall, Pomfret Centre, Connecticut. Since then he has been an instructor at Loyola University, New Orleans.

Father Fichter began writing for publication in 1933, and received inspiration and encouragement (also acceptance slips) from Father James M. Gillis of *The Catholic World,* Michael Williams of *The Commonweal,* and Father Wilfrid Parsons of *America.*

His first book, *Roots of Change,* published in 1939 is an appraisal of the thoughts of people from Vincent de Paul to Sidney Webbs, whom he considered the intellectual roots of the social, economic and political changes that have taken place since 1500. The idea for this book came from an enthusiastic seminar on Social Reformers conducted in 1938 at St. Louis University by the late Father Raymond Corrigan, S.J., Ph.D., then head of the History Department.

The social philosophy of Francis Suarez and its neglect by social thinkers and historians in general, were the compelling reasons for the next book, entitled *Man of Spain: a Biography of Francis Suarez.* Published in the summer of 1940, it is the only life of Suarez to appear in the English language.

Then Father Fichter started a work on a life of Ignatius Loyola, stressing his social theories and practices, but he has not yet finished it.

In 1942 appeared his third book, *Saint Cecil Cyprian,* the only biography of the saint written in English by a Catholic. The saint (and his first name) are very popular with the Anglicans who revere him as the great exponent of their "branch theory" of Church government and authority. Father Fichter stresses the active social work done by Saint Cyprian in Africa in the third century.

The next book, *James Laynez, Jesuit* was published in 1944. It is the life story of the great Jewish Jesuit, who succeeded Ignatius Loyola as General of the Society of Jesus, a brilliant theologian at the Council of Trent, adviser of Popes and organizer of Jesuit education. For almost ten years Father Fichter worked on this book—the only book on James Laynez in the English language.

Christianity, the fifth book by Father Fichter, is an outline of dogma for laymen. This book, published in 1945, grew out of notes made for the comprehensive examination taken at the end of the course in theology, May, 1943. It is based on a conviction that Catholic lay people are starving for a positive and readable explanation of Catholic dogma.

Father Fichter has contributed articles to *The Catholic World, America, The Commonweal, Ave Maria, The Queen's Work, Sign, Columbia* and other periodicals under his own name and also a pen name.

M. H.

Reverend Gerald M. Fitzgerald, C.S.C. 1894-

Writing occasionally under the pen name of "A Page on Father Page"—"chosen with reference to Our Blessed Mother's Service"—Father Fitzgerald's greatest inspiration to write is his three mothers, The Blessed Virgin Mary, Holy Mother the Church, and his own little mother.

The second and oldest living of the eight sons of Michael Edward Fitzgerald and Elizabeth (Brassil) Fitzgerald, Father Fitzgerald was born at South Framingham, Massachusetts, in 1894. His father is superintendent of the public schools of Cambridge, Massachusetts.

After graduating from the Weymouth High School in 1912, he entered Boston College and then St. John's Seminary. He was ordained for the Boston Archdiocese in 1921. From 1921 to 1933 he was a curate at Our Lady of the Presentation Church, Boston. In 1933 he joined the Congregation of the Holy Cross and was professed in 1934. He was rector, until 1943, of Our Lady of the Holy Cross Seminary in North Easton, Massachusetts, where high school graduates are given preliminary training before entering the novitiate. In 1943 he volunteered to serve as a chaplain but was given a post in the Military Ordinariate, which helps hundreds of Catholic chaplains in their spiritual and religious needs. Later he was made secretary at the Military Ordinariate in New York City. Then he served as Post Chaplain of the Normoyle Ordnance Depot in San Antonio, Texas. He is a brother of Brassil Fitzgerald (short story writer and essayist), and of John C. Fitzgerald, Dean of the Law School of Loyola University, Chicago.

His books are: *Paths From Bethlehem; Juxta Crucem; God's Rainbow; Letters of Father Page; Streets In Nazareth* (Poetry), and *Path of Love,* which contains counsels and spiritual direction. His devotional booklet, *The Holy Face and the Way of the Cross,* is very popular.

M. H.

Ella Marie Flick

One of the third generation to be born on Pine Street, Philadelphia within the shadow of old St. Mary's and within the sound of the old Liberty Bell, Miss Ella Marie Flick is the daughter of Lawrence Francis Flick, M.D., LL.D. (an internationally known tuberculosis specialist), and Ella J. Stone Flick—both deceased. She is called Ella Marie to distinguish her from her mother and grandmother, whose first names were also Ella. The grandfather of her mother was called upon to help mend the crack in the Liberty Bell. He made four bells from the shavings. These bells are still in the family and are valued highly as heirlooms.

Miss Flick was placed in the hands of a governess until nine years of age and spent all her remaining school years—with the exception of one year in the mountains of Pennsylvania, under the Sisters of Mercy—at the Academy of Notre Dame, Rittenhouse Square.

Her first attempt at writing was a sentimental story for *St. Xavier's Journal.* This fired her ambition to write. When she was still in high school, her father enrolled her as a life member of the American Catholic Historical Society. To encourage her to write, her father offered $25.00 for every historical manuscript she had published in the records of the Society. During the next three years some half-dozen manuscripts were published. At first the author was not partial to history, but from months of research required for each article, and from her father's patient guidance, she won a facility for biographical writing that caused her to make it her life's work.

The Benziger magazine published her first "real" story. She put into the poor box, for luck, the $9.00 she received for it. Her best articles have been written for *The Catholic World* and *America.* She wrote about one hundred articles for thirteen magazines.

About 1932 she gave up magazine writing to become secretary to her father and remained with him almost day and night until his death.

In between office hours she wrote *Chaplain Duffy* at the request of Archbishop Mitty. *The Life of Bishop McDevitt* was written at the request of Mr. Galbally, lay editor of *The American Ecclesiastical Review.* Since the death of her father she has specialized in research. Most of it centers around him or his tuberculosis work. For the White Haven Sanatorium Association, she wrote a biography of her father. It was published in 1940. Four years later she brought out a larger volume on the life of her father, entitled *Beloved Crusader: Lawrence F. Flick, Physician.*

M. H.

Reverend Paul Joseph Foik, C.S.C. 1880-1941

As a specialist in the field of history, Dr. Paul Joseph Foik for many years carried on research. He is the founder and was president of the Texas Catholic Historical Society. Through his efforts, more than 70,000 documents have been collected.

Dr. Foik was born at Stratford, Ontario in 1880. He received his early education there. His preparatory training was received at the Collegiate Institute. In 1900 he was attracted to the University of Notre Dame where he continued his studies. In 1901 he entered the Congregation of the Holy Cross and was professed in 1904. He graduated with a Ph.B. degree in 1907. During that year he became a naturalized citizen. While he pursued his studies in theology, he majored in history and the social sciences. He was ordained in 1911. In 1912 he obtained the degree of Ph.D. from Catholic University.

His first assignment to duty as a priest and a professed religious of the Congregation of the Holy Cross was that of Librarian of Notre Dame University in 1912. From 1916 to 1917, he supervised the erection of a new library building at Notre Dame. At this time he made a survey of existing conditions in Catholic libraries. A strong appeal was made for cooperation and united effort by all librarians and educators. Through his efforts authorization was given to found the library section of the National Catholic Education Association. In 1920 the first formal assembly of librarians and other interested persons was held in Philadelphia. For nine consecutive years, Dr. Foik held the chairmanship of the library section.

He left Notre Dame in 1924 to become librarian at St. Edward's University, Austin, Texas.

In 1931 the operations of the library section of the National Catholic Education Association were transferred to the Catholic Library Association at the suggestion of Dr. Foik.

He was chosen a member of the committee for the restoration of the library of the University of Louvain, Belgium.

At St. Edward's University he was head of the foreign languages department, professor of German and American history and Dean of the College of Arts and Sciences.

Among his writings are: *The First Catholic Newspaper* (1914) (brochure); *Pioneer Catholic Journalism; Martyrs of the Southwest; Early Catholic Explorers of the Southwest; Fray Juan de Padilla.* He was editor of *Our Catholic Heritage in Texas* (7 vols.).

I. C.

Jeremiah Denis Mathias Ford   1873-

Professor Jeremiah Denis Mathias Ford, for forty-eight years professor of Romance Languages at Harvard University, has an imposing two-thirds of a column devoted to him in *Who's Who in America.* It lists his many degrees (including honorary) and his writings, beginning with his first printed article, which appeared when he was twenty-four, in French in the *Annales du Midi*, an organ of the University of Toulouse (the same University which was to give him an honorary degree).

His father, Jeremiah Ford, was deeply concerned with the rebellion against British inhumanity in Ireland when he was a lad of twenty and because of his Fenian activities had to flee from Ireland in 1861. He came to the United States and enlisted in the Union Army at the opening of the Civil War for the usual period of three months. At the end of that time he enlisted in the Navy and served to the end of the war. Then, with others, he took a ship of arms to Ireland to help in the Fenian uprising in 1867. The rising failed and he again escaped to America, married Mary Agnes Collins and settled in Cambridge, Massachusetts. Jeremiah was born in Cambridge, Massachusetts on July 2, 1873. In 1886 his father did the reverse of what many Irishmen were doing at that period. He took his wife and five children back to Cork and remained there for four years. It was at this time that young Jeremiah Ford was sent to the Christian Brothers at the North Monastery in Cork. He speaks now with affection and praises highly the wonderful education and inspiration he received from their teaching.

Professor Ford was particularly devoted to his grandfather who did not share some of the extreme views concerning the Fenians held by his five sons. Young Jeremiah specialized in languages with the Christian Brothers (English, Latin, French, German and Italian). He took the Intermediate Education Boards annual examination each year and was a Junior Exhibitioner in 1888, the fourth highest in all Ireland out of thirty-five hundred contestants, and was awarded the English Gold Medal in 1889. America now won what England and Ireland lost, for instead of his wealthy bachelor uncle's sending him to Oxford University as planned, his father in the spring of 1890 decided to return to America with his family and settled in Cambridge. In 1891 Professor Ford entered

Harvard University. In 1894 he received his A.B., his A.M. in 1895 and his Ph.D. in 1897. He taught there for forty-eight years until his retirement in 1943.

He proudly boasts that his family has been Catholic, back through the ages. His youngest sister has been a Dominican nun for thirty-six years. Two of his sons were in the service in World War II. Robert, who graduated with high honors from Harvard, was with the U.S.N.R. until 1933 when he became a captain for the Pan-American Airways, flying over South American routes for five years; over the Atlantic for two and over the Pacific for five, saving his clipper plane from the Japanese in 1941 and commended for saving American lives in a ship blown up by Japanese. Richard, who graduated magna cum laude from Harvard, is a surgeon and was a major in the Army Medical Corps. For three years he served in the Pacific as Commanding Officer of the Fourth Portable Surgical Hospital and has been decorated with the Legion of Merit for saving very many lives at the front in the Burma Campaign. Professor Ford's daughters, Anna and Elizabeth, both distinguished themselves in educational circles before they were married. His wife was Anna Winifred Fearns. They were married on January 1, 1902.

Professor Ford has contributed a great many articles on the literature of Spain and Spanish-America to the *Catholic Encyclopedia*. From 1908 to 1921 he was chief examiner for Spanish under the College Entrance Examinations Board. From 1927 to 1936 he was editor-in-chief of *Speculum*. He likes to recall that the Superior General of the Christian Brothers who, in his youth, had been his best teacher in Ireland used to visit him in Cambridge, Massachusetts when on his trips around the world to inspect his colleges and schools and became "uncle" to his children. President Eliot of Harvard met and admired him.

Professor Ford is five feet ten and one-half inches in height, has a gentle voice and bright blue eyes that twinkle as he talks. He has a deep devotion to Spanish and Portuguese literature. As long ago as 1914 he visited South America on a good will tour with a group of representative Bostonians, doubtless one of the earliest Pan-America good will gestures. His lovely home in Cambridge is built in such a way that the moment you enter the door you know that you are in the house of a scholar who loves his books. The folding doors of his library are wide open and the books are on shelves that reach to the very high ceiling. They seem a very part of the life of his house. A visitor to the Ford home is dear old Professor Gulick, now blind. Professor Ford was awarded the Laetare Medal by the University of Notre Dame in 1937. In 1945 he was elected to the French Academy as a foreign member in the section called Academie des Inscriptions et Belles Lettres, a distinction that rarely comes to the United States and one which, being a truly modest scholar, he did not expect.

He devotes himself now entirely to his writing and it has been hinted that he may be persuaded to write his autobiography. Among his works are: *The Old Spanish Sibilants* (Vol. VII of Harvard Studies and Notes) (1900), and *Main Currents of Spanish Literature* (1919).

A. F.

Mrs. Anthony Formolo   *see* Rosemary Obermeyer

Pamela Frankau   1908-

A convert to the Catholic Church since 1942, Pamela Frankau is the granddaughter of the Victorian novelist "Frank Danby" and the daughter of the novelist Gilbert Frankau. She was received into the Church in Edinburgh.

Miss Frankau's early years were spent at Windsor with her mother and sister, Ursula. Her mother, a journalist, formed her literary tastes. Chesterton, Belloc, Compton Mackenzie (a great personal friend) and Evelyn Waugh, were the authors Pamela read most. She was educated at Stapleton and while there won first scholastic honors. She had no university training, which she regrets.

At eighteen she began her literary career with the Amalgamated Press. A year later she wrote her first novel, *Marriage of Harlequin*. In these early days she was under the influence of Michael Arlen. "His outlook," she said, "certainly colored all my writing and I would never put anyone into my novels that did not use a foot-long cigarette holder, drive a Hispano Suiza and have peaches for breakfast."

In 1931 she became a copywriter. During an illness when she was in her twenties, she wrote her autobiography. "That's one of the few of my books, that I still like," she said. It was published in 1935 under the title *I Find Four People*. It is an account of the successive phases of her career. The novel, in her opinion "is the one place where one can tell the absolute truth without having to subscribe to anybody's policy."

She is the author of: *Three* (1929); *She and I* (1930); *Letters from A Modern Daughter to Her Mother* (1931); *Born at Sea* (1932); *Women Are So Serious* (1932); *I Was The Man* (1932); *Foolish Apprentices* (1933); *Fifty-Fifty and Other Stories* (1936); *The Devil We Know* (1939), and *Appointment With Death* (1940). She also is known as a broadcaster.

M. H.

Theodore Penrose Fry 1892-

Theodore Penrose Fry was born in Yorkshire in 1892. He comes of Quaker stock as the names of his father and mother bear witness—Sir John Peace Fry and Margaret Fox. Yet even in childhood, he tells us in the story of his conversion—*The Church Surprising,* he longed for something more than that austerity of worship practised by the Friends. It was always a better Sunday when he was taken to Chapel, for he loved the singing and the mild ceremony and the dignity.

Mr. Fry attended Winchester and King's College and received an M.A. from Christ's College, Cambridge. Here at the university he was drawn to the Catholic Church and often went to Mass. How honestly and humbly he looks back upon this period. "Perhaps if I had had more 'guts' at this point, or had been more fully developed, I should have been clearer in my mind, and seized upon what I needed." But he chose the alternative, Anglicanism. After serving as lieutenant in the first World War, he was ordained in the Church of England in 1921.

During the next eight years he was assistant in various Anglo-Catholic parishes, returning to Rome along the path that his ancestors had taken away from her. "Like them," he writes, "I passed through the Church of England but found there 'no abiding city.'" Since he was never exposed to low church opinions, he was better disposed to the reception of Catholic theology. With his wife, the novelist Sheila Kaye Smith, whom he had married in 1924, he was received into the Church in 1929. Mrs. Fry tells the story again in *Three Ways Home*—how St. Thérèse of Lisieux had wrought her sweet influence upon them and how they had said that they would be received into the Church by anyone but a Jesuit. Yet Father Martindale, S.J., instructed them both and wrote the preface to *The Church Surprising.*

Penrose Fry's second book since his conversion, *The Making of a Layman,* was published in 1938. The home of the Frys is called Little Doucegrove. The Frys have no children. During World War II, Mr. Fry was an officer in the National Fire Service.

Stanislas Fumet   1896-

One of the leaders of the Catholic social movement in France is Stanislas Fumet, editor-in-chief of *Temps Présent* since 1937. Up to the time of the German occupation, this weekly paper and its supporters, grouped under the title "Amis du temps présent," wielded considerable influence. Fumet described his movement as "the expression of authentic Catholic action, above the outside party strife." His groups were established not only in Paris, but throughout the provinces where they continued to function even after the armistice. The paper *Temps Présent*, is extremely well edited and counts among its contributors many of the best known French Catholic writers. François Mauriac contributes a weekly column for it.

Fumet, like Maritain, was a fervent disciple of Leon Bloy, about whom he wrote an excellent book. He is a very able journalist with experience in the field of social work and a knowledge of international affairs. One of his earlier undertakings was the direction of a small paper, literary in content, called *Aux écoutes du silence*. He was a frequent contributor to *L'Intransigeant,* one of the largest Parisian secular dailies. He was also associated with Maritain in various publishing enterprises, among them the editorship of two excellent collections of Catholic books: *Le Roseau d'Or* published by Plon and *Les Villes* by Desclee de Brouwer.

Himself an able writer, among his works are: *Notre Baudelaire; Ernest Hello ou le Drame de la Lumière; Le Procès de L'Art; Qui est La France?; Mission de Leon Bloy; Jeanne d'Arc,* and *Thérèse de Lisieux.* In collaboration with Georges Fedotov he wrote, *Le Renouveau Spirituel en France et en Russie.* His *Saint Martin de Porres* was translated into English by Father Norbert Georges, O.P., and published in this country by the *Torch,* the organ of the Dominican Fathers.

Publication of *Temps Présent* in Paris was suspended after the fall of France. After the armistice of 1940, he edited another weekly, at Lyons, which took the place of *Temps Présent* and was called *Temps Nouveau.* On August 15, 1941, while making a retreat at La Salette, Fumet was notified of its suppression by Admiral Darlan, along with a number of other Catholic papers and magazines. After only eight months, *Temps Nouveau,* the only organ of the open Resistance Movement in the so-called "free zone" was suppressed by the Vichy government "on account of its general tendencies." Afterwards he started, also at Lyons, another editorial venture, *Les Editions du Livre Français* which was to go to Paris after the liberation.

He and François Mauriac, after the liberation of France from the Germans, reproached the Church leaders for showing respect for the Vichy government. The Episcopate contended that it had "to regard the Vichy government as a legitimate government, regularly invested with power by the National Assembly in July 1940; that the Sovereign Pontiff kept a Nuncio at Vichy, a fact which, for Catholics, abolished any discussion of legitimacy; that the United States of America kept an ambassador with Marshal Petain" to quote *The Catholic Register.*

From 1940 to 1944 Fumet was in close contact with all the resistance movements, especially with "Combat," "Liberation," and "Temoignage Chretien." While working on clandestine publications he was arrested by the Gestapo in 1943, and after three months' imprisonment was released for lack of proof.

In August 1944, during the insurrection at Paris, he again undertook the direction of *Temps Présent* which continues to be one of the French weeklies most appreciated by the people.

Son of the composer Dynam-Victor Fumet, Stanislas Fumet was born on May 16 in 1896 at Lescar in the Lower Pyrenees. He studied at the College of Juilly in Seine-et-Marne, later at the College Massillon at Paris and finally in the Lycée Charlemagne.

At the age of 13 years, he began to write poems, essays, and dramatic pieces. A little later he worked on many artistic literary magazines of that period. He founded the magazine *Echoes of Silence* a little while before 1914 but it had only a few issues. In 1915 he was drafted into World War I as an auxiliary infirmarian and served in the stretcher-bearer division at the front. After the armistice he was sent to Tarente, Italy and stayed there six months where he met the friend to whom he dedicated his work *Le Proces de L'Art.* He was married in 1919 and has two children.   J. K.

Reverend Paul Hanly Furfey 1896-

One of the leading Catholic sociologists of the United States, the Reverend Paul Hanly Furfey, has been a professor of sociology at the Catholic University of America and head of the department since 1940. He was born in Cambridge, Massachusetts, in 1896, and was educated there in the parochial schools and at Boston College Preparatory School and Boston College, where he received his A.B. in 1917. After a semester as a Knights of Columbus Fellow at the Catholic University, specializing in psychology, he went to St. Mary's Seminary, Baltimore, in 1918, and then to the Sulpician Seminary, Washington, D. C. Following his ordination in Baltimore in 1922, he pursued his graduate studies at the Catholic University and received a Ph.D. in 1926. He was an instructor in sociology at the University from 1925 to 1931, when he became associate professor, and for a year he did special work at the Universities of Berlin and Frankfort.

Father Furfey published his first book, *The Gang Age,* in 1926. Then followed *The Parish and Play* (1928); *Social Problems of Childhood* (1929); *You and Your Children* (1929), and *The Growing Boy* (1930).

In 1931 he became a member of the Committee on the Pre-School Child and of the Committee on Recreation and Physical Education of the White House Conference on Child Health and Protection, and he is co-director of the Catholic University of America Center for Research in Child Development. Surveys of Catholic recreation in Cincinnati, Dayton and Scranton were made under his supervision.

His book, *New Lights on Pastoral Problems,* is planned to aid the priest in his parochial duties and the Sister in her classroom. *Fire on the Earth* is a challenge to all Christians to turn to things of the spirit to prevent social chaos. Next he presented *Three Theories of Society.* His book, *This Way to Heaven,* encourages a high standard of perfection in imitation of Christ's life. *History of Social Thought* was published in 1942 and *Mystery of Iniquity* in 1944.

Father Furfey has also written several monographs and contributes to various periodicals. He is a member of the Editorial Council of the *Journal of Educational Sociology* and an associate editor of the *Journal of Experimental Education, Studies in Psychology and Psychiatry, Camping Magazine, Character,* and *Social Science Monographs.* Dr. Furfey has done research in the sociology of childhood, social statistics and the history of social thought; he is likewise very active in lecturing, giving retreats, and conducting days of recollection in various parts of the country. He is interested in "personalistic social action" as exemplified by the Catholic Worker movement and the Baroness de Hueck's work in Harlem, and by such action particularly as in Il Poverello House, and Fides House in Washington, with which he is closely connected.

Dr. Furfey is on the faculty of the National Catholic School of Social Service as well as Catholic University. He is a former vice-president of the American Catholic Sociological Society, and is a member of the Catholic Biblical Association and of various committees. He was elected a Fellow of the American Association for the Advancement of Science.

C. M. N.

Reverend Edward Francis Garesche, S.J. 1876-

Sodality and medical mission work, to which he has dedicated his priestly life, have not precluded a vast literary output from the pen of the Reverend Edward Francis Garesche, S.J. Writings of devotion, counsel and discipline, of special application to sodalists, were followed by books of a similar nature for nurses, and a score of other religious works as well as seven volumes of verse: forty-four books and ten booklets in all.

Born in St. Louis, Missouri, in 1876, Father Garesche graduated with an A.B. from St. Louis University in 1896, and then studied law at Washington University, where he was given his LL.B. in 1898, receiving an M.A. from St. Louis University the same year. For two years he practised law in St. Louis and federal courts and then entered the Jesuit novitiate at Florissant, Missouri. He taught in Cincinnati, Ohio, and St. Marys, Kansas, and took his philosophy and theology at St. Louis University from 1908 to 1912, when he was ordained priest.

During this time he had written verse and prose for many Catholic periodicals. In the summer of 1912 he was appointed to the staff of *America,* and he then returned to St. Louis to found a magazine for the Sodality of the Blessed Virgin. *The Queen's Work* was begun and continued under Father Garesche's editorship until 1922, attaining a circulation of 160,000. His articles from *The Queen's Work* form several volumes of inspirational reading published from 1918 to 1923: *Your Soul's Salvation; Your Interests Eternal; The Things Immortal; Your Neighbor and You; Your Own Heart; The Paths to Goodness; Life's Lessons; The Values Everlasting,* and *Ever Timely Thoughts.* A book of meditations on the Blessed Virgin was entitled *The Most Beloved Woman.* In 1921 he wrote on *Social Organization in Parishes* and *Communion with the Spirit World,* the latter treating of the true communion with the departed through the Church, in contrast with the false claims of spiritism. In 1924 he published *Great Christian Artists,* a book on the life and work of Michelangelo, Raphael, Da Vinci, Fra Angelico, Murillo, Rubens and Van Dyck. In 1925 he published *The Teachings of the Little Flower.* Two series of *Sodality Conferences* appeared, 1924 to 1925.

A book of poetry was among his earliest works, and it is as a poet that Father Garesche is perhaps best known in the literary field. *The Four Gates* (1913) contains one hundred poems of spiritual emphasis grouped around the four seasons, gates to eternity. Here is ardent contemplation of the beauty of nature as the handiwork of God, and also essentially religious verse. Of children he writes tenderly. His Eucharistic and Marian poems are notable. All these and everyday themes, too, are treated in his subsequent volumes, *The World and the Waters* (1918) and *The Torrent and Other Poems* (1929). His longer lyrics are especially fine, such as *War Mothers,* the title poem of a small volume (1918) dedicated to Joyce Kilmer, "one lately gone." In 1942 appeared *Niagara:* four seasonal anthems with a prelude. Priest and poet, Father Garesche through his verse raises our thoughts to the Divine.

From 1925 to 1928 Father Garesche edited *Hospital Progress.* His books for nurses belong to this period: *Vade Mecum, Couriers of Mercy* and *Ethics and the Art of Conduct for Nurses.* The last has been widely used as a textbook in non-Catholic schools. He also wrote for educators, *Training for Life,* and *Training of Writers. God in His World* and *Mirrors of God* are respectively contemplative works on points of historic interest in Europe and on reflections of the Deity in history, science and the souls of men. *The Soul of the Hospital* and a book on pastoral theology, *Modern Parish Problems,* appeared in 1929. *The Will to Succeed* and a book of prayers, *Moments with God,* appeared in 1931.

Since that time Father Garesche has been more than occupied with the Catholic Medical Mission Board, of which he is president and director; he is also editor of *Medical Mission News,* but he has continued to do much writing, preparing new editions and contributing to periodicals.

Thus a new edition of *Moments with God,* his prayerbook, was published in 1941, and a second edition of *Ethics and the Art of Conduct for Nurses,* in 1944. In 1918 he established the Knights of the Blessed Sacrament in the United States, and in the same year he set on foot the movement for a Catholic Young Men's Association in America, and was spiritual director of their pilgrimage to Rome in 1925. He is spiritual director of the International Committee of the Catholic Federation of Nurses, and of the Daughters of Mary, Health of the Sick, a community established at his initiative in 1935, to work for medical missions.

C. M. N.

Reverend Gilbert Joseph Garraghan, S.J.
1871-1942

Born in Chicago, in 1871, when the west side of the city was little more than a vast prairie, the Reverend Gilbert Garraghan, S.J., became interested in the westward movement and the factors inherent in it. Of these he wrote in several of his books, showing that there were not only economic, but non-economic and spiritual factors in the making of the West. Missionaries, educators, churchmen, had their influence in the final result, as well as the seekers after free land. In the settlement of the Midwest, Father Garraghan's family had a part. His maternal grandfather, Michael Kehoe, arrived in Chicago in 1839 and only seven years later held a seat in the city council. His mother, born in Chicago in 1843, was baptized in old St. Mary's, then the only Catholic church in the city, and in her *Reminiscences of Early Chicago* Mrs. Gilbert Garraghan gives an interesting and vivid account of pioneer days there.

Father Garraghan was educated at old St. Ignatius College, now Loyola University, taking his A.B. there in 1889. He entered the Society of Jesus in 1890, and was ordained in 1904. He served on the faculties of St. Xavier College, Cincinnati, Creighton University and St. Louis University Normal School, as professor of English and classics. In 1919 he received his Ph.D. degree at St. Louis University. From 1911 to 1921 and 1927 to 1928 he was Assistant Provincial of the Missouri Province of the Society. During this time he began to write. Two textbooks in English study, on Newman, were his first publications. Then followed *Catholic Beginnings in Kansas City, Missouri* (1920) and *The Catholic Church in Chicago, 1673-1871* (1921). Thereafter all his writings were devoted to frontier history, and the place of the Catholic Church, and particularly the Jesuits, in the westward movement. *St. Ferdinand de Florissant* is religious history of a typical trans-Mississippi Creole settlement.

From 1929 to 1934 Father Garraghan was editor of the historical quarterly, *Mid-America,* and since 1935 he had been research professor of history at Loyola University. He was a member of the Institute of Jesuit History. In 1934 he published *Chapters in Frontier History,* one of the Science and Culture series, and *Catholic Beginnings in Maryland.* Especially interested in Marquette and LaSalle, he wrote *LaSalle's Jesuit Days* and *Marquette, Ardent Missionary, Daring Explorer,* and published their letters which he discovered in the Jesuit archives in Rome. The Marquette letters were the only autographed ones of the missionary known to exist and the most interesting Marquette material brought to light since the publication of his journal in the 1850's.

After years of extensive personal research in the archives of the United States, Canada and Europe, in 1938, Father Garraghan published his chief work, three volumes on *The Jesuits of the Middle United States.* The period covered is the one hundred years from 1823 to 1923, and the territory embraced is the Great Lakes region and the Upper Mississippi Valley, with apostolic activities reaching outward to Louisiana and the Pacific coast. *The Jesuit Relations* are, as it were, here continued into the nineteenth century, for the author derives his source material from hundreds of Jesuit letters and reports, sometimes presenting the entire document to the reader. During this period missionary endeavors of earlier years are developed along diversified lines of permanent settlement, and the characters who play a part grow up with the western country, so their story partakes of the romance and glamour of the advancing frontier. The books are a notable contribution to American history.

In 1940 Father Garraghan completed fifty years in the Society of Jesus, and his golden jubilee was celebrated, on September 1st, with a solemn Mass at St. Ignatius Church, Chicago, at which Cardinal Stritch, then Archbishop, preached the sermon, commending the priestly life and literary achievements of the jubilarian. He died on June 6, 1942.

C. M. N.

Reverend Reginald Marie Garrigou-Lagrange, O.P. 1877-

One of the foremost exponents of Thomism in the world and probably the greatest living Dominican theologian is the Reverend Reginald Marie Garrigou-Lagrange, S.T.M. He represents a school of philosophy which reaches out for a grasp of reality to which the expressions of St. Thomas can render valuable aid.

Father Reginald Marie Garrigou-Lagrange (in the world, Gouteau) was born February 21, 1877 at Auch Gerst, France. He is the nephew of the famous Father Lagrange, who was the founder of the Biblical School of Jerusalem, at the Convent of St. Stephen, and also the founder of the *Revue Biblique* in 1892. After finishing his classical course, he studied medicine for two years at Bordeaux, and then entered the Dominican Order in 1897. He was professed April 20, 1900, which indicates that he entered the Dominican Institute of higher ecclesiastic studies in Rome, Italy, in 1899.

Since 1905 he has been continually engaged in the teaching of philosophy and theology. From 1904 to 1905 he was professor in the Dominican province of Paris; in 1909 in the Angelicum at Rome. He has taught fundamental theology, moral theology of St. Thomas, dogma and ascetic theology.

Father Garrigou-Lagrange first attracted attention in the first decade of this century, during the troubled days of the modernist crisis. Since then he has done much to advance the cause of Catholic thought. In the year 1909, he published his first book *Le Sens Commun: la Philosophie de l'Etre et les Formules Dogmatiques*. This work was published in four editions. It carefully examines the fundamental principles of the modernist position "relative to the validity and the precision of the basic principles of metaphysic and of dogma" as the Reverend Dr. Joseph Fenton puts it. Since then Father Garrigou-Lagrange has written prolifically and profoundly. In 1916 appeared his *Dieu, Son Existence Et Sa Nature* (*God: His Existence and His Nature*). This work which went into eight editions up to 1936, was translated from the fifth edition by Dom Bede Rose, O.S.B. It is a comprehensive study of the classical proofs for the existence of God, His nature, attributes, the problem of free will, etc. Father Garrigou-Lagrange's work, *La Prédestination des saints et la grâce, Doctrine de S. Thomas comparée aux autres systèmes théologiques*, was translated into English by Dom Bede Rose, O.S.B., under the title *Predestination*. The Dominican nun, Sister M. Timothea Doyle, translated his *Christian Perfection and Contemplation According to St. Thomas Aquinas and St. John of the Cross*. This book, *Perfection Chrétienne et Contemplation selon S. Thomas d'Aquin et S. Jean de la Croix*, which went into seven editions in French prior to 1936, was translated into Italian by Father Nivoli, O.P., and into German by Father Obersiebrasse, O.P. Among the other books that were translated into English are: *Providence* (1937), and *Three Ways of the Spiritual Life* (1939). *La Providence et la confiance en Dieu, fidélité et abandon* was also translated into German, Polish and Italian. *Les Trois Conversions et les Trois Voies*, was translated into Polish, Spanish and Italian.

His book, *Le Sens du mystère et le clair obscur intellect, Nature et Surnature,* was translated into German. Other books by Father Garrigou-Lagrange are: *De Revelatione per Ecclesiam Catholicam Proposita* (1918); *L'amour de Dieu et la Croix de Jesus, Etude de théologie mystique sur le problème de l'amour et les purifications passives d'après les principes de S. Thomas d'Aquin et la doctrine de S. Jean de la Croix,* published in two volumes; *Le réalisme du principe de finalité* (1932) and *De Deo Uno, Commentarium in Primam Partem S. Thomae. Trait de Theologie Ascétique et mystique; Les Trois Ages de la Vie Intérieure Prélude de Celle du Ciel,* 2 vols. (1938). *Le Sauveur et son amour pour nous* (1934); *Mère Françoise de Jésus, fondatrice de la Compagnie de la Vierge.*

Father Garrigou-Lagrange's only appearance in this country was on October 13, 1939 when he delivered the Jubilee Theological Lecture at the Catholic University of America before a capacity audience of theologians from Catholic institutions of the East, at the time when the organization of the Angelico Alumni took place.

The Reverend R. M. Garrigou-Lagrange is a qualificator of the Holy Office and a consultor of the Sacred Congregation of Studies.

M. H.

Robert Esmonde Gordon George   *see* Robert Sencourt

Henri Ghéon   1875-1944

The avocation of his youth had become to Henri Ghéon a life-work. He found artistic expression through his pen and in the theatre. Moreover he wrote with a purpose. The deeply moving tragedy of losing in World War I the friend responsible for his return to the Faith was the dramatic episode which stirred him to write the stories of the saints for which he is famous. He felt that could he establish a closer contact between men still striving here below and those whose heroic service to God has won them heaven he would be achieving an end to be desired. He speaks of it as "re-tablir le va-et-vient entre le ciel et la terre."

He was born Henri Vangeon, at Bray-sur-Seine, France, in 1875, and was brought up in the Faith by a devout mother. But religion was not made vital to him: lectures in Christian Doctrine did not stir him as did his studies in art and letters when he attended the Lycée at Sens. It was there, when in his teens, that he lost his Faith, influenced by the books he read, the anti-clericalism of his country, his free-thinking companions and his father's agnosticism.

He wished to become an artist, but decided to take up the medical profession as a means of livelihood, and went to Paris in 1893 to study medicine. There André Gide became his friend, and he began to write. His early works are marked by the enthusiasm of youth. In 1901 he obtained his degree, and from then until 1909 he practised medicine in his native village, and found literary expression in verse. Moving to Orsay, he founded the *Nouvelle Revue Française* and to it contributed fine critical essays. The study of music, painting and finally drama engaged his interests. He wrote *Le pain* and *L'eau-de-vie*. Travel took him to Italy and the Orient.

With the outbreak of World War I he entered military service and thus came to know lieutenant commander Pierre Dupouey. This young officer won many friends by his unaffected holiness, high intellectual attainments and delightful companionship. Vangeon deeply admired him. In 1915, at Easter, Dupouey was slain on the Yser. To Vangeon this was a severe loss. He sought an introduction to Madame Dupouey, who realizing the young man's distress and touched by his admiration for her husband lent him the diaries and notebooks wherein Dupouey had written his innermost thoughts. The New Testament and other books he commented on, Vangeon read. All this impressed him profoundly and gradually Faith was restored. By Christmas 1915 he had returned to the Church. He abandoned the name by which he had been known when an atheist and took that of Henri Ghéon. The story of his conversion, *L'hommé né de la guerre. Le témoignage d'un converti,* he wrote while in the trenches.

After the war he resumed his place in the literary world, but as a Christian writer. Seeking to make known the beauty and richness of the lives of men and women devoted to God, he decided the most realistic way to present them was on the stage, through the medium of miracle plays. For this purpose he founded in 1925 the "Compagnons de Notre Dame," later known as the "Compagnons de jeux." He wrote and produced fifty plays, among them, *Les trois miracles de Ste. Cécile; Le mystère de l'invention de la croix; Le mort à cheval,* and in some he acted himself. They have been presented in France, Belgium and Switzerland. *The Marvellous History of St. Bernard* and *The Comedian* were translated into English and produced successfully before sophisticated London audiences. *The Marriage of St. Francis* has also been translated and so has *Le Noel sur la place.* The latter play was translated into English by Sister Marie Thomas, O.P. of Rosary College under the title *Christmas on the Village Square.* This play illustrates the difficult combination best achieved in medieval plays: naive humor and religious fervor.

The Cure d'Ars is the central figure of his three-volume novel, *Le Jeux de l'Enfer et du ciel.* He also wrote the life of the saint under the title *The Secret of the Cure d'Ars,* which established him as a notable hagiographer. This same descriptive title he has given to his books on St. Thérèse of Lisieux: *The Secret of the Little Flower; St. Margaret Mary,* and *St. John Bosco. St. Vincent Ferrer* appeared in 1939 and *Secrets of the Saints* in 1944. Gheon's saints are real people, men and women of flesh and blood with human failings and weaknesses as well as virtues, and their story is told with unusual interest.

Outside the field of hagiography he wrote a book on Mozart. He also contributed to leading reviews and gave lectures. Gheon was an Academy member of the Gallery of Living Catholic Authors. He was a Chevalier de la Legion d'honneur and was decorated with the Croix de Guerre.

C. M. N.

Floyd Phillips Gibbons   1887-1939

The war correspondent and radio commentator, Floyd Gibbons was born in Washington, D. C. on July 16, 1887, the son of Edward Thomas and Emma Theresa (Phillips) Gibbons.

He was educated at Gonzaga College and Georgetown University. At the latter institution he studied law, but he left in 1917 before completing the course, to work as a reporter on the Milwaukee *Daily News*. His first assignment was the federal court. The prosaic legal proceedings were reported too colorfully for the city editor, so Floyd Gibbons was discharged. Later he worked on the Milwaukee *Free Press* and on the Minneapolis *Tribune*. In 1912 he went with the Chicago *Tribune*. While with this paper, he became internationally known. He began his spectacular career in December, 1914 when he was sent as a war correspondent to the Battle of Naco on the Arizona-Sonora frontier. He reported Villa's raid on Columbus, New Mexico, March, 1916 and accompanied both General Pershing on his march into Mexico and General Funston on his last inspection of American troops on the border and in Mexico.

For his fearless reporting of the Mexican trouble he was selected in 1917 as the London correspondent for the Chicago *Tribune*. In February of that year, the steamer Laconia, on which he was en route to France, was torpedoed two hundred miles off the Irish coast. After a night in a small boat, he was rescued and soon after the rescue he cabled a four thousand word dispatch of the disaster in which Americans lost their lives.

While covering the war front in France, he lost his left eye at Belleau Wood in the battle of Château-Thierry, trying to observe too closely a German machine gun. Upon his recovery, he habitually wore a patch over the wound. For his bravery, he was awarded the French and Italian Croix de Guerre with palm and was an Officer of the Legion of Honor. After his injury, he was put in charge of the foreign bureau of the Chicago *Tribune*.

Ever restless and looking for thrills, Floyd Gibbons covered the Irish rebellion against Great Britain, the revolutions in Germany and Russia, the Spanish War against the Riff tribes in Morocco, the Civil War in Spain, the Italian War in Ethiopia, and the Sino-Japanese War. Shortly before his death he was making plans to return to Europe to cover World War II for the Hearst papers.

Floyd Gibbons was noted as a radio commentator. Sponsored by the now defunct magazine *The Literary Digest* he broadcast his experiences at a rate of 217 words a minute on the average. His fast talking appealed to thousands of listeners. His connection with radio broadcasting began when he went to the National Broadcasting Company to seek information for his story "The Red Napoleon" which he wrote for *Liberty* magazine. He was engaged as a news commentator.

In 1923 Gibbons went to Algiers and Timbuktoo to investigate the sheiks at the request of Colonel Robert McCormick, owner of *The Tribune*. While there he remembered what a former editor had told him when he dismissed him from the Milwaukee *Daily News*—"Go to Timbuktoo!" He took advantage of his presence there to wire this editor, "Dear Bill, here I am in Timbuktoo carrying out your instructions."

Floyd Gibbons died of a heart attack at his home at Saylorsburg, Pennsylvania near Stroudsburg, on September 24, 1939. At his own request, he was buried from Dahlgren Chapel at Georgetown University, where a Requiem Mass was celebrated for him.

He is the author of *How the Laconia Sank; Militia Mobilization on the Mexican Border* (1917); *And They Thought We Wouldn't Fight* (1918); *The Red Knight of Germany* (1927), and *The Red Napoleon* (1929).

M. H.

John Stephen Reynolds Gibbons 1882-

Seeing the world on foot, and writing books on his experiences as "unwilling payment" for the fun, has been the literary occupation of John Gibbons since 1928. It was then that he tramped to Lourdes.

He was born in 1882 in Upper Norwood, England, of an Italian mother and an Anglican father, who was a provincial lawyer, descended from a line of yeomen farmers dating back to 1400. Though baptized, he was not brought up a Catholic, and was educated in a public school, St. Peter's, at York. On his seventeenth birthday he came into the Church.

He married at twenty-one and, faced with the necessity of making a living, became a "professional reader" at the British Museum doing research for other people's books. By his first wife, Mabel Woodhead, he had two daughters. He volunteered for military service at the end of 1914 and served four years in the ranks in France and Flanders, refusing promotion. Shell shock necessitated a year's hospitalization, during which time he became a friend of his doctor, who having been under Freud in Vienna, diagnosed Gibbons as an extreme "sensitive." This, he says, gave him a permanent inferiority complex. The death of his wife in 1922 grieved him deeply.

In 1926 he married Mrs. Louisa Vincent, and they had two daughters. The first child was not in good health, and his wife suggested that he go to Lourdes and walk there. This he did, walking for six weeks to the famous shrine in the South of France; and the child recovered. Under the advice of a reader of Methuen & Co., he rewrote in fourteen days an account of this pilgrimage, previously rejected by other publishers. It was entitled *Tramping to Lourdes* and was most successful. His first literary venture had been a dictionary of slang in collaboration with Fraser in 1919, called *Soldier and Sailor Words and Phrases.*

A London magazine called *The Wide World* gave him a three years' contract to write on foreign places, and he went first to Rome in 1929, going from Sicily across the Straits of Messina up through Calabria. After *Afoot in Italy* he wrote *London to Sarajevo,* prompted by a desire to see where the World War started. He also traversed the United States, from New Orleans to New York, by road. In all, he has written twenty books within ten years, and has been in twenty-eight countries and on four continents. Of his writings he considers the best to be *Tramping to Lourdes, I Wanted to Travel,* a biography of Pierre Foucauld in *Great Catholics,* and *Roll On, Next War.* The last flared through two of the great London popular papers as the book of the week, but was suddenly dropped, apparently discouraged by the government. It is a true account of his army days, not without criticism of the English military machine.

Gibbons spent the winter of 1938 to 1939 in a remote Portuguese mountain village and liked it. "The Portuguese peasant and myself were doing our thinking on exactly the same lines," he says. "There are no metaphors, no exaggerations, no anything but plain truth." And the village's verdict as told him by an educated Portuguese in London was, "Senhor John-ee was much respected." When he was taken ill he went to the British hospital in Porto. The other patient was a British stoker who lamented the fact that the true story of the stoker could never be written because no writing man could do the stoker's work. But he complimented Gibbons by saying he came nearer the stoker's mind than any "educated man" he had ever met. His book relating the experiences of these months, *I Gathered No Moss,* was the Portuguese Government's Camoens Prize Book.

Apparent are the genuineness of Gibbons and his detestation of sham. Also he hates responsibility, which induces worry. He has a great love of the Latins and would like to live in a small town in Italy, Spain, or Portugal. Gibbons has much to say and writes spontaneously with little effort toward literary style or perfection of technique. As a lecturer he talks informally and holds the interest of his audiences. He has also given occasional broadcasts and writes for magazines. Foreign timetables have a fascination for him, and he takes many a dream-journey with them, working out exactly where "I'd be now, what it would look like, what sort of food I'd be eating, and all that."

Mr. Gibbons' other books are: *Tramping Through Ireland; Afoot in Portugal; Twenty-four Vagabond Tales; Fun and Philosophy; To Italy at Last; The Truth About the Legion; Fiddler of Lourdes; Suburban Columbus; What Is This Lourdes?; Abroad in Ireland; Playtime in Portugal; The Road to Nazareth; My Own Queer Country,* and *Ireland, the New Ally.*

C. M. N.

Sir Philip Hamilton Gibbs   1877-

Journalism, fiction, history, and occasional essays have provided busy years for Sir Philip Gibbs. He began writing at the age of sixteen—a description of the sea gulls in winter at London Bridge, which was printed in the *Daily Chronicle,* one of the newspapers on whose staff he later served with distinction. His father was the former Henry Gibbs, of the Board of Education, and his mother was Helen Hamilton. All four sons bore the mother's name of Hamilton as their middle name, and Cosmo adopted this as his surname by deed poll. The brothers were all literary; Cosmo is a novelist and dramatist; Philip collaborated with him in one of his plays *Menders of Nets,* which had a good run at two London theatres; Frank wrote books on the west coast of Africa; Major Arthur Gibbs is the author of *The Hour of Conflict* and other books.

Philip Gibbs was born in 1877, and educated privately. At nineteen he wrote his first book, *Founders of the Empire,* and at twenty-one he became one of the editors of Cassell and Company and wrote his first novel, *The Individualist.* In 1901 he was editor of Tillotson's Literary Syndicate. On his twenty-first birthday he married Agnes, daughter of the Reverend W. J. Rowland. Their one son, Anthony, is a novelist. Lady Gibbs died in 1939.

Entering journalism in 1902, Gibbs was successively literary editor of the *Daily Mail,* the *Daily Chronicle* and the *Tribune,* and later special correspondent for the *Daily Chronicle* and other London papers. Among his notable stories was that revealing the cruel treatment of enemies of the Republic during the revolution in Portugal, which exposure resulted in the release of 1,500 prisoners. He also scooped an interview with Dr. Cook on his return to Copenhagen from the Arctic and despite public acclaim, courageously questioned the veracity of his story of the discovery of the North Pole that was later proved to be false.

In 1912 Gibbs was war correspondent with the Bulgarian army and in 1914 with the French and Belgian armies. He then served with the British armies at the front from 1915 to 1918 as correspondent for the *Daily Chronicle* and *Daily Telegraph.* His dispatches from the Allied fronts of 1914 to 1918 constitute one of the classic chronicles of World War I. So ably did he fill this post that for his services he was knighted by the King in 1920, and he was also made a Chevalier de la Legion d'honneur. G. K. Chesterton called him "the Ambassador of Fleet Street at the Front."

In his book, *The Street of Adventure,* Gibbs gives a lively and interesting account of the newspaper world in Fleet Street. In *A Master of Life* he depicts the manufacturer who, through courageous unselfishness triumphs over many difficulties caused by hatred between employer and employees. *Heirs Apparent* is a story of post-war Oxford, introducing the Anglican clergyman's problem of faith. *Age of Reason* is an exposition of the failure of science to satisfy man's aspirations and the tragic consequences of materialism. *Ordeal in England* (1937) tells the story of the year in which England saw three kings on her throne and faced a world of gathering chaos.

In his books, Sir Philip Gibbs is chiefly concerned with the many social and moral problems which followed the first World War and are now threatening civilization. *This Nettle Danger, Broken Pledges, Sons of the Others, The Amazing Summer,* and *The Long Alert,* carry events forward to the present chaos. Thus he uses fiction as well as historical works to comment on world affairs. In the novel, though he addresses a largely non-Catholic public, he ably conveys the message of Catholicity, showing that the only real sanity in the world is the philosophy preached by the Catholic Church.

Gibbs' historical writings include a history of the French Revolution as well as several books on war and Europe in the twentieth century.

His skill as a journalist is perhaps responsible for the lucidity notable in his writings. On the other hand, his gift of phrase and easy, flowing style, lend a literary flavor to his journalism, and to this in great part is due his pre-eminence as a correspondent. He is a master of description and in delineation of character, and is interested in the inner and wider significance of affairs. His varied journalistic experiences afford abundant material for his novels, which are numerous.

Sir Philip Gibbs is well known as a lecturer in the United States. He is a slim figure of a man, reflective and sensitive, and the intensity of spirit that has marked so active a career is evident in an eagerness and charm of manner. He has both humor and understanding, and modesty and sincerity are among his notable characteristics.   C. M. N.

Eric Gill   1882-1940

Eric Gill is well known as both artist and author. His writings are closely associated with his art, and are also of a religious nature, for to him work and religion were one. He liked to trace the relation between whole and holy, and certainly he was "a whole man" as well as a "holy" one in the best sense of the word.

He was born at Brighton, England, in 1882, the son of an Anglican clergyman, the Reverend A. T. Gill. He attended the Preparatory School at Brighton and then studied under G. H. Catt at the Chichester Art School, London, continuing there until 1902. Though he designed a few buildings, he never practised architecture independently. From 1903 to 1910, he worked as a mason and letter cutter, producing inscriptions and sometimes heraldic shields for tombstones. During this time (1904) he married Ethel Moore. In 1910 he began his work as a sculptor, for which he is best known, and settled at Ditchling. He also continued his work as a letterer and took up wood-engraving. Through August John, whom he met in 1911, he arranged for his first exhibition at the Chenil Gallery, Chelsea.

Although an agnostic Gill had made a study of the Catholic faith and he talked of it at great length with the Abbot of Louvain. In 1913 he was received into the Church, with his wife and children, three daughters and a son. He became a member of the Third Order of St. Dominic, and set up the St. Dominic's Press for the printing of the woodcuts which he did so beautifully. After 1924 he made wood-engraving for the Golden Cockerel Press, and in 1927 he became type-designer for the Monotype Corporation of London. His Gill Sans type font is very popular, and other types of great beauty are Perpetua and Bunyan. Gill wrote a fine book on *Typography* in 1931, and was director of Hague & Gill, Ltd., printers and publishers.

Among his stone-carvings are the Stations of the Cross in Westminster Cathedral, the war memorial at Leeds University, "The Driving Out of the Money Changers," panels for the League of Nations Building, Geneva, and sculptures at Broadcast House, London. Other works are in the Tate Gallery and Victoria and Albert Museum.

His first book appeared in 1929, entitled *Art and Nonsense*. Another book widely read in the United States was *Beauty Looks after Herself* (1933). Many of his later works are concerned with the problem of man in society, which became of increasing interest to him as the years passed and in view of world conditions. These writings include pamphlets on "Unemployment" and "Social Action and the Stations of the Cross" and the books: *Money and Morals* (1934); *Work and Leisure* (1935); *Work and Property* (1937); *Clothes* (1931); *The Necessity of Belief* (1936); *Sacred and Secular* (1940), and *Autopsychography* (1940). His subjects are controversial and his style vigorous. In regard to the war which began in Europe in 1939, he urged a quick peace, viewing the Allied war aims as a continuation of the Versailles policies and to make the world safe for big business.

Eric Gill was a man of strong convictions and hence considered argumentative and given to invective, yet he was willing to listen to the opinions of others and had a surprising humility and great kindness. Many honors came his way and these he considered evidence of generous appreciation. He was an associate of the Royal Academy and an honorary associate of the Royal Institute of British Architects, and he received the new and exclusive designer-for-industry honor (R.D.I.) and an honorary LL.D. degree from Edinburgh University in 1938. In appearance he was unusual, for he wore a monk-like robe and a beard.

For a while Gill had a studio at Capel-y-ffin, in Wales, after leaving Ditchling, and he then settled at High Wycombe. It was there that he wrote his autobiography, at the request of his publishers. He called it an "autopsychography," and said, "It feels to me as though I really ought to die now. I don't know how I shall be able to face the world after stripping myself more or less naked as I have done." It is indeed an honest account of a most interesting life, and Gill died before its publication. Death apparently was due to collapse after an operation and it occurred on November 17, 1940. Years before, he had designed his own tombstone for exhibition, with the following epitaph: "Remember me. E. G., the stoneworker, 1936. Woe is me." He will be long remembered as one of the outstanding men of his time, an unusually talented artist and writer.

C. M. N.

Reverend John Thomas Gillard, S.S.J.
1900-1942

Recognized as an authority on the Negro problem in the United States, Father John Gillard wrote for many Catholic and secular magazines and published four books in their defense. He conducted many retreats, especially for colored Catholics.

Father Gillard was born in Scranton, Pennsylvania on July 10th, 1900, the son of Robert Joseph Gillard and Mary Ann (Cummings) Gillard. His early education was received in the parochial schools of Scranton. In 1921 he entered the Society of St. Joseph's at Epiphany College, Walbrook, Maryland. A year later he entered St. Joseph's Seminary, Baltimore and pursued his philosophical and theological studies for the priesthood at St. Mary's Seminary. It was from St. Mary's Seminary and University that he received his A.B., M.A., S.T.B., and Ph.D. degrees—the latter summa cum laude, in 1931.

After his ordination to the priesthood in 1928, Father Pastorelli, the Superior General of the Society of Saint Joseph, appointed him his secretary and also Editor of the *Colored Harvest,* the official organ of the society, and a magazine which promotes interest in the work of the colored missions.

Father Gillard also served at Saint Frances' Academy, Baltimore, Maryland, as Chaplain of the Oblate Sisters of Providence, the first community of colored Sisters in the United States.

As a Josephite Father, his life was dedicated to the great Catholic work among the colored in the United States. He labored unselfishly, and untiringly for the spiritual education and social advancement of the Negro, until his death in 1942.

Father Gillard is the author of: *The Catholic Church and the American Negro* (1930); *The Negro American* (1934); *Christ, Color and Communism* (1938), and *Colored Catholics in the United States* (1941).

M. H.

Reverend James Martin Gillis, C.S.P. 1876-

The zeal of a modern Savonarola attacking political corruption and religious and moral indifference gives the Reverend James Martin Gillis, C.S.P., a foremost place in our modern Catholic world. An acclaimed editor, preacher, lecturer, radio speaker and writer, Father Gillis has many points of vantage from which to launch his attacks on the evils of today and to present the Catholic answer to the world's ills. Born in Boston, reared in the classical atmosphere of "the Athens of America," he attended the well-known Boston Latin School from which he graduated with high honors in 1895. From there he went to St. Charles, the Sulpician College in Maryland, where he obtained his B.A. in 1896. He pursued further studies at St. John's Seminary, Brighton, Massachusetts, and at St. Paul's College, Washington, D. C. From the Catholic University of America he obtained his degree of S.T.L. in 1903. An honorary degree of Litt.D. was bestowed upon him by the College of Mt. St. Vincent in 1934, in following year by both Fordham University and St. Francis College, in 1940 by St. Benedict's College, Atchison, Kansas and in 1941 by Boston College. In 1940 he was honored also by a degree of LL.D. from the University of Detroit.

Attracted to the work of the Paulist Fathers, the young Bostonian joined the Congregation in 1898, ten years after the death of its founder, Father Hecker. He was ordained in New York in 1901. Recognizing Father Gillis' scholarly attainments, his superiors shortly after his ordination made him a member of the faculty of St. Paul's College, Washington, D. C. In the ensuing years he not only instructed aspirants to the priesthood but also increased the vast store of historical and literary knowledge which has distinguished him among his contemporaries.

In 1910 Father Gillis was appointed to the Paulist Fathers Mission Band and for twelve busy, fruitful years his work for souls took him to every section of this country and Canada. In 1922 he succeeded Father John J. Burke, C.S.P., as editor of *The Catholic World*. Founded in 1865 by Father Hecker, from its earliest days *The Catholic World* has held a place in the front ranks of Catholic publications, and under the leadership of Father Gillis has not only maintained that position but has increased its prestige and its influence.

His column, "Sursum Corda: What's Right with the World," syndicated by the N.C.W.C. News Service weekly since 1928, enables Father Gillis to reach a large audience. There he comments as priest and scholar, and in the trenchant style that marks his editorials, on varied subjects of live and compelling interest to the Catholic mind.

Since 1930 he has broadcast an annual series of addresses on the Catholic Hour radio program, in which Catholic doctrine and all it implies in Christian living has been clearly and eloquently expressed. On

WLWL the Paulist Radio Station, his "Timely Topics" was a favorite program from 1925 until the station signed off the air in 1937.

Despite Father Gillis' editorial work and his activities as preacher and lecturer on platforms throughout the country, he has found the time to write several books: *False Prophets* published in 1925 showed up the would-be "intellectuals" and the illogic and lack of erudition which mark their line of thought. In 1928 he published *The Catholic Church and the Home,* and in 1931 *The Ten Commandments.* From his pen in 1932 came *Christianity and Civilization* and *The Paulists,* a sketch of the Congregation of St. Paul. *This Our Day* which appeared in 1933, is a collection of his editorials in *The Catholic World,* reviewing in prophetic vein the passing world scene.

Father Gillis was a valued contributor to *The Catholic Encyclopedia.* He is a member of the Catholic Press Association, the Interracial Council, the Academy of Living Catholic Authors and a member of the Board of Editors of the Catholic Book Club.   C. M. N.

Naomi Gilpatrick 1918-

It was at the University of Michigan at Ann Arbor that Naomi Gilpatrick wrote her first novel, *The Broken Pitcher.* Along with the writing of the book, she finished up work on her Master's degree and served as an assistant in the English department.

Naomi Gilpatrick was born in Holyoke, Massachusetts on June 15, 1918 and is the oldest of seven children. Her four brothers served in the Armed Forces of World War II. Her sister Consuelo at the age of 18 was the Broadway producer and director of the revival of *Outward Bound* and another sister is Sister Rose Imelda, a Sister of St. Joseph, teaching at Pennsgrove, New Jersey.

Six months after Naomi's birth, her father took her and her mother to Wyoming where he started a sheep ranch. In 1929 they moved to Oakland, New Jersey. While attending the local grammar school she began to write, in the seventh grade, and had her short stories and poetry published in the Paterson, New Jersey *Morning Call, The Newark Sunday Call* and other New Jersey and Massachusetts papers. She started playwriting at the age of twelve "mainly because her voice was so low and she was so shy the teacher would never give her a part—so she wrote daring roles for herself." Eight of her one-act plays were produced.

After attending Butler and then Pompton Lakes High School, she entered the College of St. Elizabeth, Convent Station, New Jersey. Here she studied, for her two latter years, under C. John McCole until his death in 1939. For the St. Elizabeth Year Book of which she was business manager, she wrote a sonnet "In Memoriam" in his honor. In that same year she was graduated summa cum laude and was nominated into the Kappa Gamma Pi, National Catholic Woman's Honorary Society. That fall she was awarded the 1939 three-hundred-dollar scholarship of The American Woman's Association at the annual Friendship Dinner of forty-seven women's professional groups of New York. This enabled her to spend one and a half years at Columbia University to learn radio and script writing. In 1941 she went to the University of Michigan, at Ann Arbor to work under Professor Roy W. Cowden, the director of the Avery Hopwood awards given each year in poetry, drama, essay and fiction, for the new and unusual, to writers studying at that University. Of Professor Cowden, Naomi Gilpatrick says, "He has a warmth and depth of humanity that is inspiring." For two years she studied under him and during that time, she worked twelve hours a day on her novel, *The Broken Pitcher.* The novel won the Avery Hopwood Fiction Award in 1943, a prize of $800.00, on the basis of the evaluation of a national judge, Struthers Burt. Whit Burnett, the editor of *Story Magazine* and *This Is My Best,* took the novel to George Joel of the Dial Press who published it in the spring of 1945. Six days after *The Broken Pitcher* was released, the first edition was sold out. It is a psychological study of Sharon O'Dell who finds her ideal in the Christian and discerning Mr. Stuart who has just become her mother's second husband. On the appearance of her first novel she was made an honorary member of the Eugene Field Society by virtue of a vote of the governors that *The Broken Pitcher* "is a contribution to contemporary literature." The novel was sponsored by the Cancer Drive in New Jersey "as the fiction novel to enlighten the public on the subject of cancer."

On receiving her Master's degree, she was invited into Phi Beta Kappa. Naomi Gilpatrick has contributed articles to *The Catholic World, The Catholic Library World* and her poems have appeared in *Columbia Poetry, Spirit, The Sign* and *The Hartford Times.*   M. H.

Etienne Henri Gilson   1884-

The history of philosophy, especially medieval philosophy, is the subject of Etienne Gilson's writings and lectures. Born in Paris in 1884, he was educated at the Petit Seminaire de Notre Dame des Champs, the Lycée de Henri IV and the University of Paris where he graduated in 1907. He took his doctorate in letters at the Sorbonne in 1913 with a thesis on "Lá Liberté chez Descartes et la théologie." He then taught successively at the Universities of Lille, 1913 to 1919, Strasbourg, 1919 to 1921, and Paris, 1921 to 1932. From 1926 to 1929 he was a half-time professor at Harvard University. In 1929 the Institute of Medieval Studies, of which he is director of studies, was founded, through his stimulation, at St. Michael's College, in the University of Toronto, and was erected into a Pontifical Institute by Pope Pius XII in 1939. Since 1932 he has held the chair of the history of philosophy in the Middle Ages at the Collège de France. In 1941 he lectured in unoccupied France.

Dr. Gilson writes and lectures in English as well as in French. He is Doctor honoris causa of the Universities of Oxford, Aberdeen, St. Andrew, Montreal, the Collegio Angelico (Rome), and Milan. The Gifford lectures which he gave at the University of Aberdeen are contained in his *The Spirit of Mediaeval Philosophy*. At the Harvard Tercentenary Conference he delivered an address on "Mediaeval Universalism." In 1936 he delivered the William James lectures. These were published under the title *The Unity of Philosophical Experience*. Both received notable commendation. Other books written in or translated into English are: *Philosophy of St. Bonaventure* (1937); *Mystical Theology of St. Bernard; Christianity and Philosophy; Reason and Revelation in the Middle Ages,* and *God and Philosophy*. His works are distinguished for their sound scholarship and remarkably readable style. His first book on the history of mediaeval philosophy was *La philosophie au moyen âge* (2 vols., 1922), which was followed by a volume on St. Thomas, *Thomisme*.

Dr. Gilson is a corresponding member of the British Academy, the American Academy of Arts and Sciences, the Mediaeval Academy of America, a member of the Roman Academy of St. Thomas Aquinas, and an Academy member of the Gallery of Living Catholic Authors. He was decorated with the Croix de guerre in World War I. He was a lieutenant in the French Army Machine Gun Company at Verdun and is a Chevalier de la Legion d'honneur. At the San Francisco Conference in 1945 he was technical adviser to the French Delegation.

In 1908 Dr. Gilson married Thérèse Ravisé. They have one son and two daughters.   C. M. N.

Caroline Giltinan (Mrs. Leo P. Harlow) 1884-

An active and varied life has never been a deterrent to Caroline Giltinan in the writing of poetry. Born in Philadelphia, Pennsylvania, in 1884, she was educated at the Sacred Heart Convent of Atlantic City, New Jersey, in the public schools and at the University of Pennsylvania. After World War I, she was with the Paris and New York headquarters of the Associated Press. During the war Caroline Giltinan served with the A.E.F. in France as secretary at the U. S. Base Hospital, No. 38 (Jefferson College Unit), and at the Chief Surgeons Medical Headquarters, Sick and Wounded Division. She also served with the Herbert Hoover American Relief Administration. In 1920, Caroline Giltinan married Leo P. Harlow, an attorney-at-law, of Alexandria, Virginia. Their daughter, Faith, was born two years later.

Her loveliness of song is widely recognized. She is a member of the Poetry Society of America and the Poetry Society of Virginia, and is an Academy member, and has acted as vice-president of the Catholic Poetry Society of America. She also belongs to the Women's Overseas League.

One of the founders of *The Carillon,* a quarterly of verse, Mrs. Harlow was its editor from 1929 to 1934. She is a contributor of verse to magazines and has published three volumes of poems, *The Divine Image* (1917); *The Veiled Door* (1929), and *Testimony* (1931). Her tender poem, *Communion,* is included in Joyce Kilmer's *Anthology of Catholic Poets.* And *Contrition Across the Waves,* her deeply pious verses inspired by Father Damien of Molokai, is included in Blanche Jennings Thompson's anthology, *With Harp and Lute.*   C. M. N.

Igino Giordani   1894-

Tivoli (Roma), the town dear to Horace and famous for its travertine stone, is the birthplace of Igino Giordani, who was born there in 1894. In his early years he worked as a mason, until his good landlord encouraged him to study in the Diocesan Seminary. In 1915 he went to war and was badly wounded. After the war he took part in politics and wrote some essays on Lacordaire, Montalembert and on the Greek Fathers of the Church. Apologetics, however, became his main interest.

For daily papers he wrote several political articles, defending the Christian Democracy of the Partito Popolare (Popular Party) against Fascism. At that time he used to walk almost daily with Don Luigi Sturzo to whom he gave first lessons in English for his trip to England.

When Giordani was compelled to withdraw from politics in 1927, he went to the United States for a year to study Library Science at the University of Michigan and Columbia University. He calls it "an unforgetable year of observations and study" and considers the United States as his second country.

While in the United States he finished his book *La prima polemica cristiana (Apologeti greci del 2° secolo);* compiled *Contemporanei nordamericani,* an anthology of modern American authors, and began a novel *America Quaternaria* of American interest on a humorous subject. This last mentioned book is now (1945) in its fourth edition and was translated into German but the Nazis did not permit its publication.

As editor of *Fides,* a monthly review, published by the Vatican, to show the papal work for the preservation of the Faith, he wrote voluminously on apologetics and polemics.

Giordani edited the social encyclicals of the popes from Pius IX to Pius XII which is now (1945) in its third edition. His principal work, however, is *Il messagio sociale di Gesu* (1935) (four editions), followed by *Il messagio sociale degli Apostoli* and *Il messagio sociale dei primi Padri.* All of these were reprinted in 1944 in Milan and in Rome. The first volume was published in English by the Catholic University of America.

All of these works, written while he was working at the Vatican Library as Chief of the Cataloging Department and Principal of the Vatican School of Library Science, show that the author had a sustained interest in social and political questions. In his *messagio sociale,* Giordani had gone back to the source of Christian social thought where he found "the purest water of life and avoided the suspicious fascist censure," which in its last years used to keep Giordani's books under survey for several months, imposing cuts which were often very foolish. Because of this fascist hostility, the author confined himself to historical studies and wrote a second novel, under the title *La Città murata* (1939), laid in the time of Pope St. Gregory VII.

In his book *Segno di contradizione* he explains why the Catholic Church encounters enemies. The particular reason for the persecution is dealt with in another book called *Christus patiens,* which rapidly went into a third edition. Now that fascism has been abolished, Giordani is reprinting his first polemic work *Rivolta cattolica,* a book that was on Mussolini's index of forbidden books.

His other books include *La Repubblica dei marmocchi,* a joyful book dealing with the domestic deeds of four children, who are in reality the author's sons, but might be the boys of all the families in the world. In the field of hagiography, Giordani has written the lives of St. Ignatius of Loyola, Mary of Nazareth, St. Paul, and Maddalena di Canossa. His *Il Sangue di Cristo* is a mystical book. *Norme per la Catalogazione degli stampati* is a volume of catalog rules which has been translated into English, Spanish and other languages.

In 1944 Giordani returned to the work of his youth—to journalism. He is the director of *Il Quotidiano,* a daily paper for Catholic action in Italy.   M. H.

Right Reverend Paul Joseph Glenn 1893-

Born in Scottdale, Pennsylvania, in 1893, Monsignor Paul Joseph Glenn, educator and author, received his preliminary education in the town of his birth, at St. John the Baptist School, from 1900 to 1908. He then went to Latrobe, Pennsylvania, to study under the Benedictines at St. Vincent's Preparatory School and St. Vincent's College, where he received his A.B. in 1915, his M.A. in 1917 and his Ph.D. in 1928. Studies for the priesthood were followed at St. Vincent's Seminary, where his outstanding scholastic attainments continued, and he received the degrees of S.T.B., in 1917, S.T.L., in 1918 and S.T.D., in 1922. In December, 1918, he was raised to the dignity of the priesthood, and for the next several years Monsignor Glenn occupied important posts in the classroom at his Alma Mater, St. Vincent's College, Latrobe; as professor at the Sacred Heart Seminary, Detroit; and as lecturer in philosophy at the University of Notre Dame during the summers, 1924 to 1926. Since 1927 he has been professor of philosophy at the College of St. Charles Borromeo, Columbus, Ohio and since 1930 vice-president of the Board of Trustees. In November 1945 he was named a Domestic Prelate by Pope Pius XII.

Monsignor Glenn had an urge to write from early childhood. He received encouragement when he went to St. Vincent's and was chosen for the staff of the college *Journal* in his freshman college year. He remained with the paper until he was ordained, and for the last few years he was editor-in-chief. Monsignor Glenn was urged to write by his pastor Reverend Michael A. Lambing and Reverend Gerard Bridge, O.S.B. the moderator of the *Journal*. "The old crowd in the *Journal* sanctum was an inspiration too," writes Father Glenn.

His books are textbooks, although his tastes and early efforts all tend to fiction or verse. They were born of his conviction "that pupils need very plain guides and directives in their journey towards intellectual eminence."

In 1929 Father Glenn wrote the *History of Philosophy,* and during the next ten years he published nine books of great value to students of scholastic philosophy. His background as a teacher and his deep understanding of psychology have equipped him to write a text within the comprehension of students and the man of average intelligence. His series are: *Dialectics* (1929); *Ethics* (1930); *Apologetics* (1931); *Criteriology* (1933); *Sociology* (1935); *Psychology* (1936); *Ontology* (1937); *Theodicy* (1938); *Cosmology* (1939), and *An Introduction to Philosophy* (1944).

D. D.

Oliver St. John Gogarty   1878-

Dublin's witty Oliver St. John Gogarty, M.D., Fellow of the Royal College of Surgeons in Ireland, was born in 1878. In that most vocal of all cities, talk is the national art and pastime. He was educated at Trinity College, Dublin, the Jesuit College of Stonyhurst and studied at Oxford University. He married Martha Duane in 1906. They have two sons and one daughter. After settling in Dublin to practice medicine he became a distinguished throat specialist. He indulged his wit and rare gifts not only in conversation but in the writing of verse and prose. He prefers drink to food, for it interrupts conversation less. In 1922 he was nominated as one of the original senators of the Irish Free State, and held the office until 1936.

His friend "A.E." appraises Oliver Gogarty as "the wildest wit in Ireland from which nothing in heaven or earth is immune," and with an "imagination brimful of Rabelaisian fantasy." Yet he adds, "the ideal of Oliver's genie is beauty and mystery achieved by precision, his beauty must shine in the sun not in a shade, and its mystery must be its own perfection."

Some fifteen years ago, Horace Reynolds, New York critic, made a three thousand mile "pilgrimage" to Dublin to satisfy his curiosity to meet in the flesh "this man whose volatile and grotesque name seemed the mirror of his mind," yet "whose wit was as Gothic as a gargoyle writing lyrics, as cool and fresh as a fountain, and delicate as a beautiful change of light." His contemporary friend and poet, Joseph Campbell, calls him, by contrast, "a Buck of the robust, devil-may-care 18th century, born out of time to our delight." His own friendship for his famous fellow-townsman and poet, William Butler Yeats, was a mixture of reverence for his genius, joy in his foibles, appreciation of his kindness and delight in the subtle manner Yeats possessed.

He first visited the United States in 1907 and made his next trip in 1929. Then a lecture tour brought Oliver Gogarty to the United States in the winter of 1939 and this chance to travel from coast to coast opened new vistas of thought and fresh enthusiasms—for him culture is an adventure. Except for an occasional trip to England and Ireland he has been here ever since.

His works are several. Among them are *Hyperthuliana; Poems and Plays,* and *An Offering of Swans. Wild Apples* was published in 1929. Some of the material of this last was included in his volume of *Selected Poems,* in 1933. *As I Was Going Down Sackville Street,* which he calls "a fantasy in fact" and which is semiautobiographical, followed in 1937. *I Follow St. Patrick* appeared in 1938. *Tumbling in the Hay,* a novel, was published in 1939. *Going Native* in 1940, continued the autobiographical reminiscences of *As I Was Going Down Sackville Street,* which a critic calls: "contributing once more to the gaiety of nations," and says, "the satire keen but gentle . . . fast the dart and thrust of innuendo, the reader has to keep on his toes." *Mad Grandeur,* a novel set in 18th Century Ireland, was published in 1941, and *Mr. Petunia* appeared in 1945.

To those who know Oliver St. John Gogarty, the poet emerges from the chrysalis of his wit. His personality is dynamic and through his poetry future generations will come to know the essence of his personality.

C. M. N.

David Goldstein   1870-

David Goldstein was born in London, England on July 27, 1870 of poor Netherlands Jewish parents, who were married in London. In 1871 the family came to America to live in New York City where his father worked as a cigar maker.

All his schooling was obtained in the Henry and Fifth Streets public school of New York City, the Hebrew Free School and the Spanish Jewish Synagogue where he studied Hebrew. When he was eleven years of age he went to work as a cash boy in a dry goods store on Grand Street. Work in a hardware store and a cigar factory followed. Because he was the son of a cigar maker he was permitted to attend the meetings of the Cigar Makers International Union, with which he became affiliated, and in which he has ever since continued his membership. This experience developed in him a desire to work for better economic conditions.

In 1888 the Goldstein family moved to Boston where the wages were higher and the cost of living lower. David again worked in a cigar factory, first as an apprentice then as a journeyman. The cigar makers, who sit opposite each other on long benches in the factory, would discuss various topics while working. The socialists made the greatest impression on him as being the best arguers. These radicals continually read papers and books to spread their propaganda. Mr. Goldstein wrote, "I look back to-day to the zeal of those ardent propagators of error with the thought uppermost in my mind of the wonderful power for good such a propaganda spirit would be, if it filled the minds and hearts of the many Catholics I have met who are morally a credit to their Church and to their country."

Imbued with their spirit and because it promised the material betterment of society, David joined The Socialist Labor Party. Within a few weeks after joining the party he was selected as one of the seven members of its National Board of Appeals. It was as a member of this Board that he met Mrs. Martha Moore Avery, the first American woman of prominence in the socialist movement. To her he is indebted for the understanding of the principles that led him, by God's grace, into the Catholic Church.

In his autobiography, Mr. Goldstein gives the reasons why he became a Catholic. He was baptized in the Immaculate Conception Church of Boston, on Sunday, May 21, 1905. The little he knew about the church, strange to say, was gleaned from socialist writings. When he understood the meaning of free will, "I was back to God," he writes. In 1903 he resigned from the party, after eight years of active work upon the soap box, on the lecture platform and in debate.

Some months after his resignation he wrote *Socialism—The Nation of Fatherless Children*. It was an exposé of the false doctrines of Social-ism. It was written with the help of Mrs. Martha Moore Avery, and was the start of Goldstein's book writing career. His next book, *Bolshevism: Its Cure,* appeared at a time when Americans did not realize that Bol-shevism is but another name for Socialism applied on a national scale. And in 1945 *Suicide Bent: Sangerizing Mankind* appeared.

The same untiring zeal that he showed as a Socialist, he displays now as a Catholic. After five years of being publicly inactive Cardinal O'Con-nell invited him to conduct a series of public educational meetings for workingmen on the basic principles that effect their interests, and to show them the value of the remedies the Church proposes.

A year later the Central Bureau of the Central Verein in St. Louis, Missouri, engaged him to take up work nationally in defense of the Church against socialist propaganda. He left the cigar factory to do this work and thus became the first Catholic layman to devote full time to defend the Church against the socialist attack.

Campaigning for Christ is the third book written conjointly by Mrs. Avery and David Goldstein. Mrs. Avery joined the Catholic Church in 1903. The purpose of the book is to encourage others to take up the work of spreading the knowledge of things Catholic among people assembled in streets and parks. *Campaigning for Christ* told the story of seven years' work done by Mrs. Avery, by him and by associated speakers. Since Mrs. Avery's death in 1929, David Goldstein has continued the work to which she was so devoted. In 1932 he published *The Campaigner for Christ Handbook*. Its aim is to furnish the answers to the questions asked at open air meetings. At the request of Cardinal O'Connell he wrote the *Autobiography of a Campaigner for Christ.*

To carry on his lectures for the Church, he refused an offer of $7500.00 a year from a Southern University to teach sociology especially to ten groups of business men, to keep them informed on the principles and activities of various radical organizations.

The charge that David Goldstein entered the Catholic Church for money is false. For the first six years of his Catholic life, he worked as a cigar maker. His income did not come through the Church. Through his lectures many have started on their way into the Church, and many of those who had fallen away have been reclaimed.

The Jewish Panorama is an attempt to give Catholics a well-balanced view of present-day Jewry, in the United States in particular.

In 1942 he published a companion book to *The Jewish Panorama,* entitled *Letters of a Hebrew-Catholic to Mr. Isaacs.* These letters were written "to make plain to Jews (and Christians as well) that conversion from the Synagogue to the Church means love for, not denial of the faith of their fathers of old in Israel; it means passing from the caterpillar to the butterfly stage of Judaism, as Catholic Christianity is Judaism full blossomed."

Niagara University conferred upon him the honorary degree of Doctor of Laws and in 1946 he received the Catholic Action Medal which is conferred annually by St. Bonaventure's College upon a lay person who is outstanding in the field of Catholic Action. M. H.

Brigadier Martin Louis Alan Gompertz 1886-

Priding himself on providing clean adventure yarns with a touch of out-of-the-way color and knowledge, Brigadier Martin Gompertz produced one or two books a year during all his war service. He comes from a soldier family. His father was the late Major Alfred Gompertz of the Hampshire Regiment.

Martin Gompertz was born in 1886. He was educated at St. Edmund's College, Ware and passed the Staff College of Quetta. In 1903 he served with the Third Battalion of the Hants Regiment (Militia); with the First Battalion, Yorks Regiment in 1904 and with the Indian Army in 1906. In 1913 he became a captain and in 1919 a major. He served in the first World War in Europe from 1914 to 1918. In the Mahsud Waziristan Campaign, 1919 to 1920, he was wounded. He saw further service in India in 1930 and in the Burmese Rebellion, in 1931 to 1932. In 1938, he was Commander of the Thal Brigade in India. The following year (1939) he retired.

His adventure and exploring stories are of the Rider Haggard kind. He usually wrote under the pseudonym "Ganpat." According to *Blackwood's Magazine* (1916) " 'Ganpat' was the sobriquet the sepoys had bestowed on the Captain when, as a very callow second lieutenant, he had been posted to an Indian infantry regiment. He was long and thin, and it would have been difficult to conceive any one more unlike the conventional presentment of the jovial, pot-bellied, elephant-headed deity of good fortune known to India at large as 'Ganesh' and to the Mahrattas as 'Ganpat.' But it was the nearest his men's tongues could get to his real name, and so it stuck."

He first attracted attention as a writer by his stories in *Blackwood's Magazine*. These were later published by Hodder. Some of the books that appeared under the pseudonym "Ganpat" are: *Harilek; Road to Lamaland; Snow Rubies* (1925); *High Snow* (1927); *Magic Ladakh; Roads of Peace;* and *Fairy Silver*. One of the books published under his own name is *The Sleepy Duke* (1938). It is a very solid yarn of the Crusades with the blending of the Norman and the Saxon. It has a strong Catholic flavor.

In 1921 he married Beryl Constance Fitch. They have one son and one daughter. In World War II, he went down to Devon, where he farms.

M. H.

Most Reverend Alban Goodier, S.J. 1869-1939

Years of notable service in India as well as many literary works distinguished the career of the Most Reverend Alban Goodier, S.J. He was born at Great Harwood in Lancashire in 1869 and entered the Jesuit Preparatory School, Hodder, in 1881, moving on to Stonyhurst College in 1882. These school years gave indication of the high degree to which his literary gifts would attain in later years. His Latin and Greek prose brought him honors and he won the Senior English Essay prize. While still a boy he began to write essays or descriptive accounts of historic places he had visited, for the *Stonyhurst Magazine*.

He left college with a scholarly knowledge of the classics, the love of English literature and a sensitiveness in the use of words which characterized his writings. There was also impressed on his deeply religious soul the noble Catholic ancestry of Stonyhurst and similar colleges which stemmed from a recusant past in an atmosphere redolent of the ancient Faith preserved through martyrdom and suffering.

In 1887 at the age of eighteen, the future archbishop sought admission to the Jesuit novitiate and was received at Manresa House, Roehampton. He obtained his B.A. at the University of London in 1891 and shortly after returned to Stonyhurst to teach for six years. Those who had him for master remember his unusual gifts. As one expressed it, "I found Alban Goodier the best master I had at Stonyhurst. He really educated us." A keynote of his nature showed distinctly in this relation, that of unfailing courtesy, kindness and patience, never descending to a lower level but rather bringing to his those of whom he had charge.

Ordained in 1903, Father Goodier's first permanent appointment was to the Roehampton novitiate. There he spent nine years which were among the happiest of his life. During these years he acted as chaplain to the Sacred Heart Convent at Roehampton and met Mother Janet Stuart, a soul kindred to his own.

During those years the Everyman Series came into being and Father Goodier conceived the idea of a Catholic series to be published along similar lines. He was able to bring his idea to fulfilment to the extent of some eighteen volumes or so under the title of "The Catholic Library," but it was discontinued because of World War I and his own call to Bombay, which began another and the most important period of his life.

Due to the war a most delicate situation had arisen at St. Francis Xavier's College, Bombay, then in charge of the German Jesuit Fathers. The government's decision to intern these Fathers brought an appeal to the English Jesuit Provincial to send a priest to be principal of the college and director of studies. Father Goodier was chosen, a choice which results showed to have been ideal. The new principal had been all his life engaged in education. His judgment was well balanced. His learning and tact and his gift of understanding served him in good stead and he carried through a period full of difficulties and real suffering for one of his nature.

He was rector from 1915 until 1919 when Pope Benedict XV appointed him Archbishop of Bombay. This high office he also bore with great distinction through situations even more delicate and trying. Conflicting ecclesiastical authority through a long past patronage given by the Popes to the Crown of Portugal created two archbishops in the See of Bombay, which resulted in intolerable contradictions. The strain reacted on Archbishop Goodier severely, and in 1926 he felt it best to resign, while a solution was worked out in Rome to relieve this overlapping authority. The solution finally arrived at was the one recommended by the Archbishop at his *ad limina* visit in 1925.

In October 1926, he was transferred to the titular see of Hierapolis in Phrygia and the remaining thirteen years of his life were spent in England working for souls in many channels. Cardinal Bourne held him in great esteem and named him Auxiliary Bishop of Westminster in 1930. Two years later, however, he resigned this position and retired to the Benedictine Convent of Teignmouth where he spent the last seven years of his life writing, preaching and giving retreats. In 1935 he gave his support to the effort to establish a Catholic Summer School in Cornwall, which, though it was sustained for but three summers, was a brave attempt and gives hope that it may sometime again be revived. His great gift with souls had been early recognized and now he was in overwhelming demand for retreats and preaching, but his health had long been failing and he could accept only a limited amount of such work.

Archbishop Goodier wrote prolifically, with deep devotion and erudition. It was said of him during his life that he was "the greatest living authority on the life of Christ." Revered for his deep religious sense, and recognized holiness, he had a strong spiritual influence on the life of the people of Great Britain, both Catholic and non-Catholic. Through his books he became known beyond the borders of his own nation, and his beautiful portrayals of Our Lord have given him a place unique in the Catholic literary world. The Gallery of Living Catholic Authors at Webster Groves, Missouri, elected him an Academy member. His distinguished record in the scholastic field was also recognized and caused him to serve on many committees and boards and he was a member of the Advisory Committee for Education in the Colonies.

The numerous books of the Archbishop are devotional and spiritual in nature. Perhaps his most widely known work is *The Public Life of Our Lord Jesus Christ,* in two volumes. This was followed by *The Passion and Death of Our Lord Jesus Christ,* also widely read. Other works are: *The Risen Jesus; The Life That is Light; Inner Life of a Catholic; The Word Incarnate; About the Old Testament; The Bible for Every Day; Witnesses to Christ; The Crown of Sorrow; Introduction to Ascetical and Mystical Theology; The Prince of Peace; History and Religion,* and *The Meaning of Life* and other essays. *St. Ignatius Loyola and Prayer* was published after his death.

He died on March 13, 1939.   C. M. N.

Mrs. Carl Görres *see* Ida Friedrike Coudenhove

Reverend Louis Gougaud, O.S.B. 1877-1941

A born Celt, Dom Louis Gougaud, O.S.B., early directed his studies to Celtic history. His first important work was *Les Chrétientés celtiques* and it appeared in 1911. A second edition, *Christianity in Celtic Lands* was published in 1932 and won for him renown as a student of the Celtic Church. In recognition of his services in this connection, the National University of Ireland conferred upon him the degree of Doctor of Celtic Literature, honoris causa, in 1926. Monastic history also interested him but his *Ermites et reclus* (1928) and *Anciennes coutumes claustrales* (1930) represent only a fraction of his knowledge on this subject.

Dom Louis Gougaud was born at Malestroit, Morbihan in 1877. He was educated at Ploërmel (Brittany), St. Vincent's College, Rennes and studied law at the University of Rennes. He obtained his licentiate in that faculty in 1900.

In 1902 he went to the Appuldurcombe House (Isle of Wight) where the monks of Solesmes Abbey were in exile. He was professed in 1904 and ordained a priest in 1909. Since 1907 until his death in 1941, he spent his life, with the exception of the years 1914-1919, when he was mobilized in the French Army, at St. Michael's Abbey, at Farnborough, Hants, England. The abbey possesses the commemorative medal he received in 1907 at the end of his first year as a student in law at Rennes for the prize in "Economic politique."

A confrere writes, "There are good reasons to suppose that Dom Gougaud's vocation as a Benedictine was also a vocation as an historian, for, after his first profession he was permitted to write on historical matters concerning Old Brittany and Celtic Lands. He wrote then his first article which was much appreciated by professionals, 'Un point obscur de l'itinéraire de saint Colomban venant en Gaule' published in January 1907, in *Les Annales de Bretagne*, Rennes, Volume 21."

His numerous contributions to historical reviews both in England and abroad made him known and respected in learned circles. He had "an exceptional command of detail combined with an exacting and sound critical faculty." He was known for his keen sense of humor and his willingness to help and encourage others. Dom Benedict Steuart, O.S.B., who knew him for years, described him as "very small and neat; he had a round smiling face and twinkling eyes which made one think irresistibly of an elf. He had none of the "dry-as-dust" appearance and manner connected with learning such as his, in the popular mind, though he could be serious and grave when he chose. He had, too, plenty of practical good sense."

For the last twenty years of his life he was devoted to his little flock at Bowlhead Green, Thursley, Surrey that he took care of every Sunday. He died on the 24th of March 1941.

His principal works are: *Les Chrétientés celtiques* (1911); *Gaelic Pioneers of Christianity* (1923); *Confessions de St. Augustin; Traduction nouvelle* (1923); *Devotions et pratiques ascetiques du Moyen âge* (1925); (English edition, 1927); *Ermites et reclus* (1928); *Modern Research with special Reference to Early Irish Ecclesiastical History* (1929); *Anciennes coutumes claustrales* (1930); *Christianity in Celtic Lands* (1932); *In the Tracks of Irish Wandering Monks and Scholars* and *Les Saints Irlandais hors d'Irlande,* (1936).   M. H.

Georges-Pierre-Louis-Theophile-Goyau 1869-1939

French Academician, historian and biographer of repute, Georges Goyau chose as the subjects of the majority of his works, the Church and its great figures. Fittingly, his last book was *Le Christ,* the climax as it were of his scholarly writings, distinguished for their forceful logic and clarity.

Born in Orleans in 1869, he was educated there at the Lycée, and then in Paris, at the Lycée Louis-le-Grand and l'Ecole Normale, from which he graduated in 1888. He received a university degree in history in 1891 and then began to write. From l'Ecole Française in Rome he sent remarkable letters to Débats. In 1893 he wrote *Le Pape, les Catholiques et la question social* and later a five-volume work, *Autour du Catholicisme social.* Brunetière sent him to Germany to study the religious situation there, and for his *L'Allemagne religieuse: le protestantisme* he received the Bordin Prize of the French Academy in 1898. This was followed by two more volumes, on *L'Allemagne religieuse: le catholicisme.* He also wrote *Bismarck et l'Eglise.* His book *Valiant Women: Mother Mary of the Passion and the Franciscan Missionaries of Mary,* was translated into English by George Telford.

Goyau had a filial devotion to the papacy and enjoyed the friendship of Leo XIII. He wrote books on *Le Vatican Papauté et chrétienté sous Benoît XV, Pie XI,* and *Pie XII.* Other biographies were those of St. Louis, St. Jeanne d'Arc, Cardinal Mercier and Ozanam. He also wrote *Missions et missionaires.* In 1908 he received the Prix Vitet. His *Histoire religieuse de la nation française* opened to him the doors of the French Academy in 1922, and he was elected perpetual secretary of the Academy in 1938.

In the United States, Goyau was known for his contributions to the *Catholic Encyclopedia.* His books on Canada also aroused special interest here, his argument being that French Canada had a definite religious purpose in the history of colonization.

He married twice, once in 1903, and in 1917. His first wife, Lucie Felix Faure, was a woman of extraordinary sanctity. She died in 1913. During the war while serving with the Red Cross, he married Mlle. Heuzey. She published *Le Christ*—his last work, posthumously, and received from Pope Pius XII a letter of commendation and consolation. Goyau died Oct. 25, 1939.

Of his magnum opus *L'Allemagne religieuse* special mention must be made. Goyau consecrated twenty years of his life to its production, with a studiousness and incessant labor that the appellation "a lay Benedictine" has been deservedly applied to him. This exhaustive study of the soul of the German nation and the reactions of Catholicity upon it was not only an epochal historical work in itself, but also served as the "motif" for his subsequent writings and studies. He discusses and analyses the history of the Germans but he is really speaking to the French people, "Fas est ab hoste doceri."

He was an editor of *Le Figaro* and the *Revue des Deux Mondes*, to which he long contributed. He held the chair of the history of missions at the Institute Catholique, Paris, and was a consultor on history for the Congregation of Rites, president of the Publicistes Chrétiens, and director of the Réunion des Etudiants. He was a Chevalier de la Legion d'honneur and a Commander of the Order of St. Gregory the Great and of the Order of Leopold.   C. M. N.

Reverend Ernest Graf, O.S.B.   1879-

St. Benedict's pungent observations about idleness, a vice which he very properly describes as an enemy of the soul, is partly responsible for the writings of Father Ernest Graf. His life has been that of the ordinary Benedictine monk—Prayer and Work.

For a good number of years he was in charge of the small private school, the Alumnate of St. Mary's Abbey, Buckfast, where he taught all sorts of subjects but mostly the classics. Later he taught philosophy. He is now teaching Holy Scripture. His chief external work has been the giving of retreats throughout England and Ireland. What time is left over is given to writing.

In 1920 the editors of the *Homiletic and Pastoral Review* asked the late Abbot Anscar Vonier to contribute, and to have his monks contribute, articles on the Liturgy to their *Review*. Abbot Anscar asked Father Ernest "to take the lion's share of the task," but that he himself or others might contribute. These articles appeared under the title "By the Monks of Buckfast." With the exception of two papers, every one of the monthly installments from 1920 to about 1930 were written by Father Ernest.

The editors suggested to the publisher that the papers be brought out in book form. Thus Father Ernest's first book *The Priest at the Altar* was published.

In 1930 Father Ernest went to Jerusalem and spent two years in the Holy Land sharing his time between teaching in the Syrian Seminary on the Mount of Offence and serving as the Officiating Chaplain to the R.A.F. In this way he came to travel extensively, both by road and by air. It afforded him unique opportunities to see and to study the Holy Land and the interesting country beyond the Jordan ruled over by the Emir Abdullah. While in Palestine, he went to Nablus to give a retreat to the American Carmelite Fathers who conduct a college in that ancient city nestling between Garizim and Hebal. His surprise was both great and pleasant to hear the reader in the dining room read from his book *The Priest at the Altar*.

Father Ernest's other books are: *Blessed Richard Reynolds Bridgettine Monk of Synon, Martyred at Tyburn* (1935); *Church's Daily Prayer* (1938); *In God's Own Country* (1937), and *In Christ's Own Country* (1944). He translated Schneider's *Church of the Multiplying,* and Wohrmuller's *Royal Law.* He edited the last ten volumes of the *History of the Popes from the Close of the Middle Ages* from the German of Ludwig Freiher von Pastor. A member of the famous Buckfast Abbey in England, he was professed as a Benedictine in 1897 and was ordained to the priesthood in 1902.   M. H.

Dorothy Fremont Grant   1900-

An earnest advocate of the "Apostolate of the Pen," both by word and example, is Dorothy Fremont Grant. "Financial returns will not likely reach the height of a certain publicized tree which grows in Brooklyn," she says to aspiring Catholic authors, "but God has a way of keeping his apostles decently clothed and sufficiently fed."

She is "wife, mother and writer," she notes, in that order. Born in New York City, October 8, 1900, daughter of Francis Murray and Henrietta Addison Fremont, Mrs. Grant has had the urge to write from her high school days, when for compositions, she turned in "wild west thrillers or sob-stories of the New York slums." On her eighteenth birthday she enlisted in the Navy as a yeoman, second class, and while there, gained her first practical "printer's ink" experience as assistant to the editor of the U.S. Naval *Medical Bulletin.* In May 1922, she married Douglas M. Grant of Oakland, California. Their one child, Reta Langdon Grant was born in 1930. In 1932 and again from 1936 to 1938, the "ink in her blood" prompted her to found, edit, publish, write and circulate a bi-weekly newspaper *The Patter* of Manhasset, Long Island.

She has said that, though for many, the proposition "life begins at forty" holds good, for her "it really began at thirty-three. For it was then that I received the greatest gift, that of the true Faith." After selling her newspaper, she began writing for the Catholic press, receiving her first check, from a Catholic editor, Father Gillis of *The Catholic World*. As the conversion to the Faith of her uncle, John Moody, noted financial analyst, preceded hers, so her conversion preceded that of her husband. Her book, *What Other Answer?*, an enlightening revelation of the Catholic religion for non-Catholics, without being formally an apologia, was written, in 1943, as an act of thanksgiving for Mr. Grant's conversion. *Margaret Brent, Adventurer*, an exciting historical novel of early Maryland, appeared from her pen in the autumn of 1944. *And War is my Parish*, an acknowledgment of the valiant work of the Catholic chaplains in the war—rather a compilation of accounts of them—appeared later in the same year. *Night of Decision*, a novel of colonial New York at the time of Col. Thomas Dongan, only Catholic colonial governor, appeared in 1946; and *So! You Want to Get Married!* written for high school and college girls, appeared in 1947. Other works in preparation include factual, historical biographies of John England, first bishop of South Carolina, and Archbishop Hughes of New York.

Mrs. Grant lives in Waynesville, North Carolina, her primary interests and activities still remaining those kindred to the vocation of marriage. J. M.

Clotilde Graves *see* Richard Dehan

William Whites Graves 1871-

Born in a log farm house between Bardstown and Loretto, Nelson County, Kentucky, in 1871, William Graves spent his boyhood in Marion and Washington Counties, near Hardins Creek, which he used in his historical story, *The Broken Treaty* (1935). Thus he grew up absorbing the atmosphere and history of the pioneer and Indian periods. This was further deepened when in 1881 the family moved to Osage Mission, Kansas, and he attended St. Francis Institution for Boys, started in 1847 by the Jesuit, Father Schoenmakers, for Osage Indian children, there still being a few Indians among young William's schoolmates at that time. Several of his books are the result of historical data collected about this mission and its founder: *The Early Jesuits at Osage Mission* (1916); *The Life and Letters of Father John Schoenmakers, S.J.* (1928), and *The Annals of Osage Mission* (1935).

In 1884, the thirteen year old boy went to Parsons, Kansas, to become a druggist apprentice, but after a year returned to Osage Mission, graduating from its public school in 1889. He spent two more years at St.

Francis Institution until he was graduated in 1891, when the school was moved to St. Marys, Kansas. After a few years of clerking in a store and teaching in the parish school, William Graves in 1893 went to Pittsburg, Kansas, there beginning his successful career in the newspaper field as an apprentice in the office of the *Daily World*. He was soon sent to Girard as county correspondent, remaining there until the paper was suspended in 1895. In that year he married Emma Hopkins, and the young couple went to Osage Mission, renamed St. Paul, where they made their home until her death in 1936, and where Mr. Graves still lives. The years following were active and successful. From an interest in the *Neosho County Journal* he succeeded to the ownership in 1896, and is still the editor. In 1902 he established the *Anti-Horse Thief Association Weekly News*, continuing it until 1933, when he sold it. He also established the *Kansas Knight*, official organ of the Knights of Columbus of Kansas, and continued that until he sold it in 1938. *The Degree of Honor Messenger* and *Inter-State Veterinary Journal* were also published by him. He was active in the Anti-Horse Thief Association from 1905, when he was one of the incorporators, until as national president he retired in 1926. As one of the committee, in 1929 he organized the Kansas Catholic Historical Society, of which he is now president; and in 1926 he organized the St. Paul Building and Loan Association, of which he remains secretary. Mr. Graves has also held high posts in the Kansas Knights of Columbus. As a "side-line" he writes fire insurance; he was a member of a firm of harness dealers; he now owns a plumbing establishment.

Besides the books referred to, he has written: *Legend of Greenbush* and *The Poet Priest of Kansas*, both in 1937; and *History of the Kickapoo Mission and Parish* and *Life and Times of Mother Bridget* in 1938. He has always been a student and now owns one of the largest non-professional libraries in Kansas containing many rare volumes of history.

D. D.

Mary Agatha Gray   1868-

"To begin with, I am a back number. You see I can tell you this safely because I passed my seventy-eighth birthday on February 6. At that age one scarcely counts." Thus wrote Mary Agatha Gray of herself in February, 1946.

A Catholic writer of pious novels, juvenile tales and short serials, Mary Agatha Gray earned her living by her pen in New York around the period of 1900 to 1917. Her last novel, *The Towers of St. Nicholas* was published just prior to the first World War.

One of a family of nine, she was born in Woolwich, England, on February 6, 1868, and came to America in young womanhood. Her father, a non-Catholic of literary tastes, was a bit of a naturalist, and her mother was an artist who became a convert to the

Church at the age of sixteen. Mary Agatha, somewhat of an artist by inclination and talent, was herself an intense lover of nature and cites among the keenest of her delights the enjoyment of the sunsets on the Kentish coast.

She was educated at the Convent at Notre Dame (The Namur Sisters) in Plymouth, England, and took postgraduate work at a branch of the South Kensington School of Art in her home town. She took examinations at Cambridge University, where she gained distinctions for French and Botany. Later, she took the Queen's Scholarship examination for teachers and gained the rank of fourth in the First Class. But, deciding that teaching was not her calling she abandoned the idea.

Her first writing was done for Catholic magazines in England entirely without recompense, but when she came to America she began to make literature her life work. Her first novel, *The Turn of the Tide* (1910), was written during a period of convalescence at Lakewood, New Jersey. It was sold within six weeks to Benziger Brothers of New York for whom she had been doing short stories. Within the next five years she had placed *The Tempest of the Heart,* and *Like Unto a Merchant,* with the same publishers. Then she wrote *Derfel the Strong,* a historical novel of a Welsh shrine, with the life and death of Blessed John Forrest and the ancient prophecy which connected his death with the wooden statue of Derfel Gadarn (The Strong) as its theme.

During those and the following years she did editorial work on *Truth, Benziger's Magazine,* and *The Paraclete.* For the last named—a magazine published by the Holy Ghost Fathers—she had a contract calling for a story a month, and she filled this assignment for thirteen years. She also did some work for the Fathers of the Divine Word, of Techny, Illinois, writing for their monthly three serials in three consecutive years. During the last few years she has done a few translations. *My Little Missionary:* the biography of a saintly boy written by Father Letourneau, O.M.I., has been done into Braille by St. Francis Xavier's Library for the Blind. The same society has done her *Tempest of the Heart* and two or three of her *Stories of the Sacraments,* written for the I.C.T.S. A pamphlet on the Mass, *Your Sacrifice and Mine,* written at the request of Monsignor McGinnis, Editor of *Truth,* has had a large sale on Church book racks in many places. This pamphlet was also issued by the I.C.T.S. *The Vicar Apostolic of Keewatin,* also a translation, from the French of Father J. M. Penard, O.M.I., was published in 1939 by the Maison Beuchemin of Montreal, Canada, and Canon Helleu's *Life of Jeanne Jugan* Foundress and first superior of the Little Sisters of the Poor was published by B. Herder Book Co. of St. Louis in the same year.

Toward the end of World War I, Mary Agatha Gray held a position on the Brooklyn *Daily Eagle.* A fall on an icy sidewalk put a stop to her newspaper work until 1939, when she undertook to do the publicity for the centennial celebrations of the Little Sisters of the Poor in North America.

She writes rarely now except for occasional articles in magazines that are especially interesting to her, but her books are still being printed and sold in this country.

Graham Greene 1904-

An ascending scale of merit marks the literary output of Graham Greene, one of England's young Catholic intellectuals. He was born in 1904, the son of Charles Henry Greene and Marion Greene, and was educated at Berkhamsted, where his father was headmaster, and Balliol College, Oxford. He is a cousin of Robert Louis Stevenson. During his student days he indulged his wanderlust by traveling through England. In the absence of funds, he was forced to do barrel-organing, disguised as a tramp. He had a brief business career of ten days with the British-American Tobacco Company after he left Oxford and then he took up journalism, on the staff of the *Nottingham Journal* and as sub-editor of the *London Times,* from 1926 to 1930. In 1925 he published a volume of verse called *Babbling April* and this was followed by several novels dealing with the problem of good and evil of which the first was *The Man Within* (1929) and the most popular *Brighton Rock* (1938), a strange religious melodrama, an action-story of rare adventure, mystery, and psychology, well called "An Entertainment," and which Sean O'Faolain described as "one of the finest danses macabres in the literature of ghastly true." Charles A. Brady says of him in *America,* January 25, 1941, "Only Graham Greene, among contemporary melodramatists, fights the battle of Augustine in the mantle of Buchan and Conrad and Dostoievski."

Between writings, he roamed afar, aided by publishers' royalties. *Another Mexico* is outstanding among his unconventional travel books. There where revolution and persecution flourishes he is distressed and yet fascinated by what he sees, and he transmits to the printed page his keen observations of the country and life-like portraits of its people. This journey gave him the hero and the plot of his finest work, *Labyrinthine Ways,* a soul-searching story of a Mexican priest outlawed, afraid, compassionate toward his fellowmen, ground down to the dust of sin, yet heroically fulfilling his sacred trust. The book received the encomiums of the critics. *A Gun for Sale* (1936) is a thrilling detective story. He always holds the interest of the reader with his streamlined style. William Rose Benét said of him, "No man writing today is more a master of suspense." Also that "he has now proved himself one of the finest craftsmen of story-telling in our time."

Greene writes with brilliance and art. From 1935 to 1939 he was film critic of *The Spectator.* Arthur Calder-Marshall said in *Horizon* that "few English novelists derive more material from the daily newspapers than Graham Greene." The themes of his books include the Nazi Underground and the Fifth Column of organized Marxism, English race-track gangs and the persecution of the Church in Mexico.

He married Vivien Dayrell-Browning in 1927; they have one son and one daughter.

He has written the following books: *The Name of Action* (1930); *Rumour at Nightfall* (1931); *Stamboul Train* (1932); *It's a Battlefield* (1934); *The Old School (Editor)* (1934); *The Bear Fell Free: England Made Me* (1935); *The Basement Room* (Short Stories), *Journey without Maps* (1936); *A Gun for Sale* (1936); *The Lawless Roads: A Mexican Journey* (1939); *The Confidential Agent* (1939); *The Power and the Glory* (1940); *The Ministry of Fear* (1943). (Paramount bought the motion picture rights for *The Ministry of Fear*.)

C. M. N.

Padraic Gregory 1886-

Poet, dramatist, folk-lorist and ecclesiastical architect, Padraic Gregory is essentially Catholic and Irish. Born in Belfast, in 1886, he was educated in the United States and by the Christian Brothers and private tutors in Ireland. His first wife, Madeline Crothers, died in 1920, three years after their marriage. His present wife was born Sara MacKeown. He has five sons and five daughters and makes his home in Belfast.

This is the background of "the best living writer of ballads," in the words of Aodh de Blacam, and such he is generally acknowledged to be. He published his first volume of verse, *The Ulster Folk*, in 1914. Then followed *Old World Ballads* (1913); *Love Sonnets* (1914); *Ireland: A Song of Hope* (1917), and *Ulster Songs and Ballads* (1920), which last definitely established him as one of Ireland's greatest poets. Notable are his powerful poem, "The Rebel," his lovely "Mary's Song to Jesus" and the fine "Ballad of Master Fox," remarkable for its beauty and fidelity to medieval technique. Gregory's national verse is intensely fervid. His is the true voice of Ulster, rich in faith and patriotism, and warming the heart of the exile. He handles dialect extremely well and, whether humorous or pathetic, his poems have a melodic quality. His *Complete Collected Ballads* were published in 1935. On balladry, in which he is a master—he has both studied its origins and attained perfection in its composition—he has lectured before learned societies in England and Ireland, among them the Royal Society of Literature of which he is a Fellow. Some of his historical ballads are set forth in Irish school texts and have been translated into Danish.

From its inception until 1916 Gregory was connected with the Ulster Literary Theatre. He is greatly interested in the revival of sacred drama, and for this movement he has written plays, essays and criticisms. *The Coming of the Magi* is a blank verse drama of dignity, beauty and spirituality. He also wrote *Bethlehem* and *Calvary*. Gregory began in Ireland what Gheon and others have done for France, in presenting in the theatre that which is noble, spiritual, and enjoyable in contrast with the prevailing scepticism and sensuality.

His folk songs are known the world over, many were popularized by John McCormack. Perhaps the most famous is *Padraic the Fiddler*. Volume I of *Anglo-Irish Folk Songs of Padraic Gregory* was published with settings by Charles Wood; volume II, with settings by Carl G. Hardebeck.

Gregory contributes prose and verse to *Studies* and other periodicals, and from 1926 to 1927 he was literary editor of the *Catholic Monthly Review*. His poems are included in many modern anthologies. He is vice-president of the Catholic Poetry Society of England.

In stone as well as in letters he has earned immortality. Through his architecture he has participated in the restoration of liturgical life in Ireland, for his work is characterized by an absence of non-essentials and due regard for the exigencies of the ceremonies of the Church. In particular, his altars are notably fine. He has designed many ecclesiastical buildings in Ireland, including several churches in Belfast. He is a Fellow of the Royal Institute of British Architects and a member of The Royal Institute of the Architects of Ireland and other professional bodies. From the National University of Ireland, he received an LL.D. degree.

Gregory believes religion to be "the mother of all art; and without religion, without morality, no great and lasting art is possible."

His first American published book is *When Painting was In Glory*. It is the result of twenty-five years of study of painting in European galleries and Churches, great and small.   C. M. N.

Theophilus Stephen Gregory   1897-

T. S. Gregory, as he is generally known, was born in Benares, India in 1897 and was educated in Kingswood School and New College, Oxford. He served in World War I and was awarded the Military Cross. In 1921 he entered the Methodist ministry. Four years later he was received into the Catholic Church.

He is the author of *The Unfinished Universe*. In his preface, he says: "I wrote this book as a Methodist minister and began work upon it without any suspicion that I should ever become anything else. There are questions—so it seemed to me—which must assail any sincere Christian in these days, some of faith and others of practice, and it was in attempting to find a Christian answer to them that I was led into the Catholic faith. This book is therefore the story of my conversion."

He is editor of the *Dublin Review*.

Margaret Rose Grennan

Margaret Rose Grennan, born in New York City, received her A.B., magna cum laude, from Hunter College in 1934, and an M.A. and a Ph.D. in English and Comparative Literature from Columbia University. As an undergraduate, she read for honors with Dr. Joseph J. Reilly, distinguished Catholic scholar, author, and teacher. The year's intensive reading and discussion determined her major field of interest, Victorian literature, and the privilege of studying with a Newman authority resulted in her first publication— *The Heart of Newman's Apologia,* an abridged edition of one of the world's greatest spiritual autobiographies, brought out by Longmans, Green & Co. in 1934. In the same year she was awarded the Helen Gray Cone Fellowship. In 1935 she received her Master's degree at Columbia University. Her thesis on Aubrey De Vere reflected her interest in Irish literature—an interest that led to several articles on Celtic legends, the most recent of which is a study of the influence of the Irish imagination on Swift's *Gulliver's Travels,* published in ELH (English Literary History), the Johns Hopkins University Quarterly.

Dr. Grennan, now an assistant professor, has been a member of the English Department of Hunter College since 1935. At the request of Loyola University Press, she edited a text of Shakespeare's *Julius Caesar,* published in 1942. She was awarded a Columbia University Fellowship and devoted a year to her book, *William Morris, Medievalist and Revolutionary,* in which she shows the relationship between Morris' medieval studies and his social theories. She places the poet in a tradition of particular interest to Catholic readers,—the revaluation of the social history of the Middle Ages clearly begun as early as Cobbett's *History of the Protestant Reformation* and dominant in our own day in the lively studies that have inspired the Distributism of Belloc and G. K. Chesterton. Dr. Grennan also contributed the section on Victorian literature, with its historical and literary introduction, to the fourth volume of *The Catholic High School Literature Series* published under the auspices of the Committee on Affiliation of the Catholic University of America for the Revision of English Curricula. Dr. Grennan is a member of Sigma Tau Delta, of Phi Beta Kappa, and of the English Graduate Union of Columbia University.

Beatrice Grimshaw

Many persons dream of travel in far places, but their dreams remain dreams. Beatrice Grimshaw's materialized, however, and she has spent years in the places which are only alluring names to most of us. The South Seas, Fiji, the New Hebrides, the Solomons, the cannibal country of Papua, New Guinea, Celebes, Borneo, the Moluccas, New Britain, Burma, New Caledonia, Java— she has seen all of them. She has written almost forty books out of her experiences and life in these far places.

Miss Grimshaw, the third daughter of Nicholas Grimshaw, was born at Cloona, County Antrim, Ireland. She belongs to a well known Northern Ireland family, Lancashire in origin. Members of the family settled in Ulster in 1760. They were largely instrumental in starting the spinning and weaving industries of Belfast. They were noted for philanthropic treatment of their workers in a day when such treatment was almost unknown. Though the family was not Catholic, Miss Grimshaw came into the Church when she was about twenty-three, during a stay in Dublin.

Her early life was spent in the country, in a pleasant home, with kind parents and loved brothers and sisters. "Riding was the chief amusement in those days, and command of a horse was in later life to prove most useful, as uncivilized travel was largely conducted on horseback."

She was taught by private governesses and tutors. Later she attended the Pension Retaillaud, Caen, Normandy; Victoria College, Belfast; and Bedford College, London. She specialized in the classics, and it was intended that she become a classical lecturer at a woman's college. Very early, however, she decided that she wished to write. Her parents, somewhat reluctantly, allowed her to go to Dublin when she was twenty-one and she took up journalism. She edited a Society journal, sub-edited a sporting paper, did leaderwriting and special reporting. Later she did newspaper work in London. She enjoyed this work immensely, but her dreams of travel persisted—despite the staggering prices of the shipping companies. She finally managed to make her first trip around the world by promising the shipping companies newspaper publicity in return for passes. She provided for her other expenses by commissions for articles from various newspapers. "I do not think for a minute that this sort of thing could be done now; the world before the War (I)—long before—was simpler."

On this tour she first visited the Pacific Islands. That quarter of the world eventually became her home as it had an irresistible attraction for her. "I visited and stayed in all the principal groups, but settled finally in the Western Pacific, in New Guinea, where I lived for many years. I had

very many adventures; in short, a life of adventure and incident. I owned
two plantations and managed one. In the intervals I wrote thirty-seven
books. Adventure, strange places, wild and unknown tribes have always
attracted me more than the civilized and better known travellers' haunts.
In early days I occasionally accompanied exploring parties into entirely
unknown country."

, In March and April 1923 she travelled up the Sepik River, the first
white woman ever to do so. She went on the launch of the missionary
Fathers of the Divine Word. "The missionary Fathers are, in their quiet
way, the most complete daredevils in the Territory." On this trip, however, they took many precautions, for head-hunting flourished at this
time along the Middle Sepik. It was the one topic of interest in all the
villages. A high point of the trip was the rescue by the Fathers of a young
boy who had been taken in a recent raid and whom the head-hunters
were holding for torture and slaughter. "Nothing is more astonishing on
the wild unbroken Sepik than the constant use of pidgen-English. It
seems to have become a general means of communication among tribes
who speak different tongues." In February 1926 another opportunity to
see unknown country presented itself. She made a trip up the notorious
Fly River. In the eighty years since its discovery less than a score of white
persons had travelled it, and she was the first white woman to see it.
There is only one plantation along this river and after that is left behind
one travels through hundreds of miles of country "ever stranger and
lonelier" before one finds any native villages. These tribes are head-
hunters, too. The Fly River man is an artist and everything he uses is
highly carved and decorated. Miss Grimshaw finds that the head-hunters
are more intelligent and more alert than other native tribes. She foresees
a wonderful future for them when they are weaned from their murderous
customs.

Miss Grimshaw has never had any difficulty finding publication
for her work. Readers often write her that they enjoy the strange and adventurous lives in her stories. Many find in these release from confined and
monotonous lives. Her books are great favorites with men. Besides her
novels she has written travel books and many short stories. "As a Catholic,
I am glad to say that I have been able to make a literary success without
using the easy lures of sensual plot and coarse treatment." She has done
a fair amount of broadcasting and has several times refused engagements
to lecture in America, "on account of the cold of American winters,
which would be difficult to endure after a lifetime in the tropics."

One of her chief interests is tropical colonization, another is Catholic
missions in the Pacific, especially in New Guinea and Papua. This adventuring author proclaims, "In all my travels, young and old, the Church
has always been my shield and safeguard, and my greatest happiness."
She is the author of: *In the Strange South Seas* (1907); *From Fiji to the
Cannibal Islands* (1907); *The New New Guinea* (1910); *Guinea Gold*
(1912); *The Sorcerer's Stone* (1914); *Nobody's Island* (1916); *The Coral
Queen* (1919); *The Coral Palace* (1921); *The Little Red Speck* (1921);
Conn of the Coral Seas (1922); *The Sands of Oro* (1924); *The Candles of
Katara* (1925); *The Paradise Poachers* (1927); *Eyes in the Corner* (1928);

My Lady Far-Away (1929); *Star in the Dust* (1930); *Isles of Adventure* (1931); *The Long Beaches* (1933); *The Victorian Family Robinson* (1934); *Pieces of Gold* (1936); *Rita Regina* (1939); *Lost Child* (1940); *South Sea Sarah* (1940).

M. S.

Reverend Hartmann Grisar, S.J. 1845-1932

An authority on Martin Luther and author of the first volume of the scientific *History of Rome and the Popes in the Middle Ages,* Hartmann Grisar was born on September 22, 1845 at Coblenz on the Rhine, Germany, the son of a baker. He studied in Münster (with A. Stockl) and at Innsbruck.

After his ordination to the priesthood in Rome, he entered the Austrian Province of the Society of Jesus. During his two years of novitiate, he familiarized himself with the churches and other places of interest in Rome. In 1871 he became a Professor of Church History at Innsbruck. What spare time he had he devoted to writing. In 1877 he became one of the founders of the *Zeitschrift für katholische Theologie.*

After attracting attention with his monograph on Galileo, he published the important addresses of Father James Laynez, S.J., which he had given at the Council of Trent. This work, *Jacobi Lainez Disputationes Tridentinae* in two volumes was a difficult task, because of Laynez's illegible handwriting and his peculiar abbreviations.

A frequent visitor to Rome, Father Grisar wrote several historical articles for the Roman monthly, *Civilta Cattolica.* Later he was transferred to Rome where he could devote all his time to historical and achaeological studies. As a result of his labors he published, in 1908, the first volume of the monumental *History of Rome and the Popes in the Middle Ages.* It covers the period from the close of the fourth century to the beginning of the pontificate of Gregory the Great. It was immediately translated into English and French. The English translation is in three volumes. On account of his health, the work was never continued despite repeated attempts. Ill health and the Roman climate compelled him to return to Innsbruck.

He then devoted himself to the study of the "Reformation." After ten years of labor he published his *Luther* (three volumes in the original German, six in the English translation) under the title *Martin Luther, His Life and Work.* A writer in the Augsburger Postzeitung calls it the best work on Luther which we Catholics possess. This exhaustive, accurate study of Luther, because of its fairness, won for its author the praise even of Lutherans.

Father Grisar caused quite a stir at Munich when he gave his lecture

"Church History and the Critical Spirit" before the Scientific Congress being held there in September, 1900. His address which pleaded for genuine historicity in describing the lives of the saints even at the sacrifice of edification, met with opposition.

Father Grisar has been described by Father Martin Harney, S.J., as "small in stature and ascetical looking. He was always the perfect gentleman, always the soul of kindness, having a most pleasant smile and patient attention for every visitor or historical inquirer."

Father Grisar died in 1932 at the age of eighty-seven.

M. H.

Reverend Romano Guardini 1885-

When after the first World War the Church in Germany came "to life in the souls of men" (to use Guardini's own words), Guardini was one of the foremost German leaders instrumental in that "religious process of incalculable importance." If there be hope for the Church in Germany after the second World War, it will be due, to a large extent, to the seed sown by the Catholic Youth Movement and the liturgical movement under the inspiring leadership of Guardini and others.

Born in Verona, Italy, February 17, 1885, the son of a merchant, Romano Guardini grew up in Mainz, Germany. He was ordained a priest in 1910, and was admitted to the faculty of the School of Divinity of the University of Bonn, Germany, in 1920, on the basis of a thesis dealing with the idea of redemption according to St. Bonaventure. In 1923 he was appointed a professor of dogmatic theology at the University of Breslau and at the same time was given leave of absence to teach as a "Professor für katholische Weltanschauung" something like a visiting lecturer in Catholic philosophy) at the University of Berlin. This device was used by the German republic to provide Guardini with an appropriate teaching platform, which the University of Berlin, a relatively independent corporation like all German universities before 1933, would not have given to a Catholic priest. His first lectures were attacked by the ex-Jesuit Count Paul v. Hoensbroech and his appointment sharply criticized by anti-Catholic groups in the German capital. But soon Guardini's courses of instruction, in and outside the University of Berlin, were regarded as one of the most notable educational phenomena of Germany at that time. In 1945 he was given a chair of philosophy at the University of Tuebingen, Wuerttemberg.

A. N. Raybould, Reverend Dr. Francis de Hovre, Irene Marinoff, and others, rightly stress that he unites the Classicism of the South with the problematic leanings and philosophical mind of the North, and that he has depth of thought with perfection of expression. A master of intuitive psychology, he was the leader of the German Catholic Youth Movement, a movement "born, not made," setting the "elan vital" of youth against the spuriousness of bourgeois civilization, making war on dead words and stereotyped concepts, insincere conventions and habits of life not in keeping with nature. Such books by Guardini as *Neue Jugend und katholischer Geist* (1920) (The New Youth and the Catholic Mind); *Aus einem Jugendreich* (1920), dealing with the new philosophy of life of the young generation after the first World War; *Gottes Werkleute* (many editions) (God's workmen); *Vom Geist der Liturgie* (1918); *Vom Sinn der Kirche* (1922) (The Church and the Catholic—The Spirit of the Liturgy) now available in English translation; *Von heiligen Zeichen* (Sacred Signs, tr. by G. H. Pollen, S.J., 1930); *Ehe und Jungfräulichkeit* (Matrimony and Virginity), etc., exercised a tremendous influence upon the younger post-war generation in Germany. This applies also to his numerous, yet exceedingly profound articles in *Die Schildgenossen,* a very fine periodical published by the "Quickborn," a prominent group within the Catholic Youth Movement, of which Guardini was the spiritual leader. Very significant Catholic intellectual events were also the "tings," sessions, and retreats on Burg: Rothenfels, a medieval castle on the Main river, by the "Quickborn," the heart of which were the talks given by Father Guardini, whom the Catholic youth regarded as an elder brother.

Other books by Father Guardini are: *Liturgische Bildung* (1923) (Liturgical Education); *Der Gegensatz, eine Philosophie des Lebendig-Konkreten* (1925), outlining Guardini's dialectical philosophy; *Briefe über Selbstbildung* (Letters on Self-education 1921-24) (1930); *Briefe vom Comer See* (Letters from Lake Como) (1927); *Auf dem Wege* (1923); (Theses; two books dealing with different topics); *Das Gute, Das Gewissen und die Sammlung* (1929-31) (The Good, Conscience, and Meditation—translated); *Wille und Wahrheit* (Spiritual Exercises) (1933); *Der Kreuzweg vom lebendigen Gott* (1930) (The Way of the Cross—translated); *Essays on Pascal, Dostoievski, Kierkegaard, Dante: Im Spiegel und Gleichnis* (In Pattern and Parable); *Der Herr, Betrachtungen über das Leben und die Person Jesu Christi* (1937) (The Lord, Meditations on the Life and Person of Jesus Christ); and *Das Gebet des Herrn* (1932) (The Lord's Prayer).

He has been residing near Biberach since his Berlin home was destroyed in an air raid. During World War II, Professor Guardini completed several new books. They are: *The Death of Socrates,* an interpretation of Platonic Philosophy, and *Beginning,* an analysis of the *Confessions of St. Augustine.* Two additional volumes await publication. They are: *Freedom, Grace, Destiny* and *The Year of Our Lord.*

F. M.

Right Reverend Peter Guilday 1884-1947

Church history had been the chosen field of the Right Reverend Monsignor Peter Guilday throughout his academic years as student and professor, and he is widely known as an historian of the Church in the United States.

Monsignor Guilday was born in Chester, Pennsylvania, on March 25, 1884, of Irish parents. After graduation from the Catholic High School in Philadelphia, he entered St. Charles Seminary at Overbrook in 1902. He was granted a scholarship to the University of Louvain in 1907, and upon completion of his theological studies, he was ordained there by Bishop Gabriels of Ogdensburg in 1909. Five years of research in Church history followed, with special studies in Rome and at the Universities of Bonn and London. At Louvain he became known as "l'Abbé Washington." He wrote his doctoral dissertation, "The English Catholic Refugees on the Continent, 1559-1795" while serving for two years as assistant priest at the Church of St. Mary of the Angels, Bayswater, London, and from Louvain he received the degree of Docteur-en-Sciences Historiques in 1914. He was also awarded a Fellowship in the Royal Historical Society of England. The honorary degree of LL.D. was given him by Notre Dame in 1925, Mt. St. Mary's in 1929 and Loyola (Chicago) in 1931. Marquette University awarded him an L.H.D. in 1928, and Georgetown University the degree J.U.D. in 1930. He was awarded the Litt.D. by Fordham University at its Centennial exercises in 1941.

His teaching career began in 1914 when he became instructor in history at the Catholic University of America, where he received every encouragement from Bishop Shahan and with which he was associated until his death in 1947. In 1915 he founded the *Catholic Historical Review*, of which he was editor-in-chief, and which became in 1922 the official organ of the American Catholic Historical Association, founded by him in 1919. During World War I he served as secretary of the National Catholic War Council, and assistant director of the Student Army Training Corps of the Middle States, from 1917 to 1918. Promoted to an associate professorship in history in 1919, he held this post until 1923, after which he was professor of American church history at the University. In that department he developed a seminar, productive of stimulating discussion, interested research and important writings by both professor and students.

Dr. Guilday has had a great influence on Church historiography in the United States. He published numerous articles: the manual, *An Introduction to Church History;* the brochure, *Graduate Studies in American Church History;* monographs on *The Catholic Church in Virginia, 1815-1822,* a documentary treatment of the Norfolk schism, and *The Life of John Gilmary Shea,* the great pioneer in the field whose distinguished successor he became; as well as several books. *The Life and Times of John Carroll* and *The Life and Times of John England* are scholarly accounts of important periods of American church history in Maryland and the Carolinas. The early years of the New York diocese were to be treated in a book he was writing on Archbishop Hughes. *The History of the Councils of Baltimore (1791-1884)* records ecclesiastical legislation in the United States as enacted in these assemblies. Monsignor Guilday had also edited various historical works.

For his work in the restoration of the library at Louvain he was made a Chevalier of the Order of Leopold II by the Belgian government. At many celebrations of historic events Dr. Guilday had delivered significant addresses, notably that on "Three Centuries of American Catholicism," at the Maryland Tercentenary in Baltimore in 1934. He was made a domestic prelate by Pope Pius XI in 1935 "in recognition of your scientific attainments shown in the works on history which you have published and which have won on all sides the highest appreciation of your productive scholarship." In 1934 he celebrated the silver jubilee of his ordination as a priest.   C. M. N.

Waldemar Gurian 1902-

From the time of St. Paul onwards, it has been a characteristic of converts from Judaism to Catholicity to be able to perceive keenly the issues in the conflicts between world philosophies. The challenge of Marxism to the Catholic philosophy of life and of history in the modern era is ably met by the writings of the gifted Jewish convert to the Church, Waldemar Gurian. In a span of life which has been lived from the Czarist days in old Russia to the American home front on the Notre Dame campus, Doctor Gurian has seen and felt the vast changes of the past forty years.

Waldemar Gurian was born in Russia, in the then capital city of St. Petersburg, in 1902. Educated mostly in Germany, first at the Dominican Collegium Albertinum, then at the Universities of Bonn, Munich, Breslau, and Cologne, he obtained a Ph.D. at the last named institution. The kaleidoscopic events of post-war Germany were witnessed by him as a student of sociology and philosophy under Max Scheler and later on as an editor on the staff of the *Kölnische Volkszeitung.* In 1937 he came to Indiana to be associate professor of politics at the University of Notre Dame. In 1939 Gurian became editor of the *Review of Politics,* published by the aforesaid university.

The works of Scheler, Maritain, Leon Bloy, Max Weber and Berdyayev have particularly influenced Gurian. The trends of modern thought translated into the term "totalitarianism" have ever been his field of study. Marxism and the ideas of both French and German Nationalism have found him an analyst and critic of literary and philosophic ability.

His best known books have been translated into English and enjoy a wide area of appeal. They are *Bolshevism* (1932); and the *Future of Bolshevism* (1936), translated by E. I. Watkin. Also in English are his *Hitler and the Christians* (1937), and *The Rise and Fall of Marxism* (1938), translated by E. F. Peeler. Besides the books already mentioned, he has written *Die Politischen und Socialen Ideen des Franzoesischen Katholizismus 1789-1914* (1929); *Charles Maurras und die Action Française* (1931), and *Um des Reiches Zukunft*, a study of German Nationalism (1932).

His aim is, in his own words, "to understand Bolshevism as a historical phenomenon." The general conclusion of his writings is that Marxism has burned itself out. As a Christian writer on political philosophy, Dr. Gurian is already held in international esteem.   J. M.

Denis Rolleston Gwynn   1893-

In the midst of an active life as soldier, journalist, editor, special correspondent and literary advisor, Denis Rolleston Gwynn nevertheless found time to write a number of books which entitle him to an honored place among Irish Catholic writers. Born in Ireland in 1893, the son of Stephen Gwynn, he was educated at St. Enda's College, founded by Patrick Pearse; at the London University, and at the National University of Ireland, where he received his degrees of B.A. and D.Litt.

As lieutenant in the Royal Munster Fusiliers he served in France during the first World War and was attached to the Ministry of Information. In 1915 he founded and edited *New Ireland* and also edited *The Irish Soldier,* a record of the Irish Regiments in the War. From 1918 to 1919 he was assistant editor of *Everyman* and the *Review of Reviews,* and in 1920 he became editor of the *National Press Agency.* In France from 1921 to 1923 he was special correspondent for various papers. He then went to London where he was correspondent on *Freeman's Journal* in 1924, and in 1925 he was on the editorial staff of the *Westminster Gazette.* The publishing firm of Burns, Oates and Washbourne procured him as literary adviser from 1933 to 1939 and he was made a director in 1934.

Shortly after the outbreak of World War II, he retired from active service with Burns, Oates and Washbourne. His place was taken by Christopher Hollis. He did national service by growing things on his bit of land, but kept up his literary output. Besides serving on the editorial committee of the *Universe,* he wrote the weekly comments and many of the leading articles for that paper. Mr. Gwynn is small, gentle and apparently shy, yet with an incisive style in debate. He is on the committee of the Guild of St. Francis of Sales (for Catholic writers and journalists).

Mr. Gwynn is a contributor to periodicals here and abroad and his books include: *The Catholic Reaction in France; The 'Action Française' Condemnation; The Irish Free State, 1922-1927; The Struggle for Catholic Emancipation; A Hundred Years of Catholic Emancipation; Daniel O'Connell; Cardinal Wiseman; Edward Martyn and the Irish Revival; The Life and Death of Roger Casement; John Keogh; Pius XI; The Life of John Redmond; De Valera; The O'Gorman Mahon; The Vatican and War in Europe* (1940), and *Second Spring, 1818-1852* (1942). To Catholics in all English-speaking countries the "Second Spring" denotes that sudden revival and expansion of the Catholic Church in England which reached its climax with the restoration of the Hierarchy in 1850 and the Synod at which Newman preached the most famous of his sermons.

D. D.

Most Reverend Francis Joseph Haas
1889-

When on May 28, 1943 President Roosevelt issued an executive order setting up a new Committee on Fair Employment Practice, he appointed the then Monsignor Haas, Dean of the School of Social Science at Catholic University, as chairman of this committee. Its aims were to prevent racial discrimination in war industry employment. This problem, demanding diplomatic and tactful handling, is but the latest of many such delicate undertakings which the United States Government had requested Monsignor Haas to dispose of in the last decade, until he was made a bishop. The prelate has a record of success in conciliating labor disputes which very few other men can approach. Since 1935 he has borne the title of Special Commissioner of Conciliation. As the most respected and eminent of its trouble shooters, the United States Conciliation Service calls him in from time to time on especially tough cases.

Bishop Haas, one of a large family, was born in Racine, Wisconsin, March 18, 1889. His father, Peter F. Haas, a merchant, was of German and French descent; his mother, Mary L. O'Day Haas, of Irish descent. He attended the Racine High School and then St. Francis Seminary. He was ordained June 11, 1913. Besides his nine years as a student he has spent much time at St. Francis Seminary, as professor of English from 1915 to 1919, professor of Sociology and Dean of the College Department, 1922 to 1931, and as Rector, 1935 to 1937. From 1919 to 1922 he was at the Catholic University studying under Doctors John A. Ryan, Kerby, O'Grady, O'Hara, and Monsignor Pace—a brilliant faculty. He also attended the Economics Seminar at Johns Hopkins University from 1920 to 1921. He received his Ph.D. from Catholic University in 1922.

Busy years in Milwaukee followed. Besides his St. Francis affiliation he was professor of Sociology at Marquette University, 1922 to 1931, and lecturer at the Milwaukee School of Social Work, 1925 to 1931. Editing *The Salesianum* (quarterly) from 1922 to 1931 was another responsibility. Yet the energetic priest found time for such civic duties as membership on the Examining Board of the county Civil Service Commission; Impartial Chairman, Newspaper Industry, Milwaukee (1925); and prior to the enactment of the Old Age Pension law in Wisconsin he was secretary for the county Association for Promotion of Old Age Pensions. He served a term as President of the Catholic Association for International Peace, 1929 to 1931; member of the Advisory Council of the American Association for Social Security since 1927 (director since 1933); director of the Carnegie Church Peace Union since 1926; Advisory Council of the League of Nations Association since 1927; member of the Committee on Cultural Relations with Latin America since 1929.

In 1931 Father Haas left Milwaukee and returned to Washington where he became the Director of the National Catholic School of Social Service, 1931 to 1935. Soon after the start of the Roosevelt administration he became a national figure when Secretary of Labor Perkins named him a member of the Labor Advisory Board of the NRA, June 21, 1933. A few months later he was made a member of the National Labor Board. In 1934 he was appointed to the General Code Authority. Harry Hopkins selected him for the Labor Policies Board of the Works Progress Administration in 1935 and he served for four years. From 1937 to 1939 he was an active member of the three-man Wisconsin Labor Relations Board. In 1940 and again in 1941 he spent a month in Puerto Rico as chairman of committees set up by the Wage and Hour Division of the Department of Labor to determine minimum wages for the workers on the island. He has since been a member of the Puerto Rico Wage Committee. In 1940 the Monsignor accepted a place on the Commission on Long Range Work Relief Policies of the National Resources Planning Board, which in 1943 issued the famous "five pound" report recommending the American Beveridge Plan. He is a founder of the Catholic Conference on Industrial Problems. Congressional hearings, industrial conferences, conciliation meetings, conventions, forums, crowd his days. He was professor of Economics at Catholic University until 1937 when he was made Dean of its newly established School of Social Science.

Three honours have come to him in the last decade. Pope Pius XI made him a Domestic Prelate on August 6, 1937. And his native state recognized his secular achievements when the University of Wisconsin conferred the LL.D. on him in 1936. On November 18, 1943, he was consecrated Bishop of Grand Rapids, in St. Andrew's Cathedral.

He is a regular contributor to several journals. In addition he has found time to write pamphlets for the National Conference of Catholic Charities, the Catholic Association for International Peace, and the National Catholic Welfare Council, and also several publications for the NRA and the WPA. He is the author of: *Shop Collective Bargaining* (1922) and *Man and Society* (1930).   M. S.

Rosamond Edwards Haas   1908-

For her slender first volume of poetry, *Delay Is the Song*, Rosamond Edwards Haas won a $1,000 award—the Avery Hopwood Poetry Award for 1942-43 at the University of Michigan, in 1943.

Rosamond Edwards Haas was born in Kalamazoo, Michigan on July 1, 1908. She was educated at the Western State High School, from which she was graduated in 1926; at the Western College of Education from which she received her A.B. degree in 1929, and at the University of Michigan from which institution she received her M.A. degree in 1934.

After reading many books by Catholic authors the most influential of which was John Henry Newman, she became a member of the Catholic Church in 1933.

She has held various secretarial positions. At present (1946) she is secretary to the News Service at the University of Michigan.

The book *Delay Is the Song*, published in 1944, is made up of poems on love, identity, creativeness and the spiritual life. The delay is the hesitation between the notes of music (the setting of the poem is a concert and the sentiment love—earthly love). In the latter half of the poem, "delay" becomes the intervals between the words spoken by the two lovers (still the concert-goers). It was written during a practice blackout when the only light in her bedroom was the luminous garland of letters on her alarm clock's face. William Rose Benét says of her work: "This is a new talent emerging. Here is a young poet of delicate apprehension and often forcibly modern phrase."

"Midnight" seems to be one of the best-liked poems in her book, at least in Ann Arbor, Michigan where everyone knows the carillon. It was read over the air on one of the University broadcasts. Miss Haas wrote it because day after day she found herself listening for the bell-tower to strike the quarters. The bells seemed to be building a design (fourfold) in the sky. Of course, the square was completed each hour—but for dramatic reasons she took the last hour and finished the pattern of midnight.

"Of the Redbird" is one of her "pet" poems. It's just a simple love poem—two lovers, one wakened by the bird's song, watching the awakening of the other—a soldier.

"When My Song Named You" is one of several poems in the book which describe creative activity—the making of a poem. This one: the integrating activity of love—the power of a particular name to make the atoms of one private being fuse into song.

"Orion Rising" was written from a real experience, waking in early morning to see Orion rising opposite Taurus, and both thrilling and comforting her.

"Minotaur" is another waking in the night poem—in fear and nightmare distress—this time the comfort comes from the sound of milk bottles and the milkman's wagon in the street.

Miss Haas has a particular fondness for "The Humming Bird," a descriptive poem, and "Atlantic Perspective," portraying the effect of the moon on the tides under the image of a finger plucking on the harpstrings.

M. H.

Reverend Marion A. Habig, O.F.M.   1901-

The history and activities of the Franciscans are the chief subject and inspiration of the literary works of the Reverend Marion Habig, O.F.M. He was born in 1901 in St. Louis, Missouri, and educated there at St. Anthony's School and at St. Joseph's College, Teutopolis, Illinois, where he entered the Franciscan novitiate in 1920. He studied at the seminaries in Cleveland, St. Louis and Teutopolis and was ordained in 1927. After a year as instructor at Quincy College Academy, he was director of St. Anthony's Fraternity of the Third Order, Chicago, from 1929 to 1933, in which year he received his M.A. at Loyola University. From 1929 to 1932 he was associate editor of *Franciscan Herald* and of *Third Order Forum*. Until 1935 he was instructor of history at St. Joseph's College, Mayslake, Westmont, Illinois. He then continued his graduate studies and research at the Catholic University of America and the University of California, Berkeley. From 1938 to 1942 he was instructor of history at Quincy College, chronicler of the Franciscan Province of the Sacred Heart and editor of the *Annals* of the province. He has also edited *Franciscan Studies* (made a quarterly review in 1941) since 1935, and is a member of the executive board of the Franciscan Educational Conference. In July 1942 he was transferred to St. Francis Friary on West 31st Street, New York to serve as the secretary at the headquarters for all Franciscans in North America. He is an honorary member of the Eugene Field Society and an honorary corresponding member of the Conseil Historique at Heraldique de France.

His first book was *Pioneering in China,* the story of Father Engbring, first American-born priest in China. He next wrote of La Salle missionary companion, Father Membre, *The Franciscan Pere Marquette.* The biography of Margaret Lekeux, in the form of a novel, *Maggie,* has reached its fourth edition. *Heroes of the Cross* is the history of the Franciscan martyrs of North America. In addition to his several books and pamphlets, Father Marion has contributed over two hundred articles to twenty-four different periodicals.

C. M. N.

Miecislaus Albin Francis Joseph Haimann
1888-

An authority on early Polish settlers in America and historian on Polish immigrant life in the United States, Miecislaus Haimann was born in Zloczow, Poland, March 31, 1888. His parents Wilhelm Haimann and Susan (née Ziolkowska) were also born in Poland. He married Casimira Nigbor, April 17, 1918, and is the father of two children: Adam and Theresa Mary. In 1913, at the age of twenty-five he came to the United States, and became a naturalized citizen in 1925. In his youth he travelled extensively as a seaman for five years, from 1908 to 1913. Not knowing the English language he worked as a laborer for four years just like many immigrants who came to the United States. His love for writing was directed towards journalism. From 1917 to 1935, he was editor of numerous Polish-American newspapers. In 1935 the Polish Roman Catholic Union of America appointed him curator of the Polish Archives and Museum in Chicago. This museum serves as a repository for historical documents. It is devoted to collecting and preserving materials on American Polish history and Polish Culture in general. He is a member of the Illinois State Historical Society, the Polish Historical Society (Lwow, Poland), The Society of American Archivists, American Catholic Historical Society and the American Historical Society. Under his supervision the Polish Archives and Museum have increased enormously.

For his numerous historical books and monographs he was presented with the "Silver Laurels," a literary award given by the Polish Academy of Literature, and Polonia Restituta by the Polish Government. Other awards soon followed. The Polish Roman Catholic Union of America decorated him with a Gold Cross; the Polish Army Veterans Association of America bestowed on him a Cross of Merit. In recognition of his literary work he was elected a member of the Legion of Honor of the Polish National Alliance in the United States. The Gallery of Living Catholic Authors elected him to its membership in 1942. He is also a member of the Polish Academy of Arts and Sciences in America and chairman of the Research Commission on Polish Immigration in the United States.

He is the author of the following books in English: *Poland and the American Revolutionary War* (1932); *The Fall of Poland in Contemporary American Opinion* (1935); *Poles in the Early History of Texas* (1936); *Polish Pioneers of Virginia and Kentucky* (1937); *Poles in New York in the 17th and 18th Centuries* (1938); *Polish Past in America, 1608-1865* (1939); *Polish Pioneers of California* (1940); *Polish Pioneers of Pennsylvania* (1941); *Kosciuszko in the American Revolution* (1943).   S. U.

Oscar Halecki 1891-

Historian, professor of history, lecturer and author, Oscar Halecki was born in Vienna, Austria, May 26, 1891. He studied at the Schottengymnasium in Vienna. In 1913 the Jagiellonian University in Cracow awarded him a degree of Doctor of Philosophy. He was a lecturer of History at the University of Cracow from 1916 to 1918; professor of History at the University of Warsaw since 1918 and he served twice as dean of the Philosophy Department at the University of Warsaw during the years 1920 to 1921 and 1930 to 1931. Since 1931 he has been dean and a professor at the Warsaw School of Political Science. His specialty is the Jagiellonian era and Eastern Europe. He lectured at various universities of Europe and was a delegate to several International Congresses of Historical Studies. Besides being a member of the Polish Academy of Arts and Sciences, he is also a member of numerous Polish and foreign societies. At the Peace Conference in Paris, 1918 to 1919, he served as an expert of the Polish Delegation, and was a member of the League of Nations Secretariat, 1921 to 1924.

Through the efforts of the Kosciuszko Foundation, he came to the United States in 1938 to lecture at various American universities. After serving as Rector of the Polish University, Paris, France, from 1939 to 1940, he again came to the United States in the summer of 1940, and became visiting professor at Vassar College, Poughkeepsie, New York. Since he came to the United States he has lectured on Poland and Eastern Europe in numerous American universities and also in the universities of Canada. When in the summer of 1941, the Polish Government decided to grant a subsidy in order to make possible the creation of a Polish center of science and learning in America, the Polish Ambassador asked Professor Oscar Halecki to organize a Committee which would assure the realization of a new institute, based upon the scholarly tradition of the Polish Academy of Arts and Sciences. The members of the Polish Academy residing in America were invited to serve on the Committee. The result of this was the founding of the Polish Institute of Arts and Sciences in America with headquarters in New York City. Professor Halecki was elected Director of the Institute for the period 1942 to 1945.

He is the author of the following books: *The History of Poland: An Essay in Historical Synthesis* (1942) which a year later appeared in an American edition (almost unchanged) as *A History of Poland.* It was published in England. In 1943 he also published *The Crusade of Varna.*

Among his Polish books is the *History of the Jagiellonian Union* (2 vols.) (1919-20). Two of his principal French works are: *Un Empereur de Byzance a Rome* (1930) and *Rome et Byzance au temps du grand schisme d'occident* (1937). He is also a co-editor of *The Cambridge History of Poland,* and as a contributor to many periodicals, he wrote over three hundred articles on history and international relations.

In 1927 His Holiness Pope Pius XI made him a Knight Commander of St. Gregory. In 1931 he was elected an honorary member of the "Pax Romana" and a Vice-President of the "Union Catholique d'Etudes Internationales" (Fribourg). From 1933 to 1936 he was President of the Association of the Catholic Writers of Poland and in 1943 he received an honorary doctor's degree from the Catholic "Université de Montreal" in Canada. In 1934 he had received a similar degree from the University of Lyons, France.

In recognition of his literary work he was elected to membership in the Gallery of Living Catholic Authors in 1943.

In March 1944 Dr. Halecki was appointed professor of Eastern European History in the Graduate School of Fordham University in New York. It is a new professorship created in response to the shifting historical emphasis in Europe.

S. U.

Cecily Hallack   1898-1938

If ever there was a Catholic writer of our time who should have been popular, it might be supposed that it would be this tall, beautiful, gay and witty novelist, Cecily Hallack. Yet her life was a long struggle with financial difficulties—increased no doubt by her habitual generosity. She was unable to earn her living entirely by writing.

She was born in Sussex in 1898, the daughter of a Congregationalist minister. At the age of twenty she was received into the Church and soon afterward became a Franciscan tertiary, about the same time writing the first of her books, *Beardless Counsellors.* It was a success and was followed by: *Candlelight Attic; The Sunny Wall; Sword Blade of Michael; Mirror for Toby; The Bliss of the Way; All about Salina; To Miranda; The Small Person's Mass-Book; Lady Georgy's House; The Adventure of the Amethyst; Miss Becky O'Toole,* and *Common as Daisies.* Her last book *The Legion of Mary* was published after her death. She also produced a few small biographies and left several unfinished novels at the time of her death in 1938. This came after a long illness caused by a tumor on the brain. She was buried in the cemetery adjoining the Franciscan Friary at Crawley.

Her friend Peter Anson contributed three articles entitled "Cecily Hallack and Her Writings" to the *Franciscan Annals* for May, June and July, 1939. Seeking for the reason for her failure to obtain the recognition she deserved, he says, "Perhaps it was that, rightly or wrongly, the public found them so cheerful as to strike the note of unreality. The legacy of Nonconformist upbringing and the result of valiant resistance to bad health gave Cecily an almost morbid cult of happiness, reminding one of Robert Louis Stevenson. Someone once remarked of *The Sunny Wall,* that 'no real people are ever so cheerful and lively before breakfast.' Yet you had to know Cecily Hallack to grasp the fact that *she* was, and that her gaiety was genuine, and that she had great good sense and balanced outlook underneath." This probably does explain part of the matter. At the same time it must be remarked that the public did her an injustice. Prolific as she was, she was a careful writer, scrupulous for the exact word. Her novels and short stories are well constructed and always entertaining. Her poetry is rated by some people even higher than her prose.

To maintain herself she found it necessary to accept various positions. At one time she was secretary of the Brighton Eye Hospital. For one term she taught at a school for boys. She was in turn secretary to H. G. Wells and Lord Baden-Powell, and she held positions with the publishing houses of Cassells as well as with Burns, Oates and Washbourne. All this time she went on with the production of her books and a good deal of competent and sprightly journalism. In order to help her, the Downside Benedictines established her in a house acquired from Lord Cowdray, and there in her beloved Sussex she received as paying guests those who were in need of quiet and rest. But she had a way of never charging her guests enough and sometimes she never charged them anything at all. So that which was intended as a means of support resulted in a loss rather than an income. Under the strain of keeping things going, her health, which had never been good, finally broke and an appeal had to be issued to friends for her support during her last long illness.

In America, Cecily Hallack attracted less attention than she did in England, though even there it was little enough. The reason for the American neglect is possibly that her point of view and her characters were too thoroughly English. So was her humor. Yet one book at least, *To Miranda* was written especially for an American constituency. She tried to give it what she considered an American tone of "snappiness."

It would have been better perhaps had she kept to her English vein, which was sparkling enough. There is no need to claim for Cecily Hallack that she was a great writer. "She herself would have been the last to bother her head about such a trivial matter," wrote Peter Anson.

But she did much sound literary work, and it may well be that in time a popularity greater than was ever hers during her lifetime will be given to at least some of her amazing novels. At her best, Cecily Hallack in Peter Anson's opinion "is vastly superior to most of her contemporary Catholic writers."

When in the spring of 1934 she had a private audience with the Holy Father she was glad that the Holy Father received her not as a Franciscan Tertiary—not as a convert—but as an "English writer."

Enrica von Handel-Mazzetti   1871-

Representative of the historical novel in Austria is Enrica von Handel-Mazzetti, who was born in Linz, Austria on January 10, 1871. Her father was an historian of firm Catholic conviction and a captain in the Austrian General Staff; her mother was the Baroness Carolina Mazzetti di Roccanuva of an aristocratic Hungarian family. The name of Mazzetti was added in 1841 to the family name of Handel.

Enrica was educated at the Institut der Englischen Fraulein at St. Pölten, a religious order founded by Mary Ward and known as the Institute of Mary. Two of her teachers were the enthusiastic and pious Countess Castiglione, a girlhood friend of her mother, and Maria Francisca von Zimmermann, a sister of the Viennese professor of aesthetics.

In 1887 she left the Institut to which she had become attached, to assist her ailing mother and to live with the sister of her father. With the help of private tutors she continued her studies in French and German literature and also in music and art. The greatest influence on her creative work was exerted by Robert von Zimmermann, the rector of the University of Vienna and Wiedenhofer, professor of German literature.

In her teens she began to write, being encouraged by Franz Mair, also one of her teachers, who discovered her talent. She wrote poems, folklore and children's plays. Her first book to be published was *Die Braut des Lammes* (The Bride of the Lamb)—the martyrdom of St. Agnes.

In 1901 her mother died. In 1906 she moved to Steyr in Upper Austria, the old part of the city, which has preserved its medieval character and which gave her the inspiration for her historical tales. Here she lived with her father's brother and sister. In 1911 she moved to Linz, where during World War I, she left her seclusion to help the wounded soldiers in the hospital. Most of the royalties from her books she turned over to war relief and other charities.

In the December, 1946 issue of the *Monatshefte* (published by the University of Wisconsin), Father Alcuin A. Hemmen, O.S.B. describes Handel-Mazzetti's appearance as "somewhat delicate: for years, especially after 1928, she suffered from migraine headaches. In meeting the public which consists of her few visitors, she possesses the poise and simple graciousness of generations of nobility. Her small face and high, well-formed forehead reflect her emotions, particularly when she speaks. . . . She never married." In an interview published in the *Oberösterreichische Nachrichten,* October 17, 1946—a copy of which Handel-Mazzetti sent the editor of this book—one reads, in translation, "The poetess receives her callers in the parlor: there we see two petrol-lamps; since Miss Handel-Mazzetti suffers from an inflammation of the retina she prefers to work under the mild glow of these lamps. This eye sickness forces her to appear to the visitors covered with a dense veil. Soon she retires completely behind a curtain. The room is crammed with old, antique furniture, a desk loaded with books and letters, the walls covered with old pictures." A devout Catholic and daily communicant, her predominant virtue is charity.

Handel-Mazzetti's writing is done at night and she never reveals to anyone the plans of her next book. As Eduard Korrodi states: "She emphasizes characters more than action and explains that she never constructs a plot but that it must find its origin in the characters."

Father Alcuin Hemmen, O.S.B., in his dissertation "The Concept of Religious Tolerance in the Novels of Enrica von Handel-Mazzetti" remarks: "There is little description and narration in most of her novels but an abundance of lively conversation. In all her novels, plots build up to dramatic and melodramatic climaxes. . . . She has a high concept of the poet's mission which is to delight and indirectly to edify. . . . She considers it her duty to influence society by writing good literature."

All of her historical novels are based on an extensive study of the history of that period of which she writes and the characters, most of which are taken from the baroque period, are realistically portrayed. She also adopts the idioms of the period in which her characters live. Her most important works are *Meinrad Helmpergers denkwürdiges Yahr* (1900), of which 98,000 copies were sold in the first thirty years; *Jesse und Maria,* an epic novel of 1658 published in 1906, 86,000 copies of which were sold in the same period of time. The latter book was translated into English by George N. Shuster in 1931. *Die Arme Margaret* published in 1910 sold 117,000 copies. Her fourth greatest work is *Stephana Schwertner* (1912-1914).

During the Nazi occupation of World War II she wrote *Graf Reichard III* but was unable to publish it since her entire work was boycotted and forbidden by the Nazis according to a letter sent to Father Alcuin Hemmen, O.S.B. In her letter of April 19, 1947 to the editor of this book she wrote: "My art was boycotted from 1940 to 1945 as dangerous for national socialism—not the slightest allowance of paper was granted. My books, out of print since 1940 were not allowed to be reprinted. The book that irritated Goebbels the most was the second volume of my novel *Graf Reichard,* which appeared in 1929. . . . The Rex Publishing Co. of Lucerne, Switzerland will not only publish *Graf Reichard III* and *Tagebuch* but also all my novels which have been out of print for many years."

The main theme of her writings is: "magna res est caritas" taken from the *Imitation of Christ.* Another theme is personal tolerance in the struggle of the soul consecrated to God. Karl Muth who died early in 1945 in Munich after unspeakable sufferings which the National Socialist regime inflicted upon him proclaimed Handel-Mazzetti "as an exponent of the highest ideals of Catholic thought and literature."

Mrs. Leo Harlow   *see* Caroline Giltinan

Mary St. Leger Harrison   (Lucas Malet)
1852-1931

Mary St. Leger Harrison, youngest daughter of Charles Kingsley, inherited the literary gifts of her father and for half a century wrote prolifically, attaining a well-deserved popularity. Born in 1852 at the rectory of Eversley, Hampshire, her education began at home and was continued at the Slade School and University College, London. In 1876, the year after Charles Kingsley's death, she married William Harrison, a young Anglican clergyman in whom her father had been much interested. The couple settled at Clovelly, Devonshire, amid scenes of her father's boyhood, where her husband had been appointed rector.

Mrs. Harrison took as her literary pseudonym "Lucas Malet" and her first book, *Mrs. Lorimer* was written in 1882. This was followed by *Colonel Enderby's Wife, The Wages of Sin* (1891), and *Carissima* (1896).

Reverend William Harrison died in 1897 and his widow travelled extensively in the period following, visiting the Continent, America and India in search of health. Two of her books were written at this time, *Gateless Barrier,* and *The History of Sir Richard Calmady,* the latter considered her finest novel and revised after her conversion. For this daughter of Reverend Canon Charles Kingsley, "muscular Christian," who had provoked the writing of Cardinal Newman's *Apologia,* made her submission to Rome in 1903, and until her death twenty-eight years later she remained a faithful child of the Catholic Church.

In the succeeding years "Lucas Malet" wrote many books, among them: *The Score; Adrian Savage; The Golden Galleon; Damaris,* and *Deadham Hard.* In 1919 she published *The Far Horizon,* which is held to be a story worthy to take its place among the great English novels. Increasing years did not lessen her talents, and in 1922 Mrs. Harrison wrote *The Tall Villa,* and *Da Silva's Widow,* followed in 1923 by *The Survivors. Dogs of Want* was published in 1925.

She commenced her last book *The Private Life of Mr. Justice Syme* when she was over seventy-five years of age. It was completed by her cousin and adopted daughter, Gabrielle Vallings, who is a great-niece of Charles and Henry Kingsley.

Lucas Malet once told Gabrielle Vallings that: "I never believe a book alive until the characters stand on the other side of the table and defy me. They go their own way, not mine and that is delicious!"

In 1931 at the age of seventy-nine she died. Up until the end "her intellect remained unimpaired as did her keen wit, her indomitable sense of humor, her beauty and her charm."

The Critic, in the December 28, 1895 issue states: "Her novels bear the stamp of an originality that refuses to be classified, of a powerful poetic imagination, and of strong, meditative humor."

D. D.

F. W. Harvey 1888-

One of the soldier poets of World War I, Mr. Harvey has a fine sense of local patriotism for Gloucestershire. Besides the blazing piety of these war poems for Gloucestershire, they are also known for the simple magic of the scene they conjure up. In the strictly war-verses, he sees and feels both sides of the argument: "Because of you, I hate . . . I love the name of war." He said, "Poetry is a conjunction of inspiration and technique. Anything of any use or beauty which came out of me was first put into me. God originated it all using many channels such as a loving father and mother, brothers, sisters, friends, and breeding in an English country home—a farm in Gloucestershire—where first I saw the ducks although 'Ducks' (the poem) resulted more than 20 years later drawn upon the walls of a German prison cell. God gives all. Poets patiently prepare themselves for the inspiration so not lazily to employ the sacred gift."

Harvey was born on March 26th, 1888 at Gloucestershire, England. As a little boy he was taught "after the nursery days," by the canons of Gloster Cathedral at their school. Later he went to Rossal Lancs and then studied law. He became a solicitor in 1912. Two years later he joined the army. He was sent to France in 1915 and won the D.C.M. decoration. While a prisoner of war in Germany he wrote *Ducks and other Verses.* In 1919 he returned home. In 1921 he married. They have one boy and one girl. The boy Patrick now (1947) 21 years of age was wounded twice while serving in the Royal Forces in World War II.

F. W. Harvey became a Catholic in 1915 and was influenced by the writings of Chesterton and Belloc. He had been instructed and received into the Church by an army chaplain on Salisbury Plain. "In the Catholic Church he found the discipline which his orderly mind appreciates," writes his wife.

His publications include: *A Gloucestershire Lad at Home* (1916); *Gloucestershire Friends* (1917); *Farewell* (1921); *September and Other Poems* (1925); *Comrades in Captivity* (1920), and *Pillow Well Woods* (about 1927).

Right Reverend Edward Hawks   1878-

The author and lecturer, Monsignor Edward Hawks, was born in Wales in 1878 of English parents. He has lived in the United States since 1900. His family on both sides were members of the Church of England "stiff and conventional Anglicans" in the words of the Monsignor.

Brought up in a home where definite religion was little known, of parents who were not church goers but believed in sending their children to service, the family nevertheless considered themselves average Christians. As a child he attended a private school where "scripture" was one of the subjects and he went rather indifferently for a short while to "Bible Class" which, though held in the rector's drawing room, was not in charge of the rector.

His first interest in Catholic beliefs came through the accidental attendance at a ritualistic church where from that day forward he and his brother became adepts.

On a visit to Canada in 1900 Edward was selected for the Anglican ministry by the Lord Bishop of Quebec. For several years following, he attended Lennoxville University but later moved to Wisconsin because the Bishop was more "Catholic." He finished his studies at Nashotah Seminary near Milwaukee where he was ordained "Anglican Priest." His first appointment was tutor of New Testament Greek.

When the modernist movement became acute, his eyes were opened to the necessity of a visible infallible Church. With twenty of his Episcopal brother ministers he came into the Catholic Church (1908).

He intended to return to England but was induced to enter the seminary at Overbrook by Archbishop Ryan. He has been stationed in the Philadelphia Archdiocese ever since.

Monsignor Hawks is the only member of his family in America. At the time of his conversion he was not aware that a single member of his family had become a Catholic or Non-conformist since the days of Queen Elizabeth. Later research on his part, however, has revealed a distant relative on his father's side who became a nun in Portugal, and a convert cousin who was well-known in Rome one hundred years ago; also a Quaker convert among his mother's people.

Most of his family in England have since become Catholics. His mother, brother (with eight children and grandchildren) and his unmarried sister, have all followed in his footsteps.

Monsignor Hawks is opposed to writing about his conversion, because he has never been able to analyze its phases. Speaking generally, he said: "I would not if I could." He added: "I can only say, like the blind man: once I was blind, now I can see. In this vision I pray I may be kept.

It has been a supreme satisfaction always. I cannot even suppose anything else."

Monsignor Hawks is the author of *Conversions of 1908* (1930); *Wm. McGarvey and the Open Pulpit* (1935); *Difficulties of Myron Digby* (1936); *Pedigree of Protestantism* (1936); *History of the Parish of St. Joan of Arc, Harrogate, Philadelphia,* (1937); *Difficulties of Fr. Callaghan* (1939), and *How It Looks Now* (1940).

He has been an editorial writer on the Philadelphia *Catholic Standard and Times* for twenty-four years. His column, known as the "Third Column" is recognized for style and treatment of difficult subjects. In it he discusses matters which relate to the contacts of the Church with the non-Catholic world. It has become famous as a column to be copied in out-of-the-way places. On one occasion a bishop in England reproduced one article in the form of a Lenten Pastoral. On another occasion a check came from the *Catholic Digest* by way of *G. K.'s Weekly*. As a lover of history and as an Englishman, he has many times verbally crossed swords in defence of his native land.

Right Reverend Monsignor Edward Hawks is pastor of St. Joan of Arc's Church, Philadelphia. He is known far and wide for his work with converts and the promotion of street speaking.

E. F.

Carlton Joseph Huntley Hayes 1882-

History has been not only the life-work of Carlton Hayes, but also the source of his conversion to the Catholic Church. He was born in 1882 in Afton, New York, of an old American family who moved from Connecticut to New York at the time of the Revolution. His parents, Dr. Philetus A. and Permelia Mary Huntley Hayes, were Baptists. He went to Columbia to study law, but in his junior year his interest in history led to further studies in this subject. He was received into the Church in 1904, the year of his graduation. Graduate work in medieval and modern history won him his M.A. in 1905 and his Ph.D., under James Harvey Robinson, in 1909. From Columbia University he also received an honorary Litt.D. in 1929 and the same degree was awarded him by Marquette University in that year and by Williams College in 1939. Notre Dame gave him an honorary LL.D. in 1921 and Niagara University in 1936. He was successively lecturer in history at Columbia University from 1907 to 1910; assistant professor, from 1910 to 1915; associate professor, 1915 to 1919, and professor, 1919 to 1934. He has been Seth Low professor at Columbia since 1934. During brief leaves of absence he taught at the University of Chicago, the University of California, Johns Hopkins University and Stanford

University. He served in World War I as captain in the United States Army Military Intelligence Division, was on the General Staff from 1918 to 1920 and from 1928 to 1933 was a major of the Officers Reserve Corps. In 1920 he married Mary Evelyn Carroll of New York; they have a son and a daughter.

Dr. Hayes is widely known as an authority on history and also on nationalism, of which, since World War I, he has made a special study, clearly distinguishing modern nationalism, or undue exaltation of the state, from patriotism. He treats of this dangerous movement in *Essays on Nationalism, France, A Nation of Patriots,* and *Modern Evolution of Nationalism,* and has given many lectures on it. As co-author with Parker T. Moon he published the following standard textbooks of history: *Modern History, Ancient and Medieval History* and *World History.* His books fall generally into two classes, those written for colleges and those for high schools, of which the first are more widely used. *Political and Social History of Modern Europe* and *Political and Cultural History Of Modern Europe* are scholarly works. *Generation of Materialism* was published in 1941 and *Wartime Mission in Spain* appeared in 1945. Essentially a scholar, Professor Hayes has also an extraordinary vitality which invigorates his lectures and writings. He has a great distaste for prejudice. To him history is fundamentally true and never biased. Hence his works are particularly valuable in the cause of Catholicity, which has no fear of truth. Under the auspices of the Confraternity of Christian Doctrine, for which he serves on a committee, he is planning to bring out a series of works on historical subjects concerning the Church.

Dr. Hayes has been active as Catholic co-chairman of the National Conference of Christians and Jews, as president of the American Catholic Historical Association, and in the Catholic Association for International Peace, and is on the board of trustees of the National Catholic Social Service School, the College of New Rochelle and Canterbury School. He is a member of Phi Beta Kappa, Alpha Chi Rho, the Council of Foreign Relations and many historical associations and an Academy member of the Gallery of Living Catholic Authors.

On April 3, 1942 Dr. Hayes was appointed Ambassador to Spain, by President Roosevelt, to succeed Mr. Alexander W. Weddell. After arranging with President Butler for a six months' leave of absence from Columbia, for what he believed would be a brief emergency service, he flew to Spain with his family. He arrived in Madrid on May 16, 1942, and until his resignation in December 1944 he handled our diplomatic relations with skill in a difficult period.

He is back now (1947) as Seth Low Professor of History at Columbia University. He was the recipient of the Laetare Medal for 1946 and in the same year was awarded an honorary LL.D. by Fordham University.

C. M. N.

Reverend Harold J. Heagney 1890- •

"I have always loved to read and to listen to stories as a very small child, such wonderful tales as 'Dapple Grey,' 'The Magic Horse,' 'Jack, the Giant Killer,' 'Peg Bearskin,' which my grandmother loved to relate, word for word, as she heard them herself as a little child in Ireland," writes Father Heagney.

During his high school days he entered a prize contest in the Brooklyn *Daily Eagle*. He won the contest and his story appeared in the paper. His next sale was to Benziger's magazine, while he was a college student. After he was ordained, he began to write stories of the life around him in his mission at Van Buren, Arkansas, close to the Oklahoma border. They appeared in the *Southern Guardian,* his diocesan paper.

For more than ten years, he wrote in a haphazard fashion, now and then, while his main activities and interests centered around his priestly duties as seminary teacher, pastor and missionary. He built the first Catholic Church in El Dorado, Arkansas, when oil was struck there in 1921—saw a tiny provincial hamlet grow overnight into a teeming, lawless, turbulent oil centre, then gradually settle into a fine, orderly, modern community of 20,000.

In 1926 he sold his first Catholic juvenile story to the *Sunday Companion* and received an encouraging letter from the editor, Miss M. A. Dailey. Shortly thereafter Father Winfrid, S.D.S., editor of *Manna,* juvenile monthly magazine, and *The Savior's Call,* adult monthly, accepted another juvenile. His letter was an invitation to write for both these fine Catholic publications and Father Heagney gladly accepted it. Since then he has become a staff writer for *Manna* and the *Call* which have published many of his short stories and serials. *Manna* carries a regular feature, "Fact Stories for Little Folks" each month.

About the same time (1926) he sent a short story to Mrs. Mary Pflaum Fischer, editor of *The Young Catholic Messenger* and received an acceptance. From that time on she started using his stories and he became an associate editor of the magazine some years ago. Many of his adventure serials have appeared in this splendid juvenile weekly.

In the summer of 1927 he sent his first book, *Ted Bascomb in the Cow Country,* to Benziger Brothers. It was a tale of adventure and mystery with the western setting with which he had become familiar while pastor of Van Buren. "The Bascomb Boys" series followed. The Junior Catholic Book of the Month Club selected each of these three stories as the best book of the month for Catholic children shortly after they were published.

Several years ago he started a series of short stories in *The Savior's Call* based on the lives of the saints. The stories pleased both the editor and the readers. He continued writing historical stories for adult readers.

He wrote a serial novel in *The Savior's Call,* which is based on the life of the founder of the Salvatorian Society, the Reverend Father Francis Jordan. This was selected by the Catholic Literary Guild for publication in the fall of 1941. In the background of this book lies the struggle of German Catholics with the Kulturkampf of Bismarck. Its title is *Victory.*

Fact Stories for Little Folks also started him writing in a similar vein for younger readers. From this he developed the idea of writing an adventure novel for children that would have for its inspiration the boyhood of a great American Catholic, Father Tabb, the famous poet-priest of Virginia and the Confederacy. His research disclosed many hitherto unknown and interesting facts about Father Tabb, who ran the blockade during the war between the states on the famous "Robert E. Lee," the greatest of all blockade runners. *Blockade Runner* ran in serial form in the year 1939 in *The Young Catholic Messenger.* It has been enlarged to twice the original size and appears in book form.

Father Heagney was born April 4, 1890 in New York, the son of Dennis D. and Mary (Masterson) Heagney. He was educated at Rockville Centre High School; St. John's College; Seminaire du Sacré-Coeur; Dunwoodie Seminary and St. John's Seminary. He was ordained at Little Rock, Arkansas, December 21, 1913.

He has received the honorary title of Doctor of Literature from Little Rock College, Arkansas, in recognition of his contributions to the Catholic field of writing. The Historical and Heraldic Institute of France has nominated him an honorary corresponding member in recognition of his historical stories.

Occasionally he writes a story outside the Catholic field—a horse or dog story for magazines. But his ambitions center around religious writing and he writes always with the main idea of spreading the Gospel of good will and good cheer—the perfect law of charity and the golden rule.

M. H.

Right Reverend Hugh Thomas Henry
1862-1946

Noted in his early priestly career as a raconteur of rare ability, Dr. Henry was reminded by one of his long-ago listeners a few years before his death, of his feat of telling to a child audience, week by week, chapter by chapter, all of *Alice in Wonderland* and making it so alive that when read in later years the book was very disappointing. Monsignor Henry replied: "No fairy tales I ever told could equal those we see unfolding before our eyes in Europe today." He referred to World War II.

Right Reverend Hugh Thomas Henry, Catholic educator, writer, historian and poet is the author of: *Eucharistica; Hints to Preachers; Poems of Pope Leo XIII* (translation); and *Catholic*

Customs and Symbols. For over thirty years he had been a contributor to the *American Catholic Quarterly Review, The American Ecclesiastical Review, The Catholic World, Records of the American Catholic Historical Society,* and *The Catholic Encyclopedia.* For many years he was editor of *Church Music;* he also conducted "The By-Paths of History," in the Records of the Philadelphia Catholic Historical Society. It is for his writings in the Records that he is perhaps best known.

He was born in Philadelphia in 1862; educated at St. Patrick's School, La Salle College, University of Pennsylvania, Overbrook Seminary, all in the city of Philadelphia. He was ordained a priest in 1889.

Initiated into the writing field at La Salle College, as a boy of fifteen, he helped edit *The La Salle Advance,* contributed to its editorials and poems and always looked forward to a literary career.

He received from the University of Pennsylvania the degree of Doctor of Literature (1902). In view of the fact that he had studied at the University only three years, leaving it at the end of his Junior year in order to enter Overbrook Seminary, and that he had published in the *American Quarterly Review* a rather scathing review of certain issues of its history department, he always considered the degree a "rare distinction" and one of great credit to the University of Pennsylvania.

He spent his entire life from then on as a professor. He was professor of English and Latin at Overbrook Seminary of St. Charles, 1889 to 1894; professor of music and Shakespeare at the same institution from 1889 to 1917.

He was appointed principal of the Roman Catholic High School, Philadelphia, in 1902 and held this position until 1919 when he became Professor of Homiletics at the Catholic University of America. In 1915 he was made a Domestic Prelate by Pope Benedict XV.

Monsignor Henry was known as an authority on Church Music and Hymnals. A forceful speaker and writer in younger days, his castigating pen was a weapon to strike fear in an antagonist. A great defender of historical truth he carried on two famous historical controversies: on the air of "The Star Spangled Banner," and on "Adeste Fideles." A poet in training, temperament and aspirations he wrote many odes for anniversaries of historical importance. His best known, perhaps, is "Columbus, the Man."

The oldest priest in the Archdiocese of Philadelphia, he died at the home of a nephew in Jessup, Pennsylvania on March 12, 1946.

E. F.

Reverend Winfrid Herbst, S.D.S. 1891-

The writing career of Father Herbst began about the year 1917, when his superior sent one of his manuscripts and one by a fellow scholastic to Father Joseph Husslein, S.J., asking the Jesuit which of the two men was a potential writer. Father Husslein selected Father Winfrid's manuscript. He was the potential writer! From this time on, things literary were turned over to him.

Ever since his ordination, Father Herbst has been extremely busy as a home missionary, retreat master, editor and author. He is editor of the two Salvatorian monthlies, *Manna* (for children) and *The Savior's Call*. He has written over thirty books and many pamphlets and brochures. Over three hundred and fifty thousand copies of his books have been sold and several millions of his pamphlets.

The author's one wish is that his writing may be conducive to the glory of God and the sanctification and salvation of souls. All his writings are devotional or instructive in the things of religion. He has no literary ambitions. He is a slow and careful writer as he is a reader. He has little fluency in writing but labors over everything. He writes a rough copy, corrects it carefully, and then recopies. He declares that he has no originality of thought, but some of presentation. He believes that books are made from books. One of his hardest tasks was the translation from German of *The Life of Father Francis Jordan,* the founder of the Society of the Divine Savior. This highly documented book demanded a severely literal translation, which was yet correct English. He received sharp criticism for his literalness.

Father Herbst was born in Poygan, Wisconsin, August 13, 1891, the seventh son in a family of sixteen children. His parents, Frank and Mary Jungwirth Herbst, were sterling Catholics. He grew up as a hunter-trapper-trader boy,—a farmer lad who could swim, skate, hunt, fish and handle a boat and iceboat with the best of them. After his graduation from the Poygan schools he ran his father's two hundred and fifty acre farm almost single handed. Then came the call to the priesthood. He went to the Salvatorian Seminary at St. Nazianz, Wisconsin, in September 1910, in the second year of its existence. He became a member of the Society of the Divine Savior in 1915 and was ordained by Bishop Rhode of Green Bay on August 28, 1921.

Father Herbst is six feet tall, bald-headed, and bearded. He never takes a vacation and his only diversion is a vigorous walk in the woods and open spaces. When time permits he gives missions and retreats, and in fact likes nothing better than to give retreats or conferences to Sisters.

Two of his brothers are also priests: Father Leo Herbst, S.D.S., stationed at St. Nazianz, and Father Clarence Herbst, S.J., at Creighton University, Omaha, Nebraska.

His works include: *Boyhood's Highest Ideal* (1924); *Girlhood's High-*

est Ideal (1924); *Just Stories* (1929); *Tell Us Another* (1929); *Eucharistic Whisperings* (eight volumes) (1923-1938); *Talks to Boys and Girls* (1931); *Holy Mass* (1932); *The Divine Savior* (1932); *Follow the Saints* (1934); *Jesus And His Mother* (1936); *Saintly Children* (1936); *Questions of Catholics Answered* (1938); *Ready Replies on Religion* (1939); *The Savior of the World* (1942), and *Christ's Little Ones* (1943).   M. S.

Right Reverend Ildefons Herwegen, O.S.B.
1874-1946

As leader of the liturgical movement in his country (Germany), mentor of the great organization Katholischer Akademikerverband, outstanding connoisseur of Christian art, an inspiring orator, Abbot Ildefons Herwegen was many times honored by Popes Pius XI and Pius XII. The German Catholic people considered him one of their most powerful intellectual leaders.

Abbot Ildefons Herwegen was born at Junkersdorf, near Cologne in Germany, November 27, 1874, the son of Peter Herwegen, headmaster of the grammar school at Köln-Lindenthal. He was educated in Cologne; the abbey of Seckau, Austria; the abbeys of Maria-Laach and Beuron, Germany, and at S. Anselmo, Rome. He became a monk in the abbey of Maria Laach (Rhineland) in 1895. While at S. Anselmo, he studied Christian archaeology under the direction of the well-known scholar Orazio Marruchi and the future Cardinal—Archbishop of Milan, Ildefons Schuster, O.S.B.

The following years, he spent at the abbey of Maredsous in Belgium where his interest in the history of the ancient Church, monasticism, and the liturgy was rapidly developed by the famous Benedictine scholars, Ursmar Berlière and Germain Morin. He returned to Germany to continue his historical research and to study law at the University of Bonn.

In 1913 the abbey of Maria Laach elected him for its abbot to succeed Abbot Fidelis de Stotzingen, who had been elected Abbot Primate of the Benedictine Order. As abbot, he fostered the higher studies among the monks of his monastery, leading the way by his example. He took pains to have the young monks of the abbey specially trained so that they would be equipped for research in the field of liturgy.

In 1930 the abbot announced the foundation of the Benedictine Academy for Monastic and Liturgical Studies. He also did the pioneer work for Pius Parsch in Klosterneuburg in Austria, who popularized the liturgy. Over thirty books and pamphlets have been published over his name. Some of these were translated into English. His *St. Benedict: A Character Study,* first published in 1917, is the best known. A book on the Holy Rule of St. Benedict was published during World War I.

In 1911 the abbot started a collection of monographs under the title of *Beiträge zur Geschichte des alten Mönchtums und des Benedicktinerordens,* in 16 volumes. This collection was followed by a series of liturgical books under the title *Ecclesia Orans,* in 19 volumes. For the *Catholic Encyclopedia* he wrote the article on Maria Laach. The University of Tübingen conferred an honorary S.T.D. degree on him, and the University of Bonn a J.C.D. degree.

He died in 1946.   M. H.

George Coulehan Heseltine 1895-

As a squadron leader of the R.A.F. during World War II, George Coulehan Heseltine had little time to write or to indulge his pastime, reading. At school he was a voracious reader, and as soon as the stage of adventure books was passed, he was keen on poetry, especially Shakespeare, Marlowe, Shelley, Herrick, and Campion—but all English poetry was grist to his mill. Among the contemporaries, Belloc and Chesterton came first.

George Heseltine was born at Kingston-upon-Hull in 1895, the eldest son of the late Arthur Heseltine. He was educated at St. Charles' School and Hymers College, Hull and London University. His schooling had to be done at night, because he had to earn his own living. His parents were too poor to maintain him. He left school at fourteen. When he was seventeen or eighteen years of age, he went to London to work as a clerk. Although he had a five years' free scholarship, he continued to study at night schools for a science degree. His free time was spent at the Queenshall concerts and plays where he occupied a seat in the gallery.

When World War I broke out, he joined the Territorial (volunteer) Army. After three months, he was commissioned. He saw service in Gallipoli with the 29th Division. Then he joined the Royal Flying Corps as an observer in Egypt. He served later as a pilot in France and was wounded.

When the war was over he wanted to earn his "bread and butter by the sweat of my brow on a little farm and in my spare time to say what I felt I must say in prose and poetry without the restriction, which obtains if one must write for money." He failed to make a good enough living, chiefly because his capital was quite inadequate, being only a small war gratuity. So he was forced to write for money. "Nevertheless," he states, "I can honestly say I never wrote for money alone—what I felt I had to say and ought to say, came first, and I sold it, if I could."

Encouragement came from the late Gilbert Keith Chesterton. Chesterton published Heseltine's first little essay in the *New Witness* in 1918. Heseltine wrote what he thinks was his best for *G. K.'s Weekly.* Although his work for Gilbert Chesterton was gratuitous, he felt amply repaid in the honor he had in being allowed to work in such company. He wrote, too, for *America, The Commonweal, The Sign,* and *Columbia.* When the depression came in America and family needs increased, Mr. Heseltine accepted an offer to edit an agricultural journal in London in order to relieve his financial anxiety. At the outbreak of World War II, he was given a commission in the Intelligence Branch of the Royal Air Force, and served with the rank of Squadron Leader.

Mr. Heseltine's first little book of country essays was prefaced by Gilbert K. Chesterton. It was a collection of reprints from London dailies. He published *The Change* in 1927. His *Christmas Book* (1928), edited with D. B. Wyndham Lewis, was written at the invitation of the publishers. He edited Sydney Smith's *Letters of Peter Plymley* (1929), as a tribute to that fine broad-minded Anglican Churchman who sacrificed his career in the Church of England to do political justice to Catholics, and as a tribute to his mastery of vigorous English prose. He wrote *Great Yorkshiremen* (1932) as a tribute to what he held good and great in the character of men of his own country and kind, and incidentally to do justice to some great, unknown or maligned Catholics. It was not a financial success. *William of Wykeham* (1932) was written with the idea of restoring a proper balance to English views of their own history of the fourteenth century and to correct a prejudiced and inaccurate standard "Life of Wykeham." The *English Cardinals* (1931) originally appeared as articles in the *Universe*. In *Selected Works of Richard Rolle* (1930), he published his attempts at modernizing and translating the works of the English mystic "Richard Rolle" who came to his notice as a Yorkshireman. He also translated R. Rolle's *Fire of Love*. His translation—the 1931 version of *Kalendrier des Berges: Kalendar and Compost For Shepherds*, from the original edition, published in 1493, was done because he liked the book and incidentally drive home a sly dig at the moderns. **M. H.**

Reverend Cuthbert Anthony Hess, O.S.F.C. *see* Father Cuthbert

William Heyliger 1884-

Writing for boys over a period of thirty-five years, Mr. William Heyliger has been termed "The Horatio Alger of Today." There is however, more substance to the works of William Heyliger.

He was born at Hoboken, New Jersey in 1884 and was educated in the public schools there and at the Sacred Heart Academy. At fourteen he became enamoured of the tales of Richard Harding Davis and Jesse Lynch Williams. These stories directed his life work. His first attempt at a yarn was what has come to be known as the school-athletic story. He has been writing boys' stories ever since. Looking back, he calls that first venture a masterpiece in some ways at least. Ignorant of the mechanics of authorship then, he wrote on both sides of the sheets of fools-cap, punched a hole in the top, tied the sheets together with a blue ribbon and mailed the masterpiece to the *Saturday Evening Post*. It was rejected.

At the end of the seventh grade his father's business failed and William Heyliger went to work, continuing his education by attending night school. He still had the urge to write, however. But the very first time he publicly exhibited the talent, it cost him his job. He wrote a newspaper article concerning the New York drygoods house that employed him. The newspaper liked the story but his boss did not.

His first actual paying job in the writing line came in the form of newspaper reporting. He worked for many years for the *Hudson Observer* (now the *Jersey Observer*) and gave up newspaper work only when story writing for boys became a definite business. He has been paid $300 for a single short story and $3,000 for just the magazine rights to a serial, which makes it look as though his "urge to write" had not let him down. While still in newspaper work he wrote his first book *Bartley, Freshman Pitcher,* in 1911. Its instant success mapped out his writing career.

Most of Heyliger's early books ran in series: *St. Mary's Series; Boy Scout Series; Lansing Academy Series,* and the *Fairview High School Series*. His early stories were school and sports stories. His latest books are stories of character and careers. Today he takes pride in presenting authentic pictures of the industry against which his stories are thrown. Before writing *Johnny Bree* in 1931 he spent weeks in a mining camp, living in a miners' boarding house. While working on *Ritchie of the News* in 1933 he spent more weeks in the office of a Virginia country weekly; *Dark Conquest* was written in 1936 after a long visit at The Seeing Eye of New Jersey, where dogs are trained to be the companions and guides of blind people. *Dark Conquest* was his first novel.

In 1906, Mr. Heyliger married Catherine McDermott. They have eight children. The Heyligers love the outdoors. "Before the first of the tribe drifted into business we spent twelve weeks every summer under canvas in a forest of second growth timber. We were completely off the beaten track and sometimes for an entire summer, never saw a tourist."

William Heyliger likes writing about boys because he knows boys. And loves them. The popularity of the Heyliger books is explained by that author's attitude on boys' books in general. He says: "If I have a philosophy of writing it is this: there is no such thing as writing down to the boy; a man is fortunate indeed if he can write up to him. For he represents an audience in the world."

William Heyliger is an idealist. He also calls himself a "romantic realist." His stories do not move in the sense of physical action; they do move through the medium of psychological action. He tries to reach the boys' emotions. That he succeeds is shown in the fact that boys who began to write to him twenty years ago still drop in on him with an occasional letter. In 1944 he joined the staff of the Westminster Press as associate editor in the fiction department to specialize in juveniles.

He says he has one pet literary quarrel. Let him speak for himself: "I am out of all patience with those superior persons—often writing folk —who seem to think that boys' books are a sort of literary poor relation to be sent around to the back door. True, the book of fiction for the adolescent lacks the tradition that surrounds the novel. Nevertheless, it has its own dignity, fine and stalwart, and need not lower its head in the best of literary company. Give it time. The man who writes a real book for a boy has written a book that has no age limitation. He has fashioned a piece of art. No writing man can do more than that—very few have achieved that much."

Some of his works are: *Boys Who Became President* (1932); *Gallant Crosby* (1933); *Silver Run* (1934); *Steve Merrill, Engineer* (1935); *Mill in the Woods* (1936); *Brave Years* (1937); *Backfield Play* (1938); *River Man* (1938); *Son of the Apple Valley* (1940); *You're on the Air* (1941); *Gasoline Jockey* (1942); *Top Lineman* (1943). E. F.

Daniel Whitehead Hicky 1902-

Daniel Whitehead Hicky is one of the most accomplished and popular of our American lyric poets today. He was born in Social Circle, Georgia, in 1902, but educated chiefly in the Catholic schools of Memphis, Tennessee, where his father was engaged in the cotton and cottonseed products business for many years. In due time the young Mr. Hicky himself entered the parental industry —which, by delightful paradox, became so successful that the destined poet was able to desert "business" and devote his life to poetry and the things of which poetry is made. Travel by land and sea has emphatically been among these things, and in happier days Daniel W. Hickey wandered much about Europe and the Mediterranean countries, also through South America and the West Indies. How sensitively and humbly his spirit has absorbed the beauty of "God's earth" is evident in the poetry by which he reflects it—sonnets of fine emotion and craftsmanship and songs in the romantic tradition of our language. These have been published in practically all of our most-read magazines both Catholic and secular, and have been collected in the volumes: *Bright Harbor; Thirteen Sonnets of Georgia; Call Back the Spring,* and *Wild Heron.*

"Jack" Hickey, as he is known to his friends, makes his home in Atlanta, Georgia, where his hospitality has long been famous and his weekly column in the *Atlanta Constitution* eagerly welcomed. It was characteristic that when the war crisis came upon us the man who had wished to turn from the "gaunt machines" of our modern world to the white clouds floating "with all the feathered silence of a swan" should have enlisted promptly in the United States Army Air Forces. He is back in Atlanta now (1947) and still writes a Sunday column for the *Atlanta Constitution.* K. B.

Dietrich von Hildebrand   1889-

The philosopher, moralist and educator, Dietrich von Hildebrand was from his very youth directed toward philosophical problems and at the age of 16 years was convinced that philosophy was his vocation. His first decisive philosophical inspiration came from "Logische Untersuchungen" by Husserl, that is to say from the early Husserl, who broke through the widespread subjectivism and relativism to an objectivism and realism. The turning of the later Husserl to idealism brought Hildebrand in opposition to him. After his conversion to Catholicity in 1914 his philosophy became deeply formed by the Catholic conception of life and the universe and developed into a Catholic philosophy which cannot be classified in any definite school.

Dr. von Hildebrand was born in Florence, Italy, October 12, 1889. His father, Adolf von Hildebrand was a famous sculptor. After graduating from the Theresian Gymnasium in Munich, in 1906, he studied philosophy at the University of Munich with Theodor Lipps, Alexander Pfaender, and Max Scheler. Later he attended the University of Göttingen with Edmund Husserl and Adolf Reinach. In 1912 the University of Göttingen conferred the Ph.D. degree upon him. In 1918 he became a privat-dozent at the University of Munich, and in 1924 associate professor at the same institution.

Since he was an irreconcilable enemy of National Socialism from its very beginning he had to flee from Germany in March 1933. He went to Vienna where he founded and edited for five years a Catholic review *Der Christliche Ständestaat,* in which he carried out the most bitter fight against Nazism. In 1935 he became professor at the University of Vienna. He escaped from Vienna on March 11th, 1938, just 5 hours before the Gestapo came to arrest him, and went to Fribourg, Switzerland.

In 1939 he became a professor at the Catholic University of Toulouse and at the same time lectured at the Grand Seminaire. When France fell in 1940, Dr. von Hildebrand was again on his way. This time he went to Lisbon, Portugal. In November 1940 he left Portugal for Rio de Janeiro, Brazil, and the following month he left Brazil for New York where he now resides.

He is Associate Professor at Fordham University. He has been honored with the Presidency of the German Institute for Educational Research.

His first work was *Die Idee der sittlichen Handlung* (1916); *Sittlichkeit und ethische Werterkenntnis,* followed in 1921. *Reinheit und Jungfraueulichkeit* (1927) was translated into English under the title *In Defense of Purity,* in 1931. *Die Ehe—Marriage* which appeared in 1928 was translated into English in 1942. Then followed *Metaphysik der*

Gemeinschaft—The Ontology of Community (1930); *Zeitliches im Lichte des Ewigen—Actual Questions in the Light of Eternity* (1931); *Katholisches Berufsethos—Catholic Professional Ethics* (1931); *Liturgie und Persönlichkeit—Liturgy and Personality* (1933), in English translation 1943; *Ethische Grundhaltungen—Fundamental Moral Attitudes* (1933); *Vom Wesen des Philosophischen Fragens und Erkennens—The Essence of Philosophical Research and Knowledge* (1934); *Die Umgestaltung in Christus—The Transformation in Christ,* published under the nom-de-plume, Peter Ott (1939).   M. H.

Katharine Hinkson   *see* Katharine Tynan

Pamela Hinkson

The only daughter of Henry A. Hinkson, and Katherine Tynan, Pamela Hinkson was born in London but spent much of her childhood in Brookhill, County Mayo, Ireland, where her father was appointed Resident Magistrate by Lord Aberdeen, the Home Rule Viceroy. Her mother Katherine Tynan Hinkson was a poet and novelist. Miss Hinkson was educated in private schools and learned much from the literary celebrities who visited the Hinkson home. She traveled in France for one year and in Germany for two years.

At the age of fifteen Lord Grey succeeded in having a poem of hers accepted by the *United Empire Review* "as a delightful surprise only to find that the poem had already gone into the *Queen.*" For several years she was her mother's literary secretary. Her mother suffered from violent headaches and failing eyesight. Like her mother she regards friendship as one of the great gifts in life and the "making of a friend the most satisfying adventure."

During the spring of 1944 she visited the United States for the first time. For the British Information Service, she toured the country, lecturing on such topics as "India Seen Through Irish Eyes," "Women and Children of India," "Villages—the Rural India," "Education in India" and "The Face of India."

A trip to India in 1938 provided the material for her book *Indian Harvest* and for half of the scene of *Golden Rose,* published in 1944. The latter book written in London, during the bombing of the city, was the November selection of the Catholic Book Club in New York. Miss Hinkson's chief interest has always been in the life of the village and the farm.

She is the author of *St. Mary's* (1927); *Schooldays at Meadowfield* (1930); *Patsy at School* (1930); *Wind from the West* (1930); *Ladies' Road*

(1933); *Victory Plays the Game* (1933); *Deep Rooted* (1935); *Light on Ireland* (1935), and *Golden Rose* (1944). *Irish Gold* is in preparation.

During World War II, Miss Hinkson was associated with the Office of the British Ministry of Information.   **M. H.**

Ross John Swartz Hoffman   1902-

The psychological and spiritual interpretation of history is the theme of Ross Hoffman's writings. Primarily an educator, he has also incorporated his opinions and studies in several books, notably *Great Britain and the German Trade Rivalry, 1875-1914,* which won him the George Louis Beer prize of the American Historical Association in 1934, and *Tradition and Progress,* from which aspects, as expressed in his title, he views the historic scene in a group of essays.

He was born in 1902, of Protestant parentage, in Harrisburg, Pennsylvania, his forebears having settled in that state in 1759, and was educated at Lafayette College, taking his A.B. in 1923. From the University of Pennsylvania, where he was assistant instructor in history from 1924 to 1926, he received his M.A. in 1926 and his Ph.D. in 1932. In 1926 he married Hannah McCruden and in the same year was appointed instructor in history at New York University, which post he held until 1935 when he became assistant professor. From 1938 until 1944 he was associate professor of modern European history at Fordham University and in April 1944 he was designated professor of European history. He lives at Rye, New York, with his wife and daughter.

Dr. Hoffman had been an agnostic, but reflection on the history of the last three or four centuries turned his mind irresistibly to the Catholic religion and he came into the Church in 1931, being received by the Reverend John P. Monaghan, S.J., of Fordham. To explain this step to his friends who considered it "rather strange behavior," he wrote his book *Restoration,* called by some critics an essay in the philosophy of history.

In 1935 and 1939 he published two critical studies of modern politics, analyzing the weaknesses that arose in the democratic state and assessing the merits and demerits of the new fascist political forms that flourished during the decade of the 'thirties. His book, *The Great Republic,* a study of international community, reveals perhaps more completely the general tendency of his political and historical work. It has been done against a broad background or perspective of the history of Christendom, and aims at the revival of the values that underlie constitutional democracy, freedom, right authority in the state, and an international order based on Christianity. In 1944 he wrote *Durable Peace.*

Dr. Hoffman contributes frequently to periodicals. He was awarded an honorary Litt.D. by Villanova College in 1936 and an honorary LL.D. by Marquette University in 1937. The following year he was elected president of the American Catholic Historical Association. His favorite recreations are golf and gardening, and in reading he delights in detective stories, P. G. Wodehouse and Hilaire Belloc. C. M. N.

Reverend Robert Emmet Holland, S.J.
1892-1946

"I consider my most valuable work with the pen to be *The Song of Tekakwitha* (Fordham University Press, 1942). It is the life of Venerable Kateri Tekakwitha in the verse-form of *The Song of Hiawatha*. It came in its first inspiration as if leaping at me out of an obscure footnote in the copy pages of that monumental work I was preparing for press, in 1938: *The Positio of the Historical Section of the Sacred Congregation of Rites, on the Introduction of the Cause for Beatification and Canonization, and on the Virtues of the Servant of God, Katherine Tekakwitha* (in English translation: Fordham University Press, 1940). There I read the fact so well known to every American school child, that the Iroquois Nation had been in the poem of Henry Wadsworth Longfellow, *The Song of Hiawatha*. This was the beginning of my hardihood to do for the real heroine of our American forest, what Longfellow had done for his Indian youth of legendary prowess." Thus stated Father Robert Holland. The poem of which he wrote is "of the Life and Virtues, the Dying, and the Burial of Venerable Kateri Tekakwitha, an Indian maiden of the Mohawks, born in 1656, at Ossernenon; died in 1680 at Kanawake, where repose the relics of this first child born in our country to be elected for the Honors of the Altar."

When his editorial work on *The Positio* and his writing of *The Song of Tekakwitha* were explained to the present-day brethren of Kateri Tekakwitha, who live at Caughnawaga, Province of Quebec, these modern Mohawks admitted him as an honorary chief of the tribe and named him Ronwasennowanatha—"One who causes her name to be considered great."

Father Holland was born on February 21, 1892, at Olympia, Washington. He received his elementary schooling in Washington, D.C., and then entered Gonzaga High School, also in Washington, D.C. On August 14, 1908, he entered the Society of Jesus at St. Andrew-on-Hudson, Poughkeepsie, New York. For his classical, scientific, philosophical, and theological studies he attended Woodstock College, Woodstock, Maryland. Archbishop Michael J. Curley, D.D., ordained him a priest at Dahlgren Chapel, Georgetown University, on June 28, 1923.

He taught the classics and English literature at Boston College High School; Canisius High School, Buffalo; St. Joseph's High School, Philadelphia; served as a missionary in the Philippine Islands and was principal of Canisius High School, Buffalo, New York, from 1928 to 1932. He was director of the Fordham University Press and a member of the American Institute of Graphic Arts.

"My first discovery of the desire to become a writer was made when one of my teachers in high school praised a weekly English composition. I have had the good fortune to like to write and to have been undismayed by the drudgery I soon found that serious and ambitious writing imposes. No number of rejection-slips kept me from continuing to try, for whether I was published or not, I enjoyed what I did," said Father Holland.

While teaching at Boston College High School, Father Holland found an unusual group of American boy characters. These went into a series of three juveniles, *Reardon Rah!; Dan's Best Enemy;* and *Dan's Worst Friend*. The late Father Francis J. Finn, S.J., did him the honor to read the first of these in manuscript. The electric lights failing, Father Finn lit a candle and finished the story at one sitting. After twenty years these juveniles are still in print.

Father Holland's first book was the *Life of St. John Francis Regis, S.J.* He died August 2, 1946.   M. H.

Christopher Hollis   1902-

At forty years of age, Mr. Hollis had written sixteen books. He is continuously busy writing for important English, Irish and American periodicals. For *The Tablet* (London) of which he is a director, he conducted a column Men and Movements. In it, he reviewed books and made reflections. He is at all times nimble in logic.

His articles in *The Commonweal* on the monetary system, on war in general and World War II in particular, are thought-provoking. He thinks the bombardment which London received for a whole month, resulting in 6000-odd killed, is trivial in comparison with the 400,000 casualties of the few days' blood bath of the Somme in World War I.

Judging from the experience of his own children and that of others he has seen, he believes the psychological effect of having a sort of sense, however illusive, of a share in the general risks of the day, is good. Upon his return home one day in December 1940, his son, aged three, described with ecstasy the spectacle of an air-battle that had taken place over his house and the landing of a German airman by parachute some three miles away. It was a spectacle more thrilling than any encounter in sport. He says, "This incident will save my son forever afterward from that inordinate fuss about the incidents of mortality—which is the most tiresome of human traits."

Biographer and historian, Christopher Hollis came into the Catholic Church at the age of twenty-two. He was born in 1902 at Aldridge, Somerset, England, the second son of the Right Reverend George Arthur Hollis, Bishop of Taunton, and was educated at Eton and Balliol College, Oxford.

"When I was a boy at school," he wrote, "I was taught by Mr. Aldous Huxley, and he used to tell us that in the modern world the scale of the stage was so great that there would never again be great figures as were the figures of the Victorian and previous centuries. We had to write essays on this. Mr. Huxley was a very good teacher. I learnt much from him, and it has taken me all the rest of my life to discover that everything that I learnt was untrue."

In 1922, and 1924 to 1925 he toured the United States, New Zealand and Australia as a member of the Oxford University Debating Society. He is an ex-president of the Oxford Union. From 1925 to 1935 he was assistant master at Stonyhurst College. In 1929 he married Margaret Madeline King by whom he has two sons and a daughter. He engaged in economic research at Notre Dame University, 1935 to 1937, during which time he lectured in the United States and Canada, and he was a member of the faculty of Notre Dame for the second semester of 1938 to 1939. In 1939 he was a master at the famous Downside School, conducted by the Benedictines. He has also been a member of the editorial board of *The Tablet* since 1937 and a literary director of Burns, Oates & Washbourne since 1939. During World War II he served as flight lieutenant in the Royal Air Force. Most of his work was in London but he flew on several missions to Greece. In the elections of 1945, he won the constituency of Devizes and is proving himself to be an able M.P.

Hollis' most stimulating books are his biographies. These include: *Erasmus; Thomas More,* and *Lenin* of the Science and Culture Series; *Dryden; Dr. Johnson,* and *St. Ignatius.* In *American Heresy* he offers an interpretation of the course of democracy in the United States. *The Monstrous Regiment* corrects the popular misconception of Elizabethan days. *Breakdown of Money* is an interesting sally into economics.

His latest books: *Foreigners Aren't Fools; We Aren't So Dumb; Foreigners Aren't Knaves,* and *Our Case,* aim at a better understanding between peoples. His most popular book is *The Death of a Gentleman.*

C. M. N.

Lloyd B. Holsapple 1884-

After serving for more than twenty years in the ministry of the Protestant Episcopal Church, Lloyd B. Holsapple was converted to the Catholic Church.

The positions he has held as well as the education he has received reflect his earlier environment. Mr. Holsapple was born at Hudson, New York, on February 16, 1884. His parents were William Frank Holsapple and Charlotte Taylor (Burdwin) Holsapple. He was educated in the public schools at Hudson, New York; St. Paul's School, Concord, New Hampshire; Yale University (B.A. 1905), and Oxford University, England (St. John's College) (B.A. 1910 and M.A. in 1914). He became a master in St. Paul's School,

Concord, New Hampshire, and the following year headmaster of the Kent School, in Kent, Connecticut—the first year of this school's existence.

From 1910 to 1914 he was stationed in Salina, Kansas, as the assistant pastor at Christ Cathedral (P.E.). In 1914 he became rector of St. Barnabas' Church at Omaha, Nebraska, and held this post until 1925. Part of this time, November 1918 to June 1919, he spent as a U.S.A. chaplain with the 134th Infantry, the 34th Division, at Camp Cody, New Mexico, and Camp Dix, New Jersey. He was post chaplain at Bourges (Cher) France from 1919 to 1920. In 1915 he married Mary Langford Peck. He was rector of St. Peter's (P.E.) Church at Peekskill, New York, from 1926 to 1929. In 1931 he was received into the Catholic Church at Assisi, Italy.

Since becoming a Catholic his publications are: *Latin for Use, An Anthology of Latin Through the Ages Arranged as a College Course with a Practical Purpose* (1936), and *Constantine the Great* (1943), a biography of the emperor—presenting him in relation to the Christian Church.

From 1931 to 1932, Dr. Holsapple was an instructor in the classics at Manhattanville College of the Sacred Heart and in the Fordham University Graduate School, where he taught Mediaeval History. He was associate professor of Latin and Greek at the Manhattanville College of the Sacred Heart from 1932 to 1935. Since then he has been professor of Latin and Greek there. He was the official lecturer of The Odyssey Cruise to Greece and the islands of the Aegean in 1938.

M. H.

Helen Walker Homan

From journalism, Helen Walker Homan, author, lawyer and publicist, turned her facile pen to literature of an epistolary style. Her *By Post to the Apostles,* a choice of the Catholic Book Club, is an original and informal approach which gives the reader a speaking acquaintance, as it were, with St. Peter and the other Twelve. This was followed by *Letters to St. Francis and His Friars,* conveying a similar knowledge of the early Franciscans as individuals. Pursuing the theme of hagiography, she then wrote *Little St. Agnes,* a juvenile life of the child martyr. These three works are quite different in treatment and material from her first book, *Presenting Mrs. Chase-Lyon,* a collection of satirical dialogues and sketches, published in 1927, about the time she resigned from the staff of *The Commonweal,* on which she had been an assistant-editor from its foundation.

Mrs. Homan is the daughter of James Blaine and Mary (Scannell) Walker, is a grand-niece of James G. Blaine, and was born in Helena, Montana. She was educated at Notre Dame of Maryland, Baltimore, and the Pensionnat Cyrano, Lausanne, Switzerland, and obtained the degree of LL.B. from New York University Law School in 1919. She then embarked on a journalistic career and was successfully editor of the Pelham *Sun* 1919 to 1920, managing editor of *The Forum,* 1920 to 1922, on the editorial staff of the *New Republic,* 1924, and assistant editor of *The Commonweal* 1924 to 1927. Two of her plays, *He Has His Moments* and *Plaza 3-0901* have been presented by little theatre companies and on the radio. In 1938 she became director of the School of Journalism at Notre Dame College, Grymes Hill, Staten Island. In 1940 she was sworn in as a member of the New York State Bar.

She contributes to periodicals and has been heard on the radio, specifically in a series of broadcasts on "Eternal Heroines as They Walk in the Twentieth Century," given under the auspices of the National Council of Catholic Women. She is a resident of New York City, active on Catholic and political committees, and a member of the Junior League of New York.

C. M. N.

John Joseph Horgan 1881-

John Joseph Horgan comes from a well-known and highly esteemed Cork family. He was born on the 26th of April 1881 the eldest son of M. J. Horgan. At his father's wedding Charles Stewart Parnell, the Irish political leader, was best man. John was educated at Clongowes Wood College and Queen's College, Cork, Ireland. He was a Law Scholar and Prizeman, Gold Medallist, and incorporated in the Law Society of Ireland in 1901.

He has been a solicitor since 1902. From 1902 to 1903, he was Secretary of the Catholic Shareholders Committee of the Great Southern and Western Railway, and was instrumental in having clerical appointments on that railroad made by competitive examination. Since 1914 he has been Coroner for the County of Cork. In 1915 he held an inquest on the Lusitania victims. During the year of 1924 to 1925 he was Chairman of the Cork Harbour Commission; then Chairman of the Cork Public Library Commission from 1924 to 1928; Member of the Rules Committee for Irish Circuit Courts of Justice Act, 1924 to 1941; Chairman of the Irish Free State Liquor Commission, 1925 and 1929; Member of the Town Tenants Commission, 1927; President of the Cork Literary and Scientific Society, 1928-1931; and President of the Cork Inc. Chamber of Commerce and Shipping from 1936 to 1938.

In 1908 he married Mary Katherine Windle, the eldest daughter of Sir Bertram Coghill Windle. They have two sons and one daughter. In 1920 his wife died. Three years later he married Mary Brind.

They have one son and one daughter. John Horgan has an attractive personality with much Irish charm. He has great influence as a Catholic layman.

Besides writing numerous biographical, social and economic articles in *Studies* and other periodicals, John Horgan is the author of the following books: *Great Catholic Laymen* (1908) (personally presented to Pope Pius X); *Home Rule: A Critical Consideration; The Complete Grammar of Anarchy* (1918), and *The Cork City Management Act—Its Origin, Provisions, and Application* (1929).

M. H.

Paul Horgan   1903-

The award of the Harper prize in the fiction contest of 1933 to Paul Horgan's *The Fault of Angels* drew special attention to this young Catholic novelist—author of a previous book, *Men of Arms* —and his future output was eagerly awaited. He was then thirty years of age, having been born in Buffalo, New York, in 1903. He was educated there at Nardin Academy, and then in the public schools of Albuquerque, New Mexico, and the New Mexico Military Institute where he was a student from 1920 to 1923. From 1923 to 1926 he was with the production staff of the Eastman Theatre, Rochester, New York, which was the scene of his prize-winning novel. *No Quarter Given* was his next book. Then followed *Main Line West* and others.

Since 1926 he has been librarian at the New Mexico Military Institute, at Roswell, and interest in the history of the Southwest is reflected in his writings. With Maurice Fulton he wrote *New Mexico's Own Chronicle* in 1937. *Habit of Empire* is a stirring account of the siege of Acoma in the conquest of New Mexico. *Figures in a Landscape* appeared the year of the Coronado Quatrocentennial. In these sketches he faithfully portrays the Church as the inspiration of the many heroes in those early days of exploration and settlement. Horgan's style is distinctive and brilliant. *The Common Heart* (1942) is his most recent novel. Laid in Albuquerque, the town where he spent most of his youthful years, it is a story about "the good that remains . . . in terms of a wide range of characters. It is an intimate comedy in the classic sense. It faces the tragic chances of life with spirit and conscience. It affirms a dignity in man which we are rediscovering as one of our humblest and most powerful weapons of today."

Horgan is devoted to music. He was one of the earliest serious phonograph "fans" in the country; likes to draw, and to study pictures; plays tennis for exercise, which he says he does "badly but ardently," and has been coach of the Institute tennis team for over ten years, during which it held the annual regional championship seven times.

"Am I a regional writer? By a geographical accident, probably yes, since so much of my life has been lived in New Mexico, to which I am devoted. But my earlier roots are in New York State, and my activities have taken me back and forth from East to West every year. Possibly I am a transcontinental American. As for the regional accent, if I looked at life truly, wherever I might be, the place I looked at would be reflected in my books. Perhaps regionalism is a result, not a goal. In any case, I am grateful for the land where I live—the Southwest—and if I can contribute truly to its understanding and can sketch its beauties, I am glad enough to be called a regionalist."

In 1942 Horgan was granted leave of absence by New Mexico Military Institute to go on active duty as an officer in the Army of the United States during World War II.

C. M. N.

Caryll Houselander

"When I was a small child," writes Caryll Houselander in her book *The Reed of God,* "someone for whom I had a great respect told me never to do anything that Our Lady would not do; for, she said, if I did, the angels in heaven would blush. For a short time this advice 'took' in me like an inoculation causing a positive paralysis of piety. It was clear to me that all those things which spelt joy to me were from henceforward taboo— blacking my face with burnt cork, turning somersaults between props against the garden wall, putting two bull's-eyes into my mouth at the same time—all that was over! But even if I faced a blank future shackled with respectability, it was still impossible to imagine Our Lady doing anything that I would do, for the very simple reason that I simply could not imagine her doing anything at all.

"The inoculation of piety wore off quickly, and so completely that when the sunset warmed the sky over our tangled garden with a pink glow, I thought that it must be the faint reflection of the rosy blush that suffused all heaven!

"This would not be worth recording but for one thing, namely, that the wrong conception of Our Lady which I had is one that a great many other people have, too; a very great many people still think of Our Lady as someone who would never do anything that we do." Hence *The Reed of God,* 1944 was written to contemplate the Blessed Virgin Mary that we may imitate her.

In her book *The Flowering Tree* (1945), the theme is the flowering of Christ in man. "The idea that I have in mind," Miss Houselander says "is that we are really part, as it were, of a vast rhythm and that when we become more recollected we become more and more conscious of it. It cuts two ways. We can, I think, cultivate recollection by deliberately saying rhythms or poetry; and when we do this, those thoughts expressed within us rhythmically are heard by our minds in everything round us, even in the traffic in the street."

Strange to say it was the agnostic George Spencer Bower, a barrister, who led her into the Catholic faith. Anent this she wrote to Sister M. Angeline, S.S.N.D., "As a small child I used to stay with him for weeks on end at his house in London, and during the law vacations he always came to stay with his family in our house in Brighton. He was a magnificent classical scholar, and he made us children (I have one sister) familiar with the ideas of Plato long before we ever heard the word philosophy. He used to read Shakespeare to me and then I had to act it to him! His ways were unconventional. He took us to the theatres, and when he was pleading in a big case he took me, if I was in town, to the courts with him. I sat at the back making dreadful drawings of the Judge, and in court I wrote the first poem that I ever wrote with my hand—a eulogy to him. Incidentally, or perhaps I should say above all I owe the fact that I am a Catholic to him. He was an agnostic and though he so admired the Catholic Church that he longed to be a Catholic, he never did in fact receive the gift of faith. But he influenced my mother to have us brought up as Catholics. We were received into the Church as small children, and for some time remained the only Catholics in the family. Though later my mother became one, no other members of the family ever did. I think the fact that I owe my own faith to an agnostic and learned to love it very largely from him in early childhood, has given me a respect, even reverence for the spiritual experience of people outside of the Church, and I am always ready to be grateful for the grace of their good example."

Miss Houselander was educated at the French Convent of Our Lady of Compassion in Olton, Warwickshire, England. Her two last years at school were spent at the English Convent of the Holy Child, St. Leonard's Sussex. During 1945 she worked in an advertising office, and did layout for advertisements, being skillful with her hands. She likes to draw with pencil and chalk. Her illustrations appear in many books, her latest being Joan Windham's *New Six O'Clock Saints*. In 1936 she drew the pictures for the book *A Retreat with St. Ignatius in Pictures for Children* by Reverend Goeffrey Bliss, S.J.

She prefers carving to painting and is planning to carve crucifixes for a Belgian firm.

Much of her spare time was devoted to occupational therapy for the benefit both of child refugees from the Continent, whose nerves had been jarred, and shell-shocked soldiers, in the war.

She is the author of *This War is the Passion* (1943), and is co-author with Maisie Ward of *This Burning Heat* (1941).

M. H.

Esme William Baron Howard of Penrith
1863-1939

A diplomatic career of over thirty years took Sir Esme Howard to such interesting posts as Rome, Crete, Budapest, Geneva, Stockholm and finally Washington, where he was stationed as British Ambassador to the United States from 1924 to 1930, the first Catholic to occupy this post. He had earlier been councilor of the Embassy there, from 1907 to 1909. The many experiences of this eventful period provide interesting reading in the second volume of his autobiography, *Theatre of Life,* entitled *Life Seen from the Stalls (1905-36).* In the first volume, subtitled *As Seen from the Pit (1863-1905),* he records his earlier years, which were also replete with activity.

He was born at Greystoke Castle, Cumberland, in 1863, the fourth son of Henry Howard of Greystoke, and was educated at Harrow. At his birth his father was sixty and his mother forty, and he later became the companion of her widowhood. It was not until after his mother's death in 1898 that he married Lady Isabella, daughter of Prince Giustiniani-Bandini, of a noble Scottish family that went into exile with the Stuart kings. Sir Esme was then interested in the planting of rubber in the West Indies, a project to which he devoted several years but without success. However, that laid the scene for his reception into the Church. In compliance with the request of his fiancée he received instructions in the Catholic religion from Monsignor Merry del Val, and found no obstacles to faith, with knowledge of its tenets, but rather a tremendous conviction of truth. Especially was he attracted by the Sacrifice of the Mass. It was just then necessary for him to leave for Trinidad, and upon his arrival he sought Father Coveney, head of the Benedictines at Port of Spain, who there received him into the Church. Going on to Tobago, he received Holy Communion for the first time, at Scarborough, from Father Reginald, O.P. Upon his return to Rome he was quietly married. Five sons were born. The death of one, Esmetto, at the early age of twenty-three (1926), was a great sorrow to him.

Sir Esme's diplomatic career began in 1885, when, after several years spent abroad mastering languages, in Florence, Dusseldorf and Paris, and special studies in London, he passed the competitive examination for diplomatic service, and was successively assistant private secretary to his brother-in-law, the Earl of Carnarvon, Lord Lieutenant of Ireland, attached to the Embassy in Rome, and third secretary to the Embassy in Berlin. In 1892 he retired temporarily, returning to the diplomatic service after he had launched his West Indies venture and had seen service as a trooper in the Imperial Yeomanry in the Boer War, in which he was captured, invalided and escaped.

During the first World War he was Minister to Sweden, and he was appointed a member of the British delegation to the Paris Peace Conference in 1919 and British Commissioner on a Special Interallied Mission to Poland in the same year. He was next assigned to the Embassy in Madrid and then to Washington. Upon his retirement in 1930 he was created First Baron Howard of Penrith. He received many other honors from the Crown, among them Knight of the Grand Cross of the Bath and Knight of the Grand Cross of St. Michael and St. George, and he was given the honorary degree of LL.D. by Trinity College, Hartford, Connecticut, and Georgetown University.

In 1931 Lord and Lady Howard traveled to the Holy Land. In 1932 he was made a member of the Council and foreign secretary of the Royal Geographical Society. Bookbinding was one of the interests of his leisure years. He successfully put through legislation to prevent capture of wild birds (1933) and actively endeavored to preserve the Lake District from the inroads of utilitarian improvements.

In Cumberland, at Lyulph's Tower, Ullswater, Penrith, he began and completed his 2-volume autobiography, *Theatre of Life,* published in 1935 and 1936. He concludes with a plea for law and security to support justice and peace, which must be welded together by "that greatest of all alloys—Christian charity and understanding of our fellow-men." Lord Howard died at his home in Hindhead, Surrey, August 1, 1939, at the age of seventy-five.   C. M. N.

Reverend Bernard Rosecrans Hubbard, S.J.
1888-

During his years at the University of Innsbruck, Father Bernard Hubbard, S.J., was awarded distinctions for climbing the Tyrolean Alps, which well fitted him for his career as "The Glacier Priest" in Alaska. When he was in the Tyrolese Alps the Catholics there could not understand why he, a Catholic priest, had no parish. Pointing to the Alps, Father Hubbard said: "These are my parishioners." The people exclaimed, "Oh, a glacier priest!"

Born on November 24th, 1888, in San Francisco, California, the son of a Protestant minister, he attended St. Ignatius College in that city and from there went to Santa Clara University, until 1908 when he entered the Jesuit novitiate. He was given his A.B. at Los Gatos in 1913. At Gonzaga University, Spokane, he obtained his M.A., and the D.Sc., *honoris causa* at Marquette University in 1937; also an additional D.Sc. at Trinity College, Hartford, Connecticut, in 1941. The years 1921 to 1925 were spent in Austria at the University of Innsbruck. He was ordained abroad.

Father Hubbard was professor of geology at Santa Clara when in 1926 the chance came to go to Alaska, and since then he has made constant scientific explorations there. His party was the first to scale the Taku Ice Cap, Aniakchak Crater, Shishaldin Volcano, etc. In 1931 to 1932 he made scientific studies in volcanology. Lowell Thomas calls him "a modern Jesuit explorer, who studies geology in Alaska." Judge Hellenthal, Alaskan historian calls Father Hubbard "the most observant of living geologists."

It is a matter of pride for Father Hubbard that he has never had a backer for he feels that to have a backer "makes one a yes-man." He raises funds for his scientific adventures by lecturing and writing, though most of his income goes to the support of the Jesuit Missions in Alaska. As a result of his many lectures he says he spends more nights on a pullman than a porter does. It has been said of him that he is a "natural" with the pen, though he claims it less of a task to mush through metres of snow than through metres of words and would rather straighten out the fights of his malemutes than spin a smooth tale. But writing has at times been a real necessity and his *Saturday Evening Post* stories were written in Alaska on yellow paper in order to get the money to return home.

Another successful method he uses to raise funds is through educational films, which he makes available to schools and organizations. A feature film of 10,000 feet, entitled "Aniakchak," has had world-wide distribution, and 20th Century Fox short subjects under the title "Adventures of Father Hubbard" are very popular and appear frequently each year in the theatres, while "Alaska's Silver Millions," has been distributed throughout the United States and South America and seen by over sixteen million people. At Santa Clara University, libraries of Father Hubbard's Educational Films have been established, and he now has available for distribution over 200 subjects in sound of every country in the world as well as complete coverage of everything possible in Alaska. In twenty years he has taken over a million feet of motion pictures and well over one hundred thousand still pictures. With their arrival in San Francisco, California, on June 11, 1947, he and Father Calvert Alexander, S.J., completed a 35,000 mile trip around the world, studying and filming the Catholic missions of the American Jesuits. On this trip which took seven months, Father Hubbard took almost ten miles (53,000 feet) of colored movie film and nearly 3,000 colored photographs.

His book, *Mush, You Malemutes,* was published in 1932, followed in 1935 by *Cradle of the Storms.* He is also a contributor to magazines.

Father Hubbard courts danger not for love of adventure but to fulfill his mission for science, to increase human knowledge, and primarily for God and on behalf of his fellow priests working in Alaska. That he and his party have never had a serious accident he attributes to Our Blessed Mother to whom he confides the care of his expedition.

During World War II, he was an auxiliary chaplain to the armed forces in Alaska and gave courses of lectures to the armed forces on orientation and geo-politics. Father Hubbard's meteorological data of the Bering Sea, and his wealth of photographic records of Alaska terrain have been eagerly studied by army officials who consider the material very valuable.

In 1945 Father Hubbard was sent to Europe to help study the extent of damage done during the war to the educational institutions of the Society of Jesus. **C. M. N.**

Margaret Ann Hubbard   1909-

Margaret Ann Hubbard was born on the North Dakota prairie on a large farm near the town of Souris, half way between the Turtle Mountains and the Souris River. In the stormy winters it was impossible for her and her sister to reach school, and so their mother was their tutor until they were in junior high school. Moving in 1924 to Duluth, Minnesota, Miss Hubbard graduated from Central High School, and from the State Teachers College in 1927. With a teacher's diploma at seventeen, she was too young to teach; but the next year she was engaged for the city schools of Superior, Wisconsin, and taught there until 1930, at which time she entered the University of Minnesota and received her Bachelor of Science degree in 1932.

Her career as an author was inspired by an English instructor at the University who told her that she had a definite talent for children's writing. Returning to Duluth, she began to write plays which were produced by the Children's Theatre, then accepted by the national office of the Junior League for distribution to their own children's theatres, and in 1935, along with an adult play, *The Bethlehem Road,* were published by Walter H. Baker. In 1941 Baker brought out her last play, *He Passed This Way,* an original interpretation of the part played by the two thieves in the crucifixion of Our Lord.

Little Whirlwind, Miss Hubbard's first fiction, had its inception in a short paragraph she came upon while working with other writers on a history of the diocese of Duluth. The village of Pembina, North Dakota, just over the mountains from her own birthplace, had had a discouraging beginning. Maintained by the Hudson Bay Fur Company, its livelihood was withdrawn when the traders, finding the Pembina was below the Canadian border, withdrew to their own territory. The settlers were left on the verge of starvation. Forsaking the homes they had built with great hardship, some went north to St. Boniface, some to found the new town of St. Francis: but Miss Hubbard, using this background, invented a family who moved south along the Red River and settled in an Indian village. Already familiar with the Crow Indians of the mountains, she lived for a summer at the Leech Lake Indian Reservation and became familiar with the Chippewas, and many of the adventures of her young heroine are based on stories told her by the Indian women.

Little Whirlwind was published in 1940, when the author was in Texas and at work upon her second book, *Seraphina Todd.* The story is also based upon historical fact. About the year 1775 the hulk of an English sailing vessel was discovered at the mouth of the San Antonio River, and there was no indication of the fate of the crew or passengers. Taking this as the nucleus of her story, Miss Hubbard supplied two families who were coming out to Texas and who were cast adrift when the fierce Karankawa Indians attacked the ship at the river mouth. There was no solution but for them to make their way up the river to the Villa of San Fernando, now the city of San Antonio, the last outpost of civilization in that country north of Mexico. In the settlement where English people were hated by the Spaniards, it was easy to furnish adventure for two young people. This book was published in 1941.

In 1942, *The Hickory Limb,* which is the story of the tall Watauga boys of Tennessee, was brought out; and in 1943 *Lone Boy,* which had been born in Texas. Living in an apartment house in San Antonio, Miss Hubbard used to hear the restless pacing back and forth of the tenant above her and often wondered what it was that made him so nervous. One day his wife explained the mystery. Her husband was an oil well promoter and was financing his latest project on his own, an undertaking which they called "lone boying." The name stuck in the author's mind. Oil wells did not appeal to her, but the Lone Boy would be a perfect name for a gold mine. Accordingly, in the summer of 1942, she went to Helena, Montana, and gathered material first-hand for the book.

Miss Hubbard's main interest is in historical writing, which she considers has a definite value in the painless teaching of history to children as well as in preserving pictures of the times. During World War II she was engaged as a radio operator by an airline in her home town of Duluth, but she did not discontinue writing. She applied for and was awarded a fellowship by the Regional Writers' Committee of the University of Minnesota for a book based on the history of Duluth, her first adult historical novel. In 1946 she won the Bruce Publishing Company scholarship for her manuscript *The Flight of the Swan,* a fictionized biography of Hans Christian Andersen.

Miss Hubbard is a member of the Gallery of Living Catholic Authors and the Pen and Brush Club, New York City.

Reverend Philip Hughes 1895-

Born in Manchester, England, in 1895, Father Philip Hughes received his primary schooling in his native city and was graduated from the Seminary of Leeds in 1920. Shortly after his ordination to the priesthood, his bishop, the Right Reverend Casartelli, sometime professor of oriental languages in the University of Louvain, sent him to Louvain where he became a member of the Seminar Historique, and in 1921 received his Lic. en sciences hist.

From 1921 to 1923 Father Hughes did research work in Rome. While there he received direction from his Eminence Cardinal Gasquet, O.S.B., the Vatican archivist and author of many well-known works in English ecclesiastical history. On October 20, 1923, he arrived at the College of St. Thomas in St. Paul, Minnesota, to take over the professorial duties of Reverend Nicholas M. Moelter, who was granted a leave of absence for studying English history and problems of medieval history at Cambridge University, England.

Just previous to his coming to the United States, Father Hughes had served as private secretary to Bishop Casartelli. He did parish work in Manchester, England, from 1924 to 1931 and from 1934 to 1939 was the archivist of Westminster.

His works include: *The Catholic Question, 1688-1829; A Study in Political History; History of the Church* (Vol. 1 The Church and the World in which It was Founded; Vol. 2 The Church and the World It Created; Vol. 3 of his History of the Church); *St. John Fisher; Pope Pius XI* (1937); *The Faith in Practice* (1938); *A Popular History of the Church,* and *Popes' New Order* (1943). M. H.

Right Reverend Sir David Oswald Hunter Blair, Bt., O.S.B. 1853-1939

From his happy childhood days at Dunskey Castle, "on the very edge of the rugged and beetling Wigtownshire cliffs" of Scotland, to his closing years at the Benedictine Abbey of Fort Augustus, on Loch Ness, the Right Reverend Sir David Oswald Hunter Blair, Bt., O.S.B., had an active life of nearly nine decades, and was well known both at home and on the European and American continents. His several published books of *Memories* are full of interesting events and people, and, though none are strictly autobiographical, they contain much biographical material. His diary of the last thirty odd years is neatly recorded in long hand in twenty-five volumes.

He was born at Dunskey Castle, Wigtownshire, in 1853, the eldest son of Sir Edward, 4th Baronet of Dunskey, and Elizabeth (Wauchope) Hunter Blair. There were thirteen children, and their delightful family life at Dunskey and their father's Ayrshire estate, Blairquhan, is described in *Country House Life in Scotland Seventy Years Ago,* as in his *In Victorian Days*. When he was nine, David was sent away to school at May Place, Malvern. To this good preparatory training, or to "chance," he attributes the fact that when he went to Eton, at the age of eleven, he was with boys much older than he, not an "unmixed blessing."

He left before he was seventeen, and in September 1870 went to Rome, where he witnessed the brave defense of the city by the Papal forces before their defeat by Cadorna's troops, and aided in caring for the wounded Zouaves. Again in 1871 he traveled abroad with a tutor, this time to Bavaria where he saw the Passion Play, to Austria where he enjoyed the gaiety of Vienna, and to Saxony where, in Dresden he heard all of Wagner's operas sung and each Sunday assisted at High Mass in the Court Church.

In 1872 he went to Magdalen College, Oxford. Among his closest friends there was Oscar Wilde. It is refreshing to read in *In Victorian Days* his first-hand account of the brilliant young student untarnished by the literary artificialities which are responsible for his fame. When "Dunskey," as they called him at Oxford, made his decision to enter the Catholic Church, Wilde, unlike many fellow students as well as professors, was sympathetic, confessing his own interest in Catholicism, against which militated the threat of disinheritance. Together they went to Rome and had an audience with Pius IX in 1876. In later years their ways parted, but at Wilde's death in Paris in 1900, Hunter Blair received assurance that the Reverend Cuthbert Dunne, C.P., had received him into the Church and administered the last rites. There were many other interesting associates of those college days, all well recorded in his books.

Hunter Blair was twenty-one when in Rome, on leave of absence from Oxford for the Lenten term, and was received into the Church, March 25, 1875, by Father Edward Douglas and confirmed by Archbishop Howard. He then returned to Oxford for the summer term and was graduated in 1876, receiving his M.A. from the university in 1878. He obtained a commission in the Prince Regent's Royal Ayrshire Militia, being appointed captain in 1876, and the same year was made a Privy Chamberlain of the Sword and Cloak to Pius IX, and later to Leo XIII. Of his wealth he contributed generously for the building of churches in Galloway and toward the erection of the monastic buildings at Fort Augustus and St. Bede's College, Manchester. In 1878 he gave up his million dollar patrimony to enter the Benedictine Order. He was clothed as a novice at Belmont Priory, Hereford, and took the name in religion of Oswald. In 1882 he went to Fort Augustus, then declared independent, to complete his studies for the priesthood, and he was ordained in 1886.

From 1890 to 1895 Father Oswald was rector of the Abbey School at Fort Augustus, and was then sent to Brazil to help in the restoration of Benedictine life there. A most impressive description of the three Christmas Masses in and near Pernambuco is given in Chapter VI of *In Victorian Days*. The death of his father in 1896 necessitated his return to Scotland, and he became Fifth Baronet. Three years of educational and religious work in Brazil followed.

In 1899 Dom Oswald became master of Blair's Hall at Oxford, the first hall for Catholic students at the university, and he was influential in establishing the present status of the Catholic Oxonian. After nine years he retired from these academic labors. In 1912 he was made prior of Fort Augustus and in 1913 was solemnly blessed as abbot. He resigned in 1918, was made titular abbot of Abington and took up his residence on Caldey. Ordered to return to Brazil, he remained there four years, but when his health failed, he came back to Scotland. He was made titular Abbot of Dunfermline and, except for a brief period spent at Hereford, he resided at Fort Augustus until his death, September 12, 1939.

Abbot Oswald's first literary work was *The Rule of Our Holy Father St. Benedict,* published in 1886, the year of his ordination. He then translated from the German, Canon Bellesheim's four-volume *History of the Catholic Church in Scotland,* to which he appended notes and made many additions. In the early years of the twentieth century he contributed numerous articles to *The Catholic Encyclopedia.* While in Brazil and later at Fort Augustus he wrote his many volumes of *Memories,* in essay and narrative form, all pleasingly informal, and some containing articles published in the *Universe* and *Scottish Catholic Times* under his pen name of "Nestor."

Right Reverend Sir David Hunter Blair's physical and mental activity did not decrease with the years, and frequently he journeyed from Fort Augustus to various destinations. He had a great love of music and was especially interested in antiquarian and genealogical studies. The story of the Loch Ness monster in 1937 was substantiated by his testimony to its appearance. To his monastery and his order Abbot Oswald had an unswerving loyalty and devotion, as he had also to the Church and his native Scotland. He had simplicity, piety and a rare understanding, loving this life and unfalteringly directing his ways toward eternity.

C. M. N.

Doran Hurley   1906-

Clergy and parishioners of the Catholic parish of New England, not unlike those in many other parts of these United States, come to life under the pen of Doran Hurley. Here is a fertile field for story-telling, and Hurley uses it to good advantage. He was born in 1906 in that section, in Fall River, Massachusetts, of which he writes, and was educated in the high school there and at Providence College (1923-1925) and Brown University, where he took his A.B. in 1926. From reporting for various New England papers, including the Springfield *Republican* and the Nassau, Long Island *Daily Review* he turned to radio work, first, as announcer with NBC's station WJZ and then as program director for stations WLTH and WBBC in Brooklyn. It was his voice on that historic Saturday afternoon in 1927 that announced the arrival of Colonel Lindbergh in his plane the Spirit of St. Louis at Le Bourget flying field, and he presented George M. Cohan, Walter O'Keefe, Frank Crummit and Ethel Shutta in their first radio appearances.

Under the name of McGregor he wrote for the *New Yorker* and kindred magazines, and without nom de plume he is now a frequent contributor to periodicals. In 1936 he published his first book, *Monsignor.* This was followed by *The Old Parish.* He then introduced to the world *Herself: Mrs. Patrick Crowley,* who has become well known and has since delighted readers in many episodes connected with the matriarch of the parish, published as: *Says Mrs. Crowley, Says She.* This last book was the choice of the Pro Parvulis Book Club, and his first two works of fiction, *Monsignor* and *Herself*, were chosen by the Catholic Book of the Month Club. The latter was dramatized and played on the road with an all-star cast. Excellent characterization and a sense of humor are Hurley's forte, and he perpetuates in the American scene, the Irish heritage. At the time of the New York World's Fair, in 1939, he was invited to participate in the interior decoration of the Irish pavilion, and for the inscription on one of the panels he compiled a list of names of Irishmen who had fought in the War of American Independence. Another compilation of his was the roster of men of Irish birth or ancestry in the United States Army or Navy who had received the Congressional Medal of Honor. He is active in the American Irish Historical Society, of which he is a member, and makes his home in New York City.

In 1942 he was inducted into the United States Army. At the time of his release in 1944 he was serving in the Public Relations Office at the Headquarters at Fort Knox, Kentucky. Afterwards he joined the *Courier-Journal* of Louisville as a public relations liaison man. He was until 1946 a member of the copy editing staff of the New York *Herald Tribune*. He is now United States correspondent for Radio Eireann. To them he sends a weekly news letter each Tuesday which is broadcast in Eire. This work enables him to resume free-lancing.   C. M. N.

Reverend Joseph Husslein, S.J.   1873-

As dean of the "university in print," the Science and Culture Series, the Reverend Joseph Husslein, S.J., is widely known. He also has written several books and achieved a notable place in the educational field as director of the School of Social Service at St. Louis University, which post he resigned to devote full time to his editorial duties.

Born in Milwaukee, Wisconsin, in 1873, he was educated at the primary and secondary schools there and at Marquette University, where he received his A.B. in 1891 and entered the Society of Jesus at St. Stanislaus Seminary, Florissant, Missouri. He studied philosophy at St. Louis University, receiving his M.A. in 1897, and taught there, 1897 to 1899, and at the Jesuit Scholasticate at Florissant, Missouri, 1899 to 1902. His theological studies were completed at St. Louis University and he was ordained in 1905. From 1906 to 1907 he taught at the Jesuit Normal School in Brooklyn and then at John Carroll University in Cleveland from 1907 to 1911, when he became associate editor of *America*. This post he held until 1927, teaching also at Fordham University, from 1916 to 1921 and from 1927 to 1929. He received his Ph.D. from Fordham in 1919. Since 1929 he has been professor of sociology at St. Louis University and was also director of that department and dean of the School of Social Service until 1941.

In 1931 Father Husslein launched the Science and Culture Series and in 1934 the Religion and Culture Series. They are published by Bruce,

and offer scholarly works in all branches of literature and learning. Manuscripts are solicited from authors in all parts of the world who represent
the best Catholic thought and literary ability. The works are submitted
to authorities in particular fields for criticism, in so far as there is need of
this, and edited by Father Husslein, who has achieved notable success in
presenting more than one hundred and twenty volumes of cultural value.
It is a forceful movement within the Catholic literary revival. To the
series the general editor has contributed *The Christian Social Manifesto*
which has reached a fifth edition, and *The Spirit World About Us.*

Among other books by Father Husslein are: *The World Problem;
The Church and Social Problems; The Reign of Christ,* and *Evolution and
Social Progress.* His works are important contributions to sociological
study. In 1941 he edited, arranged and annotated the fourteen epochal
encyclicals of Pope Leo XIII, entitling the collection, *Social Wellsprings.*
On August 17 of that year he celebrated his golden jubilee as a member
of the Society of Jesus.   C. M. N.

Edward Hutton   1875-

Until World War II began, Mr. Edward Hutton
lived in Italy. "I was first attracted to Italy," he
writes, "when a boy at Blundell's School. My
imagination was touched by Virgil's 'Praise of
Italy' in the Second Georgic. So much so, that,
as soon as I was twenty-one and my own master,
I started out for that country, and until this war
began, I have never been more than about six
months, on end, out of Italy. Though I always
kept a home in, and a firm hold on England,
Italy is certainly responsible for my being a Catholic. Though not actually pious, I was much too
happy to think formally of entering the Church till I was getting on in
years. No doubt this was a grave oversight. I do not think it at all wonderful that from the very first, I was attracted to the Catholic religion
while in Italy, because I am convinced that anyone who has the luck to
come in contact with it, in its very own country, cannot, or but hardly,
fail to be attracted to it. I do not believe I should ever have become a
Catholic in England, partly because it would have been unlikely that I
should ever have found myself in contact with Catholicism there. My
gate was what Father Vincent McNabb, O.P., has called 'the Gate of
Beauty' and that is not very wide open in Roman Catholic England."

Edward Hutton was born in London on the twelfth of April 1875.
He is the son of J. E. Hutton of London and Sheffield, and was educated
at Highgate School and Blundell's School in Tiverton.

He travelled on foot through Italy and Spain. He has studied especially Italian history, literature and art. The results are to be found in his
numerous and excellent books. He was awarded the British Academy Gold
Medal for Italian Studies in 1924. Italy honored him by making him a
Cavaliere of the Order of the Crown of Italy. Mr. Titterton says, "He

has an uncanny sense of the atmosphere of places and a passion for Italy and the English countryside."

In 1898 he married Charlotte Miles. They have one son. In 1928 Mr. Hutton was received into the Catholic Church. Some years ago, Mr. Hutton came into considerable prominence on account of his criticism of the mosaic decorations of Westminster Cathedral. As a result, Cardinal Hinsley made him a member of his advisory committee for the decoration of Westminster Cathedral. In the winter of 1943, Mr. Hutton was at the Benedictine Abbey of Buckfast, Devon, England, where he made a "Byzantine" mosaic pavement in the sanctuary on the same lines as the one he made in a chapel of Westminster Cathedral in 1940. Mr. Hutton spent many years studying such pavements in Rome, Ravenna and Palermo.

He is the author of: *Italy and the Italians* (1902); *Studies in the Lives of the Saints* (1902); *The Cities of Umbria* (1905); *The Cities of Spain* (1906); *Florence and Northern Tuscany* (1907); *Country Walks About Florence* (1908); *In Unknown Tuscany* (1909); *Siena and Northern Tuscany* (1910); *Venice and Venetia* (1911); *Highways and Byways in Somerset* (1912); *Milan and Lombardy* (1912); *Ravenne* (1913); *The Cities of Romagna and the Marches* (1913); *Naples and Southern Italy* (1914); *Cities of Sicily* (1926); *The Franciscans in England* (1926); *The Valley of Arno* (1927); *A Glimpse of Greece* (1928), and *Catholicism and English Literature* (1942).

Mr. Hutton says: "As to my favorites among the books I have written, I always like the last the best. At present this is *Catholicism and English Literature.* Among my older books, my favorites are: *Cities of Umbria, Cities of Spain* and *Highways and Byways in Somerset.*"

His latest book, *Catholicism and English Literature,* surveys briefly the attitude of English novelists, from Defoe onwards, to the Church. It also describes the succession of Catholic writers and poets throughout English history.   M. H.

Reverend James A. Hyland, C.S.Sp.   1888-

Not since the appearance of *Uncle Tom's Cabin* in the late fifties—until the year 1944, has the novel been used so aptly to bring before the public the crying need of the application of elementary justice to the solution of the Negro question in the United States. The Civil War and the vast social changes since that time, far from settling this vexed problem, have but served to throw it into a more clear perspective. In 1944 two novels dealing with this problem received a startling amount of publicity in the United States; one, *Strange Fruit* by Lillian Smith, besides being the center of a large amount of controversy, leaves the whole question of readjustment up in the air. The scenes and characters missing from

Strange Fruit, together with a vibrant appeal for a just understanding of the Negro, are presented in *The Dove Flies South* by Reverend James A. Hyland, C.S.Sp. Father Hyland, by means of a plot whereby an arrogant white lawyer-aristocrat is changed—by some vague scientific magic—into a Negro and as an escaped prisoner flees into the deep South, shows the wide reading public what it must be like to be on the receiving end of the many injustices the Negro has to suffer. A clarion call this book, to awaken America to the gravity of the interracial problem!

"Jim, my darling, now let us say three Hail Marys for the conversion of the Negroes." Such was the urging of an Irish mother, some fifty years ago in Ballacolla, Ireland, after her children had said their evening rosary. Today Jim is the Reverend James F. Hyland of the Holy Ghost Fathers, prominent missionary to the Negroes in the United States and author of *The Dove Flies South.*

Father Hyland was born in Abbeylix, County Leix, Ireland, in 1888. After attending Black Rock College, near Dublin, from 1905 to 1910, he went to the Seminary of the Holy Ghost Fathers in Paris because as he says, "I wanted to be sent to Africa. I never got there. Because of the first World War, our Seminary shifted to Norwalk, Connecticut. I wound up in the bayou country of Louisiana." From 1914 to 1916 he was a student at Holy Ghost Seminary at Ferndale near Norwalk. Duquesne University in Pittsburgh, Pennsylvania, awarded him a Master's degree in 1917 and then, as a priest, he was engaged in missionary work for nineteen years among the colored people of the deep South. For nine years he was pastor of the little parish of Opelousas in the heart of the Louisiana share-croppers land.

Al Smith's memorable presidential campaign in 1928 provoked the first book from Father Hyland's pen, *Rome and the White House.* Continuing his writing as a "sideline career" he completed a play about the Negro share-croppers of Arkansas which was staged at Chippewa Falls, Wisconsin, in 1938. From the plot of this play he wove his novel. The Dove in the title, he says was suggested by Tom Moore's poem "The Dove." He has lately been at the missionary house of the Holy Ghost Fathers, giving retreats, missions and lectures throughout the United States. In 1945 he received the degree of LL.D. from his Alma Mater, Duquesne University.

Speaking seriously on the question of the colored man, he says, "The white man must regard the Negro as a human being . . . we leaders seem to be refusing to face the question. The lighted fuse is getting shorter all the time."

J. M.

Helen Douglas Irvine   *see* Douglas Irvine, Helen

Helen Iswolsky 1896-

Although Russian born and bred, Helen Iswolsky spent thirty years in France. Her father, Alexander Iswolsky, was the former Russian Minister of Foreign Affairs from 1906 to 1910, and the Russian Ambassador to France during the first World War. He played an important part in establishing the entente between Russia, France and England. He died in 1919. Her mother, Mrs. Marguerite Iswolsky, née Countess Toll, was the descendant of General Toll who fought against Napoleon during the latter's invasion of Russia in 1812, and figures in Tolstoy's *War and Peace*. Mrs. Iswolsky died in 1942 in her eightieth year, at Reed Farm, the Russian community founded in New York by Countess Alexandra Tolstoy, the great writer's youngest daughter.

Helen Iswolsky was educated at the University of Paris, where she studied law and economics, and took an early interest in political and social problems. But like many Russian girls of her generation she did not pursue a purely scholarly life, because of the great international turmoil which marked her youth. First there was the first World War, and Miss Iswolsky worked for three years from 1914 to 1917, in the Russian Red Cross Hospital in Paris. Then came the Russian Revolution which deprived her family of their former ease and comfort; her father died, and she had to give up her studies to work for a living: as a private secretary and typist, and later as a journalist.

In 1923, when twenty-seven years of age, she became a Catholic of the Eastern Rite. She was formerly an Orthodox Russian. Her first spiritual awakening came during the war when she served as a nurse. A soldier from Brittany, a humble peasant, was dying and called a priest. "There were three of us in that room; the priest, the dying man and myself. That day, I believe, my soul really awakened to spiritual life as a reality. Later I began to read the works of Péguy, and they made a deep impression on me." In his works, she found the answer to all her burning questions, and it was her first initiation to Catholic social thought. What actually made a Catholic of her was a visit she made to the Benedictine convent of St. Scholastica at Dourgne near Castres, France. She had been invited by Mother Eustochie, a convert from Russian Orthodoxy and a member of the community. With permission of the bishop she spent ten days with the cloistered nuns. Though converted in this Latin community, Helen Iswolsky remained in the Eastern Rite, of which she has been an active promoter. She considers herself a disciple of the great Russian religious thinker Wladimir Soloviev, who renounced schism and who was an apostle of union and one of the outstanding figures of Russian Catholicism.

Upon her return to Paris, after her conversion, Helen Iswolsky became a writer and free-lance journalist. In the first years of her career, she worked mostly in the purely literary field, translating Russian authors, writing literary reviews and contributing to a series of Paris periodicals, such as the *Revue des Deux Mondes,* the *Revue de Paris,* the *Revue de France,* the *Nouvelle Revue Française* and *Commerce.* The two latter reviews were at that time the centre of French cultural life, comprising among others in their editorial staffs the most distinguished French writers and critics, poets and philosophers: Paul Valéry, Paul Claudel, André Gide, Jacques Rivière and Leon Paul Fargue. "They taught me to think clearly and to write concisely," she relates, "and they taught me especially to love my profession."

With the young writer Joseph Kessel, who had been awarded a prize for his book devoted to the war, *L'Equipage,* she started writing a historical novel, *Les Rois Aveugles* (translated into English under the title of *Blind Kings*). It dealt with the years preceding the Russian Revolution. Helen Iswolsky's special task was to collect all the data concerning this period, questioning eye-witnesses and the chief actors of the drama who had survived in the Russian emigration abroad. This work kindled her interest regarding Russian political and social problems. The history of the revolution itself was also absorbing to her. In the *Life of Bakunin,* published a few years later, she gave an exhaustive study of the sources of the Russian revolutionary movement.

After *Bakunin,* Helen Iswolsky gave up literature, devoting her writings to social, historical and religious problems. In 1930, she met two outstanding social and religious thinkers, Jacques Maritain, the Thomist philosopher, and Nicholas Berdiaev, the promoter of Russian religious revival. These two men became her spiritual leaders and during the ten years preceding the second World War she continually worked with them. She became identified with the French Catholic social revival and contributed to various publications devoted to these problems, such as *Etudes, Temps Present, La Revue Intellectuelle* and *Esprit.* The latter edited by Emmanuel Mounier, the founder of the "personalist movement," stimulated Christian life among young intellectuals, and Helen Iswolsky took an active part in this movement.

At the same time, she kept in close touch with the Russian intellectual circles of Paris, and published a number of articles in Russian: "I continually held in mind my country's tragic ordeal," she writes in her recollections, "and I tried to serve Russia as best I could." Both in her French and Russian articles, she closely studied the evolution of Soviet Russia, and summed up her conclusions in *L'Homme Sovietique* and *Femmes Sovietiques,* two books published in Paris in 1936-37.

For many years, Helen Iswolsky was on the board of the administration of the Russian library in Paris, known as the "Turguenev Library" and containing over a hundred thousand volumes. When the Germans occupied Paris, they expropriated the entire collection of books, among which were many valuable volumes and rare copies of Russian periodicals. The Turguenev Library was shipped to Munich where Hitler had founded a "centre of Russian studies," in preparation for his invasion of Russia.

At the time when the Nazis pillaged this sanctum of books, Helen Iswolsky had already fled to the free zone where she remained for a year after the French collapse before sailing to America. Because of her connections with French and Russian anti-totalitarian thinkers, she was on the Nazi black list, and the Gestapo agents visited her Paris apartment. From Pau, in the Pyrenees, she corresponded with her friends in America who obtained for her and for her mother a visa for the United States, where they arrived in June 1941. In New York, Helen Iswolsky became a contributor to *The Commonweal* and the *Torch,* and went on several lecture tours, speaking on "The Soul of Russia." Miss Iswolsky makes a distinction between the Russian people and the Communist regime, and is profoundly convinced of Russia's spiritual revival, in alignment with Pope Pius XI's encyclical on "Atheistic Communism." She feels that to work in the spiritual field means working with and for the Russian people. She is also pursuing her work on behalf of union between the Catholic and the Orthodox Churches. From 1943 to 1945 she worked in the OWI (Office of War Information).

Miss Iswolsky has three books published in English: *Soviet Man Now,* translated from her French work; *Light before Dusk,* a book of recollection which she wrote in America, devoted to her work in France with Maritain, Berdiaev and French Catholic youth, and the *Soul of Russia* published in the fall of 1943.

Naomi Ellington Jacob 1889-

The English novelist, Naomi Ellington Jacob, is a prolific writer of light fiction and confesses to "two novels a year." She also writes articles on cookery and lectures on literature, the theatre and political matters.

Born of mixed Christian and Jewish parentage, on July 1, 1889, at Ripon, a very ancient town in the West Riding of Yorkshire, her life has been varied. Educated in Middlesborough, England, after completing her high school course, she was employed as a teacher in an elementary school in the same vicinity. Miss Jacob was at that time a member of the Church of England. She became a Catholic when she was eighteen years of age. Disliking teaching, she turned to being secretary to Marguerite Broadfoote, the variety artiste. Later she became an officer in the Women's Legion and was supervisor of a munition factory.

In 1920 she went on the stage and would no doubt have continued in that profession had it not been for her ill health which was growing worse. Finally she became so ill she went to Italy. Here she was entirely cured of her ailment by the sunshine, simple life and fresh air. Realizing the nature of the disease with which she was suffering, she gave up the idea of a stage career and began to write. "Any writing ability I may have, I inherit from my mother, Nina Abbott," she writes. Mrs. Abbott was an extraordinarily fine journalist and wrote three books.

In 1942 Naomi Jacob acted in the play, *The Nutmeg Tree,* by Marjorie Sharp, which had a successful run of seven months in London.

Among her books are: *That Wild Lie; Me—Me Again; Our Marie; Straws In Amber; This Porcelain Clay; Full Meridian; Lenient God; Cap Of Youth,* and *Four Years.* This last mentioned is of interest to the Catholic reading public because it is the diary of her cousin Brian Bulman, who died tragically just after the completion of his first novel. It is a story of youth, a boy's soul, his struggles and submission. Of Brian Bulman (who gained the Faith in the end) the author writes: "It has always seemed to me a rather tragic thing for young people to have no faith." No one could read the final pages of this diary unmoved. Naomi Jacob's novels are chiefly an attempt to delineate character.   M. H.

Very Reverend James *see* Very Reverend James O'Mahony

Stanley Bloomfield James 1869-

Stanley Bloomfield James was born at Bristol, England, in 1869. At eighteen he was studying for the Congregational ministry and while doing so came under the spell of such poets as Emerson and Whitman. These writers and others he learned to "appreciate . . . in proportion as they glorified rebellion." To be himself at all hazards became his determination.

This quest for his "real self," upon which he then set out, led to his abandoning the ministry. He sought employment in various fruitless enterprises, going to far western Canada, becoming successively a sheep-herder, journalist, cowboy, tramp, and soldier for Uncle Sam in the Spanish-American War, returning to England, marrying, then taking up again, where his father, a Congregational minister, left off, the work of the ministry.

During the next score of years he filled several ecclesiastical benefices principally in London, where for two years he was curate to Dr. Orchard of the King's Weigh House, then a "priest" of the "Free Catholic" movement (an attempt to combine Catholicism and Protestantism). But uncertainty, doubt, and confusion regarding questions of doctrine and jurisdiction made him turn more and more to the Catholic Church. There, like some shipwrecked sailor thrown up by the waves on a friendly beach, he found that peace and security, that intellectual freedom and social tolerance in search of which he had travelled for thirty-five years, the highways and byways of the world.

The quest of his "real self" had indeed proved "elusive." In 1923 he was received into the Church of Rome at Haverstock Hill. Though he had "walked in backwards," he knew he had reached "home" at last. The conversion of his wife and two youngest sons followed four years later.

He is now (1947) assistant editor of *The New Catholic Herald*. For that paper "he has contributed a series of layman's comments on the Sunday epistles and gospels (showing the connection between the two) and now (1946) he is writing on the significance of each week's liturgy," writes Michael de la Bedoyere. "He's a journalist—one who loves to write and argue about events and their significance, who looks outward to the making and moulding of the things he loves, who instinctively detests pretence whether in himself or in others," also writes Michael de la Bedoyere. His books include: *The Adventures of a Spiritual Tramp* (1925); *The Evangelical Approach to Rome* (1933); *Back to Langland* (1935); *Franciscan Fables* (1937), and *Christ and the Workers* (1938) which deals with the J.O.C. and kindred Catholic Action Groups. In 1945 Stanley James published a sequel to his autobiography *The Adventures of a Spiritual Tramp* under the title *Becoming a Man*. His new book he says is both an extension, covering the intervening years, and an interpretation of that narrative.   S. J. M.

Francis Jammes   1868-1938

Flowers, birds and beasts, all animate things aroused a response in the mind and heart of Francis Jammes. Nature was his great inspiration always, and with the years came joy also in the spiritual, his return to the Church being marked by the dominant influence of Catholic faith and practice in his poems. The transition was not clearly defined by any rebellion of youth, for his had been an indifference, a doubt, that sapped the wellsprings of faith not deeply imbedded by early teaching. His Catholic mother had taught him the faith with too great "moderation," and he was influenced by the fact that his father was reared a Huguenot, and by the philosophy of Rousseau. He was, however, conscious of the appeal of Catholicism even when he wrote of it as an observer, and he experienced a lassitude, a nostalgia, until he returned "home." The interval was a period of seventeen years.

Francis Jammes was born in 1868 at Tournay. At the age of five he left his native village and with his family lived at Pau where for two years he attended a "dame school," conducted by two ladies. He began to write verse at the age of eight.

The government transferred his father to Orthez, St. Palais and Bordeaux. There Francis attended the Lycée, but of his studies only literature appealed to him, and he failed to attain his baccalaureate. His greatest interest was in old maps and marine charts, and his favorite haunt was the busy quays of the port whence ships were ever sailing. Especially he dreamed of their destination in the luxuriant, sun-bathed isles where his grandfather had lived. All his father's mementoes of life in the West Indies he cherished and the exotic charm of these tropical islands, of which he heard so much, is woven into many of his writings.

When his father died in 1888, they laid him to rest at Orthez, and in his father's old home there he and his mother and sister settled. The rusticity of the little village held a charm for him always. In the fields and woods he wandered daily, becoming familiar with each plant, each creature. Even to inanimate objects, such as minerals and vegetables, his all-embracing love of nature extended, endowing them with feeling. For several years he worked as a clerk in a lawyer's office, but this was distasteful to him. The pettiness, the meanness of life thus experienced, he records in his first novel in verse, *Existences*.

This was preceded by his *Vers*, published in 1893. It is a book of poems about common things of every day life. In 1898 he presented a larger collection of verse under the title *De l'Angelus de l'aube à l'Angelus du soir*. Humorous, sensual, romantic, morose and gay poems are in this work. Jammes had left the practice of his faith ten years before so the preface of this book is significant. It indicates the spirit with which he wrote the poems: "My God, you have called me among men. Here I am. . . . I pass upon the road like a laden ass at whom the children laugh and who lowers his head. I will go where you will, when you will. The Angelus rings." In the same year he printed at Orthez, *Quatres Prieres*.

Writing now consumed all his time. Within the rose-covered cottage, set in a garden, by day twittering with birds and humming with bees, and by night quiet under a moon over the magnolia trees, he sat in the old tapestry room, smoking his pipe, and weaving a tale of bygone days, for love of the past enriches his works. His first prose novel, *Clara d'Ellebeuse* was published in 1899. It is an extravagant tale of a young girl of long ago, and was praised by many, including Paul Claudel who wrote the author from Hankow, China. His *Almaide d'Estremont* is a story of another young rural aristocrat. The two early novelettes appeared together in 1903 in a volume of tales and essays with the title story, *Le roman du lièvre*. This typifies Jammes' sympathy with St. Francis, his naivete recalling the "Fioretti." He writes of the wild animals who were followers of St. Francis, telling of their life, death and hereafter. All animals had a fascination for Jammes, but especially dogs and donkeys. *Pensées des Jardins* (1906), in both prose and poetry, is full of flowers and animals, its seven concluding poems being entitled "Some Donkeys."

The most perfect of his rural pictures is *Alexandre de Ruchenfleur,* the kind-hearted old village notary. It is an "Eclogue of Spring," a tranquil description, the style sustained, the stanzas of unequal length, composed in couplets. *Peasant Woman* is an "Eclogue of Summer." This is the type most revered by Jammes, the toil-worn country woman, living in "grandeur of simplicity," whose "heart loves neither dreams nor lies." In his *Picture of Autumn* is another old peasant woman in France to whom news is brought of the death of her son in the service of his country, in Algiers. She sets forth to find him. *Winter Picture* is a moving portrait of Jean Defau, a simple man not good for much but trout fishing but aware of the mysterious force of nature. These four eclogues are contained in his *Oeuvres* published in 1921. This collection also includes *En Dieu* and *L'eglise habillée de feuilles,* which mark the completion of his conversion.

Jammes returned to the Church in 1905, after a visit from Claudel. The latter's conversion eighteen years previous interested Jammes and he asked him to come to see him upon his return to France. In 1906 Jammes married a Soissonaisse. This was probably the Mamore to whom he addressed his love poems, which are many-mooded, fresh and sensuous. *La poete et sa femme* breathes a sense of contentment that now characterized his work. *Ma fille Bernadette* is a small book in prose recounting the birth and babyhood of his daughter. Seven children were born.

Perhaps his best known work is *Les Georgiques Chrétiennes* (1912), a long pastoral poem in rhymed couplets, dealing with the agricultural labors of the year and the church festivals. In a note at the beginning he writes: "On the threshold of this book I confirm that I am a Roman Catholic, submitting very humbly to the decisions of my Pope, His Holiness Pius X, who speaks in the name of the true God and that I do not adhere closely or at a distance to any schism, and that my faith does not permit any sophism." In 1917 he received the French Academy grand prize for literature. In 1919 appeared *La Vierge et les Sonnets.* His *Memoirs* (1921) comprise three volumes. They are full of a kindly humor, a love for simple people and simple things.

There is a beautiful freshness, a striking originality, a great simplicity to Jammes' verse. He followed no accepted school, maintaining that his line is classical and admitting a harmony of soul with Virgil. Free verse he criticized for lack of form and the symbolists for their obscurity. He was akin to the romanticists as well as to the realists, but stood alone. His prose is poetic. He has a great mastery of words and a keen sense of their loveliness. There is a perfection of detail in his descriptions, in which colors and sounds are effectively used. Frequently he introduces a personal note with the use of the first person. In defiance of tradition he refused to live in Paris, though he had many friends of prominence in arts and letters who endeavored to persuade him. He made visits there and travelled as far north as Amsterdam and as far south as Algiers. But all his life he remained the woodsman and villager. He became known as the "Patriarch of Hasparran," for there he lived in his closing years, and died, November 1, 1938, at the age of seventy. According to his wish he was buried in a Franciscan habit. Certainly he had always practised Franciscan simplicity and humility. On the day of his death one of his daughters took the veil as a White Sister at Lyons. Jammes refused the Legion d'honneur. C. M. N.

Very Reverend Bede Jarrett, O.P.   1881-1934

"A shining figure and a very generous soul" is the eulogy of Father Bede Jarrett, O.P., given by an old schoolmaster. Born in 1881, the youngest of the five sons of Colonel H. S. Jarrett, C.I.E., and Agnes Delacour Beaufort, from his earliest days he showed a brilliance of mind and a radiance of soul. He was educated at Stonyhurst but in 1898 at the age of seventeen left there to enter the Dominican novitiate at Woodchester Priory, Gloucestershire, and was ordained at Hawkesyard Priory, Stafford, in 1904. Studies at Louvain followed and after obtaining the degree of Lectorate in Theology he went to Hunter Blair's Hall, Oxford, where he received his M.A.

At the early age of thirty-three he was made Prior of Haverstock Hill, London, and two years later at the exceptional age of thirty-five was appointed Provincial of the English Dominicans. This high office he held from 1916 to 1932 being re-elected four times, so important and successful were his attainments during these years of office. To him goes the honor of taking the Dominicans back to Oxford after centuries of exile, eight hundred years after their establishment there in 1221, only five years from their founding by St. Dominic. Father Jarrett held firmly to the tradition of his order, that of linking the Dominicans with the old universities. He was further able to accomplish this by founding the Friary in Edinburgh to serve as a chaplaincy to the University there. He made other foundations, including the restoration of an old Dominican mission in Persia.

At the end of his long term as provincial in 1932 he was made Prior of Blackfriars, Oxford, where he remained until his death two years later. He was the founder and latterly the editor of the Dominican review, *Blackfriars.* Though so much of his life was of necessity spent in administrative work his zeal and unusual abilities enabled him to combine frequent preaching engagements with considerable writing. Bishop Couturier of Alexandria, Ontario, his fellow-Dominican and close friend, spoke of him as one who "loved truth with his whole soul, so much so that he became almost truth itself." This shining trait showed in all his sermons and writings. Another friend who had lived with him for years, Father Vincent McNabb, O.P., said of him: "Light seemed to be a quality of his body as of his soul, this light was a spiritual flame." Direct, sincere and simple, his influence was unbounded, and his early death in 1934, at the age of fifty-two, was a severe loss to the Dominicans and to the Catholic world. Nor was his influence confined to his co-religionists, for his spiritual qualities and gifts of mind and character were recognized and appreciated equally by the non-Catholics with whom he came in contact.

Father Jarrett was well known in the United States. He came several times to preach at Our Lady of Lourdes Church, New York, at the invitation of its pastor, Monsignor McMahon. Once he travelled from England to give a retreat to the Dominican Sisters of California. While here he was in great demand for preaching and lecturing and left a lasting impression on those who heard him. His books, *House of Gold* and *Salve Regina,* are collections of sermons given during his visits at Our Lady of Lourdes. Similarly, *No Abiding City* is the collection of Lenten Conferences given at Our Lady of Victories, London, in 1932. His other writings include: *Medieval Socialism; San Antonio and Medieval Economics; Social Theories of the Middle Ages; Living Temples; The Space of Life Between; The English Dominicans; A History of Europe,* and *Emperor Charles IV.* In his life of St. Dominic it was felt that Father Bede had unconsciously revealed a portrait of himself and as he writes of his own great founder so is he remembered: "a friend to all, but you feel, as you read, that his friend was God."

C. M. N.

Douglas Jerrold   1893-

Mr. Jerrold wrote his autobiography *Georgian Adventure* when he was only forty-four. In the preface of this book, he wrote: "My Georgian Adventure was the adventure of the whole generation whose fate it was to come to manhood amid these portents and to spend the first twenty-five years of their adult life amid changes so rapid and continuous as to leave of the world in which they had been brought up little but a memory." He believes the Georgian Epoch ended with the death of King George V on January 18th, 1936.

Douglas Jerrold was born at Scarborough in 1893. He went to Westminster School in 1906, and entered New College, Oxford, in 1911. He was secretary of the Oxford Union. He was born into a literary family. His two paternal greatgrandfathers, Laman Blanchard and Douglas Jerrold were associated with *Punch.* The latter was also editor of *Lloyd's Weekly News.* They were friends of most of the great literary figures of the early and middle Victorian periods.

Like most of the Englishmen of his generation he went into service in 1914. He joined the famous Naval Division conceived by Winston Churchill and fought with the division in the ill-fated Gallipoli campaign in 1915. He considers that the failure of Gallipoli altered the tempo of European history, and prolonged the war. It caused the resurgence of the Mediterranean powers and quickened the collapse of European prestige in Asia. In May 1916 he went to France with the Division and was wounded in battle on November 13, 1916. Hospitalization in London in

1917, followed. Returning to duty in January 1918, he took command of the Naval Division Officers' School in Aldershot. He tried to be assigned to the United States on a propaganda tour. But America was not for him then, nor for eighteen more years. In midsummer 1918 he entered the Ministry of Food, the busiest of all the war-time ministries.

Complaints of hoarding and profiteering flooded the Ministry. The first sugar rationing had already failed when Jerrold joined the Rationing Division of the Ministry in June 1918. The second scheme which was a coupon and counterfoil system had many flaws. The coupon was done away with when Jerrold put his own rationing scheme into effect in 1919. "Had we reintroduced the coupon in 1919 there would have been a public outcry at the reimposition of war-time restriction. Doing without it, we reintroduced an infinitely more rigorous and exacting control without anyone saying a word. Ask anyone today if they remember the peace-time rationing system and they will tell you that there wasn't one. And there, if you like, is proof of a real miracle of staff effort." The scheme tied the consumer to one shopkeeper for the commodity. Jerrold had discovered that sugar might pass through three or four hands and sometimes travelled as far as from London to Liverpool and back again before going back to a point half a mile from its starting place. He cut the whole of this maze of wandering foods and distributed direct from the nearest wholesaler to the surrounding retailers. He became Director of Rationing and Distribution in 1919, and kept the post until he left the Ministry in 1920. Then he went to the Treasury where he remained until 1923.

Jerrold served in the Navy, Army and Civil Service. The eight years of government service gave him an interest in government and public affairs. Several of his books have been written on these topics and most of his magazine and newspaper articles. His thesis is that it is only by a return to Christian social and political theory that the world can be saved.

In 1923 Mr. Jerrold became a book publisher. He was completely ignorant of the business but became a director of Ernest Benn, Ltd. He was just beginning to write. His first book, *The Royal Naval Division,* had been published just as he left the Treasury. He claims that a publisher makes less out of a book than the author and the bookseller and that it is only by manufacturing his books he can make a regular living. He said there is a thrill in picking up a manuscript and finding that you are looking at a piece of literature, "and it is only diminished by the knowledge that if it be indeed literature it will not sell in very large quantities. The best novel I have ever published was Perez de la Ossa's *Maria Fernanda* in Allison Peers's translation. It is one of the greatest short novels in European literature. It sold about four hundred copies. I did not really expect it to sell as many, because I knew that none of the people whose names mean much to the book-reading public would understand it. Algernon Cecil's *Metternich* was another thrill. Here was that rarest of all things—a scholarly biography by a man of the world who is also a great stylist. It was called, and rightly, the best biography of the year. Yet I lost money on it because I imagined, in my ignorance, that English people were sufficiently interested in the greatest statesman of the nineteenth century (if we except Cavour) to justify publication at

8s.6d. The Americans were wiser in their generation. They never published it at all."

In 1928 he became a director of Eyre and Spottiswoode, Ltd. He is now (1947) chairman of Burns, Oates and Washbourne. From 1931 to 1936 he was editor of the *English Review*. During the Spanish Civil War, he with others formed a small committee to study and get full reports on Spanish affairs. He condemns both the British and American Press for their attitude during this war. The papers ceased to print news and sought only to influence opinion. Jerrold helped supply his Spanish friends with fifty machine guns and a million rounds of ammunition. He made the arrangements to have the airplane in the Canaries, in which General Franco flew to Morocco, where he raised his standard. Jerrold wished first-hand information and motored throughout the length and breadth of Nationalist Spain in March 1937.

He is the author of: *The Royal Naval Division* (1923); *The Hawke Battalion* (1925); *The War on Land* (1928); *The Lie About the War* (1935); *England* (1935); *They That Take the Sword* (1936); *Georgian Adventure* (1937); *The Necessity of Freedom* (1938); *The Truth About Quex; Storm Over Europe; Britain and Europe* (1941), and translated from the French, *The Soldier's Testament*, by René Quinton.

M. S.

Reverend Vernon Cecil Johnson 1886-

After nineteen years' ministry in the Church of England, "Father Vernon," well-known "Anglo-Catholic" preacher, was received into the Catholic Church in 1929 by Father Vincent McNabb, O.P. Peace then came to a soul long in travail, and a new period of ministry as a Catholic priest followed.

Born in 1886, Vernon Cecil Johnson was educated at Charterhouse and Trinity College, Oxford, where he received his B.A. From there he entered Ely Theological College where he was ordained for the Anglican ministry in 1910. He was appointed curate at St. Martin's, Brighton, where he remained for three years and then entered the Society of the Divine Compassion, Plaistow.

There followed fruitful years of work until in 1925, at the close of a retreat Father Vernon was conducting, an Anglican mother superior put into his hands a book on the life of St. Thérèse, the "Little Flower." A visit to Lisieux resulted from reading this autobiography of a soul, and a second visit was made during the four years of spiritual struggle which ensued. Finally he made his submission, recognizing the Catholic Church as the custodian of truth and the See of Peter as the recipient of Christ's divine authority.

Studies at Beda College, Rome, followed and in 1933 Father Johnson was ordained for the Archdiocese of Westminster. As a Catholic priest he continued his preaching and fruitful ministry. In 1941 he was appointed chaplain to the men undergraduates of Oxford University, a post held by many distinguished priests including his fellow-convert, Monsignor Ronald Knox. In 1946 he resigned because of ill health.

As an Anglican, Father Johnson wrote many small devotional books, the best known being *Happiness,* many times reprinted. As a Catholic, in the hope of helping other souls he wrote the story of his own conversion in *One Lord, One Faith* in 1929. This work has been translated into eight languages. In 1936 he published *The Message of St. Thérèse of Lisieux.* His other books are: *The Prayer of St. Thérèse* and *Our Guiding Star.*

C. M. N.

Mother M. Francis Johnston, O.S.U.   1900-

The Ursuline Sister, Mother M. Francis, writer of stories, verse and feature articles, is a convert to the Catholic Church. Of an old Maryland and Virginia family she is entitled to wear the insignia of the Colonial Dames, the Daughters of the Revolution, Daughters of 1812 and Daughters of the Confederacy. Her mother was a second cousin to Robert E. Lee.

Always interested in writing, a long illness from tuberculosis brought her the first chance to develop her talent. At present (1946) she is doing her writing in odd moments while acting as principal of a little Mexican public school west of the Pecos, Texas, "where law leaves off and order forgot to begin. It is in the land of coyotes, gorgeous sunsets, rattlesnakes and dust storms, and I like it," she writes.

She was born into a family of Protestants. Her direct American forefather, John Johnston, brother of the first governor of the two Carolinas, came to America in the seventeenth century due to some trouble he had had with the English Crown. Mother M. Francis, whose mother died when she was but four years old, was brought up on her father's large cotton plantation in North Texas. She loved the outdoors and was a good horsewoman. She was educated at home by a governess and at the age of nine entered the local school. At fifteen she submitted her first story, written for a contest for school children, to the Dallas *Morning News.* For this published story she received $5.00.

Her young life was void of religious influence and she boasted of being an atheist. A Catholic service attended in girlhood made such an impression that she stated to a friend, "If I ever believe in God I am going to be a Catholic." Then one day just for a lark she decided to attend a convent boarding school. Up to this time she had never seen a nun. She selected the Ursuline Boarding School at Dallas, Texas. She fell in love with the nuns and also with God. By the end of the year, she became a Catholic and at the end of the next year entered the Ursuline sisterhood.

She is the author of: *Ellen of the Plains Country; Sonny; Girl of the Riverland; Overlord; Light Shining,* and *Winning Through.* She has contributed to *Outlook, Scribner's, Yale Review, Magnificat, Sacred Heart Messenger* and other periodicals.

E. F.

Elizabeth Jordan 1868-1947

"The day of my graduation from the Convent of Notre Dame in Milwaukee was the turning point of my life," wrote Elizabeth Jordan. Truly it was the turning point of the life of this seventeen-year-old valedictorian. Born in "America's Munich," Milwaukee, Elizabeth Jordan became, even in her school days, an accomplished musician as well as something of a writer. Advised by her father to defer entering the convent—such was her intention that memorable graduation day— she yielded to his desire that she allow herself five years to decide the question, during which period she should try to win her spurs doing newspaper work in Milwaukee, Chicago, and New York.

In a series of ventures, mostly journalistic, success followed success, and within five years she became a member of the editorial staff of the New York *World,* when Joseph Pulitzer owned that American daily. Her "True Stories of the News," one of which appeared every morning in the *World,* told of the happenings in New York. Strong business sense, ready adaptability to meet new situations, and personal charm won for her distinction in a great metropolitan newspaper world. From 1897 to 1900 she was assistant editor of the Sunday *World.* During those three strenuous years, what she had sought when setting out in pursuit of a literary career, she found in abundance—"human interest in plenty, human contacts, increasing knowledge of life." Among others associated with her in her work were Arthur Brisbane and Colonel George Harvey, later president of Harper and Brothers and subsequently ambassador to Great Britain.

In 1900 Elizabeth Jordan resigned from the Sunday *World* to become editor of Harper's *Bazaar* when Colonel Harvey had become president of Harper's. For thirteen years she filled this post, that is, until the magazine, after a long but futile struggle for existence, was sold to William Randolph Hearst. Immediately the editor went over to Harper's literary department as literary adviser, a post she held till 1918. During this time she accepted Sinclair Lewis' first novel, *Our Mr. Wrenn*. Lewis inscribed a copy, thanking her for "her inspiring and creative finishing touches."

As literary adviser, she was free to devote half of every week to creative work of her own, particularly in drama and fiction, supplementing it with dramatic criticism and essays. During those eighteen years spent in the office of a great publishing firm her literary powers enjoyed their fullest scope. Her works of fiction, produced in the past forty years, total thirty-nine. In addition she had written two plays, a novel in collaboration with Henry James, William Dean Howells, and others, a biography, and her autobiography—an impressive list certainly. Moreover, she had been a staff editorial writer for a chain of American newspapers and for many years dramatic critic of *America*.

Following a brief experience with the Goldwyn Company, well-known moving picture producers, the author threw herself into war work, "serving on committees, making speeches, and selling bonds." At the termination of the war she resumed her writing and had the satisfaction of seeing three of her novels put into Braille, others made into moving pictures, and a dozen of them translated into various languages—French, Spanish, Italian, Norwegian, Swedish, and Danish.

For thirty years Miss Jordan was a resident of Gramercy Park, New York, being president of the Gramercy Park Club and a member of the Executive Committee of the Gramercy Park Association. She was likewise a member of Mayor Mitchell's Committee of Women in New York, the Big Sisters Association, The National Institute of Social Sciences, the Authors' League of America, the American Committee of Mercy, the Society of American Dramatists and Composers, the American P.E.N., and the Notre Dame Alumnae Association (vice-president). She was also a member of the Colony Club and the Cosmopolitan Club, New York, and the Northampton Country Club, Massachusetts. In 1932 her alma mater, now Mount Mary College and University, Milwaukee, honored her with the degree of Doctor of Letters. Her special recreational interests were music, travel, golf, and conversation.

She is the author of: *Tales of the Cloister* (1901); *Tales of Destiny* (1902); *May Iverson, Her Book* (1904); *Many Kingdoms* (1908); *May Iverson Tackles Life* (1913); *May Iverson's Career* (1914); *Lover's Knots* (1916); *Wings of Youth* (1917); *The Blue Circle* (1920); *The Lady of Pentlands* (1923); *Red Riding Hood* (1924); *Miss Blake's Husband* (1925); *Miss Nobody from Nowhere* (1927); *The Devil and the Deep Sea* (1928); *The Night Club Mystery* (1929); *The Fourflusher* (1930); *Playboy* (1931); *Young Mr. X* (1932); *Page Mr. Pomeroy* (1933); *Daddy and I* (1934); *The Life of the Party* (1935); *The Trap* (1936); *Three Rousing Cheers* (autobiography) (1938); *After the Verdict* (1939); *First Port of Call* (1940); *Faraway Island* (1941); *Young John Takes Over* (1942); *Herself* (1943); *Miss Warren's Son* (1944), and *The Real Ruth Arnold* (1945).

S. J. M.

Max Jordan 1895-

When the National Broadcasting Company decided to set up a separate division of religion, Dr. Max Jordan, its former Continental-European manager and dean of American foreign radio correspondents, was appointed on February 1, 1943, director of the newly-created Division of Religious Broadcasts.

The son of a chemist, Max Jordan was born at San Remo, Italy, on April 21, 1895, and was educated in the grammar and high schools of Italy, Switzerland and Germany. Further studies were made at the Universities of Frankfort, Jena and Berlin. It was from the University of Jena that he received his Ph.D. in religious philosophy. He is a convert to the Catholic Faith.

His career as a newspaper reporter began in Italy as a free lance writer. In 1920 he joined the Berlin daily *Tageblatt* as associate foreign editor. In this capacity he covered many of the major diplomatic post-war conferences. In 1923 he joined the Hearst organization as a member of their Berlin staff and was transferred to New York and Washington the following year. After circling the globe as a writer and lecturer, Max Jordan became European representative for NBC in 1931. From that year on he was also Central European correspondent of the National Catholic Welfare Conference News Service.

The ten years that followed brought Jordan fame as NBC's European chief as he reported world-stirring events from more than twenty countries on the continent. Some of the more outstanding among Jordan's exclusive broadcasts were: The first stratosphere flight, by Professor Auguste Piccard in Switzerland; Christmas services from the Roman Catacombs of St. Domitilla in 1937, fifty feet beneath the soil of the Eternal City; the first broadcast of the Bells of Bethlehem, Palestine—ringing from the Church of the Holy Nativity on Christmas Eve in 1934; the Zeppelin flights to Brazil and Chicago with programs relayed directly from aboard the giant dirigibles; an actual eruption of Mt. Vesuvius; the Oberammergau Passion Play; addresses by Popes Pius XI and Pius XII; Hitler's march on Austria; the famous Munich agreement, which was reported to the world by Jordan ahead of all other news services and radio networks; the invasion of Norway and Denmark by the Germans; the first broadcast from the Siegfried Line and the story of the ill-fated "City of Flint." There is hardly a place in the world that Jordan does not know from personal experience and he has met many of the important personalities in the countries he has visited.

For many years Jordan has been a contributor to Catholic magazines such as *The Sign, The Commonweal* and *Liturgical Week Proceedings.* His first and only book thus far is *Beyond All Fronts* in which he explains the whys and hows behind World War II, and tells of his thirty years' experience as a newspaperman and radio commentator. The book was a selection of both the Catholic Literary Foundation and the Catholic Book Club.

As NBC's director of religious broadcasts, Dr. Jordan inaugurated many new features, among them the first reading on the air of the Gospel in the language spoken by Our Lord in His lifetime (Aramaic), the pealing of the oldest church bell in America, the first series of lay speakers on the "Catholic Hour," and daily radio prayers from coast to coast. Early in 1945 Jordan undertook his twenty-fifth crossing of the Atlantic Ocean to resume his regular correspondence for the National Catholic Welfare Conference News Service and the Catholic Press. He is still (1947) in Europe covering the news for the National Catholic Welfare Conference.   M. H.

Johannes Jörgensen   1866-

Svendborg, Denmark, the island home of Johannes Jörgensen, has been ever dear to him. There he was born and spent his childhood. His father was a seafaring man and his mother of gentle birth. He and his sisters loved to roam the woods and meadows, gathering flowers. To do this, among familiar dear ones was joy "pure and deep and calm like the blue sky above the old trees and the red roofs round about—that, and the longing for it, became the fundamental note in my life, perhaps the deepest—it grew into that longing for home which brought me back from even the furthest wanderings into the wilderness. Never, I think, have I been really happy outside that old garden." The religion of the family was Lutheran Christianity and Christmas was the joyous feast round which tender memories clung. Goethe's *Faust* and Longfellow's *Golden Legend,* from his uncle's library, made a deep impression on the boy, and he also delved deep into kabbala and theosophy. The mystery of the world stirred him and he sought the truth not only in theology but in the natural sciences, especially astronomy.

After completing his studies at the secondary school he left Svendborg at the age of sixteen for Copenhagen, where he had obtained a scholarship at a grammar school. He had cheap lodgings in the attic of a shoemaker's house across the town, and daily trudged back and forth. His loneliness found no solace in the companionship of his schoolmates who mocked the "new boy," and this aroused in him a hatred of the privileged, the rich and the handsome, for he was convinced that he was ugly and also loathed himself. "I suffer, therefore I am," summed up his experiences after three months. He read copiously and wrote incessantly, chiefly poems of revolt, becoming socially and politically a rebel.

He became a student at the university, 1884-1890, in the days of the great opposition. Radicalism was the vogue. Ibsen, Strindberg and Zola influenced him. He studied philosophy under Höffding, who taught free thought, and took an intermediate degree in philosophy, with honors. In 1886 he left the small group of liberals in the Students' Association to join the newly formed Students' Society, and in June of that year walked in a socialist procession. This, and his neglect of studies and lectures for walks and discussions, brought a severe reprimand from the university authorities in the summer of 1886. This letter, received when he was at home, greatly distressed his parents. "The red star had led me outside the pale of society and a long way towards the abyss."

Upon his return to Copenhagen, he left his conservative landlord, and moved from lodging to lodging. He took up zoology and evolution. Haeckel and Huxley were his favorite authors. At this time he formed his life-long friendship with Viggo Stuckenberg and Sophus Claussen, all of them to become known in the literary world. The young men were all ardent followers of the amoralist Georg Brandes, who lectured at the university. Like his associates, Jörgensen strayed from the path of virtue to his unending regret. "At the end of the nineteenth century in Denmark, such a state of spiritual ignorance had been reached that no one knew what love was." The thought that there was no after-life filled Jörgensen with despair, and frequently he turned to God in anguished dependence, but doubt persisted. Nature was his constant source of comfort and he was attracted to pantheism.

In 1888 he published his first book of prose, *Legends of Spring,* written about Svendborg. Excluding himself from all society in the spring of 1889 he wrote verses for the *Illustrated News,* studied Russian nihilism and endured hunger. He completed his tenth term at the university that year and under Ernst Brandes, editor of the Copenhagen *Bors-Tidende,* became a permanent contributor to the paper.

After eighteen months he was sub-editor, and in 1891 he married. Theirs was the typical home of a young literary couple. In 1892 he published *Summer,* and *Moods,* and the same year his first son was born. When *Bors-Tidende* came to an end that summer with the death of Ernst Brandes, Jörgensen obtained some work on *Politiken.* The gospel of a new idealism now became popular. "All the old moods awoke, our hearts swelled with the longing and with the yearning of romanticism and its dreams." From Georg Brandes the young Danes turned to Baudelaire and Verlaine and made a cult of intoxication. Nights of dissipation left poverty in their wake. *The Tower,* a review of art and literature, which Jörgensen began to publish in 1893, brought no monetary returns. His *Tree of Life* had aroused criticism as "a Catholic book," and his paper was declared to be "Christian." This alienated him from his former friends. In 1894 he uttered his first prayer since childhood.

That year brought him into close relationship with Mogens Ballin and Carl Ewald. In contrast with the latter's paganism was the zealous Catholicism of the recently converted young Jewish artist, Ballin. He introduced Jörgensen to the works of Hello and Bloy, and with Jan (later Dom Willibrod) Verkade, enabled him to go abroad to Germany and Italy, thus bringing him to the threshold of the Faith. After months in Assisi and La Rocca and years of almost despairing inner struggle, re-

counted in his Autobiography, Jörgensen came into the Catholic Church
at Stenosgade, Denmark, in 1896. He was received by Father A. Brinkmann,
S.J., who instructed him. That year he published *Truth and Falsehood.*
It had been preceded in 1895 by *The Book of the Journey,* compared
to Huysmans' *En Route,* and *Bekendelse,* a collection of poems including
Chaldea and *Confiteor.* A daughter was born to him, he buried his second
son, and later had three other sons. During this time he wrote *Foes of
Hell,* a defense of the Home Mission; *The Last Day,* a story; *Parables;
Conversion* and a collection of poems dating from 1894, and did journalistic work. He was a member of the staff of *Tiden* until it was withdrawn,
and then undertook the publication of *The Catholic,* a literary supplement to *Nordish Ugeblad for katolske Kristne.*

In 1899 he was awarded the Anker Bequest for traveling, and took his
family to Italy. With his wife he was received into the Third Order of
St. Francis. He translated the *Little Flower of St. Francis,* sent articles
home to *The Catholic* and wrote *The Book about Rome,* a two-volume
work of Catholic apologetics; *Roman Mosaics* and *Pictures of Roman
Saints.* An audience with Leo XIII deeply impressed him, and after his
return to Denmark he was rejoiced by the great encyclical, "Rerum
Novarum," for in it he found a reconciliation of his beliefs in Catholicism
and human progress, harbinger of a new era, and he ardently took up
the cause of social justice. In *Our Lady of Denmark* a novel loosely
threaded through a chain of philosophical, political and religious essays,
his hero is a Christian democrat. He was frequently attacked by his
erstwhile associates, especially in *Politiken,* and called a "renegade." This
disturbed him deeply.

He traveled alone to Belgium in 1901, and in the summer of 1902
went with his family to Sweden, his wife's country. That fall they went
again to Rome. *The Catholic* had ceased publication and he sent home
a weekly article to *Vort Land.* In the archives of the Vatican he began
research for his book on St. Francis and he went also to Assisi. *The
Pilgrim Book,* relating this journey, was published upon his return to
Denmark.

There they lived in Charlottenlund. He gave lectures and wrote
newspaper articles under the name of "Unicus," meaning "alone," for
he felt himself isolated in thought from those around him. Frequently
he went to Beuron to write, and also visited Reichenau, Maria Laach
and Monte Cassino. He was engaged by *Nationaltidende* to write a weekly
article on literature and send "Wayside Notes" from abroad, and he
travelled extensively, lecturing throughout Europe and suffering nostalgia.
In France he had become known by an article in *Revue des Deux Mondes,*
and visiting Hoskier in Paris he there met the French Catholic literary
lights through Jean Brunhes. He wrote a book about "Lourdes" after
a journey there in connection with his "Story of a Hidden Life," on
Fraulein Paula Reinhard, whom he had visited in Germany at Villa
Emmaus. His books were translated into German by the Countess Hol-
stein Ledreborg. *St. Francis of Assisi* was translated into English by T.
O'Conor Sloane and also into Spanish and French. Other English translations of his writings are by Ingeborg Lund.

In 1912 there was a notable gathering at Copenhagen to celebrate the twenty-fifth anniversary of the publication of his *Verses,* Jörgensen's first book. Old friends of a common youth were present and there were also young students, among them Peter Schindler, who, addressing Jörgensen, said: "You have taught us Danish Protestants to make the sign of the cross; you have taught us to bend the knee before the holies!" Henriette Brunhes wrote him: "Your books have the effect of deliverance and help . . . young men and young women . . . breathe the air of a new Christianity in your writings refreshing and vivid like yourself."

Shortly before the first World War he accepted a chair in the University of Louvain, but the war prevented him from ever taking it up. He lived for many years at Assisi in Italy and is living there now (1947). Bishop Theodore Suhr, O.S.B., of Denmark in his article "Johannes Jörgensen" in the Danish *Foreign Office Journal,* No. 1, 1947, writes: "But throughout his exile he remained a writer of Danish about whom the critics at home repeatedly wrote that no Dane with the language ringing in his ears every day wrote it with such perfect purity as he did. On the approach of the second World War having shown in the title of one of his books that the axis of his life was not the Berlin-Rome Axis, he was obliged to return home. During most of the war he lived in Sweden, where he wrote the great work of his old age on the supreme saint of Scandinavia, St. Bridget of Sweden. The cultural world described by Johannes Jörgensen is twofold: first, the lives of the great saints, such as St. Francis of Assisi and St. Catherine of Siena, in whose footsteps he travelled, living for years at the places where they lived, and second, modern Catholicism in literature, in which he was widely read, and in the daily life of ordinary men and women."

Some years before the war he married a rather young Austrian woman. The last years of the war he spent with her in Vadstena in Sweden. C. M. N.

Reverend George Hayward Joyce, S.J.
1864-1943

Born the son of Reverend Francis Hayward Joyce, the Vicar of Harrow-on-the-Hill, Father George Hayward Joyce came into the Catholic Church at Farm Street, London, on October 21, 1893, when he was nearly thirty years of age. From his clerical home and his training in an Anglican seminary, he acquired personal characteristics which never changed. He was educated at the Charterhouse, Godalming and Oriel College, Oxford. From the latter institution he received an M.A. degree. One year was spent in Germany studying for six months at the University of Leipzig and six months at the University of Bonn. After a further year of study for the ministry at the Leeds Clergy School, he was ordained for the Anglican

Church in 1890. His first curacy was at Holy Trinity Church, Shrewsbury, from September 1889 to June 1892 and for the following six months he was assistant curate at Harrow-on-the-Hill. Then he spent six months travelling. He entered the novitiate of the Society of Jesus at Roehampton, on November 4, 1893. He studied philosophy at St. Mary's Hall, Stonyhurst, and theology at St. Beuno's College, St. Asaph. He was ordained at St. Beuno's on September 20, 1903, and returned there in 1909 to become professor of theology where he remained until 1926.

Later he became professor of theology at Heythrop College, where he was also prefect of studies and dean of the Faculty of Theology. The great majority of Jesuit priests in Britain studied under Father Joyce. On account of a throat ailment, his teaching was occasionally interrupted. While his diction was slow, he was known for his lucid exposition of theological truth. He had a genial personality.

Despite the fact that he had entered his eightieth year a few days before his death, on November 15, 1943, he displayed a vigor of mind and body that was astounding. For nearly thirty years he spent the months of August and September helping at the Farm Street Church of the Jesuits.

To the Stonyhurst Series of books, Father Joyce contributed *Natural Theology* and *Principles of Logic*. His *Christian Marriage* is the first book of the Heythrop Theological Series. He is also the author of *The Question of Miracles,* and *The Catholic Doctrine of Grace.*

M. H.

Henri Antoine Jules-Bois   1869-1943

Idealist, scholar and profound thinker, Henri Antoine Jules-Bois wrote dramas, novels, essays, poetry and works of erudition on psychology and trends of thought. A strong creative urge led to great and diversified activity in the fields of literature and philosophy, and this with an abundant interior life made his years rich in achievement. He was born in Marseilles, France, in 1869, and educated there at the College of St. Ignatius at Aix-en-Provence and Montpellier where he received his A.B. and B.Sc. degrees, and at the College de France and the Sorbonne which awarded him his Ph.D. and Litt. D. degree. At the Sorbonne where he studied under Dr. Berillon, he received the degree of Doctor of Psychology for his researches in the "superconscious field." Like other young men of his day he was influenced by naturalism when he began to write in the 'nineties, and he attained spiritually only by sincerely searching for the true meaning of life.

He first wrote symbolic plays in verse, and then based several novels on woman's emancipation, which was being agitated at the time, and in

The Eternal Doll, The New Era, Restless Womanhood, The New Sorrow and *The Future Couple* he extols woman's place in the world as an influence for good upon man, advocating a single standard of morality for both sexes and the ideal marriage as a means of regenerating society.

His interest in preternatural manifestations in man prompted the *Mysteries of Evil* and *Lesser Religions of Paris,* the former prefaced by Huysmans, his intimate friend. At the close of the century Jules-Bois travelled to the Near and Far East, to Greece, Turkey, Egypt, Syria, Palestine and India. He became the friend of Venizelos and of Vivekananda and met Rabindranath Tagore. His *Visions of India* describes his search for the truth in Hindu philosophy, and, disillusioned, he writes in the last pages: "Vivekananda and the spectacle of Benares has brought me back to Bethlehem."

While in Rome, in 1902, on his journey home he had a private audience with Leo XIII, to whom he recounted his spiritual pilgrimage. This he describes as one of the two great moments of his life, which were "the facing of two great altitudes: materially, the view of the Himalayas; and spiritually, my interview with Leo XIII." Upon his return to Paris he was active in the Astronomical Society, the Society for Psychological Research of Paris, of which he was later president, and the Institute of Psychophysiology, where he spent many hours in the clinics. He became deeply interested in experimental psychology, and his studies resulted in the discovery of the superconscious, or that liaison between God and man represented by the action of divine grace within us, on the one hand, and the inspiration of the poet and the scientist, on the other. At the School of Psychology he later held the chair of head professor of the superconscious. In 1903 he wrote of occultism, spiritism and theosophy in *The Invisible World.*

Drama next occupied his talents. In 1904 appeared *Hyppolitus Crowned* and in 1905 *The Fury,* both plays in verse adapted from antiquity. The first was adopted by the Odeon and the second was accepted by the Comedie Française, the highest honor awarded to French dramatists. Then followed his masterpiece, *The Two Helens,* produced in 1929 at Columbia University, New York City. *Nail,* a French-African drama, was put to music and played at the Opera Comique and Convent Garden Monte Carlo applauded the presentation of his lyric drama, *Lelilah,* a tale of Persia.

Meanwhile he had written also *The Modern Prodigy,* a scientific work in which he considers "metaphysical" phenomena as projections of the medium's subconscious personality, and *The Divine in Man,* a volume of verse expressing his philosophy. Two novels, *The Ship* and *The Eternal Return,* followed.

During World War I Jules-Bois was sent as a lecturer to Spain and then to the United States, where he made his home. He came here as a good-will ambassador of his government to counteract German propaganda. He was the general delegate for North America of "L'Idee Française a l'Etranger." In America he found inspiration and a latent idealism, and he wrote a book on it in English, entitled *Essay on Democracy.* For the post-war world he visioned an "interpatriotism," a word which he coined to express something more than internationalism. He was heartily in accord with his friend Briand's plan for a United States of Europe, and his name is included with that of Briand and Boncour and other states-men and diplomats in a "Who's Who" that was published of the "first Europeans," or workers for a federation of Europe.

Correspondent for several papers and contributor to magazines, espe-cially *The Catholic World* and *The Commonweal,* Jules-Bois through his writings as well as his lectures interpreted men and events with spiritual insight, charity and learning. At his death on July 2, 1943, he was working on a book *The Psychology of the Saints.* Many honors were bestowed on him. He was an Officer of the Legion of Honor of France, and Officer of the Order of the Savior and a Commander of the Phenix Order of Greece, Knight of the Order of Leopold of Belgium and Commander of Nichan-Ifticar of Tunisia. In 1940 Providence College, Providence, Rhode Island, gave him an honorary LL.D. for his remarkable achievements of high literary and scientific value, and preeminently for his great contri-butions to Catholic humanism in spreading the knowledge of the super-conscious, that "apex of the soul" where spiritual light and grace are infused and man is enlivened toward the attainment of supernatural perfection.

C. M. N.

Sister Julie, S.N.D. 1868-1947

Few who read *Rabboni* or *Vigil* (1929) the best known perhaps of the little spiritual books of "Sister Julie," as she signed herself, know anything of the author, a member of the Sisters of Notre Dame de Namur, West Rittenhouse Square, Philadelphia.

Born in Fort Leavenworth, Kansas, in 1868, the daughter of a rank-ing army man she became a Sister of Notre Dame de Namur in 1892.

For twenty-five years Sister Julie was moderator of the Children of Mary and at the same time mistress of boarders at the Academy as well as head of the French department until her appointment as secretary to the Provincial in 1915, with residence at Waltham, Massachusetts.

In 1919 she was transferred to Reading, Ohio to become mistress of boarders. She returned to Philadelphia in 1921 to become again Moder-ator of the Children of Mary. When illness forced her to relinquish this post in 1930 she gave private conferences to people of every class up until a week before her death. She died on February 25, 1947.

Beloved of a large following Sister Julie wrote *Rabboni* and *Spiritual Pastels* (1934) without any thought of publication. She had jotted down thoughts for instructions, which as Mistress of the Children of Mary she gave once a month in informal talks to her sodality. Somebody caught sight of her jottings and decided they should be given a wider audience than the little group within the convent walls. She had never received, or desired, benefits of any kind from her publications except the reward of knowing that she was working for God.

A few lines on the jacket of *Lucent Clay* (1932) read: "*Lucent Clay* is dedicated to sensitive souls living in the world. Each chapter of the book is self-contained and whether it be that the author writes on the Light of the World, on suffering, or on the Cross, we find both nobility of thought and graciousness of expression. The wooden style of many religious books here blossoms into a lovely living tree. Here indeed is beauty, rare and delicious."

The books of Sister Julie are but the fruit of a long cloistered life. Years before she began writing, her "talks" crowded the convent hall at retreat time. Because of her spirituality, tact and understanding of the human heart, she had gained the confidence of many. She had helped heal broken hearts, counseled troubled minds and led erring souls back to God. Her little spiritual books are real pages from the book of life.

She is also the author of *Vine and Branch* (1927); *Cresting the Ridge* (1927); and *Wonder World of the Soul.* E. F.

Sheila Kaye-Smith 1887-

Books have always formed an essential part of the life of Sheila Kaye-Smith. From her earliest years she was determined to be an author, and she wove stories about the children on the Sussex farms where she and her sister spent their holidays. Her imagination was not stirred by the accustomed daily life of a small daughter of a hard-working doctor in a seaside town, her father being a surgeon at Battle near St. Leonards-on-Sea, where Sheila grew up and went to school. She was born in Hastings, in 1887, her father of East Anglican stock and her mother of French and Scottish ancestry, a widower and widow who married each other in middle life. They accompanied their daughters on their holidays in Scotland and in Devonshire; and this country also deeply roused the imagination of the youthful authoress. The background of her tales was always carefully chosen and often came first, with the characters created for the place.

Composing became a habit of declaiming aloud, in solitude, from a book from which she pretended to read. It was sheer art for art's sake. During her last two years at school she wrote thirteen novels of 22,000 words each, all but two or three historical. This vast literary output preceded the appearance of her thirty-one published books.

Religion was a part of Sheila Kaye-Smith's every-day child life. God was a rather distant Father and she had a deep devotion to His Son, and strangely enough, a belief in the Pope as the Head of the Church, though her parents were Low Church Anglicans. The reading of the Victorian classics, *Line upon Line* and *The Peep of Day* and the hell-fire sermons she heard in Scotland disturbed not at all her secure hope for heaven, and she relinquished less regretfully her belief in fairies with the assurance of the existence of angels. She endured a brief period of great unhappiness when in reading Edna Lyall's *We Too* she came across the word "atheist" and became aware that there were some who did not believe in God; but her "faith" was restored with the feast of the Conversion of St. Paul, who, she felt, had "first-hand information" of God's existence. When the weight of morality bore down on her, though with no urge to transgress the law of good conduct, it nevertheless destroyed her delight in religion. That was temporarily renewed with her happiness in Confirmation, but as her parents opposed her desire to attend High Church, for years religion did not sway her.

This was the interval between her first book, *The Tramping Methodist,* and *The End of the House of Alard.* When she finally decided to write for publication she chose the itinerant preacher as a means of portraying the country she loved best. *Starbrace,* a story of highwaymen and their desperate deeds, was written entirely from imagination. Wanting to be a man, male characters had always interested her. The books were sentimental and unreal but received a good press and a fair sale especially for one of her youth.

At twenty-one she was allowed to stay in London unchaperoned, to seek the experience her publishers advised. It was however definitely limited.

Her first encounter with Catholicism was an evening at Alice Meynell's home where the artistic cultured atmosphere deeply impressed her but made her feel somewhat alien. She developed a will to disbelieve, to be progressive. She read Nietzsche and Biblical exegesis by modern scholars, and then Swedenborg and Madame Blavatsky. Their influence was evident in her next novel, *Spell Land,* on the advance payment for which she went to Paris. But she contracted pneumonia there and upon her return home she was ill for several months. At the age of twenty-four she found herself sixteen years old in experience. Then with new interests in life she wrote verse. Her fourth novel, *Isle of Thorns,* appeared in 1913. The heroine is in many ways herself as she would like to be. W. L. George, a French novelist, gave her the suggestion for *Sussex Gorse* and procured her a publisher. From him she also acquired a plan of writing that was a great economy of time and she enjoyed the facility of the new technique, as well as escape from the unhappiness around her, in writing the book. World War I had begun and the war hysteria left her comparatively unmoved though emotionally uneasy, disliking both propagandists and pacifists. *Sussex Gorse* was totally different from her other books, the story of a man who sacrifices himself to the land he cultivates and succeeds in the end. It sold extremely well. She had "arrived."

In 1918 Sheila Kaye-Smith made her first confession in the Church of England. *Joanna Godden* (1921), her first book with a woman as the central character, was undertaken reluctantly at the suggestion of W. L. George, and was her most successful work. In *The End of the House of Alard* she sought expression of her restored enthusiasm in religion. Though the reviewers received it unfavorably, it became a best seller both in England and America and brought her commissions for articles and short stories. It also brought her religious as well as literary fame, and she was asked to address Anglo-Catholic meetings and congresses. She further bound herself to that Church by marrying, in 1924, an Anglo-Catholic clergyman, the Reverend T. Penrose Fry, though this was a disappointment to her coreligionists who believed in celibacy of the clergy. Her husband's rector would not employ a married curate and they were obliged to leave Hastings and make their home in London.

George and the Crown, a novel with the scene laid in the Channel Islands, appeared in 1925. Then followed *Anglo-Catholicism,* and its religious propaganda impaired her literary success. For her next books her thought fled to Sussex and Kent for inspiration. In *Saints in Sussex, Joanna Godden Married, Iron and Smoke, The Village Doctor* and *Shepherds in Sackcloth* she wrote of the country she loved while homesick for it in London. *Saints in Sussex* was partly a reissue of verse written after her return to religion and included also two mystery plays by which the author says she would best like to be remembered. They are Gospel stories of the Nativity and Passion staged in the countryside of her youth. *Shepherds in Sackcloth* was her last novel as an Anglican. It is a tribute to the English clergyman and his wife whom she considers the worthiest and most misunderstood members of the community.

From her husband's curacy at Notting Dale they were transferred to the mediocre prosperity of South Kensington. There seemed to be too much worship and magnificence in the new church, so that the soul was squeezed out. Moreover the constant disputes of Anglo-Catholics with the Church of England disturbed her. She found herself taking the part of Roman Catholics against their critics. The same unrest of spirit was felt by her husband, and in 1928 they decided to go to Italy as a cure for this "Roman fever." Their cruise to Sicily and their visit to Palermo cathedral greatly impressed them. Cut off from Anglicanism they realized where they really belonged. This second conversion of Sheila Kaye-Smith was of the mind rather than the heart as the first had been. It was the result of observation and deduction, a change of allegiance not of belief. As they were financially independent of her husband's curacy their conversion was facilitated materially. He resigned and after six months, during which they received religious instruction from the Reverend C. C. Martindale, S.J., they were received into the Catholic Church, in 1929.

They then settled at Little Doucegrove, a farm they bought in Sussex. As they were nine miles from a Catholic Church they arranged for a visiting priest to say Mass each Sunday for the scattered Catholics of the district, and, for the first time since the Reformation, Mass was publicly offered there in 1930. A small church was built in a neighboring field and Sheila Kaye-Smith undertook more parochial work than she had done as a parson's wife. She cared for the sanctuary, answered the prayers of the Mass, took up the collections, taught the children, rounded up the backsliders and visited the sick. After four years there was a resident priest.

In 1946 she told an audience in London that more important than her conversion is the fact that she has remained a Catholic for seventeen years without a moment's regret.

Her first novel after conversion was *Susan Spray,* a story of the visit to England of a notorious American woman evangelist. It was said to be an exposure of the evils of Protestantism and an attack on women preachers, but was meant as neither. *Mirror of the Months* is a book of meditative essays on the religious significance of each month. The *Ploughman's Progress* dealt with agricultural conditions during the slump. Her first really Catholic novel was *Superstition Corner,* an historical work, as was also *Gallybird* which followed. She considers her later books too objective and detached. There was no longer the connection between herself and her works as in earlier years, and Sussex too had changed and her feeling for it was more external. But her novels, *Rose Deeprose, The Valiant Woman, Ember Lane, The Secret Son* and *Tambourine, Trumpet and Drum* (1943), a war novel, continue to hold her readers' interest; and great sincerity and simplicity characterize her religious autobiography, *Three Ways Home.* In 1944, she and G. B. Stern published *Speaking of Jane Austen.* It is a critical study of the great English novelist. *Kitchen Fugue,* her experience with life in war-time rural England, appeared in 1945. She is an Academy member of the Gallery of Living Catholic Authors.   C. M. N.

Reverend John Kearney, C.S.Sp.   1865-1941

The early years of the priesthood of Father John Kearney, of the Congregation of the Holy Ghost, were devoted to educational work to the training of students for the missionary priesthood, and the preaching of retreats. The latter years were devoted to writing spiritual books.

Born in 1865 at Clonmel, Ireland, the son of Michael Kearney and Elizabeth St. John, he was educated at Blackrock College, University College and the Holy Ghost Seminary in Paris. While at Blackrock College he was an exhibitioner in the first public examination held under the Intermediate Scheme in 1879. On his ordination to the priesthood in 1894 he was appointed to the staff of Blackrock College. He specialized in physics and mathematics while also cultivating his talent for music as organist and orchestra director. *The Holy Ghost Hymnal* is almost entirely his work.

From 1918 to 1937 he was director of the Senior Scholasticate (philosophy and theology) at Kimmage, Dublin, Ireland. During that period, he was active also in planning and elaborating the program of catechetical instruction now in use.

He is the author of *The Meaning of the Mass; You Shall Find Rest; My Yoke Is Sweet; Learn of Me;* and *As You Have Loved Me.* He collaborated with Archbishop Sheehan in the revision of the latter's *Apologetics and Catholic Doctrine.*

He died in 1941.

Reverend Joseph Keating, S.J.   1865-1939

For a quarter of a century, *The Month,* a Catholic magazine of London was in charge of Father Keating. For that work he is best known. He directed its policy and wrote many of the editorials.

Father Keating was born on March 6, 1865, at Dundee, Scotland. After attending private schools in Scotland and Ireland, he entered Stonyhurst College in Blackburn, England. After three years of philosophy he studied theology for four years at St. Beuno's College in North Wales. Before going to St. Beuno's, he was a master at Beaumont College from 1891 until 1896. After his course in theology, tertianship (a third year of noviceship) was spent at Tronchiennes, which is not far from Ghent. He taught again for six years—the first three, 1901 to 1904, at the newly established school of Stamford Hill, where he was also prefect of studies—the second triad at Stonyhurst, from 1904 to 1907.

From 1907 until 1912, he went to London as assistant to Father John Gerard, editor of *The Month,* and then from 1912 on he was in full control. *The Month* is only one year older than Father Keating.

Father Keating's interests in Catholic activities were wider than is sometimes supposed. He was associated with the Social Guild, Plater Dining Club, and Catholic Truth Society. With Father Cuthbert Lattey, S.J., he undertook a fresh translation of the New Testament from the Greek original. Upon its completion, Cardinal Hinsley sent him a letter of congratulation which he received four months prior to his death.

He was the author of *The Drink Question; Catholics and the Problem of Peace, The Catholic Conscience* and various pamphlets published by the Catholic Truth Society and other organizations. In collaboration with Father Gruggen, he wrote *Stonyhurst College: Its Foundation and History.* Five articles were written for *The Catholic Encyclopedia*

His Eminence Cardinal Hinsley spoke of him as "a friend to grapple to one's soul, for he was wise, frank and ever helpful. Many were the times I sought his advice in difficult matters, and his assistance was unfailing . . . To some who casually came in contact with him, he seemed in outward respect reserved and somewhat stern, but those who knew him even on terms of passing intimacy learned the warmth of his large heart."

After an illness of about nine months, he died on March 5, 1939, in St. Augustine's Nursing Home at St. Leonards-on-Sea.

M. H.

Sister Jerome Keeler, O.S.B.   1895-

Writing French as easily as she writes English, Sister Jerome, author of *Catholic Literary France,* a Science and Culture book was elected an honorary corresponding member of Institut Littéraire et Artistique de France, and received a diploma from that society.

She was born at Maryville, Missouri, 1895, the daughter of Patrick John and Mary Jane (Brady) Keeler. She was educated in the grade schools there until ten years of age when she went to the Academy and Junior College of the Sacred Heart in St. Joseph, Missouri, from 1905 to 1912, graduating at sixteen, one of the youngest ever to do so. She attributes her knowledge of French to the fact that her teachers (Religious of the Sacred Heart) had at that period several members who were just expelled from France and could scarcely speak English.

In 1913 she entered the Benedictine Convent at Atchison, Kansas. She attended St. Benedict's College in that city in the summer sessions from 1920 until 1924. She taught in the parish grade and high schools in Kansas and Iowa from 1915 until 1924. She went to the Catholic University in Washington in 1924, won her A.B. 1925, majored in French, and received a Ph.D. there in 1930. Her dissertation was: *Etude sur la poésie et sur le vocabulaire de Loys Papon, poéte Forézien du seizieme siecle.* The summer of 1929 was spent in a convent in Quebec, where English was not spoken at all.

Sister Jerome was made dean of Mount St. Scholastica College, Atchison, Kansas, in 1930, where she was also professor of French. She spent a sabbatical year doing research at Columbia University in New York, 1937. From 1940 to 1944 she was principal of Lillis High School in Kansas City, Missouri, but in September 1940 resumed her duties as dean at Mount St. Scholastica College.

Sister Jerome is a contributor to *The Catholic World, Thought, Month, Irish Studies,* and many other religious magazines. She also writes for the *American Journal of Philology, Philological Quarterly, Modern Language Journal,* and other periodicals. She is a member of the summer school faculty of Catholic University of America as an instructor in French. Her *Catholic Literary France,* published in 1938 is a study of contemporary French writers. Another one of her books is a text, an *Intermediate French Reader.* She has also written a one-act play, *White Lie.*

E. F.

Most Reverend Francis Clement Kelley 1870-

On October 18, 1905, in Archbishop Quigley's house in Chicago, a young priest, Father Francis Clement Kelley, saw his dream of many years come to birth, the founding of The Catholic Church Extension Society of the United States of America. Years later, in 1939, in his memoirs, *The Bishop Jots It Down,* that young priest, now Bishop Kelley of Oklahoma City and Tulsa, tells the story of those early years lived with his dream, while he lectured all over the country to raise funds to further it.

Bishop Kelley began life on Prince Edward Island, Canada, November 24, 1870. The parish record of Vernon River, King's County, gives the date as October 23rd, but he remarks, "Like many other things that are official, it is incorrect." The education of the future Bishop started with the Island schoolmaster. Then moving to Charlottetown the young boy went to "Miss Fennessy's Select Academy for Advanced Studies in Alphabetics." The Christian Brothers of St. Patrick's continued his education for awhile and he entered St. Dunstan's College. It was during the last year at St. Dunstan's that Francis Kelley "knew that God had called me to be one of His priests." Through the kindness of Bishop Rogers of Chatham, New Brunswick, he went to the Seminary of Chicoutimi in the Province of Quebec, a pioneer outpost of Laval University. After a year there studying philosophy, he returned home, stopping at Chatham to see Bishop Rogers who suggested that the young aspirant spend a year in his house under his tutelage. This year Bishop Kelley recalls as "lonesome as the desert and worse but worth at least any five years of my life . . . and the outstanding one."

Anxious to fulfill his vocation without adding strain to the then straitened finances of his father, Francis Kelley obtained a teaching position at Nicolet Seminary, but before entering there he learned from an ex-Islander, the pastor of a church in Baltimore, that any American bishop would pay for his studies if he were willing to join his diocese on ordination. This interested the Canadian seminarian, and Father Broydick recommended him to Cardinal Gibbons, who not then needing students passed him on to his best friend, Bishop Foley of Detroit, who accepted the prospective priest.

Ordained in the Nicolet Seminary chapel, August 24, 1893, he said his first Mass on the Island and after a few weeks' vacation set out for Detroit "to open the mysterious casket that is called Life, the key to which for me was the priesthood." He acknowledges to being frightened at exile in an unknown land, but having overcome so much, "poverty, loneliness, a feeling of inferiority and more than ordinary labor," he went forward bravely.

His first parish was Lapeer, Michigan, and its missions. A town mostly Protestant meant great loneliness to the young priest accustomed to almost wholly Catholic society, and a constant trial was the fact that a former pastor lived there in apostasy. Bishop Kelley calls his thirteen years as country pastor years of peace and poverty, but "the honey of one sweetened the hard bread of the other." In 1898 he found himself to his own surprise chaplain in the United States Army in the Spanish-American War. Returning to his parish a year later, he discovered a way to make money for parochial needs and in 1899 he became a Lyceum lecturer between Sundays, enduring this "form of torture" until 1906. But from it came rich fruits, enabling him to finish his church, and his journeys among "the scattered people and into the churchless places, gave me also the inspiration for a dream that became the central interest in my life. . . . For twenty years it was almost my only thought." This was The Catholic Church Extension Society, the story of whose growth, in the United States and Canada, was marked by unremitting zeal, constant labor and difficulties overcome. The "church on wheels" brought gratifying results, and the *Extension* magazine came into being, with Father Kelley its editor. It was while wielding the editorial pen that he wrote *Letters to Jack,* advice to young men (1917). *Charred Wood* was published the same year—*The Last Battle of the Gods* and *City and the World* had preceded. The Extension work expanded into Puerto Rico and the Philippines, and Canada started on its own.

Then Father Kelley crossed the Atlantic with the hope of starting it in England and studying similar works in France and Germany, and also to visit Rome. In 1922 he wrote *The Story of Extension.*

A close observer of the post-war conference and the League of Nations, Monsignor Kelley, as he then was, strove unsuccessfully to have a Liberty of Conscience clause inserted in the Covenant. In June 1924 came his appointment as Bishop of Oklahoma. Feeling that "change" was indicated on his personal barometer, and knowing that the mission work to which he had given so many years and so much labor, and traveled widely to consolidate, was now secure, he accepted the honor and in October he was consecrated Bishop of Oklahoma; later the title of the Diocese became Oklahoma City and Tulsa.

During nearly two decades in the episcopate, despite many other activities, Bishop Kelley has found time to write several books: *Dominus Vobiscum* (1922), advice to seminarians; *Forgotten God* (1932); *Blood-Drenched Altars* (1935), on the persecution of the Church in Mexico; *Problem Island* (1937), a novel; *The Bishop Jots It Down* (1939), and *Sacerdos et Pontifex* (1940), letters to a bishop-elect. In 1942 he published his eighteenth book *Pack Rat.* Father Parsons in reviewing it says, "It is a fable for grownups, grim and gripping. . . . The pack rat, need I say? is a thieving animal who takes things for the sake of taking them, who makes them move one way, his way." The reader will not be astonished that when this particular pack rat makes his way to Russia, Germany, France, and our own country, he finds that other pack rats, bigger and rattier ones have cornered the market of greed and power.

Bishop Kelley has received many honors: Knight of SS. Maurice and Lazarus (Italy); Knight Grand Cross of the Order of the Holy Sepulchre (Papal); Great Golden Cross of Merit (Austria); Prelate of St. Lazarus (Jerusalem), and Catholic Grand Cross of Isabel from the Spanish Government. He also received the Medals of the American Orders of the Spanish War and the Military Order of Foreign Wars.

On August 23, 1943, Bishop Kelley completed fifty years in the priesthood.

D. D.

Reverend Bernard W. Kelly 1872-

The busy life of a parish priest has not prevented the Reverend Bernard W. Kelly from writing extensively. He is the author of some twenty books of biography, history, Christian Doctrine and homiletics, of which the best known is *The Cardinal Duke of York.*

Born at Rotherhithe, London, in 1872, the son of the late Dr. Bernard Kelly, he was educated at Weybridges and George's College and then studied for the priesthood at St. John's Seminary, Wonersh, receiving Holy Orders in 1900.

He served the missions of Mitcham, Waterloo, S.E., Deptford, Cheam, Sutton Court, Effingham, Letherhead and Englefield Green, and since 1929 has been parish priest of Corpus Christi Church, Brixton Hill, London.

In 1931 he became a Fellow of the Royal Historical Society and in 1936 a corresponding member of the Canadian Catholic Association. His works include: *A Short Survey of Church History* (Sixth edition); *Notes on English Catholic Missions; Some Great Catholics of Church and State; Catholics in the British Army; The Fate of Glengarry of the Expatriation of the Macdonalds; The Fighting 'Frasers of the 'Forty-five and Quebec; Synoptical Sermons; Supplementary Volume to Butler's Lives of the Saints; Priest Heroes of the 'Forty-five; Our Faith,* in the seventh edition, a popular apologetics; *A Short History of the English Bar,* and *Some Famous Advocates and Their Speeches.*

C. M. N.

Blanche Mary Kelly 1881-

Of Irish heritage, Blanche Mary Kelly has often used her gifts to best advantage in richly human and deeply spiritual writing of the land of her ancestors, portraying an Ireland whose greatness has been sanctified by suffering. Her knowledge of literature received an early foundation in a home where the cultured things of life were part of the atmosphere. She was born in Troy, New York, in 1881, and educated at the Convent of the Sacred Heart, Kenwood, near Albany.

Upon graduation Miss Kelly was admirably equipped to take a position on the editorial staff of *The Catholic Encyclopedia* where she remained for fifteen years as contributor, translator, and general editorial assistant. In 1909 she was made chief of staff and began the compilation of the Index which was completed five years later. Supervision of the Encyclopedia Supplement followed and the work of the Catholic Dictionary was begun. She is listed as one of the five editors engaged in the revision of the Encyclopedia, and she was a collaborator in the "Catholic Builders of the Nation" series.

Her loyalty and affection for her alma mater were shown by the founding and editing of the *Signet*, the Sacred Heart Alumnae organ.

For nearly five years she acted as literary secretary for the Cardinal Hayes Literature Committee, writing a weekly critical article that was syndicated throughout the Catholic Press of the United States and editing the widely quoted quarterly survey of books approved by the Committee.

Touched with the gift of poetry Blanche Mary Kelly has written much and in 1917 published *The Valley of Vision,* a volume of verse, followed by *Mary the Mother.* A great deal of her later poetry has been included in anthologies. Her outstanding prose work is *The Well of English,* a survey of English literature, published in 1936. In 1939 she wrote *The Sudden Rose. The Eternal Purpose* published in 1943, is intended to guide the sorrowful and the bereaved to the sources of strength and hope to be found in the Scriptures. Dr. Kelly also contributes critical work to magazines.

Since 1920 she has been professor of English and journalism at the College of Mt. St. Vincent which bestowed upon her the degree of Litt.D. and where she is now head of the English Department. In conjunction with her college work she lectures on cultural subjects.

In the opinion of faculty and students who have worked with and studied under Doctor Kelly over a period of years, her greatest gift is her power to teach and inspire. Her grasp of Catholic philosophy, her wide and critical knowledge of English and her broad, fearless spirit combine to lift her teaching into the realm of inspiration.

D. D.

Reverend John Bernard Kelly 1888-

Associated with the Catholic Writers Guild of America for more than twenty-two years as spiritual director, succeeding Reverend John Talbot Smith, the founder, the Reverend John Bernard Kelly has closely identified himself with Catholic literature. He was born in New York City in 1888, and educated in the public schools, City College and Cathedral College. In 1907 he entered St. Joseph's Seminary, Dunwoodie, New York. After his ordination in 1913, he was stationed for four years at the Church of our Lady of Good Counsel in New York City. He was then spiritual director of the Catholic Big Brothers, until designated by Cardinal Hayes as his representative in the Archdiocese of New York among writers for the press, screen, stage and radio. The Catholic Writers Guild and work in connection with it has since occupied Father Kelly.

He is also chaplain of the Good Shepherd Auxiliary and the Father Duffy Post of the Catholic War Veterans. His books include *The Son of Man and Other Poems and Essays; The Romance of Truth,* and *Cardinal Hayes: One of Ourselves.* The last is an appreciation of the late Archbishop of New York, to whom Father Kelly was closely bound by ties of affection as well as priestly service, and he shows the great kindness of this shepherd toward his flock and his zeal in work for God.

It was Father Kelly who introduced Joyce Kilmer to Chaplain Francis P. Duffy of the "Fighting Sixty-ninth" Regiment—later called the 165th Infantry. Chaplain Duffy mentions the event in his book, *Father Duffy's Story.*   C. M. N.

Reverend Joseph George Kempf 1893-

Professor of sociology at St. Mary-of-the-Woods College, Indiana, where he also conducts classes in religion and the psychology of adolescence in summer sessions for resident and guest sisters, Father Kemp, author of *The Questions of Youth* (1937) and *Helping Youth to Grow* (1941), is especially interested in adolescents. He likes to work for them and with them. But even more important than his everyday classes, in his estimation, is the training of teachers of religion. While many educators were arguing about what ought to be taught along these lines, and how it should be taught, St. Mary-of-the-Woods launched out with a course itself, directed by Father Kempf. What was proposed as a tentative program has been found to be just what is wanted, and the program continues in the summer sessions without change.

Reverend Joseph George Kempf was born in Evansville, Indiana, September 27, 1893, the son of Joseph and Katherine (Daum) Kempf. He was educated in parish and public schools of Evansville, 1899 to 1907; St. Meinrad's Minor Seminary, St. Meinrad, Indiana, 1907 to 1912, and Major Seminary, 1912 to 1918, winning his A.B. in 1914. He attended the Catholic University of America from 1925 to 1926; Fordham, 1923 to 1924 and 1926 to 1927, received his M.A. in 1924; his Ph.D., 1927.

He was ordained at St. Meinrad's, April 24, 1918. He did parish work from 1918 to 1923 and from 1927 to 1930. In 1930 he was appointed professor of sociology at St. Mary-of-the-Woods where he still remains (1947).

Besides his teaching, Father Kempf is also assistant chaplain for teachers and pupils. In its summer sessions, St. Mary-of-the-Woods has some 1,100 pupils, mostly Sisters of Providence. Father Kempf has given several series of lectures to the whole community, on various psychological aspects of the spiritual life. These have been published in the book *New Things and Old* (1942).

He started his writing in 1926 with a paper on *Scruples*, worked out at the Catholic University. Several articles on *Scruples and Psychology* appeared in *The American Ecclesiastical Review* in 1930. Two papers on this subject were also prepared and published at the request of officials of the NCWC during 1937. He has also written along these same lines for *Homiletic Review*, *Journal of Religious Instruction*, *Catholic School Journal*, and *Catholic Family Monthly*. But most of his articles deal with youth and the problems of youth.

Besides publishing his own books, Father Kempf is translator of *Religious and Ecclesiastical Vocation* from the Latin of the Reverend A. Vermeersch, S.J., the first edition of which appeared in 1926.

E. F.

James Francis Kenney 1884-

The Director of Historical Research of the Public Archives of Canada, Dr. James Francis Kenney was born at Marysville, Hastings County, Ontario, on the 6th of December, 1884, the son of Martin Kenney and Mary (McCullough) Kenney. His parents are Canadians of Irish descent.

James Kenney was educated in the local public school and at Belleville High School. In 1903 he was matriculated in the University of Toronto. He took the honour matriculation examination in all subjects and ranked third in general proficiency among the candidates, receiving the Second Edward Blake Scholarship. Throughout his four years at the University of Toronto, he obtained first-class honours in the honour course of English and history (with classical option) and was ranked first in the last three years. He also took the honour course of classics during the first three years, obtaining first-class honours in the first year and second-class honours in the second and third years. In 1906 he was awarded the Frederick Wyld Prize in the English essay contest.

After receiving the B.A. degree (1907), he became a part-time assistant —two hours a week—in history, at the University of Wisconsin, from 1907 to 1908. At the same time he took a full year's postgraduate course in history and received the degree of M.A. in 1908.

For the following year he was the Alexander Mackenzie Fellow in history at the University of Toronto and did research in Canadian history. Then he became a University Fellow in history at Columbia University, New York City, 1909-1910, where he took postgraduate courses for a full year. His major subject was medieval history; his first minor, American history; his second minor, Celtic languages. He passed the examinations in these subjects and in the Latin, French and German languages, for the degree of Ph.D. in 1910. The final examination on his dissertation was passed in 1927.

Dr. Kenney received the honorary degree of Doctor of Laws from the University of Ottawa in 1936 and the honorary degree of Doctor of Letters from the National University of Ireland in 1937.

In 1932 Dr. Kenney received the Aonach Tailteann (sometimes called "The Irish Olympic Games") award for his work, *The Sources for the Early History of Ireland,* which was selected as "the most important contribution of Scholarship on the part of one of Irish descent in the period 1928-1931."

The Canadian Catholic Historical Association was founded by Dr. Kenney in 1933 and since that time he has been its secretary. In 1931 he was vice-president of the American Historical Association and in 1932, president. For the years 1937-1939, he was president of the Irish Historical Society of Canada. Other offices held by Dr. Kenney were: editor of the Canadian Historical Association, 1922-1925 and treasurer of the Canadian Authors' Association, 1925. He has been honorary vice-president of the Inter-American Bibliographical and Library Association since 1937, and Honorary Secretary of the Royal Society of Canada since 1943. In 1938 he was appointed a member of the National Battlefields Commission.

He has published many articles and reviews in various learned periodicals. He contributed the article "Catholic Education in Canada" to the *Encyclopaedia Americana,* 2nd edition.

His books include: *Catalogue of Pictures in the Public Archives of Canada* (1925); *Catalogue of Lantern Slides in the Public Archives of Canada* (1931), and *The Founding of Churchill* (1932).

Since 1912 he has been on the staff of the Public Archives of Canada as a specialist in historical research.

In 1916 Dr. Kenney married Dympna Byrne of Toronto, Canada.

M. H.

Reverend Michael Kenny, S.J. 1863-1946

Born in Tipperary, Ireland, in 1863, the Reverend Michael Kenny, S.J., after completing the Royal Irish University A.B. course at Mungret College, came to the United States and entered the Jesuit Province of New Orleans in 1886. He became a naturalized citizen in 1892, went through the regular Jesuit curriculum, and was ordained in 1897. He studied sociology at Ghent, Belgium, and Fordham University, where he obtained his Ph.D. His teaching activities at Spring Hill College, Alabama, Loyola University, New Orleans, Louisiana, and Creighton University, Omaha, Nebraska, were interrupted in 1902 by a year devoted to the negroes and poor whites near Macon, Georgia. He bought a church for them from the Episcopalians and set up a school for the negroes, conducting both thrivingly, without pew rent or church collections.

After five ensuing years of rhetoric and philosophy at Augusta, Georgia, where he preached at the funeral of James Ryder Randall, he was asked to write for the *Messenger of the Sacred Heart* an account of Joel Chandler Harris, who had just died. This and an essay on Mrs. Green's "Making of Ireland and Its Undoing" put him, in 1908, on the founding staff of *America,* where he remained as associate editor until 1915. His writings for the magazine were deemed rather militant, especially a series of articles on Masonry and those on the "Irish Players." The failure of the latter, Yeats', upon his return to Ireland, attributed to "a certain Father Kenny." *America* pamphleted many of his contributions, including "Masonry" and "Justice to Mexico," which had frequent reissues. Father Kenny has contributed to *Studies, Thought, The Catholic World, The Sign, Ave Maria,* and he collaborated in *The Catholic Encyclopedia.*

Transferred in 1915 to Loyola University, New Orleans, he taught philosophy and sociology, and jurisprudence in the Law School which grew large under his regency, furnishing many distinguished judges and lawyers to the state. Among them was the then governor of Louisiana, who presided at a banquet given by two hundred and fifty of Father Kenny's Loyola law graduates for his golden jubilee as a Jesuit, in 1936.

Father Kenny was assigned to Spring Hill College departments of philosophy and sociology from 1924 to 1940, and in 1930 wrote *Spring Hill's Cemetery Story.* This was his first book, and undertaken reluctantly, he says, but the subject proved so thrilling that he had finished it in six months without neglecting his classes. It was very favorably reviewed as a college history, and was reissued as *The Torch on the Hill.* Spring Hill awarded him a Litt.D. degree.

In 1934 Father Kenny wrote *The Romance of the Floridas,* a story of pioneer missionaries and explorers, including the eight Spanish Jesuits who came to Virginia in 1570 and there gave their lives for the Faith in 1571, slain by the Ajacan Algonquin Indians whom they had befriended. Following publication of this book the Diocese of Richmond erected a tablet to the eight Jesuit martyrs of Virginia at Aquia Cemetery, and at the request of Bishop Ireton, Father Kenny issued a brochure about them and a prayer for their beatification. In Professor Bolton's *Rim of Christendom* the author refers to *The Romance of the Floridas* as the authentic foundation history of Spanish-American achievement. The Florida WPA issued an edition in Braille. Popular legends disproved in Father Kenny's book are Ponce De Leon's "Fountain of Youth," which has no historic basis, and the rescue by Pocahontas of John Smith, who had fabled the story from an actual happening in the De Soto expedition ninety years previous. In 1939 Father Kenny wrote a brochure on *Pedro Martinez, S.J., Martyr of Florida,* Jesuit proto-martyr of the New World, slain on the present Fort George Island, Florida, in 1566.

Having championed the cause of Catholics persecuted in Mexico, in a pamphlet written in 1914, and an enlarged edition in 1927 entitled *Mexican Crisis: Its Causes and Consequences*—translated and circulated in France and Belgium—Father Kenny was sent to Mexico in 1934 to investigate conditions there. He managed to get through in lay apparel, interrogate everyone worth while and make wide observations which were published in the Baltimore *Catholic Review*. These articles were issued in book form under the title *No God Next Door, or Red Rule in Mexico* (1935), which had a wide distribution in Spanish, French, and Italian, as well as English, and was personally commended by Pope Pius XI.

Father Kenny was appointed on the Jesuit International Committee to combat Communism. One of the Committee of three, appointed by Bishop Gannon on the part of the Hierarchy to prepare the causes of American Martyrs for presentation to Rome, he had submitted some thirty accepted cases. He died on November 22, 1946.   C. M. N.

Right Reverend William J. Kerby   1870-1936

Recognized as one of the great outstanding authorities in this country on sociology and social service work, Monsignor Kerby was acclaimed "the pioneer of organized Catholic charities in the United States" by the National Conference of Catholic Charities when it met in Seattle, August 1936. Three Presidents selected him as a member of the Board of Charities of the District of Columbia.

William Joseph Kerby, the son of Daniel and Ellen (Rochford) Kerby, was born at Lawler, Iowa, on February 20, 1870. His high-school and college education was received at what is now Loras College, Dubuque, Iowa. From there he went to St. Francis Seminary, in Milwaukee, Wisconsin, to study for the priesthood. After his ordination on December 21, 1892, he was sent to the Catholic University of America for graduate work. Two years later he obtained the Licentiate in Theology and then returned to teach in the college at Dubuque.

In 1895 he joined the faculty of Catholic University where Dr. Thomas Bouquillon took an interest in him and urged him to enter the field of sociology. In April of that year, Father Kerby went to Europe to study advanced social legislation. He did graduate work at the Universities of Berlin, Bonn and Louvain in Belgium but did his main work at Louvain and from that institution he received his degree of Doctor of Social and Political Sciences in 1897. His book written as a partial requirement was *Le Socialisme aux Etats-Unis*. Since 1897 Dr. Kerby had taught sociology at the Catholic University, first as assistant professor and since 1906 as professor, until his death in 1936.

When Trinity College for women was founded in 1900, Dr. Kerby became one of the professors and its first chaplain. He held this latter post until his death. When in 1934 the Holy See elevated him to the rank of Domestic Prelate with the title of Right Reverend Monsignor he selected the beautiful chapel of Trinity College for his investiture.

Dr. Kerby was in demand as a Retreat Master. He was booked years ahead for the diocesan retreats to priests.

At his suggestion, in 1904, Dr. Charles P. Neill of Catholic University, arranged the first scientific exhibit of American Catholic charities for the World's Fair in St. Louis.

Dr. Kerby's writings are principally in the sociological and spiritual fields. His sociology was always imbued with the Christian spirit. He was editor of the *St. Vincent de Paul Quarterly* from 1911 to 1917. In 1913, he contributed his first article to *The American Ecclesiastical Review*. When death called its editor, Dr. Heuser, in 1927, Dr. Kerby succeeded him. Dr. Kerby was one of the most distinguished contributors to *The Catholic World*. From 1905 to 1927 he contributed about forty-five articles to that magazine. He also wrote for the *American Catholic Quarterly Review, The Dolphin, The Annals of the American Academy of Political and Social Science*.

He is the author of: *The Social Mission of Charity* (1921) and *Prophets of the Better Hope* (1922).

In honor of the late Monsignor Kerby there has been established in Washington the "William J. Kerby Foundation." Its purpose is primarily to supply funds for scholarship for competent lay students in the field of social work and to permit experts in various fields to study and devise solutions, in accordance with Catholic principles, of pressing social problems, and to become leaders in this field.

M. H.

Thomas Dickenson Kernan 1903-

Four years in Paris, in the publishing field, came to a climactic end in 1941 when Thomas Kernan found it impossible to continue his work under German domination in France. It was not until every effort had been expended, however, that he gave up trying to combat obstacles of all sorts placed in his way since the Nazi occupation of Paris in June 1940. After more than six months in *France on Berlin Time,* as he entitles his book giving an account of the conquest of France after the armistice, he returned to the United States. Publication of the French edition of *Vogue* was suspended indefinitely, though he still retains his nominal position as representative of the Condé Nast Publications in Europe. It was in this capacity and as vice-president of the French magazine *Jardins des Modes* and director of the Dorland Advertising Agency that he had had successful and interesting years in Paris. During the evacuation of the city, June to July 1940 he served as a special delegate of the American Red Cross.

Born in Roanoke, Virginia, in 1903, Thomas Kernan was educated at Georgetown University, where he was graduated with a B.A. magna cum laude, in 1922 and received his M.A., summa cum laude, the following year. In 1925 he entered the employ of Condé Nast Publications in New York City, as a member of the staff, and from 1929 to 1937 was circulation manager of *Vogue, Vanity Fair* and *House and Garden,* then becoming publisher of the French edition of *Vogue.* After his return to America from Paris, in 1941, he continued with the New York office for a year, resigning in January 1942 because of his unwillingness to do fashion work while his country was at war. Since then he has been writing articles under contract for various magazines, and he worked part time in the War Department, Washington, D. C. He has also resumed his activities with the Catholic Book Club, of which he was president from 1928 to 1937.

He is a member of Squadron A. Association, having served with the New York National Guard from 1932 to 1937. He has been a frequent contributor to periodicals, and his book which has been extremely successful, *France on Berlin Time,* gives a brief survey of causes which led to the collapse of France, an authentic account of German methods of economic conquest, and a glimpse of the possibilities of the future. He collaborated with Father John J. Considine on his book *Across A World,* a survey of the Catholic Mission field. In August 1942 he returned to unoccupied France with the American Red Cross, and in November was interned with the American diplomatic corps at Lourdes. In January 1943 the group was taken to Baden Baden, Germany, where he remained for thirteen months. He is now back in the United States. "Internment in Germany failed to hush my typewriter," he said, "and I have come out of Germany with the manuscript of a novel." The novel appeared under the title *Now With the Morning Star.*   **C. M. N.**

William Fergus Kernan   1892-

In the early part of 1942 when Americans were clamoring for an allied offensive, William Kernan published his book, *Defense Will Not Win The War*. It was hailed by all as a timely book.

Kernan, who was promoted to lieutenant colonel in the Army on August 9, 1940 and later colonel, had published his first book, *History of the 103d Field Artillery*, in 1937. His other books are: *We Can Win This War* (1943); a translation of Foch's *The Conduct of War*, and *A Primer For Peace Makers*.

Kernan's army career dates from August 9, 1917, when America entered World War I. At that time he was an instructor in medieval philosophy at Harvard, from which institution he was graduated with the degree of Master of Arts in 1916. His B.A. degree (1912) was earned at Tulane University.

Kernan was born in New Orleans, Louisiana, on June 4, 1892, the son of Fergus and Elizabeth (Nevers) Kernan. When he enlisted in the regular army, he was commissioned as a second lieutenant. He had the unique experience of being promoted to first lieutenant the same day. His first assignment was at Camp Stanley, Texas, with the 21st Field Artillery. It was only after the Armistice that he reached France—in June. In the fall of 1919, he went to Coblenz, Germany, in connection with railway transportation. Later he served with the American Relief Administration at London, England, and then spent a year in Novorossisk and Alexandrovsk, Russia, in the same capacity. On his return to the United States, he joined the 9th Field Artillery at Fort Des Moines, Iowa.

He married Xenia Babkin of St. Petersburg, Russia, on December 7, 1922. They have two children, one son and one daughter.

His only teaching experience, while in the army, has been at Ball High School, Galveston, Texas, where he was a teacher of military science and tactics from September 1939 until November 1940.

Before entering the army Colonel Kernan was an instructor in modern languages at the Georgia School of Technology, 1912 to 1914; an instructor in the history of medieval philosophy and metaphysics at Harvard University, 1915 to 1916, and an instructor in ethics at Boston University, 1915 to 1916.

In 1931 he entered the Catholic Church—a convert from Methodism.

Upon leaving the Army after 30 years of service he bought a farm at Highlands, North Carolina.

In May 1947 he was elected president of the North Carolina Catholic Laymen's Association.

                                                                    M. H.

Lady Anne Kerr 1883-1941

"Although she was a titled and highly cultured lady, she spoke the language of common people and put herself on a level with women of the working class, for whom she worked ceaselessly," said *The Glasgow Observer and Scottish Catholic Herald* of Lady Anne in its issue of Friday, the 22d of August 1941.

Lady Anne Kerr was the daughter of Major-General Lord Ralph Drury Kerr, K.C.B. (Knight Commander of the Bath) of the 7th Marquess of Lothian who married Lady Ann FitzAlan Howard, daughter of the fourth Duke of Norfolk. She was born at York in 1883 when her father was Inspector of Cavalry there. Five years of her childhood were spent in Ireland at Curragh, her father's last post before his retirement. When her father retired he settled at Dalkeith near Newbattle Abbey estate, the family home in Scotland.

After her brother succeeded to the title of Marquess of Lothian, at the death of his cousin, his sisters were given the rank and precedence of the daughters of a marquess. From then on Lady Anne took a great interest in the work of the Newbattle Abbey estate. Later she served on the committee which was formed for the purpose of handing over the abbey to the trustees in whose hands her brother placed the building and grounds when a residential college for adult education was founded there in 1937. Her principal work, however, was one of service for her less fortunate fellow-beings. For many years she was a health visitor under the Edinburgh Welfare Scheme.

Lady Anne died at an Edinburgh nursing home in August 1941. Her resting place is in St. David's Church, Dalkeith, where her grandmother, the foundress of the Church, also lies. Cecil, Marchioness of Lothian, a convert of the Oxford Movement, named the Church after the son of St. Margaret, Queen of Scotland, King David, who founded the original Newbattle Abbey.

She is the author of: *Cecil, Marchioness of Lothian* (1922); *Life of Ven. Philip Howard, Earl of Surrey and Arundel* (1926); *Bishop Hay* (1927); *Memoir of a Sister of Charity: The Life of Lady Ethelreda Fitz Alan Howard, Sister of the Duke of Norfolk* (1928); *Child's Book of Great Popes; Teresa Helena Higginson: Her Complete Life; Edith Feilding: A Sister of Charity; From Scotland's Past,* and *Sister Mary Martha Chambon of the Visitation.*

With her brother, Philip Kerr, she wrote *Growth of the British Empire* in 1911; when a new edition was published in 1937 it was retitled *Growth of the British Commonwealth.*

M. S.

Frances Parkinson Keyes 1885-

"The essential joyousness of Catholicism" in contrast to Calvinistic Protestantism was one of the main reasons which brought Frances Parkinson Keyes into the Church in 1939. For years she had been drawn to Catholicity and felt sure she would eventually embrace it, but the actual moment of decision came at the Shrine of St. Anne de Beaupré in Canada. There, one mid-winter afternoon in a church empty of pilgrims, raising her eyes to the altar she received "in one blinding flash" the conviction which transformed her life. In August 1939 she travelled to Lisieux and, in the Chapel of the Benedictines where Thérèse Martin made her First Communion, she was received into the Church by the Bishop of Bayeux and Lisieux. Sixteen years earlier Mrs. Keyes, more by accident than by design, had been in the Basilica of St. Peter's when this saintly child of Lisieux had been raised to the altar as St. Thérèse, the "Little Flower of Jesus." And two years before her conversion, in 1937, she wrote *Written In Heaven,* the story of this little saint of our own times.

Born in 1885, in the Monroe House at the University of Virginia where her father, John Henry Wheeler, was professor of Greek, Frances Parkinson received her education in private schools here and abroad. Her marriage in 1904, at the age of eighteen, to Henry Wilder Keyes, interrupted her formal education. But in 1921 George Washington University bestowed the degree of Litt.D. upon her and Bates College, Lewiston, Maine, gave her the same honor in 1934.

Mrs. Keyes' life has been a very full and colorful one. As wife of the Governor of New Hampshire and later a Washington hostess during her husband's term of office in the Senate, 1919 to 1937, she had a prominent official and social position. A wide traveller, she has been around the world, made many trips to Europe, and has visited Persia, South America and Mexico. The locale of her travels has often been woven into her works.

The literary achievements of Mrs. Keyes are many. Beginning in 1919, she wrote *The Old Gray Homestead. The Career of David Noble* in 1921 and her *Letters From a Senator's Wife* in 1924, found her with a large reading public. In 1930 came *Queen Anne's Lace* and the following year *Silver Seas and Golden Cities.* From then on, almost yearly a book came from her pen, and in 1940 the story of Bernadette of Lourdes, *The Sublime Shepherdess.* In the same year she wrote the story of her conversion, which she calls *Along a Little Way. The Grace of Guadalupe,* published in 1941, tells the touching story of Juan Diego and the apparition of Our Lady of Guadalupe, patroness of Mexico. Her book *All That Glitters* is a novel of Washington. *Crescent Carnival* is a story of New Orleans. Her book *Also the Hills,* is a novel of wartime

Washington. *The River Road* (1945) is a novel of the Louisiana sugar plantation.

Besides writing her books, Mrs. Keyes was for years a contributor to *Good Housekeeping* magazine and an intermittent contributor to other periodicals. From 1937 to 1939 she was editor of the *National Historical Magazine,* published by the D.A.R., but she resigned her membership in the Society in 1939 because of differences in policy and aims. She is a member of many patriotic societies and is frequently in demand as a lecturer.

Mrs. Keyes was widowed in 1938. She has three sons, two grandsons and a granddaughter. Her hobbies are collecting dolls, fans, costumes, and crucifixes.

In September, she was awarded the Theta Phi Alpha Siena Medal for 1946. The award is made annually to a Catholic woman who has made a distinctive contribution to Catholic life in the United States. The face of the medal bears the motto of St. Catherine of Siena: "Nothing great is ever done without much enduring," over the Theta Phi Alpha crest. C. M. N.

Mary Frances Kiely

Children's literature has always been the main interest of Mary Kiely, dating from her childhood love of books and developed later in her work as children's librarian. She was born in Boston, Massachusetts, of an old Maine family that is deeply Catholic and holds the New England tradition in letters. She grew up in Providence, Rhode Island. She won the Anthony Medal and attended the Providence Classical High School, and the Library School of the Rhode Island College of Education. In 1930 she became children's librarian in the Providence Public Library, continuing in this position until 1937 when she came to New York as editorial secretary of the Pro Parvulis Book Club. The preceding year she had assumed her duties with Pro Parvulis, a national book club for Catholic children, formed in December 1935, with headquarters in Stamford, Connecticut, later transferred to Providence and then to New York, and she has been a prime mover in its success.

Members of the club receive books selected by the editorial board and also a quarterly, *The Herald,* edited by Mary Kiely. In 1936 she compiled a *Catalog of Selected Books for Catholic Boys and Girls,* of which a first revised edition, entitled *New Worlds to Live,* was published in 1939, and a second revised edition in 1942. In 1941 she wrote *Traffic Lights: Safe Crossways into Modern Children's Literature from the Catholic Point of View,* a valuable handbook for parents, educators and librarians, that is required reading on the Columbia Library School syllabus. She is also the author of *O'Donel of Destiny,* the story of the life and adventures of Prince Red Hugh, of wide popular appeal, and on several state required reading lists. A dramatization of it for radio use was made by Robert Speaight, and is transcribed. Mary Kiely also lectures on children's literature and was made chairman of the Elementary School Section of the Catholic Library Association in 1940 and of the Committee on Juvenile Literature of the Gallery of Living Catholic Authors in 1941.

C. M. N.

Reverend Vincent Ferrer Kienberger, O.P.
1893-

Since 1926 the meditative articles for the "Hour of Adoration" which appear each month in *Emmanuel,* the organ of the Priests' Eucharistic League, have been written by Father Vincent Kienberger, O.P.

Father Vincent began his career as a writer with an article on St. Vincent Ferrer, for the *Baltimore Catholic Review* in 1914. At the request of its editor, he wrote a series on the saints. He also wrote a series on the saints for *The Sentinel of the Blessed Sacrament.* These articles as well as some for *The Missionary* attracted such attention that he was asked in April 1919 to contribute an article to *The American Ecclesiastical Review* commemorating the seven hundredth anniversary of St. Francis of Assisi. Inasmuch as he was ordained only one year, at the time, this was a signal honor.

When the Eucharistic Congress was held in Philadelphia in 1920, Father Vincent was invited to read a paper on "The Mass and the Priests' Personal Sanctification." Later the paper was printed in *The American Ecclesiastical Review.*

From August to September 1934, Father Vincent was the speaker on the Catholic Hour of the National Council of Young Men, delivering over the National Broadcasting Company radio network six talks on "Faith." These were later published by the *Sunday Visitor Press* with a foreword by His Excellency, Archbishop Joseph Schrembs, Bishop of Cleveland.

One of the consultors of the National Eucharistic Congresses, he was also one of the organizers of the First Eucharistic Congress of the Oriental Rites held in Chicago in 1941. Father Vincent has been for some time associated with the bishops and priests of the Ukrainian Rite in their work among their people.

His own personal hobby has been the fostering of the Blessed Martin Porres Centre for Catholic negro children in Chicago.

Father Vincent, born January 27, 1893, at Oconomowoc, Wisconsin, the son of Anthony George and Catherine (Mead) Kienberger, was educated at the Visitation School in Chicago and St. Anthony's Seminary in San Antonio, Texas. After his ordination in 1918, he received an M.A.

degree from Catholic University, and then in 1920 began to teach German and Church History at Providence College, Rhode Island. In 1925 he joined the Dominican Missionary band and later from 1926 to 1933 he served as the first pastor of St. Dominic's parish in Detroit, Michigan. The following year he became an assistant to the National Director of the Holy Name Society. He then worked as a missionary with the Southern band until 1935. Since 1935 he has been with the Western band of Do-minican missionaries. On May 9, 1943, he celebrated a Mass of Thanks-giving to commemorate his Silver Jubilee of ordination.

Father Vincent Kienberger's first book, *Benediction from Solitude* was published in 1926. It was a revision of Eucharistic articles that had appeared in the Providence *Visitor*. In 1927, *At Mass,* a book of instruction and explanation for children appeared. This went into seventy-five printings. *Tabernacle Talks* followed in 1928. His newest book, *The Way of the Blessed Christ* contains thirty-three meditations on the life of Christ from His birth to death and resurrection. It is a Spiritual Book Associates selection.   M. H.

John Francis Kieran   1892-

"Information Please," a weekly radio program, has made John Kieran known to a nation-wide audience for his phenomenal memory and a mind which is a storehouse of literature and innumerable interesting facts. He attributes his varied knowledge to his interest in so many things. His taste for reading was acquired in childhood, when he was fed on classics, his father being president of Hunter College and his mother a student of literature and an accomplished musician. At four John Kieran picked out melodies on the piano and has since continued his acquaintance with music. He was born in New York City in 1892 and lived for several years on a farm where he acquired a remarkable knowledge of birds. His college education comprised three years at the College of the City of New York and one year at Fordham University, where he graduated with a B.S., cum laude, in 1912.

He taught for a year and then became timekeeper on a construction gang, learning French on his subway ride to work. During college he had been a correspondent for the New York *Times,* which printed several of his stories and these won him his position as sports writer on the paper in 1915. His was the first signed column in the *Times.* These inimitable daily reviews of sports in general under the caption "Sports of the Times" were remarkable not only for their keen sports analysis but for an admixture of rare learning.

In January 1943 Mr. Kieran left the New York *Times* to write a column "One Small Voice" for the New York *Sun.* He can write on anything for this column. He has to write only 700 words a day, which is

500 less than the number of words required by the New York *Times*. The column "One Small Voice" is distributed through the Bell Syndicate. Kieran's main reason for making the change is that other duties prevent him from covering sports events. Since the New York *Times* does not want a general column, he accepted the offer of the New York *Sun*.

During the first World War he was overseas for two years. In 1919 he married Alma Boldtmann who died in 1944. They had two sons and a daughter. In 1947 he married Margaret Ford, a writer for the Boston *Herald*.

Kieran reads constantly, at all spare moments, carrying with him dog-eared copies of the classics and volumes of poetry. He memorizes at length and stores quotations and facts away for future reference, which are invaluable during moments before the microphone as a member of the Board of Experts on "Information Please."

He contributes to magazines and has written chapters in the books, *We Saw It Happen* and *America Now,* and articles on philology and natural history. In 1936 he published *The Story of the Olympic Games,* and in 1941 appeared *John Kieran's Nature Notes,* of intriguing content copiously illustrated, and *The American Sporting Scene,* a description of the world of sport with pictures by Joseph W. Golinkin.   C. M. N.

Aline Kilmer   1888-1941

While there are some people who know Mrs. Aline Kilmer only as the wife of Joyce Kilmer, the author of "Trees," she was also well known as a poet in her own right. By her husband's testimony, she was a better poet than he.

Mrs. Kilmer had several published poems before her marriage, even before she met Joyce Kilmer. These were published under her maiden name, Aline Murray. Several appeared in the *St. Nicholas Magazine* and some were reprinted by other papers. *The Landmark,* a newspaper, printed the poem "Christmas" in its December 14, 1903 issue when Aline Murray was only fifteen. Her very first poem was sold to the *St. Nicholas Magazine* when she was eleven years of age.

When her husband was alive, Mrs. Kilmer contributed an occasional poem to periodicals. After his death she began to lecture on poetry at schools and clubs. Her first book, *Candles That Burn,* was published in 1919. *Vigils* followed in 1921; *Hunting a Hair Shirt* and other essays in 1923; *The Poor King's Daughter* in 1925; *Selected Poems* in 1929; *Emmy, Nicky and Greg* in 1927; and *A Buttonwood Summer* in 1929. Her children frequently appear in her poems. Some of her poetry has a delicate humor. Most of it deals with actualities. Mr. John Bunker would describe her poetry as a sort of ironic disillusionment. Her best-known poem often quoted in sermons, speeches and lectures was written soon after Joyce, her husband, left for France, but before his death. The poem was entitled "I Shall Not Be Afraid" and was included in a volume dedicated to him. For a time she conducted, with Robert Cortes Holliday, her husband's biographer, a correspondence course for writers. Slight as the output has been, it has given Mrs. Kilmer a definitely assured place among American poets of our time. Being a true poet she waited the spontaneous inspiration. And being already laurelled, she had no need to seek new fame.

Mrs. Kilmer was born at Norfolk, Virginia, in 1888, the daughter of Kenton and Ada Foster Murray. Her father was an editor. Her mother was later married to Henry Mills Alden, who was editor of *Harper's* magazine for fifty years, and she herself wrote poetry under the name of Ada Alden.

Mrs. Kilmer was educated at Rutgers Preparatory School in New Brunswick, New Jersey, and at the Vail-Deane School, Elizabeth, New Jersey, from which she was graduated in 1907. One year later she married Joyce. It was while he was a student at Rutgers University and Aline was a student at Rutgers Preparatory School that they met. Five children were born. Two of them, Michael and Rose, died. Deborah, the daughter, is a Benedictine nun working as a laboratory technician at the Benedictine hospital at St. Cloud, Minnesota. Kenton is working at the Library of Congress as a consultant on English poetry. He is the eldest son. He also edits the poetry column for the Washington *Post* which uses a poem a day. Christopher was with the old "Fighting Sixty-Ninth," his father's old regiment, during World War II. Aline Kilmer's sister, Mrs. Stanley Greene, is a lecturer on literary subjects.

In 1913 Mr. and Mrs. Joyce Kilmer left the Episcopal church to become Catholics. Mrs. Kilmer was a great lover of birds and flowers. Her daughter has her bird book in which she tells when and where she saw a new bird and sometimes a note about its activities. At Stillwater, New Jersey, where she lived in a Revolutionary house, she had about two acres given over to raising flowers.

She died on October 1, 1941.   M. H.

Frederick Joseph Kinsman   1868-1944

At the age of fifty, after twenty-three years, from 1896 to 1919, as an Anglican clergyman, during eleven of which he was Bishop of Delaware, Frederick J. Kinsman became a Catholic. His conversion—the second time in American history that a Protestant Episcopal Bishop became a Catholic—caused a stir because of his episcopal tenure, and cost him great distress in realizing the effect it had upon his spiritual subjects, both clerical and lay, and the certainty that he would give pain to those dear to him. He came of Puritan stock, his American ancestors dating from the Mayflower in 1620, and none later than 1680. "Along every line," he wrote, "we are descended from the New England Puritans. . . . In our world the Roman Catholic Church did not exist save as a phenomenon in European travel, a bogey in history and an idiosyncrasy of Irish servants." From New England Congregationalism two generations had come into the Episcopal Church, and his immediate family settled in Ohio, where he was born, at Warren, in 1868, the son of Frederick and Mary Louisa Marvin Kinsman.

He was educated at St. Paul's School, Concord, New Hampshire, where Dr. Coit taught him the doctrine of the Real Presence, and his interest in the work of the Church was aroused. He then went to Oxford and spent three years at Keble College, stronghold of Tractarian Anglicanism, and a postgraduate year of study at Pusey House. In vacation time he wandered through the cathedral towns, absorbing Anglican tradition. He was much influenced by Gore, and at Vincent Coles' rectory he "learned what clerical life and parochial work should be." In 1896 he was ordained in the Church of England. His years at Oxford were the happiest of his life. From the university he received his A.B. in 1894, his M.A. in 1898 and an honorary D.D. in 1911. Berkeley Divinity School awarded him an honorary S.T.D. in 1908.

After ordination he was a master at St. Paul's School, Concord, until 1898, when he became rector of St. Martin's Church, New Bedford, Massachusetts. From 1901 to 1904 he was professor of church history at Berkeley Divinity School and then occupied the same chair at the General Theological Seminary, New York City. He went abroad in the summer of 1905, visiting Oxford once more and going to Constantinople, Asia Minor, Athens, Corinth and Rome. Christian archeology had a great fascination for him and on another trip in 1913 he spent much time among the ruins of Carthage.

In 1908 he became Bishop of Delaware. His consecration sealed his doom as an Anglican. "Below the surface, during almost my whole episcopate, I was increasingly troubled, passing through successive stages of disappointment, disillusion, doubt and disbelief, owing to the waning of faith in the church system which I was set in Delaware to represent. . . . Abandonment of my work did not signify in my case repudiation of Protestant principles, for these I had never held, but the loss of belief in the Catholic interpretation of the Anglican position." The toleration of doctrinal laxity also created an insuperable difficulty for him, and because he found Protestantism "drearily unchristian" he thought of resigning at the General Convention of 1913. He had "not the least touch of Roman fever" at the time, he said, but he was suffering from "Protestant chills."

Turning to reconsider the history of the English Reformation, he found Gairdner and Gasquet illuminating, and at length he came to agree with Cobbett's verdict that "the Reformation was engendered in lust, brought forth in hypocrisy and perfidy and cherished and fed by plunder, devastations and rivers of innocent English and Irish blood." Next he considered the vexed question of Anglican Orders, his thought upon the subject being marked by four stages: "(1) That they were schismatical; (2) that they were futile to guarantee some of the purposes of Orders; (3) that they were dubious; (4) for this reason and because of breaks in Catholic continuity, invalid."

His prejudices against Rome remained to be overcome, and the sum of various experiences and investigations finally dissipated them. During his first year at Oxford he had gone to the lying-in-state of Cardinal Manning at Westminster, and while there the forcible suggestion came to him that some day he might be a Roman Catholic. In 1895 he spent four weeks of Lent in Italy. The memory of this and a conversation he had with a Belgian Capuchin priest remained with him. He was interested in Loisy and Pius X's condemnation of Modernism. The influence of Catholicism on American life led him to read the books of Cardinal Gibbons. These and *The Catholic Encyclopedia* and the works of great continental scholars, especially the Benedictines, impressed him. He came to know the Visitation nuns in Wilmington and realized that they were a spiritual power-house in his diocese. From their chaplain, an Oblate Father, he learned much of the training and discipline of a Catholic priest. And finally, considering the Petrine claims, he recognized Our Lord's formal commission of St. Peter.

All this is revealed in Dr. Kinsman's spiritual autobiography, *Salve Mater*. He resigned his see to enter the Catholic Church in 1919. As he was not married it was expected that he would become a Catholic priest but he remained a layman. Other books written since his conversion are *Trent, Americanism and Catholicism* and *Reveries of a Hermit*. They are distinguished by lucid and vigorous prose. Dr. Kinsman was awarded an honorary LL.D. by Washington College, Maryland, in 1910 and by Seton Hall College, New Jersey, in 1923. He resided in Maine.

When asked for biographical data in 1939, Dr. Kinsman, after stating there was a record of his personal experiences in *Salve Mater,* continued, "My own preference, if anything at all has to be said, is that it should be reduced to lowest terms, e.g., F.J.K. was born in 1868, was received into the Church in 1919 and will probably die during the next five years." He died in 1944.   C. M. N.

Sally Bruce Kinsolving 1876-

The saying "all roads lead to Rome" is well verified in the life story of Sally Bruce Kinsolving. In her case the road led through a life passed for the greater part in the rectories of Protestant Episcopal parishes. Mrs. Kinsolving (the wife of Reverend Dr. Arthur Barksdale Kinsolving, now rector emeritus of St. Paul's Episcopal Church in Baltimore, Maryland, was born Sally Bruce in Richmond, Virginia, in 1876, the daughter of Thomas Seddon Bruce and Mary (Anderson) Bruce. Her ancestral family, the product of a plantation culture at once remote and romantic, had produced historians, novelists and biographers. A niece of Thomas Nelson Page, and a cousin of Ellen Glasgow, she was also related to the Cabells through the Bruces. The summers of girlhood she spent in her grandfather

Bruce's home and enriched her mind from its excellent library. Poetry, queen of the arts, has claimed Sally Bruce. Her husband's family, the Kinsolvings, celebrated in song, as well as story, has long been identified with the University of Virginia and the Episcopal Church. Three brothers, the Right Reverend George H. Kinsolving, Bishop of Texas, Right Reverend Lucien L. Kinsolving, missionary bishop in Brazil and Reverend Dr. Arthur Kinsolving (husband of Sally Bruce), were stanch and colorful figures in modern Episcopalian history.

During her husband's tenure of rectorship amidst the busy hum of Brooklyn and Baltimore, Mrs. Kinsolving found time while raising a family of seven children—one of them, the Reverend Arthur Lee Kinsolving, Oxon, M.A., now Episcopalian rector of Trinity Chuch, Princeton, was formerly at the head of Boston's famous Trinity Church—to take interest in contemplative and creative writing. She has also graced the lecture platforms and has inspired others in the art of poetry. One of her daughters, Anne Seddon Kinsolving, now Mrs. John Nicholas Brown, a critic and writer in her own right, first discovered her mother's hidden treasure of poems and encouragingly urged their publication. "Magdalen," "Empty House" and "Stillness," appeared in the *North American Review* in 1925 and "Spring" another poem, in the same review, in 1928. The magazine *Poetry* carried her poems "Surprise" in 1927 and "Tranquil" in 1930. She was selected to write the Phi Beta Kappa poem Founders' Day at William and Mary College, Williamsburg, Virginia, on December 5, 1935.

Founder of the Poetry Society of Maryland, she was a pioneer in bringing noted poets to Baltimore: Robert Frost, Amy Lowell, Edna St. Vincent Millay and Carl Sandburg as well as de la Mare from England, and George Russell and Padraic Colum from Ireland. She is a member of the Edgar Allan Poe Association in Maryland and Virginia and also belongs to the Phi Beta Kappa Society of the College of William and Mary. Her noted literary correspondence has been incorporated in the Enoch Pratt Free Library in Baltimore, as the "Sally Bruce Kinsolving Collection."

Her connections with Johns Hopkins University have been varied. She regards the Percy Turnbull Memorial Lectures at Johns Hopkins as a main cultural opportunity. She has also been chosen to succeed Lizette Woodworth Reese as a member of the Tudor and Stuart Club of the same university.

Though bound by ancestral and domestic ties to the Protestant religion, Mrs. Kinsolving was gradually led by her reading and meditation towards the Catholic Faith. She declares that much of her inspiration towards this end came from the perusal of the books of Hilaire Belloc which led her to attend Mass on Fisher's Island and in Baltimore when opportunity offered. Further inspiration she gathered from reading Newman's *Apologia,* St. Francis of Sales' *Spiritual Letters to Women,* in the use of offices contained in an English translation of the Benedictine Book of Day Hours known as *The Monastic Diurnal* and finally in her acquaintance with the *Saint Andrew Daily Missal.* The culmination of this trend of her mind came in 1940, when she was received into the Catholic

Church. That she has found peace and rest therein she well expresses in her poem "Benediction."

> "The autumn trees are sparse and thin
> Gold is shattered at my feet,
> And yet I have deep calm within
> Nothing of earth can now defeat:
>
> For I have felt a Presence blessed,
> Holy, miraculous, and strange,
> That brings the human heart to rest
> Beyond the powers of death and change.

In an appreciation of her, Joseph Auslander says that "Sally Bruce Kinsolving is a poet of fine perception and spiritual power, whose work belongs to the upper levels of our time." She is the author of: *Depths and Shadows* (1921); *David and Bathsheba, and Other Poems* (1922); *Gray Heather* (1930), and *Many Waters* (1942).

J. M.

Reverend Felix Marie Kirsch, O.F.M. Cap.
1884-1945

Education, and the teaching of it, as well as writings on that subject, and three volumes on *Catholic Faith* were the zealous work of the Reverend Felix M. Kirsch, O.F.M. Cap. He was born in Wheeling, West Virginia, December 31, 1884, attended St. Alphonsus' School there and St. Fidelis' Preparatory Seminary, Herman, Pennsylvania, and entered the Capuchin Order in 1902. After philosophical and theological studies at SS. Peter and Paul's Seminary, Cumberland, Maryland, he was ordained priest at Baltimore by Cardinal Gibbons in 1909. Until 1924 he taught the classics in St. Fidelis' Seminary. He was an instructor in education for two sessions of the Mount Alvernia Summer School, Pittsburgh, Pennsylvania, and for one session of the summer school of St. Bonaventure's College, New York. From 1924 to 1930 he taught homiletics, and from 1927 to 1930 also secondary education, at the Capuchin College, Washington, D.C. At the summer school of the Catholic University of America he gave courses in the philosophy of education in 1925, 1926 and 1928. From 1930 to 1931 he was on the research staff of the International College of San Lorenzo, Assisi, Italy. Since 1926 he was instructor in secondary education at Trinity College, and from 1932 until his death, professor of religious education at the Catholic University of America, Washington, D.C.

Father Kirsch had conducted diocesan teachers' institutes in Boston, Providence, Green Bay, Louisville, Baltimore, Wheeling, Trenton, and Milwaukee, and had addressed diocesan teachers' meeting in Brooklyn, Pittsburgh, and Chicago. He had also given many retreats for priests, sisters, and the laity. In 1927 he was awarded an honorary Litt.D. by St. Bonaventure College and in 1930 he received his Ph.D. from the Catholic University.

In 1924 Father Kirsch wrote *The Catholic Teacher's Companion*, which has been most popular, and from 1928 to 1935 with Sister M. Aurelia, O.S.F., he published *Practical Aids for Catholic Teachers* (3 vols.). A difficult work in the writing and very valuable is *Sex Education and Training in Chastity*. From 1935 to 1939 Father Kirsch collaborated with Sister M. Brendan, I.H.M., on the three-volume Catholic University Catechism, *Catholic Faith,* and the three teacher manuals, *Catholic Faith Explained. The Meaning of the Mass* written in collaboration with Reverend Paul Bussard, was published in 1942. *The Religion Teacher's Library,* an annotated bibliography for teachers of religion, was published in 1940. Father Kirsch translated Willmann's *The Science of Education* and Ehl's *The Spiritual Direction of Sisters.* He edited *Franciscan Studies* (1924-30), *The Classics,* in 1928, and *Franciscan Education* in 1929, and has contributed articles to various periodicals on Franciscan and educational subjects. He was a member of the National Catholic Educational Association and the Franciscan Educational Conference. He was also a director of the Third Order of Fraternity of the Catholic Evidence Guild of Washington and a member of the Confraternity of Christian Doctrine.

C. M. N.

Elizabeth Kite 1864-

For about thirty-five years, Miss Kite's forte has been a study of the historical events which have contributed to establish, between the United States and France, a friendship that has lasted to this day. Her researches have brought to light many hitherto unknown documents from the archives of Europe and America. She has been instrumental in placing in the Library of Congress photostats of documents from the French archives. In recognition of her work, the French Government awarded her the Cross of Chevalier de la Legion d'honneur.

Miss Kite ardently desires to finish a four- or five-volume set of books dealing with the Catholic principles that directed the policy of Louis XVI and his Minister of Foreign Affairs in aiding America to shake off the allegiance of Britain. Most of her work was done in the Library of Congress where for years she has had a study room.

Miss Kite was born in Philadelphia, a Quakeress, and was brought up in a conservative Quaker atmosphere. Her mother, though a Quakeress, was of French ancestry. She attended the Quaker boarding school at West-town, Chester County, and for the next six years took university courses in England, France, Germany, and Switzerland. In 1906, while studying in England, she was received into the Catholic Church, and was baptized at Notting Hill Gate, London, at the Church of St. Mary of the Angels. Eight members of her family including her father, a Quaker preacher, followed her into the Church.

She was at one time principal of a Quaker private school in Phila-delphia. Then she went to California to teach science in a private school. After that she taught botany, French, and German in a school at Nan-tucket, Massachusetts.

Miss Kite did psychological research at Vineland, New Jersey. During this period, she published *The Kallikak Family* and *A Social Survey of the People of the Pines.* She also made translations from the French, of Alfred Binet's *Development of Intelligence in Children* and Simon's *Intelligence of the Feeble-Minded.*

Until recently, Miss Kite was a member of the staff of the Villanova extension and summer school department. She is the first woman to have the degree of Doctor of Literature conferred upon her by Villanova.

During World War I, she was engaged in social welfare work around Camp Dix. Since 1932 she has been the Archivist of the American Catholic Historical Association.

Besides the works already mentioned, Miss Kite is the author of: *Beaumarchais and the War of American Independence* (2 vols. 1917); *L'Enfant and Washington* (1929); *Correspondence of General Washington and Comte De Grasse* (1931); *Lebegue Duportail, Comdt. of Engineers, 1777-1783* (1933); *Lafayette and His Companions on the Victoire* (1934); *Catholic Part in the Making of America* (1936).   M. H.

Reverend Andrew F. Klarmann (Virgil B. Fairman) 1866-1931

Father Klarmann's first book *The Crux of Pastoral Medicine* was in reality a thesis written for his M.A. degree. After its publication his clerical friends teased him about its solid logical content and dared him to write a book which would re-quire the exercise of his imagination. That very evening he drew up the outline for *The Princess of Gan-Sar,* his first novel. Thus began a writing career which never interfered with Father Klar-mann's pastoral duties. Besides his books, a large brick church, a school, a convent, and an audi-torium, completed shortly before his death, are his monuments. He left the entire parish debt-free.

Father Klarmann was born of humble and God-fearing parents,

Andrew and Barbara (Sauer) Klarmann, in the village of Oberhaid, near Bamberg, Bavaria. He received his primary education in the village school. After his Confirmation he went to Bamberg and worked as a hod carrier and mason's helper. The few pennies he earned were a big help to his family. In 1881 he and his brother Charles left Bavaria to set sail for the United States, to enter the Abbey of St. Vincent in Latrobe, Pennsylvania. The ship developed boiler trouble and most of the thirty days' voyage was made under sail. Shortly after their arrival the college was destroyed by fire and the students were dismissed to find means of support elsewhere. The two brothers worked at a nearby hospital until it was possible to resume their studies. After entering the novitiate, Andrew contracted malaria. While convalescing, he decided that his vocation was for the secular priesthood rather than the monastic. He continued his studies for the diocese of Brooklyn and was ordained on June 16, 1892. He was an assistant at All Saints Church in that city for nine years. Then he became pastor of St. Elizabeth's, Woodhaven. While in this small parish he began to write. After eight years as pastor here he was assigned to found a new parish in a rapidly growing section near his old church. For many years he served both parishes but the daughter-church, St. Thomas the Apostle, outgrew the mother church and became one of the largest parishes in Queens. After twenty years of labor in this parish Father Klarmann died, March 24, 1931.

Besides the works already mentioned, he is the author of: *Felix Aeternus* (The Christian Bride) a play; *Fool of God; King's Banner; Lark's Creek; Life in the Shadow of Death; Lost Ring*, a play; *Matrimonial Primer; Nizra* (3rd edition); *Vision* (Romantic operetta); and *St. Rita's Treasury*. He wrote under the pseudonym of Virgil B. Fairman.

M. S.

Reverend Felix Klein   1862-

America has no better friend or more ardent apologist for Franco-American friendship than Abbé Felix Klein. A Frenchman, born at Chateau-Chinon, in 1862, Abbé Klein has had a life rich in literary attainments. Unusually blessed from his earliest days with the friendship of eminent men and close participation in important happenings, his brilliant mind responded to the stimulus. At Saint Sulpice he was a disciple of the famous Sulpician, Father Hogan, well-known in America as the first rector of the Seminary of St. John in Boston. As fellow students and close friends he had men such as Archbishop de Guebriant, Superior General of the Foreign Missions, and the future Archbishop of Westminster, Cardinal Bourne. Their recreation was spent together and the young seminarians struggled to converse in each other's language in order to acquire that which was unfamiliar. While a student at the Catholic Institute of Paris, the young man was fortunate also in having such masters as Monsignor Duchesne, Albert de Lapparent, Eduard Branly and Cardinal Baudrillart. The rector of the Institute at that time was Monsignor d'Hulst, known deservedly as one of the greatest priests of France. Courses at the Sorbonne were also followed during this period. There Abbé Klein was trained in the great traditions of French literature. After receiving his university degree he was obliged to take a year of rest which he spent in Algeria, and was again fortunate in having the companionship at that time of the great Cardinal Lavigerie of whose life and great work in Africa he later wrote.

On his return to France, Abbé Klein taught at a college in his Diocese of Meaux, but Monsignor d'Hulst soon recalled him to Paris to teach literature at the Catholic Institute, the most active center of Catholic learning in France. As professor he won the sympathies of his students, ecclesiastical and lay, many of whom on leaving attained high positions in the Church or in the intellectual and political life of France. His influence was not confined to the class room; he also wrote articles for the press and stirring books such as the *Nouvelles tendances en religion at en littérature; Autour de Dilettantisme,* and *Quelques motifs d'espère.* Even this early his books reflected the renewed spirit of hope which the great encyclicals of Pope Leo XIII gave to the working man through his principles of social justice. Abbé Klein accepted these ideas enthusiastically and found a kindred spirit in Archbishop Ireland of St. Paul whose discourse in 1894 he translated and put in book form under the title of *The Church and the Century.* The Archbishop returned the compliment, saying later that the Abbé's work had given him the idea for his own book, *The Church and Modern Society,* published in 1897.

Abbé Klein in his writings tried as he himself expresses it "to throw a bridge across the profound valley which separates the Age from the Church . . . to give the Church to the Age and the Age to the Church." At this troubled period for the Church in France he endeavored to create courage and hope by recommending the attitude of the Catholic Church in America towards the State, from which it is separate, accepting the republic and democracy as advocated by Archbishop Ireland. Inevitably it met with much opposition among certain groups of French Catholics. Recognizing this, the abbé did not attempt to push his ideas, at least in that form, but tried dissemination by gentler, more subtle ways. To further this he made two trips to the United States at this time, and going home wrote two volumes about what he had seen of the benefits in liberty and progress of the Church in the American Republic. The French Academy crowned these works, *Au pays de la vie intense* and *L'Amerique de démain,* and they were translated into English. The latter in its English title, *In the Land of Strenuous Life,* he dedicated to President Theodore Roosevelt whose friendship he enjoyed.

During this American visit he made many valuable friends, among them Cardinal Gibbons, Bishop Spalding, Archbishop Ireland and Archbishop Glennon and made long visits to the Paulists in various cities. Also he lectured from coast to coast. Later, as a counterpart to this visit, he wrote of an imaginary visit of a young American to France under the title, *La Decouverte du Vieux-Monde par un Etudiant de Chicago.*

In view of his American sympathies and understanding, it was natural that when America entered World War I and troops arrived in France the Archbishop of Paris assigned Abbé Klein as chaplain to the American Field Hospital at Neuilly. General Pershing confirmed the appointment in a letter of recommendation and here he devoted himself to the care of the badly wounded French and Americans, until after the Armistice. During this time he also tried to further the cause of the Allies by writing for the *Revue des Deux Mondes, La Guerre vue d'une ambulance,* and for the *Correspondant, Les Douleurs qui espèrent.* The French Academy crowned these two volumes of touching memoirs, and they were translated into English under the title *The Diary of a French Army Chaplain* and *Hope in Suffering.*

In September 1918 Abbé Klein was sent on a mission to the United States by the French Government with Monsignor Julien, Bishop of Arras, Monsignor Baudrillart, Abbé Patrick Flynn and the Bishop of Nevers. His book, *En Amerique a la fin de la guerre* (also crowned by the French Academy), tells of this mission. Noting the signs of coolness and misunderstanding which were beginning to show, he made a plea to his compatriots for continued friendship between the two nations, not "to be obscured by vain clouds, childish difficulties, passing and individual mistakes" . . . but "to believe in the disinterestedness, the idealism, the youthful strength of enthusiasm which make the foundation of the American soul." Thus did he ever serve to the best of his powers Franco-American friendship, striving to overcome prejudice and misunderstanding. Tribute is paid to this unfailing effort on his part by the *Bulletin of the American Library in Paris.*

But transcending his great success in the various fields of his labor and the honors it brought him, Abbé Klein remained true to his first and only real ambition, that of fulfilling his priestly duty to make God known and loved and to shed the light of the Gospel on all his activities and through all his writings. His works comprise some thirty books as well as many contributions to French and American periodicals. *Jesus and His Apostles,* appearing in 1931, received a special letter of commendation from Archbishop Verdier of Paris. His little work published in 1934 in the *Spes Editions* under the title. *Nouvelles croisades de jeunes travailleurs,* brought him a letter from Cardinal Pacelli in the name of Pope Pius XI, accepting it with much satisfaction. Again in his book, *Le Dieu des Chretiens; Notre foi en la Trinite,* translated into English and published in New York as *The God of Christians; Our Faith in the Trinity,* won him commendation from Cardinal Pacelli for the Holy Father, then almost at the end of his Pontificate. And so Abbé Klein, crowned by the French Academy repeatedly, receiving the commendation of two great Popes, recognized by his ecclesiastical colleagues and the public as a great littérateur of France, yet remains primarily a priest using his gifts and wide experience in work for God and souls.

C. M. N.

Anthony Ferdinand Klinkner 1880-

Named the first Poet Laureate of Iowa in 1933 by the Poet Laureate League of America, Anthony Klinkner represents a state rich in poetry. To use his own words, he feels that "creating a poem is much like raising flowers, or painting a picture, bringing beauty into being." And with his poetic gift he brought much beauty into life through his innumerable writings. It was an old Civil War veteran, a great lover of Byron but a poor hand in penning his own thoughts, who helped to turn young Anthony Klinkner's inclination toward putting his thoughts in rhyme.

A native Iowan, he began life at Cascade in 1880, received his education there and was graduated from the Cascade High School. In 1896 he became an apprentice on the Cascade *Courier*. The following year, jointly with his brother Henry, he founded *Young America,* which ran for seven years and of which he was editor. One of the two complete bound volumes of this amateur journal is now housed in the Benjamin Franklin Memorial building in Philadelphia as part of the collection of the Edwin Hadley Smith-Fossil collection of amateur newspapers. The Fossils were a society of amateur journalists of forty years ago, counting many distinguished members.

During 1903 Mr. Klinkner was a reporter on the Dubuque *Telegraph-Herald* and in 1904 he became editor of the Farley *News,* where he remained until 1910. The year after going to Farley, he married Margaret Wallace of Cottage Hill. Two children were born to them. From 1912 to 1919, he was with the Waukegan *Republican* and Cascade *Pioneer.* Since 1909 he has been with the Catholic Printing Company and from 1926 was the state and fiction editor of the *Daily Tribune,* the only Catholic daily in the United States excepting the foreign language papers, until it ceased publication in 1942.

Mr. Klinkner has had stories, articles and verse in over two hundred newspapers and magazines here and abroad. He is represented in anthologies, and his poems have been broadcast and used for school programs. In 1921 he published *Ten Nights in Fairyland.* Then followed *My Baby,* and *Selected Poems* in 1935. He is a member of the Gallery of Living Catholic Authors, Catholic Poetry Society of America and many similar societies throughout the United States. In 1937 he was the only layman on the newspaper publicity committee for the centennial of the Archdiocese of Dubuque. Two of his most touching poems are written to the memory of his wife and mother, and he says one of the biggest thrills of his life was hearing a Father of the Divine Word, at the end of his sermon for a First Mass, read his lines, "To A Priest." Mr. Klinkner makes his home in Dubuque. **C. M. N.**

H. Edward Knoblaugh 1904-

At the outbreak of the Civil War in Spain, H. Edward Knoblaugh was stationed at Madrid as correspondent for the Associated Press. His work had brought him into close contact with conditions in that country since 1933 and he knew the leading political figures, including Largo Caballero, Manuel Azana, Gil Robles and Alcala Zamora, and also General Francisco Franco. Friendships among groups of all political persuasions gave him an insight into developments and a forewarning of the great conflict in which he had many friends on both sides. Of the war and circumstances leading up to it he gives an authentic account in his book, *Correspondent in Spain.*

Born in Peoria, Illinois, in 1904, Knoblaugh was educated there in the grade schools, Spalding Institute and St. Viator College, where he received his A.B. in 1925. He also studied at the Havana National University, Madrid University and the Instituto de Estudios Historicos in Madrid. He began his career as a journalist with the Peoria *Journal-Transcript* in 1925. From 1929 to 1937 he was with the Associated Press, serving as foreign correspondent in Cuba for two years and in Spain for four years, and in the Intercontinental News Division of the New York office. He is a member of the International Journalists' Federation.

Knoblaugh left Spain in 1937 when his life was threatened because of his faithful reporting of news from the Loyalist front. This brought him into extreme disfavor with the Loyalist foreign office and his work was frustrated by the officials. Warned that "an accident was looking for him," he secured exit from the country by obtaining passage on a British warship from Valencia to Marseilles. Upon his arrival in the United States, the NCWC News Service featured a series of his articles later used as part of the material for his book. The truth about Spain was difficult to obtain and *Correspondent in Spain* provides a vivid narrative destined to endure as history. In 1937 Knoblaugh returned to his home in Illinois to take a position with the Peoria *Journal-Transcript.* He has written articles for magazines and finds relaxation in books, woodcraft and sports.

C. M. N.

Right Reverend Ronald Arbuthnott Knox
1888-

At the age of ten, Ronald "Hard" Knox began his literary career by writing Latin and Greek epigrams. He was born in England in 1888, the fourth son of the late Right Reverend Edmund Arbuthnott Knox. Motherless at four, he and an older brother went to live for the greater part of the next three years in a country rectory under the care of his father's mother, brother, and sisters. "I cannot imagine," he was to write years later—referring to life in the parsonage when, like Aeneas of old, he terminated a course of high adventure during which he knew not even where his port lay—"I cannot imagine circumstances better calculated to impress the mind with that form of Protestant piety which the modern world half regrets, half derides, as 'old-fashioned.'" Its marks he describes to be "a strong devotion to and belief in Scripture; a careful observance of Sunday; framed texts, family prayers, and something indefinably patriarchal about the ordering of the household." His father, an Evangelical champion who subsequently became the Anglican Bishop of Manchester, always shared his confidence, and continued to be a kindly, sympathetic parent even after his son "went over" to Rome.

At twelve years of age, following a private school education, he went to Eton, to historic Eton whose pious founder was Henry VI and whose chapel was dedicated to Saint Nicholas and Saint Mary. "Thus I had a strong sense of the patronage of the Mother of God. . . . I already thought of her as having a special interest in me and a special influence on my life." Here he became a Ritualist and Tractarian. His hobbies were a great devotion to Gothic architecture and an insatiable love of the pre-Raphaelites. He contributed to the Eton *College Chronicle,* the *Cornhill,* and the *World.* Of the *Chronicle* he became editor.

Having won a Balliol Scholarship—and that a year earlier than he need have—he went up to Oxford in the fall of 1906. There he threw himself into the manifold activities of university life, becoming a leader in intellectual circles, engaging in debates—"I must have acquired an unenviable reputation for defending the indefensible"—attending the meetings of many-hued political and clerical groups, and taking honors by winning first the Hertford (1907), then the Ireland and Craven Scholarships (1909), and capturing first place in "Greats."

In 1910 he left Balliol to take up residence at Trinity, to which he had been elected fellow. In 1911 he was ordained a deacon and in 1912, a priest in the Church of England. In preparation for each of the latter steps he spent several weeks living in the monastery at Caldey, which was then Anglican.

During his student days and again later he made several visits to the Continent, to Rome, Germany, and Belgium, which last was the "country of his dreams," Bruges captivating him by the extraordinary devotion of its people—"an immeasurable contrast to the churches of one's country, half-filled on Sundays, shadowily peopled on week-days by a faithful few."

From 1912 to 1917 while carrying on his work as chaplain at Oxford, he devoted his study almost exclusively to examining into the question of authority in religion. This led him to investigate fully the claims of the Bishop of Rome and the validity of Anglican Orders. On May 28, 1915, his brother, newly-ordained, was "celebrating" for the first time. Ronald, who was present, suddenly was seized with an overpowering doubt. He had "seen a ghost," so to speak, that is, the "other side of the picture." From then on he realized more and more the impossibility of his position in the Church of England. Acting on advice given in the apprehension that his case might be simply one of "war nerves," he waited two years, finally making his submission at Farnborough Abbey in September 1917 and was received into the Catholic Church by Abbot Cabrol, O.S.B. In 1919, completing his theological studies at St. Edmund's College, he was ordained priest.

Appointed chaplain at Oxford in 1926, Father Knox, an acknowledged satirist from his early days as a young don at Trinity, continued in the literary role, devoting his pen to polemical writings chiefly, though now and then diverting his readers with a first-class detective story. In this year (1926) Father Knox scared England over the radio just as Orson Welles scared the United States in 1938; he broadcast a lurid account of a revolution in London. He visualized the blowing up of the Big Ben Tower, and had the National Gallery ablaze. In 1936 he was created a Monsignor. Three years later he resigned his Oxford chaplaincy when commissioned by the bishops of England to take up the responsible and scholarly task of preparing a new translation of the Vulgate. Monsignor Knox's work on the translation of the Douai Bible had practically immured him from the world of public affairs. To carry on this work he was offered the Shropshire home of Lord Acton at Aldenham Park, where there is a library of more than 15,000 volumes. He served on the Committee, however, which in 1940 produced the new Westminster Hymnal and he was appointed, in 1939, president of the Committee for providing Catholic books for men in the Forces.

On September 24, 1942, Monsignor Ronald Knox completed twenty-five years in the Catholic Faith.

Besides the well-known parody on Trollope's manner and style, *Barchester Pilgrimage,* he is the author of: *Some Loose Stones* (1913); *Reunion All Round* (1914); *A Spiritual Aeneid* (1918); *Memories of the Future* (1923); *The Viaduct Murder* (1925); *Other Eyes Than Ours* (1926); *The Three Taps* (1927); *The Belief of Catholics* (1927); *An Open Air Pulpit* (1928); *The Footsteps at the Lock* (1928); *The Mystery of the Kingdom* (sermons) (1928); *Essays in Satire* (1928); *On Getting There* (1929); *Difficulties* (with Arnold Lunn) (1932); *Broadcast Minds* (1932); *The Body in the Silo* (1933); *Still Dead* (1934); *Heaven and Charing Cross* (sermons) (1935); *The Holy Bible: An Abridgement and Rearrangement* (ed. 1936); *Let Dons Delight* (1939); *Captive Flames* (1940), and *Nazi and Nazarene* (1940).

In 1943 Monsignor Knox completed his translations and commentaries on the Epistles and Gospels for the liturgical year. His new translation of the *New Testament* received official approval by the Hierarchy of England and Wales. Explaining, in *The Universe,* how he went about the work, Monsignor Knox said: "I translate it onto a typewriter, trying to forget that anybody has ever translated the Bible into English before. It would give only an ugly, piebald effect if one tried to make a hash of the versions other people have done. My aim is to produce a translation in English (not colloquial but literary English) which is current to-day, and at the same time to avoid words and turns of phrase which were not equally current in the 17th century. The idea is that you want a kind of timeless English."

He was awarded the 1944 Catholic Literary Award given by the Gallery of Living Catholic Authors for his book *The New Testament . . .* newly translated from the Vulgate Latin.   S. J. M.

Reverend Andrew John Krzesinski 1884-

 Philosophy is the special field of Dr. Krzesinski, who was born near Cracow, Poland, November 20, 1884. From 1906 to 1910, he studied Thomist philosophy and theology in the theological department of the University of Cracow, and from 1919 to 1923, he studied philosophy, psychology and anthropology at the same university. There he obtained his Doctorate in Theology in 1919 and in 1923 his Doctorate in Philosophy. Then he continued his studies in Paris, London, Rome, Leipzig and Berlin. In October 1924 he was appointed Professor Agrégé of Philosophy in the University of Cracow where he remained until the outbreak of the second World War in 1939. From January 1925 to June 1928, he was a member of the faculty of the University of Warsaw, where he lectured on philosophy. As a philosopher he "represents a system of order and harmony comprising within it the external reality, the man and the whole spiritual world."

In 1936 and 1937 Dr. Krzesinski travelled extensively through Japan, China, the Malay States, Thailand (Siam), Indo-China, Burma, India, Ceylon and Tibet to study the native religions and cultures of these nations. He also visited Palestine and Egypt.

In India he held lengthy conferences and discussions with Mahatma Gandhi, Rabindranath Tagore, and Pandit Nehru, the President of the Indian National Congress. While in India he was invited to lecture at twenty universities and in some Buddhist scientific institutions.

In October 1939 he came to the United States. During the summer session of 1942, he became visiting professor at Villanova College, Villanova, Pennsylvania. Later he was visiting professor of Philosophy in Laval University and he is now teaching philosophy at Montreal University, in Canada.

Professor Krzesinski is a member of various philosophical and scientific societies in Poland and the United States of America, a member of the Polish Institute of Arts and Sciences and in 1942 he was elected a member of the Gallery of Living Catholic Authors.

He is the author of the following books: *Is Modern Culture Doomed?* (1942—2nd ed. 1944); *The Church and National Cultures (The Race and Nation,* 2 vols., 1944); *The Dangers of the Nazi Culture* (1944); *Heroic Poland* (1944); *Bleeding Poland and Our Conscience* (1944); *Christianity's Problem in the Far East* (1944) (English and French); *The Future of Western Culture* (1944); *Poland's Culture and its Character* (1944); *National Cultures: Nazism and the Church* (1945), *Poland's Rights to Justice* (1946).   S. U.

Erik Maria Ritter von Kuehnelt-Leddihn
1909-

Impressed by the horrors of the world today and the abyss of misery towards which materialism tends, Erik von Kuehnelt-Leddihn lends his pen to vivid portrayal of present conditions and portents of the future. He was born in Tobelbad, Styria, in 1909, of Austrian parents, and his childhood was shadowed by World War I. His father became a pioneer in X-ray in Vienna and a victim of it, dying as the result of his experiments. At ten, Erik traveled to Denmark, and later visited England. He studied at the Theresianic Academy of Vienna, and while there was Vienna correspondent of the London *Spectator,* 1926 to 1927, thus beginning journalism at a very early age. Continuing his studies at the University of Budapest, he received his Ph.D. there in 1937. Meanwhile he had travelled throughout Europe and Western Asia, and twice visited Russia, legally and illegally, where he was correspondent for some Hungarian publications. In Finland he spent three summers in the Petsamo region of Lapland, and in England he taught for a year at Beaumont College. In 1937 he came to the United States as professor in the Graduate School of Georgetown University. He married Countess Christiane Goess, and they were both in Europe when war was declared in 1939. By devious routes they separately found their way to the United States and are now residing here. Kuehnelt-Leddihn has lectured throughout the country and since 1943 has been teaching at Chestnut Hill College in Philadelphia, Pennsylvania.

His first book, *Die Anderen* (The Others), was published in Vienna, in 1931, under the pseudonym of Tomislav Vitezovic. His *Gates of Hell* in the original German, was given second prize as the best novel on Bolshevism, in an international competition conducted by the Academy of Social Education in Paris in 1936. *Gates of Hell* has been translated into English, Dutch, Polish, Hungarian, Italian and Spanish. A second book on Russia, *Moscow 1979*, written in English in collaboration with his wife, is a fantasy of the future based on wide observation of trends of the present. It depicts the hideous results of the subservience of the individual to the masses, the "utilization" of man, in a Europe under Soviet dominion, with Satan astride the world. *Night Over the East*, published in this country, appeared in 1936. He also wrote, *Murder in Blue Light.*

C. M. N.

Reverend John LaFarge, S.J.   1880-

"Most people become writers through trying to become writers and making great effort in that direction. Personally, I have never felt inclined that way. My whole life has been simply that of the missionary" writes the tall, stooped, soft-spoken Father LaFarge, S.J. He is the son of the distinguished American mural painter, John LaFarge, and comes of a gifted family, his brother Bancel being a painter, and another brother, Christopher Grant, an architect. A long line of distinguished American ancestors is also his heritage, these include Benjamin Franklin and Commodore Oliver Hazard Perry of Lake Erie fame. His mother was Margaret Mason (Perry) LaFarge. John LaFarge was born at Newport, Rhode Island, in 1880. He attended Harvard University, where he received his A.B. in 1901. The next four years were spent at the University of Innsbruck, Austria, and there in 1905 he was ordained by the Prince-Bishop of Brixen.

On his return to the United States, he entered the Society of Jesus at Poughkeepsie on November 12, 1905, and later taught at Canisius College, Buffalo, and Loyola College, Baltimore. For a year, from 1910 to 1911, Father LaFarge was chaplain at the hospital and penal institutions on Welfare Island, New York City. The following fifteen years, spent in educational and pastoral work in the old Jesuit missions in Southern Maryland, were among the happiest of his life and there he became familiar with social problems, rural and racial. The missionary's life and trials appeal to him most but, as he expresses it, "Superiors pulled me out of the mission life and launched me on the magazine *America*." And there, as associate editor, he remained until July 1942 when he was made executive editor.

His first literary venture was at the early age of ten, when with two companions he started a monthly. While at Cambridge he contributed to and edited the *Harvard Monthly*. As a priest he has written for many periodicals and published three books, *The Jesuits in Modern Times*, and ten years later, in 1937, *Interracial Justice. The Race Question and the Negro* appeared in 1943. "Unfortunately, for my peace, however, I have always had considerable facility in writing" he wrote in 1939. He writes now, he says, because there is so much to say, so many to say it to. In the matter of rural problems and interracial relations he has devoted much time to study and writing and has worked constantly for their improvement. He is in demand as a lecturer and retreat master.

He has made a hobby of languages. He reads Russian, Slovenian, Bulgarian, Polish, Czech and Slovak with equal facility. And for those who have ambition to write he gives this advice: "I think it is most important to have one thing, naturally, something human, concerning which you have done much spade work in the matter, and study, and can feel very sure of. Without that there is always a certain vagueness and some floundering."

He is chaplain of the Catholic Interracial Council and chaplain of the Liturgical Arts Society, the liaison body between Catholic craftsmen and the Church, also first vice-president of the National Catholic Rural Life Conference and has affiliation with many other associations and societies.   D. D.

Reverend Thomas Aquinas Lahey, C.S.C. 1886-

A weekly page, "Bits of Life," is the regular contribution to the *Ave Maria* by the Reverend Thomas Aquinas Lahey, C.S.C., associate editor of the magazine. He was born in Michigan City, Indiana, in 1886, and received his Litt.B. from the University of Notre Dame in 1911. Entering the Congregation of the Holy Cross, he was ordained a priest in 1915, and the same year received his S.T.B. from the Catholic University of America, Washington, D.C. Father Lahey took his M.A. at Notre Dame in 1918 and his Ph.D. there in 1923, after graduate studies at the New York University School of Salesmanship in the summer of 1921 and at Columbia University in 1922.

For four years he was a member of the faculty of the University of Notre Dame, from 1924 to 1928, and then became vice-president of the University of Portland, returning to his alma mater as professor of advertising in 1929. He has since held that post, and has also served as associate editor on *Ave Maria*. In 1924 he published a book on *The Morals of Newspaper Making*. In 1935 he wrote *Twisted Trails* and in 1937 *King of the Pygmies. God's Heroes* and *God's Wonder-World* are part of a prospective series for children. Father Lahey has also written a number of pamphlets, among them *Religion and Business; Between Acts* and *A Death Cell Vigil.*

C. M. N.

Raymond E. F. Larsson   1901-

While still a high school student in Green Bay, Wisconsin, Raymond Larsson secured a job on the Green Bay *Press-Gazette.* The job consisted chiefly in running a daily column. Once, when he satirized certain irregularities at the school in his column, too thinly veiling the names of those involved, he was temporarily expelled. He left school in his senior year to work for a newspaper in Appleton, Wisconsin. Subsequently he worked on newspapers in Marquette, Michigan; Clarksburg, West Virginia; Milwaukee, Wisconsin; Chicago, Illinois; Boston, Massachusetts, and New York City. He edited a weekly newspaper at Clearwater, Florida.

His urge to write poetry came while he was reading poems in a magazine of poetry and was unimpressed by the poems. Putting down the magazine, he "went to my desk, wrote five poems, posted them to the magazine. They were accepted, printed and fortunately long since forgotten." From 1923 until its suspension in 1928, he contributed poems to *The Dial.*

He went to France in 1926, where he "lived through trials and vicissitudes, poverty and a meagre periodic affluence." After brief visits to England and Belgium, he returned to America in 1928. Some months after his return, his first book *O City, Cities!* was published. Much of this book had been put in order on the voyage to the United States. In 1929 he became an advertising manager for a firm selling the most expensive chocolates in the world. When the firm dissolved, Mr. Larsson's impoverishment began anew.

Under the direction of the Jesuit and Paulist Fathers, he entered the Catholic Church in 1932. His conversion began in 1930 while working on a long and never-completed poem, "The Various Tree." Work on the Green Bay *Press-Gazette,* the California *Pacific Weekly* and life on a plantation in Georgia followed. Back in New York, he published *Selected Poems* and *Weep and Prepare.* In 1941 Coward-McCann published his collection of prayers of the Saints, *Saints At Prayer,* which he began to compile in consequence of his own devotions. With August Derleth he published in 1937 an anthology of verse and poems by residents and natives of Wisconsin under the title *Poetry Out of Wisconsin.* Among his other publications is *Wherefore: Peace.* A long litany poem "Perfect Vessel" was published in 1941.

Mr. Larsson was formerly editor of *Lirica,* the Italian review suspended during the World War II. Among the magazines he has contributed to are: *The Dial, The Criterion,* (London) *Transition,* (Paris) *Augustea,* (Rome) *The Bookman, The Commonweal, The New Republic, The Nation, Prairie,* and several others.

M. H.

Reverend Francis Xavier Lasance 1860-1946

After but seven years of zealous labors following his ordination, Father Francis Xavier Lasance in 1890 was forced by ill health to retire from active ministry. He accepted an appointment the following year as chaplain to the Sisters of Notre Dame of Namur at Our Lady's Summit, East Walnut Hills, Cincinnati, Ohio, where he spent the greater part of his life writing many devotional books. This retirement has been called a dispensation of Providence for had Father Lasance been engaged in active pastoral work there would not have been time for his valuable literary output.

Born in Cincinnati, Ohio, in 1860, he was educated by the Brothers of Mary, at St. Mary's Parochial School there. Following his graduation he went to the Jesuit Fathers at St. Xavier's College in the same city. When the call to the priesthood came he took his studies at St. Meinrad's Abbey, Indiana, under the Benedictines. Ordained in 1883 by Archbishop Elder in St. Peter's Cathedral, Cincinnati, he served several parishes in the archdiocese for the next seven years. At Monroe, his last appointment, the Church of Our Lady of Dolors was built under his supervision.

When his always frail health definitely broke he went to Europe where he travelled extensively seeking aid, natural and supernatural, at spas and shrines, including a visit to the white Madonna of the Pyrenees, Our Lady of Lourdes. But returning home his condition was unchanged, so he accepted it as God's will and bore the cross of suffering thereafter. His poor health did not deter what was to be his life's work, the apostolate of the pen. Father Finn, contemporary Jesuit writer, said of him that he had shown how "happiness and holiness are brought together." Through his writings he has shown the sunlight of understanding on earthly darkness and discouragement, often utilizing the thoughts of the greatest minds to interpret it. He might well be called an apostle of God's benignity.

Father Lasance has a long list of books to his credit, all devotional: little treatises on the Holy Eucharist as *Visits to Jesus in the Tabernacle,* devotions for Mass and devotions to the Sacred Heart, Our Blessed Mother and the saints. Perhaps his best-known work is *My Prayer Book.* He also compiled missals in several forms, for daily use, for Sundays and holydays and for children. He wrote, too, for religious as well as for the young. Laboring untiringly with his pen he worked through a long life to help souls, to encourage the timid and to show the way to greater perfection and love of God. In May 1927 the Holy Father Pope Pius XI in recognition of his devotional works bestowed on him his special blessing. He died December 11, 1946. **D. D.**

Reverend Cuthbert Charles Lattey, S.J. 1877-

Known and recognized as one of the greatest living authorities on St. Paul, Father Cuthbert Lattey, S.J., has summed up in his book *Paul* (1939), thirty years' study of the doctrine and theology contained in the Pauline epistles. He calls it his "most characteristic work," embodying the favorite study of his priestly years. It is the keynote to the main work of his life, Holy Scripture and Fundamental Theology (Apologetics).

Mainly of Scottish ancestry, Cuthbert Charles Lattey was born in London in 1877, his great height of six feet, three-and-a-half inches, showing his Highland blood. One of his earliest influences was a pious French nurse, from whom he learned French and absorbed piety almost before he could speak English. Later he had considerable contact at the Jesuit novitiate at Canterbury with the French Fathers of the Society, and France, he feels, still leads the modern world in the teaching of sanctity and learning through her predominance of saints and scholars.

Sensitive to inspiration, the young boy, Cuthbert, responded to the beauty of his preparatory school, St. John's, Beaumont, near Windsor, and recognized it as an important beginning for his life. This sensitiveness of spirit he carried into the Jesuit novitiate which he entered in 1894. There he was impressed with the realization of being among the first in the Society trained to go to Oxford from the noviceship. Campion Hall was opened in 1896, only a year after permission had been given for Catholics to reestablish themselves at the university. At Oxford he took a first class in Classical Moderations and a first in the final School of Litterae Humaniores. Finally a fifth year of postgraduate work prepared him for his scholarly destiny.

Father Lattey was ordained in 1908. He then taught Holy Scripture at St. Beuno's College, 1911 to 1926, and after that Scripture and Fundamental Theology at Heythrop in Oxfordshire. In conjunction with Father Keating, S.J., his former master at Beaumont, he began, in 1912, the Westminster Version of the Holy Scriptures. The New Testament has been completed in four volumes, and a few parts of the Old Testament have appeared. In 1915 Father Lattey edited the pulpit edition of the Epistles and Gospels for Sundays and Festivals. He was the most active factor in founding, 1919 to 1920, the Catholic Conference of Ecclesiastical Studies, composed of Catholic professors of philosophy and theology—it has been held yearly since—and for a long time he served on the committee. He helped to organize the Cambridge National Bible Congress of 1921, to commemorate the fifteenth centenary of St. Jerome in accordance with the wish of Pope Pius XI. Out of this grew the Cambridge Summer School of Catholic Studies, for the continuance of which his labors have been of much service. Eighteen volumes of lectures, delivered there since 1921, have been published, including Father Lattey's papers; most have been edited by him.

Besides editing and collaborating in the writing of many books, he has published several himself: *Back to Christ; Thy Love and Thy Grace,* which is a retreat manual; *First Notions of Holy Writ; Readings in First Corinthians: Paul,* and *Back to the Bible* (1945). Father Lattey has also written many pamphlets, chiefly for the Catholic Truth Society, and has contributed articles to many periodicals, mostly on biblical subjects.

For years this learned Jesuit has been a member of the undenominational Oxford Society of Historical Theology, before which he read a paper, and he has long served on the committee. He is also a member of the undenominational Society for Old Testament Study, composed of the outstanding scholars of Great Britain and including a few Catholics, has long served on the committee and has read two papers.   D. D.

Clifford J. Laube 1891-

On December 8, 1937, there was established a small printshop and bindery in the cellar of a Richmond Hill, New York, home. Its owner, Clifford James Laube, named it The Monastine Press in honor of St. Augustine, his patron saint, and Augustine's mother, St. Monica. Here Mr. Laube hand-set, illustrated and bound his first book, which he published on September 1, 1938, in an edition of one thousand copies, under the title *Crags.*

Father Leonard Feeney, writing in *America,* said of the volume: "This book unquestionably would win the Pulitzer Prize if the Pulitzer Committee had any sense of sympathy or discovery." Christopher Morley found in Mr. Laube's workmanship "a sure hand for the strange and sudden phrase." John Kieran wrote: "Your feat of writing, printing, binding a book has me standing in awe before you." The magazine *Coronet* commented: "Clifford J. Laube is unique and envied among poets in a world which has thousands of them." Sister Madeleva said: "The craftsmanship of Mr. Laube's book is as unobtrusive and sure as beauty itself."

Clifford Laube was born on August 28, 1891, at Telluride, Colorado, the fifth of eight children of Adolph and Alma (James) Laube. Living at St. Vincent's Orphanage in Denver from his sixth to his twelfth year, he breathed the atmosphere of Catholic life at its purest and best. From there he went to live at Rico, Colorado, where he obtained a position as a printer's apprentice on the Rico *News.*

Then came an opportunity to go to high school at Durango, Colorado. The four-year course was completed in three years. Returning to Rico, he assisted his father in establishing the weekly Rico *Item* in 1907. In 1916, when only twenty-five years of age, he was elected to the Colorado state legislature.

With the salary earned as legislator he was able to take a trip to Los Angeles and there marry Miss Dora E. Weber, an Ohio girl who taught school first at Rico and then at Los Angeles. Later he became statehouse reporter for the Denver *Times* and the *Rocky Mountain News*. When his father died in 1919, Clifford sold the *Item* and two years later joined the staff of the New York *Daily News* (tabloid). He served that paper as assistant city editor and Brooklyn editor until 1929, then moved to a position on the New York *Times,* where he soon became suburban editor. Since 1942 he has been day telegraph editor, a post from which he daily directs the handling of approximately 400,000 words of national news dispatches.

Mr. Laube is one of the founders, and was, until 1945, associate editor, of *Spirit,* the national Catholic poetry magazine. After ten years of service, he resigned his *Spirit* editorship in order to devote himself more freely to creative writing. Besides contributing poetry and reviews to Catholic periodicals, he has done important textbook work, notably as a collaborator for the Committee on Affiliation of the Catholic University of America for the Revision of English Curricula. He is a lecturer in journalism at Georgian Court College, Lakewood, New Jersey, and at Fordham University, New York.
M. H.

Maura Laverty

In his review of Maura Laverty's book *Touched by the Thorn* (1943), Thomas Sugrue asserts: "Maura Laverty has all the equipment to make a first-rate novelist. Her prose is delicate, well-pruned and clear. Her description of the Irish countryside through the seasons, of the individual details of woods and meadows, of Irish cooking and Irish kitchen life, are suberb and moving. Her characters come easily to life. They move, without awkwardness through situations which at times are quite unlikely. With a more exciting and believable plot—and with a purpose beyond the exposition of sadism, selfishness and ignorance—this young writer could show her heels to all but the best of the pack." *Touched by the Thorn* appeared in England as *Alone We Embark*. When it was published it became an immediate success. This was followed by the novel *Never No More* which is partly autobiographical. In it she relates some of her early life.

Maura Laverty lives in Dublin. She is married to a journalist and has two daughters. Before her marriage she spent some years in Spain where she worked as secretary for Princess Bibesco and did some foreign correspondence for a bank and had various newspaper jobs on *El Debate*. On this experience she drew when her third book, *No More Than Human* (1944) was written. It contains the episodes of Delia Scully whose earlier life is related in *Never No More*. Her fourth book *Gold of Glanaree* (1945) is for children.

Besides editing a woman's magazine and contributing plays, stories, interviews and cookery talks to Irish radio programs, Maura Laverty is running a weekly radio feature for women.   M. H.

Emmet Lavery   1902-

The theatre, and especially the Catholic theatre, is the richer for the work of Emmet Lavery. As a dramatist he has had the unique experience of receiving an instant hearing for plays that have a religious background, and in 1937 he organized, with the Reverend Urban Nagle, O.P., the Catholic Theatre Conference. Born in Poughkeepsie, New York, in 1902, the son of Katherine T. (Gilmartin) and James A. Lavery, widely known editor and lecturer, and first president of the New York State Federation of Labor, he was educated by the Marist Brothers in their grade school there and in the Poughkeepsie High School, from which he graduated at the age of fifteen. He immediately entered newspaper work as a reporter and then took up the study of law at Fordham University, where he received his LL.B. in 1924, and in 1925 he was admitted to practice before the Bar of the State of New York. In that same year he married Genevieve Drislane; they have a son and a daughter.

From 1925 to 1935 Emmet Lavery was city editor of the Poughkeepsie *Sunday Courier,* and from 1929 to 1933 he also served as president of the Board of Aldermen in that city. He entered upon his dramatic career via the Experimental Theatre of Vassar, as an actor in some of Hallie Flanagan's productions, and also through the summer theatres in the neighborhood of Poughkeepsie. In 1934 he went to Broadway with *The First Legion,* a drama of the Jesuits, produced by Bert Lytell. It ran for three months in New York and six months on the road, and has been translated into ten languages and played abroad in Rome, Milan, Prague, Zurich, Budapest, Vienna, London, Paris (250 performances at the Vieux Colombier, 1938-1939), and Latin America.

In 1935 he went to Hollywood as a scenario writer, remaining until 1937 when he issued the first call for the Catholic Theatre Conference at Chicago and presided as its first temporary chairman. In the Conference he sees the great bridge between the professional and non-professional theatre, with many Catholic drama groups doing the same good plays the same years, and thus building up a theatre at once national and local. In the fall of 1937 he became identified with the Federal Theatre at the invitation of Hallie Flanagan. He supervised the Federal Theatre's Catholic Drama Survey, the first inventory of its kind ever undertaken in the theatre, and was director of its National Service Bureau until the Federal Theatre Project was dissolved. He then became associated, on a grant from the Rockefeller Foundation, with the Theatre Research Project at Vassar College, to classify and correlate the records of the Federal Theatre. He also conducted drama seminars at Fordham University and lectured extensively on the theatre.

While he was in Hollywood his play, *Brief Music,* or *Daisy Chain,* dealing with seven girls in three years of life at Vassar, was tried out at the Pasadena Playhouse, in the summer of 1936. *Monsignor's Hour,* a short peace play, was first published by *Stage* in 1935. It was produced with great success in Vienna in 1936 and in Budapest in 1937. Its first Catholic presentation in America was at the opening session of the Catholic Theatre Conference, at the Loyola Community Theatre, Chicago. Since then Lavery has published: *Second Spring,* a play on Cardinal Newman, produced by Boston College in 1939; *Brother Petroc's Return,* a dramatization of the novel by S.M.C., the first play to have its premiere within seminary walls in America, having been produced at Mundelein Seminary, Chicago, in 1938; *Kamiano,* an adaptation of a play on Damien by Grace Murphy, produced by the Catholic Theatre Guild of Pittsburgh in 1939; produced but not as yet published are *Pie in the Sky,* based on the Catholic perspective in labor problems; and *Tarquin,* the first contemporary Catholic opera, the story of dictator vs. saint-in-the-making, for which Ernst Krenek composed the music, and Emmet Lavery played the lead at its premiere at Vassar College in May, 1941.

In 1940, he edited *Theatre for Tomorrow,* in which he gives a special survey of the Catholic tradition in drama and includes three plays that "bring into focus the full sweep of the resurgence of spiritual drama in the theatre." These are historical dramas on Damien, Savonarola, and Campion, of the first of which he is the author. In the theatre, Lavery sees "an art form historically Catholic, distinctively Catholic, in which we and the world are well met." He believes the Catholic theatre is "a life-giving force which has no part with mediocrity," animating "the culture of the world for some thirteen centuries at least," the forerunner of the Catholic revival. As to its influence for good, he says: "Even if the world does not change its way of life after pretending for two hours that our way of life is its way, isn't it important that the world learn to like our way of life?" In the summer of 1941, Emmet Lavery was elected president of the National Catholic Theatre Conference and was also named drama consultant for the National Catholic Community Service.

RKO Studios called Mr. Lavery back to Hollywood in 1941 and while at RKO he adapted Gregor Ziemer's *Education for Death* for production by Edward A. Golden under the title *Hitler's Children.* After winding up a year's contract with RKO in the fall of 1942. Mr. Lavery returned East with his family and took up residence at Smith College, Northampton, Massachusetts, as resident playwright, on a grant from the Rockefeller

Foundation. While at Smith College, Mr. Lavery revised *Murder in a Nunnery,* which he had adapted from the novel by Eric Shepherd, and began work on a new play about Justice Holmes, titled *The Magnificent Yankee.*

RKO Studios called Mr. Lavery back to Hollywood once more in the spring of 1942 and this time he adapted for the screen James R. Young's *Behind the Rising Sun,* a film that scored a success almost equal to that of *Hitler's Children.* He remained under contract to RKO until the spring of 1943 when he became affiliated with Walter Wanger (Universal), to whom he is presently under contract.

In the spring of 1944 Pasadena Playhouse revived *Murder in a Nunnery,* which was first tried out by the Catholic Theatre Guild of Los Angeles in 1942, and the same season saw the play published by Samuel French *The Magnificent Yankee,* which in 1946 was produced on Broadway.

Mr. Lavery, who now makes his home in Los Angeles, is president of the Screen Writers Guild.   C. M. N.

Mary Lavin (Mrs. William Walsh) 1912-

Born in June, 1912, in East Walpole, Massachusetts, U.S.A., the daughter of Thomas Lavin and Nora (Mahon) Lavin, Mary Lavin, as a child, made several trips to Ireland with her parents, and when about ten years old stayed in Ireland. "I was just old enough," she writes, "to be powerfully impressed with the influences of a new country, but still young enough to feel a fierce childish resentment for the loss of what was always home—New England. I suffered a child's nostalgia for tangible things—for the white violets in the woods, the sleigh rides in winter, the croaking of the bull-frogs at nights in the swamps. I remember how for years the sight of the Atlantic in Galway made my heart ache, and how, above all things I loved to stand barefoot at the window of my room on moonlit nights because something of the black and white quality of the moonlight made it possible for me to pretend that I was looking out over a black and white landscape of pines under snow."

Mary Lavin was educated in the Loreto Convent in Dublin and afterwards at the National University, also in Dublin. Her B.A. degree was followed later by a First Honors M.A. degree, with a thesis on Jane Austen. She did some postgraduate work, including a long thesis on Virginia Woolf which she abandoned near its point of completion to do a short story which was published in the *Dublin Magazine.* "Until 1938," she writes, "I never thought of writing. I was perhaps too busy reading, or as my father used to put it 'too busy idling' but after returning from a four months' visit to Boston in that year, I suddenly began to write.

Seumas O'Sullivan published a story in the *Dublin Magazine*. Lord Dunsany read it, and became from then on my friend and adviser. It was he who first sent my work to the editor of the *Atlantic Monthly*." Thereafter she wrote steadily. Of her, Lord Dunsany says: "To me she seems reminiscent of the Russians more than any other school of writers, and, with the exception of the gigantic Tolstoy, her searching insight into the human heart and vivid appreciation of the beauty of the fields are worthy in my opinion to be mentioned beside their work."

"The second great influence of my life," Mary Lavin says—her first was Ireland by adoption—was when "in 1926 my father undertook to look after an estate in County Meath which was bought by Charles Sumner Bird of East Walpole, Massachusetts. Bective House, on the banks of the Boyne, looking out across the plains of Tara Hill, is one of the loveliest places in Ireland. In this lovely, lonely old desmesne I spent . . . many of the hours that should have been spent in the classroom and lecture hall, and yet I owe no greater debt to either than the debt I owe to the woodland paths and river bank at Bective. Even to the empty rooms and passageway of the house where I wandered on wet days I owe those stirrings of the heart that grow rarer with the years. Here I was always alone and always glad to be alone, wandering with idleness and aimlessness unaware then, but grateful now, to think that every leaf and bud and bird, was forming those images that the heart can never forget."

Tales From Bective Bridge, published in 1942 is her first book. It contains ten short stories about Ireland and its people. This book won for her the James Tait Black Memorial prize. Her other books are *The Long Ago* and *The House In Clewe Street*. The latter is a book of 529 pages, her first novel and tells the story of three generations of an Irish family. The book is moral in its demonstration of sin and punishment.

Since 1942 Mary Lavin has been married to William Walsh, a lawyer in Dublin. They live in Meath and have one daughter, Mary.   M. H.

Pat Lawlor   1893-

The Australian journalist and publisher's representative, Pat Lawlor, author of *Confessions of a Journalist*, names among his proud achievements as editor of the *New Zealand Artists' Manual* that his magazine was probably the first periodical to introduce Eileen Duggan to an international audience. He is the founder of the Catholic Writers' Movement in New Zealand, and founded the New Zealand Ex Libris Society in 1929. He contributes to many Catholic journals under the nom de plume "Christopher Penn."

Born in Wellington, New Zealand, in 1893, of Irish Catholic parents, he was educated at the Marist Brothers School and St. Patrick's College in Wellington.

His best known books are: *Maori Tales; The Poetry of Dick Harris; Templemore; Wellington in Verse and Picture; The Last First Friday and Other Poems,* and *The Mystery of Maata. Templemore* is a novel of Irish colonial life.

Pat Lawlor is one of the best known journalists of Australia and New Zealand. His *Maori Tales* series (three books) sold to the extent of nearly 40,000 copies. His last book *Confessions of a Journalist* covers the whole gamut of a journalistic endeavor in his country over the last quarter of a century.

His journalistic career started young when as a lad in knickers he got his first job on the Wellington *Post;* later he joined the Wellington *Dominion* and later still the provincial press, *The Hawke's Bay Herald.*

In 1917 he joined the Defence Stores but being ineligible for active service he went back to journalism. For a time he was the youngest man in the Parliamentary Press Gallery. For two years he was sub-editor of New Zealand *Truth* and then went on to the Sydney *Daily Telegraph.* His subsequent connection with the *New Century Press* lasted for ten years.

For the past thirteen years Pat Lawlor has moved between the two countries, New Zealand and Australia. In 1923 he inaugurated the New Zealand edition of *Aussie* which gave New Zealand's greatest creative writers and artists their first real outlet in that country; in 1926 he published the first number of the *New Zealand Artists' Manual.* He formed, at the request of London headquarters, the New Zealand branch of the world famous P.E.N.

He is a representative of the *Sydney Bulletin* and also commercial representative of the *New Zealand Railways Magazine.*

A book collector in recreation hours, Mr. Lawlor has one of the finest private libraries in New Zealand.

E. F.

Reverend Francis Peter Le Buffe, S.J.   1885-

Known to thousands of readers as the author of *My Changeless Friend,* Father Francis P. Le Buffe, S.J., began this pocket-edition series of twenty-six volumes in 1915 after a physical breakdown following ordination, and traces his career as a writer directly to this illness, "one of the greatest graces of my life." He was born in Charleston, South Carolina, in 1885, and educated at Gonzaga College, Washington, D.C., 1897-1901, after which he entered the Society of Jesus at Frederick, Maryland. He took his philosophy and theology studies at Woodstock College, where he received his M.A., and was ordained there in 1915, taking his final vows in 1920. His illness lasted three years, but in spite of it he has led a most active life.

From 1920 to 1922 Father Le Buffe was regent of the Fordham University School of Law. It was at Fordham in 1922 that he received his Ph.D. After one year as associate editor of *America,* he returned to Fordham as dean of the School of Social Service and remained there from 1923 to 1926. In 1926 he founded the Eastern Jesuit Philosophical Association and became business manager of *America* and managing editor of *Thought,* holding the first post until 1938 and the latter till 1939. He was also science editor for *Thought* from 1933 to 1937. In 1936 he founded the Jesuit Anthropological Association, and in 1939 he was elected president of the Catholic Anthropological Conference, of which he had been director from 1933 to 1936, and vice-president from 1936 to 1938. From 1926 to 1938 he was moderator of the New York Circle of the International Federation of Catholic Alumnae. In 1928 he was chosen moderator of the Catholic Evidence Guild of New York and in 1936 moderator of the Alumnae Catholic Evidence Guild of New York, and is still moderator of both Guilds which were made into one in 1939. From 1936 to 1938 he was director of the Catholic Press Association. Since 1932 he has been Eastern Secretary of Sodalities and at present devotes all his time to Sodality work as Secretary for Sodalities in the Middle Atlantic States, this association and work with the Catholic youth being greatly to his liking.

As a young Jesuit, he loathed writing and determined never to set pen to paper. He blames his loathing on the artificial, mechanical way composition and rhetoric were taught. He was suddenly roused one day by the words of the rector of Woodstock College, Father Anthony J. Maas, S.J., saying to the Jesuit seminarians: "If you want to write, take your pen in hand and write, write, write!" Thereupon he "was struck down as Paul on the Damascan road—and began writing." Besides *My Changeless Friend,* which has sold over 800,000 copies, Father Le Buffe has written the five-volume series, *Let Us Pray,* beginning in 1930, and the three-volume series, *As It Is Written,* beginning in 1931, both of which have sold many thousands of copies. In 1927 he wrote an interpretation of *The Hound of Heaven,* and in 1938 he was co-author, with J. V. Hayes, of *Jurisprudence.* He is also the author of *Human Evolution and Science* and many other pamphlets on religious subjects, and is a frequent contributor to Catholic periodicals. In 1941 he edited the masterly notes of Reverend Timothy Brosnahan, S.J., under the title: *Prolegomena to Ethics.*

C. M. N.

Reverend Jacques Leclercq 1891-

Among the alumni of the renowned Catholic University of Louvain, there have been many who have been eminent students of the "philosophia perennis" of the Christian Church. Some of these sons of this great Catholic University have greatly enhanced the literature of philosophy by their writings. Among them stands the figure of the Reverend Jacques Leclercq, a noted Belgian priest and doctor.

Father Leclercq, a son of the Procurator General of the Belgian Supreme Court, was born in 1891. Retarded in early life in his progress in faith and spirituality, perhaps from the fact that his parents were none too practical Catholics, Jacques for some years after his first Communion, was not a close follower of Catholic belief and practice. After being taught at home by a special tutor, at the age of fifteen he enrolled as a student at the University of Brussels, where a strong trend of rationalism and anti-clericalism permeated the intellectual air. However, he returned to the Faith and since has given great signs of a continuous growth in spirituality.

He entered the University of Louvain as a student of civil law, and there earned the degree of Doctor of Law in 1911. Then he entered the Institut supérieur de philosophie, Louvain, gaining a doctorate in Thomistic philosophy, maxima cum laude, in 1914. He was a leader of student groups and editor of a students' paper during his course. After completing his ecclesiastical studies at the Seminaire Léon XIII and at the Malines Seminary, he was ordained a priest in 1917. After ordination he taught philosophy at the Collège Saint Louis in Brussels and later at his own alma mater, the Institut supérieur de philosophie. Gifted with a brilliant mind and endowed with the grace of a spiritual outlook, he has shown in his works the fruits of his frequent personal meditations. He has exerted a fine influence on his students and has been chaplain of the J.U.C. (Jeunesse Universitaire Catholique) (Catholic University Youth).

He is the author of: *Mystique de L'apostolat; St. Catherine de Sienne, Catholique romains* (1923); *S. Francois de Sales, docteur de la perfection* (1929); *L'Etat on la politique* (1929); *Back to Christ,* from *Essays in Catholic Morals,* translated by Reverend Francis Day (1932); *Depouillement* (1933); *La Famille* (1933); *Retour a Jesus* (1933); *Albert, Roi des Belges* (1936); *Vie Interieure* (1936), and *Dialogue de l'homme et de Dieu* (1939).

Dr. Leclercq has written four large volumes on social philosophy. In 1941 Reverend Dr. Thomas R. Hanley, O.S.B., brought out a revised and enlarged edition in English of the third volume published in French in 1933.

J. M.

Very Reverend Edward Leen, C.S.Sp.
1885-1944

While a student at Rome from 1912 to 1916, Father Edward Leen of the Congregation of the Fathers of the Holy Ghost at Chevilly, Paris, France, was ill for some time and looked for something "to read less taxing than my theology tests. In the library I lighted on Père Lemén's *La Grace et la Gloire*. The title did not attract, for the word grace was associated with arid discussions in the schools. But scarcely had I read the first chapter when I was gripped and read through the two volumes with intense interest. I here and there had formed the resolution to give to the ordinary Catholic reader, should I ever get the chance, a glimpse into the wonderful life, that God offers for souls," wrote Father Leen.

When his studies were ended, he returned to Ireland and after a few years there, he was, for reasons of health, sent to South Nigeria, on the west coast of Africa, as secretary to the Most Reverend Dr. Shanahan, the Vicar Apostolic of South Nigeria. For nearly two years, from 1920 to 1922, he and Bishop Shanahan toured the vast vicariate together. "The continual catechizing and instructing," wrote Father Leen, "gave me scope for outlining, to the unencumbered native nuns, the wonders of the divine life of grace. The results were very gratifying. They listened eagerly and absorbed the teaching." This work directed Father Leen's attention to catechetics and education. The sight of the fetish sacrifices provoked consideration on the Christian sacrifice.

On returning to Ireland he wrote some articles for the *Irish Ecclesiastical Record* on Catholic education, the catechism and the Mass. In the summer of 1923 he was invited to give a course on the outlines of the Christian Faith. This was given to an audience composed mainly of nuns from different parts of the country. The lectures were given in the University College, Dublin and attracted some attention. This was the first opportunity Father Leen had had of putting before a European audience the ideas that had germinated through the reading of Père Lemén's work. The Dominican Convent, Cabra, Dublin, first, and later the Sacred Heart Convent, Mt. Auville, Dundrum, Dublin, asked for a series of lectures on the spiritual life on the lines of the university lectures. These were copied and circulated widely. After the year 1927, applications for retreats began to pour in from religious houses in Ireland, England and Scotland.

Father Edward Leen was born in Ireland, at Abbeyfeale, County Limerick, in 1885. He was educated at Rockwell College, Cashel, County Tipperary, conducted by the priests of the Congregation of the Holy Ghost. Entering that Congregation, he took his ecclesiastical studies at Chevilly, near Paris, and at the Gregorian University, Rome. He was ordained in 1914. The National University of Ireland, Dublin, gave him his A.B. in 1921 and his M.A. in 1917. He received his D.D. degree, summa cum laude, in 1916.

From 1925 to 1931, Father Leen was president of Blackrock College. He then went to Kimmage Manor, Dublin, to become professor of philosophy, ethics and psychology. For nearly ten years he lectured regularly at the Sacred Heart Convent at Mount Auville and gave many retreats. When in 1935 Father Leen perceived that these retreats and the more formal spiritual conferences seemed to appeal so profoundly to widely different audiences, he determined to prepare for publication the material that had accumulated during the twelve years of his experience as a lecturer. The manuscript on *Progress Through Mental Prayer* was offered to Sheed and Ward in 1935. The response was favorable and the other books followed in quick succession. These are: *In The Likeness of Christ* (1936); *The Holy Ghost* (1937); *Why The Cross?* (1938); *The True Vine and Its Branches* (1938); *The Church Before Pilate* (1939); and his last book, *What Is Education?* (1943).

In 1939 Father Leen visited the United States and was in demand as a lecturer and preacher. The advent of World War II shortened his stay. In October of that year he took a plane to Eire. He died in Dublin, Ireland, on November 11, 1944.

D. D.

Dom Gaspar Lefebvre, O.S.B.   1880-

A devotee of the liturgy, Dom Gaspar Lefebvre was born in Lille, France, on June 17 in 1880. He was educated in the Maredsous Abbey School where he completed his study of the humanities. Later he entered the novitiate in Maredsous and was professed a Benedictine monk on April 6, 1900. Four years afterwards he was ordained to the priesthood.

When Pope Leo XIII entrusted the task of the restoration of the monasteries of the Brazilian congregation to Bishop van Caloen, Dom Gaspar Lefebvre was sent there to help in this work. After spending several years in Brazil—in the later years serving as prior of the Parahiba Priory—he returned to Europe at the beginning of World War I. During the war he was stationed at Lille, France. It was here he started his liturgical work and began preparing his *Daily Missal*, the French edition of which was first published in 1919. In a short time it met with great success and was used, not only in France and Belgium, but also in Canada, Switzerland and in other French-speaking countries. Later he published various editions of the same missal, more or less complete, in different sizes. Translated into English, Dutch, Polish, Spanish, Italian, and Portuguese it became famous throughout the world.

Soon after the *Daily Missal* was published he started a magazine, *Bulletin Paroissial Liturgique,* which is now published under the title *Paroisse et Liturgie.* Its purpose is to popularize the liturgy for priests, religious, and laymen. He also helped spread a knowledge of the liturgy by giving lectures and retreats especially in France. A firm believer in visual education, Dom Gaspar Lefebvre has also stimulated liturgical information by pictures, many of which appear in his missals and books. He was probably the first to introduce pictures into the missal for the laity.

The increasingly large number of Catholics using the daily or Sunday missals today give ample proof of the popularizing of the holy liturgy. In this contribution to a fuller Catholic life, practiced by millions today, Dom Lefebvre has had no small part. His importance in this field is due to his success in bringing down to the average lay mind, by approved psychological means, the age-old words and phrases which present the Holy Sacrifice as the drama of the Mass.

Dom Lefebvre's latest work is *La Redemption par le sang de Jesus,* the first volume of which was published in 1942. The English title of his principal work is *Catholic Liturgy, Its Fundamentals and Principles.* He is a member of the Abbey of St. André in Belgium.

M. H.

Gertrud von Le Fort 1876-

In the Catholic Church, to which she is a convert, Gertrud von Le Fort finds inspiration for her novels and her poetry. She is of French heritage, born in Westphalia, at Minden in Germany on October 11, 1876. Her father was Lothar Frederick Francis Peter Le Fort. The Barons Le Fort were Protestants who fled France because of their religion. From Savoy to Switzerland to Russia to Germany her branch of the family migrated, finally settling in Prussia where they were landowners for two centuries. The Baroness Le Fort lives in Bavaria, at Baierbrunn, near Munich. She was educated at the Universities of Heidelberg and Berlin, studying philosophy under Ernst Troeltsch. As upon Christopher Dawson so upon Gertrud von Le Fort the thought of this Protestant philosopher had a profound influence and she edited and published his theological writings after his death. This work brought her to the threshold of the Church which she entered in 1925.

Her *Hymns to the Church* which rank with the poetry of Claudel were first published in 1924, one year before her conversion. Many passages reflect the struggle of her mind with the doctrine of the Church. For that reason these passages can be considered as autobiographical. A new edition came out in 1929, with a few hymns added. Among these was the Litany of the Sacred Heart which can be truly regarded as one of the most beautiful pieces of modern literature. The hymns resemble the power of the psalms. They are free from any sentimentality and they praise in quietly flowing rhythm the efficiency, beauty and perpetuity of the Church, which she says "is the only symbol of the eternal on this globe." The hymns may be compared to waves which strike with force against the land.

The Veil of Veronica which was her first novel translated into English and which aroused much favorable comment, first appeared in a Catholic literary periodical, *Das Hochland*. In 1929 the German edition appeared under the title *Das Schweisstuch der Veronika*. In 1934, the English translation by Conrad M. R. Bonacina was published by Sheed and Ward. It is the story of a modern woman who visits St. Peter's Church in Rome on a Good Friday. When the veil of Veronica is shown to the people, this makes such an impression on her that she looks upon Rome as the dearest spot on earth and thereafter makes several visits to Rome.

The Song From the Scaffold (Die Letzte Am Schafott) appeared in 1933. The story is based on the history and legend of the sixteen Carmelites belonging to a convent in Compiègne, which had enjoyed special favors under the old regime, but who were executed at the outbreak of the French Revolution. The novel is written in the form of a letter.

In *The Pope From the Ghetto* (1930), she tells the story of the family of Pier Leone. The historic background is the struggle over investitures, with Henry IV and Henry V in conflict with papal authority. Spiritual and material forces have full sweep on the broad canvas whereon Gertrud von Le Fort depicts the action of her novels. She sees all the contributory elements that make for drama in human life and these she skillfully depicts: her books are essentially Catholic.

C. M. N.

Sir Shane (John Randolph) Leslie, Baronet
1885-

An associate of the Irish Academy of Letters, Sir John Randolph Shane Leslie is the author of notable and numerous literary works. He was born in London, England, the eldest son of Sir John Leslie, an Irish baronet of Glaslough, County Monaghan, and Leonie Jerome, daughter of Leonard Jerome of New York whose daughter, Jenny, became the mother of Winston Churchill. Sir John Leslie died in 1944 and Shane succeeded him to the baronetcy. After graduation from Eton he went to the University of Paris and to King's College, Cambridge, where he received his M.A. In 1907 he made a trip to Moscow and St. Petersburg in search of communion—"If the Greek authorities allowed me to receive Holy Communion as an Anglican according to the Greek Rite I would remain where I was, but if they refused me, I would seek entry into the Church of the Popes. . . . When I returned to England, I studied and accepted the full Catholic creed." He entered the Church in 1908. Of his conversion he writes: "My strongest feeling then and today is an acute desire to die in the Catholic fold, and to be laid in an anonymous but consecrated monastery corner."

While in Russia he visited Tolstoy whose literary genius he admired. Though of Protestant heritage, he was descended also from the adopted daughter of Mrs. Fitzherbert, Catholic wife of King George IV. In 1911 he visited America, where he met his future wife, Marjorie Ide, daughter of the Honorable H. C. Ide, United States Minister to Spain and Governor of the Philippines. They were married in 1912; two sons and a daughter were born. All three children came safely through war service: John (Irish Guards), Desmond (R.A.F.), Anita (M.T.C.). During World War II he served as a gas officer on the Home Guard Staff and edited Cardinal Vaughan's *Letters to Lady Herbert,* Archbishop Ullathorne's *Autobiography* and a work dedicated to Irish reconciliation called *The Irish Tangle.*

Shane Leslie served also in World War I, in which his brother, Norman, was killed, and, while invalided in a hospital, he wrote a book of essays, *The End of a Chapter.* Here are family reminiscenses, entitled "Links with the Past," and comment on "Society in Decay," "The Religion of England," "Ireland and the Irish," and other subjects. His first book was a volume of verse, *Songs of Oriel,* published in 1908. *Verses in Peace and War* appeared in 1916, *Poems* in 1928, and *Poems and Ballads* in 1933, and in 1925 he compiled *An Anthology of Catholic Poets.* Among his prose works are: a life of *Henry Edward Manning* (1921); *Studies in Sublime Failure* (1932), which includes Cardinal Newman and Charles Stewart Parnell, to whom he is related, Patmore, Curzon, and Frewen; and *The Oxford Movement, 1833-1933,* a concise and comprehensive survey which is one of The Science and Culture Series, *The Skull of Swift* is a dramatic story of the great satiric dean. Five studies of late Victorian biography are included in *Men Were Different.* One of his early books was *The Celt and the World* (1917), a study of the relation of the Celt and Teuton in history. *The Irish Issue in Its American Aspect* was a contribution to the settlement of Anglo-American relations during and after the Great War.

From 1911 to 1935 Shane Leslie made four lecture tours in the United States. In 1935 he was invited by the University of Pennsylvania to come to this country and deliver, under the Rosenbach Fellowship, a series of lectures which was later published in book form, under the title *The Script of Jonathan Swift and Other Essays,* by the University of Pennsylvania Press under the auspices of The Rosenbach Fellowship. It was during this visit to America that the University of Notre Dame awarded him an LL.D.

In *American Wonderland* (1936), he writes his memories of these visits. He believes it is better to interest or amuse people than to make them rich or prosperous. He served as editor of the *Dublin Review* from 1916 to 1925.

His interest in Mrs. Fitzherbert has prompted four volumes: *George the Fourth* (1926); *Mrs. Fitzherbert* (1928), a drama; and a two-volume biography (1930-1940), also entitled *Mrs. Fitzherbert,* for which he had access to family archives, Windsor Castle documents and other authoritative sources that had been carefully guarded from public scrutiny. These make a well-documented story of one of the most interesting women in history; letters and connected papers are comprised in the second volume. Other books by Leslie are: *The Oppidan* (1922); *Life of Sir Mark Sykes* (1922); *Doomsland* (1923); *Masquerades* (1924); *The Cantab; The Anglo-Catholic* (1929), and his autobiography *The Film of Memory* (1938).

In 1921 Shane Leslie was a Privy Chamberlain of the Sword and Cape to His Holiness Pope Pius XI. He has served the Church with loyalty and learning. He is a first cousin of Winston Churchill. Rowing, forestry, walking, bird sanctuaries, and Irish archeology are his hobbies. His home is at Castle Lesley, Glaslough, Eire. He is an Academy member of the Gallery of Living Catholic Authors.

C. M. N.

Dominic Bevan Wyndham Lewis   1894-

Possessing the "Catholic attitude," as he calls it, D. B. Wyndham Lewis presents the foibles of men with a richness of satire and a refreshing cleverness that appeals to a large reading public. The two million subscribers to the London *Daily Mail* have for several years enjoyed his weekly article "of an alleged light nature," written under the nom de plume of "Beachcomber," which he assumed when he first entered journalism and conducted the "By the Way" column in the *Daily Express.* This was after military service in the first World War had prevented his reading law at the University of Oxford.

Lewis was born in 1894, of Welsh heritage, "a family reasonably old, but lately decayed, rooted in the counties of Carmarther and Pembroke." A notable ancestor was Rhys ap Lewis, counsellor of Llwellyn ap Griffith, the last ruling Prince of Wales, slain in 1282. He notes with regret the decline of the clan to obscure small squires and clergymen. It was in a country rectory that he passed his boyhood and at an early age he read the sermons of Jewell and the "Ecclesiastical Polity" of Hooker, which he declares were, and are, "awful." Educated "at reasonable expense," he gave up proposed studies at Oxford to enlist as a private in the British Infantry on September 1, 1914. Early in 1915 he went to France and into the trenches, which he "disliked." Without influence he rose to the rank of second lieutenant. He was shell-shocked twice, and at the Macedonian

Front, from 1916 to 1918, was many times the victim of malaria. By way of Malta he was invalided home early in 1918, and when recuperated sufficiently for further service, the Armistice was signed and he was demobilized.

In 1919 he turned to journalism and until 1923 was on the staff of the London *Daily Express,* for which he wrote a column similar to those conducted in American papers by Morley and Broun. In 1921 he was received into the Catholic Church, and at about this time his career as an author began. His first book, *A London Farrago,* appeared in 1922. In the foreword he introduces the author as follows: "I will say Mr. Beachcomber stands head and shoulders over his contemporaries as a writer of fine, sincere, brilliant, subtle, pure, exquisite, flexible and uplifting English and that he is personally one of the greatest men, morally, spiritually and intellectually it has ever been my good fortune to meet." Almost annually thereafter he produced a volume of satire or humor: *At the Green Goose; At the Sign of the Blue Moon; At the Blue Moon Again* and *On Straw and Other Conceits.* After leaving the *Daily Express* he contributed a weekly article to the *Daily Mail* and continued to do so from Paris where he retired to write biography. This he called a "luxury" and he excelled in it. His *François Villon; King Spider; Some Aspects of Louis XI of France,* and *Emperor of the West* (Charles V) or *Charles of Europe* are well known. In 1944 he brought out a life of Pierre de Ronsard, the French poet, 1524-1585, under the title *Ronsard,* in which he displays "scholarship, wit, Gallic irony, enthusiasm, a true ear for the music of poetry, and that religion which enables men to see Europe from the inside. I think he is the biographer Ronsard would have chosen for himself," wrote J. B. Morton in reviewing the book for the London *Tablet.* In 1928 he translated Barbey d'Aurevilly's *Anatomy of Dandyism.* One of his latest books is *Nonsensibus.* In the dramatic field he writes skits, burlesques and film scenarios. He has also written verse and compiled the literary blunders of well-known poets in *The Stuffed Owl: An Anthology of Bad Verse.* His method of deflating pronounced ego he describes in the preface to this amusing book.

Few escape his pungent satire. "Progressive" thinkers in the professorial chair or the fields of science and literature, the big business men and the stupid rich fall victim to his pen. Often the individual is mentioned by name, sometimes under slight disguise as "George Bernard Bagshaw." Against his "hates" he arrays his "loves." These embrace all things Catholic, especially the lowly poets and saints, "dago" culture, Celtic peoples, the Mendicant Orders and Thomism, "the only philosophy with a 'hoot.' " It is a tribute to him that these opinions appeared in non-Catholic papers. His sophistication is enriched by a cultural background. According to Stanley James, he provides "good food for the soul, refreshment for the pensive mind and consolation against all the million charlatans and spellbinders who infest this unhappy age." Of himself Lewis says that he is "impulsive, lazy, easily imposed upon (except by the grave and good), temperamental, distinctly Celt, full of strong loves and hates."

C. M. N.

Right Reverend Luigi Gino Ligutti   1895-

Monsignor Ligutti's homestead project at Granger, Iowa, has drawn the attention of the nation. The success of this venture has enkindled hope in many victims of economic misfortune and has inspired new confidence in the ability of the Church to cope with the agrarian question. Through Section 208 of the National Industrial Recovery Act, the pastor of Assumption Church, Granger, was allotted a $200,000 loan by the Subsistence Homesteads Division (now the Resettlement Administration) of the Department of the Interior in 1934. Onto the property he bought and into the houses he built with this fund, fifty families moved in December 1935. The average acreage per homestead is 4.02. This small acreage is for subsistence farming, for the owners have occupations which provide on the average an income of about $800 a year. Each year, as their skill and knowledge has grown, for none of them are farmers, the homesteaders have increased the diversified harvest from their few acres. The fruits of this acreage have meant an almost unbelievable rise in the standard of living for these folk, and the beginning of repayment of their debt to the government. Granger Homesteads celebrated the fifth anniversary of its foundation in December 1940.

Monsignor Ligutti has been for years a leader in movements to better the conditions of rural folk and their communities. *America* stated recently, "Monsignor Ligutti will soon count, as a curiosity, places in this country and Canada where his tireless rural-life apostolate has not yet led him to speak." He has also travelled in Europe, studying agrarian problems from the farmsteads of Finland to the reclaimed homesteads of Littorio. He pioneered in religious vacation school work, and the recently established Rural Life School.

He has been especially interested in the education of rural youth. Bishop Ryan of Bismarck said in the opening address at the National Catholic Rural Life Conference convention in 1940, "The chief cause of the farmers' plight is the lack of the right sort of education in the schools where rural youth is taught. For two generations urban-minded teachers and urban-tainted textbooks have glorified the city for our rural youth. The curriculum of our rural schools neglected entirely the things necessary for successful farm operation. The curriculum was designed for city rather than rural living." Monsignor Ligutti is one of the first to take steps to remedy this condition. He has adopted a curriculum in Assumption High School that is planned to make rural girls and boys eager and happy to stay on the land.

Monsignor Ligutti was born near Venice, Italy. His parents were Spiridione and Teresa Ciriani Ligutti. He came to the United States in 1912. He received his A.B. at St. Ambrose College, Davenport, Iowa, in

1914; his S.T.D. at St. Mary's, Baltimore, 1917; and M.A. at Catholic University, 1918. He also studied at Columbia University and the University of Chicago. He was ordained in 1917, and appointed pastor in Granger in 1926. He helped found the National Catholic Rural Life Conference, and was its president from 1937 to 1939. St. Ambrose honored her son with an LL.D. in 1938. He was made a Domestic Prelate by Pope Pius XI in 1938. He is an active member of the Iowa Tenancy Commission and the Executive Secretary of the National Catholic Rural Life Conference. In January 1941 he was relieved of his pastoral duties to enable him to devote all his time to the administrative headquarters of the N.C.R.L.C. and to editing *Land and Home*. If rural America becomes Catholic, much of the credit must go to Monsignor Ligutti.

With the Reverend John C. Rawe, S.J., he wrote *Rural Roads to Security—America's Third Struggle for Freedom* (1940).   M. S.

Reverend Peter Lippert, S.J.   1879-1936

Deeply touched by the beauty of the human soul, Father Lippert was a keen observer and discerner of human nature. He had a deep insight into human character. As a spiritual director he was held in highest esteem for his almost infinite patience, sympathy and understanding of the human soul. Those in need of spiritual help received the greatest comfort from his advice. It was said of him: "Whoever came close to Father Lippert came closer to God." Many of his books are the result of his exhortations given to troubled souls. Although Father Lippert confined himself to theological works, his writings have literary value. Dr. Wurm calls his works "jewels of German prose." Max Picard, an authority on the German language, says: "If I had to select 100 pages of the best German prose, I would certainly include Peter Lippert's 'Die Lieblinge Gottes' in these 100 pages." Karl Adam, a classmate says: "There was no pen in Catholic Germany which knew how to write so discreetly and tenderly, so intimately, so psychologically true, so full of faith and courage as his pen." Theodore Kappstein, a Protestant, in a letter to the publishers, B. Herder Book Company, says: "Peter Lippert is the classic religious writer of our present time." In the beginning, his writings explained fundamental truths of the Catholic faith; later he covered all the fields of Catholic theology. He was a prolific writer. He was the author of thirty-four volumes and wrote over one hundred articles for various magazines, particularly *Stimmen der Zeit* and *Seele*.

Peter Lippert was born on August 23, 1879, at Altenricht near Amberg, Bavaria. He was the youngest child of his pious parents. They had eight children. For his mother he had a great filial devotion and referred to her as a living saint. His father had a small farm. As a boy

Peter tended geese. In these early years he showed a love for books. His father often chided him because he read books during meals.

Soon after Peter entered the Latin school in Amberg, his father sold the farm in Altenricht and purchased a small dairy farm outside of Amberg. While on his way to school, Peter not only carried his books but also delivered milk to his father's customers. He attended Mass daily. In his early years he was not a good student. With the help of a private tutor, however, he was graduated among the best students. Shortly before graduation from school in 1898 he made a retreat at Altötting. There he received the Divine Call for the priesthood. Undecided whether to join a religious order or to become a secular priest, he entered the seminary at Ratisbon on October 2, 1898. The spiritual director, Father Freiherr von Pelkhoven, S.J., advised him to join the Jesuits. A year later, (September 30, 1899) he entered the novitiate of the Jesuits at Feldkirch, Austria. In 1901 he went to Exaeten, Holland, for his humanities and in the summer of 1902 he was sent to the college of St. Ignatius, Valkenburg, for philosophy. Upon finishing his philosophical studies he taught mathematics for several years as a Jesuit scholastic. In 1906 he began his theological studies and was ordained on August 28, 1909. He took his final vows on February 2, 1916. In 1912 he was sent to Munich. There he had great success as a lecturer and a writer. For 25 years he was a member of the staff of *Stimmen der Zeit*. His Lenten sermons delivered in 1912 in the concert hall created a sensation. Well versed in all branches of learning he was in demand as a lecturer, retreat master and radio speaker. His radio talks, which were given over the Munich Catholic Hour, appeared later in book form. He gave countless lectures in the principal cities of Germany, Austria and Holland. When interest in lectures waned he turned to writing.

From his early youth, Peter Lippert was of delicate health. His voice was thin, nasal and raucous. Notwithstanding this fact he filled the largest auditoriums in Munich and Berlin and held thousands spellbound. To improve his voice he took lessons from an actor in Munich.

Despite his fame as a theologian, philosopher, psychologist, poet, retreat master and radio speaker his dominant trait was humility. He used to joke about his ugliness. He was oddly shaped. He was of small stature. His head which was flat was bent forward. His face was sunken in. He had a love for solitude and lived a deep interior religious life.

On account of failing health and the conditions of the time he left Munich to spend the last few years of his life in Switzerland and South Tyrol. On Easter 1936 he returned to Munich to undergo an operation on his throat by Dr. Lebsche, his good friend. Upon his recovery he went to Locarno, Switzerland and while there contracted grippe. On December 10, he entered the Clinica S. Agnese. The next day pleurisy and pneumonia set in. He died on December 18, 1936. His body is interred at Immensee, Switzerland.

Der Mensch Job redet mit Gott was the last of Father Lippert's works and he considered it his best work. It was translated into English by George N. Shuster under the title, *Job the Man Speaks with God*. His books in German include: *Zur Psychologie des Jesuitenordens; Kredo,*

Darstellungen aus dem Gebiet der Christlichen Glaubenslehre, 6 vols.; *Das Wesen des Katholischen Menschen* (1923); *Von Seele zu Seele* (1924); *Die Kirche Christi* (1931); *Vom guten Menschen* (1931); *Zwierlei Menschen* (1931); *Briefe in ein Kloster* (1932); *Von Wundern und Geheimnissen* (1933); *Von Christentum und Lebenskunst* (1933), and *Einsam und Gemeinsam* (1936).

In 1938 the Reverend Joseph Kreitmaier, S.J., published a life of Father Lippert under the title, *Peter Lippert: Der Mann und Sein Werk*, and gives a complete bibliography of his works. A more personal biography of Father Lippert was edited by Dr. Alois Wurm under the title, *P. Lippert zum Gedächtnis*, in 1937. M. H.

Prince Hubertus zu Loewenstein 1906-

Prince Hubertus zu Loewenstein-Wertheim-Freudenberg was born October 14th, 1906, at Castle Schoenwoerth, near Kufstein in the Austrian Tyrol. His parents are Maximilian, Prinze zu Loewenstein-Wertheim-Freudenberg, and Constance Pirbright. Loewenstein-Wertheim is the elder branch of the Royal House of Bavaria. He was educated by private tutors until the year 1916. Then the young prince attended the Gymnasium at Bamberg and Munich from 1916 to 1917. The next four years were spent at the Realgymnasium, Gmünden, Upper Austria, and from 1922 to 1924 at the Realgymnasium, Klagenfurt in Carinthia.

He then studied law and political science at the Universities of Munich, Hamburg, Geneva, and Berlin. After a state examination at the Supreme Court of the State of Prussia, in November 1928, he was appointed Referendar. Hamburg University awarded him the degree of Doctor of Law in 1931. Hamline University, St. Paul, Minnesota granted him a Litt.D. degree, honoris causa. Appointed Visiting Professor to the United States of the Carnegie Endowment for International Peace, in 1937, he taught history and political science at Swarthmore, the University of Virginia, Knox College, the University of Nebraska, Iowa State College, Brown University, Syracuse University, Assumption College and many other colleges and universities and continued in that appointment up to 1946. He ascribes to this work "not only the major part of my knowledge of America but also a continued educational influence upon my whole life." Prince Loewenstein's first visit to the United States was made in 1935. Since then he has made five additional trips here.

In 1930 he became a member of the German Catholic Center Party, and in 1932 a leader of the Republican Youth Movement on a democratic non-partisan basis. In 1929 he married Helga Maria Mathilde Schuylenburg, who was born in Norway, of Dutch parents. They have two daughters, Maria Elisabeth, born in New York in 1939, and Konstanza Maria, born in 1942. When Hitler came into power in 1933, Prince Loewenstein left Germany in April for the Austrian Tyrol where the family castle was situated and where he continued the fight for constitutional government.

Prince Hubertus zu Loewenstein's earliest attempt at literature was a Christmas fairy tale written for his father when he returned on furlough from the Russian front in 1916. A drama came next. His first poems were written at the age of ten. When the prince was twenty-four years of age, he wrote his first political article called "The Third Reich," prompted by the realization of the growing neo-pagan menace of National Socialism for Christianity and world peace. His writings since then have dealt mainly with political, religious and social questions. For the *Nineteenth Century Review*, London in 1934, he wrote the article "Rome and Neo-Paganism"; for *Contemporary Review*, London in 1938, he wrote the article "The Church in Germany," and for the *Atlantic Monthly* the three articles "Catholicism at the Cross Roads" (September 1938); "Christian World Revolution" (January 1942), and "Fascism and Christianity" (March 1943).

Prince Hubertus zu Loewenstein has a novel almost completed. It is tentatively called *The Night Is Far Spent*. Its hero is a German bishop, and the story deals with his life, fight and death as a martyr by the Nazi neo-pagans.

His other books are: *The Tragedy of a Nation* (1934); *After Hitler's Fall, Germany's Coming Reich* (1934)—it was this book that deprived him of his German citizenship and of his property; *A Catholic in Republican Spain* (1937); *Conquest of the Past*, an autobiography (1938); *On Borrowed Peace* (1942), and *The Lance of Longinus* (1946).

While in the United States the Loewensteins lived in Newfoundland, New Jersey, thirty-two miles from New York, in a region famous for its lakes and hills. The house built in 1749, was chosen by them after his wife had seen a photograph of it in a real estate office in New York.

After thirteen years in exile, Prince Hubertus zu Loewenstein returned to Germany in September 1946 with his wife and two children.

M. H.

Reverend Valentine Long, O.F.M.   1902-

Born October 28, 1902, in Cumberland, Maryland, Father Valentine was christened William George Long, receiving the name Valentine upon reception in the Franciscan Order. The Shockey side of his maternal ancestors, dating back to the Revolutionary War, were Pennsylvania Protestants from whom came "a convert, my grandmother, and the most human-saintly Catholic I have ever met or ever hope to meet," writes Father Valentine.

His early training in a Catholic home, and in a parochial school at the hands of Ursuline nuns, introduced the boy to the beauty of the Faith. "I shall always feel unworthy," he says, "to have had parents and a convert grandmother who attended Mass daily and who, after the decree of Pope

Pius X, received Holy Communion daily. If the eight of us children fail to make heaven, the fault will certainly not lie in a bad start."

In 1914 he took his first step toward the priesthood by entering a preparatory seminary, near Butler, Pennsylvania. There he came under the influence of the well known Capuchin educator, a professor at the Catholic University. Dr. Felix Kirsch. It was the personality of this instructor in English, with his large dark eyes and shaggy brows, that drew the heart of young William George toward the subject. "Who wouldn't love the classics after his rich deep voice got finished with them?" is the way Father Valentine remembers it.

In June 1921 he graduated from St. Fidelis Seminary and went home, to settle an important doubt, among the hills of western Maryland. He was sure he wanted to be a priest. But in what diocese? In what order? He finally decided to join the Friars Minor and journeyed to the novitiate in Paterson, New Jersey. He was received August 15th of the same year.

After the novitiate year he resumed studies at St. Bonaventure, New York, taking the prescribed courses in philosophy and theology. He was ordained to the priesthood, May 29, 1927.

He has taught English ever since, first at St. Joseph's Seminary, Callicoon, New York, then at Aquinas Institute, Rochester, New York, and finally at St. Bonaventure College, St. Bonaventure, New York.

Much of his leisure Father Valentine spends writing for magazines. He has published three books: *Not on Bread Alone* (1934), now in its fifth printing; *They Have Seen His Star* (1938); *Youth-Springtime of Love* (1944).

Reverend Daniel Aloysius Lord, S.J. 1888-

A remarkable gift of understanding the viewpoint and needs of youth has made the Reverend Daniel A. Lord, S.J., a general favorite with young people and a great influence in the lives of many. Especially in his capacity as national organizer of the Sodality of Our Lady, and editor of its publication, *The Queen's Work,* he reaches great numbers, and his numerous pamphlets are widely read. He was born in Chicago, Illinois, in 1888, and educated at Holy Angels Academy, De La Salle Institute, St. Ignatius High School and Loyola University, where he was leader of the dramatic societies and editor of the school paper, and from which he graduated with an A.B. in 1909. In that year he entered the Society of Jesus at St. Stanislaus Seminary, Florissant, Missouri. In 1913 he was assistant editor of *The Queen's Work.* His graduate studies in philosophy were made at St. Louis University, where he received his M.A. in 1915. From 1917 to 1920 he was professor of English there. He was ordained in 1923 and professed in the Society in 1925. Since 1926 he has been editor of *The Queen's Work* and national director of the Sodality of Our Lady. Under his editorship the magazine has increased in circulation from 3,000 to 100,000.

Father Lord has a love of music and the theatre as well as of literature and all these he has used to advantage. A college musical comedy, "Full Steam Ahead," which he wrote, with Reverend J. F. Quinn, S.J., was a success, and he decided to use "music, comedy and dancing to achieve a definite goal in social philosophy." "The Dreamer Awakes" was the first of many pageants that became widely known. Hollywood asked his services as consultant on Cecil de Mille's "King of Kings," and at the request of the Hays Office and under the patronage of Cardinal Mundelein, he went to Hollywood "to write for the motion picture industry a code under which could be produced motion pictures that would not be detrimental to American life, pictures that would truly present American living and the virtues and achievements that have characterized our land."

Six One-Act Plays were published in 1923. In all, he has written over twenty plays. In 1936 he produced *Social Order Follies*, and for *The Matrimonial Follies of 1939* he also wrote the words and music. Other "Follies" are to follow. Among his hymns are "For Christ the King" and "Mother Beloved."

As a pamphlet writer, he is indefatigable and covers a wide variety of subjects pertinent to social, economic and religious problems of the day. So successful are the "Queen's Work" booklets, of which he wrote one a month for more than ten years that their circulation had reached 5,000,000 in 1940, and they have helped pay the cost of the sodality movement. "The Months with Mary," "How to Stay Young," "It's Christ or War," "When Sorrow Comes," "The Call of Christ," "Marry Your Own," "Forward America," "These Terrible Jesuits," "My Faith and I" are a few of his more than 100 pamphlets.

His first book, *Armchair Philosophy*, was published in 1918. *Our Nuns* appeared in 1921. Then followed *Religion and Leadership; Our Part in the Mystical Body,* and a book on his mother, *My Mother.* In 1940 he wrote *Our Lady in the Modern World,* and in 1944 *The Glorious Ten Commandments.* His first book for children, *I'd Like You to Meet My Family,* was published in 1941. His versatility includes mystery novels. Many of his writings appear serially in *The Queen's Work,* and he also contributes to other periodicals.

Under his direction Summer Schools of Catholic Action, attended by directors, faculty moderators, and parish and school sodalists from every part of the country, have been held, in collaboration with universities in Boston, Chicago, St. Louis, New Orleans, Milwaukee, New York, Buffalo, St. Paul, Denver, San Antonio, and Washington. Father Lord is also a popular retreat master and lecturer. He is an Academy member of the Gallery of Living Catholic Authors.

C. M. N.

Reverend Robert Howard Lord 1885-

Most of what Father Lord has written was published before he became a Catholic in 1920. His numerous routine duties while a professor of church history and vice-rector of a metropolitan seminary gave him little time for writing.

For sixteen years, Father Lord taught history at Harvard University. From 1910 to 1916 he was an instructor in history; an assistant professor from 1916 to 1922; an associate professor from 1922 to 1924 and a professor from 1924 to 1926.

Because of his knowledge of history he was chosen one of the two American representatives on the inter-allied commission sent to Poland in 1919 to assist the new republic. He was also chief of the department of Polish affairs in the American Commission to Negotiate Peace. At the Versailles Peace Conference he was largely responsible for the creation of the boundaries of Poland as then existed before World War II.

During his stay in France, he was impressed by the work of the Catholic Church there. This impression, though a minor factor, helped him to embrace the Faith. Another factor was his knowledge of history. "The more I studied secular history," he says, "the more I realized that religion is the most important cause a man can work for, and that the highest calling for a man who is free to devote himself to it is the priesthood." Dr. Lord said "My conversion is due to private study and not to outside influence. The more I studied religion, the more I became convinced of the truth of Catholicism." After six years of study and meditation, he took the final step. He was ordained a priest in 1929. When he sang his first Mass in St. Paul's Church, Harvard Square, Cambridge, not a few of the faculty of Harvard attended.

Father Lord was born at Plano, Illinois, July 20, 1885, the son of Frank Howard and Julie Marie (Custin) Lord. He was educated at the Plano High School, attended Northwestern University from 1902 to 1903, and graduated from Harvard with an A.B. degree in 1906. He also received his A.M. and Ph.D. degrees from Harvard in 1907 and 1910 respectively. From 1908 to 1910 he studied at the Universities of Vienna, Berlin and Moscow. The University of Lemberg in Poland conferred an honorary Ph.D. degree on him. He was a student of St. John's Seminary, Brighton, Massachusetts, from 1926 to 1929.

For one year, he was a curate at St. Cecilia's Church in Boston, 1929 to 1930. From 1930 until 1944 he was a professor of church history at St. John's Seminary, and from 1933 to 1944 Vice-Rector.

In November 1944 he was appointed pastor of St. Paul's Church, Wellesley, Massachusetts.

He is the author of *The Second Partition of Poland* (1915) (with Prof. Haskins); *Some Problems of the Peace Conference* (1920); *The*

Origin of the War of 1870 (1924) (with H. J. Coolidge); *Archibald Coolidge: Life and Letters* (1932), and with Reverend John E. Sexton and Reverend Edward Harrington, *History of the Archdiocese of Boston, 1604-1943* (3 volumes).   M. H.

Frater M. Louis, O.C.S.O.   *See* Thomas Merton

Marie Adelaide (Belloc) Lowndes
(Mrs. Frederic Sawrey Archibald Lowndes)
1868-1947

During early years spent between France and England, Marie Adelaide Belloc gained an intimate knowledge of the literature of both countries, and also that of America. Certainly, she says, *Rollo* was her first sweetheart and *Little Women* were her first girl friends. Practically her only formal education was two years spent at Mayfield, the English convent of the Sisters of the Holy Child. She was born in 1868 of a French father, Louis Swanton Belloc, barrister, and an English mother, Bessie Rayner Parkes, and until she was fifteen years of age she lived with her French grandmother. "My heart is all French," she writes.

Her ancestors were distinguished in the history of both countries, among them the last colonel of the famous Berwick Brigade, the regiment raised in Scotland and Ireland to fight for the Stuarts. Her great-uncle, Colonel Baron Chasseiran, led the famous charge of the Cuirassiers at Waterloo, and her great-grandfather was one of Napoleon's staff officers. She was also proud that her English mother was the great grand-daughter of the Unitarian minister, Joseph Priestley, called the Father of Modern Science, who, claiming that all men are free and equal, was ill-treated by British Tory mobs and fled to America. His descendants are still living in the United States, she and her brother Hilaire being the only ones in Europe. Mrs. Belloc Lowndes' husband was Frederic S. A. Lowndes of the staff of the London *Times*, who died in 1940. A son and two daughters were born to them.

She began writing at sixteen. Her first literary effort was published then in Meynell's magazine, *Merry England*. It was a short story called "pastel." Her first book, published when she was twenty-one, was a biography, *Life and Letters of Charlotte Elizabeth, Princess Palatine*. Though she early developed a plot mind she did not begin the writing of her many novels until later in life. Her interest in crime, she said was wholly psychological, and she disliked being known as a mystery story writer. *The Lodger,* however, which has been translated into many languages, has been called the best book on murder written by any living author. It was the result of a chance dinner conversation. Her books are many. Among them are: *The Heart of Penelope* (1904); *The Uttermost Farthing* (1908); *When No Man Pursueth* (1910); *The Chianti Flask* (1935); *The House by the Sea* (1937); *The Marriage-Broker* (1937); *Motive* (1938); *And Call It Accident* (1939); *Lizzie Borden* (1940); *I, Too, Have Lived in Arcadia* (1941); *What of the Night?* (1943).

The second section of the author's autobiography takes her back to her seventeenth year and is entitled, *Where Love and Friendship Dwelt* (1943). Mrs. Belloc Lowndes also wrote three plays: *With All John's Love* (1932); *The Second Key* (1935); *What Really Happened* (1936).

Although Mrs. Lowndes' first book was published after the death of Queen Victoria, there was much in her style and general background that savored of the Victorian era. She disliked the vicious type of woman who preys on man, and dealt devastatingly with her in her books. One of these was *Ivy*, recently seen here as a film. In spite of this she was an early champion of women's rights.

Mrs. Belloc Lowndes claimed no literary preferences, liking anything that is good in belles lettres and she was proud of the fact that she discovered authors who later became famous, such as Theodore Dreiser, Arnold Bennett, Willa Cather, Walter de la Mare and Sinclair Lewis. Games had no interest for her. Reading, writing and knowing people were her pleasures. She had a genius for friendship.

Born into the Catholic Church, she was firm in her adherence to the tenets of her faith. Petite of figure and vivacious, she resembled "a small bird perched on the window sill," as the Boston *Transcript* described her on her visit to Boston in 1933. In London her home was on a little street curving back of Westminster Abbey with a piece of the old medieval wall on one side. In summer she went to Wimbledon.

Marie Belloc Lowndes died November 14, 1947 at the home of her daughter, Countess Iddesleigh, in Hampshire, England.   D. D.

Clare Boothe Luce   1903-

The increasing prominence of women in public life is a salient feature of the current American scene. It is not only in literary and dramatic fields that women have gradually gained a position, which more than fulfills the prophecies of "woman's rights" advocates of generations ago. Everywhere people have become familiar with the careers of women who are mayors, senators and even cabinet members; so it could not be called a sensation when, in 1942, a conservative New England Congressional district, for the first time, sent to Washington, a woman as its representative. The election of this lady, however, was first page news in November of that year. Clare Boothe Luce, already well known in the social and literary world, had also made her mark as a keen observer of public affairs and a courageous critic of the "mores" of contemporary life. Young, famous and successful, she had already reviewed intelligently, both from within and without, many of the contrasting "isms" which make up the sum total of modernistic philosophy.

The daughter of a concert violinist, William F. Boothe, and his wife, the former Ann Snyder, Clare Boothe was born in New York City, April 10, 1903. Later the family lived for a while in Memphis, Tennessee, but had returned to New York, before a divorce separated the father from the mother and daughter. About a year before the outbreak of the first World War, Mrs. Boothe took her young daughter to Paris, where they stayed till hostilities forced a return home. They then made their home in Greenwich, Connecticut, and Clare, now twelve years old, was sent to St. Mary's Episcopalian School at Garden City, Long Island, and later she became a boarding scholar at Castle School, Tarrytown, New York. At the age of nineteen she was married to George Tuttle Brokaw, some twenty years her senior. The next year, a daughter, Ann Clare, was born. Five years after this, the couple were divorced. Mr. Brokaw died several years later, and after his death, Clare Boothe married Henry R. Luce, the son of a famous Presbyterian missionary, and the publisher of *Time, Life* and *Fortune.*

Interested in the drama and literature from an early age, she had even written and produced a play in high school. After her first marriage ended Mrs. Luce secured a position with the late Condé Nast on the editorial staff of *Vogue,* a job "which was to lead to a career dazzlingly divided into three epochs, in which she shone successfully as a magazine editor and literary hostess, as a playwright and as a political crusader." By 1931 she was associate editor of *Vanity Fair.* With a pen which turned towards satire, she had written a novel *Stuffed Shirts,* a caricature of the society in which she had lived, and several plays—one of them, *O, Pyramids,* was a critical study of the NRA. In this field she was at home for she was a member of the Code Authority in the early days of the New Deal. The dissolution of the NRA balked plans for the play's production. Her first production to make Broadway was *Abide With Me,* opening a few days before her second marriage in 1935. This venture, a failure, did not daunt her efforts and three of her later dramatic pieces were successes, *The Women, Kiss the Boys Good-bye* and *Margin for Error. The Women,* called a most brilliant social satire, takes her own sex to task mercilessly.

After a trip to Europe during the early war years, Clare Boothe Luce recorded her impressions in a book named *Europe in the Spring,* published in 1941. In 1940 public affairs engaged her attention as a campaign speaker for Wendell Willkie. The next year, with her husband, she made a visit to the Chinese war front, from where she sent dispatches and articles to the press. Elected to Congress as a Liberal Republican from the 4th Connecticut District, she was reelected in 1944. A vigorous critic of many totalitarian governmental policies during the war, she has been no less vocal in upholding what she believes to be the principles of a just peace. In 1946, although offered the Senate nomination by her party, she declined further service in Congress.

Clare Luce has long been dissatisfied with the answers or the lack of answers to her quest for happiness. The Protestant churches of her youth had affected her religious thinking very little. She saw the vacuity of a system of life without the Christian ideals. Divorce which had been so much in her background, and the mad race for money and pleasure which characterized the boom, served further to unsettle her mind. The years of depression followed by the war only increased her realization of the nothingness which the various religious or semi-religious groups had to offer to a soul seeking the meaning of life. At Christmas in 1943 her only daughter, Ann Clare, on whom she had centered her love and ambitions, was killed in an automobile accident. From this time on, gradually but surely her steps led her to the portals of the Catholic Church. In 1940, on her visit to Europe, she had an audience with Pope Pius XII. Impressed as she was with his kindly appearance, and sensing, together with many non-Catholics the Pope's great influence on world thought, she does not attribute her progress to the Church to this meeting. Rather, very humbly, she ascribes it to the prayers of her Catholic friends, many unknown to her. After a course of instructions by Monsignor Fulton Sheen, she was received into the Church in St. Patrick's Cathedral, New York in February 1946.

Since her coming into the Church Mrs. Luce has written a detailed account of her conversion called "The Real Reason" which began to appear in *McCall's* magazine in February 1947. She and her husband make their home at Ridgefield, Connecticut, at their estate, called "Sugar Hill." They also have a large plantation near Charleston, South Carolina. Her pleasant appearance plus her resourceful mind have contributed to her popularity and have helped make her one of the personalities in America today. That she has added to this the willingness to share with others what she calls "the inexhaustible generosity of Almighty God" is indicative of the wide influence she can bring to bear on the future of her country.

J. M.

Reverend Alphonse Lugan 1869-1931

Someone once said of *Le Mouvement,* the pacifist and democratic journal which Abbé Lugan founded and edited, that it would probably die with him since he wrote almost every word of it himself. Along with this the publicist was correspondent for papers in Austria, Belgium, and Spain. Despite these tasks and his extensive travels he managed to publish twenty-seven books.

The Abbé especially devoted the labors of his pen to opposing L'Action Française, the ultra monarchist party in France. For over twenty-five years, almost single-handed, he fought against this faction. In 1909, he wrote *Action Française Et L'Idèe Chretienne* to show from L'Action Française writings that the movement was agnostic and non-moral. The accuracy of his analysis was demonstrated by the decree of Pope Pius XI in 1927 against the party and its daily. The hostile and insubordinate reception of this condemnation by the party and its supporters completely justified the Abbé's long-continued battle against it. In 1929 he published *Fin D'Une Mystification,* a history of L'Action Française, its teachings and its policies. While his opposition was bitter he never felt hostile toward the party's leader, Charles Maurras. His charity has been fruitful for it is said that Maurras died reconciled to the Church.

While never classed as an agrarian, Abbé Lugan did advocate a sound land policy as the base of stability in a nation. "To understand social and economic crises, one should not look first of all at the eddying tides of industry and commerce, but at the land. For, the land is the original and indispensible source from which man derives his livelihood, and in proportion as he clings to it and finds in it satisfaction for his essential needs, is he at peace with the world, and—I will venture to say—a conservative. Take each one of the great revolutions in their turn, including the Russian Revolution, and anyone can see that in the beginning, all of them had an agrarian character and origin. No one can ever count on the security of a country where the land question has not been settled to the satisfaction of the majority of its inhabitants."

The author was an ardent democrat. This was a source of his interest in America and Americans. He made three or four visits to the United States and was travelling here and in Mexico when his last illness seized him. He wrote *Catholicisme Aux Etats Unis* in 1930. He felt that the position of the Church in this country was to be envied by European Catholics who could not rid themselves of historical ties and ideologies unsuited to the contemporary age. Yet, he thought that the Church in America was not planning as effectively for the future as it should.

He joined the Jesuits and took his philosophy and theology courses in Spain, where he acquired the Spanish culture which was one of his chief characteristics. He not only spoke Spanish, but had an intimate knowledge of Spanish literature. The politics of a divided country like Spain could not but arouse his interest. Through study and travel he was thoroughly at home in the complicated political situation of the country. He was also at home in the affairs of Mexico, Peru and Argentina. Few statesmen in either Europe or America had his grasp and understanding of political situations.

Abbé Lugan was a priest of the diocese of Albi. He was born in that city in 1869 and died there in 1931. He was educated at Castres. In 1905 he left the Jesuits and went to Paris, which he made his headquarters for many years. His three great interests were religion, social welfare, and peace. He loved the working people and admired their champions like Manning, Von Kettler and Gibbons. He believed the most fruitful work to be done in this age is to reconcile the laboring classes to the Church. Rather than by his brilliant political writings he preferred to be remembered by his vast seven-volume treatise on the *Social Teaching of Jesus in the Gospel.* A volume of this work under the title of *Social Principles of the Gospel* was translated into English by the late Reverend T. Lawrason Riggs in 1928.

On his deathbed after saying something about failures, he added, "But my poor life has been filled by the love of Christ."

He is the author of: *Balmes, La Vie Et L'Oeurve* (1911); *Egoisme Humain* (crowned by the French Academy); *Enseignment Social De Jesus Dans L'Evangile* (7 vols.) (1929); *Esprit Public Aux Etats-Unis Apres La Guerre* (1927); *Fray Luis De Leon* (1925); *Grand Eveque Francais Realisateur* (1929); *Horizons D'Ames* (1926); *Jesus Et Le Peuple* (1930); *Precurseur Du Bolshevisme: Fransisco Ferrer* (1921); *Grand Poete-Moine Du Siecle D'Or Espagnal: Luis De Leon* (1930). He also translated into French Allan Sinclair Will's *Life of Gibbons*.

M. S.

Arnold (Henry Moore) Lunn 1888-

Arnold Lunn has travelled so much about Europe that a continental railroad carriage seems to him a natural habitat, and the railroad stations tug at his heartstrings. "No country-bred exile returning from the towns could listen with greater rapture to the farmyard sounds of his home than I to the metallic noise when wheels are tested with a hammer, and to the slow hiss of escaping steam." Travel is in his blood; his father owned a tourist and travel agency.

His father, Sir Henry Lunn, a Methodist minister, had married Miss Ethel Moore, the eldest daughter of Canon Moore, the head of the Middleton College in Ireland. They were married May 12, 1887, and went to India. Their son, Arnold, was born at Madras, April 18, 1888. After a year in India, Henry Lunn's ill health forced his return to England. He became involved in a controversy over mission policy and left the Methodist ministry but remained a lay preacher. Turning to journalism he founded *The Review of the Churches* to promote Christian unity—unity was also of interest to young Arnold. In 1892 Mr. Lunn summoned a conference at Grindelwald, Switzerland, to discuss reunion. This conference was to change his life and his son's. He made the travel arrangements for the conference and from this gradually drifted into the travel and hotel business. The conference gave his son his first glimpse of the Alps which have played such a big part in his life.

From the age of four Arnold Lunn spent almost all his summers, and from the age of eight, practically every winter in the Alps. Here, two of his biggest interests, mountain climbing and skiing, were born. He was a ski-mountaineering pioneer and made the first ski ascents of a number of Alpine peaks. His book *Alpine Skiing* is recognized as a classic study of snow and avalanche craft. He has also played an important part in the development of ski racing. He initiated a campaign for the international recognition of downhill ski racing and invented the modern slalom race. Thanks largely to his efforts downhill ski racing was introduced into the Olympic programme. He was referee for the first slalom to be included in the Winter Olympic games.

Lunn spent five happy years at Orley Farm School and then entered Harrow where he remained from 1902 to 1907. As a boy he read conventional school stories and decided that adults soon forgot their school days. To guard against a like forgetfulness he kept a journal recording with great care conversations and actions of his contemporaries. This diary furnished the material for his first novel, *The Harrovians,* which was an immediate best seller. It outraged the sentimental but was rapidly acclaimed by others as the first realistic account of public-school life. In 1907 he entered Balliol College, Oxford. He became secretary of the Oxford Union and editor of the *Isis.* He regarded his appointment as editor as the first step in a distinguished literary career. He was passionately anxious to attain literary fame. Now he finds it rather amusing to reflect that if he is remembered after death he will be rememberd not as a writer but as the inventor of the slalom race. He believes that social historians may consult the *Harrovians,* and skiers use *History of Skiing* as a work of reference, but that his only book which will perchance be read for its own sake fifty years hence is *The Mountains of Youth.*

Much of his important writing has been controversial and hence slated for a short life. "Nothing, of course, is so ephemeral as controversial writing. The Catholic apologist can add little of value to the old arguments for the old Faith. His principal concern is with the fashionable heresy of the moment, and there is nothing as dead as a dead fashion, and few forms of literature as uninteresting save to specialists, as the refutation of extinct heresies." He has collaborated in three books of controversial letters. *Difficulties* (with R. A. Knox) and *Is Christianity True?* (with C. E. M. Joad) were written before his conversion; *Science and the Supernatural* (with J. B. S. Haldane) after it. He invented this type of controversy. He admits its disadvantages but thinks editing the letters would destroy spontaneity and human interest. "But to my mind the main value of a correspondence controversy is the possibility of reaching a public which would never open a book of Christian apologetics. It is difficult today for the Christian to reach the non-Christian public, but a straight fight between a Christian and a leading secularist will be read with interest by those who enjoy a scrap, and by secularists who will read a book of this type, in the hope that the Christian will be knocked out in the first round."

The year 1909 brought Arnold Lunn both good and bad fortune. On the eve of his twenty-first birthday he met Miss Mabel Northcote, the younger daughter of Prebendary Northcote. He proposed to her the next day and went on proposing at intervals for four years. They were married in 1913.

The summer after he met Miss Northcote while mountain climbing in Wales a great piece of rock came away on top of him. He fell for a hundred feet onto a little ledge just above another drop of two hundred feet. His leg was not only broken but crushed and shattered. He was alone for the next three hours. "As I lay on that ledge I vowed that I would never again climb without companions, for the horror of finding oneself alone with a broken leg must be experienced to be understood." Twice preparations were made for amputation. Two years later, however, he resumed his climbing and alone. "I did not want to be reminded by the presence of climbers rejoicing in their fitness of all that I had lost."

After the accident he returned to Oxford. He never obtained his degree. He always found it hard to interest himself in any subject in which he was to be examined. Instead of reading history he read philosophy and theology. He could argue pragmatism backwards and forwards and was well posted in English and Continental Modernism. "I took my views of orthodox Catholicism from the Modernists, who convinced me that an intelligent man need not waste five minutes' thought on the fundamental Catholic doctrines."

He left Oxford in 1912. His father was determined to make a barrister of him and entered him for the Inner Temple. He passed the first of his bar examinations but never became reconciled to his father's wishes. It would have meant the sacrifice of two ambitions—the first, to write, and the second, to shape the development of British skiing.

Early in 1915 he went to Flanders with a Quaker ambulance. He arrived just after a disagreement with the Army Medical Corps shut the Quaker hospitals. He made vain efforts to obtain a commission, first with the Army, then the Navy. "Medical authorities looked at my right leg, which was short and misshapen, and at my open wound and shook their heads." Shortly after his rejection by the Army and Navy he got a job in connection with the interned British prisoners at Müren and the French prisoners at Montana where his father's company owned hotels. Thus he spent most of the war years in Switzerland.

In 1924 he wrote the anti-Catholic *Roman Converts*. "*Roman Converts* had no sooner been published than my friends began to prophesy my conversion. I was much annoyed by the forecast, and replied petulantly to my father that I was just as likely to become a Buddhist as a Catholic." His brother-in-law, the Earl of Iddesleigh, became a Catholic in 1927. Lunn was received into the Church in 1933 by Father Ronald Knox. He has written his apologia in *Now I See* and *Within That City*. "I spent many years in the examination of the available evidence. I entered the Church along the road of controversy and by the gate of reason. I clarified my mind by three controversial books, in the first of which, *Difficulties*, I attacked, and in the second and third of which I defended, the Catholic position. And I did not become a Catholic till I had satisfied myself that I had found a satisfactory answer to the worst that could be said against the Church."

His elder son, Peter, the Captain of the British Olympic Skiing team, followed his father into the Chuch. He has contributed articles to *America* and the London *Tablet*.

Lunn paid the first of four long visits to the United States in 1935. He has lectured in more than fifty cities and has crossed the continent from New York to San Francisco and from Montreal to New Orleans. In 1937 he was appointed assistant professor of apologetics at Notre Dame.

He visited Spain in 1937 and again in 1938 when he witnessed the final phases of the battle for the sea. He acted as war correspondent. He supported General Franco and gave his reasons in *Spanish Rehearsal.*

When England went to war in 1939 he became war correspondent for *America.* He spent the winter, 1939 to 1940, in eastern and southern Europe journeying through Turkey and the Balkans. Late in 1940 he revisited the United States. A mission which he was to have carried out under British Government auspices to South America had been cancelled.

His brother, Hugh Lunn, writes under the name of Hugh Kingsmill. He is one of Britain's foremost literary critics, the author of *The Return of William Shakespeare,* and the editor of the anthology, *Invective and Abuse.*

Arnold Lunn is the author of: *Guide to Montana* (1907); *Oxford Mountaineering Essays* (ed.) (1912); *The Englishman in the Alps* (1912); *The Harrovians* (1913); *The Alps* (1914); *Was Switzerland Pro-German?* (nom de plume, Sutton Croft) (1918); *Loose Ends* (1919); *Cross Country Skiing* (1920); *The Alpine Ski Guides* (1920); *Auction Piquet* (nom de plume, Rubicon) (1920); *Alpine Skiing* (1921); *Skiing for Beginners* (1924); *Roman Converts* (1924); *The Mountains of Youth* (1925); *A History of Skiing* (1927); *Switzerland, Its Literary, Historical and Topographical Landmarks* (1927); *Things That Have Puzzled Me* (1927); *John Wesley* (1928); *The Complete Ski-Runner* (1930); *Flight From Reason* (1930); *Family Name* (1931); *Within the Precincts of the Prison* (1932); *The Italian Lakes* (1932); *Venice, Its Story, Architecture and Art* (1932); *Difficulties* (with R. A. Knox) (1932); *Is Christianity True?* (with C. E. M. Joad) (1933); *Now I See* (1933); *A Saint In the Slave Trade* (1934); *Science and the Supernatural* (with J. B. S. Haldane) (1935); *Within That City* (1936); *Spanish Rehearsal* (1937); *Communism and Socialism* (1938); *The Science of World Revolution* (1939); *Whither Europe?* (1940); *Come What May* (autobiography) (1940); *And The Floods Came* (1941); *Mountain Jubilee* (1943); *The Good Gorilla* (1944), and *The Third Day* (1945).

M. S.

Reverend John W. Lynch 1904-

Stationed as an assistant pastor in St. Patrick's Rectory, Binghampton, New York, Father John W. Lynch spent his evenings working on his first and only book thus far, *A Woman Wrapped in Silence.* The purpose of this book is to present a human story of the Mother of Christ. When possible he tried to set the hours from nine to eleven or possibly nine to twelve each night as a working period. "Holidays, such as the Fourth of July and New Year's I found very helpful, as it seems nobody rings rectory doorbells on these days," he wrote.

At first, Father Lynch intended to state merely the dramatic and appealing scriptural incidents previous to the birth of the Child. Frequent meditation on Our Lady's life, however, to prepare his sermons for a novena devotion to Our Lady of the Miraculous Medal, opened the vista. As to sources, he consulted one or two kind mothers in the parish as to the facts about how a child develops from a baby into a boy. The "details of serving for the Marriage Feast of Cana were taken from some Confirmation and Forty Hours dinners. A very kind rabbi in the Jewish building at the World's Fair explained to me his model of the Temple in Jerusalem for the details of scenery and location."

Father Lynch was born in Oswego, New York, on January 25, 1904. He was educated in St. Paul's Parish School and the local public high school. He was graduated with a B.A. from Niagara University. His seminary training was received at Our Lady of the Angels, Niagara Falls, and he was ordained for the Diocese of Syracuse in 1929.

He contributed articles to *The Catholic World, The Commonweal, America* and *Columbia.*

At present he is the editor of the *Catholic Sun* and is assistant pastor of St. John the Baptist Church in Syracuse, New York.

M. H.

Anna Shannon McAllister 1888-

Of early American heritage on her mother's side, it is not surprising that Anna Shannon McAllister chose for the subject of her writing the study of Catholic women in American history. She was born in Cincinnati, Ohio, in 1888. Her mother was a descendant of Patrick Stewart who came from Argyll, Scotland, to North Carolina in 1739. Though reared a staunch Presbyterian, Mrs. Shannon brought up her children scrupulously in the Catholic religion of their father, who was of Irish descent. Three years before her death, she too became a Catholic.

Living in a home where reading and travel were major interests, Anna Shannon acquired naturally a love of books and the cultural joys of life. She was educated first by the Sisters of Notre Dame de Namur and then was graduated from the Columbus School for Girls. In 1909 she obtained her B.A. from the Ohio State University. Two years later she married Earl Sadler McAllister, who after being admitted to the Ohio Bar, forsook his profession to enter business. Until she started to write in 1934, Mrs. McAllister's interest centered in her home with considerable social, parochial and charitable work to add diversion.

Her first book, *Ellen Ewing, Wife of General Sherman,* was inspired by the reading of Lloyd Lewis' *Sherman—Fighting Prophet.* Lewis' picture of the charming and devout Ewing home, in which Tecumseh Sherman grew up, created a keen desire in Mrs. McAllister to learn more of the vivacious Ellen Ewing, who became the wife of the future Civil War General. Published data was completely lacking, and it was only after corresponding with Ellen Sherman's son, the late Mr. P. Tecumseh Sherman, and gradually overcoming his reticence that Mrs. McAllister was able to secure sufficient material to attempt the biography. A granddaughter, Miss Eleanor Sherman Fitch, and several other Ewing relatives eventually lent their aid, furnishing family letters, diaries, and scrapbooks, from these unpublished sources the author wove her story. *Ellen Ewing* was the choice of the Catholic Book of the Month Club for June 1936. The book received wide and favorable recognition in the Catholic and secular press, and was awarded the third prize in the 1938 nonfiction contest of the National League of American Penwomen.

Encouraged by this success, Mrs. McAllister wrote a second biography, this time taking for her subject the colorful history of Sarah Worthington King Peter, a distinguished convert who gave generously of herself, her wealth and her talents in behalf of the Church and the poor. The book *In Winter We Flourish* was published in the fall of 1939. The title was taken from the family crest of Sarah Peter's grandmother—an evergreen tree bearing the motto: "In Winter We Flourish." The book was well received by reviewers, who termed it a valuable contribution to the history of notable American Catholic women.

Mrs. McAllister's third book, *Flame In the Wilderness,* was published in November 1944. It is the life of Mother Angela Gillespie, C.S.C., the American Foundress of the Sisters of the Holy Cross. Mother Angela was a cousin and a life-long friend of Ellen Ewing Sherman. Material for the book is based on original research by the author, together with data gathered from the archives of Saint Mary's Convent, Holy Cross, Indiana.

Prior to the publication of her first book, Mrs. McAllister had written occasional book reviews and magazine articles. Her husband, who became a Catholic soon after their marriage, retired from business in 1933. He, too, is a student of American history and shares his wife's liking for historical research. He not only gives sympathetic encouragemen to her writing, she says, but also lends aid in compiling and typing the manuscript. Their home is in Bexley (Columbus) Ohio. Anna McAllister is a member of the Gallery of Living Catholic Authors, the Daughters of the American Revolution, the American Association of University Women, and the Columbus Chapter of the National League of American Penwomen.

D. D.

Reverend David McAstocker, S.J.   1884-

Occupying a sort of penthouse apartment at the top of his devoted sister's house in a peaceful sunny spot a few miles out of Riverside, California, Father David McAstocker, an invalid, spent many years writing poems, magazine articles, book manuscripts and the daily column for the Tacoma *News-Tribune*. Since the use of a typewriter would be too much of a strain on his chest, most of what he wrote was done by hand and while propped up in bed. The work was sent to a friend for typing.

For over nine years, Father McAstocker was a semi-invalid—suffering from tuberculosis. And yet he could write in his letter: (1939) "Possibly the most interesting time of my life for me has been the last seven years when I have been a semi-invalid in my sister's home in Riverside, California. These years have given me the mental strength to think and to plan whatever I have written."

Father David McAstocker was born of Scotch-Irish parents, in the village of Guelph, Ontario, on August 6, 1884. While he was still young his folks moved to Nelson, British Columbia.

While of robust health in his youth, his health broke when he was about nineteen, soon after he completed his studies in the juniorate of the Jesuits. He was advised by doctors to give up all thought of remaining in the Society. He refused. His younger brother took him to a sanatorium in Pennsylvania where he rested in bed for eighteen months living principally on milk and eggs. At the end of that time, he felt strong enough to go to Woodstock, Maryland, where for seven years he continued with his theological studies. On June 29, 1913, he was ordained at Baltimore, Maryland, by Cardinal Gibbons, somewhat in advance of his time, to allow him as his superiors thought "to say a few Masses before he died."

Following his ordination, Father McAstocker, then in his twenty-ninth year, went to live in Havre, Montana. Four years were spent here, writing, studying and discharging his priestly duties. In 1918, he went to Los Gatos to complete what is known as the Jesuit tertianship or third year of probation.

Then he became interested in the tubercular patients at the City and County Hospital of San Francisco. It is quite probable that while working among these unfortunate people he got his inspiration to write the clear and consoling books he does for the sick.

His next assignment was at the Government Indian School, Arlington, California. Here he taught and preached for eight years. From Arlington he went to Tacoma. Besides being the founder and first rector of Ballarmine College, Tacoma, Washington, he wrote: *A Friend of Mine* (1930); *Flashlights* (1929); *Himself* (1930), all during a period of six years.

He returned to Arlington to take charge of the small parish there, but because of his physical handicap he had to give up even this tiny parish. He is back again now in parish work as pastor of Christ the King parish for colored, in San Diego, California.

Besides the books already mentioned, he is also the author of: *My Ain Laddie* (1924); *Once Upon a Time* (1926); *Current Catholic Verse* (1926); *Herself* (1934); *The Carpenter* (1934); *The Joy of Sorrow* (1936); *Little Virtues* (1940), and *Speaking of Angels* (1946).   M. H.

Reverend Paul McCann   1909-

A desire to advance the cause of social justice prompts the recently ordained Father McCann to write. He is also eager to write Church History in such a manner "that the whole truth is told, leading to the inevitable conclusion in readers' minds that the only hope of salvation for men and women is to identify themselves with the mind and spirit of Christ in the Church as well as with the Mystical Body which is the Church."

Father McCann was born at Cambridge, Massachusetts, November 9, 1909, the son of Charles James and Margaret Josephine (Burns) McCann. He was educated at Cambridge High School, Latin School, Boston College, St. John's Seminary and St. Paul's Seminary. He also attended the Curry School of Oratory.

In 1935, he was an instructor at the Cambridge Evening High School; in 1936, instructor in history and English at the Rindge Technical School and Cambridge High School. It was natural for him to enter the teaching profession since his three sisters and brother are all educators.

Having been invited by the Most Reverend Archbishop Murray to continue his studies at St. Paul Seminary, he accepted and left for St. Paul, Minnesota, in 1939. Bishop Francis P. Keough of Providence, Rhode Island, ordained him on June 7, 1941, for the Archdiocese of St. Paul.

Father McCann's first writings consisted of poetry and educational articles for magazines such as *The Grade Teacher, The American School Board Journal,* and *The Catholic School Journal.* From that he progressed to short stories which appeared in *The Grail, The Miraculous Medal* magazine and several western story secular magazines. His best poem, perhaps, is "The Court Jester" which appeared in *The Magnificat.*

For his life of St. John Fisher, *A Valiant Bishop Against a Ruthless King,* published in 1938, he received the Apostolic Blessing of Pope Pius XI; and the Apostolic Blessing of Pope Pius XII for his book *The Circle of Sanctity.*

At present, he is writing a one-volume but full-length history of the Catholic Church, emphasizing those things he considers important in her development.   M. H.

Reverend Raphael McCarthy, S.J.   1889-

In his priestly duties, Father Raphael McCarthy often came in contact with the mentally ill. Finding such a dearth of Catholic writing on mental hygiene, he decided to specialize in this field.

With the permission of his superiors, he attended St. Louis University School of Medicine for a year and then the University of London, London, England. There he received his Ph.D. in psychology in 1925. Upon his return to the United States, he was associate professor of psychology at St. Louis University until 1928, when he was advanced to professor in this same department. He relinquished this post in 1936 when he was appointed president of Marquette University. His many duties then forced him to relegate mental hygiene to the status of a hobby. He keeps up his interest, however, by giving numerous talks on the subject. In the summer of 1938, he conducted a course of mental hygiene in the summer school of Marquette University.

In the summer of 1944 he resigned as President of Marquette University to become a Navy chaplain. He returned to the University in September as head of the Department of Psychology.

His two best known books, *Training the Adolescent* (1934) and *Safeguarding Mental Health* (1937), were written to present the Catholic point of view on the problems of child psychology and to give sane, sensible advice to those confronted with mental abnormalities, either in their own lives or in the lives of those under their charge. His other book, *The Measurement of Conation,* was published in 1926.

Father McCarthy was born in Marquette, Michigan, January 20, 1889, the son of Dennis Patrick and Catherine Agnes (Heaphy) McCarthy. His early education was received at the Spalding Institute in Peoria, Illinois, from 1902 to 1903. In 1903 he attended Regis College, Denver, and was there until 1906. In August of that year he entered the Society of Jesus. His A.B. and M.A. degrees were received from St. Louis University in 1911 and 1913 respectively.

M. H.

C. John McCole   1905-1939

C. John McCole was born in Sagola, Wisconsin, on April 25, 1905, the oldest son of his witty father, Patrick, and gracious mother, Blanche. After the death of his parents and brother, an aviator, he spent his holidays in Green Bay with his aunt, Miss Mary McCole, slender, hospitable and spirited and dedicated to others—a former school principal, who is as feminine as he was manly. Everything about him was expansive: his appearance, mature and compelling—stalwart in his tweeds with his candid brow, long grey hair, dynamic grey eyes and his leisurely gait. His understanding of all kinds of people and ideas; his capacity for work, made him a central figure in all the eastern colleges where he lectured on the drama, novel and creative writing.

He attended St. Norbert's College near Green Bay, Wisconsin, and received his M.A. at the University of Notre Dame where he taught. On the urging of Reverend James M. Gillis, C.S.P., he came East in 1934 as a member of the faculty of St. John's University in Brooklyn. He was also English lecturer at the College of St. Elizabeth, Convent Station, New Jersey, the College of Notre Dame, Staten Island, Seton Hall College, South Orange, New Jersey, and Hunter College. He taught article writing at the Bread Loaf School of English.

As a critic, McCole wished to praise in literature those fundamental and enduring qualities which proclaim "the invincibility of the human spirit" and do justice to the high courage and "the legitimate hungers of the human heart." In his book of essays on contemporary authors, *Lucifer At Large*, he castigated those authors whose characters, instead of falling nobly like Lucifer from a high place, have not even Lucifer's dignity but start out with no divine heritage to "fall from the floor." His purpose was unique and independent: to wound with irony and acumen the vulnerable heel in the writing of defeatism. He believed in the inviolable dignity of the human spirit which it is the purpose of art to mirror and not distort. He held that men live by a definite system of values, "and that these values are absolute and objective." His geniality was disarming.

Lew Sarett, poet and professor at Northwestern University, wrote of "Mac": "If he lived, I am confident McCole would become the most effective Catholic critic of literature in this country. I always felt like smiling when I looked at him. It was a smile not merely at him but also with him—with affection in it. I remember the fun and the boyish heart in him whenever we spoke of the earthly, wholesome life and earthly, honest and good people we both liked and his sober, scholarly look when we talked of the great causes for which good men fight. Mac was at once gentle and courageous, sweet and strong. He was liberal and tolerant in his attitudes but ruthless and uncompromising when the issues challenged the codes that govern good men and decent living. He was a most unusual Catholic crusader because of his tolerance and awareness combined with his unshakeable and intelligent faith. He did not fight solely in the name of authority; but he built on the *logic* under that authority; on the reasons and the reasonableness behind that authority; on the decent codes, the fine moral standards, the good taste, the concepts of truly Christian living which at bottom moved authorities to make decisions and hand them down. For clergymen to study Mac, his life and his way of crusading is to profit."

Dr. Joseph J. Reilly, professor at Hunter College, wrote: "He was utterly free from vanity. He had the tolerance of a great mind." Dr. Blanche Colton Williams of Hunter College wrote: "Students and his fellow instructors recognized in him a gentleman, genial, upright, fearless for the truth."

He was a member of the reviewing staff of *The Catholic World* and was a frequent contributor to *The Writer, The Commonweal, America, Contemporary American Literature* and *Spirit.* His books include *On Poetry,* a critical study of prosody on which, at twenty-five, he collaborated with Andrew Smithberger, and in 1937 his book of criticism, *Lucifer At Large.* He was Executive Chairman of the Catholic Poetry Society of America and a member of the Third Order of St. Norbert when he died suddenly on January 14, 1939, in New York City following an operation for appendicitis. He shared the life-span on earth of Him he served. His funeral services were held in Our Lady's Chapel of St. Patrick's Cathedral and he was buried in Iron Mountain, Michigan.

Katherine Bregy wrote: "C. John McCole's early death has left in our literature a chasm hard, indeed, to fill." For achieving an integrated mind, a selfless scope of activity, a character of inviolable purity and sensitiveness—thirty-three years were not too few.   N. G.

Anne O'Hare McCormick

Designated the "Woman of 1939," by the New York Career Tours for Women, sponsored by thirty-three women's organizations, Anne O'Hare McCormick received in that year not only this citation but also the American Women's Association medal for eminent achievement and the National Federation of Press Women's certificate of merit. She won in 1937 the Pulitzer Prize for foreign correspondence and the New York Newspaper Women's Club award for the best feature article of 1936, "Exploring the Hitler Legend." In 1944 she was awarded the Laetare Medal by Notre Dame University in Indiana.

Born in England and brought up from infancy in Ohio, she received her education in private schools abroad and in this country. Her B.A. degree was received from St. Mary's College, Columbus, Ohio, and her degree of LL.D. at the University of Dayton. Her mother, Teresa Beatrice O'Hare, was a poet and Anne O'Hare McCormick has also written verse, contained in *Braithwaite's Poetry Anthology*. Before and after graduation she contributed articles and stories to various magazines and was for a time associated with the *Catholic Universe Bulletin* of Cleveland. She married Francis J. McCormick, a manufacturer of Dayton, Ohio.

In 1922 she began contributing articles from abroad to the New York *Times* and soon became attached to its staff as foreign correspondent, winning distinction for her accounts of Fascism and the rise of Mussolini, with whom she had many interviews. She was made a member of the editorial council of the paper in 1936, the first woman to have a place on this influential board.

Meanwhile she had met the most important European figures, Hitler, Dollfuss, Schuschnigg, Benes, Van Zeeland, Stresemann, Blum, Chamberlain, Churchill, Eden, de Valera and Stalin. She has had several private audiences with Pope Pius XI and Pope Pius XII. Her interviews she uses for the purpose of studying personality, avoiding the distraction of taking notes. With a keen sense for news she has been on the spot when big things were about to happen, and early in 1939 within three months travelled from Cairo to Jerusalem, Rome, Budapest, Belgrade, Vienna, Berlin and Huszt, Carpatho-Ukraine, where she saw a new-born republic die in a day. In another two months she had visited five countries, for events of importance were fast accumulating. She not only saw the political leaders but talked to the people, obtaining firsthand information and storing up a knowledge that will be most valuable in post-war adjustments. In 1940 she travelled for six months on both sides of the battle line. Her column in the New York *Times* on alternate days is devoted to international affairs.

Here in the United States she has covered national conventions, made campaign surveys and met national leaders. Theta Phi Alpha gave her the Siena Medal in 1940 as the outstanding Catholic woman in the United States. She has received many honorary degrees: Doctor of Letters from Elmira College, Columbia University, New York University and Villanova College; Doctor of Humanities from Rollins College and Ohio State University; Doctor of Laws from the University of Dayton and Smith College. On January 2, 1947, she was elected to the National Institute of Arts and Letters. She was elected to the Department of Literature.

Though the recipient of so many honors, Mrs. McCormick remains extremely modest and lives quietly. Besides her newspaper work, she has also contributed to periodicals, including the *Ladies' Home Journal, Saturday Evening Post, Atlantic Monthly*, etc., and in 1928 she wrote a book on the Soviets, entitled *Hammer and Scythe: Communist Russia Enters the Second Decade*. She lectures and speaks occasionally on the radio. Her home is in New York when she is not abroad, but she remains a director of the Dayton Art Museum, art being also one of her main interests.

C. M. N.

Francis McCullagh 1874-

In 1923 when correspondent in Moscow for the New York *Herald,* Francis McCullagh sacrificed his career as a journalist to cable the true report of the proceedings of the trial of Archbishop Cieplak and fifteen priests, for teaching the catechism to Catholic children. As he knew, it meant his expulsion from Russia and though his accuracy was acknowledged by the English and American press he was not again accepted as a correspondent.

For twenty years McCullagh had concentrated on the study of Russian politics and the Russian language. His exclusion from Russia, therefore, he felt very keenly. This integrity has marked the long and varied experience of McCullagh during the years in which he covered the globe as correspondent and soldier.

Francis McCullagh was born in 1874 at Omagh, Tyrone, Ireland. He was educated by the Christian Brothers in Omagh and later went to St. Columb's, Derry. His newspaper work, begun in Glasgow, eventually took him all over the world. He was editor of the *Catholic Messenger* in Colombo, Ceylon, of the *Siam Free Press* in Bangkok and English editor of the *Japan Times* in Tokio and then took over the editorship of the *Novi Krai* in Port Arthur, Russia. While in Siam and later in Port Arthur he also represented the New York *Herald.* Witnessing the opening attack by the Japanese under Togo on Port Arthur in 1903, he managed to escape through mines and falling shells to Chefoo whence McCullagh sent the *Herald* the first description of the outbreak of the war. As war correspondent, he was taken prisoner at various times by the opposing armies, but wherever trouble started there he was to be found cabling reports to his paper of the moment.

At the outbreak of war in 1914 McCullagh was in Russia and remained with the Russian army until he received his appointment as lieutenant in the Royal Irish Fusiliers in December 1914. He saw service in Macedonia, Serbia and Gallipoli. For his work in Serbia he was decorated by King Peter and made Knight Commander of the Royal Order of St. Sava. Because of his knowledge of Russian, in 1918 he was sent to Siberia with General Knox's Military Mission, with rank of captain. The Bolshevik revolution was then spreading fast throughout Russia and only through his wit, sharpened by grave danger and helped by his long experience, did McCullagh eventually manage to escape from Russia and reach England. His book, *A Prisoner of the Reds,* published in 1921 tells of these months of danger and hardship.

Two years later, in 1922, his old paper, the New York *Herald,* sent him back to Moscow as correspondent and it was in April 1923, that he ended his journalistic career by sending out the truth from the Soviet capital. *The Bolshevik Persecution of Christianity* published in 1924 portrays Communist methods, of which he has intimate knowledge.

Mr. McCullagh's versatile talents kept him busy in other ways after that. He lectured on Russia in the United States in 1925, and then went to Australia as a guest of the American Fleet, visiting other countries as well in the course of the voyage. Later he travelled extensively in Latin America. In Brazil he accompanied the great Jesuit scientist, Father Camille Torrend, on an expedition to the province of Goyaz. He went to Mexico in 1927 to investigate President Calles' anti-Catholic policy, which he revealed in his book, *Red Mexico,* published in 1928. During the civil war in Spain he was with the Nationalist forces, and in 1937 his book, *In Franco's Spain,* told of his experiences.

From Francis McCullagh's earlier experiences as war correspondent we have: *With the Cossacks* (1916); *The Fall of Abd-Ul-Hamid* (1910); *Italy's War for a Desert* (1912); *Tales from Turkey* (1914) (with Allan Ramsay), and a pamphlet *Russia To-day* published by the *Times.* He has also contributed to many newspapers, periodicals and reviews. Now in the United States, of which country he has become a citizen, he resides in New York and continues to use his pen for the cause of truth and integrity in journalism and in the interests of the Catholic Church. His recreations are travelling, sketching, writing, painting. Practically all his journalistic work appears in London, England.   D. D.

Donagh MacDonagh   1912-

In collaboration with W. B. Yeats and F. R. Higgins, Donagh MacDonagh worked on a collection of Irish ballads, on which he is an authority.

Donagh MacDonagh was born in 1912, the son of Thomas MacDonagh, the poet and executed leader of the Irish Rising of Easter Week in 1916. He was educated by the Jesuits at Belvedere College and was graduated with a B.A. degree in Modern Languages in 1936. Called to the Irish bar that same year, he has been State Prosecutor for most of that time. From the University College in Dublin, he received his Master's degree in 1939, and wrote on "The Poetry of T. S. Eliot" for his thesis.

Donagh MacDonagh has had his verse published in many Irish, English, and American magazines, including *Criterion, Dublin Magazine, Poetry* (Chicago), *Poetry* (Scotland), *Furioso* (New York), *The Old Line* (Maryland) and *Irish Times.* For several years he was at work writing a history of the pre-Rising period, 1900-1916. Some of his short stories appear in *New Writing* and the *Faber Book of Irish Short Stories.*

He has frequently broadcast feature programs, stories and plays from Radio Eirean. He gained outstanding recognition during the twenty-fifth anniversary commemoration of the 1916 Rising, through his broadcast of "Easter Christening." From 1940 to 1942 he was Irish correspondent for the BBC.

By his wife Maire Smith, since deceased, he has a son and daughter. He is the author of *Twenty Poems* (1934), and *Veterans and Other Poems* (1941). M. H.

Michael MacDonagh 1860-

After forty years' service as a reporter for the London *Times,* Mr. MacDonagh retired in 1933. His work as a reporter for the great national newspaper was of the most varied kind. It brought Mr. MacDonagh as "Our Special Correspondent" to all parts of England and Scotland on all sorts of missions. He also reported the debates in both Houses of Parliament. Since he had about ten years' service in the Reporters' Gallery of both Houses as the special correspondent of *The Freeman's Journal* in Dublin, Mr. MacDonagh had fifty years of experience from Gladstone and Chamberlain to Lloyd George and Ramsay MacDonald.

Since he was the only Catholic on the staff of the *Times,* he was given the task of reporting all the great Catholic functions in London. He covered the memorable International Eucharistic Congress held in London in 1908 and the consecration of Westminster Cathedral by Cardinal Bourne in 1910. At the latter elaborate ceremony, Mr. MacDonagh was not only the only layman, he was the only journalist invited.

Mr. MacDonagh was born in Limerick, Ireland, in 1860, and was educated by the Christian Brothers. In 1888 he married Mary Govan. She died in 1924. They had one son.

In 1880 Mr. MacDonagh began his journalistic career working for *The Munster News.* In 1885 he joined *The Freeman's Journal* in Dublin and was sent to London on its parliamentary staff in 1887, succeeding Mr. T. P. O'Connor, M.P. (who left to found *The Star)* as writer of *Freeman's* descriptive article "In the House."

Mr. MacDonagh was one of the Freeman's staff of reporters that gave the interested world the historic debate of the Irish Parliamentary Party in December 1890, which led to the downfall of Parnell. The last important event which Mr. MacDonagh described for the *Freeman* was Parnell's funeral in Dublin in October 1891. In the following year Mr. MacDonagh took up his residence permanently in London.

His books include: *Bishop Doyle; The Book of Parliament; Irish Life and Character; Parliament; Its Romance, Its Comedy, Its Pathos; The Life of Daniel O'Connell; The Viceroy's Post-bag; The Reporter's Gallery; The Speaker of the House; The Irish At the Front; The Irish On the Somme; The Home Rule Movement; The Pageant of Parliament; The Life of William O'Brien* (1928); *The English King* (1929); *Daniel O'Connell and The Story of Catholic Emancipation* (1929); *In London During the Great War,* and *The Diary of a Journalist* (1935). M. H.

Most Reverend Alexander MacDonald
1858-1941

Alexander MacDonald was born in S. W. Mabou, Inverness County, Cape Breton, Nova Scotia, in 1858 the son of Finlay and Catharine (Beaton) MacDonald. He was educated in St. Francis Xavier College, Antigonish, Nova Scotia, where he received a B.A., 1879; an honorary LL.D., 1905; and the Propaganda, Rome, Italy, from which he had his D.D. in 1884.

From the year of his ordination in 1884 until 1903, he was successively professor of English, Latin, philosophy and Christian Doctrine at the University of St. Francis Xavier, Antigonish, Nova Scotia. In 1900 he was appointed vicar general by Bishop Cameron of Antigonish, a post he held until 1908 when he was made bishop of Victoria, British Columbia. He resigned his bishopric in 1923 and was appointed to the titular see of Hebron. He had served as pastor of St. Andrew's Church, Antigonish, Nova Scotia, from 1903 to 1908. The year 1908 to 1909 was spent visiting Rome and Ireland. He was consecrated bishop at Rome, January 3, 1909. He attended the Plenary Council at Quebec in 1909 and the Eucharistic Congress at Montreal in 1910.

The well-known Roman theologian and author, the Most Reverend Monsignor Lepicier, in an introductory letter to Bishop MacDonald's *The Apostles' Creed,* wrote: "Your claim that the Apostles' Creed was really composed by the chosen disciples of Christ and as such has been handed down to us through the ages is well established indeed, and so your work is to be considered as a most valuable contribution to Catholic literature. Other points which are treated by you in connexion with the main subject, such as, for instance, 'The Discipline of the Secret,' are of great importance in the field of critical studies and represent laborious researches, the value of which will not escape the attention of the thoughtful student."

The Single Tax Law which did not exempt the land on which churches were erected imposed an unbearable burden on the parishes of Victoria, particularly on the Cathedral which occupied a very desirable site. Other financial difficulties occasioned by the First World War brought about an acute situation implying the imminent threat of having the Cathedral property sold. To raise money Bishop MacDonald undertook a tour among the dioceses of Canada and the United States, giving public lectures, putting himself at the services of other bishops for confirmation tours, conducting seminary classes and soliciting the assistance of the faithful, all with very gratifying results. At the same time he had legal proceedings instituted to test the law taxing land occupied by churches in British Columbia. The case passed from the Supreme Court of British Columbia to the Appeal Court and finally to the Privy Council, which body by a unanimous decision declared the law in question unconstitutional.

Other books by Bishop MacDonald are: *The Symbol of the Apostles* (1903); *The Symbol in Sermons* (1904); *The Sacrifice of the Mass in the Light of Scripture and Tradition* (1925); *Religious Questions of the Day, The Mercies of the Sacred Heart* (1904) (Sermons); *Sacraments: A Course of Seven Sermons* (1906); *The Apostles' Creed* (2nd ed. enlarged); *Stray Leaves or Traces of Travel* (1915); *It is the Mass that Matters; The Primacy of Thought in Poetry* (1928), *The Mass Explained,* and a large number of pamphlets.

He lived his years of retirement at St. Francis Xavier University and until infirmity made it impossible he devoted considerable time to writing.

He died on February 24, 1941.   M. H.

Edward MacDonald 1900-

Gregory MacDonald 1903-

EDWARD MAC DONALD

The two brothers, Edward and Gregory Mac-Donald, occupy a unique place in Catholic journalism because of their unselfish and unfailing devotion to the spread of Catholic truth. American born and sons of Doctor William G. MacDonald of Boston, at an early age they went to England with their widowed mother to continue their schooling—a suggestion made by her intimate friend Louise Imogen Guiney, a former fellow-student at Elmhurst Academy, Providence, Rhode Island. They have remained in England ever since. Both boys received a Benedictine training at Douai School and early showed talent in the use of pen and ink.

In 1918 Edward joined the teaching staff of Thetford Grammar School. Two years later he was appointed Correspondence Secretary of the Catholic Social Guild at Oxford where Father Charles Dominic Plater, S.J., encouraged him to exercise his journalistic ability. In 1921 he became sub-editor of the London *Universe,* specializing later in dramatic and film criticism for London daily and weekly papers.

Gregory was an Exhibitioner at Wadham College, Oxford, where he took Second Class Honors in Modern History. In 1933 he won the Marshall Prize for Polish at London University and specialized in Slavonic studies, being the first to receive the Howard Prize for a thesis on a language other than Russian—his subject was Polish. He is now Secretary of the Anglo-Polish Society and a recognized authority in the discussion of politics, economics, and international affairs. He is the best informed English journalist on Poland.

Both brothers contributed regularly to *G. K.'s Weekly* from the first number until it became the *Weekly Review* in 1937, and never were disciples more faithful to the teachings of a Master than they to the Distributist ideas of Gilbert K. Chesterton. When His Eminence, Cardinal Hinsley established the Catholic Enquiry Bureau at Archbishop's House, Westminster, Edward was put in charge of the press department. They are jointly responsible for the two books *Cathedrals and Abbey Churches of England* and *Castles of England and Wales.* In 1933 Edward edited *G. K.'s: A Miscellany of the First 500 Issues of G. K.'s Weekly.* Gregory is a regular contributor to the London *Catholic Times* of which he was formerly editor and should be proud of the fact that he was the originator of the famous pilgrimage to Rome of three hundred unemployed men, sponsored by the London *Universe.*

Edward married Winefred Thatcher in 1927 and has four children, three sons and one daughter. Gregory married Dorothy Kay of Capetown, South Africa, and has two sons. To those who know the sacrifices demanded in the defence of truth the example set by Edward and Gregory MacDonald should prove an inspiration.   A. Mu.

Reverend William James McGarry, S.J.
1894-1941

Father McGarry was singularly devoted to Saint Paul. His book, *Paul and the Crucified,* in its first form was a course of lectures on the doctrine of Redemption as delivered in the classroom to Jesuit scholastics. His students were so enthusiastic about the beauty and clarity of the lectures that they begged their professor to publish them. He adapted the lectures for less theologically trained readers. The Spiritual Book Associates made the volume their choice in January 1940.

Father McGarry died in a New York City subway station on September 23, 1941. He had been stricken with a heart attack while riding on the subway at Columbus Circle, Manhattan. He was taken from the train and the last rites were administered by the Reverend R. E. Gilbert, C.S.P., who was summoned and Reverend William Guinan, a chaplain who had been in the subway. Doctor McGarry was on his way to the Convent of the Cenacle, Ronkonkoma, Long Island, where he was scheduled to begin a series of conferences.

The son of Edward Leslie and Julia (Burns) McGarry, he was born in Hamilton, Massachusetts, in 1894. He entered the Society of Jesus in 1911. From Woodstock College he received an A.B. in 1917; an M.A., 1918, and an S.T.D. in 1926. Fordham University conferred a Ph.D. degree on him in 1922. He was ordained in 1925. After study in Rome and Jerusalem he was made a licentiate in Sacred Scripture by the Pontifical Biblical Commission at Rome in 1930. Fordham honored him with a Litt.D. in 1938 and in the same year he received an LL.D. from Holy Cross University.

Doctor McGarry was professor of mathematics and philosophy at Fordham from 1918 to 1922. He served Weston College as professor of Sacred Scripture, 1930 to 1935. He was also dean of Philosophy from 1930 to 1933. In 1935 he became professor of dogmatic theology, dean of studies and dean of the theological faculty. He left Weston College in 1937 to become president of Boston College. He came to New York City in 1939 and assumed the editorship of *Thought* and later of *Theological Studies*.

Doctor McGarry was the author of *The Biblical Commission* (1931); *Anthropology and Knowledge of God* (1932); *Mystical Body* (1935); *Paul and the Crucified* (1939); *Unto the End* (1941). His last book, *He Cometh,* was published posthumously.   M. S.

Reverend George J. MacGillivray 1876-

The Reverend George J. MacGillivray, born in 1876 at Edinburgh, was baptized and reared a member of the Episcopal Church of Scotland. His mother had on him "the very best possible influence through her profound goodness and beauty of character." By his father he was brought up from his earliest years "in the belief that Darwin's theory was an incontrovertible fact, and that the Bible could no longer be accepted by well-informed people with the simple faith of a former generation." At school—the Edinburgh Academy, "the recognized school for the sons of Edinburgh professional men"—he learned nothing more, he declares. He was not, however, taught to regard the Catholic Church "with any sort of horror or hostility." "The impression I gathered was merely that Roman Catholicism was an old and out-of-date religion, which some people strongly clung to, but which was perfectly unreasonable."

Continuing his education at Edinburgh University, he took his M.A. there in 1895. During the following year, while studying French at Geneva—ostensibly to prepare for a position in a bank—he decided to become a minister. After four months' study in Italy he entered Trinity College, Cambridge, then became a member of the so-called Bishop's Hostel at Farnham, where a small number of candidates for the ministry received training under the supervision of Doctor Randall Davidson, Bishop of Winchester. His ministerial work began when, after receiving the Anglican diaconate, he was assigned to Portsmouth Parish Church.

The following year after ordination to the "Priesthood" he resumed his duties, until 1903, when he was transferred to Croyden, his field of labor for the next seven years. In the summer of 1908 a chance visit to Lourdes, made in the spirit of curiosity rather than of faith, left nevertheless an "extraordinarily vivid impression." . . . "It seemed that somehow I was in the presence of a supernatural power, or in a supernatural atmosphere, surrounded by supernatural forces." The experience, however, did not lead him to further enquiries.

Moved by a growing interest in foreign missions, he volunteered for service in Syria, where since 1886 the Church of England had been engaged in work chiefly educational. For four years, from 1910 to 1914, he assisted in the establishment of schools for the natives and in teaching, at the same time studying religious conditions, noting and comparing the methods and progress of such other missions as those of the Russian Orthodox Church, of the American Presbyterians, and of the French Dominicans. The result of all this experience was that his own faith in the Church of England was "considerably shaken." By the time he returned to England in 1914 he was "beginning to think that the Roman Catholic Church was the one true Church of Christ." He had not, however, reached any "settled conviction."

Assigned for parochial duty to a little suburban church in Dundee, Scotland, the Reverend George MacGillivray early in 1915 resumed his ministerial labors, only to find himself, before long, harassed by serious doubts and questionings concerning the authenticity of Anglican claims. For two years he carried on, all the time examining into the Roman Catholic position, reading the Scriptures, the early Fathers, church history, everything that could lead in any way to a settlement of his perplexities. At length, finding his position no longer tenable, he laid his case before his bishop, who advised him not yet to resign his charge but to accept a leave of absence.

World War I being in progress, he answered the appeal of the French Red Cross for volunteers to drive ambulances and was accordingly sent to Salonika, where he continued in service till after the Armistice. On returning to England, Christmas Day, 1918, having meanwhile resigned his benefice, he spent a month at Downside Abbey and was there received into the Church on Candlemas Day, 1919. In October of the same year he entered the Beda College, Rome, to study for the priesthood and in 1923 was ordained.

Since then Father MacGillivray has filled various positions. He was appointed assistant priest at Saint Anselm's, Tooting Bec, in South London; two years later he went to Saint Mary Magdalen's, Brighton; and in 1928 he was appointed chaplain to the Catholic undergraduates in Cambridge University. In 1932 he was appointed parish priest of Maidstone, where he remained until 1939. He is now rector of St. Joseph's, Brighton.

Besides articles contributed to various periodicals, *The Scotsman,* the *Tablet,* the *Month,* the *Universe* and pamphlets for the Catholic Truth Society, the author has published: *Father Vernon and His Critics* (1929), an answer to an attack on the Catholic Church made by two Cambridge dons on the occasion of the publication of Father Vernon Johnson's story of his conversion *One Lord, One Faith;* also *The Way of Life* (1931); *Through the East to Rome* (1932) his autobiography; a small *Life of Our Lord for Catholic Schools* (1932); *The Christian Virtues* (1934); *Saints You Ought to Know* (1936).   S. J. M.

John Steven McGroarty 1862-1944

Although he was not born in California—he moved there when he was nearly forty years old —John Steven McGroarty became one of California's chief historians and was its poet laureate from 1933 until his death.

Born in Foster Township, Luzerne County, Pennsylvania, on August 20th, 1862, the son of Hugh and Mary M. McGroarty, he was educated at the Harry Hillman Academy in Wilkes-Barre, Pennsylvania. In 1925 the University of California conferred an Litt.D. upon him and in 1927 the University of Santa Clara honored him with an LL.D. degree. He lived in Tujunga, California.

In 1890, he married Ida Lubrecht and in that same year became treasurer of Luzerne County, setting a new age record for that office in Pennsylvania. While serving in this capacity, he studied law and was admitted to the bar in 1894. After practising for two years, he went to Butte, Montana, to serve on the legal staff of Marcus Daly, the copper leader. After Mr. Daly's death, he went to Mexico on a mining venture and in 1901 arrived with his wife, in Los Angeles. There he joined the Los Angeles *Times*. A poem, inspired by the death of Krupp, a German munitions manufacturer, attracted the attention of the publisher of the *Times*, Harrison Gray Otis, and brought the two together to become intimate friends.

Mr. McGroarty is best known, perhaps, as the author of *The Mission Play*, which ran for twenty years at San Gabriel. During 3,200 performances, 2,500,000 spectators were present. This drama of Father Serra Junipero, colonizer of California, dealt with the history of the mission. It was presented again during the international exposition in San Diego in 1936. As early as 1901 Mr. McGroarty became a crusader for the preservation and restoration of the missions, many of which were being used to store grain and stable horses. His work for the missions was rewarded by Pope Pius XI when he made him a Knight of St. Gregory.

In 1934, Mr. McGroarty was elected to Congress and served two terms. He supported the Townsend old age pension plan, although he later introduced a bill which provided $100.00 per month instead of $200.00 to persons sixty years of age.

He was the author of *Poets and Poetry of Wyoming Valley* (1885); *Just California* (1903); *Wander Songs* (1908), and *The King's Highway* (1909). Mr. McGroarty's historical works include: *California: Its History and Romance* (1912); *Los Angeles, From the Mountains to the Sea* (3 vols., 1921), and *California of the South: A History* (4 vols., 1933). Besides *The Mission Play* (1911), his other plays are *La Golondrina* (1923); *Osceola* (1927), and *Babylon* (1927).

When he was presented with a statue of the Blessed Mother, a gift from the Catholic Film and Radio Guild on the occasion of his 81st birthday, on August 20th, 1943, he remarked: "This is the last honor I ever expect to receive and it is the one I shall cherish most."

He died on August 7, 1944, four years after the death of his wife.

M. H.

Paul Dominic McGuire 1903-

An internationally known exponent of Catholic Action, Paul McGuire was born in Peterborough, South Australia, in 1903, of an Australian pioneering family. His father, James McGuire, was for many years Railway Commissioner in South Australia, and his mother, Mary McGuire, was during her girlhood a school teacher on the remote frontiers of an Australian settlement. He was their eighth son. Five brothers served in World War I and three were killed. He was educated at the Christian Brothers College, Adelaide, and at the university of Adelaide, where he became Tinline Research Scholar in History and began to write seriously as editor of the *Adelaide University Bulletin* and as literary and dramatic critic. During his twenties he traveled extensively and contributed to numerous publications, including the *Sydney Bulletin* and *The Triad,* in Australia, and the English *Spectator, Nation and Athenaeum, G. K.'s Weekly* and *Observer.*

In 1927 he married Frances Margaret Cheadle of South Australia. They lived for one year in an Australian mountain shack and then in a thousand-year-old Somersetshire house which had once been part of a Benedictine abbey. In addition to writing several books, he lectured for University Extension movements in literature and in social history, and was special correspondent on various occasions for newspapers in various countries. In these countries he made a study of Catholic Action. With the Reverend J. P. O'Doherty, O.P., he was co-founder of the Catholic Guild for Social Studies in Australia, of which he is First Master.

During the Spanish Civil War (1937) Paul McGuire represented, in Spain, the Duke of Wellington's Committee for the Repatriation of Spanish Children. In 1938 he lectured extensively in the United States on social questions and on Catholic Action. Under the auspices of the Knights of Columbus he lectured on Catholic Action throughout the United States and Canada in 1939, and the following year Knights of Columbus councils in eighteen cities of the United States sponsored lectures by him on Catholic Action. He presents his information and ideas clearly and forcibly. With the Reverend John Fitzsimons he was joint editor and author of *Restoring All Things: A Guide to Catholic Action.*

Other published works include: (poetry) *The Two Men and Other*

Poems; (a critical essay) *The Poetry of Gerard Manley Hopkins; Australia: Her Heritage—Her Future,* published in England as *Australian Journey; Westward the Course! The New World of Oceania,* a book about the southwestern Pacific, concerned with the expansion of Western man and the Western mind in the lands under Asia, beyond the Pacific. He also wrote many novels, mostly mystery stories. Among the latter are: *The Spanish Steps; Funeral in Eden; W. 1; Cry Aloud for a Murder; Born to be Hanged; Threepence to Marble Arch; 7:30 Victoria; Murder at High Noon; Death Fugue; Murder in Haste; Murder by the Law; The Tower; Three Dead Men; The Black Rose* (1931); *There Sits Death,* and *Death Tolls the Bell.* American magazines to which he has contributed are *America, Columbia, The Sign, Extension* and *The Commonweal.*

C. M. N.

Very Reverend John Ambrose McHugh, O.P.
1880-

Like his distinguished co-worker, Father Callan, Father John A. McHugh, O.P., has been bred in the high tradition of English letters. Born in Louisville, Kentucky, on the 2nd of November, 1880, he appears during his school days to have been a boy entrenched in serious study. Early in his career he began to look for that "wisdom which ordereth all things sweetly." His school days with the Xaverian Brothers in his native city were a "remote preparation" for things to come. In 1897, St. Dominic called this young Kentuckian to the novitiate at the venerable Priory of St. Rose, the first Dominican house of the United States. The new novice became Brother Ambrose, and the tranquil years that followed were steeped in philosophy, theology and other ecclesiastical subjects; and although Brother Ambrose "filled many notebooks with the semi-annual theses, the dissertations and class disputations, which are a part of the work in the excellent Dominican course," literature was not neglected. During these student days some of his writings appeared in print—book reviews, short magazine articles, and a column in *The Rosary Magazine.*

Father McHugh was ordained at St. Joseph's Priory, Somerset, Ohio, on the feast of Sts. Peter and Paul, 1905. He was then transferred to Washington, D. C., to pursue graduate work at the then recently established Dominican House of Studies and at the Catholic University. Then ensued special theological work at the Pontifical Universities of the Minerva, Rome, and of Fribourg, Switzerland. At Rome in 1907 the Dominican College of the Minerva conferred upon him the degree of Lector of Sacred Theology.

Returning to his country, Father McHugh taught at the Washington

House of Studies between 1908 and 1915. He continued to specialize in his own fields of speculative and practical theology, in church history and patrology. Despite a heavy program, he found opportunity also for preaching and writing. At this time he prepared a number of articles for the newly established *Catholic Encyclopaedia.* Of particular scholarship at this time are his commentaries on the whole First Part of the *Summa Theologica,* so far unpublished.

In 1911, with the production of two works on the Dominican Office and rubrics for the nuns, he began his felicitous collaboration with Father Charles J. Callan, O.P. Together they have written and published some thirty volumes on the liturgy, the Scriptures, homiletical and theological subjects, devotion and literary studies. In 1914 they conceived the idea and helped to bring about the establishment of the Dominican students' attractive review *Dominicana.*

In 1915, because of impaired health Fathers McHugh and Callan had been assigned to a small country parish at Hawthorne, near New York, in order to teach at the Seminary of the Foreign Mission Society, immortalized as Maryknoll, which had just recently been founded and started on its apostolic way. These two fathers thus became members of its professorial staff, residing in their Dominican home at Hawthorne and going daily to their classes at Maryknoll. This they are still doing.

Father McHugh's first book, *The Casuist,* appeared in 1917. Such was its scientific scholarship that it was submitted to and approved by Rome along with other matter when its author passed his examination there for Mastership in Sacred Theology. He also holds a D.Litt. degree from Gonzaga College, Washington, D. C. He is a past president of The Catholic Biblical Society of America, and has been co-editor of *The Homiletic and Pastoral Review* since the summer of 1916.

A. M.

Claude McKay 1890-

Benjamin Brawley in his book, *The Negro Genius,* appraises Claude McKay as the "most vigorous of negro poets in the years immediately after the first World War."

Claude McKay was born in Jamaica, British West Indies, on September 15, 1890, the son of Thomas Francis and Ann Elizabeth (Edwards) McKay. When he was six years of age his parents sent him to live in a more refined part of the island with his brother, who though a school teacher and lay reader for an Anglican Church, was an agnostic. Four years later he was reading Huxley, Lecky, Haeckel and Gibbon whom he liked especially.

When he was sixteen years old he met the agnostic Mr. Jekyll, an English squire who was interested in the folklore of the island of Jamaica and had written a book about it. Mr. Jekyll took an interest in him and helped him as to the thought, rhyme and rhythm in writing poems in the Jamaican dialect, published in book form in 1911 under the title of *Songs of Jamaica*. In this book of fifty poems there is an appendix containing six poems set to music which Claude McKay had composed but which were written by Mr. Jekyll. Since the book was a success he was advised to come to America to widen his education, which he did in 1912.

He entered the Tuskegee Normal and Industrial Institute in Alabama organized by Booker T. Washington and which Claude McKay considers "a wonderful school of all negro students and teachers." He stayed there only a short time, however, having transferred to Kansas State College where he remained until 1914. He then left for New York. From 1915 to 1918 he worked as a waiter and a porter. In 1918 Frank Harris, the editor of *Pearsons Magazine*, engaged him to write and later Max Eastman invited him to join the staff of the *Liberator* as an associate editor. Then he went to London and while there published his little book of poems *Spring in New Hampshire and Other Poems* (1920), containing in its forty pages a number of poems on "subjects suggested by nature." Perhaps his best known collection of poems is *Harlem Shadows* which was published in New York in 1922 with an introduction by Max Eastman of the *Liberator*.

McKay went to Russia soon after the Revolution. Shocked to find there "a government and a society basically anti-human nature," he went on "to sample the rest of Europe." While in France and in Spain he says, "I had leisure for visiting and contemplation in the cathedrals. I lifted my head up at the great Gothic arches and was overwhelmed by their beauty. It was in Europe that I saw the vision of the grandeur and glory of the Roman Catholic religion. . . . In Spain," he says, "I discovered that Catholicism had made of the Spanish people the most noble and honest and humane of any in the world." After twelve years in Europe and North Africa, he returned to the United States, still an agnostic.

In 1938 he met Ellen Tarry, a convert to the Church since 1922. She worked as feature writer on the *Amsterdam News*, New York City, and is a writer of children's books. It was she who set him thinking when she said: "It is easier for an intellectual not to believe than to believe." Disliking taking things easy he started to read books about the Roman Empire and its decadence and learned that Jesus Christ fulfilled the longing of a man's heart for peace.

During the winter of 1941 to 1942 he became very ill. Ellen Tarry visited him and brought with her some girls from Friendship House to nurse him. Mary Jerdo was among them. "She was the intellectual type, and we discovered much in common," says McKay. In the spring of 1944 Mary Jerdo, through Bishop Sheil, invited him to Chicago. "That fall I was baptized by the Paulist, Father Riach of Old St. Mary's."

Besides the books already mentioned, he wrote *Constab Ballads* (1912); *Home to Harlem* (1927); *Banjo* (1929); *Gingertown* (1932); *Banana Bottom* (1933); *A Long Way from Home* (1937) (autobiographical); and *Harlem: Negro Metropolis* (1940). The novels stress certain degraded aspects of life. **M. H.**

Compton Mackenzie 1883-

At the mature age of nineteen and a half, Mr. Mackenzie founded and edited a magazine, *The Oxford Point of View*. At twenty-four he published his first book of verse. Publishers were unwilling to take a chance with his first novel, however, and seven of them returned his manuscript. In despair over gaining his livelihood by writing, he thought gardening would be more profitable and tried his hand at that. He even resorted for one week to "the intolerable boredom of acting for a living."

Martin Secker was a reader for one of these unsporting publishers. He liked the manuscript. When, soon afterward, he inherited a legacy and decided to become a publisher himself, he sought out Mackenzie to secure the novel for his first venture. *The Passionate Elopement* (1916) appeared on its author's twenty-eighth birthday and was an immediate hit. The publishing firm was off to a good start and the stage lost an actor.

If Compton Mackenzie had remained on the stage, he would have been but following a traditional family profession. His father, Edward Compton, was director of and actor for The Compton Comedy Company which toured the British Isles in old English comedy for over thirty-five years with hardly a break. His mother, Virginia Bateman, was an actress, but did not care for acting. Fay Compton, his sister, is well known on the British and American stages; she created the title role in J. M. Barrie's *Mary Rose*. Mackenzie is really the family name. In the days when the theatre was in bad repute his grandfather took the name "Compton," the maiden name of his great-grandmother, to protect the name of "Mackenzie." The author used the name "Compton" for only one of his works, a play, *The Gentleman in Grey*, which he wrote for his father's repertoire.

Mr. Mackenzie preferred to make his living by writing. After the publication of his first novel he wrote lyrics and "Potted Plays" for Harry Pélissier's revues and follies. From his management of the ladies of the ballet for a revue he got the background for his second novel, *Carnival* (1912). When this novel was also a success he decided he could depend upon writing for his support. In Fay Compton's memoirs, *Rosemary*, he writes, "We both agreed that we were neither of us as much absorbed as we ought to be in our professions and yet for some reason or other we both still work at them as hard as might enthusiastic beginners. We agreed one of the reasons we worked so hard was to make enough money to do the things we liked doing; but what seemed to us at this late hour a grave injustice was that whereas both of us groaned under our self-allotted tasks, we were always credited, by our critics, with an almost sinful facility." His output has been so great that the conclusion he is a facile writer is a natural one. The quantity seems all the more extraordinary when we know that since his early youth he has suffered from sciatica and neuritis when any worry or fatigue was present. Much of his writing has had to be done in bed or in an invalid's chair.

Edward Montagu Compton Mackenzie was born January 17, 1883, at West Hartlepool, England. He attended St. Paul's School and Magdalen College, Oxford. He received second class honours in Modern History in 1904. After he left Oxford he was reading for the bar and was to specialize in ecclesiastical and canon law. In 1905 he married Faith Stone, the youngest daughter of Edward Stone, a former master at Eton. She is the author of *Cardinal's Niece; Sibyl of the North,* and *Angle of Error,* and two autobiographical volumes, *As Much As I Dare,* and *More Than I Should.* After his marriage he gave up the bar and began to think seriously of being ordained to the Anglican ministry. He spent some time at a small country vicarage in Cornwall and lectured about the countryside. In January 1908 he became a lay reader and a short time later was licensed to preach in church. In April 1914 he was received into the Catholic Church at Capri. Many consider his trilogy, *The Altar Steps* (1922), *The Parson's Progress* (1924), and *The Heavenly Ladder* (1924), the story of his own experiences.

He had been a second lieutenant with the First Hertfordshire Regiment from 1900 to 1901, but his ill health kept him out of the Army in 1914. In 1915 he succeeded in obtaining a commission as lieutenant in the Royal Marines and he served with the Royal Naval Division in the Dardanelles Expedition. In 1916 he was made captain. He was military control officer in Athens, 1916, and director of the Aegean Intelligence Service, Syria, 1917. For his war services he was awarded the Order of the Holy Redeemer (Greek); White Eagle with Swords, 4th Class (Serbia); 1915 Star; Chevalier of the Legion of Honour, and O.B.E. He has published four volumes of his war memories. For one, *Greek Memories,* he was prosecuted under the Official Secrets Acts and was fined a hundred pounds. The hearings and trial were "in camera." The case cost him about $25,000 and left him practically penniless. He had to sell the manuscripts of nearly all his books and some treasures from his library as well. In 1939 *Greek Memories* was re-issued. *Pericles,* and *Marathon* and *Salamis* are also fruits of his service and interest in Greece.

Mrs. Mackenzie used to play the piano for him while he was writing. Then he began to use the gramophone. In 1923 he started a monthly review, *The Gramophone,* which now has a world-wide circulation. Later he founded *Vox* to criticize radio broadcasts. This magazine merged with *The Gramophone.* He has written a monthly editorial for the review all these years. From these editorial comments, which amount to almost half a million words, the material for *A Musical Chair* has geen gathered. He was also the literary critic of the *Daily Mail* for five years, 1931 to 1935.

The author can scarcely remember when he was not a perfervid Gael. He laments that when he was eight or nine he did not meet a Gaelic enthusiast at whose feet he could have sat. A gift of Scott's *Tales of a Grandfather* on his seventh birthday inflamed this interest. As a young man he was determined to obtain land in the country of his forefathers.

He was advised to learn Gaelic, but felt he must have Gaelic land before he acquired the Gaelic tongue. In 1931, after twenty-eight years of waiting, he was able to buy property in Scotland. He then began to learn Gaelic. He is a Scots nationalist and is haunted by dreams of a Scottish Free State. His Jacobite interest inspired such books as *Prince Charlie, The Lost Cause,* and *Catholicism and Scotland.* As the Nationalist candidate he won the rectorial election at Glasgow University in 1931. He was the first Catholic Lord Rector of the University since the sixteenth century.

He is the author of *Poor Relations* (1919); The *Vanity Girl* (1920); *Rich Relatives* (1921); *Buttercups and Daisies* (1931); *The East Wind* (1937); *The South Wind* (1937); *The West Wind* (1940); *West to North* (1941); *Mr. Roosevelt* (1944), and very many others.   M. S.

Cecily Mackworth   1911-

Born in 1911 at Llantillio Pertholey (South Wales), Cecily Mackworth had no proper education until she was fourteen "and thus had time" she says, "to read through the whole of Shakespeare and most of the classics at a most unsuitable age. After three years at a number of unsatisfactory schools, I went to the London School of Economics and took a diploma in Journalism. When I was nineteen I got a bad attack of Wanderlust (which has lasted ever since) and started off to get acquainted with Europe, working my passage by means of odd jobs, governessing, etc." Cecily Mackworth spent six months in Berlin, learning German and attending the Hochschule für Politik; then she went to Hungary for six months and to Switzerland for a year. After that she settled in Paris and began to write poetry as a whole-time job. Her first book was a little volume of verse published by Henry Miller—"Editions du Booster," and about the same time her first poem appeared in an English magazine— The London *Mercury.*

"My real career as a writer began in 1940," she says, "when I escaped from Paris the day before the entry of the Germans and spent three months wandering on foot around France before I was able to pass the Spanish frontier and return home by way of Lisbon. When I reached England, I wrote about my experiences and the result was my book, *I Came Out of France.*" With World War II over, Cecily Mackworth is waiting to go back to France, the country she loves. "I should like to have been born in France during the latter half of the nineteenth century," she says, "since that epoch represents for me one of the most exciting periods of artistic development in the history of mankind." Rimbaud, Mallarme and Apollinaire have influenced her writing.

She has written two books on Central European questions: *Czecho-*

slovakia, in the Crossroads Series, and *Czechoslovakia Fights Back. A Mirror of French Poetry* is soon to appear. At present (1946) she is writing her autobiography.

She has contributed poems and articles to *Horizon, Tribune, Life and Letters Today, Poetry Quarterly, Transformation* and other English journals besides various French and Czech papers.

Since 1942 she has been acting as assistant editor to *People and Freedom* for which she writes a monthly column under the name of "Rhiannon." M. H.

Reverend Clifford Alexis McLaughlin, S.J.
1867-

Clifford Alexis McLaughlin was born on 13th Street, New York City, near Lafayette Square (now Cooper Square), November 29, 1867. He was the eighth of fourteen children. With him still survive (1947) two brothers, Monsignor Lalor R. McLaughlin of Convent, New Jersey, and Leo McLaughlin, counsellor-at-law, New York City.

Moving to Jersey City in his childhood, he attended St. Bridget's School and St. Mary's Academy, and finally had five years at St. Peter's College. Here in classics and poetry he was taught by M. P. Hill, S.J., to whom he afterwards dedicated six of his sonnets.

On August 14, 1884, at the age of seventeen, he entered the Jesuit Novitiate at West Park, near Esopus, on the Hudson. But after four years of assiduous application to study and piety, his physical strength was exhausted. It was decided to release him from his vows and from the Society. But it happened that Father John O'Shanahan, Superior of the New Orleans Mission (afterward the New Orleans Jesuit Province), meeting him at Fordham and taking a fancy to him, offered to take him to the Southland on one condition: "If I cure him, I'll keep him."

After six years at Spring Hill College, Mobile County, Alabama, teaching and recuperating, he was able to study philosophy and theology, and was ordained in 1901 by Bishop Allen of Mobile.

In his recuperating rambles through the pine woods of Spring Hill, it happened one day that he sat down, wearied, on the log of a tree to rest and listen to a mockingbird. When he took out his watch and found that a whole hour had passed he started to express the rapture of that hour in the opening line of the "King-of-Warblers."

> "As glad and as gay
> As the cataract's spray
> When it leaps in the light of the sun;
> As soft and as low
> As the rivulet's flow
> When the din of the daylight is done."

For eight years he labored with great success among the poor Hoosiers of Alabama. While suffering from an injury received in one of his expeditions, he composed in his sick room, the "Midnight Sun," after studying minute descriptions of the midnight sun and the Northland.

On another occasion, when his horse and buggy had fallen into a deep pool of water, while they were being extricated by a friendly Hoosier, he completed the writing of the poem, "The Flight of the Buzzard." At this time, also, he re-wrote the poem, "Immaculata," composed in earlier years. He believes this poem is his best.

"About the year 1916," writes Dr. James T. Nix in the foreword to Father McLaughlin's only book, *Songs from the Vineyard,* "Joyce Kilmer, author and critic, was asked to give his evaluation of some few of Father McLaughlin's poems. He replied that he would like to see the author publish a book of poems declaring that 'Catholic poetry needs Father McLaughlin.' "

From 1923 to 1931 while at Loyola University, as teacher of poetry, he followed the counsel of Joyce Kilmer. He composed or rewrote most of his sonnets for the benefit of his class. The book was not published however until 1944. It contains ninety-one poems.

Father Clifford A. McLaughlin is now (1947) in his 81st year, stationed at Grand Coteau, near Lafayette, Louisiana. In this Acadian territory, where fifty years ago he started his course of philosophy he still takes walks under the Evangeline "oaks bearded with moss." Full of life and cheerfulness, he is called by his young juniors, "the youngest of all old men."

Michael McLaverty

Although he was born in County Monaghan, Michael McLaverty spent most of his life in Belfast. He was educated at St. Malachy's College, Belfast, and later at the University of that city. Having taken a Master of Science degree in physics at Queens University of that city, he adopted teaching as a profession and in his spare time began to write short stories. Part of his boyhood was passed in Rathlin Island, and out of the lives of the people of that island and of Belfast his novels and short stories are created.

When he was at college he was fascinated by mathematics and history. He had no interest whatsoever in writing, and the arid topics set for official examinations in essay writing invariably presented him with difficulty and later filled him with revolt for all prose that is impersonal and artificial.

His first story was written when he was convalescing. He was reading a book of short stories and when he had finished it he scratched out a short story of his own and sent it to the *Irish Monthly* (the Jesuit magazine which was also the first to publish some of W. B. Yeats's earlier poems). The editor, Father John Joy, liked his story and asked for more. One of these came under the notice of the late Edward J. O'Brien who introduced him to other editors and later when he had written his first novel, *Call My Brother Back,* commended him to Longmans, Green and Company. Much of his early work was fostered by Father Senan, editor of *The Capuchin Annual.*

Since 1933 he has written: *Call My Brother Back; Lost Fields; In This Thy Day* (1945), and thirty short stories. Some of his stories appeared in O'Brien's anthologies; *Pigeons,* which appeared in the 1936 volume, is regarded by Irish critics as one of the greatest short stories of the Anglo-Irish troubles. On both sides of the Atlantic passages from his work are included in prose anthologies for use in schools.

His first novel which contrasts the lyrical life of Rathlin with that of the anti-Catholic, anti-Nationalist life prevailing in Belfast, came to him when on a visit to Rathlin in an old house overlooking a lake, he discovered a faded newspaper containing an account of the 1935 Belfast pogrom. As he read it, all the twisted life of that city, which he had experienced as a boy, suddenly surged with compulsive force into his mind, and seeing a few swans in the lake below him he thought of Yeats's beautiful poem "The Wild Swans at Coole." The recollection of this poem re-illumined for him the tranquillity of the island life compared with the pitiable waste of blood that was spilt in the poorer quarters of Belfast. He appended Yeats's line ". . . they paddle in the cold companionable streams" to convey the atmosphere of the island section of his book and for the city section, lines by Louis MacNeice, the Belfast poet:

> "Frost will not touch the hedge of fuchsia
> The land will remain as it was
> But no abiding content can grow out of these minds
> Fuddled with blood, always caught by blinds. . . ."

This book was well received by the critics, especially Horace Reynolds in the New York *Times Book Review,* and Shaemas O'Sheel in the New York *Herald Tribune.*

The idea for his second novel, *Lost Fields,* which he considers his best work, was derived from a boy's essay in the Belfast school where he teaches. The boy wrote a short description of his cantankerous old grandmother who had come from the country to live with her poor relations in the city and ended her days threatening to go back to her home in the country where she had her fields, her hens and the Angelus bell. From the few words the lad wrote, Michael McLaverty created his *Lost Fields* which reveals the socially maladjusted life of country people in an industrial city and how their minds are preserved from sourness and deformity by the spiritual attitude they adopt toward their scanty livelihood. Edwin Muir wrote of it: "It is hard to describe the charm and beauty of this story which deals with people twisted into the shapes of poverty. Its virtue lies in its humanity, in a fine precision, and in a very curious quietude. Mr. McLaverty is a born artist." Robert Lynd said of it: "So much exquisitely faithful observation and human and poetic feeling distinguish this story that I rank it high among the novels of the year."

His third novel concerns a small community of people in a rural seaboard district in County Down. In a setting of pastoral brilliance he gives us the conflict between two families, caused and inflamed by the hardness and materialism of a selfish mother. By the example of a poor priest, she realizes the futility of her life when it is too late to make amends.

All Mr. McLaverty's work exhibits his passionate interest in the social regeneration and national aspirations of his own people. His prose is quietly lyrical, meticulously precise, its subtle implications being revealed only to the discriminating. *The Northman,* winter issue of 1942 to 1943, states that, "Michael McLaverty is the best novelist living in Ulster—the most exquisite novelist, indeed, that we have yet produced."

Some of his work has appeared in *The Sign, Story, Columbia,* and *The Catholic World.*

Seumas MacManus   1869-

Sitting on the side of the workbench, right under the eye of John Burns, the tailor for the MacManus family, Seumas as a youngster spent many a day reading the tailor's books. "Maybe when you grow big you'll want to make up a book yourself. Greater wonders have happened," said Mr. Burns to him. And greater wonders did happen. Seumas MacManus has written over twenty-five books and more than a dozen plays.

The locality in which he lived had much to do with his writing. He was born in County Donegal, the northwestern part of Ireland, in 1869. "It is the wildest, most remote, most rugged and mountainous, the most barren and the most beautiful, as well as the most Irish corner of Ireland," he says.

His boyhood was spent herding cattle and sheep on the hills, laboring on the farms and attending the mountain school. Nights were spent visiting neighboring cottages. Around the blazing turf-fire, he listened to the old men telling fairy stories and the ancient folk tales. At the age of seven, he could tell about one hundred of these tales. Some of these he got from the firesides, but many too he learned in Glen Cuach school. For the boys from the hills and the glens carried to school with them, and there traded, the best tales heard the night before.

When he was sixteen, he received a letter—the first letter of his life— informing him that he was appointed pupil-teacher in Iniskillen Model School in the next county, Fermanagh. After finishing this school, he had a teacher's certificate "sticking out of my coatpocket for all the world to see and ignore."

The next ten years were devoted to teaching. "More than ever during these ages did the boy's mind turn to that refuge for Donegal wild geese, America." His mind, now freed from study, ran to rhyming—mainly on Ireland and Donegal, their heroes, sorrows, and glories. Occasionally he would write on a humorous subject.

An invitation to take an appointment as assistant teacher in Kinawley National School was accepted. Later, through a competitive examination he became master of Glen Cuach School. The happiness of schoolmastering was now and then heightened by the creation of a poem. These appeared in *The Donegal Vindicator,* the first paper to appear in Donegal.

The winning of a prize offered by the Dublin paper, *The Weekly Irish Times,* for the best description of *A Ride on An Irish Jaunting Car,* fired him with enthusiasm to burst into the writing field. Soon he was writing for the other weekly story-paper of Ireland, *The Shamrock.* He found he could write stories as easily as he could teach. With time, he became less eager to teach and more eager to write. He closed his school and sailed to America—with a bag of stories. Quickly, these were accepted by *Harper's, Century, McClure's* and almost all of the story magazines of that time which numbered about fifteen. *McClure's* asked for a book. He got one out for them under the title *Through the Turf Smoke,* which he dedicated to the famed and beloved poetess Ethna Carberry, author of *The Four Winds of Eirinn,* whom he most esteemed in Ireland and later married in 1901. She died in 1902. In 1911 he married Catalina Violante Páez, of Venezuela. They have two daughters.

His publications include: *Shuilers* (poems) (1893); *The Leadin' Road to Donegal* (1895); *The Humours of Donegal* (1898); *The Bend of the Road* (1898); *In Chimney Corners* (1899); *A Lad of the O'Friels* (1903); *The Red Poocher* (1903); *Hardhearted Man* (1903); *Irish Nights* (1905); *Yourself and the Neighbors* (1914); *Ireland's Case* (1915); *Lo, and Behold Ye* (1919); *The Story of the Irish Race* (1921); *The Donegal Wonder Book* (1926); *Bold Blades of Donegal* (1935); *The Rocky Road to Dublin* (1938); *Well O' the World's End* (1939); *Dark Patrick* (1939).

His plays include: *The Woman of Seven Sorrows; Orange and Green; The Lad from Largymore; Dinny O'Dowd; Father Peter's Miracle; The Rale True Doctor; The Bachelors of Braggy; The Hardhearted Man,* and others.

M. H.

Very Reverend Vincent McNabb, O.P.
1868-1943

"Nobody who ever met or saw or heard Father McNabb has ever forgotten him," wrote his friend G. K. Chesterton. For fifty years there was no Catholic movement in England to which he had not allied himself. When he celebrated the golden jubilee of his priesthood, in 1941, he declared that in this life there is only time for fighting but there is an eternity for enjoying one's friends. He wanted to celebrate his golden jubilee by walking to Rome, but his provincial forbade it. He made the journey by boat and train.

Father McNabb was born in 1868 in Portaferry, County Down, Ireland, within a few miles of the rock that covers the bones of St. Patrick. "My father," wrote Father McNabb, "was a master 'Mariner' (to give him his noble title) and my mother, a dressmaker." Vincent, who was proud he was the seventh son and the tenth of eleven children, spent his schooldays at the diocesan seminary of St. Malachy's College, Belfast. When asked by the editor of *The Catholic Times* to lend assistance to Ireland during one of the last crises, Father McNabb wrote in his scalpel-like way that both peoples alike, the people of England and the people of Ireland have been martyred by the same imperious few. He said that he loved Ireland like a mother and England like a wife.

Except for a period of study at the University of Louvain, Father McNabb's Dominican life had been identified with the English province for which he was ordained in 1891. On November 10, 1885, he had joined the novitiate of the English Dominicans at Woodchester in Gloucestershire. He walked about London in habit and army boots. A born controversialist, he often spoke in Hyde Park for the Catholic Evidence Guild. He had a fine sense of humor and a soaring eloquence. A zealous priest, he did a lot of work among the poor. In St. Pancras, London slum, he actually lived the extreme poverty enjoined by the gospel. An admirer wrote, while Father Vincent was still alive: "It is wonderful to see that happy face with its look of smiling quizzical inquiry come from among a swirl of anxious self-absorbed London faces, the habit billowing from the lean, alert old figure like the drapes of winged victory." He practiced a rigid asceticism. While he had a chair and a bed in his room he never used them. He either stood or knelt. There were just about four books in his room, a Bible, a Breviary, the Dominican constitutions, and the *Summa of St. Thomas.*

It was during his term as prior of Holy Cross in Leicester that he visited the United States, preaching and lecturing in New York in the spring of 1913. His proficiency in the divine sciences was rewarded by the Master of Sacred Theology degree in 1917. For his indefatigable work in the interests of Belgium, he was made in 1919 a Chevalier of the Order of the Crown of that country. During World War I, while prior at Hawkesyard in Staffordshire, he brought spiritual consolation *in ex-tremis* to those two exquisite women poets, Katherine Harris Bradley and her niece, Edith Emma Cooper, whose nom de plume was Michael Field.

Between 1929 and 1934 Father McNabb lectured on the *Summa of St. Thomas* at the University of London Extension.

He is the author of about thirty books. Among them are: *Infalli-bility; The New Testament Witness to St. Peter; Oxford Conferences on Prayer; Oxford Conferences on Faith; Our Reasonable Service; Frontiers of Faith and Reason* (thirty scholarly papers on Scripture); *The Catholic Church and Philosophy; Thoughts Twice Dyed*. Father McNabb's *The Church and Reunion*, shows a long interest in the subject. On this topic he wrote numerous articles between 1902 and 1936. An authority on economics, he had long been an advocate of the "Back-to-the-Land" movement and treats of it in his book, *The Church and the Land*. The city, he said, is the graveyard of religion and the machine age is the doom of mankind. His book *Old Principles and the New Order* has for its main theme the principle that true economics must rest on true faith and morals. During the first World War, he learned practical farming in his leisure, as a recreation. He had been, also, a shining light in the Distributist Movement.

Father McNabb was, however, not only a polemic writer, but an informal essayist of undeniable charm, as shown particularly in: *Francis Thompson and Other Essays; The Wayside*, and the lovely *Path of Prayer*. Many people not of the Catholic faith read *Blackfriars*, the Dominican literary monthly published in Oxford, for which he was a regular contributor. His words are racy of the soil. Writing with his capuche on, he used the back of old letters and envelopes for his manu-script. His motto was, "produce as much as you can, consume as little as you need." He urged the scrapping of all machinery and wanted people living as members of family-owned subsistence farms. The reader is never permitted to forget that here is a son of St. Dominic, a follower of St. Thomas. His vocabulary smacked of pre-Norman times, even in such a title as *The Craft of Prayer*. More recent books have been in the field of hagiography—on St. John Fisher or on St. Elizabeth of Portugal, the patroness of peace, who rode upon her little mule between embattled armies. In *A Life of Jesus Christ Our Lord*, hitherto shadowed places in the divine chronicle are illumined by a penetrating flash.

In 1942 Mr. James Gunn, a non-Catholic, painted a portrait of Father Vincent McNabb. He proclaimed Father Vincent a wonderful "sitter"—"Actually, however, he refused to sit down at all, but remained standing for periods of an hour and a half after having walked all the way from Highgate to the studio in Pembroke Walk—to the great concern of the artist."

Despite an ailment, a disease of the throat, Father McNabb continued to live his active life until his death June 17, 1943. When he was told his end was in sight, he remarked: "I don't see why I should make a

tragedy of this—it's what I have been preparing for all my life. I am in
the hands of my doctors—or better, in the hands of my God."

In the true spirit of poverty, Father Vincent McNabb handed over
to his superior before his death what he most prized, the decoration
given him in 1919 by Albert, the King of the Belgians, for his efforts,
during the last war, for Belgian Relief, and his ring of a Master of Sacred
Theology.   A. M.

Eoin MacNeill   1867-1945

Professor Eoin MacNeill had said that the aim of
his work in research and historical writing was to
provide "a critical basis for early Irish history"—
a work of importance to all historians as well as
to the Irish race. But Dr. MacNeill has a broader
claim to fame as one of the architects of modern
Eire; he had a part in winning a large though as
yet incomplete measure of freedom for his native
land, and a still greater part in reviving the culture and cultural pride of his people.

Born at Glenarm, County Antrim, Ireland, in
1867, and educated at St. Malachy's College,
Belfast, Eoin MacNeill entered Civil Service in 1887. He was in the
Accountant-General's Office of the Law Courts, Dublin, for twenty-two
years. In 1870, he began the study of Old and Middle Irish, and was
the editor of *Irisleabhar na Gaedhilge,* organ of the Gaelic Union. But
finding this organization ineffective, MacNeill together with Dr. Douglas
Hyde and the late Father Eugene O'Growney, in 1893 founded the
Gaelic League; which, taking the cause of the native language directly
to the people, became the very root and soil of the Irish Renaissance in
literature and in politics. Eoin MacNeill was in turn vice-president and
president of the Gaelic League, and editor of its newspaper, *An Claid-
heamh Soluis.* He became a member of the Senate of the National University of Ireland and the Governing Body of University College, Dublin,
in 1908, and was professor of early and medieval history at the latter institution from 1909.

On the political side, he was chairman of the original Provisional
Committeee of the Irish Volunteers, head of that organization in 1916
when the Easter Rebellion was begun, and editor of *The Irish Volunteer*
weekly. Although due to misunderstanding of the situation, he tried to
prevent the uprising at the last minute, a British court-martial sentenced
him to penal servitude for life, and he suffered imprisonment until 1921.
Meanwhile he was elected Member of Parliament for Londonderry City
and County, and Deputy to Dail Eireann for Londonderry City and for
the National University of Ireland. He was Speaker of Dail Eireann
(1921); Minister for Education (1922); a member of the Commission that
drafted the Constitution of the Irish Free State (1922); Deputy for Clare

(1923 to 1927); Free State Representative on the Boundary Commission (1924 to 1925); and was Chairman of the Irish Historical Manuscripts Commission from 1928.

In addition to such books as: *Celtic Ireland, Celtic Religion, Early Irish Laws and Institutions* and *St. Patrick, Apostle of Ireland,* Dr. MacNeill is the author of many erudite papers printed in scholarly periodicals, and editor of several of the important historical and literary remnants of ancient Irish annals. Among his edited works may be cited: *The Annals of Tigernach, An Irish Historical Tract, A.D. 721; Duanaire Finn,* and *Historical Poems by Flann Manistrech;* while his articles include: *Notes on the Ogham Inscriptions; Early Irish Population Groups; Place Names and Family Names of Clare Island,* and *The Native Place of St. Patrick.*

Dr. MacNeill held an A.B. degree from the Royal University of Ireland, a D.Litt. degree from the National University of Ireland and an honorary D.Litt. from Dublin University. He was married to the former Agnes Moore of Ballymena, County Antrim. He died on October 15, 1945.　　　　　　　　　　　　　　　　　　　　　　　　　　　S. O.

Reverend Joseph McSorley, C.S.P.　1874-

Born in Brooklyn, New York, in 1874, the Reverend Joseph McSorley, C.S.P., has exemplified in his own career the fruits of Catholic education. It was his school years, he feels, which nourished his religious vocation and trained him for his priestly work. This is outstanding in American Catholic life. When but six years old young Joseph entered St. John's Preparatory School and at the unusual age of twelve he was ready for the College, now St. John's University of Brooklyn. Graduated at sixteen, the youngest of the class of 1891, he received his A.B., and joined the Congregation of St. Paul. While at the Paulist Novitiate in Washington, affiliated with the Catholic University, the young novice advanced further in his studies and obtained his Master's degree in 1893 and his S.T.L. in 1897. The same year he was ordained in the Church of St. Paul, New York. Being only twenty-two years old, a year younger than canon law permits, special permission had to be obtained for his ordination. His first appointment was as curate at St. Paul's but in 1899 he was sent back to Washington where he remained until 1907 when again he was appointed to the Church of St. Paul.

The next twenty-two years he spent in New York, except for a year and a half as chaplain in the United States Army during the World War. When discharged from his duties as army chaplain he was made pastor of St. Paul's until, in 1924, he was chosen for the still higher honor of Superior General of the Paulists. Relieved from this exacting office in 1929, he was appointed to St. Peter's Church in Toronto, but in 1932 returned to New York to become contributing editor of *The Catholic World*. It was while he was Superior General that the Paulists established the radio station WLWL, the first Catholic medium for broadcasting.

Ever zealous, Father McSorley has never been too busy or too absorbed in the cares of the moment to give freely of his time and counsel to those seeking it. During a period in Italy he learned the Italian language that, on his return, he might the better assist those in the parish of that nationality. With a facility for foreign tongues he has done work in six languages and uses this and all his gifts for the apostolate of souls. He is confessor, guide and counsellor to many, his kindliness and tact enabling him to overcome difficult situations and to assist those in spiritual need. Even when tied to the heavy duties of administrative work, he devoted two afternoons a week to the hearing of confessions. As retreat master, preacher and lecturer he is much sought and he answers these innumerable calls generously.

Despite these demands on his time, Father McSorley has managed to write a number of books. In 1909 he published *The Sacrament of Duty,* which was revised in 1935. *Italian Confessions,* and *Be of Good Heart* appeared in 1925; *A Primer of Prayer* in 1934; *Think and Pray* in 1936 and in 1943 he published an *Outline History of the Church by Centuries.* He also translated from the German, Bishop Keppler's *More Joy* and Dr. Hansjakob's *Grace.* He is co-author of *A Short History of the Catholic Church* and of *Spanish Confessions* by Sheerin and McSorley (1942). Besides this he has written many doctrinal and devotional pamphlets and articles for Catholic periodicals. He also contributed to the *Catholic Encyclopedia.* In 1937 his alma mater bestowed on him the honorary degree of Doctor of Letters.

D. D.

Sister M. Madeleva, C.S.C.   1887-

One of the most challenging and creative personalities in what has sometimes been referred to as our contemporary "Catholic Emergence" in English and American literature is Sister M. Madeleva, of the Congregation of the Holy Cross. She was born (1887) Mary Evaline Wolff, the daughter of a pioneering family of German descent which had settled at Cumberland, Wisconsin, and she grew into girlhood with a vigorous love of the outdoors, of long rambles and old stories and hard study. Her first collegiate experience was at the University of Wisconsin, from which—desiring a more Catholic background—she passed to St. Mary's College, Notre Dame, Holy Cross, Indiana. In 1908, while still a student there, Mary Evaline took the vows which devoted her life to religion.

Immediately after her graduation the following year, Sister Madeleva began teaching English at St. Mary's, continuing there until 1919 and meanwhile completing her studies for the M.A. degree at nearby Notre Dame University. Leaving there to teach at schools of her Congregation in Ogden, Utah, and Woodland, California, she took time out for residence and work at the University of California—from which she was the first nun to emerge as a Doctor of Philosophy. She is also the only woman to be honored by a degree of Litt.D. from Manhattan College. An honorary degree was also conferred on her at Mount Mary College in 1940.

The young Sister Madeleva had already contributed verse of music and distinction to various magazines and anthologies, but her first collection was the *Knights Errant and Other Poems* of 1923. Two years later came *Chaucer's Nuns and Other Essays,* followed shortly by *The Pearl, a Study in Spiritual Dryness,* the highly original piece of criticism which had been prepared as her doctoral dissertation. In both of these works, the insight and intuition of Catholic experience and of the religious life supplemented merely technical scholarship in interpreting problems of medievalism—a fact which secular critics were not slow to note.

In 1927 came a characteristic volume, *Penelope and Other Poems,* the title poem of which remains the favorite of its author if not always of her readers. By this time Sister Madeleva's accomplished artistry, all the way from sonnet or couplet to free verse, was as evident as her distinct and sometimes daring originality of theme. For her subject matter was by no means that traditionally expected from a nun-poet, the mysteries of Faith and the Soul, the impersonal beauties of Nature, or poignant experiences of the religious life. She was obviously determined to give human nature its due also, rejoicing in courage or tenderness wherever found and singing the interrelation of sacred and romantic love as passionately as Patmore himself. A year divided between study at Oxford and travel through Europe and the Holy Land inevitably enriched her equipment and she was fortunate in her overseas friendships, visiting the Meynells in Sussex, Edith Wharton in France and Seumas McManus' family in Donegal.

Before this happy interlude Sister Madeleva had been president of the College of St. Mary-of-the-Wasatch in Salt Lake City. She returned to assume the presidency of her own alma mater, Saint Mary's College at Notre Dame. In spite of the absorbing executive duties connected with these assignments, she has continued to publish with fair regularity; her *Question of Lovers* being issued in 1935, followed by the charming *Ballad of the Happy Christmas Wind; Gates and Other Poems; Christmas Eve;* and the *Selected Poems* of 1939, and *Four Girls,* of 1941. *A Song of Bedlam Inn and Other Poems* appeared in 1946.

That brevity and subtle irony should mark the more recent verses—many of which are cast in quatrains as masterfully wrought as those of Father Tabb or of her friend Father Charles O'Donnell—would seem to follow naturally enough from the poet's restricted leisure, perhaps also from maturity tempering the audacious ardor of earlier years.

All of Sister Madeleva's work, whether in verse or prose, is infused by strong vitality and mystical insight. It should mean much for the future makers and readers of Catholic literature that these precious qualities are now poured out so generously upon the development of our young women students.

This very dynamic nun is a member of the National Catholic Educational Association, the Medieval Academy and the Modern Language Association of America, and the Poetry Societies of America and England. From 1942 until 1947 she served as president of the Catholic Poetry Society of America, whose work she has encouraged from its inception.

K. B.

Louis Madelin   1871-

Louis Madelin, one of France's leading historians and a member of the French Academy, was born at Neufchateau, Vosges, on May 8, 1871. After completing his studies at the Ecôle Fénélon of Bar-le-Duc and the Faculty of Letters of Nancy, he entered the Ecôle des Chartes at Paris. He obtained the degree of doctor of letters at the University of Paris and was also connected with the Ecôle Français in Rome.

His earliest ambition had been to work in the field of French history especially of the Revolution and the Empire, and he patiently and laboriously prepared himself for this task. He acquainted himself fully with the methods of the various schools of historical research, refusing to remain shut up with documents alone. In preparing his books he made many visits to the localities he described and tried to recreate the life of the period with which he was dealing. In the provincial archives especially he made many discoveries concerning the origins of the French Revolution which he proved to be far more carefully organized than had generally been supposed. As a result, his historical writing is not only scrupulously exact and full of erudition but it is marked by that movement and life which create a wide popular appeal.

The works of Louis Madelin have covered almost every period of modern French history. To an important series published under the direction of Gabriel Hanotaux he contributed a study, *L'histoire politique de la nation française de 1515 à 1804*. In 1911 he wrote his brilliant history of the French Revolution which won the Grand Prix Gobert. His life of Fouché was widely read by the general public and obtained the Prix Thiers, and he won the Prix Gobert a second time with a work on Napoleon. Among his other important books are *Le Consulat et l'Empire,* a biography of Danton, and *La Fronde*. In 1935 he edited a fine edition of the letters of Napoleon to the Empress Marie Louise which was published by the Bibliothèque Nationale.

In the first World War, Louis Madelin was a sergeant in the 44th

Territorial Regiment, from 1914 to 1915; in 1916 he was attached to the general staff in Verdun; in 1917 to the staff of the Sixth Army, and in 1918 to the general headquarters of the French Army. He received the *Croix de Guerre* at the end of the war, and upon the request of Marshal Foch he wrote *La Bataille de France de 1918* which was published in 1919; he later published several other remarkable books on the first World War.

In 1924 his fellow citizens of the Vosges elected Louis Madelin to the Chamber of Deputies where he was most assiduous in his duties until 1928. He was elected to the French Academy in 1928, taking the chair of Robert de Flers.

He is a brilliant speaker. As early as the year 1907 to 1908 he came to the United States and Canada as a lecturer for the Alliance Française. He taught at the Sorbonne from 1905 to 1910 and was vice president of the Société des Gens de Lettres from 1919 to 1922. He is an officer of the Legion of Honor and has been a contributor to *La Revue de Deux Mondes* and many other papers and magazines. He is known to have had royalist leanings.

His principal works are: *Fouché* (1901); *La Rome de Napoléon* (1904); *La Révolution* (1910); *La France du Directoire* (1929); *La Fronde* (1930), and *Le Consulat et l'Empire* (1932-33).

J. K.

Helene Magaret 1906-

Miss Magaret began writing when she was about seven. She cannot remember any period when she did not intend to make writing her avocation if not her vocation. Discouragement has never been hers. She was just too busy ever to be discouraged. Nearly all her writing has had to be done at night, for she was working during the day. "For instance, when I was writing my second book, I was working very long hours at the office, often having to work on Sundays and holidays, and for a time I was also teaching a night class in creative writing at Creighton University in Omaha," she wrote.

She attended Grinnell College, Grinnell, Iowa, and was a student at the Municipal University of Omaha. For three years she was employed as a Spanish translator by commercial firms in Omaha. She was awarded a scholarship to Barnard College, New York City, and received her B.A. there in 1932, after being elected to Phi Beta Kappa, and winning the Mariana Griswold Van Rensselaer Poetry Prize. From then until 1937 she was employed in Omaha in secretarial work, first as secretary to the treasurer of the Federal Land Bank, and later as secretary to the president of the Live Stock National Bank. She has also been interpreter and social secretary to the Chilean poet, Gabriela Mistral. Miss Magaret had begun to publish lyrics in periodicals in 1929 and continued her sales throughout this period.

In 1937 she obtained a graduate assistantship at the State University of Iowa, and received her M.A. in 1938. That year the American Association of University Women granted her a fellowship. Supported by this stipend she made her first real attempt at prose writing and in two years produced a biography. *Father De Smet.* This was a selection of the Catholic Book of the Month Club. Reading some of the pioneer priest's letters one day in a library she was inspired to write his life.

She had continued her studies while writing, and obtained her doctor's degree at the State University of Iowa in 1940. In the fall of the year she went to Rockford College, Rockford, Illinois, as an English instructor. From September 1941 until 1944 she was a member of the faculty of the College of St. Teresa, Winona, Minnesota. She is now (1947) professor of English at Marymount College, Tarrytown-on-Hudson, New York.

Her first book, *The Trumpeting Crane,* came to her publishers from one who was quite unknown to them. It proved to be one of those rare discoveries in the unsolicited mail of a successful publishing house. William Rose Benét wrote of her re-creation of the prairie country in this book, "Not since Willa Cather wrote of it have I felt this essential part of the American scene as I have felt it in this poem."

Dr. Magaret was born in Omaha, Nebraska, on May 18, 1906. Her parents were Ernst Friedrich and Celia Wolcott Magaret. Her maternal ancestors had come from England in 1660 and steadily their descendants moved westward. American history has been a source of inspiration for her as Father De Smet and the narrative poem, *The Great Horse,* the story of the flight of the Mormons from Illinois to Utah, show.

On December 31, 1940, she was received into the Catholic Church by the Reverend Father Herman Strub, assistant pastor of St. Mary's Church in Iowa City, Iowa. She writes, "My rather recent conversion to the Church is indicative of a radical change in thought, interest and standards. I have just started down a new road and scarcely know what I shall find at the other end."

She is the author of: *The Trumpeting Crane* (1934); *The Great Horse* (1937); *Father De Smet* (1940); *Change of Season* (1941); *Who Walk in Pride* (1944), and *Gailhac of Béziers* (The story of the founder of the Religious of the Sacred Heart of Mary). In 1943 she was elected a member of the Gallery of Living Catholic Authors.

M. S.

Reverend James Aloysius Magner 1901-

Dr. Magner, procurator of the Catholic University of America, has written on a wide variety of subjects, religious, sociological and historical. Extensive travel in Europe, the Near and Far East and Latin America has inclined his pen also to current events over a wide field, although he is perhaps best known as an authority on Ibero-American affairs and particularly on Mexico. *America* has referred to him as "one of the foremost and soundest authorities" on our first neighbor south of the Rio Grande.

Born in Wilmington, Illinois, on October 23, 1901, the son of James and Margaret Follen Magner, he attended the public schools in his native community and later studied at Campion Academy and College at Prairie du Chien, Wisconsin. His B.A. and M.A. degrees were received from St. Mary of the Lake Seminary, Mundelein, Illinois, in 1923 and 1924. He was ordained one year ahead of schedule, in 1926, by Cardinal Mundelein. Study at the Canadian College in Rome followed. He was awarded the S.T.D. in 1928, and the Ph.D. in 1929. Service as a curate in Chicago, in St. Dominic's, then St. Gertrude's, and finally St. Laurence's parish, accompanied his work as instructor of English and Italian in the Quigley Preparatory Seminary from 1929 to 1940. In September of the latter year, he went to Washington, as assistant secretary-treasurer and procurator of the Catholic University, where he also edits the *Catholic University Bulletin*. His brother, the Most Reverend Francis J. Magner, who was Bishop of Marquette, Michigan, died in 1947.

Dr. Magner dates his first literary interest to the facilities of the library developed in his home and to the encouragement of his family, as well as to ready access to the community public library and the inspiration of speakers who appeared under the auspices of Chautauqua and lyceum programs. Participation in local literary contests was later followed by the expert counsel of the Jesuit Fathers at Campion, in debating, dramatics, and writing. A sustained interest in music during this period also contributed to broaden his interest in the arts and general culture.

As seminarian at Mundelein, he founded the Bellarmine Society, which is still functioning, and in 1926 published his first article "Blessed Robert Bellarmine—Controversialist" in *The Catholic World*. Upon his return from Rome, he became associated with the *Extension* magazine, and besides contributing frequent articles to this and other Catholic periodicals, conducted its "Question Box" and "Marriage Questions" for a period of five years. His first book, *This Catholic Religion,* appeared in 1930. He attributes much of his development during this time and later to the stimulation and counsel of the well-known editor of *Extension,* Mr. Simon A. Baldus.

Dr. Magner's interest in Mexico dates back to boyhood and was later fanned into action by Monsignor Francis C. Kelley, now Bishop of Oklahoma City and Tulsa, and by the late Father Frederic Siedenburg, S.J., then of Loyola University, Chicago. A substantial background supports his numerous articles on this and kindred subjects. While a student at Rome, he spent a summer in Spain. In the summer of 1931, he joined the Mexican seminar of the Committee on Cultural Relations with Latin America. In 1932, he traveled through South America. The summers of 1933 and 1934 he spent in Spain, studying her history and problems through the stirring days of the Republic. In 1936 he went again to Mexico. A period of commuting between Texas, California and Mexico followed. He led a seminar group in Mexico for two summers, and has seen most of that country, by rail, motor, plane, on horseback and afoot. During this time also, he visited neighboring countries such as Cuba and Guatemala, and interviewed numerous personalities, ranging from President Batista of Cuba to leading members of the Mexican Hierarchy and the American Ambassadors Ruben Clark and Josephus Daniels.

Through his articles and lectures he made the acquaintance of Señorita del Valle of Mexico, who in turn introduced him to the Reverend Miguel Dario Miranda, now Bishop of Tulancingo. As a result of their discussion of the need of a history of Mexico written in English by a Catholic, he undertook the writing of *Men of Mexico,* which appeared in 1942, after five years of special research. Cast in the form of biographical chapters on seventeen leading personalities from Montezuma to Cardenas, this book has been described as "a work of scholarship that gives a view of Mexico in the only manner in which she can be seen whole and entire. . . ."

While at St. Gertrude's parish, Dr. Magner conceived the idea of an integrated program of Catholic adult education, which he developed through the organization of a parish library and a series of home study circles in conjunction with the St. Gertrude Forum, which, during its time, attracted to its platform the leading Catholic speakers of the country. He subsequently founded the Charles Carroll Forum of Chicago, on the second centenary of the birth of the great Catholic signer of the Declaration of Independence, bringing this organization to a position of national importance. On his transfer to Washington, he established its sister organization, The Charles Carroll Forum of Washington, whose purpose is likewise stated "to make better known Christian principles and representative Catholic views on leading topics of the day." In furtherance of Catholic ideals in democracy, his book *For God and Democracy* was published in 1940. *Latin American Pattern* followed in 1944, and *Personality and Successful Living* in 1945.

Through the Forum, he became acquainted with Monsignor Peter Guilday, historian of the Catholic Church in the United States and editor of *The American Catholic Historical Review.* For three years he served on the board of advisory editors of the publication and is now its secretary-treasurer. He is also serving as contributing editor on Latin American affairs for the *Shield,* official organ of the Catholic Students Mission Crusade, and is now completing under its auspices a study outline on Latin America, shortly due for publication. Dr. Magner states that he does not regard himself as a professional writer but thinks that there must be some underlying impulse to account for his activities in this direction.

M. S.

Reverend William Augustus Maguire 1890-

Since June 1917 Father William Maguire has spent the years of his priesthood as a chaplain in the United States Navy. His first ship was the battleship U.S.S. Maine of the Atlantic Fleet, and on it, besides his spiritual duties, he was mess caterer and treasurer, entertainment officer and editor of the Maine's first weekly paper. In January 1918 he was ordered on board the U.S.S. Texas and served for a short time at Scapa Flow in the Orkneys with the British Grand Fleet. Then he was with the United States destroyers as Base Chaplain, Brest, France, until February 1919. The battleship U.S.S. Idaho—the first battleship to visit Alaska—was his next assignment. This was followed by shore duty and then he served with the destroyer squadron in Turkish waters. He also served on the carrier Langley, the battleships Arkansas and Mississippi; on destroyers for two years (China station); and on the cruiser Indianapolis as Scouting Force Chaplain, 1938 to 1940. He was Fleet Chaplain of the Pacific Fleet on board the U.S.S. California from 1940 to 1942; and was at Pearl Harbor during the Japanese attack December 7, 1941. He returned to the United States in June 1942 to serve at the Naval Training Station, San Diego, California, until 1943. After serving on the staff of the Commanding General of the Fleet Marine Force in 1943 he became District Chaplain, 11th Naval District, San Diego, California, on May 19, 1944, and is still (1947) serving in that position.

Captain William Maguire was born on December 31, 1890, at Hornell, New York. His father, John Francis Maguire was the superintendent of a division of the Erie Railroad. William was educated in the public schools until the second year of high school, when he transferred to Seton Hall Preparatory School (1905) and then passed on to Seton Hall College. He received his B.A. in 1910 and then went to Catholic University for his M.A. degree which he received in 1911. From 1911 to 1915 he studied at the American College, at the University of Louvain, Louvain, Belgium. He was ordained at Brussels, Belgium, on July 4, 1915, by the Papal Nuncio, Archbishop Tacci. Upon returning home his first assignment was St. Mary's Church in Jersey City, New Jersey. "St. Mary's was a good school for my future years in battleships. The discipline in the rectory was inflexible," writes Father Maguire. After nine months he was transferred to the Immaculate Conception parish in Montclair, New Jersey. While there he applied to join the Canadian Forces and then the American Army before we were at war, but Bishop O'Connor refused to let him go. When Father Maguire read in the New York *Times* on a Good Friday morning in the year 1917 that we had declared war on Germany, he again asked Bishop O'Connor for permission to go as a chaplain and this time permission was granted.

During his service he was awarded the Navy Cross for extraordinary heroism at Quiberon Bay, France, April 1918 and was awarded the Order of Merit, second class, by the Republic of Chile, 1921.

Both Father Maguire's books deal with his life in the Navy. *Rig for Church* was published in 1942 and *The Captain Wears a Cross* a year later.   M. H.

Reverend Arthur Maheux   1884-

Born June 22, 1884, at Ste—Julie de Mégantic in the Province of Québec, the Abbé Maheux belongs to a French-Norman family, which came to Canada towards the middle of the seventeenth century; he belongs to the tenth generation of people born in the province of Québec, without any mixture of Indian, Saxon, Irish or Scottish blood.

He studied at the high school and at the College of Arts of the Québec Seminary and obtained the B.A. degree of Laval University in 1904. He studied philosophy and theology at the Faculty of Theology of the same university and obtained the baccalaureate in canon law in 1906 and the doctorate in theology in 1908. He studied at Paris, at the Institut Catholique, at the Sorbonne, at the Ecole des Hautes Etudes, and obtained the licence ès lettres with honours in 1915 and the diploma in philology in 1917.

After teaching in the high school, from 1908 to 1913, and in the College of Arts, 1918 to 1923, at the Québec Seminary, he was director of studies from 1923 to 1927, professor at the Ecole Normale Supérieure, 1927 to 1929, and secretary-registrar of Laval University, 1931 to 1938. He was also the editor of two university periodicals, *Le Canada français* and *L'Enseignement Secondaire,* and is still editor of *Le Bulletin des Sociétés des Géographie.*

He was appointed archivist of the Québec Seminary and Laval University, and professor of history of Canada in 1938. This led him to give public lectures on history at the University.

His first book appeared in 1940, *Propos sur l'Education.* In 1941 he published another book, *Ton Histoire est une Epopée, vol. I, Nos débuts sous le régime anglais.* That book was translated into English, by

Richard M. Saunders, under the title *French Canada and Britain* (1942). In March 1943 the Abbé Maheux published *Pourquoi sommes-nous divisés?* being a study of Canadian national unity. In May 1944 he published an English counterpart of that book, under title of *What Keeps Us Apart?* and in June 1944 another book, *Problems of Canadian Unity.*

Abbé Maheux is engaged now in lecturing throughout Canada on National unity. His lectures and radio addresses have aroused a great interest amongst both English and French-speaking Canadians. Committees have been organized, in both groups, to study the problems of Canadian unity; discussions have been and are being held in the newspapers about a better understanding between the two groups; hundreds of letters sent by Canadians of all social ranks, from coast to coast, offer a variety of opinions on the debated question and will lead to another book on national unity in Canada. The quick sale of Abbé Maheux's book is sure evidence of the interest Canadians take in the question.

Lucien Lortie, member of the Québec bar, has published a book giving a detailed account (complete to March 1942) of the writings of l'Abbé Maheux; the title is *Bibliographie analytique de l'oeuvre de l'Abbé A. Maheux* (160 pages). Other works of L'Abbé are: *Le Problème Protestant; Notes Sur Roubaud; Messire Edouard Bélanger.*

Not content with these activities, Abbé Maheux has brought up two children, orphans, of whom one, Jean Gauthier, served in the Canadian Army, and the other, Claire Gauthier, was graduated with a B.A. from the Mount St. Scholastica College, at Atchison, Kansas, and obtained a diploma in dietetics at the General Hospital, Vancouver, Canada.

C. J. E.

Lucas Malet   *See* Mrs. Mary Harrison

Mary Walsh Mannix   1846-1938

A poetess who sang because she could not help it, unconsciously as a bird, Mrs. Mary E. Mannix for over half a century created joy through her poems, hymns and stories. Born in New York in 1846 in the month of Mary and named for the Queen of Heaven, Mary Ellen Walsh throughout her life kept for our Blessed Mother a tender love which sustained her in unswerving loyalty and devotion to her Catholic faith. At the age of seventeen, almost accidentally she wrote the words and music of one of the best known and loved hymns for the month of May, "Bring Flowers of the Rarest." This and others of her hymns are included in the compilations made by the Sisters of Notre Dame, *May Chimes* and *Wreath of Mary.*

Mary Ellen was the eldest of nine children. Her parents, Michael Walsh and Margaret Mansfield, moved to Cincinnati early in the little girl's life and there she grew up. Her mother's constant companion, she learned to read at the very early age of four. At five she was reading *Old Curiosity Shop* to her mother while they wept together over the sorrows of Little Nell. Educated by the Sisters of Notre Dame de Namur, she graduated from their academy at Reading, Ohio, when she was sixteen. The Civil War was then raging and she often recalled the heated feelings of the Northern and Southern girls at the passing of the soldiers through Cincinnati. Her literary skill displayed itself during her school years and she began her scholastic career writing an acrostic on the name of a new friend, a friendship thus begun which lasted until death.

Her husband, John B. Mannix, admired her as a poetess and made a collection of her poems before they met. Married in May 1873, they had a large family of seven children, one, a nun. In 1888 they moved to San Diego, California, where the remainder of her life was spent. Her love and understanding of children shows in her success in writing for the child. A unique story teller, she writes as a mother with sympathy and humor and without exaggerating childishness.

Though best known for her verses and hymns, Mrs. Mannix had great skill in prose and among her books are: *A Life's Labyrinth; Tales Tim Told Us; Child's Life of Joan of Arc; Fortunes of a Little Emigrant; Life of Sister Louise,* the foundress of the Sisters of Notre Dame de Namur in this country, written at the request of the Sisters of that congregation in Cincinnati and *Chronicles of the Little Sisters of the Poor,* her own favorite.

In a tribute to her, Maurice Francis Egan notes her gift of painting a vivid picture and calls her art "the handmaid of simplicity," her poems being written without consideration of effect except to make a "heart-string vibrate."

Living to the venerable age of ninety-two, she was constant in her work for and loyalty to her Church. At La Jolla, where many summers were passed and where her last years were lived, she and her husband were largely responsible for the building of a Catholic church dedicated to "Mary, Star of the Sea." Mrs. Mannix wrote a hymn of that name which was often sung there, and used at the dedication of a larger church shortly before her death.

She was a contributor to the *Ave Maria* from its beginning and was among the outstanding Catholic writers whom Father Hudson gathered on his roster during his half-century as editor. Other periodicals sought her poetry and prose, among them *The Catholic World,* the *Rosary,* the *Messenger of the Sacred Heart, Our Young Catholic Messenger, The Magnificat,* and *The Grail.*

She wrote under several names, among them "Sylvia Hunting," "Hope Willis," and "Sarah Frances Ashburton."

In November 1938 her long life of years rich and full came gently to a close, and she remains in the memory of those who knew her as the "valiant woman" of the Scriptures.

D. D.

Gabriel Marcel 1889-

One of the most interesting thinkers of the Catholic school which prompted religious revival in France during the last decade preceding the war, Gabriel Marcel is the son of Henry Marcel, a distinguished diplomat, who was the Director of the Fine Arts and administrator of the National Library in Paris. He was born in Paris on December 7, 1889. As a young man he studied at the Lycée Carnot and graduated from the Sorbonne, after writing a thesis on the influence exercised by Schelling's philosophy on the metaphysical ideas of Coleridge. In 1910 he received his degree in philosophy. Between 1911 and 1914 his first two works appeared.

He lived and taught for a time in Switzerland, where he started writing his *Metaphysical Diary,* and his first plays, one of which was to be staged in 1921. During the war, Marcel was in France, but was exempted from military service. He worked with the Red Cross in the bureau of research on soldiers missing in action. He wrote during that time an exhaustive study devoted to the American philosopher Josiah Royce. He taught for three years at the Lycée Condorcet in Paris and was appointed, in 1919, professor of philosophy at Sens. In 1923 he returned to Paris, where he devoted himself entirely to his philosophical research, to the writing of plays and contributed to various reviews, such as *Europe Nouvelle* and the *Nouvelle Revue Française,* both as philosopher and as theatrical critic. Moreover, he read manuscripts for two publishing houses and directed a collection of translations of non-French authors, *Feux Croises,* for the French publishers Plon.

Gabriel Marcel has an excellent command of foreign languages, and intellectuals from all over the world met at his Paris home, where many interesting debates and talks were continually going on. This man of small and frail stature with pale blue eyes and a sickly complexion, was animated with an intense and communicative vigor. He seemed to be continually "in action," either in the metaphysical, literary or dramatic field. He was and remains, what the French call *"un remuer d'ideés,"* a "mover of ideas," and when in 1930 he became a practicing Catholic, he brought to Catholic cultural circles his eager mind and his spirit of research, and was welcomed as an exceptionally generous, noble and independent character.

Gabriel Marcel presents a rare blending of intellectual activities: he is a philosopher and a playwright, and his approach to the theatre is that of a thinker and a mystic.

Influenced in his early years by the English Neo-Hegelians, James Bradley and Bosanquet, he later turned to Bergson, who—as he did for a number of men of his generation—opened for Gabriel the doors of the supernatural world. When Marcel became a Catholic thinker, he replaced Bergson's theory of intuition by religious experience (to which he had already been attracted in his pre-Catholic days through the study of William James). He centered his world—conception on contemplation and the interpretation of the universe as a *mystery*, to which Christianity and the Christian supernatural truth alone offer a key.

In the *Metaphysical Diary* which is his most important philosophical work we discover Marcel's fundamental traits. "Marcel does not offer us immediately a complete philosophy," writes his learned commentator, Professor Jean Wahl in his *Vers le Concret* (1932), "but a trend of thought which develops gradually, which destroys little by little its own hypothesis, which puts questions to itself and observes, its answers, examines them and beholds its own vision as it is revealed, not all at once, but in the element of time . . . in his eyes, if the eternal can be reached, it is first of all through the very flow of meditation, through the intense moments of feeling."

It is precisely this trend of thought born of meditation and the intensity of feeling, which form the distinctive mark of Gabriel Marcel's plays, such as the *Quatuor en Fa dièse; Le Coeur des autres; Le Regard neuf; Le Mort de Demain; L'Homme de Dieu; La Chapelle ardente; Le Divertissement posthume;* and *Le Monde cassé*, some of which have been staged in Paris, while others still await a theatre audience. But these plays do not actually require staging to be fully appreciated. They are extremely interesting in book form. Their pattern is, as writes Jean Wahl, "a mixture of the real and the abstract." They are not inspired by the cold "God of the Philosophers," but by an *ontological mystery*, that is by an invisible yet active presence of the Divine in human lives, of a God who links all human beings to each other through the Mystical Body; this means that all men *participate* in a community which is a *communion:* "To think in terms of God," writes Marcel, "means to think that God does not exist for oneself alone."

This mystical interpretation of human events, relations and feelings is most strongly felt in Marcel's play, *Le Monde Cassé* (The Broken World), where a young woman is saved from suicide by the prayers of a Benedictine novice, whom she loved when the young man was still in the world. His sacrifice to God is projected in her life and becomes a greater reality than the visible world around her. The play was published in a volume containing an exhaustive philosophical essay by Marcel in which he explains his dramatic and religious conception.

During the years immediately following his return to Catholicity, Marcel was in touch with Jacques Maritain, Charles Du Bos and the group of Catholic intellectuals surrounding them. He exercised a stimulating influence on his followers, contributed to the Catholic weekly, *Temps Présent* (directed by Stanislas Fumet) and to the Catholic periodical *Vigile.*

After the collapse of France, he settled down in the free zone, at Lyon, and gave a series of lectures on "Hope," the theological virtue, which, he declared, was to inspire the French and lead them on during these tragic days. His faith and fervor deeply impressed his audience, and his independent attitude, his loyalty to his ideals and his inflexible spiritual courage in the face of the oppressive regime were profoundly admired by all those who defend in France the values of Christian culture.   H. I.

Sister Marie Paula 1867-1940

From her earliest years, Sister Marie Paula had found her greatest pleasure in writing. She was born in New York City, in 1867, the daughter of John P. and Anna E. (Geary) Duffy. For a time she attended St. Lawrence's and later Mount St. Vincent Academy, but, owing to delicate health, the greater part of her early education was received at home. While a young girl she went to Europe and studied in Dresden, Germany, with a governess, then at the Sacred Heart Convent in Paris and finally at the Château de Neuilly, Neuilly-sur-Seine, France.

Shortly after her return to America she entered the Congregation of the Sisters of Charity of Mount St. Vincent, New York, in 1887. The years since then were spent teaching at the Mount, except for a few years at the Blessed Sacrament Academy, New York City. At first she taught in the Academy at Mount St. Vincent, but after the opening of the College, in 1910, she was a member of its faculty and was chairman of the department of English. She received the degrees of A.B. from Mount St. Vincent College in 1914 and Litt.D. in 1931. Her postgraduate work included studies at the Catholic University of America and at Fordham University, where she obtained an M.A. in 1919 and a Ph.D. in 1921. Her dissertation for the Doctorate of Philosophy was on "Psychology and Dramatic Art."

In her childhood Sister Marie Paula wrote little rhymes, which she called "jingles," and playlets, usually presented by her girl friends and herself to an audience of admiring playmates. She admitted that she even attempted a novel but added that "happily it was only begun." As a young religious she contributed poems, short stories and essays to Catholic magazines, but it was not until her more mature years that she began to publish books. These were written when she found time away from her teaching duties, and they include: *Talks with Teachers; Living for God; Shibboleths; God's Mother and Ours,* and *God's Ways.* She also dramatized stories and adapted or wrote short plays, this work being done chiefly for Le Cercle Jeanne d'Arc, the French Club of Mount St. Vincent College, of which she was moderator from 1922 to 1925. For several years she taught French, but her greatest interest was in English literature.

She was a member of the Catholic Poetry Society of America and of the Alice Meynell Poetry Society, of Mount St. Vincent's. Her hobbies were reading, writing, music, working out puzzles, and the Hail Mary Club, of which she urged her students to become members, the only obligation being to say one Hail Mary morning and evening.   C. M. N.

Sister Mariella (Gable), O.S.B.   1899-

It is often said that lovers of nature possess a certain sensitiveness and feeling for beauty. These qualities were dominant in the character of Mary Gable, the future Sister Mariella. She was born in Marine-on-St. Croix, Minnesota, in 1899. As a child her main pastime was "collecting flowers, butterflies, birds' nests, making butterfly nets, sailing up and down the river in search of new specimens and mounting them with the assistance of my younger brother," she writes. Days were spent in happy hours exploring the beauty of her town which she describes as "an exceptionally beautiful little town folded between shaggy, wild hills with a river at its back door."

At the age of fifteen, she left this utopia to attend St. Benedict's Academy from which two years later she was graduated. One month later she received the habit of St. Benedict and became known as Sister Mariella. Subsequent years were spent studying at the College of St. Benedict where she received her A.B., 1925; the University of Minnesota from which she got her M.A., 1928, and Cornell University which awarded her a Ph.D., 1934, with Phi Beta Kappa honors.

Sister Mariella began to write poetry at the age of ten. When the elder members of her family could not find an appropriate piece for her little brother John to speak at a Friday afternoon exercise of the school, she wrote a poem for him which was highly praised.

Sister Mariella's book, *The Blind Man's Stick* (1938), is a collection of her poems which have previously appeared in *The Commonweal, America* and *Spirit*. Many of these poems reflect her memories of Marine-on-St. Croix. Her poem, "Clam Digger" is almost an exact transcript from reality. The two of her poems that she likes best, however, are "The Spy" and "The Sheep Herd." Both poems are based on the thought that the beauty of the universe depends upon the recognition of God's power. One of the poems "Blue," won a cash prize from the Boston *Herald*. Another "To a Madonna in Carrara Marble," was set to music by Charles Repper, the Boston composer. Her poetry has won the praise of Professor Steeves of Columbia University, Lew Sarett of Northwestern University and Aline Kilmer.

In spite of the fact that her first love is poetry, she has become interested in fiction. Evidence of that is revealed in her critical essay "Catholic Fiction" which appeared first in *The Catholic World* (December 1940) and has since been reprinted; in *Prose Readings,* an anthology for Catholic Colleges compiled by Father Vincent Flynn, and also by her book *Great Modern Catholic Short Stories,* a Catholic Book of the Month, which she edited. Later the title was changed to *They Are People. Our Father's House* a compilation of 28 stories, appeared in 1945.

Sister Mariella prefers writing to teaching. "I like to write better than anything else in the world. I like to teach, too, but I am always jealous of the time I put in on it, and am continually pulling away from it because I feel a most compelling need to write. But I have not had time to do more than a few insignificant jottings." Much of her time is spent as a professor of English at the College of St. Benedict, St. Joseph, Minnesota, where she is also the Head of the Department of English.

"Of the various courses I teach," she writes, "Dante is the one I prefer." While at Cornell University, she studied under Lane Cooper, the noted authority on Dante. Francis Thompson is her favorite poet, and among the moderns she is very fond of Robert Frost.   S. M.

Sister Maris Stella 1899-

In 1939 the St. Anthony Guild Press at Paterson, New Jersey, brought out, under the title *Here Only a Dove,* a singularly piercing series of sonnets and other lyrics by Sister Maris Stella. It almost immediately placed this distinguished member of the Sisters of St. Joseph in the front rank of contemporary Catholic poets. Such cautious critics as Father Leonard Feeney and Clifford J. Laube have recognized in her a poet of exceptional insight, clarity and elevation.

Sister Maris Stella was born in Alton, Iowa, December 21, 1899. After grammar and high-school studies in the public schools, chiefly at Des Moines, she took a course at Derham Hall, a school preparatory to the College of St. Catherine in St. Paul, Minnesota. She entered the novitiate of the Sisters of St. Joseph of Carondelet on September 12, 1920, received the habit on March 19, 1921, and made her final profession on August 15, 1926. Meanwhile she attended the College of St. Catherine, where she received her B.A. degree in 1924. In October 1927 she was matriculated at Oxford University in England, taking her degree of B.A. in 1929 and her M.A. in 1933.

Since January 1930 she has been a member of the English Department at St. Catherine's, and since 1938 chairman of that department. At the University of Chicago, where she spent several summer sessions, she became, in the summer of 1940, a member of the Workshop in General Education. As a teacher her talents have been intensively devoted to the training of young writers and to the cultivation of intelligent Catholic reading. A beginner's course in Dante's *Divine Comedy,* which she initiated at St. Catherine's, and a beginner's course in the history of the English language, are among the projects which have flourished under her leadership.

Students in creative writing, under her direction, have won among other distinctions, first prize in the *Forum Magazine* poetry competition in 1934, and first prizes in the *Atlantic* Poetry Contests for 1936, 1939 and 1941.

Her own work has appeared frequently in *America, The Commonweal, Spirit, The Sign, The Catholic World, The Catholic Art Quarterly, Poetry: A Magazine of Verse* and other periodicals.

The textbook, *American Profile* (Sadlier, 1944), says of Sister Maris Stella: "The calmness of her spirit gives indication of the depth from which her poetry comes. Her lyrics seem to well from her spirit like water from a spring, making their own music rather than being made into music."

Sister Maris Stella is a member of the College English Association; also of the Catholic Poetry Society of America, the Gallery of Living Catholic Authors and the League of American Pen Women. Her affiliations include Phi Beta Kappa and Delta Phi Lambda. She is also a member of St. Anne's Society of Oxford. Her poems have appeared in numerous anthologies, including Alfred Noyes' *The Golden Book of Catholic Poetry*.   C. J. L.

Jacques Maritain   1882-

Jacques Maritain was born in Paris on November 18, 1882, the son of a Burgundian lawyer and of Geneviève Favre Maritain. His mother was the daughter of Jules Favre who played an important role in French politics under the Second Empire and at the beginning of the Third Republic, and was the defender of French interests in the peace negotiations with Germany at the end of the Franco-Prussian War. Maritain's mother had her son baptized by a Protestant minister and gave him an education that was rationalist, humanitarian and in the republican tradition of her family; his Catholic father played but little part in his education and religious training. He attended the Lycée Henri IV and there formed a lasting friendship with Ernest Psichari, the grandson of Ernest Renan. These ardent and studious young men matured in an atmosphere of intellectual groping and artistic experimentation; they undertook a passionate exploration of modern thought and attended the Sorbonne where they followed courses in philosophy and literature; Maritain was especially interested in biology, as well as in the social questions of the day.

It was at the Sorbonne that Maritain met his future wife, Raïssa Oumansoff, a young Russian Jewess, like himself tragically deceived by the rationalism, positivism and skepticism then being taught. They were persuaded by their friend Charles Péguy to attend Henri Bergson's courses at the Collège de France. Bergson's teaching revealed to them the fallacy at the heart of rationalism, the failure of relativist philosophy and the necessity of an Absolute; his theory of intuition, however, was not enough to satisfy the intelligence of these pupils. Jacques and Raïssa

Maritain were married in 1904, and shortly thereafter came under the influence of the strange and fiery genius, Léon Bloy. It was largely due to this ardent believer that, after years spent in fruitless search for intellectual peace, they came into the Catholic Church. Jacques Maritain, his wife, and sister-in-law were baptized June 11, 1906.

For a while, Maritain, disappointed in his quest for human wisdom, thought he had to leave philosophy for faith and devote himself entirely to the study of the saints and mystics, but he still preserved his aptitude for natural sciences and his love for experimental work. He received the Michonis scholarship to Heidelberg University and there he spent two years, 1907 and 1908, studying biology with Hans Driesch. He was the first to publicize Driesch's theory of vitalism in France, publishing in 1910 his study on Darwinism and neo-vitalism in the *Revue de Philosophie.*

While he was still at Heidelberg, and later at Versailles where he retired on his return to France to study Saint Thomas under the direction of the Dominican, Père Clerissac, Maritain's philosophical interest revived. He perceived that not only had he found in Catholicity the light of Revelation and divine guidance but also a philosophy which could foster, direct and regulate speculative thinking. He decided that henceforth his true vocation lay in the spread of Thomistic doctrines and in bringing it to grips with contemporary problems.

By his agrégation, Maritain was entitled to a chair of philosophy in one of the state lycées, but fearing that he would not be free, in that period of marked anti-clericalism, to teach as a Christian and a philosopher he gave up his career in the state universities. He secured work from one of the French publishers and taught scholastic philosophy at the Collège Stanislas from 1912 to 1914, and from 1915 to 1916.

In the light of the philosophy of Saint Thomas, Maritain reconsidered his past studies and began publishing a series of articles dealing with problems of modern thought; these were collected and published somewhat later (in 1922) under the title *Antimoderne.* In 1913 he published *La Philosophie Bergsonienne,* a trenchant criticism of Bergson's thought; and in his lectures and courses at the Institut Catholique, where he was named professor in 1914, Maritain opposed Thomism not only to the errors of Bergsonian metaphysics but to Cartesianism—"the French philosophical sin"—and to German idealism which seemed to him to spring from the same source, as well as from the Lutheran scission—another "national sin."

The Maritains' conversion to Catholicism had profound repercussions upon their intimates. Péguy announced that he, too, had come to accept Catholic teaching; although unfortunately the attitude of his family placed obstacles to his complete return to the Church. Psichari, after a period of service in the French army in Africa, was received into the Catholic Church in 1913; both he and Péguy died heroic deaths on the battlefield of the Marne. Madame Maritain's father, just before his death in 1912, was received into the Catholic Church and confirmed by the Bishop of Versailles.

In 1917 Maritain was requested by the bishops of France to begin work on a manual of philosophy for use in seminaries. This work, his *Introduction to Philosophy,* caused him to be given the title of Doctor ad honorem by a decree of the Congregation of Studies in Rome. His great activity since that time has been marked by numerous books, by courses, by lectures, the foundation of study groups in scholastic philosophy, by his support of the Thomist Society, his researches in Thomist esthetics *(Art et scholastique),* his manual of logic, his polemics with Legendre and Chevalier on Bergson, Descartes and Aristotle, by contributions to numerous philosophical reviews, prefaces to others' books, etc. In addition to his own writing he has been the editor of important books in many fields directing, for the French publishers Plon, the series "Roseau d'Or" which first introduced such thinkers as Berdaieff and Henri Gheon, and for the firm of Desclee de Brouwer the philosophical series, "Les Iles" and "Questions Disputees." While in the United States he began a similar series called the "Golden Measure Books."

In the Action Française controversy in 1927, Maritain opposed the current of political thought started by Charles Maurras. When his efforts proved hopeless and Rome condemned the movement, Maritain published his *Primauté du Spirituel (The Things That Are Not Caesar's)* to point the direction which enlightened Catholic political thinking should follow.

In the world upheavals of the past years Maritain has continually proclaimed the freedom of the philosopher to deal as a philosopher, not as a politician, with the problems of contemporary politics. He has refused to associate himself with any political party in his native France or elsewhere. Perhaps his greatest philosophical work is *Les Degrés du Savoir* (1932) which covers vast territories of speculative thought. But *True Humanism* (1938) dealing with the practical problems of our social structure, has been most widely acclaimed.

Maritain has given lectures and courses of study at, among other places, Louvain University, at the Angelicum in Rome, at Geneva, in Milan, in Germany, in Ireland and in England. For some years he has taught regularly at the Pontifical Institute of Mediaeval Studies in Toronto and at the University of Chicago. In 1936 he made an extensive lecture tour through South America.

When France fell in the Spring of 1940, Maritain was in this country lecturing. Refusing to depend in any way on the ruling government of France and determined to keep on speaking freely, he gave up the thought of returning to his home in Meudon, outside Paris. He and his wife and sister-in-law lived in New York, and while there he taught one semester each at Columbia and Princeton, with shorter courses in Toronto and Chicago. Since 1945 he is the French ambassador to the Vatican.

His books in English are: *The Angelic Doctor; Art and Scholasticism; A Christian Looks At the Jewish Question; The Degrees of Knowledge; France My Country; An Introduction to Logic; Freedom in the Modern World; An Introduction to Philosophy; Prayer and Intelligence* (with Raissa Maritain); *A Preface to Metaphysics; Religion and Culture; An Essay in Order; Scholasticism and Politics; Science and Wisdom; Some Reflections on Culture and Liberty; The Things that Are Not Caesar's; Three Reformers; Luther-Descartes-Rousseau; True Humanism; The*

Living Thoughts of St. Paul; The Twilight of Civilization (translated by Lionel Landry—an address delivered in Paris in February, 1939); *Education at the Crossroads* (1942), and *Le Songe de Descartes* translated by Mabelle L. Andison in 1944. J. K.

Raissa Maritain 1883-

Raissa Maritain was born September 12, 1883, at Rostov-on-the-Don. Of Jewish parentage, she was raised in an atmosphere of strict orthodoxy and under the influence of her grandparents. In her memoirs, *We Have Been Friends Together,* she writes of a happy childhood, of an early family move to Marioupol, a small town on the shores of the Sea of Azov, and of schooling unusual for a Jewish child at that time and place. When she was ten her parents, mindful of the future of their two little girls, went to France where they felt that greater opportunities existed. Despite their modest circumstances—the father was the proprietor of a small clothing establishment—the daughters were given every possible educational advantage. Raissa Oumansoff was a brilliant student and was registered at the Sorbonne at the age of sixteen. She followed courses mainly in the Faculty of Sciences and was for a while an ardent disciple of Bergson. It was at this time that she met Jacques Maritain to whom she was married in 1904. Together the young couple undertook the intellectual pilgrimage which in 1906 led them into the Catholic Church, and with them, many of their intimates. The Maritains' conversion was due in large part to the tempestuous, but ardently believing, Léon Bloy, who became godfather to Jacques and Raissa Maritain as well as to her sister, Vera Oumansoff.

Following their conversion, the Maritains spent two years at the University of Heidelberg. In addition to their studies they enjoyed in Germany a period of solitude and reflection which marked the beginning of the present philosophical career of Jacques Maritain. Raissa Maritain's story is inextricably bound up with the life of her husband. Seldom separated for any length of time, they have studied and written together over the years. She has collaborated in many of his philosophical writings and her name is signed with his to *Prayer and Intelligence,* translated into English by Algar Thorold, and to *Situation de la Poésie.* She has written several poetical works, especially *La Vie Donnée* and *Lettre de Nuit,* also a child's life of St. Thomas Aquinas, and *The Prince of this World,* translated by Gerald Phelan. Her memoirs, *Les Grandes Amitiés,* was translated by Julie Kernan under the title *We Have Been Friends Together.* She published more recently a philosophical essay, *La Conscience Morale et l'État de Nature,* and an essay on the painter Marc Chagall.

Madame Maritain is a small, frail woman, dark and vivacious. Intensely interested in philosophy, literature, art and music, she is a good critic and has won the devotion of many talented men and women. She is sympathetic and thoughtful, possessing a real genius for friendship. In her memoirs (which cover only the years of their life before the last war) she writes understandingly of Bergson, Psichari, Péguy, Léon Bloy, Georges Rouault and Pierre Termier. This same understanding went out to those who visited the Maritain home in later years. Until 1939 they lived in a modest villa on the rue du Parc in Meudon, a small town outside Paris, where their house became a focal point for Catholic intellectual life in France. Especially notable was a group which gathered there each fall for a week's retreat under the auspices of some Dominican preacher. As many as possible were accommodated at the Maritain home and the others nearby. They also usually received on Sunday afternoons. Many of their guests came for advice, guidance and encouragement, and one met there students from many lands as well as leaders of various youth movements.

In 1940, Madame Maritain and her sister accompanied Jacques Maritain to the United States. Events made it impossible for them to return. They made their home in New York until her husband took over his duties as French ambassador to the Vatican.

She is the author of: *Lettre de Nuit; La Vie donnée,* poems (English translation by G. B. Phelan as *The Prince of This World*); *L'Ange de l'Ecole; Vie de Saint Thomas d'Aquin racontée aux enfants;* illustrated by Gino Severini (English translation by Julie Kernan as *The Angel of the Schools*); *Les Grandes Amitiés* (English translation by Julie Kernan as *We Have Been Friends Together*); *La Conscience Morale et l'État de Nature; Marc Chagall,* and *Adventures in Grace—Memoirs* (1945), the Catholic Book Club selection for July. In collaboration with Jacques Maritain she wrote: *De la Vie d'Oraison* (English translation by A. Thorold as *Prayer and Intelligence*).   J. K.

Mrs. E. R. Marlin   *See* Hilda Van Stockum

Bruce Marshall   1899-

The author of *Father Malachy's Miracle,* a top-seller in the early thirties, Bruce Marshall is unmistakably of Scottish descent. His strong Scottish voice betrays his nationality. He was born in 1899, the son of Claude Niven Marshall of Edinburgh, and Annie Margaret Seton Bruce. He was educated at Edinburgh Academy; Trinity College, Glenalmond, till his seventeenth year and St. Andrew's and Edinburgh Universities. His M.A. degree was received in 1924 from the University of Edinburgh and a year later from the same institution he received his B.Com. (Bachellor of Commerce). In 1926 he was admitted as a member of the Society of Accountants in Edinburgh.

By choice he is a novelist but by occupation he is a continental auditor of English and American companies. He gives two reasons for entering accountancy: (a) "I wanted to get a job abroad and this was the easiest profession in which to do so; (b) I realized that it would be a long time before I was able to live by my pen." He practised this profession in Paris from 1926 until two days before the Germans entered the city in 1940.

Back in Britain, Marshall again joined the British Army and was assigned to the Royal Army Pay Corps. He finished as lieutenant colonel in the Displaced Persons Division of the British Element of the Allied Commission for Austria. In World War I, at the age of nineteen, he lost a leg as a result of wounds received in France just six nights before the armistice. He served as second lieutenant in the 3rd Royal Irish Fusiliers.

In 1928 he married Mary Pearson Clark, a Scots girl, in Paris. They have one daughter, Sheila.

He has been defined as "a dark, smiling man, slightly less than medium height, sturdily built, with blue eyes, a quick sense of humor, and definite in manner." He has been a Catholic since the first day of January 1918. When asked by Father Daniel Lord, S.J., whether Catholic literature influenced his conversion to any extent, he replied, "Yes. All the novels of Robert Hugh Benson had their effect but more especially Cardinal Gibbons' *The Faith of Our Fathers*."

When Grace Conway in an interview asked him these questions: What's wrong with the novel today? What about the novel with the Catholic background? Why are there so few of this type? He replied: "I'm glad I haven't to talk about what is misleadingly called 'The Catholic Novel.' I dislike that term. All that it conveys to me is that hateful thing propaganda which is often so badly done that it achieves the very opposite effect from the one aimed at. What I find wrong with the average novel today is the exact inverse of what is wrong with the Catholic propaganda type of book. I mean the absence of all spirituality, whose presence in the so-called Catholic novels is stultified by a complete refusal to depict the world, the flesh, and the devil. The kind of book that has all the characters kneeling down and saying the rosary on the last page, whereas in real life nothing of the sort would ever happen. No converts are made that way."

Marshall's book, *All Glorious Within* (1945), published in the United States as *The World, the Flesh, and Father Smith*, has reached its fifth edition in England with a sixth in preparation. Marshall wrote it to depict a Scots priest who had a real vocation. *George Brown's School Days* appeared in 1946.

Among his other books are: *Stooping Venus* (1926); *Prayer for the Living* (1934); *The Uncertain Glory* (1935); *Canon to the Right of Them* (1936); *Lucky-Penny* (1937), and *Delilah Upside Down* (1941). In 1943 he published *Yellow Tapers for Paris*, a pen-portrait of the disillusioned city of Paris.

Bruce Marshall dislikes verbosity. "Cliches," he says, "whether spoken or written, become soporifics rather than an incitement to thought or action." To convey his meaning he uses the fewest possible words.

M. H.

Reverend Cyril Charlie Martindale, S.J. 1879-

A brilliant mind, a tireless and capable pen, and a zealous priestly life have brought Reverend C. C. Martindale, S.J., to the knowledge of many. He was born in England, in 1879, the son of Sir Arthur Henry Temple Martindale, K.C.S.I., and Marian Isabella MacKenzie, and, after schooling at Harrow, he became a Catholic and entered the Jesuit novitiate, pursuing his studies at St. Mary's Hall, Stonyhurst, and Pope's Hall, Oxford. There he obtained the Hereford (Latin) and Craven (Latin and Greek) scholarships in 1903, and in this and the following year stood second for the Ireland Scholarship. In 1904 he won the Chancellor's Latin Verse and Gaisford Greek Verse Prizes, in 1906 the Derby Scholarship and in 1907 the Ellerton Theological Essay Prize. After his ordination in 1911, Father Martindale taught at Stonyhurst, Manresa House, Roehampton and Oxford. Since 1927 he had been on the staff of Farm Street Church, London. In 1940 he went to Copenhagen, Denmark, arriving there on April 6. On April 9th Denmark was invaded by the Germans and he was subsequently interned in a German Jesuit House. "I was very lucky not to be put under lock and key," he said. "I think that the fact that I was in a German Jesuit house somewhat baffled the Germans. They were not quite sure how to proceed." In the winter of 1941, Father Martindale became dangerously ill with angina and dropsy. He wrote occasionally. He finished a new life of Frassati, and a new life of St. Camillus de Lellis. On September 5, 1945, he returned to England.

During his life Father Martindale has travelled far. After his visits to Australia and New Zealand he wrote *The Risen Sun. African Angelus* records journeys to the Union of South Africa and Rhodesia, and he also made trips to Athens, Argentina and Again Australia. Other books are *In God's Nursery; The Waters of Twilight* about Robert Hugh Benson, and *The Goddess of Ghosts* about Bernard Vaughan, S.J. He also wrote lives of these two priests and of C. D. Plater, S.J., and a *Memoir of R. P. Garrold, S.J.* On the foundresses of the Cenacle and of the Missionary Sisters of the Sacred Heart he wrote *King's Daughters.* With the late Father C. Plater, S.J., he is co-author of *Retreats for Soldiers.* Maisie Ward says that Father Martindale keeps up his friendship with the invalided soldiers he wheeled about in chairs at Oxford. He heard their confessions and wrote theology books for them.

Among his earliest works is *The Legend of St. Christopher* (1908). *The Vocation of St. Aloysius Gonzaga* appeared in 1926, and *Man and His Destiny* in 1928. *The Mind of the Missal* (1929) and *The Words of the Missal* are well known, as are also the two volumes he published on *Prayers of the Missal.* He has rebuilt Christian apologetics about the doctrines of the supernatural life and the Mystical Body. His sermons comprise seven volumes. Some of his talks broadcast over the radio are published as *What Are Saints?*

Father Martindale is editor of the series, *Catholic Thoughts and Thinkers* and *The Household of God,* to which he has contributed respectively the *Introductory Volume* and *St. Justin* and the series, *In God's Army, Upon God's Holy Hills* and *Princes of His People.* One of his great interests is the Apostolate of the Sea, in the foundation of which he was instrumental. In work for seafarers, study of native missions, social and international relations and the liturgy he finds outlet for his zeal. He is President of the Federation of Catholic Societies in the Universities of Great Britain.

Father Martindale's health has suffered from the time of a car accident some years ago in New Zealand. Despite his present illness he has received many people into the Church and rejoices at the opportunity of "soaking and resoaking" himself in the Scriptures.   C. M. N.

Paul Martin-Dillon   1886-

Writing as "Paul R. Martin" the short form of his name, Paul R. F. Martin-Dillon is best known perhaps as the author of *The Gospel in Action* which has become a standard textbook of the Third Order of St. Francis. He is likewise the author of *The First Cardinal of the West,* the official story of Cardinal Mundelein's career as Archbishop of Chicago.

Born January 23, 1886, the son of Dr. Frank and Alfreda (Martin) Dillon, this Catholic writer was educated in the preparatory school of the University of Notre Dame and in the collegiate department of that institution. Later he did graduate work at Loyola University, Chicago. He holds the degrees of Bachelor of Philosophy and Master of Arts.

His working life has been spent in secular newspaper work, his Catholic writing being a sideline undertaken in a spirit of devotion. For years he was connected with such newspapers as the Indianapolis *Star,* the New York *Tribune,* the New York *Evening Sun,* the Washington Bureau of the Associated Press, the Chicago *Evening Post,* the Chicago *Journal of Commerce* and the Chicago *Daily News.* Although experienced in all branches of editorial work, Paul Martin-Dillon is generally thought of as a drama and music critic and editorial writer. At present he is chief editor of the evening and Sunday *Times,* Cumberland, Maryland.

During the first months of World War I, he was general director of publicity for the Knights of Columbus Committee on War Activities, resigning to enter the United States Army. While on the staff of the Chicago *Daily News* he was sent on three trips to the sub-arctic as a result of which he not only gave his newspaper the news and features it wanted but likewise wrote three series of articles which were syndicated by the NCWC News Service under the titles, "Paths and By-Paths of Catholic Quebec", "To Gaspesie and Beyond" and "Catholic Trails of the Labrador."

At an early age he became interested in all things Franciscan and joined the Third Order of St. Francis when fourteen years old. In collaboration with Reverend Maximus Poppy, O.F.M., he has written *Survey of a Decade* and *The Franciscan Heritage,* both books dealing with the Third Order. In 1931 Mr. Martin-Dillon was elected a consultor of the National Executive Board of the Third Order of St. Francis, U.S.A. He was re-elected at the expiration of his first five-year term and re-elected for a third term in 1941. In 1942 he resigned from the Board due to the pressure of his professional duties. In recognition of his contribution to Franciscan literature, Mr. Martin-Dillon was granted the unusual distinction of affiliation to the Order of Friars Minor in 1937. This was bestowed by the Most Reverend Father Leonard Bello, minister general of the Order of Friars Minor at Rome.

In 1910 Paul Martin-Dillon married Lillian Irene Buckman of Philadelphia. They made their home at Cumberland, Maryland. Mrs. Martin-Dillon died May 27, 1945. Mr. Martin-Dillon is a bibliophile and his private library contains about 3,000 volumes. Many of these are on Catholic subjects including a special collection of Franciscana. He likewise has a representative collection of books written by alumni of the University of Notre Dame, and his theatre section, comprised of theatrical history and biography, numbers about 500 volumes. Many of these are collectors' items—first editions and other rare works.

Sister Mary Angelita, B.V.M. 1878-1934

Sister Mary Angelita, B.V.M., who was Mary Agnes Stackhouse before her reception into the Congregation of the Sisters of Charity of the Blessed Virgin Mary, was born in Vincennes, Indiana, on July 16, 1878. With the exception of one sister who died in infancy, she was the youngest of nine children born to Mr. and Mrs. Samuel B. Stackhouse. Both parents were Pennsylvanians, of English, Irish, Scotch, and Welsh descent. They were married in Philadelphia, where their first child was born, but soon migrated to the West.

Sister Mary Angelita was frail from babyhood and suffered almost constantly throughout her life, but her vigorous and energetic will proved a sharp contrast to her delicate health. She was precocious in a gentle, winning way, and at the age of four was learning to read and spell from a volume of Longfellow.

She attended the Immaculate Conception Academy in Davenport, conducted by the Sisters of Charity, B.V.M., and was graduated from the high school department at the age of sixteen. For the following two years she continued her studies in a postgraduate course at St. Francis Academy, Council Bluffs, under the guidance of the same community of sisters.

Through all these years, the realization of her call to the religious life was present with her, and, on September 8, 1899, she entered the community which had educated her. Her mother accompanied her to Mount Carmel, Dubuque, and there left her youngest and, possibly, her best loved child. An older sister, Sister Mary Charlotte, B.V.M., was in the same community.

Sister Mary Angelita had been writing frequently in verse all through her girlhood years and publishing occasionally in local papers and magazines, and she continued her writing during her novitiate and throughout the thirty-five years of her life in religion.

She matriculated at Marquette University, Milwaukee, where she took her first degree, and studied also at De Paul University, Chicago; at Clarke College, Dubuque, and at the University of Notre Dame, where she received her Master's degree and where she spent one summer teaching Anglo-Saxon, a subject in which she had done considerable research.

Busy as a teacher and organizer, Sister Mary Angelita found time for her writing, and published a volume of verse, *Starshine and Candlelight,* which has gone through several editions, and she published both prose and verse in *America, The Commonweal, Spirit, The Catholic World,* and *The Catholic School Journal.* In 1932, she won the Star-Dust Prize for Religious Poetry, in a contest sponsored by *Poetry Magazine,* then edited by Edith Merrick. The poems, on prayer, were printed in *The Commonweal,* March 16, 1934. A number of her poems appear in American anthologies.

She had taught in several academies of her community, at Clarke College, Dubuque, and finally at Mundelein College, Chicago, to which she came when it was established in 1930. Here she organized the English department, over which she presided until the year of her death. The college publication, *The Tower,* a year-book which has since been discontinued, the *Skyscraper,* campus newspaper, *The Clepsydra,* now the *Mundelein College Review,* a literary magazine, and *Quest,* an anthology of student verse issued annually, all owe their inception to her keen vision and practical management. The last named volume, *Quest,* is the mouthpiece of the Charles L. O'Donnell Unit of the Catholic Poetry Society of America, organized by Sister Mary Angelita and affiliated with the National Catholic Poetry Society.

During her years at Mundelein College, Sister Mary Angelita sowed the seeds for more than ordinary artistic production, and established a tradition of literary excellence which has grown with the years. Fourteen of the students whose gifts she developed during her three years as a teacher there, have won success as writers, and today are publishing poems and articles in magazines, and writing for the stage and the radio.

Scarcely five feet tall and correspondingly slender, she had, nevertheless, a remarkable intellect, a rare poetic insight, and the unusual ability to develop in her students the same scholarly precision and creative powers which she possessed. Especially appreciated by her students were her genial wit, her facility for sparkling conversation, her sound judgment, sympathy, common sense, and skill as an organizer.

Besides launching the Mundelein publications, she organized three literary societies, enlisting the cooperation of her many literary friends to act as honorary members, critics, and lecturers and established the annual Creative Writing Contest, all of which are sponsored by the English department and judged by outstanding writers in the five fields which they cover. She inspired the drama department to foster creative ability among its members and to present student-written plays; launched a group of new successful radio writers, and gave impetus to the debating society of which she was an early sponsor.

With the years, her physical strength declined, and in the fall of 1933, Sister Mary Angelita left forever the skyscraper college where her name will always be hallowed, and returned to the motherhouse of her community, where she died in the thirty-sixth year of her religious life, on April 3, 1934.   S. M. J.

S. M. C. (Sister Mary Catherine)

Writing under the initials S. M. C., and desiring to remain anonymous, the author of the novel, *Brother Petroc's Return,* is not an easy subject for biographical study. "My name, except the nom de plume," she writes, "is of no interest to anyone, neither is my private life." A letter to her superior for more information brought the reply: "Only the details already given will be allowed to be used."

It is permissible, however, to identify S. M. C. as a Dominican nun who lives in a little town on the southwestern coast of England. She teaches in a parish school, is the organist of her community, and recites the full Divine Office in addition to her teaching duties.

Emmet Lavery, who visited S. M. C. in the spring of 1939, reports that "Sister is the very salt of the English earth: a truly stalwart person, suggesting a wonderful strength, both physical and intellectual." Her life in the school during World War II, followed much the same schedule that it did before the war. There were new problems, new responsibilities, but Sister carried on with both her teaching and her writing. Raiders had often been near but the pattern of community life went on, with even deeper intensity.

S. M. C. first came to the attention of publishers in 1925 with a little book called *Parables for Grown-Up Children.* Except for occasional articles, she was not heard from again until 1937, when she brought out her novel *Brother Petroc's Return.* It was immediately designated by the London *Daily Mail* as its book of the month selection, and shortly afterward it was re-published in the United States by Little, Brown & Company, being selected by the Catholic Book of the Month Club for October 1937. The novel attracted widespread attention in this country, without any special exploitation. Critics and readers alike gave it unstinted praise. Mr. Lavery began a dramatization of the novel in 1938 and soon thereafter it was presented in premiere performance by the seminarians of Mundelein Seminary, St. Mary of the Lake, Mundelein, Illinois. Later, the play was published by Samuel French. A German translation of the novel was made by Benziger Brothers in Switzerland and, just before the outbreak of World War II, one of the monks at Solesmes was negotiating for the French translation rights.

The power of Brother Petroc through the years seems to be that, in a way, his problems are not unlike those of today. It is the story of a young Benedictine monk of the sixteenth century, who awakens four hundred years later, to discover that he has not died, that he stands midway between the age of faith and the age of reason. In trying to adjust himself to the subjectivity of the new era, Petroc loses for a moment the objectivity of his earlier day. But in the end Petroc finds his place in time, in the eternal will of God.

In 1939 Sand's & Company published the next novel by S. M. C., *The Dark Wheel,* the rights of which were taken up in the United States by Kenedy in 1940. Kenedy also published her book *The Spark in the Reeds,* the story of a young English priest of the early nineteenth century "whose every work failed, but whose life was no failure."

Friends of S. M. C. had been urging her to jot down the day-to-day recollections of a teacher in a war-danger area, showing the relation of Catholic philosophy to Catholic life, during a period of great stress and strain. These notes appear in her book *Children Under Fire* (1943). *Once in Cornwall: Legends of Saints and Dragons* was published in 1944.

M. H.

Sister Mary Edwardine   R.S.M.

Schoolteachers, at least religious schoolteachers, have little leisure; principals have less; the teacher-principal has none. That fact accounts, in large part, for the slender literary output of Sister Mary Edwardine of the Religious Sisters of Mercy. Perhaps there is another reason, too. She is a perfectionist who will not release a line of verse that does not meet her own exacting standards.

Regina Mary O'Connor, as Sister was known before her entrance into religion, was born in West Branch, Michigan, eldest daughter of Michael and Theresa Walsh O'Connor. When she was still very small, her parents moved to Bay City in order that their children might receive a Catholic education. Her brother the Reverend Neil O'Connor is editor of the *Catholic Weekly* and pastor of St. Elizabeth's Church, Reese, Mchigan. Regina attended St. Mary's grade school and high school, which were taught by the Sisters of Mercy. Two months after her graduation, she entered the novitiate of the Order. Heredity and environment both contributed to a love of books and a love of teaching, for there were teachers on both sides of the family.

When she was asked recently how she had begun to write poetry, she laughed ruefully. "I was forced to," she confessed. "When I was a novice preparing to be a religious teacher, one of our teachers was George Sprau, head of the English department at Western State Teachers College, Kalamazoo. He came to Mount Mercy, Grand Rapids, every week for our classes. He gave us, among other courses, one in Lyric Poetry. I suppose most English students know his book, *The Meaning of Literature,* and can realize what he would do with such a course.

"He opened up a new and completely fascinating land in the reading of English lyrics. Incidentally, Palgrave's *Golden Treasury* has been my constant companion ever since. But it was not only the reading and interpretation of poetry that proved an exhilarating experience. There was the writing of poetry. Mr. Sprau asked for two lyrics each week. Of course, we gave him quantities of imitative verse. But we were writing. And for me, at least, life took on a fuller, richer meaning. The creation of beauty became at once a torment and a secret happiness. As a result I have been writing poetry, or more correctly, wanting to write it, ever since."

For twenty years Sister Mary Edwardine taught high school in Saginaw and Grand Rapids, Michigan, and in the fall of 1945 was appointed to the faculty of Mercy College, Detroit. During those twenty years the writing of poetry had, of necessity, to be limited to what could be done in vacations while attending summer school or teaching summer classes.

She received her bachelor's degree from the University of Notre Dame in 1927, her master's from the same institution in 1931. Graduate study at the University affected her writing of poetry. The critical judgment of Professor Burton Confrey helped her to formulate her own standards, and the encouragement of Professor Norbert Engels, poet and essayist, was an abiding inspiration. Later, the influence of Raymond Larsson, experimentalist, turned her interest to the newer forms and movements in poetry.

When *Our Lady's Choir,* an anthology of nuns' poetry selected by William Stanley Braithwaite, was published in 1932, it contained several of her poems which had appeared in magazines under a variety of pseudonyms. This early, facile verse has been succeeded by a slighter output characterized by a disciplined economy.

While a student at the University of Michigan 1941 summer session, Sister Mary Edwardine entered a small collection of poems, written that summer, in the Hopwood contest. These won the major award in the field of poetry. Urged to make a collection of her poems for publication in book form, she used the Hopwood title *Rising Wind* for the volume which came out late in 1942. Critics have passed favorable judgment on the volume. Most reviews praised its "modern, highly individual style and the controlled intensity of its emotion. . . . Its deceiving simplicity which is recognized as the finished technique of genuine lyric poetry."

Sister has made time also for occasional essays in educational journals, lectures on educational subjects and on poetry. A few one-act plays and two full length plays are proof of an interest in drama. "Romance in Blue" and "Cousin Judy" were written as class plays for the classes of 1943 and 1945 respectively at St. Andrew's, Saginaw. As these served their purpose in script form, they will not be published.

Sister's thesis on Adelaide Crapsey, American poet, which was the result of extensive correspondence with the family and friends of the poet, has received favorable comment as a fairly complete biographical and critical study of the poet. It is used in manuscript in several libraries, but has not been published. A promise to that effect was made to the poet's mother, Mrs. Adelaide Crapsey, from whom much important material was obtained.

Research, plays, lectures, and poetry itself are interesting, even fascinating, bypaths to one by profession a teacher. But the great highway leads through the classroom. Sister Mary Edwardine's chief concern is the welfare of the young people who make up her classes. To them goes that last full measure of devotion alone worthy of one vowed to God's service as a religious teacher.

Behind every book ever written is a person. Behind *Rising Wind* is a Sister of Mercy who reveals in its pages a love of beauty, the beauty of God's world, His creatures, Himself. The poems are not autobiographical, but they are indicative of a many-faceted personality, endowed with a temperament that finds this world a place of wordless wonder and finds in the religious life of a Sister of Mercy the perfect poetry of God.

Sister Mary Edwards *see* "Clementia"

Sister Mary James Power, S.S.N.D. 1894-

The educator and critic, Sister Mary James Power, S.S.N.D., was born in Massachusetts in 1894, educated at St. Peter's School, Cambridge, and Cambridge Latin School, and received her B.A. degree from St. John's University in 1923; her M.A., in 1926, and Ph.D. in 1936 from Fordham University. Her work within her religious congregation has taken her to teaching assignments in Brooklyn, Fort Lee, New Jersey, Baltimore and the Mid-West. At present (1947) she is the principal of Girls' Catholic High School, Malden, Massachusetts.

Sister Mary James has long had close acquaintance with many contemporary literary figures, has been in correspondence with the most significant, and has played host, at various lectures in schools and convents to which she has been attached, to their welcome visits. These have included Catholics and non-Catholics alike: Fathers Alfred Barrett, S.J., and Leonard Feeney, S.J., Theodore Maynard, John

Pick, Madame Bianchi, the executrix of Emily Dickinson, Anna Hempstead Branch, and Thomas S. Jones, Jr., among others.

As a result of her enthusiasm for the poets, particularly those of the nineteenth century and after, she has anonymously published several articles and reviews in current periodicals, and one signed paper in *The Catholic World.*

Her book, *Poets at Prayer* (1938), is a study of modern English and American figures who show an awareness of God in their work, either actively, passively or without specific definiteness. As Professor Henry W. Wells of Columbia writes in the foreword: "This survey will be found original in its critical point of view and inspiring alike to lovers of poetry, of philosophy, and of Christ. It will be best understood by those who love all three." The style of the study is felicitous and the insight exceptional. R. P. Tristram Coffin reviewed the volume by stating: "It is a great pleasure in these days to come on a treatise on poetry that puts substance above form, meaning before aesthetics."

The latest work is a study of the mind of one poet, Emily Dickinson, which she visits in her book *In the Name of the Bee* (1944). Here an attempt has been made to discover the spiritual significance of the New England singer, and to ally her outlook to that of Hopkins and other Catholic thinkers. The criticism is more feminine than that of her previous volume, but the feminine approach is, perhaps, essential to the discovery of the feminine mind. Of the work, Father Alfred Barrett has written: "A real New England nun has here shown that Emily Dickinson's inspiration was, if not to believe what the Church believes, at least to sing what the Church sings. By repeated demonstrations and without exaggerated inferences, Sister Mary James has used the poetry of Emily Dickinson to give a norm for the solution of the vexed problem, What is a Catholic poet?"   J. T.

Sister Mary Theodore, S.S.A. 1856-

The Chronicler of St. Ann's Convent, Victoria, British Columbia, the Diocesan Historian and Custodian of the Museum, Sister Mary Theodore, S.S.A., was born in Oswego, New York, in 1856. When about ten years old she showed a love for books and began by reading the *Vicar of Wakefield*. Except for one year during which she attended the Sisters' school, she went to the public school till the "teen" age. Then she prevailed on her parents to let her go to a boarding school in the Lachine Convent in Canada where an aunt, who was a nun, was stationed. That was in 1869. All these years, except one, which she spent in Alaska, she has lived in the Dominion of Canada.

At fifteen, she took the "first veil" in the Institute of the Sisters of

St. Ann. After her vows, which she pronounced when she was seventeen, she was sent to teach in the parish of Hemmingford. Her next assignment was at Rawden in the Laurentides of East Quebec. In 1878 she was appointed to the missions on Vancouver Island, British Columbia. After a few days' rest from the ten days' trip she was sent from the headquarters in Victoria to St. Ann's School for Orphans, nestled in the Cowichan Indian mission. The nearest neighbors were four Indian tribes three miles away. The convent, built of square logs, was open to the native children of the camps, and to outcasts from near and far—Sitka, Mexico, China, the Sandwich Islands and the half-breeds of the province.

Here there was abundant reading matter. When, after some years, Sister Mary Theodore returned to city life with an appointment to St. Ann's, Victoria, she discovered that intellectually she was up to date. Her propensity for letter-writing, fostered by the need to bridge the continent between "my missionary field and the homeland, developed into community journalism." From this she went into press articles and book publications. In writing *Heralds of Christ the King,* she says her "exceeding reward is the joy of having rescued from oblivion missionaries who form the galaxy of Mother Church in the North Pacific."

Her other publications are: *Pioneer Nuns of British Columbia; Seal of the Cross—Life of Mother Mary Anne, Foundress; Laurels for St. Ann's —Life of Sister Mary Loretto,* and *A Chaplet of Years.* Her monographs include: *Sketch of the Victoria Diocese; First Resident Priest in Alaska; Alaska's Debt to Victoria; The Heroic Trek of a Young Community; Treasures of St. Ann-The Orphans; The Russian Princess; A Marian Jubilee; St. Ann's in Alaska* (1888); *Hour of Adoration to Christ the King,* and *One Thousand Titles of Our Lady.*   M. H.

Sister M. Therese, Sor. D.S. 1902-

"I was a child of three loves: music, painting and poetry, to any one of which I can still bring a deep enthusiasm," writes Sister M. Therese. Her mother was the late Florence Mae Brooks (Lentfoehr), the gifted Wisconsin artist of French and English lineage. "My early years were spent in hovering— sometimes perilously—about and under her easels. It was there, I think, that I received my first impression of beauty, and my invariable answer to the question 'What will you be when you grow up?' was, I am told, 'an artist like mother.' " Her mother had planned for her a musical career and accordingly she studied the piano at the age of six. And although Sister M. Therese continued her musical training until she graduated from the Wisconsin Conservatory of Music, it was poetry, the third of her "loves" that claimed her heart.

Like Sister Madeleva, she is Wisconsin born—at Oconto Falls in 1902. Her first poems were of mountains, sunsets, and the sea—snatches of beauty she had glimpsed upon her mother's canvases.

"I remember never to have been consciously concerned with technique; the poetical lines sang themselves into my mind as if to some preconceived melody, the poem thus forming itself quite completely before a word was confided to paper. This, I find, is the method I have followed ever since with this difference, that now I revise constantly and tirelessly until at times the result surprises me with its newness. I believe that a poet achieves his fullest freedom under discipline. A poem must become a part of me, must live with me a long time, before I write it."

In her mother's library there were attractively bound copies of the works of English and American poets. These appealed to her as a child. From frequent reading she memorized long passages from the poems of Tennyson, Keats, and Shelley without grasping the meaning of the lines she read. "I loved them for their sheer music alone," she admits.

The Bible was another of her favorites—especially the Book of Psalms. "My mother's death placed an early poignancy into my life and writing; since that time, death has come to me as a familiar theme. . . . The theme of beauty, love and death, when they are dealt with in my verse are always conceived of as a part of a great unity, and contingent on the Absolute. Beauty in all its manifestations serves but to mirror in a finite way—yet ineffably winning for all that—the Infinite Beauty which is God."

Sister M. Therese thinks that her future writing will be greatly influenced by her travelling through England, France and Italy, and especially to Rome, where she spent two months and was favored with "what will be perhaps the two most poetically fruitful experiences of my life, namely, a First Mass (my brother's) in the Papal Crypt in the Catacombs of St. Callixtus, and the great privilege of being presented to His Holiness Pope Pius XII, and of an audience with him."

Sister M. Therese received her higher education at Marquette University in Milwaukee, and holds a bachelor's and master's degree, magna cum laude. At graduation, she received the Golden-key award for the highest scholastic record of her class over the four-year college course; in 1932 she was named Poet Laureate of her alma mater and in 1935 was made an honorary member of Sigma Tau Delta, National English Honor Society. In 1931 she made her final religious profession as a member of the Congregation of the Sisters of the Divine Savior. And for over twelve years she has been teaching English at the Sisters' Training School, St. Mary's Convent, the American motherhouse of her order in Milwaukee. Sister M. Therese's lectures are concerned principally with the philosophy of poetry.

Her first volume of verse *Now There Is Beauty* was published in 1940. Her second volume of verse *Give Joan a Sword* appeared in 1944.

                                                                    M. H.

Henri Massis 1886-

Considered as one of the leaders of the Catholic rightists, Henri Massis was born in Paris in 1886 and studied at the Lycée Condorcet and at the Sorbonne. He started his literary career as secretary of the editorial staff of the periodicals *Marches de l'Est* and *L'Opinion* and became a practising Catholic in 1913. He was a friend of Ernest Psichari (the grandson of Renan) whose conversion from atheism to Catholicism is one of the most moving pages in the history of French Catholic revival and who was killed in the first World War. To Ernest Psichari, gifted writer and Christian soldier, Henri Massis devoted one of his outstanding works. Massis himself fought in the first World War and was wounded. Later he was sent to the Near East. After the war, he was appointed director of the rightist periodical, *La Revue Universelle,* and was awarded the Grand Prize of Literature in 1929.

Massis wrote a number of books, essays and articles in various periodicals. His chief works are: *Les Jeunes Gens d'Aujourd'hui* (under the pseudonym of Agathon); *Jugements* (in two volumes); *Défense de l'Occident; L'Honneur de Servir; Notre Ami Psichari,* and *Les Idés Restent,* the latter published in Paris after the collapse of France and the Armistice.

Massis is representative of the extreme rightist tendencies which prevailed in certain French intellectual circles between the two wars. He was a friend of Charles Maurras, the leader of the Action Française (the extreme nationalist royalist party) and participated in the movement up to the time of its condemnation by the Holy See. Unlike the other leading spirits of the Action Française, Massis submitted, but the link was not broken between him and Maurras, and the *Revue Universelle,* directed by Massis, was still the organ of reactionary nationalism, emulated by the Catholic right wing.

The author of *Jugements* (Judgements) is a severe critic of his times. He attempted to evolve an attitude of condemnation towards what he called "Asiatic Mysticism," opposed to Christianity, which he conceived as essentially linked to the West and to the Latin world. Such an irreconcilable outlook predetermined all Massis' writings. He is a bitter enemy of democracy and of democratic individualism which he considers the fruit of this "Asiatic Mysticism." For him, not only the Far East and Russia, but Germany also, was filled with this spirit, in which he saw a threat to civilization. He places the intellect (in the bookish sense of the word) above intuition, above the attributes of the heart, and chooses as cornerstones of Western civilization: "personality, unity, stability, authority and continuity"; such are, in his mind, "the mother ideas of the West" (*Defense of the West*). This book is translated into English by E. J. Flint and is prefaced by G. K. Chesterton. A devout Catholic, his faith is however strongly tinged with the ideology of the Action Française and his world-conception suffers from the amoralism preached in politics by Charles Maurras.

Henry Massis was a staunch opponent of the Germanic spirit. He wrote pages of bitter criticism directed against Hitler's theories and the racist ideology of National-Socialism. He was, on the other hand, strongly attracted by fascism and Latin authoritative state systems, and devoted one of his books: *Chefs*, to Mussolini, Franco and Salazar, all three of whom he personally visited. Up to the second World War, he believed that Italian fascism would act as "moderator," counterbalancing the Nazi extreme ideology. Even after Hitler's visit to Rome, in 1938, he still hoped that this moderating influence would be exercised by Mussolini. This attitude towards Italian fascism, as the "savior of civilization" prompted him to issue a manifesto in favor of Mussolini's aggression against Abyssinia. The manifesto was signed by a group of extreme rightist French intellectuals, and provoked the indignation of all French liberal circles who foresaw that Mussolini's Abyssinian campaign was but the first move in a series of aggressions which were to form the current tactics of the Axis.

After the defeat of France, Henri Massis joined the Vichy Government and became one of the official ideologists of Marshal Petain's "National Revolution." H. I.

Most Reverend David Mathew 1902-

Archbishop David Mathew is a distinguished historian who like Christopher Dawson, thinks in terms of cultures rather than of nations. It is the atmosphere of Europe in the beginning of the Reformation, the pervading influence of the Celtic peoples during the early Renaissance, the mood of the Jacobean age that we feel as we read the pages of his brilliant and scholarly studies.

David Mathew's descent is English, Irish and Welsh. He was born in England in 1902, the son of Francis Mathew and Agnes Woodroffe. His brother, Father Gervase Mathew, O.P., is lecturer in Greek Patristics at Oxford. They are great-grandnephews of the celebrated temperance priest, Father Theobald Mathew; Lord Justice Mathew was a granduncle and the Orientalist, Sir John Woodroffe, an uncle.

David Mathew has always successfully combined a life of action with that of a student. Educated at the Royal Naval College, Dartmouth, he served in the first World War as a midshipman on The Tiger and was later second-in-command of an armed trawler guarding the German fleet in Scapa Flow. After the war he went to Balliol College, Oxford. Upon taking his degree in 1923, he was appointed by the University to do special research work on sixteenth and seventeenth century English history.

He held the Balliol senior studentship, 1923 to 1924, and the Preston Read Research Endowment, 1924 to 1925.

In 1924 Dr. Mathew began his studies for the priesthood at the Beda College in Rome and was ordained in 1929. He was priest in charge of Cardiff Docks, 1930 to 1934, and at the same time chaplain to University College, Cardiff. He has been chaplain at the University of London since 1934 and is in remarkably close and sympathetic touch with the activities and interests of the students with whom he is very popular. On December 21, 1938, Father Mathew was consecrated titular bishop of Aelia and auxiliary bishop of Westminster. His appointment did not mean the abandonment of his work as university chaplain, although he had to lean more heavily in these duties on his assistant, Father Vernon Johnson.

For some time before his appointment as bishop, Father Mathew had been increasingly employed by Cardinal Hinsley in the business of the Church, but had also managed, by careful economy of time, to pursue a distinguished literary career. This opened with the publication of a very remarkable study of *The Celtic Peoples and Renaissance Europe* (1933), an approach to political and social history through the study of particular groups of families in Cornwall and Wales. This was followed by a study, in conjunction with his brother, Father Gervase Mathew, of *The Reformation and the Contemplative Life* (1934). In 1936 there appeared his history of Catholicity in England, with the subtitle *The History of a Minority,* a book which won much praise, even from critics far removed from any sympathy with Catholicity. The same wide appeal is present in a later work, *The Jacobean Age* (1939), which is concerned with the opening period of the seventeenth century, its political and religious reactions and the transition from Elizabethan to Stuart England. Here Dr. Mathew considers the roots of American history against their background of early Stuart colonization. Dr. Mathew also produced a vignette, *Steam Packet,* which showed a remarkable knowledge of the actual physical details of life a hundred years ago. In 1943 there appeared *British Seamen* and in 1945 *The Naval Heritage.* All of his books are remarkable for their power of evoking the past by a systematic, artistic accumulation of physical details of scene and habit. He states that all his historical work has developed from his fascination with great stores of unexplored manuscript material, especially his realization of the hidden treasures in the muniment rooms of many historic English houses. Dr. Mathew's writings possess a character of minute discernment, which is also a characteristic of his conversation. He has a choice of words and a sense of nuances so fine that men of a more downright vocabulary are often liable to mistake or to miss the implications. He combines, in particular, a great charitableness with an intellectual appreciation of human characteristics.

Dr. Mathew received the honorary degree of Doctor of Letters from Trinity College, Dublin, in 1933, and was made a Fellow of the Royal Historical Society in the same year, and Fellow of the Society of Antiquaries in 1935. He has published articles and documents in the *English Historical Review* and the Bulletin of the *Board of Celtic Studies.* He has been a contributor to the *Dictionnaire d'histoire et de géographie ecclésiastiques* (Louvain), and is a well-known reviewer for *History, Spectator,*

Tablet, Dublin Review, Blackfriars, Pax, etc. He contributed to the volume on Church and State of the Cambridge Summer School of Catholic Studies. He is a member of the Catholic Education Council of Great Britain and Catholic representative on the League of Nations Union.

Without concerning himself with its political implications, Bishop Mathew has always been a strong advocate of Anglo-American friendship. As a member of the Institute of Historical Research he has had many opportunities to meet American scholars and has a high regard for American historical scholarship, especially in seventeenth century studies. He has lectured in the United States, at the University of Notre Dame, on sixteenth and seventeenth century history.

In 1946 he was made Titular Archbishop of Pelusium and Apostolic Delegate to Africa for Missions of the Sacred Congregation of the Propagation of the Faith.   A. M. & J. K.

Sister Maura (Mary Power) 1881-

Sister Maura was born in the pleasant sea-port city of Halifax in 1881, when the English Navy and the English Army still gave it contacts around the world. She has spent nearly all her life within sight of the sea. One of her forebears was a young Irishman who fought under Nelson, another was a German sea captain; one grandfather built his own ships and his seven sons sailed them, the other made a fortune in business and sent his merchant ships sailing the sea. The latter, Patrick Power, K.S.G., M.P., bequeathed the greater part of his money to works of charity and education. Her father, Lawrence Geoffrey Power, who completed his studies at the Catholic University in Dublin, and Harvard Law School, was a public man with a share of scholarly writing to his credit.

Mrs. Power, her mother, who was as good as she was beautiful, dedicated her daughter to the Blessed Virgin, and the child wore Our Lady's livery of blue and white until she changed it for the black habit of a Sister of Charity. At the age of six, she tried to write a story, but not succeeding very well, desisted until she was eleven and then produced a composition book of verse of various kinds, including a rhymed play. She continued to try both prose and verse and cherished the girlhood ambition of becoming a writer; but on entering the convent she put aside this desire and wished only to give her life to the service of the poor.

Sister Maura was educated at Mount Saint Vincent in Nova Scotia, won her B.A. from London University, her M.A. from Dalhousie University, and her Ph.D. from the University of Notre Dame. She found the five months spent in travelling through Europe, just before she entered religion, of special cultural value. Seven happy years of teaching at the Academy of the Assumption, Wellesley Hills, Massachusetts, have given her the mental privilege of American citizenship. For five summers, Sister gave courses at the University of Notre Dame, her subjects being Shakespearean Drama, Modern Plays and Play-making, and Lyric Poetry. Since 1925, she has been professor of English in Mount Saint Vincent College, Halifax, Nova Scotia.

Sister considers *Shakespeare's Catholicism* (Riverside Press) her most important book. Charles Phillips said, in *The Catholic World,* "this is an invaluable work for student and lay reader, a real contribution to our critical literature." *Via Vitae,* a morality published by the press of Newman's beloved Oxford, gave her the greatest thrill of her literary life. *Breath of the Spirit* is, she thinks, the most artistic of her books. The others are *Lionel Johnson's "Ireland"; Christus Vincit* (miracle play); *A Wind Through the Oaks; Rhyme and Rhythm; A May Masque; The Angelus and the Apostles' Creed* (a mystery and a prayer play).

Contributions of Sister Maura's have appeared in such magazines as: *America, The Catholic World, The Commonweal, Eikon, G. K.'s Weekly, Irish Rosary, Magnificat, Poetry Review.*

She has lectured in the United States and Canada on various subjects, including: Blessed among Women, Medieval Religious Drama, Shakespeare, the Catholic, Unser Goethe, Dante and the Gaels, Epic Stories of the Goal, Euterpe of the Goal, the Friendly Art (letter-writing), Gilbert Keith Chesterton, Making of a National Drama, the Devil as a Personage in Literature.

The only noteworthy struggle Sister Maura has had was one in her own soul with religious doubt. The realization that "Charity never falleth away, whether prophecies shall be made void, or tongues shall cease, or knowledge shall be destroyed," gave her strength in that battle; and a mystic appreciation of the sacrificial death of the Son of Man brought her at last the peace of victory. Within the compass of religious life, Providence has fulfilled her girlhood ambition of authorship by the promised hundredfold. Besides she has had practical scope for her inherited love of the poor.   C. J. E.

Francois Mauriac 1885-

"Every intelligent man as well as every critic wants to know something about the author whose book he is reading," wrote François Mauriac in *God and Mammon.* We know Mauriac's childhood and youth from *Commencements d'une Vie,* but his memoirs cease with his youth. He explains: "The true reason of my laziness, is it not that our novels express the inner of ourselves? Fiction alone does not lie. It half opens on a man's life a tiny door, through which glides, free from all control, his hidden soul." So it is in his works we must find the author, and this is to be expected with a man who believes that "writing is handing oneself over."

He is a Catholic. Of this fact there can be no doubt: "I belong to that race of people who, born in Catholicism, realize in earliest manhood that they will never be able to escape from it, will never be able to leave it or re-enter it. They were within it, they are within it, and they will be within it for ever and ever. They are inundated with light; they know that it is true. But for myself, I remained attached to the church as narrowly as a man to this planet; fleeing from it would have been as mad as trying to flee from this planet. I remember with what ardour I set about, at the age of sixteen, proving to myself the truth of a religion to which I know myself bound for all eternity."

And he is a novelist. In 1926 he was awarded the annual Prix de Roman of 5000 francs for two of his early novels, *L'Enfant Chargé de Chaînes* and *La Robe Prétexte*. In June 1933 the French Academy elected him to membership. Julie Kernan said of this election, "By believer and skeptic alike he is considered France's greatest living writer."

In English and French literary circles it has been much debated as to what extent François Mauriac may be considered a "Catholic" novelist. It is safe to say that though he never wrote his novels to make them symbolic of Christian virtue yet through them he brought out his studied conclusions that man, by imitating Christ, can gain the mastery over the effects of original sin. His frank portrayal of the habits of the most decadent section of Paris society has been shocking to some. His morbidity, introversion, and overemphasis on the dark and sorrowful make him unpopular with many. The taunt of André Gide, "this reassuring compromise which allows you to love God without losing sight of Mammon," has forced Mauriac to consider the question in *God and Mammon*. He defends his choice of subjects: "In the world of reality you do not find beautiful souls in the pure state—these are only to be found in novels and in bad novels at that. What we call a beautiful character has become beautiful at the cost of a struggle against itself, and this struggle should not stop until the bitter end. The evil which the most beautiful character has to overcome in itself and from which it has to sever itself, is a reality which the novelist must account for. If there is a reason for the existence of the novelist on earth it is this: to show the element which holds out against God in the highest and noblest characters—the innermost evils and dissimulations; and also to light up the secret sources of sanctity in creatures which seem to us to have failed." And he warns: "It is seldom that writers who distort reality and depict untrue characters so as to be sure of not being immoral attain their object. For it must be remembered that they are not the only authors of their novels; the reader himself collaborates with them and often adds horrors without their knowing it. The collaboration between the reader and the writer, varying as it does with each individual makes the question of good and bad books an almost insolvable one. For my own part, I know by experience and by confidential admission that the book in which an excessive outspokenness has been detected—and doubtless rightly— and which has been most severely censured is also the very book which has had the greatest effect on people from the religious point of view. We must not forget that the worst books as well as the best are double-edged weapons which the unknown reader plays with in a way which we never can foresee."

Probably the *Noeud de Viperes (Viper's Tangle),* brought out in 1932, marked the climax of Mauriac's progress toward a settled philosophy in his novels. In this book he paints an old man, proud, defiant and violently anti-religious, who suddenly toward the end of his life, begins to comprehend that he can free himself from the troubles and temptations which have well-nigh stifled his soul. The author here brings out clearly the Catholic teaching of the strife between the flesh and the spirit. "Man," he concludes, "is neither an angel nor a beast." He wants his characters to be conscious of their fall, but courageous enough to rise with the help of God. André Maurois has said of him: "His tragic words clarify his own life and ours."

François Mauriac was born at Bordeaux, France, in 1885, the youngest of a family of four boys and one girl. He has no memory of his father, Jean Paul Mauriac, who died when François was twenty months old. He was brought up in the home of his maternal grandmother. His family were landowners and vintners. He has a deep love of Bordeaux and the surrounding countryside where "my peasant race, which has never moved, plunges down its deep roots." He says of his birthplace: "This city where we were born, or where we were a child or a youth, it is ourselves; we carry it in ourselves. The history of Bordeaux is the history of my body and soul. It is my childhood and youth crystallized." He was educated at Bordeaux, at the institution Saint-Marie and the College Grand-Lebrun, by the Marianites to whom he has paid tribute in his memoirs. Later he studied at Paris. He began writing as a poetry critic on *Revue du Temps Present* in 1910. In 1913 he married Jeanne Lafont, the daughter of a functionary in the Ministry of Finances. World War I interrupted his career and he served in the French Army. His first two books were poetry, but then he turned to prose. Since then his only poetical work is *Orages* published in 1925. He lives in Paris during the winter, but he does most of his writing during the summer when he returns to the family estates near Bordeaux. His son is now (1947) the private secretary to General de Gaulle.

He is the author of: *Les Mains Jointes* (1901); *L'Adieu a l' Adolescence,* poetry (1911). He wrote the following novels: *L'Enfant Chargé de Chaînes* (1913); *Le Desert de l'Amour* (1925); *(Desert of Love,* 1929); *Le Noeud de Viperes* (1932) *(Viper's Tangle); Woman of the Pharisees* (1946), a religious novel, and *Thérèse* (1947). His essays and books of criticism include: *Le Jenne Homme* (1926); *La Province* (1926); *Dieu et Mammon* (1929) *(God and Mammon,* 1936); *Vie de Jesus* (1936); *(Life of Jesus* (1937).

M. S.

Reverend Joseph R. N. Maxwell, S.J.   1899-

Father Maxwell is the author of *The Happy Ascetic* (1935), a biography of Adolph Petit, S.J., *Completed Fragments* (1937) verse, and *Jesuit Education of the Sixteenth Century,* a translation from the French. He has also done critical essays and written on literary themes for *America, The Commonweal* and *Classical Bulletin.*

Father Maxwell was born November 7, 1899, at Taunton, Massachusetts, the son of Richard Everett Maxwell and Caroline (Carpenter) Maxwell. He was educated in the local schools of Taunton, both public and parochial, finishing in 1918. In September of that year he matriculated at Holy Cross. In September 1919 he entered the Jesuit Novitiate at Yonkers, New York. He completed his studies at Weston College, Weston, Massachusetts, with the degree of A.B. in 1925 and M.A. in 1926. From 1926 to 1929 he was an instructor of English at Holy Cross College, Worcester, Massachusetts. In 1929 he began his theological studies and was ordained in June 1932. From Fordham he received a Ph.D. degree in 1931 and from Weston College an S.T.L. in 1932. He taught English at Weston College for one year, 1933 to 1934. Then he went to Tronchiennes, Belgium, to do some private study at Ancienne Abbaye. Returning to America in 1935 he was appointed Dean of Boston College. He holds an honorary Ph.D. degree from the Collegio Mayor Y Real, Colombia, S. A., and Cavalier of the Royal Cross of Italy, a decoration from the Italian Government.

P. Mc.

Sara Maynard   ?-1945

Sara Maynard, daughter of Patrick and Margaret Casey, was born in Cape Colony, South Africa, and lived there for the first ten years of her life. When her family moved to Dublin, she was educated at the Loreto Abbey School at Dalkey and subsequently by Ursuline and Franciscan nuns in Cologne, Germany. Her knowledge of German was put to use during World War I by censoring letters of German prisoners for the British War Office.

Meanwhile she had begun her literary career by writing a novel which was published in London by Heinemann, and a comedy, *Brady,* which was produced by the Abbey Theatre in Dublin in 1919. But after her marriage to Theodore

Maynard in 1918 the duties of raising a family made it impossible for her to write except some short stories and poems at rare intervals. These had charm and delicacy and distinction and therefore attracted attention when they appeared in *The Catholic World, America,* and the *Ave Maria.* The last named magazine had serialized *Scott and His Men,* an account of the antarctic explorer. It appeared in 1945 as a book. *Here Come the Penguins* and *Rose of America,* a life of St. Rose of Lima, appeared in 1943.

Her recently published *Princess Poverty* tells for children the story of Saints Francis and Clare of Assisi. It will, however, be read with pleasure and profit by many adults, for it is not only based upon the contemporary accounts of the two saints but catches the spirit of the *Fioretti* to a remarkable degree. Mrs. Maynard died at her home in Westminster, Maryland, on November 26, 1945.

Theodore Maynard 1890-

Though born in India of English parents who were Protestant missionaries, and educated in England, Theodore Maynard is more American than mere citizenship papers would prove. For not only has he lived here for the greater part of his adult life, receiving all his higher education in the United States, but he has made the interpretation of American Catholic history his main province.

At his birth, his father and mother were Salvation Army officers in India and afterwards labored in that country as Plymouth Brethren. It was therefore natural that young Maynard should think of the ministry, though he early broke away from the denomination to which his parents belonged. Coming to this country in 1909, when he was nineteen, he studied for a short time with a view to the ministry, but upon taking a temporary pastorate was dismissed after his third sermon for what his congregation considered, if not heresy, at least flippancy, but which he still thinks sense.

There followed a period of a year in a textile mill in Massachusetts, and a few months of odd jobs and semi-starvation in Philadelphia, until he worked his way back to England on a cattle boat. There he intended to enter Oxford to study for the Unitarian ministry, meanwhile taking an office job. But although he was preaching from time to time in Unitarian churches up until a few weeks of his seeking admission to the Catholic Church, he soon discovered that this would be his goal. The first priest he had ever spoken to in his life was the one to whom he went for instruction, already perfectly convinced as to which was the true church.

In America he had been writing but not publishing anything. In

England he began to contribute to the *New Witness* under Cecil and Gilbert Chesterton, as well as for other papers, and at a rather alarming pace. But he still did not think of literature as his life's work; instead he entered the Dominican novitiate in 1915, and there he remained seven months.

His first book had already been published, a collection of verse entitled *Laughs and Whiffs of Song,* to which G. K. Chesterton wrote an introduction. Soon after leaving the Dominicans he published *Drums of Defeat,* another book of poems, and *Carven from the Laurel Tree,* a collection of essays. These he soon followed with *A Tankard of Ale* and his first and (thus far) only novel, *The Divine Adventure,* all produced before the end of World War I, while he was working in the Ministry of Munitions.

Meanwhile he had married Sara Katherine Casey, an Irish girl born in South Africa, who was already the author of a novel and who was soon to write a play for the Abbey Theatre. If her literary career was somewhat hampered by the family of seven children, his career received from marriage and the cares of parenthood a further stimulation. In 1920 he came to the United States, where several books of his were on the point of publication, and here he remained to teach in a California college, where he was joined by his wife and family. He remained a college professor until 1936, when ill health forced him to give up this work.

In England, Theodore Maynard had been largely under the influence of G. K. Chesterton (who was largely the unconscious instrument of his becoming a Catholic), and to some extent of Hilaire Belloc. Chesterton described him at that time as "a poet of color." Since then, his poetry has avoided decoration and has grown more austere, deeper and more metaphysical; he has discovered his own note and a means of conveying his own rich experience.

Transferring to the East in 1926, he was first a professor at Fordham, and afterwards at Georgetown. As he had no university degrees, he now set about remedying that defect, obtaining his B.A. from Fordham, his M.A. from Georgetown and his Ph.D. from the Catholic University of America, carrying meanwhile a full teaching schedule and writing books and lecturing far and wide. He says he still does not know how all this was managed.

Dr. Maynard is a man of medium height, slim in build, and ascetic in appearance, though he denies being ascetic in his habits. His eyes are in turn burning and lit with laughter, and that, together with his Van Dyke beard, makes him look like a poet, though he has said, "If a man looks like a poet, you may be sure that he isn't one."

It is as a poet that he still thinks of himself, though since 1929 he has been chiefly engaged in the writing of biography and history. The first of this new literary line was *De Soto and the Conquistadores,* and this was followed by *The Odyssey of Francis Xavier* (1936); *The World I Saw,* autobiography (1938); *The Apostle of Charity,* a life of St. Vincent de Paul (1939); *Queen Elizabeth* (1940); *The Reed and the Rock: Portrait of Simon Bruté* (1942); *Orestes Brownson: Yankee Radical, Catholic* (1943); *Too Small a World: The Life of Francesca Cabrini* (1945), and

Humanist as Hero: The Life of Sir Thomas More (1947). His *Story of American Catholicism* (1941), which is perhaps his most important work, gives in a single volume the history of the Catholic Church in the United States, and ranges from Leif Ericsson to our own time. Yet a month after the publication of that book he brought out his collection of poems, *Not Even Death*. This volume, together with his *Exile and Other Poems* (1929) and *Man and Beast* (1936) contain his later and more individual poetry.

In addition, he is the author of a book of criticism, *Our Best Poets* (1921) and the two anthologies *The Book of Modern Catholic Verse* (1926) and *The Book of Modern Catholic Prose* (1927), also a study of the meaning and technique of poetry entitled *Preface to Poetry* (1934). In addition there are almost countless articles on all kinds of subjects and many poems that he has never reprinted from the magazines in which they appeared.

While all this vast body of work in both prose and verse appears to have been produced almost without effort, he assures us that it is due only to his habit of discipline and his power of intense and prolonged concentration. The only virtue he claims is that of industry. But he also says that his aim in writing is to be interesting. When people sometimes compare him to the German mystic Rilke, he only laughs, as he is likely to laugh at anything people say about him.

Theodore Maynard has explained his method of biography as one of first gathering all the available data—a laborious process—and then waiting for the moment when the character about whom he is to write becomes as much alive to him—and perhaps a bit more so—than the people he meets every day. He is also convinced that every biography should have its own distinctive pattern, just as each life lived on earth is different from all others. It is therefore a question of psychological understanding followed by an effort of artistic creation.

In reading Theodore Maynard one is continually conscious of being in the presence of a man who has seen a great deal of life and who has himself always lived intensely. Therefore he can draw from that wide general knowledge of life and of literature without being trammelled by a narrow specialized scholarship. Of this he has more than enough for his purposes, but he would probably be the first man to disclaim the title of scholar, as he is certainly inclined to be somewhat scornful of pedantry. What he is, is a man versed in many things and with the artist's gift of enjoying them first himself and then of making others enjoy them.

On October 19, 1946, he married Kathleen Sheehan.

E. F.

Francis Joseph Meehan   1881-

Literary critic, author and former professor of literature, Francis Joseph Meehan, formerly Brother Zachary Leo, F.S.C., is an authority on Catholic letters. He was born in San Francisco, California, in 1881, the son of James and Mary Ellen (Gallagher) Meehan. In 1897 he joined the Brothers of the Christian Schools and took the name in religion of Brother Zachary Leo. After graduation from the De La Salle Institute, Martinez, California, in 1899, he went to St. Mary's College, Moraga, California, where he took his A.B. in 1903 and his M.A. in 1908. For the following six years he was instructor in English at St. Mary's and then did postgraduate work at the Catholic University of America, where he received his L.H.D. in 1915.

In that year he returned to his alma mater as professor of literature which post he held until 1941 when he received a Papal dispensation to withdraw from the Christian Brothers and to return to secular life.

As Brother Leo he was dean of St. Mary's College from 1929 to 1930, chancellor, 1930 to 1933, and trustee, 1915 to 1933. Since 1931 he had been a professor at the summer sessions of the University of California and since 1933 he had been a lecturer at the University. In 1926 he received the degree of LL.D. from the University of Santa Clara.

A student of Dante and Shakespeare, and a noted authority on them, his first book was a study of *Contrasts in Shakespeare's Historical Plays* (1915). His next work was a biography of the founder of his Institute, *St. John Baptist de la Salle. Teaching the Drama and the Essay* and *Religion and the Study of Literature* followed. In 1928 he wrote a textbook on *English Literature*. His plays include *Dante the Wing Bearer* and *Ecce Homo*. Under the name of "Will Scarlet" he wrote several novels, among them *False Gods*.

From 1906 on, he was a feature writer for the San Francisco *Monitor*, and he conducted a page of book chat in *The Missionary, Light,* and *Columbia*. He has been widely known as a lecturer. In twenty years he delivered more than 2,000 lectures outside the classroom, and critics called him "California's most polished platform speaker." He gave up this activity in 1940. The subject of his farewell discourse, delivered in December of that year, in the War Memorial Opera House in San Francisco, was "St. Thomas More and the Modern Man." In 1939 he conducted a series of four radio broadcasts over the Catholic Hour on "The Catholic Tradition in Literature." These were published in pamphlet form by the National Council of Catholic Men.

Francis Joseph Meehan recently published *Living Upstairs* (now in its seventh edition), a book of essays, in which he shares his rich experience in literature with the reader. His scholarly criticism is a guide to writers as well as readers, and to his students he had given both knowledge and inspiration.

E. P. Dutton & Co. employs him from time to time to pass judgment on manuscripts. Dr. Meehan turned down an offer from the Hays organization.

Since February 1943 Mr. Meehan has been living in a house on the shores of Lake Sherwood in southern Ventura County. The house comprises one huge room, forty feet long. Its walls and floor are of stone, and high at one end of the raftered living room is a little gallery which Dr. Meehan uses for his sleeping quarters. It is called the Casa della Madonna and was dedicated to the Blessed Virgin Mary. It had been called a one-man monastery. After five years in the world and more than three years of solitude on Lake Sherwood, Dr. Meehan married in February 1946 De Neze Clare a convert from Episcopalianism.

Max Mell 1882-

The poet and dramatist Max Mell was born in 1882 in Marburg, Austria, the son of Alexander Mell, a schoolmaster and director of the Institute of the Blind.

For many centuries religious plays were performed in the home town of the poet, either in the living rooms of the farm houses, in the stables or in the open air, and were staged without any decorations or scenery. The townspeople were the players. Max Mell produced the play *Das Wiener Kripperl* in 1919 for performances in such surroundings. *The Apostel-spiel* (1923) is the only one of his plays that has been translated into English. This was translated by Maude Valerie White and was published in London in 1934 under the title *The Apostle Play*. In this play Mell uses an archaic form of verse. He combines in his sacred plays popular Catholic sentiments with classical and medieval form. He is also a powerful novelist and lyricist. In 1937 he was awarded the Mozart Prize.

Among his works in German are: *Lateinische Erzählungen* (1904); *Jägerhaussage und andere Novellen* (1910); *Das bekränzte Jahr* (1911); *Barbara Naderes Viehstand* (1914); *Schutzengelspiel* (1923), and *Nachfolge-Christispiel* (1927).

M. H.

Louis Joseph Alexandre Mercier   1880-

Louis Mercier was born in Le Mans, the old capital of the Plantagenets in western France, a city rich in Benedictine Abbeys. St. Scholastica is its patroness. Her relics were brought there about 660 by the Abbot of the church in which Louis was baptized and are kept in the church in which he was prepared for his First Communion. Le Mans is also the foundation seat of the Congregation of the Holy Cross. Father Sorin, the founder of Notre Dame University, was born in a neighbouring village. Hence there were some migrations to the United States from this region, and, in 1890, Louis' father, François Mercier, a veteran of the Franco-Prussian war, and his mother, Marie Valliot Mercier, urged by some relatives already in Chicago, decided to emigrate to that city where it was said there was much more freedom for religious education than in France whose government was beginning to persecute the religious orders.

They found themselves in the French parish of Notre Dame de Chicago from the parochial school of which Louis passed to the neighbouring St. Ignatius College, now part of Loyola University, which then had a strictly classical course with an introduction to scholastic philosophy and practice in every form of expression. The faculty was notable, including such well-known Jesuit teachers as Fathers Cassilly, Gleason, Conroy and Furey. Much encouragement was given to the study of general literature and history through intercollegiate essay contests. Louis thus kept up his French and studied French literature and in his Junior year was given charge of a French class in which were many of his classmates. Before graduating, in 1900, he won prizes for a catechetical essay, an historical essay on Sir Thomas More, and for an oration on Louis Pasteur in a contest on the great men of the nineteenth century. Bishop Spalding of Peoria, famous as an orator, essayist, and proponent of university education, made the award and encouraged him to take up graduate work. This also led at once to publication in the Chicago *New World* to which Mercier contributed verse and prose during the editorships of Father Judge and William O'Malley. He remained as a teacher at St. Ignatius College, receiving an A.M. degree in 1902. Among his early articles was one published in the New York *Freeman Journal* calling for the preparation of an American Catholic encyclopedia.

In 1903 he was awarded a fellowship in Romance Languages at the University of Chicago where he studied with some of the best Romance scholars of the day, Pietsch, Jenkins, Dubedout, and the next year he went on another fellowship to Columbia University to continue his Romance studies with Todd, Cohen, Bargy, and to take up comparative literature under Spingarn. He returned to Chicago to become head of the French department at the Francis Parker School, the cradle of the progressive movement in American education. This laboratory school offered great opportunities for experimentation in teaching methods, and "education" thus became one of his specialties. In 1906 he made a statistical study of the Catholic colleges for the American Catholic Educational Association and in his report suggested their readjustment in conformity with the setup of the other American colleges. The same year he went to Canada to visit the French-Canadian poet William Chapman on whose work he had written in the Chicago *New World* after it had been recognized by the French Academy. After meeting many eminent Canadians he went to England and then to France where he was known to some critics through articles in a French-American magazine, and thus got in touch with the beginnings of the Catholic literary renaissance in France, meeting such men as René Bazin, Monsignor Baudrillart, Jean Lionnet, Marc Sanguier, René Doumic, Victor Giraud, Emile Baumann, and many educators. He was invited to remain to teach at the Ecole des Roches, the first French progressive school, but decided to return to university work in the United States and sailed back from Italy after a stay in Rome with some stop-overs in Spain.

He was given an instructorship at the University of Wisconsin and in 1911 was called to Harvard. He had just married Zoé Lassagne, niece of one of the early French missionaries in Minnesota, Father Pernin, some-time Vicar-General of Winona. A gifted pianist, pupil of Rudolf Ganz and a teacher in the Chicago Musical College, she was to continue her musical work in Cambridge. One of their seven children became a Carmelite nun. At Harvard and Radcliffe, Mercier developed a course in The Social Background of French Literature and advanced French practice courses. He was also called to teach at the newly founded Harvard Graduate School of Education where he was given charge of the training of teachers of modern languages. He became known among language teachers for his "Oral-Self-Expression Method" and published several textbooks: *Junior French; French Pronunciation and Diction; First French Readings; College French,* and many articles on teaching methods. He served as president of the New England Modern Language Association, of the American Association of Teachers of French, and as Chairman of the Tutorial Board of the Modern Language Division at Harvard shortly after the tutorial system was established there. He also presided for several years at the meetings of the Salon Français of Boston.

At the outbreak of the first World War he returned to France and was until 1917 interpreter with British units at the front, taking part in the 1916 Somme offensive. Sent back to the United States, he taught at West Point and in the Harvard R.O.T.C., and edited a French hand-book on trench warfare. Resuming his studies he became interested in the work of his colleague Irving Babbitt who with Paul Elmer More was challenging the principles and results of naturalism in the name of a humanism which called for the recognition in man of a control power over not only physical lusts but over those of the intellect and will. This was at least to see the need of an element corresponding to Christian grace, and moreover the critique of naturalism and of its consequences had been effectivly done. After some articles on Babbitt's work in a French review, Mercier published in Paris *Le Mouvement Humaniste aux Etats-Unis*, in 1928. It was crowned by the French Academy the following year. Shortly after, the movement gained further impetus through the publication of Norman Foerster's *Humanism and America*. There followed what came to be called "a new battle of the books" with the naturalists retorting through a symposium edited by H. Grattan, and the humanists continuing their campaign through *The Bookman* and *The American Review* under the editorship of Stuart Collins. Mercier contributed articles to these magazines and to *The Forum* and *The Commonweal*, finally publishing, in 1933, at the Oxford Press a general study of the movement compared with the point of view of neo-scholasticism under the title *The Challenge of Humanism* in which he brought out that "human integralism" must include not only rationality but grace.

This work besides being favorably reviewed in Europe attracted attention here among Protestants as well as Catholics, notably among the Unitarians, challenged to abandon even Deism by a naturalistic group calling themselves humanists. The Protestant review *Religion in Life* asked Mercier for an article clarifying the issue. This was published in 1937 under the title: "Naturalism, Humanism and Religion." As early as 1926 Mercier had proposed in *The Harvard Graduate Magazine* a method of conference for the handling of such controversies. He was now led to formulate the principles of a comparative criticism based on the fundamental alternatives of thought and their derivatives. By reducing all schools of thought to the fundamental alternatives: the monism of matter or mind, the dualism of matter and mind, and the trialism of matter, mind, and grace, the tenets of all schools may be objectively compared and the necessary consequences in all domains objectively charted. Mercier has also applied this method in the course on seventeenth century French Literature which he gave at Harvard, on the principle that there must be a philosophical approach to the study of literature, not only to understand its content but because even form depends on the psychological outlook.

In recent years he has lectured extensively from this point of view, notably at the American Catholic Philosophical Association, the National Catholic Alumni Federation, the Catholic Forums of Washington, Chicago, Harrisburg, Cleveland, Ministers Clubs and Protestant Theological Schools, Massachusetts State Colleges and Normal Schools, Teachers Conventions in all New England States, New York, Pennsylvania and New Jersey, Leland Stanford University, the University of Iowa, Western Reserve University, the Catholic University Summer School, Notre Dame University, and many Catholic colleges. At the first joint meeting of the American Philosophical Association with the American Catholic Philosophical Association Mercier represented the latter with a paper on the need of a re-examination of scholastic philosophy by American non-Catholic philosophers. He was also called on to speak on several historical occasions: in the Old North Church of Boston on the first Armistice Day, at a reception to Marshall Foch under the Washington Elm in Cambridge; at the twenty-fifth anniversary of *America* in New York, at the 400th anniversary of the Society of Jesus in St. Louis, at the Charlemagne Day Festival at St. Mary's College (California); and, for the City of Boston, at Lafayette Day and "I am an American Day" celebrations, and as "Independence Day Orator" in Faneuil Hall. He was visiting lecturer on French Catholic literature and in education at Fordham University, 1939 to 1940; lecturer at the Cliff Haven Summer School, and visiting professor at Western Reserve University Summer School. He is an associate editor of *Education* and of *The New Scholasticism,* a trustee of the Newman School, a member of the Advisory Council of the Boston College School of Social Work, a member of the Gallery of Living Catholic Authors, past-president of the Catholic Alumni Sodality of Boston, and an Oblate of St. John's Abbey (Minnesota). He received honorary degrees from Loyola University, St. Benedict's College and Boston College, was made a Knight of the French Legion of Honor, and elected Fellow of the Royal Society of Arts of London. Since 1946 he is professor emeritus of Harvard. He now (1947) teaches at Georgetown University.

His more recent writings include: Catholic Thought and the Nation *(The Catholic Mind);* Principles and Progress (The City of Boston Press); Charlemagne and Christian Civilization *(The Moraga Quarterly);* Humanistic Education (Holy Cross College Magazine); Prefaces to James Castiello's *Humane Psychology* (Sheed and Ward), and to Geoffrey O'Connell's *Naturalism in American Education* (Benziger); The Religion of Irving Babbitt (in *Babbitt, Man and Teacher,* Putnam); The Legacy of Irving Babbitt *(The Harvard Graduate Magazine);* and an illustrated gift-book: *Our Lady of the Birds* (The St. Anthony Guild Press, 1943), which tells of the spiritual adventures of a Benedictine brother in a garden of his monastery and which has been described as "giving in delightful form the Catholic philosophy of life."   M. L.

Thomas Merton (Frater M. Louis), O.C.S.O.
1915-

Thomas Merton was born in a small town in the Pyrenees near the Spanish border, in southern France, on January 31st, 1915. His father and mother were both artists, the former a New Zealander and the latter an American from Ohio. Owen Merton, the father of the poet, was beginning to be known as a powerful and original landscape painter when his career was cut short by an untimely death in 1930 in London. Mrs. Merton died ten years before in New York, where the Mertons had gone during World War I to be with Mrs. Merton's family.

Meanwhile the young artist's son travelled with his father to Bermuda, then to France where he spent some time at the Lycée of Montauban. Above all he became impregnated with the Catholic culture of the Middle Ages, traces of which surrounded them on every side. However, their interest in Catholicism was more or less confined to the cultural sphere. Owen Merton, a man of sincere faith, died an Anglican as he had been raised.

At the time of Owen Merton's death, his son was at Oakham School, in the English Midlands, where he received the usual English classical education with the addition of much French and German literature. He also learned Italian at this time, travelling in Italy, and in 1932 he won a scholarship, or rather an exhibition at Clare College, Cambridge. After a year of reading Modern Languages at the university, Merton left England to rejoin his grandparents and younger brother in the United States, where he completed his education at Columbia University, New York City. Here as an undergraduate he played an active part in campus literary activities and won a prize for poetry. Entering the graduate school of English in 1938, Merton wrote an M.A. thesis on "Nature and Art in William Blake" in the course of which he became acquainted with Jacques Maritain's "Art and Scholasticism," then passed on to the reading of St. Thomas Aquinas and other masters of Christian thought.

At the same time he renewed his interest in the poetry of men like Father Hopkins, S.J., Crashaw, and others. As a result of all this, before he had finished his thesis, Merton had presented himself to the chaplain of Catholic students, Father Ford, at Corpus Christi Church, 121st Street, and began taking instructions. He was baptized on November 16th, 1938, and received his M.A. in 1939.

After that, intending to pursue his academic career, Merton continued in the Columbia Graduate School, and taught English for a session in the University Extension. At the same time he was writing book reviews for the New York *Times* and *Tribune* Sunday Book Sections and other publications.

In the fall of 1940, Thomas Merton joined the staff of St. Bonaventure College, near Olean, New York, teaching English literature. Living in this peaceful atmosphere, among the wooded hills of the Alleghany valley, and taking full advantage of the spiritual opportunities of a secluded life among the Franciscan Friars who conduct the college, Merton began to deepen and develop an active vein of poetry and other writing, mostly of a religious character.

However, all this was only the prelude to something far more important. Sensing the need to penetrate further into the life of union with God of which he had barely touched the threshold, Merton made a retreat at Our Lady of Gethsemani in Kentucky, and then hesitated during the summer of 1941, debating various alternatives—the possibility of getting to Europe and becoming a Carthusian, or entering Gethsemani, or finally joining the workers at Friendship House in Harlem, New York.

He finally entered the strict Cistercian monastery in Kentucky in December 1941. He was clothed in the white habit of a Trappist novice on the first Sunday of Lent, 1942, and had the joy of seeing his younger brother converted to the Faith at Gethsemani where he made a retreat before going overseas with his unit of the R.C.A.F. in the summer of 1942. Sergeant J. P. Merton lost his life when his plane was wrecked in the North Sea, on a bombing flight, on the feast of Our Lady of Sorrows, 1943.

At Gethsemani Abbey, Merton, known in religion as Frater M. Louis, has continued to write verse and prose under obedience to his superiors.

The contemplative Cistercian life, steeped in the liturgy, close to the soil, wrapped in silence and peace and liberated by penance from most of the obstacles that cloud the poet's vision, has contributed immensely to the literary formation of this young writer and has, indeed made him what he is. In fact it is only at Gethsemani that Merton has really found himself as a writer, just as in Frater Louis he has discovered his own true identity as a person. Writing however can only be an exception in the life of a Cistercian whose vocation demands labor in the woods and fields rather than study and composition.

Merton made his simple profession on the Feast of St. Joseph, 1943, received clerical tonsure on Easter Monday 1946 and the minor orders in the course of the next year, finally pronouncing his solemn vows on St. Joseph's day, 1947. He is continuing his studies for the priesthood.

Besides publishing two books of verse, *Thirty Poems* (1943) and *A Man in the Divided Sea* (1946), Merton has done some translations, from the French, printed anonymously at Gethsemani and elsewhere, as well as writing various biographical studies which are awaiting publication.

Reverend Ernest Charles Messenger 1888-

A colleague of Dr. Ernest Charles Messenger describes him as "one of the most learned and most acute theologians in England, perhaps in Europe. But he looks as innocent as Gilbert K. Chesterton's Father Brown, as cheery and brisk as a holiday schoolboy, and as spruce as a cock-robin. Well, he would remind you most of all of a cock-robin, if he did not remind you equally of a cherub. He has a suave and nimble wit, and beams on his fellows with jovial good fellowship."

Dr. Messenger was born in 1888. He was educated at County High School, Ilford, St. Edmund's College, Ware, and Louvain University where he received his Ph.D., summa cum laude. He came into the Catholic Church in 1908 and was ordained a priest in 1914. In his early days, he was a Fleet Street journalist under T. P. O'Connor. He gave up journalism to study for the priesthood.

In the very year of his ordination, Cardinal Bourne made him his assistant private secretary. For five years he was a chaplain of Westminster Cathedral and taught in the Cathedral Choir School. He is a fine singer and a pianist. From 1921 to 1933 he lectured on philosophy at St. Edmund's College. From 1925 to 1938 he was chaplain to Poles, in Ware and since 1935, Westminster Diocesan Censor. He is the Theological Adviser to the Guild of Mendel and Pasteur and is able to meet the scientists on their own ground. In 1938 he became rector of the Benson Memorial Church, Buntingford, Herts where he is still located. He incorporated into his Church tower a piece of marble pavement from the

Basilica of St. John Lateran Rome; a piece of stone from the Colosseum; a piece of marble from the Catacombs, a stone from Mars Hill, Athens; stones from the Holy Land and a piece of old wood from St. Alban's Abbey.

He is the author of *Evolution and Theology* (1931); *Epistle from the Romans* (1933); *Rome and Reunion* (1934); *Lutheran Origin of the Anglican Ordinal* (1934); *The Reformation, the Mass, and the Priesthood* (1935, 1936, and 1937); *Know Your Faith* (1937); *The Sunday Epistles Simply Explained* (1938), and *The Sunday Collects* (1939).

He has a high reputation, too, as a translator. He has just completed volume one of Lebreton and Zeiller's *History of the Primitive Church*. He is the translator of several philosophical works from the French. His monumental work is *The Reformation, the Mass, and the Priesthood*. This gives the best study of Anglicanism, especially in its doctrinal aspect from 1559-1662, and of the reconciliation with Rome under Queen Mary.

Besides being editor of the Catholic Truth Society's "Religions" series, he has directed the *Universe* Enquiry Bureau since 1928. He drops into the office of the *Universe* almost every week to talk over some query and to suggest a leading article. His Enquiry Bureau has brought back lapsed Catholics into the fold; has made many converts and has cleared away many difficulties for the faithful.   M. H.

Reverend Fulgence Meyer, O.F.M.   1876-1938

After teaching for fifteen years, serving as Assistant Postulator in Rome, and becoming Commissary Provincial of his Order in the United States, where in 1925 he celebrated his silver jubilee, Father Meyer began to write. Between the years 1925 and his death in 1938 he was the author of twenty-seven books. Most of Father Meyer's writings were on purity, love, courtship and marriage. His books having the largest sale are *Plain Talks on Marriage* and *Uni Una* (retreat lectures for nuns, priests, and all who are seeking perfection. It is conservatively estimated that at least 600,000 copies of his various books have been sold.

Father Meyer was born at Remich, Luxembourg, May 30, 1876, son of Nicholas and Margaret (Sauerwein) Meyer. At an early age he came to the United States, where he was educated in the parish schools in Kansas City, Kansas. His studies for the priesthood were pursued in St. Francis Preparatory Seminary, Cincinnati, and other philosophical and theological schools under the supervision of the Franciscan Fathers of St. John the Baptist Province. He completed his theological studies in St. Anthony's International College, Rome, where he received the title Lector Generalis, qualifying him for the teaching chair in any Franciscan theological seminary throughout the world. Having joined the

Order of Friars Minor in Cincinnati, August 15, 1892, he was ordained at Rome by Archbishop Ceppetelli, July 15, 1900.

Father Meyer taught theology, Sacred Scripture, and sacred eloquence for fifteen years in schools of the Franciscan Order in Cincinnati, St. Bernard, Ohio, and Oldenburg, Indiana. From 1916 to 1917 he was rector of St. Francis Preparatory Seminary, Cincinnati, Ohio. For three years he was assistant postulator of the Order of Friars Minor in Rome, Italy, where he likewise taught dogmatic theology in St. Anthony's International College.

In 1920, upon his return to the United States, he became Commissary Provincial of the Order, a position he held for seven years. From 1920 until his death November 14, 1938, he preached missions and retreats from coast to coast in the United States and Canada.

Father Meyer possessed an unusual vocabulary. For many years he made it a point to study *Webster's Unabridged Dictionary* one hour a day. A capable linguist, he could converse fluently in English, German, French and Italian.

Along with writing books he conducted the popular "Thought for the Month" in *St. Anthony's Messenger,* and in 1927 originated the widely read department "The Tertiary Den" in the same magazine. For many years he was a regular contributor to *Der Sendbote,* a German publication issued by the Franciscans of St. John the Baptist Province.

He is the author of: *Jesus and His Pets* (1925); *The Seraphic Highway* (1926); *Forty Hours* (1926); *Youth's Pathfinder* (1928); *Back to God* (1929); *Helps to Purity* (1931); *Safeguards of Chastity* (1931); *The Door of Salvation* (1932); *Waiting for the Para-Clete* (2 Vols., 1934); *I'm Keeping Company Now* (pamphlet); *Christ-like Healing* (1935); *Solace in Weeping* (1928), and *The Cross of Christ* (1938).　　　　E. F.

Viola Meynell (Mrs. John W. Dallyn)

From her gifted parents, Wilfrid and the late Alice Meynell, Viola, their third daughter, inherited a rich literary background. From childhood she has shown a most discriminating talent of her own.

Educated in part by nuns but largely at home, she married, in 1922, John Dallyn whose practical experience as a Sussex farmer complemented his wife's ardent love of a country life. One son, Jacob, is their only child. In her father's house as well as in her own she has had many duties, not the least of which was the entertainment of visitors, for their household became a very mecca for literary pilgrims; and she is now the chief companion of her father in his old age. That writing is to her a chief necessity of life, her many publications bear witness. Among her best known works may be mentioned: *Second Mar-*

riage; Girl Adoring (1928); *Alice Meynell, A Memoir* (1929); *The Frozen Ocean and Other Poems* (1931); *Follow Thy Fair Sun* (1935); *The Poets Walk* (1936); *Kissing the Rod* (1937); *Friends of a Lifetime* (edited 1940). She is preparing for the press a volume of letters written by the late Sir James Barrie.

The memoir of her mother shows Viola's power of discrimination. Her brother, Everard's, *Life of Francis Thompson* had set a difficult standard for a second member of the family to emulate, in the portrayal of intimate biography. But her treatment of Alice Meynell combines most exquisite literary criticism of one artist appraising the work of another together with a daughter's tribute to a beloved parent. Delicate touches of humor lend vitality to the picture and make of this biography most delightful reading.

The short stories which comprise the volume *Kissing the Rod* are among Miss Meynell's finest work. For delicacy of sentiment, feminine subtlety of character diagnosis, charm and deftness of expression they are unrivalled in contemporary fiction.

Viola Meynell continues to live in her own domain at the family colony in Greatham near Pulborough, Sussex, and when in London has a flat of her own in the family residence.   A. M.

Wilfrid Meynell 1852-

Francis Thompson, in a letter to Bishop Carroll, declared very truly that "Mr. Meynell has, in my opinion, done more than any other man to educate Catholic literary opinion. I was myself virtually his pupil, and his wife's, long before I knew him." And the man who stands today as patriarch of the Catholic Literary Revival in England will be remembered in many ways and in many hearts as the angel of its earlier days.

Wilfrid Meynell, the seventh child of a famliy of eight, was born in 1852, and spent much of his youth in Yorkshire, with which county his family had been long and honorably associated. His maternal great-grandfather, William Tuke of York, had labored to ameliorate the condition of the insane in England much as Pinel did in France; his grandfather worked with William Wilberforce for the liberation of slaves; while his philanthropist uncle, James Tuke, was active in Ireland during the famine years.

True to this family tradition of idealism, young Wilfrid Meynell was received into the Catholic Church in 1870, and began working in the London slums under the direction of Father Lockhart, with whom he made his home at St. Etheldreda's. A modest allowance from his family left him free to begin the career of journalism to which he was so admirably adapted; and after reading the early poems of Alice Thompson (not a relative of Francis), he sought her out with devotion. They were married in 1877, beginning then the long and fruitful union only interrupted by her death in 1922.

Cardinal Manning requested Meynell in 1881 to become editor of the *Weekly Register,* a post which he continued to hold until 1899. Meanwhile in 1883, he had himself founded the magazine *Merry England*—designed (as his daughter Viola says in her memoir of her mother) to support "the social revolution of the Young England Movement, the revival of the peasantry, the abolition of the wrongs of the poor, and the spread of art and letters." Among its contributors were Manning, Patmore, Wilfrid Blunt, Belloc, and of course the editor and his increasingly distinguished wife, while its unique claim to immortality lies in its having carried the first published poem of Francis Thompson. For it was Wilfrid Meynell who discovered that "star crossed" candidate for immortality, and who with Mrs. Meynell rescued him from the dereliction of the London streets and devotedly coaxed him into health and the fullness of his genius.

Wilfrid Meynell's self-abnegating sympathy and infallible taste equipped him as perfect editor for the eventually collected works of Thompson and of his own exquisite Alice. His scholarship and wit found more original expression in his life of *Benjamin Disraeli: An Unconventional Biography;* in *Faith Found in London; Verses and Reverses; Aunt Sarah and the War; Who Goes There? Rhymes With Reasons,* and *Come and See.* For many years his column "Et Cetera" enlivened the London *Tablet* with characteristic comments on contemporary literature, while the Meynell homes in London and Sussex offered to the makers of this literature unfailing hospitality and inspiration.

In 1943 he was created a Commander of the British Empire in the King's Birthday Honours List. K. B.

Reverend Virgil Michel, O.S.B. 1890-1938

Founder of the Liturgical Movement in the United States, the Reverend Virgil Michel, O.S.B., was born in St. Paul, Minnesota, in 1890, and educated at St. John's High School from 1903 to 1907, and St. John's College, Collegeville, where he was graduated with an A.B. in 1912. He entered the Benedictine Order in 1909, was professed the following year, received his M.A. at St. John's Seminary in 1913 and was ordained in 1916. After graduate studies in English and philosophy at the Catholic University of America, he received his Ph.D. there in 1918. His doctoral dissertation was on "The Critical Essays of Orestes Brownson." The summers of 1917 and 1918 he attended classes at Columbia University. He then taught philosophy in St. John's University, Collegeville, 1918 to 1923, was dean of the preparatory school 1921 to 1923, and served as registrar of the university 1923 to 1924.

In 1924, Father Virgil went abroad for a year and did postgraduate work in philosophy at the College of St. Anselm, Rome, and at the University of Louvain. Becoming interested in the Liturgical Movement then well advanced in Europe, he determined to promote it in the United States as a means of fortifying Christian life and devotion. Upon his return in 1926, he founded the magazine, *Orate Fratres*, as an organ of the movement and was its editor. Simultaneously he inaugurated the Liturgical Press, for the publication of popular liturgical pamphlets and texts. Also in 1926, to advance liturgical ideals, he translated from the French *Liturgy, The Life of the Church,* and from the Italian *The Spirit of the Liturgy*. Returning to the teaching of philosophy at St. John's University from 1925 to 1929, he translated from the German *Thomas Aquinas, His Personality and Thought*.

He organized a liturgical summer school at the Abbey which culminated in the first national Liturgical Day on July 25, 1929. Overwork necessitated temporary retirement from active duty in 1929, but the following year he took up the cause of the Indian Missions in Northern Minnesota, helping to reorganize these missions in the dioceses of Duluth and Crookston. In 1932 a great Indian Congress was held, due to his labors. In 1933 he became dean of the college and in 1935 director of the Institute for Social Studies, at St. John's University. These posts he occupied at the time of his death in 1938, in his forty-eighth year.

Three books came from his pen in 1937: *The Liturgy of the Church; Christian Social Reconstruction,* and *The Christian in the World. My Sacrifice and Yours* had appeared in 1927. In collaboration with his confrère, Father Basil Stegmann, O.S.B., and the Dominican Sisters, he wrote the "Christ Life Series in Religion" (1934-35), comprising eight volumes and two teachers' manuals, and he had nearly completed an advanced volume of the series when he died. He also contributed to English and American Catholic periodicals and was in demand as a lecturer and gave liturgical retreats for priests and nuns. In the summer of 1936 he lectured at the Pius X School of Liturgical Music in New York City.

Dom Virgil Michel was prominent in the educational field and from 1937 to 1938 president of the Minnesota Catholic College Association. He upheld an idealistic approach to educational problems. At St. John's he organized a backgrounds course in contemporary social questions, and he was actively interested in the Catholic Worker groups in New York and Chicago. In the Institute for Social Studies, which he founded to train leaders in adult study groups, he dealt primarily with the social economic theory, and under his inspiration credit and cooperative unions were established. In the fall of 1938 he took part with outstanding scholastic philosophers of the United States and Europe in a Philosophical Symposium at the University of Notre Dame, and before his death he completed the first chapter of a symposium on the philosophy of St. Thomas Aquinas. He was a member of the American Philosophical Association and the American Catholic Philosophical Association. He was also moderator of St. Augustine's Literary Society at St. John's Seminary. Discussion was always of interest to him, and he was a great lover of nature. His death, on November 26, 1938, was at the height of a fruitful career.

                                                                    C. M. N.

Joseph Corson Miller 1883-

In the great tradition of the Catholic poets down through the ages, J. Corson Miller writes in praise of Christ, His Blessed Mother and His Church with the inspiration of faith and love and a felicity of expression that places him in the first rank of Catholic poets of today. He was born in Buffalo, New York, in 1883, the son of Joseph Engels and Mary (Schmid) Miller, and was educated at St. Agnes School and Canisius College, Buffalo. An early predilection for literature and composition won him the prize in English for three consecutive years at Canisius. His wide reading of literature embraced all the classics and the whole array of major and minor poets, with particular relation to English and American romanticists, past and contemporaneous. Thus imbued with the spirit of the masters, he began to write verse, but it was not until he was twenty-three that he wrote his first serious poem, with a love-nostalgic note, and sent it to a woman's magazine, which paid him the munificent sum of one dollar for it. He then made a study of the technique of verse-writing and creative poetry practice, still incessantly reading the best works of the centuries.

After leaving college in 1905, Miller was employed as assistant to corporation executives in the steam and electric railway industry. He continued in this capacity until 1926, when he became connected with the Municipal Civil Service Commission of Buffalo, and he is at present employed on the staff of the Commission. In 1936 he married Ottilia Schneider; they have one daughter.

For many years Miller has been a member of the choir of the parish church which he attended as a child, and has thus participated in all church services. This affiliation has been a source of much inspiration and spiritual emotion, the beauty of ecclesiastical music and the glory of the rituals having a tendency to stir the heart and mind of the poet.

His poetical career actually began with the acceptance of some verses by a syndicated national weekly. Shortly after, at about the age of twenty-eight, the *Magnificat* accepted a poem he wrote on the Blessed Virgin and requested more work along the same line. Therefore he wrote a large amount of religious verse, with Our Lord and Our Lady as the central themes. He has also written and published many nature poems and love lyrics and has been successful with the ballad or genre poem. His "Ballad of Simple Simon" has been set to music and is frequently sung in concerts. Several of his poems, notably "Conan of Fortingall," have been reprinted in many anthologies.

His work is included in such collections as Maynard's *Book of Modern Catholic Verse,* Walsh's *Catholic Anthology,* Rittenhouse's *Third Book of Modern Verse,* Strong's *Best Poems,* Stevenson's *Poems of American His-*

tory, and Kilmer's *Catholic Anthology.* Braithwaite also included his work in his annual magazine-verse anthologies.

Miller's first book of poems, *Veils of Samite,* was published in 1922. Diversity of rhythm and metre and a variety of theme marked this first collection, much of the verse reflecting the World War. He was hailed as "distinctively a Catholic poet." *A Horn from Caerleon* appeared in 1927. This the poet considers his most representative work. It was universally praised, as was also *Cup of Years,* published in 1934. A fourth volume is *Finger at the Crossroads.*

Many publications, including representative magazines and newspapers such as the *Bookman, Nation, Forum, Vanity Fair, Times, Post, Tribune* and *Herald,* and all Catholic and poetry magazines, have published his verse. His "Epicedium" (in memory of America's dead in the first World War) is broadcast annually on a national hook-up on Armistice Day. Miller lectures on poetry, and reads from his books before clubs, colleges and business organizations. He was elected a member of the Poetry Society of America and an Academician of the Catholic Poetry Society of America; is an honorary member of the Spring Hill College Poetry Society and the Canisius College Alumni Association; also a member of the Institut Literaire et Artistique de France (Paris). He endeavors to have his poetry reflect his basic philosophy, which is that life is directed by an all-wise, omnipotent God and its keynote is love of God and of our neighbor. In his verse he seeks to glorify God, His Saints and His Church. Of the high purposes and aspirations of man he takes due cognizance, and in the soil he believes lies the salvation of present-day civilization.   C. M. N.

Reverend Charles C. Miltner, C.S.C. 1886-

Charles Christopher Miltner, C.S.C., priest and educator, was born at Iosco, Livingston County, Michigan, April 9, 1886. The son of George and Mary Elizabeth (Lerg) Miltner, Father Miltner was educated in the public schools of Michigan and Notre Dame Preparatory School before taking the degrees of Ph.B., University of Notre Dame (1911); Ph. D., Gregorian University, Rome (1913); D.D. from Laval University, Quebec (1917). This distinguished educator entered the Congregation of the Holy Cross in September 1903 and was professed in 1907. For five months after his ordination in June 1916 he was curate at Sacred Heart Church, New Orleans. Appointed to the faculty of Notre Dame in 1917, Father Miltner advanced from instructor and professor of philosophy—1917 to 1937—to dean of the liberal arts college, 1925. He was appointed head of the graduate school of Christian apologetics in 1937. Since 1940 he has been president of the University of Portland, Portland, Oregon.

An unexcelled teacher, for many years, of moral and social philosophy, Father Miltner has exerted a tremendous influence on many teachers of philosophy. For relaxation he plays the violin or engages in a stiff game of golf.

The stimulating criticism and encouragement of the late Reverend Daniel E. Hudson, C.S.C., editor of the *Ave Maria,* and of Professor Charles Phillips, account, he says, for whatever success he has had as a writer. This modest claim accords with the admirable urbanity and gentleness of this true priest.

The works of Father Miltner include *Elements of Ethics* (1925); *Progressive Ignorance* (essays) (1925); *Introduction to Metaphysics* (with Daniel C. O'Grady) (1931), and a translation from the French of Simon Deploige's *Le Conflit de la Morale et la Sociologie* (1937). He has also contributed to outstanding magazines and is a member of the Knights of Columbus, the American Catholic Philosophic Association (president, 1933), and the National Catholic Education Association.   S. M.

Sister Miriam, R.S.M.   1886-

Though the patterned life of a nun appears uninteresting, Sister Miriam seems to have found, or made, her own fascinating, partly through the cultivation of a number of friendships—usually by correspondence. Among her friends are H. L. Mencken, Odell Shepard, Robert P. Tristram Coffin. The late Sir Granville Bantock had put to music five of her poems.

The daughter of Hugh Gallagher and Brigid (Bonner) Gallagher of County Donegal, Ireland, she was born in Hazleton, Pennsylvania, August 9, 1886. One month after her seventeenth birthday, she resigned a teaching position to enter the convent of the Sisters of Mercy at Wilkes-Barre. Since then, she says, she has never had a monotonous day. She has taught in high schools and colleges in Iowa and Pennsylvania; has taken courses or degrees from several universities, including Creighton, Iowa, Notre Dame, Chicago, and the Catholic University. Now she is professor of English at College Misericordia, Dallas, Pennsylvania, where she conducts successful courses in creative writing and edits the *Thinker's Digest.*

Her contributions to magazines, both in prose and verse, have been many, and she has edited two volumes of analecta from the writings of Canon Sheehan. Perhaps the most ambitious and valuable of her prose papers are the uncritical essay on "Richard Le Gallienne: Painter of Shadows," and the biographical and bibliographical article, "Theodore Maynard, Divine Adventurer," contributed to the *Catholic Library World,* February 1941, and later reissued in pamphlet form. Her verse was published in a volume entitled *Woven of the Sky,* with a preface by Odell

Shepard. It is full of delicately felt emotions all expressed with great simplicity and economy. It attracted the attention of many non-Catholic readers. For these John Hall Wheelock spoke when he called it "beautiful poetry from the heart of a true poet," and Victor Burr when he said, "Beauty shines in every line and sings in every word."

Sister Miriam of the Holy Spirit   *see* Jessica   Powers

Gabriela Mistral (Lucila Godoy Alcayaga)   1889-

When the Nobel Poetry Award for 1945 was announced, the name of the winner, for the first time, was that of a Latin-American. The coveted honor went to a native of Chile, a former school teacher and one who, to English-speaking readers, was then not widely known, Gabriela Mistral. The Spanish literary world had, for some years, however, been aware of the high literary ability of Miss Mistral, who can justly claim a place as an outstanding poet of the South American hemisphere.

Lucila Godoy Alcayaga, whose chosen pen name is Gabriela Mistral, was born at Vicuña in the rural depths of Northern Chile on April 7, 1889. Both parents were of Basque-Indian stock. Her father, a teacher of the primary grades, was a writer of verse of some local celebrity. At fifteen years of age, the young Lucila Godoy herself became a primary school teacher in a village near her birthplace. She taught in a succession of girls' schools from 1904 to 1914, when an event happened which changed the course of her life. She won the highest prize in a poetry contest at Santiago, the capital. The story has it that she was too shy to come forward to receive the prize—a laurel crown and a gold medal—but stayed hidden among the audience to hear her poem read amid the plaudits of the crowd. Soon, over her pen name, Gabriela Mistral, the poems began to appear in the magazines and newspapers and made friends for her among the poets of other lands.

Her first volume of collected poems, *Desolacion,* was published in New York City in 1922 by the American Teachers of Spanish. Dr. Federico di Onis of Columbia University had asked her permission to put some of her poems into a volume. This volume, perhaps Miss Mistral's best book, proved to be the foundation on which was built her fame which two decades later, won for her the Nobel Prize.

In the same year, 1922, Gabriela Mistral was invited by the Mexican government to inaugurate a school named after her. While in Mexico she published a volume called "Lecturas para Mujeres." Her Mexican stay, the first away from Chile, was followed in one year by a trip to Europe. In Madrid she published another volume, *Ternura,* a collection of poems for children. Later she was named "head of the Letters and Arts Committee of the Institute for International Cooperation of the League of Nations and in 1931 she came to the United States and taught at Barnard College, Vassar College and at Middlebury. Of her third volume of poems *Tala* published in 1938 she says: "I have nothing else to give to the Spanish children scattered to the four winds of the world." The proceeds of this book went to help the Basque orphans of the Spanish Civil War.

Since the early thirties Miss Mistral has been in the Chilean diplomatic service, holding consular posts in Madrid, Lisbon, Nice and Rio de Janeiro. In April 1946 she was appointed consul at Los Angeles, California.

Sad events of her life have influenced her poetry, the suicide of a lover when she was very young, the mysterious death of a favorite nephew and latterly, the grief which she felt at the plight of the helpless victims, especially children, of the Spanish Civil War.

A critic of her poetry, Jorge Manach, says of her: "She has become a living incarnation of the world-wide Hispanic soul." Deja Hernan Diaz Arrieta says that the distinctive note in her is her intensity and one Chilean critic thinks that "her best claim to enduring fame is her making articulate and moving the tragedy of the childless woman."

Always an admirer of some of the great mystics, St. Francis of Assisi and St. Theresa, Miss Mistral shows in her works a sense of the divine power in the human soul which makes her poetry ecstatic and profoundly powerful. Though her work has been translated into many tongues, French, Portuguese, Swedish, German—English readers are limited to two recent anthologies, a dozen Mistral poems translated by Alice Stone Blackwell, in *Some South-American Poets,* appearing in 1938.

From Immaculate Heart College in Los Angeles, California she received the Cor Mariae literary medal.

Sister Mary Monica, O.S.U.

As educator and authoress, Sister M. Monica has spent many busy years in the order of the Ursuline Sisters of Brown County, Ohio. She was born in Zanesville, Ohio, of New England and early Maryland stock, the daughter of Honorable T. J. Maginnis, a lawyer and member of the Ohio Legislature, and Mary De Gratte (Jackson) Maginnis. She was graduated from the School of the Brown County Ursulines at St. Martin, Ohio, and the Sisters' College of the Catholic University of America, where she received her A.B. in 1917. Having entered the Ursuline Sisters of Brown County, she took her graduate studies at the University of Notre Dame, where she received her M.A. in 1920 and her Ph.D. in 1926. Her book

Angela Merici and Her Teaching Idea was published in 1927. This was her first historical work and is a study in the Renaissance.

Sister Monica taught history and English at the School of the Ursulines at St. Martin, and at a private school and the Diocesan Athenaeum of Cincinnati, and taught English at the Notre Dame Summer School. For five years she was director of the Brown County School for Girls. She organized and administered the Brown County Alumnae and is a former member of the Alumnae Board of the Sisters' College of the Catholic University and the University of Notre Dame.

In 1930 she published *Cross in the Wilderness,* a study in the American background of her own order, and in 1937 a book on pre-Civil War Spain, entitled *And Then the Storm,* and a translation from the Spanish, *Jesus Silent.* In 1938 appeared *Grace of the Way,* and *Hope of Life* in 1942. She has also contributed verse and articles on literary and historic subjects to Catholic periodicals. She has lectured to Catholic women's clubs and study groups on Spain and the historic background of Spanish America and has engaged in extensive research work in European archives, being the first nun to study in the Vatican secret archives.

Her chosen field is Spanish colonial history, 1550-1600. Her research work in Spain consisted in studying the background of the Vice-royalty in Peru.   C. M. N.

N. Elizabeth Monroe   1896-

The Novel and Society, published by the University of North Carolina Press in October 1941, started a new movement in literary criticism. It is essentially Aristotelian and Thomistic in its approach to the novel, and its milieu is scholarly, penetrating, and deeply Catholic. The author, N. Elizabeth Monroe, assistant professor of English at Brooklyn College, believes that the novel cannot succeed without representing the whole of life.

Miss Monroe comes from the rich farming section of southeastern Pennsylvania. Her paternal grandfather gave up his legal practice in Scotland and came to Chanceford Township to farm the land. Her father, William Mitchell Monroe, married an English woman, Mercy Catherine Norris. Both were Presbyterians and in this faith brought up their seven children.

Miss Monroe was educated in schools of this vicinity until time for college when she won a four year scholarship for Oberlin. She received her A.B. from Oberlin in 1919 with Phi Beta Kappa honors and won a half scholarship to the University of Pennsylvania, from which she received her M.A. in 1923, her Ph.D. in 1929. She is a member of the Modern Language Association, The National Council of Teachers, the Institute of English Studies, the American Association of University Professors, and the American Association of University Women.

Her first book, *Nicholas Breton, Pamphleteer,* was published in 1919, her second, *The Novel and Society,* in 1941. She is at present finishing a novel, *Thornbend.* She has contributed articles to *College English,* the *American-Scandinavian Review,* the *Southern Literary Messenger, The Catholic World, Thought, The Sign, Educational Forum,* and to the Catholic Youth Organization magazine.

Miss Monroe was received into the Catholic Church in 1933. She says the next best thing to being born a Catholic is to become one by conversion. She spends her week-ends and holidays in her country home in St. Cloud, West Orange, where she does most of her writing.   M. G.

Maria Montessori 1870-

Not satisfied with the current educational systems, Maria Montessori, after much observation in the principal European schools, and her own experimentation, introduced the "Montessori Method." For this new educational method a knowledge of medicine, psychiatry, psychology and practical pedagogy are necessary.

The central ideas of the "Montessori Method" are that "children are best educated by allowing them to find things out for themselves; that training of the sensory faculties by handwork is of prime importance; that the teacher or parent should not impose his own personality on the child; that rewards, marks and punishments should be abolished; that discipline should be entirely free and self-imposed."

Its author, Maria Montessori was born at Chiaravalle, Ancona, Italy, the only daughter of Chevalier Alessandro Montessori and Renilde Stoppani. At the University of Rome she studied both medicine and literature. She is the first woman on whom the degree of M.D. was conferred by the University of Rome.

Her medical training was followed by a study of defective children. She was so successful with them that she was appointed directress of the Scuolo Ortofrenica, an institution for retarded children.

In 1907 she was put in charge of one of the children's houses in the slum section of San Lorenzo in Rome. Here too, she achieved excellent results. In 1919, she began training courses in London that were given every two years. Alternate courses were given in other parts of the world. In 1922 she became Government Inspector of Schools in Italy. The following years were spent in writing.

She is the author of: *Pedagogical Anthropology; The Montessori Method; The Advanced Montessori Method; Montessori's Own Handbook; The Mass Explained to Children; The Child in the Church; Psycho-Geometry; Psycho-Arithmetic; Secret of Childhood.*   M. H.

John Moody 1868-

The fifth of twelve children, John Moody was born May 2, 1868, in Jersey City, New Jersey, a city then little more than a suburban home town. "Migrating" five years later to Bayonne, a village six or seven miles south, his parents sent him to the local public school where he received his entire junior education. The family were regular church-goers, being staunch adherents of the Protestant Episcopal Church. Up to his ninth year, the *Book of Common Prayer* and the *Child's Bible* were his chief spiritual guides. Then were sown in his youthful mind seeds of doubt.

During a summer vacation passed on his uncle's farm in Connecticut, he was told that the Protestant Episcopal Church was not "right"; that it was no more than three hundred and fifty years old. This incident marked his starting point in serious thinking. His doubts grew. His faith was shaken. Perhaps, he thought, there was no God, after all. A few years later the shock of finding that the rector of the church and his bishop did not see eye to eye on points of doctrine, still further shattered his beliefs. A long course of reading in history and modern philosophy led to yet greater skepticism, so that by the time he was twenty-five or twenty-six, the last vestige of his faith in Christianity as a revealed religion had been quite destroyed.

Meanwhile, he had proved himself a "regular" boy in school, being leader of a "gang," playing truant for as long as five whole months together, and engaging in such pranks as only school boys can think of. Denied the coveted opportunity of a college education, he was obliged to seek employment at fifteen. This he obtained in a wholesale wood-ware house in New York City, where during the following seven years he worked up from errand boy to accountant, and on the side carried on other minor ventures of a commercial and literary nature, and gave himself the equivalent of a college education by taking up a course in home study. Then he went to Wall Street, where till the closing years of the century he was employed in a well-known banking firm.

His family moved to Cranford where his mother died. In 1899 he married Anna Mulford Addison. They had two children, only one now living. In 1900 appeared the first edition of his *Moody's Manual of Investments,* the first thing of its kind ever published. Through membership in the Sunrise Club, whose roster included the names of all sorts of "forward" thinkers, he became a believer in the "religion of democracy," and a leader in the political reform movement. Several years' experience in the political arena, however, proved both bitter and costly, and left him, in his late thirties, a wiser if not a richer man. Despite reverses of fortune, he and his wife made their first trip to Europe in 1906. Surprised at the emptiness of the London churches, they were equally amazed at the well-filled Catholic churches on the continent. Far from being an anachronism, the Church of Rome appeared vital, a Church thousands were still taking seriously.

In 1910 he removed his family to New York City. As his business prospered he was growing "harder and more materialistic" in his outlook on life. Years of reading in philosophy and history, mostly post-Renaissance, had made an agnostic of him, albeit an optimistic one. Optimism was so in the air even in the fatal year of 1914 that John Moody sent his family to Europe in June and he himself followed in July. It was on the high seas that he learned that war had been declared. In London he met his wife and sons and in three weeks returned, at considerable hazard but with no mishap, to America. Three years after the war, in 1921, he travelled again to Europe to study conditions. Advancing in age, he grew more and more "weary of the aimless, hedonistic drift" he saw all round him.

One day a chance reference to Chesterton found in a comment penned by Arnold Bennett led Mr. Moody to read one after another of Chesterton's works. Their influence devastated all his philosophical notions. In 1921 his eldest son, John Edmund, a student at Oxford died. The experience, he records, caused in him a "yearning for God." In August of the following year, while on a visit to Vienna, he found himself inside the Cathedral of Saint Stephen. It chanced to be the feast of the Assumption. Moved by the devotion manifested by Our Lady's clients praying before her shrine, he knelt down and prayed for "light and leading." Before he left the church he knew that he had "passed a line." On board the homebound ship, a business man in the course of a conversation anent the moral chaos of the world, remarked to him, "After all, the Catholic Church is the only hope of the world." Back in America, he determined seriously to investigate the Catholic Church "through study, research, meditation, and prayer."

By such method he arrived "at the end of the road." The year 1930 found him again crossing the ocean, this time bound for Egypt and the Holy Land. It was on the shores of the Sea of Galilee that his long conflict, with himself and his prejudices, saw its end. The following year, 1931, in the chapel of the Dominican Sisters at Saint Joseph's, in Sullivan County, New York, he made his submission and was received into the "One, Holy, Catholic, Apostolic Church."

In 1932 he was made a Knight Commander of the Order of the Holy Sepulchre. His books are: *The Truth About the Trusts* (1904); *The Investor's Primer* (1907); *The Art of Wall Street Investing* (1909); *How to Invest Money Wisely* (1912); *Masters of Capital* (1917); *The Railroad Builders* (1919); *The Remaking of Europe* (1921); *Profitable Investing* (1923), and *The Long Road Home* (1933). *Fast By the Road* (1942) was written after more than ten years in the Church, and is a sequel to *The Long Road Home.* Father Gillis states in the Preface that Mr. Moody has given us "theology with chuckles." *John Henry Newman* was published in 1945.

S. J. M.

Parker Thomas Moon   1892-1936

An authority on international affairs as well as on history, Dr. Parker Thomas Moon served on the Commission of Inquiry, appointed by President Wilson and headed by Colonel House, from 1917 till 1919. The task of this Commission was to investigate the possibilities of peace and to draft conditions and terms on which treaties could be based when World War I ended. In 1918 and 1919, Dr. Moon went to Paris to serve on the staff of the American Commission at the Peace Conference. In 1919 he was secretary to the International Commission on Territorial Questions during the Peace Conference.

Through his prolific writings and his hundreds of addresses, Dr. Moon pleaded continually for the cooperation of the United States with the League of Nations. When he delivered the address at the commencement exercises of the Catholic University of America in 1935, Dr. Moon said: "With a little wisdom we could so strengthen and improve the League of Nations and the World Court that war would become as obsolete as dueling."

When Dr. Moon finished his work in Europe, he returned to Columbia University in New York where he had been an instructor in history from 1915 to 1917. After serving two more years, from 1919 to 1921, as an instructor, he was promoted to assistant professor in 1921. Four years later he became an assistant professor of international relations, then associate professor from 1926 to 1931 and professor in 1931.

Parker Leroy Moon was born in New York City on June 5, 1892, the son of Alfred Goodrich and Mary Esther (Parker) Moon. When he became a Catholic in 1914 he took the name of "Thomas" as his special devotion was to St. Thomas Aquinas, and his favorite prayer was one of St. Thomas' which begins with: "Grant us, we beseech Thee, Almighty and most merciful God, fervently to desire, wisely to search out, and perfectly to fulfill, all that is well-pleasing unto Thee.

"Order Thou our worldly condition to the glory of Thy Name, and of all that Thou requirest us to do; grant us the knowledge, the desire, and the ability, that we may so fulfill it as we ought, and may our path to Thee be safe, straightforward, and perfect to the end.

"Give us, O Lord, steadfast hearts which no unworthy affection may drag downwards; give us unconquered hearts which no tribulation can wear out, give us upright hearts which no unworthy purpose may tempt aside.

"Bestow upon us also, O Lord, our God, understanding to know Thee, diligence to seek Thee, wisdom to find Thee, and a faithfulness which may finally embrace Thee—all which we ask through Jesus Christ our Lord. Amen."

Parker Moon was educated at the Yonkers High School where he won honors, and at Columbia College. He was graduated with a B.S. degree in 1913. He studied chiefly history, mathematics and German. The Senior class selected him to receive the Charles M. Rolker, Jr., prize awarded annually "to the member of the Senior College class who, in the estimation of his classmates, has proved himself most worthy of distinction as an undergraduate."

Through his study of history he became interested in the Catholic Church. A year after graduation he took instructions at the Paulist Church in New York City and became a Catholic.

He held the William Mitchell Fellowship at Columbia in 1913 and 1914 and the Gilder Fellowship in 1914 and 1915 at which date he began his career as an instructor at that institution.

In 1921 Dr. Moon married Edith Conway of Holyoke, Massachusetts. They have one daughter, Alice.

His first book *A Syllabus of Imperialism and World Politics* was published in 1919. This was revised and brought up to date in 1926. *Imperialism and World Politics* (1926) which was perhaps the first study of its kind, was his chief work. He was the first to develop a comprehensive course in International Relations and World Politics. In 1921 he wrote *The Labor Problem and the Social Catholic Movement in France,* which earned for him the Ph.D. degree.

At the time of his death he was writing a book on the French foreign policy since World War I.

With Dr. Carlton J. Hayes, as co-author, he wrote: *Modern History* (1923); *Ancient and Medieval History* (1929); *Ancient History* (1929); with Carlton J. Hayes and J. W. Wayland as co-authors he wrote: *World History* (1932) and with Chester L. Jones and H. K. Norton he wrote: *The United States and the Caribbean* (1929).

Modern History, an American history textbook, stirred a storm of protest in 1927 and again in 1930. The national Americanization committee of the Veterans of Foreign Wars charged in 1927 that the book was "pro-British" and wanted it banned from use in New York's schools. The book was still in use however until 1930 when it was barred by the Board of Superintendents. The board acted on a complaint of a Protestant Episcopal clergyman who claimed the book exhibited undue leaning to the Catholic Church. Dr. Moon said he supposed "the clergymen did not appreciate the story of the origin of the Church of England, with its inclusion of the private life of Henry VIII and his many wives."

For fifteen and a half years—the longest continuous term in the *Political Science Quarterly's* history—Dr. Moon had been managing editor. He was secretary of the Academy of Political Science, editor of its Proceedings and ex-officio member of its Board of Trustees.

In later life his avocation was gardening. Often he would leave the typewriter when his writing refused to go smoothly and work in the garden until he obtained the phrasing he wanted. He strove for pungent phrases. He once called the land hunger of nations "a dangerous disease which I like to call 'mapitis' or inflammation of the map."

His outstanding qualities were great simplicity, humility, patience, perseverance, a sense of humor and piety.

On May 23, 1929, he caused much perturbation when he failed to appear to give his waiting class an examination. The professor was discovered at his summer home in Woodmont, Connecticut, fishing. He had forgotten about the examination.

Dr. Moon was president of the Catholic Association for International Peace from 1931; former president of the American Catholic Historical Association and vice-president of the Students International Union.

He died on June 11, 1936.

M. H.

Reverend Thomas Verner Moore, O.Cart.
1877-

Reverend Thomas Verner Moore, educator, psychiatrist, and a co-founder of St. Anselm's Priory at the Catholic University of America in Washington, the son of John N. and Charlotte McIlvain Moore, was born in Louisville, Kentucky, on October 22, 1877.

His primary education was received at a public school in Louisville. To provide better education his mother moved to New York City in the autumn of 1890. He attended Fordham University from January to June of 1891 and continued his education at St. Francis Xavier's College in New York in the autumn of 1891. In 1896 he joined the Paulists and was ordained priest on the feast of St. Thomas the Apostle, December 21, 1901. He received his Ph.D. from the Catholic University in 1903 and began a long period of association with that university as fellow in psychology, 1903, instructor in psychology 1910 to 1916, associate professor, 1916 to 1922, and professor, 1922. From 1939 to 1947 Dr. Moore had been Head of the Department of Psychology and Psychiatry at the Catholic University. In addition to his work at the Catholic University, Dr. Moore had taught at Trinity College for a number of years. He accepted an invitation from the Spanish Ministry of Education to lecture in psychiatry at the University of Madrid during the year 1947.

Dr. Moore spent the period from 1906 to 1909 as chaplain of the Newman Club at the University of California, and during the year 1904 to 1905 he studied abroad under Wundt at the University of Leipzig. He studied medicine at Georgetown University, 1911 to 1913. He went abroad again in 1913 to continue his medical studies at Munich. The outbreak of war in 1912 compelled his return and he received his M.D. from Johns Hopkins in 1915.

During World War I, Dr. Moore served as a psychiatrist with the American Expeditionary Forces, as captain and major in the Medical Corps, 1918 to 1919. He received the Benedictine habit at Fort Augustus, Scotland, on September 8, 1923. He then returned to this country as co-founder of the English Benedictine Foundation at St. Anselm's Priory at Washington, D. C. and was for several years its Prior.

In 1916 Dr. Moore became the director of the Clinic for Mental and Nervous Diseases at Providence Hospital, Washington. Since 1937 this clinic, under the name of the Child Center, has been on the campus of the Catholic University. Here are treated the mental problems of both children and adults. The work of the clinic was considerably extended by a Rockefeller grant made in 1939.

St. Gertrude's School of Arts and Crafts, a pioneer Catholic school for retarded girls, was established in 1924. In 1942 Dr. Moore opened The Priory School, a boys' preparatory day school.

The story of Dr. Moore's interests and work is revealed in his writings. In addition to his contributions to scientific, literary, and psychological publications in this country and abroad, Dr. Moore was the editor of *Studies in Psychology and Psychiatry,* a series of monographs in which is published some of his work as well as that of students of the department. Among his monographs are *The Essential Psychosis* (1933), and *Consciousness and the Nervous System* (1938). *Formal Causality and Fields of Force* was a contribution read at the meeting of the American Catholic Philosophical Association in 1939.

In the field of ethics, Dr. Moore wrote, in 1915, *An Historical Introduction to Ethics.* This was followed in 1935 by *Principles of Ethics,* a textbook for nurses. In 1943 the latest revised edition of this book appeared, containing an additional chapter on the ethics of war.

In 1931 Dr. Moore wrote *Prayer,* a book for the guidance of Benedictine Oblates. This was re-issued in 1943. *Dynamic Psychology* came out in 1924 and is still used as a standard text. *Cognitive Psychology* appeared in 1939.

In 1943 Dr. Moore's book *The Nature and Treatment of Mental Disorders* appeared. In this book he has offered to educators and psychiatrists the results of a long and rich experience in dealing with the personality problems of children and adults. A year later he published *Personal Mental Hygiene.*

On June 12, 1947, he joined the Carthusians at the Cartuja de Miraflores near Burgos, Spain, to lead the life of a hermit.

On October 17th, 1947, he received the habit. The Italian International News Company filmed the ceremony. He took the name of Pablo Maria: Pablo after St. Paul of the desert, the first hermit, to indicate that he is to be his model in Carthusian life; and Maria to signify that he now belongs wholly to the Blessed Mother.

A. M. & C. K.

Evan Frederic Morgan Tredegar (Evan Morgan) 1893-

Evan Morgan was born in London on the 13th of July 1893, the son of Viscount Tredegar, First Viscount of the second creation and Lady Katharine Carnegie, the daughter of the Ninth Earl of South Esk. He succeeded to the Viscountcy and Barony of Tredegar on the death of his father in 1934.

Evan Morgan was educated at Eton and Christ Church College, Oxford. While he was at Oxford, he began to write seriously, his chief urge being the love of literature, especially poetry. Though his output of books is not large, it is of high quality. His best work he thinks is *The Eel*. The title poem in this book, the foreword of which was written by Alfred Noyes, is but three stanzas long. Evan Morgan is also the author of *Fragments; Gold and Ochre; Sequence of Seven Sonnets; Psyche; Trial by Ordeal,* (a novel), *At Dawn,* and *City of Canals* (poems). He contributes to the Queen's Doll House Library and various periodicals. He is the founder of the Tredegar Memorial Lecture Royal Society of Literature.

In 1928 Evan Morgan married Honorable Lois Sturt, the daughter of the second Baron Alington, who died in 1937. Two years after her death, he married Princess Olga Dolgorouky. In 1915 he joined the Welsh Guards and became a lieutenant a year later. The following year, he was the private secretary to Mr. Bridgeman, the Parliamentary Secretary to the Ministry of Labor. In 1919 he was with the Foreign Press Bureau and at the Allied Peace Conference. It was during that year he became a Catholic. He was made Cameriere Segreto di Spada a Cappa (Privy Chamberlain of Sword and Cape) to their Holinesses Pope Benedict XV and Pope Pius XI respectively; Commander with Star of the Order of the Holy Sepulchre; Knight of Devotion and Honour of the Sovereign and Military Order of Malta and Knight of Justice of the Constantinian Order of St. George.

In 1929 he contested in the Conservative Cause of the Limehouse Division of Stepney, East London. A year later he adopted the Conservative candidate of the Cardiff Central Division and in the same year was made an Honorary Colonel in the 17th London Regiment. He also became an Honorary Colonel in the first Monmouthshire Regiment (1934) and in the 38th (Divisional) Royal Engineers (1940). He had membership in the Imperial Air League. From 1940 to 1942 he was a battalion commander of the third (Mon.) Battalion Home Guard and then a second lieutenant in the Royal Corps of Signals attached to the war office for special duties. He served also as a British Legion liaison officer for Wales.

Evan Morgan is interested in hospitals. He is president of the Royal

Reverend Germain Morin, O.S.B.   1861-1946

Leopold Frédéric Germain Morin was born in the ancient Norman city of Caen on November 6, 1861. A few years ago he wrote, "Among all the blessings with which God has showered me in the course of my long life, the greatest, without doubt, is that of having allowed me to be born in that corner of Normandy forming the diocese of Bayeux and Lisieux, in which the old liturgical traditions are better preserved than in any other part of the Catholic world, Lyons perhaps excepted." He grew up in a thoroughly Catholic and liturgical atmosphere and from his earliest years was in love with the venerable religious practices of a French diocese that had remained unaffected by either Jansenism or Gallicanism. He was educated by the Brothers of the Christian Schools at Caen and at Lisieux, then in the Minor Seminaries at Vire and at Villiers-le-Seu. At the age of twenty he entered the recently established Abbey of Maredsous in Belgium. He made his profession on the 15th of August 1882. Even before his ordination to the priesthood on April 10, 1886, he had begun his studies of the Fathers of the Church which have made him one of the world's greatest living patristic scholars. Until 1908, Dom Morin fulfilled the duties of Master of Ceremonies.

Dom Morin was distinguished as an author, an editor, and a discoverer of important manuscripts. Most of his writings on ancient Christian literature, especially from the fourth to the twelfth centuries, have appeared in the *Revue Bénédictine* of Maredsous from 1884 until his death. Quite different from most of his other works is his early book *L'Ideal Monastique et la Vie Chrétienne des Premiers Jours* (1912), which was not published until twenty years after it was written. It has been translated into English by C. Gunning under the title *The Ideal of the Monastic Life Found in the Apostolic Age* and into three other languages. Abbot Columba Marmion quotes from this book and refers to it repeatedly, praising it as a work of great originality and sure knowledge. Among the collections Dom Morin has edited are the three volumes of *Anecdota Maredsolana;* the second series of *Études, Textes, Découvertes* (1913); *S. Augustini Tractatus sive sermones inediti* (1917); and *S. Augustini sermones post Maurinos reperti, nunc primum disquisiti* (1930). His principal discoveries are the works of the famous ninth century monk Gottschalk; a very ancient Latin version of the epistle of St. Clement of Rome;

Commentarioli et Tractatus of St. Jerome on the Psalms; a seventh century Visigothic Lectionary of Toledo; the author of the *Te Deum,* Niceta de Remesiana; and the unpublished work of Pacien de Barcelona and of Arnobius the Younger.

The last volume of Dom Morin's monumental work, his complete and definitive edition of the writings of St. Caesarius of Arles, went to press in 1942 at the expense of the Holy Father.

Dom Morin's scholarship has won very wide recognition. Until his death in 1930, the great Protestant historian and theologian Adolph Harnack was a close and admiring friend and helper of Dom Morin. The University of Oxford conferred upon him the honorary degree of Doctor of Letters, and the Universities of Zurich, Budapest, and Fribourg in Breisgau honored him similarly with the degree of Doctor of Theology. He was a Fellow of the Royal Society of Literature and a corresponding member of the Academy of Sciences of Bavaria and of the Society of Christian Archeology of Rome.

In the fields of ancient Christian literature, liturgy, hagiography, Church and monastic history, Dom Morin is distinguished for his sensational discoveries and definitive solutions of the old problems which exercised the wisdom of the savants.

During the period between the first and second World Wars, Dom Morin made his residence at the Abbey of St. Boniface in Munich.

During World War II, he lived at Fribourg, in Switzerland and then as he weakened under the weight of age he retired to a rest house at Orselina-Locarno. He died on the 13th of February 1946. His body rests in the crypt of the Abbey of Our Lady of the Hermits at Einsiedeln which he particularly loved.

B. S.

Reverend Robert Bakewell Morrison, S.J.
1894-

A breakdown in health opened the way to writing for Father Morrison, S.J. Writing texts in religion enabled him still to give voice to the message of Christ, though, as far as his taste went, it was a much less satisfactory way than teaching and preaching. He has seven books dealing with Religion for college students — on character, on dogma, on apologetics, on marriage and a venture into the general field of moral and educational orientation for the non-Catholic. His book *In Touch With God,* a treatment of Mass, prayer and the sacraments, he considers to be the most practical and, in general, perhaps the most acceptable of his writings.

Robert Bakewell Morrison was born December 18, 1894, in St. Louis,

Missouri. He was educated, first at Barat Hall, then at St. Louis University High School. From the College of Arts, St. Louis University, he received his A.B. degree and from the Graduate School of the same University his M.A. The Gregorian University in Rome conferred the S.T.D. degree upon him.

In 1911 he entered the Jesuit novitiate at Florissant, Missouri, and as a novice lived in the same building in which Father De Smet made his novitiate. As a Jesuit scholastic, "Mr." Morrison taught the classics for four years at the University of Detroit. He was ordained June 25, 1925, at St. Louis, Missouri. With minor interruptions he has taught at St. Louis University since 1927. At present (1947) he has a varied assignment of work. He gives "counsel," teaches, preaches occasionally—sometimes on "The Sacred Heart Hour," and is Director of the Department of Religion at St. Louis University. His teaching is done in The Medical School, The School of Social Service and the College of Arts.

He is the author of: *The Catholic Church and the Modern Mind* (1933); *Marriage* (1935); *Revelation and the Modern Mind; Teachings From the Life of Christ* (1936); *Character Formation in College* (1938), and with Reverend Stephen J. Rueve, S.J., he is co-author of *Think and Live* (1937). M. H.

John Cameron Andrieu Bingham Michael Morton 1893-

Known to his intimates as "Johnny," J. B. Morton has also, since 1924, been referred to as the "Beachcomber." It was then that he succeeded D. B. Wyndham Lewis as the writer of that notable column of light comedy in the *Daily Express* signed "Beachcomber." The majority of Morton's books are in the Beachcomber vein.

Although Mr. Morton had done some good general work for the *Daily Express*, to succeed Bevan Lewis was a hard test. Mr. Lewis had made the column famous and was, and still is, acknowledged as one of the leading English humorists, whereas J. B. Morton, at the time, was an unknown man. He did not copy Lewis' style and at first received unkind letters. Soon, however, he won favor and has retained it ever since.

J. B. Morton belongs to the school of the Chestertons and Belloc. He is English to the marrow and delights in the English countryside, the English country people and their ways. He is a good companion with a hearty laugh. Slim in his earlier years, he has now acquired a majestic girth.

J. B. Morton was born in 1893 the son of Edward Morton, the journalist and dramatist, and Rosamond (Bingham) Morton. He was educated at Park House, Southborough; Harrow and Worcester College, Oxford.

In 1914 he enlisted and fought in France as a private for two years with the Royal Fusiliers and then was an officer with the Suffolk Regiment in England and in France from 1916 to 1918. Then he was connected with the Ministry of Labor. He was demobilized in 1919.

He was received into the Catholic Church in 1922. It is strange to reflect that one who has all the marks of a dyed-in-the-wool born Catholic is really a convert.

In 1927 he married Dr. Mary O'Leary of Cappoquin County, Waterford.

J. B. Morton has written a fine novel of World War I in *The Barber of Putney* (1919); an excellent travel book *Pyrenean* (1938), and several first class historical studies. Among his books are: *Enchanter's Nightshade* (1920); *Penny Royal* (1921); *Tally-Ho!* (1922); *Old Man's Beard* (1923); *The Cow Jumped Over the Moon* (1924); *Sobieski, King of Poland* (1932); *St. Martin of Tours* (1932); *Hag's Harvest* (1933); *Morton's Folly* (1933); *Who's Who at the Zoo* (1933); *The Adventures of Mr. Thake* (1934); *The Bastille Falls* (Studies of the French Revolution) (1936); *The New Ireland* (1938); *The Dancing Cabman* (Collected Verse) (1938); *Saint—Just* (1939); *A Bonfire of Weeds* (1939); *I Do Not Think So* (1940), and *Fool's Paradise* (1941).

                                                                          M. H.

Daisy H. Moseley   1892-

In Italy, during the winter of 1926, Daisy Moseley amused herself visiting scenes associated with Saint Catherine of Siena and Saint Philip Neri, and wrote an article about them entitled "Sunshine and Saints" which appeared in *The Catholic World* for December 1927. "Saint Francis of Assisi's 'Canticle of the Sun,'" she wrote, "is re-echoed in the hearts of those who spend their winters in Italy. . . . 'The sun signifies Thee, Most High One,' sang Francis. . . . It is natural to associate sunshine with saints."

This article is the source of the arrangement and title of her children's book *Sunshine and Saints*. She thought that many of the children's books on saints gave the idea that the saints were born good and beautiful, of wealthy and pious parents, and that that discouraged young readers, aware that they themselves did not start life so well equipped. She decided to write a group of biographies based on the most reliable sources, and to tell both facts and legends, trying to make evident which was which. In her original manuscript, she included a bibliography, but when the volume was published it was found necessary to omit this.

Daisy H. Moseley was born in Raleigh, North Carolina, June 26, 1892, but has lived in Glen Ridge, New Jersey, since childhood. Shortly after her graduation from the College of Notre Dame of Maryland, Father John Burke, C.S.P., then editor of *The Catholic World,* telephoned her that he had heard through a mutual friend that she might have time for an undertaking that he had in mind and asked her to come to his office to discuss it. She complied, and later, she incorporated material collected while a student at the New York School of Social Work in an article "The Catholic Social Worker in an Italian District," which was published in *The Catholic World* and also in pamphlet form. Since then she has contributed frequently to *The Catholic World, The Commonweal, Sign,* and other magazines, articles about saints or literary persons and the places associated with them.

Emmanuel Mounier 1905-

Considered as the promotor and guiding spirit of the French personalist movement among young intellectuals, Emmanuel Mounier was born at Grenoble, April 1st, 1905, from peasant stock on both sides. He studied at the University of Grenoble and at the Sorbonne in Paris where he finished in 1928 with an agrégé in philosophy (one of the eight per annum of the Sorbonne). In 1929 he got his inspiration from the writings of Péguy which led to the personalist trend of social and religious thought.

In October 1932, Mounier founded the review *Esprit* which was to play an important part in the spreading of his ideas. In the winter of 1933, the first group of friends, the "Amis d'Esprit," was formed. The members of these groups included Catholics, non-Catholic Christians, as well as non-Christians. The common basis of agreement among them was the primacy of spiritual values in human life, however different various members may have defined these spiritual values in detail. They agreed upon the fundamental importance of the human person and of personal spiritual values, and in terms of this basic starting point they discussed the current problems of life, civilization, social conditions and politics. Their criticism of the present world was trenchant and was expressed in the first issue of *Esprit* as "rupture of Christian order with modern disorder." This meant that the followers of the Esprit movement were opposed to the excesses of capitalism, as well as to the totalitarian doctrines of communism and national-socialism. They were guided by the papal social encyclicals, by Charles Péguy, Léon Bloy, Jacques Maritain and the Russian religious thinker Berdiaev. Both Maritain and Berdiaev contributed to *Esprit,* and a number of brilliant young scholars, economists, philosophers and publicists were on the review's editorial staff.

Mounier's movement did not follow a purely ideological and academic trend. Personalism demanded something more: an individual pledge, a personal contribution, a radical change in the attitude of young men and women towards life, towards their profession, personal and family interests. It meant breaking up the mould of egotism to join a common task based on comradeship and fraternity. It meant especially a humanist approach to people and institutions.

In 1936, Mounier published the *Personalist Manifesto,* which was a summary of four years of fertile discussion and meditation and an exposé of the author's doctrine. Translated into English, German, Spanish and Polish, it exercised and still continues to exercise a deep influence on spiritual-minded youth throughout the world. Mounier's *"personalist revolution,"* which is meant as a spiritual revolution, the transformation of man and society through Christian means, has been a powerful factor of social and religious revival among intellectuals of all countries.

Groups of the "Amis d'Esprit" were founded in all the principal cities of France, in Switzerland, Belgium, in the French colonies, in Canada, Egypt, Spain, England, Holland, Poland and the Argentine Republic. The "Friends" met at yearly congresses held near Paris and a continual interchange of ideas went on between the groups. However, Mounier always insisted that his movement was not guided by a fixed formulary abstract of theories, it was to serve as a flexible platform of *living ideas.*

"The Christian message, Mounier writes, did not start as did the moral schools of antiquity, as a philosophy addressed to the learned, but it was an appeal to every man: change the heart of your heart." Once given this change of inner man, a transformation of the world must follow. Personal salvation is insufficient; it would mean, in Berdiaev's words, "double-bookkeeping." Man cannot rest in peace, nor can he enjoy spiritual security as long as a more just order is not achieved.

Besides being a well-trained scholar, Mounier was a remarkable leader and organizer. Though his financial resources were more than limited, he published his review regularly, formed a militant élite of young writers and thinkers, stimulated the life of the groups and inspired them with genuine enthusiasm. This quiet, fair-haired young man with the blue eyes of a dreamer, was practical and efficient in his work, and was animated with inexhaustible energy. He was assisted by his young wife, a Belgian teacher, and by a staff of collaborators who devoted themselves to the movement in a spirit of complete self-sacrifice.

When the war broke out in 1939, Mounier was mobilized, like most of his friends, and joined an Alpine regiment. After the collapse of France, the groups of *Esprit* rallied to continue their work. The young men and women who belonged to the movement formed a nucleus of spiritual resistance. The publication of *Esprit* was resumed in Lyons, but only a few copies appeared. In 1941, the review was suppressed by the Vichy government. A year later, Emmanuel Mounier was arrested and interned. He spent many months in prison, was released, and once more arrested. His health was gravely impaired by this ordeal. In the fall of 1942, he was tried, acquitted and finally released. Two years later just before Christmas the review *Esprit* reappeared, again under his leadership.

After the *Personalist Manifesto,* Mounier published little in book form. But his numerous editorials in *Esprit,* his lectures and various essays on contemporary problems before and after the war, form a most important contribution to the development of Christian humanism and of the Catholic social ideal. But what is most remarkable in Mounier is his personality, his extraordinary energy. One must always stress the militant character of his thought which is, as he calls it himself, an "ideological pledge." It is the deep consciousness of the Christian's essential responsibility, the call to fearless action, self-sacrifice and disinterested service which alone can create a more just world, which is Mounier's continual goal.

H. I.

Franz Hermann J. Mueller 1900-

The professional interests of Franz Mueller are in the fields of social history, theoretical sociology, economic theories, and social reform. He is professor and head of the Department of Economics of the College of St. Thomas, St. Paul, Minnesota. For four years, 1936 to 1940, he was an assistant professor of sociology at St. Louis University.

Franz Mueller came to this country in 1936 from Cologne, Germany, where he was assistant director at the Institute for Research in the Social Sciences of the University of Cologne for six years, 1928 to 1934. Born in Berlin-Charlottenburg, Germany, in 1900, he was educated in the Catholic grade school in Berlin-Neukölln. In 1914 he was employed as commercial apprentice by a company for making laboratory equipment. At night he prepared himself for the college entrance examination, which he passed in 1919. He then went to night classes at the Berlin School of Commerce and at the University of Berlin, working from 8:00 A.M. to 5:00 P.M. as a clerk; later working part time at a central bank (Deutsche Bank) in Berlin. After the third semester he was appointed private secretary and assistant to Dr. W. Schücking, professor at the Berlin School of Commerce, and well-known international authority in international law, democratic member of the German Reichstag, and Judge of the Permanent Court of Arbitration at The Hague. Later he became private secretary to Dr. V. Totomianz, also a professor at the Berlin School of Commerce, and international authority on cooperativeness. Both positions not only enabled him to drop all work other than his college and university duties as an assistant and student, but also provided unusual opportunities to widen his intellectual horizon. In 1922 he received the degree of "Diplom-Kaufmann" (equivalent to Master of Business Administration). His thesis dealt with the social theories of St. Thomas Aquinas and was written under the supervision of Werner Sombart, then the leading German economist.

During his studies in Berlin he met and made friends with Father Heinrich Pesch, S.J., famous Catholic economist, and came in close contact with Romano Guardini, professor of theology, and renowned leader of the German liturgical and Catholic youth movements. They, as well as Professor F. W. Foerster and Professor W. Sombart, influenced Franz Mueller greatly. To Father Guardini he owes his first book, which dealt with the life and work of the great German social reformer, Reverend Franz Hitze, *Franz Hitze und sein Werk* (Hamburg, 1928). It was Father Guardini who suggested to the publisher that Franz Mueller be asked to write the book which gained him recognition.

From 1923 to 1925, Franz Mueller studied economics and sociology at the University of Cologne, Germany, under such famous men as Max Scheler and L. V. Wiese. During those years and later he took courses in scholastic philosophy at the Albertus Magnus Academy in Cologne and with the Dominican Fathers there. In 1925, he received the degree of "Doctor rerum politicarum" of the University of Cologne; the title of his dissertation was *Der kapitalistische Unternehmer* (published at Würzburg, in 1926), dealing with the psychology and the functions of the capitalistic entrepreneur. From 1920 to about 1930, Franz Mueller was a leader in the Catholic youth movement in Germany and co-editor of one of its organs, *Vom frohen Leben,* a monthly which fought against a bourgeois interpretation of Christianity, for international reconciliation, against capitalism, for genuine art and for a religious revival. In 1930 he married Therese Geuer of Cologne (Dr. rer. pol., M.A. in Econ.), also active in the Catholic youth movement. Much of Mr. and Mrs. Mueller's religious development was shaped by the spirit of the Benedictine Abbey of Maria Laach in Germany. Mrs. Mueller is well known in this country for her writings in the field of liturgical life in the home.

After his graduation from the University of Cologne, Franz Mueller was appointed director of a welfare agency of the Catholic Charities in Berlin, in 1926; assistant to Professor G. Briefs (now at Georgetown University) at the Graduate School of Engineering in Berlin in 1927 and an assistant to Dr. T. Brauer at the Graduate School of Engineering in Karlsruhe in 1928. He followed Professor Brauer to Cologne and later to St. Paul, Minnesota. While at the University of Cologne, he also lectured at the Christian Trade Union Colleges in Cologne and Königswinter; during those years he was a member of the Round Table Conference of German Catholic social reformers, and vice-chairman of the German Ecumenical Conference for the re-union of the Christian churches. In 1935 Franz Mueller spent several months in England, partly as a guest of the Catholic Workers' College in Oxford.

After the death of Dr. Brauer, he became the latter's successor as chairman of the department of economics of the College of St. Thomas. He is now a member of the editorial board of the *American Catholic Sociological Review* and general editor of *Social Studies: College Series.* He is a member of the American Catholic Sociological Society, the American Sociological Society, the Catholic Economic Association, Alpha Kappa Delta (national honorary sociological fraternity).

Other publications by Franz Mueller are: *Zur Überwindung des modernen Kapitalismus* (overcoming of modern capitalism) (1925); *Alkoholismus und Kapitalismus* (an inquiry into the relationship between alcoholism and capitalism) (1929); *Das Schicksal des alternden Arbeiters* (an extensive factual study on the situation of older workers in industry); *Sozialrechtliches Jahrbuch* (1930); with Reverend W. Schwer, Dean of the School of Divinity of the University of Bonn, *Der deutsche Katholizismus im Zeitalter des Kapitalismus* (German Catholicism in the age of capitalism) (1932); *Heinrich Pesch and his Theory of Christian Solidarism* (1941); with Reverend S. A. Sieber, S.V.D., *Social Life of Primitive Man* (1941); *Economic Aspects of Industrial Decentralization* (1943); *Person and Society according to St. Thomas,* in: *Thomistic Principles in a Catholic School* (1943); edited and annotated W. Schwer's *Catholic Social Theory* (1940), and L. V. Wiese's, *Sociology* (1941). He contributed to the following encyclopedias: *Internationales Handwörterbuch des Genossenschaftswesens; Handwörterbuch der Betriebswirtschaftslehre; Staatslexikon der Görresgesellschaft; Encyclopaedia of the Social Sciences* as well as to many periodicals.

M. H.

Reverend Charles J. Mullaly, S.J. 1877-

For three years Father Charles J. Mullaly was assistant editor of *The Messenger of the Sacred Heart* and for nearly twenty-two years its editor. During his editorship, The Apostleship of Prayer Building was completed, 1922 to 1923. It contains the presses on which *The Messenger of the Sacred Heart* is printed. "Nothing is printed in the building which does not directly pertain to the promotion of the interests of the Sacred Heart." Nearly twenty-five of his forty-nine years as a Jesuit, Father Mullaly spent in the work of the League of the Sacred Heart, and during these years he had the happiness of consecrating two million families to the Sacred Heart and of introducing the First Friday Communion of Reparation into many parishes in the United States.

Father Mullaly was born in Washington, D. C., September 19, 1877, the son of Charles W. and Catherine (Croghan) Mullaly. He was educated at the Immaculate Conception School, Gonzaga High School, and Gonzaga College in Washington, D. C. In the fall of 1893, when he was sixteen years of age and attending "Old Gonzaga," he wrote a poem in honor of the golden jubilee of the Civil War chaplain, Father Francis McAtee, S.J., which appeared in *The Catholic Church News* of Washington, D. C.

In 1895, Father Mullaly joined the Jesuits and studied in the Scholasticates at Frederick and Woodstock, Maryland, and at Tortosa, Spain. While at Frederick, Maryland, in 1899, his first short story appeared in *The Messenger of the Sacred Heart.*

From Tortosa, Catalonia, while a student of theology at the Jesuit Scholasticate in 1909, he sent an article entitled "The Spanish Situation," a vivid story of actual revolution in Catalonia. This won for him a place among the contributors to *America,* and, from 1909 until 1912, he was the Spanish correspondent for *America.*

When he returned to the United States in 1912, he was assigned a professorship at Gonzaga College in Washington, D. C. In 1914 he was transferred to Fordham University, where he became Dean of Discipline, and in 1916 he was a missionary pastor in Reading, Jamaica, British West Indies. The following year he was recalled to New York to become assistant editor of *The Messenger of the Sacred Heart.* In 1920, he began his long term as editor, relinquishing it in 1941 on account of ill health. He also retired as National Director of the Apostleship of Prayer. He was appointed spiritual director of the Jesuit scholastics at the Novitiate of St. Isaac Jogues, Wernersville, Pennsylvania, a post which he now holds in addition to being head of the Spanish department.

Father Mullaly is the author of: *The Priest Who Failed* (1936); *The Bravest of the Virginia Cavalry* (1937); *Spiritual Reflections for Sisters* (Vol. I, 1936, Vol. 2, 1938, and translated into four languages); *Could You Explain Catholic Practices?* (1937). About 180,000 copies of his books have been sold. He was a contributor to *The Catholic Encyclopedia* and has published various pamphlets. He has also written for Spanish and American reviews. During his many years as editor of *The Messenger of the Sacred Heart* he constantly encouraged young Catholic authors, and his own output of articles, stories, etc., was so great that he wrote under three names: his own, and the two pseudonyms, "Paul Winslow" and "Francis Goodwin." Much to his amusement he received, under these three names, pressing invitations to join various literary societies.

M. H.

Reverend Alexander Murphy, O.F.M.
1854-1941

Half a century ago, a young seaman sailed through the Golden Gate into San Francisco, the city so named by pious Spaniards to honor the gentle saint of Assisi. This youth was John Murphy of Greenock, Scotland, serving before the mast. He found his way to the Church of St. Francis and there kneeling, looking up into the face of the saint, he felt insistently "God calls me to His altar." Some time was to pass before this desire was consummated, and in the interim John Murphy returned to Scotland from his one and only sea voyage, which lasted twelve months, sought out a private tutor of Latin and Greek, and for the following six years studied keenly, although engaged in teaching. He then began the study of law, showing brilliant promise. But the call to serve God as a Franciscan persisted and was finally realized when, in 1881 he made his profession at Thielt, Belgium, and was ordained there five years later becoming Father Alexander, O.F.M. A long life followed in the service of God.

Born in Greenock, Scotland, in 1854, the oldest of nine children of Mr. and Mrs. Robert Murphy, Father Alexander from his early years showed diversified talents. His gift for art brought favorable comments from some of Scotland's finest painters. A gift for writing resulted in his leaving several books, touched by the grace and skill of his pen which he used only to write of God and His Blessed Mother, which caused him to be appointed editor of the *Franciscan* magazine. His talent for organization and administration was recognized by his Order, and for two years he was Provincial Definitor, and he also held the post of Commissary for the Third Order.

While stationed at various cities in Scotland and England, chiefly Manchester and Glasgow, he travelled throughout Britain giving retreats, for he had a wonderful gift of uniting people in the battle against evil and a vast understanding and sympathy. His tender love for the Mother of God imbued him with outstanding reverence for motherhood, and one of his gentle prides was that he inspired love and confidence in the children. In 1904 one of his great desires was fulfilled when he was sent as director of a pilgrimage to the Holy Land. From 1918 till 1921 he was rector of the Franciscan College at Buckingham. Service in other parts of England followed, until in 1930 he was appointed to Forest Gate, London. After seven years he was transferred to Glasgow, where he remained, thus attaining his longing to die in the city he loved best. The reward of a long and valued life came in August 1941 when he had reached his eighty-seventh year.

Father Alexander left a number of books, among them: *Veni, Sancte Spiritus; A Catholic Home; A Mother's Letters; The Way of Youth; The Seraph of Assisi;* and *Lives of Franciscan Lay Brothers.* He also wrote the only play in English of the life of St. Lawrence, staged by the boys of his native parish, St. Lawrence, Greenock.

His brother, Robert, died in Australia where he had entered a monastery in his later years, as a brother. Two of Father Alexander's sisters followed him into the Franciscan Order, but of the large family only a married sister, Mrs. Rose Anne O'Donnell survives.

D. D.

Reverend Edward Francis Murphy, S.S.J.
1892-

Born in Salem, Massachusetts, on July 21, 1892, in the shadow of a literary tradition, Edward Francis Murphy attended St. Mary's School, directly opposite the birthplace of the great novelist, Nathaniel Hawthorne. He continued his studies at Epiphany College, Newburgh, New York; St. Joseph's Seminary; St. Charles Seminary, Baltimore; Catholic University, and at the Sorbonne, Paris. In an interview with Mary Frances Putnam of the Associated Press, Father Murphy said: "When I learned that most of Salem's beautiful old mansions were built with the proceeds from that area's early Negro slave traffic and that the first slave ship was constructed in Marblehead, Massachusetts, I felt that New England owed the Negro a debt for having been a factor in his misery, and sought a way of paying my share. I entered the Society of St. Joseph devoted to the evangelization of Negroes in the South."

Father Murphy was ordained to the priesthood in 1919, one year after joining the Josephites. He chose writing as his avocation. In this capacity he has given us a treatise on behaviorism, *New Psychology and Old Religion* (1933); two juvenile books entitled *Two Brothers* (1923) and *Just Jack* (1924); *Between the Golden Lines; Handclasps with the Holy* and a humanized study of the Negro, *The Tenth Man* (1936-37). The novel, *The Scarlet Lily* was written between Christmas, 1943 and Easter, 1944. When he had penned the 80,000 words (in longhand) he entered it in the Bruce-Extension novel contest for the best Catholic novel of the year. He won first place. Father Murphy gives this explanation for writing the novel: "When my last book, *Handclasps with the Holy,* was published, one reviewer remarked that I should have included a vignette of St. Mary Magdalene. I decided to make up for the omission by writing a book on her." When asked for the reason of the title, he said: "The lilies to which Christ referred in His most beautiful parables were scarlet and bent their heads, as if offering their blood to God and their beauty to the earth. In fancy I personified one of them, and the result was that somehow I glimpsed the Magdalene." This novel under the title "Mary Magdalene" will be the first movie produced under the newly formed partnership of David O. Selznick and J. Arthur Rank, an Englishman. Plans are being made to film it against a Palestine background and in the London studios of the new company. In 1946 he published *Road From Olivet,* a sequel to *The Scarlet Lily.* To the Jesuit weekly *America,* the *Extension* magazine and *The Sign,* he became a frequent contributor, while *The Catholic World* and *The American Ecclesiastical Review* are indebted to him for many fine essays.

But life has not left him any too free to transcribe his impressions. As a member of the Society of Joseph for the evangelization of the American Negro and as dean of philosophy and faculty adviser at Xavier University, in New Orleans, Louisiana, he has been able to seize his pen only in rare moments.

To him "the short story is the medium most alive and suitable to the expression of a truth of life or a comment on it." He is impressed that the Greatest of Teachers used this form.

S. M. & P. Mac.

Rosalind Murray (Mrs. Arnold Toynbee)

At the age of eighteen, Rosalind Murray published her first novel, *The Leading Note*. Two other books, *Moonseed* (1911) and *Unstable Ways* (1914), followed. In 1926, the novel *The Happy Tree* was published, and in 1929, the novel *Hard Liberty*. Her most recent book is *Time and Timeless*.

She is the daughter of the distinguished Professor Gilbert Murray and Lady Mary Henrietta Howard (eldest daughter of the ninth Earl of Carlisle). Her father's family was Catholic and Irish. Her great-grandfather emigrated from the County of Limerick after the Napoleonic Wars in which he fought, to escape from the penal laws, under which a Catholic was debarred from promotion in the British Army. This family history made a strong impression on Rosalind as a child.

Rosalind Murray was educated principally at home but spent a good deal of her childhood at the homes of her maternal grandparents in Yorkshire and Cumberland and in Italy.

In September 1913 she married Arnold Joseph Toynbee, an author. The Toynbees have two sons living, Theodore Philip, born in June 1915 and Lawrence, born December 1922.—A son, Anthony, was born September 1914, but died in March 1939.

During World War I, Rosalind Murray was entirely occupied with her children and her domestic duties. She accompanied her husband to the Peace Conference in Paris—her husband being a member of the British Delegation. While there she was an assistant to the Manchester *Guardian* correspondent. Apart from writing, Mrs. Toynbee has never done any professional or public work.

After World War I, she travelled with her husband in the Near East and Central Europe. On one occasion in 1929, she drove by car, with her two children, to Constantinople and back.

In World War II she assisted her husband in his war-time organization of the Royal Institute of International Affairs, of which he has been director since 1925.

In 1932, Rosalind Murray was received into the Church. Her Apologia, in the form of a general consideration of the place of the Christian religion in human experience and of the insufficiency of the humanistic alternative, was written in 1939, under the title *The Good Pagan's Failure.*

M. H.

T. C. Murray 1873-

The "T" stands for Thomas, but the real father of realism in the Irish drama has always preferred to be known simply as T. C. Murray. Born in Macroom, County Cork, 1873, and educated at St. Patrick's College, Dublin, T. C. Murray's avocation has been educational work, but his vocation is the drama.

The beginnings of Irish drama at the Abbey Theatre were poetic. Yeats and Lady Gregory transferred their poetry from legendary kings and heroes to the peasantry, but it was still poetry. Synge, at first mistaken for a realist, merely made his peasants more earthy, but his interest was in poetic speech, and his plots were fantasies, with the exception of *Riders to the Sea,* which alone dealt with tragic realities of the toiling people's lot. But T. C. Murray in all but one of his plays, grapples with typical, potentially tragic problems which beset toiling peasants whose perpetual insecurity breeds narrowness and covetousness and shuts the door against beauty and art and lightness of heart. In *The Pipe of the Fields,* written before 1911 though not published until 1928, Murray projected one of these struggles very feebly indeed; but with *Birthright* (1911) he suddenly arrived at full stature as a great tragic dramatist. *Birthright*—in which unintended fratricide grows out of the conflict between an older son who looks beyond the daily round of toil, and a father and younger son who can think of nothing else—remains a great landmark in the Irish drama; it really brought realism to the Abbey.

A résumé of Murray's subsequent plays is impossible here; but it may be said that excepting *A Spot in the Sun,* they continued to deal grippingly with the lives, hopes and tragedies of the Munster peasantry among whom he was born. It may be said too that from the first he has been a master dramaturgist; and that his reproduction of the peasant speech may be taken as the most authentic in literature, as charming as Synge's and Lady Gregory's transcriptions, but more veracious. Space may be spared for one example—a mother thinking about her son soon to be ordained: "And I often say to myself, whenever the death'll come after, 'twont be so hard at all. 'Twould be a great joy thinking of him saying the Mass for your soul, and all the priests and they chanting the great Latin."

All of Murray's typical plays are shot through with Catholic feeling; the reactions and instinctive customary works of an immemorially Catholic people. And it may be said that at least *Birthright* and *Autumn Fire* are truly great tragedies, which—except for the absence of the machinery of the "gods,"—would satisfy the requirements of Sophocles.

A Spot in the Sun, published in 1938, finds T. C. Murray essaying a drawing-room tragedy, with very feeble results. Murray has also published one work of fiction, *Spring Horizon,* and has contributed extensively to the *Irish Independent, Irish Press,* and *Dublin Magazine.* He is headmaster (retired) of Inchicore Model Schools, Dublin; member of the Irish Academy of Letters; President of the Irish Playwrights' Association; member of the Film Censorship Appeal Board. He married Christina Moylan, and has five children. His recreations are gardening and swimming.

His other books are: *Maurice Harte* and *Stag at Bay* (plays, 1912); *Sovereign Love* and *The Briery Gap* (1917); *Spring* (1918); *Aftermath* (play, 1922); *The Blind Wolf* (1928); *A Flutter of Wings* (1929); *Michaelmas Eve* (1932), and *Illumination* (play, 1939).   S. O.

Benjamin Francis Musser   1889-

Throughout his life Benjamin Musser has been a life time friend and champion of men and things Franciscan as well as the author of many writings on Franciscan subjects and of Franciscan flavor. His special interest is poetry. "Poetry is as necessary for the spirit as is bread for the body," he says, and his output of poetry has been prolific. Moreover, he early entertained the hope of a religious vocation. He was born in Lancaster, Pennsylvania, in 1889, the son of Willis Benjamin and Katharine (Kaufman) Musser, and was educated at the Yeates School and the Episcopal Academy at Philadelphia, being at the time a member of the Episcopalian Church of his parents. Wishing to enter the ministry he began studies at the seminary at Nashotah, Wisconsin, in 1907, but left the following year to become a convert to the Catholic Church (April 18, 1908). His desires then turned toward the Order of Friars Minor, but ill health prevented his fulfilling them. He had attended St. Joseph's Seraphic Seminary, Callicoon, New York. In 1909 he became a member of the Third Order of St. Francis at Camden, New Jersey. In 1921 he married Helen Laning of Wilkes-Barre, Pennsylvania, by whom he has two sons and a daughter.

His first book of verse, *Chiaroscuro,* was published in 1923. Then followed *Untamed* (1927); *Riding at Anchor* (1928); *Selected Poems* (1930); *Bucolics and Caviar* (1930), and *Poems* (1930-33). In 1930 he published two books of prose, *Passion Called Poetry* and *Straws in the Wind;* and in 1932 two others, *One Man Show* and *De Re Franciscana.* Essays on *Franciscan Poets* appeared in 1933. In all he has published some forty volumes, of which the latest is *The Bird Below the Waves,* a collection of spiritual poems. He is the first Poet Laureate of New Jersey, appointed in September 1934. The appointment was ratified by the United States Congress and approved by the Governor of New Jersey. He is represented in one hundred and seven poetry anthologies. He is an Academy member of the Catholic Poetry Society of America.

An outstanding recognition of his allegiance to things Franciscan was the proclamation of the Minister General of the Friars Minor in December 1940 affiliating Benjamin Francis Musser with the First Order, with the right, without taking vows, to use O.F.M. after his name, to wear the complete habit and to other privileges.

C. M. N.

Reverend Urban Nagle, O.P. 1905-

Father Urban Nagle, O.P., has made the name of Blackfriars stand out as the most important Catholic little theatre movement of this generation. Launched at Washington in 1932, the Guild is synonymous with drama wherever Catholic theatre interests are most active. With his aide-de-camp and fellow founder, Father Thomas Carey, O.P., Father Nagle has persuaded the Catholic clergy and laity that, as Bernard Shaw says, "after religion the theatre is the most potent form of propaganda." The Blackfriars now boast guilds in twenty American cities and affiliate chapters in fourteen others. On Broadway in New York the plays are a success.

Father Nagle is not only an organizer but a dramatist in his own right. His first production was a Passion play called *Barter* which was awarded first prize in a drama contest sponsored by Longmans, Green & Company. The next plays may be called a Dominican's concrete thoughts on two of the most dramatic, perhaps melodramatic characters in the history of the order—St. Catherine of Siena and Savonarola. Both have been published, *Catherine, the Valiant* (1931), and *Savonarola,* which has since been included in *Theatre for To-morrow,* a survey of the Catholic tradition in drama and chosen by the Pro Parvulis Club.

Edward John Nagle, Jr. (Father Urban Nagle, O.P.) was born in Providence, Rhode Island, on September 10, 1905. His parents were Edward John, Sr., and Elizabeth (Keefe) Nagle, both Providence born and bred. He received his early education from the School Sisters of Notre Dame and from the Christian Brothers. He won a scholarship to Providence College.

Entering the Dominican order in 1924, he was ordained in Washington in 1931. Two years were spent at Catholic University studying psychology for his Ph.D. degree which he received in 1933. For his dissertation, *Religious Thinking in Boys from 12 to 16 Years Old*, he used the diary examination method and read ten thousand diary entries. For his Lectorate in Sacred Theology, a Dominican degree, Father Nagle wrote on *Psychological Monism.*

From 1933 to 1939, Father Nagle taught at Providence College during the winters and at the Catholic University Summer School, where with Father Carey, he founded the Institute of Dramatic Arts which has since developed into the Department of Speech and Drama. Touring the East in the interests of Blackfriars has absorbed that part of Father Nagle's time that is not given to his present editorial work on the *Holy Name Journal*. The headquarters of the Blackfriars is the office in the same building with their New York little theatre—316 West 57th Street.

A. M.

Esther Neill   1874-

As a daughter of the successful Catholic novelist, Mary T. Waggaman, and the wife of Charles P. Neill, former Commissioner of Labor, who was awarded the Laetare Medal (1922) by Notre Dame University for his outstanding work in the Labor World, Esther Neill is loath to talk of her own work.

She was born in 1874 in Washington, the daughter of Samuel and Mary T. Waggaman. Her father was in the Confederate Army, and later studied medicine. While her father was trying to establish himself in his profession her mother, Mary Waggaman, undertook to finance the family by writing for the secular press. Her mother's example and success seemed to make story telling seem worth while and thus implanted in her daughter Esther a real urge to write.

She was educated by governesses and later sent to Georgetown Visitation Convent. Her first writing was done for the Boston *Pilot* and local papers. Most of her work has been for the Catholic press. For years she was a regular contributor to *The Catholic World* and *Ave Maria*.

Four of her novels have appeared in book form: *The Red Ascent; Barbara's Marriage and the Bishop; Miss Princess;* and *The Tragic City.* Of these, Esther Neill's favorite is *Barbara's Marriage and the Bishop.*

In 1901 she married Charles Patrick Neill, then organizer of the Department of Economics of the Catholic University of America, Washington, D.C.

As the wife of a public man and the mother of four sons, Mrs. Neill says she now lists writing as "one of her hobbies."

She is a woman much interested in charity and her recreations consist in reading and travelling. She resides in Washington, D.C.

E. F.

Covelle Newcomb

Writing "novelized biographies" for the 'teen age group is the forte of Covelle Newcomb. She calls them novelized rather than fictionized biographies because "fiction is more or less associated with untruth. To novelize a 'life,' I merely add backdrops and stage properties. I never consciously falsify a fact. I see nothing gained by it."

This very young author has already written three of these juvenile biographies and one for all ages. *Black Fire,* her first, was published in 1940. It is the story of Henri Christophe, the slaveking of Haiti. Her second appeared in 1941. *The Red Hat* is the story of John Henry Newman. Both were selections of the Pro Parvulis Book Club. Her third, *Vagabond in Velvet,* a life of Cervantes, was published in the fall of 1942, and *Larger Than the Sky: A Story of James Cardinal Gibbons* appeared in 1945. With her husband, Addison Burbank, she brought out *Narizona's Holiday* in 1946. *The Secret Door* also appeared in 1946.

She prefers biography to fiction "because I feel that it has a more permanent value in the reader's later experience whether he is conscious of it or not. Actually, every book of fiction has its hero or heroine; his or her life composes the story, but there are so many great men and women whose lives make dramatic reading that I prefer biography from every standpoint."

In selecting her subject for a biography, Covelle Newcomb is influenced primarily by the character of the man. If she likes his personality, she will "do" his story.

Her decision to write for juveniles was made while studying at New York University. She had just earned her M.A. degree and was a candidate for a Ph.D. degree when she joined a writing class at New York University. Here she wrote her first four or five pieces of fiction "for adult consumption, all of which were about children." Upon reading these pieces, the instructor suggested: "You could write for children, as well as about them. Why don't you?" This encouragement sent her to Dr. Mabel Robinson, an authority on juvenile writing at Columbia University. She began by writing stories, but Dr. Robinson predicted that she would start a book before the term was over. During this spring term in Dr. Robinson's class, she wrote the first five chapters of *Black Fire.* Before the fall term opened, she had sold the novelized biography.

Covelle Newcomb believes that biographies for juveniles should end with the climax of a life. She sees no point in dragging out a story to a man's death, once the dramatic peak has been reached. She considers details, especially sensuous details—texture, smell, sound, etc., important in books for juveniles. She maintains that dialogue and illustrations are of greatest importance.

Covelle Newcomb was born in San Antonio, Texas, of a well-known family. Her paternal grandfather, Colonel James P. Newcomb, was a newspaper veteran in Texas and California. He was a friend of Mark Twain, Bret Harte and O. Henry, and was Secretary of State for seven years under Governor Davis and helped make Texas history. She is also related to the late Professor Simon Newcomb, the only Canadian elected to the American Hall of Fame, and official United States Naval astronomer and mathematician.

Of the three R's in grammar school she liked "reading" best, because it was easiest. This love for reading was never lost. Her high school training was received at the Incarnate Word High School which she liked better than the public grammar school because she got more personal attention. It was here that she was first encouraged to write. Sister M. Clement, C.C.V.I., suggested that she enter an essay contest conducted by the University of Texas. Her essay, based on her grandfather's newspapers, won. She accepted the check but refused the scholarship to the University of Texas. When she moved on to the college (Incarnate Word) she tried another state-wide essay contest and won it, too.

Suddenly beset with a desire to study medicine, she left Incarnate Word College to enter Washington University in St. Louis. Changing her mind about the "pre-med" course, she developed an interest in juvenile delinquency. She hoped to be a child psychiatrist. Deciding, however, that it was not her work, she returned to Incarnate College for another year and then came to New York. It was while taking a postgraduate course in "Nineteenth Century Prose Writers" that Covelle Newcomb became profoundly interested in Newman. Her attachment to him persuaded her to drop the idea of writing her master's thesis on T. S. Eliot in order to write on Newman instead. She chose as her subject *John Henry Newman—A Romantic.*

Covelle Newcomb spent her summers travelling. She prefers the tropics: Dutch West Indies, Haiti, South America, Mexico and Guatemala.

She works best on the crest of a heat wave. Propped up on a day-bed, she holds the typewriter on her knees. She has tried varieties of tables, but is persuaded that her brain works only when her knees hurt. She loves to work, especially after the first draft is down. She begins at six hours a day and works her way up to ten, twelve, sixteen, eighteen, and, during the last mile, works twenty-two hours a day.

Covelle Newcomb is a convert. She came into the Church April 11, 1925. In 1942 she married Addison Burbank.

She collects ancient musical instruments, bells, and owls (stuffed owls *out*) and she spends her spare time in art galleries.

She is an Honorary member of the Eugene Field Society, the Authors' League of America, and a member of the Gallery of Living Catholic Authors. On December 8, 1942, she was presented with the first annual Downey Medal for the Finest American Children's Book of 1941, written in the Catholic tradition. The Downey Medal was established in memory of the Reverend Francis X. Downey, co-founder with Mary Kiely of the Pro Parvulis Book Club.

Douglas Newton 1884-

As Douglas Newton himself modestly confesses, he has the special correspondent's knack for being on the spot, or dropping in just when big news breaks. Thus he happened to be at Vienna during one of its revolutions, at Danzig when British Navy men were attacked, in Yugoslavia when King Alexander was assassinated, and at Sarajevo at the moment that made it famous in history.

He has remained primarily a newspaperman, though he has written twenty-six novels under his own name and ten others under various pen-. names. He has also written several short stories and serials. His short stories appeared in *The Saturday Evening Post, Liberty, Harper's, The Catholic World, The Sign,* and many others. He always had the urge for writing both in school and after. The arts were in his blood, for though his father's family was made up of engineers, chemists and builders, on his mother's side he springs from a family of musicians and actors.

He describes his boyhood as a mingling of music and blue prints. The fireside conversation embraced everything from painting to geology, and from engineering to music and the latest books. But above all, the topic under constant discussion was that of the Faith. Now he seems to have passed the same thing on to his seven children (one son and four daughters are living), whom he says are all "infected with Catholic Action" while their mother (Winifred Henna, whom he married in 1912) is "valiant in the Faith." Theirs sounds like a tumultuous and busy and happy household.

Born in London on September 9, 1884, of Irish and Scots extraction, he was educated first at St. Aloysius' College, Highgate, and then, as a lay boy at St. Edmund's College, Ware, Herts. He then tried his hand in an engineering shop, at architecture, insurance and many other occupations. While he learned much from them he didn't like any of them. But because of his itch to write he managed to get out of the steady job that followed, exchanging a seven-hour day of drudgery in an office for a twelve-hour day of "freedom." This went on until, wishing to marry, he again sought a job that would bring in a salary, and so in turn edited a suburban paper, acted as private secretary to Arnold Bennett, and as assistant to T. P. O'Connor on T. P.'s weekly.

World War I gave him his chance. He fell in with the future Lord Tweedsmuir, then John Buchan, who found use for his services in the writing of propaganda at the War Office. At the close of the war, he went to the Peace Conference as liaison for the American war correspondents and afterwards was employed by the London *Daily Chronicle,* his work being syndicated to The New York *Times* and other American and

Canadian newspapers. Later he was one of the five correspondents who accompanied H.R.H. the Prince of Wales (now Duke of Windsor) throughout his tour through Canada and the U.S.A.

All this time he was still wedded to his first love, fiction, writing a novel or two a year. Some of his novels are social studies, such as: *Low Ceilings; Sookey; Eyes of Men;* and *Infinite Morning.* He also produced his "Savaran" series and a highly exciting adventure thriller of the Bela Kuhn episode in Hungary under the title of *The Red Judas.* *Dr. Odin* was a thriller, prophetic of Hitler's mad Nordicism not then grasped by the world. And he wrote, "I have got a great deal of fun out of writing adventure and thriller stories, and a certain amount of solid satisfaction over my more serious work. His first novel was *War.* The manuscript was rejected by thirteen publishers, because, in those days, "people were quite sure there would never be another large scale war, and certainly, as a critic said, after Methuen had published the book, never a war as terrible as I had made it—we'd become far too civilized."

His finest novel is *Dark Pathway.* This is the history of several generations of Sussex ironfounders. The power of the book is the sombre sculpturing of the figures and the quiet narrative of their doom.

Meanwhile short stories and articles poured from his never silent typewriter. If Catholic papers got some of them, more went to such publications as the *Saturday Evening Post, Liberty,* the *Pictorial Review* and *Harper's.* His range was from the "pulps" to the *Dial.* And several of them were bought for the movies. The only trouble about these was that there seemed to be no relation between the work for which he had received his pay cheque and what he eventually saw upon the screen. He says himself that he has "no special vein," but writes leaders, humor, thrillers, realism, fantasy and social studies with equal impartiality. His work has something more than journalistic facility. Its professional competence often conceals from the unprofessional reader the fact that it has been produced by a man of genuine literary gifts.

Living now at Ealing, a London suburb, he is extremely active on various Catholic and journalistic committees. He was one of the foundation members of the English Catholic Writers Guild of St. Francis de Sales, of which he is now chairman and he makes it his hobby to encourage Catholics to read books by Catholics. He "writes and circulates reading lists to this end wherever and whenever possible—and even oftener." As a member of the editorial board of the Catholic weekly, the *Universe,* he is able to do a good deal in this direction.

Others of his books are: *Westward With the Prince of Wales* (the fruit of his going with the present Duke of Windsor on his tour through Canada); *The Jade Green Garter; The Golden Cat,* and *The Beggar.* He also helped T. P. O'Connor in editing his *Journal of the Great War.* Everything, in short, is grist that comes to his mill. And his mill grinds without ceasing. Douglas Newton has served the Catholic cause well, especially in his efforts to create a public that, in his own words, "will support and encourage our craftsmen, particularly the young, and so build up a body of healthy literature strong enough to fight the pagans in their own field and, please God, beat them."

Most Reverend John Francis Noll   1875-

Born in Fort Wayne, Indiana, in 1875, the Most Reverend John Francis Noll received Baptism, Confirmation, First Communion and Holy Orders and was consecrated Bishop of the Diocese of Fort Wayne in its Cathedral of the Immaculate Conception. He is therefore closely identified with his city and state, of which his father, John G. Noll, was also a native. His mother, Anna (Ford) Noll, was born in London, of Irish parentage. As a boy, Bishop Noll attended the Cathedral Brothers' School, and in 1888 went from there to St. Lawrence College, Mount Calvary, Wisconsin, where he completed his classical studies in 1893. He then went to Mt. St. Mary's Seminary in Cincinnati, Ohio, for his philosophy and theology, and was ordained in 1898.

After the young priest had served nine months as assistant at Elkhart and Logansport, he held pastorates at Kendalville, 1899 to 1902; Besancon, 1902 to 1906; Hartford City, 1906 to 1910, and Huntington, 1910 to 1925. He wrote his first book, *Kind Words from Your Pastor* (1904), while at Besancon. In 1912 he founded *Our Sunday Visitor,* which has become a nationally read weekly and he remains its editor-in-chief. His *Father Smith Instructs Jackson* was published in 1913, and in 1914 appeared *The Fairest Argument.* He was appointed Domestic Prelate in 1921, and in 1923 he built a Training School and Novitiate for the Society of Missionary Catechists, founded in Huntington in 1918. This organization now has one hundred sixty professed catechists and its members are working in New Mexico, California, Nevada, Texas, Utah, as well as in Indiana. In addition to this large structure Bishop Noll's personally directed building projects have included the largest Catholic printing plant in the United States, two large high schools, a modern orphanage, a preparatory seminary. Through *Our Sunday Visitor* he raised a large fund for the erecting of a colossal statue of Christ, the Light of the World, and the façade of the new headquarters of the National Catholic Welfare Conference in Washington, D.C.

Bishop Noll has been head of the See of Fort Wayne, since June 1925. As a member of the episcopate, he has served on the Administrative Board of the National Catholic Welfare Conference and is now Chairman of the N.C.W.C. Department of Lay Organizations, also of the Committee on Clean Literature, the Committee on the Census, and a member of the Committee for Catholic Refugees and of the Legion of Decency. For seventeen years he was treasurer of the American Board of Catholic Missions. In 1941 he was made an Assistant at the Pontifical Throne.

His other books are: *Our National Enemy Number One* (1942); *The Decline of Nations* (1940); *It Is Happening Here; Civilization's Builder and Protector; Catholic Facts,* and *History of the Diocese of Fort Wayne.* He also wrote about thirty pamphlets.   C. M. N.

Mrs. George Norman *see* Melesina Mackenzie Blount

Kathleen Thompson Norris 1880-

A small house in the heart of a redwood forest, near San Francisco, was the childhood home of Kathleen Norris, the daughter of James Alden and Josephine (Moroney) Thompson. There, with her brothers and two sisters, she lived the simple, emotional and united life of a big family until the death of her parents within a month of each other. The years had been rich in faith, goodness and mutual love, but there was little of material wealth. The sudden bereavement left Kathleen, at the age of nineteen, with the responsibility of caring for the others.

They moved to a small apartment in San Francisco, and her oldest brother helped with the support of the family. Kathleen worked first in a hardware store and then in a library. Here she was in the midst of the books she loved which had whiled away so many earlier carefree hours. Of those childhood days in the country she writes: "We raked books off the shelves by the dozen and hauled them along on picnics, to haylofts, up oak trees, to bath and to bed. The one terrifying possibility was to find oneself without a book." During winter evenings in San Francisco one of the six would be a storyteller for the others who gathered around a lamp to listen. "For whole years of winter evenings this was my proud responsibility," writes the storyteller for a now much larger audience.

Settlement work next occupied the future writer, and she grew to know well the old San Francisco: the tangled buildings of Chinatown, the tree-shaded streets of the Mission and the Spanish houses on Nob Hill. But these last were more especially the background for her work as Society Editor of the San Francisco *Bulletin*. Her association with this paper marked the beginning of her writing career. After some discouragement, her first story, *The Colonel and the Lady,* appeared in the San Francisco *Argonaut,* in 1904.

At a skating party, while reporting for the San Francisco *Call,* she met Charles Norris, then with *Sunset Magazine.* Their romance was enhanced by their eager hopes for literary success. Charles Norris went East, and Kathleen followed. They were married in New York in 1909. He was then on the *American Magazine.* She was at first hesitant about writing for fear of the criticism she might receive, but she was encouraged when a short short-story was awarded a prize by the New York *Evening Telegram.* Many rejection slips preceded the final acceptance of her stories by the magazines: *Atlantic Monthly, McClure's, American Magazine* and *Munsey's.* Her big success came with the publication of *Mother* by *American Magazine.* So warmly was it received that she enlarged the story into a book, which was published in 1911. "I wheeled a baby carriage past those bookstore windows," writes Kathleen Norris, "and stood enraptured looking at the dark blue cover and the neat little box on which the single word 'Mother' was stamped." Its appearance was signalled by an unprecedented offer from Edward Bok, editor of the *Ladies' Home Journal,* to publish it in serial form. This was a departure from editorial custom and won the story innumerable readers. The book has sold over a million and a half copies and has appeared in twenty different editions.

Though the author felt she had poured all she had to give into this book, others quickly followed: *Saturday's Child* (1914); *The Story of Julia Page* (1915); and *The Heart of Rachel* (1916), were early predecessors of the much later: *Certain People of Importance* (1922); *Passion Flower* (1930), and *Younger Sister* (1932)—about seventy novels in all. *My San Francisco* (1932), and *My California* (1933), describe her beloved city and state, where she and her husband returned to live.

Mr. Norris died on July 25, 1945. In her Palo Alto estate in California, she welcomed many friends as well as the family, sons, nephews and nieces. In 1946 she sold this place to buy a modern home in San Francisco.

Her short stories are numerous. So facile is her pen that her manuscripts bear few corrections. Easily written and easy to read, her works are very popular but not distinctively great. Family relationships are her favorite theme, studies of people in everyday life, in love, in joy and sorrow, in hope and fear. Her characters are real. They are typical Americans, often of Irish stock. She has faith in human nature and in God. She has sentiment, wit and a skill in picturesque phrasing. Unfortunately, in recent years there is an occasional leniency toward divorce. As a columnist Mrs. Norris has taken a definite stand against divorce. An excellent collection of her works is presented in *These I Like Best* (1941), which contains her three favorite novels: *Little Ships, Barberry Bush,* and *Mother;* five short stories and an essay, *Beauty in Letters.* This last shows how keenly she appreciates the finest in literature.

She is the author of: *Angel In the House* (1933); *Beauty and the Beast* (1928); *Walls of Gold* (1933); *What Price Peace?* (1928); *Wife for Sale* (1933); *Dina Cashman* (1941); *An Apple for Eve* (1942); *Corner of Heaven* (1943); *Burned Fingers* (1944).

C. M. N.

Alfred Noyes 1880-

Poet, essayist and novelist, Noyes is best known as a poet, perhaps the most notable of the Catholic poets. He began writing verse while at Exeter College, Oxford—where he was also a skilled oarsman—and published his first volume, *The Loom of Years* (1902) at the age of twenty-two. He had the rare experience of being immediately hailed as a genius and the popularity of his verse: *The Flower of Old Japan* (1903); *Poems* (1904); *The Forest of Wild Thyme* (1905), secured him a public which few poets can obtain. Another unusual feature of his early success was the publication serially, 1906 to 1908, in *Blackwood's Magazine* of his long poem, *Drake: An English Epic*. During this time there also appeared a fifth volume of verse, *Forty Singing Seamen* (1907) and a sixth, *The Enchanted Island* (1909), followed.

In 1907 he married Garnett Daniels, daughter of Colonel B. G. Daniels of the United States Army. Noyes was born in Staffordshire, but during his childhood lived near the coast. His love of the English countryside and the sea find expression in his verse. From America, too, he drew inspiration. In 1913 he came to the United States to deliver a series of lectures at Lowell Institute, Boston, on *The Sea in English Poetry*. Yale awarded him an honorary degree of Litt.D. From Glasgow he received an honorary LL.D. He became visiting professor of English literature at Princeton, from 1914 to 1923, where he enjoyed great popularity, and edited a *Book of Princeton Verse* (2 vols., 1916-19). He was temporarily attached to the British Foreign Office in 1916, and was appointed Commander of the Order of the British Empire in 1918. A horror of war prompted his writing *The Wine-Press: A Tale of War,* the epilogue of which, a plea for peace, had the singular honor of being included in the *Congressional Record* (1913). In *Lucifer's Feast* he describes the hideous carnage of war so soon to follow in the years 1914 to 1918.

In 1913 he published *Tales of the Mermaid Tavern,* tales of Will Shakespeare, Kit Marlowe, Ben Jonson and others, as heard by

> "A leather-jerkined pot-boy to these gods,
> A prentice Ganymede to the Mermaid Inn."

Narrative and description are enriched by the color and romance of Elizabethan days. Diverse mood is expressed in interwoven refrains. The blank verse is supple, the ballads rollicking. *Drake* is a poem of the same historic era: twelve books of blank verse narrate the exploits of England's great Admiral. Interspersed are fine lyrics which obviate monotony, the metre being suited to the variant theme. Swinburne called it "a noble work . . . a gifted painter, skilled in his craft, has, with signal success, made of the sky a studio; and for a canvas upon which to paint his picture, he has taken the sea."

The greatest of Noyes' works is *The Torchbearers,* a trilogy narrating the discoveries of science, which he conceives as a torch to be carried through the ages. The idea of the epic narrative came to him when in the Sierra Madre Mountains he observed the trial of the new one hundred-inch telescope, and his first volume, *The Watchers of the Sky* (1922), tells of the astronomers, Copernicus, Tycho Brahe, Galileo, Newton and the Herschels, each receiving and adding to the light of his predecessor's discovery. In the second book, for which he first received inspiration from the marvelous wonder of the Grand Canyon, he writes of the physical scientists: Pythagoras, Aristotle, Avicenna, Lamarck, Linnaeus, Goethe, Darwin. The light of the torch still held aloft by Lamarck is later nearly extinguished, for too close to the earth is the vision of modern scientists, and *The Book of Earth* (1925) ends on a tragic note of frustration. In the prologue to the third volume the poet writes:

"—when it was darkest I came to a strong city."

This is the City of God. Long a Catholic at heart, Noyes took the final step into the Church in 1927, and in the last of the trilogy, *The Last Voyage* (1930), he writes with the conviction of faith. Here enter the medical scientists and metaphysicists. All the marvels of modern science lend aid toward the recovery of a child dying on a ship at sea. The wireless operator obtains for the doctor who operates on the child consultation with a skilled surgeon many miles away. The discoveries of Harvey, Lister and Pasteur all play a part, but the child dies. Then comes the spiritual climax of the Mass following the tragedy, and the vision of an ordered universe, with Christ the Light of the World.

A deep spirituality is noted throughout Noyes' writings, even from his earliest poem, *The Symbolist.* Of rare beauty, tender and sweet, are *Slumber Songs of the Madonna* to her Divine Child. His *Creation* is a profound, mystical poem. In answer to those who doubt the true origin of life he wrote *Before the World,* which ends:

"You found on that dark road you trod
In the beginning—God."

Favorites among his collected poems, now published in three volumes, are *The Highwayman* and *The Barrel-Organ* with its lilting refrain, "Come down to Kew in lilac-time." The story of *Robin Hood* he fashioned into a five-act play (1911), and another play, in one act, is *Rada: A Belgian Christmas Eve* (1914).

In *Orchard's Bay* (1939) forty poems are interspersed amid reflections in his garden. Other essays are contained in *Pageant of Letters* (1940) in which eighteen writers from Chaucer to Meynell are ably and critically appraised; the discussion on "poetry and reality" was delivered as a lecture before the Royal Institution of Great Britain. Also, critical writings in prose are: *Some Aspects of Modern Poetry* (1924), and *The Opalescent Parrot* (1929). "Poetry is music," says Noyes, and in his own adherence to nineteenth-century traditions as well as in outspoken criticism he holds "modern" verse unworthy of the poetic muse. Some find fault with his romantic diction and conformity with an outmoded poetic style. Yet he is a master of rhythm and new metres. His verse reveals such variations as internal rhyme with another word in the same stanza, rhymes at the beginning instead of at the end of a line, and ten stanzas with the same rhyme.

In 1934 he wrote *The Unknown God*, the story of his conversion, which has been described as "the spiritual biography of a generation." In 1936 he wrote *Voltaire*. His portrayal of the French unbeliever surprised his readers. In 1938 it was censored by the Holy Office until certain emendations were made. It was then submitted to a Westminster Board of Censorship, and Noyes expressed his willingness to abide by their decisions. In conformity with their recommendations a new edition appeared in 1939, in which no alterations were made in the text but in a new Preface to the book the author explains certain passages the meaning of which it is possible to misconceive, and thus makes clear that he holds no unorthodox views.

He wrote a novel, *The Sun Cure*, in 1929. In 1940 another novel, *No Other Man*, was published. This is a remarkable book visioning the possible final catastrophe when man's hate for man, let loose in war, exterminates all peoples. Only two, a man and a woman, survive to carry on the human race. The conditions leading up to and attending this destruction are powerfully limned by the author through the eyes of his hero and heroine, and the closing chapter is as balm to the tortured world. His poem, *If Judgment Comes* (1941), is an indictment of Hitler as arch villain in the tragedy on the world's stage of the twentieth century. *Shadows on the Down* and other poems (1941) is the first collection of his poems in sixteen years. In *Poems of the New World* (1943), Dr. Noyes "has collected all his verse about America, as a tribute from an Englishman to the New World." His latest book is *The Golden Book of Catholic Poetry* (1946).

Noyes during 1940 to 1941 lectured in Canada and the United States. In 1927 he married Mary Angela Mayne, widow of Richard Weld-Blundell, his first wife having died in 1926.

In 1944 he was awarded the Downey Award made annually by the Pro Parvulis Book Club for his book, *The Secret of Pooduck Island*.

C. M. N.

Rosemary Obermeyer (Mrs. Anthony Formolo)
1903-

"I was born in the little town of Iron Mountain, Michigan, about the time the last big lumber drive went down the Menominee in 1903. My childhood was a happy one. Living in the outskirts of the town, as we did, we had an unrivalled view of a little lake surrounded by hills, and that reflected all the moods of the western sky. Sometimes it lay becalmed, like a magical green mirror. At other times, wild and white with fury, its tossing waves showed like angry teeth. During a sunset, the most exquisite ferny green, wild rose and saffron bloomed upon it," writes Rosemary (Obermeyer) Formolo. She was educated at St. Mary's, Notre Dame, the University of Michigan and Columbia University. From the latter institution she received her Master's degree in English. While at the University of Michigan she wrote a fairy tale called "The Fairy Philosopher" which has been the nucleus for almost everything she has done since. After graduation she taught English at Mooseheart, Illinois.

For a hobby she wrote plays, short stories, fairy tales and novels. "Finally there grew and matured within me," she says, "a fantastic sort of yarn that gave me a good many chuckles and a most deep satisfaction. I mulled over it for about five years, filling notebooks and reconstructing the plot hundreds of times. When I felt ready, I resigned my job, entered the Hopwood Awards contest at the University of Michigan and wrote *Golden Apples of the Sun* in six months." Published in 1943, this first novel is the story of the orphaned gypsy girl, Rhona, and her adventures.

Rosemary Obermeyer is married to Anthony Formolo. They have a daughter, Mary Angela.   M. H.

Edward Joseph Harrington O'Brien   1890-1941

Though born in the United States in Boston in 1890, Edward J. O'Brien left this country in 1922 and went to England to live. For some years he lived in Switzerland. When, in 1937, he became European Story Editor for the Metro-Goldwyn-Mayer British Studios, he returned to London. He resigned in 1939. Two years later he died at his home, Garrard's Cross, Buckinghamshire, February 25, 1941.

He was educated at Boston College and Harvard (non-graduate), and was married twice, first to Romer Wilson, the novelist, of Sheffield, England, who died in 1930, then to Ruth Gorgel of Hamburg, Germany. By his first wife he had one son; by his second wife, two daughters. He was assistant editor of the *Poetry Journal,* 1912 to 1915, and of *Poet Lore,* 1914 to 1915, and published two volumes of verse, *White Fountains* and *Distant Music.* His prose works are: *The Forgotten Threshold; The Advance of the American Short Story; Hard Sayings; The Dance of the Machines,* and *Son of the Morning.* He also wrote two plays, *The Flowing of the Tide* and *The Bloody Fool* and translated works from the French. But he is best known as an editor and anthologist, and especially as an authority on the short story. From 1915 until his death he annually edited *The Best Short Stories.* The 1941 edition was published posthumously with a memorial introduction by Martha Foley who carries on the series. With John Cournos he edited the first four volumes of *Best British Stories* which he published from 1921 to 1940. He also edited *The Fifty Best Short Stories* (1914 to 1939); *The Twenty-Five Finest Short Stories; The Great Modern English Stories; Modern English Short Stories; New English Short Stories; Modern American Short Stories,* and *The Guest Book.* He did not consider the large circulation magazines a final authority on choice of material and consistently pushed the unknown writer. His choice is therefore controversial, but his judgment sincere and generally sound. He had a system, known as the "Yearbook of the American Short Story," of grading the merit of selected stories by stars, such as a tabloid newspaper grades motion pictures. Other books edited by him are: *Poems of the Irish Revolutionary Brotherhood; The Masque of Poets; The World's History at a Glance,* and *Walks and Talks about Boston.*

C. M. N.

Reverend Isidore (George) O'Brien, O.F.M.
1895-

For his regular contributions to the *Anthonian,* quarterly publication of St. Anthony's Guild, the Reverend Isidore O'Brien, O.F.M., is known to the large Guild membership, and his numerous pamphlets and many books are also widely read.

He was born in 1895 in Braid, County Antrim, Ireland, where it is said St. Patrick learned to speak Gaelic and began his conversion of the Irish. After he had completed his education in the National Schools and St. Louis College, County Westmeath, George O'Brien came to the United States in 1921, and entered the Franciscan Order at St. Bonaventure Monastery, Paterson, New Jersey, on August 15th of that year. Professed in simple vows in 1922 and in solemn vows in 1925, he pursued the study of philosophy at St. Stephen's Monastery, Croghan, New York, and St. Bonaventure College, Alleghany, New York, where he completed his theology.

He was ordained priest in 1928 and afterwards taught at St. Bonaventure College. He was stationed at St. Francis of Assisi Monastery, New York City, and its affiliate School of Sacred Eloquence, and is now back at St. Bonaventure College.

Among his books are *Enter St. Anthony,* a vivid biography of the wonderworker of Padua; *The Life of Christ* written for the laity in general and recommended by the Confraternity of Christian Doctrine, and *Mirror of Christ, St. Francis of Assisi,* 1944. This biography of St. Francis was selected by the Spiritual Book Associates as the book of the month for October. The most recent of his more than twenty booklets is *The Plain Truth,* an outline of the Catholic religion, demonstrating the main teachings of the Church. Father O'Brien also contributes to many periodicals, and lectures on Catholic subjects.

C. M. N.

Reverend John Anthony O'Brien   1893-

Ever since the day of Father O'Brien's graduation from college, he hoped "that in some way, I might be privileged to study and teach—a hope that was to be realized beyond my fondest dream."

John A. O'Brien was born in Peoria, Illinois, on January 20, 1893, the son of John Francis and Elizabeth T. (Powers) O'Brien. His early education was received at St. Patrick's School in his native city of Peoria and at Spalding Institute, founded by John Lancaster Spalding, the first bishop of Peoria. "For four years," he tells us, "I was engaged in an unremitting fight for first place against two more gifted rivals. I had to burn the midnight oil and work like a galley slave to emerge valedictorian by the skin of my teeth."

From Spalding he went to Holy Cross College at Worcester, Massachusetts. Here he felt "the love of literature, first kindled in me by my mother, growing into a consuming flame." Since he was only seventeen years old at the time and a thousand miles away from home he suffered from nostalgia and longed for spring.

In the fall he went to St. Viator's College in the quaint French village of Bourbonnais to study philosophy with the Clerics of St. Viator. During these days he had the supreme joy to lead a debating team over to Notre Dame to vanquish the "Irish" in old Washington Hall.

After graduation he decided to study for the priesthood, and his first thought was to enter the Society of Jesus. He was twenty then and since ordination in the Society does not ordinarily occur much before one is thirty-three he turned to the diocesan priesthood as his father, none too well, hoped to live to see him ordained.

At twenty-three he was ordained by Bishop Edmund M. Dunne of Peoria. He then took up studies for the doctorate at Catholic University. A year later, when the Catholic students at the University of Illinois petitioned Bishop Dunne for a chaplain, Father O'Brien was selected to minister to them. As the attendance of Catholic students was less than three hundred Father O'Brien found time to complete his studies and to receive the Ph.D. degree in psychology being the first priest to receive that doctorate from that institution. While there he discovered that there was a grotesquely small percentage of Catholics on the faculty of this institution of higher learning supported by the taxes of all the citizens of the State. From then on he proclaimed in season and out of season that Catholics in their proportionate numbers should be on the faculties of such universities. It was this profound conviction that led him to project and publish a symposium *Catholics and Scholarship,* in which this question and kindred ones are thoroughly explored by a variety of eminent scholars.

While at the University, he also deplored the fact that students were receiving instruction in all the fields of culture save religion. One day he called upon two of the leading ministers on the campus, Dr. James C. Baker of the Wesley Foundation and Dr. Stephen E. Fisher of the Christian Foundation and suggested that they present a united front in petitioning the university for the granting of credit for courses in religion to be offered by the respective churches or foundations. They and their colleagues were quick to respond. The faculty studied the plan for about six months and then adopted it. The religious foundation determines the content of the courses while the university has the right to see that the academic standards maintained by the university are met by the religious foundation, as by all other educational institutions which she has accredited.

To meet the requirements of the university authorities, Father O'Brien organized the Newman Foundation. He secured a frame house and tore down the partitions between the rooms to make a classroom, a library and a weekday chapel. Then began the teaching of systematic courses in religion, apologetics, ethics and church history to the students at Illinois, particularly to those of the Catholic faith. In a few years it was necessary to build a new church, and resident halls.

Catholic students brought their problems to Father O'Brien. One of the difficulties confronting the students was the general doctrine of organic evolution. Father O'Brien made an exhaustive study of this subject for fifteen years and embodied his results in his book *Evolution and Religion.*

For those who wished to know the teaching of the Catholic religion and the credentials of her divine origin, enquiry classes were established and met two nights per week for three months. Priests who had achieved success in convert work were asked to detail their methods of procedure and to make suggestions based on their experience. The symposium was published in 1925 under the title *The White Harvest.*

Then realizing that a book was needed which would present the doctrines and credentials of our Faith to gear into the intellectual mood of our day, Father O'Brien wrote *The Faith of Millions*. Fifteen years of labor were expended on this book but its sale surpassed all anticipations. In a period of five years, the amazing mark of 150,000 has been reached. In 1945 it had reached 200,000 sales.

During Father O'Brien's twenty-two years at Illinois he instructed about eight hundred members of the inquiry classes.

When the Catholic enrollment at the university had grown to 1,500, Father O'Brien urged his ecclesiastical superiors to turn over the student parish and the Newman Foundation to a religious order. The offer was accepted by the Benedictines.

Father O'Brien's long delayed sabbatical year came at last, in the summer of 1939. He spent it at Oxford University, England. Since his return in 1940 he has been teaching the philosophy of religion at Notre Dame University.

The summer of 1942 was spent in Mexico renewing acquaintances with prelates, priests and Indians he had met in his travels there six years previously. The results of his observations and study were embodied in his *Discovering Mexico,* written in a popular, journalistic style.

Although Father O'Brien is the author of some fifteen volumes in the field of philosophy, religion and science, he has never found writing easy. "It has always been the fruit of mental travail and painful gestation. After twenty-five years of rather copious writing, this still remains true."

He is the author of: *Silent Reading* (1921); *Reading: Its Psychology and Pedagogy* (1924); *Priesthood in a Changing World* (1938); *The Power of Love* (1938); *Religion in a Changing World* (1938); *The Church and Marriage; Pathways to Happiness; Thunder from the Left, Truths Men Live By* (1946).

M. H.

Kate O'Brien   1898-

Kate O'Brien, journalist, novelist and playwright is one of the best stylists of contemporary English fiction. She was born in Boru House, Limerick, Ireland, the daughter of Thomas and Catherine (Thornhill) O'Brien and was educated at Laurel Hill Convent in that county and at University College, Dublin. Her writing career began on the staff of the Manchester *Guardian*. Her first novel, *Without My Cloak* (1931), won the Hawthornden Prize that year. It is a family chronicle, the scene of which is Ireland in the Victorian period. The strength and beauty of its prose and the forceful-ness of its character portrayal show Kate O'Brien's power. The next story, *The Anteroom,* published in 1934, is a romantic novel in which three days in the life of a prosperous Irish family, the Mulqueens, are portrayed. In it she makes the most of a dramatic situation.

In *Pray for the Wanderer* (1938) there is a "conflict of two moralities that of the 'individualistic' artist and that of puritanism" as a reviewer in the *New Yorker* puts it.

Miss O'Brien has also written three plays: *The Bridge, The Schoolroom Window* and *Distinguished Villa* (1927). The travel book *Farewell Spain* (1937) recalls the things that delighted her during her many visits to Spain in the years before the war. The description of the Spanish countryside and of Spanish architecture leaves a vivid impression. Miss O'Brien lived in Bilbao in 1923.

The novelist's love for Spain was earlier shown in a story of the Abelard-Heloise genre, *Mary Lavelle* (1936). *The Land of Spices* (1941) is exquisitely written. "The land of spices—something understood" was Henry Vaughan's lovely, poet's description of prayer. "The scene is an Irish convent, a branch of a French order for the training of young ladies." The time is the early 1900's. And the flavor of the seventeenth century blends with the thoughts of its nun heroine Mother Helen Archer whose scholar father had bred in her the literary tradition. Too, the character of Helen Archer shows, in the truest sense of the author of the *Imitation,* a noble nature moving towards perfection by grace. So the fine gifts of Kate O'Brien lead us to hope that in her writing career she will follow the precepts set forth in that rugged Chapter Fifty-four.

In her book *The Last of Summer,* Miss O'Brien gives us a study of an emotional, psychological crisis in the lives of several individuals during the summer, 1939." The dramatic episode takes place in neutral Ireland. *Diaries and Journals* was published in 1945. *For One Sweet Grape* (1946) is a deeply moving novel based on the life of Ana de Mendoza, sixteenth century Spanish heiress.

Kate O'Brien lives in England.

A. M. & M. H.

Michael Joseph O'Brien   1870-

Michael Joseph O'Brien was born at Fermoy, County Cork, Ireland, April 5, 1870, the son of Michael and Hannah (O'Mullane) O'Brien. He was educated at the Christian Brothers' School and St. Colman's College, both in Fermoy. He did not graduate from college owing to the necessity of obtaining employment. He has three daughters. His wife died in 1935.

Employed as a clerk in the office of the Crown Prosecutor, Fermoy, 1888, Michael J. O'Brien was simultaneously a member of a patriotic revolutionary society. When he discovered a letter in which British Prime Minister Lord Salisbury directed the Crown Prosecutor to secure without fail the conviction of two popular leaders then on trial, namely William O'Brien, M.P., and the Reverend Canon Keller, young Michael sent an impression copy of the letter to Timothy Healy, M.P., who in turn gave it to the Irish Parliamentary leader Parnell; the latter made dramatic use of it in the House of Commons. Suspicion falling on the young clerk, he fled to England and thence to America. Arriving in New York on July 4, 1889, Michael J. O'Brien secured employment with the Western Union Telegraph Company, with which he remained until his retirement in 1935.

In the early 1900's Mr. O'Brien began systematic research into the history of the Irish in America. His first essay in this field appeared in the *Journal of the American Irish Historical Society* for 1910. From 1912 to 1932 he was Historiographer of that society. He has not only written but lectured extensively on his chosen subject. In 1932 the National University of Ireland conferred upon Michael J. O'Brien the honorary degree of Doctor of Laws. Dr. O'Brien is a member of various state and regional historical societies. In 1920 he was made an honorary member of the Friendly Sons of St. Patrick.

While he has had predecessors and contemporaries in the field of Irish-American history, Michael J. O'Brien is universally conceded pre-eminence. His principal work, *A Hidden Phase of American History* (1919), establishes forever the facts about the very large Irish population in the Thirteen States at the time of the Revolution, and the leading part they played in the establishment of our independence. This book, distributed to all members of Congress, greatly influenced the two houses of that body toward the passage of resolutions supporting Irish claims to self-determination. Dr. O'Brien's writings are distinguished by the most meticulous documentation. All his vacations, holidays and spare time for many years were spent in research among original records and documents of the Colonial and Revolutionary periods. Avoiding all unsubstantiated claims, he has compelled recognition, which many biased and bigoted historians tried to withhold, of the numerical, political and moral importance of the Irish in laying the foundations of our Republic. He is now working on a book to be called *Celtic Footprints In the Mohawk Valley.*

He wrote the following: *A Hidden Phase of American History; Early Irish Settlers in Kentucky; In Old New York; The McCarthys in Early American History; An Alleged First Census of the American People, 1699; Irish Pioneers in Connecticut; Irish Schoolmasters in the American Colonies; George Washington's Associations with the Irish; Hercules Mulligan, Confidential Correspondent of General Washington; Pioneer Irish in New England; Timothy Murphy, Hero of the American Revolution;* and numerous articles in the *Journal of the American Irish Historical Society* and elsewhere, not yet gathered into book form.

                                                                    S. O.

Seumas O'Brien 1880-

Of Seumas O'Brien's book *The Whale and the Grasshopper, and Other Fables,* the astute American critic H. L. Mencken said that it redeemed the Irish Literary Revival from Celtic gloom and for his part, he preferred it to many a more pretentious product of that revival. The whimsical thought and witty dialogue which fascinated Mencken are the most marked literary qualities of one who might be called a "Renaissance man," since he is at once poet, fabulist, dramatist, novelist, sculptor, and painter.

Born at Gleenbrook, County Cork, Ireland, April 26, 1880, son of John J. and Elizabeth Harding (Aherne) O'Brien, young James (as he was christened) was educated at the Presentation Brothers School; the South Monastery, Cork; the Cork School of Art; Cork School of Music; National College of Art, Dublin; and Royal College of Art, London. He received a silver medal for sculpture in the National Competition (Board of Education), London, in 1912, exhibited at the Royal Hibernian Academy, and had a specimen of his work entitled "The Rising of the Moon" placed in the foyer of the Abbey Theatre, Dublin, by Lady Gregory. His famous teacher, Oliver Shepherd, R.H.A., was so much impressed with his statuettes that he had one placed in his private collection, and said that Seumas O'Brien could do in sculpture what J. M. Synge did in literature. W. B. Yeats said his bust of the Irish dramatist Lennox Robinson was as like Robinson as any of Rodin's were like the originals.

During the time he spent in Dublin—1910 to 1912—like many other Irishmen of his generation, he changed the English form of his name to the Gaelic form, becoming Seumas, pronounced Shaemas. In 1912 he wrote the comedy *Duty,* one of the most successful plays in the repertoire of the Abbey Theatre. It was published in book form in 1916 with four other one-act comedies. *Duty* is a robust farce comedy mercilessly lampooning the pompous venality of the Royal Irish Constabulary, the police of other days. The four other farce-comedies subsequently published in the same volume with it: "Jurisprudence"; "Magnanimity"; "Matchmakers," and "Retribution," are likewise broad but witty commentaries on Irish social weaknesses. *The Black Bottle* and *The Cobbler's Den* are Seumas O'Brien's other contributions to the drama; in addition to which he has written a number of slight plays chiefly notable for ingenious stagecraft. The high point of his whimsy, *The Whale and the Grasshopper,* was published in 1916. Mr. O'Brien is a frequent contributor of poems to the New York *Sun* and other publications while he continues a useful career as an instructor in painting and sculpture. His statuette, *The Leprechaun*—the Irish fairy cobbler who will tell you where the pot of gold is hidden, if you can catch and hold him—has been widely distributed throughout this country. Early in 1913 Seumas came to the United States for a visit and remained. Mr. O'Brien is unmarried.

Besides the other books mentioned, he wrote: *Blind* (a comedy) (1918); *The Bird Catcher* (a play) (1918); *The Wild Boar* (a play) (1927); *Christmas Eve* (a play) (1928); *The Well* (a play) (1937), and *Queen Puff-Puff* (a play) (1937).

S. O.

William Henry Cardinal O'Connell 1859-1944

Seventy years of the life of this great prelate of the Catholic Church are interestingly recounted in his autobiography, *Recollections of Seventy Years*. His parents John O'Connell and Bridget (Farley) O'Connell, finding living conditions in Ireland difficult, came to the United States and settled in Lowell, Massachusetts, where the eleventh child and seventh son, William, was born. The family life was intensely religious, and soon after graduating from high school he decided to become a priest. From 1876 to 1878 he studied at St. Charles Seminary, Baltimore, where the poet, Father John Tabb, was among his teachers. Ill health necessitated his return home. After an interval, he attended Boston University, where he obtained his A.B. in 1881, with high honors. He was then sent to Rome to pursue his studies for the priesthood at the North American College. While there he was director of the college choir, and also painted and wrote some verse, only "of passing significance," he says in his autobiography, but the inspiration was "quickened to life by the atmosphere of sublime thought and the exquisite beauty of my environment." Ordained in 1884 in St. John Lateran, he was assigned to St. Joseph's parish in Medford, Massachusetts, and then transferred to St. Joseph's, Boston in 1886. In 1895 he delivered a series of lectures at the Catholic Summer School on Lake Champlain. These were published in book form. *His Sermons and Addresses* on particular needs of the time, totaled eleven volumes. He translated the *Life of Christ* by Cardinal De Lai.

Appointed rector of the North American College in November of that year (1895) he rehabilitated the College financially and made friends in Rome. Some of the most delightful pages in his book give reminiscences of important and interesting people there. He returned to the United States as Bishop of Portland, Maine, in 1901, having been consecrated in Rome. Pope Pius X sent him to Japan in 1905 as Papal Envoy to Emperor Mutsuhito. Upon his arrival in Japan, he was received by the Mikado and the Empress, and was so successful in his mission of restoring relations with Japan that he was decorated with the Grand Cordon of the

Sacred Treasure by the Mikado. Many other honors and decorations were given him.

Appointed Coadjutor Archbishop of Boston in 1906, he succeeded to the See upon the death of Archbishop Williams in 1907, and during his episcopacy greatly advanced parochial, educational and charitable works in his archdiocese. He was elevated to the cardinalate in 1911.

Besides being honored by the Vatican, he possessed the Lebanese Grand Medal of Merit, the grand Crosses of the Order of Malta, of the Crown of Italy, of the Constantinian Order of St. George, of the Holy Sepulchre, and of the Legion d'honneur.

In 1934 Catholic University made Cardinal O'Connell an honorary Doctor of Laws. In 1937 Harvard University awarded him the honorary degree of Doctor of Letters. He had both knowledge and love of music, and composed the *Holy Cross Hymnal*. He was also a great reader. In his own words, "Music has always been to me a precious gift and on occasion I enjoy to the fullest the works of the great masters of art whether old or modern; but books—these are my real silent friendly companions wherever I happen to be."

The Cardinal died on April 22, 1944.

C. M. N.

John J. O'Connor   1904-

The writing career of John J. O'Connor began in 1932 with the publication of his book *Twenty-Five in Ireland*. It came to be written as a result of a first trip to Ireland.

Dr. O'Connor's journalistic career began a year later. In that year (1933), he published eight articles and received a total remuneration of $48.00. In subsequent years and until the war, he averaged about two articles and a book review a month with rapidly growing success.

His next two books were texts on sociology and written in collaboration with Dr. Walter L. Willigan. The inspiration for the second book, *Sociology* (1940), came from Dr. Willigan, who had been collecting sociological material for years. They were given a contract for their book *Social Order* (1941)—designed for more advanced students in sociology—before they had a word on paper. These two books are being used in about twenty-four colleges in various parts of the country.

Dr. O'Connor's fourth book was written at the invitation of Dr. Ross Hoffman of Fordham University who urged him to contribute a volume to the Christendom Series. It is entitled *The Catholic Revival in England* and was published in 1942.

Dr. O'Connor was born in Washington, D.C., November 9, 1904, the son of John Daniel and Mary Ellen (Roche) O'Connor. All of his degrees are from Georgetown University. The A.B. degree was received in 1926; the A.M. degree in 1927; the LL.B. degree in 1931; and the Ph.D. degree in 1936. In October of that year (1936) he married Eleanor Louise Crowley. They have three daughters.

His teaching career began in 1927 as an instructor and assistant professor of history at Georgetown University. In 1936 he transferred to St. John's University, Brooklyn, New York, to become associate professor of history in the Graduate School and Teachers College. Two years later, he became professor of history and Chairman of the History Department in the Graduate School and Teachers College.

His other posts have been and are: Catholic editor, *Religious News Service,* New York City, 1937 to 1938; managing editor of *The Commonweal,* 1938 to 1939; member of the book review staff of *America,* New York City, since 1939; member of the editorial staff of the *Magnificat,* Manchester, New Hampshire, since 1941; member of the advisory staff, *Books on Trial,* Thomas More Library, Chicago, Illinois, since 1942; conductor of the column "Inter-American and Interracial" for the *Interracial Review,* New York City, since 1942; editor of *International Correspondence,* New York City, 1942, and Councillor of the United States Catholic Historical Society since 1943. In 1943 Dr. O'Connor was elected a member of the Gallery of Living Catholic Authors, Webster Groves, Missouri.   M. H.

Violet O'Connor (Mrs. Armel O'Connor)
1867-1946

The English *Catholic Who's Who* tells us that Violet O'Connor's father, Henry Bullock-Webster, hunted with no less than fifty packs of hounds! Her Catholic mother was Gwladis Mary Powel of Craig-y-nos Castle Breconshire, Wales— a castle which was sold to Madame Adelina Patti, after whose death it became a sanatorium for consumptives. The Powels claim to be able to trace their descent back fourteen hundred years, to the days of King Arthur.

Violet was born in Devonshire, England, on the twenty-fifth of April 1867. Her Christian names were Lucy Violet, but when she began to write for print and when she signed cheques, she used only the second of these. As a girl she studied art at a pension in Paris, and later at the School of Art in Cheltenham and still later at the Herkomer School at Bushey. Upon her return to the world, after a trial at religious life in a Dominican convent in Devonshire, she rented a cottage in Watford and while there taught for a year in the Infant school.

After Violet Bullock-Webster's marriage to the poet and musician Armel O'Connor on December 24th, 1908, they went to live in a house near Ludlow designed by Mrs. O'Connor, and this they named "Mary's Meadow." It has an entrance porch specially arranged with a seat and a table where Christ, in the person of the poor, could always be given a welcome and a meal. It was the home life of Mary's Meadow that was woven into many of Violet O'Connor's popular books. Among these are *The Idea of Mary's Meadow* (written to let her husband know what sort of life to expect); *The Songs of Mary's Meadow,* and *Mary's Meadow Papers,* with another book, written mainly for her little daughter Catherine Elizabeth (who is now married) entitled *Thoughts for Betty from the Holy Land.* Her other child, Aelred, is a doctor.

But Mrs. O'Connor was by no means confined to Mary's Meadow. Others of her books are : *The Door,* which treated of the women's suffrage question; *The Sport of the Past and the Future,* where she pays a beautiful tribute to her father, a fox-hunting squire of the old school; *Thoughts for a Busy Woman; A Girl's Ideals,* and *Great Saints for Little Children.* Her first book, published on her twenty-first birthday, was called *Flower Stories and Allegories.* All of them have the charm that comes from a limpid and simple style. Though she has contributed to most of the leading American magazines, she is not nearly so well known in America as she is in England, perhaps because her work is too distinctively English.

Violet O'Connor has had a wide appeal and has produced work that is unique of its kind, full of touching piety expressed in a manner at once homely and marked by true style. She has an appreciation of musical, rhythmical sentences and a natural taste for phrases and cadences. It was her feeling for words that made her abandon the art career she had begun at Paris and Florence, as it was her hunger for faith that led her into the Catholic Church very early in life, in 1897.

In 1933, The Marquis de Farémont, in recognition of the merit of her literary work, presented her with the Diploma of the Institut Historique and Heraldique de France. The payment she received for one short article in *The Illustrated Sporting and Dramatic News* was sufficient to purchase all the novels Disraeli had written. She loved buying books. They enabled her to live for many hours a day in a world apart—a world of romance.

She wrote: "There is not a single word—deliberately not—in any of my books which could offend the eye of a contemplative nun." She used to sit by Our Lady's statue and read what she had written aloud to her, to see if there was any sentence which she would like to have changed.

For *Punch* she produced a joint article with P. G. Wodehouse on otter-hunting. She also contributed to *The Pall Mall Gazette, The Pilot* and *The Ladies' Pictorial.*

Her life *My Dear Mummy* (Mrs. Armel O'Connor)—by "Michael" appeared in 1946. "The reader is asked to suppose that Mrs. Armel O'Connor has been dead for more than twenty years and that this account of her life and work was published on April 25th, 1967 to commemorate her centenary." Mrs. O'Connor died in October 1946.

Reverend Charles Leo O'Donnell, C.S.C.
1884-1934

The parents of Reverend Charles O'Donnell possessed the same surname before their marriage, and both were born in Donegal, Ireland. Charles, their youngest son was born in Greenfield, Indiana, on November 15, 1884. His education began when his family moved to Kokomo.

In the fall of 1899, at the age of fourteen, Charles went to Notre Dame and presented himself as a candidate for the Congregation of the Holy Cross. He remained there for his college education. After graduating from Notre Dame, he studied four years of theology at Holy Cross College, in Washington, D.C., and was ordained to the priesthood in 1910. He received his Ph.D. degree the same year. Later in 1910 he attended Harvard. He found time to contribute to the better magazines of the day.

For eighteen years, 1910 to 1928, he was professor of English at Notre Dame—save from February 1918 to May 1919, when he served as chaplain in the Rainbow Division and worked side by side with Father Francis P. Duffy of the "Fighting Sixty-Ninth," in World War I.

A year after Father O'Donnell's return to Notre Dame, he was elected Provincial of the Congregation of the Holy Cross in the United States and six years later was made Assistant Superior General. In 1928 he was appointed President of the University of Notre Dame. It was during his administration that the new law school and new stadium were built.

Father O'Donnell's first book appeared in 1916 under the title, *Dead Musician and Other Poems*. Its title poem was in memory of Brother Basil, the saintly organist of Notre Dame. Subsequent volumes were: *Cloister and Other Poems* (1922); *A Rime of the Rood and Other Poems* (1928), and *Notre Dame Verse*. His dissertation for the Ph.D. degree was *The Prose of Francis Thompson*. Father O'Donnell contributed to the *Atlantic Monthly, Harper's, Ave Maria* and other magazines. Like Father Tabb, he was a master of the quatrain. He was noted for his ready wit and for his ability as a story teller.

His nephew, Father Charles Carey, C.S.C., described him as "a man of medium height and a robust constitution. Though gifted with heavy bushy hair, his forehead gradually loomed high and intellectual. The nose was well chiseled though not conspicuous, the lines of his face were ascetic yet florid. His eyes loomed cavernous and penetrating; his thin lips were taut with discipline. About him there was a reserve that it would not do to overstep."

At the age of 49, just as he completed his term as President of Notre Dame (1934), Father O'Donnell died after an illness of over a year.

M. H.

Sean O'Faoláin 1900-

For those who "have no Gaelic" the explanation is needed that O'Faoláin is pronounced "o fwhaylawn," and for good measure be it noted that Sean is "shawn." Thus it is not mysterious that the son of Denis and Bridget (Murphy) Whelan, christened John, grew up in the days of reborn pride in things Gaelic, to be Sean O'Faoláin, as he would have been had Irish names never been distorted to English forms.

A native of Cork, educated first at the Presentation Brothers' School in that city, the future novelist took his first M. A. at the National University of Ireland, and his second at Harvard University, to which he came as a Commonwealth Fellow (1926 to 1928), lingering as a John Harvard Fellow (1928 to 1929). While teaching Gaelic at Harvard, he lectured on Anglo-Irish Literature at Boston College (1929). His latest term in what he found to be the uncongenial task of teaching was as lecturer in English at St. Mary's Training College, Strawberry Hill (1929 to 1933). During that time he found himself as a writer. His book of stories *Midsummer Night Madness,* dealing with Irish life, particularly in the days of "the troubles," 1916 to 1924, was one of three works nominated for the English Femina Prize, and brought him an invitation to charter membership in the Irish Academy of Letters.

O'Faoláin had fought for his country's freedom during the Irish Revolution (1918 to 1921). In the ensuing civil war he took the Republican side (1922 to 1924) and was Director of Publicity for the Irish Republican Army. "My American Trip," he subsequently wrote, "did one good thing for me—it readjusted me out of the bitter disillusionment following the Irish Civil War." And in the same article—printed in the spring 1932 issue of the English magazine *Now and Then*—he struck the keynote of his work in fiction, which is to picture "my own people, the simple, poor farming-stock whose lives go on and on through it all, the simple middle-class people of the towns whose lives are a slow tale of pathetic endeavour." He adds, "That is a story worth telling," and the reading public has judged that O'Faoláin has told it stirringly. His first novel, *A Nest of Simple Folk,* established his fame wherever English is read.

O'Faoláin at first wrote in Gaelic; but not having been born to the ancestral speech, having learned it at school, he felt that he "did not have absolute control. . . . Besides, to write in Irish accentuates the great difficulty confronting all Irish writers—lack of cricticism."

In his article "About Myself" in the magazine *Now and Then,* O'Faoláin touched on another theme which has haunted him—"how a nation lives within itself a double life, each life in that duality thwarting the other." In an article, "The Gamut of Irish Fiction," published in *Saturday Review of Literature* (1936), he longs for a greater sharing of knowledge between "the people" and the "big houses" and between the writers who speak for these two social classes. In the same article he says:

"We may dream of romance. But we know that it must be made out of what we have—rags and bones, moonlight, limed cabins, struggle, the passion of our people, a bitter history, great folly, a sense of eternity in all things, a courage 'never to submit or yield.' "

Malcolm Cowley (*New Republic,* February 15, 1939) credits O'Faoláin with "slow and rhythmical eighteenth-century style that survives only in Dublin," and O'Faoláin himself has written, "I have been mainly interested in form," and points out the musical form of his story entitled *Fugue.* But it appears to others that his compassionate understanding of Irish life and of simple folk is his forte, rather than mere form. *Midsummer Night Madness,* in writing which he thought much of form, is verbose, and slow at times in movement. *A Nest of Simple Folk* is certainly a better book; its tense interest derives from its integration with life; it has construction, character interest and masterly dialogue. Of *A Purse of Coppers,* one reviewer has written, "This Sean O'Faoláin is more than a spinner of ingenious tales. He is a very keen and many-faceted intelligence, whose business it is restlessly to pierce and reflect many aspects of life in his native land; and moreover to understand and reveal their relation to the greater currents of life in the whole Western World." His biographies of the contemporary Constance Countess Markievicz and of that giant of other days, Daniel O'Connell, reveal O'Faoláin's possession of no small competence as an historian.

Mr. O'Faoláin was married in 1928. They have one daughter.

He wrote the following books: *Lyrics and Satires from Tom Moore* (edited) (1929); *The Life Story of Eamon DeValera* (biography) (1933); *Constance Markievicz; or The Average Revolutionary* (1934); *There's a Birdie in the Cage* (story) (1935); *A Born Genius* (short story) (1936); *Bird Alone* (novel) (1936); *The Autobiography of Wolfe Tone* (edited) (1937); *The Silver Branch* (anthology of early Irish poetry) (1937), American edition 1938; *King of the Beggars* (biography of Daniel O'Connell) (1938); *She Had To Do Something* (play) (1938); *An Irish Journey* (travel book) (1940), and *Come Back to Erin* (novel) (1940).   S. O.

Lenore Glen Offord 1905-

Of the six books Mrs. Lenore Glen Offord has written, four are mystery stories. Her first book, *Murder on Russia Hill,* was written in 1936 but was not published until the spring of 1938. Two non-mystery novels, *Cloth of Silver* and *Angels Unaware,* followed in 1939 and 1940. In 1941 Mrs. Offord decided that she preferred mystery writing to any other kind. In this year she published *The Nine Dark Hours,* and a year later *Clues To Burn. The Glass Mask* was published in 1944.

Mrs. Offord writes: "The only observations I can think of to make about my first book are these: if I'd known before I started how complicated, how well-documented and how well-rounded a mystery story has to be for present-day taste it's possible that I might never have begun; but once having started, I developed a taste for writing as well as reading mysteries, and now it seems to me the most fascinating type of light novel writing—controlled by a set of rules and ethical canons more definite than those for any other type of novel and yet offering all the latitude the author can wish, in the way of background, character development, and the opportunity for good craftsmanship in writing. Also when I discovered how much miscellaneous information one must possess about every point in one's detective novel, and how accurate that information must be, I discovered at the same time that the persons who possessed the knowledge I needed were delighted to help me. All one has to do, it seems, is to say 'I am writing a detective story,' and then *ask*. I have been readily and generously helped by the police of two cities, by doctors and lawyers and priests, by officials of the telephone company, the gas company, the fire-prevention division of the City Hall, the Ground Observation Corps, the Government Weather Bureau, the Southern Pacific Railroad, and every one of these persons has laughed heartily when he learned what I wanted and then gone to infinite trouble to give me the information. The same is true of all my books, and by this time I never have any hesitation in asking for help, having learned that people really like to give it."

Mrs. Offord is primarily a housewife. Yet she finds time to write about one book a year. She works at her writing, as most professional writers do, as if it were a trade, though it is at the same time her chief hobby.

Mrs. Offord was born Lenore Frances Glen, October 24, 1905, in Spokane, Washington, the daughter of Robert Alexander and Catherine (Grippen) Glen. She graduated from Mills College, California, in 1925 with a B.A. degree. She did graduate work for a year (1925 to 1926) at the University of California. In September 1929 she was married to Harold R. Offord. Three of her books were published in England. During World War II, Mrs. Offord did warden service in Berkeley and was with the Aircraft Warning Service of the Fourth Fighter Command.   M. H.

Thomas O'Hagan   1855-1939

Thomas O'Hagan was born near Toronto, Canada, on March 6, 1855. After studying at St. Michael's College, Toronto, he completed his college education at Ottawa University, graduating in 1882. He received the degree of Doctor of Philosophy from Syracuse University in 1889 and later studied at Cornell University and the Universities of Wisconsin and Chicago in the United States and the Universities of Louvain, Grenoble, Bonn, and Freiburg in Europe. He travelled extensively in Europe, studying modern languages and art.

From 1884 to 1893, Dr. O'Hagan taught English, classical and modern languages in a number of Canadian high schools. He took a deep interest in the welfare and development of the Catholic schools of Ontario, and he organized the first Provincial Separate School Teachers' Association and served as its first President. Subsequently he taught in many convent schools in different parts of the United States.

He was a member of the staff of the Duluth, Minnesota, *Daily Tribune* in 1891 and was editor of the Chicago Catholic weekly, *The New World,* from 1910 to 1913. He was the International Sponsor for the Mark Twain Monument in 1935 and an Honorary Corresponding Member of the Historic Institute of Paris.

Dr. O'Hagan is best known as a poet and as a critic. His first volume of poems, *A Gate of Flowers,* appeared in 1887. His second book, *In Dreamland* (1893), contained his much quoted lyric, "The Song My Mother Sings." His other volumes of poetry are: *Songs of the Settlement* (1899); *In the Heart of the Meadow* (1914), and *Songs of the Heroic Days* (1916). He published his *Complete Poetical Works* in 1922, and this was followed by *Chap Book,* a volume of selected poems, in 1928. Besides contributing a number of articles to the *Catholic Encyclopedia,* he is the author of the following prose works: *Studies in Poetry* (1900); *Canadian Essays* (1901); *Essays, Literary and Historical* (1909); *Chats by the Fireside* (1911); *Essays on Catholic Life* (1916); *With Staff and Scrip* (1924); *Genesis of Christian Art* (1926); *Intimacies of Canadian Life and Letters* (1927); *Dudheen Dreams* (1930); *Spain and Her Daughters* (1931), and *What Shakespeare Is Not* (1936). He also wrote *Dean Harris* in the *Makers of Canadian Literature Series* (1924); *Father Morice* in the *Ryerson History Readers* (1927); and *Tide of Love* in the *Ryerson Poetry Chap Books* (1933).

Dr. O'Hagan was popular as a lecturer and reader. In his career as a teacher and on the lecture platform he always attached the greatest importance to the cultivation and proper use of the voice and he was outstanding for the excellence of his vocal interpretations of poetry. He died on March 2, 1939.   B. S.

Ernest James Oldmeadow   1867-

For many years editor of *The Tablet,* Ernest Oldmeadow is also the author of many books. He was born in Chester, England, in 1867 and educated there at King's School and also privately. In 1897 he married Annie Cecilia Dawson, the daughter of an Anglican clergyman but a convert to Catholicism. Oldmeadow entered the Church in 1900. He was editor of *The Dome* from 1897 to 1900, in which year he became music critic of *The Outlook.* He published his first book, *Lady Lohengrin,* in 1897, and in 1898 he wrote *The Little Christian Year.* After 1904 he gave all his time to writing, and numerous works came from his pen. The conclusion of his career as music critic was marked by the publication of short lives of Schumann and Chopin, in 1905. A later book was *Great Musicians*. Before 1909, he had published: *The North Sea Bubble; Susan—The Scoundrel; Aunt Maud,* and *Antonio. A Babe Unborn* appeared in 1911. World War I then intervened before his next publications: *Coggin; The Hare; Wildfang,* and *Miss Watts,* although in 1915 he had written *Home Cookery in War Time.*

In 1923 he assumed the editorship of *The Tablet,* and ably conducted this paper until 1936 when he resigned. He is best known for his work as editor of *The Tablet.* He made that Catholic review a national organ in a Protestant country. He was always combative like Dimond of the *Catholic Herald* and he always kept his dignity. He was invariably obedient to the hierarchy and Cardinal Bourne thought most highly of him.

The following year he wrote *In Town Tomorrow* and in 1938 *A Layman's Christian Year.* With the death of Cardinal Bourne he became his official biographer. The first volume, *Francis Cardinal Bourne,* was published in 1940 and a second in 1944. Others are to follow. Oldmeadow has been a frequent contributor to the *Standard, Westminster Gazette, Nineteenth Century and After, Saturday Review,* and *Morning Post.* His books have been translated into French, German, and Norwegian. He is a member of the Westminster City Council and was created a Knight Commander of St. Gregory, in 1934. He is particularly interested in ecclesiology.   C. M. N.

Reverend James Edward O'Mahony, O.F.M. Cap.
1897-

Father James O'Mahony was born at Mitchelstown, County Cork, Ireland, in the year 1897, the son of James O'Mahony and Ellen O'Callaghan. His father, besides being a builder and contractor, was an athlete of standing, and a maker of violins. He was educated by the Christian Brothers at Mitchelstown and later at the Capuchin Franciscan College, Rochestown, County Cork. One year here sufficed to qualify him for entry into the Capuchin branch of the Franciscan Order, which he entered at the early age of sixteen. He attended University College, Cork, where he had a brilliant record. In 1918 he took his B.A. with First Honours in Mental and Moral Science and was awarded a postgraduate scholarship. In that year he obtained the Pierce Malone Scholarship in competition with the other constituent colleges of the National University. In 1919 Father James received his M.A. with First Honours and the following year he was awarded a travelling studentship in philosophy.

After one year's stay in Rome, at the Gregorian University, he was ordained priest and won his S.T.B. degree. He then went to the Catholic University of Louvain for the purpose of further studies. In 1925 he was awarded a Licentiate in Philosophy with first place (solus), and the following year was awarded the Ph.D. again "avec la plus grande distinction." Father James' special study for the Ph.D. was in Experimental Psychology. Such was his success that he was invited to return to Louvain where, in 1928, he was promoted "Agrégé" of the Higher Institute of Philosophy. For this coveted distinction Father James wrote his first book, *The Desire of Good in the Philosophy of Saint Thomas.*

On his return to Ireland, in 1928, Father James was appointed President of St. Bonaventure's University Hostel, Cork. He has been Provincial Definitor on several occasions; he is at present Provincial of the Irish Province of Capuchins. While yet Provincial Definitor, he made canonical visitations of the Foreign Mission in Africa and of the various houses of the Irish Province in America. In 1935 he was elected to the governing body of Cork University, and has since been twice re-elected; he was appointed professor of philosophy in 1937. On the death of the late president of University College, Cork, he was unanimously elected acting-president until the successor, Dr. Alfred O'Rahilly, was appointed.

During this time Father James has been in frequent demand for sermons, lectures and retreats. This has not interfered with his literary activities. Already he has written eighteen books, some of which have reached several editions. These books are at once philosophical and religious, and among the most popular are the following: *Where Is thy God?; Christian Philosophy; The Person of Jesus,* and *The Music of Life.*

Reverend George O'Neill, S.J.   1863-1947

Weary of the Irish discord in 1922, Father George O'Neill got permission from his superiors to leave his native country and to go to Australia.

Father O'Neill was born at Dungannon, Ireland, in 1863. His father was a barrister-at-law. When he had completed six years of his education at St. Stanislaus College, Tullabeg, he entered the Jesuit novitiate in 1880. Later he studied at the Irish universities—the Royal and National—where he earned degrees and professorships. He majored in English and other modern languages. He studied German and French in Prague and Paris. He was one of the founders of the Jesuit review *Studies.*

On his arrival in Australia he taught church history and the modern languages at Corpus Christi College, Werribee, the seminary for the province of Melbourne. In Ireland, he was a member of the Feis Ceoil Committee and in his new home in Australia he took a practical interest in the musical work of their students and in other art-matters.

Father O'Neill had frequently contributed to Catholic periodicals "being unwilling to refuse requests for contributions. A similar unwillingness has been largely responsible for the variety of subjects on which I have appeared in print. And I have learnt from experience that the great public prefers specialists and resents this variegated kind of appeal to its favor."

Father O'Neill's first book *Blessed Mary of the Angels,* a life of a Carmelite nun appeared in 1911. The Catholic Press in various countries praised it. The companion biographies: *Life of Mother Mary of the Cross,* an Australian Educational foundress, and *Life of the Reverend Julian T. Woods,* scientist and Australian pioneer and missionary, were highly praised by the Australian critic, Dr. Beovich, the Archbishop of Adelaide.

When Father O'Neill published his book *Essays on Poetry* in 1919, *The Daily Telegraph* said: "This little book of essays is full of quality and of warm human sympathy. Father O'Neill is enough of an academician to retain his reverence for the great figures of English poetry, but he is open to new impressions and sensitive to fresh impulses. He interprets rather than criticizes and his interpretations are full of personal insight."

His two Scriptural volumes—translations and commentaries, *The Psalms and the Canticles* (1937), and *Job* (1938), were written at the request of an American editor and publisher. A more modest enterprise was *Scripture Readings for Times of Retreat* (1926).

When his eyesight became impaired he was forced to resign and went to Sydney. There he died on July 19, 1947, after a year of inactivity.

Besides the works already mentioned Father O'Neill is the author of: *Five Centuries of English Poetry* (1912); *The Golden Legend* (selections) (1914); *Readings from Newman* (1923); *The Servant of the Sacred Heart* (1933), and *Golden Years on the Paraguay* (1934).   M. H.

Sister Mary Agatha O'Neill, R.S.M.

One of six thousand Religious Sisters of Mercy in this country governed by a Mother General, Sister Mary Agatha O'Neill—pen name, Beatrice Gaule—is, despite multifarious duties, author of three works: *Guide to the Study of Dante; Poets and Catholic Fiction Writers;* and *Idaho in Song and Poetry,* for which Governor Chase A. Clark has written the foreword.

Born in Parkhill, Ontario, Canada, she received degrees from the Universities of Oklahoma, Creighton, and Saint Louis, and is at present principal and superior of Our Lady of Victory Academy, Council Bluffs, Iowa.

Perhaps the first to suggest, in her column of the *Southwest Courier,* a "Catholic Book-a-Month Club," she was chosen one of five on the first Editorial Board of this kind in the United States, that of the *Catholic Booklover.*

The offices of State Historian for the N.C.C.W. in Oklahoma, and of State Parliamentarian for Iowa's State Nurses' Association fill many hours of this busy sister. She considers her greatest moment that of her reception of the habit of a Sister of Mercy.

As a member of the Dante League of America, she has awakened interest in worth-while literature by her lectures on Dante in the Oklahoma City College. She was invited to contribute to Monsignor Slattery's *My Favorite Passage from Dante.*   S. M.

Reverend Nicholas O'Rafferty

Born in County Sligo, Ireland, Father O'Rafferty prides himself on belonging to that part of Ireland into which the Irish were driven by Oliver Cromwell whose motto was: "To Hell or Connaught." Nicholas O'Rafferty was the fifth of a family of nine children. His father's name was Patrick and his mother's name Honora, née Hunt. His studies, begun in Ireland, were completed in Italy where he was ordained to the Holy Priesthood.

Father O'Rafferty came to Seattle, Washington, in the fall of 1911. After serving fifteen months as curate at Our Lady of Good Help Church in that city, he was placed in temporary charge of a small parish in southwestern Washington. Three months later he was appointed by the Right Reverend Edward J. O'Dea, D.D., Bishop of Seattle, as pastor of St. Anthony's parish, Renton, a suburb of Seattle. During the first twelve months of his pastorate at this latter place, he built two churches in two of his many missions, Kirkland and Bellevue, and left them free of all debt on the day of their dedication.

Before coming to Seattle as pastor of St. Edward's, where he has been for the past twenty-three years (1947), Father O'Rafferty served three years as the first pastor of St. Joseph's Church, Leavenworth, during which he built St. Francis Church and Hall at Cashmere; and six years as pastor of Sacred Heart Church at Enumclaw. In every place he has been, he paid off the parish debts.

Despite his many pastoral duties, including church building and financing, Father O'Rafferty interested himself in the study of languages and writing. For his life's work in the field of writing, Father O'Rafferty selected Christian doctrine. This subject interested him even as a child and his interest in it grew with the years. Another factor which contributed much to his decision was the fact that he came upon an old Italian work in three volumes by the Reverend Father Bressanvido, O.F.M., which served not only as a model but also as a fruitful source of excellent doctrine. It was one of the first of its kind, if not the first, written after the Council of Trent, and it followed closely the *Catechism of the Council of Trent*. But the most weighty motive of all was the encyclical *Acerbo Nimis* of Pope Pius X in which he enjoins on all pastors, and others having the care of souls, the duty of giving to the faithful a four or five years' course of catechetical instructions, comprising the Apostles' Creed, the Sacraments, the Commandments of God, the Lord's Prayer, and the Precepts of the Church. All this resulted in Father O'Rafferty's "Complete Course of Instructions on Christian Doctrine." The work consists of four volumes, covering the four parts into which the subject is usually divided. The first part treats of the Apostles'

Creed; the second of the Sacraments; the third of the Commandments of God; the fourth of Prayer, the Precepts of the Church, Sin and its Kinds, Virtues.

According to Father O'Rafferty there are three occasions of joy in the life of one who writes a book: the first is when one begins and while one is engaged in writing it, for only those who have had the experience are in a position to know the satisfaction derived from writing; the second is when the book is accepted for publication; and the last but not least is when the book finally makes its appearance. "And to these joys," he adds, "there are three sorrows which correspond: one of these is experienced during the writing of the book when the writer's headaches become too acute; another is when one begins to negotiate with the publishers who return one's work with the usual 'thanks for giving us the privilege of examining your manuscript'; and the last is when the book finally appears and both the author and his work become the innocent victims of unjust and sometimes incompetent critics."

Pope Benedict XV, through his Secretary of State, Peter Cardinal Gasparri, graciously permitted Father O'Rafferty's entire work of Instructions on Christian Doctrine to be dedicated to the Vicar of Christ. And he also received commendation from Pope Pius XII, through his Secretary of State, L. Cardinal Maglione.

The four volumes: *The Apostles' Creed; The Sacraments; The Commandments of God; Prayer, Precepts of the Church, Sin and its Kinds, Virtues,* are a complete course of popular theology, doctrinal, moral, and sacramental. The work is intended for teachers and students of religion. Its primary purpose, however, is to serve as an aid to seminarians and young priests in their preparation of catechetical sermons and catechetical instructions for their life's work of preaching God's word. *Discourses on Our Lady,* for the month of May, our Lady's Feasts, and other such occasions, is Father O'Rafferty's latest work.

Reverend William Edwin Orchard 1877-

The Catholic Church has had every possible type of convert. Yet, rarely, if ever, has it welcomed to its fold anybody quite like Father Orchard. Most of those it receives in England enter via High Anglicanism; Father Orchard came in through Nonconformity.

Even his Nonconformist experiences were of a unique sort. For after a "liberal" phase—in which, however, he never abandoned the "evangelicism" of his youth—he was appointed minister of the King's Weigh House Chapel in London, and there he "Catholicized" a congregation made up of the large personal following he attracted from all over the great city. This could only have been possible among Congregationalists, where each church has its own independence. Because of that independence of Dr. Orchard and his assistant, Stanley B. James (who preceded him into the full acceptance of the Faith), "Mass" was said, the "Blessed Sacrament" was reserved, and confessions were regularly heard. The story is related by Dr. Orchard himself how one Saturday evening he was walking, attired in soutane and biretta, in front of his confessional, waiting for penitents, when a lady came in; but despite the many signs of Catholicism, something aroused her suspicions. Going up to the little black-robed figure, she asked, "Father, is this a Catholic church?" He answered, "Madam, honesty obliges me to admit that it isn't. But I'm doing my best to make it one. I think you are probably looking for Farm Street."

Catholicism itself was not reached except after a long search and arduous struggles. Born in 1877 of poor parents, with eight children, the boy's formal education ended at the age of twelve. At fourteen he became, like his father, a railway clerk. At sixteen, following his conversion (in the evangelical Protestant sense), his artistic instincts were awakened, and he began to paint and to compose music and poetry. For him, however, his main artistic outlet was then, as it still is, in preaching. This was at first in the open air and in mission halls, but it made him wish to enter the ministry. As the Presbyterians demand a university degree of candidates, he took private lessons in Greek and Latin, rising early in the morning and studying late at night, working as usual in his office by day. At the age of twenty-one he was appointed lay minister of a derelict church in East London. It was while there that he met a lady who was the superintendent of a social settlement. They fell in love and were married. Two years later he was admitted to the Presbyterian College as a "special case." Eventually he obtained his B.D. at London University and later his D.D. But it was all accomplished mainly by a heroic instance of self-education.

He came into prominence during the time of Dr. R. J. Campbell's New Theology Movement. But he had far more learning and intellectual substance than the more flashily famous man, and in time he veered towards the "Free Catholic Movement," which was attracting many of the more brilliant Nonconformists. Of this, he and Dr. Lloyd Thomas became the recognized leaders.

Meanwhile, he (together with Mr. James) received schismatic ordination. Not until twelve years after the death of Mrs. Orchard in 1920 did the "Free Catholic" resign the pulpit of Weigh House, where his preaching had attracted so large a congregation. Then, at length, he presented his case to the Holy See with the result that, after a year's delay, he was conditionally ordained after a brief course of study under Dr. Arendzen, and—again as a special case—he was ordained, not to a diocese or under his own patrimony, but to the service of the Church. The orders were all conferred within five successive days; since then Dr. Orchard has been a free-lance, devoting himself especially to work among Nonconformists.

The title of his fascinating autobiography, *From Faith to Faith*, published in 1933, indicates not so much a renunciation of faith but rather the fulfillment of evangelicalism discovered in Catholicism. His understanding of Nonconformity, at once in its vagaries and its sincere groping for truth, has made him uniquely effective in approaching people whose incipient Catholicism he appreciates better than they do themselves. Under Cardinal Hinsley's direction he began a "Catholic Evangelistic Campaign" which was carried not only to the universities and industrial centers of England, but also along similar lines to the United States. His endeavor is to reach those without religious beliefs or denominational attachments—which of course opens a very wide field.

In 1940, Dr. Orchard, together with his friend, Dr. Richard Roberts, the well-known Presbyterian theologian and one time moderator of the United Church of Canada, appeared at a series of joint lectures at Yale University. This was not intended to be a debate but a conference for mature and well-educated audiences.

Father Orchard is not primarily a writer, but a speaker. The living voice and the personal contact are his instruments. In addition to his autobiography, which will probably gain a permanent place among books of its type, he has published *The Way of Simplicity, The Inevitable Cross,* and *The Cult of Our Lady.* His own devotion to the Blessed Virgin bore its fruit when, following a visit to Lourdes, his apparently broken health was largely restored. Certainly it has since been robust enough to enable him to do an immense amount of extremely exhausting work. His book *The Necessity for the Church,* published in 1940, is intended for prospective converts, but unlike so many apologetic works, it bears always in mind that the cut-and-dried answer to religious difficulties is not as a rule the persuasive answer. Having a special vantage-point, Dr. Orchard seeks to get around to the other side of the reader's mind, to the unconscious prejudice that commonly remains even after the formal objection has been removed. His apologetic method is an effort to show all Christians that they are already at least imperfect Catholics, and that all men of good will are at least potentially Christians. The success of the method is proved by the many converts it has made. The book *Humanity: What? Whence? Whither?* appeared in 1944.

Edith Coues O'Shaughnessy 1870-1939

Much of the world's interesting literature is that which is in the diary form, or is enriched by the broadening experiences of travel. This total has been felicitously enlarged by the life work of Edith O'Shaughnessy. The diplomatic career of her distinguished husband, of course, made available to her the approach to famous persons and places.

Edith Louise Coues was born in Columbia, South Carolina, the daughter of Elliot and Jeanie Augusta (McKinney) Coues. She was educated in the Convent of Notre Dame in Maryland as well as under private tutors. Always possessed of a delightful and fascinating personality, she was favored by being given the opportunity to travel in Europe. In Rome, in 1901, she married Nelson

O'Shaughnessy who was in the American diplomatic service. Besides being the United States Ambassador to Mexico in the troublous days of 1914, Mr. O'Shaughnessy held diplomatic posts in Berlin, St. Petersburg, Vienna, and Bucharest.

Though she had been the author of several sophisticated short stories, Mrs. O'Shaughnessy's first venture into adventure and travel literature began with the appearance of *A Diplomat's Wife in Mexico* (1916). The unrest and turmoil which prevailed in that country during Ambassador O'Shaughnessy's tenure there, with the effect on American relations, are here vividly portrayed. Mrs. O'Shaughnessy had unexcelled opportunities to observe firsthand what went on behind the scenes. This she relates in her book, which is a series of letters written from the American Embassy from October 1913 until April 23, 1914, culminating with an account of the occupation of Vera Cruz. The doings in Mexico of John Lind, President Wilson's somewhat enigmatical special envoy, figure very largely in her report.

Others of Mrs. O'Shaughnessy's works in chronological order are: *Diplomatic Days* (1917); *My Lorraine* (1918); and *Intimate Pages of Mexican History* (1920) where she chronicles her firsthand observations of four Mexican presidents: Diaz, De la Barra, Madero, and Huerta. Also in 1920 there came out *Alsace in Rust and Gold,* a picture of that much disputed French province during the war. Her other books were: *Viennese Medley* (1924); *Married Life* (1925); *Other Ways and Other Flesh* (1929), and *Marie Adelaide* (1932). The last is a sympathetic study of the young but unhappy ruler of the little principality of Luxembourg during the years from 1912 to the Armistice in 1918.

Mrs. O'Shaughnessy was honored by the French Republic by being made an "Officer de l'Instruction Publique." Her husband died in 1932, and she followed him on February 18, 1939, dying in New York City. Surviving them is one son, Elim, now connected with the United States Department of State.

J. M.

Right Reverend George Barry O'Toole
1886-1944

As secretary to Bishop Joseph Schrembs of Toledo, Ohio, canonist, pastor, professor, military chaplain, co-founder of the Pontifical Catholic (Fu Jen) University of Peking and author, Monsignor O'Toole had a varied career.

He was born at Toledo, Ohio, December 11, 1886, the son of George Joseph O'Toole and Catherine Anne (Downey) O'Toole. In 1900 he matriculated at St. John's High School in Toledo, Ohio, and upon graduation in 1904 attended St. John's University also in Toledo (1904-1906) and received an M.A. degree in 1908. His other degrees are a Ph.B., a Ph.L., a Ph.D., an S.T.B., S.T.L., and an S.T.D. from the Urban University of the Propaganda in Rome, Italy. He took courses in biology, geology and chemistry at Columbia University in the summers of 1918 and 1924 and in the winter session of 1922 to 1923.

It was after his ordination to the priesthood at Rome in 1911 that he became secretary to Bishop Joseph Schrembs of Toledo, Ohio, holding this office until 1915. During this time (1913 to 1915) he also served as diocesan canonist. In 1915 he became pastor of St. Aloysius' Church, Bowling Green, Ohio, leaving this parish in 1917 to become professor of philosophy at St. Vincent Seminary, Latrobe, Pennsylvania (which is under the supervision of the Benedictine Fathers). On July 23, 1918, he was commissioned as a first lieutenant chaplain in the United States Army. On May 8, 1919, he was promoted to the rank of captain. His honorable discharge came at his own request on August 21, 1919, after which he served ten years as a captain chaplain in the United States Army Reserve Corps. In the fall of 1919 he returned to St. Vincent Seminary, Latrobe, to resume his professorship of philosophy and to become professor of animal biology in Seton Hill College, Greensburg, Pennsylvania, from 1919 to 1920 and 1923 to 1924.

In 1920, Monsignor O'Toole, while travelling in China, met Mr. Vincent Ying, K.S.G., Catholic journalist and scholar. As early as 1912, Mr. Ying had sent a letter to His Holiness, Pope Pius X imploring the Holy Father to start a Catholic University at Peking. In 1917 Mr. Ying wrote his *Exhortation to Study,* which was an appeal to the hierarchy and clergy of China to enter the field of higher education. From Mr. Ying, Monsignor O'Toole received translations of his "Letter to the Pope" and *Exhortation to Study* and came to share their author's enthusiasm to start a Catholic University in China.

Returning to America by way of Europe, Monsignor O'Toole visited Rome and recounted his experiences to Pope Benedict XV and to the Abbot Primate of the Benedictine Order, Dom Fidelis Stotzinger, O.S.B. He also spoke of his experiences to the late Right Reverend Ernest Helmstetter, O.S.B., of St. Mary's Abbey in Newark, New Jersey, the President of the American Cassinese Congregation of the Benedictine Order and to Right Reverend Aurelius Stehle, O.S.B., of St. Vincent Archabbey where Monsignor O'Toole was appointed to teach dogmatic theology.

When the twenty-first General Chapter of the American Cassinese Congregation decided to open a University in Peking, St. Vincent Archabbey was chosen the consignee. On January 15, 1925, Archabbot Aurelius Stehle, O.S.B., appointed Monsignor O'Toole, who was an Oblate of St. Benedict, rector of the Catholic (Fu Jen) University of Peking. During the latter's rectorship a beautiful university building in Chinese style was built, of which the great Benedictine artist Dom Adelbert Gresnigt was the architect. Monsignor O'Toole continued as rector until the American Benedictines left Peking in 1933.

Returning to the United States he became professor and head of the department of philosophy at Duquesne University in Pittsburgh in 1934. It was in this year, too, that he was appointed a Domestic Prelate.

In 1937 he left Duquesne University to become a professor in the School of Philosophy at Catholic University in Washington, D.C.

In 1939 he was appointed Treasurer-Secretary of the Sponsoring Committee of the tour of the Chinese flyers, Misses Yen and Lee, for China's Civilian Relief Fund. In the same year, he became editor-in-chief of *The China Monthly*.

Monsignor O'Toole is the author of *The Case Against Evolution* (1925); *An Enemy Sowed Cockle* (in collaboration with Theodore F. Mac-Manus, C.K.S.G.) (1926); *Logic, A Bilingual Test* (in collaboration with Ignatius Ying) (1931); *The Last Romans* (a translation of Ostatni Ryzmianie, and historical novel by Theodore Jeski-Choinski) (1936); *Race: Nation: Person* (an international symposium of which he is editor and a contributor) (1944). Some brochures and pamphlets are: *Craniotomy and Abortion from a Moral Standpoint* (1920); a translation of Cardinal Billot's *Liberalism* (1922); *Psychology and the Catholic Teacher* (1925); *Christian Wheat and Marxian Cockle* (1937); Louis Veuillot's *The Liberal Illusion* (1939); *War and Conscription at the Bar of Christian Morals* (1941).

In March 1944 Monsignor O'Toole died of coronary thrombosis.

Posthumously, the Chinese government has conferred the Order of Brilliant Star, with cravat, on the Right Reverend G. Barry O'Toole for his work as co-founder of the Catholic University of Peking. The honor is conferred only upon Chinese cabinet members and upon foreigners who have given outstanding service to the Chinese people.

M. H.

Fulton Oursler   1893-

The author, playwright, editor and commentator Fulton Oursler was born in Baltimore, Maryland, on January 22, 1893, the son of William Clarence and Lillian Phillips (Sappington) Oursler. He was educated in the public schools and studied law for two years. From 1910 to 1912 he was a reporter for the Baltimore *American*, and from 1912 to 1918 the music and dramatic critic for the same paper. Then he began to write short stories for magazines. In 1920 he came to New York as the editor of *The Music Trades* and two years later became editor-in-chief of *Metropolitan Magazine* and in that same year (1922) he became a writer of novels, plays and short stories. From 1931 to 1942 he was editor-in-chief of the Macfadden Publications which included the weekly *Liberty* and ten other monthly magazines with a circulation of sixteen million a month. As editor of *Liberty* he introduced the condensation of novels. In 1941 he became vice-president and editorial director of the Macfadden Publications. In July 1944 Oursler became senior editor of the *Reader's Digest*, which post he holds at present (1947).

He is the author of ten novels: *Behold the Dreamer* (1924); *Sandalwood* (1925); *Stepchild of the Moon* (1926); *Poor Little Fool* (1928); *The World's Delight* (1929); *The Great Jasper* (1930); *Joshua Todd* (1935); *A Skeptic in the Holy Land* (1936); *The House of Leorwood* (1944), and *Three Things We Can Believe In* (1942).

His detective stories, the hero of which has been the Police Commissioner, were written under the pseudonym of "Anthony Abbot." Oursler is one of the few detective novelists who has worked successfully with the police in solving actual crimes. Before the National Academy of the F.B.I. he lectured on methods of criminal deduction. His detective stories include: *About the Murder of Geraldine Foster; About the Murder of the Choir Singer; About the Murder of the Night Club Lady; About the Murder of the Circus Queen; About the Murder of a Startled Lady* (1935); *About the Murder of a Man Afraid of Women* (1937); *The Creeps* (1941), and *The Shudders* (1943).

He wrote the following plays: *Behold This Dreamer; The Spider* (1927); *All the King's Men* (1929); *The Walking Gentleman* (with Grace Perkins Oursler) (1941). Besides writing many motion picture scenarios, he contributed to *American Mercury, Atlantic Monthly, Cosmopolitan, Liberty, Reader's Digest* and *Good Housekeeping* and many other magazines.

He has been described as "a medium-sized stocky man, with a cultivated voice and a large aquiline nose." On September 7, 1925, he married Grace Perkins, an author and former actress. A convert to the Catholic Church, he gave many addresses on the Catholic Hour radio program. His favorite hobbies are ventriloquism and sleight of hand. M. H.

Maggie Owen *see* Mrs. Thomas Wadelton

Giovanni Papini 1881-

The Life of Christ, published in 1920, "was impelled by a sincere need to help some of my brethren," said its author, Giovanni Papini. It was more than just a new presentation of our Lord's life, it was an outpouring of faith resulting from his conversion. "When it was finished there faced me the need of belonging to the society founded by Christ," he said.

Born in Florence, Italy January 9, 1881, of an atheist father, he had hitherto been without faith and was a professed atheist and revolutionary. He lived an unhappy childhood. He had no classical education, only that of the common and normal school. From 1887 to 1899 he was at school in Florence and in 1898 published in a student paper his first article on Manzoni's *Inno Del Natale*. From 1900 to 1902, he studied at the Instituto di Studi Superiori, and while there he wrote *Teoria Psicologia della Previsione* in *Archivio per l'Antropologia*. He then taught Italian for a year in the Anglo-Italian school and from 1902 to 1904 was librarian at the Museum of Anthropology. While librarian, when he was only twenty-three years of age, he founded the review, *Leonardo,* to which he contributed articles under the pseudonym of "Gian Falco." He was a representative of the Italian pragmatists at the Congress of Philosophy in Geneva, of which he was long the ablest living expounder. During the next six years he wrote several books, including *Il Crespuscolo dei Filosofi* (The Twilight of the Philosophers) (1905), his first book; *Tragico Quotidiano* (Tragic of Everyday) (1906); *Le Memorie d' Iddio* (1911), and *Vita di Nessuno.* The review *La Voce* was founded in 1908 with his collaboration, and in 1913, with A. Soffici, he founded the review *Lacerba.* Other books that came from his pen during these years were: *Ventiquattro Cervelli* (1912) and *Pragmatismo* (1913). He wrote with brilliancy and daring. His fiction has a philosophical basis.

For three years, 1913 to 1916, Papini was literary correspondent in Italy for the *Mercure de France* of Paris. When the war started he began in the review *Lacerba* a campaign for Italian intervention, which he continued at the invitation of Benito Mussolini in *Popolo d' Italia* in Milan. Twice he offered his services to the military officials but was refused by the medical authorities. For the year 1916 to 1917 he was literary critic for *La Nazione* of Florence. Again with A. Soffici, he founded in 1918 the review *La Vrai Italie* and published his third volume of poems, *Giorni di Festa.* The following year the beginning of his conversion is manifested in two articles "Amore e Morte" (Love and Death) and "Esistono Cristiani?" (Are There Any Christians?). And in 1920, after years of opposition and atheism, he made his submission and was received into the Catholic Church.

Since his conversion, Giovanni Papini's most important Catholic books are: *The Life of Christ* (1920); *Gli Operai Della Vigna* (Laborers in the Vineyard) (1929); *Sant' Agostino* (1929); *Gog* (1931); *Dante Vivo* (1933); *I Testimoni della Passione* (1937), and *Lettere agli Uomini del Papa Celestino VI* (1946). The last named work has been translated into English under the title *The Letters of Pope Celestine VI* and will be published in January, 1948. It is "a series of letters from a mythical Pope bearing upon problems similar to those of our own times."

Notwithstanding the unfavorable criticisms and reservations of some of his readers, either in good or bad faith, Papini is generally considered the greatest, the most powerful and most original Catholic writer of Italy in this century.

In 1907 he married Giacinta Giovagnolia. They have two daughters.

Katharine Olive Parr

Katharine Olive Parr, "Beatrice Chase, the Lady of the Moor" to the English literary world, writer of passion tales of fighting men, was born in London. She is a descendant of Katharine Parr, the sixth Queen of Henry VIII, a granddaughter of General Chase Parr, and a niece of Admiral Chase Parr, who was naval aide-de-camp to Queen Victoria. Her family were warriors since the days of the Wars of the Roses. William Parr, from whom she is directly descended, apostatized from the Catholic Church. A devout Catholic, Katharine Parr says of herself: "As far as I know I am the next of the family to return to the Church." She was educated at Holy Child Convent, London, where her agnostic parents—lost in a sea of doubt rather than scoffers—had her baptized, believing that, if there were a God, the Catholic Church must be His Church. She had the happiness of seeing her parents become Catholics before they died.

Special interest attaches to her work because most of her tales are based on truth, many of them centering around her chapel in Dartmoor and her White Knight Crusade, founded during the first World War by herself and her poet-friend, "John Oxenham," to keep the souls and hearts of men white by friendly interest and religious services. Many of her stories come straight from her record sheet of the "Shrine" at Venton House, at Widecombe-in-the-Moor.

In her book, *The Twelfth an Amethyst,* "Beatrice Chase" describes this chapel and its priestess. In *White Knights On Dartmoor* she recounts the incentive and progress of her White Knight Crusade. Katharine Parr, known generally as a writer of prose, also writes verse, occasionally in her own name, but more often under her pseudonym of "Beatrice Chase."

E. F.

Reverend Wilfrid Parsons, S.J. 1887-

A notable editorial career and distinguished library work preceded the professorship in political science at the Catholic University of America now held by the Reverend Wilfrid Parsons, S.J. He was born in Philadelphia, Pennsylvania, in 1887, and after attending grade and high schools there entered the Society of Jesus in 1903. He studied for three years at Louvain, Belgium, where in 1910 he received his Ph.D. In 1918 he was ordained to the priesthood. Awarded his S.T.D. at Woodstock in 1919, he then went abroad for two years' postgraduate study at the Gregorian University, Rome. He received his S.T.M. degree in 1921.

In 1925 he was appointed editor of the Jesuit weekly *America*, which celebrated its twenty-fifth anniversary during his editorship. In May 1936 he was transferred to Georgetown University, Washington, D. C., and was professor of political science in the Graduate School until 1940, when he became professor of political science at the Catholic University of America. While at Georgetown he was made librarian and archivist, in 1938, and dean of the Graduate School in 1939. As archivist he compiled a valuable, monumental work on *Early Catholic Americana,* comprising over one thousand titles of all books written by Catholics, on Catholic and non-Catholic subjects, from 1729 to 1830 inclusive, and their location in various libraries of the country. An introduction gives the history of the publishers and printers, and in the appendix are listed Catholic periodicals of the time.

Father Parsons' first book, published in 1929, was *The Pope and Italy*. The authority of the Church in relation to political regimes is of particular interest to him, as witnessed by his other works: *God and Governments; Church and State,* and *Mexican Martyrdom*. In the last book he gives a vivid portrayal of the sufferings of the Church in Mexico during recent years. A keen analysis of the problems of democracy, its basic strength in industrial, racial, and international justice, and the threats of communism, fascism, socialism, and liberalism, is given in *Which Way, Democracy?* published in 1940. In the field of periodical literature, in addition to being editor of *America* for eleven years, Father Parsons began the publication of *Thought* and has contributed to *Etudes* of Paris, the London *Month* and other journals here and abroad. He is well known as a lecturer. The honorary degree of Litt.D. was conferred on him by St. Joseph's College, Philadelphia, in 1929, and St. Francis College, Brooklyn, in 1934.   C. M. N.

Frances Taylor Patterson

Lecturer on motion pictures in the English Department of Columbia University, Frances Taylor Patterson is also the author of several books, a poet and a frequent contributor to magazines. "I can't remember a time when I wasn't writing something," she says. Her inspiration took the form of verse, a diary, a novel and even a newspaper at the tender age of twelve.

She was born in Dobbs Ferry-on-Hudson and her father, James Leo Taylor, owned and edited two Westchester County newspapers. In one of them she made her first appearance in print with a poem entitled "A Wreck," which the press foreman smuggled in when her father was in Europe. She was then eleven and knew all the men at the shop, which was her favorite haunt. Finally she herself became the proud possessor of an old printing press given her by the Reverend Joseph F. Flannelly after it had been discarded from use for parish notices. On this she printed each Friday the *Dobbs Ferry Gazette,* news items collected during the week and laboriously typed on a toy type-writer. Subscribers were chiefly the professors at St. Joseph's Seminary, Dunwoodie.

With Father Flannelly in those early days of literary endeavor she sometimes went on river picnics in his launch "Tegaquita." These out-ings she considered far better than Alice in Wonderland's picnics. Some twenty years later there recurred to her the name "Tegaquita," which had then engaged her fancy, and she determined to learn the story of this "little Indian saint" after whom her childhood friend had named his boat. Thus *White Wampum* came to be written.

Meanwhile she had completed her studies at the Masters School at Dobbs Ferry, received her A.B. at Trinity College, Washington, D. C., taken postgraduate work at Columbia University, and married Rowland Patterson of New York City. While at preparatory school she wrote for its paper *The Masterpieces* and later she contributed to the *Trinity College Record*. Andrew Carnegie wrote her in praise of an article in the *Record* on the Disarmament of Nations, and one of her poems evoked a letter from the present Cardinal Spellman of New York, then exchange editor for the *Fordham Monthly*, the literary paper there.

After college she wanted to do newspaper work, and a friend of her father's, Dr. Albert Shaw, editor of the *Review of Reviews,* gave her some leads for special articles. She also met H. V. Kaltenborn, who was on the City Desk of the Brooklyn *Eagle,* and he started her in reporting. At college she had majored in English and her dislike of the way the movies garbled the classics made her wish to become an influence in that field. So she decided to take some courses at Columbia. Given a position on the faculty as a member of the English Department, she has since lectured there on that "constantly changing, constantly progressing, ever fresh subject, the motion picture," studying it in its relation to the other arts, to architecture and painting and music and drama, and in its rela-tion to the audience as a far reaching social and moral influence. She has come to believe that it is not possible to adapt classics to the screen any more than it is possible to translate a statue into music. Her chief interest is in helping to build up a medium of story telling completely independent of the stage and fiction, of which the basic appeal is pic-torial motion, aided and enriched, but not dominated by sound in its dual use, music and dialogue; a medium of pictures, not words.

She has had two leaves of absence, one to work at Oxford, the other to work at Hollywood, the two extremes between which she keeps the "via media." At Oxford she took special courses, and lived at St. Hilda's College. Some impressions of the university were published in *The Commonweal* (1938) under the title "Sketch in Charcoal." Numerous articles on the movies, among them "Bread and Cinemas," "A New Art in an Old University" and "Descent into Hollywood," have appeared in the *New Republic,* the *North American Review,* the New York *Times* and other publications. She has also written three books: *Cinema Craft-manship* (1920); *Scenario and Screen* (1928); and *Motion Picture Con-*. *tinuities* (1929). She is a member of the National Board of Review of Moving Pictures.

Mrs. Patterson's first short story, "The Ghostways," published in *Scribner's,* was included in Edward J. O'Brien's *Best Short Stories of 1928* with four stars. He also starred "Gesture," a later story in *Scribner's* and "Table for One," in *Harper's,* July 1940. Her poetry has been printed in many magazines and newspapers. In 1928, sponsored by the poet Edwin Arlington Robinson and Robert Bridges, editor of *Scribner's,* she was made a Fellow of the MacDowell Association, with the privilege of spending a portion of each summer with other artists at the MacDowell Colony at Peterborough, New Hampshire. She and her husband have a summer home at Mt. Washington, Massachusetts, in the Berkshires.

While doing research for her book on Kateri Tekakwitha she lived for a time at the Indian Reservation of Caughnawaga, near Montreal. "When I went there, I intended to live with an Indian family in one of their cabins in order to get to know better these blood relations of Kateri Tekakwitha. But the Jesuit Father in the old French 'Presbytère,' whom I went to call on while I was still at the hotel in Montreal, gently suggested that I ought to go to the hospital. I was about to explain that I wasn't ill when he added that he thought it would be healthier living with the sick Indians in the hospital than with the well Indians in their cabins."

She wrote of it in an article in *The Commonweal,* "The Praying Castle." The book, *White Wampum,* was published in 1934. In appreciation of her work she was presented by Father John J. Wynne, S.J., vice-postulator of the cause for beatification of Tekakwitha, to the Apostolic Delegate who offered his congratulations and felicitations on her book. A deep interest in the American Indians and in the missionaries who lived among them in the seventeenth century has led her to a new subject, a life of St. Jean de Brébeuf.   C. M. N.

Hertha Pauli 1909-

The starting point of Hertha Pauli's literary career was the theatre. As a young actress, trying to live other people's lives on the stage, she came to think of writing them. Her first book, *Toni,* published in 1936, was a biographical novel about Austria's great dramatic poet, Ferdinand Raimund. He also started as an actor. Miss Pauli says, "This may be the reason why I still regard my first biography as my 'most representative.'" Her next, published in 1938, was *Only a Woman,* a fictional biography of Bertha Von Suttner, the apostle of world peace and friend of Alfred Nobel whose life story the author was to write some years later, in America.

Miss Pauli was born in Vienna, Austria, September 4, 1909, the daughter of Dr. Wolfgang and Bertha (Schuetz) Pauli. She attended the Doeblinger Gymnasium and the Academy of Dramatic Arts in Vienna from 1920 to 1926, and began her theatrical career in Breslau, Germany, with Shakespeare's Juliet as her first part. She later was a member of the Reinhardt Theatre in Berlin and appeared on the stage in Paris and Vienna, in films and in radio plays, some of which she wrote herself. In 1929 she married a colleague, Carl Behr, who died in 1934.

Immediately after Hitler's rise to power, Hertha Pauli left Germany and returned to Vienna, to devote herself entirely to writing. Besides her books, she wrote stories, articles and poems. "Whatever I wrote," says Miss Pauli, "was in some way a protest against Nazism. So I had to flee Austria when the Germans arrived in 1938." She went to France and remained there for two years. Her books, banned in Germany, were published in translations throughout Europe. When France collapsed in the summer of 1940, she spent five weeks in flight from Paris to Marseille, mostly on foot and occasionally under German bombs. In Marseille, she received one of the American rescue visas obtained for a group of anti-Nazi European writers by a committee headed by Thomas Mann; unable to get an exit visa from Vichy-France, she walked across the Pyrenees and managed to get to Lisbon where she boarded a Greek freighter and arrived in the United States in September 1940.

In New York she did secretarial work for a short time. In the spring of 1941 she went to Hollywood as an assistant to an M.G.M. writer but did not like it, so returned to New York when her manuscript, *Alfred Nobel: Dynamite King—Architect of Peace,* was accepted, and she has lived in New York ever since. Her biography of the inventor of high explosives and donor of the Nobel Prizes, Alfred Nobel, was published in 1942. In *Silent Night: The Story of a Song,* she wrote a history of the celebrated Christmas carol and published it in 1943. This was the first children's book ever to be condensed in *The Reader's Digest.* Hertha Pauli's book, *The Story of the Christmas Tree,* appeared in 1944 and *St. Nicholas Travels* in 1945.   P. H.

Anton Charles Pegis   1905-

The educator and philosopher, Anton Charles Pegis, was born in 1905 in Milwaukee, Wisconsin, the son of Costas and Euphrosyne (Stacey) Pegis. He received his bachelor's degree from Marquette University in 1928; his M.A. there the following year, and completed his Ph.D. studies at the University of Toronto in 1931. That year he married the poet, Jessie Donaldson Corrigan. They have four children.

He owes his teaching inspiration and some of his philosophical outlook to the work of two men for whom he has the highest regard: the late Reverend J. F. McCormick, S.J., in whose honor he edited a memorial volume, *Essays in Modern Scholasticism* (1944), and Étienne Gilson, in

exposition of whose thought he has written several papers. Dr. Pegis
served as assistant professor of philosophy at Marquette from 1932 to
1937, and at Fordham until 1940. After four years as associate professor,
he was advanced to professor in 1944. Concurrently, he holds the chair
of the history of philosophy at the Pontifical Institute of Mediaeval
Studies in Toronto, and spends his weeks alternately in New York and
in Canada. In 1946 he was appointed president of the Pontifical Institute
of Mediaeval Studies.

He is a Fellow of the Institute, president of the American Catholic
Philosophical Association, and a member of the American Philosophical
Association, the Conference in Science, Philosophy and Religion and the
Mediaeval Academy. He is also one of the editors of the newly projected
philosophical texts to be known as the *Christian Wisdom Series,* and
serves on the editorial boards of *The New Scholasticism* and *Thought.*

While Professor Pegis has taught and written on the whole stream of
Western philosophical thinking, his particular interests have been Greek
thought and the contribution of St. Thomas Aquinas. He combined the
two in his published Aquinas lecture, *St. Thomas and the Greeks* (1939).
He has also written *St. Thomas and the Problem of the Soul in the
Thirteenth Century* (1934), and is the editor of the two-volume *Basic
Writings of St. Thomas Aquinas* (1945), containing a completely revised
English translation of large parts of the *Summa* and of the *Contra
Gentiles,* with an introduction and a detailed author index. This project
has been the work of several years, and was born of the recognized need
for an accurate translation of the philosopher to whom so many writers
refer, but whom so few know in actuality. Articles, papers and reviews,
some of which are to appear in book form, have been published in
*America, The Commonweal, Journal of Religion, Mediaeval Studies, The
New Scholasticism, Speculum, The Thomist, Thought, Traditio,* and in
Canadian journals.

He is an invigorating and stimulating lecturer, and has toured this
country and Canada several times. The same traits appear in the forceful
thinking and sturdy style of his printed convictions.

On the press (December, 1947) is *An Introduction to St. Thomas
Aquinas*—essence of his thought from the *Summa Theologica* and the
Summa Contra Gentiles for the Modern Library Series.

He is at present (1947) engaged in writing a volume entitled *The
Wisdom of Catholicism* for the Lifetime Library Series of Random House.

J. T.

Hilary Douglas Clark Pepler 1878-

Hilary Douglas Clark Pepler comes of Quaker stock. He was received into the Catholic Church in 1916, and at about that time became a leading member of the famous Ditchling (Sussex) Catholic Colony of craftsmen and small farmers. Eric Gill was there too but some years later broke away. The St. Dominic's Press, with which Pepler's name is chiefly associated, was established "after His Majesty's medical advisers had decided that I and a coalheaver were unsuited to the trade of war" as Hilary Pepler tells us in an introductory note to a list of publications issued by the Press. The printing press used was a handpress. It made his publications distinctive. Mr. Pepler aimed at being a craftsman and not a mechanic. He was opposed to mass production and had no ambition to produce cheap and shoddy work. Pepler's type was worthy of ranking with William Morris' Kelmscott Gothic, but was simpler. He also wrote and published with Gill's illustrations, many spirited, audacious, and fervent Catholic squibs.

Since "aesthetic minorities are apt to engender an unhealthy kind of conceit" a chapel was erected in the centre of the settlement as a corrective. The members of the community with one or two exceptions were Dominican tertiaries and at fixed times during the day they left their work for prayer. Father Vincent McNabb, the famous Dominican preacher and writer was their Spiritual Director. The zeal of Gill and Pepler may be judged by the fact that finding that the Angelus was not rung at Ditchling they ransacked the by-ways for a worthy bell, and then rang it daily.

During the period of World War I, it became necessary to do farming. Six hundred acres were secured and tilled. "During 1917 and 1918," wrote Pepler, "we could have stood a close siege without lack of food." Soon other crafts were added. A weaving shed was set up. Statuary and cabinet making were undertaken. The community assumed the proportions of a tiny village.

After Pepler had done all he set out to do as a printer, he left the press to one of his sons (another son is a Dominican) and a Distributist friend, and launched out on a new career. This was only a few years before World War II, when Pepler was nearly sixty. He wrote and produced miming plays, himself expressing the gamut of the emotions in a nicely stylised dumbshow, and training a company to approach the same pitch. His triumph was *The Field Is Won*, a mime of the life of St. Thomas More, produced at a London theatre not long after the canonization. He was highly successful with his mimes on a visit to the United States.

At about the time when he took on miming in public, he was for a short while secretary of the Distributist League, and went down to Beaconsfield to be "knighted" by Gilbert K. Chesterton with the famous sword-stick.

Although, no doubt, still ready to do a job of printing or a job of miming, Pepler has in fact embarked on a new career. He is a director of *The Weekly Review,* a child of *G. K.'s Weekly,* and a busy member of the editorial staff, writing on economics and public entertainment. Now and then he indulges himself with a squib in verse. Since this *Weekly Review* is the only independent paper left in England, it may afford him sufficient outlet for his vast energies.

Hilary Pepler was born at Eastbourne, borough of Sussex, England, in 1878, and was educated at Bootham School, York. In 1905 he married Clare John Whiteman. They have three sons and three daughters.

Stanley B. James said of his writings: "It is true he is more poet than playwright; I think there is sometimes a lack of dramatic movement in his compositions. But the austere beauty of his writing cannot be denied. It is entirely free from superfluous ornament and sentimentalism. The intellectual quality is high; the lines are packed almost too closely with thought."

He is the author of: *Justice and the Child; Care Committees; The Devil's Devices; Pertinent and Impertinent; Plays for Puppets; The Hand Press,* etc. Also the following mimes: *The Passion; St. Joan,* and *Everyman.*   M. H. & W. T.

Mary Perkins (Mrs. John Ryan) 1912-

Mary Perkins was born on April 10, 1912, and is the youngest of a hard working family. Her father, Charles Bruen Perkins, was an architect. Her mother, Elizabeth (Ward) Perkins, worked with Dr. Thomas Edward Shields at the Catholic University, and with Charles Woodbury, the painter and etcher. She also wrote for various publications. Her brother, Francis D. Perkins, is music editor for the New York *Herald Tribune.* One sister, Dr. Anna Perkins, is a country doctor and her other sister, Mrs. Lewis P. Mansfield, taught the Ward Method (Gregorian Chant) started by her aunt, Mrs. Justine B. Ward. Both her grandfather and grandmother were converts to the Faith and she can count Quakers, Unitarians, Presbyterians and Episcopalians among her immediate ancestors as well as, in distant perspective, Charles Carroll of Carrollton, the only Catholic signer of the Declaration of Independence.

Mary's education began in the Boston schools. When she was thirteen she went to the Convent of the Sacred Heart, Noroton, Connecticut, and was graduated from high school in 1927. She travelled in Europe for a summer with her brother and sister, visiting her aunts who had married abroad, and attended the Finishing School of the Convent of the Sacred Heart, West Hill, London, for a year. When she returned to the United States, her parents thought she was still too young for college so she went to the Bouve School of Physical Education for a winter.

In 1929 she entered the College of the Sacred Heart, Manhattanville, and graduated in 1932. She majored in English and edited the college magazine *The Essay* during her senior year. In 1933 she went to live with her brother in New York and to look for a job that would have some connection with literature or journalism. She was advised to take a secretarial course as the first step but before she completed the course her teacher of religion at Manhattanville College, Reverend John J. Hartigan (now 1947 a Monsignor and pastor of St. John the Evangelist Church in White Plains, New York) informed her that Sheed and Ward were about to open an American Office and that he had recommended her for a position, and she worked for them until the early part of 1934. Odd secretarial jobs for the rest of the winter followed. The summer found her in Santa Fe, New Mexico, working for Alice C. Henderson who was for many years on *The Poetry Magazine* with Harriet Monroe. She had the opportunity of watching an experienced writer at work, collecting material, organizing it and finally writing and rewriting.

When she returned to Boston she wrote some short stories but was unsuccessful in marketing them. A year of illness gave her much time for reading. When she recovered, she again went to New York and for the second time met Reverend Leonard Feeney, S.J. She had made his acquaintance when working for Sheed and Ward. He asked her what she was going to do next and she told him that she was not strong enough for a nine-to-five job and wanted to write but did not know how to make a start. Father Feeney gave her the idea and title of her first book, *At Your Ease in the Catholic Church.*

After a summer in California she came home and wrote the book, which was published in 1938. Two years later, in 1940, *Your Catholic Language* was published. The idea of this second book is to show the reader by means of the Latin of the Mass, supplemented with familiar prayers and hymns, how much Latin he already knows unconsciously and to make correlation and extension of his knowledge as interesting and fruitful as possible.

Mary's ever increasing interest and knowledge of the Liturgy brought her to four Liturgical Week meetings in Chicago, St. Paul, St. Meinrad's Abbey in Indiana and Denver. In this field alone she believes that she has enough material for several lifetimes of writing. She has written articles on the Liturgy for the *Catholic Woman's World, The Sign* and other magazines.

On August 2nd, 1942, Mary Perkins married John Julian Ryan of Boston, Massachusetts. Father Leonard Feeney, S.J., performed the ceremony. Mr. and Mrs. Ryan live in Cambridge, Massachusetts, where he is a member of the Holy Cross faculty in Worcester.

In her latest book, *Speaking of How to Pray*, published in October 1944 she has tried to make a layman's guidebook to the glorious possibilities of our life in Christ in the Church. She shows how the flower of the Church's theology, the liturgy, can be integrated into everyone's life and how rich life and prayer can become through such an integration. The title of the book is from a poem of Father Feeney's. The whole sentence runs:

"And, by the way,
Speaking of how to pray,
Dogmas come first, not liturgies."   C. P.

Reverend Gerald Bernard Phelan 1892-

Writing almost exclusively on philosophy and psychology, Father Gerald Phelan has always had a predilection for these subjects. His early interest in modern philosophy and psychology was stimulated by reading the works of Cardinal Mercier.

Gerald Phelan was born in Halifax, Nova Scotia, on August 26, 1892, the youngest of twelve children of Edward Phelan and Margaret (Connolly) Phelan. He was educated in St. Patrick's Common and High Schools and St. Mary's College in Halifax, graduating from the last named institution in 1909. His theological studies were under the direction of the Eudist Fathers at Holy Heart Seminary, Halifax, and he was ordained to the priesthood on December 27, 1914. After doing some graduate work at the Catholic University of America, Washington, D.C., where he obtained his S.T.B. degree, Father Phelan was appointed to do parochial work among the Acadians in Nova Scotia, afterwards going as curate to the parish of Hamilton, Bermuda, and subsequently to the Cathedral at Halifax. While in Bermuda he had much leisure and used it to study philosophy; and, on his return to Nova Scotia, took up further graduate work in philosophy at St. Francis Xavier University, Antigonish, where he received his M.A. degree. In 1917 he was appointed Lecturer in Philosophy at St. Mary's College, Halifax, an appointment which fulfilled a long-felt wish, for, he desired teaching as his life-work. He left St. Mary's College in 1922 to go abroad to pursue further studies at the famous University of Louvain, Belgium, where he earned his Ph.D. degree. Later he was made an Agrégé of this world famous university, for special research in psychology. He prepared in the psychological laboratories of the University of Louvain, Cambridge University in England and the University of Würzburg in Germany. Upon his return to Canada in 1925 he was appointed professor of psychology in St. Michael's College, University of Toronto. He collaborated with Professor Etienne Gilson and the Basilian Fathers at St. Michael's College in the establishment of the Institute of Mediaeval Studies, of which institution he was successively librarian, 1929 to 1932, director, 1932 to 1937, and president, 1937 to 1946. During his second year as president, the Institute was granted a Papal Charter and became the Pontifical Institute of Mediaeval Studies, with power to grant special degrees, created for the Institute by the Holy See, the Licentiate and the Doctorate in Mediaeval Studies.

During his early priesthood Father Phelan founded the Newman Club at Dalhousie University and gave an annual course of thirty lectures on Medical Ethics to Catholic students of that university. He also edited a local Catholic weekly, *The Cross,* from 1917 to 1922.

Father Phelan is a member of a number of learned societies including the British Institute of Philosophy, the British Psychological Society and the American Catholic Philosophical Association. He was president of the last named society in 1931. He is also a Fellow of the Canadian Academy of St. Thomas Aquinas, a Corresponding Fellow of the Mediaeval Academy of America and a Fellow of the Royal Society of Canada. He holds an honorary LL.D. from Duquesne University and is Chairman of the Committee on Grants in Aid of Research of the Canadian Humanities Research Council.

Although he has contributed numerous articles to reviews and many of the studies have appeared in the volumes of the *Proceedings* of the learned societies to which he belongs, Father Phelan has written only three books: *Feeling Experience and Its Modalities* (Louvain and London, 1925) (an experimental research in psychology); *Jacques Maritain* (New York, 1937) (in which he gives a brief sketch of Maritain's life and a clear exposition of his philosophical thought), and *St. Thomas and Analogy* (1941) (a study in metaphysics given as the Aquinas Lecture at Marquette University for the year 1941). He has also translated into English St. Thomas Aquinas' *Opusculum de Regimine Principum* which he published, with an analytical introduction, under the title of *The Governance of Rules* (1935), and Raissa Maritain's *LePrince de ce Monde (The Prince of This World)* privately printed at Toronto (1933) and published in England (1936).

In 1946 he organized and became director of the Mediaeval Institute at the University of Notre Dame.

Charles Phillips 1880-1933

During his years at Notre Dame (1924 to 1933), Charles Phillips was probably the best known and best loved of all the professors. By incoming freshmen he was referred to as "that pleasant-looking prof." He founded the University Theatre, and helped to found the William Mitchell prize for playwriting. Father O'Hara (afterwards Bishop O'Hara) said of Phillips, "He enriched the literary traditions of Notre Dame."

He was born in New Richmond, Wisconsin, November 20, 1880, the son of Patrick and Martha (MacConaghy) Phillips. He received his early education at De La Salle College, Toronto, and New Richmond High School, where he was graduated in 1899.

For several years following high school he worked in the office of a railroad, using spare moments to study Shakespeare and Dante. He received a degree from St. Mary's College, Oakland, California, in 1914; took special work at Catholic University, Washington and at Oxford, and spent two years in Florence studying Dante.

He arrived at Notre Dame and the chair of literature by way of newspaper work. He had never been a professor until his return from the World War I. He even surprised himself that he could teach. Phillips was famous at Notre Dame for being able to hold interest. Men never before keen on literature signed up for his classes. He never went for a walk without a group of young men accompanying him to pick up wisdom from his good-natured lips. During his Notre Dame days he was also an associate editor of *The Catholic World.*

He loved Notre Dame to such an extent that all through Europe he dragged his friends to visit any church, convent, hospital, or shrine with that name attached. He said Notre Dame kept him young. Shortly after his arrival he remarked, "Since coming to Notre Dame I have aged ten years younger." He remained all his life unmarried and retained much of his boyish look and manner.

After several successful editorships in St. Paul, Washington, and in his own town, New Richmond, he was made editor of the *Monitor,* the official organ of the Archdiocese of San Francisco, California, 1907 to 1915. All through these years, since his railroad job at nineteen, he had been writing poetry. In 1908 he published his first book *Back Home.* It ran into five editions and was written to commemorate his father's eightieth birthday. The fifth edition he dedicated to the memory of his father who was called "back home" in 1913.

In the early *Monitor* days he was well known in San Francisco. He arrived there at the time of the earthquake when everything was in mad confusion. Brother Leo, one of his dearest friends, and so long connected with the *Monitor,* liked best to recall Charles Phillips in his destitute, temporary quarters of the newspaper, a tired, calm young man sitting amidst the ruins, taking life as it came. While in California, he so loved the beauty of the Greek drama that he frequently crossed the bay to attend the Greek theatre in Berkeley. A friend once called him "a pagan with a crucifix around his neck."

During 1918 to 1919 he volunteered for secretarial war work with the Knights of Columbus. He was assigned to European duty, and sailed for an eastern post in October 1918. The Armistice was signed while he was on the way over, but he did not know it until he reached England. He had his bag packed to return home when he was put on relief work in France and Germany, 1918 to 1919; and in Poland, 1919 to 1922. Phillips was so touched with the sad plight of the Polish people that he resigned from the Knights of Columbus and remained in Europe to do welfare work in Poland with the American Red Cross. He came home with the rank of captain. He was an American delegate to the International Congress of Young Men's Societies, Rome, in 1921.

Phillips' interest in Poland dated back to the early days in San Francisco when he had met Helena Modjeska, the renowned Polish actress, and had listened to her story of her people. He was a lover of Poland's art and culture. His fascinating personality drew the Polish people to him just as he felt drawn to them. He met Paderewski, the Polish Prime Minister in Warsaw and met there, also, his Eminence Cardinal Ratti (afterwards Pope Pius XI) and went to the estate of Premier Grabski, Pilsudski's cousin, to sleep in the bed of Napoleon.

Pilsudski said he wished Poland had a few sons of her own like Phillips. In explanation of his deep study and vast writings on Poland, Phillips said he liked the Polish people better than any in Europe, adding, "something so homelike and American about them."

He came back from the war duty in 1922, a broken man. After a rest of two years, he started what many believe the greatest of his works, the biography of Paderewski, taking ten years in its preparation and three months writing it. He always wrote in long hand as he could not use the typewriter and he refused to dictate. As the book ran on and on he used to remark: "I intended this to be a biography of Paderewski . . . not another history of Poland." *Paderewski* was his last work and was published one month after his death which occurred December 29, 1933.

In 1925, after a first-hand survey of Mexico, he had written for N.C.W.C. a series of articles bringing the attention of the public in this country, for the first time, to the bitter persecution of the Catholic Church in Mexico.

Professor Phillips was an authority on comparative literature, drama, creative writing, and the Polish people. He wrote on drama, fiction, poetry and biography. The religious drama *The Divine Friend,* a beautiful tale of Mary Magdalen, was produced in October 1915 by the celebrated Margaret Anglin, Laetare Medalist, and she enacted the stellar role. He met Miss Anglin while he was editor of the San Francisco *Monitor* writing drama criticisms. To her he dedicated his poem *Antigone.* He also wrote *Tarcissius* (drama) (1917); *A Saint for Soldiers* (1918); *A Buccaneer of Christ* (1918); *The New Poland* (1923); *The Teacher's Year* (1924); *The Doctor's Wooing* (a novel) (1926); *High in Her Tower* (1929) (collection of poetry).

Phillips was a member of the Poetry Society of America. He was co-founder of the magazine *Pan* which had the subtitle *Poetry and Youth.*

E. F.

John Pick 1911-

One of the younger literary critics and scholars is John Pick who was born in West Bend, Wisconsin, on September 18, 1911. His deepest interest lies in literary criticism which is at the same time scholarly and thoroughly Catholic.

After graduating from the University of Notre Dame in 1933, he took graduate courses and did special research at Harvard University, the University of Wisconsin, and Oxford. In 1938 he was granted his Ph.D. by the University of Wisconsin.

Having taught a short time at the University of Wisconsin, he was anxious to devote himself to Catholic education, and in 1939 he joined the faculty of Boston College, Chestnut Hill,

Massachusetts, as assistant professor of English. There he gave a full schedule of courses but especially devoted himself to mediaeval literature and to Shakespeare. His articles and reviews may be found in such periodicals as *The Month, America, The Commonweal, Thought,* and *The Catholic World.*

Gerard Manley Hopkins: Priest and Poet, his most important work, was published in London in 1943 and in New York in 1944. It was praised by non-Catholics as well as by Catholic reviewers. The London *Times Literary Supplement* greeted it as "the first study to be based on a real understanding of the unity of poet, priest, and Jesuit in Hopkins . . . the most informing which has yet been written," while the reviewer in *America* summed it up in these terms: "This is a thorough piece of work, and ought to answer, once for all, the charge Dr. Pick sets himself to disprove, namely that Hopkins' genius grew hampered and tortured because he became a Catholic, a priest, and, above all, a Religious . . . the whole tone of the slim volume is one of restrained enthusiasm for one who is without doubt, despite his obviously limited audience, one of the language's greatest religious poets."

In 1943 Mr. Pick took leave of Boston College and is at present an English master at Groton School, Groton, Massachusetts.

Reverend Maximin Piette, O.F.M.   1885-

Father Maximin Piette, O.F.M., is known to students of religious movements for his definitive work, *John Wesley in the Evolution of Protestantism.*

He was born, October 8, 1885, on a farm near Longueville, in the Walloon province of Brabant, Belgium, close by the battlefield of Waterloo. He was next to the youngest of seven children. The father died when Maximin was four.

What made the deepest impression on his childish consciousness was the heroism displayed by his mother in providing for her numerous family. Of the seven, four—two boys and two girls—followed religious vocations; the rest found their place in the business world.

After attending primary school in his native village, the boy was sent to St. Anthony's College, Lokeren, in East Flanders (1899). Here he studied the classics, together with French, Flemish, English and German. In 1904 he joined the Franciscan Order and, after distinguishing himself above his fellows in philosophy and theology, was appointed to the theological faculty of Louvain University.

During the first World War, he served as a Red Cross stretcher bearer, and then as a military chaplain during the siege of Liege. On August 8, 1914, the young priest, in the course of his sacred ministry, made the rounds of the frontline trenches three times under a withering fire. He was taken prisoner, and stood up before a firing squad the same evening in the barracks yard at Aix-la-Chapelle. A drunken brawl among the soldiers saved his life, but it did not spare him the anguish of mind, the torment of soul, that accompanies the certainty of death. "Were I to be shot now, I would not be afraid," he remarks. "I have already gone through the experience—save only the crumbling into a senseless heap on the ground."

Escape from death, however, did not prevent his serving a prison term in Hanover (from 1914 to 1915) and later, in the fortress border town of Gross-Strelitz in Upper Silesia (1916).

He was later released and served as chaplain in the occupied parts of Belgium. Busy though he was, he spent whatever spare time came his way making a study of the life of John Wesley, who had assumed almost the proportions of a hero to him, despite his differing religious views. He had started this work in 1913 at the suggestion of Professor Alfred Cauchie, the founder of *La Revue d'Historie Ecclesiastique*. In recognition of his work the theological faculty granted him, two years later, his licentiate and doctorate in theology. Then followed five years' assiduous work in Belgian and English libraries; a labor crowned by the publication of the first edition of his book *John Wesley et sa Réaction dans l'Évolution du Protestantisme* in 1925. As a reward for his untiring efforts, the University of Louvain granted him the exceptional title of Doctor and Master of Theology.

The work was warmly received and accorded many honors, including the Belgian Inter-University Government Prize in 1926, and the Marcellin Guérin Prize accorded by the French Academy in 1927 upon the appearance of a second edition. The same year, the C.R.B. (Commission for Relief in Belgium) Educational Foundation of New York, now known as the Belgian American Educational Foundation voted the author a traveling purse and made him a graduate fellow.

And so he spent two years in America from 1927 to 1929, winning his Master of Arts degree from Harvard in 1928 for research conducted on the role of Methodism in the religious evolution of the United States and Canada. Since that time, Father Piette has twice returned to the United States to put the final touches on this work of critical research. With the help of a Model T Ford he visited practically every State in the Union, and every library of any note. In 1945 he became an American citizen.

During the fall of 1937, an English translation of his book appeared, translated by the Very Reverend Joseph Bernhard Howard. It bears the title *John Wesley in the Evolution of Protestantism*.

Father Piette is a laureate of the French Academy, and in 1937 was appointed professor of history at the University of Brussels.

Happening to be in the United States for further research in 1939 when war broke out in Europe, thus rendering his return home impossible, Father Piette was prevailed upon to undertake the collecting and editing of the *Letters of Fray Junipero Serra*, Apostle and Founder of California. The translation of these letters has been entrusted to the Very Reverend Joseph B. Howard. Father Serra's letters are of a directness, simplicity and sincerity almost unique in the field of literature.   P. O.

Very Reverend Thomas Plassmann, O.F.M.
1879-

Well known and esteemed as one of the leading figures in education in the United States, as well as author of books, and contributor to many periodicals of high standing, Father Thomas Plassmann was born in Avenwedde, Germany, on March 19, 1879. After the completion of his elementary studies, he attended a private school for a year, and then, in 1894, came to the United States, where he entered St. Francis Solanus College, Quincy, Illinois, from which institution he received the M.A. degree. In 1898, he joined the Order of Friars Minor, at Paterson, New Jersey, and continued to study there for the priesthood, which was conferred on him in 1906, by the Apostolic Delegate, the Most Reverend Diomede Falconio, O.F.M., at Washington, D.C. Completing his studies at Catholic University in Semitic languages and literature, he was awarded his Ph.D. degree in 1907. The period from then until 1910 was spent in Rome, in visiting the Holy Land, and in further studies at the Universities of Louvain, Bonn, and others in Germany. In 1909, the University Appolinaris in Rome conferred on him the S.T.D. degree. He holds honorary degrees of Litt.D., LL.D., and Lector General of Sacred Scripture.

Since 1910 he has been a member of the faculty of St. Bonaventure's College and Seminary, St. Bonaventure, New York, teaching a number of subjects and holding various offices. In addition, he has served the Order as Secretary, as Definitor, as Prefect of Studies for the Holy Name Province, and as Visitor General.

The educational societies with which he has been, or is connected include the Seminary Department of the National Catholic Education Association of which he is a life member, the Association of Colleges and Universities of New York State, the Catholic Biblical Association of America, the Franciscan Educational Conference, of each of which he has been president, the Regents' College Council for New York State and the Catholic Historical Association.

He is Consultor for the Catholic Biblical Association of America, and a member of the Editorial Board for the Revision of the Douai Version. He belongs to the "Goerresgesellschaft" and the "Conseil Historique et Heraldique de France." Articles of his have appeared in the *American Ecclesiastical Review; The Catholic Educational Review;* the *Pastoral and Homiletic Review; Archivum Franciscanum Historicum;* the *Catholic Biblical Quarterly; Franciscan Studies;* the *Catholic Encyclopedia,* and other publications. His works include: *The Signification of Beraka* (1913); *Bartholomaeus Anglicus* (1917); *The Book Called Holy* (1937);

The Priest's Way to God (1938); *The Seven Words of Mary* (1939), and *From Sunday to Sunday* (1942).

The esteem in which he is held, both at St. Bonaventure's College and by the Franciscan Order generally, is shown by the fact that in 1947 he celebrated his twenty-seventh year as president of St. Bonaventure College and Seminary, and he has been president of the Franciscan Educational Conference since its organization in 1918. Buildings added to St. Bonaventure's College during his administration are The Alexander Hickey Memorial DeVereux Hall, and the Friedsam Library.

In June 1945 he received the honorary degree of Doctor of Laws from Niagara University, and in January 1946 he was appointed Visitor General of a German province of the Franciscan Order.

R. F.

Reverend Joseph Conrad Plumpe 1901-

Fully in proportion to their numbers, the German-American Catholics have contributed to the educational and organizational strength of the Church in the United States, particularly in the mid-western area. A goodly part of this contribution has come from the Pontifical College Josephinum, near Columbus. From here hundreds of priests, trained with the thoroughness of the German Gymnasium, have gone forth to their apostolic labors in many parts of the land. Among the contemporary educators and scholars is Reverend Joseph Conrad Plumpe, an alumnus of Josephinum.

Father Plumpe was born April 12, 1901, on a farm near Cloverdale, Ohio, oldest of the eight children of August and Mary (Gerding) Plumpe. He attended the small parochial school of St. Barbara, in a rural district close to the Indiana line, where the combination of Catholic and German was not above suspicion by the descendants of the New England Yankees. Here the future priest received the groundwork of his education in English and German, and the zealous parish priest gave him his first acquaintance with the Latin declensions. From 1916 to 1928 he pursued his studies for the priesthood at Josephinum. Of this period of his life he writes: "It was a rugged schooling we received at the old Josephinum on East Main Street, Columbus. We came from a great many states, and to these there was a steady regression owing to the standards and discipline maintained. Christmas vacation was spent there, and not even a rural Kansan's son was in any way spoiled by the comforts provided. However, besides all else it gave us, the institution must have sheltered us with a combined motherliness and fatherliness that have made the love and loyalty of its alumni outstanding." He received both the A.B. and M.A. from Josephinum and was ordained on June 2, 1928, at Toledo, by Bishop Stritch, now Cardinal.

After his ordination he went abroad and studied classical philology at the German universities of Münster and Berlin, from 1928 to 1932. His Ph.D. was obtained at Münster in 1932. Returning to the United States, he taught Latin, Greek, and German for nine years at the school from which he received his first degrees. Since 1941 he has served on the faculty of the Catholic University in Washington, D.C., where he is associate professor of Latin. He is a member of the American Philological Association, The Catholic Historical Association, The Classical Association of the Middle West and South, and serves on the Executive Committee of the Classical Association of the Atlantic States.

As a classical scholar, Dr. Plumpe did research on Cicero and the Attic orators. This is evidenced by his published Münster dissertation: *Wesen und Wirkung der auctoritas maiorum bei Cicero* (1935), and by a number of articles in classical journals. In recent years he has veered more and more to a study of early Christianity, especially as seen against the ancient pagan background. The results of this occupation have been published in various papers and in his latest work, *Mater Ecclesia: An Inquiry into the Concept of the Church as Mother in Early Christianity* (1943).

The years he spent as a college teacher show his abiding interest in the history of the German-American Catholics. He is co-author of *Monsignor Joseph Jessing (1836-1899); Founder of the Pontifical College Josephinum* (1936); and wrote a translation of Father Peter Lemcke's *Life and Work of Prince Demetrius Augustine Gallitzin* (1940), a Catholic Book Club selection. Both Prince Gallitzin and his Benedictine biographer labored long during the nineteenth century among German and Irish Catholics in the Alleghenies.

Dr. Plumpe recalls fondly his travels in Europe, especially in Germany, where he made every effort to become acquainted at first hand with German life and problems. As a lone American student there during the final fateful years of the Weimar Republic, he found admission everywhere. Thus, too, he treasures not least his memories of an active membership in one of the colorful German student confraternities. In a nostalgic vein he writes: "In August 1932 I left good Westphalian Münster, Catholic Münster of more than a thousand years, that had weathered fire and pestilence and heresy, but that lies a shambles now, only one more monument to the infamy that came later. I left on the very day that Heinrich Brüning, Münster's own son, resigned as Chancellor of the Reich." It may well be that men of Father Plumpe's training and erudition will be needed in the future to help make Germany understood in America and America in Germany.

                                                                    J. T. & J. M.

Reverend Raoul Plus, S.J. 1882-

Popularly known and admired as a writer on mystical and ascetical theology, Father Raoul Plus was born on January 22, 1882, at Boulogne-sur-Mer. He entered the Jesuit college of his native city where he also took his secondary school studies. When he finished his philosophical studies in July 1899 he went to the novitiate then located at Amiens (St. Acheul).

The persecutory laws against the religious orders in 1901 constrained him to leave France, and except for ten months of military service at St. Mihiel, he had to pass ten years in exile: two years of literary studies at Arbon, Belgium; three years of scholastic philosophy in Gemert, Holland; three years as a professor in the French refugee college at Florennes in Belgium, where he taught Humanities and Rhetoric successively; four years of theology at Englien near Brussels.

During his three years of philosophy, he had the rare honor of having as his spiritual father, Father Foch, the brother of the well-known marshal. Father Plus heard him explain in his private and public conferences the wonders of the Divine life in us and of our incorporation in Christ, this in a fashion so incisive and eloquent that he resolved to make a special study of it. "If all this be true," he said, "it should be proclaimed to the world."

His four years of theology, spent in studying dogma, the Gospels and the Fathers strengthened his firmness in the doctrines enunciated by Father Foch, so that at the end of his theology course, he published two articles in the Revue Apologetique: "Our Times and the Knowledge of the State of Grace."

At the beginning of World War I, in August 1914, Father Plus was mobilized as a simple soldier at first and later as a chaplain. Twice cited and decorated with the Croix de guerre, he obtained the medaille militaire. During the stagnant hours in the trenches he put in writing the talks he gave to the soldiers and priests. Out of these came his first two books, *Dieu en nous* and *L'Idée réparatrice*. Soon these two books had a large circulation, especially the first, and he was asked to have them translated. In its original edition, 140,000 copies of *Dieu en nous* were sold and it has been translated into Russian, English, Polish, Bohemian, German, Dutch, Italian, Portuguese, Spanish, Chinese and Japanese.

When he was at Lille, as professor of religion at the Catholic Institute of Arts and Sciences, he produced the book *Notre histoire divine* which is a synthetic resumé of his teaching. Despite his manifold duties at the Catholic University as spiritual director of the students, as a teacher and preacher, Father Plus continued to write. Always it was on the great subject of which Father Foch formerly had shown him the grandeur. He made a serious study of the problems of our Divine life. To give to souls in an accessible way a knowledge of the Mystical Body, Father

Plus published the two volumes which he considers the centre of his entire work: *Dans le Christ Jesus* and *Le Christ dans nos freres*, and then afterwards to fulfill the needs of souls, *Marie dans notre histoire divine* and *Rayonner le Christ*, written for his students; *Comment toujours prier; Comment bien prier; Vivre avec dieu; Comment trouver Dieu au-dedans,* this to aid souls to find in their own hearts the Most High who accompanies them to the borders of the well of Jacob. Impressed by many remarkable examples of the interior life, Father Plus published many biographies of which the most expressive is that of *Marie- Antoinette de Gueser.*

During vacations, Father Plus gives retreats especially to seminarians and priests not only in his native country but also in England, Poland, Rome and Budapest.

During World War II, he lived from 1940 to 1946 in a retreat house. In 1946 he returned to Lille where he is the "spiritual father" of the community, and is busy with his work of preaching and writing.

Convinced that without the practice of prayer, there is no authentic life here below, Father Plus also wrote some brief meditations for young people, *Face a la vie,* and *Mon Oraison* for priests. He wrote too some meditation books for religious, seminarians and married people. In all he has written over forty books.

Among his popular works translated into English are: *God Within Us* (1924); *How to Pray Always* (1926); *Baptism and Confirmation* (1930); *Christ in His Brethren; Eucharist* (1931); *Progress In Divine Union; Mary In Our Soul-Life; Jesus—the Model of Religious* and *Radiating Christ* (1939).   M. H.

Very Reverend Hugh Pope, O.P.   1869-1946

An effort to get biographical data directly from Father Hugh Pope, O.P., brought this response: "Do not think me churlish. But I have had to refuse all similar applications for years past. The truth is that life is too short and my hands are very full—too full, I fear." Again: "I am never photographed. I am afraid of breaking the camera."

This well-known English Biblical scholar was born at Kenilworth in 1869, the son of Richard Vercoe Pope, a convert to the Faith. He was educated at the Oratory School, Birmingham, and studied medicine at Queen's College, Birmingham, from 1888 to 1891. In that year (1891) he entered the Order of Preachers—the Dominicans or Blackfriars. After his ordination to the priesthood in 1896, he went to Louvain and received the degree of Lector in Theology two years later. From 1898 to 1909, he was a professor at Hawkesyard, Rugeley. After taking his Licentiate in Holy Scripture in Rome, he remained to take his Doctorate of Scripture before the Pontifical Biblical Commission at the Vatican in 1910. In 1911 he was created Master of Theology.

At the Dominican Collegio Angelico in Rome he was professor of New Testament Exegesis from 1909 to 1913. The following year, he became prior of the Dominican Novitiate House, Woodchester, Glos. Upon relinquishing this post in 1920, he was made regent of studies in the Dominican House of Studies at Hawkesyard, Rugeley. When he terminated his ninth year in this office, he was transferred to Blackfriars, Oxford to serve in the same capacity for five more years. From 1935 to 1941 he was prior of Hawkesyard. From 1942 until his death in 1946 he was vicar of St. Albert's, Edinburgh.

His first book was the *Life of Father Thomas Burke, O.P.,* written in 1895. *The Date of Deuteronomy* appeared in 1909. Then followed his best work, *The Catholic Student's "Aids" to the Bible,* in five volumes. Other books are *The Layman's New Testament* (1928 and 1934); *The Church and the Bible* (1928); *St. Augustine on Prayer and the Contemplative Life* (1935), and *St. Augustine of Hippo* (1937) which is a collection of essays to afford light relief to the more formal addresses delivered in honor of the saint in the Cathedral Hall, Westminster, in September 1930. The book is valuable for its depiction of Christian life in Roman Africa in the fourth and fifth centuries and for its clearness in explaining the Donatist Schism. He also wrote *Prayer and the Contemplative Life, According to St. Thomas Aquinas;* and *The Friar Preacher Yesterday and Today* (translated from the French of Pere Jacquin, O.P.). Besides various translations, Father Hugh Pope has written articles for several theological and Biblical Reviews. M. H.

Henri Pourrat 1887-

Though he belongs to the most gifted and brilliant representatives of Paris literary circles, Henri Pourrat can be described as a typical regional author, for he has devoted most of his works to his native Auvergne. Born in the little city of Ambert, Puy-de-Dome on May 7, 1887, Pourrat spent his childhood years there, then went to Paris where he completed his studies at the Lycée Henri IV, and was admitted in 1905 to the Agronomical Institute. But his frail health obliged him to give up his studies. At that time he was already a fervent admirer of the Catholic poets, Paul Claudel, Charles Peguy and Francis Jammes. He shared with the latter a deep love for nature, and of the countryside and of the rustic farm life. With his friend, Jean Angeli he started on a literary career, writing essays and poems, and worked for a time at the *Nouvelle Revue Française* reading manuscripts for the review. During the war, Jean Angeli was killed and this tragic death robbed young Pourrat of a devoted and stimulating companion. His own health was rapidly failing, and he had to give up Paris and return to Ambert, where he made his home with his wife and three children.

Pourrat's most famous work is *Gaspard des Montagnes,* a rustic epic, which has been called the "Auvergnat Somma." The hero, Gaspard and his beloved cousin Anne-Marie, are typical of the peasantry which lived in the Auvergne some one hundred years ago, an Auvergne full of rebellions, melodrama, superstitions and ghosts. Gaspard himself can be described as a peasant-paladin, defender of the oppressed and continually out for romance and adventure. It has been said of this novel that it is "a wild book"; it is inspired by the stubborn and primitive people of Auvergne, who have changed little since the days of Gaspard and Anne-Marie. The book is rich in dramatic situations: kidnappings, fights, ambushes and flights through underground passages to secret strongholds. Like all Pourrat's writings, it would make an excellent movie-script.

Yet there is something more in *Gaspard* than romance and adventure. There is genuine poetry and inspiration, the deep feeling of nature, of the sacred and almost mystic values represented by the soil tilled by the hands of man. One might say that Pourrat was one of the first promoters of the "back to the land" movement, at a time when it was fashionable in French intellectual circles to spend one's time in Paris cafés and not to venture beyond the Luxembourg Gardens or the Tuileries.

Besides *Gaspard,* followed by *A la Belle Bergère, le Pavillon des Amourettes* and *La Tour du Levant,* Henri Pourrat wrote *Les Montagnards, LaVeillée de Novembre, Les Jardins Sauvages* dedicated to his friend Jean Angeli, *Le Mauvais Garçon, La Colline Ronde,* written in collaboration with Jean d'Olagne, and *Liberté,* a book of poems. Most of his works are devoted to his native Auvergne. Yet he makes a point of not turning "provincial" or "regional" in an artificial and conventional way. He stresses that to be a genuine regional author does not mean to dress up in peasant costume and dance the peasant dances for the benefit of the tourist. It means getting close to the soil, to the woods and fields, to the peasant at work among his crops and the humble artisan plying his profession. He compares himself to the sky lark, soaring high above the cornfields, yet always dropping back to earth to regain his strength and impulse.

Henri Pourrat, who received the literary award of the "Figaro" (1922) is a typical Catholic writer, both by birth and inspiration. The "wildest" pages of his *Gaspard* are penetrated with the Christian spirit: he is the poet of evangelical solidarity, of true love and friendship, of devotion, "outside which," as he writes, "nothing exists." And he is also the poet of joy, of healthy and communicative gaiety. "If Rabelais came back," he declared in an interview, "how a little laughter would purify the air of our century!"

H. I.

Sister Mary James Power *see* <u>Mary</u> James Power

Jessica Powers (Sister Miriam of the Holy Spirit)

The greater part of the life of Sister Miriam of the Holy Spirit (Jessica Powers) was spent in Mauston, Wisconsin, where she was born. Encouraged by a Dominican sister, she began to write verse in grade school. Later she was aided much by a course in poetry conducted by Father John Danihy at Marquette University. Her attraction for reading poetry fostered her desire to write and her country environment afforded her leisure and inspiration for verse. At a later period, a few years in New York and contact with those who wrote was conducive to much writing. She admits a debt to modern poetry, even to the newer forms. To have a seemingly perfect modern poem before her is of the greatest assistance in trying to create her own verse, though her inspiration may lead far afield and rest upon a totally different topic from that of the poet.

In 1941 she entered the Order of Discalced Carmelite Nuns in Milwaukee, where she made her profession. During her novitiate she did not write for publication.

Her book of verse, *The Lantern Burns,* was published in 1939.

P. J.

Arthur Preuss 1871-1934

Of Protestant ancestry on both sides and baptized in the Lutheran Church, Arthur Preuss was raised a Catholic. His father, Dr. Edward Preuss, D.D., Ph.D., who before his conversion was a professor of Lutheran theology and exegesis, was received into the Catholic Church in 1872.

Arthur was born on March 22, 1871, at St. Louis, Missouri. His mother was Concordia (Schuricht) Preuss, a native of St. Louis. He was educated in the parochial schools of St. Louis and for about one year he attended Canisius College at Buffalo, New York. Both his A.B. and M.A. degrees were received from St. Francis College (now Quincy College). He refused to accept honorary degrees.

On May 3, 1893, he married Marie Dohle, by whom he had one daughter. After her death he married Pauline Beuckman of East St. Louis, on October 23, 1900. They had eleven children, nine of whom are alive.

Arthur began his active life as a newspaper reporter in St. Louis and then in Chicago, where in 1892 he became the editor of the *Weltbuerger,* a Catholic weekly. This weekly was published in the German language.

Soon after his arrival he changed the name of the weekly to *Katholisches Sonntagsblatt*. The following year (1893) he established the *Chicago Review* (1894). The title was subsequently changed to *The Catholic Fortnightly Review* (1905) and finally to the *Fortnightly Review* in 1912.

Arthur was the leader in the United States in the fight against "Americanism" and later Modernism. Both were condemned publicly by the Pope.

During the last two years of his father's life and for some time thereafter Arthur, in addition to his other work, carried the whole burden as editor-in-chief of the daily *Amerika*. For a number of years he also wrote the editorials of the Buffalo *Echo*, the chronicle of current events for the *Christian Family* of Techny, Illinois, and was an occasional contributor to other journals in America and abroad.

In his later years, he spent his winters in Florida because of failing health, being a frequent guest, at such times, of his friend Abbot Charles Mohr, O.S.B., at St. Leo Abbey, St. Leo, Florida.

Three of Arthur's brothers are priests. Joseph, the oldest is a secular priest, the other two, Francis and James, are Jesuits.

Arthur is the author of: *The Fundamental Fallacy of Socialism* (1907); *A Study in American Freemasonry* (1908) (a fifth edition was published in 1924); *Dictionary of Secret and Other Societies* (1924). With the Reverend Joseph Pohle, Ph.D., D.D., formerly professor of Apologetics at the Catholic University of America and subsequently professor of Dogma in the University of Breslau he brought out "The Pohle-Preuss Series of Dogmatic Textbooks" in twelve volumes. He published *Moral Theology* by Dr. Anthony Koch (five volumes) (1918-1921), and *Handbook of Fundamental Theology* (Lehrbuch der Apologetik) by Reverend John Brunsmann (four volumes).

Arthur Preuss died on December 16, 1934.   M. H.

Reverend Erich Przywara, S.J. 1889-

Father Erich Przywara, S.J., does most of his writing in the fields of philosophy and theology.

He was born on October 12, 1889, at Kattowitz in the Province of Silesia, Germany, the son of Matthias and Bertha (Peiker) Przywara. His father was a merchant. Erich entered the Society of Jesus on June 2, 1908, and went to Valkenburg, Holland, to study philosophy and theology. Ordained a priest in 1920, he became active as an associate editor of several magazines. Since 1922 he has been a member of the editorial staff of *Stimmen der Zeit*. Most of his writing was done at Munich. Father Przywara is also known for his courses in philosophy and theology. With Joseph Kreitmaier he published in 1915, *Unsere*

Kirche, the seventeenth edition of which appeared in 1931. His other works include: *Eucharistie und Arbeit* (1917); *Himmelreich der Seele* (1922); *Kirchenyahr* (1923); *Gottgeheimnis der Welt* (1923); *Liebe* (1924); *Wandlung* (1925); *Majestas Divina* (1925); *Gott* (1926); *J. H. Newman, Christentum* (mit O. Karrer, 8 Bde.) (1922); *Religionsbegrundung* (1923); *Geheimnis Kierkegaards* (1929); *Christus lebt in mir* (1929); *Kant Heute* (1930), and *Karmel* (1932). *A Newman Synthesis* arranged by Erich Przywara is a translation in one volume of the original German edition which appeared in six volumes.

M. H.

Richard J. Purcell 1887-

History is the special field of Dr. Richard J. Purcell of Catholic University where he is a professor and head of the history department.

Born in Minneapolis, Minnesota, in 1887, he was educated in the public schools of his native city and at the University of Minnesota where he received his B.A. degree in 1910 and M.A. degree in 1911. Five years later he received his Ph.D. from Yale University. Georgetown University conferred an LL.B. degree in 1939. He is a member of the bar of the District of Columbia.

From 1911 to 1912 he was an assistant in history at the University of Minnesota. From 1912 to 1916 he was a fellow and an assistant in history at Yale and left when he received his degree (Ph.D.) to become head of the department of history and government at St. Thomas College, St. Paul, Minnesota. He left there in 1920 to become an instructor in history at Catholic University. Two years later he became an associate professor and in 1929 professor. From 1927 to 1928 he was a Guggenheim Memorial Fellow to study Irish immigration and to do research abroad. He has been head of the department of history at Catholic University since 1931. From 1930 to 1935 he was general secretary of the University. In 1941 Dr. Purcell was elected President of the Middle States Association of History and Social Science Teachers.

In 1923 Dr. Purcell married Clara A. Fick, B.A., M.A., of Lake City, Minnesota. They have three children, Richard, Mary, and Pat.

He is the author of *Connecticut in Transition.* This won for him the coveted Justin Winsor Prize of the American Historical Association. He also won the Addison-Porter prize in 1916 for the best doctoral dissertation submitted during the year at Yale. *American Nation,* passing through several reprints, was published in 1929. To the *Dictionary of American Biography* (20 vols.), Dr. Purcell contributed one hundred and seventy-five biographical sketches. He has contributed numerous articles to the revised *Catholic Encyclopedia, World Book Encyclopedia* and *Dictionary of American History,* and many periodicals.

He has contributed 50 annotated articles on the Irish and Catholic contribution to America to the *Catholic Educational Review, Columbia, Studies* (Dublin), *Thought, Journal of American Irish Historical Society;* a number of articles on teaching the social sciences, and about 500 book reviews in secular and Catholic publications.

He has directed, in whole or in part, about forty doctoral dissertations and one hundred and thirty masters' essays at the Catholic University. He is an historiographer of the American Irish Historical Society and a member of the advisory editorial board of the Bulletin of the Association of American Professors and of *Social Education.*

M. H.

Reverend Johannes Quasten   1900-

Johannes Quasten was born at Homberg-Niederrhein, Germany, on May 3rd, 1900, the son of Wilhelm Quasten and Sibyl Schmitz. He received his early education at the Gymnasium Adolfinum at Moers in the Rhineland. From 1921 to 1927 he attended the University of Muenster in Westphalia where he gained his doctorate in Christian archaeology in 1927. After his ordination in 1926, he devoted himself for two years to archaeological studies in Rome, Pompeii, Palermo, Syracuse and Salona and Split in Dalmatia. In 1931 he joined the faculty of the University of Muenster in Westphalia, and taught there until 1937. In 1938 he participated in excavations in Leptis Magna, Tripolis and Sabratha in North Africa. He then came to this country and was appointed professor of Christian archaeology and ancient Church history at the Catholic University of America, Washington, D.C. In 1945 he was appointed dean of the School of Sacred Theology of the Catholic University.

A number of leading publications, both here and in Europe, have published his scholarly articles. He contributed to: *Oriens Christianus; Römische Quartalschrift; Jahrbuch für Liturgiewissenschaft; Römische Mitteilungen; Byzantion; American Journal of Philology; Harvard Theological Review; Catholic Historical Review; Theological Studies.*

He is the author of the following works: *Musik and Gesang in den Kulten der heidnischen Antike und christlichen Frühzeit* (1930); *Expositio antiquae liturgiae Gallicanae Germano Parisiensi ascripta* (1934); *Monumenta Eucharistica et Liturgica vetustissima* (7 vols.) (1935-1937).

As founder and editor of the Series Studies in Christian Antiquity and the annual publication *Traditio,* Dr. Quasten has made an auspicious beginning to what bids fair to be an extensive life-work, and a rich contribution to the rapidly increasing body of the science of church history.

Arthur Hobson Quinn 1875-

Arthur Hobson Quinn is an author and scholar closely identified with the University of Pennsylvania and with the cause of American drama. He was born in Philadelphia in 1875, with a literature-loving, adventure-loving Irish heritage; his maternal grandmother, a Dublin woman, having conducted a "seminary" for boys and girls in the "Quaker City" during the 1840's. As far back as he can remember, Arthur Quinn intended to write, and many of his earliest experiments in prose and verse were contributed to the *Red and Blue,* of which he was editor-in-chief during his undergraduate days at the University of Pennsylvania. Immediately after obtaining his baccalaureate degree there in 1894, he began teaching mathematics at his alma mater. But the next year he moved into the English department—with which, as instructor, assistant professor or professor he has been associated ever since. One year was taken out for supplementary study in modern philology at the University of Munich; but it was from his own university that he received his Ph.D. in 1899.

Dr. Quinn confesses that he entered upon college teaching with the idea that it would permit leisure for creative writing. His first volume was, in fact, *A Book of Pennsylvania Stories* in 1899; and for several years he contributed fiction intermittently to the *Saturday Evening Post, Scribner's* and other magazines. But as he had in the meantime shown extraordinary ability as college executive as well as educator, the result was foreordained. He was promptly chosen as organizer and director of the Summer School and dean of the college faculty of his university, at the same time being invited as visiting lecturer for a number of summer sessions at the Universities of Chicago and California, at New York University and Columbia.

More and more the subject of American drama attracted Dr. Quinn's critical interest, and he was able to pass on to innumerable students his enthusiasm for this important and, in the earlier years, little known branch of our culture. In 1917 he edited *Representative American Plays* —beginning with the pre-Revolutionary tragedy, *The Prince of Parthia,* and ending with our own contemporaries—the first critical collection of American drama to be published anywhere. His *History of the American Drama from the Beginnings to the Civil War,* a work entailing enormous research, was published in 1923; followed four years later by his monumental *History of the American Drama from the Civil War to the Present Day.* These three works established their author as one of the leading authorities on his subject in this country, and he continues this preeminence in a field where he has had many followers. His interpretation of the problematical Eugene O'Neill, founded upon personal friendship and correspondence, has also been an outstanding achievement.

It is one of the not-uncommon ironies of literature that the book which Dr. Quinn considers his best should remain among the least known of his publications. This is *The Soul of America,* a "spiritual history" of our country and our national character, and by far the best attempt yet made to interpret American history with reference to its expression in American literature. "By simply stating the facts as I found them," Dr. Quinn declared, "I hoped to give a fairer picture of the Catholic contribution to American civilization than had previously been given." But since it was published in the midst of the 1932 depression, and was far more spiritual than the mode of the moment, the book reaped public neglect although assured of a succès d'estime by such appreciation as that of the London *Times.* In 1936 came *American Fiction, an Historical and Critical Survey,* and in 1941 Dr. Quinn continued his services to Americana by a critical biography of *Edgar Allan Poe.*

Meanwhile, in addition to a heavy teaching schedule, the author has found time to contribute half a hundred articles to scholarly and popular magazines, to prepare the Dryden article for the *Catholic Encyclopedia,* and several on American playwrights to the *Dictionary of National Biography.* He was also a contributor to the *Cambridge History of American Literature,* and acted as advisory editor of the Cardinal Readers, widely used in our Catholic schools.

Dr. Quinn has been duly elected to membership in the Phi Beta Kappa and Beta Theta Pi fraternities, and has received the honorary Litt.D. from his own University and St. Joseph's College, Philadelphia. He is a member of the Board of the American National Theatre and of the American Philosophical Society. Recently he was elected an honorary member of the Conseil Historique and Heraldique de France, and of the American Antiquarian Society.

Since 1939 Arthur Hobson Quinn has been the John Welsh Centennial Professor of History and English Literature at the University of Pennsylvania, a post which seems particularly fitting because of his late grandfather's association with the Welsh shipping interests. In 1904 he married Helen McKee, to whose sympathetic assistance in his literary work he often refers. They are the parents of two sons and three daughters—who, with their various mates and a growing group of grandchildren, are liable to foregather on Sunday afternoons at the family home in the attractive suburb of Bala-Cynwyd, Pennsylavnia. Dr. Quinn remains an indefatigable theatregoer, both in Philadelphia and New York, and is an active member of the Franklin Inn, Plays and Players, and other clubs.

K. B.

Serafín Alvarez Quintero 1871-1938

Joaquín Alvarez Quintero 1873-1944

The brothers Quintero form one of those composite personalities which from time to time have appeared in literature. All their work has been done jointly. Professor S. Griswold Morley, Ph.D., in his introduction to *Doña Clarines y Mañana de Sol,* says: "Their intellectual harmony is so perfect that on one occasion, as a test, the younger composed a copla of four lines; the first two were then given to the elder, who completed the stanza with the identical words of his brother. Their method of composition is described by them as a continuous conversation. They plan their plays while walking out of doors, in the morning; thus they discuss characters, outline the plot, division into acts and scenes, and even dialog. When the whole and the details are well in mind, the actual writing is done by don Serafín. He reads the results to his brother as he proceeds, and the latter comments or corrects. Details of style are settled in the same viva voce way, better adapted to the drama than to other forms of composition." Together with Jacinto Benavente they have dominated the Spanish theatre since the beginning of the present century.

Born in Utrera, a railway junction on the Seville-Cadiz line, at an early age the brothers removed to Seville where their first play, a farce in one act, *Esgrima y Amor,* was produced, when Serafín was 16 years old and Joaquín was 14. In 1888 their father took them to Madrid in order to give their talents a wider field. For nine years they worked in the Treasury Department, rising at dawn to do some writing before they began their office work at eight. By temperament and choice, however, they remain the poets of Andalusia, its sunny calm, its vivid coloring, the haunting melody of its songs. The distinctive contribution of the Quinteros to the world theatre has been the creation of a drama of atmosphere, free from the usual conflicts and stress of plot and violent action, but which nevertheless enchants and holds the spectator as long as laughter plays or the sun shines. They have been well called "Professors of Happiness" and their works have been translated into all the principal European languages and imitated widely in many lands.

The initial successes of the Quinteros were in the one-act form, which they continued to cultivate throughout their career. The best known of the shorter pieces is *A Sunny Morning (Mañana de Sol),* acted in this country at the Toy Theatre, Boston, in 1915 and subsequently at the Neighborhood Playhouse and the Civic Repertory Theatre, New York (1917 and 1929). Equally notable is the musical sainete *El Mal de Amores* (1905). Among the major plays: *Las Flores* (1901); *El Genio Alegre* (1907); the comedy *Las de Cáin* (1909); *Amores y Amorios* (1910); *Malvaloca*

(1912); *Cabrita que Tira al Monte* (1916); *Asi se Escribe la Historia* (1917); *Cancionera* (1924); and *Las de Abel* (1929), deserve mention, both because of success and distinction. *La Calumniada* (1919), is a vigorous attack upon the Protestant legend of a Black Spain. The brothers Quintero continued to produce for the theatre through the year 1936. The total number of their plays of all kinds exceeds two hundred and fifty. Both brothers have been elected to the Spanish Academy. In 1907 they were both presented with the cross of Alfonso *XII*.

Malvaloca was chosen as the opening day of the Actors' Theatre in New York (1922), starring Jane Cowl. Eva Le Gallienne appeared in *The Lady from Alfaqueque* and *The Women Have Their Way* at the Civic Repertory Theatre (1928 and 1929), while the Neighborhood Playhouse presented *Fortunato* (1918), and Otis Skinner *A Hundred Years Old,* both in New York and on tour (1929-1930). The plays have also been performed frequently in the British Isles.

Of the plays accessible in the English version, eight are from the hands of Helen and Harley Granville-Barker, contained in two volumes: *Four Plays* (The Women Have Their Way, A Hundred Years old, Fortunato, The Lady from Alfaqueque) (1927); *Four Comedies* (Love Passes By, Don Abel Wrote a Tragedy, Peace and Quiet, Doña Clarines) (1932). Individual plays by other translators include: *Malvaloca* (1916); *By Their Words Ye Shall Know Them* (1917); *Papa Juan* (1918); *A Sunny Morning* (1920);*The Fountain of Youth* (1922); *Widows' Eyes* (1929); *Grief* (1930).

J. G. U.

Reverend Charles Joaquin Quirk, S.J.   1889-

A southern poet whose verse is widely praised, the Reverend Charles J. Quirk, S.J., is above all a master of the quatrain. He was born in New Orleans, Louisiana, in 1889, the son of Henry Clay and Mary Louise (Shaw) Quirk. At the age of sixteen he was received into the Catholic Church, and the following year, 1906, he entered the Southern Province of the Society of Jesus. He was ordained at Louvain, Belgium, in 1922, and travelled extensively in Belgium, Holland, Germany, Switzerland, France and England before returning to the United States to teach. After several years at Spring Hill College, Spring Hill, Alabama, where he was head of the English department, he was given leave of absence in 1937 to study at St. Louis University, where he received his M.A. in English. Father Quirk also had a year of graduate work at Columbia University in New York. He is now professor of English at Loyola University of the South, New Orleans.

Father Quirk's definition of poetry, well known to those who have studied under him, is "The ecstasy of a moment snared in words." His inspiration may be religious, life and death, the universe, nature, places, things or moods. Brother Leo says his work has technical efficiency, basic reality, spiritual insight—the "vision of goodness, beauty and truth." *The American Mercury* praises his "high degree of technical skill." Edward D. Stewart in "The Poetry of Father Quirk," writes: "He is best in the quatrain, yet some of his lyrics and sonnets are of unusual beauty and power." Father Quirk also writes dramatic episodes. He is interested in drama and directed the Yenni Dramatic Society of Spring Hill. The Poetry Society of Spring Hill College, one of the pioneer Catholic poetry societies of America, which numbers such notable poets as Claudel, Chesterton and O'Donnell among its honorary members, was founded and directed by him, as was also the Spring Hill Short Story Society. He is a member of the Poetry Society of America, The Mark Twain International Society, Modern Language Association, one of the founders of the Delta Epsilon Sigma, a learned scholastic organization, an honorary member of the Poetry Society of Alabama, and an honorary member of the Eugene Field Association. His favorite poets are, John Bannister Tabb, Gerard Manley Hopkins, S.J., and Alice Meynell. He is a connoisseur of art, a lover of nature and fond of reading, writing and walking.

Poems by Father Quirk have been published in many current anthologies such as *The Catholic Anthology*, edited by the late Thomas Walsh, and he is a frequent contributor to English and American periodicals. Some of his best poems are "New Orleans," "The Countersign," "Fontainebleau," "The Cathedral, Aix-la-Chapelle," "Slumber Song of Bethlehem," "After Calvery," "Queen Guinivere's Song," which has been compared to Tennyson's "Idylls of the King," verses about his mother including "Dream Avenues of Thought," and "Pilate and Claudia," a dramatic episode. His first book was *Sails on the Horizon* published in 1926. Others are: *Interlude; Candles in the Wind; Gesture Before Farewell,* and *Full Circle.*

C. M. N.

Reverend Sidney Albert Raemers   1892-

Translations which he undertook in order to earn his seminary expenses, started Father Raemers on his writing career. His readers range from the small children who find delight in the colored illustrations of *A Children's Bible History,* to the seminarians who use his translation of Tixeront's *Handbook of Patrology.* This was his first translation. It took him a year to do the work and he received $300 for it. He says, "Have never had a manuscript turned down. First publication accepted, but since I had no name, my name was omitted and the mere caption inserted 'Authorized Translation from the French.'" The handbook is already in its sixth edition and is used in most seminaries.

The son of Thomas Francis and Elizabeth (Shemmings) Raemers, he was born in London, May 2, 1892. He was educated in the London County Council Schools, and began his higher studies at the Lyceum, Luxembourg, and the University of Louvain. "I gained my love of translation from the strenuous translation work demanded at the University of Louvain. Remember once we were compelled to translate into Latin verse a poem by Alfred De Musset and only given three hours to do it. Accomplished the feat in two hours." His work was interrupted by the war. He served from 1914 to 1916 in the Hospital Corps in France. In 1916 he came to the United States and continued his studies at the Catholic University, where he received his A.B. and M.A. degrees. He was ordained here in 1921. In 1929 Notre Dame awarded him a Ph.D., and in 1934 Leland Stanford his Ed.M.

Father Raemers has taught in high school, college, and university. From 1921 to 1926 he taught at the Catholic High School, Portland, Maine. He also served Bishop Walsh of Portland as assistant chancellor and secretary during this time. He was head of the department of Philosophy, Nazareth College, Kalamazoo, Michigan, 1926 to 1928; assistant professor of philosophy, Notre Dame, 1928 to 1933; professor of philosophy, St. Mary's, California, 1934 to 1935. From 1938 to 1939 he assisted Bishop O'Hara of Great Falls in the foundation of Great Falls College. His work as teacher has influenced the direction of many of his books. For years he wished to see better religious texts in the schools and to help supply this need he wrote his Bible history and church history. Many of his translations were made especially to aid American seminarians. Of particular interest to educators are his translations of the works of De La Vaissière and Allers.

Several of the Hollywood studios have employed Father Raemers as technical adviser in many pictures with Catholic backgrounds. Among these pictures have been "Mary of Scotland" (RKO), "Garden of Allah" (Selznick), "Prisoner of Zenda" (Selznick), "The Prince and the Pauper" (Warner Bros.), and "The Hurricane" (United Artists).

Father Raemers confesses that he loves to "work on books that will bring more glory to the Church." His favorite theme is church history. At present he is interested in the translation from the French of *History of the Catholic Church* in twenty-four large volumes, each volume contributed by an expert. He would like to make this work the crowning effort of his life.

His hobby is music, and he has been, since 1939, Director of Music at St. Joseph's Cathedral, San Diego, California. Portland, Maine, is his diocese by affiliation.

His works include: (Sicard-Raemers) *The Mass;* (Sicard-Raemers) *The Soul of Sacred Liturgy;* (Lebreton-Raemers) *The Living God;* De La Vaissière-Raemers) *Experimental Psychology;* (De La Vaissière-Raemers) *Educational Psychology;* (Poulet-Raemers) *Church History;* (Brunner-Raemers) *Questions of Psychology;* (Allers-Raemers) *Sex Psychology in Education;* (Froget-Raemers) *Indwelling of the Holy Ghost in the Souls of the Just; The Science and Philosophy of Matter; The Youth of the Blessed Virgin.*

M. S.

Arthur Benjamin Reeve 1881-1936

Writer of mystery stories and creator of "Craig Kennedy, the American Sherlock Holmes," Arthur Benjamin Reeve occupies a rank in this form of literature not far below that enjoyed by A. Conan Doyle. The stories centered around a character named Craig Kennedy, who called science to his aid in solving baffling mysteries of the criminal world.

Mr. Reeve was born in Patchogue, New York, in 1881, the son of Walter F. and Jennie (Henderson) Reeve. While a student at Princeton University, during vacations, he edited the Cape May (New Jersey) *Daily Star*. When he was graduated from Princeton University in 1903, he studied law at the New York Law School, but in spite of his training, he decided to follow his original bent toward writing. In 1906 he married Margaret A. Wilson. Until 1906 he was assistant editor of *Public Opinion;* from 1906 to 1910 he was editor of *Our Own Times* and was a member of the staff of *The Survey*.

His early stories were rejected, but with the creation of "Craig Kennedy," the *Cosmopolitan* magazine decided to use his work. Shortly after this, his stories became best sellers.

He wrote, in all, forty novels. Most of these are mystery stories. His most famous non-mystery book was *The Golden Age of Crime*—a historical study of racketeering written in 1931.

Mr. Reeve became a Catholic in 1926. His conversion was brought about by the illness of his wife who, while being cared for by the Daughters of Wisdom in a Catholic hospital, asked for instruction in the Faith. Mr. Reeve also became interested in the Faith, and before long, Mr. and Mrs. Arthur B. Reeve and their two children were received into the Church.

During the last fifteen years of his life, Mr. Reeve covered murder trials for newspapers. He had been ill since he undertook the job of covering the Hauptmann trial for a newspaper syndicate. He died of cardiac asthma on August 9, 1936, at his Trenton, New Jersey, home.

He is the author of: *The Silent Bullet* (1912); *The Black Hand* (1912); *Adventures of Craig Kennedy, Scientific Detective* (in Cosmopolitan) (1910-1918); *The Dream Doctor* (1914); *Guy Garrick* (1914); *The Exploits of Elaine* (1915); *Craig Kennedy Listens In* (1923); *Craig Kennedy on the Farm* (1925); *The Clutching Hand* (1934); *Enter Craig Kennedy* (1935), and *The Stars Scream Murder* (1936).

M. H.

Joseph John Reilly 1881-

Literature is the subject to which Joseph J. Reilly has devoted the greater part of his life, as professor, editor and author. Born in Springfield, Massachusetts, in 1881, he was educated in the public schools and at Holy Cross College, Worcester, Massachusetts, from which he graduated with an A.B. in 1904. He became instructor in English, first at Fordham University, 1904 to 1907, and later at the College of the City of New York, 1907 to 1910. At the same time he pursued graduate studies in English and comparative literature at Columbia University and received his M.A. in 1909. Granted a leave of absence from City College, he entered the graduate school of Yale in 1910, was appointed a University Fellow there in 1911 and received his Ph.D. in English in 1912. An instructorship in English at Yale University was then offered him, but instead Dr. Reilly accepted an appointment as Chief Examiner for the Massachusetts Civil Service Commission, continuing in this post from 1912 to 1921, when he resigned to return to the field of education.

He had been active in promoting civil service matters, and from 1919 to 1920 was vice-president, and 1920 to 1921 president of the National Association of Civil Service Commissioners. From 1921 to 1926 he was superintendent of schools at Ware, Massachusetts. Since then he has taught at Hunter College in the City of New York. He was associate professor of English from 1926 to 1927, when he was promoted to a full professorship. In 1928 he was appointed librarian and he has since held this position in addition to his professorial work. From 1927 to 1931 he was professor of English at Fordham Summer School.

Dr. Reilly's first book was *Lowell as a Critic* (1915). Ten years later, in 1925, he wrote *Newman as a Man of Letters*. This volume brought him recognition as one of the foremost authorities on Newman in America. In a later book entitled *The Fine Gold of Newman* he culled brief excerpts from his writings that reveal Newman's thought and power of expression. Designed for all readers, it portrays a spiritual leader and great literary figure. In 1930, Dr. Reilly edited *Masters of Nineteenth Century Prose* and in 1932 he published *Dear Prue's Husband* and *Other People. Of Books and Men,* twenty-three literary essays written in a conversational vein, was published in 1942. His book, *The Fine Gold of Newman,* is being translated into Portuguese for South American readers.

As a lecturer Dr. Reilly has appeared before prominent organizations in the East and Middle West, including the Catholic Summer School at Cliff Haven, New York. Virtually all the Newman Clubs in the East have invited him for lectures, knowing his deep sympathy with the movement. In August 1945 he read a paper on "Newman's Place in Literature" at the Newman Centenary Conference that was held from August 15 till

August 22 in London under the sponsorship of the Archbishop of Westminster. He is a frequent contributor to periodicals.   C. M. N.

Agnes Repplier 1858-

There is no contemporary American Catholic
writer who has won more universally recognized
distinction than Agnes Repplier. Born in Philadelphia in 1858 of French-Alsatian ancestry, she has
remained practically all her life a resident of that
city of taste and traditions, with long, intimate
visits to the Old World of even longer traditions
and taste. The most happily remembered of her
girlhood years seem to have been spent at Eden
Hall, Sacred Heart Academy in a suburb of the
"quondam" Quaker City, an experience amusingly
recorded in her volume of 1905, *In Our Convent
Days*. And it is characteristic of this grande dame's care for the quiet
amenities of life that she found time as late as 1932 to devote another
volume to the history and praise of tea-drinking!

It must be reckoned among the many services of Father Isaac Hecker
—founder of the Paulist Congregation and then editor of *The Catholic
World*—to have guided the young Agnes Repplier away from short story
writing into that field of the essay which she was to develop so expertly
and so felicitously. Her first collection, *Books and Men*, published in 1888,
showed practically all the qualities which have since brought her fame:
the scorn of cheap sentiment, the French incisiveness of phrase, the
satire which would cut deeply were it not blended with urbanity—which
indeed has often cut deeply. These epigrammatic rambles were duly
followed by: *Points of View; Essays in Miniature; Essays in Idleness;
Varia;* the *Compromises,* of 1904, enriched by memories of much far-
flung travel; and the autobiographical *Happy Half Century,* of 1908.

Miss Repplier had broken in upon this series—many of which were
first contributed to the *Atlantic Monthly* under the friendly editorial
encouragement of Thomas Baily Aldrich—with her tender and understanding interpretation of the cat dynasty in *The Fireside Sphinx*. It
remains her own favorite volume, and may easily be that of many readers,
warmth of enthusiasm being always more contagious than even the most
unerringly cool criticism. But indeed, her criticism has not always been
unerringly cool: devotion to her "star of the first magnitude," Jane
Austen, having brought her into none too gentle controversy with the
exquisite judgment of Alice Meynell.

During the first World War, Agnes Repplier's interest shifted from
life-in-literature to life-in-the-living, and her sympathy for the Allied
cause flamed like a torch. Readers of *Counter Currents* (1916), will not
easily forget her arraignment of "the cost of modern sentiment," nor of
our modern "loss of nerve," nor the quotations from St. Thomas Aquinas
upon just and unjust warfare which she flung out to readers of every

shade of opinion, along with her finely reasoned reply to the old, old charge of a "bankrupt Christianity."

By the time peace returned with all its own problems, Miss Repplier had reached that maturity of art and experience wherein one scarcely looks about for "pastures new." She was the ranking essayist in the United States and one of the ranking essayists in the English language. Then she turned quietly but capably to the fresh and increasingly popular field of historical biography. It might almost be called, in fact, the field of hagiography, since her life of *Père Marquette* (1929) was followed by *Mère Marie of the Ursulines* and *Junípero Serra.* These were admirable examples of the biographical method—factual, graceful, sympathetic, rarely emotional. For instance, writing as she did for a general rather than a strictly Catholic audience, the author was more concerned with the French nun's share in founding Quebec than with her personal religious experiences.

While the autobiographical *Eight Decades* of 1937 is likely to remain Agnes Repplier's final volume, there is a sense in which the culmination of her work may rather be found two years earlier in that penetrating collection of essays *In Pursuit of Laughter.* No one could be better equipped to pursue it than this author, who had always enjoyed a good joke. Here, along with her habitual scorn for the "cheerful clan"—who insist upon wearing an "appalling grin" even in their photographs—goes her devotion to true merriment down the ages, not forgetting the laughter of the saints. "Those who listen to the laughter of the Middle Ages," she observes, "instead of writing about them with undue horror and commiseration, can hear the echo of laughter ringing from every side, from every hole and corner where human life existed. Through the welter of wars and famine, through every conceivable disaster, through an atmosphere darkened with ignorance and cruelty there emerges clear and unmistakable that will to live. . . . It seems strange that so little attention should have been paid to the gaiety of the Middle Ages, which is as characteristic as the passionate devotion of their saints or the callous cruelty of their sinners."

Miss Repplier has taken small pains to hide the many disenchantments which come to any thoughtful observer of life, but she believes that "the wit and wisdom of humanity are permanent." She has herself been a memorable example of this wisdom and this wit. And while touching so rarely upon explicitly Catholic themes, she has brought the message of Catholic sanity and security with consummate art before our groping modern world.

It is heartening to see how cordially even the secular world responded to this combined scholarship and spirituality. For Agnes Repplier has been awarded both the Laetare Medal and the gold medal of the American Academy of Arts and Letters, and has received honorary doctorates from Yale, Columbia, Princeton, Marquette and the University of Pennsylvania. Until age and illness quieted her indomitable activities she was an able, if unwilling, itinerant lecturer, and a member of the Acorn, Cosmopolitan, College and Contemporary Clubs of her native city.   K. B.

Reverend Thomas Lawrason Riggs 1888-1943

In the front rank of literary Catholics, who in the past two decades have contributed greatly to make the Church and its priesthood better understood and appreciated, stands Father Thomas Lawrason Riggs. Well known as one of the original directors of the Calvert Associates and as a member of the Editorial Council of *The Commonweal*, he is perhaps best known as the Catholic Chaplain for over twenty-one years to the Catholic students of Yale University.

As Chaplain of the Catholic Club at Yale from 1922 until 1938, and its successor The More Club from 1938 until 1943, Father Thomas Lawrason Riggs founded the St. Thomas More Association for Catholic students at Yale in 1937, and through the Association he was instrumental in the building of St. Thomas More Chapel. Thus came to pass a dream Father Riggs entertained for years, "to build for the Yale students a church that would combine the best in modern design, colors and materials with the classic austerity of his own faith," writes his friend Philip Berstein.

Mrs. Margaret M. Link of Yale University writes: "Father Riggs loved beauty. His little church at East Haven, as well as the Yale Chapel, were models of what a Catholic Church should be both as to decoration and the conduct of the services. His choirs always sang Gregorian music and his servers were so carefully trained that his Masses were artistic as well as religious experiences of the first order."

By Special Rescript from the Sacred Congregation of Rites, permission was granted to keep the Patronal Feast in October. This was a more convenient date since the feast day, which occurs in July, came during the vacation period of the University. Since many Protestant visitors attended the solemn celebration of the Feast, Father Riggs distributed mimeographed copies of the order of the Mass so that they could follow in English what was being said in Latin.

Concerning Father Riggs, Mrs. Link states further: "The drama had always been one of his major interests and the last years of his life he produced every spring one of Shakespeare's plays which he had edited, arranged, and personally coached. These productions were among the best dramatic work done by Yale undergraduates and were very popular."

Thomas Lawrason Riggs was born in New London, Connecticut, on June 28, 1888, the son of Elisha Frances and Medora (Thayer) Riggs. From 1899 to 1903 he attended the University School in Washington, D.C., and from 1903 until 1906 the Westminster School in Simsbury, Connecticut.

After receiving his A.B. degree from Yale in 1910, he travelled abroad for a year. Upon his return to the United States he entered Harvard and received his M.A. degree in 1912. He was an assistant professor of English at Yale from 1912 to 1913 and an instructor in English at the same institution, 1916 to 1917.

On June 27, 1917, he enlisted in Mobile Hospital No. 39 (Yale unit) and went overseas on August 22, 1917, remaining with that unit until July 27, 1918. After serving at Limoges and Aulnoissous-Vertuzey (Meuse), he was transferred to Mobile Hospital No. 3 Paris, and then was attached to the American Mission, Bureau Interaillié in Paris. Commissioned a second lieutenant in the Infantry, he was assigned to the 866th Company, Transportation Corps at Bordeaux. After his discharge on July 15, 1919, he attended the Catholic University of America for a year. Then he entered St. Joseph's Seminary at Yonkers, New York, for the year 1920 to 1921 and St. Thomas' Seminary, Hartford, Connecticut, for the year 1921 to 1922. Here he was also ordained. He was appointed chaplain for the Catholic Club at Yale, and for the same length of time—1922 to 1938—he was the administrator of the Church of Our Lady of Pompeii, East Haven, Connecticut. From 1925 to 1943 he was a member of the advisory council of Albertus Magnus College and an instructor in religion from 1925 to 1938. He served on the Executive Committee of the National Conference of Christians and Jews from 1928 to 1943; was an associate fellow of Calhoun College; a trustee of the Newman School of Lakewood, New Jersey, a director of the Calvert Associates and governor of the Yale Publishing Association.

When Father Riggs died on April 26, 1943, in New Haven, Connecticut he left a large sum in trust for the upkeep of St. Thomas More House.

He is the author of: *The Book of Kildare and other Verses* (1911); *Mr. Goodenough on Christianity* (pamphlet) (1930), and *Saving Angel* (1943), the title of which was taken from a poem by St. Thérèse of Lisieux —Father Riggs died before this last book was published.

He is the translator of *The Social Principles of the Gospel* by Alphonse Lugan (1928), and *The Last Night of Don Juan.* He was an editor of *The Christendom Series* and contributed to *The Harvard Illustrated Magazine, Yale Alumni Magazine, Yale Scientific Monthly, The Catholic World, La Revue des Jeunes* (Paris), *Ecclesiastical Review, The Symposium* and other publications.   J. M. & M. H.

Reverend George Cyril Ring, S.J.   1890-

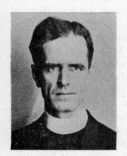

Although Father George Cyril Ring, S.J., has, according to his own account, lived "innocent of outstanding adventures and interesting struggles," his research studies have widened considerably his mental horizon.

Born in St. Louis, Missouri, December 2, 1890, to James John Ring and E. Agnes McEnnis Ring, he attended St. Rose School, Barat Hall, and St. Louis University High School, before receiving A.B. and A.M. degrees from the same University. He entered, in 1910, the Society of Jesus, and fourteen years later was ordained. He studied at Chicago University and was awarded the degrees of S.T.D. and "Magister Aggregatus" at the Gregorian University in Rome where he was inspired by the authoritative Fathers de la Taille, Bea, and Pinard de la Boullaye.

Since 1931 he has been associate professor of fundamental theology at St. Louis University. His only book, *Gods of the Gentiles,* is an outgrowth of his lectures on ancient beliefs. It is popular in style, and reliable; in spirit, simple, vivid, and fair-minded. Critics call it "a standard work based on solid historical science and intimate archeological research."

S. M.

Most Reverend Paschal Robinson, O.F.M.
1870-

 Noted Franciscan scholar and writer, the Most Reverend Paschal Robinson, O.F.M., is Titular Archbishop of Tyana and Apostolic Nuncio to Ireland. He was born in Dublin in 1870, the son of Nugent Robinson, a well-known-writer, and was given in baptism the name of Charles. He received his early education in London and then studied for the bar, but he gave up a legal career to be a writer. For some time he was a London correspondent and then became associate editor of the *North American Review* (1892 to 1895). Imbued with a desire for the religious life, he went to St. Bonaventure's College, Allegany, New York, for his studies, in 1896, and was received there into the Franciscan Order, taking the name Paschal. During his clericate he taught rhetoric and founded *The Laurel,* the oldest campus publication. In 1901 he was ordained priest in Rome, and a year later received the degree of Lector General. For two years he was master of clerics and professor of history and philosophy at the Franciscan Monastery of Mount St. Sepulchre, Washington, D.C., and was then recalled to Europe to take part in historical research work at Quaracchi, near Florence. In 1907 he became associate editor of the *Archivum Franciscanum Historicum,* and he catalogued several archives hitherto unknown to the outside world.

In 1909, Father Paschal made an extended visitation to the Franciscan missions in the Near East. Later recalled to Washington, he was professor of medieval history at the Catholic University from 1913 to 1919 and lectured on this subject at many Catholic and non-Catholic universities. Subsequent honors were: election to the Royal Historical Society of England; invitation to participate in the Roger Bacon Commemoration in England; the degree of S.T.D. awarded him by the Pope, and membership in the American Delegation to the Peace Conference at Paris (March-July, 1919). In this last capacity he was called upon in connection with certain questions concerning the holy places to visit Palestine from September to December. He then became Apostolic Visitor for the

Custody of the Holy Land from July 1920 to April 1921, and for the Latin Patriarchate of Jerusalem and the Uniate Churches in Palestine, Transjordan and Cyprus, 1925 to 1928. He also visited Greece, Syria and Egypt on special missions for the Vatican, and in 1927 he was elevated to the dignity of Titular Archbishop of Tyana and consecrated in Rome.

In 1929, Archbishop Robinson was sent as Apostolic Delegate to Malta to settle threatening difficulties between the English government and the ecclesiastical authorities, and he successfully reestablished harmony in the island. In January 1930 he was sent as Apostolic Nuncio to Ireland, the first official papal representative in Ireland since 1645 when the country was subjugated under Cromwell. In addition to the distinction of this office which he now occupies, His Excellency is also Consultor of the Sacred Congregations of Religious, of Studies, of the Propaganda and for the Oriental Church. In 1939, he received an honorary LL.D. from the Catholic University.

To his brilliantly successful official duties, the Most Reverend Paschal Robinson has added notable literary achievement. He was a contributor to *The Catholic Encyclopedia* and *The Encyclopedia of Education* and has written for the *Dublin Review, Historical Review, The American Ecclesiastical Review* and other publications. His books embody the result of extensive research work on Franciscan life and literature. They include: *The Real St. Francis; The Writings of St. Francis of Assisi; Some Pages of Franciscan History; The Golden Sayings of Brother Giles; the Life of St. Clare,* and *An Introduction to Franciscan Literature.*   C. M. N.

Carlos Pena Romulo   1901-

Until the outbreak of the war in December 1941, Carlos P. Romulo was the editor and publisher of the newspapers D-M-H-M—*Debate* (Spanish morning paper); *Mabuhay* (a Tagalog morning paper); *Herald* (an English evening paper); *Monday Mail* (an English tabloid); and was the managing director of two radio stations in the Philippines. The Romulo-signed editorials on the front page of the *Philippines Herald* on national and international events were regarded as strikingly representative national opinion; many were cabled by news service to the United States. For the best interpretative correspondence of 1941, he won the Pulitzer Prize. This covered a series of articles reporting his observations on an eight-day tour through China, Burma, Thailand, French Indo-China, British Malaya and the Dutch East Indies on the eve of the attack on Pearl Harbor, in which he predicted the imminent outbreak of war in the Pacific and exposed the fifth column activities in these countries. "I can tell you now that those articles never would have won the Pulitzer Prize if I had told all of my experiences in the Orient," he said. The awarding of the Pulitzer Prize to Mr. Romulo was the first time this coveted journalistic award has ever gone to one outside continental America. These articles were published in his own newspapers in the Philippines and in leading American newspapers.

For a number of years, Carlos P. Romulo was the editor of the Manila *Tribune* and eventually became the editor-in-chief of the chain of newspapers generally styled the "T-V-T" organization. This chain of papers included an English daily, the Manila *Tribune,* a Spanish daily, The *Vanguardia,* and a Tagalog daily, The *Taliba.*

When World War II broke out, Romulo, who was a reserve officer in the Philippine Army, was called to active service by General MacArthur, who made him his personal aide. According to his rank in the Reserves he was commissioned as a major. He was immediately assigned to the work of Press Relations Officer. In this capacity he did much to uphold the morale of the people of the Philippines during the trying days of the Philippine Campaign. General MacArthur awarded him the Silver Star for gallantry in action, two Oak Leaf Clusters, and Lieutenant General Wainwright awarded him the Purple Heart for bravery under fire during the Battle of the Philippines. He was rescued by plane, by order of MacArthur, the night that Bataan fell (two hours before the surrender). MacArthur knew that Romulo was marked for death by the Japanese for his work of broadcasting over the Corregidor Radio as "The Voice of Freedom." He took with him only the farewell letters of the trapped soldiers and the diary on which he based *I Saw the Fall of the Philippines.*

On March 5, 1943, he was made a lieutenant colonel and on July 7, 1942, he received a cable from General MacArthur elevating him to the rank of colonel. In 1944 he was made a brigadier general and Philippine resident commissioner to the United States. With President Sergio Osmeña, the president of the Philippine Commonwealth, and the other five cabinet members, Romulo returned to the Philippines in 1944 to take part in the conquest of Leyte. Five days after landing, the schools were reopened and Romulo was named Commissioner of Education.

In his book, *I Saw the Fall of the Philippines,* he writes simply of what he and his friends in the fortress of Corregidor or the fox-holes of Bataan experienced. The book was the January selection of the Catholic Book Club. In an interview, Romulo said he visited Japan eighteen times before the attack on Pearl Harbor. On these visits the Japs tried to win him over to their side.

As a speaker Romulo is perhaps even better known to Americans than as a writer. He was Vice-President of Rotary International and has visited the United States often. In 1940, at the Rotary International Convention in Cleveland, Ohio, an audience of 14,000 stood up and cheered him in what was one of the greatest ovations ever given a speaker there. In the 1942-1943 lecture season, he appeared in over two hundred and eighty-nine different cities in the United States and spoke about three hundred and fifty-six times. To tell the story of the Fall of Bataan, Romulo traveled 99,000 miles through the United States and has talked in 466 cities.

Romulo was born in Camiling in the Philippine Islands in 1901, the son of Gregorio Romulo, a leader under the rebel, Aguinaldo, and of Maria Pena. He was educated in the public school system in the Philippines. His first two years of college were spent in the University of the Philippines in Manila. He completed the last two years at Columbia University in New York City, where he received the Master of Arts degree in Comparative Literature.—He also holds an honorary LL.D. degree from Notre Dame University and Columbia University (1935). In 1921 he returned home and became an assistant professor of English at the University of the Philippines and later became the head of the English department. In 1922 he was made a member of the Philippine Independence Mission. In 1934 he was awarded a medal as the "most distinguished alumnus" by the Board of Regents of the University of the Philippines for his work in journalism and letters.

In 1937 before the outbreak of the Sino-Japanese War, he flew to Nanking from Shanghai and secured a world scoop in a personal interview with Chiang Kai-shek revealing China's intention of fighting Japan. Another world scoop was Romulo's exclusive interview with President Roosevelt—one of two granted by the American President—in which Roosevelt outlined the Philippine policy for the Filipino editor as later developed in the Tydings-McDuffie Act. For this interview in 1939, Romulo flew from Manila to Washington.

Colonel Romulo is married to the former Virginia S. Llamas, a one-time Manila Mardi-gras Queen. They have four sons.

At the time of the Japanese invasion of the Philippines, Romulo was a member of the Board of Regents of the University of the Philippines; member of the Board of Directors of the Manila Hotel Company; member of the Philippines Charity Sweepstakes Board; vice-president of the Boy Scouts of the Philippine National Council; president of the Philippine Gun Club; president for seven years of the Philippine Columbia Association; president of the Manila Rotary and member of the Board of Directors of Rotary International; vice-president (elected in Nice, France) of Rotary International; member of the Tau Kappa Alpha, Phi Gamma Mu, Phi Kappa Phi, and Sigma Delta Chi.

Romulo was given an opportunity to serve his country still further when he was appointed a member of the War Cabinet of President Quezon as Minister of Information and Public Relations. At the same time, Quezon awarded him the Distinguished Conduct Star, the highest decoration in the gift of the Commonwealth Government of the Philippines.

He is the author of *Daughters For Sale and Other Plays* (1924); *Better English* (1924); *College Composition* (1925); *Rizal: A Chronicle Play* (1926); *Juli, and Other Plays* (1927); *Mother America* (1943), the story of the benefits the United States brought to the Philippines; and *My Brother Americans* (1945).

T. C. & M. H.

Philip Rooney 1909-

In 1939 Philip Rooney wrote: "I have the dubious distinction of being known among bank clerks as a writer, and among writers as a bank clerk. The position has its advantages. The bank clerks forgive my clerical shortcomings by generously conceding abilities in authorship. The writers condone my literary lapses by supposing that my banking technique is less faulty than my literary craftsmanship." The comment shows Mr. Rooney to have humor as well as modesty. In 1943 he gave up his job in the bank to work as a free-lance journalist, radio-script writer, short story and novel writer. His first book to be published in America is *Captain Boycott.*

Mr. Rooney was born in 1909 in the Connaught village of Collooney, County Sligo, Ireland. Both his parents and all four of his grandparents were school teachers, "so my early education was rather a family affair." Later he went to the college of the Jesuit Fathers at Mungret, County Limerick, Ireland and there first tried his hand at writing.

In 1933 he married. His wife, who is a musician and a well-known 'cellist, persuaded him to try his luck with more ambitious stories than he had been attempting. He wrote the short story, *Irish Fortune,* in the Donn Byrne manner and entered it in an international short story competition. "I had forgotten all about the yarn six months later, when one night on the radio I heard the result announced. Out of 6000 entries, I had been lucky enough to win the First Prize, a cash prize of £100— ($500)." This success started him off to write with great gusto.

Further encouragement followed. Mr. Aodh de Blacam, well known as a critic and publicist, who was then acting as associate editor of a new Irish magazine, used several of his short stories and persuaded him to try his hand at a novel on fox hunting and horse racing. This theme had been used very charmingly by the ladies who wrote under the names of Somerville and Ross, but his book was unlike theirs in that it avoided the "Big House" atmosphere or any suggestion of British ascendency. Though a second novel was less successful, the one that followed, *The Red Sky At Dawn,* which dealt with smuggling adventures, after the rising of 1798, made something of a hit both in Ireland and in the United States. Mr. Rooney's fourth novel deals with the outlawed Irish landowners of the Ulster counties who, in the days after Cromwell, took to the hills and lived as highwaymen on their despoilers. In 1946 *Captain Boycott* was published. It is the story of the famous character who gave the word "boycott" to the English language. "Away back in the eighteen-eighties when Captain Boycott was at the height of his fame, my mother's father and mother were school-teachers in the little schoolhouse in the village of The Neale. From them and my mother, I had been hearing, since I was a very small boy, tales and stories of Captain Boycott and of the wild doings at Lough Mask. I decided to tell the tale of Captain Boycott as it was told to me." Mr. Rooney believes in packing a story full of action and making the yarn go from start to finish.

His home is in Bray, a seaside resort on the Wicklow coast where he says he manages to do a very full day's work, working from breakfast-time till luncheon at fiction; in the afternoon at journalistic commissions and radio-scripts; reserving the evenings for amusement, a trip into Dublin thirteen miles away with his wife, for a visit to the Abbey Theatre, or the cinema; walks and talks with his two boys, Sean and Ben.

Eva Jeany Ross

Prior to 1923 Eva Ross' studies were chiefly centered on English, French and Spanish literature, with a view to becoming a novelist. She left college before taking the French and Spanish degree for which she was studying and began a business career which lasted for seven years. She was for nine months foreign correspondent to John Whitworth and Company, affiliate of the Royal Niger Company. From January 1924 to June 1925 she was assistant to the managing director and works' manager of a Leeds engineering firm. Two years were spent as secretary and staff manager of the chief European office of Moody's Investors' Service at London. In 1928 she went to Paris to be head of the Information Department of Dillon, Read and Company's principal European office. Miss Ross is an Associate Member of the Chartered Institute of Secretaries in London, whose membership qualification is the passing of an advanced examination in economics, accounting, corporation law and the like, and at least six years of experience in responsible positions with large corporations.

In 1930 Miss Ross turned her back upon business, came to the United States, and started teaching economics, sociology and Spanish at Nazareth College, Michigan. From Nazareth College she went to St. Louis in 1932. She taught the same subjects at Maryville and Fontbonne Colleges, both corporate colleges of St. Louis University, until 1935. At the College of St. Elizabeth, Convent Station, New Jersey, she was a professor of economics and sociology from 1936 to 1939. She has also given summer courses in these subjects at the College of the Holy Name, Oakland, California, Rosemont College, Pennsylvania, St. Benedict's College, Minnesota, and College Misericordia, Dallas, Pennsylvania.

Her book, *Social Origins* (1936) is the substance of a short series of lectures she gave at the Catholic Social Guild Summer School, Oxford, England, in 1935.

After a brief lecture tour of the United States and Canada in the beginning of 1939 she returned to Europe for an extended vacation. While in Europe, she represented the American Catholic Sociological Society at the summer school of the Catholic Social Guild held in Oxford, and was one of the leading speakers at the Summer School of Catholic Action, held in London at the request of Cardinal Hinsley in 1939. While abroad she made a study of the Catholic social movements in Belgium, France, Great Britain, and Holland. After her return to the United States she entered upon her present teaching position at Trinity College, Washington, D.C., in 1940.

In the summer of 1931 she decided to devote her time to writing a much needed sociology college textbook, *A Survey of Sociology* (1932). That it filled a need is attested by its adoption by many of the major colleges, universities and seminaries. It went into a fourth edition and was then replaced by the author's *Fundamental Sociology* (1939).

Doctor Ross was born in Northern Ireland, of Scottish-English parents, Charles Alexander Ross and Eva Woodland Ross. She was baptized in the Church of England but later became a Catholic. She attended a Catholic convent school from 1914 to 1921 and won the first prize in the Catholic Social Guild school examinations in 1920 and again in 1921. Her busines career interrupted her studies, but in 1930 she took her Bachelor of Commerce degree from the University of London. After she came to the United States she resumed her scholastic work and in 1933 she received an A.M. from St. Louis University and in 1937 a Ph.D. in sociology from Yale University.

She is also the author of: *Rudiments of Sociology* (1934); *What is Economics?* (1939); *Belgian Rural Cooperation* (1940), and *Sound Social Living* (1941).

She is the co-author of *Devant la Crise Mondiale* (1942) and co-author of *American Democracy* (1944).

During 1943 she was president of the American Catholic Sociological Society. Since 1940 she has been one of the editors of the *American Catholic Sociologic Review* and since 1943 she has been one of its book review editors. M. S.

Reverend John Elliot Ross, C.S.P.   1884-1946

To Catholics in non-Catholic colleges the Reverend J. Elliot Ross dedicated many years of his life and he worked zealously to better the relations and understanding between Catholics, Protestants and Jews. He was born in Baltimore, Maryland, in 1884, and educated at Loyola College where he was graduated with an A.B. in 1902; at George Washington University, where he received his M.A. in 1908; the Catholic University of America which conferred upon him his degrees of S.T.B. and Ph.D. in 1912, and the Papal University of Rome where he was awarded his S.T.D. in 1913. Ordained as a Paulist at New York in 1912, he spent a year abroad and was then stationed at St. Mary's Church, Chicago, from

1913 to 1914. He then became chaplain and approved lecturer to Catholic students at the University of Texas. This work continued until 1923. From 1916 until 1923 he was pastor of St. Austin's Chapel, Austin, Texas, and from 1921 to 1923 lecturer in social ethics at Our Lady of the Lake College in San Antonio. During the succeeding year he was professor of moral theology at St. Paul's College at the Catholic University, Washington, D. C. He then became chaplain to Catholic students at Columbia University and lecturer in religious education at Teachers College, New York City, from 1925 to 1929, when he went to the State University of Iowa as professor and associate administrative director of the School of Religion. From 1930 to 1931 he was lecturer in religion at the Newman Foundation of the University of Illinois.

In 1932 Father Ross travelled some 10,000 miles throughout the United States, speaking from the same platform as the Reverend Edward R. Clinchy and Rabbi Morris Lazaron in a plea for amity and understanding between the three great religious groups. This was the first time a priest, a Protestant minister and a rabbi had made a tour of this sort.

His first book was his dissertation at the Catholic University on *Consumers and Wage Earners* (1912) and after more than a quarter of a century he returned to the keynote position of the consumer on securing social justice.

His last book, published in 1941, was on *Cooperative Plenty*. In the interval, about a dozen volumes have come from his pen. Among them are: *The Right to Work* (1917); *Christian Ethics* (1918); *Sanctity and Social Service* (1921); *Indulgences as a Social Factor in the Middle Ages* (1922); four series of *Five Minute Sermons* (1925-37); *Truths to Live By* (1929); *Ethics from the Standpoint of Scholastic Philosophy* (1938); and *Not by Bread Alone* (further sermons) (1940). The American Library Association listed his *How Catholics See Protestants* as one of the fifty most important religious books of 1928. His work on Cardinal Newman, *Faith that Conquers Fear, John Henry Newman,* was published in 1933, and according to a reviewer reflects "Father Ross' interest in religion as a vital part of college and university life."

In 1941 he collaborated on a book sponsored by the National Council of Christians and Jews, *The Religions of Democracy,* which was featured during Brotherhood Week, February 22-28 of that year. Rabbi Louis Finkelstein and the Reverend William Adams Brown of the Union Theological Seminary, were the co-authors. Each presented his faith, in creed and life, with a view to united action among the three major religions for the defense and preservation of the democratic way of life. In 1933 Father Ross was awarded the Gottheil Medal for distinguished service to the cause of Jewry. This was notable recognition of his work for concord between peoples of all faiths. He was a member of The Ark and the Dove Society, advocating the principles of early settlers who sought religious freedom in Maryland.

He died September 18, 1946, at the Mother House of the Church of St. Paul the Apostle in New York City.

C. M. N.

Right Reverend Camille Roy 1870-1944

That the descendants of the "habitants" of French Canada are little in danger of becoming extinct through race suicide is axiomatic. Multiple examples of the children of the large families of the Province of Quebec who have strengthened the growth of both Church and Nation can be cited. The twenty children of Benjamin Roy and Desanges (Gosselin) Roy of Berthier, Montmagny County, Province of Quebec, may be instanced as a notable case in point. No less than five sons of Mr. and Mrs. Roy were distinguished members of the Canadian clergy, one of whom was Most Reverend Paul Eugene Roy, Archbishop of Quebec, and another Right Reverend Monsignor Camille Roy, the noted educator and litterateur.

(Joseph) Camille Roy was born at Berthier, Province of Quebec, on October 22, 1870. He took his classical studies at the Quebec Seminary where he received a B.A. degree in 1890. After pursuing his theology at Laval University, he was ordained a priest by Bishop Labrecque of Chicoutimi in the Quebec Basilica in May 1894. The following year he received a Ph.D. from Laval University. Later he studied at the Sorbonne where he was graduated with an M.A. degree in 1900. Returning to Canada, he taught rhetoric in the Quebec Seminary till 1918 and French literature at Laval University till 1927. In 1924 his years of service were recognized when he was called to be rector of the university. He occupied the post for two terms and then devoted himself to his literary work till 1940, when he was again elected rector of the university. He remained to guide the fortunes of Laval till a week before his death which occurred on June 22, 1944. He served the Archdiocese of Quebec for many years as vicar-general and was honored by the Holy See in 1925, by being made an Apostolic Protonotary.

He received many honorary academic degrees from various universities and numerous distinctions were conferred upon him, chief of which may be considered his citation as an Officer of the French Legion of Honor in 1928.

The remarkable loyalty of the French Canadians to the Faith of their ancestors who came from the land of the Eldest Daughter of the Church has ever been made more firm by the tenacity with which the language and traditions of the French have been preserved in Canada. To continue this tradition and give it a literary standing was the life work of Camille Roy. From 1902 on, there flowed from his pen historical and literary works appreciatively critical of his people's life-story and traditions. Chief of these may be mentioned *Histoire de la Littérature canadienne-francaise,* which appeared in seven editions from 1907 to 1930. This work was translated into English under the title *French Canadian Literature* (1913).

Monsignor Roy contributed the article "Literature, French-Canadian" to the *Encyclopedia of Canada*.

Besides his many duties as an educator and writer, he was a great pulpit orator and defended French rights in the Catholic tradition in the pulpits of Montreal, Quebec and Paris. A leading figure, if not the leading figure, in the literary renascence of Quebec, he has with the finest grace presented to the minds of his readers and hearers the French-Canada from the days of Nouvelle France to the vigorous and healthy Province of Quebec in the twentieth century Dominion of Canada.

He is the author of: *Essais sur la Littérateur Canadienne* (1907); *Nos Origines littéraires* (1909); *Propos Canadiens* (1912); *Nouveaux Essais* (1914); *La Critique littéraire au XIX siecle* (1918); *Erables en Fleurs* (1923); *A l'Ombre des Erables* (1924); *Etudes et Croquis* (1928); *Les Leçons de notre Histoire* (1929); *Regards sur les Lettres* (1931), and other works.

J. M.

Reverend David Rubio, O.S.A.   1884-

Now that Latin-Americanism, influenced by the culture of old Christian Spain is greatly encouraged in the United States, where amicable relations with South America are essential, the presence of Dr. David Rubio, a native of Spain, with years of experience among our Latin neighbors, is fortunate for Washington, D.C. At the Library of Congress he is consultant in Hispanic Literature and Curator of the Hispanic Foundation. Since 1938 Dr. Rubio has been head of the Romance Language Department of Catholic University of America.

Born in León, Spain, December 29, 1884, Dr. Rubio received his M.A. from St. Augustine College, Valladolid, Spain, in 1904; S.T.L. at La Vid, Burgos, 1908; Ph.D., University of San Marcos, Lima, in 1912, and also from the University of Madrid in 1926. In 1900, he joined the Augustinian Order and was ordained at La Vid, Burgos, on July 25, 1907.

He has taught at St. Augustine College, Lima, Peru; St. Augustine Lyceum, Santiago de Chile, 1915; St. Augustine College, Havana, Cuba, 1918 to 1919, and since 1920 in the United States at Villanova College, Pennsylvania, and the University of Pennsylvania, 1922 to 1926.

Dr. Rubio is a corresponding member of the Spanish Royal Academy and the Hispanic Society of America; also a member and former president of the Washington Chapter of Spanish Teachers and the Geographical and Historical Society of America; honorary member Mediaeval Academy of America; on the Advisory Council of the Inter-American Bibliographical Association and vice-president of the Institute de las Espanas, Washington.

The following standard works have come from his pen: *Symbolism and Classicism in Modern Literature* (1924); *Hay una Filosofia en el Quijote?* (1924); *Spanish Anthology* (1928); *Spanish Fables* (1930); *Spanish Wit and Humor* (1932); *Peralvillo de Omana* (1932); *La Universidad de San Marcos de Lima durante la colonizacion Espanola* (1933); *Classical Scholarship in Spain* (1934); *A Glossary of Technical Library and Allied Terms in Spanish and English* (1936); *La Filosofia del Quijote* (1945). He was formerly the editor of Catholic University Romance Language Series, and has contributed to reviews and periodicals in Spain and Latin America.

In 1940, Dr. Rubio was awarded the Spanish Government's annual Cervantes Day prize in recognition of his contribution in spreading the knowledge of Spanish and Spanish literature in the United States.

I. H. C.

Reverend Leo Rudloff, O.S.B. 1902-

It was when the suppression of religious life by Hitler and his followers made the future of monastic communities in Germany increasingly dark and doubtful, that Reverend Leo Rudloff, O.S.B., was sent to America by his Abbot, Dom Raphael Molitor, O.S.B., Abbot of St. Joseph's Abbey, Gerleve in Westphalia, and President of the Congregation of Beuron of the Order of St. Benedict. He arrived in the United States on September 9, 1938, and became an American citizen on November 13, 1944. From 1938 to 1941 he was professor of theology and philosophy in the Immaculate Conception Seminary at Darlington, New Jersey, the major seminary of the Archdiocese of Newark. In October 1941 he took part, with two confreres of the Abbey of Maria Laach (Rhineland), in the foundation of St. Paul's Priory, Keyport, New Jersey.

Born Alfred Felix von Rudloff, the youngest of eight children, Father Leo is the son of a public official (Regierungsrat) of Germany. He was born in Dueren, Rhineland, on January 31, 1902, and was educated in the Domschule and the Paulinisches Gymnasium at Muenster, Westphalia. He entered St. Joseph's Abbey, Gerleve near Muenster, in 1920, taking the name of Leo. He made his religious profession on February 22, 1922, and was ordained priest on August 6, 1926. His philosophico-theological studies were made in Gerleve and in the International Benedictine College of Sant' Anselmo in Rome, Italy, where he won his S.T.D. in 1928. He did further studying at the University of Muenster. After his return from Rome he taught philosophy in his Abbey, 1928 to 1938, where he was also subprior from 1934 to 1938. He was professor of religion at the College for Nurses and Social Workers (Westphaelische Frauenschule fuer Volkspflege) in Muenster from 1933 to 1936.

His name became known upon publication, in 1934, of his *Kleine Laiendogmatik,* which within a few years reached a distribution of 30,000 copies and was translated into five languages. An American edition was published in 1942 under the title *Everyman's Theology.* The book is the result of numerous conferences and lectures the author had given to various audiences all over Germany on theological matters. Besides, he made many contributions to magazines and theological periodicals. *Das Zeugnis der Vaeter* (The Testimony of the Fathers), which he published in German in 1936, is a collection of excerpts from the Church Fathers applied to the various chapters of dogmatic theology, with introductions and short commentaries. In the collection *Heilige Feiern der Ostkirche* (Sacred Rites of the Eastern Church), edited by the monks of St. Joseph's Abbey, Gerleve, he wrote the first volume, *Taufe und Firmung in Byzantinischen Ritus* (Baptism and Confirmation in the Byzantine Rite), published in 1938, just before his departure for the United States.

Before his return to Germany early in 1947 he gave lectures, retreats and summer courses.

Reverend William H. Russell   1895-

Well known as educator, writer and speaker, Dr. Russell was born at Michell, South Dakota, in 1895, and received his education in the parochial school at Lawler, Iowa, Loras Academy and Loras College, Dubuque, Iowa, all Catholic institutions. After the completion of his studies for the priesthood at the Grand Seminary, Montreal, he was ordained to the priesthood in December, 1919. His first appointment was to the Cathedral at Dubuque, and from there he went to Loras to teach in the Diocesan College. After a year at the Catholic University at Washington, where he received his M.A. degree, he returned to Loras to teach education, but exchanged this subject for religion, which has since remained his chief interest. His contention that there should be full-time teachers of religion in Catholic high schools and colleges was supported by the then president of Loras, now Archbishop of Oregon, and this idea he has steadily urged for many years. He became the first principal of Loras Academy in 1925, which position he retained until 1931, when, at the invitation of the Catholic University, he left for Washington to teach religion. Having finished his work for the Ph.D. degree in 1934, he spent the summer of 1935 in Palestine, in preparation for his *Life of Jesus,* which was published in 1937.

In 1936, he became chaplain and head of the department of religion at Trinity College, Washington, and remained till 1943. At present he gives a graduate course at the University on the life of Christ. He teaches also in the undergraduate college at the University, and at De La Salle College of the Christian Brothers at Washington.

In 1939, he gave a course of five lectures on the "Catholic Hour" over a nationwide network of the National Broadcasting Company.

Among his published works are his dissertation for the Ph.D. degree: *The Function of the New Testament in the Formation of the High School Teacher,* published in 1934, and later republished as *The Bible and Character,* containing a history of Bible reading. His *Life of Jesus,* issued in 1935 as a work book for upper grades, was followed in 1937 by a life of Christ, under the title of *Christ the Leader,* intended as a textbook for college freshmen. His first book, *Your Religion,* appeared in 1926, as a text to be used during the last year of high school, and is still being printed; his *Chats with Jesus,* designed to bring to the attention of students of religion the personal traits of our Saviour, was published in 1941, the second volume in 1942. The third volume appeared in 1944, as did a new work entitled *Jesus The Divine Teacher.*

In addition to his chief work as religious instructor, Dr. Russell has been active in mission work in Iowa and Idaho and has given lectures and retreats in all parts of the country, including a course on the life of Christ, at Johns Hopkins University. Since 1933, he has spent much time as a member of the Catholic Evidence Guild in Washington, being one of the two instructors of the Guild, and a frequent speaker in the streets of the city.

He is a regular contributor to many periodicals, including *The American Ecclesiastical Review, Journal of Religious Instruction,* and the *Catholic School Journal.* Since 1921, despite his many activities, the teaching of religion has continued to be his chief interest, and from that time, he has been urging that the Personality of Christ should be given more prominence in our religion courses, and that the teaching of religion should center around the figure of our Lord.   R. F.

Reverend Edwin Ryan 1883-

Since 1916, Reverend Doctor Edwin Ryan has been interested in the South American Republics, especially Chile and Argentina, and now he is devoting all his time to these countries. He made frequent visits to them between 1929 and 1940. In 1934 he flew around South America and it was said at the time that he was the first priest to do so. A description of his Andean flight was published in *The Catholic World* and *The Voice.* These articles attracted such attention that many readers eager to read more on that subject sent for his book *The Church in the South American Republics* (1932). Since 1940, he has been executive secretary of the Institute of Ibero-American Studies at Catholic University.

Born in New York in 1883, the son of Thomas Meagher and Mary (Brennan) Ryan, Dr. Ryan was educated at St. Francis Xavier College from which he was graduated in 1901 with an A.B. degree. From 1901 to 1906 he attended the Dunwoodie Seminary and was ordained in 1906. He received the degrees S.T.B. and S.T.L. in 1906 and 1907, respectively, from Catholic University; his D.D. degree was conferred on him by Apollinare in Rome in 1908. His teaching career began in 1910 as professor of ecclesiastical history at Dunwoodie, where he taught until 1920. In 1922 he went to the Catholic University to become professor of English literature, a post he held until 1931. In this same year he went to Roland Park (Baltimore) to teach modern history, the subject in which he had been interested for a considerable number of years. Since 1939 he has been professor of South American history at Catholic University.

Other posts held by Dr. Ryan were: secretary, Catholic Historical Association, 1923 to 1924; Member of the Board of Directors, Liturgical Arts Society, 1933 to 1937; first lieutenant in the U.S. Army, attached to aviation, 1918 to 1919.

His other books are: *A College Handbook to Newman* (1929); *The Liturgical Construction of the Altar* (1931); *The Monstrance* (1933); and *Candles in the Roman Rite* (1933). He has also contributed to many periodicals.

M. H.

Brother Ernest Ryan, C.S.C.   *see* Brother Ernest, C.S.C.

Right Reverend John Augustine Ryan
1869-1945

To the cause of social justice Right Reverend Monsignor John A. Ryan devoted his life, working consistently to improve labor and social conditions both by active endeavor and in his writings. He was born in 1869 in Vermillion, Dakota County, Minnesota, the son of William and Mary Elizabeth Luby Ryan. Both his parents had come from Ireland. He was educated in the district schools and at the Christian Brothers' High School, 1886 to 1887. In his boyhood his interest in industrial problems was aroused by the *Irish World and American Industrial Liberator* and Henry George's *Progress and Poverty*. Later the encyclical of Leo XIII On the Condition of Labor made an ineradicable impression. Archbishop Ireland, who was deeply concerned with social questions, also greatly influenced him. From the Archbishop he received Holy Orders in 1898, after completing his preparatory studies at St. Thomas College where he was from 1887 to 1892, and taking his ecclesiastical training at St. Paul Seminary, 1892 to 1898. He was then sent to the Catholic University of America for a four year period of postgraduate studies in moral theology. For his optional courses Father Ryan chose economics, sociology and English. In 1902, Archbishop Ireland appointed him professor of moral theology of St. Paul Seminary. His chair later included ethics and economics and he remained there till 1915. In that year Dr. Ryan returned to Washington, and became nationally known as a social welfare authority.

At the Catholic University, from which he received the degree S.T.D. after the completion of his dissertation in 1906, he was first professor of political science, and then professor of moral theology and industrial ethics, from 1916 to 1937, and subsequently professor of sociology, until his retirement in 1939 in conformity with the rule of compulsory retirement of instructors at the age of seventy. He retained his post as professor of social ethics at the National Catholic School of Social Service, which assignment he accepted when the school first opened in 1921, and also the chair of political science at Trinity College, held since 1917, following two years as professor of economics.

Since 1920, Dr. Ryan had been director of the Social Action Department of the National Catholic Welfare Conference, which he considered "one of the most satisfying and fruitful experiences of my life." Throughout the years since 1907, he had been active in social reform and he sought to apply the Christian principles of morality to industrial conditions and relations. His first interest was wages, which was the subject of his doctoral dissertation, *A Living Wage: Its Ethical and Economic Aspects*. This was the first systematic discussion of the question in the United States and the book has since been the standard work on the subject. The first edition of 1906 was revised and abridged in 1920. Through his advocacy minimum wage legislation was enacted, and he drafted the Minimum Wage Law passed by the Minnesota State Legislature. "A minimum just wage, the alleviation of poverty, and relief for needy individuals, are interrelated concepts."

Dr. Ryan took considerable interest also in the theory and practice of organized charity. For several years, until he left for Washington in 1915, he served as vice-president of the Minnesota Conference of Charities and Corrections, and he was founder in 1917 of the *Catholic Charities Review*, of which he was editor and manager for four years and afterwards contributing editor.

For the reform of industrial or economic conditions and institutions he delivered many lectures and wrote numerous articles. The right of labor to organize had been strongly defended by him, and he favored public control of monopolies and utilities and the formation of cooperative societies with labor sharing in the management, profits and ownership. He would have a system of industrial democracy established which would interest the worker in his work, restrict interest to a rate sufficient to induce investment and award the surplus gains of industry to the producers, both wage-earners and managers. Expounding these principles, he wrote: *Distributive Justice; Social Reconstruction; The Catholic Church and the Citizen; A Better Economic Order,* and other volumes. In collaboration with the Reverend Joseph Husslein, S.J., he also wrote *The Church and Labor,* and he is co-author with the Reverend Moorehouse F. X. Millar, S.J., of *The State and Church,* of which a second and revised edition in joint authorship with the Reverend Francis Boland, C.S.C., appeared as *Catholic Principles of Politics.* Pius XI's encyclical, *Quadragesimo Anno,* he hailed as a powerful papal pronouncement on the social question and implicit approval of the socio-ethical doctrines he had been defending for nearly forty years. Bishop Shahan, then rector of the Catholic University, referring to the encyclical, observed, "Well, this is a great vindication for John Ryan."

With the election of President Roosevelt, Dr. Ryan saw new hope for the advancement of his principles in the field of sociology and economics, and was a faithful adherent to the policies of that administration. The President had recognized his ability and he was appointed to the committee of three who made up the Industrial Appeals Board of the National Recovery Administration. Dr. Ryan declared, "I still believe that if the N.R.A. had been permitted to continue, it could readily have developed into the kind of industrial order recommended by Pope Pius XI." For the first time at inaugural ceremonies for the President of the United States a benediction was pronounced when the late President Roosevelt took the oath of office for the second time, in 1937, and Monsignor Ryan gave this blessing, the first priest on record to participate in a presidential inauguration. When Franklin D. Roosevelt was sworn in for the fourth time as President of the United States at brief inauguration ceremonies at the White House, January 20, 1945, Right Reverend John A. Ryan again offered the benediction. At national conventions Dr. Ryan's views and principles were received with profound respect and his expert knowledge was sought by members and committees of Congress.

In 1933, Pope Pius XI conferred upon him the honor of domestic prelate with the title of Right Reverend Monsignor. Honorary degrees bestowed on him are LL.D. from the University of Notre Dame (1917); Seton Hall College (1923); and Loyola University, Chicago (1933); and Litt.D. from the National University of Ireland (1930). Non-Catholic sociologists and economists have spoken in the most generous terms of the value of his work, which was recognized abroad as well as in the United States. On his seventieth birthday he was given a testimonial dinner which was one of the most distinguished banquets ever held in Washington. Some 500 persons attended, and notable guests included justices of the Supreme Court, cabinet ministers, congressmen, Monsignor Corrigan, rector of the Catholic University, and Monsignor Ready, secretary of the N.C.W.C. Messages of congratulation were received from the Apostolic Delegate, the President and others.

In *Social Doctrine in Action: A Personal History,* published in 1941, Monsignor Ryan records his social and economic beliefs and activities.

He died in 1945.

C. M. N.

Reverend John K. Ryan 1897-

On philosophy and allied subjects the Reverend Dr. John K. Ryan has written numerous articles and several books. He was born in Caledonia, Minnesota, October 29, 1897, the son of Judge Thomas F. and Mary (Kelly) Ryan. His early studies were taken at the Christian Brothers' School and St. Thomas Academy in St. Paul, Minnesota. He attended Holy Cross College from 1916 to 1920, receiving the B.A. degree. He was ordained in 1924 after studying at the St. Paul Seminary and the American College in Rome. He received his Ph.D. degree from the Catholic University of America in 1933. The academic year 1939 to 1940 was spent by Dr. Ryan in research in the Harvard University library. He has also pursued special researches in the Vatican Library and at the British Museum. From 1924 to 1930 Dr. Ryan taught philosophy at the College of St. Teresa, and St. Mary's College, Winona, Minnesota, and since 1931 he has been a member of the faculty of the School of Philosophy at the Catholic University of America.

Dr. Ryan's first book was *Modern War and Basic Ethics*, published in 1933, a revised edition appearing in 1940. He is also the author of: *Anthony Legrand (1629-1699); Franciscan and Cartesian* (1935); *A Bibliography of Logic, Deductive and Inductive* (1939), and *Basic Principles and Problems of Philosophy* (1939). With the Reverend Dr. Joseph B. Collins, S.S., he is the author of *My Communion* (1935), and *God and My Heart* (1938), both of which have passed through several editions. To *Essays in Thomism* (1942) he contributed "The Problem of Truth," and to *Essays on Catholic Education in the United States* (1942) he contributed "Philosophy and Catholic Education." He contributes to various periodicals. His article "Are the Comics Moral?" in *The Forum*, May 1936 was the first published criticism of the comic strips. His article "Of Pacifists" in *The Washington Post*, May 6, 1941, was reprinted in the *Congressional Record* (Vol. 87, No. 94) and in many magazines and newspapers. Dr. Ryan is associate editor of *The New Scholasticism*. He is treasurer of the Catholic Association for International Peace, a member of Pi Gamma Mu and the American Catholic Philosophical Association, and of the Religious Books Committee of the American Library Association.

C. M. N.

Mrs. John (Perkins) Ryan *see* Mary Perkins

Anna Teresa Sadlier   1854-1932

Daughter of a well-known writer, Anna Teresa Sadlier also became a Catholic novelist of importance. She was born in Montreal, Canada, in 1854. Her father, James Sadlier, was a pioneer Catholic publisher who came to New York in 1860 and established partnership in the publishing house of D. and J. Sadlier & Company. He owned a weekly paper, *The Tablet,* and his wife, Mary Anne Madden Sadlier, contributed editorials and stories to its columns. She was the author of several books, and a compiler. In this literary household their daughter Anna Teresa early absorbed a taste for literature and soon developed a talent for writing. She attended St. Mary's School and the Holy Cross Academy of the Sisters of Charity and showed a great ability for languages. At a French school, fashionable at the time, she perfected her French. She also studied Italian and German. This knowledge of foreign languages she later directed to translation of standard works and religious treatises that were thus made accessible to American Catholics.

Anna Sadlier completed her education at a boarding school in Montreal, the Villa Maria Convent, and at eighteen began to write. She had known the most distinguished men and women of Catholic literary New York, of which the Sadlier home was the centre. Soon after her father's death in 1869 she returned with her mother to make her home in Montreal. Her mother died in 1903 and thereafter Miss Sadlier resided in Ottawa.

Harper Brothers published her earliest work. George William Curtis, who was a reader there at the time, recognized her talent, as did also John Boyle O'Reilly who praised her first book. *Seven Years and Mair* appeared in 1878. She then launched into an active literary career, publishing some forty volumes and over two hundred short stories and other contributions to periodicals. Most of the Catholic magazines in the United States and Canada carried her work, for she dedicated her talents to Catholicism. Her books were popular as premiums at Catholic schools of the time. Among them were *Gerald de Lacey's Daughter* (1916), an historical romance of colonial days, and *Ethan Allen's Daughter* (1917). The former appeared in *The Irish Catholic,* as did also *The Monk's Pardon* and *Carmelita.* Other novels were: *Master Gerard; The Pilkington Heir; The Red Inn of St. Lyphar,* and *The Last Jewel of the Mortimers.* In her *Women of Catholicity* she gives memoirs of Margaret O'Carroll, Isabella of Castille, Margaret Roper, Marie de l'Incarnation and Marguerite Bourgeoys. Her stories for children were very popular and her magazine work included verse as well as articles on religious, literary and historical subjects, and fiction. Some of her numerous translations from the French, German and Italian are: *Matilda of Canossa; The Wonders of Ligouri,* and *The Sayings of St. Alphonsus Ligouri.*

Miss Sadlier was an active member of the International Federation of Catholic Alumnae and spoke at their meeting in Niagara in 1928 and at the diamond jubilee celebration of her alma mater, Villa Maria, in 1930. She also gave much time to charity, in work for the poor and for the Tabernacle Society. At the first International Eucharistic Congress held in North America, at Montreal in 1910, she delivered an address on the Altar Societies. To the missions in the great Northwest she gave aid and she was elected president of the Society of Work for Poor Missions. In 1922 she received the honorary degree of Litt.D. from the College of Mount St. Vincent, New York. She died in 1932, after many years of active service in the apostolate of Catholic letters.   C. M. N.

Arthur Saint-Pierre   1885-

Although author of some twenty works on economic and social problems of French Canada, Arthur Saint-Pierre is best known for his *History of St. Joseph's Oratory,* famous Holy Cross Fathers' Shrine, founded by the beloved Brother André. This book, original title of which is *L'Oratoire Saint-Joseph du Mont-Royal,* was translated into English by Barry O'Neill (1923). It first appeared in 1922, with a preface by the Archbishop of Montreal. It became not only a best seller in French Canadian literature but won for its author a letter of commendation from Pope Benedict XV and a gold medal from the French Academy.

Arthur Saint-Pierre, a self-made man of farming stock, son of Jean-Baptiste and Azilda Lapierre Saint-Pierre, French-Canadian emigrants, was born September 30, 1885, in Walkerville, Ontario.

With very little schooling, snatched between family movings, he went to primary class in Detroit, made his First Communion in Montreal, and before he had acquired sufficient French or English to make progress in either language he was forced by poverty to go to work; illness and hard luck carried him in and out of many cities and many jobs before he started his writing career.

In 1914 he married Leatitia Desaulniers, also a writer. They have a family of six children.—He himself is one of a family of thirteen.

Saint-Pierre was born with a great love of good literature and a desire to write. Since seventeen he has kept a "scribbling note book." Three of his brothers became journalists. One of his brothers supplied him with books, English books, while his parish library opened to him the world of French classical literature.

His first literary efforts were published in the women's column of the newspaper *La Patrie.*

As president of a little study group, under guidance of a Jesuit leader, he became very much interested in the economic and social problems of his country. One of his first papers read before the group was entitled "L'Avenir du Canada Français" or "The Future of French Canada." It later appeared in *La Revue Canadienne*.   E. F.

Erin Marie France Samson

Born in Washington, D. C., the daughter of Rene Jean, a Frenchman, and Oona (Scanlan) Samson, an American of Irish parentage, Erin Samson has travelled back and forth across the Atlantic since she was nine months old.

She was educated at Central High School in the District of Columbia. When eighteen years of age she went to the Catholic University of Angers where she spent two years and obtained the French Baccalaureat. Then she spent two years at Trinity College in Washington to receive her A.B. and A.M. degrees. She also spent two years at the University of Oxford, and for her B.Litt. thesis wrote on Maria Edgeworth, that typical and almost forgotten woman-of-letters of the closing eighteenth century.

She taught for a year (1925) at Trinity College, then went to Paris for un-academic education and some free-lance writing on the Catholic renaissance in France. While there she interviewed such figures as Jacques Maritain, François Mauriac and Maurice Denis, and published articles on their work in *The Commonweal, America, The Catholic World,* and *Columbia.* In 1928 she founded the Paris Study Group an organization for college girls who spent their junior year at the Sorbonne and lived with French families. Occasionally she wrote an article or a short story but her life was too full for serious writing. World War II put an end to foreign study. "I returned home," she writes, "to my American home—for I shall always have two, one in Virginia and one in France—in the spring of 1940."

In June 1945 her first novel *Claire* was published. "My dual heritage," she writes, "will explain its French background and interweaving of American and French characters. *Claire* was born of the wish to present a well-balanced, loving and lovable woman—moderns speak of an integrated personality—one who possessed inner resources and yet who reached her full stature through human relations. Perhaps I wanted, subconsciously, to react against the frustrated heroes of our day, those familiar rebels against society and their times."

Miss Samson reads with especial sympathy Henry James, Virginia Woolf, Elizabeth Bowen, Georges Bernanos and François Mauriac. She is keenly interested in the visual arts, has written and lectured on modern painting and religious art in contemporary France. Her first novel gives evidence of her sensitivity to color and rhythmic form.   M. H.

William Franklin Sands 1874-1946

The main interest of William Franklin Sands was the affairs in the Far East in their relation to the United States. This interest began in 1896 when President Grover Cleveland and the Secretary of State, Richard Olney, appointed him second secretary of the Legation at Tokyo, to study the "Pacific basin." To Cleveland and Olney, the "Pacific basin" meant, to quote them "the Asiatic coastal peoples of Asia, with special emphasis on China and Japan; the West Coast of America from Alaska to the Strait of Magellan; the islands of the Pacific; and above all, the key to it all, the unknown quantity of Russia which is both Asia and Europe, Atlantic and Pacific." He thus became the first appointee under the Cleveland-Olney plan for a trained foreign service.

William Franklin Sands was born in Washington, D.C., on July 29, 1874, the son of James Hoban and Mary Elizabeth (Meade) Sands. He was educated in the College de St. Michel, Fribourg, Switzerland; the German Gymnasial-Kurs, Feldkirch, Austria, and received in 1896 an LL.B. degree from the Georgetown Law School in Washington, D. C. That same year he was appointed to the diplomatic service to be second Secretary of the Legation at Tokyo. From 1899 to 1904, he served as vice-consul general and deputy-consul general and secretary of the legation in Korea. In 1900, the Emperor of Korea asked him to be his general adviser, with full powers—which post he held for four years. His assassination was ordered three times by the Imperial Japanese government but in each case he was warned by the Japanese, even by high Japanese officers. Expelled from Korea by Japan in 1904, he was reappointed to the United States Foreign Service, serving in Panama, Central America and Mexico; secretary of the Embassy; charge d'affaires; envoy extraordinary and minister plenipotentiary; with special missions for Presidents Theodore Roosevelt and William Howard Taft.

In 1911, he represented James Speyer & Co. of New York in Ecuador for the projected construction of the Guayaquil waterworks as a safeguard against the last west stronghold of yellow fever and bubonic plague. While in Ecuador he made a study of the Alfaro-Estrada revolution there. During the year 1915 to 1916 he represented George McFadden & Company of Philadelphia at London for the solution of the British naval seizures of non-contraband cotton. When that was settled, Basil Miles of the State Department sent him a cable to ask him to help organize the relief of the German and Austrian prisoners of war in Russia—about 1,000,000 prisoners of war and over 500,000 interned civilians. After the United States entered the war, this work was turned over to the Scandinavian countries. Sands, however, remained in Russia to observe the series of revolutions. He represented the American International Corporation of New York—studying what eventually became the Soviets' series of Five Year Plans. When American business was driven out by Trotsky, he returned to the head office of his firm in New York and served as executive secretary.

With Huntington Wilson and Alvah A. Adee, assistant secretaries of state, he helped set up a diplomatic school within the State Department, in training diplomatic secretaries after appointment. He also helped to prepare candidates for the State Department's examination for appointment to foreign service. At Georgetown University's School of Foreign Service in Washington, D.C., he held the chair of diplomacy.

In recognition of his part taken in the Boxer Rebellion and the halting of Chang Tso Lin's raids into Korea, he was decorated with the Chevalier of the Legion of Honor.

Mr. Sands was married to Edith Gertrude Keating in 1909. Their four sons served in the Armed Forces.

Mr. Sands is the author of *Undiplomatic Memories,* the first book to be published by Whittlesey House, New York (when McGraw-Hill branched out from purely scientific and technical publications and set up their own Whittlesey House for general literature) in 1930. The book is an account of his early days (1896 to 1904) as a "career" diplomat in the Far East. Of his other book, *Our Jungle Diplomacy,* published in 1944, Mr. Sands says: "Diplomacy is very like the jungle. You cut your way through, only to find the trail grown up within twenty-four hours. However, it is not the big things in the jungle that worry you, those you can see. It is the thousands of tiny poisonous insects that bite and sting and which pass unnoticed until after the burning and itching begins, which are the real trouble—it is the same in diplomacy. The small things which pass unnoticed at the time cause the real troubles."

Mr. Sands died on June 17, 1946.   M. H.

Daniel Sargent   1890-

"I am a poet, I believe, by nature," says the historian, biographer, and poet, Daniel Sargent. Resigning his professorship at Harvard in 1937 to give himself entirely to writing, the author of *Thomas More,* which is considered his masterpiece, prefers poetry to prose. His book, *Christopher Columbus,* verifies his statement that he was born a poet. His gifted pen depicts colorful scene after scene of old Genoa, land of beauty, in true epic style, in which there is no trace of fiction.

Born in Boston, 1890, he was educated at Groton School and Harvard (A.B., A.M.). He has been associated with Harvard many years and taught there for one year under Barrett Wendell.

In 1916 he joined the ambulance corps of the French Army. When the United States declared war he served with the Artillery in the First Division, as a first lieutenant, in France. After the war he did part-time work at Harvard as instructor in history and literature and devoted himself to writing.

A convert to the Catholic Church (1919) from Unitarianism, Mr. Sargent credits his love for and interest in Dante for his first awakening to Rome. He had been brought up in ignorance of the Catholic faith and was drawn to it by the study of medieval literature at Harvard.

In 1920 he married Louise Collidge. They have two children.

A lover of travel, Mr. Sargent, while in France, became interested in the Catholic trend of thought and feels greatly indebted to Professor Maurice de Wulf of Louvain, who first introduced him to scholastic philosophy and to Jacques Maritain, to whom he was attracted in 1925.

In addition to *Christopher Columbus,* Mr. Sargent has written, in prose: *Thomas More; Four Independents; Catherine Tekakwitha; Our Land and Our Lady; All the Day Long; Mitri,* or The story of Prince Demetrius Augustine Gallitzin; and in verse: *The Door; The Road to Welles-Perennes; The Song of the Three Children; God's Ambuscade; My Account of the Flood; Our Gleaming Ways.*

Sargent is at his best in the dual role of historian and poet, interpreting world events and depicting world characters. In his *Four Independents,* a study of Peguy, Gerard Hopkins, Claudel, and Orestes Brownson, we have an illustration of his various talents at their best, prose that is very close to the art of song.

During 1936 to 1937 he was president of the Catholic Poetry Society of America, also president of the American Catholic Historical Association. At present, along with his writing, Mr. Sargent is a member of the Art Commission of the City of Boston.   E. F.

Hilary Aidan St. George Saunders 1898-

The London *Daily Telegraph* of October 2, 1941, referred to Mr. Saunders as "a genial man of the world who in no way resembles the popular idea of a librarian." The article was in praise of Mr. St. George Saunders as assistant librarian of the House of Commons, a post he had held since 1938.

He was born January 14, 1898, the elder son of the late Reverend G. W. St. George Saunders and the late Sybil K. Somers Clarke. His father was a curate of St. Paul's, Grighton, Sussex, and was converted in 1904 with his wife and children. St. George Saunders was educated at Downside and Balliol College, Oxford. His first wife, Helen Foley, died in 1937. His second wife is Joan Bedford. They have one son and one daughter.

In World War I he served with the Welsh Guards from 1916 to 1918, and in 1918 was awarded the Military Cross. The years from 1920 to 1937, he spent in the League of Nations Secretariat at Geneva and "kept his sense of humor undimmed." From 1921 to 1923 he was private secretary to Doctor Fridtjof Nansen. In 1939 he worked in the Admiralty. Later he was attached to the Ministry of Information and had his headquarters in Paris, where he helped Mr. Childs, the press attaché at the Embassy. After the capitulation of France, in World War II, he gave valuable aid to the British jouralists stranded in France. In 1940 he was attached to the Air Ministry. He became Great Britain's official reporter and historian of World War II.

He is the author of *The Battle of Britain; Bomber Command* (1941); *Coastal Command* (1942), and *Combined Operations* (1943). With John Palmer, under the pen name "Francis Beeding" he has written numerous novels. Among these are: *The Seven Sleepers; The Six Proud Walkers; Death Walks in Eastrepps;* and *Eleven Were Brave.* Also with John Palmer under the pen name of "David Pilgrim": *So Great a Man,* and *No Common Glory* (1941). For *Life* magazine he wrote the article "The Flying Bomb," which appeared in the November 20, 1944, issue, and for the July 9, 1945, issue, he wrote "The Queens," the sister ships, the "Queen Mary" and the "Queen Elizabeth."

M. H.

Alma Savage 1900-

Born in St. Louis, Missouri, Miss Savage was educated at a Catholic convent school and the Soldan High School. After receiving an A.B. degree from Washington University, she did graduate work at the University of Wisconsin and Columbia University. With the exceptions of a brief teaching experience and her present work as head of her own lecture bureau, she has been associated with the publishing business—as publicity director for Macmillan Company in their Boston office from 1928 to 1931; in the promotion department the following two years with *The Publisher's Weekly;* and, from 1934 to 1946 as sales manager for Sheed and Ward in New York. In this capacity Miss Savage travelled 10,000 miles a year and was the only saleswoman to cover the entire country for a publishing house.

Although innumerable stories come to Miss Savage from her many contacts, it was while vacationing in Juneau in southeastern Alaska in 1940 that she discovered a tale that just had to be written. From people who had lived in the interior, from isolated herders, from lone airplane pilots flying the trail from Fairbanks down the Yukon River, from trappers working in the foothills of Mt. McKinley, there came to her the story of one, *Smoozie,* an Alaskan reindeer fawn, far off in the herd at Holy Cross Mission.

"I began to realize," she states in speaking of her Alaskan experience, "that those who lived away from the cities and either in or near the wilderness, had a habit of talking of animals much as we talk of our next door neighbors." *Smoozie* was like any human being adventuring in a frightening but glorious world.

The next summer found Miss Savage at the Holy Cross Mission, 250 miles south of the Arctic Circle on the Yukon River. Here she met *Smoozie,* and so his story came to be written. At once it became a best seller in the juvenile field, praised by critics as an "Alaskan Bambi" and by wild life authorities as a thoroughly authentic piece of natural history.

It was during this second trip to Alaska that Miss Savage collected data for *Dogsled Apostles,* a book on Bishop Crimont and the Alaska missions. *Eben the Crane,* an Alaskan animal story, was published in 1944, and *Holiday in Alaska,* an elementary school reader telling of a boy's travels through Alaska and his friendships with Indians, pilots, and surveyors, appeared later.

From time to time she contributes articles to various magazines and newspapers, and when time permits, gives talks on vocations, on Alaska, and on Catholic books and authors.

Her feminine grace, charm, modesty and talents assure her latest venture, the opening, in 1946, of the Alma Savage Lecture Service, of success.

T. V.

Courtenay Savage 1890-1946

In 1937, a prosperous playwright and radio executive was very busy directing a large broadcasting network, with his spare time given in great part to enjoying himself. Typically unreligious, he had given, throughout his forty-seven years, little thought to the meaning of life. Popular, with years of success behind him, as an author, dramatic critic, Broadway playwright and public relations official, he had busied himself with the many cares and pleasures such a career brings with it. Caught up suddenly by a Catholic friend of his who asked him the question, "Where are you going?" he started a train of thought seeking to answer not only this question but "Why?" Courtenay Savage, guided and encouraged by his friend, learned of the Catholic faith and found the direction in life that he needed. Upon his reception into the Church, he zealously strove to change his pattern of life and undertook the apostleship of the Catholic press.

Courtenay Savage was born in New York City, July 20, 1890, the son of Episcopalian parents, Charles Edward and Frances (Hennessy) Savage. He was educated in public and private schools and took a special course in writing at Columbia University. From his adolescence he had a gift for expression. Oddly enough, his first encouragement as a writer came from a story "Rainmaker" which he sold to *Columbia,* the Knights of Columbus magazine. This beginning of his literary career was followed by the production of a great many short stories, magazine articles and fourteen plays—many Broadway successes—among the most notable of which were *Home is the Hero,* a dramatization of the life of Robert Louis Stevenson; *They All Want Something* and *The Little Dog Laughed.* With the advent of the radio, he did dramatic and public relations work in New York, Chicago and Europe.

After becoming a Catholic, Mr. Savage devoted most of his time and efforts to the Catholic press, the Catholic radio and the Catholic theater. At America's entrance into the war in 1941, he became Director of Public Relations for the National Catholic Community Service. While in Chicago, at this work, he founded the Catholic Actors Guild of that city. Here, too, in Chicago he met so many servicemen who asked for information about St. Christopher, that he gathered together all the facts and legends he could about this saint and turned his material into *The Wayfarer's Friend,* a book which may be said to be a life of St. Christopher in fiction.

In 1946 Mr. Savage went to Europe on special work for the National Catholic Welfare Council. He was to direct publicity for the War Relief Services. Within a month after his departure from the United States, he died unexpectedly of a heart attack in the Grand Hotel, Rome, August 23. In the last nine years of his life he used the talents and training of the first forty-seven years to give widespread testimony of the Faith that he had embraced.

J. M.

Albert Paul Schimberg   1885-

Like most authors, Albert Paul Schimberg finds writing hard work but cannot resist it. At the early age of fourteen he contributed to *The New World,* Chicago, when Charles J. O'Malley was its editor, and to *Our Young People,* Milwaukee, Wisconsin. Later he contributed to *The Magnificat, The Christian Family, Columbia, Queen's Work, The Catholic World, America,* and other periodicals.

Albert Schimberg was born in Appleton, Wisconsin, on March 7, 1885, the son of Henry and Josephine (Frantz) Schimberg. After attending St. Joseph's and Sacred Heart parish schools he worked successively in a photographer's studio; a furniture factory; for the Appleton *Daily*

Crescent; as secretary to a member of the House of Representatives, and for a small-town newspaper in Kaukauna, Wisconsin. He then attended Marquette University and was graduated in 1923 with a Bachelor of Literature degree. He worked on *The Catholic Tribune* (now defunct), Dubuque, Iowa, when it became a daily in 1920. Two years later he became a member of the staff of *The Catholic Herald,* Milwaukee, and served till its merger with *The Catholic Citizen,* in 1935; since then he has been on the staff of *The Catholic Herald Citizen,* Milwaukee, Wisconsin.

Schimberg's first translation, *Theresa Neumann,* which was published in 1929, led to correspondence with the author, Friedrich Ritter von Lama. Two other von Lama books on Theresa Neumann, *Further Chronicles of Theresa Neumann* and *Theresa of Konnersreuth* were published in 1932 and 1935 respectively. Then Schimberg translated Dr. Linus Bopp's *Liturgical Education* (1937) and in 1929 Leo Weismantel's *Die Guten Werke des Herrn Vinzenz,* under the title of *The Mantle of Mercy.*

In 1942, Schimberg wrote his first book, *The Larks of Umbria,* which he undertook at the suggestion of his publisher, to whom he said after having translated *The Mantle of Mercy:* "I wish Weismantel had written a life of St. Francis of Assisi so I could translate it." The publisher asked: "Why don't you write your own?"

The life of Frederick Ozanam, the founder of the Society of St. Vincent de Paul, was written in 1946.

Schimberg is working on a life of St. Coletta, reformer of Poor Clares. He hopes to write a history of Luxembourg, his father's native land and biographies of Jean Nicolet, the first white man in Wisconsin, and Father René Menard, the Lost Black Robe of New France.

M. H.

Reverend Wilhelm Schmidt, S.V.D. 1868-

Spurred on by letters from his missionary confreres, the German ethnologist Father Wilhelm Schmidt took an early interest in the religions, languages and customs of primitive peoples. Arnold Janssen, the founder of the Society of the Divine Word, had sent young Schmidt to the university to study natural science but the young priest showed a greater interest in linguistics. Consequently, when permission was granted him to enter this field he took up the studies of Hebrew, Aramaic and Arabic.

Wilhelm Schmidt was born at Hoerde in Westphalia on February 16, 1868, and was educated in the missionary seminary of Steyl. He entered the Society of the Divine Word in 1890. In 1892 he went to St. Gabriel's missionary college at Mödling near

Vienna where, until 1938, he lectured to the students and directed the Anthropos Institute, which he founded. When the Nazis seized Austria, Father Schmidt and his co-workers went to Froideville near Fribourg in Switzerland. There he became a professor at Fribourg University and director of the Anthropological Institute.

Father Schmidt gave particular attention to the languages of Southern Asia, Australia and Oceania. In his first published book (1899) he proved that the Melanesian and Polynesian languages were related. Then he proved that the Monkhmer tribes formed the link between the peoples of Central-Asia and Australia.

When in 1898, Andrew Lang published his book, *The Making of Religion*, and proved from historical facts that the monotheism of certain primitive people was part of the original inheritance of the human race, Father Schmidt made use of this material and built upon these conclusions to bring out his series of books, *The Origin of the Idea of God*.

In 1907, Father Schmidt compiled the *Anthropos-Alphabet*, an artificial alphabet by means of which the sounds of all languages of the world can be represented. It is used only in *Anthropos*, the international magazine to which learned writers contribute in more than a dozen languages. It was founded to offer missionaries an organ of their own in which to publish the result of their researches. Soon it became the best-known ethnological-linguistic journal, with articles in French, English, German, Polish, Italian, Spanish, Dutch and even Latin.

Father Schmidt is largely responsible for the inauguration of the courses in religious ethnology that were held twice at Louvain and once in Austria, at Tilburg in Holland, and in Milan.

When the Vatican Mission Exhibition took place, Father Schmidt was asked to organize the ethnological section. In 1927 he was nominated director of the Ethnological Department of the Lateran Museum, and he was given membership in the newly re-organized Pontifical Academia delle Scienze in 1937.

Despite his achievements in science he is also very active in priestly work, especially in giving retreats. For years he was choir-master at the Seminary. Among the compositions which he wrote are: a *Salve Regina; Magnificat; Miseremini; Popule Meus;* the *Eight Beatitudes;* and a *Compline*.

In 1928 Father Koppers, S.V.D., compiled the *Schmidt Festschrift* in honor of Father Schmidt's 60th birthday. Besides the articles on linguistics, ethnology and comparative religion, there is an authoritative list of one hundred and fifty of his scientific publications.

The following books are available in English: *The Origin and Growth of Religion* (1931), translated by H. J. Rose; *Primitive Revelation,* translated by Joseph J. Baierl (1939); *The Culture Historical Method of Ethnology,* translated by S. A. Sieber, and *High Gods in North America* (1933).

M. H.

Reverend Edgar Schmiedeler, O.S.B. 1892-

Rural life, the family and the religious training of the child in the home have been the chief interests of the Reverend Edgar Schmiedeler, O.S.B., in the socio-religious field, where his achievement has been notable. Born in Kansas City, Kansas, in 1892, one of seventeen children whose parents lived to celebrate their sixtieth wedding anniversary—early influenced by his own home life, and by his priestly studies in the Order of St. Benedict, which is built upon the ideal of the family—he began his life work with this foundation. His parents had been educated in the schools of France and Luxembourg and often contrasted social aids given to the poorer classes in Europe with the lack of those activities in earlier years in the United States. With the problems of rural life he became familiar during the years spent in the country. He took his early studies in the parochial schools in Kansas City; at St. John the Evangelist School, Argentine; at Holy Name School, Rosedale; and then attended St. Benedict's High School, 1907 to 1910, and St. Benedict's College, Atchison, Kansas. His senior college work was done at St. Vincent College, Latrobe, Pennsylvania, where he received his A.B. in 1914. He entered the novitiate of the Benedictine Order in 1912, taking the name of Edgar, his baptismal name having been Louis. In 1916 he pronounced his solemn vows. He received his M.A. from St. Vincent's Graduate School of Theology in 1915 and his S.T.L. in 1917. Because of the need for chaplains in World War I, ordination was advanced one year so that he received holy orders in 1918 and did not complete his work for the Doctorate in theology.

From 1919 to 1921 Father Edgar taught dogmatic theology at St. Benedict's Seminary, Atchison. The following year was spent in parish work, and in the summer of 1922 he studied at Notre Dame University. From 1922 to 1925 he taught sociology at St. Benedict's College, Atchison, introducing a special course on the family and one in rural sociology, the first to be offered in these fields in any Catholic educational institution in the United States. Two years' graduate study at the Catholic University of America from 1925 to 1927, won him his Ph.D. During the summer of 1927 he studied at Harvard. Other summer periods were spent doing parochial work, alternately in rural and urban parishes. From 1927 to 1930 he was professor of sociology at St. Benedict's College, Atchison, and headed the sociology department. From 1930 to 1941 he served as director of the Rural Life Bureau and of the Family Life Section in the Social Action Department of the National Catholic Welfare Conference, Washington, D.C. In 1941 the Family Life Section became the Family Life Bureau, and was placed under the Executive Department of the Welfare

Conference. Continuing direction of the family work in this bureau he has devoted most of his time since 1941 to this field of activity. He is a member of the National Catholic Rural Life Conference and is the founder (1933) and liaison officer of the National Catholic Conference on Family Life. From 1932 to 1935 he was instructor in sociology at the Catholic University and since 1937 has been a lecturer in the School of Social Sciences there, giving courses on the family, in rural sociology, agricultural economics and cooperatives.

As a student he began writing for the college publication, *Abbey Student.* His thesis, "The Industrial Revolution and the Home," was a comparative study of city, country town and farm families. While teaching, Dr. Schmiedeler wrote articles for such periodicals as *The American Ecclesiastical Review* and the *Catholic Educational Review.* In 1930 his first book appeared. It was written as a text and entitled *An Introductory Study of the Family.* As supplementary readings to this text he published *Readings on the Family* in 1931. With Sister Rosa McDonough, child psychologist, he was co-author of *Parent and Child* (1935), setting forth Catholic viewpoints in the various fields of child-care and training. In 1937 he revised the volume of Dr. Thomas J. Gerrard, *Marriage and Parenthood; The Catholic Ideal.* His most recent books are: *A Better Rural Life* (1938); *The Sacred Bond* (1940) on happiness and holiness in family life; *Cooperation: a Christian Mode of Industry* (1941), and *Marriage and the Family* (1946). He has contributed to various symposia, encyclopedias and other works.

Dr. Schmiedeler is also the author of many booklets on rural life, agriculture, cooperatives, the family, the parent, the child. *Balanced Abundance* received special commendation from former Secretary of Agriculture, Henry A. Wallace. *Christian Marriage* is an analysis of and commentary on the marriage encyclical. Dr. Schmiedeler lectures extensively and has spoken on the radio, appearing on such programs as the "Catholic Hour," "Church of the Air" and "Farm and Home Hour." He is associate editor and contributes regularly to *The Catholic Family Monthly,* organ of the National Catholic Conference on Family Life and has also written numerous articles for many other Catholic periodicals. During the past decade he has averaged more than an article or an address each month. He has constantly placed emphasis upon the necessity for religious training of the child in the home, and through his efforts stress is now being brought to bear upon this. He is a member of the National Commission on Family and Parent Education, the Conference on Conservation of Marriage and the Family, the National Conference on Family Relations, and the American Sociological Society.

Since 1941 he has been an associate editor of *Rural Sociology,* a publication of Harvard University.

C. M. N.

Reverend Paul Schulte, O.M.I. 1895-

The speediest transportation devised by man has been put to the service of God through Reverend Paul Schulte, O.M.I., widely known as the "Flying Priest." The last scion of an age-old Westphalian farmer family, Schulte-Holtermann, he was born in Magdeburg, Germany, in 1895, and educated at the Rectoratschule Luedinghausen, Westphalia, and the Collegium Carolinum of the Oblate Fathers at Valkenburg, Holland, where he graduated in 1913. The following year he entered the novitiate of the Oblates of Mary Immaculate and in 1915 studied at the Askanisches Gymnasium in Berlin. He then enlisted in the German Army and learned to fly, receiving his commission and decoration for valor in service. This was providential in view of his future life work, for his knowledge of aviation equipped him to undertake missionary work aided by flights over difficult terrain or vast areas.

After World War I he resumed his theological studies and was ordained at Huenfeld, Hessen Nassau, in 1922. A few years later, in 1925, he suffered a great personal loss in the death of his best friend, the Reverend Otto Fuhrmann, O.M.I., in Ovamboland, South West Africa. Thus was acutely brought home to him the realization that proper transportation which might have saved the life of his friend was greatly needed on the missions. This Father Schulte endeavored to impress on his superiors, but it took several years to effect recognition of the plan of the "flying missionary." It came through Cardinal Schulte, Archbishop of Cologne, in whose archdiocese in 1927 Father Paul Schulte founded the "Missions Verkehrs Arbeitsgemeinschaft," and with the MIVA he has since been identified. The same initials represent the organization in Latin terminology, "Missionalium Vehiculorum Associatio"—in Dutch, "Missie Verkehrs Aksie"—in English, "Missionary International Vehicular Association." Its object is to modernize the missions through vehicular aid or rapid communication.

Throughout Germany Father Schulte gave lectures in cathedrals and crowded halls, seeking prayer and financial aid for the success of the organization. He also came to America, where he made many friends and was entertained at the wealthiest club in the United States, Boca Raton, Florida, of which he was elected an honorary member. Some 800,000 members, contributing at least two dollars annually, came to the support of the Association in Germany, and the membership spread to Switzerland and all over Europe. Since its foundation MIVA has had in use over three hundred automobiles, fifteen motor boats, twelve airplanes, twenty wireless stations and hundreds of bicycles, and where vehicles could not travel, horses and mules have been bought and put to use.

In 1930, Father Schulte went to South West Africa to establish there on behalf of MIVA a combined water, land and air transportation system for the service of the Catholic missions. Motion pictures were taken of the trip to spread knowledge of the vicissitudes of the missionaries and how they could be aided by modern transportation supplied by MIVA. His varied experiences during six months travelling in the jungles, through sand and mud, and in lands and on waters infested by dangerous animal life are recorded in *The Flying Missionary,* his first book.

The following year the African film, "Legacy of a Missionary," was shown before the Congregation for the Propagation of the Faith and many other interested audiences in Rome, and Father Schulte was received in audience by Pope Pius XI, who said to him of his work: "You do not have to arouse my enthusiasm—I am enthusiastic!" In a second audience the Holy Father said to Father Schulte: "Go to the poorest and most isolated of all missionaries, those in the Arctic—my blessing accompanies you. May everyone help you to carry out your task."

In 1936, the Flying Priest crossed the Atlantic, in the Hindenburg, and on May 8 he celebrated Mass on the airship, the first Mass ever said in the air. Since then, the Flying Priest has travelled thousands of miles in his missionary work in the frozen North, covering the Hudson Bay area, far into the Arctic region. In 1938, he saved the life of a French missionary, Father Julien Cochard, who was near death at Arctic Bay, the flight of 2,200 miles bringing him where hospitalization and medical aid could be provided. Many other lives and countless souls have been saved by Father Schulte piloting The Flying Cross, as he called his airplane. Of his labors and those of other heroic missionaries among the Eskimos, and the lives of these people, he writes in *The Flying Priest over the Arctic.* By his lectures he raised funds to finance the mobilization of the Arctic missions where the work of the MIVA is successfully organized.

When World War II broke out, Father Schulte sold his plane, and is now occupied in writing. He writes in English, having learned the language since coming to the United States, but he is rewriting his second book in German under the title, *The Flying Cross over the Arctic,* stressing the religious aspects which, he says, they need in Germany today. His third book will be entitled *Our Lady of the Snows.* Magazine articles too come from his pen. Father Schulte took out United States citizenship papers in 1937. He is of fine physique and pleasing personality, and the warmth of his smile will be well remembered in far places.

C. M. N.

Reverend Henry C. Schuyler 1876-

All four of Father Schuyler's little volumes comprising his *Virtues of Christ* series have been translated into French, and sell as well in Europe as they do in America.

Born in Pottstown, Pennsylvania, on the 20th of April, 1876, Henry C. Schuyler was educated at the Hill School, Pottstown, where he was graduated in 1896. While there he played on the football team. The fall following graduation (1896) he entered St. Charles Seminary, Overbrook, where he was ordained December 16, 1903. The two years following, 1903 to 1905, were spent at Catholic University, Washington, D.C., where he received the degree of Licentiate in Sacred Theology in June 1905.

His first writing interest came through his love of history, in which he majored while at the Catholic University. He wrote two biographical articles for the *Catholic Encyclopedia,* and later became a member of the Board of Directors of the American Catholic Historical Society, Philadelphia.

Early in his course at the University he conceived the idea of presenting in popular language and in the form of small and low-priced books, studies of the human side of the life of Christ. At that time there were very few, if any, publications of this character in English. His idea took form in four books, one each, on the four virtues of Courage, Charity, Obedience, and Friendship, under the titles: *The Courage of Christ; The Charity of Christ; The Obedience of Christ,* and *A Divine Friend* (1913). *The Sacrament of Friendship* appeared in 1916. The noted English writer, Monsignor Robert Hugh Benson, wrote an introductory chapter to *A Divine Friend.*

The appointment of Father Schuyler as pastor to St. Agnes, West Chester, Pennsylvania (1919), brought a halt to his writing for a time. After an interval of eighteen years of silence, in 1934, while on a leave of absence at Lourdes, he completed a long contemplated book on the virtues of the Blessed Virgin. It is entitled *Mary, Mother Most Admirable.* It was reprinted one year later. His latest book, *Life's Final Goal,* a work on philosophy "charting a course by the light of reason," was published in 1939.

E. F.

Reverend Martin Jerome Scott, S.J.   1865-

Outstanding apologist, Reverend Martin J. Scott, S.J., is the author of some thirty books, of which the majority are in defense or exposition of Catholic truths. He was born in New York City in 1865. Soon after, his family moved to Utica, New York, where he attended Assumption Academy, 1872 to 1879, and Utica Academy, 1879 to 1883. After a year at Holy Cross College, Worcester, Massachusetts, where he received his A.B., he entered the Jesuit novitiate at Manresa-on-Hudson, New York, August 15, 1884. From 1891 to 1893 he was professor of Latin at Holy Cross College. Completing his philosophy and theology studies at Woodstock, Maryland, he received his M.A. there in 1899, and was ordained priest that year. He was appointed dean of discipline at St. Francis Xavier's College, New York, and was then assistant pastor at St. Ignatius Loyola Church in that city, 1901 to 1914. In 1915 he was a lecturer at Boston College, and until 1924 assistant pastor of the Immaculate Conception Church, Boston. Since 1924 he has been lecturer in apologetics at the Postgraduate School of Fordham University and instructor in religion at the College of St. Francis Xavier, New York City.

In this metropolis he has come in contact with all classes of people and every type of mind, and thus knows human nature well. Moreover, he has the priest's knowledge of the human soul. His preaching soon attracted attention, but he delayed writing until after his fiftieth year. Zeal for souls and literary skill have since then borne abundant fruit in numerous books which are the product of a mature and scholarly mind. His first work, *God and Myself,* published in 1917, is a simple explanation of Catholic belief. It was followed by *The Hand of God,* which answers questions often proposed by the inquirer. In *Credentials of Christianity* he presents evidence for the divine origin of the Church. Subsequent works in the field of dogma and apologetics are: *Man; Christ or Chaos; The Virgin Birth; Religion and Common Sense; Christ's Own Church; Why Catholics Believe; Religious Certainty; The Church and the World; Answer Wisely,* and *Introduction to Catholicism.* In 1927, he gave answers to *Things Catholics Are Asked About,* and his broadcasts over Station WLWL, 1927 to 1928, defining the Catholic position on various questions, were published in book form as *Father Scott's Radio Talks.*

A description of dedication to God's service in a religious community is given in *Convent Life,* and the Christian home is portrayed in *Your and Yours: Practical Talks on Family Life.* Some novels, too, have come from his pen: *The Boy Knight; For Better or Worse; Mother Machree,* and *The Altar Boys of St. John's. The Divine Counsellor* is helpful to those in trouble, and he also wrote a treatise on *Happiness.* Of our future life he writes in *What Is Heaven?* In 1940, he published *Jesus As Men Saw Him,* portraying Christ through the eyes of those who knew Him. It was extremely popular. At the same time he began a series of ten pamphlets on God and our relation to Him. He has also written other pamphlets. The sales of his books have exceeded one million copies.

C. M. N.

Ann Scott-Moncrieff 1914-1943

The distinguished critic, Edwin Muir, wrote in *The Scotsman,* at the time of Ann Scott-Moncrieff's death in 1943 that "she had great gifts, and if she had lived might have been one of the best Scottish writers of her time. A few short stories, which she wrote for *The New Alliance* raised high hopes in those who admired her work. Two children's stories, *Aboard the Bulger* (1936) and *Auntie Robbo,* and a volume of short stories, *The White Drake and Other Tales* (1937), make up her published work. She was planning a book of Scottish saints for children when she died."

Her book, *Auntie Robbo,* was rejected by London publishers as "too Scottish." It was accepted and successfully published in New York.

Ann Scott-Moncrieff (Agnes Millar Shearer) was a native of the Orkney Islands, having been born in Kirkwall in 1914, the daughter of Major John Shearer. When she was seventeen years old Agnes Shearer (as she was then—she changed her name to Ann, later) worked on the local paper, *The Orcadian.* To pursue her literary career, she went to London. There she met George Scott-Moncrieff. She returned to Scotland and was married to him in 1934. She was received into the Church with her husband at Easter, 1940.

A friend remarked: "During all my long friendship with Ann, she seemed to be fighting for an inner peace and purity of spirit—sometime the goal was lost sight of but never for very long. I believe she achieved it when she entered the Catholic Church."

M. H.

George Irving Scott-Moncrieff 1910-

As Secretary to the Scottish Council of the National Buildings Record in World War II, George Irving Scott-Moncrieff has written no books since he was received into the Catholic Church in 1940. He has on hand, however, a pamphlet on "Rebuilding Scotland" and a history of Edinburgh. He is a regular writer for broadcasting.

He was born in Edinburgh, Scotland, in 1910, the second son of the Reverend C. W. Scott-Moncrieff, an Episcopalian minister, and was educated at the Aldenham School. His grandparents were Presbyterians and his ancestors Covenanters.

His uncle, Charles Kenneth Scott-Moncrieff, a translator of Proust, Pirandello and Stendhal, was a convert to Catholicism.

From 1929 till 1932 George Scott-Moncrieff did editorial and journal-istic work in London. After publishing his first novel, *Café Bar* with a London underworld setting, he returned to Scotland. From 1939 till 1941, he was joint editor of the *New Alliance*, a Scottish cultural bi-monthly with Irish sympathies. He is an active supporter of the Scottish Nationalist Cause.

In 1934, he married Agnes Millar Shearer (Ann Scott-Moncrieff). They have three children, a girl and two boys. Mrs. Scott-Moncrieff died on February 17, 1943, at the age of twenty-nine.

He is the author of: *Tinkers' Wind* (Novel); *A Book of Uncommon Prayer* (verse); *The Lowlands of Scotland,* and *The Wind in the East* (1942) (a one-act play).

He edited two volumes, *Scottish Country* and *The Stones of Scot-land,* dealing respectively with the land and its buildings.   M. H.

Sister Blandina Segale   1850-

Faithfully keeping a diary all during her life helped Sister Blandina Segale to bring out a book about the Southwest of territorial days. In the fore-word of this book Archbishop McNicholas states that it "rivals in many of its pages the most thrilling romances written of that period."

When Sister Blandina was sent to Trinidad, Colorado, on November 27, 1872, she came in contact with frontier life in all its pristine glory. Her twenty years of labor at Trinidad, Colorado, Santa Fe and Albu-querque, New Mexico, are recorded in her book, *At the End of the Santa Fe Trail.* Permission was granted to a moving picture concern to use the scene of her first encounter with Billy the Kid.

Sister Blandina, formerly Rose Segale, was born in 1850 at Cicagna, a town about fifteen miles from Genoa, Italy. When four years of age, she came with her parents, to the United States, landed at New Orleans and moved the same year to Cincinnati, Ohio. Here she received her early education from private tutors and in the public schools. In 1864 at the age of fourteen she was a nurse in the Battle of Nashville.

The work of the Mother Seton Sisters of Charity, caring for the orphans and nursing the sick in hospitals, attracted her to join them, at the age of sixteen on September 13, 1866. After her novitiate of two years, she made her vows and was sent to teach in the parish schools at Dayton and Steubenville, Ohio.

In 1897, Archbishop Elder had become aware of the great proselytiz-ing work that was being done among the Italians. He called upon Mother Mary Blanche Davis to suggest some plan to keep them within the fold. Mother sent Sister Blandina and her own sister who had also entered the community and had taken the name Sister Justina. With five dollars in their purse and relying on the help of God they succeeded in their laborious endeavors and saved the faith of hundreds of Italians. Through their efforts, centers were established in many of the parish schools of the city. A bequest of $2,000 for an Italian Charity had been willed by

Christian Moerlein of Cincinnati if the Italian work was organized. This
was done on December 8, 1897, under "The Santa Maria Italian Educational and Industrial Home." Since then most of her time has been spent
teaching in Ohio. Now over ninety years of age, she has retired from
public life.

Besides furnishing all the data for Anna C. Minogue's story of "The
Santa Maria Institute" Sister Blandina also wrote: *Indulgenced Prayers;
Souvenir of My First Holy Communion; Lay Missionary League; Hymns
of Our Eucharistic Lord,* and *Facts About the Catholic Church.*

M. H.

Monica Selwin-Tait

Catholic literature has meant—and still means
Catholic Action to Monica Edith Selwin-Tait. Her
work is published principally in *The Ave Maria,*
the *Prairie Messenger,* Saskatchewan, Canada, and
The Messenger of the Sacred Heart. For the last
mentioned publication she wrote over a hundred
short stories. Her books: *Three Ships Come Sailing* (1931); *Uncharted Spaces* (1932); *Wings of
Lead,* and *Winding Ways* appeared serially in
The Ave Maria, before coming out in book form.

Miss Selwin-Tait was born in London. Her
father, James Selwin-Tait, was a banker and finan-
cier by profession but was devoted to literature. He wrote four novels.
Her mother, Augusta Edith Meynell, was a cousin of Wilfrid Meynell,
the husband of Alice Meynell. She was a linguist, musician and artist.

Monica was educated privately—and much of her education was received by reading and travelling. At the age of sixteen she had a desire
to go on the stage, but suppressed it when she learned her mother did
not like the idea. Instead, she turned to the lecture platform and to writing. Cardinal O'Connell sent her to Auriesville, New York, for an article
on the shrine dedicated to the North American martyrs. This was printed
in the *Pilot,* the Boston diocesan paper, over her own name. The article
was later incorporated in the literature on the shrine. Lectures on
Auriesville at schools and colleges followed.

Miss Selwin-Tait is a free-lance writer, principally for Washington
and New York papers. Some of her articles have appeared in the Boston
Transcript. While she does research writing on secular matters, her main
interest is Catholic literature. Her advent into this field came about
through an eight-days' retreat at a convent. When it was over, she said to
the Reverend Mother who had guided her: "Mother, perhaps I could
write a pamphlet to help others know what I have gained from this
retreat." With permission granted, Miss Selwin-Tait went to work but
instead of writing the pamphlet, she wrote a triple love story, *Three Ships
Come Sailing.*

Miss Selwin-Tait is interested in painting and interior decorating. Her recreations are: music, the theatre and reading. She is a member of the Gallery of Living Catholic Authors.

M. H.

Reverend Isidore Joseph Semper 1883-

All of Father Semper's writing is based on his professional work and on his two hobbies, reading and travel. His experience as a teacher inspired four textbooks: *Questions and Exercises on Newman's Idea of a University* (1929); *A Shakespeare Study Guide* (1931); *An Approach to Poetry* (1933), and *The Fine Gold of the Old Testament* (1938). All four books were written for college students. Three other books: *The Return of the Prodigal and Other Essays* (1932); *So You're Going to College* (1934), and *In the Steps of Dante and Other Papers* (1941), are collections of his lectures and articles.

Father Semper was born in Dubuque, Iowa, the son of Lomer O. and Louise (Latour) Semper, on January 11, 1883. He received his early education in the parochial and public schools of his native city, graduating from St. Patrick's school in 1897. His classical studies were made at St. Joseph's College, now Loras College. After graduation in 1905, he studied theology in the North American College, Rome, Italy, and was ordained in the Basilica of St. John Lateran on June 13, 1908. On Trinity Sunday, June 14, he celebrated his first Mass at the tomb of St. Peter.

Since 1908, he has been teaching at Loras College, and became head of the department of English in 1924. In 1921, he was granted a sabbatical year of absence which he spent at the University of Oxford, pursuing graduate studies under the direction of such eminent English scholars as the late Sir Walter Raleigh, Percy Simpson, David Nichol Smith, A. J. Carlyle and H. F. B. Brett-Smith.

In 1910, Father Semper organized the college dramatic club and from 1910 to 1925 he staged over forty plays. Besides teaching at Loras College, Father Semper has also taught English literature at St. Clara's College, Sinsinawa, Wisconsin; for three years at Mount Carmel, Dubuque; and for seventeen years at Clark College.

He has been much in demand as a lecturer on educational and literary subjects. As a teacher and a writer he says he owes more to *Newman's Idea of a University,* than to any other book which he has read. He is a firm believer in the doctrine that a professor of English literature should justify his right to teach by his ability to write. His textbooks have been adopted for class use at Notre Dame and Marquette Universities and other institutions.

Father Semper is the author of three dramatizations, including *Oliver Twist* and *Joseph, the Dreamer*. His articles have appeared in *The Witness, Telegraph-Herald, Catholic World, The American Ecclesiastical Review, Columbia, The English Journal* and the *Homiletic Review*. He writes principally to combat the forces of skepticism and materialistic science.

M. H.

Robert Sencourt (Robert Esmonde Gordon George) 1894-

Under the pseudonym of "Robert Sencourt," Robert Esmonde Gordon George has made a valuable contribution to Catholic letters, particularly in the historical field. He was born in New Zealand in 1894 and educated there at St. John's College, Tamaki, and later went to St. John's College, Oxford for his M.A. and B.Litt. (1918). He gave his services in the first World War, serving with the Central India Horse from 1915 to 1916 and with the General Staff in Simla-Delhi from 1917 to 1918. Later he was with the India Office, 1919 to 1920.

Since the war Mr. George has had important posts in the scholastic world, occupying the chair of English at Lisbon, and Lahore, India. He was vice-dean of the faculty of arts and professor of English literature at the University of Egypt, 1933 to 1936.

The opportunities which his many contacts gave him have enabled him to write with knowledge of the facts and philosophy which make history. Among his numerous books are: *Purse and Politics* (1921); *Outflying Philosophy* (1904); *Life of George Meredith* (1929); *Life of the Empress Eugenie* (1931); *Napoleon III, the Modern Emperor* (1933); and *Conversations with Napoleon III* (1934) (with Sir Victor Wellesley). In 1932 he wrote *Spain's Uncertain Crown*, an able exposition of the history of the Spanish monarchy and the causes of its collapse and his belief in and hope of its restoration. *The Genius of the Vatican* (1935) gives in pleasant and popular style the historical background of the papacy from its beginning until 1870, while the second part of the book takes up in more detail the discussion of subsequent history in its relation to the papacy. He published two books in 1938: *Italy*, a discussion of Italy of today as evolved from the past, especially as to the Risorgimento, the World War and the Post-war period; and *Spain's Ordeal* in which he does the same thing for Spain, showing the causes and giving the historical background which brought about the Civil War of 1936-39, and taking the reader up to the recapture of Teruel in 1938.

In 1942 *King Alfonso* appeared. This life of the late King of Spain, Alfonso XIII, was written in the interval between finishing his life of Mr.

Churchill and before writing his life of St. John of the Cross. The life of the Spanish 16th century mystic was published in 1944 under the title *Carmelita and the Poet.* He is now (1947) working on a life of Cardinal Newman.

Mr. George has also contributed widely to periodicals, among them the *Times Literary Supplement,* Edinburgh *Review,* London *Times, Spectator,* and outstanding American reviews.

D. D.

Reverend Antonin-Gilbert Sertillanges, O.P.
1863-

This well-known French moral theologian and Thomistic philosopher was born at Clermont-Ferrand on November 16, 1863. His father was an industrialist and bitterly opposed his son's early ambition to become an artist. When Antonin Sertillanges was twenty he entered the novitiate of the French Dominicans which because of the anti-religious laws of the time, had been removed to Belmonte in Spain. He finished his theological studies in Corbara and, after securing his doctorate in 1890, remained three further years as professor of theology.

Father Sertillanges then spent some years in Italy—in Florence, Pisa and Milan—and drew upon his travels for his first book *Un pélerinage artistique* (1896). Then, established at the Dominican convent in Paris on the Faubourg St. Honoré, he became managing editor of *La Revue Thomiste,* and in 1900 took the chair of philosophy at the Institut Catholique of Paris soon becoming one of the leading spirits in the revival of Thomistic studies for which the Institut has become famous. He soon began work upon his masterly treatise on St. Thomas Aquinas which was published in two volumes in 1910. In 1916 he published *La philosophie morale de Saint-Thomas;* in 1928, *Les grandes thèses de la philosophie thomiste,* and at various times a number of less extensive works upon various points of Thomistic teaching.

In all of his writings upon "neo-Thomism," Father Sertillanges has not only restated and affirmed the principles of Saint Thomas' doctrine, but has brought out their application to the problems of our own day; it is in this sense that he can be called "modern." He has used the same methods in his religious writings, in his social studies and in his treatises on esthetics which show that a love for art still burns strongly within him.

He became a popular preacher at the Madeleine and at Notre Dame. His eloquence was dry and flowing and abounded in picturesque words and images and he never hesitated to treat of the most burning questions of the hour, interpreting them in the light of Christian teaching and belief. His personality is original and striking and his looks and carriage commanding. On November 30, 1918, Father Sertillanges was elected a member of the Institut de France, but would accept only a seat in the section devoted to moral and political sciences. In 1934 he was decorated with the Legion of Honor.

Among his works are: *Jésus; Nos luttes; Nos vrais ennemis; La politique crétienne; Socialisme et christianisme; Féminisme et christianisme; L'Art et apologétique; Saint Thomas d'Aquin* (2 vols.); *La philosophie morale de Saint Thomas d'Aquin; L'Eglise* (2 vols.); *Ce que Jésus voyait du haut de la croix; Les plus belles pages de saint Thomas d'Aquin.* He collaborated in the production of the treatise on "God" in the translation of the *Summa. Saint Thomas and His Work* was translated into English by Father G. Anstruther, O.P.

J. K.

Most Reverend Thomas Joseph Shahan
1857-1932

An outstanding scholar and educator, professor at the Catholic University of America for eighteen years and its rector for a subsequent period of nineteen years, Most Reverend Thomas J. Shahan was also an authority and writer on ecclesiastical history. He was born of Irish parentage in Manchester, New Hampshire, in 1857, and studied at Montreal College and at the North American College, Rome, where he was ordained in 1882. In that year he received the degrees of S.T.D. from the Propaganda College, Rome, and J.U.L. (Juris Utriusque Legum) from the Roman Seminary. Following ordination he studied at the New Sorbonne and Institut Catholique, Paris, with the Abbé Duchesne. In 1883 he returned to the United States and was chancellor of the Diocese of Hartford, Connecticut, and secretary to Bishop McMahon until 1888, meanwhile also undertaking parochial work. He then pursued graduate studies in the universities abroad for three years. In 1891 he joined the faculty of the Catholic University, Washington, D. C., where he was professor of church history and patrology until 1909, when he became rector of the university. In 1928 he retired from the rectorship, and was rector emeritus until his death at Holy Cross Academy, Washington, D. C., March 9, 1932.

Papal recognition of his valued service was given in his elevation to the episcopate in 1914. He was named Titular Bishop of Germanicopolis and consecrated by Cardinal Gibbons in the Baltimore Cathedral, on November 15, 1914. In 1928 he was named an assistant at the pontifical throne. Honorary degrees were conferred by the University of Louvain, which, by unanimous vote of its faculty of theology, bestowed on him in

1923 the Doctorate of Theology, honoris causa, and by Georgetown University which gave him in 1928 the Doctorate of Canon and Civil Law. The French Government made him a member of the Legion of Honor.

A tribute to him by the hierarchy of the United States, when he resigned as rector of the Catholic University, was voiced by Archbishop Dowling of St. Paul in a resolution unanimously adopted by the bishops at their annual meeting, and was, in part, as follows: "He has been in the forefront of every progressive educational movement in the Church in this country for the last thirty-five years. With Monsignor Pace—*par nobile fratrum*—he was a member of the original Board of Editors of the *Catholic Encyclopedia.* He had an outstanding part in encouraging the establishment of the first Catholic woman's college. He was the inspiration of the Catholic Educational Association. He brought into existence the Catholic Social Conference. He was the first mover in the work of the Catholic Teachers' College. I venture to say he has to his credit the establishment of more than a half dozen learned periodicals, covering the fields of philosophy, of history, of pedagogy, of charity, and bringing recognition to the labors of Catholic scholars."

The Catholic Encyclopedia owed to him much of its inspiration. He was associate editor from 1905 until its completion in 1913 and contributed many articles. He was also one of the editors of *Universal Knowledge,* which began publication in 1927. For nearly twenty years he was president of the Catholic Educational Association, and he founded the *Catholic University Bulletin* in 1895 and continued as its editor until 1909. As rector of the university, he was responsible for the erection of many of its great buildings and for the foundation of its library, to which, upon his retirement he contributed his own fine collection of volumes. Under his rectorship the university library grew from 34,000 to the total of 305,000 volumes. The religious houses of study in conjunction with the university were encouraged by his welcome.

He was essentially an "Apostle of Encouragement," giving this needed stimulus in many worthy causes. A special and tender devotion to the Mother of God envisioned the National Shrine of the Immaculate Conception, the foundation of which on the university grounds was begun in his lifetime, and it will endure as a monument to his love for Mary Immaculate. One of his earliest works was *The Blessed Virgin in the Catacombs.* Other books include: *The Beginnings of Christianity; The House of God; The Middle Ages,* and *St. Patrick in History.* His love of Ireland led him to constant study of its history, and the Celtic revival was to him a source of great joy. Bishop Shahan was a man of culture as well as of learning, gentle and well-loved. Perhaps his two dominant traits were a passion for books and a devotion to young students.

Retiring after an evening spent in reading and writing, he arose in the night to call a priest to anoint him as he knew he was dying. There was but time for a single anointing. He died soon after.

C. M. N.

Francis Joseph Sheed 1897-

Publishing has been successfully carried on by Francis Joseph Sheed in England and the United States during the last decade. Not only are the best Catholic writers of Britain on his list, but also continental scholars such as Karl Adam, Rudolf Allers, Paul Claudel, Henri Gheon and Jacques Maritain, whose publications in English are an important contribution to the literary world. Frank Sheed is himself a well-known translator and writer. He was born in Sydney, Australia, in 1897, of Irish ancestry. After graduation from Sydney University, where he received first-class honors in Latin, French and English and the degrees of B.A. and LL.B., he went to England to practice law. He became interested in the Catholic Evidence Guild of Westminster, and was Master of it from 1922 to 1924, 1927 to 1928 and 1935 to 1936. In 1925 he was Master of the Catholic Evidence Guild of Sydney, Australia, and wrote a book on the organization. As a Guild speaker he has addressed over 3,000 street-corner and indoor meetings. He also became well known in the lecture field, and his able exposition of Catholicity from the lecture platform includes both its literary and doctrinal aspects.

In 1926 he married Mary Josephine (Maisie) Ward. Together they founded the Catholic publishing house of Sheed & Ward in London, in 1927, and after six years established the New York office in 1933. Their plan was to provide a medium of expression for the whole Catholic world, and this they have done despite the difficult years of depression and war, in which their London office was twice bombed. They have a daughter and a son. His wife and children are residents in this country. Mr. Sheed travels back and forth between England and America.

On January 23, 1944, he received the Christian Culture Award. This annual award medal is an outgrowth of the "Christian Culture Lecture Series" of Assumption College, Worcester, Massachusetts, and is bestowed each year by Assumption College on "some outstanding lay-exponent of Christian ideals."

The house organ of the firm, *This Publishing Business* (since changed to *Sheed & Ward's Own Trumpet*) which Frank Sheed issues several times annually, provided material for a book he published in 1940, under the title, *Sidelights on the Catholic Revival*. This includes articles, in the style of publishers' blurbs, on authors and writings of the period. Earlier works include: *Nullity of Marriage; Map of Life; Ground Plan for Catholic Reading,* and *Communism and Man.* In 1938 he edited *The Irish Way* and in 1946 *Theology and Sanity.*

C. M. N.

Mrs. Frank Sheed   *see* Maisie Ward

Reverend Maurice Stephen Sheehy   1898-

Father Maurice S. Sheehy is one of several priests who have come from Columbia College, Dubuque, to the Catholic University and attained distinction in educational or literary accomplishment.

Born in Irwin, Iowa, in 1898, he was educated at Columbia (A.B.), St. Paul Seminary (S.T.B.) and the Catholic University (M.A. and Ph.D.), where he became head of the department of Religious Education. He has been a member and president of the Eastern Association of College Deans and Advisors of Men, and chairman of the Committee on Racial Attitudes, a division of the Catholic Association for International Peace.

In 1936, Dr. Sheehy was appointed by President Roosevelt one of the Board of Visitors to the Naval Academy at Annapolis. In 1939, on the "Church of the Air" program, he had the honor of interviewing His Eminence, Arthur Cardinal Hinsley, Archbishop of Westminster, on world peace, a subject of great interest to Dr. Sheehy. Among his many broadcasts were two from South America—Rio de Janeiro and Buenos Aires—during an unofficial tour with Bishop James Ryan, former rector of the Catholic University.

So intensively has Dr. Sheehy studied inter-American politics that Sumner Welles, when Under-Secretary of State, commended him for his contribution to our understanding of inter-American policies.

Father Sheehy was commissioned a lieutenant commander in the Naval Reserve in 1938 and was called to active duty early in 1941. In 1942 he was promoted to the rank of commander. In 1945 he held the rank of captain and was cited for his "excellent performance of duty as district chaplain." He was awarded the Navy Bronze Star Medal for meritorious service as Chaplain aboard the carrier U.S.S. *Saratoga*. After fifty-six months as Navy chaplain he returned to Catholic University to his pre-war position as head of the Department of Religious Education.

Besides two pamphlets entitled "Some Spiritual Problems of College Students" and "The Popes Condemn Anti-Semitism," his works include: *Christ and the Catholic College,* and *College Men—Their Making and Unmaking.* His latest book is *Problems of Student Guidance.*

J. M.

Right Reverend Fulton J. Sheen 1895-

Renowned as a preacher and lecturer, Dr. Fulton J. Sheen has become familiar to millions of Americans as the outstanding speaker on the radio program, "The Catholic Hour," a venture which began in 1930. The London *Universe* called him "the most popular of American preachers who have come to England." Many of his addresses have been published in book form.

Shortly after his birth at El Paso, Illinois, on May 8, 1895, his parents moved to Peoria, Illinois, where he attended the parochial school. After secondary education at Spaulding Institute, conducted by the Christian Brothers, he entered the Brothers' College of St. Viator, Bourbonnais, Illinois, where he received his B.A. degree in 1917, and his M.A. in 1919. That same year he was ordained a priest and went to St. Paul's Seminary, Minnesota, leaving there to enter the Catholic University of America, at Washington, D. C., which awarded him the S.T.B. and J.C.B. degrees together in 1920. He studied at Louvain University, obtaining the Ph.D. degree in 1923, and the D.D. at Rome in 1924. During 1925 he taught dogmatic theology at St. Edmund's College, Ware, England, and the following year was honored by Louvain, being made Agrégé en Philosophie. For his dissertation, *God and Intelligence,* a critical study in the light of the philosophy of St. Thomas, he was awarded the Cardinal Mercier prize for philosophy, the first American to receive this award, which had been conferred only eleven times since 1894.

Returning to America, laden with honors and invited to teach at the Catholic University of America, his bishop sent him to a poor, little parish in Peoria, where he served as an assistant priest for one year.

Honorary degrees have been conferred upon Dr. Sheen; an LL.D. by St. Viator, Loyola (Chicago), and St. Bonaventure (New York), and the Litt.D. by Marquette University. He is a member of the Catholic Philosophy Association and the Mediaeval Academy. Pope Pius XI made him a Papal Chamberlain in 1934 and a Domestic Prelate the following year. In 1936 he won the Cardinal Mazella Medal in Philosophy, and now holds the chair of Philosophy of Religion at Catholic University.

Monsignor Sheen has delivered lectures in England and Scotland, and in many parts of the United States. He has a natural talent as an orator, and in addition, the valuable gift of being able to deal with religious and ethical subjects in language that the average mind can readily grasp. His speaking engagements have been numerous, and for many years he spoke during Lent at the Church of the Paulist Fathers in New York, and since 1931 has been the Lenten preacher at St. Patrick's Cathedral in the same city.

In three of the most modern ways of spreading religious instruction and information, Dr. Sheen has taken a leading part. Chosen as the first priest to deliver a course of lectures when the Catholic Sunday Hour was inaugurated in 1930, he has returned to this work each year. His ability to attract and hold the attention of radio listeners to religious broadcasts has been amply demonstrated. Though he has at all times dealt with Catholic teaching without compromise, many of the letters sent him have come from ministers of various denominations. Monsignor Sheen receives as many as 6,000 letters a day. In February 1941 he received his 100,000th letter. One-third of these letters have come from Protestants. As a result of one broadcast, requests for his *Prayer Book for our Time* totalled more than 50,000.

With television in a more or less experimental stage, Monsignor Sheen conducted the first religious service ever to be telecast, early in 1940. The following year he acted as narrator for the first full-length motion picture made within the boundaries of Vatican City, which was presented as *The Story of the Vatican* by The March of Time. His vivid description covered everything of interest, a view of the Holy Father receiving pilgrims in audience, the civil administrators of the Vatican, the life and work of humble artisans, the industries of the tiny state, the Vatican palaces, churches, gardens, museum, Swiss guard, the spot where St. Peter was crucified, and all the other historical and interesting places.

When the New York World's Fair was officially opened in 1940, he was a principal speaker at the inaugural ceremonies in the Temple of Religion.

His books number about thirty, many of which were also delivered as sermons. Among these are: *Life of All Living* (1929); *God and Intelligence* (1925); *Old Errors and New Labels* (1931); *The Philosophy of Science* (1934); *The Eternal Galilean* (1934); *The Mystical Body of Christ* (1935), and *Whence Come Wars* (1940). His *Freedom Under God* (1940), was produced in Braille type for distribution to the blind, *Philosophies at War,* was published in 1943 and in 1944, *Love One Another* and *The Seven Pillars of Peace.*

About the same number of pamphlets have come from his pen, most of them having been delivered as addresses during the Catholic Hour. Though some of his early writings had a distinct flavor of G. K. Chesterton's style, so as to cause him to be referred to as "the American Chesterton," he has, in his later works, developed a distinctive style of his own. Particularly severe in his condemnation of communism, which he considers the chief enemy of mankind, he has also roundly denounced fascism, and "monopolistic capitalism." He contributes regularly to periodicals such as *Commonweal, America,* and *New Scholasticism.* General opinion of his gifts as a writer may well be summed up in the words of the New York *Herald Tribune:* "Dr. Fulton J. Sheen's pen is recognized as the most trenchant and potent now at the service of the Catholic Church."

In the primary work of every priest, the conversion of souls, Dr. Sheen has been singularly blessed. His radio addresses and writings have brought many to the Church, and he has personally instructed many people, unknown as well as well-known, among the most recent and celebrated, being the late Heywood Broun, the former newspaper writer and Clare Boothe Luce. His main purpose is to teach that "the kingdom of God and its justice is the only important concern of life," and he is convinced that lasting world peace can be achieved only through the efforts of the Pope, "the only moral authority that is left in the world."

R. F.

George Nauman Shuster 1894-

The many and exacting tasks as president of Hunter College, the world's largest college for women, gives George Nauman Shuster little time for writing books. Yet in the very year of his appointment, he managed to bring out *The English Ode From Milton to Keats*.

Dr. Shuster was born in Lancaster, Wisconsin, August 27, 1894, the son of Anthony and Elizabeth (Nauman) Shuster. His father's people were German Catholics, his mother's people were German Lutherans. He received his secondary education at St. Lawrence's College, Fond du Lac, Wisconsin; from there he went to Notre Dame and graduated in 1915. He hoped to enter West Point, but when the war came he took up journalism. After one year as a reporter, he entered military service, and his eighteen months with the A.E.F. were served first as a sergeant of the Intelligence Section, G.H.Q., and then as an interpreter in the Army of Occupation. During his stay in Germany he saw much of the hunger, the fighting in the streets, the first electoral campaign and the effect the heavy pressure of the armistice terms was having on the German people. Later he attended the University of Poitiers, France, and received a Certificate d' Aptitude in 1919. This experience in Europe awakened his interest in modern Europe.

Returning to the United States with his health somewhat impaired, he decided to accept the invitation to teach at Notre Dame, thinking that the quiet life he had known there while a student would be beneficial to him. Instead he found himself very busy and interested in teaching. Along with his teaching he took graduate work in French literature and received his Master's degree. In 1920 he became the head of the Department of English and associate editor of the *Ave Maria,* and remained at Notre Dame until his marriage in 1924 to Doris Parks Cunningham of Los Angeles, California. They have one son, Robert, and two foster daughters.

He then went to New York and matriculated in the graduate school of Columbia University. While in New York he came into contact, quite accidentally, with the newly-formed *Commonweal* group, bent on starting a weekly magazine similar in character to the *Nation* and the *New*

Republic but dedicated to religious principles. When, at the end of the year 1924, the magazine began publication, Dr. Shuster was writing editorials for it. After six months he severed his academic connections and accepted the arduous position of associate editor and later managing editor. For eight years, from 1929 to 1937, he held the post, and also taught English at Brooklyn Polytechnic Institute, at St. Joseph's College for Women, and at Immaculate Conception Seminary. He is now a contributing editor to *The Commonweal.*

During his years as editor, he received two grants for study in Germany, one from the Vereinigung Carl Schurz and another from the Oberlaender Trust. In 1937 the Carnegie Corporation awarded him a two year fellowship in the study of the Weimar Republic and in particular of the Center Party. At the invitation of Reynal & Hitchcock, publishers, he edited their edition of *Mein Kampf* by Adolf Hitler.

In 1939 the Board of Higher Education of the City of New York invited him to become academic dean and acting president of Hunter College. After a year of service he became president, and was the first to occupy that office in their new sixteen-story, $6,500,000 building on Park Avenue. In this same year he earned his Ph.D. at Columbia University.

Dr. Shuster's hobbies are rose-growing, carpentry and tennis.

He is the author of *The Catholic Spirit in Modern English Literature* (1922); *Newman—Prose, Poetry* (1925); *English Literature* (1926); *The Hill of Happiness* (1926); *The Catholic Spirit in America* (1927); *The Catholic Church and Current Literature* (1929); *The Germans* (1932); *Strong Man Rules* (1934); *Like a Mighty Army* (1935); *Brother Flo* (1938), and *Look Away* (1939). He is co-author of *Pope Pius XI and American Public Opinion* (with Robert Joseph Cuddihy) (1939). He is editor of *Century Catholic College Texts in English* (1932-   ), and translator of *Jesse and Maria* by Handel-Mazzetti (1931); *Job the Man Speaks with God* by Lippert (1936); *The Vatican as a World Power* by Bernhart (1938). He wrote *The World's Great Catholic Literature* in 1943. In 1944, with Arnold Bergstraesser, he wrote: *Germany: A Short History*. He has contributed numerous articles to magazines here and abroad, and has written regularly for the New York *Times* and New York *Herald Tribune.*

He is a member of the General Advisory Committee of the Division of Cultural Relations of the State Department and a member of the advisory committee of the Office of the Co-ordinator of Inter-American Affairs.

On April 11, 1944, he was elected president of the Catholic Association for International Peace. In 1945 he went on a special mission to Germany.

                                                                        M. H.

Yves Simon 1903-

When, in the spring of 1938, Yves Simon received an invitation from the head of the department of philosophy at Notre Dame University to teach philosophy there, he accepted at once. He had been teaching at the Catholic University of Lille, France, since 1930. He came to the United States in August accompanied by his wife and four children. He is still teaching philosophy at Notre Dame.

Mr. Simon was born in Cherbourg, France, in 1903, the son of Auguste and Berthe Simon. He received his secondary education in his native city. He went to Paris in 1920 where, for one year, he attended a class of "rhétorique supérieure" at the Lycée Louis-le-Grand. (The so-called "rhétorique supérieure" is an upper form attended by literary students already provided with the degree Bachelor of Letters.) In the winter of 1921 he left the Lycée Louis-le-Grand and became a university student with the purpose of taking degrees in philosophy. During the school year of 1921 to 1922, he attended courses both at the Sorbonne and at the Catholic Institute of Paris. There he came under the influence of Jacques Maritain. In July 1922 he received his "licence-ès lettres, série philosophie" at the Sorbonne. "From then on it was perfectly clear that I should be a student of philosophy all my life," said Mr. Simon. In 1922 to 1923 he prepared for and obtained the degree called "Diplôme d'études supérieures de philosophie" with a dissertation on the economist, Charles Dunoyer. At the same time he kept attending Maritain's course at the Catholic Institute and even did some work in biology at the College of Sciences of the Sorbonne. Most of his time, however, was spent in libraries doing research. In 1923 he began to prepare, as a dissertation for a doctor's degree at the Sorbonne, a book on the *Philosophy of Proudhon,* which remains unfinished. For three years he worked on it assiduously. In 1926 to 1927, however, he was again working at the College of Sciences. The following year he studied medicine but kept increasing his knowledge of philosophy. From the College of Philosophy of the Catholic Institute he received the degree "lector philosophiae."

In 1930, he obtained his first professorship in philosophy. The Catholic University of Lille appointed him instructor with a complete schedule. Simultaneously, he was appointed lecturer at the Catholic Institute of Paris. He kept both these positions until 1938. Mr. Simon finished his dissertation in the fall of 1933. It was accepted on April 18, 1934. Desclée De Brouwer Publishing Company brought it out the next day under the title *Introduction à L' Ontologie du Connaitre* (An Introduction to the Ontology of Knowledge). Also in the spring of 1934 the same publisher brought out his *Critique de la connaissance morale.*

In 1935 an outburst of indignation against the attitude of the French

Right regarding the Fascist aggression against Ethiopia prompted him to write *La Campagne d'Ethiopie et la Pensée politique Française.* (*The Ethiopian War and the French Political Opinion*) (1936). In the meantime, he had become managing editor of the *Revue de Philosophie* and the editor of a set of philosophical books called *Cours et documents de Philosophie.* For this collection, he wrote a little book on the philosophy of work, *Trois leçons sur le Travail* (1938).

In 1930 he married Paula Dromard of Nozeroy, France. They have six children. Vincent and Michael were born in the United States at South Bend. Mr. Simon is a cripple.

Besides the books already mentioned Mr. Simon wrote *Nature and Functions of Authority* in 1940. In 1942 appeared *The Road to Vichy.* This was published in French in 1941 under the title *La Grande Crise de La République Française.* He is preparing a French book on *Liberty and Authority* (Qù est ce que La Liberte? Recherches sur le libre-arbitre, le principe d' autonomie et le principe d'autorité); also *An Introduction to the Metaphysics of Love* (in English). The English translation (The March to Liberation) of *La Marche a la Delivrance* appeared in December 1942. Mr. Simon has another book out, *Community of the Free.*

M. H.

Richard Dana Skinner   1893-1941

Dramatic critic, essayist, lecturer and economist, Richard Dana Skinner was born at Detroit, Michigan, April 21st, 1893, the son of Henry Whipple and Henrietta Dana Skinner. He was educated at Sts. Peter and Paul School, Detroit, Michigan; the Newman School, Hackensack, New Jersey, from 1908 to 1909; and Carlton Academy, Summit, New Jersey (1910). He graduated from Harvard College with an A.B., cum laude, in 1915. He received an honorary LL.D. from the University of Detroit in June 1936.

While at Harvard, he married, on April 2nd, 1913, Margaret Hill of Washington, D. C. Twin daughters, Henrietta Dana (Mrs. Irving Woodworth Raymond) and Eleanora Carroll were born March 25th, 1914. A third daughter, Margaret Hill, was born December 13th, 1919.

Mr. Skinner, upon graduation, took up newspaper work on the Boston *Herald,* going to Washington in 1916 as its special Washington editorial writer. He sailed for France June 2nd, 1917, where he joined the American Aviation Corps as first lieutenant and later became captain. He became the American secretary of the Inter-Allied Advisory Committee on Aviation. He was cited by the Commander-in-chief of the A.E.F. for "conspicuous and meritorious service" and was made a Chevalier of the Legion of Honor by the French Government. He also received the Italian decoration of Cavaliere SS. Maurizio E. Lazaro.

Returning to civil life in April 1919, he was associated with the Guaranty Trust Company of New York, where he edited one of their economic survey publications. After some years in advertising work he returned to financial and economic research, and at the time of his death was a partner in Townsend-Skinner and Company, New York, advisors to industrial concerns, banks and insurance companies on basic trends in business and investment.

In addition to his financial work, during the ten years from 1924 to 1934, Mr. Skinner was drama critic of *The Commonweal*, a weekly magazine published by Catholic laymen, which he had been instrumental in founding. In 1935 and 1936, he was associate editor of the *North American Review*, which was founded a hundred and twenty years before by his great-grandfather, Richard Henry Dana and others. Besides writing for these two magazines, Mr. Skinner contributed many articles on Latin-American relations, on economics and on sociology, as well as history, literature and the theatre to leading magazines, including the *Atlantic Monthly, The Forum,* New York *Times Magazine, The Coliseum, Barron's, The Sign* and many others.

Mr. Skinner's first book, *Our Changing Theatre* (1931) incorporated his experiences and observations while acting as dramatic critic for *The Commonweal*. A second, *Eugene O'Neil—A Poet's Quest,* was published in 1935. A work on economics, *Seven Kinds of Inflation* followed in 1937. At the time of his death, on November 6th, 1941, Mr. Skinner was collaborating with his son-in-law, Professor Irving Woodworth Raymond, on a book to be entitled *Traditions of European History;* and was also working on a fifth book, *Free Men Must Answer,* dealing with the need for responsible freedom in economic life. E. C. S.

Lady Eleanore Furneaux Smith 1903-1945

As the daughter of the first Earl of Birkenhead, Lord Chancellor of England in the post-war years, Lady Eleanore Smith could have lived the conventional life of a girl of the British upper classes. She preferred, however, a more glamorous and unique life. She was born in Birkenhead in a little "cottagy" house, and at her birth, two doctors pronounced her dead. The midwife, defiant of the doctors, slapped her violently. After a long time, Eleanore moved, cried, and showed herself alive.

After attending the day school in Queen's Gate for a short time, she entered a boarding school for a year, but disliked her lessons so much that instead of busying herself with them, she wrote stories. Later she went to two French schools. When her parents discovered that the majority of girls at the second school at Meudon were English, they thought that she must, by speaking a queer kind of French, be undoing the good of her more childish days. She was, therefore, sent to live with the family of a certain Baron de Halleville, living outside Brussels so that she could attend a convent day school in Brussels. The forest of Soignies, near his home, was written about in her book *The Spanish House.*

After living for some years in Belgium, she returned to England and felt herself a stranger in her own country. While she was away she had become familiar with the French language; she had grown interested in French literature and even in Belgian politics.

At seventeen, after completing her book *The Tents of Shem* (eighty thousand words), she left the manuscript with a well-known agency. About two weeks later the principal of the typing agency sent for her and told her that Mr. John Lane, the publisher, had read it and thought it had promise and would like to meet her. Miss Smith said, "I walked out of his office in such a daze that I was nearly run over five times. Policemen shouted at me, taxi drivers swore and errand boys were abusive. But I was oblivious." A few days later, she had her interview with Mr. Lane but nothing came of it as Mr. Lane died shortly afterwards and Eleanore destroyed the manuscript.

Her father loved Madeira and he took the family there every Christmas for some years. It was there that Lady Eleanore Smith found a job as a journalist and received three pounds a week. She was engaged to write "Women's Gossip" twice a week. After six months at this job she left to write a weekly gossip column in a leading Sunday paper. Hating gossip writing she left after a year to accept a job as film critic on another weekly. One day while attending a film lunch in honor of the actor, Adolphe Menjou, she sat next to an elderly man who interested her in the circus. He induced her to resign her job as film critic and to go off with the circus as a writer. She roamed all over the British Isles. While with the circus she began to write *Red Wagon,* her first published novel, which, when it appeared, was an immediate success. It had been previously refused by two well-known publishers.

She then began to write short stories. Her mind was also active in the matter of another novel, prompted by her love for gipsies. She was an authority on gipsy life and traditions. The novel *Flamenco,* was based on the influence of Spanish gipsy blood, and it was to be dominated by the Spanish gipsy music that had impressed her when she was in Spain. She usually allowed herself six months in which to write a book.

After watching Pavlova dance the "Swan," Lady Eleanore Smith decided to write *Ballerina.* The book is not based upon Pavlova's art entirely. Two other great dancers—Shura Danilova and Alicia Markova—contributed unconsciously to the technical side of *Ballerina.*

Her other books are: *Satan's Circus; Christmas Tree; Tzigane* (1935); *Portrait of a Lady* (1936); *Life's a Circus* (1939) (her autobiography); *Lovers' Meeting* (1940); *Caravan* (1943), which has "its entertainment value vitiated by its glamorizing of adultery," and *Magic Lantern* (1945), which is also objectionable from a moral standpoint.

During the war she worked as a volunteer helper in a London canteen. With her sister Lady Pamela Smith, she was received into the Catholic Church at Westminster Cathedral in 1931. After a long illness, she received the Last Sacraments from Reverend Francis Devas, S.J., of Farm Street, London, and died on October 20, 1945. She left instructions with her father that she was to be buried according to the rites of the Catholic Church. M. H.

John George Snead-Cox 1855-1939

For thirty-six years, 1884 to 1920, John George Snead-Cox was editor of the London *Tablet*. On his retirement in 1920, he received a gold medal from Pope Benedict XV.

Born April 4, 1855, he was the eldest son of the late Colonel Richard Snead-Cox and was a grand-nephew on his mother's side of Cardinal Weld. He was educated at Stonyhurst and admitted to the Bar Middle Temple in 1881. Three years later he became editor of the London *Tablet*.

In 1891 he married Mary Porteous of New Orleans, Louisiana. Three of their four sons were killed in World War I.

For his book, *Life of Cardinal Vaughan,* he received an autographed letter of thanks from Pope Pius X. This work first appeared in two volumes in 1910. Later it was abridged into one volume. Mr. Snead-Cox also wrote *Jubilee Tide in Rome*. He was an occasional contributor to *The Nineteenth Century* and other periodicals.

He died December 30, 1939. M. H.

Henry Somerville 1889-

Born in Leeds, England, October 2, 1889, Henry Somerville is the son of working-class parents and had seven brothers and three sisters. He went to elementary schools in the Cathedral parish of Leeds and started work in a factory as soon as he was 13 years old. At 21 he got a job as sub-editor on a Catholic weekly newspaper and after a few months there got a scholarship at Ruskin College, Oxford, through the interest of the late Father Charles Plater, S.J. While still in the factory and before there was any national movement of the kind, Henry Somerville had started a social study club in Leeds and when the Catholic Social Guild was established the methods of this club became the model for clubs all over Britain. He was one of the earliest and most active workers for the Catholic Social Guild and had a good deal to do with establishing it in the industrial centres. At Oxford he obtained the Diploma in Economics and Political Science with Distinction.

After leaving Oxford he devoted himself to writing on social questions and to lecturing for the Catholic Social Guild for a time, and then joined the staff of the Manchester *Guardian* as sub-editor. In November 1915 he went to Toronto at the invitation of the late Archbishop Neil McNeil and spent nearly three years in the Archdiocese, engaged in the promotion of social work and social study among Catholics. In the fall of 1918 he gave a course in sociology at St. Francis Xavier's College, Antigonish. He returned to England, at the beginning of 1919, and became Organizing Secretary of the Catholic Social Guild, a position which he held until the summer of 1922.

It was during this period that *The Christian Democrat* was started as the monthly organ of the Guild, the annual summer schools at Oxford were begun and week-end schools in other parts of England, and the Catholic Workers' College was founded. Mr. Somerville then became London correspondent for the Toronto *Daily Star* in which capacity he visited many European countries, including Soviet Russia. In 1933 he returned to Toronto to assist in the editorship of *The Catholic Register,* now *The Canadian Register,* work in which he is still engaged.

He has published three books: *Civics: A Manual for Schools* (1929); *Britain's Economic Illness* (1931), and *The Catholic Social Movement* (1933). In addition he has written booklets and pamphlets and has contributed to almost all the leading Catholic reviews published in the English language. He was awarded the Cross Pro Ecclesia et Pontifice. In 1947 he was named a Knight Commander of St. Gregory of His Holiness Pope Pius XII.

C. J. E.

Robert William Speaight 1904-

The theatre gave Robert Speaight inspiration for his book on *Thomas Becket,* written in 1938 after he had been playing the part for three years in *Murder in the Cathedral.* He began his career as an actor with the Oxford University Dramatic Society in 1924 and several years later began to write novels, achieving success in the literary field as well as on the stage. The eldest son of Frederick William Speaight, J.P., he was born at St. Margaret's Bay, England, in 1904, and educated at Haileybury and at Lincoln College, Oxford. In the year 1925 to 1926 he played Peer Gynt and Falstaff for the O.U.D.S., of which he was honorary secretary. The following year he was with the Liverpool Repertory Theatre, and in 1927 toured Egypt in Shakespeare with Robert Atkins. There ensued several years in the theatre in London. At the Savoy and the Prince of Wales he created the part of Hibbert in *Journey's End,* 1929 to 1930, and from 1931 to 1932 he took various Shakespearean roles, including Hamlet, at the Old Vic. He frequently acted under William Poel for the Elizabethan Stage Society. In the Long Vacation of 1926 he visited the Benedictine Abbey of Ampleforth. It was his first introduction to Catholicism in action and it made an impression on him that he never forgot. He was received into the Catholic Church in 1930.

Speaight's first book, *Mutinous Wind,* appeared in 1932. Then he wrote *The Lost Hero; The Angel in the Mist,* and *Thomas Becket,* meanwhile acting the parts of Judas Iscariot in *Caesar's Friend,* Muller in *The Ace,* Lassels in *The Rose without a Thorn,* the Refugee in *Nurse Cavell,* Cameron in *A Sleeping Clergyman,* the Daimyo in *Two Kingdoms* and Becket in *Murder in the Cathedral.* This last play ran in London from 1935 to 1936, made provincial tours in 1937 and came to the United States in 1938, with Speaight in the leading role. In Boston, Philadelphia and Washington, Speaight also played in *Five Kings* and in Washington in 1939 he acted the part of Genesius in *The Comedian.*

In this same year he wrote *The Unbroken Heart,* which established him as one of the foremost young Catholic novelists. Three lectures that he delivered to the Guild Theatre Studio were published in book form under the title, *Acting: Its Idea and Tradition.* Recently he published *The Voice of the Vatican,* a pamphlet giving an account of the Vatican Radio's work in wartime. It contains a representative selection of statements and gives the lie to many anti-Catholic propagandists.

Speaight is also a broadcasting artist and a producer and has staged plays for the Catholic Stage Guild. Articles by him have been published in various magazines here and abroad. From 1939 to 1940 he was on the faculty of the University of Notre Dame, inaugurating the first summer theatre to be held on the campus. He married Esther Evelyn Bowen in 1935. They have one son and make their home in Kew Gardens, Surrey, England, where his favorite recreations are walking and riding. In 1942 he became a director of Hollis & Carter, Ltd., publishers, and in 1946 was elected a Fellow of the Royal Society of Literature.

C. M. N.

Frank Hamilton Spearman 1859-1937

Author of about twenty volumes of essays, short stories and novels, many of the latter adapted to the screen, Frank Spearman was also outstanding in his scholarly devotion to his Catholic faith. Of early American heritage, he was born in Buffalo, New York, in 1859, and was educated at public and private schools and at Lawrence College, Appleton, Wisconsin. Reared in the Congregational Church, he became a convert to Catholicism at the age of twenty-five, and in the same year, 1884, married Eugenie Lonergan of Chicago, by whom he had six children. One of his four sons is a Jesuit. He was outstandingly a family man devoted to his wife and children. He took up selling, banking and politics, in which he was an independent. Although best known for his stories of railroad life, he was never a railroad man, but began to write about railroad men and their colorful life at the turn of the century, largely because he knew and admired them. Railroad and mountain men were ever the sincerest admirers of his work because, as they said, "he knows our kind."

His first published volume of short stories, *The Nerve of Foley,* appeared in 1900. The following year he published another series of stories of railroad life, *Held for Orders.* Then in successive years came the three novels: *Dr. Bryson; The Daughter of a Magnate,* and *The Close of the Day.* In 1904 he also published a book of essays *The Strategy of Great Railroads.* This became a standard reference for students of economics, being a critical study of the major period of development of transportation by rail in the United States. Between 1897 and 1904, Frank H. Spearman's short stories and essays appeared in most of the leading secular, as well as Catholic magazines of the United States.

His western railroad novel *Whispering Smith,* which appeared in 1906, was one of his most popular books, a best seller and the first of his works to be put on the screen. It was filmed nine years after publication, in 1915, and again in 1926, starring H. B. Warner. In the latter year *The Runaway Express,* from *The Nerve of Foley,* was also shown on the screen, and in 1927, *The Yellow Mail,* from *Held for Orders,* was dramatized for the movies. In 1917 *Nan of Music Mountain,* written the preceding year, was filmed, starring Wallace Reid, who also appeared in *The Love Special,* in 1919, an adaption for the screen of *The Daughter of a Magnate.* Spearman also lent his pen and name to the serial photoplays, *The Girl and the Game* and *Whispering Smith Rides.*

The majority of his books, like *Whispering Smith,* were Western stories, among them *Laramie Holds the Range; Flambeau Jim; Hell's Desert,* and *Gunlock Ranch.* In defense of the sanctity of marriage he wrote *Robert Kimberly* (1911), and in *The Marriage Verdict* (1923) he deals with the canon law regulating the Pauline privilege, with the labor problem and high finance. *Merrilie Dawes* (1913) has a Wall Street background and *Selwood of Sleepy Cat* (1924) is a novel of American frontier life. *Spanish Lover* (1930) is a sixteenth-century historical romance of Don John of Austria. His last book, *Carmen of the Rancho,* is a romance of early California. It appeared the year of his death, which occurred at Hollywood, December 29, 1937, at the age of seventy-eight.

Two years previous Spearman had been awarded the Laetare Medal by the University of Notre Dame. He received the honorary degrees of LL.D., from Notre Dame in 1917 and from Santa Clara University in 1924, and Litt.D. from Loyola University, Los Angeles, in 1931. For many years he had made his home in California. In addition to his books and photoplays, he wrote two brochures, *The Road to Sodom* and *Your Son's Education,* a plea for Catholic education, and contributed stories and articles to Catholic and secular periodicals. He was a member of the Society of Colonial Wars, the Sons of the Revolution, Knights of Columbus and the St. Vincent de Paul Society, and an honorary member of the Newman Club of Los Angeles.

C. M. N.

Inez Specking 1895-

One of the truly industrious people is Inez Specking. She was born in 1895 at Washington, Missouri, the daughter of Bernard J. and Anna (Comer) Specking. Her father was the headmaster of St. Borgia's Catholic School. She had very little formal education in her early years, but despite having to take care of a family of ten, found herself at the age of eleven able to speak and write four languages and to play piano. At fifteen, after one year of high school, she graduated five units above the nearest ranking member of her class and was awarded the honor scholarship for four years to her State university and the gold medal for being the honor student in the entire high school. She did not accept the scholarship, on account of financial conditions at home. Instead she became a teacher in the far Southwest of Colorado. While in Colorado, she had the opportunity to attend college, which she completed in two years, receiving an A.B. degree. Then she returned home to St. Louis to teach, becoming finally a full professor in 1931. Since 1923 she has been a graduate lecturer in English and adviser on M.A. and Ph.D. theses at St. Louis University.

Her first short stories were published in *Queen's Work, The Sacred Heart Messenger,* and *The Salvatorian.* In 1929 they were gathered together and published in one volume, *So That's That.* Her first book *Missy* is the most widely known. It has been adopted for seventh and eighth grade reading—at least in the Missouri schools. All of her boarding-school stories are founded on actual fact. So is the Stanford story, *It's All Right.* Among her other books are: *The Awakening of Edith* (1924); *Boy* (1925); *Martha Jane* (1926); *Mirage* (1926); *Martha Jane at College* (1926); *What Else Is There?* (1929); *Martha Jane, Sophomore* (1929); *I Get Married* (1933); *Martha Jane Abroad* (1933); *Go West, Young Lady* (1941). In 1935 she edited *Literary Readings in English Prose.* What she herself considers her best work from the literary point of view is *What Else Is There?* Many of her books have been serialized. In fact, *What Else Is There?* has been serialized no less than four times. In 1936 she had an essay published in the *Atlantic Monthly* and re-published later by *Fiction Parade.* Besides all this she somehow managed to find time to do graduate work at the Sorbonne and at Oxford and she has a Ph.D. from St. Louis University.

Francis Cardinal Spellman 1889-

If we except such figures as Gibbons, O'Connell, England, Spalding and a few others, it is probably safe to assert that the American Catholic hierarchy has not been so prolific of literary lights as has the Church in Europe, both in modern and former years. The reason is not hard to discover. The strong and energetic characters, who have been leaders in the guidance of the Church in the United States, have lived in a pioneer age and have had to meet pioneer problems in the organization and the development of Catholicity here. Such men have, as a rule, had little time to write. Their task was building and administering. Signs are not wanting that this condition is in process of passing. One of the indications of such a passing is the work, even within the past few years, of His Eminence Francis Cardinal Spellman. The energy and assiduousness which have marked his labors since assuming direction of the most important see in the country, are nothing short of phenomenal. Besides being directly concerned with the details of the government of his great archdiocese and having had the spiritual jurisdiction, in World War II, over some 11,000,000 members of the armed forces, he found time to travel to the outposts of the far-flung Army and Navy, advise and consult with the Holy Father in person, and to be at the same time the author of five works, which have had inestimable value in stiffening the morale and clarifying the ideals of the man in the ranks as well as the citizen on the home front.

These five books are: *The Road to Victory* (1942); *Action This Day* (1943); *The Risen Soldier* (1944); *Fruits of Freedom* (1945), and *No Greater Love* (1945), a story of our soldiers. Doubtless, in the mind of many a GI and many of those who remained in civilian life, there were, at the outset of American participation in the war, the questions, "What are we fighting for?" and "When and how shall we win?" These questions the *Road to Victory* sets out to answer. The answer is, that only by keeping in mind religion and the principles of religion, in a world at war, does one see and follow the road to victory, a victory which will be worthwhile.

When Cardinal Spellman was in London, as the guest of the Prime Minister, Mr. Churchill brought him into the cabinet room, the same room where England declared war on the American Colonies. He gave the Cardinal one of the slips customarily attached to documents demanding immediate attention. "The slip, which intrigued me," said the Cardinal, "is bright red; stamped in black letters upon it is: Action This Day." Thus was the title for the second book conceived. *Action This Day* was originally a series of letters to his father, written by the Cardinal while he was making a tour of the fighting fronts, supervising the work of the chaplains.

The Risen Soldier is a little tone poem, wherein the Cardinal recalls that "the first battle is to be won in man's own heart" and that "the idealists of today are the realists of tomorrow" and that since Jesus on the cross said "It is finished," the corollary is that "it is time for man to begin."

Francis Joseph Spellman was born in Whitman, Massachusetts, in 1889, educated there in the public schools and at Fordham University, where he received his A.B. in 1911. Upon his making known his desire to become a priest of his native archdiocese, he was sent by Cardinal O'Connell to the North American College in Rome, where he was ordained and received his S.T.D. in 1916. After his return to Boston he was an assistant at All Saints Church from 1916 to 1918; served on the editorial staff of the Boston *Pilot*, 1918 to 1922; was Assistant Chancellor, 1922 to 1925, and attaché to the Secretary of State's office in the Vatican, 1925 to 1932. His immediate superior was Cardinal Pacelli, now Pope Pius XII. The next year he was given the title of Monsignor, and for six years thereafter he served the Holy See in an outstanding way. He translated and broadcast papal encyclicals in English, took care of American business in the Papal Curia, and, being an accomplished flier, he made a plane trip to Paris in 1931, there to release the words of the encyclical "Non abbiamo bisogno," which condemned Fascist tactics in Italy. He returned to Boston in 1932, after being the first American to be consecrated bishop in the Basilica of St. Peter, and took up the post of Auxiliary Bishop of Boston. After serving nearly seven years in this position, as well as holding the pastorate of Sacred Heart Church in Newton, Massachusetts, he went to New York in 1939 as successor to Cardinal Hayes, as Archbishop of New York. In December 1939 he was appointed by the Holy See to be the Ordinary of the "Diocesis Castrensis," which gives him spiritual jurisdiction over the Catholics in the Army and Navy.

In December 1945, after being officially informed of his elevation to the Cardinalate, he paid a visit to his native town of Whitman, Massachusetts, to celebrate Christmas with his father. Asked on this occasion whether this would be his happiest homecoming, he said, "The happiest was the day I came home ordained after five years away and said Mass for my father and mother."

In February 1946 at a consistory Pope Pius XII created Archbishop Spellman a Cardinal of the Holy Roman Church.

He is the translator of two books from the Italian: Monsignor Borgongini-Duca's *The Word of God* and *In the Footsteps of the Master*. Still a young man, Cardinal Spellman gives promise of a life replete with activity for God and country.

J. M.

Louis Stancourt 1900-

A constant urge to write which led Louis Stancourt into newspaper work and produced three novels, finally bore fruit in the story of his subsequent conversion. For light as to whether he should finish this work he prayed to St. Thérèse, the Little Flower, and asked for a sign, one of her roses, as a token that his prayer was heard. This was given him in a most unexpected way, a red rose of unusual loveliness, and thus he entitles his book *A Flower for Sign*.

He was born of Italian parents in Brooklyn, New York, in 1900. One of his earliest recollections is of the happy spirit of the Italian festa in the tenement district where he lived, and of the Madonna, "heart of the festa." But he lost this image, ceased going to church and grew up an atheist. He loved the droll and beautiful tales of old Italy that he heard at home and those of paradise he longed to accept, but the stories of hell he discarded, though dreams of the devil haunted his sleep. When he was at school he felt himself an American, while at home he was the son of people of Italy. So torn was he by this dual allegiance that at this early age he wrote a book with the theme "that the first generation born of foreign people in a new land is a lost generation."

When World War I began, he joined the Army, and came back from France with "a spring in his step and the great glow that is youth in the sun." He had a vague picture of the one woman for whom he must wait, and he married an American girl soon after. Though a Catholic she consented to be married by his war chaplain, an Episcopalian. His marriage estranged him from his parents, but with his first baby, a son, he brought his wife and child to their home. A daughter was born later.

Stancourt tried clerical work, bookkeeping, construction and railroad work and selling, and was then a postman. Finally he sold a story. The newspaper gave him a position in its subscription department and when he got a news story in the paper he was put on assignments, which he successfully handled. Asking to be transferred to the day staff in Long Island, he left Brooklyn in 1926 for the "grass" of a provincial news-area. There he hoped he would be able to write, but in seven years he had only tangled versions of three books: one a novel, another his tenement story, and the third a portrait, *A Woman Named Brown*. When his newspaper dropped the Long Island staff he went with another, but quit this job in 1932 and was on the relief rolls.

He sought some meaning to life, but his hatred of the Catholic Church barred his way to the truth. His children were unbaptized but he then had them confirmed in the Episcopalian Church. At the suggestion of the minister he read the *Bible*, and to the *Old Testament* he gave complete acceptance. Bruce Barton's *The Man Nobody Knows* made him wish to "know" Christ, and for this he prayed. Through a fellow-worker at the relief headquarters where, in December 1933 he obtained a position as investigator, he visited a Catholic church. Afterwards the "stillness that was never empty" drew him frequently. He read the *New Testament,* Stoddard's *Rebuilding a Lost Faith, The Question Box* and Gibbons' *Faith of Our Fathers.* Finally he sought instruction and after seven months made his profession of faith at the Queen of the Most Holy Rosary Church, Roosevelt, Long Island, in 1934. His daughter, taken suddenly ill, was baptized a Catholic. His son was placed under instruction and then his wife, too, joined him in the household of the Faith. His book, completed two years later, was published in 1937.

In 1943 he published, *Her Glimmering Tapers,* in which he depicts the spiritual struggle of our age. Mr. Stancourt also served in World War II.   C. M. N.

Walter Fitzwilliam Starkie   1894-

When the British Council established the British Institute in Madrid, Spain, in 1940, as a cultural center, Professor Starkie was made the first director—a post which he still holds.

Professor Starkie was born on August 9, 1894, the oldest son of the late Right Honorable W. J. M. Starkie, P.C. (Privy Councillor) for Ireland and Resident Commissioner of National Education; his mother was May (Walsh) Starkie. In his book, *The Waveless Plain,* he says: "Anglo-Irish I was born and Aglo-Irish I wish to be, for was it not a fact that the Anglo-Irish have always been the salt of the British Empire?"

He was educated at Shrewsbury School in England and Trinity College, Dublin. He was awarded the Classical Foundation Scholarship, and won the gold medal for excellence in the classics. He was also the gold medallist in history and political science. His musical education was received at the Royal Irish Academy of Music. In 1913 the Vandeleur Academy Violin Scholarship was bestowed upon him. Since 1924 he has been a Fellow of Trinity College, Dublin. At Dublin University, he is professor of Spanish and has also served as lecturer in Italian literature at the same University and as lecturer on Spanish literature at Stockholm and other cities in Sweden. From 1929 to 1931 he made lecture tours in the United States and Canada, including lectures at Harvard, Princeton, Columbia, Chicago and Toronto universities.

In 1927 he was appointed by W. B. Yeats and Lady Gregory a director of the Irish National (Abbey) Theatre. He can talk expertly on the Irish drama and Hollywood films. He serves on Ireland's Film Censorship Appeals Board. The summer of 1927 he spent in Rome and had an interview with Benito Mussolini.

Professor Starkie, who is small of stature but stocky, startled London about seven years ago by appearing armed with a huge spear of the Abyssinian Galla tribe—a curved native sword—and his fiddle.

Since 1919 he has associated with gypsies and has travelled as one of them during the summer vacations in the caravans—with his fiddle—through many European countries. In this way he learned their folklore and folk music. The first night he ever spent in a gypsy camp was with the gypsies in Apulia. Ever since, he has felt at certain moments a longing to be away on the plain, near the tents of the wandering folk. He also travelled on foot through Hungary, Transylvania and Rumania as far as the Black Sea, collecting stories and songs, playing the fiddle for his meals (and straw).

He has had twenty years acquaintance with Italy, and it was Genoa that initiated him into Italian life. This love of Italy was first engendered when he was fourteen years of age, when he happened to read Shelley's poem written among the Euganean hills. Years later the love of music linked his life to Italy by stronger bonds.

Professor Starkie is married to Italia Augusta, the second daughter of the Italian Professor, Cav. Alberto Porchietti of Genoa, Italy and Buenos Aires, Argentina. Starkie met her when he was lent to the Red Cross by the Y.M.C.A., which he had joined after being rejected for military service on the fourth of August, 1914 because of chronic asthma. His day was occupied giving lessons in French to the soldiers he was helping in Y.M.C.A. huts and playing to the patients in the wards of hospitals. Italia Augusta was a Red Cross nurse who daily came into the wards to sing the songs the wounded soldiers liked. Italia was born in South America. After their marriage in Genoa, they spent three months roaming about Spain. They have a son and a daughter.

Starkie is a Chevalier of the Legion of Honor and a Knight of the Order of Alfonso XII and the order of the Crown of Italy.

His publications include: *Jacinto Benavente* (1925); *Il Teatro Contemporaneo Inglese* (1926); *Writers of Modern Spain* (1929); *Raggle Taggle* (1934); *Don Gypsy* (1936); *Luigi Pirandello* (1937); *The Waveless Plain* (1938); *Grand Inquisitor* (1940); *Abridged Translation of Don Quixote* (1941); *In Sara's Tents* (1942).

He has written several articles on gypsy folklore, and has contributed to Dent's *Dictionary of Modern Music*. M. H.

William Force Stead 1884-

Born in Washington, D. C., in 1884, William Force Stead was fortunate in growing up in a house full of books and pictures. His father, who is still alive, is an architect and a collector of books and etchings. His mother was an accomplished pianist. She died in 1894 when William was only ten years of age. Lightning struck the Stead home. William's mother, who was expecting a child, suffered a shock which brought on premature labor and she died in child-birth the next day. His mother's sister, called Innie, reared William.

In the winter the Steads lived in Washington, D.C.; in the summer they moved to Elk Ridge in Maryland. It was the latter home which was one of the chief influences in his life. One spring evening when he was 15 or 16 his father read him Pope's "Ode On Solitude":

> "Happy the man whose wish and care
> A few paternal acres bound,
> Content to breathe his native air,
> In his own ground."

"The result," states William Stead, "was an explosion, the fire of my country sentiments falling into the dry powder of a dormant but inherited taste for literature. I came down early the next morning and read the poem over and over to myself, and from that moment I, who had never cared for books, became a voracious and insatiable reader of poetry —and, of course, a would-be poet."

At the age of 19, William Stead left the Friends School in Washington and entered the University of Virginia, for which he has a deep affection. While there he won a gold medal for the best poem of the year.

Having no taste for study and feeling an urge to do something, he applied to the State Department, and was appointed American Vice Consul at Nottingham, England, once the town of Robin Hood, but since the industrial revolution, the centre of a coal-mining district and the lace manufacturing trade. He was not happy there. He longed for a country life and an opportunity to write poetry, but he was too tired in the evening and his surroundings were distasteful.

In 1913, Mr. William J. Bryan, then Secretary of State, promoted him to Vice Consul at Liverpool where he remained during most of the first World War.

When the war was over, Mr. Stead resigned the consular service and entered Oxford University. He was 34 years of age then but he did not feel out of place, surrounded by a number of men well up in their twenties or early thirties whose careers had been changed by the war.

At Oxford he quickly became acquainted with three outstanding poets, W. B. Yeats, John Masefield and Robert Bridges. Yeats was living at Oxford, and Masefield and Bridges on Boar's Hill just outside. Stead's friends included Edmund Blunden, Alan Porter, Richard Hughes, Louis Golding and Robert Graves, all of whom have made some stir in the world of letters. While he was supremely happy, he was poor and overworked.

In 1916 William Stead was ordained in the Anglican Church and had services and sermons at Littlemore (Newman's last Anglican Church) and these kept him busy over the week-end, while his work for a degree pressed heavily on him throughout the week; especially were Latin and Greek necessary as he had neglected them at Virginia. Also he had a wife and child to support. His B.A. was finally attained and later an M.A. and B.Litt.

When the United States entered World War I, he volunteered, was rejected, and then resumed his post in the consular service at Liverpool.

In 1922 William Stead was appointed assistant chaplain of the English Church in Florence, Italy, where he arrived in time to witness the fascist revolution. He studied Italian, read some Dante, found opportunities to visit Rome, Venice, Siena and in fact much of Italy. Italian art and architecture were a great delight to him, and the Catholic Church began to cast a spell upon him.

In 1926 he returned to Oxford, and in this year baptized the Anglo-American poet T. S. Eliot and later introduced him to the Bishop of Oxford by whom he was confirmed.

In 1927 he was appointed chaplain of Worcester College, Oxford, and was elected a Fellow of Worcester College in 1930. Three years later Father Bede Jarrett received him into the Catholic Church. Mr. Stead resigned his Oxford appointments. He is at present lecturer at Trinity College, Washington, D.C.

All of Mr. Stead's books of verse were published in England. *The Sweet Miracle* was published in 1922 and *The Shadow of Mt. Carmel* in 1926 (an approach to the Catholic Church).

Some specimens of his work can be seen in *The Oxford Book of Modern Verse* edited by W. B. Yeats, and the *Oxford Book of Christian Verse* edited by Lord David Cecil. Mr. Stead's best work of poetry is contained in *Uriel, A Hymn in Praise of Divine Immanence,* published in London in 1933.

Mr. Stead's chief work in scholarship is found in the introduction and notes to a manuscript, which he discovered, written by the crazy eighteenth century poet, Christopher Smart, author of the glorious *Song to David.* This was published under the title of *Rejoice in the Lamb.* Jonathan Cape brought it out in London in 1938 and Henry Holt produced an American edition in 1939.

Mr. Stead wrote many reviews for *The Times Literary Supplement,* London, the chief being a front page article entitled "Dryden's Conversion," published about 1937.   M. H.

Reverend Robert H. J. Steuart, S.J.   1874-

For four centuries the Steuarts have preserved an unbroken male succession from Sir John Steuart of Sticks, County Perth, a son of James II of Scotland. In this family was born in 1874 Robert H. J. Steuart, S.J., third son of John Steuart, K.S.G. (Knight of St. Gregory), J.P. (Justice of the Peace), D.L. (Deputy-Lieutenant), of Ballechin Perthshire, and of Caroline, daughter of Sir Albert de Hochpied-Larpent, Bt. (Baronet). The future Jesuit received his education with the Benedictines at Fort Augustus and at the Royal Military Academy at Woolwich. In 1893 Robert Steuart entered the Society of Jesus and in 1896 went to Campion Hall, Oxford, for further studies. He was ordained in 1907 and during the first World War was an army chaplain in France, 1916, connected with a Highland regiment and with the Army of Occupation in Cologne in 1919. Returning to England he was made superior of St. Aloysius, Oxford, in 1921, and was superior of Farm Street Church, Mayfair, from 1926 to 1935. The year of his ordination also saw raised to the priesthood a younger brother who had entered the Benedictine Order, Dom Benedict, O.S.B. His oldest brother is Captain John Malcolm Steuart who married an American, a native of Iowa.

In the midst of a busy life of study, teaching, army chaplaincy and as superior of large and active parishes, Father Steuart has found the time to write many books, among them: *The Book of Ruth; A Map of Prayer; The Inward Vision; March, Kind Comrade; Temples of Eternity; World Intangible; Diversity in Holiness; In Divers Manners;* and in 1940, *The Four First Things,* the fundamentals which, as he says, "set out in detail the duties of knowing, loving and serving God." Father Steuart is also well known as a director of souls and during the heavy bombings of London in World War II, he refused to leave Farm Street, feeling that there were some there who might need him.   D. D.

William F. P. Stockley 1859-1943

Urged by "intelligent young scribblers" to join their ranks in writing papers for debating societies, William Frederick Paul Stockley, then a student in Trinity College, Dublin, began his writing career.

Mr. Stockley was born in 1859 at Templeogue, County Dublin, Ireland, the son of John Surtees Stockley and Alicia Gabbett Stockley. He was educated at Rathmines School and Trinity College, Dublin, at which college he came under the influence of the Irish critic and poet, Professor Edward Dowden, to whom he attributed his interest in religious and literary history.

From 1886 to 1902, he was a professor of English in the University of New Brunswick, Canada, holding a similar position from 1902 to 1903 in the University of Ottawa. It was in Montreal in 1894 that he was received into the Church. Of his conversion he writes, "As Brownson says for me, 'That is the most rational act a thinking man can perform.' " From 1903 to 1905 he was headmaster at St. Mary's College, Halifax, Nova Scotia. When he was in the United States, he numbered among his close friends John Boyle O'Reilly, the former revolutionist and author whom he had known in Ireland, and William James of Harvard University.

In Ireland, from 1905 to 1930, he was professor of English in University College, Cork. He was prominent, too, in civic life, being Alderman of Cork from 1920 to 1929, president of the Cork Literary and Scientific Society, 1913 to 1915, and Deputy to Dail Eireann from National University 1921 to 1923. He was a member of De Valera's first government, but later disagreed with the leader and retired from politics.

The author of over five hundred articles for American, Irish, English, and Canadian reviews and periodicals, he ranged in subject matter from a eulogy on the personal charm of the patriot, John Boyle O'Reilly to scholarly articles on Burke and Religion, Wordsworth and Patriotism, Wordsworth and Catholicism, the Faith of Tennyson's *In Memoriam,* and Faith and Morals in Browning. Among his published works, too, are: a pamphlet, *How to Read a Shakespeare Play* (Julius Caesar); a *Commentary on the Dream of Gerontius* (a poem by Cardinal Newman); *English Visitors from Raleigh to Newman* and *Newman, Education, and Ireland.* In 1933 he published a book *Studies in Irish Biography,* a work valuable to students of Thomas Moore, Canon Sheehan, and Dr. Henebry.

His first wife was Violet Osborne, daughter of William Osborne, R.H.A. She died in 1893. He married, in 1908, Marie Germaine Kolb, daughter of the sometime superintendent of the Royal Botanical Garden in Munich.

Professor Stockley died in 1943.   T. V.

John Lawson Stoddard   1850-1931

"On the threshold of my eightieth year I pause to look back on the latest stadium of my life, a period of fourteen years . . . because it is the only one in which I have consciously lived in the presence of eternity." Thus wrote John Lawson Stoddard in 1930, a year before he passed into the eternity of which his entrance into the Catholic Church in 1917 gave him a foretaste. Born at Brookline, Massachusetts, in 1850, the son of Lewis Tappan Stoddard and his second wife Sarah H. (Lothrop) Stoddard, of Puritan stock, his early training was in very devout Calvinism. After attending public school in Boston, he entered Williams College, from which he graduated in 1871.

When he was but thirteen his mother died, "leaving a blessed memory of piety and love." His father, "also eminent in Godliness," followed her two years later. Just after that, he had a "conversion" and was baptized in the Congregational Church, which brought about an ardent desire to become a missionary. This was not strange, as he had many ministers and missionaries in his ancestry. In his university years, surrounded by religious influences, he led a nominal Christian life and at twenty-two "without remarkable enthusiasm, yet equally without misgivings or regret" entered the Yale Divinity School, in 1871, to prepare for the Congregational ministry. However, doubts began seriously to assail him, but seeking advice and intellectual assistance he found none to satisfy or solidify his wavering faith. So it was inevitable that when a change of circumstances made it possible he left and entered upon a career of teaching in the Boston Latin School from 1873 to 1874. When the year ended he was still uncertain and hesitant about renewing his theological studies, so he determined to make a tour of Europe and the Orient, hoping to find light and surety. But it was not vouchsafed and for forty years he wandered in a spiritual wilderness and agnosticism. Yet for him rationalism did not mean indifferentism and together with other young and questing souls he traversed many paths of thought ever seeking for the Truth.

Much of Stoddard's life was spent abroad and he became a distinguished traveller and lecturer. "From the moment his slender, erect figure appeared on the platform, his audience was won by his eloquence and personal magnetism." He was a pioneer in the use of the stereopticon. In this period, he wrote *Red Letter Days Abroad* (1884), and in 1892 *Glimpses of the World*. In 1897 he retired from the lecture platform to write of his travels. These comprised fifteen volumes. He published his *Lectures* in 1909, and in 1913 and 1914 respectively, *Poems* and *Poems on Lake Como*. Then came the war and he found himself caught in one of the belligerent countries where circumstances kept him for the duration of hostilities. These he calls "five years of well-nigh universal wretchedness and sometimes of complete despair," but he adds, "This encampment at the gates of hell, this sojourn in the valley of the shadow of death, slowly but surely drew me back to God." And thus on the 28th of September 1922, the eve of the Feast of St. Michael, quietly and unobtrusively he and his wife made their submission and were received into the Catholic Church. Tranquility followed tumult and until his death in Merano, Italy, in 1931, he walked in firmness of Faith and surety, having found the way home after nearly seventy years of seeking.

The story of his conversion, written in 1922, *Rebuilding a Lost Faith,* sold over 100,000 copies. Sentiment he distrusted, and there is little of the personal in this logical discussion of those years of travail. Then the year before his death, when already eighty, he wrote *Twelve Years in the Catholic Church,* his last book and testimonial to the Faith which he had received. After his conversion in 1922, he gave his time almost wholly to religious study and writings. He translated Dr. Hilarin Felder's *Jesus Christus;* he translated Prat's *The Theology of St. Paul* (2 volumes) from the French; *The Evening of Life* was translated from the French of Louis Baunard, and *Yesterdays of an Artist Monk* was translated from the German of Willibrord Verkade. D. D.

Edward Adam Strecker 1886-

Catholics, perhaps, know Dr. Strecker best as the co-author of *Discovering Ourselves,* which has run into seven editions. Edward Adam Strecker, psychiatrist, educator, physician, was born October 16, 1886, in Philadelphia, Pennsylvania, the son of Adam and Maria (von Weiler) Strecker.

When the city of Frankfort, Germany, was deprived of its charter as a free city, his father, with a group of young men, left their native Germany in protest and came to the United States. His mother was descended from an old German family of the lesser nobility, who lost their fortune in the Napoleonic Wars by refusal to supply troops and money to Napoleon.

Dr. Strecker was educated at St. Joseph's College, La Salle College, Jefferson Medical College, A.B. (1907); M.A. (1911); M.D. (1911). St. Joseph's conferred a Sc.D. degree on him in 1934 and La Salle College a Litt.D. degree in 1936. In 1915 he married Elizabeth Kyne Walsh of Philadelphia.

He served as an interne and chief resident physician at St. Agnes Hospital, Philadelphia, from 1911 to 1913. He was a member of the Pennsylvania Hospital staff, Department for Nervous and Mental Diseases, from 1913 to 1917, Medical Director of the same Department, from 1918 to 1925. Since 1918 he has served as neurologist and psychiatrist for most of the principal hospitals in and around Philadelphia. During World War II, he was constantly engaged by the government.

At various periods from 1924 until the war began, he was teaching psychiatry and neurology at Yale University, Jefferson Medical College and the University of Pennsylvania. Just prior to the war, though deep in important work in Washington in connection with the program of National Defense, he was busy with the preparation of a book on morale.

During World War I, Dr. Strecker served as first lieutenant (Neuro-psychiatrist) in the United States Army, 28th Division, and was in the combat zone until the Armistice. He was promoted to captain and then major.

In 1939 he was named the Salmon Memorial Lecturer. Lectures were also delivered at the New York Academy of Medicine and at the University of Toronto in April and May 1939.

At a Catholic Book Week display, along with Dr. Strecker's other books, was shown a Swedish translation of *Discovering Ourselves*. His little paper edition of *Alcohol—One Man's Meat* was so popular that at the time of publication it was to be found in every liquor store in Philadelphia. It has been considered a great boon to both the Catholic priest and the Catholic physician in the proper understanding of the use and abuse of alcohol.

Dr. Strecker wrote the following books: *Practical Examination of Personality and Behavior Disorders* (1936); *Beyond the Clinical Frontiers,* and *Their Mother's Sons* (1946).

In collaboration with others, he wrote: *Clinical Psychiatry* (1925); *Clinical Neurology* (1937), and *Discovering Ourselves* (1931).

Dr. Strecker says that among his hobbies is "observing human beings."

E. F.

Francis Stuart 1902-

To this author life is an adventure, the greatest game of all. The truth is more romantic to him than any of his childish dreams. He claims that for him there has been no such thing as disillusionment. "Always in life the nearer I have approached the truth the more inspiring I have found it."

Francis Stuart was born in 1902 at Queensland, Australia, of Ulster parents, Henry and Elizabeth Stuart. The family returned to Ireland when he was too young to remember the long journey. He became a Catholic at the time of his marriage in 1920 to Iseult Gonne. "We eloped together to London because of our families' opposition." They have two children and live at Glendalough, which he has described in *Pigeon Irish*. Stuart took part in the Irish Civil war in 1922 and was captured during the street fighting in Dublin. He was sent to Maryborough Military Prison where conditions were so appalling that the prisoners tried to burn down the prison as a protest. A whole wing was gutted but the prisoners had to live in it anyway. After six months the prisoner was sent to an internment camp. It was worse than the prison. Illness sent him to the hospital. A few days after he left the hospital, despairing of release, he went on a hunger strike. After eleven days the strike was called off. Apparently it had failed, but from then on, prisoners began to be released.

Horse racing is one of Mr. Stuart's hobbies. He has owned his own racers and has written of the turf in *Racing for Pleasure and Profit*. Tinkering with automobile and airplane engines is another amusement. He learned to fly in one of the first civil airplanes to come to Ireland. He was a poultry farmer for some years but gave it up devote more time to writing.

His first work, *We Have Kept the Faith,* a book of poems, was published when he was twenty-one. It was awarded an American prize, and a prize by the Irish Royal Academy, W. B. Yeats and George Russell (AE) being judges. In his first novel, *Women and God,* he tried to write of the secret Lourdes, the Lourdes of Bernadette. He feels now that he was too near to it then. "Few novels can have had such shockingly bad reviews. I had craved for success. It was a knock all right. But it was one of the knocks that has done me most good. Since that day I have never cared a damn what sort of reviews my books have got." The next afternoon the whole idea of his second novel came to him. He began to write *The Coloured Dome* that night.

The author says, "In writing I have felt the exaltation of creation; in my novels I have at times exalted because it seemed to me I had made permanent in them some part of the truth wrested from the chaos around me." He has always put himself in his books. "That is part of the fun of it. Putting oneself against this background and against that, with these people and with those. I have made myself a general, a bookie's clerk, a race horse trainer, an aeroplane pilot. I live in my books the things I have not time to live in life."

In 1935 he set down his notes for an autobiography, *Things to Live For.* He has since written: "If I were now to write an autobiography I should insist more on the help to me as a writer the Church is. I believe that today in the midst of so much sensationalism and emotionalism a writer must have the inspiration and discipline of some spiritual or mental goal."

C. C. Martindale's book about Bernadette had fired him with the desire to visit Lourdes. He made a pilgrimage. "All day from six I worked in the Asile, in the baths, at the grotto, tending the sick pilgrims and wheeling them on their stretchers. I have felt an ecstasy of happiness working in the hospital there." On his next visit to the shrine the author found himself completely dead to all religious emotion, completely cold. He forced himself to stay and continue his work as a brancadier. Gradually he began to see there was a strange secret joy in doing what was most difficult, "in holding on to a dark faith without feeling an emotional inspiration. For the first time in my life I began to know a joy that was not dependent on any dream. I had lost that sense of expectancy and was living in the present. But it was not easy." Before Mr. Stuart left Lourdes this time he knew that one part of life was over for him, and another about to begin, that he could not go back. A miracle had happened. "The sense of loneliness from which all my life in one mad way or another I had tried to escape had now left me. And it seemed to me that life had been planned on a grand scale. And far from being tired of it I felt more in love with it than ever."

Besides the works already mentioned he is the author of: *Try the Sky; Glory; In Search of Love; The White Hare; The Silver Ship; The Bridge; Julie; The Great Squire; The Angel of Pity* (philosophy); *Men Crowd Me Round* (play, produced at Abbey Theatre).   M. S.

Reverend Don Luigi Sturzo 1871-

An exile from his native country, Italy, since October 1924 because of his opposition to fascism, Don Luigi Sturzo lived in the United States until his return to Italy in August 1946. For over thirty years he had been a student of the political and social life of Italy and other European countries.

Don Sturzo was born on November 26, 1871, at Caltagirone (Sicily), Italy. His early studies were made in the seminaries of Ac'reale and Noto, Sicily. From the Lyceum of Caltagirone he received his Classical Licentiate. He completed his studies of philosophy and theology at the diocesan seminary of Caltagirone, in eastern Sicily.

After his ordination to the priesthood in 1894, Don Luigi Sturzo went to Rome to follow his philosophical avocation. He enrolled in the

Thomistic Academy and the Gregorian University, where he received the doctorate degrees in philosophy and theology.

While in Rome in 1895, he heard for the first time of Christian Democracy. He soon became attracted to Catholic social activities. "What impressed me most," he writes, "was the sight of unheard of miseries in the workers' quarters of Rome (where the old Ghetto used to be) which I completely covered on Holy Saturday in 1895, as I had been asked by the parish to bless the homes. For several days I felt sick and did not eat. I got hold of some social literature. I sought out what the socialists and humanitarians were doing and tried to get acquainted with workers' leagues and cooperatives."

When Don Sturzo returned to his native Caltagirone for the vacation, he went to work at once to ameliorate the condition of the working class. After founding a Catholic Diocesan Committee, workers', farmers', and students' associations, he returned to Rome to complete his studies. His interest in social problems gradually drew him into political life. Returning to Caltagirone, Don Sturzo taught literature, history, philosophy and sociology in the ecclesiastical seminary. His free time was devoted to the social movement.

In 1897, Don Sturzo founded a weekly newspaper *La Croce di Constantino* (Constantine's Cross), and helped found a daily paper at Palermo, *Il Sole* (The Sun), in 1899. Journalism gave him little time for creative work. It helped him, however, to achieve fame as a social worker. In 1899 he was appointed Municipal Councilor of his town, later Provincial Councilor, governmental authority of Caltagirone. The Christian democratic workers of Caltagirone placed his name in the municipal elections. He was elected Mayor in 1905 and held this office for fifteen years. He was also elected National Councilor and vice-president of the National Association of Italian Municipalities.

After the Armistice, Don Sturzo founded on January 18, 1919, a new political party, The Italian Popular Party, composed of Catholic Christian democrats. In November 1919, in the general political election, the Italian Popular Party won 99 of the 508 seats available in the House, ranking second among the parties represented. When the fascists seized power in 1922, The Popular Party began to wane until in 1926, the party was dissolved by Royal Decree.

Don Sturzo attributes his interest in Christian Democracy to Giuseppe Toniolo, who attracted him by one of his famous lectures. He was carried away by Toniolo's spiritual inspiration and his economic-social doctrine.

Don Sturzo founded in Paris with the help of the French Popular Democratic Party an International Secretarial Center of the Christian democratic parties in Europe. Now he is one of the three vice-presidents of the International Christian Democratic Union in London.

He is the author of many works. Among them are: *L'Italie Et Le Fascisme* (Italy and Fascism), translated by Barbara B. Carter in 1926); *La Communaute Internationale et Le Droit De Guerre* (International Community and the Right of War, translated by Barbara B. Carter in 1928); *Essai de Sociologie* (translated by Juliette Bertrand in 1935);

L'Eglise Et L'Etat (translated as *Church and State* by Barbara Barclay Carter in 1939); *Politique et Morale* (translated as *Politics and Morality,* by Barbara Barclay in 1938); *Sociology of the Supernatural* (The True Life) (1942); *Inner Laws of Society* (1944); *Italy and the Coming World* (1945); *Spiritual Problems of our Times* (1945); *Man in History and Society* (1946).   M. H.

Aloysius Michael Sullivan   1896-

A successful businessman and a poet do not ordinarily fuse in one human being, but such is the case in the person of Aloysius Michael Sullivan. Not only is Mr. Sullivan the advertising manager of the firm of Dun and Bradstreet in New York City, and the Associate Editor of *Dun's Review,* but he is also a poet and past president of the Poetry Society of America. He is especially well known for his pioneering in radio presentation of poetry and poets and for inspiring young people in creative effort.

Born in Harrison, New Jersey, in 1896, Mr. Sullivan attended school at Oxford Furnace, New Jersey, and was graduated from St. Benedict's Preparatory School, in Newark, New Jersey, in 1913, to which latter alma mater he attributes, "my understanding of the classic tradition." It was at St. Benedict's that Mr. Sullivan wrote his first poem which found its way into the school paper, thus marking the first publication of its author.

Upon graduation Mr. Sullivan obtained a position with the General Electric Company and then with the Submarine Boat Corporation, as editor of their house organ. Aroused by the Easter Rebellion in Dublin, Ireland, in 1916, he began reading widely on the history and literature of Ireland, and studying Gaelic. Later, in New York, he founded an Irish cultural society, The Companions of Brendan.

In answer to the challenge of a friend Mr. Sullivan attempted the writing of his first sonnet. This led to determined experimentation in verse forms. Then came: *Sonnets of a Simpleton* (1924); *Progression and Other Poems* (1928); *Elbows of the Wind* (1932); *Ballad of a Man Named Smith* (1940); *New Jersey Hills* (1940); *A Day in Manhattan* (1941) (narrative poems written for radio presentation and choral speaking); *The Ballad of John Castner* (based on an unrecorded incident of the American Revolution), and *Stars and Atoms Have No Size* (1946).

Mr. Sullivan's poetry has been commended for originality of statement, and for the vibrant, staccato picturing of modern America in the realistic tradition of Carl Sandburg.

Beginning in 1933 and continuing for seven years, Mr. Sullivan conducted a highly successful poetry program over the Mutual network.

Concerning influences that have shaped his writing, Mr. Sullivan states, "I know that modern industrial life is reflected in many of my works. I also feel that life in the middle-class Irish-American family has flavored many of the things I have attempted to do."

Mr. Sullivan is married to Catherine Veronica McNamee. They have two children. T. V.

Richard Sullivan 1908-

In American folklore "the expectant father has become a standard joke," as W. A. S. Dollard observed in reviewing, in the New York *Herald Tribune*, Richard Sullivan's novel *Summer After Summer*. But, continued the reviewer, in the character of Eddie Nails, Richard Sullivan has created "an almost religious figure of the father, with 'the dignity of St. Joseph.'" Certainly this first novel dignifies the family, not by dealing with great figures and heroic actions, nor by artful writing and graces of style; but by relating how the coming of a second child to a low-paid white-collar worker and his simple housekeeping wife, brought first strains and fears, then new courage, new love and new acceptance of the goodness of life.

Summer After Summer is the first full-length work of a man who has contributed stories and verse to *Atlantic Monthly, The Catholic World, Columbia, Frontier and Midland, New Republic, Scribner's* and other periodicals. One of his short stories *Jubilee At Baysweek* is in *Great Modern Catholic Short Stories* compiled by Sister Mariella Gable, O.S.B.

Richard Sullivan, born in Kenosha, Wisconsin, on November 29, 1908, of Irish descent on his father's side and German on his mother's, is a graduate of a parochial grade school and a public high school, and an A.B. of Notre Dame (1930). He hesitated for three years between painting and writing. He studied at the Art Institute of Chicago and the Goodman School of the Drama, a department of the Institute. The call to literature prevailed. From 1931 to 1936 he wrote stories, stage plays, radio plays and blood-and-thunder books for boys. More than one of his stories have appeared on the late Edward O'Brien's honor roll. Since 1936 he has been teaching playwriting and poetry as a member of the department of English at Notre Dame. In 1932, he married Mabel Constance Priddis, and is the father of two daughters.

Richard Sullivan may be expected to develop a richer style and a firmer hand in creating character in the round, but his evident intention to study life as it is experienced by the great inarticulate masses, and to search out heroism among small people, makes him a writer to watch. He can create gripping episodes, as in his picture of Eddie Nails' anxieties during the last few tense hours before the miracle of birth. As a contribution to Catholic fiction, his manner of dealing casually with the simple Catholic round of prayers, going to Mass and so forth, with no display or emphasis, is something which other Catholic writers will study.

In 1943 he published *The Dark Continent*. This was serialized in *Cosmopolitan* magazine. *The World of Idella May* appeared in 1946.

He was named the 1946 recipient of the Notre Dame Lay Faculty award for outstanding achievement during the 1945-1946 school year. The award carries with it an honorarium of $500. Mr. Sullivan is a book critic for the New York *Times* and the Chicago *Tribune*.   S. O.

Halliday Gibson Sutherland 1882-

The story of Dr. Halliday Sutherland's life has been told in his *The Arches of the Years* (1933), an autobiography to the end of World War I; in his *A Time to Keep* (1934)—further autobiography, and in his *In My Path*—reminiscences in his medical career.

Dr. Sutherland is a Scot, having been born in Glasgow, June 24, 1882. He is the eldest son of the late Doctor J. F. Sutherland. His mother was the daughter of the clergyman, Reverend John MacKay. All the summers of childhood and boyhood were passed in the Highlands. In his boyhood, he learned the superstitions of his race. He was educated at Glasgow High School and the Merchison Castle School which he entered when thirteen years of age. To this latter school he credits "the physique that comes from playing compulsory games." He was not good at games, however. He excelled in writing essays and in mathematics.

At the age of fourteen he wrote his first article for the Press, and entitled it "Training in Rugby Football." It appeared in *The Glasgow Evening Citizen*.

After he finished high school, he attended the universities of Edinburgh and Aberdeen. To make up a deficiency in anatomy, his father sent him to an uncle, a surgeon, in Spain, for tutoring in this subject. When he returned to Edinburgh he passed the examination in anatomy. For the *Aberdeen Free Press,* he wrote three articles on Spain.

After taking his degree at Edinburgh he went to the seaport town of Huelva to assist his uncle in his clinic. While there he tried to find a cure for leprosy.

Returning to Scotland the following year (1908) he took a post as clinical assistant at Craig House, Edinburgh, a mental hospital, at his father's suggestion. After six months' asylum experience, he decided he was unsuited for this branch of medicine. Within a year (1910) of leaving the asylum, he became medical superintendent of the Westmoreland Sanatorium. He was then 28 years of age. In his spare time, he edited *The Control and Eradication of Tuberculosis,* a book to which the leading authorities in Europe and America contributed. The book took a year to compile and was sold at fifteen shillings. There were no profits to divide.

The following year, he became a medical officer at St. Marylebone Tuberculosis Dispensary and held this post till 1914. Dr. Sutherland is a leading specialist in tuberculosis. In 1912 he founded Regents' Park Bandstand School, the first open air school in a London park.

Then the war came—World War I. He applied as an emergency surgeon in His Majesty's Fleet. He was put aboard the armed merchant cruiser "Empress of Britain." Their commission was to protect British commerce and to look for German raiders. When the "Empress of Britain" paid off at Liverpool, he obtained a week's leave and returned to London. Since there was little or no medical work aboard the ship, he decided to ask for a hospital billet ashore. Instead, he was appointed bacteriologist to the naval hospital at Pembroke Dock. It was there in October 1915, that Dr. Sutherland discovered the aetiology of cerebro-spinal fever. In February 1916 he was transferred to the Royal Marine Depot at Deal. The two cases of spotted fever that had occurred in the barracks gave him the opportunity to test his theory as to how the disease spread.

In 1919 Dr. Sutherland, after reading Belloc's *Path to Rome,* made a commonsense investigation of the claims of the Catholic Church and entered it. In 1920 he married Muriel Fitzpatrick. They have five sons and one daughter. Dr. Sutherland's first broadcast took place in 1935. He relates his experience in *In My Path.* His first twenty minutes' talk gave him at least three days' work. The doctor confesses that before any long speech to a large audience he suffers from stage fright.

Some have asked the Doctor if his books are true. To that he answered, "Yes, they are true, but they are paintings not photographs." He accentuates some lines and attenuates others and always tries to give a life-like portrait. His other books are: *Pulmonary Tuberculosis in General Practise* (1916); *Tuberculosis: A Story Lesson for Children* (1918); *Use and Abuse of Alcohol* (1930); *Laws of Life* (1935). (This book was banned in Ireland as the Board considered it of peculiar value, only for a limited class of readers.) Also: *Hebridean Journey* (1939); *Southward Journey* (1941); *The Tuberculin Handbook* (1935).

During World War II, Dr. Sutherland served as a medical attendant in tin hat at an A.R.P. post. His daughter Joan and four of his sons served as A.R.P. wardens.   M. H.

Reverend Jon Sveinsson   1857-1944

For each individual to whom he is known as Father Jon Sveinsson, S.J., it is estimated that a thousand know him as "Nonni." He is "Nonni" to everyone in his native Iceland and to countless readers of the eighteen languages into which his books have been translated.

Priest, writer, humanitarian, traveller and lecturer, Father Sveinsson's life of eighty-seven years spanned three European wars, two of which he survived. Born in a land where Catholicism was not then tolerated, he was later expelled from two countries because of his religion. When he was a Jesuit novice in 1880, he and his brothers in the Society of Jesus were driven out of France. In 1942, when he was an old man, Hitler's

S.S. troops stormed the Jesuit House where he lived in Holland and transported him and all the residents to Germany. Interned in Cologne, Father Sveinsson died there on November 1, 1944, within a few days of his eighty-eighth birthday.

"Nonni"—the name he was called in childhood and the name he gave to his most widely read books—was born November 16, 1857, at Modruvellir in north Iceland, close to the Arctic Circle. He was the oldest son of Svein Thorarinsson and Sigridur Jonsdottir. His father farmed his own estate and was also secretary to a sub-governor of the area.

Like all Icelanders of the time, "Nonni" was reared as a Lutheran. But he was destined to become the second Icelander to embrace the Catholic faith since Reformation days. Through a French priest, who was befriended by a neighbor of "Nonni's" parents when the Icelandic Government sought to deport him for ministering to Catholic sailors on fishing vessels anchored in Iceland harbors, "Nonni," at thirteen, was given the opportunity to complete his schooling in France.

He sailed from Iceland with another boy who had just been converted to Catholicism. This was Gunnar Einarsson, first Catholic in Iceland since 1551. He grew up to become the father of the first native Catholic Bishop in Iceland since the Reformation, the present (1947) Vicar Apostolic, Most Reverend Johannes Gunnarsson.

The boys had reached Denmark when the Franco-Prussian war halted their journey to France. In Copenhagen, where they lived and studied with the Apostolic Prefect, young Jon Sveinsson was received into the Catholic Church. Years later, he wrote an article published in *La Croix* (France), in which he said his conversion was due to Gunnar Einarsson's example.

After a year in Denmark, "Nonni" went to Amiens, France, where he remained as a student until 1878. Then he decided to enter the Society of Jesus.

His novitiate, interrupted at Acheul, France, he continued at Louvain, Belgium. Returning to Holland in 1883, he taught until 1888 at St. Andrew's, Jesuit college near Copenhagen. He was ordained in 1891 in England, where he had been sent for theological studies. The following year, after a visit home, he went back to Copenhagen, where he taught in Jesuit institutions until 1912.

A break in his health at that time necessitated a rest, during which he penned the first of the world-famous "Nonni" books, remembrances of his boyhood in the Arctic.

He had already published two volumes. The first was *Iceland Flowers,* a collection of essays dealing with ancient Icelandic literature and the sagas. The second, *Journey Through Iceland,* he wrote in 1894 after he had revisited his homeland.

It was during this period also, that he personally collected in Denmark a large sum to build a leper hospital in Reykjavik, capital of Iceland, where the plague had been brought by sailors from foreign ships. His second great humanitarian endeavor was during World War I, when he remained in Austria, ministering to the spiritual and material needs of French prisoners of war.

After years of travelling and lecturing in Europe, Father Sveinsson made his first voyage to the United States and Canada in 1937. Then he went to Japan, where he became a popular speaker, drawing large audiences of Japanese who already knew him through his books. He was in Valkenburg, Holland, when World War II broke out. As an Icelandic citizen and a neutral, he might have returned to his own country but elected to remain with his companions in religion.

Father Sveinsson was distinguished by a gentle sense of humor and a simplicity of manner that became more pronounced through the years. He wrote copiously in several languages for literary and religious periodicals issued in Europe. His books have been published in English, Icelandic, French, Czech, Dutch, Spanish, Italian, Portuguese, Polish, Croat, Norwegian, Chinese, Japanese, Hungarian, Slovene, Flemish, German, Danish and Esperanto, the "international" language. They include: *Nonni; Stadt Am Mer* (City of the Sea) story of Nonni's early days in Copenhagen; *Sonnentage* (Sunny Days); *Nonni Erzahlt* (Story of Nonni); *Wie Nonni Das Gluckfand* (How Nonni Was Converted and Won His Happiness); *Der Kleine Bote Bottes* (The Little Messenger of God); *Nonni und Alis; Nonni und Manni* (story of his brother who followed him into the Church and died while a Jesuit novice); *Eyjafjordur* published in English as (*Lost In The Arctic*); *Die Feurinsel Im Nordmeer* (*The Island of Fire in the North Atlantic*): published in English as *A Visit To Iceland* and *Aus Island* (*From Iceland*). E. L.

Harry Sylvester 1908-

Harry Sylvester was born in Brooklyn, New York, January 19, 1908, the son of Harry Aaron and Margaret (Curtin) Sylvester. His grandfather was Jeremiah Crimmins Curtin, well known as a translator and editor a generation ago. Sylvester was graduated from Notre Dame in 1930, with an A.B. degree in journalism. He started to write in his senior year under the encouragement of the late Charles Phillips and sold his first story while still an undergraduate. He returned to Notre Dame in 1931 and stayed there a few months doing graduate work in English, where he received the advice and encouragement of John T. Frederick, sometime editor of *The Midland*.

Sylvester wrote for the New York *Herald Tribune,* the New York *Evening Post* and the Brooklyn *Daily Eagle*. He resigned from the *Post* in 1933 to free-lance, which he has done successfully ever since. His work has appeared in the following Catholic periodicals: The *Commonweal, The Catholic Worker, Columbia, America* (under the editorship of Wilfrid Parsons, S.J.), and The *Catholic Digest*. His work has also appeared in the following secular magazines: *Collier's, Scribner's, Cosmopolitan, Story, Esquire, American, Pictorial Review, This Week* and

The Midland. According to Paul F. Kneeland of the Boston *Daily Globe,* he is the highest paid fiction writer on *Collier's* magazine since Damon Runyon died.

His work has also been reprinted in the following anthologies: *The O. Henry Memorial Prize Stories* for 1934; the *O'Brien Best Short Stories* for 1935; the *O'Brien Best Short Stories* for 1939.

In March 1938 Sylvester went into the interior of Mexico and interviewed General Saturnino Cedillo in his stronghold at Las Palomas. Sylvester was the last journalist to interview Cedillo before the revolt in May and, on coming out of Mexico, predicted this revolt fifty days before other news sources. While at Palomas, Sylvester was under guard at all times. He was accompanied on this journey by William M. Callahan, managing editor of *The Catholic Worker* and by Daniel Kern, a painter.

In 1936, Sylvester married Rita Ryall Davis, a graduate of Manhattanville College. They have four children.

His success in writing comes from the encouragement of Messrs. Frederick and Phillips, of Notre Dame, and from an intense reading and study (for style alone) of Ernest Hemingway, Edward Garnett, James Joyce, William Faulkner, Georges Bernanos (in translation) and William McFee. It comes also from a cursory reading of most types of American Catholic writing. He is an associate compiler of *Joy in Reading* (1941).

His first novel, *Dearly Beloved,* was published in 1942. It is a race story in which, as Mr. Lewis Gannett said in his "Books and Things," "Mr. Sylvester looks at the relations of black man and white in southern Maryland through the eyes of Jesuit priests." *Dayspring* was published in 1945. "I wanted a change of scenery when I did my last book," Sylvester explained to Paul Kneeland of the Boston *Daily Globe,* "so the whole bunch of us went to Guatemala City where I worked 90 days straight in a hotel knocking out 100,000 words on a typewriter for *Moon Gaffney.* He's my most expensive character, by the way—the trip cost me $12,000."

With eleven others he founded the Committee of Catholics to fight Anti-Semitism, which published *The Voice.*   M. H.

Mary Synon

Mary Synon, writer and editor, is one of the group of Midland authors who served a writing apprenticeship on the Chicago newspapers. Born in Chicago of a family who had been pioneers in that dramatic city, bred in the great hospital neighborhood of the West Side, she naturally gravitated to the human interest frontier of newspaper reporting after a brief teaching career with the Dominican Sisters of Sinsinawa, Wisconsin.

In a time of some of Chicago's wildest excitements she worked on the Chicago *Journal,* covering fires, police, City Hall, teamster strikes, murder trials and almost everything else but society and woman's page assignments. It was the great strike at the Union Stock yards that gave her the opportunity to become a reporter. In those days there was a prohibition against women working as reporters. One day she went to the managing editor of the Chicago *Journal* and said, "If I prove to you that I can do a man's work, will you give me a man's chance?" He gave her the chance. The city editor sent her out with no instructions except the address of the union headquarters. Not until later did she learn that she was sent because the strikers threatened to kill the next *Journal* reporter who came on the scene, the *Journal* being unfriendly at the time to the cause of the strikers. At the gate she saw Mary McDowell, head of the University Settlement. She was walking very rapidly. Miss Synon tried to overtake her for she knew Mary McDowell would have real news. She was the friend of the strikers and trusted by the plant operators. Before Miss Synon could overtake her she found herself in a big hall where the men cried, "What do they say?" when they saw Miss McDowell. She told them the terms for settlement of the strike from the owners of the big plants in the yards and they accepted the terms. Miss Synon got back as fast as she could to the *Journal* and wrote her story. This scoop made her a newspaper reporter. From coverage of national political conventions she went into foreign correspondence. She was correspondent in Ireland and London for the New York *World* and a special correspondent for International News Service. Her interest in World War I led her back to Washington as an executive officer of the National Woman's Liberty Loan Committee.

Meanwhile, in realization that fiction could present life more truly than reportorial articles, Mary Synon had gone into the short story field with two groups of stories, one in Catholic periodicals, the other in secular magazines. Her first story, *The Friar in the Doorway* won first prize in a contest conducted by the Chicago Catholic weekly, *The New World*. Her second, *A Beacon on a Hill* won first prize in a contest of *Extension* magazine. In the same year she finished a series of stories on the Canadian north country for *Scribner's* magazine. From that time she has been a contributor to nearly all the leading fiction magazines.

Her interest in Catholic education, particularly as a builder· of a better national way of life, drew her to her present work as editorial consultant for the Commission on American Citizenship of the Catholic University of America. In this work she has edited the "Faith and Freedom Series" of readers for Catholic schools, and has written much of the text for the upper grades.

In recognition of her work in the cause of Catholic education, Rosary College at River Forest, Illinois, conferred on her, on May 27, 1943, the honorary degree of Doctor of Laws.

Her best known novels are: *The Good Red Bricks* (1929), and *Copper Country* (1931). Her best known short stories are: *The Fleet Goes By; My Grandmother and Myself; None So Blind,* and *Back to Ballyquinn.*

Marion Ames Taggart   1860-1945

Marion Ames Taggart became a Catholic in Boston when she was fourteen years old, "in spite of an adulterated New English Puritan blood" she wrote.

She was born in Haverhill, Massachusetts, in 1860, the daughter of Alfred G. and Sarah P. (Ames) Taggart. Her family on the paternal side was of Scotch descent being originally MacTaggarts; on the mother's side she was of English descent. She was an only child. Because of ill health, she was educated at home and thus deprived of companions of her own age.

"I had no Catholic influences," she wrote, "but as I had never been baptized, it was clear to me that there must be authoritative Truth somewhere and that I must find it. Protestantism repelled me; no one interfered with me when I began going every Sunday to the Jesuit Church of the Immaculate Conception and studying the Catechism of the Council of Trent, recommended to me by the Father to whom I applied for answers to questions, answers he would not give to my profound disgust. I did not realize that I was but a little girl, appearing unflanked by my mother, whom, under those conditions, he would not instruct." Persisting in her desire to become a Catholic she again went to the Jesuit superior of Boston College, Father Fulton and he yielded to her wish. Her home on Dorchester Bay in Boston, which her family purchased and moved into when she was a little child, was lost the following year; exceedingly practical problems were hers. While her health was partly restored through the frequent use of the rowboat she had at Dorchester Bay, her usual ill health and her serious reverses of fortune changed the little girl to a practical young woman. Following her father's death, she supported herself and her mother by needlework and writing.

Since she loved books, she read almost constantly. "I was allowed to browse as I would in the best English books." Naturally, she tried to write. She was first published in the *The Catholic World* and was encouraged by Father Hudson. "Then I did," she says, "what I had vowed to do when I was but seven. Inspired by *Little Women,* I am sure, for I dearly loved that book, I have written some forty stories for young girls. They went to Century Company, Appleton, etc., but Doubleday, Doran & Company published most of them. I did Catholic work, too, most of it was handled by Benziger Brothers. Now I write no more; am unable to walk; arthritis had destroyed the power of the knee cartileges," wrote Miss Taggart in 1939. She died on January 19, 1945, at the age of 84, at Harrisburg, Pennsylvania, where she lived with her bosom and intimate friend Miss Elizabeth E. Clark, M.D.

Since 1882 Miss Taggart was a writer of juveniles; since 1920 a writer of novels. Her best known work, perhaps, is *Loyal Blue and Royal Scarlet,* a tale of the American Revolution. She is also the author of: *The Blissylvania Post Office* (1897); *Bezaleel* (1899); *Miss Lochivar* (1902); *The Doctor's Little Girl* (1907); *Nut Brown Joan* (1905); *Six Girls Grow Up* (1912); *Beth's Old Home* (1915); *A Pilgrim Maid* (1920); *The Annes* (1921); *No Handicap* (1922); *The Cable* (1923); *By Branscombe River; The Little Grey House,* and *The Windhan Girls.* She also translated German adventure stories.   M. H.

Very Reverend Francis Xavier Talbot, S.J.
1889-

The distinguished Jesuit, Father Talbot, S.J., biographer of Isaac Jogues (*Saint Among Savages*), as a child always wanted to write about Indians. He got his wish and a little something besides. His research has led him into the archives of Orleans, Quebec, Montreal, and New York. He travelled every mile of the trail made by Jogues 300 years ago, and is considered an authority on everything pertaining to the Jesuit martyrs.

Born in Philadelphia, Pennsylvania, January 25, 1889, the son of Patrick Francis and Bridget (Peyton) Talbot, he received his early education at the School of St. Edward the Confessor. He attended St. Joseph's Preparatory School and entered St. Joseph's College. In 1906 he joined the Society of Jesus. His early studies were completed at St. Andrew-on-Hudson, Poughkeepsie, New York, with three years at Woodstock College, Maryland, studying philosophy. He obtained his M.A. in 1913. He was ordained on June 29, 1921.

All his teaching career, as his career to follow, ran along literary lines. He served four years as instructor at Loyola School, New York, and from there was transferred to Boston College, Chestnut Hill, Massachusetts, where he became professor of English literature.

After he was ordained to the priesthood (1921) he spent an added year in the study of theology. In 1922 to 1923 he was engaged in the study of ascetical theology, that is in the tertianship or third year of novitiate. In 1923 he was appointed literary editor of *America,* the national Catholic weekly, and served in that capacity until 1936. From 1936 to 1944 he was editor-in-chief of *America.*

Some of his best writing has been done for *America.* During the thirteen years in which he served as literary editor his main objective was that of stimulating and encouraging Catholic authors, especially bright young men and women who showed promise.

During his *America* years he became widely known as a critic. His many articles and books dealing with literature were accepted as authoritative. Under his guidance, *America* became the most quoted and most influential Catholic weekly in this country.

In 1925 Father Talbot was made a trustee of the United States Catholic Historical Society, where for many years he served as chairman of the publication committee.

In 1928 he organized the Catholic Book of the Month Club of which he is editorial secretary. In 1932 he developed the idea and founded the Spiritual Book Associates, a book of the month club, devoted to spiritual reading. In 1934 he collaborated in the organization of the Pro Parvulis Book Club for children.

In 1930 he conceived the idea of uniting the poets of the United States in an organized body, and with the cooperation of a small representative group, he formed the Catholic Poetry Society of America, which now has the largest membership of any poetry society in the United States.

In 1932 he published a series of poetic miracle plays, *Shining in Darkness*. He also inaugurated in *America* discussions upon the possibilities of Catholic poetry and the Catholic novel. As was fitting, he was chosen chaplain of the Catholic Poetry Society of America, and from 1924 till 1936, was chaplain of the National Motion Picture Bureau of the International Federation of Catholic Alumnae, as well as adviser. He is Chairman of the Editorial Board of the Spiritual Book Associates.

Father Talbot has written for the *Encyclopaedia Britannica* since 1935. Among his writings was an historical survey of the Society of Jesus, which replaced the very objectionable article on that subject which the *Encyclopaedia Britannica* had carried for years. He has also written articles for the *Encyclopaedia Britannica* on the life of Pius XI and Pius XII. When the *Encyclopaedia Britannica Book of the Year* was first published in 1936, Father Talbot was deputed to write the articles dealing with the Catholic Church. He is the writer on "Catholicism" in the *Britannica Book of the Year* for 1939, 1940 and subsequent years. He was also chosen to contribute the chapter on Catholicism in America for the symposium *America Now* (Scribner's), a book in which thirty-six prominent Americans offered their comments on American life at the present time. He has continued to write for various Catholic and secular magazines.

His best known books are: *Jesuit Education in Philadelphia* (1927); *Richard Henry Tierney* (1930); *Shining in Darkness* (plays) (1932); and *Saint Among Savages* (a biography of St. Isaac Jogues) (1935). Besides his own writings he has edited several books: *The Eternal Babe* (1927); *American Anthology* (1929), and *Fiction By Its Makers* (1929).

He is a popular and much sought-after speaker. He has appeared on platforms in every big city in the United States to speak to Catholic audiences, and as a Catholic representative, to non-Catholic audiences. During the Spanish Civil War he became the champion of the Nationalists' cause, under General Franco. He organized the American Spanish Relief Fund which collected and forwarded to Spain nearly one hundred thousand dollars for the relief of the children and the aged in war-torn Spain.

In 1926 Father Talbot was granted the degree of Doctor of Literature by his alma mater, St. Joseph's College, on the occasion of the seventy-fifth anniversary of that institution. In 1937 he was honored with the degree of Doctor of Literature by Boston College, Chestnut Hill, Massachusetts, and in June 1941 was granted the honorary degree of Doctor of Humane Letters by Holy Cross College. In September 1941 Fordham University granted him a degree of Doctor of Letters.

In July 1944 Father Talbot was freed from editorial duties in order to engage in organizational work as Regional Director of the Institute of Social Order. Father Talbot's appointment brought to a close twenty-one years of continuous association with *America*.

In 1947 he was appointed president of Loyola College in Baltimore, Maryland.

Father Talbot was also president of the America Press and Superior of Campion House, Manhattan, New York.

E. F.

Mary Dixon Thayer 1896-

If poetry is the language of soul speaking to soul, Mary Dixon Thayer is indeed a poet. An artist in words, her verse has music, is without age, and will live. One of an old and prominent family, she was born December 16, 1896, in Philadelphia, Pennsylvania, daughter of Russell and Mary Homer (Dixon) Thayer. She was educated in private schools. An athletic type of girl, "Molly" Thayer, as she was known to her old tennis fans, is as famous for her love of sports as for her love of poetry. She was holder of the tennis championship of Pennsylvania and Eastern United States for 1920, 1924, and 1927 and stood thirteenth in the National Tennis ranking for 1928, while for some years previous to this she was ranked in the first ten.

She was a staff writer on the Philadelphia *Bulletin* from 1926 to 1928. In 1928 she married Dr. Maurice Tremont-Smith of Boston, where she now makes her home. She is the mother of three sons.

Her writing career began in 1915 with the contribution of verses and short stories to current magazines. Her name has appeared in *Saturday Evening Post, Ladies' Home Journal, Forum, The Commonweal,* and a host of Catholic magazines. She is author of several volumes of verse and one novel. In order of publication they are: *Intellectuals* (1921); *Songs of Youth* (verse) (1922); *New York and Other Poems* (1925); *The Child On His Knees* (1926); *Foam* (novel) (1926); *Ends of Things* (prose) (1927); *A Child's Way of the Cross* (prose) (1928); *Songs Before the Blessed Sacrament* (1932); *Sonnets* (1933).

The excellence of her poetry was recognized when she received the Contemporary Verse Prize for the long poem, "New York," noted for its strength and vision; and again in 1928 when she won the Browning Medal for another poem "If Dying I Do Never See" (entitled, A Prayer), a poem of sweetness and meditative restraint.

In her one novel *Foam* (1926), she interprets staid Philadelphia society in a leisurely Philadelphia manner. The same awareness of life and its secrets, which characterizes her poetry, marks her novel, and the same beauty of words.

Her most important role is in Catholic letters. Mary Dixon Thayer is a Catholic poet in the sense that her poetry could have been written only by a Catholic. She has a distinct place and a large following in the Catholic poetry movement in America since the war. Hers is religious poetry in the best sense of the word, lofty in theme and holy in treatment. She has in her "songs" a blending of youth and piety seldom to be found; a spontaneous outburst from a soul brimming with song. One reads much of her poetry with a sense of reverence akin to a prayer.

E. F.

Blanche Jennings Thompson

Lecturer and leader of discussion groups on poetry, travel and children's literature, Blanche Jennings Thompson, the author of *Bible Children,* had the unique pleasure of seeing her book selected as the 1937 book of the month by the Pro Parvulis Book Club where she serves upon the editorial board.

She is a specialist in juvenile literature. Her *Silver Pennies,* an anthology of poetry which has become a children's classic, has been reprinted forty-three times since its first appearance in 1925.

Blanche Jennings Thompson was born in Geneseo, New York, attending Geneseo schools and Normal School. She received her B.S. from Columbia University (1921); her M.A. (1931) from the University of Rochester and her D.Litt. (honorary) from Nazareth College, Rochester, New York. At present she is head of the English Department at the Benjamin Franklin High School in Rochester.

She began to write early in her teaching career, writing educational articles and children's plays, many of which she helped to produce.

The Holy Year Pilgrimage in 1935 brought about her start in Catholic writing. Upon her return she commenced a Catholic Anthology and began to write for Catholic magazines.

She is also the author of: *Golden Trumpets* (1927); *With Harp and Lute* (1935); *More Silver Pennies* (1937); *All Day With God* (in form of a prayer book), and *A Candle Burns For France* (1946). Since 1925 she has had poems, articles, essays, and one-act plays appearing in contemporary magazines. She has contributed to *The Commonweal, America, Ave Maria,* and *The Catholic World.* In *Ave Maria* she published a serial.

Her hobby is collecting ornamented crosses. She has over one hundred and fifty of them from many parts of the world.

Very happy in her writing career, and grateful to God for her gift of song, Blanche Jennings Thompson says of herself and her poetry: "I just depend upon the Holy Spirit for imagination and guidance."

She is a member of the Third Order of St. Francis.

E. F.

Charles Willis Thompson 1871-1946

One of the most popular fields of literary endeavor in late years has been biography. More indeed than formal histories of great figures of the past, life-stories of contemporary prominent men written by their intimates have proved attractive to the reading public. When these writings are of political figures they form a most suitable background for the story of our times. At the very topmost place among political writers in the United States stood Charles Willis Thompson. His work as a Washington correspondent and in the editorial rooms of metropolitan dailies furnished him an opportunity to present to an extensive public unparalleled observations on men and things.

Born March 15, 1871, at Kalamazoo, Michigan, he was the son of Charles A. Thompson who had been a Union Army captain in the Civil War, and of the former Emily Leslie Logie. His father's health had been impaired by imprisonment during the war, and he died when his son was a year old. His mother took the child to Perth Amboy, New Jersey, and later to Brooklyn, New York, where he grew up.

To support his mother and himself, he had to go to work as an office boy at the early age of fifteen. He became expert at stenography and typing and studied law at night, obtaining a Bachelor of Laws degree from New York University in 1892. Three years later he got his first newspaper job with the New York *World.* In 1897 he began work with the New York *Times* and in two years advanced to become assistant Washington correspondent for that paper. Until 1912, when he became editor of the New York *Times Book Review,* he was associated with various metropolitan dailies at Washington headquarters. There he came into contact with most of the prominent figures of that era. He was made editorial writer for the *Times* in 1914. In 1922 he struck out as a freelance writer for many of the leading magazines, which work he continued until ill health forced him to relinquish active writing about three years before his death.

Mr. Thompson never married. A childhood romance, begun when he was a small lad in Perth Amboy, was broken off when his mother took him to live in Brooklyn. "Lizzie," the object of his attentions when he was so small, never left the thoughts of his adult years. In a revealing story of his life called *Autobiography at Seventy,* in *The Catholic World* (1941), he gives the details of this life-long attachment. The little playmate "Lizzie" of his younger years, the Perth Amboy boys had nicknamed "Tom." When Thompson was seventeen, nearing manhood, earning a little money he managed to save thirty-five cents for a trip from Brooklyn to Perth Amboy to seek "Lizzie"—but without avail. "A gossipy old woman," he says, "whom I had known in childhood, told me as I arrived that 'Lizzie' had married and moved to another city, so I turned and went right back to Brooklyn." Thus ended the first part of his life story. In 1929, after he had published his work *Presidents I Have Known,* among the letters of congratulations was one which, he says, "electrified me; it bore no return address, was only one sentence long and was signed, 'Your friend of the seventies, Tom.'" This set him on another five years of search which was ended in February 1934 when a sixty-three-year-old man and woman excitedly faced each other in an apartment she and her brothers had taken in New York City for the winter. She was not a wife, neither had she moved from Amboy but merely to another street and the gossipy old woman's story proved false. The close intimacy of the years 1876 to 1881 was resumed between the two where it had left off, and for the remaining three years of "Lizzie's" life she proved a most helpful friend and guide in Thompson's declining years.

An omniverous reader and prolific writer, "Charlie" as he was known to nearly all members of the "Fourth Estate," had a particularly apt way of illustrating happenings of the day by allusions of the past. He had the happy characteristic of being able to portray the deeds of men, featured in the headlines, without resort to the merely sensational or scandalous. His work was used plentifully by Mark Sullivan in his standard historical work *Our Times.* He has left thousands of letters, which, though not yet collected and edited, are believed to contain a vast supply of material for contemporary Americana. During the latter years of his life, Mr. Thompson lived with a Catholic family. The example of a mother and daughter awoke in him a spiritual chord. This, together with a copious reading of Catholic literature urged him to seek from a priest instructions in the Catholic faith. After a few meetings, the priest threw down the book he had been following, with the remark, "There's no use giving you instructions. I wish one half of my parishioners knew as much as you know about Catholicity."

In 1927, at Our Lady of Mercy Church in the Bronx, Mr. Thompson was received into the Church by the Right Reverend Monsignor Patrick Breslin. After his conversion he was ever an ardent supporter of the Catholic press. A member of the Washington Gridiron Club, he was also one of the founders of the National Press Club.

Early in his career in 1900, he scored a newspaper "beat" of international proportions. He had learned exclusively that an Allied Expeditionary Force was marching on Peking to rescue the Americans and

Europeans besieged there by the Chinese Boxers. This news story of the Boxer incident gave to the world advance notice of the battle which proved the beginning of western intervention in China. How he obtained this information, Mr. Thompson would never reveal.

Four books written by Charles W. Thompson are indicative of the scope of his life's work. In 1906, he published *Party Leaders of the Time,* character studies of public men. In 1918 appeared *The New Voter,* a book on the inside of politics. *Presidents I've Known and Two Near-Presidents* (1929) is probably his most widely appreciated work. In its pages McKinley, the first Roosevelt, Wilson, Harding, Coolidge, Mark Hanna and Bryan live again. *The Fiery Epoch,* which came out in 1931, is an interpretative history of the Civil War.

Mr. Thompson died September 8, 1946, at Fordham Hospital, New York City. Mourned by his friends of the newspaper and political world, he was laid to rest in Gate of Heaven Cemetery, Hawthorne, New York.

J. M.

Reverend Joseph Francis Thorning 1895-

Dr. Joseph F. Thorning is one of the most indefatigable priest writers in the United States. His work is by no means confined to Catholic circles because he believes that "nine-tenths of our own excellent Catholic literature is wasted upon ourselves or upon people already convinced of the truth." He is therefore emphatically opposed to our hiding under a bushel, for we are a city seated upon a hill and, as he says, it is our duty to bring about personal contacts with the directors of important vehicles of public opinion. He has been special correspondent for the Washington *Post* as well as for the National Catholic Welfare Conference. During the disarmament conference at Geneva in 1932, Father Thorning was the first priest to deliver a transatlantic radio broadcast over the National Broadcasting Company. He was the first priest ever to lecture at the Universities of either North Carolina or Duke.

Joseph Francis Thorning comes from what foreign scholars call the real America—the Middle West. He was born in Milwaukee on the 25th of April, 1895. His parents were Cully M. Thorning and Julia Theresa Hallissey. His early education was received at Marquette Academy. Undergraduate work at Holy Cross was followed by an M.A. degree from St. Louis, then Father Thorning pursued studies at Oxford and the Catholic University in Washington, where in 1932 he received his Ph.D. Ordained in 1928, he is a priest of the archdiocese of Baltimore. A former professor of sociology at Mt. St. Mary's College, Emmitsburg, Maryland, he is now (1947) rector of St. Joseph's Church, Carrollton Manor, Maryland, and special lecturer on sociology at the Catholic University of Chili.

Dr. Thorning's interest in sociology began in St. Louis when he embarked upon graduate work in anthropology and paleontology. His doctoral dissertation *Religious Liberty in Transition* (1931) has been recommended by Carlton Hayes as one of the most significant and scholarly pieces of research in the story of religious toleration. Its author's appeal to those without the fold is nowhere more noticeable than in the choice, in 1928, by a non-Catholic teacher, of the *Primer of Social Justice,* as a textbook at Von Steuben High School, Chicago. *Builders of the Social Order,* published in 1941, was considered by the Catholic Literary Guild of New York its most important current book. The theme is social reconstruction according to the papal encyclicals and put into practice by leaders whom Father Thorning personally knows and whose methods he has inspected at first hand—among them: Eamon De Valera, Salazar of Portugal, General Franco, and former Chancellor Brüning of Germany.

A writer who has travelled as foreign correspondent and one who speaks several languages, Dr. Thorning has had many intimate contacts with the most colorful personalities of our time. Friendship with writers in continental key cities keeps him abreast of the contemporary scene. In the words of Archbishop Curley, "he is one of the greatest authorities in the nation today on Spanish affairs."

A few years ago no Catholic voice was more ringing than that of Dr. Thorning's in its insistence upon the truth about Mexico, for whose cause he worked with untiring zeal and enthusiasm. Today he pours out innumerable articles every month on the politics, culture and social conditions of "our good neighbors to the south."

Father Thorning's reviews and articles—particularly in the cause of International Peace—have appeared in magazines from Bombay to Brisbane. He is associate editor of *World Affairs* and advisory editor of *The Americas.* His swift energetic style carries one along on a buoyant tide and his yearly rereading of Shakespeare lends resiliency to his language. But Father Thorning's own vibrant personality would give charm and distinction to anything he might write.

He was the director of the first Spiritual Seminar to South America at the University of San Marcos, Lima, Peru, in 1941, and director of the Seminars at the Universities of Havana and Mexico in 1942 and 1943.

In 1942 he was elected an Honorary Fellow of the Historical and Geographic Institute of Brazil. In the same year he was elected a Director of the American Peace Society and a Fellow of the American Geographic Society. In 1944 The Catholic University of Chile conferred upon him the honorary degree of Doctor of Divinity, and in 1946 he was presented the Grand Cross of the Order of Isabella the Catholic, with the rank of "Comendador" by the Spanish government. Also in 1946 he was invested with the insignia of the national decoration of the Republic of Ecuador known as the Order of Merit.

A. M.

Algar Labouchere Thorold 1866-1936

Speaking French and Italian as fluently as English, with a good working knowledge of German, Algar Labouchere Thorold produced many translations of books dealing with mystical theology. One of these was a translation of selections from Blessed Angela of Foligno, a complete version of the Dialogues of St. Catherine of Siena. Later he translated several volumes from de Caussade.

His best work, however, is the life of his uncle Henry Labouchere, in which he concentrates his attention just on Labouchere. Otherwise, instead of the five hundred and forty pages he devotes to Labouchere "it would have been necessary to write at least a dozen volumes." His sense of humor and satire are happily blended in the life of his uncle who was an outstanding personality of the later Victorian Age. Entertaining anecdotes are mingled with political history to give the biography verve.

Algar Labouchere Thorold was born in 1866, the only son of the late Right Reverend Anthony Thorold, Bishop successively of Rochester and Winchester, by his second wife Emily Labouchere, the sister of the famous proprietor of *Truth*. Mr. Thorold was educated at Eton and Christchurch, Oxford. While still an undergraduate at Oxford, he was received into the Catholic Church in 1884. To find out whether he was called to the monastic life, he went to the Grand Chartreuse. Later he tried out for the secular priesthood at the London Oratory. Being convinced he was not called to the monastic life nor the secular priesthood, he married, in 1894, Theresa Mary Mansel. They had two sons and two daughters.

From 1912 to 1917 he was on the editorial staff of *Truth* and was a regular contributor to the *Edinburgh Review*. In 1917 he joined the Foreign Office (Information Department) and was placed in charge of a propaganda mission to Italy where he remained until the end of 1918. In 1919 he became a member of the British Peace Delegation in Paris. Later he was put in charge of the press section. He was the first press attaché at the British Embassy, in Paris, in 1920. From 1926 to 1934 he was editor of the *Dublin Review*.

Mr. Thorold's long friendship with Downside Abbey began in the early nineties when he met Dom Edmund Ford, then newly elected to his second term of office as Prior. Except for the years he was a resident in Italy, he was a frequent visitor to Downside. He died on May 31st, 1936.

Besides the books already mentioned, Mr. Thorold is the author of: *Catholic Mysticism,* and *Six Masters in Disillusion.*

M. H.

Reverend Herbert Thurston, S.J. 1856-1939

An authority on spiritualism, the falsity of which he combated, and a writer on this and ecclesiastical subjects, the Reverend Herbert Thurston, S.J., was a well-known British Jesuit scholar. Born in London, in 1856, the son of G. H. Thurston, M.R.C.S., he was educated at Mount St. Mary's College and at Stonyhurst, received his A.B. and was an Exhibitioner of London University. He took his vows in the Society of Jesus, served as Master at Beaumont College, from 1880 to 1887, and was ordained in 1890. The greater part of his life was spent at the Farm Street Jesuit Church in London and was devoted to writing.

Father Thurston was a frequent contributor to Catholic reviews and wrote numerous books. In 1898 he published *The Life of St. Hugh of Lincoln*. This was followed by a book on *The Holy Year of Jubilee* in 1900. *Lent and Holy Week* appeared in 1904 and *The Stations of the Cross* in 1906. At the time of World War I he wrote *The War and the Prophets* and *The Memory of Our Dead*. He was a keen student of spiritualism, its frauds and deceptions, many of which he exposed. Admitting the possibility of genuine spiritual manifestations, he brought such phenomena into their proper perspective, and warned that the subject requires a cautious approach. He wrote *Modern Spiritualism* in 1919 and *The Church and Spiritualism* in 1933. Other books were: *Christian Science; The Church and the Confessional; The Eucharistic Fast; Indulgences for Sale; No Popery; Superstition; Beauraing and Other Apparitions,* and his latest volume was *Miss Kate,* published in 1938.

One of his outstanding works was the revision of Butler's *Lives of the Saints,* which was enlarged and modernized. The twelve volumes of the revised edition appeared almost annually from 1926 to 1939. He also edited the folio edition of Bridgett's *History of the Holy Eucharist* and many of Mother Loyola's devotional works, and with Bishop Ward was co-editor of the Westminster Library Series of Catholic books. Many articles were contributed by him to the *Catholic Encyclopedia* and the *Encyclopaedia of Religion and Ethics.*

At the time of his death Father Thurston was the only surviving English Jesuit who had been the subject of indictment in the English Courts for being an "undeclared Jesuit," that is, for not having registered in accord with the Catholic Emancipation Act. The case fell through, for it was settled that no common informer, but only the Attorney General could prosecute. He died, after several months' illness, at Hampstead, near London, on November 6, 1939, at the advanced age of eighty-three, a great loss to Catholic letters and to the Church he had so long and so well served.

C. M. N.

William Richard Titterton 1876-

The son of a shipmaster, William Richard Titterton early in life became a public official. Later he became an artist's model in Paris and posed for George Gray Barnard and Jacob Epstein. Returning to his native London in 1876, he wrote an article every week for the *Daily News* and then became a staff reporter. In his column "The Discovery of Britain" he described England's beauty spots. He worked for *New Age* (Guild Socialism) and then for *Vanity Fair* with Frank Harris. A great admirer of Isadora Duncan, he was responsible for her coming to Frohman in London. He also covered music halls for *London Opinion* and for some years the *Pall Mall Gazette.* When the *Daily Herald* was run by London compositors, Mr. Titterton became a first leader-writer. For five years, he wrote the homely leader "Uplift" each day for the *Daily Sketch.* Then he became the dramatic critic for the *Sunday Herald* (now the *Sunday Graphic*) and *Lloyds.* A job, as publicity manager for Basil Dean, and after him for most of the London managers, followed. Returning to Fleet Street, he wrote a series of interviews, which appeared in many papers and began with "What Are We Here For?" in the *Daily Herald.* Through these articles Mr. Titterton became well known. For years, he wrote "Uplift" for the *Sunday Graphic,* under the caption "Uncommon Sense, by John Straight." Then he joined the staff of *The Universe.*

Mr. Titterton occasionally writes interview articles with George Bernard Shaw, who likes him for the sake of Chesterton. G. K. Chesterton had run like a thread through Titterton's career. They were on the *Daily News* together, both having been Socialists. They were fellow club members. They both wrote for the *Eye Witness* and the *New Witness,* and Titterton became Chesterton's assistant on the *New Witness* and afterwards on *G. K.'s Weekly.* It was through Chesterton that Mr. Titterton became a Distributist and it was largely owing to Chesterton that he became a Catholic in 1931. In 1936 Mr. Titterton wrote a life of Chesterton under the title: *G. K. Chesterton, a Portrait.* His other books are: (verse) *Love Poems and River Music; Guns and Guitars; The Madness of the Arts;* and *Drinking Songs;* (prose) *Studies in Solitary Life; An Afternoon Tea Philosophy; Me As a Model; From Theatre to Music-Hall; London Scenes; A Candle to the Stars* (1932), and *Have We Lost God?* (1933).

In 1944 his book of poems *London Pride* was the first publication of the new firm of Douglas Organ. In this work Mr. Titterton gives "a picture of the courage and faith with which London stood up to its long ordeal of bombing."

In prose, his best work has been in impressions of things seen. It is as journalist, however, that he is best known and his reputation rests on:

(a) his music-hall criticism, where his devotion lent him insight; (b) uplift, where his love for the commonplace and his liking for simple people gave him the key to their hearts; (c) interviews, where again his liking for people helped him to write intimately of people.

Mr. Titterton is married to a hospital nurse who contracted arthritis from serving under fire among muck and vermin in World War I. She is now a total cripple but still gay. The Tittertons have four children. Two boys were in the forces and one of the girls is a nurse. When their boys were at Douai, the Benedictine school, Mr. Titterton wrote a hymn to Saint Benedict which is now sung in the Abbey Church on the Saint's Feast Day.

                                                                          M. H.

Agnes Tobin   1863-1939

In these days of bustling, highly efficient literary practitioners, it is something of a relief to come across a figure like Agnes Tobin, shy, remote, almost evanescent. The general public has hardly so much as heard her name, though she and her work made a deep impression on some of the leading figures of her time. To her, Alice Meynell addressed her poem, *The Shepherdess,* which was inspired by the charm of Miss Tobin's personality; to her, Joseph Conrad dedicated his *Under Western Eyes,* paying his tribute to "her genius for friendship," and Yeats once declared her to be the finest poet America has produced since Whitman.

Yet very little of her work is in existence. In fact the only original poem from her pen that survives is the one printed by Theodore Maynard in his *Book of Modern Catholic Verse.* We have no more than the exquisite translations she made from Petrarch's Latin works and a privately printed volume containing her rendering of John Milton's Italian sonnets. But we know of a translation of Racine's Phèdre made for the English actress, Mrs. Patrick Campbell, as we also know of other works—in translation, and those that sprang from direct personal inspiration. The slim volumes of her poems are collectors' items today. Her many friends, who included such dissimilar writers as Sir Edmund Gosse, Francis Thompson, Arthur Symons, Katharine Tynan, Aubrey de Vere, E. V. Lucas, Richard Le Gallienne and Ezra Pound, were firmly convinced of her great talent.

She was not urged on by any economic necessity to write, inasmuch as she belonged to a well-to-do San Francisco family that includes Richard Tobin, American Minister to The Hague under President Hoover and now president of the Hibernia Savings and Loan Society in San Francisco. She wrote leisurely, therefore, and with scrupulous attention to perfection. But the reason for the disappearance of most of her work was that she was ill during the last years of her life so that such manuscripts as she had were either destroyed or were mislaid. This illness lasted until her death in San Francisco in 1939.

Born of California stock at San Francisco, Miss Tobin spent most of her years after graduating from the Convent of Notre Dame, San Francisco, in London and Italy. She returned to San Francisco in 1924 when her mother became mortally ill.

Most of her time in London was spent with the Meynell family at Palace Court and later in their charming place in Sussex. In that family she was always known as "Lily" because she was so exquisite and innocent of soul. But judging from what little survives in print, it may be said that Agnes Tobin proved her literary metal in the difficult task of translation, perhaps about the most exacting test of literary skill that there is. The overtones and the passion of Petrarch are caught by her more successfully than by anyone else who has attempted to turn him into English. The enchantment of her personality is still a kind of legend among those who knew her, and we may be sure that, though Miss Tobin is never likely to become popular, she will from age to age be a discovery of the discriminating in literature. The only general article about her work is one that appeared in the Autumn number of the *Mundelein College Review* for 1939.

Her translations of Petrarch into English verse are entitled *Love's Crucifix; Nine Sonnets,* and a *Canzone from Petrarch* (1903); *The Flying Lesson; Ten Sonnets; Two Canzoni; A Ballata; A Double Festina from Petrarch* (1905); *On the Death of Madonna Laura* (1907).   M. H.

James Edward Tobin   1905-

The educator and writer, James Edward Tobin, is the son of William J. J. Tobin and Mary L. (Kelleher) Tobin. He was born in Fall River, Massachusetts, January 17, 1905. He attended Boston College, where he was student correspondent for several newspapers. He also organized an intercollegiate news bureau and assisted in the foundation of the New England Intercollegiate Newspaper Association. Following graduation in 1925, he owned and edited a newspaper on Cape Cod, wrote sports and features for the Boston *American,* and served on the staff of The Associated Press in the Boston and Baltimore offices. A short pamphlet on the architecture of Charles D. Maginnis and a study of the stained glass of Earl Edward Sanborn are indicative of his interests at this period. Encouraged by Reverend Francis X. Talbot, S.J., and by Mrs. Helen Walker Homan, he published considerable verse in newspapers and magazines.

In 1927 he joined the faculty of Fordham University, and obtained his A.M. there in 1928, and his Ph.D. in 1933. He married Lorraine Walsh of South Boston in 1929, and is now the father of five children.

In 1932, a bibliographical pamphlet on eighteenth century literature was issued, and in 1933 a collection of early poems, *Ardent Marigolds*. Professor Tobin taught Latin, history, government, and English literature at the University, and in 1936 became head of the Department of English at the Fordham Graduate School of Arts and Sciences. He published *An Approach to Graduate Study* in 1937.

A stimulating lecturer as well as an accurate and discerning scholar, he has maintained for the past twelve years a consistent crusade against romanticism as a prevailing system of thought. The romantic delusion of evaluation by the emotions alone he has singled out for special attack in all his lectures and articles. A strong traditionalist, he believes implicitly in the existing standard, the inherited rule, which have stood the test of time and critics, as opposed to the so-called "originality" of the moderns. A growing faith in the positive value of satire as a preservative and a corrective has led him with perfect consistency to an intensive study of the work and thought of Pope and Swift, of More and Erasmus. Among the moderns, D. B. Wyndham Lewis and Belloc seem to him to be carrying on most effectively the fight for principles which their satiric work presupposes. Professor Tobin has tried to preach "truths which the weight of inherited nonsense will not permit the wide acceptance they deserve." For this reason, he has been accused not infrequently of cynicism. In the last analysis, however, he is an idealist who, in the face of much misdirected human endeavor, has found a critical approach, particularly the satiric, "the most comforting of all expressions, since it at once demolishes human pretense and highlights the ideal."

In poetry as in prose, he holds to thought as the most important element in the allegiance to truth as well as in the defeat of incoherence. He writes a direct and vigorous prose, highly concentrated and allusive. He exemplifies in his later verse a fine restraint, a balance of the emotional and the intellectual which make for strength as for effective imagery. In all forms of expression, he insists, clear thinking leads inevitably to correct standards, both ethical and artistic.

Professor Tobin is co-editor of *Contrast and Comparison*, a collection of essays published in 1931, and of *To An Unknown Country*, which he brought out with Francis X. Connolly in 1942. He is on the editorial board of *Thought* and of the *Comparative Literature News Letter*, and is associate editor of the forthcoming *Guide to Comparative Literature and Intercultural Relations*. He is well known in academic circles for his valuable contributions to bibliography. In 1939 he published *Eighteenth Century Literature and Its Cultural Background*, and he is now engaged on a continuation of the *Short Title Catalogue* of Pollard and Redgrave, a listing of all publications in England from 1701 to 1735. He has contributed prose and verse to *Philological Quarterly, Classical Bulletin, Notes and Queries, The Commonweal, America, The Catholic World, Catholic Library World, Spirit* and *Best Sellers*. He is a member of the Bibliographical Society of America, The Catholic Poetry Society, Medieval Academy, Modern Humanities Research Association, Modern Language Association, and the National Council of Teachers of English.

Mr. Tobin is now (1947) editor-in-chief of the Trade Book Department of the Declan X. McMullen Co.

Most Reverend Tihamer Toth 1889-1939

From his youth Most Reverend Tihamer Toth was of marked spirituality and outstanding scholastic aptitude, and in later years he was known as a saintly priest and prelate, a scholar and great orator. He was born of an illustrious family, at Szolnok, Hungary, in 1889. Aged seven when his father died, the grief of his mother, left alone to provide for him and four other sons, made a deep impression on him. He frequently sought the solitude of the church near his home or took long walks along the banks of the River Tisza, his keen observation and love of nature in those early days bearing fruit in later lectures on the wonders of God's creation and especially in his notable book, *God's Amazing World*. With his childhood companions he liked to "play" Mass, thus already yearning for the fulfilment of his religious vocation.

After he had studied six years at the Gymnasium at Szolnok, the archbishop of Eger accepted him into the diocesan preparatory seminary, and he was then sent to the Central Seminary at Budapest to continue his theological studies at the university. The rector in a letter to his bishop spoke of the young seminarian as "an exemplary cleric . . . a promising satellite of the Church."

Following ordination, Father Toth travelled through Europe, everywhere keenly observant of people. With the outbreak of the World War I he served as chaplain for fifteen months, but was then recalled by his bishop, as the strain was too much for him, and he became professor of theology at the seminary in Eger. Deciding to devote his life especially to the care of young men and boys, he began by delivering a series of sermons, "Letters to My Boys," at the university church. He edited papers and magazines concerned with youth, organized boys' clubs and headed Boy Scout activities. By 1918 he had become a noted pulpit orator, and the social unrest following the conclusion of the war gave him much scope for his zeal. In 1924 he was offered an instructor's chair at the University of Budapest, becoming head of the catechetical, homiletical and pedagogical departments the following year. Several books were written during this time, and he visited England and America.

His radio sermons, which made him known far and wide, were begun January 31, 1926, from the pulpit of his beloved city church. Thousands of letters gave evidence of their apostolic fervor and of his remarkable ability to present ancient truths, convincingly and appealingly, to modern minds. His sermons were printed in book form, and translated into English by V. G. Agotai. Among them are: *Great God,* on the Divine attributes; *Great Redeemer,* on the Passion and death of Christ; *Great Teacher,* on Christ the Divine Teacher; *The Kingship of Christ; The Risen Christ; The Catholic Church; Life Everlasting,* on the mysteries of death and the life beyond.

In 1931, Father Toth was made rector of "Old Central," the seminary he had attended and loved. His consecration as bishop took place in 1938. During the International Eucharistic Congress of that year at Budapest, the papal legate, Cardinal Pacelli, now Pope Pius XII, presented him with a papal bull appointing him Bishop of Vezprem. He did not long occupy this important see, for death, following a brief illness, closed his apostolic career on May 5, 1939. Though the voice that reached so many souls is stilled, his words are printed for all to read. His more than twenty books have been translated into ten languages. C. M. N.

Mrs. Arnold Toynbee *see* Rosalind Murray

Vera Marie Tracy 1895-1940

Writing is for most authors a laborious task but for Vera Marie Tracy it was even more so. When she was twelve years of age, paralysis twisted her body and confined her to a wheel chair. Only one of her fingers was capable of movement. With this one finger she typed out all her work. Hours which should have been given to rest, she devoted to writing.

Born in Indiana in 1895, she spent her happy childhood days in Texas. When she was twelve years of age, her malady was declared incurable. Her grandmother took her to Colorado in search of specialists, still hoping she could be cured. It was of no avail. She became a patient in the Glockner Sanatorium in Colorado Springs, where she spent the remaining years of her invalidism. Undaunted by her affliction, she satisfied the urge within her to write.

"I wrote twenty poems before I dared show them to any one," she said. And like most beginners, rejection slips came often at first. Determination to do better and the will to succeed prevailed.

Her writings reflect a Catholic attitude on life and sparkle with humor. Her pain and disappointment transformed her into a "saint of the sick room." Her smile and merry laugh earned for her the name "Sunnie" from nurses and friends. This merriness manifests itself in her literary work. She shows that through tears one can smile and that pain can be met with a song.

She was made an Academy member of The Catholic Poetry Society which counted her among the thirty leading Catholic poets of America. One of her stories, *Lavender's Purple*, was rated by *Extension* magazine as the second best of the year in 1928.

Besides the poems and stories which she contributed to *The Catholic World, Far East, Extension* magazine, *America* and *Ave Maria*, she wrote the following books: *Incense* (1926) (Poems); *Blue Portfolio* (1933) (short stories); *Burnished Chalices* (ten touching hospital sketches) (1931), and her last, *Gold Dusty* (1938) (82 short poems). She died in 1940. M. H.

Evan Frederic Morgan Tredegar *see* Evan Morgan

Most Reverend William Turner 1871-1936

Only two books came from the pen of the late Bishop Turner, and these were textbooks on *The History of Philosophy* and *Lessons in Logic.* Both of them, however, were accepted and regarded highly not only in Catholic colleges and seminaries but in many secular institutions.

Most Reverend William Turner, D.D., sixth Bishop of Buffalo, was born in Kilmallock, County Limerick, Ireland, April 8, 1871, the son of Patrick and Bridget (Carey) Turner. He received his early education in the public schools of his native town, and at an early age was sent to the Royal University of Ireland in Dublin, from which he was graduated with honors in 1888. In 1893 he was ordained to the priesthood by Cardinal Parocchi and was graduated, with the degree of Doctor of Sacred Theology, from the American College at Rome. In the autumn of 1893 he entered the Institut Catholique in Paris where he continued his study of philosophy and other subjects helpful to him in his chosen vocation. In 1894, in his twenty-fourth year, he returned to the United States to teach Latin and logic at St. Thomas College, St. Paul, Minnesota, where he remained for one year. In 1895 he was offered, and accepted, the chair of philosophy at the St. Paul Seminary, one of the youngest men ever to be given such an important post. Dr. Turner taught philosophy at St. Paul for eleven years. It was during this period that he wrote his *History of Philosophy* which was published in 1903. His second book, *Lessons in Logic,* was published in 1911.

In 1906 Bishop Turner accepted the invitation of the Catholic University of America to become professor of logic and the history of philosophy there. This honored position he retained until made Bishop of Buffalo in 1919.

While at the Catholic University, Dr. Turner held many other important roles: Librarian of Catholic University and editor of the *Catholic University Bulletin* (1906). From 1911 to 1913 he was a lecturer in the Brooklyn Institute of Arts and Science, and also served as a lecturer at Trinity College, Washington, the Catholic Summer School of America at Cliff Haven, and at various other summer schools.

From 1914 to 1919 he was editor of *The American Ecclesiastical Review.* He was also associate editor of *The Catholic Historical Review.*

Dr. Turner's knowledge of German, Italian, and French made him at home in all groups. During his years in Washington he came to be known and admired by men high in the government and diplomatic corps. He was a member of the Dante Society of Washington and also of various American and Irish patriotic organizations.

Besides his two books he was a frequent contributor to Catholic and non-Catholic educational publications. Among them: *American Catholic Quarterly; Irish Theological Quarterly; The American Ecclesiastical Review; Philosophical Review,* and *Review of Philosophy and Psychology.* As one of the editors of the *Catholic Encyclopedia* Bishop Turner contributed several articles on philosophy, which are being retained in the revised edition of the set now being printed.

Colleges, societies, and numerous learned organizations honored Bishop Turner. The King of Italy awarded him the decoration of Commander of the Royal Crown of Italy. After serving sixteen years in the See of Buffalo, he departed this life, July 10, 1936.

E. F.

Katharine Tynan 1861-1931

When Katharine Tynan was sixty she remarked one day, looking back over her forty years of industrious writing, "It is a real sorrow to me that my novels have never been accepted by America." She was not speaking with any resentment, but she was puzzled. Her novels have been described as "models of simple story-telling." They gave much pleasure and never did any harm. Her first impulse towards authorship, as she herself writes in her autobiography, "was because of a slight. Someone had been preferred before me and I wanted to show that I was that other's superior. In Celtic Ireland, although they may not buy books, there is always a certain respect for literary achievement."

She began her writing career at the age of seventeen. Her quiet life in Clondalkin, County Dublin, where she was born in 1861 and where she lived most of her life until she married, at the age of thirty-two, no doubt helped to bring out her talent at such an early age. She was born in the house which had once been lived in by Sarah Curran, who was engaged to Robert Emmet. Her education was received at the Convent of St. Catherine in Drogheda. She left school at the age of fourteen, owing to bad eyesight. Her father, Andrew Tynan, helped her in the continuation of her studies. Her mother had become an invalid at a very early age.

Her poems are simple and direct; they deal with her religion, her country—"golden Ireland"—her friends, her children. One theme may be repeated in several poems, but without ever a note of staleness. "Sheep and

Lambs" is probably her best known religious poem. Many of her poems about Ireland were written when she had gone to live in England after her marriage. She sang of her homesickness for the things intrinsically Irish: the characteristics of her own people, the mist, the thrush and blackbird—birds which sing in Ireland as in no other country. Her collected poems were published in 1930.

Many of her early poems were brought out by Father Matthew Russell, S.J., in *The Irish Monthly*. Father Russell encouraged her in every way, and introduced her to the literary people of the day. She wrote of him in her book *Twenty-five Years: Reminscences*, "My first important literary event was the beginning of my friendship with Father Matthew Russell, S.J."

Her first volume of poems *Louise de la Vallière and Other Poems* appeared when she was twenty-four (1885). A few years later this was followed by the first of her long list of novels. She seemed to have no difficulty in producing three or four novels a year. In spite of her enormous literary output she was domesticated, in the sense that she was deeply attached to her husband, Henry Hinkson, the classical scholar and writer of boys' stories, whom she married in 1893 and converted to Catholicism, and to her three children. Her marriage brought her happiness, but financially it did not seem to bring her much security. Her husband died in 1919.

In 1913 she published *Twenty-five Years: Reminiscences* and followed it in later years by four similar volumes. These stories of her life are pervaded by the charm and humor she possessed so abundantly; and they are interesting because of her literary friends—the Rossettis, Alice Meynell, Francis Thompson, W. B. Yeats, Douglas Hyde, George Russell, better known as A.E., and Lionel Johnson. Dora Sigerson was her closest friend.

By nature she was a sincere, kind, warm-hearted woman, and intensely loyal. All her intimates called her K.T. She had a passionate love for Ireland, Parnell being her political hero. In the later sixties she had ulcers of the eyes from which she suffered for two years. Her recreations were talking to a good listener, collecting china and the society of her children.

Her long busy life came to an end in London in April 1931. She had published well over a hundred volumes. Her literary reputation rests mainly on her poems, but indirectly her glowing and very "Irish" personality is essentially a part of the Irish Renaissance movement.

Among her books are: *Shamrocks* (1887); *Ballads and Lyrics* (1890); *A Cluster of Nuts* (1894); *The Way of a Maid* (1895); *The Dear Irish Girl* (1899); *Love of Sisters* (1902); *Miss Mary* (1917); *Wives* (1924); *The Rich Man* (1929); *The Other Man* (1932), and *An International Marriage* (1933).

Sigmund Uminski   1910-

Starting his journalistic career at the early age of sixteen, Sigmund Uminski for several years was contributing editor and columnist of the *Alliance Daily* and the weekly *Zgoda* published in Chicago, Illinois. For nine years he was associate editor of the *Polish Morning World, Nowy Swiat,* a daily published in New York City.

He was also a contributing editor to the American Slav magazine published in Pittsburgh, Pennsylvania, for which magazine he also wrote book reviews, and to many other periodicals. His poems have appeared in several anthologies. Two of his lyrics have been set to music.

His monographs, *How To Study, Planning Your Life* and *Making Good in High School* have been printed serially in the *Polish Morning World* (1942 and 1943). Two other monographs: *Why Go To College?* and *Planning to be a Leader* were published serially in the *Alliance Daily* and the Weekly *Zgoda.*

He was born February 6, 1910, and studied at St. John's University, Brooklyn, New York, Columbia University and Pace Institute. From 1933 to 1942 he was director of the Polish National Alliance Youth Camps in Connecticut, New Jersey and New York.

He is the author of several textbooks on youth leadership, published in Polish and English by the Polish National Alliance of the United States of North America, used by the Alliance Youth Movement.

Besides the monographs mentioned, he is the author of the following books: *The Progress of Labor in the United States* (1939); *Poland's Contribution to the World's Civilization* (1942); *Avenging Eagles.* He is co-editor of *Who's Who in Polish America* (Third Edition) (1943).

He holds membership in the Research Commission on Polish Immigrants organized by the Polish Institute of Arts and Sciences in America, The Catholic Poetry Society of America, The League to Support Poetry and The Gallery of Living Catholic Authors.

Sigrid Undset 1882-

From the Middle Ages and from modern life, Sigrid Undset has woven stories with a master hand. Her essays have the touch of genius, and in her appreciation of the saints she is moved by a deep spirituality. It is ageless humanity that is her theme, and of it she has a rare understanding that, combined with literary skill, makes her one of the outstanding writers of the twentieth century. She was born in 1882, in Kallundborg, Denmark, of a Danish mother and a Norwegian father, the distinguished archeologist, Dr. Ingvald Martin Undset, author, and a professor at the University of Oslo. In that city, then called Christiania, they made their home, and she was educated at a private school. Her father died when she was only eleven years old, and after attending a commercial school she did clerical work in business offices and became a secretary, in this way supporting herself from 1899 to 1909.

In her free time she studied fiction writing, and in 1907 she published her first novel, *Frau Marta Oulie,* written in the form of a diary. It was a story of marriage, parenthood and human relationship, the family saga on which Madame Undset builds her works. With the publication of her second book in 1909 she decided to devote all her time to writing, but it was not until the appearance in 1911 of *Jenny,* a study in feminine psychology, that she received popular acclaim. In 1912 she wrote her most famous short story, *Simonsen.*

In that year she married Anders C. Svarstad, a Norwegian artist. Three children were born of the union. Her marriage to him was declared invalid and she had to leave him before she could be received into the Catholic Church, as Mr. Svarstad's first wife was still living. In 1924 she made her profession of faith in the Catholic Church. She had come to know this ancient stronghold of the truth through her research. Moreover, she realized that only on the sacrament of matrimony could the sanctity of the married state be built. The sanction of divorce, within the Lutheran Church, in which she was reared, was partly influential in leading her to this step.

Meanwhile, she had written the great trilogy, *Kristin Lavransdatter* (1920-1922), which in *The Bridal Wreath, The Mistress of Husaby,* and *The Cross,* gives the story of this erring daughter who in sorrow expiates her sin. It is an epic of fourteenth-century Catholic Norway, a powerful drama of faith and the weakness of human nature. Madame Undset writes for the mature mind, with a direct candor that leaves no glamor to evil done. The book has been translated into most European languages and has sold over 300,000 copies in the United States alone. The medieval tetralogy, *The Master of Hestviken,* followed. The first volume was published in 1925. It is of equal literary status with the preceding trilogy. Madame Undset was the first writer to apply the technique of modern

psychological and realistic fiction to a vanished period. In 1928 the Nobel
Prize for Literature was awarded her, the citation especially commending
her remarkable depiction of medieval life. This prize she gave to charity.

Her modern novels frequently treat of the disillusion that married
life may bring. In *The Wild Orchid* and *The Burning Bush* the hero
becomes a Catholic, and through his religion finds strength to bear with
an unhappy marriage and to withstand the temptations of an unlawful
love. In *Ida Elizabeth* it is the natural bond that ties. *The Faithful Wife*
was published in 1937, and her novel *Madame Dorothea,* is a story of
eighteenth-century Norwegian life, to which she plans a sequel. *Saga of
Saints* and *Stages on the Road* are biographies of holy men and women,
such as Robert Southwell, Margaret Clitherow, Ramon Lull and St.
Angela Merici. She treats further of the saints in *Saints and Places.* In
1939 she published *Men, Women and Places,* a book of essays, on blas-
phemy, with a strong indictment of the spiritualists; on a landscape in
Gotland and on Glastonbury, "holiest of holy places in England"; and
on Marie Bregendahl, Leo Weismantel, Margery Kempe, D. H. Lawrence
and three heroes of religious wars. Her keen insight into human nature
and true sense of values are especially shown in her analysis of Lawrence.

The subject of Madame Undset's *Return to the Future* (1942) is her
hazardous flight from her homeland, invaded by the Nazis, via Sweden,
Russia, Japan and across the Pacific to San Francisco. It is a tragic story
of treachery within Norway by the Germans to whom hospitality had
been given, of the marauding army, the destruction of her own home
among many others, and the death of her eldest son, Anders, fighting
in defense of his country. Her books were among the first to be banned
by the Nazis in Norway and Germany. *Happy Times in Norway* (1943),
is a book about her own country as it was. Then followed *Sigurd and His
Brave Companions;* a tale of medieval Norway, and *True and Untrue
and Other Norse Tales.*

During the war in Norway, she worked with the Army at the Norwegian Free Broadcaster. She went to Sweden in the hope of getting back
to Northern Norway, where "our army still fought on—my son went with
me also, in the hope of getting back to the fight, and returned to the Norwegian Army as soon as it was re-formed in Scotland. Before I could
get back over the frontier the Norwegians had to give in, as our Allies
withdrew their troops during the last fighting in France. Then it would
have been useless for me to return to Norway, so I went on to America."

The United States gave her a warm welcome. Under the auspices of
America, national Catholic weekly, she lectured throughout the country.
From Assumption College, Windsor, Ontario, came recognition in the
1941 Christian Culture Award, conferred on her as the outstanding lay
exponent of Christian ideals during the previous year. On May 30, 1943,
Smith College conferred on her the honorary Litt.D.

Madame Undset resided in Brooklyn, New York, during World War
II. She returned to Norway in 1945. She is an Academy member of the
Gallery of Living Catholic Authors. Recently King Haakon VII of Norway
bestowed on her the Grand Cross of the Order of St. Olaf. This marks the
first time in its one hundred year history that this honor has been conferred on a woman not of the royal blood.   C. M. N.

Hilda van Stockum 1908-

A painter and lecturer as well as a writer, Hilda van Stockum first gained recognition at the age of twenty-one, when she was commissioned to illustrate a booklet for a school run by the method of Dr. Maria Montessori, an Italian educator.

She was born in Rotterdam, Holland, on February 9, 1908, the daughter of Olga Emily (Boissevain) and Abraham John van Stockum. When Hilda was sixteen years old, her family moved to Ireland where she attended the Dublin School of Art. Later she was sent to the Academy of Art in Amsterdam, Holland, and while studying there she was assigned to do a number of portraits.

In 1932 Miss van Stockum married Ervin Ross Marlin, and they are the parents of five children, three girls and two boys.

She came to the United States in 1934 and spent her first year in this country lecturing at the Child Education Foundation, New York City, on the Montessori Method of Education, a system of teaching introduced in 1907 by Dr. Maria Montessori, applied to children by directing rather than controlling their activity.

Miss van Stockum became a Catholic in 1938.

She writes fiction exclusively for children, and explains her choice in these words: "I write for children because I wouldn't know what to write for grown-ups. I always wanted to be the mother of a large family, and the fulfillment of that wish makes me very happy. My talents come next. I owe it to God to use them; but none of my books are as nice as my children."

She has written six books, in each of which the illustrations are her own: *A Day on Skates* (1934); *Cottage at Bantry Bay* (1938); *Francie on the Run* (1939); *Kersti and St. Nicholas* (1940); *Pegeen* (1934); *Andries* (1942), and *Gerrit and the Organ* (1943).

Miss van Stockum is fond of water sports and gardening.

G. M. A.

Reverend Gerald Vann, O.P. 1906-

The work of Father Gerald Vann, O.P., is the result of an almost exclusively Dominican training. He was born in 1906, the fourth son of William S. and Alice Marshall Vann, and his early school days were spent at an English Dominican preparatory school. He received his lectorate in theology at the Dominican Collegio Angelico in Rome and then studied for a B.A. in politics and philosophy at Oxford. Continuing in the Blackfriars atmosphere, he now unites a life of writing and teaching at the English Dominican School, Laxton, with the stimulus of outside lecturing.

As a writer, Gerald Vann is chiefly concerned with the problems of religion and culture and with the Thomist view of modern conditions and problems, particularly in regard to ethics in its personal, social and political aspects. In his book, a metaphysical study of the principles of *St. Thomas Aquinas*, he reminds us that in the Middle Ages it was the office of the theologian "to expound the 'principia suprema' of life in accordance with which the everyday affairs of life were ultimately to be governed."

Father Vann approaches things with a direct simplicity, an engaging frankness, adding to scholarship a broad sympathy which would have delighted that prince of humanists, Saint Thomas More. His literary descendant (if we may use the phrase) shows himself to be of the line royal in *On Being Human*. This essay is a synthesis of the purely natural phases of humanism and their completion in the Thomist outlook: "The Catholic ideal is the consummation of the ideal of pagan humanism." The humanism of Saint Thomas does not lead to negation or to sterility but is constructive and fertile. In 1944 *The Heart of Man* was published and *The Divine Pity: A Study in the Social Implications of the Beatitudes* appeared in 1945. This was followed by *His Will Is Our Peace* and *Eve and the Gryphon*—a study of the vocation of women.

Like the author of *Utopia*, Father Vann is keenly interested in the moral problem of war as *Morals Makyth Man* testifies. He has also a number of dynamic pamphlets on this intricate subject, also a book *Morality and War*. In 1936, he founded the *Union of Prayer for Peace*, which he calls an international crusade of daily prayer. He has been a delegate to the Catholic International Peace conferences held at Dublin in 1937 and at The Hague in 1938. A forceful contributor to English Catholic magazines, Father Vann's penetrating and vigorous articles are found in such American periodicals as *The Commonweal, The Catholic World*, and *The Torch*.

Father Vann is now in this country (1947) to lecture, preach retreats and conduct a series of conferences for religious communities.

A. M.

Dom Willibrord Verkade, O.S.B. 1868-

"Down the labyrinthine ways" from the bleak world of no faith to entrance into the Benedictine cloister at Beuron, Germany, is the life story of Dom Willibrord Verkade as told in his autobiography *Yesterdays of an Artist Monk.*

Born in 1868 in Zaandam near Amsterdam, Holland, of Mennonite parents, he was not baptized, but, strangely enough, even in his childhood, Catholicity seemed to be close to him. Manifesting early a desire to become a painter, he left the commercial school in Amsterdam and entered the National Academy of Fine Arts, spending two and a half years there.

Always spiritual matters crowded his consciousness. After having read Tolstoi's *My Confessions* and such Catholic authors as De Maistre, Lacordaire, Baudelaire and Verlaine, he said, "These writers brought me nearer to the Catholic Church, since what is good and beautiful in their books is an emanation of Catholic culture."

Subsequently in Paris in 1891, he studied under the painter, Gauguin, at a period when a strong reaction against realism and naturalism in both art and literature was setting in. At this time he read Balzac's *Seraphita* and "drank for the first time from the fountain of Christian mysticism." Under the spell of the world's great art treasures, he came to the conclusion that "without religion, there is no really great art." This perception, he said, caused him to seek a "religious philosophy of life."

Whether painting in Brittany, Paris, or Italy, his interest in things religious became of paramount importance to him. Among the books which profoundly appealed to him was a catechism which contained "the whole doctrinal structure of the Catholic Church."

Finally on August 26, 1892, he was baptized in the Jesuit College at Varnnes, and soon received the Sacraments of Holy Eucharist and Confirmation. When in Copenhagen, in 1894, he held a Jan Verkade Exposition of paintings, it proved a brilliant success and established his reputation as a distinguished artist. That same year he entered the Benedictine monastery of Beuron.

In Quest of Beauty, a second book by Father Verkade, continues his life's story as artist and monk. Commissioned to decorate churches, he travelled throughout Europe and the Holy Land, and in his book comments wisely on "what is modern in art, economics, and politics," as well as his main interest, religious art.

T. V.

Grenville Vernon   1883-1941

When Grenville Vernon died suddenly in New York on November 30, 1941, there passed a writer and a personality who had long occupied a unique place among Catholic dramatic critics; for he had a special competence in music. It was in fact as music critic that he worked for the New York *Times* for a year, beginning in 1908, and left to take a similar position with the *Herald Tribune,* one that he held until 1921. It was also as a writer on music that he started contributing to *The Commonweal* in 1926. He succeeded Mr. Dana Skinner on the same paper as dramatic critic, a position that he maintained until his death. In fact the very issue of *The Commonweal* (that for December 12, 1941) which contained an obituary article about him, also contained a long article from his pen on the present state of the stage.

Vernon was born in Providence, Rhode Island, on July 22, 1883, of a well-known New England family. After graduation at Harvard in 1905 he came to New York and started to write for various papers, also holding, for ten years, beginning in 1928, the post of editor for the Dial Press. In the interval he had served as foreign correspondent for several New York papers in London and Paris. Even so he managed in 1926 to publish a novel, entitled *Image in the Path;* to write several plays, among which was *The Dictator's Wife,* as well as to compile a collection of pre-Civil War American folk-songs, which appeared as *Yankee Doodle Doo.* At the time of his death he was working on a biography of Gladstone.

It is, however, as a dramatic critic that Grenville Vernon will be best remembered. As such he was honest, sensitive, and discerning and brought to his work an immense knowledge of the stage. His writing had the same grace and charm that were so much in evidence in the clubs and literary circles he frequented.

Grenville Vernon's wife was Miss Valentine d'Orn of Martinique, French West Indies, a sister-in-law of Elisha Walker, a partner of Kuhn, Loeb & Co. They had two children, a boy who died at the age of ten, and a daughter who is now Mrs. Edward C. Craig, whose husband served in World War II as a captain in the United States Marine Corps. Captain Craig served at the invasion of Guadalcanal. Mrs. Vernon's death occurred two years before that of her husband. His passing, almost simultaneously with that of Dana Skinner, leaves a gap among Catholic dramatic critics that will be very hard to fill.

Dom Anscar Vonier, O.S.B.   1875-1938

Hardly had he been elected Abbot of Buckfast, at the age of thirty, to take the place of Dom Boniface Natter who was drowned at sea, while Dom Vonier escaped, than he announced to his astounded community that they would rebuild the ancient church of Buckfast, crumbled to ruins in the 360-odd years since Henry VIII had dissolved England's monasteries. They must have supposed that he had lost his wits, for all the funds they were able to obtain was a gift of £5 to buy stone, and the loan of a horse. Yet for twenty-five years the abbot and his monks labored until Buckfast —the sole English abbey that goes back to pre-Reformation times—at last stood again in its stately beauty. The foundation goes back even further than to the time of King Canute (as was once supposed) to St. Petrock of the sixth century. It is, therefore, at once, the most ancient and the newest of English abbeys. And it was all done by the work of the monks themselves, kept to their task by Abbot Vonier.

It is a marvel how funds were always forthcoming for the purchase of materials for the building of the great church. In part they were raised by the monks making and widely advertising their "Buckfast Tonic." But another source of income was that visitors from far and wide flocked to gaze on the bee-hive industry of the community and were so impressed as generally to leave contributions. And, of course, the Duke of Norfolk, and Lord Clifford of Chudleigh, and other wealthy Catholics gave large donations. What eventuated was a building that is one of the best examples of Norman Gothic. The monks had, it is true, a good architect, but the actual art of construction had to be learned from a former stone-mason who had become a lay-brother. The soul of the enterprise was Abbot Vonier himself.

If the abbey church is one of Anscar Vonier's monuments, he also built himself another, though in both cases he would probably have been surprised to learn that what he was doing was anything of the kind. He was the author of a number of remarkable books, which included: *The Human Soul and its Relations with Other Spirits* (1913); *The Personality of Christ* (1915); *The Christian Mind* (1921); *The Divine Motherhood* (1921); *A Key to the Doctrine of the Eucharist* (1925); *The Life of the World to Come* (1927); *The Angels* (1928); *The New and Eternal Covenant* (1929); *Death and Judgment* (1930); *Christ the King of Glory* (1932); *Christians* (1932); *The Spirit and the Bride; The People of God; The Art of Christ; Christianus.* Abbot Vonier knew how to bridge the gulf which so often divides theology from the common understanding, certainly not by thinning out the more difficult elements of dogma but by making clear their application to the life of all Catholics. It was a work that needed to be done, and no man did it more successfully than Abbot Vonier. But that his standing as a scholar was high is indicated by his serving for some years at the University of Oxford as an examiner in philosophy.

Dom Vonier was born at Ringschnaitt in Würtemberg in Germany in 1875. He spent the whole of his active life in England, except for a year in France and a period of studying in France and a period of study in Rome at the International Benedictine College of Sant' Anselmo. Later he became a professor of the same college for a year. Moreover, his voluminous writings, which give him a special place among contemporary spiritual authors, were in English.

On December 26, 1938, this really great Benedictine died at the age of sixty-three. During the thirty years as Abbot of Buckfast, he had made a deep impression upon the religious life of England. His work will stand. He will also be remembered as a man in whom great geniality and humor were added to profound piety.

Hugh Mason Wade 1913-

Mr. Wade first began doing editorial and literary work at the age of fourteen and has never stopped. He presided over the destinies of the school newspaper at Choate, and at Harvard the literary magazine, *The Advocate*. Upon leaving college he went into the book-publishing business as a reader and editorial assistant, and has worked for Viking Press (1935), Harcourt, Brace & Co., Little, Brown Co., Reynal and Hitchcock, and John Day, from 1937 to 1938. He has also contributed articles and book reviews to many magazines.

Mr. Van Wyck Brooks' *The Flowering of New England* first set him to thinking about Margaret Fuller. This transcendentalist, feminist, and friend of every literary figure of the day, was the most widely known woman in nineteenth century America. Today her name is little remembered. In 1938 Mr. Wade began to unearth her from obscurity and in 1940 *Margaret Fuller, Whetstone of Genius*, was published. Mr. Wade's first book was The Catholic Book Club choice for April 1940.

In his work Mr. Wade is particularly interested in the conflict of Puritanism and Catholicism in America, being a Bay Stater of 300 years' standing on his father's side, and Catholic through his mother's Pennsylvania Dutch ancestry.

Mr. Wade was born in New York City, July 3, 1913. He attended the Allen-Stevenson School there, the Choate School, and Harvard. During his college vacations he travelled in Scotland, England, Holland and France. He had early become interested in medieval architecture and literature. He did college work in these fields and planned his trips abroad to further this interest. He lives now at Cornish, New Hampshire, a state which gives him ample opportunity to pursue his favorite sports, mountain-climbing and skiing.

Besides his book *Margaret Fuller, Whetstone of Genius* (1940), he has edited *The Writings of Margaret Fuller* (1941) and in 1942 he published *Francis Parkman: Heroic Historian.* It is considered by such an eminent authority as James Truslow Adams to be the best life of Parkman. He also says of it: "The book is not only very interesting and easy to read, but obviously of first-rate importance for the understanding of one of our greatest literary figures and of his period." In 1946 Mr. Wade published *The French Canadian Outlook.*

M. S.

Thomas Dorrington Wadelton   1926-

With the exception of the three years spent in Indianapolis, Tom Wadelton spent his entire life in one or another Army Post—Georgia, Tennessee, Maryland, Texas and Kansas. Surprising enough, life on an army post can become quite dull at times, so dull that one wishes he could get away. Such boredom started Thomas Dorrington Wadelton on his literary career. When he was eleven years of age, he rode his bicycle out of bounds. For punishment his mother told him he would have to do "something fancy" to get it back. His "something fancy" was a story about his life on the army post and especially an account of the act which had deprived him of his bicycle. This was his first story. He sold it to the *Cavalry Journal* for $6.50. The story attracted the attention of one of the editors of *Country Life,* who bought a story and later a second story. Some publishers urged him to write a book. He wrote his first book when thirteen years of age, the second when he was fourteen.

This young writer was born in the Borough of Paddington, London, England, on September 4, 1926. When a very young lad he came to America with his parents. His father was lieutenant-colonel Thomas Dorrington Wadelton, U.S.A. (he died May 29, 1945), and his mother is the well-known writer, Maggie-Owen Melody Wadelton. She was born Margret Kearns in Roscommon, Ireland. She lived all her young life with her great-aunt, Kate Holt Melody, and bore her name.

Tommy is six feet two inches tall and weighs one hundred and ninety eight pounds. He appears older than his years. He has an I. Q. rating two points below genius. He has brown hair, brown eyes and is handsome. The movies made two offers and his photographs have been used extensively in advertising. He likes to sleep, read and eat. His mother says, "stress the latter." While in high school, he discovered there are girls in the world but he preferred boys. He disliked dancing and other socials. He is known to be very even tempered, cheerful and endowed with a "grand sense of the comic." He plays piano well, but is much better on drums. He belonged to two swing bands. While in Tennessee, he attended the Miss

Mamie Bright's private school in Chattanooga, Tennessee, and later the Baylor Military School in the same town. In June 1944 he graduated from the Shortridge High School in Indianapolis and then entered Butler University in Indianapolis. After the completion of his sophomore year, he was inducted into the army at Camp Atterbury, Indiana, and took basic training with the signal corps at Camp Crowder, Missouri.

He is the author of: *My Mother is a Violent Woman; My Father is a Quiet Man,* and *Army Brat* (1943). Metro Goldwyn Mayer purchased the film rights for *Army Brat*. His fourth book *Silver Buckles on His Knee* appeared in 1945.

P. Mac.

Maggie-Owen Wadelton (Mrs. Thomas Wadelton) 1895-

Born in Roscommon, Ireland, as Margret Kearns, Maggie-Owen Melody lived all her young life with her great-aunt, Kate Holt Melody, and bore the name of Melody. Her great-uncle was Father Hugh Melody, one time instructor at Maynooth and later made a Bishop of an Australian diocese. Another great-uncle was Father Philip Kearns, a parish priest of St. Brigid in Athlone.

She was educated at Sacred Heart Convent, Paris, France, from 1909 to 1911, and at Carshallton House, Carshallton, Surrey, England, 1911 to 1912. Her Uncle Malcolm taught her geography, arithmetic and especially to know and value great men of letters. The convent in Roscommon taught her lace-making, painting and drawing.

After several years in the United States she returned to Paris to continue her studies. But her plan did not materialize because Germany declared war on France, and England declared war on Germany. She therefore, offered her services as a nurse at the clinic of St. Vincente. Compelled to leave this work, she entered the Service as a chauffeur. After the war she again returned to the United States and became a naturalized citizen, in 1917. That same year she married lieutenant colonel Thomas Wadelton. They have one son who is also an author. Since her husband elected to remain in the service of his country her dream of returning to Ireland was not fulfilled. From one army garrison to another she had moved. Her husband died in 1945.

Yet she found time to write. Under the name of Melody she wrote *Shelia* and *Ponobscot Ferry*. Under her own name she wrote *The Book of Maggie Owen* (1941); *Maggie No Doubt* (1943). In the dedication of this latter book, she writes: "Perhaps *Maggie No Doubt* will more fully explain to them (her husband and son) the sometimes unexplainable woman with whom they dwell." *Sarah Mandrake* appeared in 1946.

M. H.

Mary Teresa Waggaman 1846-1931

When Mary T. Waggaman died in 1931, Dr. William J. Kerby eulogized her in these words: "Mrs. Waggaman, in her works of fiction, has truly translated the Gospel of Christ to the hearts of little children." Perhaps no other Catholic story-teller was as well known a generation or two ago. But such is her spell over young minds that most of her books—and she wrote over forty—are still in circulation. Some have been transcribed into Braille and others have been dramatized.

Mrs. Waggaman began writing during her school days. When she was twenty-five years of age one of her poems, "The Legend of the Mistletoe," was the feature article of the Christmas number of *Harper's Magazine*. This success launched Mrs. Waggaman on her professional career. Her desire to write for children began in 1894. When her eldest son was preparing for First Communion, Mrs. Waggaman searched the stores and libraries for some books that would "sugar coat" piety and yet be interesting. Not finding any, she decided to write a story herself. *Little Comrades, A First Communion Story,* was an immediate success. Her daughter writes that it was "an entrancing experience to live in the house with a born story-teller . . . and when she began to write for children, we were her critics." As the young keep older minds perennially keen, Mrs. Waggaman's facile pen never flagged. In 1923, when she was seventy-seven years old, she was the winner of a secular short story contest in which three thousand authors competed. Irving Cobb, one of the judges, paid a high tribute to her talent. Even in her 85th year she was busy on her last book, *The Trevelyn Twins.* Two of Mrs. Waggaman's outstanding books are historical novels about early days in Maryland: *Carroll Dare* (1903) and *The Strong-Arm of Avalon* (1904). The latter is an enthralling tale of a young Catholic cavalier embroiled in the religious and political struggles of the new country. *Buddy* is a boy's tale of World War I, *White Eagle, Carmelita,* and *Billy Boy* are western stories. *The Secret of Pocomoke* deals with the coal mining districts. *Lorimer Light* is a story of the sea. Her books in later years were written with a desire to strengthen the religious faith of young Catholic readers. Her plots prove the wealth of her imagination. Her style is easy and natural.

In a paper she contributed to *The Commonweal* some years ago she wrote: "To the casual reader, juvenile writing may seem light and easy work, and of course it can be made so by writers who feel that it is unnecessary to expend any great effort on stories for children, that almost any simple thing will do. But I have never taken this viewpoint. I can truthfully say that I have given my juvenile readers the best that is in me. And I think that they may have been, in some subtle way, conscious of this sincerity, so warm and sweet and altogether charming have I found their response."

Mrs. Waggaman was born in Baltimore in 1846. Her father, a native of Ireland, joined the gold rush to California in 1849, made a fortune and became a shipbroker in New York. Her mother, Esther (Cottrell) McKee, was the daughter of an Anglican clergyman and died when Mary was six years of age. Upon the death of her mother, Mary was sent to Mount De Sales Convent, Catonsville, Maryland. When the Civil War broke out, her father took her to New York to live in the home of friends. Here Mary spent much of her time in the well filled library to supplement her education. In 1864 she returned to the convent to be valedictorian of her graduation class.

In 1870 she married Dr. Samuel J. Waggaman. They had eleven children. Dr. Waggaman died in 1913. Mrs. Waggaman's death occurred in 1931.

Among her other books are: *Tom's Luck-Pot* (1897); *Little Missy* (1900); *Corinne's Vow* (1902); *Grapes of Thorns* (1917); *The Finding of Tony* (1919); *Barney's Fortune; Ben Regan's Battle; Captain Ted* (1910); *Eric* (1910); *Jerry's Job; Nan Nobody; Sergeant Tim;* and *Shipmates* (1914).

A. M.

Mervyn Wall 1908-

Mervyn Wall, the son of a member of the Irish Bar, was born in Dublin in 1908 and educated at the Jesuit College of Belvedere and at Bonn in Germany where he spent some years of his boyhood. He entered University College, Dublin, in 1925 and graduated from the National University in 1928 with a degree in literature and philosophy. He studied medicine for a year, but found that his tastes did not lie in that direction. Since 1934 he has been in the Irish Civil Service. His first play, "Alarm Among the Clerks," was produced by the Abbey Experimental Theatre, under the auspices of the Abbey Theatre, Dublin, in 1937, and has since been revived. In 1941 a second play, "The Lady in the Twilight," was produced also at the Abbey Theatre but has not yet been published. Other plays of his are "The Wine Flows Over" which made a tour in Ireland in 1944, and "Black Harvest" which was produced in Dublin in the summer of 1944.

His first short story, "They Also Serve—," was published in *Harper's* in June 1940. Since then he has been a regular contributor of short stories to *The Capuchin Annual,* Dublin. He has had a considerable number of stories, critical essays, and autobiographical sketches broadcast in Ireland and America, and has been a contributor of essays and dramatic criticism to various literary and other periodicals since 1935.

His first novel, *The Unfortunate Fursey* (1947), is a mixture of fantasy and satire, depicting a bitter war between hell and the Irish clergy.

He was a founder and director of the University College Dramatic Society, was active in the Dublin Drama League and founded in 1941 a Library of Drama in Dublin. He has been for many years a member of Irish P.E.N. and its Honorary Treasurer since 1943.

W. J. W.

Reverend Edmund A. Walsh, S.J. 1885-

One of the great authorities in the United States on the Russian question is Dr. Edmund A. Walsh. For the past eighteen years he has made a close study of Russian affairs, and has written several books, articles, and pamphlets on the subject. He has lectured on Russia over 2,000 times, having appeared in practically all the leading cities of the United States. His library contains over 3,000 books on foreign affairs, and his office is full of maps, pictures, and posters that betray his interest in the Soviet State.

Reverend Edmund Aloysius Walsh was born in Boston, Massachusetts, on October 10, 1885, and received his education at the Jesuit colleges in that city, in Woodstock, Maryland, and in Pough-keepsie, New York. Then he went abroad and studied in London, Dublin. and Innsbruck, returning in 1920 to receive his Ph.D. from Georgetown University. His mother, with her ready Irish wit, congratulated him with the remark, "You must have been hard to educate, it took so long."

He had been ordained a priest of the Society of Jesus in 1916, and two years later became dean of the College of Arts and Sciences at Georgetown University. Soon after, however, the War Department called him to be a member of a special commission to administer the Student Army Training Corps to supply officers to the army. In 1919 we find him back at Georgetown organizing the School for Foreign Service, of which he became regent, as well as vice-president of the University.

While Father Walsh was at Paray-le-Monial, France, for his tertian-ship in 1921, General William Haskell, who was in charge of the American Relief Administration in Russia, wrote to him frequently, arousing his interest in the work and urging him to lend his aid. The following year Father Walsh was appointed Director General of the Papal Relief Mission, and entered Russia in March 1922. At that time a terrible famine was ravaging the country, threatening twenty-three millions with death by starvation. During the twenty months that Father Walsh was there, he fed the Russian people some twenty-eight million meals, as many as

160,000 a day. In spite of the terrific cold—it was often forty degrees below zero—he travelled to all parts of the country, learning the language and ways of the people while he brought them relief. He established a tuberculosis hospital and an institution for the blind at Moscow.

From 1924 to 1928 Father Walsh visited practically all the states bordering on Russia or affected by the revolution, and his *Fall of the Russian Empire* appeared in 1928. It is a clear and unbiased picture of the outstanding personalities and major events of the revolution. He published *The Last Stand, an Interpretation of the Soviet Five-Year Plan* in 1931. In addition he has written two other books in English, one a discussion of the merchant marine in national economy, *Ships and National Safety* (1934), and the other a prose poem entitled *The Woodcarver of Tyrol* (1935), the brief tragedy of Maria Manzel, who was saved from despair by gazing on the figure of Christ in the unfinished Pietà carved by her husband. He also edited *The History and Nature of International Relations* (1922), a collection of lectures given by eminent scholars at the National Museum at Father Walsh's request.

Although Father Walsh's principal interest has been in Russia, he has accomplished much in other fields. With Dwight Morrow, he assisted in bringing about peace between the Catholic Church and the Mexican government in 1929. In 1931 he made a journey to Bagdad, Iraq, and negotiated an agreement with the government of King Feisal for the establishment of an American College there. He has been decorated for services in the field of international relations by the governments of Spain, Chili, Venezuela, Roumania, Jugo-Slavia, Hungary, Finland and Czechoslovakia. He has crossed the ocean twenty-seven times, and speaks German, Russian, Spanish, and French fluently. In fact, a book of his *Les Principes fondamentaux de la Vie internationale,* was published in Paris in 1936. For five years he served as president of the Catholic Near East Welfare Association, and he is an active member of a dozen learned societies in Washington.

During World War II he was at Georgetown University, which the army had taken over for the duration, teaching future officers in the Foreign Service School. Later he lectured at the Command and General Staff School at Fort Leavenworth and at the Judge Advocate General's School at Ann Arbor. In October 1945 he was in Nuremberg, Germany, serving as adviser on geopolitics to Justice Robert A. Jackson's Council for the Prosecution of Axis War Criminality.

For the past sixteen years, Father Walsh has studied the rise of the German school of geopolitics under Professor Haushofer of the University of Munich. Geopolitics is a science that studies the relation of geography to the development of peoples and states.

S. J. K.

Very Reverend Francis Augustine Walsh, O.S.B.
1884-1938

When the Northeastern Clergy Conference on Negro Welfare met at the Catholic University of America on November 21, 1939, it presented to the University a bronze tablet in memory of the late Very Reverend Francis Walsh, O.S.B., educator and philosopher, who organized the Conference in 1931 and was its first chairman.

This was just one of the varied and many activities in which Father Walsh was interested and labored. He was the director of the Institute of Apologetics at the Catholic University Summer School of 1932, from which grew the Confraternity of Christian Doctrine. He became its director in 1933 and held this position until his death in 1938.

Born in Cincinnati, Ohio, on the Feast of St. Benedict, March 21, 1884, Father Walsh attended St. Charles Borromeo School in that city and then St. Francis Xavier Academy and College receiving his A.B. degree in 1903. He later studied at St. Mary's Seminary, Cincinnati, and the Gregorian University in Rome, Italy. He was ordained to the priesthood in 1907. He received the degree of Doctor of Philosophy from Xavier University, Cincinnati, in 1922.

Following his ordination, Father Walsh served as a curate at St. Andrew's Church, Cincinnati, 1907 to 1908, and at Sacred Heart Church, Dayton, from 1908 to 1911. He was vice-president and professor of philosophy at Mt. St. Mary's Seminary from 1911 to 1922. During World War I his superiors allowed him to enter the army as chaplain. He was assigned to the base hospital at Camp Taylor, Kentucky, during the influenza epidemic of 1918. Later he served at Camp Humphreys and received his discharge at Camp Beauregard. From 1920 to 1923 he was professor of philosophy and ethics at the College of Mt. St. Joseph-on-the-Ohio. From 1921 to 1923 he was professor of philosophy and the philosophy of education at Summit Normal School, Cincinnati, and at the Summer School of Xavier University from 1920 to 1923.

Father Francis Walsh was also Pro-synodal and Synodal Examiner of the Archdiocese of Cincinnati from 1916 to 1923, Censor Librorum from 1920 to 1923, and irremovable rector of St. Andrew's Church, Cincinnati, from 1920 to 1923.

In 1923 he was transferred to the Catholic University of America, where he became associated with a group of scholars who were planning the establishment of a Benedictine monastery near the University, and in that same year he went with them to St. Benedict's Abbey at Fort Augustus, Scotland, to make his novitiate. On their return this group founded St. Anselm's Priory and its members took up their teaching duties at the University. From 1924 until his death he was assistant professor of philosophy at the Catholic University. From 1931 to 1937 he was regent of the, seminary of the University. In 1924 he became professor of ethics at Trinity College.

He also served as chaplain of the Newman Club of Howard University and as chaplain of the Brothers of the Christian Schools at St. John's College in Washington. Father Francis Walsh died at the age of fifty-four. The funeral services were held in the crypt of the National Shrine of the Immaculate Conception.

Among the writings of Father Walsh are *Religion and Liturgy* (1933); *Manual for Seminarists* (1934); *The Priest of God and The World* (1937); *The Missal of Every Day* (written with Fr. Lasance); and *Integral Philosophy* (1937). He was editor of the *Placidian* from 1923 to 1929 and became editor of *New Scholasticism* in 1937.   M. H.

Reverend Gerald Groveland Walsh, S.J. 1892-

Dante is the deepest interest in the literary life of Father Walsh, and he has endeavored to arouse others to his own enthusiasm by articles in numerous periodicals and lectures before many audiences. He even lectured about Dante at Rome— in Latin, before an international assembly.

This American Dantean was born in South Norwalk, Connecticut. His father, Michael Francis Walsh, was a member of a publishing firm that brought out what was once the rather famous *Library of the World's Best Literature*. Gerald Walsh's first years at school, 1898 to 1902, were passed in Hamilton, Ontario. The year 1903 was spent in England with his father as his tutor. Six years at the Boulevard School at Kingston-upon-Hull in Yorkshire followed. "There used to be tremendous competition in an English school in those days because in the last two years the examinations were of a national character, being set and marked by examiners of Oxford and Cambridge. The Royal Geographical Society used to offer a medal to the best candidates in the Junior and Senior examinations in physiography and ordinary geography. My brother and I set a sort of record by getting the two medals not only for the same school, but for the same family." Gerald Walsh took First Class Honors in his four successive examinations, and twice received the nationally awarded Cobden Club Prize for Political Economy. The future editor of *Thought* was the editor of his school magazine.

In 1910 he was supposed to follow his brother to Cambridge. He felt, however, that he had a vocation to the priesthood, and despite his father's opposition, entered the Jesuit novitiate at Roehampton. Fellow-novices were James Brodrick, who was later to be distinguished by his lives of Bellarmine and Canisius, and Thomas Roberts who is now Archbishop of Bombay. The summer of 1912 he spent with the French Jesuits at Canterbury where he perfected his power of handling French with ease.

The next year he repeated Latin, Greek and English under Father Alban Goodier, who was later to be Archbishop of Bombay, and a famous writer of spiritual books. "Then philosophy at Stonyhurst under Michael Maher and John Rickaby. St. Mary's Hall, Stonyhurst, was in those years an international college. Germans like Heuvers who has now a distinguished position in Tokio, and Portuguese like Duaro who became the Provincial in Lisbon, and Belgians like Delannoye, and many others, Irish, French, Italian and Dutch were there." A year was spent at the University of London getting an A.B. degree.

World War I interrupted his Superiors' plans to send him to Oxford. There was a great shortage of qualified teachers so he spent four years in teaching various subjects, but finally went to Oxford in 1921. "Campion Hall at Oxford had an enviable reputation. Men like Martindale and Martin D'Arcy had carried everything before them. The Spiritual Father at Campion Hall was Father Joseph Rickaby, and it fell to my lot to serve his Mass daily for three years. I grew extremely fond of him, but I could never have dreamed that when I returned to America he would send me, as he did, a great parcel of his notes and, above all, his precious spiritual diary. This, some day, I hope to publish." His tutors at Oxford were Mr. Mowat, author of many historical works; Mr. J. H. R. Weaver, editor of the continuation of the *Dictionary of National Biography;* and Mr. J. E. A. Jolliffe, who has written so much on Anglo-Saxon institutions. At Oxford he won the Marquis of Lothian Prize and the Gibbs Scholarship in modern history, and was awarded First Class Honors in his finals.

Four years of theology lay ahead. The first was passed at St. Beuno's College in North Wales, where he had as professors Father Cuthbert Lattey, Father Joyce, well known for his works on logic and on marriage, and Father Henry Davis, the great moral theologian. He returned to the United States and did the last three years at Woodstock College, Maryland. He was ordained at Woodstock in 1926.

He spent the year 1928 to 1929 in Italy and then returned to Woodstock where he remained as professor of history for five years. In 1934 he was called to the Graduate Faculty of Ecclesiastical History in the Gregorian University, Rome. The Italian climate proved too trying and he returned to the United States in 1936. Since then he has been at Fordham University, where he was head of the Department of Italian Studies, and is now graduate professor of medieval history.

Father Walsh began to read translations of Dante as far back as 1913; from them he went to the original and by the time he went to Oxford, Dante was sort of a passion with him. In the history schools he specialized in the Age of Dante and sat at the feet of the great Oxford Dantean, Cesare Foligno. In his four years in Italy he managed to meet many of the Italian Dantean like Busnelli and Pietrobono. He is interested in Dante mainly as an integrally Catholic humanist. "I like him because he is ever so much more than merely a poet."

A contributor to *Thought* almost from its beginning, he later became the associate editor for *History,* and when the review was taken over by Fordham University in 1939 became the editor-in-chief.

Father Walsh's first published article appeared in 1910 in the *West-*

minster Review. While still in England he contributed to the *Month,* and while in Rome to *Gregorianum* and *Studium.* Many of his articles have appeared in *The Catholic Historical Review, The Historical Bulletin, The Modern Schoolman, America* and *Thought.* His first book *The Emperor Charles IV, A Study of Holy Roman Imperialism,* appeared in 1924. He published *Medieval Humanism* in 1942 and *Dante Alighieri, Citizen of Christendom,* in 1946. He is the co-author of *The Catholic Philosophy of History* (1936), and *Faith for Today* (1941). He has also published "bits of verse" here and there.   M. S.

Most Reverend James Anthony Walsh, M.M.
1867-1936

Chiefly remembered as the co-founder of Maryknoll and its first Superior General, the late Bishop James Anthony Walsh, M.M., is known also as the first editor of Maryknoll's magazine, *The Field Afar,* established in 1907. Bishop Walsh was the author of several books and of mission short stories, these latter being written under a pseudonym, "Father John Wakefield." The Bishop's books: *A Modern Martyr* (1907); *In the Homes of Martyrs* (1922); *Thoughts from Modern Martyrs* (1908) (edited and arranged by him), and *Observations in the Orient* (1919) form a representative section of Maryknoll Bookshelf literature. Sympathetic keenness, simplicity, lucid thought, power of observation and wit characterize all of Bishop Walsh's writings.

He was born in Cambridge, Massachusetts, on February 24, 1867, the son of James and Hannah (Shea) Walsh. He was educated in Boston schools, at Boston College, 1881 to 1885; at Harvard University, 1885 to 1886, and at St. John's Seminary, Brighton, Massachusetts, 1886 to 1892, where he was ordained to the priesthood. The first eleven years of his priesthood he spent as curate at St. Patrick's Church, Boston.

From 1903 to 1911 he was director of the Propagation of the Faith in Boston. In 1907 he began, with the assistance of other priests, *The Field Afar,* which later became the official magazine of the Catholic Foreign Mission Society of America.

When the International Eucharistic Congress met at Montreal in 1910, Father Walsh met the Reverend Thomas Frederick Price of Wilmington, North Carolina. They decided to found an American society devoted to missionary work. In 1911 they chose Hawthorne, New York, as their home but later moved to the present property in Ossining which they called Maryknoll. In 1918 four missionaries were sent to South China, with Father Price in charge.

On June 29, 1933, Father Walsh was consecrated Titular Bishop of Siene, Egypt, in the College of the Propaganda in Rome.

Although the Society is only about thirty-five years old, it has had a phenomenal growth. The present (1947) enrollment totals almost nine hundred priests, brothers and students while the Maryknoll Sisters, a separate community though a part of the Maryknoll "family," number almost seven hundred.

Bishop James Anthony Walsh died on April 14, 1936.   J. C.

Most Reverend James Edward Walsh, M.M.
1891-

Eighteen years of mission experience in South China combined with literary skill are the store-houses on which Bishop James Edward Walsh are drawn for the writing of his three published books: *Father McShane of Maryknoll; Mission Manual of the Vicariate of Kongmoon* and *Tales of Xavier* (1946). Bishop Walsh is likewise the author of numerous editorials, essays, and short stories—the subject of the latter being St. Francis Xavier. "Distinctive charm, pithy directness, originality of thought and expression, a very fine appreciation and understanding, characterize Bishop Walsh's individual style as an author," writes Father Considine. The Bishop is the second Superior General of Maryknoll, having been elected to succeed the late Bishop James Anthony Walsh, first Superior General of Maryknoll, in 1936. Nine years previous he had been consecrated bishop, the first missioner to be raised to the episcopate off the Sancian Island on the coast of China where St. Francis Xavier died. When, in 1946, he completed the established term of ten years, he was succeeded by Bishop Raymond E. Lane.

Born at Cumberland, Maryland, on April 30, 1891, the son of William E. and Mary (Concannon) Walsh, he attended St. Patrick's School at the same place and later, Mt. St. Mary's College where he received his A.B. in 1910. He entered as a student at Maryknoll on September 15, 1912, and was ordained on December 7, 1915. From 1916 to 1918 he was director of Maryknoll Preparatory College at Clark's Summit, Pennsylvania. He left for China as one of Maryknoll's first four pioneer missioners on September 8, 1918. *The Catholic World* states: "The Reverend Thomas F. Price, co-founder of the Society, was head of that pioneer band. He died the following year and Father Walsh, then only twenty-eight, was placed in charge. He opened the first Maryknoll missions in South China at Yeung-kong and Loting, and in 1921 started Wuchow which is now a separate Apostolic Prefecture. Three years later he was named Prefect Apostolic of Kongmoon, the first American-born priest to hold such an office in China, and when he was consecrated a Bishop in 1927 he became the first American Bishop in China."

In 1926 he founded the Little Flower Seminary and the Native Congregation of Sisters of the Immaculate Heart of Mary in 1927, both at Kongmoon, South China.

Bishop Walsh has a brother and a cousin in the Society, and three sisters in different religious communities in this country.   J. C.

James J. Walsh 1865-1942

One of New York's most distinguished Catholic laymen, Dr. James J. Walsh, whose versatility was exercised in the medical profession, on the lecture platform, and in the writing of books, in each of which he won a solid reputation, died February 28, 1942.

Born at Archbald, Pennsylvania, in 1865, the son of Martin and Bridget (Golden) Walsh, he received his early schooling in one of the little country schools where all the grades were taught in one room. At the age of twelve he went to the parochial school of the Sisters of Mercy in Wilkes-Barre. He did his high school work at St. John's College, now Fordham University. He graduated with honors from Fordham University at the age of nineteen and remained there for a year teaching and studying for his Master's Degree. Entering the Jesuit order in 1885 he remained there for six years until poor health obliged him to return to secular life. Upon the restoration of his health, he studied at the medical school of the University of Pennsylvania, where in 1895 he was graduated, following this with postgraduate work in Paris, in bacteriology at the Pasteur Institute, and in neurology at the Saltpêtrière. From there he went on to Vienna, devoting himself particularly to pathology and to the study of autopsies for which such magnificent opportunities were offered by the university. In 1897 he attended the International Medical Congress in Russia, acting as correspondent for the American medical journals.

Upon his return to the United States he practiced medicine in New York City, acting also as instructor and then adjunct professor at the New York Polyclinic School for Graduates. From 1905 to 1913 he was a professor at the Fordham University Medical School and from 1906 he taught physiological psychology at Cathedral College.

Meanwhile he had begun to lecture extensively, his vast fund of varied information and his genial personality making him a notable success on the platform. And as though these activities did not suffice, he had begun to write his long series of books. In 1915 he married. He was the father of two children.

The list of his books includes: *The Popes and Science* (1908); *Education; How Old the New* (1911); *The Thirteenth the Greatest of Centuries* (1913); *Success in a New Era* (1919); *Health Through Will Power* (1920); *What Civilization Owes to Italy* (1923); *The World's Debt to the Catholic Church* (1924); *The World's Debt to the Irish* (1926); *These Splendid Priests* (1926); *These Spendid Sisters* (1926); *Our American*

Cardinals (1926); *Laughter and Health* (1927); *The Church and Healing* (1928); *Mother Alphonsa* (1930); *A Golden Treasury of Medieval Literature* (1931); *American Jesuits* (1934); *High Points of Medieval Culture* (1937). He is also the co-author of several works not mentioned here and has contributed to magazines a countless number of articles in the fields of medicine, apologetics, history and literature. During his life he published more than fifty books.

In addition to everything else he served as a trustee of the Carnegie Church Peace Union, the Catholic Summer School of America, the Catholic Institution for the Blind, and The College of New Rochelle, and as a member of the board of the Catholic Book Club. As will be seen from the titles listed above, Dr. Walsh addressed himself to the general public rather than to specialists, his aim being to make known Catholic contributions to science, education and philosophy. But to do this he did much solid research, and his findings have been presented in an eminently readable style. Especially in the case of medicine he wrote with authority.

His services had been recognized by the Holy See by his inclusion among the Knights Commanders of the Papal Order of St. Gregory and the Knights of Malta.

Of all his books the one best known is *The Thirteenth the Greatest of Centuries.* Dr. Walsh's book has gone into ten editions, a special large edition being issued by the Knights of Columbus, and following its publication, he was more in demand than ever as a lecturer. The closing of the Fordham Medical School, occurring about this time, left him more free for this work. During the troubles in Mexico, he often made speeches setting forth the true state of affairs in that country. In fact, there have been few aspects of Catholic Action in which he has not taken his part.

Dr. Walsh established the Fordham University Press.

During his long illness he examplified his thoroughly Catholic attitude by giving every sign of fortitude, patience, and resignation to the Divine Will.

Louis J. Walsh 1880-1942

"All my life I have loved and yearned for the mountains and wished to wander over them as it pleased me without thought of time or tide." Thus begins chapter one of Louis J. Walsh's book *On My Keeping and in Theirs,* his book of prison memories.

His day dream came true when in 1920 the English Parliament met, determined to quell the clamor in Ireland for freedom. "And they did me the honour," wrote Mr. Walsh, "of thinking that Ireland would not be finally conquered whilst even poor, insignificant I was left to bleat my pettifogging plea for Irish freedom. So their soldiers raided my office that morning, and I, having been informed of what was taking place and realizing what it all meant, felt myself at last free to turn, without any qualms of conscience for my unfulfilled tasks, to the hills I loved." There he met hospitality at every door. Later when he was arrested, a crowd gathered "and I got the greeting and send-off that the big hearts of our common people love to bestow on everyone who is privileged to suffer for Ireland." From December 1920 to May 1921, he was interned as a political suspect at Ballykinlar Camp.

Mr. Louis Walsh was born in Maghera County, Derry, Ireland, in 1880. He was educated at St. Columb's College, Derry, and the University College, Dublin, from which institution he received his A.B. in 1902. He became a solicitor in 1905, practicing in Armagh and Derry. Appointed a district judge in 1922, he had been the first magistrate to conduct courts in County Donegal since the Ulster Plantation. He was the first magistrate to conduct his courts in Irish and to state a case for the High Court entirely in Irish.

In 1908 he married Mary McKenna. They had two sons and five daughters.

Mr. Walsh was a writer and lecturer on Ulster rural life. He is author of: *Yarns of a Country Attorney* (1917); *The Next Time* (1919); *Twilight Reveries; Our Own Wee Town* (1929); *Old Friends; Life of John Mitchel; The Pope in Killybuck* (a satire on Ulster Orange bigotry); *Nothing In His Life; The Guileless Saxon; The Deposit Receipt,* and *The Grand Audit Night.*

He died in 1942.

M. H.

Maurice Walsh 1879-

Reminiscent of William Carleton's sketches of nineteenth century Irish life, and of James Stephens' *Crock of Gold,* are the sketches and novels of Maurice Walsh in their "astonishing understanding of the Gael." Mr. Walsh was born at Ballydonohue, County Kerry, Ireland, on May 2, 1879, "the son and the grandson and the great-great grandson of farmers and rebels," as he puts it. His father was John Walsh, a farmer and land-leaguer; his mother, Elizabeth (Buckley) Walsh.

He worked on the farm until well in his teens and during this time began writing short stories which were published in the weekly *Freeman,* a Dublin paper. "I wrote," he confesses, "about Australian bushranging and Klondike gold digging and the Boer War, and other subjects with which I was closely acquainted at a distance."

Mr. Walsh received his early education at Lisselton, Ballybunion, and later at St. Michael's College in Listowel. At the age of twenty-one, to satisfy his mother's wish, he took the British Civil Service Examination at Dublin, entering the Customs Excise Service in 1901. As customs officer, he traveled widely in Ireland, Scotland, Wales and England, learning "the vagaries of human nature, and the contours of the Highlands of Scotland," and receiving that wealth of impressions which was to crystallize later in a series of romantic novels and sketches.

"He learned how beer was brewed in breweries; he worked in tobacco factories; and with rod and rule in the wine-fragrant vaults of bonded warehouses, performed the mysteries of gauging; and often roved the countryside on excise-license work. But it was mostly in distilleries of the Scottish Highlands that Maurice Walsh spent the earlier years of his service."

In 1908 he married Caroline I. J. Begg of Dufftown, Banffshire, whom he describes as "Scotch, red-haired, and having a temperament." His first book, *Eudmon Blake,* appeared in 1909, but it was not until 1923, when he published *The Key Above the Door,* that his literary reputation was established. Returning to serve his own country after the Irish Treaty, Mr. Walsh found an Ireland torn by civil war. In trying to "recapture the atmosphere of the Highlands and shut out the restlessness of Dublin," he wrote a romance of the outdoors in which the charm of the Scottish countryside vies in interest with the plot—primitive conflict engaging "three sophisticated moderns."

Introduced to the *Saturday Evening Post* by Eugene Manlove Rhodes, the New Mexican cowboy who was also a contributor to the *Post,* Mr. Walsh began publishing the "Thomasheen James" sketches, to the chuckling delight of American readers. In telling of the origin of his character, Mr. Walsh says, "My Thomasheen James, man-of-no-work, turned up out of nowhere like the Ancient Mariner. I was on top of the summer house nailing a board, and the hammer slipped and fell out. A bony freckled fist appeared over the edge with a hammer in it. 'Lucky me skull was hard,' said Thomasheen James. I had never seen him before. The look in his eye held me, and his method of manipulating language. In no time at all I was in his spider's web."

Other books by Mr. Walsh are: *While Rivers Run* (1926), a love story of Scotland; *The Small Dark Man* (1929), a romantic tale of Ireland; *Blackcock's Feather* (1932), "a story of rapiers, fine fellows, and bold ventures" having for its setting 16th century Ireland in its struggle against Queen Elizabeth; *The Road to Nowhere* (1934); *Green Rushes* (1935); *And No Quarter* (1937); *Sons of the Swordmaker* (1938); *The Dark Rose* (1938); *The Hill Is Mine* (1940), an old Irish folk story retold; *Thomasheen James, Man-of-no-work* (1941) collected sketches; *The Spanish Lady* (1943); *Nine Strings To Your Bow* (1945).

In 1938 Mr. Walsh was president of the Irish P.E.N. In appearance he is described as robust, below medium height with a shock of iron-grey hair and a weather-beaten countenance, and of unusual vitality. Retired from the Irish Free State Service now, he lives outside of Dublin where, "I write a little, shoot a little, fish a little, garden a lot, and go on talking." He has three sons, one a doctor, one a banker, one a medical student, and two grandsons.

T. V.

Michael Walsh   1897-1938

Among the many poets Ireland has given to the world, the late Michael Walsh holds no mean place. His poems manifest the profound influence on his life of his much loved mother's religious instruction. He was always deeply but unobtrusively pious and this piety influenced much of his writing. He is typical of the cultured Catholic layman dreaming at first of the priesthood but abandoning the thought when his health broke down while at the Apostolic School of Mungret. His devoted friend, Father Joseph McDonnell, S.J., editor of the *Irish Messenger of the Sacred Heart,* explained to him that his delicate health made such a life impractical and that his gift for writing so well on devotional subjects fitted him for Catholic journalism.

The wide extent of his literary contributions is shown by such magazines as the *Irish Monthly, Irish Rosary, The Irish Catholic, The Standard, The Leader, Cork Examiner, Westmeath Examiner, Irish Press, Irish Independent,* and other periodicals. When Michael was about twelve years of age, he won first prize for his first published poem "A Welcome to Summer" in the *Irish Catholic.*

Born in 1897 at Ben-of-Fore in the heart of the beautiful lake country of North Westmeath, Walsh was deeply influenced by the loveliness of his surroundings and found in this enchanting countryside the inspiration for most of his poems and essays. Fore is an historic spot rich in the folklore of centuries and hallowed by religious association of more than a thousand years. He himself tells us in his autobiography: "These remain still at the root of my poetry: the reeds in the bog, summer coming in clouds of white daisies to the sloping fields at the back of the house, and the Hill of Ben itself like some eternal symbol amid the suns and mist of change."

His mother's death and the consequent break-up of the family life permanently saddened him and is responsible for the note of melancholy so characteristic of many of his poems. His father's influence on the boy was deep and abiding and to him was dedicated Michael's first book of poems *Brown Earth and Green.* In his wife, a Wexford school teacher and also a writer, Walsh found an ideal mate. For twelve years of happy married life he wrote incessantly despite his trials and ill-health. His keen sense of humor, his domestic happiness, books and a few chosen friends made his earthly paradise. The Catholic religion in all its aspects was very often discussed at his fireside. His family was brought up in the true Irish and Catholic tradition and the family rosary never omitted. His inward life of communion with God was intense and he gave alms regularly out of his scanty means. When his death occurred on December 1, 1938, at the early age of forty-one, Ireland mourned a devoted son and gifted poet.

His other books are: *Heart Remembers Morning* (1931), and *Red on the Holly* (1934).   A. Mu & M. H.

William Thomas Walsh 1891-

Probably no Catholic American author has had so instantaneous a success with his non-Catholic public as William Thomas Walsh, says Frank Sheed. Born in 1891 in Waterbury, Connecticut, he was educated in his own state, has an A.B. (1913) from Yale and an honorary Litt.D. from Fordham (1933). He taught one year in a Hartford public high school, and directed the English department of Roxbury School, Cheshire, Connecticut for fourteen years. Since 1933, he has been professor of English at Manhattanville College of the Sacred Heart. This varied teaching experience, and his newspaper reporting during World War I, account for what the critics call his "swift, pliant, vivid, vigorous style."

His literary efforts, particularly in the field of historical research with a Spanish background, are extremely readable. The London *Times* regards *Philip II* (1937) with its vast and fascinating theme, more gripping than fiction. The New York *Times* says his *"Philip II* is so thoroughly documented that it must stand as a calm and realistic portrayal of a man and an era, often more exciting to the imagination than fiction, while the suavity of his impeccable literary style offers constant delight." *Isabella of Spain* (1930), a picturesque biography, was published in French in 1932, and subsequently in German and Spanish translations. The book was a great success in Spain just before and during the Civil War. The publishers, Espasa Calpe, are bringing out *Philip II* in Spanish at Buenos Aires and his *Characters of the Inquisition* at Madrid. His latest biography is a *Life of St. Teresa of Avila* (1942), a choice of the Catholic Book Club.

His prize-winning short story, "Gold;" his thoroughly Catholic novel, *Out of the Whirlwind* (1935); the blank-verse play *Shekels* (1937); *Lyric Poems* (1939), and *Characters of the Inquisition* (1940), attest his versatility. The novel *Out of the Whirlwind* has appeared in London, Holland and Hungary as well as in New York. The Dutch translation was published just before the invasion of Holland. A poetical play on the Carmelite martyrs of Compiegne is in preparation. This Laetare Medalist of 1941 is an "enemy of corroding ease."

In 1914 he married Helen Gerard Sherwood of Derby, Connecticut. One of his six children is a Sister of Mercy, Sister Mary Concepta at the Sacred Heart Convent, Belmont, North Carolina.

On October 28, 1944, in a double ceremony, Dr. Walsh was awarded the highest cultural honor given by Spain when he received the Cross of Comendador of the Civil Order of Alfonso the Wise and the 1944 Catholic Literary Award of the Gallery of Living Catholic Authors. In conferring the award of his government, the Spanish Ambassador, Senor Don Juan Francisco de Cardenas, remarked that for the first time the recipient of the honor was a North American writer. "When the

State Department forwarded me the official notification from Madrid," says Dr. Walsh, "I asked if there was any reason why a loyal citizen of the United States should not accept this honor. The State Department offering no objection, I then wrote the Minister of Education my acceptance. I was glad to further, even in this small way, the friendly relations of our country with all the Spanish nations."   S. M.

Barbara Ward 1914-

To Americans, Miss Barbara Ward is better known as a lecturer than as an author. Coming to America on her first visit in the latter part of 1942, she lectured on "The Sword of the Spirit," "Democracy and Christianity in Britain," "Christian Voice of Europe" and "The New Economics and Catholic Teaching." Miss Ward also gave an address over the NBC network on October 20, 1942. In 1947, under the auspices of the *Economist,* for which she is to do a series of articles on the trends of the United States, she made her second visit to the United States. Of medium height, with brown hair, brown eyes and unaffected smile and manner, and rather slender build, Miss Ward is a vivacious speaker. In 1944 a well-known Poll rated her second in popularity among the nation's public speakers. She asserts she has "a horrible facility with words." She has an attractive radio personality but had to give up broadcasting when she went on the BBC's Board of Governors in 1946.

To Britons, Barbara Ward is best known for her part on the British Broadcasting Company's Brain Trust program—the equivalent of the Information Please program in America. She can hold her own with the males on the program.

Barbara Ward was born at York, England, in 1914, the daughter of Walter and Teresa Mary Ward. She was educated at the Convent of Jesus and Mary in her native Felixstowe and also in Dresden, the Lycée "Moliere," Paris and Somerville College, Oxford. From 1936 to 1939, she was a University Extension Lecturer on international affairs. Though she wanted to become a singer she studied international economics at Somerville College and took first-class honors in philosophy, politics and economics—the only woman to do so in her year—and decided economics was more interesting than singing. She had the distinction of being the first woman to deliver one of the Dallas lectures to the Glasgow Junior Chamber of Commerce.

In October 1943 A. C. F. Beales, joint secretary of "The Sword of the Spirit" Movement in England, an organization for international peace and social justice, paid tribute to her upon her retirement as co-secretary, having served the maximum period of three years in office. He described her work as "that which no one but herself, with her particular gifts and talents could have done."

In 1938 Miss Ward wrote her first book, *The International Shareout,* which dealt with the colonial problem. Since that time she has written *Turkey* and is co-author of *Hitler's Route to Bagdad* and *Christian Basis for Construction.* She wrote two pamphlets—*Russian Foreign Policy* and *Italian Foreign Policy.* She has been an assistant editor of the London *Economist* and the *Dublin Review* since 1939. Miss Ward lives in a London flat by herself. Her hobby is music. M. H.

Josephine Mary Ward 1864-1932

The well-known English Catholic novelist, Josephine Mary Ward, was born in 1864, the second daughter of James Robert Hope Scott of Abbotsford, Scotland, by his second wife, Lady Victoria Howard, daughter of Henry Granville, the fourteenth Duke of Norfolk. James Hope had married first the granddaughter of Sir Walter Scott and changed his own name to Hope-Scott, but the children of his second marriage reverted to the original "Hope." Josephine's maternal grandmother was the austere Duchess of Norfolk, and from childhood she heard of the Oxford Movement, the spirit of which was to be the inspiration of her life. In 1887 she married Wilfrid Ward, son of William George Ward, first of the Oxford Movement converts, for he preceded Newman into the Church by a year. She and her husband were of the Transition Period, 1870 to 1920, within which the Catholic Church in England renewed contact with the outside world. Of this period Wilfrid Ward was the historian and philosopher.

The literary great who formed their circle are intimately portrayed in *The Wilfrid Wards and the Transition,* written by their daughter, Maisie. There we read of ideas in conflict and the personages who waged the battle. She tells of Wilfrid Ward's walks with Huxley and Tennyson —the latter caught in an off-guard moment, saying, "Stop up your ears, Josephine Ward, I am about to tell your husband an improper story"— of the correspondence of Ward with Baron Von Hugel and with Lord Halifax; the meetings of the Synthetic Society frequented by diverse personalities such as Oliver Lodge, Bishop Gore and Father Tyrrell, of the intimacy with Newman and Manning; and Cardinal Newman enduring the puns of Mrs. Ward's father, Hope-Scott, and endeavoring without success to give an impromptu speech. These were the friends of Josephine Mary Ward.

She was one of the literati who surrounded her, and is recognized as "the first really considerable and significant English Catholic novelist." Her first book, *One Poor Scruple,* was published in 1899. Then at intervals of two or three years she wrote: *The Light Behind; Out of Due Time; Great Possessions; The Job Secretary,* and *Horace Blake.* After her husband's death in 1916 there was an interim before she published *Not Known Here* (1920). This was followed by *The Plague of his Own*

Heart in 1925 and *The Shadow of Mussolini* in 1927. Her last book *Tudor Sunset* deals with the Elizabethan persecution and was published the year of her death. The manuscript is preserved in The Gallery of Living Catholic Authors, Webster Groves, Missouri, of which Mrs. Ward is a member. Some of her novels appeared in the *Catholic Times* and the *Catholic Fireside*. All are marked by a vigorous Catholicity and a love and understanding of human nature.

In her later years, Mrs. Wilfrid Ward became a member of the Catholic Evidence Guild and in behalf of the Faith spoke from street-corner platforms. She made her home in London and died there, in a nursing home, after an operation, in November 1932.   C. M. N.

Reverend Leo Richard Ward, C.S.C. 1893-

Gaunt, over six foot in height, with a strikingly ascetic face, a philosopher who is a farmer with roots fixed deeply in the soil, a scholar of European education who has retained strong human sympathies for rural people and rural living as a way of life—so is Father Leo Richard Ward, assistant professor of philosophy at Notre Dame University, described by his friends.

Father Ward, considered an authority on scholastic philosophy, has written two volumes to explain the Catholic viewpoint on philosophical problems, in a style that makes the thought accessible to the lay reader. His books on philosophy are: *Philosophy of Value* (1930), and *Value and Reality* (1935), "concerned with the application of the ethical principles of Plato and St. Thomas to modern problems and their contacts with the ideas of modern American philosophers." He is also the author of numerous articles for magazines on such subjects as: "The Content of a Philosophy of Value," "The New Humanism and Standards," "Search for a Usable Concept of Value," and "Faith of a Philosopher." Others of his books are: *God in an Irish Kitchen* (1930), depicting the "social life and religion of the Irish peasants, especially those of the Galway coast"; *Holding Up the Hills,* characterized as his "most autobiographical book," which grew out of his experiences with rural life and people when he was a boy; and *Nova Scotia: Land of Co-operatives* (1942). He tells what he saw when he "traversed the Maritimes, talked in kitchens and fisher huts, seeing the dyeing, spinning, and weaving of rugs in a family, learning how houses were built, how study clubs were organized." *Ourselves, Inc.,* was published in 1945.

Telling of his youth, he writes, "I was brought up on the land, in a close-knit family of five boys and two girls in a neighborhood that was very much a community. Everything was, of course, known to everybody, and young and old played together and worked together and worshipped together. In other words, we had an organic life and a totally organic community. . . . A priest set up a Catholic library of six hundred books which was surely and is surely a rare institution in a country parish."— This rural community into which he was born was Melrose, Iowa, which state was likewise the birthplace of his mother Catherine (Morrison) Ward and his father Richard M. Ward.

His high school and college education was obtained at Notre Dame University from which he received the B.A. Degree in 1923. Higher degrees he obtained in quick succession—a Ph.M. from Catholic University in 1927, and a Ph.D. in 1929. In 1934 and 1935 he studied at Oxford University, England, and in 1935 and 1936 at the University of Louvain, Belgium. Since 1928 Father Ward has been a teacher of philosophy at Notre Dame.

It is to certain of the men at Notre Dame that he attributes the encouragement for writing which he received when he was in the seminary there. Among these were Father Charles O'Donnell, C.S.C., and George N. Shuster, one of his teachers. "Trying to write," he confesses, "gives me a special delight, once I get well started at any piece. But the starting is a trial and is always painful."

To bring to the Catholic lay person the essence of Catholic philosophy, to apply it to modern problems of living—and this in a language understandable to him—is one of the finest achievements a teacher could accomplish. This Father Ward has done.   T. V.

Maisie Ward (Mrs. Francis Joseph Sheed)
1889-

A rich literary heritage and life-long association with the intellectuals have admirably equipped Maisie Ward Sheed as a writer, lecturer and publisher. She was born in Shanklin, Isle of Wight, England, the eldest daughter of Wilfrid Ward, philosopher of the Catholic intellectual revival in England and biographer of its leaders, and of Josephine Ward, novelist. Her grandfather first married Sir Walter Scott's granddaughter, and afterwards Lady Victoria Howard, mother of Josephine Hope, whose childhood was spent at Abbotsford. Josephine Hope became Mrs. Wilfrid Ward, mother of Maisie Ward, who grew up among the literati of the early twentieth century and as secretary to her father came in contact with the leaders of European Catholic thought. In 1926 she married Francis Sheed, then interested in the Catholic Evidence Guild, as she was also. She spoke from outdoor platforms and edited *Catholic Evidence Training Outlines,* an important handbook in this form of Catholic apologetics. She also edited *The English Way.*

Mr. and Mrs. Sheed decided to establish a publishing house for the growing output of Catholic letters, and this they did in 1926 when they opened the London office of Sheed & Ward. Encouraged to expand their activities, they opened a New York office in 1933. Frequent transatlantic trips were made by both of them, and in 1940 she with their son and daughter took up their residence in the United States. Mr. Sheed travels back and forth between the United States and England.

In addition to fulfilling her duties as vice-president of the publishing firm, Maisie Ward has lectured throughout the country, having appeared in some seventy cities of England and America, and she also continues her Guild work, being chairman of the Practical Training Committee of the Catholic Evidence Guild. She has written three biographies, *St. Bernardino: The People's Preacher; Fr. Maturin: A Memoir;* and *Gilbert Keith Chesterton* (1943); the important biographic-historical works, *The Wilfrid Wards and the Transition,* and *Insurrection versus Resurrection;* and a book on England in wartime, *This Burning Heat,* made up of letters from those under enemy fire in the British Isles. Her royalties from the last she divides between the work in England of the Grail and the Catholic Worker. In both these movements Mrs. Sheed is actively interested, and the book portrays the great opportunity the Church now has through these and other forms of Catholic Action to reach all those suffering the tragedy of war. In 1945 she brought out *The Splendor of the Rosary.*

The years 1870 to 1920 are covered by Maisie Ward, under which name she writes, in her two books on English Catholic thought and letters in that period. In the first volume on *The Wilfrid Wards* she tells of the intellectuals of the late nineteenth century, with a great deal of personal anecdote that enhances the interest and value of the book. In the second volume, beginning with the twentieth century, her main theme is "The Modernist movement set against the Catholic Intellectual Revival," hence the title, *Insurrection versus Resurrection* and again she gives sidelights on outstanding characters. They form a valuable record of people and events strongly affecting English Catholicism.

She is a frequent contributor to Catholic periodicals.   C. M. N.

Mrs. Wilfrid Ward   *see* Josephine Ward

Edward Ingram Watkin   1888-

Truth has been always the objective of E. I. Watkin, and his books convey his thoughts and convictions. He was born at Stand, near Manchester, England, in 1888, the son of Edgar and Emmeline (Ingram) Watkin, and was educated at St. Paul's School, London, and at New College, Oxford, where he received his M.A. While studying at Oxford he became convinced that Christ had established one Church undivided, which the Anglican Church did not even claim to be, and he was received into the Catholic Church at Stratton-on-the-Fosse in 1908. "For me," he writes, "Catholicism has been the fulfillment of all I learned and prized as an Anglican," and to the Church of England he says he owes "an appreciation of liturgical worship and prayer which has enabled me to find treasures in the Catholic liturgy I might otherwise have failed to discover."

In 1913 he married Helena, daughter of Philip C. Shepheard, J.P., of Abbot's Hall, Aylsham, Norfolk. They have a son and four daughters and live quietly in the country. The son is a Benedictine monk of Downside Abbey. One of the daughters married a convert to the Church in 1942. Edward Ingram Watkin writes his books in the country and enjoys the wild plants which are one of his hobbies. Church architecture is also of especial interest to him.

The book which Watkin regards as his most personal thought, the expression of that which he desires most to say, is *The Philosophy of Form.* There he seeks "to reconcile the view that truth is attained by intuition and the view that it is attained by reasoning, by showing that all thought is intuition or the discrimination of intuitions, the sole difference being between abstract and clear intuitions, of which the most perfect example is the quantitative apprehensions of the sciences and the dimmer and more concrete intuitions such as the aesthetic." His own thought, he says, "naturally works by short flashes such as would find expression in a 'penséé' rather than a sustained train of reasoning."

He has been influenced by the philosophy of Wust and that of Lossky, though he recognizes the latter's tendency to extravagances that must be discounted. To Christopher Dawson, with whom he has had a personal friendship and association for many years, he acknowledges a profound intellectual debt though their fields of work are different. At Oxford, when he first became a Catholic, he knew the late Father Joseph Rickaby, S.J., whose spirituality and depth and originality of thought he greatly admires, and to which he feels due recognition is not given. From Father Rickaby he learned, among much else, the fundamental Catholic truth of the Mystical Body of Christ, which deeply impressed him and was then strangely neglected by Catholics.

His present thought, Watkin says, is "dominated by the passionate realization that the world is now the stage of a conflict between those who genuinely believe in a Divine Creator and those who avowedly or implicitly deify man, especially some social group, state, race or class. In this battle the Church with her fulness of truth should be our leader." He believes that if the Catholic Church is to exercise her full power today, it must be seen and presented "more organically and more inwardly." He advocates instead of so much learning of catechetical formulas that children be educated in the liturgy and brought to enter into its life." Herein, he claims, lies the remedy for leakage from the Church. It was to present this standpoint that he wrote *The Catholic Centre.* In contemplative prayer based upon the liturgy he envisions a renewal of Catholic life in the face of an increasingly godless world.

In the Essays in Order series Watkin has written *The Bow in the Clouds.* He also contributed two essays to *God and the Supernatural,* edited by Father Cuthbert, O.S.F.C., and two essays to *The English Way,* edited by Maisie Ward. *Men and Tendencies* are essays on H. G. Wells, Galsworthy, Havelock Ellis, Aldous Huxley, J. B. Haldane, Santayana,

Karl Marx. He sees the hidden points of agreement with these men, with whom he disagrees, and ably sums up the case as would a judge rather than a litigant. Other works by him are: *Some Thoughts on Catholic Apologetics; The Philosophy of Mysticism; Theism, Atheism and Agnosticism;* and *An Essay on Catholic Art and Culture.* In this book, Watkin traces the rise and fall of the Catholic Religion Culture which was Christendom. He puts forward the idea of a Catholic humanism, theocentric and integral, combining the vertical movement towards God and the horizontal movement towards man and other creatures, detachment with appreciation, and realized by a Church of contemplatives.

Another book published in the United States is *The Praise of Glory,* a devotional commentary on Lauds and Vespers. A book of verse entitled *Poplar Leaves,* and *A Little Book of Comfort in Time of War,* were written during the first World War. His books: *The Balance of Truth,* and *Catholic Art and Culture* appeared in 1944.   C. M. N.

Reverend Lewis Watt, S.J.   1885-

Father Lewis Watt, S.J., was born in the industrial town of West Hartlepool in the northeast of England, the eldest son of G. A. Watt, L.D.S. He began his education at a preparatory school at the age of four. A few years later, he was transferred to a private day-school for boys, and later to a boarding school. When nearly seventeen, he entered a solicitor's office to begin his studies for the profession of solicitor. He qualified when he was twenty-one years old but practised only about two years.

About this time he became very much interested in various religions. He was discontented with the "vague Anglicanism" in which he had been brought up. One day, in a shop window, he saw a little book by Faá di Bruno, *Catholic Belief.* He bought it and read it. It convinced him completely. He was received into the Catholic Church on November 1, 1906. This step caused great sorrow to his parents. Haunted by the idea that he ought to become a religious, he sought the advice of his Carmelite confessor. After long thought, he applied and was accepted by the Provincial of the Society of Jesus and entered the Noviceship in 1908 at the cost of still further pain to his family. In 1910 he began his course in philosophy. Feeling that he would like to take on some extra work, he consulted Father Michael Maher, S.J., his Superior. Father Maher suggested he should study social economics in his spare time. "I began this," writes Father Watt, "and as I went on became conscious of a growing sense of indignation at the injustices inflicted on the British workers during the nineteenth century, and I should like to say here that without some emotional stimulus I should have found it difficult to persevere with a subject which seemed dry indeed."

Father Watt was sent to the London School of Economics (University of London), and secured the degree B.Sc. (Econ.). After the usual four years' course of theology, he went to Louvain to the Jesuit College to spend two years in the study of moral philosophy there and at Paris. He was ordained a priest in 1920. In 1923 he became professor of moral philosophy, first at Stonyhurst and later at Heythrop College, when this was opened by the Society as a Collegium Maximum in 1926. He also taught history of philosophy for about five years.

Under the aegis of or in connection with the Catholic Social Guild and its associated Catholic Workers' College, Father Watt lectured in various towns in Great Britain and Ireland. He gave a course of lectures at practically every one of the Catholic Social Guilds' Summer Schools, at which visitors from the United States frequently attended.

In order to give him more time to devote to social economics, Father Watt was set free from the duties of teaching ethics at Heythrop in 1937 and was sent to Campion Hall, Oxford, a constituent part of the University. There he gives public lectures on Catholic social teaching, which are attended by non-Catholic as well as Catholic undergraduates.

Father Watt is the author of: *Capitalism and Morality; Catholic Social Principles; The Future of Capitalism; Pope Pius XII on World Order,* and a booklet on *Quadragesimo Anno,* as well as some pamphlets on similar topics published by the Catholic Social Guild.   M. H.

Evelyn Waugh 1903-

That Evelyn Waugh became a writer is not remarkable when one remembers that he came of a literary family, his father being Arthur Waugh, the critic and publisher, and his brother Alec Waugh, a novelist who wrote a best-selling novel while hardly more than a boy. Evelyn himself produced at the age of seven a five-hundred-word novel in nine chapters. It was entitled *The Curse of the Horse Race.*

Born in 1903 at London, and educated at Lancing School and Oxford, he was successively a student of painting, a schoolmaster and a journalist before beginning his literary career. This was with a life of Rossetti, which hardly indicated his future course. But the same year (1928) saw the publication of his first novel, the amazing *Decline and Fall,* which was followed in rapid succession by *Vile Bodies, Black Mischief, A Handful of Dust,* and *Scoop.* This last came out of his experience as a war-correspondent in Ethiopia. As might be expected from Waugh, it is savagely and at the same time light-heartedly satirical.

Already he had written a novel about Ethiopia, his *Black Mischief,* a fantasia on an Abyssinian theme. And works that are nearer to being travel books are: *Labels, a Mediterranean Journal* (published in America as *A Bachelor Abroad*); *Remote People* (relabelled here *They Were Still*

Dancing), and *Ninety-two Days.* In 1939 he published his *Mexico: An Object Lesson.* All of these are marked by a fine sense of style which is sometimes overlooked by those who enjoy them for their hilarious and somewhat "pixilated" humor.

Most of Evelyn Waugh's writing has been done since he became a Catholic in 1930. His road to the Church was a somewhat surprising one, judging from his novel *Vile Bodies,* which would be a horrifying account of the smart upper-class English set just after the war, were it not so amusing and also so full of profound implications.

There is in Waugh little of that slow acrid disgust that is in Aldous Huxley's treatment of a similar scene. Instead the antics of his bright young people are seen as a pure—well, perhaps hardly "pure"—fount of absurdity. But Evelyn Waugh perceives the underlying tragedy of these lives and indicated it again in *A Handful of Dust,* a novel which made Alexander Wollcott say that he was "the nearest thing to a genius among the young writers who have arisen in post-war England." Though the opinion—as was commonly the case with those vented by Mr. Wollcott—may be excessive, there can be no doubt that Waugh is at least one of the cleverest of contemporary writers. Though he lacks the "saeva indignatio" of Swift and of all really great satirists, this very fact makes him all the more readable and entertaining.

But that his mind is fundamentally serious is abundantly proved by the books themselves, and still more by the fact of his acceptance of the Catholic Faith. If an explicit statement of his religious beliefs is wanted it may be found in his little book on *Edmund Campion,* the Jesuit martyr of Elizabeth's time. It was deservedly crowned with the Hawthornden prize. Though he disclaims making any attempt at fresh research and confessedly bases himself upon Simpson's monumental study, he has exhibited the charming and heroic Campion in sharper lines and brighter colors than have been found before. And a strong, supple, noble prose gives it such distinction as to place the book among the half-dozen best Catholic biographies of our time. Here he turns from flies in amber to a saint enaureoled, but a saint whose lineaments have nothing of the stiff conventionality of the older school of hagiography. The book is dedicated to Father Martin D'Arcy, S.J., provincial of the Society of Jesus in England, who received him into the Catholic Church in 1930. When, in 1947, the Very Reverend Francis X. Talbot, S.J., the new president of Loyola College, Baltimore, awarded an honorary degree to Waugh, it was accepted on Mr. Waugh's behalf by Father D'Arcy.

In February 1940 he wrote of himself, "I am proud to say that I have ceased to be a writer and am now a second lieutenant in the Royal Marines. Any information about my previous career which I wish to make public, may be found in the ordinary English works of reference—'Who's Who' and 'Kelly's Handbook of the Titled, Landed and Official Classes.'" *Life* magazine for November 17, 1941, published an article by Evelyn Waugh on the work of the Commandos of which he was a member, with the rank of major. (They were small bands of specially trained volunteers who raided Axis-held territory.) He narrowly escaped death when a transport plane in which he was flying crashed and burned.

Despite the war he managed to write *Put Out More Flags* (1942), a novel which was the March choice of the Book Society in England. It deals with England's smart set during the war. In 1945 he produced *Brideshead Revisited* which an anonymous reviewer in *The Tablet* (London) for June 9, 1945, acclaims as "the finest of all his works, a book for which it is safe to prophesy a lasting place among the major works of fiction." Waugh himself considers *Brideshead Revisited* his best book. His favorite hitherto had been *A Handful of Dust* which dealt entirely with behavior. "It was humanist and contained all I had to say about humanism." *Brideshead Revisited* is the story of a great British Catholic family through the decades between World War I and World War II. Commenting on the criticism Mr. Edmund Wilson, the American critic, gave his book *Brideshead Revisited,* Waugh writes in *Life* for April 8, 1946: "He was outraged (quite legitimately by his standards) at finding God introduced into my story. I believe that you can only leave God out by making your characters pure abstractions. . . . They (modern novelists) try to represent the whole human mind and soul and yet omit its determining character—that of being God's creature with a defined purpose. So in my future books there will be two things to make them unpopular: a preoccupation with style and the attempt to represent man more fully, which, to me, means only one thing, man in his relation to God." For his work, *Brideshead Revisited,* he was selected for the 1945 Catholic literary award given by The Gallery of Living Catholic Authors.

Since 1937 he has been married to Laura Herbert. They have four children and live in a Gloucestershire Manor named Piers Court.

D. M. and M. H.

Leo Weismantel   1888-

In his autobiographical novel, *Die Hauser meines Lebens,* Leo Weismantel tells us he spent his youth between poverty and distress among starving weavers. Day after day the weavers sat at their looms. For them there was no comfort save the meditation on the sufferings of Christ whose picture they wove in their linen with great devotion. Leo, as a boy, listened to their stories and in this way got his impetus to write. He determined to train himself, like a soldier does, with the purpose of fighting the threefold enemy—the World, the Flesh, and the Devil.

Born on June 10, 1888, in the small village of Obersinn on the Rhön, he studied in Würzburg and obtained a Ph.D. in philosophy. He became a teacher, poet, and dramatic coach. He directed plays in various towns—plays on the style of those shown in the Middle Ages. His dramas were something new for the German stage. They are not similar to the plays of Shakespeare nor are they like the plays of Schiller, Goethe or Kleist. They are modelled more after the Greek and Spanish theatres.

The characters are personifications of ideals. Among his best plays are: *Die Reiter Der Apokalypse* (1919), which reminds one of Dürer's famous picture of the three horsemen; *Der Totentanz* (1921), written under the influence of a post-war revolution and inflation; *Das Spiel Vom Blute Luzifers* (1921), a religious festival play, and another festival play, *Wallfahrt Nach Bethlehem*, written for the "Quickborn" (The Catholic Youth Movement of Germany). He had a leading part in the revival of the marionette shows and he published a work-book for them. He also did some work on the shadow play.

His first book, *Maria Madlen*, a novel, was published in 1917. His other works include *Die Hexe* (1919); *Das Unheilige Haus* (1922); *Die Blumenlegenden* (1922) (a children's book), and *Musikanten Und Wallfahrer* (1923) (a collection of short stories of his life and others).

His best work perhaps is *Das Alte Doof* (1928). This three-volume novel about the history of Sparbrot from the 1840's to the post-war period is, says Sigrid Undset in her book, *Men, Women, and Places* "an exceedingly beautiful and varied picture of life, besides being a regular gold mine for the folklorist."

His life of St. Vincent de Paul was translated into English by Albert Schimberg in 1939 and was published under the title, *The Mantle of Mercy.*

Leo Weismantel became a Senator in his home State and lives at Marktbreit on the Rhine.   M. H.

Reverend Will W. Whalen   1886-

A popular writer of short stories, novels, articles and skits, Father Whalen, who publishes under the signature of Will Whalen, has been pastor of a little church in the Blue Ridge Mountain district at Orrtanna, Pennsylvania, site of the Old Jesuit Mission in Buchanan Valley. He started writing at fourteen and has been at it ever since. About his work he says: "I am first and foremost a playwright."

Will Wilfred Whalen, a son of Michael and Alice (Debo) Whalen, was born May 7, 1886, in a village outside Mt. Carmel, Pennsylvania, a mining town which he labels "a village without a name."

He received his ecclesiastical education at St. Charles College, Ellicott City, Maryland, St. Charles Seminary, Overbrook, Pennsylvania, and Mt. St. Mary's, Emmitsburg, Maryland, where he was ordained June 13, 1911.

When very young he had a flair for drama. As a small boy he went on the stage as "The Boy Patti," being blessed with an unusual soprano voice. He looks back upon himself as a sort of Jackie Coogan or Jackie Cooper in the pre-movie days of entertainment.

A prolific writer of very light stories, he names among his many books: *Twilight Talks to Tired Hearts; The Ex-Seminarian; The Slate*

Picker Soprano; The Girl from Mine Run; The Ex-Nun; The Girl Who Fought; The Golden Squaw; Bridget Or What's in a Name?; Strike; Co-Stars: Cecil Spooner and Oscar Wilde; The Forbidden Man; Priests; The Celibate—Celibate Father; What Priests Never Tell; Give Me a Chance!; The Irish Sparrow; Ill-starred Babbie.

Father Whalen writes in a semi-humorous style peculiarly "Will Whalen." He likes this approach and apparently so do his followers. Under his melodramatic titles he tells very human stories. He always teaches sound doctrines and good always triumphs over evil, oftentimes in a dime novel thriller style. Under his light words is a deep piety. His rapid output of popular style books was born of dire need in a hillbilly country where part of everyday life of a priest is to "keep the wolf from the door."   E. F.

Helen C. White   1896-

Apart from consideration of the great value of her literary work, Helen C. White is remarkable for at least two other reasons. One is that she is a Catholic woman who is a full professor in a large state University—that of Wisconsin; the other is that she manages to combine scholarship of a high order with the creative impulse. In two distinct fields she has won recognition. Yet her scholarship is all the better because it is that of an artist, and her novels are written on the basis of a wide and deep historical knowledge. Therefore, though distinct, they are related.

Helen Constance White was born at New Haven, Connecticut, on November 26, 1896. She took her Bachelor's Degree at Radcliffe College at the age of nineteen, obtaining her Master's Degree the following year. After two years of teaching at Smith College, she went to Wisconsin University as an instructor in English, and took her doctorate there in 1924, being appointed a full professor in 1936. There she still teaches in a way that combines solid scholarship with charm and wit. In 1940 she had a fellowship at the Huntington library to do research.

She first attracted attention with her book on *The Mysticism of William Blake* (1927). But unlike other young teachers, who produce one good book and are content to rest upon their laurels, she followed it up with others, still better. Her *English Devotional Literature, 1600-1640* (published in 1931), examines the writings of the Anglican divines, Baxter, Lancelot Andrewes, Donne and Taylor, tracing in their work the Catholicism from which all these men so freely drew. She performs much the same service for the poets of the period in her *Metaphysical Poets* (1936), which deals with the work of Donne, Herbert, Vaughan, Crashaw and Traherne. Again all were largely Catholic in their inspiration, and though Donne left Catholicity for Anglicanism, Crashaw, led by the writings of St. Teresa, found his way into the Church. This study is interesting for its examination of the relationship between mysticism and poetry.

These books, however, though widely recognized as important contributions to literary criticism, were mainly read by scholars, and of these attracted more attention outside Catholic circles than within them.

But Miss White was not satisfied with being nothing except a scholar. Her first novel appeared in 1933. This was *A Watch in the Night* and has as its central figure Jacopone da Todi, the fine thirteenth-century gentleman who left the world to become a Franciscan. He is remembered as the reputed author of the *Stabat Mater,* and in Helen White's story we see him as one of the leaders of the "Spirituals" who got at odds with Pope Boniface VIII.

An even finer novel was *Not Built With Hands* (1935). Here we have the story of the conflict between Hildebrand (Pope Gregory VII) and the Emperor Henry IV, which culminated in the submission at Canossa. Countess Matilda of Tuscany, to whom Dante gave such a noble function in the *Divine Comedy,* is among the leading characters.

But probably the novel by Miss White that received the widest recognition was *To the End of the World* (1939). Again the scene is set with the most scrupulous adherence to historical accuracy. In fact, Miss White is so careful with regard to her details that the story itself is somewhat slowed down at times in consequence. Nothing is here of the melodrama of red-capped mobs and the grim knitting-women sitting under the guillotine. Rather, we see the quiet heroism of Father Emery, the Superior General of the Sulpicians, who at a time when so many of the French clergy had taken the Constitutional Oath and had, therefore, fallen into heresy, worked from his prison in the Conciergerie towards a reasonable adjustment of affairs, under which the Church would accept the accomplished fact of the Revolution and the Republic would give freedom to the Church. Talleyrand and Grègoire appear as characters, along with many others who played their part in history, but the central figure is fictional. This is Michel de la Tour d'Auvergne, the nephew of the Cardinal de la Rochefoucauld. Refusing all offers of rapid ecclesiastical preferment, much to his uncle's dismay, he buries himself in the ancient abbey of Cluny, until the Revolution brings about the dispersion of the monks. After that, he works as a curé in the Vendée and is among the peasants during their revolt against the despotism of Paris, afterwards being one of that band of priests who, in disguise, often gave absolution at the very foot of the scaffold. It is for him and men of his type to maintain the Faith to the end of the world.

In none of these books do we have what can be described as propaganda. Rather Miss White prefers to allow a faithful and moderate statement of the truth, without any overstatement of romantic gilding, to achieve its object. In fact, she seems almost to lean backwards in this matter, often avoiding the obvious dramatic opportunity and understating her case. However, it must be added that Helen White for this very reason obtains a hearing in quarters where Catholic writing is commonly dismissed as being merely apologetic in purpose. The distinction of her style and the general sound craftsmanship of her books go a long way towards making compensations for anything she may lack as a teller of exciting "yarns." Perhaps with a greater mastery of her instrument, she will be able in future work to subdue setting to the story, and give us even better historical fiction. A excellent biographical and bibliographical study of Miss White was contributed by Dr. Austin App to the *Catholic Library World* for April 1940, and has been reissued as a pamphlet.

In 1942 she was awarded the Laetare Medal of the University of Notre Dame. She is the thirteenth woman to receive the medal which is awarded each year to an outstanding member of the laity in the United States, who has reflected glory upon the Catholic Faith in a particular field of endeavor.

In 1943 she was visiting professor of English at Barnard College and in 1944 she published *Social Criticism in Popular Religious Literature of the Sixteenth Century.*

In 1945 she was re-elected to the presidency of the American Association of University Women. In 1947 she was named vice-president of a board of educators which will administer government-subsidized scholarships in foreign universities for American students.

The Theta Phi Alpha Siena Medal, an award given anually to a Catholic woman who has made a distinctive contribution to Catholic life in the United States, was conferred on her in 1944.

Olive Bernardine White   1899-

Out of her research on various aspects of the cultural history of the Middle Ages and of the Renaissance in England, have come the imaginative works of Olive B. White, who writes with sound scholarship and dispassionately of the position of Catholics in England during the sixteenth century. There is something about the sincere faith revealed in both her novels that is especially appealing; it satisfies the mind and, while full of sentiment, is unsentimentalized.

Born on May 28, 1899, the second child of John and Mary (King) White, in New Haven, Connecticut, she moved early to Roslindale, a suburb of Boston, Massachusetts, which place has been her home since.

Miss White's writing dates from her freshman year at the Girls' High School in Boston, where she contributed to the school magazine, becoming editor-in-chief of that paper in her senior year. From Radcliffe she was graduated in 1918, magna cum laude, with highest honors in English; she took her M.A. in 1919 and Ph.D. in 1926. For both her bachelor's thesis and her doctoral dissertation she received the Wilby Prize for "the best original work in any department."

After teaching for several years in high school in Boston and in Wellesley College, Miss White, in 1927, became an instructor in English at Bradley Polytechnic Institute, Peoria, Illinois, where she is now (1947) a full professor of English and Dean of Women.

Since she leads a very active and full life in her profession as an educator, the writing can have only what may be legitimately called leisure time. The longest stretches of her writing have filled summer vacations. The place she knows best for work is the front porch at her own home. "There, a folding drawing-table, my portable typewriter, plenty of paper, and a straight, hard chair—the better to writhe on the edge of and almost tip over—are my equipment."

At the Widener Library at Harvard, the British Museum, and Bodleian Library at Oxford, the Public Records Office in London, and the Huntington Library, Olive White has engaged in the fine scholarly research for which her novels have been so widely praised.

It is with the utmost frankness that Miss White tells of her growth as a writer of fiction. Of her first novel *The King's Good Servant* (1936) which deals with the story of Sir Thomas More and his "struggle against political dictatorship in matters of religion," she writes that it "hugged the facts of biography and history, taking only the liberty of filling the gaps in the extant records"; of *Late Harvest* (1940) she says, "I wondered whether I could invent the central people and give them a drama closer to the orthodox concept of fiction than the first book had been. Of course, many of the auxiliary characters in the story are historical people, and the happenings that make the chronicle of the Collingridges and the Winbournes are all matchable in the official records of the age."

In Olive White the reader feels that there is not only the promise of a fine historical novelist, but a highly respected contributor to Catholic culture. She is the sister of Helen C. White, distinguished scholar and author of *A Watch in the Night* and *Not Built With Hands.* Helen says of her, "Olive has always been a close companion and sharer in all my interests. . . . She is the most unfailing of friends and the most delightful of companions for either work or play."

Olive White is a member of the Modern Language Association of America, Modern Humanities Research Association, Phi Beta Kappa, and The Gallery of Living Catholic Authors, as well as of many professional and education organizations. In Peoria she is engaged in many varieties of work, civic, cultural and educational.   T. V.

Reverend Joseph John Williams, S.J.   1875-1940

Keep the Gate (1923), a work of the late retreat master and missioner, Father Williams, is rated among the most popular of retreat readings. He was born December 1, 1875, at Boston, Massachusetts, the son of Nicholas Mark and Mary Jane (O'Connor) Williams. Privately tutored for Boston College High School, which he entered in 1887, he followed on to Boston College in 1892. At the end of his Freshman year (1893) he entered the Society of Jesus. He was ordained priest in June 1907. He received his A.B. at Woodstock in 1901; his A.M. in 1903 and his Ph.D. in ethnology in 1909. He specialized in anthropology. Boston College conferred an honorary Doctor of Literature on him in 1929.

His work as a Jesuit was varied. He was registrar at Xavier College, New York, from 1897 to 1900, and was on the original Board of Editors of *America* and managing editor from 1909 to 1911. From 1912 to 1917 he was engaged in mission work and ethnological research in Jamaica, British West Indies.

Upon his return to the United States he was appointed treasurer of Woodstock College, 1917 to 1918, and of Holy Cross College from 1918 to 1922. From 1922 to 1934 he devoted himself to ethnological research and writing and then served as professor of cultural anthropology at Boston College Graduate School until his retirement in 1939.

As a Missionary in Jamaica, British West Indies, he made exhaustive studies of racial characteristics and customs of the natives, gathered material which in later years he put into several books including *Hebrewisms of West Africa* (1930), and *Voodoos and Obeahs* (1932). He visited Jamaica five times, devoting from two to six months to research on each occasion.

Father Williams was a member of all the important societies devoted to the study of ethnology and anthropology; president of the Jesuit Anthropological Association, and a member of the African Society and International Institute of African Languages and Culture, of London.

He had held important posts at St. Francis Xavier College, New York, Holy Cross, Worcester, and Boston College, Boston, Massachusetts.

Besides the books already mentioned he wrote: *Yearning for God* (1923); *Whisperings of the Caribbean* (1925); *Whence the Black Irish of Jamaica?* (1932); *Psychic Phenomena of Jamaica* (1934); *Africa's God* (1936-1938); *The Maroons of Jamaica* (1938); and *Thoughts on Evolution* (1939).

E. F.

Mother Margaret Williams, R.S.C.J. 1902-

When Mother Margaret Williams of Manhattanville College began the study of Old English literature, she became deeply impressed by the spectacle of faith and grace working so spontaneously in the writings of the newly converted Anglo-Saxons. As a teacher, to make manifest to her classes the living power of this early Christian literature, she translated much of the Old English writing, using mimeographed copies for her college courses. After four years there was evolved from this work her book, *Word-Hoard* (1940), which consists of translations of Old English poetry and prose together with studies of the history and culture of the period. One very commendable feature is that it makes accessible to the modern reader what was previously available only to the scholars and translators of Old English. In preparation is another volume of similar plan in which Mother Williams picks up the thread of her work at the Norman Conquest, the concluding period of *Word-Hoard,* and continues the pattern of interpretation down to the Renaissance.

The daughter of Michael Williams, author and former editor of *The Commonweal,* and Harriet Margaret (Olmsted) Williams, Mother Williams was born in Manchester Green, Connecticut, July 15, 1902. Significantly her early years were spent in California at Carmel-by-the-Sea, a very beautiful little town near the old Spanish Mission where Father Junipero Serra, the Missionary of the Indians is buried. The town at that time was largely a colony of artists and writers. At the age of eleven she became a Catholic, after the return to the Church of her father, who was converted "through special graces received through St. Teresa of Lisieux in 1913." While her early education was obtained in California at the Sacred Heart Academies in San Francisco, and in Menlo Park, she received her B.A. from Manhattanville College of the Sacred Heart in New York in 1923. The next year she entered the novitiate of the Religious of the Sacred Heart at Kenwood, making her final profession in Rome in 1933. Oxford University conferred on her the degree B.A.Oxon, in 1939. At present Mother Williams is a professor of English at Manhattanville College of the Sacred Heart where she lectures on Old and Middle English literature.

Her new book is *Second Sowing,* the life and work of Mary Aloysia Hardey, one of the pioneer Religious of the Sacred Heart in America.

Small in stature, Mother Williams impresses one indelibly by her fine scholarly mind. She is a member of the Medieval Academy of America and the Modern Language Association of America.

T. V.

Michael Williams 1877-

One of the outstanding Catholic laymen of the United States and a leading literary figure, Michael Williams is well known both as journalist and author. He was born in Halifax, Nova Scotia, in 1877, the eldest of six children, five boys and one girl. His father was a seafaring man, who fell victim to yellow fever, leaving his mother the care of the family when Michael was thirteen. He studied with the Jesuit Fathers in New Brunswick and gave great promise as a scholar, when his academic career was cut short by the necessity of taking a position offered him in a warehouse. During five years in this environment his life was "as solitary as a pigeon in a flight of crows." Books were his only companions. Making the acquaintance of a book-seller who wanted to start a little magazine, he was given the editorship, and the thrill that accompanied publication of the first issue foreshadowed that later editorship which filled so many profitable years. This small paper, which was short-lived, cost him his warehouse position but gave him brief emancipation of the spirit.

Removing to Boston with his family, he lived there for several years in grinding poverty, earning a mere pittance as a clerk in a ten-cent store. Again he found consolation in books, in art and in music. He continued to write without recognition until one of his stories was accepted by Philip Hale, columnist in the Boston *Journal.* A poem was then printed in the *Transcript,* and other stories signed the "Quietist" were accepted by Hale. This writer whose literary skill he admired and who had given him encouragement in a bleak world became his good friend, and after him Michael Williams in later years named his son. When ill health seized him, Hale enabled him to leave Boston for recuperation in North Carolina. Edward Thompson of the *Youth's Companion,* for whom Williams also wrote, assisted. A vigorous constitution which underlay an organism weakened by a "hole in his lung" restored him to health and after eighteen months he returned to Boston.

There followed a difficult period of transition from his own serious style to commercialized writing. For a time he was a literary hack for the *Black Cat,* rewriting short stories of popular variety and concocting them, and then he drifted into newspaper work. When a cub reporter on the Boston *Post,* in 1900, he married Margaret Olmstead of East Hartford, Connecticut, by whom he had a daughter and a son. They moved to New York and he was a reporter there for the *World* and *Evening Telegram* and also sold stories to the *Sunday Sun* and other papers and to *McClure's Magazine.* In 1904 his old illness necessitated leaving the city and in sun-drenched San Antonio, Texas, he fought his way back to health.

With his family he then went to San Francisco and there resumed newspaper work, becoming city editor of the *Examiner* in 1906. In his autobiography, *The High Romance,* he vividly describes the earthquake of that year which disrupted the city the day after he took over his editorship. After several months he returned East and earned his living writing short stories and serials. Joining the "cooperative home colony" of "advanced thinkers" established by Upton Sinclair at Englewood, New Jersey, he found congenial company there at Helicon Hall but was not formally a Socialist. The encountering of a strange mixture of ideas among the oddly assorted colonists and also solitary periods of thought stimulated his quest for an answer to the meaning of life and opened spiritual vistas. He had completed an accepted novel and several thousand words of another book when these and all his manuscripts, as well as clothes, furniture and books, were wiped out by a fire which destroyed Helicon Hall. Destitute, he faced life anew.

He again took up free-lancing in New York and then after a summer at Martha's Vineyard he went to Bermuda, where, with Upton Sinclair, he wrote *Good Health and How We Won It.* But ill health pursued him, and the following year he took his family West, settling in California at Carmel. It was here that he found the answer to all his years of search for the truth among cults and religious movements. He returned to the Faith of his childhood. This came about through the Archbishop of San

Francisco and the Prioress of the Carmelite Convent there, who became his good friends. He was received anew into the Church in 1912.

He had been doing newspaper work and in 1913 when war threatened between Mexico and the United States he went to Mexico as special correspondent for the International News Service. Upon his return he resumed his former contacts and continued in journalism until 1915 when he did publicity for the Panama-Pacific Exposition and then became organizing secretary of the San Francisco Institute of Art. In 1917 he completed his spiritual biography and went East to find a publisher. *The Book of the High Romance* was brought out in 1918.

Returning to San Francisco, Michael Williams took part in the war work of the United Welfare Organizations, making speeches and writing publicity, and in 1919 he undertook similar work for the National Catholic War Council, later the Welfare Conference. He edited its Bulletin and traveled throughout the country and in Canada, Panama, the West Indies and Europe. His book on *American Catholics in the War* appeared in 1921. That year he covered the coronation of Pope Pius XI for the N.C.W.C. News Service. Eighteen years later, in 1939, he went to Rome again for the N.C.W.C., to write of the election and coronation of his successor, Pius XII.

The intervening years witnessed his founding, in 1924, of a Catholic weekly published by laymen, *The Commonweal*. The magazine continued under his editorship until 1935, when the Calvert Associates founded for the purpose of this publication was dissolved. Several books have come from his pen. In 1926 he wrote of both *The Little Flower of Carmel* and *Little Brother Francis of Assisi*. Then followed *Catholicism and the Modern Mind, The Shadow of the Pope* and *The Catholic Church in Action*. Gonzaga College of Washington, D.C., awarded him an honorary Litt.D., and in 1935 he received the Catholic Action Medal from St. Bonaventure's College. He resides at Westport, Connecticut.

C. M. N.

Valentine Williams   1883-

A keen zest for life, action and adventure and a well-established position in the newspaper world enabled Valentine Williams to "write his way across the globe," transmitting his experiences through Reuter's and later Lord Northcliffe's *Daily Mail*. Touching at first hand the great happenings of momentous years, he has recorded much of these periods of history and the men who made them in his *World of Action,* which he published in 1938. Philosophizing as well as narrating, the author brings out, time and again, "the continuity of history."

Born in London in 1883, through his mother Williams comes of ancient Irish Catholic heritage: "The Skerrets of Finavara, in the County

Clare, were one of the so-called Fourteen Tribes of Galway, settled on the shores of Galway Bay since the thirteenth century." And branches of the clan have migrated throughout the world, including the United States.—He was educated at the Benedictine School of Downside and privately in Germany.

The Williams were a "Reuter family." For three decades his father, Douglas, had his desk in the window of the editorial room at 24, Old Jewry; his uncle Harry was Reuter's General Manager at Bombay; his brother Douglas was the representative in the United States. In that same old-fashioned editorial room, in 1902, Valentine started "subbing" telegrams, after his return from a year in Germany, where he had gone after he left school, to acquire proficiency in the language. Three years later Baron Herbert, son of "the old Baron," founder of Reuter's Agency, "the world's greatest news bureau," appointed him Berlin correspondent. There he remained until 1909 and there met his future wife, Alice Crawford, when in 1907 she came with Sir Herbert Tree and his company to play a season of Shakespeare in Berlin.

In 1909 Williams received from Lord Northcliffe the offer of the post of *Daily Mail* correspondent in Paris. To remain indefinitely in Berlin he felt would end in a rut, so reluctantly he severed his connection with Reuter's and went to Paris to stay until 1913. During that time he covered special assignments in Portugal, Spain, Austria, Russia, and the Balkans. When hostilities broke out in 1914, Northcliffe made him chief of the war service and he was the first accredited correspondent at British G.H.Q. and in March 1915 wrote the official account of the battle of Neuve Chapelle. In December of that year, wearied by the obstacles put in the way of accurate news transmission by censorship and official opposition, he enlisted in the Irish Guards. On September 25, 1916, in the battle of the Somme "a shell landed beside me and blew me sky-high. I went up an experienced newspaper man, and came down a budding novelist." While convalescing in Scotland, the book, *The Man with the Clubfoot,* was born. It was published in 1918. Williams was in the Army of Occupation and billeted in Cologne for some months, until he returned to England and demobilized in February 1919. Three days later he was rushed across the Channel to take charge of the *Daily Mail* staff at the Versailles Peace Conference, which brought him in close contact with the chief actors of that drama.

He was asked to represent Reuter's Agency in Egypt in 1923, at the excavation of the tomb of Tutankhamen, Pharaoh of the XVIIIth Dynasty at Luxor. Following that were assignments to the United States, Morocco and Tunisia, and in 1930 a prolonged visit to the United States where he and his wife remained for three years and a half. While here he covered the country and writes keenly and sympathetically of his impressions. He wrote and acted in four plays for the National Broadcasting Company and has broadcast extensively both here and in England. *The Clock Ticks On* is his New York crime story.

Up to 1947 Valentine Williams had written twenty-seven works of fiction, using often the locale of the places he was visiting and the native types. Among them are: *Fog,* which ran in the *Saturday Evening Post,* written in collaboration with Dorothy Sims; *Mr. Ramosi,* based on material collected in Egypt and dealing with stolen Egyptian antiques; *The Key Man,* a Foreign Legion story resulting from a summer in the Basque country; *Dead Man's Manor,* following a trip to the Province of Quebec. *The World of Action* (1938) is his autobiography, and *The Fox Prowls* came in 1939. *Courier to Marrakesh* appeared in 1945.

He also wrote: *With Our Army in Flanders; Adventures of an Ensign; The Secret Hand; The Yellow Streak; The Return of Clubfoot; The Three of Clubs; The Red Mass,* and others. His pseudonyms are Douglas Valentine and Vedette.

Valentine Williams makes his home with his wife in London. His clubs are: Guards, Pratt's, and his recreations are lawn tennis, squash and ice skating. For his war services he received the M.C. (Merit Cross), and was made Chevalier of the Order of the Crown of Belgium.

D. D.

Reverend Benedict Williamson   1868-

Father Benedict Williamson is one of the most versatile of men, his activities extending from architecture to the re-establishment of the Bridgettine Order, and from the writing of biographies to works on mysticism. And to cap it off, he somehow found time to edit the *Catholic Review* from 1912 to 1917.

He was born near London on June 7, 1868, and was received into the Church in 1896. Already he had studied and discarded law, his artistic temperament leading him to architecture. Among his buildings are those of St. Ignatius' Church, Stamford Hill (together with its college), St. Michael's College, Leeds, the Lithuanian Church, Hackney Road, as well as churches at Slough, Frimley, Cowley, Shanklin, Portslade, Southwold and Royston. The Benson Memorial Chapel at Hare Street is also his. In most of these the style is Byzantine, severe and distinguished.

The study of architecture served to lead him towards the Church, but he did not abandon its practice even after becoming a priest in 1909. After his ordination in Rome, where he had gone to study for the priesthood in 1907, he returned to England and was rector of St. Gregory's, Earlsfield, till the end of 1915. Thereafter, he was rector of Cobham till he went to the front as army chaplain and took part in the principal engagements in France and Belgium until the end of the first World War.

His literary work has been of various kinds. In *Happy Days in France and Flanders,* he gave an account of his experience as a chaplain in the war. As he had been through some of the fiercest engagements, it was very popular with ex-soldiers. About the same time he wrote *The*

Straight Religion, which, as he says, was a rendering in untechnical language of the theological course at the Gregorian University at Rome. This was followed by *Supernatural Mysticism* and *The Triumph of Love* (which he considers his best book). Both set out the doctrine of the Spanish mystics in simple language. *The Real Thing* is on similar lines to *The Straight Religion* and is effective apologetics. More recently Father Williamson has contributed several volumes to the growing literature on the Little Flower. Of these, *The Sure Way* is a study of her teaching.

But Father Williamson still found other literary territories to cultivate. In *The Treaty of the Lateran* he gives the full text of the Treaty and of the Law of Guarantees, so often referred to but so seldom read, and offers an examination of the historical circumstances that brought about the arrangement between Italy and the Holy See. In strong contrast are his *Maria of Padua,* the story of an Italian schoolgirl; *Cecilia,* a contemporary of Maria's, and *Fernanda,* a student at the university of Turin. *The World and the Cloister* takes us to the Italy of the 'fifties, and tells the story of a young Carmelite of S. Maria Maddalena de' Pazzi. *Anglioletta* is also concerned with the same period and is about a Tuscan country girl, while *Antonito* shows us the life of a young Spaniard just before the civil war. All have been very popular, especially in India, and have been translated into several languages.

Though Benedict Williamson has written twenty-five books, he began his career of authorship in middle age and almost by accident. *Supernatural Mysticism* is hardly more than the amplification of the notes taken by one of the nuns at the Tyburn Convent during one of Father Williamson's retreats. In the same way *The Straight Religion* was written during convalescence and set down the instruction he was accustomed to give his converts. Being unable to see them then, he wrote out what his living voice would have said. The purpose of such books was practical rather than literary in the ordinary sense. But the object aimed at—the clear presentation of Catholic piety and thought—has certainly been achieved.

Of one book, *The Triumph of Love,* Father Williamson tells us that it was finished in a little over two weeks. His pen has always been a ready one and used most industriously, but literature has not been to him an art, as architecture has been an art. It is no more than one of the sidelines of an immensely active life. Yet Father Williamson is an artist, however casually, in all that he has done.

In his youth, before his ordination, he did much for the propagation of plain-chant according to the Solesmes tradition, working with his friend the celebrated Benedictine, Dom Mocquereau, when the monks of Quarr Abbey and the nuns of St. Cecilia's found refuge in England. Though his most notable contribution to contemporary Catholic culture is the beauty of the churches he has designed, he has found a wide audience for his books. Among others of a long list not mentioned are his *Bridgettine Order* and *The Story of Pius XI.* It is a remarkable record for a man who did not become a priest until he was past forty and who did not begin to write until still later.

Reverend Claude Williamson, O.S.C.   1891-

Life stories of thirty-seven *Great Catholics,* edited by Father Claude
Williamson, O.S.C., and highly acclaimed by critics, is the latest publication of this English religious. Vivid sketches by the biographers, well
known American and English writers, have been compiled into an interesting handbook on Catholics now world famous.

Priest, historian and writer, Father Williamson, born in 1891 in England, followed the usual path of an English student with a university
education. During early school days he showed proneness for no particular studies, but as an undergraduate at King's College developed an
enthusiasm for historical and geographic studies resulting in his election
as Fellow of the Royal Geographic Society and the Royal Historical
Society. Life as a religious began in 1925 when Father Williamson entered the novitiate of the Congregation of the Oblates of Saint Charles.

He is the author of: *Human Concerns* (1915); *Some Aspects of Men
and Things* (1915); *Writings of Three Centuries* (1920); *Writers of Many
Centuries* (1918); *Problems and Facts; As They Were; Greek Aesthetics;
Stations of the Cross,* and other books.

Showing the same enthusiasm for his work as for his specal studies,
Father Williamson occasionally contributes timely articles to seventy
American and English magazines including *The Catholic World* and the
Magnificat.

George Charles Williamson   1858-1942

The indefatigable convert and authority on certain aspects of archaeology, George C. Williamson, was born in Guildford, Surrey, in 1858, educated privately and at London University (LL.D.). In 1883, he married
Louisa May Lethbrige; he had two sons and one daughter. He began his
literary career with newspaper articles on local archaeological subjects. His
deep interest in coins resulted in a small book, *Coins of the Bible;* after
its completion, he began unceasing work on art. He had travelled extensively, visiting the public and private picture galleries of Europe and
for many years had been art editor for George Bell and Sons. For recreation he collected miniatures and portrait drawings in pencil. He was a
Fellow Royal of the Society of Literature, of the Zoological Society, and
Chevalier of the Legion of Honor.

He wrote over one hundred books. Among his varied publications
are: *Trader's Tokens; Perugino; The History of Portrait Miniatures;
Fra Angelo; Raphael; The Cities of Northern Italy; Life of Milton;
Catalogue of the Pierpont Morgan Collection of Miniatures;* and *The
Book of Ivory* (1938).

He was a frequent contributor to the London *Tablet* and edited the new edition of *Bryan's Dictionary of Painters and Engravers* (5 volumes).

S. M.

Reverend André Wilmart, O.S.B.   1876-1941

Dom André Wilmart was born at Orleans, France, on January 28, 1876. After brilliant success as a student in his native city and at the Sorbonne, from which he was graduated at the age of nineteen, he entered the École des Hautes Études, where he studied under Louis Havet and Monsignor Batiffol. It was the latter who initiated him into the study of early Christian literature, to which he devoted thirty-five years of his life. He entered the Seminary of St. Sulpice in 1897 to take up theology, but withdrew two years later and joined the Order of St. Benedict in the Abbey of Solesmes, where he made his profession on June 24, 1901. Upon the expulsion of the religious from France in 1901, he went with the other monks of Solesmes into exile on the Isle of Wight, and in 1906 he became a member of St. Michael's Abbey at Farnborough, where Abbot Fernand Cabrol had been blessed as the first abbot three years before.

Dom Wilmart recognized the fact that Ludwig Traue was inaugurating a new era in Latin paleography and he himself made important contributions to this science. His interests were chiefly in three fields: patristics, liturgy, and the devotional literature of the Middle Ages. His patristic studies are characterized by exact learning and sobriety of judgment and are comparable to the work of his illustrious confrère, Dom Germain Morin. Dom Wilmart was also eminent as a liturgiologist, and his monograph on the *Missal of Bobbio* will stand as a model of its kind.

But it was in medieval devotional literature, a subject that had been more or less overlooked by other medievalists, that Dom Wilmart was at his best. Besides solid learning and the power of careful critical analysis, he had a sympathetic understanding and a warmth of admiration for the simplicity and piety of the Middle Ages that enabled him to bring to life again and interpret medieval devotional works in the spirit that produced them. A few of his studies of this kind were published at Paris in 1932 in a volume entitled *Auteurs Spirituels et Textes Dévots du Moyen Âge Latin*. Other recent publications are his editions of *Meditationes* by Guigues du Chastel (Paris, 1936) and *De Vera Pace* by John de Trastevere (1938). *Mediaeval and Renaissance Studies*, I, no. 1 (1941) contains his study of the *Florilège mixte de Thomas Bekynton*. Among English writers who were the subjects of special studies are St.

Anselm, St. Aelred, Eadmer, Osbert of Claire, Richard Rolle, and Master Adam the Carthusian.

Dom Wilmart was a Corresponding Fellow of the Mediaeval Academy of America. He was not only a savant whose learning was encyclopedic, but he was also a writer with a style of unusual charm. A collection of his more than four hundred monographs and essays would make quite a series of volumes. It seems unfortunate that he never undertook to reduce his vast knowledge to a synthesis and that he never tried to write a history of medieval literature or even of medieval piety. His erudition was so extensive that he saw more clearly than others the need of further research before the whole story of the literature of the Middle Ages could be told.

The Vatican Library invited Dom Wilmart to Rome in 1929 and commissioned him to prepare a catalogue of the vast collection of Latin manuscripts bequeathed to the Vatican by Queen Christina of Sweden. The first fruit of his work on this subject was the *Analecta Reginensia,* which appeared in 1933. He published the first volume of the catalogue in 1937, and the second volume was in press when the outbreak of the second World War compelled him to leave Rome in May, 1940. On his way back to Barnborough he was detained in Paris by the German invasion and was not permitted to return to England. He spent the last year of his life in cataloguing Latin manuscripts in the Bibliotheque Nationale. He died in Paris on April 21, 1941.

B. S.

Genevieve Wimsatt

Probably the only contemporary Catholic writer specializing in the social and literary aspects of Chinese life is Genevieve Wimsatt. As a child she lived in her native Washington, D.C., where she attended the Visitation Convent in Georgetown, studying poetry under that venerable individualist Sister Paulina—who at an earlier date had taught Harriet Monroe. At the end of her school days she travelled extensively, and during World War I served with the Red Cross. After the war she went to China, where in Tientsin, she edited the woman's weekly, *Woman in China.* Later she rented a house in the native section of Peking and began a serious study of the people and the language and the literature—the women poets in particular.

Number Two Wife, a novel published in London in 1933, is the story of a foreign educated Chinese girl who is constrained to follow the social tradition of her people. In 1934 Columbia University Press brought out *Lady of the Long Wall,* a metrical translation of one of the oldest and most widely known Chinese folk songs, with illustrations from old

Chinese masterpieces. *Selling Wilted Peonies* is the biography and a translation of the poems of tragic Yü Hsuan-chi, frail and futile T'ang exponent of woman's rights who, quite understandably, considering her period, lost her head on the execution grounds beyond the walls of Ch'ang An. *Chinese Shadow Shows,* which appeared in 1936, was the first full account of a medieval folk art which still flourishes in forgotten corners of the Chinese Republic.

She has written other books on China: *A Griffin in China; The Bright Concubine; Apricot Cheeks and Almond Eyes.* This deals with the Empress Yang (not Yang Kuei Fei) of the Southern Sung; and *A Well of Fragrant Waters* (1944). This last volume completed the trilogy of the Taoist-nun, the Sung Empress and T'ang adventuress Hung-Tu, first female private secretary of China. *A Lady Like the Moon* (1945) is an historical novel of seventeenth century China, and relates the rise of the dancing girl, Round Moon, to become the wife to the last of China's Ming Emperors.

Genevieve Wimsatt's house in Georgetown contains many interesting curios and art objects, including a number of paintings by the masters of Chinese Christian art—Chang Shat-tzu and Luke Ch'en, Art Director of the Catholic University of Peking.

Her small adopted Chinese son lives with her in Washington, D.C.

D. M.

William Kurtz Wimsatt, Jr. 1907-

There is one Catholic writer who in one sense may be said to be head and shoulders over all Catholic writers of our day (or for that matter over all writers of any period) as he is six feet ten inches tall. He is William Kurtz Wimsatt who was born at Washington on November 17, 1907. He took his Bachelor's Degree at Georgetown University in 1928 and his Master's Degree there the following year. From 1929 to 1930 he taught at Gonzaga High School, Washington, and was Head of the English Department at Portsmouth Priory School, Portsmouth, Rhode Island, 1930 to 1935. The next year he studied at the Catholic University and was an instructor in English. After taking his Ph.D. at Yale University in 1939 he became an instructor in English there and Fellow of Silliman College in 1940, and assistant professor in 1943.

He is the author of two books, the first of which, *Shapes from Dusk and Winter,* won the Yale University Prize for Poetry in 1938. It has a certain austere distinction. But Mr. Wimsatt is primarily a scholar, rather than a creative artist, though he is all the better a scholar for having some insight into the artistic process. His doctoral dissertation, *The Prose Style of Samuel Johnson,* was published in 1941. In it he attempts to explain how style ought to be discussed in terms of meaning and seeks to analyze Johnson's style consistently with his own theory of criticism. Mr. Wimsatt is also the contributor of learned articles to such periodicals as *Speculum, American Literature, College English, Modern Language Notes* and *Publications of the Modern Language Association.* His work is likely to remain mainly within the field of specialized research and theory of criticism but it may not be wholly confined there. From time to time he produces a poem and once published a short story. It would not be surprising if one day he even produced a novel.   D. M.

Mary Fabyan Windeatt 1910-

After graduating from the San Diego State College with an A.B. degree in 1934, Mary Fabyan Windeatt came to New York to find work in advertising. Nowhere was work to be had in this field. Not knowing anyone and having a lot of spare time, she decided to write a story. When it was finished, she sent it to a Catholic magazine. It was accepted.

Although Miss Windeatt always liked to write in school, she had never considered doing it professionally. Encouraged by the acceptance of her first story in 1934 she has continued writing stories and sending them out to various Catholic publications. She has written for thirty-three magazines, contributing verse, articles, book reviews, etc., along with her short stories. Miss Windeatt makes a living free-lancing, in this fashion, for the Catholic press.

Born in Regina, Saskatchewan, Canada, in 1910, she was interested as a child in music and at the age of fifteen graduated with first class honors from the Toronto Conservatory of Music (1926). The following year, she received the degree of Licentiate of Music from Mount Saint Vincent College, Halifax, Nova Scotia. In this same year (1927) she came with her family to the United States, settling in San Diego, California. In 1940 she received an A.M. degree from Columbia University.

Miss Windeatt feels indebted to the Dominican Fathers, especially the editors of *The Torch,* for in 1936 they gave her the chance to write a monthly "Children's Page" in their magazine. She has been doing it ever since. Her first book bears the title *Saints In the Sky.* It is a life of St. Catherine of Siena. The six chapters of this book appeared in the "Children's Page" of *The Torch.* Another children's book is *Lad of Lima.* This also was published in serial form in *The Torch.* It is a biography of Blessed Martin de Porres, the celebrated South American Negro lay brother of the Dominican Order, and is the first book to be written for children on the great patron of interracial justice. To obtain material for this book, Miss Windeatt made a trip to Peru in the summer of 1941. *Hero of the Hills* (1943) is a dramatic story of St. Benedict. *My Name*

Is Thomas (1943) is an imaginary autobiography of St. Thomas Aquinas for young readers. *Warrior In White:* the story of John of Magdala a Dominican lay brother of Peru, contemporary of Blessed Martin, was published in 1944.

Other books are: *Little Queen; Saint Thérèse of the Child Jesus* (1944); *Little Sister; The Story of the Blessed Imelda, Patroness of First Communicants* (1945); and *Northern Lights* (1945).

In the last six years, *Columbia* published over fifty of her verses.

The Ave Maria Radio Hour of the Franciscan Friars of the Atonement has produced eighteen of her thirty-minute radio plays based on the lives of the saints.

At the present time (1947) she is contributing to different magazines under six names, her own and five pseudonyms.   M. H.

Reverend Francis Woodlock, S.J.   1871-1940

When the Reverend Francis Woodlock, S.J., died at Farm Street Church, Mayfair, in April 1940, at the age of sixty-nine, the English Jesuits lost one of their distinguished members, and Catholic literature the gifted author of several books.

Born in County Dublin, in 1871, the son of Thomas and Emilia (Moran) Woodlock, Francis Woodlock was a great-nephew of Dr. Woodlock, Bishop of Ardagh and of Reverend Francis Mahony ("Father Prout"). He was educated at the Jesuit College of Beaumont and entered the Society of Jesus in 1889. Ordained a priest in 1903, he did missionary work in Leeds, and later was professor of logic, psychology, ethics, and metaphysics at Stonyhurst. When the first World War came, Father Woodlock received a commission as chaplain in the British Army and was later decorated with the Military Cross of an Officer in the Portuguese Order of Christ.

He was among the distinguished preachers invited by Monsignor Joseph McMahon to give the Lenten course at the Church of Our Lady of Lourdes in New York City. His brother, Thomas Francis, had long been a prominent figure in the New York financial world, for many years a member of the New York Stock Exchange, an Interstate Commerce Commissioner, and contributing editor of *The Wall St. Journal* before his death in 1945.

Among Father Woodlock's books are: *Lourdes Miracle; The Anglican Church and Reunion; The Reformation and the Blessed Eucharist; Catholicism and the True Rationalism,* an apologetic handbook; *Constantinople, Canterbury and Rome; Modernism and the Church of Christ.* Besides these, Father Woodlock wrote pamphlets and articles on points of Anglican controversy.   D. D.

Thomas Francis Woodlock   1866-1945

One of the leading financial writers in this country for fifty years, Thomas Francis Woodlock also wrote unashamedly on moral issues. Born in Ireland in 1866, the son of Thomas and Emilia Jane (Moran) Woodlock, he was educated at Beaumont College, Windsor, England, and London University. After serving as a clerk with a London brokerage firm, he joined his father and brother in the London Stock Exchange house of Woodlock Brothers.

In 1892 he came to America and joined the Dow-Jones News Service, specializing in American railroads. After the death of Mr. Dow in 1902 he became the editor of the *Wall Street Journal.* He resigned the editorship in 1905 to become a member of the New York Stock Exchange, in partnership with Schuyler N. Warren. Here he remained until 1918. He then joined the American International Corporation. He served as director of the St. Louis and San Francisco Railway from 1922 to 1924 and the Pere Marquette Railway from 1923 to 1924. In 1925 he was appointed by President Coolidge to serve on the Interstate Commerce Commission and served until 1930, returning then to the *Wall Street Journal.* President Hoover in a public statement regretted his resignation from the Interstate Commerce Commission and said that Mr. Woodlock had rendered "very distinguished service to his country."

For the *Journal,* he wrote the column "Thinking It Over." At the age of 29 he wrote *Anatomy of a Railroad Report* (1895), which remained for several decades the standard work in its field. Four years later he published *Ton Mile Cost* (1899). In 1942 he wrote his apologetic work *The Catholic Pattern.* In it he traces the pattern of Catholicism and shows at the same time that the world, in casting aside the pattern, has worked its way out of order into chaos. For many years Mr. Woodlock conducted the column "By Way of Comment" for the New York *Sun.* In the early days of *The Catholic News* he contributed editorial articles. He contributed the article on Father Prout to *The Catholic Encyclopedia* and was a member of its Board of Directors. His articles appeared frequently in Catholic magazines.

He was a former president and one of the organizers of the Laymen's League for Retreats and Social Studies. From St. Francis College in New York City he received an honorary Master of Arts degree in 1905 and from Fordham University, in 1906, a Doctor of Laws degree. In 1943 Mr. Woodlock was awarded the Notre Dame University Laetare Medal as the outstanding Catholic layman of the year.

In an editorial about him in the New York *Times* (August 27, 1945), the writer states: "Those who were privileged to know him were unfailingly impressed by the depth, solidity and range of his culture. He might illustrate a point in economics by quoting some thirteenth century Pope, or some scrap of wisdom from an obscure figure in the eighteenth century. He retained to the last his intellectual resilience and curiosity. Perhaps most striking of all was the sense he gave his listeners (certainly without any conscious effort on his part to give it) of rare moral stature."

Mr. Woodlock died on August 25, 1945. His wife, the former Miss Josephine Byrne, whom he married in 1893, died in 1932.

M. G.

(John) Douglas Woodruff 1897-

"A large burly person who might be a country squire or a barrister-at-law, John Douglas Woodruff is in fact one of the foremost English journalists," writes one of his friends. He made his name while writing leaders for the London *Times* with his "Plato's American Republic," an acute and witty analysis of the United States.

Douglas Woodruff was born at Wimbledon, Surrey, England, in 1897. He is the son of the late Cumberland Woodruff and the late Emily Louisa (Hewett) Woodruff. He was educated at St. Augustine's, Ramsgate; Downside School, and New College, Oxford (Lothian prizeman, 1921, with First Class Honors in History).

After graduating from New College, Oxford, he lectured in history at Sheffield University for one year, 1923 to 1924. The following year he visited the United States as leader of the Oxford University Debating Team (he was president of the Oxford Union in 1923). It was as the result of these visits that he wrote his best known book *Plato's American Republic* (1926). He was on the editorial staff of the London *Times* from 1926 to 1938. From 1931 until 1933 he was in charge of press publicity for the Empire Marketing Board and from 1934 until 1936 he was on the staff of the British Broadcasting Corporation.

Since 1936 Mr. Woodruff has been editor of the *Tablet,* which many think is England's leading Catholic weekly review. He is also chairman of the Tablet Publishing Company. His fine staff includes Christopher Hollis and Monsignor Ronald Knox. Mr. Woodruff conducts the "Talking at Random" column and signs it "D. W." It is a witty charivari and bubbles with the Catholic spirit.

Of late years he has shown himself a brilliant speaker for all kinds of Catholic societies and on the radio in broadcast debates. Several years ago he followed in G. K. Chesterton's footsteps by taking the part of Dr. Johnson in a charity pageant at Daly's Theatre.

In 1933 Mr. Woodruff married Marie Immaculée, the daughter of the second Lord Acton. Mrs. Woodruff succeeded Lady Winefride Elwes as president of the Catholic Women's League, England's leading organization for women, which has founded so many huts for soldiers and has mothered the Union of Catholic Mothers.

Other books by Mr. Woodruff are: *The British Empire* (1929); *Plato's Britannia* (1930); *Charlemagne* (1934); *Contributor to Early Victorian England* (1934); *Great Tudors* (1935); *European Civilisation; The Grand Tour* (1935); (Editor of) *Dear Sir* (1936), and *Talking at Random* (1941). In 1943 he edited the book *For Hilaire Belloc,* essays in honor of his 71st birthday. The authors of the essays—eleven in all—are Catholics.

M. H.

Cuthbert Wright   1899-

The childhood of Cuthbert Wright was spent in that historic section of New Jersey that is redolent of Revolutionary atmosphere. His father, the Reverend William Wright, an Episcopal clergyman, was attached to old St. Peter's Church in Freehold, near the battlefield of Monmouth, Cuthbert was born in Elmira, New York, on March 20, 1899.

He was educated at the Kent School in Connecticut, conducted by the (Episcopal) Order of the Holy Cross, and at Harvard, where he came under the temporary influence of Santayana and of the late President Neilson of Smith College, Northampton, Massachusetts. *The Harvard Monthly* published his first work and at this time he was associated with such men of future talent as Gilbert Seldes and John Dos Passos. In 1916 he wrote his first book, *One Way of Love* (verse).

In 1918, he joined the 103rd Regiment Infantry in the Twenty-Sixth, or New England Division, and engaged in the battles of Chateau-Thierry and St. Mihiel in the first World War. "It was under these conditions," he writes, "that I learned to love France wholeheartedly. I also saw for the first time how the Catholic religion operates at such a moment though I had long since attended its services, especially, at the Paulist Church in New York City, attracted by its glorious harmonized plain chant and the great humanity of its atmosphere. A practising Anglican in 1918, convinced that my father's church was a true branch of the Catholic one, I found I could only go to Mass in ruinous French churches, near the lines, or in stables, etc., on the eve of action. My own church was one of several sects, operating feebly at the Front. While there I brooded over the ruined country, over the very Europe we were engaged in 'saving,' a mighty universal religion in which I already felt at home." Wright, however, did not become a Catholic until 1936.

After the Armistice, he went to the Sorbonne for two years to study the French Revolution. He did a great deal of "extracurricular travelling" in France, Germany, Italy and the Near East where he witnessed the Holy Week ceremonies at Jerusalem in 1920. In 1922, while in Paris, he supported himself by writing for the *Dial* (extinct), the *Freeman* (extinct), the *Smart* Set (extinct) and other periodicals.

On returning to the United States, he taught history at his old school. He wrote in one term, and published in 1926 *A Short History of the Catholic Church,* which he says "was the kind of book that pleases nobody."

Wright's only "hobby" is teaching. He also enjoys lecturing in public and has had the honor of being included in the Catholic Culture Series, given at Assumption College, Windsor, Ontario. Among the poets his favorite is T. S. Eliot. He is a frequent contributor to *The Commonweal.*

A. M. & M. H.

John Chin Hsung Wu 1899-

One of the greatest intellectual converts of China since Candida Hsu, Dr. John C. H. Wu recently drafted China's new Constitution, and at the same time awakened his country not to the love of science but to the science of love.

Born in 1899 in Chekiang, China, this convert from Methodism, led to Catholicity by a reading of the autobiography of the Little Flower, studied law at Shanghai (L. B. with honors), took a D.D. from the University of Michigan, and as Fellow of the Carnegie Foundation for International Peace, studied at both the Sorbonne and the University of Berlin. Resigning the presidency of the Provisional Court in 1929, he began lecturing at the Law School of Northwestern University and was later invited to join the faculty of the Harvard Law School. Acceptance was prevented by the illness of his wife, so he returned to China, becoming advisor of the Shanghai Municipal Council, 1931. He then became vice-chairman of the commission for drafting a permanent constitution.

Baptized as late as 1937, this proud father of twelve children had the joy of converting them one by one, thus giving twelve little apostles to the Lord. His wife's conversion followed the cure of their daughter Therese by St. Thérèse. Dr. Wu, who was confirmed at Chungking during an air raid, is a daily communicant and a member of the Third Order of St. Francis. He has successfully convinced some of the learned ones of China that it was a little French girl who died in her twenties, and who used to say that "books she read gave her headaches," who discovered the only science that would bring peace and happiness to the human soul.

In April 1940, *T'ien Hsia,* the national Chinese secular magazine devoted to culture and education, printed *The Science of Love: A Study in the Teachings of Thérèse of Lisieux.* Editions in French, English, and Spanish followed. In this essay Dr. Wu holds that the true conception of Catholicism, according to St. Thérèse, is not that of a mere bargain with God, or a dry series of "don'ts" with heavy sanctions, but a falling in love with God, "but a kiss for a kiss" as he puts it, "or rather a small kiss for a big kiss" between the soul and its Redeemer. This keynote of love in the writings of the Little Flower led him not only to embrace her religion, but to induce China, too restless in her efforts, to be inspired by this saint who wanted no rest till the end of the world.

At the request of Chiang Kai-shek, Dr. Wu is translating the Catholic *New Testament* into Chinese in classical style.

In China, where only one per cent of the people are Catholics, after three hundred years of missionary work, Dr. Wu hopes by making an intellectual approach to an intellectually inclined nation, to effect a "blitz" surrender of the Chinese to the love of Christ. At present (1947), Dr. Wu is the Chinese Minister to the Vatican.

Among his other books are *The Art of Law* and other essays, juridical and literary; with M. C. Liang he wrote *Essays in Jurisprudence and Legal Philosophy.*

S. M.

Peter Wust   1884-1940

Peter Wust was one of the most distinguished of contemporary German Catholic philosophers. He was born of poor parents at Rissenthal, a village in the Saar Region, on August 28, 1884. After finishing at the Gymnasium in Trier in 1907 (he had given up the idea of becoming a priest in 1905), he continued his studies in philology at the universities of Berlin and Strassburg. At both institutions he also attended lectures in philosophy, under Friedrich Paulsen at the former, under Klemens Bäumker at the latter. Having passed the state examination in 1910, he taught English, German, and other subjects in the Gymnasia at Berlin, Neuss, Trier, and Cologne. While at Neuss, he made the acquaintance of Oswald Külpe, of Bonn University under whom he took his doctorate in 1914, with the dissertation, *John Stuart Mill's Logische Grundlegung der Geisteswissenschaft.* This volume was followed in 1917 by *Die Oberrealschule und der moderne Geist.*

Early in his career Wust succumbed to the influence of Neo-Kantianism, prevalent in Germany at the time. But late in the year 1918, affected by the defeat of Germany and after meeting the profound thinker and scholar, Ernst Troeltsch, he gradually returned to Catholic thinking. Of this thinking, metaphysics of the mind was the core, and in 1920 he published *Die Auferstehung der Metaphysik*. His acquaintance the following year with Max Scheler, professor of philosophy and sociology at the University of Cologne, was another milestone in his development. Soon after, in 1923, Wust returned, as he wrote, "into the arms of Una Sancta Ecclesia."

There followed years of fruitful literary productivity during which he, still Gymnasial professor at Cologne, published the following volumes: *Naivität und Pietät* (1925); *Die Rückkehr aus dem Exil* (1926), in which he described the return of Catholicism to the intellectual life of Germany; the monumental *Die Dialektik des Geistes* (1928); and *Die Krisis des abendländischen Menschentums* (also in 1928). The last named work has been translated into English, French, Dutch, Italian, and Portuguese.

In 1930 Wust accepted a call to the University of Münster as professor of philosophy. The method of his appointment had been unusual, for which reason he was made to suffer a great deal from an arrogant ostracism practiced by many of his colleagues. However, beginning with his first lecture the student body recognized in the gentle little Studienrat from the Saar an outstanding Christian apostle and teacher. The Auditorium Maximum was never so completely filled by students from all faculties, as when Peter Wust set forth and defended Catholic wisdom and truth. His regained faith was that of a child, and heroic was his fortitude as its protagonist, when during the following years of the Third Reich he remained at his post, until in 1939 a fatal illness forced him to resign. He died April 3, 1940.

Father Joseph Plumpe, usually one of the group that accompanied Peter Wust on his famous Saturday walks, describes him as "a very little man, with black kindly eyes. He was most humble, gentle, kind, with a fine bass voice, with a wonderful smile alternating with a very serious set of features. If ever a man loved his fellow-man, Wust did. He had a very happy family life. This is reflected in the touching dedications in his books—"Meiner Lieben Tochter Lotti," "Meiner lieben Tochter Else gewidmet."

The earlier of Dr. Wust's books especially were well received, and he was acclaimed as a herald of a needed return to metaphysics, at least in its application to some of the practical problems of life. Credit for making Peter Wust known in England and America is largely due to the English philosopher, E. I. Watkin.

Although it is merely a sketch of a vast subject, *Crisis in the West* is as good an analysis of Western civilization and of the Western mind as has been made. Written fifteen years ago, midway between the two World Wars, it seems surprisingly up-to-date. It is optimistic and at times eloquent, and it ends on a note of hope.

Wust published his chief work, *Ungewissheit und Wagnis,* in 1932. To his friends he often spoke of his hope of publishing a work that would certainly characterize the entire decade of his activity at Münster, "Weisheit und Heiligkeit" (Wisdom and Holiness). This hope was not realized. But on his deathbed he completed his beautiful autobiography, *Gestalten und Gedanken* (1st and 2nd editions, 1940). Likewise on his deathbed, when cancer had paralyzed his tongue, he wrote "Ein Abschiedswort," his farewell to his students: . . . "and if you should ask me before I go, whether I do not know of a magic key to open the final and ultimate portal of the wisdom of life, I would answer, 'Indeed, I do.' And this magic key is not reflection, as you might expect to hear from a philosopher, but it is prayer. Prayer induces stillness, it makes one childlike, it makes one objective. . . . The great things of existence are given only to those minds that pray."

B. S.

Euphemia Van Rensselaer Wyatt   1884-

"Background is the essential qualification for dramatic critics, as well as enthusiasm for the theatre," says Euphemia Van Rensselaer Wyatt, the distinguished dramatic critic of *The Catholic World.* A descendant of illustrious forbears, Mrs. Wyatt is the great-granddaughter of Stephen Van Rensselaer, the founder of the Van Rensselaer Polytechnic Institute. She is descended from a long line of non-Catholics, including clerics in the Church of England.

Born on April 1st, 1884, of George and Elizabeth Van Rensselaer Waddington, in New York City, Mrs. Wyatt was educated by private governesses at home, with one year at Miss Spence's School and Miss Davidge's Private Class. She was graduated from the New York School of Philanthropy (now the New York School of Social Work), later doing graduate work at Columbia University in philosophy and sociology. In 1906 she was married to Christopher Billop Wyatt by the Patriarch of Venice in his own chapel.

Active for many years in social service in New York City, she organized and directed the Caritas Club for Working Girls in the parish of St. Francis Xavier, and is a vice president of the Carroll Club, and a director of the Catholic Big Sisters.

In 1924 Mrs. Wyatt, the author of several one-act plays, became dramatic editor of *The Catholic World.* In addition she is a frequent contributor to *Commonweal* and occasionally to *Liturgical Arts,* and the *Franciscan.* Whether she is comparing John Gielgud's interpretation of Hamlet with that of Maurice Evans, or writing about archaeology in Yucatan, or Petrarch's fame, or the efficacy of prayer, she brings to her subject an illuminating mind, rich in knowledge and breadth of sympathy. Always she discovers evidences of the spiritual in a materialistic world; always she manifests the charm of gentle humor.

She has lectured on American history for the New York Board of Education and the City History Club, and is a member of the advisory board of Albertus Magnus College in New Haven, Connecticut.

Tall, with greying hair and quiet, hooded, grey-blue eyes, Euphemia

Van Rensselaer Wyatt impresses one as a lady of genuine culture and charm.

She has four children: Elizabeth (Mrs. William A. Russell), Jane (stage and screen star), (Mrs. Edgar Bethune Ward); Christopher Billop, and Monica.

T. V.

Right Reverend Peter M. H. Wynhoven
1884-1944

To syndicate weekly articles to forty-eight Catholic papers would seem a full-time job for most men, but to the Right Reverend Monsignor Peter Wynhoven it was just one activity out of a multiplicity of labors. Besides being president of the Catholic Press Association, Monsignor Wynhoven was editor of *Catholic Action of the South,* a diocesan weekly, and author of a series of sermons on the Gospels and Epistles, and of several books among which the two best known are *The Sincere Seeker,* "a streamlined and almost colloquial *Faith of Our Fathers,*" and *Wild Wisdom,* a collection of essays selected from his newspaper column, that "explain the relations of the man in the street to his religion."

Highly respected as a sociologist, Monsignor Wynhoven was appointed in 1941 as chairman of the Gulf Shipbuilding Stabilization Conference, having served formerly as chairman of the United States Regional Labor Board, and the Louisiana State Cotton Textile Industrial Relations Board. His personal efforts in the field of social work, based on the idea of "social restitution" include the founding of Hope Haven, orphanage and industrial school for homeless boys—known as "the South's rival of Nebraska's Boys' Town"—at Marrero, Louisiana; Madonna Manor, a home for younger children; Chinchuba Deaf-Mute Institute; St. Vincent's Hotel and Free Labor Bureau, and a Catholic Woman's Club for working girls. In addition he was also the organizer and first director of the Associated Catholic Charities.

Father Wynhoven was born December 31, 1884, in Venray, Holland, the son of John and Mary (Theuws) Wynhoven. Begun in Holland, his formal education was completed at Kenrick Seminary, St. Louis, Missouri. He was ordained to the priesthood in June 1909 and was pastor of Our Lady of Lourdes Church, New Orleans, Louisiana. In July 1934 he was made Domestic Prelate by Pope Pius XI. In 1943 the rank of Prothonotary Apostolic was conferred on him. He died on September 13, 1944.

T. V.

Reverend John J. Wynne, S.J. 1859-

Encyclopedist and editor of note, the Reverend John J. Wynne, S.J., has had a distinguished career of some sixty years in the service of the Catholic Church. He was born in New York City in 1859 and educated there by the Christian Brothers and by the Jesuits at the College of St. Francis Xavier, from which he graduated in 1876, in his seventeenth year, with an A.B., cum laude. Entering the Society of Jesus at West Park, New York, he made his novitiate and classical studies there from 1876 to 1879, studied philosophy and science at Woodstock College, Woodstock, Maryland, 1879 to 1881, was professor of science and languages at St. Francis Xavier College, New York City, 1882 to 1886, and professor of mathematics at Boston College, 1886 to 1887. He was ordained by Cardinal Gibbons in 1890.

In 1892, Father Wynne was appointed director of the Apostleship of Prayer in the United States. For many years he was editor of the *Messenger of the Sacred Heart,* and he was the founder and the first editor of the Jesuit national weekly, *America.* Placed in charge of the Shrine of Our Lady of the Martyrs, Auriesville, New York, he there became deeply interested in the cause of the Jesuit martyrs, Isaac Jogues and his companions, of which he was later vice-postulator. They were canonized by Pope Pius XI in 1930. At the time of their beatification, five years previously, Father Wynne wrote his book, *The Jesuit Martyrs of North America,* vividly recording their heroism. In 1939 he was influential in the erection at Lake George, New York, of the statue of St. Isaac Jogues, discoverer of the lake. For fifty years he has been interested in the cause for canonization of the Indian maiden, the Venerable Kateri Tekakwitha, "Lily of the Mohawks," now in process at Rome, with Father Wynne as vice-postulator.

The great work of his life was the publication of *The Catholic Encyclopedia,* a monumental achievement that owed its origin to misstatements about the Church in *Appleton's Universal Encyclopedia and Atlas,* since revised. Following the publication of the brochure, *Poisoning of the Wells,* which showed the gravity of this misinformation, Father Wynne, with the Reverend Thomas J. Shahan, the Reverend Edward A. Pace, Dr. Charles Herbermann and Mr. Conde Pallen, formed an editorial board in 1905 for the publication of an encyclopedia which would give the truth about all subjects of Catholic interest. Appleton & Company became the publishers. The first volume of *The Catholic Encyclopedia* was published in 1907, and the fifteenth and final volume in 1912. It was the first work of its kind in English and outstanding Catholic scholars from all over the world contributed articles. The Index appeared in 1914.

A book on *The Encyclopedia and Its Makers* followed. A *Supplement to the Catholic Encyclopedia* was published in 1922.

Two years later Father Wynne undertook another encyclopedic work that would include all topics. Associate editors were Bishop Shahan, Monsignor Pace and Dr. Pallen. Only the first two volumes of *Universal Knowledge* were published, the years of the depression making it impossible to continue. A one-volume *Catholic Dictionary* was meanwhile completed under Father Wynne's supervision and published in 1929. A revised edition of *The Catholic Encyclopedia* has been begun but only one volume issued.

Other literary activities of Father Wynne's were the editing of *The Encyclicals of Leo XIII* and the translation of *The Mass Every Day in the Year* and *The Mass, Sundays and Holydays.* His pamphlet *The Friars Must Stay* was instrumental in preventing the expulsion of the Franciscan and Augustinian Missionaries from the Philippines after the American occupation of the Islands. He was the organizer of the League of Daily Mass and of the Holy Hour. He now devotes his time to spreading devotion to Kateri Tekakwitha, through the Tekakwitha League, and advancing her cause.

Father Wynne has received many honors. For protecting the Belgian Congo Missions he was made a Knight of the Order of Leopold II. The Catholic University of America conferred on him the degree of S.T.D. and Fordham University gave him an honorary degree of Litt.D. The Holy Father sent him a special blessing on the completion of his sixtieth year as a Jesuit, and the occasion was celebrated by a dinner attended by six hundred of his friends and the presentation to him of a bas-relief portrait of himself and a set of resolutions adopted by the alumni of the College of St. Francis Xavier, his alma mater. Four years later, in 1940, he observed the golden jubilee of his ordination to the priesthood. He is resident at Fordham. C. M. N.

Thomas Russell Ybarra 1880-

Thomas Russell Ybarra was born in Boston, Massachusetts, in 1880, the son of Nelly Russell, a Bostonian, and of General Alejandro Ybarra of Caracas, Venezuela. His first trip to Europe was made when he was twelve years of age. Since then he has made about twenty-five round trips. He has been to Venezuela again and again and has visited Cuba, Puerto Rico and other West Indian islands several times. He took trips to Egypt, Morocco, Algeria, Tunisia, and Asia Minor. Until he was twenty, he shuttled back and forth between the United States and South America according to the rise and fall of political powers in Venezuela.

While he was living in Caracas, "Tommy" attended two schools there. Later, in Boston he went to the Roxbury Latin School, as well as to the Cambridge, Massachusetts, Latin School and, finally, to Harvard. No matter in what school or country he happened to be he had a strong leaning toward journalism and scribbling verses. His resolve to enter Harvard marked the decisive victory of his North American self over his South American self.

While a student at Harvard, Ybarra wrote light verse for the New York *Times*. Later he became a staff member of that paper, rising from a cub reporter to Acting Sunday Editor. His first post-Harvard job was as a translator from Spanish into English for New York concerns. In the meantime, he sent some poems to the New York *Times* which were accepted. Mr. Carr V. Van Anda, the Managing Editor of the *Times,* gave him a reporter's job on the strength of these verses. In 1934 Mr. Ybarra became head of the Berlin Bureau of the *Times.* Two years later he was sent to London to head the New York *Times* Bureau there. In 1927 a roving commission from the same paper enabled him to cover fifteen European countries in fifteen months.

In 1908 Mr. Ybarra published a book called *Davy Jones's Yarns and Other Salted Songs. Bolivar, the Passionate Warrior,* appeared in 1929; *Cervantes* in 1931; *Hindenburg, The Man With Three Lives,* in 1932; *America Faces South* in 1939; *Young Man of Caracas* (autobiography) in 1941, and the continuation of his autobiography, *Young Man of the World,* in 1942.

From 1931 to 1937, Mr. Ybarra worked for *Collier's* weekly as European editor. He travelled all over Europe and the Near East and made an extensive tour of South America. In 1940 he became a commentator on foreign affairs for the National Broadcasting Company over Station WJZ.

R. K.

Margaret Yeo   1877-1941

From Margaret Yeo herself there came these words: "I suppose the two most vivid and spiritual forces in my own life have been my conversion to the Catholic faith and my irresistible desire to spoil paper."

She was born at Canterbury, the daughter of Charles Routledge, His Majesty's Inspector of Schools, and Honorary Canon of Canterbury Cathedral, and of Dorothy, his wife, daughter of Charles Blomfield, Bishop of London. She was educated at home by a governess until she was fourteen, when she was sent to school in Northamptonshire and Lausanne. She spent a year at Lausanne.

Very early she showed an interest in the "strange" religion of Catholics, and while at school in Switzerland got herself into trouble for "sneaking off to Mass on Sundays." To correct this tendency, her father gave her a book entitled *Thirty-nine Reasons Against Joining the Church of Rome,* with the result that her conviction was strengthened that *it* was the only true Church. Yet, it was not until ten years after her marriage, in 1906, to Eric Yeo, member of a distinguished Irish legal family, that she finally came into the Church. She was living in Ireland at the time of the Sinn Fein rising in 1916; and, though English, strongly took the Sinn Fein side. The final decision was reached that year after a pilgrimage to Lough Dearg. The moment she set her bare feet on the island, she knew "I was for it."

The first money that she earned had been for an article on an old leper hospital near Canterbury. This article was revised by her father, a keen archaeologist. Most of the five pounds went on a marble bust of Napoleon, bought at Naples "on my way to an Archaeological Congress at Athens." Three volumes of short stories had been published by a "high-church" firm, but not until after Margaret Yeo's conversion did her literary career really begin. Then she produced in rapid succession her novels: *Salt* (1927); *King of Shadows* (1928); *Wild Parsley* (1929); *Uncertain Glory* (1930), and *Full Circle* (1933). All were competently written and were well received. But she still had not yet found her true metier, that of biography. To this she turned in 1931 with the publication of her *St. Francis Xavier.*

If this book was somewhat over-drenched with local color, it is hardly possible to write about the Xaverian adventures in so many strange lands without being dazzled by the bright light and the vivid hues that are everywhere. The action itself does not suffer, and the saint is made a living person. Margaret Yeo must certainly be grouped with the new school of hagiographers who combine sound scholarship with a keen dramatic sense. Perhaps the fact that she was a novelist enabled her to make the most of character and conversation.

The *St. Francis Xavier* was followed by: *Don John of Austria* (1934); *The Greatest of the Borgias* (1936); *Reformer, St. Charles Borromeo* (1938), and *These Three Hearts* (1940). The last mentioned, which was also her last book, was an attempt to tell simultaneously the story of St. Margaret Mary and Blessed Claude de la Colombiere. The third heart is of course, the Sacred Heart. She was a Benedictine Oblate of Prinknash, formerly the Anglican community of Caldey.

Her hobbies, she said, were collecting Stuart prints, portraits and biographies, and gardening. Being a woman of considerable private means, she was able to travel widely. She produced her work under the spur, not of economic, but artistic necessity. She confesses to being influenced by her surroundings, and in these she was fortunate. The stately beauty of Canterbury was succeeded, after her marriage, by a Tudor manor-house in a lovely Devonshire setting. Ireland followed, and after Ireland came an old house at St. Alban's, the cellars of which were part of the medieval abbey. At the time of her death—she had been a widow since 1929—she was living in the small modern house at Harpenden, Hertfordshire. There she did most of her writing in the garden. These settings, though they are not as a rule the actual scenes about which she wrote, nevertheless are reflected in the distinguished style of her work. She had a remarkable gift for conveying atmosphere and for presenting her great scenes with the maximum of effectiveness.

After completing a motor tour through Italy in 1939, which took her to out of the way places "where nothing has changed for many thousand years," she wrote, "it seemed that only two things last in this world, the Catholic Church and cultivating the earth. Perhaps the drift away from these two is the major cause for the decadence of our materialistic, mechanistic 'civilization.'"

Mrs. Margaret Yeo died in Egland in 1941.

Reverend John Stanislaus Zybura   1875-1934

For nineteen years, Father Zybura was stricken with tuberculosis, and was confined first to the Glockner Sanatorium and later to St. Francis Hospital, Colorado Springs, Colorado, until his death on October 7, 1934. It was during this illness that he did most of his literary work in philosophy. He continued to write up to a year before his death. While a patient at Glockner Sanatorium, he wrote to Father Lelen of Falmouth, Kentucky, on January 6, 1925, "there is nothing like suffering to teach one the sacrificial attitude of mind and the ideal of reparation."

John Stanislaus Zybura was born in Subkau, Prussian Poland, July 21, 1875, and was educated at St. Ignatius College, Cleveland, Ohio, and at St. Mary's Seminary, Cleveland, Ohio. He completed his theological course at the North American College, Rome, Italy, and was ordained there April 17th, 1898, by Cardinal Parocchi for the Diocese of Cleveland. Because of ill health, he did not receive an appointment until April 1902 when he was appointed Assistant Pastor of St. Anthony's Church, Toledo, Ohio, where he served until May 1903. He was then appointed Assistant Pastor of St. Stanislaus Parish, Cleveland, Ohio, and served until December 1904. He was on sick leave until his appointment as Pastor of St. Stanislaus Parish, Lorain, on August 19th, 1908. He was the first resident pastor of St. Stanislaus, and during his administration built the first church and organized the parish school. He left St. Stanislaus Parish, Lorain, on September 22, 1911, when he went to the Columbus Diocese to accept an appointment there. He retired from active service in 1915.

In 1928 he was awarded an Honorary Ph.D. from the congregation of Seminaries and Universities in Rome. Five years later the Polish Government awarded him the Medal of Merit.

He is the author of *Contemporary Godlessness* (1924). He edited *Present-day Thinkers and the New Scholasticism*. He translated Reverend Francesco Olgiatti's *Key to the Study of St. Thomas,* from the Italian and Gerado Bruni's *Progressive Scholasticism,* also from the Italian, and Otto Zimmermann's *Problem of Evil* from the German. In 1930 he published *Introduction to the Theological Summa of St. Thomas* and in 1931 *The Perennial Vitality and Timeliness of the Philosophy of St. Thomas.*

In 1941 he was elected a member of The Gallery of Living Catholic Authors, the only Polish author to receive that distinction up to that time.

M. H.

U.I.O.G.D.

(Ut In Omnibus Glorificetur Deus)